Collins English Dictionary

Collins

Collins English Dictionary

HarperCollins Publishers
Westerhill Road
Bishopbriggs
Glasgow
G64 2QT
Great Britain

First Edition 2006

ISBN-13 978-0-00-777413-5
ISBN-10 0-00-777413-3

www.collins.co.uk

A catalogue record for this book is available from the British Library.

Designed by Mark Thomson

Typeset by Wordcraft

Printed in Great Britain by Clays Ltd, St Ives plc

Acknowledgements
We would like to thank those authors and publishers who kindly gave permission for copyright material to be used in the Collins Word Web. We would also like to thank Times Newspapers Ltd for providing valuable data.

CONTENTS

EDITORIAL STAFF

EDITORS
Cormac McKeown
Elspeth Summers

FOR THE PUBLISHERS
Morven Dooner
Elaine Higgleton
Lorna Knight

This dictionary is easy to use and understand. Its layout is refreshingly clear and clutter-free, taking you straight to the information you want with a minimum of fuss. Every definition is presented in straightforward English. Where a word has more than one sense, the one given first is the most common meaning in today's language. Other senses of a word – for example, historical and technical senses – are explained after the main present-day meaning.

As you would expect, entries show the spelling and meaning of each word. Other features which make this dictionary particularly helpful include simple pronunciations for words that may be unfamiliar or confusing. Over 100 spelling tips are also included, with useful advice on how to avoid common errors.

In compiling this dictionary our lexicographers have been able to consult an unparalleled 2.5-billion-word database of written and spoken English from a huge variety of sources around the globe. By analysing this data, lexicographers have ensured that you, as a dictionary user, are given the most up-to-date information about how English is really used today. Examples have been taken from real English to help illustrate meaning within the definitions.

New words and senses have been gathered through close analysis of our database, as well an extensive reading, listening, and viewing programme, taking in all kinds of broadcasts and publications. There is also specialist vocabulary from subjects such as science, technology, and computing.

An added bonus is the supplement of new words for 2005. This section of the dictionary gives a snapshot of the ever-evolving language, listing some of the more interesting neologisms brought to light recently by our various language monitoring programmes.

These features mean that this dictionary is one of the most up-to-date and user-friendly small dictionaries available.

Main Entry Words	printed in large bold type, eg **abbey** All main entry words, including abbreviations and combining forms, in one alphabetical sequence, eg **abbot** **abbreviate** **ABC** **abdicate**
Variant spellings	shown in full, eg **adrenalin, adrenaline** *Note:* where the spellings **-ize** and **-ization** are used at the end of a word, the alternative forms **-ise** and **-isation** are equally acceptable.
Pronunciations	given in square brackets for words that are difficult or confusing; the word is respelt as it is pronounced,

with the stressed syllable in bold type, eg

antipodes [an-**tip**-pod-deez]

Parts of Speech

shown in italics as an abbreviation, eg

ablaze *adj*

When a word can be used as more than one part of speech, the change of part of speech is shown after an arrow, eg

mock *v* make fun of; mimic ▷ *adj* sham or imitation

Parts of speech may be combined for some words, eg

alone *adj, adv* without anyone or anything else

Cross References

shown in bold type, eg

doner kebab *n* see **kebab**

Irregular Parts	or confusing forms of verb, nouns, adjectives, and adverbs shown in bold type, eg

begin *v* **-ginning, -gan, -gun**
regret *v* **-gretting, -gretted**
anniversary *n, pl* **-ries**
angry *adj* **-grier, -griest**
well *adv* **better, best**

Meanings	separated by semicolons, eg

casual *adj* careless, nonchalant; (of work or workers) occasional; for informal wear; happening by chance.

Phrases and Idioms	included immediately after the meanings of the main entry word, eg

hand *n* ... *v* ... **have a hand in** be involved **lend a hand** help ...

Related Words shown in the same paragraph as the main entry word, eg

absurd *adj* incongruous or ridiculous **absurdly** *adv* **absurdity** *n*

Note: where the meaning of a related word is not given, it may be understood from the main entry word, or from another related word.

Compounds shown in alphabetical order at the end of the paragraph, eg

ash *n* ... **ashtray** *n* receptacle for tobacco ash and cigarette butts
Ash Wednesday first day of Lent

ABBREVIATIONS USED IN THIS DICTIONARY

AD	anno Domini
adj	adjective
adv	adverb
anat	anatomy
archit	architecture
astrol	astrology
Aust	Australia(n)
BC	before Christ
biol	biology
Brit	British
chem	chemistry
C *of* E	Church of England
conj	conjunction
E	East
eg	for example
esp	especially
etc	et cetera
fem	feminine
foll	followed
geom	geometry
hist	history
interj	interjection
lit	literary
masc	masculine
med	medicine

ABBREVIATIONS USED IN THIS DICTIONARY

meteorol	meteorology
mil	military
n	noun
N	North
naut	nautical
NZ	New Zealand
obs	obsolete
offens	offensive
orig	originally
photog	photography
pl	plural
prep	preposition
pron	pronoun
psychol	psychology
®	trademark
RC	Roman Catholic
S	South
S Afr	South Africa(n)
Scot	Scottish
sing	singular
US	United States
usu	usually
v	verb
W	West
zool	zoology

a

a *adj* indefinite article, used before a noun being mentioned for the first time

AA Alcoholics Anonymous; Automobile Association

aardvark *n* S African anteater with long ears and snout

AB able-bodied seaman

aback *adv* **taken aback** startled or disconcerted

abacus *n* beads on a wire frame, used for doing calculations

abalone [ab-a-**lone**-ee] *n* edible sea creature with a shell lined with mother of pearl

abandon *v* desert or leave (one's wife, children, etc); give up (hope etc) altogether ▷ *n* lack of inhibition **abandoned** *adj* deserted; uninhibited **abandonment** *n*

abase *v* humiliate or degrade (oneself) **abasement** *n*

abashed *adj* embarrassed and ashamed

abate *v* make or become less strong **abatement** *n*

abattoir [**ab**-a-twahr] *n* place where animals are killed for food

abbess *n* nun in charge of a convent

abbey *n* dwelling place of, or a church belonging to, a community of monks or nuns

abbot *n* head of an abbey of monks

abbreviate *v* shorten (a word) by leaving out some letters **abbreviation** *n* shortened form of a word or words

ABC[1] *n* alphabet; basics of a subject

ABC[2] Australian Broadcasting Corporation

abdicate *v* give up (the throne or a responsibility) **abdication** *n*

abdomen *n* part of the body containing the stomach and intestines **abdominal** *adj*

abduct *v* carry off, kidnap **abduction** *n* **abductor** *n*

aberration *n* sudden change from what is normal, accurate, or correct; brief lapse in control of one's thoughts or feelings **aberrant** *adj* showing aberration

abet *v* **abetting, abetted** help or encourage in wrongdoing **abettor** *n*

abeyance *n* **in abeyance** not in use

abhor *v* **-horring, -horred** detest utterly **abhorrent** *adj* hateful, loathsome **abhorrence** *n*

abide *v* endure, put up with; *obs* stay or dwell *eg abide with me* **abide by** *v* obey (the law, rules, etc) **abiding** *adj* lasting

ability *n, pl* **-ties** competence, power; talent

abject *adj* utterly miserable;

lacking all self-respect **abjectly** *adv*

abjure *v* deny or renounce on oath

ablative *n* case of nouns in Latin and other languages, indicating source, agent, or instrument of action

ablaze *adj* burning fiercely

able *adj* capable, competent **ably** *adv* **able-bodied** *adj* strong and healthy

ablutions *pl n* act of washing

abnormal *adj* not normal or usual **abnormally** *adv* **abnormality** *n*

aboard *adv, prep* on, in, onto, or into (a ship, train, or plane)

abode *n* home, dwelling

abolish *v* do away with **abolition** *n* **abolitionist** *n* person who wishes to do away with something, esp slavery

abominable *adj* detestable, very bad **abominable snowman** large apelike creature said to live in the Himalayas **abominably** *adv*

abomination *n* someone or something that is detestable

aborigine [ab-or-**rij**-in-ee] **aboriginal** *n* original inhabitant of a country or region, esp (**A-**) Australia **aboriginal** *adj*

abort *v* have an abortion or perform an abortion on; have a miscarriage; end a plan or process before completion **abortive** *adj* unsuccessful

abortion *n* operation to end a pregnancy; *Informal* something grotesque **abortionist** *n* person who performs abortions, esp illegally

abound *v* be plentiful **abounding** *adj*

about *prep* concerning, on the subject of; in or near (a place) ▷ *adv* nearly, approximately; nearby **about to** shortly going to **not about to** determined not to **about-turn** *n* complete change of attitude

above *adv, prep* over or higher (than); greater (than); superior (to) **above board** in the open, without dishonesty

abracadabra *n* supposedly magic word

abrasion *n* scraped area on the skin

abrasive *adj* harsh and unpleasant in manner; tending to rub or scrape ▷ *n* substance for cleaning or polishing by rubbing

abreast *adv, adj* side by side **abreast of** up to date with

abridge *v* shorten by using fewer words **abridgment, abridgement** *n*

abroad *adv* to or in a foreign country; at large

abrogate *v* cancel (a law or agreement) formally **abrogation** *n*

abrupt *adj* sudden, unexpected; blunt and rude **abruptly** *adv* **abruptness** *n*

abs *pl n* *Informal* abdominal muscles

abscess *n* inflamed swelling containing pus

> SPELLING There is a silent *c* in the middle of **abscess** that's easy to forget

abscond *v* leave secretly

abseil [**ab**-sale] *v* go down a steep drop by a rope fastened at the top and tied around one's body

absent *adj* not present; lacking; inattentive ▷ *v* stay away **absently** *adv* **absence** *n* being away; lack **absentee** *n* person who should be present but is not **absenteeism** *n* persistent absence from work or school

absent-minded *adj* inattentive or forgetful **absent-mindedly** *adv*
absinthe *n* strong green aniseed-flavoured liqueur
absolute *adj* complete, perfect; not limited, unconditional; pure *eg absolute alcohol* **absolutely** *adv* completely ▷ *interj* certainly, yes **absolutism** *n* government by a ruler with unrestricted power
absolve *v* declare to be free from blame or sin **absolution** *n*
absorb *v* soak up (a liquid); take in; engage the interest of (someone) **absorption** *n* **absorbent** *adj* able to absorb liquid **absorbency** *n*
abstain *v* choose not to do something; choose not to vote **abstainer** *n* **abstention** *n* abstaining, esp from voting **abstinence** *n* abstaining, esp from drinking alcohol **abstinent** *adj*
abstemious *adj* taking very little alcohol or food **abstemiousness** *n*
abstract *adj* existing as a quality or idea rather than a material object; theoretical; (of art) using patterns of shapes and colours rather than realistic likenesses ▷ *n* summary; abstract work of art; abstract word or idea ▷ *v* summarize; remove **abstracted** *adj* lost in thought **abstraction** *n*
abstruse *adj* not easy to understand
absurd *adj* incongruous or ridiculous **absurdly** *adv* **absurdity** *n*
abundant *adj* plentiful **abundantly** *adv* **abundance** *n*
abuse *v* use wrongly; ill-treat violently; speak harshly and rudely to ▷ *n* prolonged ill-treatment; harsh and vulgar comments; wrong use **abuser** *n* **abusive** *adj* **abusively** *adv* **abusiveness** *n*
abut *v* **abutting, abutted** be next to or touching
abysmal *adj Informal* extremely bad, awful **abysmally** *adv*
abyss *n* very deep hole or chasm
AC alternating current
a/c account
acacia [a-**kay**-sha] *n* tree or shrub with yellow or white flowers
academy *n, pl* **-mies** society to advance arts or sciences; institution for training in a particular skill; *Scot* secondary school **academic** *adj* of an academy or university; of theoretical interest only ▷ *n* lecturer or researcher at a university **academically** *adv* **academician** *n* member of an academy
acanthus *n* prickly plant
ACAS (in Britain) Advisory Conciliation and Arbitration Service
ACC (in New Zealand) Accident Compensation Corporation
accede *v* consent or agree (to); take up (an office or position)
accelerate *v* (cause to) move faster **acceleration** *n* **accelerator** *n* pedal in a motor vehicle to increase speed

> SPELLING The commonest misspelling of **accelerate** in Collins Word Web has a double *l*. In fact there should be only one *l*

accent *n* distinctive style of pronunciation of a local, national, or social group; mark over a letter to show how it is pronounced; stress on a syllable or musical note ▷ *v* place emphasis on
accentuate *v* stress, emphasize **accentuation** *n*
accept *v* receive willingly; agree to; consider to be true **acceptance** *n* **acceptable** *adj* tolerable;

satisfactory **acceptably** *adv* **acceptability** *n*

access *n* means of or right to approach or enter ▷ *v* obtain (data) from a computer **accessible** *adj* easy to reach **accessibility** *n*

accession *n* taking up of an office or position

accessory *n, pl* **-ries** supplementary part or object; person involved in a crime although not present when it is committed

accident *n* mishap, often causing injury; event happening by chance **accidental** *adj* happening by chance or unintentionally ▷ *n music* symbol indicating that a sharp, flat, or natural note is not a part of the key signature **accidentally** *adv*

acclaim *v* applaud, praise ▷ *n* enthusiastic approval **acclamation** *n*

acclimatize *v* adapt to a new climate or environment **acclimatization** *n*

accolade *n* award, honour, or praise; award of knighthood

accommodate *v* provide with lodgings; have room for; oblige, do a favour for; adapt or adjust (to something) **accommodation** *n* house or room for living in **accommodating** *adj* obliging

> SPELLING Collins Word Web shows that people usually remember that **accommodation** and **accommodate** have two *cs*, but they often forget that these words have two *ms* as well

accompany *v* **-nying, -nied** go along with; occur with; provide a musical accompaniment for **accompaniment** *n* something that accompanies; *music* supporting part that goes with a solo **accompanist** *n*

accomplice *n* person who helps another to commit a crime

accomplish *v* manage to do; finish **accomplishment** *n* completion; personal ability or skill **accomplished** *adj* expert, proficient

accord *n* agreement, harmony ▷ *v* fit in with

accordance *n* **in accordance with** conforming to or according to

according *adv* **according to** as stated by; in conformity with **accordingly** *adv* in an appropriate manner; consequently

accordion *n* portable musical instrument played by moving the two sides apart and together, and pressing a keyboard or buttons to produce the notes **accordionist** *n*

accost *v* approach and speak to, often aggressively

account *n* report, description; business arrangement making credit available; record of money received and paid out with the resulting balance; person's money held in a bank; importance, value ▷ *v* judge to be **on account of** because of **accountable** *adj* responsible to someone or for something **accountability** *n*

accounting *n* skill or practice of maintaining and auditing business accounts **accountant** *n* person who maintains and audits business accounts **accountancy** *n*

accoutrements *pl n* clothing and equipment for a particular activity

accredited *adj* authorized, officially recognized

accretion [ak-**kree**-shun] *n* gradual growth; something added

accrue *v* **-cruing, -crued** increase

gradually **accrual** *n*
accumulate *v* gather together in increasing quantity **accumulation** *n* **accumulative** *adj* **accumulator** *n* *Brit & Aust* rechargeable electric battery
accurate *adj* exact, correct **accurately** *adv* **accuracy** *n*
accursed *adj* under a curse; detestable
accusative *n* grammatical case indicating the direct object
accuse *v* charge with wrongdoing **accused** *n* **accuser** *n* **accusing** *adj* **accusation** *n* **accusatory** *adj*
accustom *v* make used to **accustomed** *adj* usual; used (to); in the habit (of)
ace *n* playing card with one symbol on it; *Informal* expert; *tennis* unreturnable serve ▷ *adj Informal* excellent
acerbic [ass-**sir**-bik] *adj* harsh or bitter **acerbity** *n*
acetate [**ass**-it-tate] *n chem* salt or ester of acetic acid; (also **acetate rayon**) synthetic textile fibre
acetic [ass-**see**-tik] *adj* of or involving vinegar **acetic acid** colourless liquid used to make vinegar
acetone [**ass**-it-tone] *n* colourless liquid used as a solvent
acetylene [ass-**set**-ill-een] *n* colourless flammable gas used in welding metals
ache *n* dull continuous pain ▷ *v* be in or cause continuous dull pain
achieve *v* gain by hard work or ability **achievement** *n* something accomplished
Achilles heel [ak-**kill**-eez] *n* small but fatal weakness
Achilles tendon *n* cord connecting the calf muscle to the heel bone
achromatic *adj* colourless; *music* with no sharps or flats
acid *n chem* one of a class of compounds, corrosive and sour when dissolved in water, that combine with a base to form a salt; *slang* LSD ▷ *adj* containing acid; sour-tasting; sharp or sour in manner **acidic** *adj* **acidify** *v* **acidity** *n* **Acid (House)** *n* type of funk-based electronically edited disco music with hypnotic sound effects **acid rain** rain containing acid from atmospheric pollution **acid test** conclusive test of value
acknowledge *v* admit, recognize; indicate recognition of (a person); say one has received **acknowledgment, acknowledgement** *n*
acme [**ak**-mee] *n* highest point of achievement or excellence
acne [**ak**-nee] *n* pimply skin disease
acolyte *n* follower or attendant; *Christianity* person who assists a priest
aconite *n* poisonous plant with hoodlike flowers; poison obtained from this plant
acorn *n* nut of the oak tree
acoustic *adj* of sound and hearing; (of a musical instrument) not electronically amplified **acoustics** *n* science of sounds ▷ *pl* features of a room or building determining how sound is heard within it **acoustically** *adv*
acquaint *v* make familiar, inform **acquainted** *adj* **acquaintance** *n* person known; personal knowledge
acquiesce [ak-wee-**ess**] *v* agree to what someone wants **acquiescence** *n* **acquiescent** *adj*
acquire *v* gain, get **acquisition** *n* thing acquired; act of getting

acquisitive *adj* eager to gain material possessions **acquisitiveness** *n*

acquit *v* **-quitting, -quitted** pronounce (someone) innocent; behave in a particular way **acquittal** *n*

acre *n* measure of land, 4840 square yards (4046.86 square metres) **acreage** [**ake**-er-rij] *n* land area in acres

acrid [**ak**-rid] *adj* pungent, bitter

acrimonious *adj* bitter in speech or manner **acrimony** *n*

acrobat *n* person skilled in gymnastic feats requiring agility and balance **acrobatic** *adj* **acrobatics** *pl n* acrobatic feats

acronym *n* word formed from the initial letters of other words, such as NASA

across *adv, prep* from side to side (of); on or to the other side (of) **across the board** applying equally to all

acrostic *n* lines of writing in which the first or last letters of each line spell a word or saying

acrylic *n, adj* (synthetic fibre, paint, etc) made from acrylic acid **acrylic acid** strong-smelling corrosive liquid

act *n* thing done; law or decree; section of a play or opera; one of several short performances in a show; pretended attitude ▷ *v* do something; behave in a particular way; perform in a play, film, etc **act of God** unpredictable natural event **acting** *n* art of an actor ▷ *adj* temporarily performing the duties of **actor, actress** *n* person who acts in a play, film, etc

ACT Australian Capital Territory

actinium *n chem* radioactive chemical element

action *n* process of doing something; thing done; lawsuit; operating mechanism; minor battle **actionable** *adj* giving grounds for a lawsuit **action replay** rerun of an event on a television tape

active *adj* moving, working; busy, energetic; *grammar* (of a verb) in a form indicating that the subject is performing the action, eg *threw* in *Kim threw the ball* **actively** *adv* **activity** *n* state of being active *pl* **-ties** leisure pursuit **activate** *v* make active **activation** *n* **activator** *n* **activist** *n* person who works energetically to achieve political or social goals **activism** *n*

actual *adj* existing in reality **actually** *adv* really, indeed **actuality** *n*

actuary *n, pl* **-aries** statistician who calculates insurance risks **actuarial** *adj*

actuate *v* start up (a device)

acuity [ak-**kew**-it-ee] *n* keenness of vision or thought

acumen [**ak**-yew-men] *n* ability to make good judgments

acupuncture *n* medical treatment involving the insertion of needles at various points on the body **acupuncturist** *n*

acute *adj* severe; keen, shrewd; sharp, sensitive; (of an angle) less than 90° ▷ *n* accent (´) over a letter to indicate the quality or length of its sound, as in café **acutely** *adv* **acuteness** *n*

ad *n Informal* advertisement

AD anno Domini

adage *n* wise saying, proverb

adagio *n, pl* **-gios,** *adv music* (piece to be played) slowly and gracefully

adamant *adj* unshakable in

determination or purpose **adamantly** *adv*

Adam's apple *n* projecting lump of thyroid cartilage at the front of the throat

adapt *v* alter for new use or new conditions **adaptable** *adj* **adaptability** *n* **adaptation** *n* thing produced by adapting something; adapting **adaptor, adapter** *n* device for connecting several electrical appliances to a single socket

add *v* combine (numbers or quantities); join (to something); say or write further

addendum *n, pl* **-da** addition; appendix to a book etc

adder *n* small poisonous snake

addict *n* person who is unable to stop taking drugs; *Informal* person devoted to something **addicted** *adj* **addiction** *n* **addictive** *adj* causing addiction

addition *n* adding; thing added **in addition** besides, as well **additional** *adj* **additionally** *adv* **additive** *n* something added, esp to a foodstuff, to improve it or prevent deterioration

addled *adj* confused or unable to think clearly

address *n* place where a person lives; direction on a letter; location; formal public speech ▷ *v* mark the destination, as on an envelope; make a speech; give attention to (a problem, task, etc) **addressee** *n* person addressed

> SPELLING If you spell **address** wrongly, you probably miss out one *d*. Remember to double the *d* and the *s*

adduce *v* mention something as evidence or proof

adenoids [**ad**-in-oidz] *pl n* mass of tissue at the back of the throat **adenoidal** *adj* having a nasal voice caused by swollen adenoids

adept *adj, n* very skilful (person)

adequate *adj* sufficient, enough; not outstanding **adequately** *adv* **adequacy** *n*

adhere *v* stick (to); be devoted (to) **adherence** *n* **adherent** *n* devotee, follower **adhesion** *n* sticking (to); joining together of parts of the body that are normally separate, as after surgery

adhesive *n* substance used to stick things together ▷ *adj* able to stick to things

ad hoc *adj, adv Latin* for a particular purpose only

adieu [a-**dew**] *interj lit* farewell, goodbye

ad infinitum [ad in-fin-**eye**-tum] *adv Latin* endlessly

adipose *adj* of or containing fat

adj. adjective

adjacent *adj* near or next (to); having a common boundary; *geom* (of a side in a right-angled triangle) lying between a specified angle and the right angle

adjective *n* word that adds information about a noun or pronoun **adjectival** *adj*

adjoin *v* be next to **adjoining** *adj*

adjourn *v* close (a court) at the end of a session; postpone temporarily; *Informal* go elsewhere **adjournment** *n*

adjudge *v* declare (to be)

adjudicate *v* give a formal decision on (a dispute); judge (a competition) **adjudication** *n* **adjudicator** *n*

adjunct *n* subordinate or additional person or thing

adjure *v* command (to do); appeal earnestly

adjust *v* adapt to new conditions; alter slightly so as to be suitable **adjustable** *adj* **adjuster** *n* **adjustment** *n*

adjutant [**aj**-oo-tant] *n* army officer in charge of routine administration

ad-lib *v* **-libbing, -libbed** improvise a speech etc without preparation ▷ *n* improvised remark

admin *n Informal* administration

administer *v* manage (business affairs); organize and put into practice; give (medicine or treatment)

administrate *v* manage (an organization) **administrator** *n*

administration *n* management of an organization; people who manage an organization; government *eg the Bush administration*

administrative *adj* of the management of an organization

admiral *n* highest naval rank **Admiralty** *n* (in Britain) former government department in charge of the Royal Navy

admire *v* regard with esteem and approval **admirable** *adj* **admirably** *adv* **admiration** *n* **admirer** *n* **admiring** *adj* **admiringly** *adv*

admissible *adj* allowed to be brought in as evidence in court **admissibility** *n*

admission *n* permission to enter; entrance fee; confession

admit *v* **-mitting, -mitted** confess, acknowledge; concede the truth of; allow in **admittance** *n* permission to enter **admittedly** *adv* it must be agreed

admixture *n* mixture; ingredient

admonish *v* reprove sternly **admonition** *n*

ad nauseam [ad **naw**-zee-am] *adv Latin* to a boring or sickening extent

ado *n lit* fuss, trouble

adobe [ad-**oh**-bee] *n* sun-dried brick

adolescence *n* period between puberty and adulthood **adolescent** *n, adj* (person) between puberty and adulthood

adopt *v* take (someone else's child) as one's own; take up (a plan or principle) **adoption** *n* **adoptive** *adj* related by adoption

adore *v* love intensely; worship **adorable** *adj* **adoration** *n* **adoring** *adj* **adoringly** *adv*

adorn *v* decorate, embellish **adornment** *n*

adrenal [ad-**reen**-al] *adj* near the kidneys **adrenal glands** glands covering the top of the kidneys

adrenalin, adrenaline *n* hormone secreted by the adrenal glands in response to stress

adrift *adj, adv* drifting; without a clear purpose

adroit *adj* quick and skilful **adroitly** *adv* **adroitness** *n*

adsorb *v* (of a gas or vapour) condense and form a thin film on a surface **adsorption** *n*

adulation *n* uncritical admiration

adult *adj* fully grown, mature ▷ *n* adult person or animal **adulthood** *n*

adulterate *v* spoil something by adding inferior material **adulteration** *n*

adultery *n, pl* **-teries** sexual unfaithfulness of a husband or wife **adulterer, adulteress** *n* **adulterous** *adj*

adv. adverb

advance *v* go or bring forward;

further (a cause); propose (an idea); lend (a sum of money) ▷ *n* forward movement; improvement; loan ▷ *pl* approaches to a person with the hope of starting a romantic or sexual relationship ▷ *adj* done or happening before an event **in advance** ahead **advanced** *adj* at a late stage in development; not elementary **advancement** *n* promotion

advantage *n* more favourable position or state; benefit or profit; *tennis* point scored after deuce **take advantage of** use (a person) unfairly; use (an opportunity) **advantageous** *adj* **advantageously** *adv*

advent *n* arrival; (**A-**) season of four weeks before Christmas **Adventist** *n* member of a Christian sect that believes in the imminent return of Christ (also **Seventh Day Adventist**)

adventitious *adj* added or appearing accidentally

adventure *n* exciting and risky undertaking or exploit **adventurer, adventuress** *n* person who unscrupulously seeks money or power; person who seeks adventures **adventurous** *adj*

adverb *n* word that adds information about a verb, adjective, or other adverb **adverbial** *adj*

adversary [**ad**-verse-er-ree] *n, pl* **-saries** opponent or enemy

adverse *adj* unfavourable; antagonistic or hostile **adversely** *adv* **adversity** *n* very difficult or hard circumstances

advert *n Informal* advertisement

advertise *v* present or praise (goods or services) to the public in order to encourage sales; make (a vacancy, event, etc) known publicly **advertisement** *n* public announcement to sell goods or publicize an event **advertiser** *n* **advertising** *adj, n*

> SPELLING Some verbs can be spelt ending in either *-ise* or *-ize*, but **advertise** and **advise** always have an s

advice *n* recommendation as to what to do **advise** *v* offer advice to; notify (someone) **advisable** *adj* prudent, sensible **advisability** *n* **advisory** *adj* giving advice **advised** *adj* considered, thought-out *eg ill-advised* **advisedly** *adv* deliberately

> SPELLING Collins Word Web shows that people sometimes write **advise** where they ought to write **advice**. The verb is **advise** and the noun is **advice**

adviser, advisor *n* person who offers advice, eg on careers to students or school pupils

advocaat *n* liqueur with a raw egg base

advocate *v* propose or recommend ▷ *n* person who publicly supports a cause; *Scot & SAfr* barrister **advocacy** *n*

adze *n* tool with an arched blade at right angles to the handle

aegis [**ee**-jiss] *n* sponsorship, protection

aeolian harp [ee-**oh**-lee-an] *n* musical instrument that produces sounds when the wind passes over its strings

aeon [**ee**-on] *n* immeasurably long period of time

aerate *v* put gas into (a liquid), as when making a fizzy drink **aeration** *n*

aerial *adj* in, from, or operating in the air; relating to aircraft ▷ *n* metal pole, wire, etc, for receiving or transmitting radio or TV signals **aerial top dressing** spreading of fertilizer from an aeroplane onto remote areas

aerobatics *pl n* stunt flying **aerobatic** *adj*

aerobics *n* exercises designed to increase the amount of oxygen in the blood **aerobic** *adj*

aerodrome *n* small airport

aerodynamics *n* study of how air flows around moving solid objects **aerodynamic** *adj*

aerofoil *n* part of an aircraft, such as the wing, designed to give lift

aerogram *n* airmail letter on a single sheet of paper that seals to form an envelope

aeronautics *n* study or practice of aircraft flight **aeronautical** *adj*

aeroplane *n* powered flying vehicle with fixed wings

aerosol *n* pressurized can from which a substance can be dispensed as a fine spray

aerospace *n* earth's atmosphere and space beyond

aesthetic [iss-**thet**-ik] *adj* relating to the appreciation of art and beauty **aesthetics** *n* study of art, beauty, and good taste **aesthetically** *adv* **aesthete** [**eess**-theet] *n* person who has or affects an extravagant love of art **aestheticism** *n*

aether *n* same as **ether**

aetiology [ee-tee-**ol**-a-jee] *n* same as **etiology**

afar *adv* **from afar** from or at a great distance

affable *adj* friendly and easy to talk to **affably** *adv* **affability** *n*

affair *n* event or happening; sexual relationship outside marriage; thing to be done or attended to ▷ *pl* personal or business interests; matters of public interest

affect¹ *v* act on, influence; move (someone) emotionally

affect² *v* put on a show of; wear or use by preference **affectation** *n* attitude or manner put on to impress **affected** *adj* displaying affectation; pretended

affection *n* fondness or love **affectionate** *adj* loving **affectionately** *adv*

affianced [af-**fie**-anst] *adj* *old-fashioned* engaged to be married

affidavit [af-fid-**dave**-it] *n* written statement made on oath

affiliate *v* (of a group) link up with a larger group **affiliation** *n*

affinity *n, pl* **-ties** close connection or liking; close resemblance; chemical attraction

affirm *v* declare to be true; uphold or confirm (an idea or belief) **affirmation** *n* **affirmative** *n, adj* (word or phrase) indicating agreement

affix *v* attach or fasten ▷ *n* word or syllable added to a word to change its meaning

afflict *v* give pain or grief to **affliction** *n*

affluent *adj* having plenty of money **affluence** *n* wealth

afford *v* have enough money to buy; be able to spare (the time etc); give or supply **affordable** *adj*

afforest *v* plant trees on **afforestation** *n*

affray *n* *Brit, Aust & NZ, law* noisy fight, brawl

affront *v, n* insult

Afghan *adj* of Afghanistan or its language **Afghan hound** large slim dog with long silky hair

aficionado [af-fish-yo-**nah**-do] *n,*

pl **-dos** enthusiastic fan of something or someone
afield *adv* **far afield** far away
aflame *adj* burning
afloat *adv, adj* floating; at sea
afoot *adv, adj* happening, in operation
aforesaid, aforementioned *adj* referred to previously
aforethought *adj* premeditated *eg with malice aforethought*
Afr. Africa(n)
afraid *adj* frightened; regretful
afresh *adv* again, anew
African *adj* of Africa ▷ *n* person from Africa **African violet** house plant with pink or purple flowers and hairy leaves
Afrikaans *n* language used in S Africa, descended from Dutch
Afrikaner *n* White S African whose mother tongue is Afrikaans
Afro- *combining form* African *eg Afro-Caribbean*
aft *adv* at or towards the rear of a ship or aircraft
after *prep* following in time or place; in pursuit of; in imitation of ▷ *conj* at a later time than ▷ *adv* at a later time **afters** *pl n Brit, Informal* dessert
afterbirth *n* material expelled from the womb after childbirth
aftercare *n* support given to a person discharged from a hospital or prison; regular care required to keep something in good condition
aftereffect *n* result occurring some time after its cause
afterglow *n* glow left after a source of light has gone; pleasant feeling left after an enjoyable experience
afterlife *n* life after death
aftermath *n* results of an event considered together
afternoon *n* time between noon and evening
aftershave *n* lotion applied to the face after shaving
afterthought *n* idea occurring later; something added later
afterwards, afterward *adv* later
Ag *chem* silver
again *adv* once more; in addition
against *prep* in opposition or contrast to; in contact with; as a protection from
agape *adj* (of the mouth) wide open; (of a person) very surprised
agaric *n* fungus with gills on the underside of the cap, such as a mushroom
agate [**ag**-git] *n* semiprecious form of quartz with striped colouring
age *n* length of time a person or thing has existed; time of life; latter part of human life; period of history; long time ▷ *v* **ageing** *or* **aging, aged** make or grow old **aged** *adj* [**ay**-jid] old [rhymes with **raged**] being at the age of **ageing, aging** *n, adj* **ageless** *adj* apparently never growing old; seeming to have existed for ever **age-old** *adj* very old
agency *n, pl* **-cies** organization providing a service; business or function of an agent; *old-fashioned* power or action by which something happens
agenda *n* list of things to be dealt with, esp at a meeting
agent *n* person acting on behalf of another; person or thing producing an effect
agent provocateur [azh-**on** prov-vok-at-**tur**] *n, pl* **agents provocateurs** [azh-**on** prov-vok-at-**tur**] person employed

by the authorities to tempt people to commit illegal acts and so be discredited or punished

agglomeration *n* confused mass or cluster

aggrandize *v* make greater in size, power, or rank **aggrandizement** *n*

aggravate *v* make worse; *Chiefly Informal* annoy **aggravating** *adj* **aggravation** *n*

> SPELLING The biggest problem with spelling **aggravate** is not how many *g*s there are at the beginning, but that there is an *a* (not an *e*) in the middle

aggregate *n* total; rock consisting of a mixture of minerals; sand or gravel used to make concrete ▷ *adj* gathered into a mass; total or final ▷ *v* combine into a whole **aggregation** *n*

aggression *n* hostile behaviour; unprovoked attack **aggressive** *adj* showing aggression; forceful **aggressively** *adv* **aggressiveness** *n* **aggressor** *n*

> SPELLING Collins Word Web shows that **aggressive** is quite a common word and that *agressive* is a common way of misspelling it

aggrieved *adj* upset and angry

aggro *n Brit, Aust & NZ, slang* aggressive behaviour

aghast *adj* overcome with amazement or horror

agile *adj* nimble, quick-moving; mentally quick **agility** *n*

agitate *v* disturb or excite; stir or shake (a liquid); stir up public opinion for or against something **agitation** *n* **agitator** *n*

aglow *adj* glowing

AGM annual general meeting

agnostic *n* person who believes that it is impossible to know whether God exists ▷ *adj* of agnostics **agnosticism** *n*

ago *adv* in the past

agog *adj* eager or curious

agony *n, pl* **-nies** extreme physical or mental pain **agonize** *v* worry greatly; (cause to) suffer agony **agonizing** *adj* **agony aunt** journalist who gives advice in an agony column **agony column** newspaper or magazine feature offering advice on personal problems

agoraphobia *n* fear of open spaces **agoraphobic** *n, adj*

agrarian *adj* of land or agriculture

agree *v* **agreeing, agreed** be of the same opinion; consent; reach a joint decision; be consistent; (foll. by *with*) be suitable to (one's health or digestion) **agreeable** *adj* pleasant and enjoyable; prepared to consent **agreeably** *adv* **agreement** *n* agreeing; contract

agriculture *n* raising of crops and livestock **agricultural** *adj* **agriculturalist** *n*

agronomy [ag-**ron**-om-mee] *n* science of soil management and crop production **agronomist** *n*

aground *adv* onto the bottom of shallow water

ague [**aig**-yew] *n old-fashioned* periodic fever with shivering

ahead *adv* in front; forwards

ahoy *interj* shout used at sea to attract attention

AI artificial insemination; artificial intelligence

aid *v, n* (give) assistance or support

aide *n* assistant

aide-de-camp [aid-de-**kom**] *n, pl* **aides-de-camp** [aid-de-**kom**] military officer serving as personal assistant to a senior

AIDS acquired immunodeficiency syndrome, a viral disease that destroys the body's ability to fight infection

AIH artificial insemination by husband

ail *v* trouble, afflict; be ill **ailing** *adj* sickly **ailment** *n* illness

aileron *n* movable flap on an aircraft wing which controls rolling

aim *v* point (a weapon or missile) or direct (a blow or remark) at a target; propose or intend ▷ *n* aiming; intention, purpose **aimless** *adj* having no purpose **aimlessly** *adv*

ain't *not standard* am not; is not; are not; has not; have not

air *n* mixture of gases forming the earth's atmosphere; space above the ground, sky; breeze; quality or manner; tune ▷ *pl* affected manners ▷ *v* make known publicly; expose to air to dry or ventilate **on the air** in the act of broadcasting on radio or television **airless** *adj* stuffy **air bag** vehicle safety device which inflates automatically in a crash to protect the driver or passenger when they are thrown forward **airborne** *adj* carried by air; (of aircraft) flying **airbrush** *n* atomizer spraying paint by compressed air **airfield** *n* place where aircraft can land and take off **air force** branch of the armed forces responsible for air warfare **air gun** gun fired by compressed air **air hostess** female flight attendant **airlift** *n* transport of troops or cargo by aircraft when other routes are blocked ▷ *v* transport by airlift **airlock** *n* air bubble blocking the flow of liquid in a pipe; airtight chamber **airmail** *n* system of sending mail by aircraft; mail sent in this way **airman** *n* member of the air force **air miles** miles of free air travel that can be earned by buying airline tickets and various other products **airplay** *n* broadcast performances of a record on radio **airport** *n* airfield for civilian aircraft, with facilities for aircraft maintenance and passengers **air raid** attack by aircraft **airship** *n* lighter-than-air self-propelled aircraft **airspace** *n* atmosphere above a country, regarded as its territory **airstrip** *n* cleared area where aircraft can take off and land **airtight** *adj* sealed so that air cannot enter

air conditioning *n* system that controls the temperature and humidity of the air in a building **air conditioner**

aircraft *n* any machine that flies, such as an aeroplane **aircraft carrier** warship for the launching and landing of aircraft

airing *n* exposure to air for drying or ventilation; exposure to public debate

airline *n* company providing scheduled flights for passengers and cargo **airliner** *n* large passenger aircraft

airworthy *adj* (of aircraft) fit to fly **airworthiness** *n*

airy *adj* **airier, airiest** well-ventilated; light-hearted and casual **airily** *adv*

aisle [rhymes with **mile**] *n* passageway separating seating areas in a church, theatre, etc, or row of shelves in a supermarket

ajar *adj, adv* (of a door) partly open

akimbo *adv* **with arms akimbo** with hands on hips and elbows outwards

akin *adj* **akin to** similar, related

alabaster *n* soft white translucent stone
à la carte *adj, adv* (of a menu) having dishes individually priced
alacrity *n* speed, eagerness
à la mode *adj* fashionable
alarm *n* sudden fear caused by awareness of danger; warning sound; device that gives this; alarm clock ▷ *v* fill with fear **alarming** *adj* **alarmist** *n* person who alarms others needlessly **alarm clock** clock which sounds at a set time to wake someone up
alas *adv* unfortunately, regrettably
albatross *n* large sea bird with very long wings
albeit *conj* even though
albino *n, pl* **-nos** person or animal with white skin and hair and pink eyes
album *n* book with blank pages for keeping photographs or stamps in; CD or long-playing record
albumen *n* egg white
albumin, albumen *n* protein found in blood plasma, egg white, milk, and muscle
alchemy *n* medieval form of chemistry concerned with trying to turn base metals into gold and to find the elixir of life **alchemist** *n*
alcohol *n* colourless flammable liquid present in intoxicating drinks; intoxicating drinks generally **alcoholic** *adj* of alcohol ▷ *n* person addicted to alcohol **alcoholism** *n* addiction to alcohol
alcopop *n Brit, Aust & SAfr, Informal* alcoholic drink that tastes like a soft drink
alcove *n* recess in the wall of a room
aldehyde *n* one of a group of chemical compounds derived from alcohol by oxidation
alder *n* tree related to the birch
alderman *n* formerly, senior member of a local council
ale *n* kind of beer
alert *adj* watchful, attentive ▷ *n* warning of danger ▷ *v* warn of danger; make (someone) aware of (a fact) **on the alert** watchful **alertness** *n*
alfalfa *n* kind of plant used to feed livestock
alfresco *adv, adj* in the open air
algae [al-jee] *pl n* plants which live in or near water and have no true stems, leaves, or roots
algebra *n* branch of mathematics using symbols to represent numbers **algebraic** *adj*
ALGOL *n computers* programming language for mathematical and scientific purposes
algorithm *n* logical arithmetical or computational procedure for solving a problem
alias *adv* also known as ▷ *n* false name
alibi *n* plea of being somewhere else when a crime was committed; *Informal* excuse
alien *adj* foreign; repugnant (to); from another world ▷ *n* foreigner; being from another world **alienate** *v* cause to become hostile **alienation** *n*
alight[1] *v* step out of (a vehicle); land
alight[2] *adj* on fire; lit up
align [a-line] *v* bring (a person or group) into agreement with the policy of another; place in a line **alignment** *n*
alike *adj* like, similar ▷ *adv* in the same way
alimentary *adj* of nutrition **alimentary canal** food passage in the body

alimony *n* allowance paid under a court order to a separated or divorced spouse

A-line *adj* (of a skirt) slightly flared

aliquot *maths* ▷ *adj* of or denoting an exact divisor of a number ▷ *n* exact divisor

alive *adj* living, in existence; lively **alive to** aware of **alive with** swarming with

alkali [alk-a-lie] *n* substance which combines with acid and neutralizes it to form a salt **alkaline** *adj* **alkalinity** *n* **alkaloid** *n* any of a group of organic compounds containing nitrogen

all *adj* whole quantity or number (of) ▷ *adv* wholly, entirely; (in the score of games) each **give one's all** make the greatest possible effort **all in** *adj* exhausted; (of wrestling) with no style forbidden ▷ *adv* with all expenses included **all right** *adj* adequate, satisfactory; unharmed ▷ *interj* expression of approval or agreement **all-rounder** *n* person with ability in many fields

Allah *n* name of God in Islam

allay *v* reduce (fear or anger)

allege *v* state without proof **alleged** *adj* **allegedly** *adv* **allegation** *n* unproved accusation

allegiance *n* loyalty to a person, country, or cause

allegory *n, pl* **-ries** story with an underlying meaning as well as the literal one **allegorical** *adj*

allegretto *n, pl* **-tos,** *adv music* (piece to be played) fairly quickly or briskly

allegro *n, pl* **-gros,** *adv music* (piece to be played) in a brisk lively manner

alleluia *interj* same as **hallelujah**

allergy *n, pl* **-gies** extreme sensitivity to a substance, which causes the body to react to it **allergic** *adj* having or caused by an allergy **allergen** *n* substance capable of causing an allergic reaction

alleviate *v* lessen (pain or suffering) **alleviation** *n*

alley *n* narrow street or path; long narrow enclosure in which tenpin bowling or skittles is played

alliance *n* state of being allied; formal relationship between countries or groups for a shared purpose

alligator *n* reptile of the crocodile family, found in the southern US and China

alliteration *n* use of the same sound at the start of words occurring together, eg *moody music* **alliterative** *adj*

allocate *v* assign to someone or for a particular purpose **allocation** *n*

allot *v* **-lotting, -lotted** assign as a share or for a particular purpose **allotment** *n* distribution; portion allotted; small piece of public land rented to grow vegetables on

allotrope *n* any of two or more physical forms in which an element can exist

allow *v* permit; set aside; acknowledge (a point or claim) **allow for** *v* take into account **allowable** *adj* **allowance** *n* amount of money given at regular intervals; amount permitted **make allowances for** treat or judge (someone) less severely because he or she has special problems; take into account

alloy *n* mixture of two or more metals ▷ *v* mix (metals)

allspice *n* spice made from the berries of a tropical American tree

allude *v* (foll. by *to*) refer indirectly to **allusion** *n* indirect reference **allusive** *adj*

allure *n* attractiveness ▷ *v* entice or attract **alluring** *adj*

alluvium *n* fertile soil deposited by flowing water **alluvial** *adj*

ally *n, pl* **-lies** country, person, or group with an agreement to support another ▷ *v* **-lying, -lied** **ally oneself with** join as an ally **allied** *adj*

alma mater *n* school, university, or college that one attended

almanac *n* yearly calendar with detailed information on anniversaries, phases of the moon, etc

almighty *adj* having absolute power; *Informal* very great ▷ *n* **the Almighty** God

almond *n* edible oval-shaped nut which grows on a small tree

almoner *n Brit* formerly, a hospital social worker

almost *adv* very nearly

alms [ahmz] *pl n old-fashioned* gifts to the poor

aloe *n* plant with fleshy spiny leaves ▷ *pl* bitter drug made from aloe leaves

aloft *adv* in the air; in a ship's rigging

alone *adj, adv* without anyone or anything else

along *prep* over part or all the length of ▷ *adv* forward; in company with others **alongside** *prep, adv* beside (something)

aloof *adj* distant or haughty in manner **aloofness** *n*

alopecia [al-loh-**pee**-sha] *n* loss of hair

aloud *adv* in an audible voice

alpaca *n* Peruvian llama; wool or cloth made from its hair

alpenstock *n* iron-tipped stick used by climbers

alpha *n* first letter in the Greek alphabet **alpha male** dominant male animal or person in a group

alphabet *n* set of letters used in writing a language **alphabetical** *adj* in the conventional order of the letters of an alphabet **alphabetically** *adv* **alphabetize** *v* put in alphabetical order

alpine *adj* of high mountains; (**A-**) of the Alps ▷ *n* mountain plant

already *adv* before the present time; sooner than expected

alright *adj, interj* all right

Alsatian *n* large wolflike dog

also *adv* in addition, too **also-ran** *n* loser in a race, competition, or election

alt. *combining form Informal* alternative: *alt.rock*

altar *n* table used for Communion in Christian churches; raised structure on which sacrifices are offered and religious rites are performed **altarpiece** *n* work of art above and behind the altar in some Christian churches

alter *v* make or become different **alteration** *n*

altercation *n* heated argument

alter ego *n* second self; very close friend

alternate *v* (cause to) occur by turns ▷ *adj* occurring by turns; every second (one) of a series **alternately** *adv* **alternation** *n* **alternator** *n* electric generator for producing alternating current **alternating current** electric current that reverses direction at frequent regular intervals

alternative *n* one of two choices ▷ *adj* able to be done or used instead of something else; (of

medicine, lifestyle, etc) not conventional **alternatively** *adv*
although *conj* despite the fact that
altimeter [al-**tim**-it-er] *n* instrument that measures altitude
altitude *n* height above sea level
alto *n, pl* **-tos** *music* short for **contralto:** (singer with) the highest adult male voice; instrument with the second-highest pitch in its group
altogether *adv* entirely; on the whole; in total
altruism *n* unselfish concern for the welfare of others **altruistic** *adj* **altruistically** *adv*
aluminium *n chem* light silvery-white metal that does not rust
alumnus [al-**lumm**-nuss] *n, pl* **-ni** [-nie] graduate of a college **alumna** [al-**lumm**-na] *n fem, pl* **-nae** [-nee]
always *adv* at all times; for ever
alyssum *n* garden plant with small yellow or white flowers
am *v* see **be**
AM amplitude modulation; (in Britain) Member of the National Assembly for Wales
a.m. ante meridiem: before noon
amalgam *n* blend or combination; alloy of mercury and another metal
amalgamate *v* combine or unite **amalgamation** *n*
amandla [ah-**mand**-lah] *n SAfr* political slogan calling for power to the Black population
amanuensis [am-man-yew-**en**-siss] *n, pl* **-ses** [-seez] person who writes from dictation
amaranth *n* imaginary flower that never fades; lily-like plant with red, green, or purple flowers
amaryllis *n* lily-like plant with large red, pink, or white flowers
amass *v* collect or accumulate
amateur *n* person who engages in a sport or activity as a pastime rather than as a profession; person unskilled in something ▷ *adj* not professional **amateurish** *adj* lacking skill **amateurishly** *adv*
amatory *adj* relating to romantic or sexual love
amaze *v* surprise greatly, astound **amazing** *adj* **amazingly** *adv* **amazement** *n*
Amazon *n* strong and powerful woman; legendary female warrior **Amazonian** *adj*
ambassador *n* senior diplomat who represents his or her country in another country **ambassadorial** *adj*
amber *n* clear yellowish fossil resin ▷ *adj* brownish-yellow
ambergris [**am**-ber-greece] *n* waxy substance secreted by the sperm whale, used in making perfumes
ambidextrous *adj* able to use both hands with equal ease
ambience *n* atmosphere of a place
ambient *adj* surrounding
ambiguous *adj* having more than one possible meaning **ambiguously** *adv* **ambiguity** *n*
ambit *n* limits or boundary
ambition *n* desire for success; something so desired, goal **ambitious** *adj* **ambitiously** *adv*
ambivalence *n* state of feeling two conflicting emotions at the same time **ambivalent** *adj* **ambivalently** *adv*
amble *v* walk at a leisurely pace ▷ *n* leisurely walk or pace
ambrosia *n myth* food of the gods

ambrosial *adj*
ambulance *n* motor vehicle designed to carry sick or injured people
ambush *n* act of waiting in a concealed position to make a surprise attack; attack from a concealed position ▷*v* attack from a concealed position
ameliorate [am-**meal**-yor-rate] *v* make (something) better **amelioration** *n*
amen *interj* so be it: used at the end of a prayer
amenable *adj* likely or willing to cooperate
amend *v* make small changes to correct or improve (something) **amendment** *n*
amends *pl n* **make amends for** compensate for
amenity *n, pl* **-ties** useful or enjoyable feature
American *adj* of the United States of America or the American continent ▷*n* person from America or the American continent **Americanism** *n* expression or custom characteristic of Americans
amethyst [**am**-myth-ist] *n* bluish-violet variety of quartz used as a gemstone
amiable *adj* friendly, pleasant-natured **amiably** *adv* **amiability** *n*
amicable *adj* friendly **amicably** *adv*
amid, amidst *prep* in the middle of, among **amidships** *adv* at or towards the middle of a ship
amino acid [am-**mean**-oh] *n* organic compound found in protein
amiss *adv* wrongly, badly ▷*adj* wrong, faulty **take something amiss** be offended by something
amity *n* friendship
ammeter *n* instrument for measuring electric current
ammonia *n* strong-smelling alkaline gas containing hydrogen and nitrogen; solution of this in water
ammonite *n* fossilized spiral shell of an extinct sea creature
ammunition *n* bullets, bombs, and shells that can be fired from or as a weapon; facts that can be used in an argument
amnesia *n* loss of memory **amnesiac** *adj, n*
amnesty *n, pl* **-ties** general pardon for offences against a government
amniocentesis *n, pl* **-ses** removal of some amniotic fluid to test for possible abnormalities in a fetus
amniotic fluid *n* fluid surrounding a fetus in the womb
amoeba [am-**mee**-ba] *n, pl* **-bae, -bas** microscopic single-celled animal able to change its shape
amok [a-**muck**, a-**mock**] *adv* **run amok** run about in a violent frenzy
among, amongst *prep* in the midst of; in the group or number of; to each of *eg divide it among yourselves*
amoral [aim-**mor**-ral] *adj* without moral standards **amorality** *n*
amorous *adj* feeling, showing, or relating to sexual love **amorously** *adv*
amorphous *adj* without distinct shape
amortize *v* pay off (a debt) gradually by periodic transfers to a sinking fund
amount *n* extent or quantity ▷*v* (foll. by *to*) be equal or add up to
amour *n* (secret) love affair
amp *n* ampere; *Informal* amplifier
ampere [**am**-pair] *n* basic unit of

electric current
ampersand *n* the character (&), meaning *and*
amphetamine [am-**fet**-am-mean] *n* drug used as a stimulant
amphibian *n* animal that lives on land but breeds in water; vehicle that can travel on both land and water **amphibious** *adj* living or operating both on land and in water
amphitheatre *n* open oval or circular building with tiers of seats rising round an arena
amphora [**am**-for-ra] *n, pl* **-phorae** two-handled ancient Greek or Roman jar
ample *adj* more than sufficient; large **amply** *adv*
amplifier *n* device used to amplify a current or sound signal
amplify *v* **-fying, -fied** increase the strength of (a current or sound signal); explain in more detail; increase the size or effect of **amplification** *n*
amplitude *n* greatness of extent
ampoule *n* small sealed glass vessel containing liquid for injection
amputate *v* cut off (a limb or part of a limb) for medical reasons **amputation** *n*
amuck *adv* same as **amok**
amulet *n* something carried or worn as a protection against evil
amuse *v* cause to laugh or smile; entertain or divert **amusing** *adj* **amusement** *n* state of being amused; something that amuses
an *adj* form of **a** used before vowels, and sometimes before *h*
anabolic steroid *n* synthetic steroid hormone used to stimulate muscle and bone growth
anachronism [an-**nak**-kron-iz-zum] *n* person or thing placed in the wrong historical period or seeming to belong to another time **anachronistic** *adj*
anaconda *n* large S American snake which kills by constriction
anaemia [an-**neem**-ee-a] *n* deficiency in the number of red blood cells **anaemic** *adj* having anaemia; pale and sickly; lacking vitality
anaesthetic [an-niss-**thet**-ik] *n, adj* (substance) causing loss of bodily feeling **anaesthesia** [an-niss-**theez**-ee-a] *n* loss of bodily feeling **anaesthetist** [an-**neess**-thet-ist] *n* doctor trained to administer anaesthetics **anaesthetize** *v*
anagram *n* word or phrase made by rearranging the letters of another word or phrase
anal [**ain**-al] *adj* of the anus
analgesic [an-nal-**jeez**-ik] *n, adj* (drug) relieving pain **analgesia** *n* absence of pain
analogous *adj* similar in some respects
analogue *n* something that is similar in some respects to something else ▷ *adj* displaying information by means of a dial
analogy *n, pl* **-gies** similarity in some respects; comparison made to show such a similarity **analogical** *adj*
analysis *n, pl* **-ses** separation of a whole into its parts for study and interpretation; psychoanalysis **analyse** *v* make an analysis of (something); psychoanalyse **analyst** *n* person skilled in analysis **analytical, analytic** *adj* **analytically** *adv*
anarchism *n* doctrine advocating the abolition of government
anarchist *n* person who

advocates the abolition of government; person who causes disorder **anarchistic** *adj*

anarchy [**an**-ark-ee] *n* lawlessness and disorder; lack of government in a state **anarchic** *adj*

anathema [an-**nath**-im-a] *n* detested person or thing

anatomy *n, pl* **-mies** science of the structure of the body; physical structure; person's body; detailed analysis **anatomical** *adj* **anatomically** *adv* **anatomist** *n* expert in anatomy

ANC African National Congress

ancestor *n* person from whom one is descended; forerunner **ancestral** *adj* **ancestry** *n* lineage or descent

anchor *n* heavy hooked device attached to a boat by a cable and dropped overboard to fasten the ship to the sea bottom ▷ *v* fasten with or as if with an anchor **anchorage** *n* place where boats can be anchored **anchorman, anchorwoman** *n* broadcaster in a central studio who links up and presents items from outside camera units and other studios; last person to compete in a relay team

anchorite *n* religious recluse

anchovy [**an**-chov-ee] *n, pl* **-vies** small strong-tasting fish

ancient *adj* dating from very long ago; very old **ancients** *pl n* people who lived very long ago

ancillary *adj* supporting the main work of an organization; used as an extra or supplement

and *conj* in addition to; as a consequence; then, afterwards

andante [an-**dan**-tay] *n, adv music* (piece to be played) moderately slowly

andiron *n* iron stand for supporting logs in a fireplace

androgynous *adj* having both male and female characteristics

android *n* robot resembling a human

anecdote *n* short amusing account of an incident **anecdotal** *adj*

anemometer *n* instrument for recording wind speed

anemone [an-**nem**-on-ee] *n* plant with white, purple, or red flowers

aneroid barometer *n* device for measuring air pressure, consisting of a partially evacuated chamber in which variations in pressure cause a pointer on the lid to move

aneurysm, aneurism [**an**-new-riz-zum] *n* permanent swelling of a blood vessel

anew *adv* once more; in a different way

angel *n* spiritual being believed to be an attendant or messenger of God; person who is kind, pure, or beautiful **angelic** *adj* **angelically** *adv*

angelica *n* aromatic plant; its candied stalks, used in cookery

Angelus [**an**-jell-uss] *n* (in the Roman Catholic Church) prayers recited in the morning, at midday, and in the evening; bell signalling the times of these prayers

anger *n* fierce displeasure or extreme annoyance ▷ *v* make (someone) angry

angina [an-**jine**-a] *n* heart disorder causing sudden severe chest pains (also **angina pectoris**)

angle[1] *n* space between or shape formed by two lines or surfaces that meet; divergence between these, measured in degrees; corner; point of view ▷ *v* bend or place (something) at an angle

angle² *v* fish with a hook and line; (foll. by *for*) try to get by hinting **angling** *n*
angler *n* person who fishes with a hook and line
Anglican *n, adj* (member) of the Church of England **Anglicanism** *n*
anglicize *v* make or become English in outlook, form, etc
Anglo- *combining form* English *eg Anglo-Scottish*; British *eg Anglo-American*
Anglo-Saxon *n* member of any of the W Germanic tribes that settled in England from the fifth century AD; language of the Anglo-Saxons ▷ *adj* of the Anglo-Saxons or their language
angophora *n* Australian tree related to the eucalyptus
angora *n* variety of goat, cat, or rabbit with long silky hair; hair of the angora goat or rabbit; cloth made from this hair
Angostura Bitters *pl n* ® bitter tonic, used as a flavouring in alcoholic drinks
angry *adj* **-grier, -griest** full of anger; inflamed *eg an angry wound* **angrily** *adv*
angst *n* feeling of anxiety
angstrom *n* unit of length used to measure wavelengths
anguish *n* great mental pain **anguished** *adj*
angular *adj* (of a person) lean and bony; having angles; measured by an angle **angularity** *n*
anhydrous *adj chem* containing no water
aniline *n* colourless oily liquid obtained from coal tar and used for making dyes, plastics, and explosives
animal *n* living creature with specialized sense organs and capable of voluntary motion, esp one other than a human being; quadruped ▷ *adj* of animals; sensual, physical
animate *v* give life to; make lively; make a cartoon film of ▷ *adj* having life **animated** *adj* **animation** *n* technique of making cartoon films; liveliness and enthusiasm **animator** *n*
animism *n* belief that natural objects possess souls **animist** *n, adj* **animistic** *adj*
animosity *n, pl* **-ties** hostility, hatred
animus *n* hatred, animosity
anion [an-eye-on] *n* ion with negative charge
anise [an-niss] *n* plant with liquorice-flavoured seeds
aniseed *n* liquorice-flavoured seeds of the anise plant
ankle *n* joint between the foot and leg **anklet** *n* ornamental chain worn round the ankle
annals *pl n* yearly records of events
anneal *v* toughen (metal or glass) by heating and slow cooling
annelid *n* worm with a segmented body, such as an earthworm
annex *v* seize (territory); take (something) without permission; join or add (something) to something larger **annexation** *n*
annexe *n* extension to a building; nearby building used as an extension
annihilate *v* destroy utterly **annihilation** *n*
anniversary *n, pl* **-ries** date on which something occurred in a previous year; celebration of this
anno Domini [an-no **dom**-in-eye] *adv Latin* (indicating years numbered from the supposed year of the birth of Christ) in the year of

our Lord
annotate *v* add notes to (a written work) **annotation** *n*
announce *v* make known publicly; proclaim **announcement** *n* **announcer** *n* person who introduces radio or television programmes
annoy *v* irritate or displease **annoyance** *n*
annual *adj* happening once a year; lasting for a year ▷ *n* plant that completes its life cycle in a year; book published once every year **annually** *adv*
annuity *n, pl* **-ties** fixed sum paid every year
annul *v* **-nulling, -nulled** declare (something, esp a marriage) invalid **annulment** *n*
annular [an-new-lar] *adj* ring-shaped
Annunciation *n Christianity* angel Gabriel's announcement to the Virgin Mary of her conception of Christ
anode *n electricity* positive electrode in a battery, valve, etc **anodize** *v* coat (metal) with a protective oxide film by electrolysis
anodyne *n* something that relieves pain or distress ▷ *adj* relieving pain or distress
anoint *v* smear with oil as a sign of consecration
anomaly [an-**nom**-a-lee] *n, pl* **-lies** something that deviates from the normal, irregularity **anomalous** *adj*
anon *adv obs* in a short time, soon
anon. anonymous
anonymous *adj* by someone whose name is unknown or withheld; having no known name **anonymously** *adv* **anonymity** *n*
anorak *n* light waterproof hooded jacket
anorexia *n* psychological disorder characterized by fear of becoming fat and refusal to eat (also **anorexia nervosa**) **anorexic** *adj, n*
another *adj, pron* one more; different (one)
answer *n* reply to a question, request, letter, etc; solution to a problem; reaction or response ▷ *v* give an answer (to); be responsible to (a person); respond or react **answerable** *adj* (foll. by *for, to*) responsible for or accountable to **answering machine** device for answering a telephone automatically and recording messages
ant *n* small insect living in highly organized colonies **anteater** *n* mammal which feeds on ants by means of a long snout; same as **echidna, numbat** **ant hill** mound built by ants around their nest
antacid *n* substance that counteracts acidity, esp in the stomach
antagonist *n* opponent or adversary **antagonism** *n* open opposition or hostility **antagonistic** *adj* **antagonize** *v* arouse hostility in, annoy
Antarctic *n* **the Antarctic** area around the South Pole ▷ *adj* of this region

SPELLING Almost one in every hundred references to the **Antarctic** in Collins Word Web is written without its first *c* as *Antartic*. Note there is a *c* after the *r*

ante *n* player's stake in poker ▷ *v* **-teing, -ted** *or* **-teed** place (one's stake) in poker
ante- *prefix* before in time or position *eg antedate; antechamber*

antecedent *n* event or circumstance happening or existing before another ▷*adj* preceding, prior
antedate *v* precede in time
antediluvian *adj* of the time before the biblical Flood; old-fashioned
antelope *n* deerlike mammal with long legs and horns
antenatal *adj* during pregnancy, before birth
antenna *n, pl* **-nae** insect's feeler *pl* **-nas** aerial
anterior *adj* to the front; earlier
anteroom *n* small room leading into a larger one, often used as a waiting room
anthem *n* song of loyalty, esp to a country; piece of choral music, usu set to words from the Bible
anther *n* part of a flower's stamen containing pollen
anthology *n, pl* **-gies** collection of poems or other literary pieces by various authors **anthologist** *n*
anthracite *n* hard coal burning slowly with little smoke or flame but intense heat
anthrax *n* dangerous disease of cattle and sheep, communicable to humans
anthropoid *adj* like a human ▷*n* ape, such as a chimpanzee, that resembles a human
anthropology *n* study of human origins, institutions, and beliefs **anthropological** *adj* **anthropologist** *n*
anthropomorphic *adj* attributing human form or personality to a god, animal, or object **anthropomorphism** *n*
anti- *prefix* against, opposed to *eg anti-war*; opposite to *eg anticlimax*; counteracting *eg antifreeze*
anti-aircraft *adj* for defence against aircraft attack
antibiotic *n* chemical substance capable of destroying bacteria ▷*adj* of antibiotics
antibody *n, pl* **-bodies** protein produced in the blood, which destroys bacteria
anticipate *v* foresee and act in advance of; look forward to **anticipation** *n* **anticipatory** *adj*
anticlimax *n* disappointing conclusion to a series of events
anticlockwise *adv, adj* in the opposite direction to the rotation of the hands of a clock
antics *pl n* absurd acts or postures
anticyclone *n* area of moving air of high pressure in which the winds rotate outwards
antidote *n* substance that counteracts a poison
antifreeze *n* liquid added to water to lower its freezing point, used esp in car radiators
antigen [**an**-tee-jen] *n* substance, usu a toxin, causing the blood to produce antibodies
anti-globalization *n* opposition to globalization
antihero *n, pl* **-roes** central character in a book, film, etc, who lacks the traditional heroic virtues
antihistamine *n* drug used to treat allergies
antimacassar *n* cloth put over a chair-back to prevent soiling
antimony *n chem* brittle silvery-white metallic element
antipathy [an-**tip**-a-thee] *n* dislike, hostility **antipathetic** *adj*
antiperspirant *n* substance used to reduce or prevent sweating
antiphon *n* hymn sung in alternate parts by two groups of singers **antiphonal** *adj*

antipodes [an-**tip**-pod-deez] *pl n* any two places diametrically opposite one another on the earth's surface **the Antipodes** Australia and New Zealand **antipodean** *adj*
antipyretic *adj* reducing fever ▷*n* drug that reduces fever
antiquary *n, pl* **-quaries** student or collector of antiques or ancient works of art **antiquarian** *adj* of or relating to antiquities or rare books ▷*n* antiquary
antiquated *adj* out-of-date
antique *n* object of an earlier period, valued for its beauty, workmanship, or age ▷*adj* made in an earlier period; old-fashioned
antiquity *n* great age; ancient times **antiquities** *pl n* objects dating from ancient times
antiracism *n* policy of challenging racism and promoting racial tolerance
antirrhinum *n* two-lipped flower of various colours
anti-Semitism *n* discrimination against Jews **anti-Semitic** *adj*
antiseptic *adj* preventing infection by killing germs ▷*n* antiseptic substance
antisocial *adj* avoiding the company of other people; (of behaviour) harmful to society
antistatic *adj* reducing the effects of static electricity
antithesis [an-**tith**-iss-iss] *n, pl* **-ses** [-seez] exact opposite; placing together of contrasting ideas or words to produce an effect of balance **antithetical** *adj*
antitoxin *n* (serum containing) an antibody that acts against a toxin
antitrust *adj Aust & SAfr* (of laws) opposing business monopolies
antler *n* branched horn of male deer
antonym *n* word that means the opposite of another
anus [**ain**-uss] *n* opening at the end of the alimentary canal, through which faeces are discharged
anvil *n* heavy iron block on which metals are hammered into particular shapes
anxiety *n, pl* **-ties** state of being anxious
anxious *adj* worried and tense; intensely desiring **anxiously** *adv*
any *adj, pron* one or some, no matter which ▷*adv* at all *eg it isn't any worse* **anybody** *pron* anyone **anyhow** *adv* anyway **anyone** *pron* any person; person of any importance **anything** *pron* **anyway** *adv* at any rate, nevertheless; in any manner **anywhere** *adv* in, at, or to any place
Anzac *n* (in World War 1) a soldier serving with the Australian and New Zealand Army Corps **Anzac Day** 25th April, a public holiday in Australia and New Zealand commemorating the Anzac landing at Gallipoli in 1915
AOB (on the agenda for a meeting) any other business
aorta [eh-**or**-ta] *n* main artery of the body, carrying oxygen-rich blood from the heart
apace *adv lit* swiftly
apart *adv* to or in pieces; to or at a distance; individual, distinct
apartheid *n* former official government policy of racial segregation in S Africa
apartment *n* room in a building; flat
apathy *n* lack of interest or enthusiasm **apathetic** *adj*
ape *n* tailless monkey such as the chimpanzee or gorilla; stupid, clumsy, or ugly man ▷*v* imitate
aperient [ap-**peer**-ee-ent] *adj*

having a mild laxative effect ▷ *n* mild laxative
aperitif [ap-per-rit-**teef**] *n* alcoholic drink taken before a meal
aperture *n* opening or hole
apex *n* highest point
APEX *Brit, NZ & SAfr* Advance Purchase Excursion: reduced fare for journeys booked a specified period in advance
aphasia *n* disorder of the central nervous system that affects the ability to speak and understand words
aphid [**eh**-fid] **aphis** [**eh**-fiss] *n* small insect which sucks the sap from plants
aphorism *n* short clever saying expressing a general truth
aphrodisiac [af-roh-**diz**-zee-ak] *n* substance that arouses sexual desire ▷ *adj* arousing sexual desire
apiary *n, pl* **-ries** place where bees are kept
apiculture *n* breeding and care of bees
apiece *adv* each
aplomb *n* calm self-possession
apocalypse *n* end of the world; event of great destruction **the Apocalypse** book of Revelation, the last book of the New Testament **apocalyptic** *adj*
Apocrypha [ap-**pok**-rif-fa] *pl n* **the Apocrypha** collective name for the 14 books of the Old Testament which are not accepted as part of the Hebrew scriptures
apocryphal [ap-**pok**-rif-al] *adj* (of a story) of questionable authenticity
apogee [**ap**-oh-jee] *n* point of the moon's or a satellite's orbit that is farthest from the earth; highest point
apology *n, pl* **-gies** expression of regret for wrongdoing; (foll. by *for*) poor example (of) **apologetic** *adj* showing or expressing regret **apologetically** *adv* **apologetics** *n* branch of theology concerned with the reasoned defence of Christianity **apologist** *n* person who formally defends a cause **apologize** *v* make an apology

> SPELLING Remember that the correct way to spell **apology** is with one *p* and one *l*

apoplexy *n med* stroke **apoplectic** *adj* of apoplexy; *Informal* furious
apostasy [ap-**poss**-stass-ee] *n, pl* **-sies** abandonment of one's religious faith or other belief **apostate** *n, adj*
a posteriori [eh poss-steer-ee-**or**-rye] *adj* involving reasoning from effect to cause
Apostle *n* one of the twelve disciples chosen by Christ to preach his gospel; (**a-**) ardent supporter of a cause or movement **apostolic** *adj*
apostrophe [ap-**poss**-trof-fee] *n* punctuation mark (') showing the omission of a letter or letters in a word, eg *don't*, or forming the possessive, eg *Jill's car*; digression from a speech to address an imaginary or absent person or thing
apothecary *n, pl* **-caries** *obs* chemist
apotheosis [ap-poth-ee-**oh**-siss] *n, pl* **-ses** [-seez] perfect example; elevation to the rank of a god
appal *v* **-palling, -palled** dismay, terrify **appalling** *adj* dreadful, terrible

> SPELLING The verb **appal** has two *p*s, but only one *l*. If you extend it with an ending beginning with a vowel, you must add another *l*, as in **appalling**

apparatus *n* equipment for a particular purpose
apparel *n old-fashioned* clothing
apparent *adj* readily seen, obvious; seeming as opposed to real **apparently** *adv*

> **SPELLING** It's quite common to spell **apparently** with three *a*s, but there should only be two - and then an *e*

apparition *n* ghost or ghostlike figure
appeal *v* make an earnest request; attract, please, or interest; request a review of a lower court's decision by a higher court ▷*n* earnest request; attractiveness; request for a review of a lower court's decision by a higher court **appealing** *adj*
appear *v* become visible or present; seem; be seen in public **appearance** *n* appearing; outward aspect
appease *v* pacify (a person) by yielding to his or her demands; satisfy or relieve (a feeling) **appeasement** *n*
appellant *n* person who makes an appeal to a higher court
appellation *n formal* name, title
append *v* join on, add **appendage** *n* thing joined on or added
appendicitis *n* inflammation of the appendix
appendix *n, pl* **-dices, -dixes** separate additional material at the end of a book; *anat* short closed tube attached to the large intestine.

> Extra sections at the end of a book are *appendices*. The plural *appendixes* is used in medicine

appertain *v* (foll. by *to*) belong to; be connected with
appetite *n* desire for food or drink; liking or willingness **appetizer** *n* thing eaten or drunk to stimulate the appetite **appetizing** *adj* stimulating the appetite
applaud *v* show approval of by clapping one's hands; approve strongly **applause** *n* approval shown by clapping one's hands
apple *n* round firm fleshy fruit that grows on trees **in apple-pie order** *Informal* very tidy
appliance *n* device with a specific function
applicable *adj* relevant, appropriate **applicability** *n*
applicant *n* person who applies for something
application *n* formal request; act of applying something to a particular use; diligent effort; act of putting something onto a surface
appliqué [ap-**plee**-kay] *n* kind of decoration in which one material is cut out and attached to another
apply *v* **-plying, -plied** make a formal request; put to practical use; put onto a surface; be relevant or appropriate **apply oneself** concentrate one's efforts **applied** *adj* (of a skill, science, etc) put to practical use
appoint *v* assign to a job or position; fix or decide *eg appoint a time*; equip or furnish **appointment** *n* arrangement to meet a person; act of placing someone in a job; the job itself ▷*pl* fixtures or fittings
apportion *v* divide out in shares
apposite *adj* suitable, apt **apposition** *n* grammatical construction in which two nouns or phrases referring to the same thing are placed one after another without a conjunction *eg my son the doctor*

appraise *v* estimate the value or quality of **appraisal** *n*

appreciate *v* value highly; be aware of and understand; be grateful for; rise in value **appreciable** *adj* enough to be noticed **appreciably** *adv* **appreciation** *n* **appreciative** *adj* feeling or showing appreciation

apprehend *v* arrest and take into custody; grasp (something) mentally **apprehension** *n* dread, anxiety; arrest; understanding **apprehensive** *adj* fearful or anxious

apprentice *n* someone working for a skilled person for a fixed period in order to learn his or her trade ▷ *v* take or place (someone) as an apprentice **apprenticeship** *n*

apprise *v* make aware (of)

appro *n* **on appro** *Brit, Aust, NZ & SAfr, Informal* on approval

approach *v* come near or nearer (to); make a proposal or suggestion to; begin to deal with (a matter) ▷ *n* approaching or means of approaching; approximation **approachable** *adj* **approach road** smaller road leading into a major road

approbation *n* approval

appropriate *adj* suitable, fitting ▷ *v* take for oneself; put aside for a particular purpose **appropriately** *adv* **appropriateness** *n* **appropriation** *n*

approve *v* consider good or right; authorize, agree to **approval** *n* consent; favourable opinion **on approval** (of goods) with an option to be returned without payment if unsatisfactory

approx. approximate(ly)

approximate *adj* almost but not quite exact ▷ *v* (foll. by *to*) come close to; be almost the same as **approximately** *adv* **approximation** *n*

appurtenances *pl n* minor or additional features

Apr. April

après-ski [ap-ray-**skee**] *n* social activities after a day's skiing

apricot *n* yellowish-orange juicy fruit like a small peach ▷ *adj* yellowish-orange

April *n* fourth month of the year **April fool** victim of a practical joke played on April 1 (**April Fools' Day**)

a priori [**eh** pry-**or**-rye] *adj* involving reasoning from cause to effect

apron *n* garment worn over the front of the body to protect the clothes; area at an airport or hangar for manoeuvring and loading aircraft; part of a stage in front of the curtain

apropos [ap-prop-**poh**] *adj, adv* appropriate(ly) **apropos of** with regard to

apse *n* arched or domed recess, esp in a church

apt *adj* having a specified tendency; suitable; quick to learn **aptly** *adv* **aptness** *n* **aptitude** *n* natural ability

aqualung *n* mouthpiece attached to air cylinders, worn for underwater swimming

aquamarine *n* greenish-blue gemstone ▷ *adj* greenish-blue

aquaplane *n* board on which a person stands to be towed by a motorboat ▷ *v* ride on an aquaplane; (of a motor vehicle) skim uncontrollably on a thin film of water

aquarium *n, pl* **aquariums, aquaria** tank in which fish and other underwater creatures are kept; building containing such tanks

aquatic *adj* living in or near water; done in or on water **aquatics** *pl n* water sports

aquatint *n* print like a watercolour, produced by etching copper

aqua vitae [ak-wa **vee**-tie] *n obs* brandy

aqueduct *n* structure carrying water across a valley or river

aqueous *adj* of, like, or containing water

aquiline *adj* (of a nose) curved like an eagle's beak; of or like an eagle

Arab *n* member of a Semitic people originally from Arabia ▷ *adj* of the Arabs **Arabic** *n* language of the Arabs ▷ *adj* of Arabic, Arabs, or Arabia

arabesque [ar-ab-**besk**] *n* ballet position in which one leg is raised behind and the arms are extended; elaborate ornamental design

arable *adj* suitable for growing crops on

arachnid [ar-**rak**-nid] *n* eight-legged invertebrate, such as a spider, scorpion, tick, or mite

Aran *adj* (of sweaters etc) knitted in a complicated pattern traditional to the Aran Islands, usu with natural unbleached wool

arbiter *n* person empowered to judge in a dispute; person with influential opinions about something

arbitrary *adj* based on personal choice or chance, rather than reason **arbitrarily** *adv*

> SPELLING The spelling *arbitary* appears 22 times in Collins Word Web. But the correct spelling, **arbitrary** appears 1959 times: it has three *r*s

arbitration *n* hearing and settling of a dispute by an impartial referee chosen by both sides **arbitrate** *v* **arbitrator** *n*

arboreal *adj* of or living in trees

arboretum [ahr-bore-**ee**-tum] *n*, *pl* **-ta** place where rare trees or shrubs are cultivated

arboriculture *n* cultivation of trees or shrubs

arbour *n* glade sheltered by trees

arc *n* part of a circle or other curve; luminous discharge of electricity across a small gap between two electrodes ▷ *v* form an arc

arcade *n* covered passageway lined with shops; set of arches and their supporting columns

arcane *adj* mysterious and secret

arch[1] *n* curved structure supporting a bridge or roof; something curved; curved lower part of the foot ▷ *v* (cause to) form an arch **archway** *n* passageway under an arch

arch[2] *adj* superior, knowing; coyly playful **archly** *adv* **archness** *n*

arch- *combining form* chief, principal *eg archenemy*

archaeology *n* study of ancient cultures from their physical remains **archaeological** *adj* **archaeologist** *n*

archaic [ark-**kay**-ik] *adj* ancient; out-of-date **archaism** [**ark**-kay-iz-zum] *n* archaic word or phrase

archangel [**ark**-ain-jell] *n* chief angel

archbishop *n* chief bishop

archdeacon *n* priest ranking just below a bishop

archdiocese *n* diocese of an archbishop

archer *n* person who shoots with a bow and arrow **archery** *n*

archetype [**ark**-ee-type] *n* perfect specimen; original model **archetypal** *adj*
archipelago [ark-ee-**pel**-a-go] *n, pl* **-gos** group of islands; sea full of small islands
architect *n* person qualified to design and supervise the construction of buildings **architecture** *n* style in which a building is designed and built; designing and construction of buildings **architectural** *adj*
architrave *n archit* beam that rests on columns; moulding round a doorway or window
archive [**ark**-ive] *n* (often pl) collection of records or documents; place where these are kept **archival** *adj* **archivist** [**ark**-iv-ist] *n* person in charge of archives
Arctic *n* **the Arctic** area around the North Pole ▷ *adj* of this region; (**a-**) *Informal* very cold
ardent *adj* passionate; eager, zealous **ardently** *adv* **ardour** *n* passion; enthusiasm, zeal
arduous *adj* hard to accomplish, strenuous **arduously** *adv*
are[1] *v* see **be**
are[2] *n* unit of measure, 100 square metres
area *n* part or region; size of a two-dimensional surface; subject field
arena *n* seated enclosure for sports events; area of a Roman amphitheatre where gladiators fought; sphere of intense activity
aren't are not
areola *n, pl* **-lae, -las** small circular area, such as the coloured ring around the human nipple
argon *n chem* inert gas found in the air
argot [**ahr**-go] *n* slang or jargon
argue *v* **-guing, -gued** try to prove by giving reasons; debate; quarrel, dispute **arguable** *adj* **arguably** *adv* **argument** *n* quarrel; discussion; point presented for or against something **argumentation** *n* process of reasoning methodically **argumentative** *adj* given to arguing

> SPELLING There's an *e* at the end of **argue**, but you should leave it out when you write **argument**. A lot of people get that wrong

argy-bargy *n, pl* **-bargies** *Informal* squabbling argument
aria [**ah**-ree-a] *n* elaborate song for solo voice, esp one from an opera
arid *adj* parched, dry; uninteresting **aridity** *n*
aright *adv* rightly
arise *v* **arising, arose, arisen** come about; come into notice; get up
aristocracy *n, pl* **-cies** highest social class **aristocrat** *n* member of the aristocracy **aristocratic** *adj*
arithmetic *n* calculation by or of numbers ▷ *adj* of arithmetic **arithmetical** *adj* **arithmetically** *adv*
ark *n old testament* boat built by Noah, which survived the Flood; (**A-**) *Judaism* chest containing the writings of Jewish Law
arm[1] *n* either of the upper limbs from the shoulder to the wrist; sleeve of a garment; side of a chair **armful** *n* as much as can be held in the arms **armchair** *n* upholstered chair with side supports for the arms **armhole** *n* opening in a garment through which the arm passes **armpit** *n* hollow under the arm at the shoulder
arm[2] *v* supply with weapons;

prepare (a bomb etc) for use **arms** *pl n* weapons; military exploits; heraldic emblem
armada *n* large number of warships
armadillo *n, pl* **-los** small S American mammal covered in strong bony plates
Armageddon *n New Testament* final battle between good and evil at the end of the world; catastrophic conflict
armament *n* military weapons; preparation for war
armature *n* revolving structure in an electric motor or generator, wound with coils carrying the current
armistice [**arm**-miss-stiss] *n* agreed suspension of fighting
armour *n* metal clothing formerly worn to protect the body in battle; metal plating of tanks, warships, etc **armourer** *n* maker, repairer, or keeper of arms or armour **armoury** *n* place where weapons are stored
army *n, pl* **armies** military land forces of a nation; great number
aroma *n* pleasant smell **aromatic** *adj* **aromatherapy** *n* massage with fragrant oils to relieve tension
arose *v* past tense of **arise**
around *prep, adv* on all sides (of); from place to place (in); somewhere in or near; approximately
arouse *v* stimulate, make active; awaken
arpeggio [arp-**pej**-ee-oh] *n, pl* **-gios** *music* notes of a chord played or sung in quick succession
arr. arranged (by); arrival; arrive(d)
arraign [ar-**rain**] *v* bring (a prisoner) before a court to answer a charge; accuse **arraignment** *n*
arrange *v* plan; agree; put in order; adapt (music) for performance in a certain way **arrangement** *n*
arrant *adj* utter, downright
arras *n* tapestry wall-hanging
array *n* impressive display or collection; orderly arrangement, esp of troops; *poetic* rich clothing ▷*v* arrange in order; dress in rich clothing
arrears *pl n* money owed **in arrears** late in paying a debt
arrest *v* take (a person) into custody; stop the movement or development of; catch and hold (the attention) ▷*n* act of taking a person into custody; slowing or stopping **arresting** *adj* attracting attention, striking
arrive *v* reach a place or destination; happen, come; *Informal* be born; *Informal* attain success **arrival** *n* arriving; person or thing that has just arrived
arrogant *adj* proud and overbearing **arrogantly** *adv* **arrogance** *n*
arrogate *v* claim or seize without justification
arrow *n* pointed shaft shot from a bow; arrow-shaped sign or symbol used to show direction **arrowhead** *n* pointed tip of an arrow
arrowroot *n* nutritious starch obtained from the root of a W Indian plant
arse *n vulgar slang* buttocks or anus **arsehole** *n vulgar slang* anus; stupid or annoying person
arsenal *n* place where arms and ammunition are made or stored
arsenic *n* toxic grey element; highly poisonous compound of this **arsenical** *adj*
arson *n* crime of intentionally

setting property on fire **arsonist** *n*

art *n* creation of works of beauty, esp paintings or sculpture; works of art collectively; skill ▷ *pl* nonscientific branches of knowledge **artist** *n* person who produces works of art, esp paintings or sculpture; person skilled at something; artiste **artiste** *n* professional entertainer such as a singer or dancer **artistic** *adj* **artistically** *adv* **artistry** *n* artistic skill **arty** *adj* **artier, artiest** *Informal* having an affected interest in art

artefact *n* something made by human beings

arteriosclerosis [art-ear-ee-oh-skler-**oh**-siss] *n* hardening of the arteries

artery *n, pl* **-teries** one of the tubes carrying blood from the heart; major road or means of communication **arterial** *adj* of an artery; (of a route) major

artesian well [art-**teez**-yan] *n* well bored vertically so that the water is forced to the surface by natural pressure

Artex *n* ®, *Brit* textured plaster-like covering for ceilings and walls

artful *adj* cunning, wily **artfully** *adv* **artfulness** *n*

arthritis *n* painful inflammation of a joint or joints **arthritic** *adj, n*

arthropod *n* animal, such as a spider or insect, with jointed limbs and a segmented body

artichoke *n* flower head of a thistle-like plant, cooked as a vegetable

article *n* written piece in a magazine or newspaper; item or object; clause in a document; *grammar* any of the words *the, a*, or *an*

articled *adj* bound (as an apprentice) by a written contract

articulate *adj* able to express oneself clearly and coherently; (of speech) clear, distinct; *zool* having joints ▷ *v* speak or say clearly and coherently **articulately** *adv* **articulated** *adj* jointed **articulated vehicle** large vehicle in two separate sections joined by a pivoted bar **articulation** *n*

artifice *n* clever trick; cleverness, skill **artificer** [art-**tiff**-iss-er] *n* craftsman

artificial *adj* man-made, not occurring naturally; made in imitation of something natural; not sincere **artificial insemination** introduction of semen into the womb by means other than sexual intercourse **artificial intelligence** branch of computer science aiming to produce machines which can imitate intelligent human behaviour **artificial respiration** method of restarting a person's breathing after it has stopped **artificially** *adv* **artificiality** *n*

artillery *n* large-calibre guns; branch of the army who use these

artisan *n* skilled worker, craftsman

artless *adj* free from deceit or cunning; natural, unpretentious **artlessly** *adv*

arum lily [**air**-rum] *n* plant with a white funnel-shaped leaf surrounding a spike of flowers

arvie *n SAfr, Informal* afternoon

as *conj* while, when; in the way that; that which *eg do as you are told;* since, seeing that; for instance ▷ *adv, conj* used to indicate amount or extent in comparisons *eg he is as tall as you* ▷ *prep* in the role of, being *eg as a mother, I am concerned*

asafoetida *n* strong-smelling plant resin used as a spice in Eastern cookery

a.s.a.p. as soon as possible

asbestos *n* fibrous mineral which does not burn **asbestosis** *n* lung disease caused by inhalation of asbestos fibre

ascend *v* go or move up **ascent** *n* ascending; upward slope **ascendant** *adj* dominant or influential ▷ *n* **in the ascendant** increasing in power or influence **ascendancy** *n* condition of being dominant **the Ascension** *Christianity* passing of Jesus Christ from earth into heaven

ascertain *v* find out definitely **ascertainable** *adj* **ascertainment** *n*

ascetic [ass-**set**-tik] *n, adj* (person) abstaining from worldly pleasures and comforts **asceticism** *n*

ascorbic acid [ass-**core**-bik] *n* vitamin C

ascribe *v* attribute, as to a particular origin **ascription** *n*

aseptic [eh-**sep**-tik] *adj* free from harmful bacteria

asexual [eh-**sex**-yew-al] *adj* without sex **asexually** *adv*

ash[1] *n* powdery substance left when something is burnt ▷ *pl* remains after burning, esp of a human body after cremation **the Ashes** cricket trophy competed for in test matches by England and Australia **ashen** *adj* pale with shock **ashtray** *n* receptacle for tobacco ash and cigarette butts **Ash Wednesday** first day of Lent

ash[2] *n* tree with grey bark

ashamed *adj* feeling shame

ashlar *n* square block of hewn stone used in building

ashore *adv* towards or on land

ashram *n* religious retreat where a Hindu holy man lives

Asian *adj* of the continent of Asia or any of its peoples or languages ▷ *n* person from Asia or a descendant of one; person from the Indian subcontinent or a descendant of one **Asian pear** apple-shaped pear with crisp juicy flesh.

Use *Asian* for 'someone who comes from Asia'

aside *adv* to one side; out of other people's hearing *eg he took me aside to tell me his plans* ▷ *n* remark not meant to be heard by everyone present

asinine *adj* stupid, idiotic

ask *v* say or write (something) in a form that requires an answer; make a request or demand; invite

askance [ass-**kanss**] *adv* **look askance at** look at with an oblique glance; regard with suspicion

askew *adv, adj* to one side, crooked

aslant *adv, prep* at a slant (to), slanting (across)

asleep *adj* sleeping; (of limbs) numb

asp *n* small poisonous snake

asparagus *n* plant whose shoots are cooked as a vegetable

aspect *n* feature or element; position facing a particular direction; appearance or look

aspen *n* kind of poplar tree

asperity *n* roughness of temper

aspersion *n* **cast aspersions on** make derogatory remarks about

asphalt *n* black hard tarlike substance used for road surfaces etc

asphodel *n* plant with clusters of

yellow or white flowers
asphyxia [ass-**fix**-ee-a] *n* suffocation **asphyxiate** *v* suffocate **asphyxiation** *n*
aspic *n* savoury jelly used to coat meat, eggs, fish, etc
aspidistra *n* plant with long tapered leaves
aspirate *phonetics* ▷ *v* pronounce with an *h* sound ▷ *n* *h* sound
aspire *v* (foll. by *to*) yearn (for), hope (to do or be) **aspirant** *n* person who aspires **aspiration** *n* strong desire or aim
aspirin *n* drug used to relieve pain and fever; tablet of this
ass *n* donkey; stupid person
assagai *n* same as **assegai**
assail *v* attack violently **assailant** *n*
assassin *n* person who murders a prominent person **assassinate** *v* murder (a prominent person) **assassination** *n*
assault *n* violent attack ▷ *v* attack violently **assault course** series of obstacles used in military training
assay *n* analysis of a substance, esp a metal, to ascertain its purity ▷ *v* make such an analysis
assegai [**ass**-a-guy] *n* slender spear used in S Africa
assemble *v* collect or congregate; put together the parts of (a machine) **assemblage** *n* collection or group; assembling **assembly** *n, pl* **-blies** assembled group; assembling **assembly line** sequence of machines and workers in a factory assembling a product
assent *n* agreement or consent ▷ *v* agree or consent
assert *v* declare forcefully; insist upon (one's rights etc) **assert oneself** put oneself forward forcefully **assertion** *n* **assertive** *adj* **assertively** *adv*
assess *v* judge the worth or importance of; estimate the value of (income or property) for taxation purposes **assessment** *n* **assessor** *n*
asset *n* valuable or useful person or thing ▷ *pl* property that a person or firm can sell, esp to pay debts
asseverate *v* declare solemnly
assiduous *adj* hard-working **assiduously** *adv* **assiduity** *n*
assign *v* appoint (someone) to a job or task; allot (a task); attribute **assignation** *n* assigning; secret arrangement to meet **assignment** *n* task assigned; assigning
assimilate *v* learn and understand (information); absorb or be absorbed or incorporated **assimilable** *adj* **assimilation** *n*
assist *v* give help or support **assistance** *n* **assistant** *n* helper ▷ *adj* junior or deputy
assizes *pl n* *Brit* court sessions formerly held in each county of England and Wales
associate *v* connect in the mind; mix socially ▷ *n* partner in business; friend or companion ▷ *adj* having partial rights or subordinate status *eg associate member* **association** *n* society or club; associating
assonance *n* rhyming of vowel sounds but not consonants, as in *time* and *light*
assorted *adj* consisting of various types mixed together **assortment** *n* assorted mixture
assuage [ass-**wage**] *v* relieve (pain, grief, thirst, etc)
assume *v* take to be true without proof; take upon oneself *eg he assumed command*; pretend *eg I*

assumed indifference **assumption** *n* thing assumed; assuming

assure *v* promise or guarantee; convince; make (something) certain; insure against loss of life **assured** *adj* confident; certain to happen **assuredly** *adv* definitely **assurance** *n* assuring or being assured.

> When used in the context of business, *assurance* and *insurance* have the same meaning

astatine *n chem* radioactive nonmetallic element

aster *n* plant with daisy-like flowers

asterisk *n* star-shaped symbol (*) used in printing or writing to indicate a footnote etc ▷ *v* mark with an asterisk

astern *adv* at or towards the stern of a ship; backwards

asteroid *n* any of the small planets that orbit the sun between Mars and Jupiter

asthma [ass-ma] *n* illness causing difficulty in breathing **asthmatic** *adj, n*

astigmatism [eh-**stig**-mat-tiz-zum] *n* inability of a lens, esp of the eye, to focus properly

astir *adj old-fashioned* out of bed; in motion

astonish *v* surprise greatly **astonishment** *n*

astound *v* overwhelm with amazement **astounding** *adj*

astrakhan *n* dark curly fleece of lambs from Astrakhan in Russia; fabric resembling this

astral *adj* of stars; of the spirit world

astray *adv* off the right path

astride *adv, prep* with a leg on either side (of)

astringent *adj* causing contraction of body tissue; checking the flow of blood from a cut; severe or harsh ▷ *n* astringent substance **astringency** *n*

astrolabe *n* instrument formerly used to measure the altitude of stars and planets

astrology *n* study of the alleged influence of the stars, planets, and moon on human affairs **astrologer** *n* **astrological** *adj*

astronaut *n* person trained for travelling in space

astronautics *n* science and technology of space flight **astronautical** *adj*

astronomy *n* scientific study of heavenly bodies **astronomer** *n* **astronomical** *adj* very large; of astronomy **astronomically** *adv*

astrophysics *n* science of the physical and chemical properties of stars, planets, etc **astrophysical** *adj* **astrophysicist** *n*

astute *adj* perceptive or shrewd **astutely** *adv* **astuteness** *n*

asunder *adv obs or poetic* into parts or pieces

asylum *n* refuge or sanctuary; old name for a mental hospital

asymmetry *n* lack of symmetry **asymmetrical, asymmetric** *adj*

asymptote [**ass**-im-tote] *n* straight line closely approached but never met by a curve

at *prep* indicating position in space or time, movement towards an object, etc *eg at midnight; throwing stones at windows*

atavism [**at**-a-viz-zum] *n* recurrence of a trait present in distant ancestors **atavistic** *adj*

ate *v* past tense of **eat**

atheism [**aith**-ee-iz-zum] *n* belief that there is no God **atheist** *n*

atheistic *adj*

atherosclerosis *n, pl* **-ses** disease in which deposits of fat cause the walls of the arteries to thicken

athlete *n* person trained in or good at athletics **athletic** *adj* physically fit or strong; of an athlete or athletics **athletics** *pl n* track-and-field sports such as running, jumping, throwing, etc **athletically** *adv* **athleticism** *n*

athwart *prep* across ▷ *adv* transversely

atlas *n* book of maps

atmosphere *n* mass of gases surrounding a heavenly body, esp the earth; prevailing tone or mood (of a place etc); unit of pressure **atmospheric** *adj* **atmospherics** *pl n* radio interference due to electrical disturbance in the atmosphere

atoll *n* ring-shaped coral reef enclosing a lagoon

atom *n* smallest unit of matter which can take part in a chemical reaction; very small amount **atom bomb** same as **atomic bomb**

atomic *adj* of or using atomic bombs or atomic energy; of atoms **atomic bomb** bomb in which the energy is provided by nuclear fission **atomic energy** nuclear energy **atomic number** number of protons in the nucleus of an atom **atomic weight** ratio of the mass per atom of an element to one twelfth of the mass of a carbon atom

atomize *v* reduce to atoms or small particles

atomizer *n* device for discharging a liquid in a fine spray

atonal [eh-**tone**-al] *adj* (of music) not written in an established key

atone *v* make amends (for sin or wrongdoing) **atonement** *n*

atop *prep lit* on top of

atrium *n, pl* **atria** upper chamber of either half of the heart; central hall extending through several storeys of a modern building; main courtyard of an ancient Roman house

atrocious *adj* extremely cruel or wicked; horrifying or shocking; *Informal* very bad **atrociously** *adv* **atrocity** *n* wickedness *pl* **-ties** act of cruelty

atrophy [**at**-trof-fee] *n, pl* **-phies** wasting away of an organ or part ▷ *v* **-phying, -phied** (cause to) waste away

attach *v* join, fasten, or connect; attribute or ascribe **attached** *adj* (foll. by *to*) fond of **attachment** *n*

attaché [at-**tash**-shay] *n* specialist attached to a diplomatic mission **attaché case** flat rectangular briefcase for papers

attack *v* launch a physical assault (against); criticize; set about (a job or problem) with vigour; affect adversely ▷ *n* act of attacking; sudden bout of illness **attacker** *n*

attain *v* achieve or accomplish (a task or aim); reach **attainable** *adj* **attainment** *n* accomplishment

attar *n* fragrant oil made from roses

attempt *v* try, make an effort ▷ *n* effort or endeavour

attend *v* be present at; go regularly to a school, college, etc; look after; pay attention; apply oneself (to) **attendance** *n* attending; number attending **attendant** *n* person who assists, guides, or provides a service ▷ *adj* accompanying **attention** *n* concentrated direction of the mind;

consideration; care; alert position in military drill **attentive** *adj* giving attention; considerately helpful **attentively** *adv* **attentiveness** *n*

attenuated *adj* weakened; thin and extended **attenuation** *n*

attest *v* affirm the truth of, be proof of **attestation** *n*

attic *n* space or room within the roof of a house

attire *n formal* fine or formal clothes

attired *adj* dressed in a specified way

attitude *n* way of thinking and behaving; posture of the body

attorney *n* person legally appointed to act for another; *US & SAfr* lawyer

attract *v* arouse the interest or admiration of; draw (something) closer by exerting a force on it **attraction** *n* power to attract; something that attracts **attractive** *adj* **attractively** *adv* **attractiveness** *n*

attribute *v* (usu foll. by *to*) regard as belonging to or produced by ▷ *n* quality or feature representative of a person or thing **attributable** *adj* **attribution** *n* **attributive** *adj grammar* (of an adjective) preceding the noun modified

attrition *n* constant wearing down to weaken or destroy

attune *v* adjust or accustom (a person or thing)

atypical [eh-**tip**-ik-al] *adj* not typical

Au *chem* gold

aubergine [**oh**-bur-zheen] *n Brit* dark purple tropical fruit, cooked and eaten as a vegetable

aubrietia [aw-**bree**-sha] *n* trailing plant with purple flowers

auburn *adj* (of hair) reddish-brown

auction *n* public sale in which articles are sold to the highest bidder ▷ *v* sell by auction **auctioneer** *n* person who conducts an auction

audacious *adj* recklessly bold or daring; impudent **audaciously** *adv* **audacity** *n*

audible *adj* loud enough to be heard **audibly** *adv* **audibility** *n*

audience *n* group of spectators or listeners; formal interview

audio *adj* of sound or hearing; of or for the transmission or reproduction of sound **audio typist** typist trained to type from a dictating machine **audiovisual** *adj* (esp of teaching aids) involving both sight and hearing

audit *n* official examination of business accounts ▷ *v* **auditing, audited** examine (business accounts) officially **auditor** *n*

audition *n* test of a performer's ability for a particular role or job ▷ *v* test or be tested in an audition

auditorium *n, pl* **-toriums, -toria** area of a concert hall or theatre where the audience sits

auditory *adj* of or relating to hearing

au fait [oh **fay**] *adj French* fully informed; expert

Aug. August

auger *n* tool for boring holes

aught *pron obs* anything whatever

augment *v* increase or enlarge **augmentation** *n*

au gratin [oh **grat**-tan] *adj* covered and cooked with breadcrumbs and sometimes cheese

augur *v* be a sign of (future events) **augury** *n* foretelling of the future *pl*

-ries omen
august [aw-**gust**] *adj* dignified and imposing
August *n* eighth month of the year
auk *n* northern sea bird with short wings and black-and-white plumage
aunt *n* father's or mother's sister; uncle's wife **auntie, aunty** *n, pl* **aunties** *Informal* aunt **Aunt Sally** *Brit, NZ & SAfr* figure used in fairgrounds as a target; target of abuse or criticism
au pair *n* young foreign woman who does housework in return for board and lodging
aura *n* distinctive air or quality of a person or thing
aural *adj* of or using the ears or hearing
aureole, aureola *n* halo
au revoir [**oh** riv-**vwahr**] *interj French* goodbye
auricle *n* upper chamber of the heart; outer part of the ear **auricular** *adj*
aurochs *n, pl* **aurochs** recently extinct European wild ox
aurora *n, pl* **-ras, -rae** bands of light sometimes seen in the sky in polar regions **aurora australis** aurora seen near the South Pole **aurora borealis** aurora seen near the North Pole
auscultation *n* listening to the internal sounds of the body, usu with a stethoscope, to help with diagnosis
auspices [**aw**-spiss-siz] *pl n* **under the auspices of** with the support and approval of
auspicious *adj* showing signs of future success, favourable **auspiciously** *adv*
Aussie *n, adj Informal* Australian
Aust. Australia(n)
austere *adj* stern or severe; ascetic or self-disciplined; severely simple or plain **austerely** *adv* **austerity** *n*
Australasian *n, adj* (person) from Australia, New Zealand, and neighbouring islands
Australia Day *n Aust* public holiday on 26th January
Australian *n, adj* (person) from Australia
autarchy [**aw**-tar-kee] *n* absolute power or autocracy
autarky [**aw**-tar-kee] *n* policy of economic self-sufficiency
authentic *adj* known to be real, genuine **authentically** *adv* **authenticity** *n* **authenticate** *v* establish as genuine **authentication** *n*
author *n* writer of a book etc; originator or creator **authorship** *n*
authority *n, pl* **-ties** power to command or control others; (often pl) person or group having this power; expert in a particular field **authoritarian** *n, adj* (person) insisting on strict obedience to authority **authoritative** *adj* recognized as being reliable; possessing authority **authoritatively** *adv* **authorize** *v* give authority to; give permission for **authorization** *n*
autism *n psychiatry* disorder, usu of children, characterized by lack of response to people and limited ability to communicate **autistic** *adj*
auto- *combining form* self- *eg autobiography*
autobiography *n, pl* **-phies** account of a person's life written by that person **autobiographical** *adj* **autobiographically** *adv*
autocrat *n* ruler with absolute authority; dictatorial person

autocratic *adj* **autocratically** *adv* **autocracy** *n* government by an autocrat

autocross *n* motor-racing over a rough course

Autocue *n* ® electronic television prompting device displaying a speaker's script, unseen by the audience

autogiro, autogyro *n, pl* **-ros** self-propelled aircraft resembling a helicopter but with an unpowered rotor

autograph *n* handwritten signature of a (famous) person ▷ *v* write one's signature on or in

automat *n US* vending machine

automate *v* make (a manufacturing process) automatic **automation** *n*

automatic *adj* (of a device) operating mechanically by itself; (of a process) performed by automatic equipment; done without conscious thought; (of a firearm) self-loading ▷ *n* self-loading firearm; vehicle with automatic transmission **automatically** *adv*

automaton *n* robot; person who acts mechanically

automobile *n US* motor car

autonomy *n* self-government **autonomous** *adj*

autopsy *n, pl* **-sies** examination of a corpse to determine the cause of death

autosuggestion *n* process in which a person unconsciously influences his or her own behaviour or beliefs

autumn *n* season between summer and winter **autumnal** *adj*

auxiliary *adj* secondary or supplementary; supporting ▷ *n, pl* **-ries** person or thing that supplements or supports **auxiliary verb** verb used to form the tense, voice, or mood of another, such as *will* in *I will go*

avail *v* be of use or advantage (to) ▷ *n* use or advantage *esp in to no avail* **avail oneself of** make use of

available *adj* obtainable or accessible **availability** *n*

avalanche *n* mass of snow or ice falling down a mountain; sudden overwhelming quantity of anything

avant-garde [av-ong-**gard**] *n* group of innovators, esp in the arts ▷ *adj* innovative and progressive

avarice [**av**-a-riss] *n* greed for wealth **avaricious** *adj*

avast *interj naut* stop

avatar *n Hinduism* appearance of a god in animal or human form

Ave. Avenue

avenge *v* take revenge in retaliation for (harm done) or on behalf of (a person harmed) **avenger** *n*

avenue *n* wide street; road between two rows of trees; way of approach

aver [av-**vur**] *v* **averring, averred** state to be true

average *n* typical or normal amount or quality; result obtained by adding quantities together and dividing the total by the number of quantities ▷ *adj* usual or typical; calculated as an average ▷ *v* calculate the average of; amount to as an average

averse *adj* (usu foll. by *to*) disinclined or unwilling **aversion** *n* strong dislike; person or thing disliked

avert *v* turn away; ward off

aviary *n, pl* **aviaries** large cage or enclosure for birds

aviation *n* art of flying aircraft **aviator** *n*

avid *adj* keen or enthusiastic; greedy (for) **avidly** *adv* **avidity** *n*
avocado *n, pl* **-dos** pear-shaped tropical fruit with a leathery green skin and yellowish-green flesh
avocation *n old-fashioned* occupation; hobby
avocet *n* long-legged wading bird with a long slender upward-curving bill
avoid *v* prevent from happening; refrain from; keep away from **avoidable** *adj* **avoidance** *n*
avoirdupois [av-er-de-**poise**] *n* system of weights based on pounds and ounces
avow *v* state or affirm; admit openly **avowal** *n* **avowed** *adj* **avowedly** *adv*
avuncular *adj* (of a man) friendly, helpful, and caring towards someone younger
await *v* wait for; be in store for
awake *v* **awaking, awoke, awoken** emerge or rouse from sleep; (cause to) become alert ▷ *adj* not sleeping; alert
awaken *v* awake
award *v* give (something, such as a prize) formally ▷ *n* something awarded, such as a prize
aware *adj* having knowledge, informed **awareness** *n*
awash *adv* washed over by water
away *adv* from a place *eg go away;* to another place *eg put that gun away;* out of existence *eg fade away;* continuously *eg laughing away* ▷ *adj* not present; distant *eg two miles away sport* played on an opponent's ground
awe *n* wonder and respect mixed with dread ▷ *v* fill with awe **awesome** *adj* inspiring awe; *slang* excellent or outstanding **awestruck** *adj* filled with awe
awful *adj* very bad or unpleasant; *Informal* very great; *obs* inspiring awe **awfully** *adv* in an unpleasant way; *Informal* very
awhile *adv* for a brief time
awkward *adj* clumsy or ungainly; embarrassed; difficult to use or handle; inconvenient **awkwardly** *adv* **awkwardness** *n*
awl *n* pointed tool for piercing wood, leather, etc
awning *n* canvas roof supported by a frame to give protection against the weather
awoke *v* past tense of **awake**
awoken *v* past participle of **awake**
AWOL *adj mil* absent without leave
awry [a-**rye**] *adv, adj* with a twist to one side, askew; amiss
axe *n* tool with a sharp blade for felling trees or chopping wood; *Informal* dismissal from employment etc ▷ *v Informal* dismiss (employees), restrict (expenditure), or terminate (a project)
axil *n* angle where the stalk of a leaf joins a stem
axiom *n* generally accepted principle; self-evident statement **axiomatic** *adj* self-evident
axis *n, pl* **axes** (imaginary) line round which a body can rotate or about which an object or geometrical figure is symmetrical; one of two fixed lines on a graph, against which quantities or positions are measured **axial** *adj*
axle *n* shaft on which a wheel or pair of wheels turns
axolotl *n* aquatic salamander of central America
ayatollah *n* Islamic religious leader in Iran
aye, ay *interj* yes ▷ *n* affirmative vote or voter

azalea [az-**zale**-ya] *n* garden shrub grown for its showy flowers

azimuth *n* arc of the sky between the zenith and the horizon; horizontal angle of a bearing measured clockwise from the north

azure *adj*, *n* (of) the colour of a clear blue sky

b

BA Bachelor of Arts

baa *v* **baaing, baaed** make the characteristic bleating sound of a sheep ▷ *n* cry made by a sheep

babble *v* talk excitedly or foolishly; (of streams) make a low murmuring sound ▷ *n* muddled or foolish speech

babe *n* baby

babel *n* confused mixture of noises or voices

baboon *n* large monkey with a pointed face and a long tail

baby *n*, *pl* **-bies** very young child or animal; *slang* sweetheart ▷ *adj* comparatively small of its type **babyish** *adj* **baby-sit** *v* take care of a child while the parents are out **baby-sitter** *n*

baccarat [**back**-a-rah] *n* card game involving gambling

bacchanalia [back-a-**nail**-ee-a] *n* wild drunken party or orgy

bach [batch] *NZ* ▷ *n* small holiday cottage ▷ *v* look after oneself when one's spouse is away

bachelor *n* unmarried man; person who holds the lowest university or college degree

> SPELLING We find *batchelor* spelt with a *t* 14 times in Collins Word Web. The correct spelling has no *t*: **bachelor**

bacillus [bass-**ill**-luss] *n, pl* **-li** [-lie] rod-shaped bacterium

back *n* rear part of the human body, from the neck to the pelvis; part or side of an object opposite the front; part of anything less often seen or used; *ball games* defensive player or position ▷ *v* (cause to) move backwards; provide money for (a person or enterprise); bet on the success of; (foll. by *onto*) have the back facing towards ▷ *adj* situated behind; owing from an earlier date ▷ *adv* at, to, or towards the rear; to or towards the original starting point or condition **backer** *n* person who gives financial support **backing** *n* support; musical accompaniment for a pop singer **backward** *adj* directed towards the rear; retarded in physical, material, or intellectual development **backwardness** *n* **backwards** *adv* towards the rear; with the back foremost; in the reverse of the usual direction **back up** *v* support **backup** *n* support or reinforcement; reserve or substitute

backbencher *n* Member of Parliament who does not hold office in the government or opposition

backbiting *n* spiteful talk about an absent person

backbone *n* spinal column; strength of character

backchat *n Informal* impudent replies

backcloth, backdrop *n* painted curtain at the back of a stage set

backdate *v* make (a document) effective from a date earlier than its completion

backfire *v* (of a plan) fail to have the desired effect; (of an engine) make a loud noise like an explosion

backgammon *n* game played with counters and dice

background *n* events or circumstances that help to explain something; person's social class, education, or experience; part of a scene or picture furthest from the viewer

backhand *n tennis etc* stroke played with the back of the hand facing the direction of the stroke **backhanded** *adj* ambiguous or implying criticism *eg a backhanded compliment* **backhander** *n slang* bribe

backlash *n* sudden and adverse reaction

backlog *n* accumulation of things to be dealt with

backpack *n* large pack carried on the back

backside *n Informal* buttocks

backslide *v* relapse into former bad habits **backslider** *n*

backstage *adv, adj* behind the stage in a theatre

backstroke *n* swimming stroke performed on the back

backtrack *v* return by the same route by which one has come; retract or reverse one's opinion or policy

backwash *n* water washed backwards by the motion of a boat; repercussion

backwater *n* isolated or backward place or condition
backwoods *pl n* remote sparsely populated area
bacon *n* salted or smoked pig meat
bacteria *pl n, sing* **-rium** large group of microorganisms, many of which cause disease **bacterial** *adj* **bacteriology** *n* study of bacteria **bacteriologist** *n*
bad *adj* **worse, worst** of poor quality; lacking skill or talent; harmful; immoral or evil; naughty or mischievous; rotten or decayed; unpleasant **badly** *adv* **badness** *n*
bade *v* a past tense of **bid**
badge *n* emblem worn to show membership, rank, etc
badger *n* nocturnal burrowing mammal of Europe, Asia, and N America with a black and white head ▷*v* pester or harass
badinage [**bad**-in-nahzh] *n* playful and witty conversation
badminton *n* game played with rackets and a shuttlecock, which is hit back and forth over a high net
Bafana bafana [bah-**fan**-na] *pl n* *S Afr* South African national soccer team
baffle *v* perplex or puzzle ▷*n* device to limit or regulate the flow of fluid, light, or sound **bafflement** *n*
bag *n* flexible container with an opening at one end; handbag or piece of luggage; *offens* ugly or bad-tempered woman ▷*v* **bagging, bagged** put into a bag; succeed in capturing, killing or scoring **baggy** *adj* (of clothes) hanging loosely
bagatelle *n* something of little value; board game in which balls are struck into holes
bagel *n* hard ring-shaped bread roll
baggage *n* suitcases packed for a journey
bagpipes *pl n* musical wind instrument with reed pipes and an inflatable bag
bail[1] *n law* money deposited with a court as security for a person's reappearance in court ▷*v* pay bail for (a person)
bail[2]**, bale** *v* (foll. by *out*) remove (water) from (a boat); *Informal* help (a person or organization) out of a predicament; make an emergency parachute jump from an aircraft
bail[3] *n cricket* either of two wooden bars across the tops of the stumps
bailey *n* outermost wall or court of a castle
bailiff *n* sheriff's officer who serves writs and summonses; landlord's agent
bairn *n Scot* child
bait *n* piece of food on a hook or in a trap to attract fish or animals ▷*v* put a piece of food on or in (a hook or trap); persecute or tease
baize *n* woollen fabric used to cover billiard and card tables
bake *v* cook by dry heat as in an oven; make or become hardened by heat **baking powder** powdered mixture containing sodium bicarbonate, used as a raising agent in baking
baker *n* person whose business is to make or sell bread, cakes, etc **baker's dozen** thirteen **bakery** *n, pl* **-eries** place where bread, cakes, etc are baked or sold
bakkie *n S Afr* small truck
Balaclava, Balaclava helmet *n* close-fitting woollen hood that covers the ears and neck
balalaika *n* guitar-like musical instrument with a triangular body
balance *n* state in which a weight

or amount is evenly distributed; amount that remains *eg the balance of what you owe;* weighing device; difference between the credits and debits of an account ▷*v* weigh in a balance; make or remain steady; consider or compare; compare or equalize the money going into or coming out of an account

balcony *n, pl* **-nies** platform on the outside of a building with a rail along the outer edge; upper tier of seats in a theatre or cinema

bald *adj* having little or no hair on the scalp; plain or blunt; (of a tyre) having a worn tread **balding** *adj* becoming bald **baldness** *n*

balderdash *n* stupid talk

bale[1] *n* large bundle of hay or goods tightly bound together ▷*v* make or put into bales

bale[2] *v* same as **bail**[2]

baleful *adj* vindictive or menacing **balefully** *adv*

balk, baulk *v* be reluctant to (do something); thwart or hinder

Balkan *adj* of any of the countries of the Balkan Peninsula: Romania, Bulgaria, Albania, Greece, the former Yugoslavia, and the European part of Turkey

ball[1] *n* round or nearly round object, esp one used in games; single delivery of the ball in a game ▷*pl vulgar slang* testicles; nonsense ▷*v* form into a ball **ball bearings** steel balls between moving parts of a machine to reduce friction **ball cock** device with a floating ball and a valve for regulating the flow of water **ballpoint, ballpoint pen** *n* pen with a tiny ball bearing as a writing point

ball[2] *n* formal social function for dancing **ballroom** *n*

ballad *n* narrative poem or song; slow sentimental song

ballast *n* substance, such as sand, used to stabilize a ship when it is not carrying cargo

ballet *n* classical style of expressive dancing based on conventional steps; theatrical performance of this **ballerina** *n* female ballet dancer

ballistics *n* study of the flight of projectiles, such as bullets **ballistic missile** missile guided automatically in flight but which falls freely at its target

balloon *n* inflatable rubber bag used as a plaything or decoration; large bag inflated with air or gas, designed to float in the atmosphere with passengers in a basket underneath ▷*v* fly in a balloon; swell or increase rapidly in size **balloonist** *n*

ballot *n* method of voting; actual vote or paper indicating a person's choice ▷*v* **-loting, -loted** vote or ask for a vote from

ballyhoo *n* exaggerated fuss

balm *n* aromatic substance used for healing and soothing; anything that comforts or soothes

Balmain bug *n* edible Australian shellfish

balmy *adj* **balmier, balmiest** (of weather) mild and pleasant

baloney *n Informal* nonsense

balsa [**bawl**-sa] *n* very light wood from a tropical American tree

balsam *n* soothing ointment; flowering plant

baluster *n* set of posts supporting a rail

balustrade *n* ornamental rail supported by balusters

bamboo *n* tall treelike tropical grass with hollow stems

bamboozle *v Informal* cheat or

mislead; confuse, puzzle

ban *v* **banning, banned** prohibit or forbid officially ▷ *n* official prohibition

banal [ban-**nahl**] *adj* ordinary and unoriginal **banality** *n*

banana *n* yellow crescent-shaped fruit

band[1] *n* group of musicians playing together; group of people having a common purpose **bandsman** *n* **bandstand** *n* roofed outdoor platform for a band **band together** *v* unite

band[2] *n* strip of some material, used to hold objects; *physics* range of frequencies or wavelengths between two limits

bandage *n* piece of material used to cover a wound or wrap an injured limb ▷ *v* cover with a bandage

bandanna, bandana *n* large brightly coloured handkerchief or neckerchief

B&B bed and breakfast

bandicoot *n* ratlike Australian marsupial

bandit *n* robber, esp a member of an armed gang **banditry** *n*

bandolier *n* shoulder belt for holding cartridges

bandwagon *n* **jump, climb on the bandwagon** join a party or movement that seems assured of success

bandy *adj* **-dier, -diest** (also **bandy-legged**) having legs curved outwards at the knees ▷ *v* **-dying, -died** exchange (words) in a heated manner; use (a name, term, etc) frequently

bane *n* person or thing that causes misery or distress **baneful** *adj*

bang *n* short loud explosive noise; hard blow or loud knock ▷ *v* hit or knock, esp with a loud noise; close (a door) noisily ▷ *adv* precisely; with a sudden impact

banger *n* *Informal, Brit & Aust* old decrepit car; *slang* sausage; firework that explodes loudly

bangle *n* bracelet worn round the arm or the ankle

banish *v* send (someone) into exile; drive away **banishment** *n*

banisters *pl n* railing supported by posts on a staircase

banjo *n, pl* **-jos, -joes** guitar-like musical instrument with a circular body

bank[1] *n* institution offering services such as the safekeeping and lending of money; any supply, store, or reserve ▷ *v* deposit (cash or cheques) in a bank **banking** *n* **banknote** *n* piece of paper money **bank on** *v* rely on

bank[2] *n* raised mass, esp of earth; sloping ground at the side of a river ▷ *v* form into a bank; cause (an aircraft) or (of an aircraft) to tip to one side on turning

bank[3] *n* arrangement of switches, keys, oars, etc in a row or in tiers

banker *n* manager or owner of a bank

bankrupt *n* person declared by a court to be unable to pay his or her debts ▷ *adj* financially ruined ▷ *v* make bankrupt **bankruptcy** *n*

banksia *n* Australian evergreen tree or shrub

banner *n* long strip of cloth displaying a slogan, advertisement, etc; placard carried in a demonstration or procession; advertisement that extends across the top of a web page

bannisters *pl n* same as **banisters**

banns *pl n* public declaration, esp in a church, of an intended marriage

banquet *n* elaborate formal

dinner

banshee *n* (in Irish folklore) female spirit whose wailing warns of a coming death

bantam *n* small breed of chicken **bantamweight** *n* boxer weighing up to 118lb (professional) or 54kg (amateur)

banter *v* tease jokingly ▷ *n* teasing or joking conversation

Bantu *n* group of languages of Africa; *offens* Black speaker of a Bantu language

baobab [**bay**-oh-bab] *n* Australian and African tree with a thick trunk and angular branches

baptism *n* Christian religious ceremony in which a person is immersed in or sprinkled with water as a sign of being cleansed from sin and accepted into the Church **baptismal** *adj* **baptize** *v* perform baptism on

Baptist *n* member of a Protestant denomination that believes in adult baptism by immersion

bar[1] *n* rigid length of metal, wood, etc; solid, usu rectangular block, of any material; anything that obstructs or prevents; counter or room where drinks are served; heating element in an electric fire; *music* group of beats repeated throughout a piece of music ▷ *v* **barring, barred** secure with a bar; obstruct; ban or forbid ▷ *prep* (also **barring**) except for **the Bar** barristers collectively **barman, barmaid** *n*

bar[2] *n* unit of atmospheric pressure

barb *n* cutting remark; point facing in the opposite direction to the main point of a fish-hook etc **barbed** *adj* **barbed wire** strong wire with protruding sharp points

barbarian *n* member of a primitive or uncivilized people **barbaric** *adj* cruel or brutal **barbarism** *n* condition of being backward or ignorant **barbarity** *n* state of being barbaric or barbarous *pl* **-ties** vicious act **barbarous** *adj* uncivilized; brutal or cruel

barbecue *n* grill on which food is cooked over hot charcoal, usu outdoors; outdoor party at which barbecued food is served ▷ *v* cook (food) on a barbecue

barber *n* person who cuts men's hair and shaves beards

barbiturate *n* drug used as a sedative

bar code *n* arrangement of numbers and parallel lines on a package, which can be electronically scanned at a checkout to give the price of the goods

bard *n lit* poet

bare *adj* unclothed, naked; without the natural or usual covering; unembellished, simple; just sufficient ▷ *v* uncover **barely** *adv* only just **bareness** *n*

bareback *adj, adv* (of horse-riding) without a saddle

barefaced *adj* shameless or obvious

bargain *n* agreement establishing what each party will give, receive, or perform in a transaction; something bought or offered at a low price ▷ *v* negotiate the terms of an agreement **bargain for** *v* anticipate or take into account

barge *n* flat-bottomed boat used to transport freight ▷ *v Informal* push violently **barge in, into** *v* interrupt rudely

barista [bar-**ee**-sta] *n* person who makes and sells coffee in a coffee bar

baritone *n* (singer with) the

second lowest adult male voice
barium *n chem* soft white metallic element
bark¹ *n* loud harsh cry of a dog ▷ *v* (of a dog) make its typical cry; shout in an angry tone
bark² *n* tough outer layer of a tree
barley *n* tall grasslike plant cultivated for grain
barmy *adj* **-mier, -miest** *slang* insane
barn *n* large building on a farm used for storing grain
barnacle *n* shellfish that lives attached to rocks, ship bottoms, etc
barney *n Informal* noisy fight or argument
barometer *n* instrument for measuring atmospheric pressure **barometric** *adj*
baron *n* member of the lowest rank of nobility; powerful businessman **baroness** *n* **baronial** *adj*
baronet *n* commoner who holds the lowest hereditary British title
baroque [bar-**rock**] *n* highly ornate style of art, architecture, or music from the late 16th to the early 18th century ▷ *adj* ornate in style
barque [**bark**] *n* sailing ship, esp one with three masts
barra *n Aust, Informal* short for **barramundi**
barrack *v* criticize loudly or shout against (a team or speaker)
barracks *pl n* building used to accommodate military personnel
barracouta *n* large Pacific fish with a protruding lower jaw and strong teeth
barracuda *n* tropical sea fish
barrage [**bar**-rahzh] *n* continuous delivery of questions, complaints, etc; continuous artillery fire; artificial barrier across a river to control the water level
barramundi *n* edible Australian fish
barrel *n* cylindrical container with rounded sides and flat ends; tube in a firearm through which the bullet is fired **barrel organ** musical instrument played by turning a handle
barren *adj* (of a woman or female animal) incapable of producing offspring; (of land) unable to support the growth of crops, fruit, etc **barrenness** *n*
barricade *n* barrier, esp one erected hastily for defence ▷ *v* erect a barricade across (an entrance)
barrier *n* anything that prevents access, progress, or union
barrister *n Brit, Aust & NZ* lawyer qualified to plead in a higher court
barrow¹ *n* wheelbarrow; movable stall used by street traders
barrow² *n* mound of earth over a prehistoric tomb
barter *v* trade (goods) in exchange for other goods ▷ *n* trade by the exchange of goods
basalt [**bass**-awlt] *n* dark volcanic rock **basaltic** *adj*
base¹ *n* bottom or supporting part of anything; fundamental part; centre of operations, organization, or supply; starting point ▷ *v* (foll. by *on, upon*) use as a basis (for); (foll. by *at, in*) to station or place **baseless** *adj*
base² *adj* dishonourable or immoral; of inferior quality or value **baseness** *n*
baseball *n* team game in which runs are scored by hitting a ball with a bat then running round four bases; ball used for this
basement *n* partly or wholly underground storey of a building

bash *Informal* ▷*v* hit violently or forcefully ▷*n* heavy blow; party

bashful *adj* shy or modest **bashfully** *adv* **bashfulness** *n*

basic *adj* of or forming a base or basis; elementary or simple **basics** *pl n* fundamental principles, facts, etc **basically** *adv*

BASIC *n* computer programming language that uses common English words

basil *n* aromatic herb used in cooking

basilica *n* rectangular church with a rounded end and two aisles

basilisk *n* legendary serpent said to kill by its breath or glance

basin *n* round open container; sink for washing the hands and face; sheltered area of water where boats may be moored; catchment area of a particular river

basis *n, pl* **-ses** fundamental principles etc from which something is started or developed

bask *v* lie in or be exposed to something, esp pleasant warmth

basket *n* container made of interwoven strips of wood or cane **basketwork** *n*

basketball *n* team game in which points are scored by throwing the ball through a high horizontal hoop; ball used for this

Basque *n, adj* (member or language) of a people living in the W Pyrenees in France and Spain

bas-relief *n* sculpture in which the figures project slightly from the background

bass[1] [**base**] *n* (singer with) the lowest adult male voice ▷*adj* of the lowest range of musical notes

bass[2] *n* edible sea fish

basset hound *n* smooth-haired dog with short legs and long ears

bassoon *n* low-pitched woodwind instrument

bastard *n offens* obnoxious or despicable person; person born of parents not married to each other

baste[1] *v* moisten (meat) during cooking with hot fat

baste[2] *v* sew with loose temporary stitches

bastion *n* projecting part of a fortification; thing or person regarded as defending a principle

bat[1] *n* any of various types of club used to hit the ball in certain sports ▷*v* **batting, batted** strike with or as if with a bat **batsman** *n cricket* person who bats or specializes in batting

bat[2] *n* nocturnal mouselike flying animal

batch *n* group of people or things dealt with at the same time

bated *adj* **with bated breath** in suspense or fear

bath *n* large container in which to wash the body; act of washing in such a container ▷*pl* public swimming pool ▷*v* wash in a bath **bathroom** *n* room with a bath, sink, and usu a toilet

Bath chair *n* wheelchair for an invalid

bathe *v* swim in open water for pleasure; apply liquid to (the skin or a wound) in order to cleanse or soothe; (foll. by *in*) fill (with) *eg bathed in sunlight* **bather** *n*

bathos [**bay**-thoss] *n* sudden ludicrous change in speech or writing from a serious subject to a trivial one

batik [bat-**teek**] *n* process of printing fabric using wax to cover areas not to be dyed; fabric printed in this way

batman *n* officer's servant in the

armed forces
baton *n* thin stick used by the conductor of an orchestra; short bar transferred in a relay race; police officer's truncheon
battalion *n* army unit consisting of three or more companies
batten *n* strip of wood fixed to something, esp to hold it in place **batten down** *v* secure with battens
batter[1] *v* hit repeatedly **battering ram** large beam used to break down fortifications
batter[2] *n* mixture of flour, eggs, and milk, used in cooking
battery *n, pl* **-teries** device that produces electricity in a torch, radio, etc; group of heavy guns operating as a single unit ▷ *adj* kept in series of cages for intensive rearing
battle *n* fight between large armed forces; conflict or struggle ▷ *v* struggle
battle-axe *n Informal* domineering woman; (formerly) large heavy axe
battlement *n* wall with gaps along the top for firing through
battleship *n* large heavily armoured warship
batty *adj* **-tier, -tiest** *slang* eccentric or crazy
bauble *n* trinket of little value
bauera *n* small evergreen Australian shrub
baulk *v* same as **balk**
bauxite *n* claylike substance that is the chief source of aluminium
bawdy *adj* **bawdier, bawdiest** (of writing etc) containing humorous references to sex
bawl *v* shout or weep noisily
bay[1] *n* stretch of coastline that curves inwards
bay[2] *n* recess in a wall; area set aside for a particular purpose *eg loading bay*
bay[3] *v* howl in deep prolonged tones
bay[4] *n* Mediterranean laurel tree **bay leaf** its dried leaf, used in cooking
bay[5] *adj, n* reddish-brown (horse)
bayonet *n* sharp blade that can be fixed to the end of a rifle ▷ *v* **-neting, -neted** stab with a bayonet
bazaar *n* sale in aid of charity; market area, esp in Eastern countries
bazooka *n* portable rocket launcher that fires an armour-piercing projectile
BBC British Broadcasting Corporation
BC before Christ
BCG antituberculosis vaccine
be *v, present sing 1st person* **am** *2nd person* **are** *3rd person* **is** *present pl* **are** *past sing 1st person* **was** *2nd person* **were** *3rd person* **was** *past pl* **were** *present participle* **being** *past participle* **been** exist or live; used as a linking between the subject of a sentence and its complement *eg John is a musician*; forms the progressive present tense *eg the man is running*; forms the passive voice of all transitive verbs *eg a good film is being shown on television tonight*
beach *n* area of sand or pebbles on a shore ▷ *v* run or haul (a boat) onto a beach **beachhead** *n* beach captured by an attacking army on which troops can be landed
beacon *n* fire or light on a hill or tower, used as a warning
bead *n* small piece of plastic, wood, etc, pierced for threading on a string to form a necklace etc; small

drop of moisture **beaded** *adj* **beading** *n* strip of moulding used for edging furniture **beady** *adj* small, round, and glittering *eg beady eyes*

beagle *n* small hound with short legs and drooping ears

beak[1] *n* projecting horny jaws of a bird; *slang* nose **beaky** *adj*

beak[2] *n Brit, Aust & NZ, slang* judge, magistrate, or headmaster

beaker *n* large drinking cup; lipped glass container used in laboratories

beam *n* broad smile; ray of light; narrow flow of electromagnetic radiation or particles; long thick piece of wood, metal, etc, used in building ▷ *v* smile broadly; divert or aim (a radio signal, light, etc) in a certain direction

bean *n* seed or pod of various plants, eaten as a vegetable or used to make coffee etc

beanie *n* close-fitting woollen hat

bear[1] *v* **bearing, bore, borne** support or hold up; bring *eg to bear gifts passive* **born** give birth to; tolerate or endure; hold in the mind **bearable** *adj* **bear out** *v* show to be truthful

bear[2] *n* large heavy mammal with a shaggy coat **bearskin** *n* tall fur helmet worn by some British soldiers

beard *n* hair growing on the lower parts of a man's face **bearded** *adj*

bearer *n* person who carries, presents, or upholds something

bearing *n* relevance (to); person's general social conduct; part of a machine that supports another part, esp one that reduces friction ▷ *pl* sense of one's own relative position

beast *n* large wild animal; brutal or uncivilized person **beastly** *adj* unpleasant or disagreeable

beat *v* **beating, beat, beaten** *or* **beat** hit hard and repeatedly; move (wings) up and down; throb rhythmically; stir or mix vigorously; overcome or defeat ▷ *n* regular throb; assigned route, as of a policeman; basic rhythmic unit in a piece of music **beat up** *v* injure (someone) by repeated blows or kicks

beatify [bee-**at**-if-fie] *v* **-fying, -fied** *RC church* declare (a dead person) to be among the blessed in heaven: the first step towards canonization **beatific** *adj* displaying great happiness **beatification** *n* **beatitude** *n Christianity* any of the blessings on the poor, meek, etc, in the Sermon on the Mount

beau [**boh**] *n, pl* **beaux, beaus** boyfriend or admirer; man greatly concerned with his appearance

Beaufort scale *n* scale for measuring wind speeds

beautician *n* person who gives beauty treatments professionally

beautiful *adj* very attractive to look at; very pleasant **beautifully** *adv*

beautify *v* **-fying, -fied** make beautiful **beautification** *n*

beauty *n, pl* **-ties** combination of all the qualities of a person or thing that delight the senses and mind; very attractive woman; *Informal* something outstanding of its kind

beaver *n* amphibious rodent with a big flat tail **beaver away** *v* work industriously

becalmed *adj* (of a sailing ship) motionless through lack of wind

became *v* past tense of **become**

because *conj* on account of the fact that **because of** on account of

beck[1] *n* **at someone's beck and call** having to be constantly available to do as someone asks

beck[2] *n n English* stream

beckon *v* summon with a gesture

become *v* **-coming, -came, -come** come to be; (foll. by *of*) happen to; suit **becoming** *adj* attractive or pleasing; appropriate or proper

bed *n* piece of furniture on which to sleep; garden plot; bottom of a river, lake, or sea; layer of rock **go to bed with** have sexual intercourse with **bed down** *v* go to or put into a place to sleep or rest **bedpan** *n* shallow bowl used as a toilet by bedridden people **bedridden** *adj* confined to bed because of illness or old age **bedrock** *n* solid rock beneath the surface soil; basic facts or principles **bedroom** *n* **bedsit, bedsitter** *n* furnished sitting room with a bed

bedding *n* sheets and covers that are used on a bed

bedevil *v* **-illing, -illed** harass, confuse, or torment

bedlam *n* noisy confused situation

bedraggled *adj* untidy, wet, or dirty

bee *n* insect that makes wax and honey **beehive** *n* structure in which bees live **beeswax** *n* wax secreted by bees, used in polishes etc

beech *n* tree with a smooth greyish bark

beef *n* flesh of a cow, bull, or ox **beefy** *adj* like beef; *Informal* strong and muscular **beefburger** *n* flat grilled or fried cake of minced beef **beefeater** *n* yeoman warder at the Tower of London

been *v* past participle of **be**

beep *n* high-pitched sound, like that of a car horn ▷ *v* (cause to) make this noise

beer *n* alcoholic drink brewed from malt and hops **beery** *adj*

beet *n* plant with an edible root and leaves **beetroot** *n* type of beet plant with a dark red root

beetle *n* insect with a hard wing cover on its back

befall *v old-fashioned* happen to (someone)

befit *v* be appropriate or suitable for **befitting** *adj*

before *conj, prep, adv* indicating something earlier in time, in front of, or preferred to *eg before the war; brought before a judge; death before dishonour* **beforehand** *adv* in advance

befriend *v* become friends with

beg *v* **begging, begged** solicit (for money or food), esp in the street; ask formally or humbly

began *v* past tense of **begin**

beget *v* **-getting, -got** *or* **-gat, -gotten** *or* **-got** *old-fashioned* cause or create; father

beggar *n* person who lives by begging **beggarly** *adj*

begin *v* **-ginning, -gan, -gun** start; bring or come into being **beginner** *n* person who has just started learning to do something **beginning** *n*

begonia *n* tropical plant with waxy flowers

begrudge *v* envy (someone) the possession of something; give or allow unwillingly

beguile [big-**gile**] *v* cheat or mislead; charm or amuse **beguiling** *adj*

begun *v* past participle of **begin**

behalf *n* **on behalf of** in the interest of or for the benefit of

behave *v* act or function in a

particular way; conduct (oneself) properly

behaviour *n* manner of behaving

behead *v* remove the head from

beheld *v* past of **behold**

behest *n* order or earnest request

behind *prep, adv* indicating position to the rear, lateness, responsibility, etc *eg behind the wall; behind schedule; the reasons behind her departure* ▷ *n Informal* buttocks

behold *v* **-holding, -held** *old-fashioned* look (at) **beholder** *n*

beholden *adj* indebted or obliged

behove *v old-fashioned* be necessary or fitting for

beige *adj* pale brown

being *n* state or fact of existing; something that exists or is thought to exist; human being ▷ *v* present participle of **be**

belabour *v* attack verbally or physically

belated *adj* late or too late **belatedly** *adv*

belch *v* expel wind from the stomach noisily through the mouth; expel or be expelled forcefully *eg smoke belched from the factory* ▷ *n* act of belching

beleaguered *adj* struggling against difficulties or criticism; besieged by an enemy

belfry *n, pl* **-fries** part of a tower where bells are hung

belgium sausage *n NZ* large smooth bland sausage

belie *v* show to be untrue

belief *n* faith or confidence; opinion; principle accepted as true, often without proof

believe *v* accept as true or real; think, assume, or suppose **believable** *adj* **believer** *n* **believe in** be convinced of the truth or existence of

Belisha beacon [bill-**lee**-sha] *n Brit* flashing orange globe mounted on a post, marking a pedestrian crossing

belittle *v* treat as having little value or importance

bell *n* hollow, usu metal, cup-shaped instrument that emits a ringing sound when struck; device that rings or buzzes as a signal

belladonna *n* (drug obtained from) deadly nightshade

bellbird *n* Australasian bird with bell-like call

belle *n* beautiful woman, esp the most attractive woman at a function

bellicose *adj* warlike and aggressive

belligerent *adj* hostile and aggressive; engaged in war ▷ *n* person or country engaged in war **belligerence** *n*

bellow *v* make a low deep cry like that of a bull; shout in anger ▷ *n* loud deep roar

bellows *pl n* instrument for pumping a stream of air into something

belly *n, pl* **-lies** part of the body of a vertebrate which contains the intestines; stomach; front, lower, or inner part of something ▷ *v* **-lying, -lied** (cause to) swell out **bellyful** *n slang* more than one can tolerate

belong *v* (foll. by *to*) be the property of; (foll. by *to*) be a part or member of **belongings** *pl n* personal possessions

beloved *adj* dearly loved ▷ *n* person dearly loved

below *prep, adv* at or to a position lower than, under

belt *n* band of cloth, leather, etc, worn usu around the waist; long narrow area *eg a belt of trees*; circular strip of rubber that drives moving parts in a machine ▷*v* fasten with a belt; *slang* hit very hard; *slang* move very fast

bemoan *v* express sorrow or dissatisfaction about

bemused *adj* puzzled or confused

bench *n* long seat; long narrow work table **the bench** judge or magistrate sitting in court, or judges and magistrates collectively **benchmark** *n* criterion by which to measure something

bend *v* **bending, bent** (cause to) form a curve; (often foll. by *down*) etc) incline the body ▷*n* curved part ▷*pl Informal* decompression sickness **bendy** *adj*

beneath *adv, prep* below; not worthy of

Benedictine *adj* of an order of Christian monks and nuns founded by Saint Benedict

benediction *n* prayer for divine blessing

benefactor, benefactress *n* someone who supports a person or institution by giving money **benefaction** *n*

beneficent [bin-**eff**-iss-ent] *adj* charitable or generous **beneficence** *n*

beneficial *adj* helpful or advantageous

beneficiary *n, pl* **-ciaries** person who gains or benefits

benefit *n* something that improves or promotes; advantage or sake *eg I'm doing this for your benefit*; payment made by a government to a poor, ill, or unemployed person ▷*v* **-fiting, -fited** do or receive good

benevolence *n* inclination to do good; act of kindness **benevolent** *adj* **benevolently** *adv*

benighted *adj* ignorant or uncultured

benign [bin-**nine**] *adj* showing kindliness; (of a tumour) not threatening to life **benignly** *adv*

bent *v* past of **bend** ▷*adj* curved; *slang* dishonest or corrupt; *Brit & Aust, offens slang* homosexual ▷*n* personal inclination or aptitude **bent on** determined to pursue (a course of action)

bento, bento box *n* thin lightweight box divided into compartments which contain small separate dishes comprising a Japanese meal

benzene *n* flammable poisonous liquid used as a solvent, insecticide, etc

bequeath *v* dispose of (property) as in a will **bequest** *n* legal gift of money or property by someone who has died

berate *v* scold harshly

bereaved *adj* having recently lost a close friend or relative through death **bereavement** *n*

bereft *adj* (foll. by *of*) deprived

beret [**ber**-ray] *n* round flat close-fitting brimless cap

berg[1] *n* iceberg

berg[2] *n SAfr* mountain

bergamot *n* small Asian tree, the fruit of which yields an oil used in perfumery

beri-beri *n* disease caused by vitamin B deficiency

berk *n Brit, Aust & NZ, slang* stupid person

berm *n NZ* narrow grass strip between the road and the footpath in a residential area

berry *n, pl* **-ries** small soft stoneless fruit

berserk *adj* **go berserk** become violent or destructive

berth *n* bunk in a ship or train; place assigned to a ship at a mooring ▷*v* dock (a ship)
beryl *n* hard transparent mineral
beryllium *n chem* toxic silvery-white metallic element
beseech *v* **-seeching, -sought** *or* **-seeched** ask earnestly; beg
beset *v* trouble or harass constantly
beside *prep* at, by, or to the side of; as compared with **beside oneself** overwhelmed or overwrought
besides *adv, prep* in addition
besiege *v* surround with military forces; overwhelm, as with requests
besotted *adj* infatuated
besought *v* a past of **beseech**
bespeak *v* indicate or suggest
bespoke *adj* (esp of a suit) made to the customer's specifications
best *adj* most excellent of a particular group etc ▷*adv* in a manner surpassing all others ▷*n* most outstanding or excellent person, thing, or group in a category **best man** groom's attendant at a wedding **bestseller** *n* book or other product that has sold in great numbers
bestial *adj* brutal or savage; of or like a beast **bestiality** *n*
bestir *v* cause (oneself) to become active
bestow *v* present (a gift) or confer (an honour) **bestowal** *n*
bestride *v* have or put a leg on either side of
bet *n* the act of staking a sum of money or other stake on the outcome of an event; stake risked ▷*v* **betting, bet** *or* **betted** make or place (a bet); *Informal* predict
betel [bee-tl] *n* Asian climbing plant, the leaves and nuts of which can be chewed
bête noire [bet nwahr] *n, pl* **bêtes noires** person or thing that one particularly dislikes
betide *v* happen (to)
betoken *v* indicate or signify
betray *v* hand over or expose (one's nation, friend, etc) treacherously to an enemy; disclose (a secret or confidence) treacherously; reveal unintentionally **betrayal** *n* **betrayer** *n*
betrothed *adj* engaged to be married **betrothal** *n*
better *adj* more excellent than others; improved or fully recovered in health ▷*adv* in a more excellent manner; in or to a greater degree ▷*pl n* one's superiors ▷*v* improve upon
bettong *n* short-nosed rat kangaroo
between *prep, adv* indicating position in the middle, alternatives, etc
betwixt *prep, adv old-fashioned* between
bevel *n* slanting edge ▷*v* **-elling, -elled** cut a bevel on (a piece of timber etc)
beverage *n* drink
bevy *n, pl* **bevies** flock or group
bewail *v* express great sorrow over
beware *v* be on one's guard (against)
bewilder *v* confuse utterly **bewildering** *adj* **bewilderment** *n*
bewitch *v* attract and fascinate; cast a spell over **bewitching** *adj*
beyond *prep* at or to a point on the other side of; outside the limits or scope of ▷*adv* at or to the far side of something
bi- *combining form* two or twice *eg bifocal; biweekly*
biannual *adj* occurring twice a year **biannually** *adv*

bias *n* mental tendency, esp prejudice; diagonal cut across the weave of a fabric; *bowls* bulge or weight on one side of a bowl that causes it to roll in a curve ▷*v* **-asing, -ased** *or* **-assing, -assed** cause to have a bias **biased, biassed** *adj*

bib *n* piece of cloth or plastic worn to protect a young child's clothes when eating; upper front part of dungarees etc

Bible *n* sacred writings of the Christian religion; **(b-)** book regarded as authoritative **biblical** *adj*

bibliography *n, pl* **-phies** list of books on a subject; list of sources used in a book etc **bibliographer** *n*

bibliophile *n* person who collects or is fond of books

bibulous *adj* addicted to alcohol

bicarbonate *n* salt of carbonic acid **bicarbonate of soda** powder used in baking or as medicine

bicentenary *n, pl* **-naries** 200th anniversary

biceps *n* muscle with two origins, esp the muscle that flexes the forearm

bicker *v* argue over petty matters

bicycle *n* vehicle with two wheels, one behind the other, pedalled by the rider

bid *v* **bidding, bade, bidden** say (a greeting); command *past* **bid** offer (an amount) in an attempt to buy something ▷*n* offer of a specified amount; attempt **bidder** *n* **biddable** *adj* obedient **bidding** *n* command

biddy-bid, biddy-biddy *n, pl* **-bids, -biddies** *NZ* low-growing plant with hooked burrs

bide *v* **bide one's time** wait patiently for an opportunity

bidet [**bee**-day] *n* low basin for washing the genital area

biennial *adj* occurring every two years ▷*n* plant that completes its life cycle in two years

bier *n* stand on which a corpse or coffin rests before burial

bifocals *pl n* spectacles with lenses permitting near and distant vision

big *adj* **bigger, biggest** of considerable size, height, number, or capacity; important through having power, wealth, etc; elder; generous ▷*adv* on a grand scale **bighead** *n Informal* conceited person **big-headed** *adj* **big shot, bigwig** *n Informal* important person

bigamy *n* crime of marrying a person while still legally married to someone else **bigamist** *n* **bigamous** *adj*

bigot *n* person who is intolerant, esp regarding religion or race **bigoted** *adj* **bigotry** *n*

bijou [**bee**-zhoo] *adj* (of a house) small but elegant

bike *n Informal* bicycle or motorcycle

bikini *n* woman's brief two-piece swimming costume

bilateral *adj* affecting or undertaken by two parties

bilberry *n* bluish-black edible berry

bilby *n, pl* **-bies** Australian marsupial with long pointed ears and grey fur

bile *n* bitter yellow fluid secreted by the liver

bilge *n Informal* nonsense; ship's bottom

bilingual *adj* involving or using two languages

bilious *adj* sick, nauseous
bill[1] *n* statement of money owed for goods or services supplied; draft of a proposed new law; poster; *Chiefly US & Canadian* piece of paper money; list of events, such as a theatre programme ▷ *v* send or present a bill to; advertise by posters
bill[2] *n* bird's beak
billabong *n Aust* stagnant pool in an intermittent stream
billet *v* **-leting, -leted** assign a lodging to (a soldier) ▷ *n* accommodation for a soldier in civil lodgings
billet-doux [bill-ee-**doo**] *n, pl* **billets-doux** love letter
billhook *n* tool with a hooked blade, used for chopping etc
billiards *n* game played on a table with balls and a cue
billion *n* one thousand million; formerly, one million million **billionth** *adj*
billow *n* large sea wave ▷ *v* rise up or swell out **billowy, billowing** *adj*
billy, billycan *n, pl* **-lies, -lycans** metal can or pot for cooking on a camp fire
biltong *n SAfr* strips of dried meat
bimbo *n slang* attractive but empty-headed young person, esp a woman
bin *n* container for rubbish or for storing grain, coal, etc
binary *adj* composed of two parts; *maths, computers* of or in a counting system with only two digits, 0 and 1
bind *v* **binding, bound** make secure with or as if with a rope; place (someone) under obligation; enclose and fasten (the pages of a book) between covers ▷ *n Informal* annoying situation **binder** *n* firm cover for holding loose sheets of paper together **binding** *n* anything that binds or fastens; book cover
bindi-eye *n* small Australian plant with burlike fruit
bindweed *n* plant that twines around a support
binge *n Informal* bout of excessive indulgence, esp in drink
bingo *n* gambling game in which numbers are called out and covered by the players on their individual cards
binoculars *pl n* optical instrument consisting of two small telescopes joined together
binomial *n, adj* (mathematical expression) consisting of two terms
bio- *combining form* life or living organisms *eg biology*
biochemistry *n* study of the chemistry of living things **biochemist** *n*
biodegradable *adj* capable of being decomposed by natural means
biodiversity *n* existence of a wide variety of species in their natural environment
biographer *n* person who writes an account of another person's life
biography *n, pl* **-phies** account of a person's life by another person **biographical** *adj*
biological *adj* of or relating to biology
biology *n* study of living organisms **biologist** *n*
biometric *adj* of any automated system using physiological or behavioural traits as a means of identification *eg biometric fingerprinting*
bionic *adj* having a part of the body that is operated electronically
biopsy *n, pl* **-sies** examination of tissue from a living body

biotechnology *n* use of microorganisms, such as cells or bacteria, in industry and technology
bioterrorism *n* use of viruses, bacteria, etc, by terrorists **bioterrorist** *n*
biped [bye-ped] *n* animal with two feet
biplane *n* aeroplane with two sets of wings, one above the other
birch *n* tree with thin peeling bark; birch rod or twigs used, esp formerly, for flogging offenders
bird *n* creature with feathers and wings, most types of which can fly; *slang* young woman
birdie *n golf* score of one stroke under par for a hole
biretta *n* stiff square cap worn by the Catholic clergy
Biro *n* ® ballpoint pen
birth *n* process of bearing young; childbirth; act of being born; ancestry **give birth to** bear (offspring) **birth control** any method of contraception **birthday** *n* anniversary of the day of one's birth **birthmark** *n* blemish on the skin formed before birth **birthright** *n* privileges or possessions that someone is entitled to as soon as he or she is born
biscuit *n* small flat dry sweet or plain cake
bisect *v* divide into two equal parts
bisexual *adj* sexually attracted to both men and women **bisexuality** *n*
bishop *n* clergyman who governs a diocese; chessman which is moved diagonally **bishopric** *n* diocese or office of a bishop
bismuth *n chem* pinkish-white metallic element
bison *n, pl* **-son** large hairy animal of the cattle family, native to N America and Europe
bistro *n, pl* **-tros** small restaurant
bit[1] *n* small piece, portion, or quantity **a bit** rather, somewhat **bit by bit** gradually
bit[2] *n* metal mouthpiece on a bridle; cutting or drilling part of a tool
bit[3] *v* past tense of **bite**
bit[4] *n maths, computers* single digit of binary notation, either 0 or 1
bitch *n* female dog, fox, or wolf; *offens* spiteful woman ▷ *v Informal* complain or grumble **bitchy** *adj* **bitchiness** *n*
bite *v* **biting, bit, bitten** grip, tear, or puncture the skin, as with the teeth or jaws; take firm hold of or act effectively upon ▷ *n* act of biting; wound or sting inflicted by biting; snack **biter** *n* **biting** *adj* piercing or keen; sarcastic
bitter *adj* having a sharp unpleasant taste; showing or caused by hostility or resentment; extremely cold ▷ *n* beer with a slightly bitter taste ▷ *pl* bitter-tasting alcoholic drink **bitterly** *adv* **bitterness** *n*
bittern *n* wading marsh bird with a booming call
bitumen *n* black sticky substance obtained from tar or petrol
bivalve *n, adj* (marine mollusc) with two hinged segments to its shell
bivouac *n* temporary camp in the open air ▷ *v* **-acking, -acked** camp in a bivouac
bizarre *adj* odd or unusual
blab *v* **blabbing, blabbed** reveal (secrets) indiscreetly
black *adj* of the darkest colour, like

coal; (**B-**) dark-skinned; without hope; angry or resentful *eg black looks;* unpleasant in a macabre manner *eg black comedy* ▷ *n* darkest colour; (**B-**) member of a dark-skinned race; complete darkness ▷ *v* make black; (of trade unionists) boycott (goods or people) **blackness** *n* **blacken** *v* make or become black; defame or slander **black magic** magic used for evil purposes **black market** illegal trade in goods or currencies **black sheep** person who is regarded as a disgrace by his or her family **black spot** place on a road where accidents frequently occur

blackball *v* exclude from a group ▷ *n NZ* hard boiled sweet with black-and-white stripes

blackberry *n* small blackish edible fruit

blackbird *n* common European thrush

blackboard *n* hard black surface used for writing on with chalk

blackboy *n* Australian plant with grasslike leaves and a spike of small white flowers

blackbutt *n* Australian eucalyptus tree with hard wood used as timber

blackcurrant *n* very small blackish edible fruit that grows in bunches

blackfish *n* small dark Australian estuary fish

blackguard [**blag**-gard] *n* unprincipled person

blackhead *n* black-tipped plug of fatty matter clogging a skin pore

blackleg *n* person who continues to work during a strike

blacklist *n* list of people or organizations considered untrustworthy etc

blackmail *n* act of attempting to extort money by threats ▷ *v* (attempt to) obtain money by blackmail

blackout *n* extinguishing of all light as a precaution against an air attack; momentary loss of consciousness or memory **black out** *v* extinguish (lights); lose consciousness or memory temporarily

blacksmith *n* person who works iron with a furnace, anvil, etc

black snake *n* venomous Australian snake

black swan *n* black Australian swan with a red beak

bladder *n* sac in the body where urine is held; hollow bag which may be filled with air or liquid

blade *n* cutting edge of a weapon or tool; thin flattish part of a propeller, oar, etc; leaf of grass

blame *v* consider (someone) responsible for ▷ *n* responsibility for something that is wrong **blameless** *adj* **blameworthy** *adj* deserving blame

blanch *v* become white or pale; prepare (vegetables etc) by plunging them in boiling water

blancmange [blam-**monzh**] *n* jelly-like dessert made with milk

bland *adj* dull and uninteresting **blandly** *adv*

blandishments *pl n* flattery intended to coax or persuade

blank *adj* not written on; showing no interest or expression ▷ *n* empty space; cartridge containing no bullet **blankly** *adv* **blank verse** unrhymed verse

blanket *n* large thick cloth used as covering for a bed; concealing cover, as of snow ▷ *v* cover as with a blanket

blare *v* sound loudly and harshly ▷*n* loud harsh noise
blarney *n* flattering talk
blasé [**blah**-zay] *adj* indifferent or bored through familiarity
blaspheme *v* speak disrespectfully of (God or sacred things) **blasphemy** *n* **blasphemous** *adj* **blasphemer** *n*
blast *n* explosion; sudden strong gust of air or wind; sudden loud sound, as of a trumpet ▷*v* blow up (a rock etc) with explosives **blastoff** *n* launching of a rocket
blatant *adj* glaringly obvious **blatantly** *adv*
blaze[1] *n* strong fire or flame; very bright light ▷*v* burn or shine brightly
blaze[2] *n* mark made on a tree to indicate a route
blazer *n* lightweight jacket, often in the colours of a school etc
blazon *v* proclaim publicly
bleach *v* make or become white or colourless ▷*n* bleaching agent
bleak *adj* exposed and barren; offering little hope
bleary *adj* **-rier, -riest** with eyes dimmed, as by tears or tiredness **blearily** *adv*
bleat *v* (of a sheep, goat, or calf) utter its plaintive cry ▷*n* cry of sheep, goats, and calves
bleed *v* **bleeding, bled** lose or emit blood; draw blood from (a person or animal); *Informal* obtain money by extortion
bleep *n* short high-pitched sound made by an electrical device ▷*v* make a bleeping sound **bleeper** *n* small portable radio receiver that makes a bleeping signal
blemish *n* defect or stain ▷*v* spoil or tarnish
blench *v* shy away, as in fear
blend *v* mix or mingle (components or ingredients); look good together ▷*n* mixture **blender** *n* electrical appliance for puréeing vegetables etc
bless *v* make holy by means of a religious rite; call upon God to protect; endow with health, talent, etc **blessed** *adj* holy **blessing** *n* invoking of divine aid; approval; happy event
blether *Scot* ▷*v* talk, esp foolishly or at length ▷*n* conversation
blew *v* past tense of **blow**[1]
blight *n* person or thing that spoils or prevents growth; withering plant disease ▷*v* frustrate or disappoint
blighter *n Informal* irritating person
blimp *n* small airship
blind *adj* unable to see; unable or unwilling to understand; not determined by reason *eg blind hatred* ▷*v* deprive of sight; deprive of good sense, reason, or judgment ▷*n* covering for a window; something that serves to conceal the truth **blindly** *adv* **blindness** *n*
blindfold *v* prevent (a person) from seeing by covering the eyes ▷*n* piece of cloth used to cover the eyes
blink *v* close and immediately reopen (the eyes); shine intermittently ▷*n* act of blinking **on the blink** *slang* not working properly
blinkers *pl n* leather flaps on a horse's bridle to prevent sideways vision
blip *n* spot of light on a radar screen indicating the position of an object
bliss *n* perfect happiness **blissful** *adj* **blissfully** *adv*
blister *n* small bubble on the skin; swelling, as on a painted surface

▷ *v* (cause to) have blisters **blistering** *adj* (of weather) very hot; (of criticism) extremely harsh

blithe *adj* casual and indifferent **blithely** *adv*

blitz *n* violent and sustained attack by aircraft; intensive attack or concerted effort ▷ *v* attack suddenly and intensively

blizzard *n* blinding storm of wind and snow

bloat *v* cause to swell, as with liquid or air

bloater *n Brit* salted smoked herring

blob *n* soft mass or drop; indistinct or shapeless form

bloc *n* people or countries combined by a common interest

block *n* large solid piece of wood, stone, etc; large building of offices, flats, etc; group of buildings enclosed by intersecting streets; obstruction or hindrance; *slang* person's head ▷ *v* obstruct or impede by introducing an obstacle **blockage** *n* **blockhead** *n* stupid person **block letter** plain capital letter

blockade *n* sealing off of a place to prevent the passage of goods ▷ *v* impose a blockade on

blockie *n Aust* owner of a small property, esp a farm

blog *n* short for **weblog**

bloke *n Informal* man

blonde *masc* **blond** *adj, n* fair-haired (person)

blood *n* red fluid that flows around the body; race or kinship **in cold blood** done deliberately **bloodless** *adj* **blood bath** massacre **bloodhound** *n* large dog formerly used for tracking **bloodshed** *n* slaughter or killing **bloodshot** *adj* (of an eye) inflamed **blood sport** sport involving the killing of animals **bloodstream** *n* flow of blood round the body **bloodsucker** *n* animal that sucks blood; *Informal* person who extorts money from other people **bloodthirsty** *adj* taking pleasure in violence

bloody *adj* covered with blood; marked by much killing ▷ *adj, adv slang* extreme or extremely ▷ *v* stain with blood **bloody-minded** *adj* deliberately unhelpful

bloom *n* blossom on a flowering plant; youthful or healthy glow ▷ *v* bear flowers; be in a healthy, glowing condition

bloomer *n Brit, Informal* stupid mistake

bloomers *pl n* woman's baggy knickers

blooper *n Chiefly US, Informal* stupid mistake

blossom *n* flowers of a plant ▷ *v* (of plants) flower; come to a promising stage

blot *n* spot or stain; something that spoils ▷ *v* **blotting, blotted** cause a blemish in or on; soak up (ink) by using blotting paper **blotter** *n* **blot out** *v* darken or hide completely **blotting paper** soft absorbent paper for soaking up ink

blotch *n* discoloured area or stain **blotchy** *adj*

blotto *adj Brit, Aust & NZ, slang* extremely drunk

blouse *n* woman's shirtlike garment

blow[1] *v* **blowing, blew, blown** (of air, the wind, etc) move; move or be carried as if by the wind; expel (air etc) through the mouth or nose; cause (a musical instrument) to sound by forcing air into it; burn out (a fuse etc); *slang* spend (money) freely **blower** *n* **blowy** *adj* windy **blow-dry** *v* style (the hair) with a hand-held dryer **blowout** *n* sudden loss of air in a tyre; escape of oil or gas from a well; *slang* filling meal **blow up** *v* explode; fill with air; *Informal* lose one's temper; *Informal* enlarge (a photograph)

blow² *n* hard hit; sudden setback; attacking action

blowie *n Aust, Informal* bluebottle

blown *v* past participle of **blow¹**

blowsy *adj* fat, untidy, and red-faced

blubber *n* fat of whales, seals, etc ▷ *v* sob without restraint

bludge *Informal* ▷ *v Aust & NZ* evade work; *Aust & NZ* scrounge ▷ *n Aust* easy task **bludger** *n* person who scrounges

bludgeon *n* short thick club ▷ *v* hit with a bludgeon; force or bully

blue *n* colour of a clear unclouded sky ▷ *pl* feeling of depression; type of folk music of Black American origin ▷ *adj* **bluer, bluest** of the colour blue; depressed; pornographic **out of the blue** unexpectedly **bluish** *adj* **bluebell** *n* flower with blue bell-shaped flowers **bluebottle** *n* large fly with a dark-blue body **blue-collar** *adj* denoting manual industrial workers **blue heeler** *Aust & NZ, Informal* dog that controls cattle by biting their heels **blueprint** *n* photographic print of a plan; description of how a plan is expected to work **bluetongue** *n* Australian lizard with a blue tongue

bluff¹ *v* pretend to be confident in order to influence (someone) ▷ *n* act of bluffing

bluff² *n* steep cliff or bank ▷ *adj* good-naturedly frank and hearty

blunder *n* clumsy mistake ▷ *v* make a blunder; act clumsily

blunderbuss *n* obsolete gun with a wide flared muzzle

blunt *adj* not having a sharp edge or point; (of people, speech, etc) straightforward or uncomplicated ▷ *v* make less sharp **bluntly** *adv*

blur *v* **blurring, blurred** make or become vague or less distinct ▷ *n* something vague, hazy, or indistinct **blurry** *adj*

blurb *n* promotional description, as on the jacket of a book

blurt *v* (foll. by *out*) utter suddenly and involuntarily

blush *v* become red in the face, esp from embarrassment or shame ▷ *n* reddening of the face

bluster *v* speak loudly or in a bullying way ▷ *n* empty threats or protests **blustery** *adj* (of weather) rough and windy

BMA British Medical Association

BO *Informal* body odour

boa *n* large nonvenomous snake; long scarf of fur or feathers **boa constrictor** large snake that kills its prey by crushing

boab [boh-ab] *n Aust, Informal* short for **baobab**

boar *n* uncastrated male pig; wild pig

board *n* long flat piece of sawn timber; smaller flat piece of rigid material for a specific purpose *eg ironing board; chess board*; group of people who administer a company, trust, etc; meals provided for money ▷ *v* go aboard (a train, aeroplane, etc); cover with boards; receive meals and lodgings in return for money **on board** on or in a ship, aeroplane, etc **boarder** *n* person who pays rent in return for accommodation in someone else's home; *Brit* pupil who lives at school during the school term **boarding house** private house that provides meals and accommodation for paying guests **boardroom** *n* room where the board of a company meets

boast *v* speak too proudly about one's talents etc; possess (something to be proud of) ▷ *n* bragging statement **boastful** *adj*

boat *n* small vehicle for travelling across water **boater** *n* flat straw hat **boating** *n*

boatswain *n* same as **bosun**

bob¹ *v* **bobbing, bobbed** move up and down repeatedly ▷ *n* short abrupt movement

bob² *n* hairstyle in which the hair is cut short evenly all round the head ▷ *v* **bobbing, bobbed** cut (the hair) in a bob

bobbin *n* reel on which thread is wound

bobble *n* small ball of material, usu for decoration

bobby *n, pl* **-bies** *Brit, Informal* policeman

bobotie [ba-**boot**-ee] *n SAfr* dish of curried mince

bobsleigh *n* sledge for racing down an icy track ▷ *v* ride on a bobsleigh

bode *v* be an omen of (good or ill)

bodice *n* upper part of a dress

bodkin *n* blunt large-eyed needle

body *n, pl* **bodies** entire physical structure of an animal or human; trunk or torso; corpse; group regarded as a single entity; main part of anything; woman's one-piece undergarment **bodily** *adj* relating to the body ▷ *adv* by taking hold of the body **body-board** *n* small polystyrene surfboard **body-boarder** *n* **bodyguard** *n* person or group of people employed to protect someone **bodywork** *n* outer shell of a motor vehicle

Boer *n* descendant of the Dutch settlers in S Africa **boerewors** *n S Afr* spiced sausage

boffin *n Brit, Aust, NZ & S Afr, Informal* scientist or expert

bog *n* wet spongy ground; *slang* toilet **boggy** *adj* **bog down** *v* **bogging, bogged** impede physically or mentally

bogan *n Aust dated & NZ, slang* youth who dresses and behaves rebelliously

bogey, bogy *n* something that worries or annoys; *golf* score of one stroke over par on a hole

boggle *v* be surprised, confused, or alarmed

bogong, bugong *n* large nocturnal Australian moth

bogus *adj* not genuine

bogy *n, pl* **-gies** same as **bogey**

bohemian *n, adj* (person) leading an unconventional life

boil¹ *v* (cause to) change from a liquid to a vapour so quickly that bubbles are formed; cook by the process of boiling ▷ *n* state or action of boiling **boiler** *n* piece of equipment which provides hot water

boil² *n* red pus-filled swelling on the skin

boisterous *adj* noisy and lively **boisterously** *adv*

bold *adj* confident and fearless; immodest or impudent **boldly** *adv* **boldness** *n*

bole *n* tree trunk

bolero *n, pl* **-ros** (music for) traditional Spanish dance; short open jacket

bollard *n* short thick post used to prevent the passage of motor vehicles

boloney *n* same as **baloney**

Bolshevik *n* (formerly) Russian Communist **bolshie, bolshy** *adj Informal* difficult or rebellious

bolster *v* support or strengthen ▷ *n* long narrow pillow

bolt *n* sliding metal bar for fastening a door etc; metal pin which screws into a nut; flash (of lightning) ▷ *v* run away suddenly; fasten with a bolt; eat hurriedly **bolt upright** stiff and rigid **bolt hole** place of escape

bomb *n* container fitted with explosive material; *slang* large amount of money ▷ *v* attack with bombs; move very quickly **the bomb** nuclear bomb **bomber** *n* aircraft that drops bombs; person who throws or puts a bomb in a particular place **bomb out** *v Aust, NZ & SAfr, Informal* fail disastrously **bombshell** *n* shocking or unwelcome surprise

bombard *v* attack with heavy gunfire or bombs; attack verbally, esp with questions **bombardment** *n*

bombast *n* pompous language **bombastic** *adj*

bona fide [bone-a **fide**-ee] *adj* genuine

bonanza *n* sudden good luck or wealth

bond *n* something that binds, fastens or holds together; something that unites people; written or spoken agreement; *finance* certificate of debt issued to raise funds; *SAfr* conditional pledging of property, esp a house, as security for the repayment of a loan ▷ *pl* something that restrains or imprisons ▷ *v* bind **bonded** *adj*

bondage *n* slavery

bone *n* any of the hard parts in the body that form the skeleton ▷ *v* remove the bones from (meat for cooking etc) **boneless** *adj* **bony** *adj* having many bones; thin or emaciated **bone-dry** *adj* completely dry **bone-idle** *adj* extremely lazy

bonfire *n* large outdoor fire

bongo *n, pl* **-gos, -goes** small drum played with the fingers

bonhomie [bon-om-**ee**] *n* cheerful friendliness

bonito [ba-**nee**-toh] *n, pl* **-os** small tunny-like marine food fish; related fish, whose flesh is dried and flaked and used in Japanese cookery

bonk *v Informal* have sex with; hit

bonnet *n* metal cover over a vehicle's engine; hat which ties under the chin

bonny *adj* **-nier, -niest** *Scot* beautiful

bonsai *n, pl* **-sai** ornamental miniature tree or shrub

bonus *n* something given, paid, or received above what is due or expected

boo *interj* shout of disapproval ▷ *v* **booing, booed** shout 'boo' to show disapproval

boob *slang* ▷ *n* foolish mistake; female breast; *Aust, slang* prison

boobook [**boo**-book] *n* small spotted Australian brown owl

booby *n, pl* **-bies** foolish person **booby prize** prize given for the lowest score in a competition **booby trap** hidden bomb primed to be set off by an unsuspecting victim; trap for an unsuspecting person, intended as a joke

boogie *v Informal* dance to fast pop music

book *n* number of pages bound together between covers; long written work; number of tickets, stamps, etc fastened together ▷ *pl* record of transactions of a business or society ▷ *v* reserve (a place, passage, etc) in advance; record the name of (a person) who has committed an offence **booklet** *n* thin book with paper covers

book-keeping *n* systematic recording of business transactions

bookmaker *n* person whose occupation is taking bets

bookmark *n* strip of some material put between the pages of a book to mark a place; *computers* marker on a website that enables the user to return to it quickly and easily ▷ *v computers* identify and store (a website) so that one can return to it quickly and easily

bookworm *n* person devoted to reading

boom[1] *v* make a loud deep echoing sound; prosper vigorously and rapidly ▷ *n* loud deep echoing sound; period of high economic growth **boomer** *n Aust* large male kangaroo

boom[2] *n* pole to which the foot of a sail is attached; pole carrying an overhead microphone; barrier across a waterway

boomerang *n* curved wooden missile which can be made to return to the thrower ▷ *v* (of a plan) recoil unexpectedly

boon *n* something helpful or beneficial

boongary [**boong**-gar-ree] *n, pl* **-garies** tree kangaroo of NE Queensland, Australia

boor *n* rude or insensitive person **boorish** *adj*

boost *n* encouragement or help; increase ▷ *v* improve; increase **booster** *n* small additional injection of a vaccine

boot[1] *n* outer covering for the foot that extends above the ankle; space in a car for luggage; *Informal* kick ▷ *v Informal* kick; start up (a computer) **bootee** *n* baby's soft shoe **boot camp** centre for young offenders, with strict discipline and hard physical exercise **boot-cut** *adj* (of trousers) slightly flared at the bottom of the legs

boot[2] *n* **to boot** in addition

booth *n* small partly enclosed cubicle; stall at a fair or market

bootleg *adj* produced, distributed, or sold illicitly ▷ *v* **-legging, -legged** make, carry, or sell (illicit goods) **bootlegger** *n*

booty *n, pl* **-ties** valuable articles obtained as plunder

booze *v, n Informal* (consume) alcoholic drink **boozy** *adj* **boozer** *n Informal* person who is fond of drinking; *Brit, Aust & NZ* pub **booze-up** *n Informal* drinking spree

bop *v* **bopping, bopped** *Informal* dance to pop music

bora *n Aust* Aboriginal ceremony

borax *n* white mineral used in making glass

border *n* dividing line between political or geographical regions; band around or along the edge of something ▷ *v* provide with a border; be nearly the same as *eg resentment that borders on hatred*

bore[1] *v* make (a hole) with a drill etc ▷ *n* (diameter of) the hollow of a gun barrel or other tube

bore[2] *v* make weary by being dull or repetitious ▷ *n* dull or repetitious person or thing **bored** *adj* **boredom** *n*

bore[3] *n* high wave in a narrow estuary, caused by the tide

bore[4] *v* past tense of **bear**[1]

boree [baw-ree] *n Aust* same as **myall**

born *v* a past participle of **bear**[1] ▷ *adj* possessing certain qualities from birth *eg a born musician*

borne *v* a past participle of **bear**[1]

boron *n chem* element used in hardening steel

boronia *n* Australian aromatic flowering shrub

borough *n Chiefly Brit* town or district with its own council

borrow *v* obtain (something) temporarily; adopt (ideas etc) from another source **borrower** *n*

borstal *n* (formerly in Britain) prison for young criminals

borzoi *n* tall dog with a long silky coat

bosh *n Brit, Aust & NZ, Informal* empty talk, nonsense

bosom *n* chest of a person, esp the female breasts ▷ *adj* very dear *eg a bosom friend*

boss[1] *n* person in charge of or employing others ▷ *v* **boss around, about** be domineering towards **bossy** *adj*

boss[2] *n* raised knob or stud

bosun *n* officer responsible for the maintenance of a ship

botany *n* study of plants **botanical, botanic** *adj* **botanist** *n*

botch *v* spoil through clumsiness ▷ *n* (also **botch-up**) badly done piece of work or repair

both *adj, pron* two considered together

bother *v* take the time or trouble; give annoyance or trouble to; pester ▷ *n* trouble, fuss, or difficulty **bothersome** *adj*

bottle *n* container for holding liquids; *Brit, Informal* courage ▷ *v* put in a bottle **bottleneck** *n* narrow stretch of road where traffic is held up **bottle shop** *Aust & NZ* shop licensed to sell alcohol for drinking elsewhere **bottle store** *SAfr* shop licensed to sell alcohol for drinking elsewhere **bottle tree** Australian tree with a bottle-shaped swollen trunk **bottle up** *v* restrain (powerful emotion)

bottom *n* lowest, deepest, or farthest removed part of a thing; buttocks ▷ *adj* lowest or last **bottomless** *adj*

botulism *n* severe food poisoning

boudoir [boo-dwahr] *n* woman's bedroom or private sitting room

bougainvillea *n* climbing plant with red or purple flowers

bough *n* large branch of a tree

bought *v* past of **buy**

boulder *n* large rounded rock

boulevard *n* wide, usu tree-lined, street

bounce *v* (of a ball etc) rebound from an impact; *slang* (of a cheque) be returned uncashed owing to a lack of funds in the account ▷ *n* act of rebounding; springiness; *Informal* vitality or vigour **bouncer** *n* person employed at a disco etc to remove unwanted people **bouncing** *adj* vigorous and robust

bound[1] *v* past of **bind** ▷ *adj* destined or certain; compelled or obliged

bound[2] *v* move forwards by jumps ▷ *n* jump upwards or forwards

bound[3] *v* form a boundary of ▷ *pl n* limit **boundary** *n* dividing line that indicates the farthest limit

bound[4] *adj* going or intending to go towards *eg homeward bound*

bounty *n, pl* **-ties** generosity; generous gift or reward **bountiful, bounteous** *adj*

bouquet *n* bunch of flowers; aroma of wine
bourbon [**bur**-bn] *n* whiskey made from maize
bourgeois [**boor**-zhwah] *adj, n offens* middle-class (person)
bout *n* period of activity or illness; boxing or wrestling match
boutique *n* small clothes shop
bovine *adj* relating to cattle; rather slow and stupid
bow¹ [rhymes with **now**] *v* lower (one's head) or bend (one's knee or body) as a sign of respect or shame; comply or accept ▷ *n* movement made when bowing
bow² [rhymes with **go**] *n* knot with two loops and loose ends; weapon for shooting arrows; long stick stretched with horsehair for playing stringed instruments **bow-legged** *adj* having legs that curve outwards at the knees
bow³ [rhymes with **now**] *n* front end of a ship
bowdlerize *v* remove words regarded as indecent from (a play, novel, etc)
bowel *n* intestine, esp the large intestine ▷ *pl* innermost part
bower *n* shady leafy shelter **bowerbird** *n* songbird of Australia and New Guinea, the males of which build bower-like display grounds to attract females
bowl¹ *n* round container with an open top; hollow part of an object
bowl² *n* large heavy ball ▷ *pl* game played on smooth grass with wooden bowls ▷ *v cricket* send (a ball) towards the batsman **bowling** *n* game in which bowls are rolled at a group of pins
bowler¹ *n cricket* player who sends (a ball) towards the batsman; person who plays bowls or bowling
bowler² *n* stiff felt hat with a rounded crown
box¹ *n* container with a firm flat base and sides; separate compartment in a theatre, stable, etc ▷ *v* put into a box **the box** *Informal* television **box jellyfish** highly venomous jellyfish with a cuboidal body that lives in Australian tropical waters **box office** place where theatre or cinema tickets are sold
box² *v* fight (an opponent) in a boxing match **boxer** *n* person who participates in the sport of boxing; medium-sized dog with smooth hair and a short nose **boxer shorts, boxers** *pl n* men's underpants shaped like shorts but with a front opening **boxing** *n* sport of fighting with the fists
box³ *n* evergreen tree with shiny leaves; eucalyptus with similar timber and foliage, and with rough bark
boy *n* male child **boyish** *adj* **boyhood** *n* **boyfriend** *n* male friend with whom a person is romantically or sexually involved
boycott *v* refuse to deal with (an organization or country) ▷ *n* instance of boycotting

> SPELLING The word **boycott** has two *t*s, whether or not it has an ending such as in **boycotting**

bra *n* woman's undergarment for supporting the breasts
braaivlies [**brye**-flayss] **braai** *SAfr* ▷ *n* grill on which food is cooked over hot charcoal, usu outdoors; outdoor party at which food like this is served ▷ *v* cook (food) on in this way
brace *n* object fastened to something to straighten or support it; pair, esp of game birds ▷ *pl*

straps worn over the shoulders to hold up trousers ▷*v* steady or prepare (oneself) for something unpleasant; strengthen or fit with a brace **bracing** *adj* refreshing and invigorating

bracelet *n* ornamental chain or band for the wrist

bracken *n* large fern

bracket *n* pair of characters used to enclose a section of writing; group falling within certain defined limits; support fixed to a wall ▷*v* **-eting, -eted** put in brackets; class together

brackish *adj* (of water) slightly salty

bract *n* leaf at the base of a flower

brag *v* **bragging, bragged** speak arrogantly and boastfully **braggart** *n*

braid *v* interweave (hair, thread, etc) ▷*n* length of hair etc that has been braided; narrow ornamental tape of woven silk etc

Braille *n* system of writing for the blind, consisting of raised dots interpreted by touch

brain *n* soft mass of nervous tissue in the head; intellectual ability ▷*v* hit (someone) hard on the head **brainless** *adj* stupid **brainy** *adj* *Informal* clever **brainchild** *n* idea produced by creative thought **brain up** *v* *Brit* make (something) more intellectually demanding or **brainwash** *v* cause (a person) to alter his or her beliefs, esp by methods based on isolation, sleeplessness, etc **brainwave** *n* sudden idea

braise *v* cook slowly in a covered pan with a little liquid

brake *n* device for slowing or stopping a vehicle ▷*v* slow down or stop by using a brake

bramble *n* prickly shrub that produces blackberries

bran *n* husks of cereal grain

branch *n* secondary stem of a tree; offshoot or subsidiary part of something larger or more complex ▷*v* (of stems, roots, etc) divide, then develop in different directions **branch out** *v* expand one's interests

brand *n* particular product; particular kind or variety; identifying mark burnt onto the skin of an animal ▷*v* mark with a brand; denounce as being **brand-new** *adj* absolutely new

brandish *v* wave (a weapon etc) in a threatening way

brandy *n, pl* **-dies** alcoholic spirit distilled from wine

brash *adj* offensively loud, showy, or self-confident **brashness** *n*

brass *n* alloy of copper and zinc; family of wind instruments made of brass; *n English, dialect* money **brassy** *adj* brazen or flashy; like brass, esp in colour

brassiere *n* bra

brat *n* unruly child

bravado *n* showy display of self-confidence

brave *adj* having or showing courage, resolution, and daring ▷*n* Native American warrior ▷*v* confront with resolution or courage **bravery** *n*

bravo *interj* well done!

brawl *n* noisy fight ▷*v* fight noisily

brawn *n* physical strength; pressed meat from the head of a pig or calf **brawny** *adj*

bray *v* (of a donkey) utter its loud harsh sound ▷*n* donkey's loud harsh sound

brazen *adj* shameless and bold ▷*v*

brazenly *adv*
brazier [bray-zee-er] *n* portable container for burning charcoal or coal
breach *n* breaking of a promise, obligation, etc; gap or break ▷ *v* break (a promise, law, etc); make a gap in
bread *n* food made by baking a mixture of flour and water or milk; *slang* money **breadwinner** *n* person whose earnings support a family
breadth *n* extent of something from side to side
break *v* **breaking, broke, broken** separate or become separated into two or more pieces; damage or become damaged so as to be inoperative; fail to observe (an agreement etc); disclose or be disclosed *eg he broke the news*; bring or come to an end *eg the good weather broke at last*; weaken or be weakened, as in spirit; improve on or surpass *eg break a record*; (of the male voice) become permanently deeper at puberty ▷ *n* act or result of breaking; gap or interruption in continuity; *Informal* fortunate opportunity **break even** make neither a profit nor a loss **breakable** *adj* **breakage** *n* **breaker** *n* large wave **break down** *v* cease to function; yield to strong emotion **breakdown** *n* act or instance of breaking down; nervous breakdown **break-in** *n* illegal entering of a building, esp by thieves **breakneck** *adj* fast and dangerous **break off** *v* sever or detach; end (a relationship etc) **break out** *v* begin or arise suddenly **breakthrough** *n* important development or discovery **break up** *v* (cause to) separate; come to an end; (of a school) close for the holidays; (of a caller) to become inaudible on the telephone **breakwater** *n* wall that extends into the sea to protect a harbour or beach from the force of waves
breakfast *v, n* (eat) the first meal of the day
bream *n* freshwater fish with silvery scales; food fish of European seas
breast *n* either of the two soft fleshy milk-secreting glands on a woman's chest; chest **breastbone** *n* long flat bone in the front of the body, to which most of the ribs are attached **breaststroke** *n* swimming stroke in which the arms are extended in front of the head and swept back on either side
breath *n* taking in and letting out of air during breathing; air taken in and let out during breathing **breathless** *adj* **breathtaking** *adj* causing awe or excitement **breathe** *v* take in oxygen and give out carbon dioxide; whisper **breather** *n* *Informal* short rest **breathing** *n*
Breathalyser *n* ® device for estimating the amount of alcohol in the breath **breathalyse** *v*
bred *v* past of **breed**
breech *n* buttocks; back part of gun where bullet or shell is loaded **breech birth** birth of a baby with the feet or buttocks appearing first
breeches *pl n* trousers extending to just below the knee
breed *v* **breeding, bred** produce new or improved strains of (domestic animals or plants); bear (offspring); produce or be produced *eg breed trouble* ▷ *n* group of animals etc within a species that have certain clearly defined

characteristics; kind or sort **breeder** *n* **breeding** *n* result of good upbringing or training

breeze *n* gentle wind ▷*v* move quickly or casually **breezy** *adj* windy; casual or carefree

brethren *pl n old-fashioned* (used in religious contexts) brothers

brevity *n* shortness

brew *v* make (beer etc) by steeping, boiling, and fermentation; prepare (a drink) by infusing; be about to happen or forming ▷*n* beverage produced by brewing

brewer *n* person or company that brews beer **brewery** *n, pl* **-eries** place where beer etc is brewed

briar[1], **brier** *n* European shrub with a hard woody root; tobacco pipe made from this root

briar[2] *n* same as **brier**[1]

bribe *v* offer or give something to someone to gain favour, influence, etc ▷*n* something given or offered as a bribe **bribery** *n*

bric-a-brac *n* miscellaneous small ornamental objects

brick *n* (rectangular block of) baked clay used in building ▷*v* (foll. by *up, over*) build, enclose, or fill with bricks **bricklayer** *n* person who builds with bricks

bride *n* woman who has just been or is about to be married **bridal** *adj* **bridegroom** *n* man who has just been or is about to be married **bridesmaid** *n* girl or woman who attends a bride at her wedding

bridge[1] *n* structure for crossing a river etc; platform from which a ship is steered or controlled; upper part of the nose; piece of wood supporting the strings of a violin etc ▷*v* build a bridge over (something) **bridgehead** *n* fortified position at the end of a bridge nearest the enemy

bridge[2] *n* card game based on whist, played between two pairs

bridle *n* headgear for controlling a horse ▷*v* show anger or indignation **bridle path** path suitable for riding horses

brief *adj* short in duration ▷*n* condensed statement or written synopsis; (also **briefing**) set of instructions ▷*pl* men's or women's underpants ▷*v* give information and instructions to (a person) **briefly** *adv* **briefcase** *n* small flat case for carrying papers, books, etc

brier[1], **briar** *n* wild rose with long thorny stems

brier[2] *n* same as **briar**[1]

brig *n* two-masted square-rigged ship

brigade *n* army unit smaller than a division; group of people organized for a certain task

brigadier *n* high-ranking army officer

brigalow *n Aust* type of acacia tree

brigand *n lit* bandit

brigantine *n* two-masted sailing ship

bright *adj* emitting or reflecting much light; (of colours) intense; clever **brightly** *adv* **brightness** *n* **brighten** *v*

brilliant *adj* shining with light; splendid; extremely clever **brilliance, brilliancy** *n*

brim *n* upper rim of a cup etc; projecting edge of a hat ▷*v* **brimming, brimmed** be full to the brim

brimstone *n obs* sulphur

brine *n* salt water **briny** *adj* very salty **the briny** *Informal* the sea

bring *v* **bringing, brought** carry, convey, or take to a designated place or person; cause to happen;

law put forward (charges) officially **bring about** *v* cause to happen **bring off** *v* succeed in achieving **bring out** *v* publish or have (a book) published; reveal or cause to be seen **bring up** *v* rear (a child); mention; vomit (food)

brinjal *n SAfr* dark purple tropical fruit, cooked and eaten as a vegetable

brink *n* edge of a steep place

brisk *adj* lively and quick **briskly** *adv*

brisket *n* beef from the breast of a cow

bristle *n* short stiff hair ▷ *v* (cause to) stand up like bristles; show anger **bristly** *adj*

Brit *n Informal* British person

British *adj* of Great Britain or the British Commonwealth ▷ *pl n* people of Great Britain

brittle *adj* hard but easily broken **brittleness** *n*

broach *v* introduce (a topic) for discussion; open (a bottle or barrel)

broad *adj* having great breadth or width; not detailed; extensive *eg broad support*; strongly marked *eg a broad American accent* **broadly** *adv* **broaden** *v* **broadband** *n* telecommunication transmission technique using a wide range of frequencies **broad bean** thick flat edible bean **broad-minded** *adj* tolerant **broadside** *n* strong verbal or written attack; *naval* firing of all the guns on one side of a ship at once

broadcast *n* programme or announcement on radio or television ▷ *v* transmit (a programme or announcement) on radio or television; make widely known **broadcaster** *n* **broadcasting** *n*

brocade *n* rich fabric woven with a raised design

broccoli *n* type of cabbage with greenish flower heads

> SPELLING You might expect **broccoli** to have two *l*s at the end, but it has only one because it comes from Italian and ends with an *i*

brochure *n* booklet that contains information about a product or service

broekies [**brook**-eez] *pl n SAfr, Informal* underpants

brogue[1] *n* sturdy walking shoe

brogue[2] *n* strong accent, esp Irish

broil *v Aust, NZ, US & Canadian* cook by direct heat under a grill

broke *v* past tense of **break** ▷ *adj Informal* having no money

broken *v* past participle of **break** ▷ *adj* fractured or smashed; (of the speech of a foreigner) noticeably imperfect *eg broken English* **brokenhearted** *adj* overwhelmed by grief

broker *n* agent who buys or sells goods, securities, etc

brolga *n* large grey Australian crane with a trumpeting call (also **native companion**)

brolly *n, pl* **-lies** *Informal* umbrella

bromide *n* chemical compound used in medicine and photography

bromine *n chem* dark red liquid element that gives off a pungent vapour

bronchial [**bronk**-ee-al] *adj* of the bronchi

bronchitis [bronk-**eye**-tiss] *n* inflammation of the bronchi

bronchus [**bronk**-uss] *n, pl* **bronchi** [**bronk**-eye] either of the two branches of the windpipe

bronco *n, pl* **-cos** (in the US) wild or partially tamed pony

brontosaurus *n* very large plant-eating four-footed dinosaur
bronze *n* alloy of copper and tin; statue, medal, etc made of bronze ▷ *adj* made of, or coloured like, bronze ▷ *v* (esp of the skin) make or become brown **Bronze Age** era when bronze tools and weapons were used
brooch *n* ornament with a pin, worn fastened to clothes
brood *n* number of birds produced at one hatching; all the children of a family ▷ *v* think long and unhappily **broody** *adj* moody and sullen; *Informal* (of a woman) wishing to have a baby
brook[1] *n* small stream
brook[2] *v* bear or tolerate
broom *n* long-handled sweeping brush; yellow-flowered shrub **broomstick** *n* handle of a broom
broth *n* soup, usu containing vegetables
brothel *n* house where men pay to have sex with prostitutes
brother *n* boy or man with the same parents as another person; member of a male religious order **brotherly** *adj* **brotherhood** *n* fellowship; association, such as a trade union **brother-in-law** *n, pl* **brothers-in-law** brother of one's husband or wife; husband of one's sister
brought *v* past of **bring**
brow *n* part of the face from the eyes to the hairline; eyebrow; top of a hill
browbeat *v* frighten (someone) with threats
brown *n* colour of earth or wood ▷ *adj* of the colour brown ▷ *v* make or become brown **brownish** *adj* **browned-off** *adj* *Informal* bored and depressed
Brownie Guide, Brownie *n* junior Guide
browse *v* look through (a book or articles for sale) in a casual manner; nibble on young shoots or leaves ▷ *n* instance of browsing **browser** *n computers* software package that enables a user to read hypertext, esp on the Internet
bruise *n* discoloured area on the skin caused by an injury ▷ *v* cause a bruise on **bruiser** *n* strong tough person
brumby *n, pl* **-bies** *Aust* wild horse; unruly person
brunch *n* *Informal* breakfast and lunch combined
brunette *n* girl or woman with dark brown hair
brunt *n* main force or shock of a blow, attack, etc
brush[1] *n* device made of bristles, wires, etc used for cleaning, painting, etc; brief unpleasant encounter; fox's tail ▷ *v* clean, scrub, or paint with a brush; touch lightly and briefly **brush off** *v slang* dismiss or ignore (someone) **brush up** *v* refresh one's knowledge of (a subject)
brush[2] *n* thick growth of shrubs
brush turkey *n* bird of New Guinea and Australia resembling the domestic fowl, with black plumage
brusque *adj* blunt or curt in manner or speech **brusquely** *adv* **brusqueness** *n*
Brussels sprout *n* vegetable like a tiny cabbage
brute *n* brutal person; animal other than man ▷ *adj* wholly instinctive or physical, like an animal; without reason **brutish** *adj* of or like an animal **brutal** *adj* cruel and vicious; extremely honest

in speech or manner **brutally** *adv* **brutality** *n* **brutalize** *v*
BSc Bachelor of Science
BSE bovine spongiform encephalopathy: fatal virus disease of cattle
BST British Summer Time
bubble *n* ball of air in a liquid or solid ▷ *v* form bubbles; move or flow with a gurgling sound **bubbly** *adj* excited and lively; full of bubbles **bubble over** *v* express an emotion freely
bubonic plague [bew-**bonn**-ik] *n* acute infectious disease characterized by swellings
buccaneer *n hist* pirate
buck[1] *n* male of the goat, hare, kangaroo, rabbit, and reindeer ▷ *v* (of a horse etc) jump with legs stiff and back arched **buck up** *v* make or become more cheerful
buck[2] *n US, Canadian, Aust & NZ, slang* dollar; *SAfr* rand
buck[3] *n* **pass the buck** *Informal* shift blame or responsibility onto someone else
bucket *n* open-topped round container with a handle ▷ *v* **-eting, -eted** rain heavily **bucketful** *n*
buckle *n* clasp for fastening a belt or strap ▷ *v* fasten or be fastened with a buckle; (cause to) bend out of shape through pressure or heat **buckle down** *v Informal* apply oneself with determination
buckshee *adj slang* free
buckteeth *pl n* projecting upper front teeth **buck-toothed** *adj*
buckwheat *n* small black grain used for making flour
bucolic [bew-**koll**-ik] *adj* of the countryside or country life
bud *n* swelling on a tree or plant that develops into a leaf or flower ▷ *v* **budding, budded** produce buds **budding** *adj* beginning to develop or grow
Buddhism *n* eastern religion founded by Buddha **Buddhist** *n, adj*
buddleia *n* shrub with long spikes of purple flowers
buddy *n, pl* **-dies** *Informal* friend
budge *v* move slightly
budgerigar *n* small cage bird bred in many different-coloured varieties
budget *n* financial plan for a period of time; money allocated for a specific purpose ▷ *v* **-eting, -eted** plan the expenditure of (money or time) ▷ *adj* cheap **budgetary** *adj*

> **SPELLING** A lot of verbs ending in *et* have two *ts* when you add an ending like *-ing*, but **budget** is not one of them: **budgeting** and **budgeted** have a single *t*

budgie *n Informal* short for **budgerigar**
buff[1] *adj* dull yellowish-brown ▷ *v* clean or polish with soft material
buff[2] *n Informal* expert on or devotee of a given subject
buffalo *n* type of cattle; *US* bison
buffer *n* something that lessens shock or protects from damaging impact, circumstances, etc
buffet[1] [**boof**-ay, **buff**-ay] *n* counter where drinks and snacks are served
buffet[2] [**buff**-it] *v* **-feting, -feted** knock against or about
buffoon *n* clown or fool **buffoonery** *n*
bug *n* small insect; *Informal* minor illness; small mistake in a computer program; concealed microphone; *Aust* flattish edible shellfish ▷ *v* **bugging, bugged** *Informal* irritate (someone); conceal a microphone in (a room or phone)

bugbear *n* thing that causes obsessive anxiety

bugger *slang* ▷*n* unpleasant or difficult person or thing; person who practises buggery ▷*v* tire; practise buggery with **buggery** *n* anal intercourse

bugle *n* instrument like a small trumpet **bugler** *n*

build *v* **building, built** make, construct, or form by joining parts or materials ▷*n* shape of the body **builder** *n* **building** *n* structure with walls and a roof **building society** organization where money can be borrowed or invested **build-up** *n* gradual increase

built *v* past of **build** **built-up** *adj* having many buildings

bulb *n* same as **light bulb**: onion-shaped root which grows into a flower or plant **bulbous** *adj* round and fat

bulge *n* swelling on a normally flat surface; sudden increase in number ▷*v* swell outwards **bulging** *adj*

bulimia *n* disorder characterized by compulsive overeating followed by vomiting **bulimic** *adj, n*

bulk *n* size or volume, esp when great; main part **in bulk** in large quantities **bulky** *adj*

bulkhead *n* partition in a ship or aeroplane

bull[1] *n* male of some animals, such as cattle, elephants, and whales **bullock** *n* castrated bull **bulldog** *n* thickset dog with a broad head and a muscular body **bulldozer** *n* powerful tractor for moving earth **bulldoze** *v* **bullfight** *n* public show in which a matador kills a bull **bull's-eye** *n* central disc of a target **bullswool** *n* *Aust dated & NZ, slang* nonsense

bull[2] *n* *Informal* complete nonsense

bull[3] *n* papal decree

bullet *n* small piece of metal fired from a gun

bulletin *n* short official report or announcement

bullion *n* gold or silver in the form of bars

bully *n, pl* **-lies** person who hurts, persecutes, or intimidates a weaker person ▷*v* **-lying, -lied** hurt, intimidate, or persecute (a weaker person)

bulrush *n* tall stiff reed

bulwark *n* wall used as a fortification; person or thing acting as a defence

bum[1] *n* *slang* buttocks or anus

bum[2] *Informal* ▷*n* disreputable idler ▷*adj* of poor quality

bumble *v* speak, do, or move in a clumsy way **bumbling** *adj, n*

bumblebee *n* large hairy bee

bumf, bumph *n* *Informal* official documents or forms

bump *v* knock or strike with a jolt; travel in jerks and jolts ▷*n* dull thud from an impact or collision; raised uneven part **bumpy** *adj* **bump off** *v* *Informal* murder

bumper[1] *n* bar on the front and back of a vehicle to protect against damage

bumper[2] *adj* unusually large or abundant

bumph *n* same as **bumf**

bumpkin *n* awkward simple country person

bumptious *adj* offensively self-assertive

bun *n* small sweet bread roll or cake; hair gathered into a bun shape at the back of the head

bunch *n* number of things growing, fastened, or grouped together ▷*v* group or be grouped

together in a bunch
bundle *n* number of things gathered loosely together ▷*v* cause to go roughly or unceremoniously **bundle up** *v* make into a bundle
bung *n* stopper for a cask etc ▷*v* (foll. by *up*) *Informal* close with a bung; *Brit, slang* throw (something) somewhere in a careless manner
bungalow *n* one-storey house
bungee jumping, bungy jumping *n* sport of leaping from a high bridge, tower, etc, to which one is connected by a rubber rope
bungle *v* spoil through incompetence **bungler** *n* **bungling** *adj, n*
bunion *n* inflamed swelling on the big toe
bunk[1] *n* narrow shelflike bed **bunk bed** one of a pair of beds constructed one above the other
bunk[2] *n* same as **bunkum**
bunk[3] *slang* ▷*n Brit* **do a bunk** make a hurried and secret departure ▷*v Brit, NZ & SAfr* be absent without permission
bunker *n* sand-filled hollow forming an obstacle on a golf course; underground shelter; large storage container for coal etc
bunkum *n* nonsense
bunny *n, pl* **-nies** child's word for a rabbit
Bunsen burner *n* gas burner used in laboratories
bunting *n* decorative flags
bunya *n* tall dome-shaped Australian coniferous tree (also **bunya-bunya**)
bunyip *n Aust* legendary monster said to live in swamps and lakes
buoy *n* floating marker anchored in the sea ▷*v* prevent from sinking; encourage or hearten **buoyant** *adj* able to float; cheerful or resilient **buoyancy** *n*
bur *n* same as **burr[1]**
burble *v* make a bubbling sound; talk quickly and excitedly
burden[1] *n* heavy load; something difficult to cope with ▷*v* put a burden on; oppress **burdensome** *adj*
burden[2] *n* theme of a speech etc
bureau *n, pl* **-reaus, -reaux** office that provides a service; writing desk with shelves and drawers
bureaucracy *n, pl* **-cies** administrative system based on complex rules and procedures; excessive adherence to complex procedures **bureaucrat** *n* **bureaucratic** *adj*
burgeon *v* develop or grow rapidly
burgh *n* Scottish borough
burglar *n* person who enters a building to commit a crime, esp theft **burglary** *n* **burgle** *v*
Burgundy *n* type of French wine **burgundy** *adj* dark-purplish red
burial *n* burying of a dead body
burlesque *n* artistic work which satirizes a subject by caricature
burly *adj* **-lier, -liest** (of a person) broad and strong
burn[1] *v* **burning, burnt** *or* **burned** be or set on fire; destroy or be destroyed by fire; damage, injure, or mark by heat; feel strong emotion; record data on (a compact disc) ▷*n* injury or mark caused by fire or exposure to heat **burning** *adj* intense; urgent or crucial
burn[2] *n Scot* small stream
burnish *v* make smooth and shiny by rubbing
burp *v, n Informal* belch
burr[1] *n* head of a plant with prickles or hooks

burr² *n* soft trilling sound given to the letter r in some dialects; whirring sound

burrawang *n* Australian plant with fernlike leaves and an edible nut

burrow *n* hole dug in the ground by a rabbit etc ▷ *v* dig holes in the ground

bursar *n* treasurer of a school, college, or university **bursary** *n* scholarship

burst *v* **bursting, burst** (cause to) break open or apart noisily and suddenly; come or go suddenly and forcibly; be full to the point of breaking open ▷ *n* instance of breaking open suddenly; sudden outbreak or occurrence **burst into** *v* give vent to (an emotion) suddenly

bury *v* **burying, buried** place in a grave; place in the earth and cover with soil; conceal or hide

bus *n* large motor vehicle for carrying passengers ▷ *v* **bussing, bussed** travel or transport by bus

busby *n, pl* **-bies** tall fur hat worn by some soldiers

bush *n* dense woody plant, smaller than a tree; wild uncultivated part of a country **bushy** *adj* (of hair) thick and shaggy **bushbaby** *n* small African tree-living mammal with large eyes

bushel *n* obsolete unit of measure equal to 8 gallons (36.4 litres)

business *n* purchase and sale of goods and services; commercial establishment; trade or profession; proper concern or responsibility; affair *eg it's a dreadful business* **businesslike** *adj* efficient and methodical **businessman, businesswoman** *n*

busker *n* street entertainer **busk** *v* act as a busker

bust¹ *n* woman's bosom; sculpture of the head and shoulders

bust² *Informal* ▷ *v* **busting, bust** *or* **busted** burst or break; (of the police) raid (a place) or arrest (someone) ▷ *adj* broken **go bust** become bankrupt

bustard *n* bird with long strong legs, a heavy body, a long neck, and speckled plumage

bustle¹ *v* hurry with a show of activity or energy ▷ *n* energetic and noisy activity **bustling** *adj*

bustle² *n* cushion or framework formerly worn under the back of a woman's skirt to hold it out

busy *adj* **busier, busiest** actively employed; crowded or full of activity ▷ *v* **busying, busied** keep (someone, esp oneself) busy **busily** *adv* **busybody** *n* meddlesome or nosy person

but *conj* contrary to expectation; in contrast; other than; without it happening ▷ *prep* except ▷ *adv* only **but for** were it not for

butane *n* gas used for fuel

butch *adj slang* markedly or aggressively masculine

butcher *n* person who slaughters animals or sells their meat; brutal murderer ▷ *v* kill and prepare (animals) for meat; kill (people) brutally or indiscriminately **butchery** *n* **butcherbird** *n* Australian magpie that impales its prey on thorns

butler *n* chief male servant

butt¹ *n* thicker end of something; unused end of a cigar or cigarette; *slang* buttocks

butt² *n* person or thing that is the target of ridicule

butt³ *v* strike with the head or horns **butt in** *v* interrupt a conversation

butt[4] *n* large cask

butter *n* edible fatty solid made by churning cream ▷*v* put butter on **buttery** *adj* **butter up** *v* flatter

butter bean *n* large pale flat edible bean

buttercup *n* small yellow flower

butterfingers *n Informal* person who drops things by mistake

butterfly *n* insect with brightly coloured wings; swimming stroke in which both arms move together in a forward circular action

buttermilk *n* sourish milk that remains after the butter has been separated from milk

butterscotch *n* kind of hard brittle toffee

buttock *n* either of the two fleshy masses that form the human rump

button *n* small disc or knob sewn to clothing, which can be passed through a slit in another piece of fabric to fasten them; knob that operates a piece of equipment when pressed ▷*v* fasten with buttons **buttonhole** *n* slit in a garment through which a button is passed; flower worn on a lapel ▷*v* detain (someone) in conversation

buttress *n* structure to support a wall ▷*v* support with, or as if with, a buttress

buxom *adj* (of a woman) healthily plump and full-bosomed

buy *v* **buying, bought** acquire by paying money for; *slang* accept as true ▷*n* thing acquired through payment **buyer** *n* customer; person employed to buy merchandise

buzz *n* rapidly vibrating humming sound; *Informal* sense of excitement ▷*v* make a humming sound; be filled with an air of excitement **buzzer** *n* **buzz around** *v* move around quickly and busily **buzz word** jargon word which becomes fashionably popular

buzzard *n* bird of prey of the hawk family

by *prep* indicating the doer of an action, nearness, movement past, time before or during which, etc *eg bitten by a dog; down by the river; driving by the school; in bed by midnight* ▷*adv* near; past **by and by** eventually **by and large** in general

bye, bye-bye *interj Informal* goodbye

by-election *n* election held during parliament to fill a vacant seat

bygone *adj* past or former

bylaw, bye-law *n* rule made by a local authority

BYO, BYOG *n Aust & NZ* unlicensed restaurant at which diners may bring their own alcoholic drink

bypass *n* main road built to avoid a city; operation to divert blood flow away from a damaged part of the heart ▷*v* go round or avoid

by-product *n* secondary or incidental product of a process

byre *n Brit* shelter for cows

bystander *n* person present but not involved

byte *n computers* group of bits processed as one unit of data

byway *n* minor road

byword *n* person or thing regarded as a perfect example of something

C

C *chem* carbon; Celsius; centigrade; century

c. circa

cab *n* taxi; enclosed driver's compartment on a train, truck, etc **cabbie, cabby** *n, pl* **-bies** *Informal* taxi driver

cabal [kab-**bal**] *n* small group of political plotters; secret plot

cabaret [**kab**-a-ray] *n* dancing and singing show in a nightclub

cabbage *n* vegetable with a large head of green leaves **cabbage tree** *NZ* palm-like tree with a bare trunk and spiky leaves

caber *n* tree trunk tossed in competition at Highland games

cabin *n* compartment in a ship or aircraft; small hut **cabin cruiser** motorboat with a cabin

cabinet *n* piece of furniture with drawers or shelves; (**C-**) committee of senior government ministers **cabinet-maker** *n* person who makes fine furniture

cable *n* strong thick rope; bundle of wires that carries electricity or electronic signals; telegram sent abroad ▷*v* send (someone) a message by cable **cable car** vehicle pulled up a steep slope by a moving cable **cable television** television service conveyed by cable to subscribers

caboodle *n* **the whole caboodle** *Informal* the whole lot

cabriolet [kab-ree-oh-**lay**] *n* small horse-drawn carriage with a folding hood

cacao [kak-**kah**-oh] *n* tropical tree with seed pods from which chocolate and cocoa are made

cache [**kash**] *n* hidden store of weapons or treasure

cachet [**kash**-shay] *n* prestige, distinction

cack-handed *adj Informal* clumsy

cackle *v* laugh shrilly; (of a hen) squawk with shrill broken notes ▷*n* cackling noise

cacophony [kak-**koff**-on-ee] *n* harsh discordant sound **cacophonous** *adj*

cactus *n, pl* **-tuses, -ti** fleshy desert plant with spines but no leaves

cad *n old-fashioned* dishonourable man **caddish** *adj*

cadaver [kad-**dav**-ver] *n* corpse **cadaverous** *adj* pale, thin, and haggard

caddie, caddy *n, pl* **-dies** person who carries a golfer's clubs ▷*v* **-dying, -died** act as a caddie

caddis fly *n* insect whose larva (**caddis worm**) lives underwater in a protective case of sand and stones

caddy *n, pl* **-dies** small container for tea

cadence [**kade**-enss] *n* rise and fall in the pitch of the voice; close of a musical phrase
cadenza *n* complex solo passage in a piece of music
cadet *n* young person training for the armed forces or police
cadge *v Informal* get (something) by taking advantage of someone's generosity **cadger** *n*
cadmium *n chem* bluish-white metallic element used in alloys
cadre [**kah**-der] *n* small group of people selected and trained to form the core of a political organization or military unit
caecum [**seek**-um] *n, pl* **-ca** [-ka] pouch at the beginning of the large intestine
Caesarean section [see-**zair**-ee-an] *n* surgical incision into the womb to deliver a baby
caesium *n chem* silvery-white metallic element used in photocells
café *n* small or inexpensive restaurant serving light refreshments; *SAfr* corner shop or grocer **cafeteria** *n* self-service restaurant
caffeine *n* stimulant found in tea and coffee
caftan *n* same as **kaftan**
cage *n* enclosure of bars or wires, for keeping animals or birds; enclosed platform of a lift in a mine **caged** *adj* kept in a cage
cagey *adj* **cagier, cagiest** *Informal* reluctant to go into details
cagoule *n Brit* lightweight hooded waterproof jacket
cahoots *pl n* **in cahoots** *Informal* conspiring together
cairn *n* mound of stones erected as a memorial or marker
cajole *v* persuade by flattery **cajolery** *n*
cake *n* sweet food baked from a mixture of flour, eggs, etc; flat compact mass of something, such as soap ▷*v* form into a hardened mass or crust
calamine *n* pink powder consisting chiefly of zinc oxide, used in skin lotions and ointments
calamity *n, pl* **-ties** disaster **calamitous** *adj*
calcify *v* **-fying, -fied** harden by the depositing of calcium salts **calcification** *n*
calcium *n chem* silvery-white metallic element found in bones, teeth, limestone, and chalk
calculate *v* solve or find out by a mathematical procedure or by reasoning; aim to have a particular effect **calculable** *adj* **calculating** *adj* selfishly scheming **calculation** *n* **calculator** *n* small electronic device for making calculations
calculus *n, pl* **-luses** branch of mathematics dealing with infinitesimal changes to a variable number or quantity; *pathology* hard deposit in kidney or bladder
Caledonian *adj* Scottish
calendar *n* chart showing a year divided up into months, weeks, and days; system for determining the beginning, length, and division of years; schedule of events or appointments
calendula *n* marigold
calf[1] *n, pl* **calves** young cow, bull, elephant, whale, or seal; leather made from calfskin **calve** *v* give birth to a calf
calf[2] *n, pl* **calves** back of the leg between the ankle and knee
calibre *n* person's ability or worth; diameter of the bore of a gun or of a

shell or bullet **calibrate** *v* mark the scale or check the accuracy of (a measuring instrument) **calibration** *n*
calico *n, pl* **-coes** white cotton fabric
caliph *n hist* Muslim ruler
call *v* name; shout to attract attention; telephone; summon; (often foll. by *on*) visit; arrange (a meeting, strike, etc) ▷ *n* cry, shout; animal's or bird's cry; telephone communication; short visit; summons, invitation; need, demand **caller** *n* **calling** *n* vocation, profession **call box** kiosk for a public telephone **call centre** office where staff carry out an organization's telephone transactions **call for** *v* require **call off** *v* cancel **call up** *v* summon to serve in the armed forces; cause one to remember
calligraphy *n* (art of) beautiful handwriting **calligrapher** *n*
calliper *n* metal splint for supporting the leg; instrument for measuring diameters
callisthenics *pl n* light keep-fit exercises
callous *adj* showing no concern for other people's feelings **calloused** *adj* (of skin) thickened and hardened **callously** *adv* **callousness** *n*
callow *adj* young and inexperienced
callus *n, pl* **-luses** area of thick hardened skin
calm *adj* not agitated or excited; not ruffled by the wind; windless ▷ *n* peaceful state ▷ *v* (often foll. by *down*) make or become calm **calmly** *adv* **calmness** *n*
calorie *n* unit of measurement for the energy value of food; unit of heat **calorific** *adj* of calories or heat
calumny *n, pl* **-nies** false or malicious statement
calypso *n, pl* **-sos** West Indian song with improvised topical lyrics
calyx *n, pl* **calyxes, calyces** outer leaves that protect a flower bud
cam *n* device that converts a circular motion to a to-and-fro motion **camshaft** *n* part of an engine consisting of a rod to which cams are fixed
camaraderie *n* comradeship
camber *n* slight upward curve to the centre of a surface
cambric *n* fine white linen fabric
camcorder *n* combined portable video camera and recorder
came *v* past tense of **come**
camel *n* humped mammal that can survive long periods without food or water in desert regions
camellia [kam-**meal**-ya] *n* evergreen ornamental shrub with white, pink, or red flowers
Camembert [**kam**-mem-bare] *n* soft creamy French cheese
cameo *n, pl* **cameos** brooch or ring with a profile head carved in relief; small part in a film or play performed by a well-known actor or actress
camera *n* apparatus used for taking photographs or pictures for television or cinema **in camera** in private session **cameraman** *n* man who operates a camera for television or cinema
camiknickers *pl n Brit* woman's undergarment consisting of knickers attached to a camisole
camisole *n* woman's bodice-like garment
camomile *n* aromatic plant, used to make herbal tea

camouflage [**kam**-moo-flahzh] *n* use of natural surroundings or artificial aids to conceal or disguise something ▷ *v* conceal by camouflage

camp[1] *n* (place for) temporary lodgings consisting of tents, huts, or cabins; group supporting a particular doctrine ▷ *v* stay in a camp **camper** *n*

camp[2] *adj Informal* effeminate or homosexual; consciously artificial or affected **camp it up** *Informal* behave in a camp way

campaign *n* series of coordinated activities designed to achieve a goal ▷ *v* take part in a campaign

campanology *n* art of ringing bells

campanula *n* plant with blue or white bell-shaped flowers

camphor *n* aromatic crystalline substance used medicinally and in mothballs

campion *n* red, pink, or white wild flower

campus *n, pl* **-puses** grounds of a university or college

can[1] *v, past* **could** be able to; be allowed to

can[2] *n* metal container for food or liquids ▷ *v* **canning, canned** put (something) into a can **canned** *adj* preserved in a can; (of music) prerecorded **cannery** *n, pl* factory where food is canned

canal *n* artificial waterway; passage in the body

canapé [**kan**-nap-pay] *n* small piece of bread or toast with a savoury topping

canary *n, pl* **-ries** small yellow songbird often kept as a pet

canasta *n* card game like rummy, played with two packs

cancan *n* lively high-kicking dance performed by a female group

cancel *v* **-celling, -celled** stop (something that has been arranged) from taking place; mark (a cheque or stamp) with an official stamp to prevent further use **cancellation** *n* **cancel out** *v* counterbalance, neutralize

cancer *n* serious disease resulting from a malignant growth or tumour; malignant growth or tumour **cancerous** *adj*

candela [kan-**dee**-lă] *n* unit of luminous intensity

candelabrum *n, pl* **-bra** large branched candle holder

candid *adj* honest and straightforward **candidly** *adv*

candidate *n* person seeking a job or position; person taking an examination **candidacy, candidature** *n*

candle *n* stick of wax enclosing a wick, which is burned to produce light **candlestick** *n* holder for a candle **candlewick** *n* cotton fabric with a tufted surface

candour *n* honesty and straightforwardness

candy *n, pl* **-dies** *US* sweet or sweets **candied** *adj* coated with sugar **candyfloss** *n* light fluffy mass of spun sugar on a stick **candy-striped** *adj* having coloured stripes on a white background

cane *n* stem of the bamboo or similar plant; flexible rod used to beat someone; slender walking stick ▷ *v* beat with a cane **cane toad** large toad used to control insects and other pests of sugar-cane plantations

canine *adj* of or like a dog ▷ *n* sharp pointed tooth between the incisors and the molars

canister *n* metal container

canker *n* ulceration, ulcerous disease; something evil that spreads and corrupts

cannabis *n* Asian plant with tough fibres; drug obtained from the dried leaves and flowers of this plant, which can be smoked or chewed

cannelloni *pl n* tubular pieces of pasta filled with meat etc

cannibal *n* person who eats human flesh; animal that eats others of its own kind **cannibalism** *n* **cannibalize** *v* use parts from (one machine) to repair another

cannon *n* large gun on wheels; billiard stroke in which the cue ball hits two balls successively **cannonade** *n* continuous heavy gunfire **cannonball** *n* heavy metal ball fired from a cannon **cannon into** *v* collide with

cannot can not

canny *adj* **-nier, -niest** shrewd, cautious **cannily** *adv*

canoe *n* light narrow open boat propelled by a paddle or paddles **canoeing** *n* sport of rowing in a canoe **canoeist** *n*

canon[1] *n* priest serving in a cathedral

canon[2] *n* Church decree regulating morals or religious practices; general rule or standard; list of the works of an author that are accepted as authentic **canonical** *adj* **canonize** *v* declare (a person) officially to be a saint **canonization** *n*

canoodle *v slang* kiss and cuddle

canopy *n, pl* **-pies** covering above a bed, door, etc; any large or wide covering **canopied** *adj* covered with a canopy

cant[1] *n* insincere talk; specialized vocabulary of a particular group

cant[2] *n* tilted position ▷ *v* tilt, overturn

can't can not

cantaloupe, cantaloup *n* kind of melon with sweet orange flesh

cantankerous *adj* quarrelsome, bad-tempered

cantata *n* musical work consisting of arias, duets, and choruses

canteen *n* restaurant attached to a workplace or school; box containing a set of cutlery

canter *n* horse's gait between a trot and a gallop ▷ *v* move at a canter

canticle *n* short hymn with words from the Bible

cantilever *n* beam or girder fixed at one end only

canto *n, pl* **-tos** main division of a long poem

canton *n* political division of a country, esp Switzerland

cantor *n* man employed to lead services in a synagogue

canvas *n* heavy coarse cloth used for sails and tents, and for oil painting; oil painting on canvas

canvass *v* try to get votes or support (from); find out the opinions of (people) by conducting a survey ▷ *n* canvassing

canyon *n* deep narrow valley

cap *n* soft close-fitting covering for the head; small lid; small explosive device used in a toy gun ▷ *v* **capping, capped** cover or top with something; select (a player) for a national team; impose an upper limit on (a tax); outdo, excel

capable *adj* (foll. by *of*) having the ability (for); competent and efficient **capably** *adv* **capability** *n, pl* **-ties**

capacity *n, pl* **-ties** ability to contain, absorb, or hold; maximum amount that can be contained or produced; physical or mental ability; position, function **capacious** *adj* roomy **capacitance** *n* (measure of) the ability of a system to store electrical charge **capacitor** *n* device for storing electrical charge

caparisoned *adj* magnificently decorated

cape[1] *n* short cloak

cape[2] *n* large piece of land that juts out into the sea

caper *n* high-spirited prank ▷ *v* skip about

capercaillie, capercailzie [kap-per-**kale**-yee] *n* large black European grouse

capers *pl n* pickled flower buds of a Mediterranean shrub used in sauces

capillary *n, pl* **-laries** very fine blood vessel

capital[1] *n* chief city of a country; accumulated wealth; wealth used to produce more wealth; large letter, as used at the beginning of a name or sentence ▷ *adj* involving or punishable by death; *old-fashioned* excellent **capitalize** *v* write or print (words) in capitals; convert into or provide with capital **capitalize on** *v* take advantage of (a situation)

capital[2] *n* top part of a pillar

capitalism *n* economic system based on the private ownership of industry **capitalist** *adj* of capitalists or capitalism; supporting capitalism ▷ *n* supporter of capitalism; person who owns a business

capitation *n* tax of a fixed amount per person

capitulate *v* surrender on agreed terms **capitulation** *n*

capon *n* castrated cock fowl fattened for eating

cappuccino [kap-poo-**cheen**-oh] *n, pl* **-nos** coffee with steamed milk, sprinkled with powdered chocolate

caprice [kap-**reess**] *n* sudden change of attitude **capricious** *adj* tending to have sudden changes of attitude **capriciously** *adv*

capsicum *n* kind of pepper used as a vegetable or as a spice

capsize *v* (of a boat) overturn accidentally

capstan *n* rotating cylinder round which a ship's rope is wound

capsule *n* soluble gelatine case containing a dose of medicine; plant's seed case; detachable crew compartment of a spacecraft

captain *n* commander of a ship or civil aircraft; middle-ranking naval officer; junior officer in the army; leader of a team or group ▷ *v* be captain of **captaincy** *n*

caption *n* title or explanation accompanying an illustration ▷ *v* provide with a caption

captious *adj* tending to make trivial criticisms

captivate *v* attract and hold the attention of **captivating** *adj*

captive *n* person kept in confinement ▷ *adj* kept in confinement; (of an audience) unable to leave **captivity** *n*

captor *n* person who captures a person or animal

capture *v* take by force; succeed in representing (something elusive) artistically ▷ *n* capturing

car *n* motor vehicle designed to carry a small number of people; passenger compartment of a cable car, lift, etc; *US* railway carriage **car park** area or building reserved for parking cars

carafe [kar-**raff**] *n* glass bottle for serving water or wine

caramel *n* chewy sweet made from sugar and milk; burnt sugar, used for colouring and flavouring food **caramelize** *v* turn into caramel

carapace *n* hard upper shell of tortoises and crustaceans

carat *n* unit of weight of precious stones; measure of the purity of gold in an alloy

caravan *n* large enclosed vehicle for living in, designed to be towed by a car or horse; group travelling together in Eastern countries

caraway *n* plant whose seeds are used as a spice

carbide *n* compound of carbon with a metal

carbine *n* light automatic rifle

carbohydrate *n* any of a large group of energy-producing compounds in food, such as sugars and starches

carbolic acid *n* disinfectant derived from coal tar

carbon *n* nonmetallic element occurring as charcoal, graphite, and diamond, found in all organic matter **carbonate** *n* salt or ester of carbonic acid **carbonated** *adj* (of a drink) containing carbon dioxide **carbonize** *v* turn into carbon as a result of heating; coat with carbon **carbon copy** copy made with carbon paper; very similar person or thing **carbon dioxide** colourless gas exhaled by people and animals **carbonic acid** weak acid formed from carbon dioxide and water **carbon paper** paper coated on one side with a dark waxy pigment, used to make a copy of something as it is typed or written

Carborundum *n* ® compound of silicon and carbon, used for grinding and polishing

carbuncle *n* inflamed boil

carburettor *n* device which mixes petrol and air in an internal-combustion engine

carcass, carcase *n* dead body of an animal

carcinogen *n* substance that produces cancer **carcinogenic** *adj* **carcinoma** *n* malignant tumour

card *n* piece of thick stiff paper or cardboard used for identification, reference, or sending greetings or messages; one of a set of cards with a printed pattern, used for playing games; small rectangle of stiff plastic with identifying numbers for use as a credit card, cheque card, or charge card; *old-fashioned* witty or eccentric person ▷ *pl* any card game, or card games in general **cardboard** *n* thin stiff board made from paper pulp **cardsharp** *n* professional card player who cheats

cardiac *adj* of the heart **cardiogram** *n* electrocardiogram **cardiograph** *n* electrocardiograph **cardiology** *n* study of the heart and its diseases **cardiologist** *n* **cardiovascular** *adj* of the heart and the blood vessels

cardigan *n* knitted jacket

cardinal *n* any of the high-ranking clergymen of the RC Church who elect the Pope and act as his counsellors ▷ *adj* fundamentally important **cardinal number** number denoting quantity but not order in a group, for example four as distinct from fourth **cardinal points** the four main points of the compass

care *v* be concerned; like (to do something); (foll. by *for*) like, be fond of; (foll. by *for*) look after ▷ *n* careful attention, caution; protection, charge; trouble, worry **careful** *adj* **carefully** *adv* **carefulness** *n* **careless** *adj* **carelessly** *adv* **carelessness** *n*

careen *v* tilt over to one side

career *n* series of jobs in a profession or occupation that a person has through their life; part of a person's life spent in a particular occupation ▷ *v* rush in an uncontrolled way **careerist** *n* person who seeks advancement by any possible means

carefree *adj* without worry or responsibility

caress *n* gentle affectionate touch or embrace ▷ *v* touch gently and affectionately

caret [**kar**-rett] *n* symbol (ʎ) indicating a place in written or printed matter where something is to be inserted

caretaker *n* person employed to look after a place

careworn *adj* showing signs of worry

cargo *n, pl* **-goes** goods carried by a ship, aircraft, etc **cargo pants, trousers** loose trousers with a large pocket on the outside of each leg

caribou *n, pl* **-bou** *or* **-bous** large N American reindeer

caricature *n* drawing or description of a person that exaggerates features for comic effect ▷ *v* make a caricature of

caries [**care**-reez] *n* tooth decay

carillon [kar-**rill**-yon] *n* set of bells played by keyboard or mechanically; tune played on such bells

cark *v* **cark it** *Aust & NZ, slang* die

carmine *adj* vivid red

carnage *n* extensive slaughter of people

carnal *adj* of a sexual or sensual nature **carnal knowledge** sexual intercourse

carnation *n* cultivated plant with fragrant white, pink, or red flowers

carnival *n* festive period with processions, music, and dancing in the street

carnivore *n* meat-eating animal **carnivorous** *adj*

carob *n* pod of a Mediterranean tree, used as a chocolate substitute

carol *n* joyful Christmas hymn ▷ *v* **-olling, -olled** sing carols; sing joyfully

carotid *adj, n* (of) either of the two arteries supplying blood to the head

carouse *v* have a merry drinking party

carousel [kar-roo-**sell**] *n* revolving conveyor belt for luggage or photographic slides; *US* merry-go-round

carp¹ *n* large freshwater fish

carp² *v* complain, find fault

carpel *n* female reproductive organ of a flowering plant

carpenter *n* person who makes or repairs wooden structures **carpentry** *n*

carpet *n* heavy fabric for covering floors ▷ *v* **carpeting, carpeted** cover with a carpet **on the carpet** *Informal* being reprimanded **carpet snake** *or* **python** large nonvenomous Australian snake with a carpet-like pattern on its back

carpus *n, pl* **-pi** set of eight bones of the wrist

carriage *n* one of the sections of a

train for passengers; way a person holds his or her head and body; four-wheeled horse-drawn vehicle; moving part of a machine that supports and shifts another part; charge made for conveying goods **carriageway** *n Brit* part of a road along which traffic passes in one direction

carrier *n* person or thing that carries something; person or animal that does not suffer from a disease but can transmit it to others **carrier pigeon** homing pigeon used for carrying messages

carrion *n* dead and rotting flesh

carrot *n* long tapering orange root vegetable; something offered as an incentive **carroty** *adj* (of hair) reddish-orange

carry *v* **-rying, -ried** take from one place to another; have with one habitually, in one's pocket etc; transmit (a disease); have as a factor or result; hold (one's head or body) in a specified manner; secure the adoption of (a bill or motion); (of sound) travel a certain distance **carry on** *v* continue; *Informal* cause a fuss **carry out** *v* follow, accomplish

cart *n* open two-wheeled horse-drawn vehicle for carrying goods or passengers ▷ *v* carry, usu with some effort **carthorse** *n* large heavily built horse **cartwheel** *n* sideways somersault supported by the hands with legs outstretched; large spoked wheel of a cart

carte blanche [kaht **blahntsh**] *n French* complete authority

cartel *n* association of competing firms formed to fix prices

cartilage *n* strong flexible tissue forming part of the skeleton **cartilaginous** *adj*

cartography *n* map making **cartographer** *n* **cartographic** *adj*

carton *n* container made of cardboard or waxed paper

cartoon *n* humorous or satirical drawing; sequence of these telling a story; film made by photographing a series of drawings which give the illusion of movement when projected **cartoonist** *n*

cartridge *n* casing containing an explosive charge and bullet for a gun; part of the pick-up of a record player that converts the movements of the stylus into electrical signals; sealed container of film, tape, etc **cartridge paper** strong thick drawing paper

carve *v* cut to form an object; form (an object or design) by cutting; slice (cooked meat) **carving** *n*

caryatid [kar-ree-**at**-id] *n* supporting column in the shape of a female figure

Casanova *n* promiscuous man

casbah *n* citadel of a N African city

cascade *n* waterfall; something flowing or falling like a waterfall ▷ *v* flow or fall in a cascade

case[1] *n* instance, example; condition, state of affairs; set of arguments supporting an action or cause; person or problem dealt with by a doctor, social worker, or solicitor; action, lawsuit; *grammar* form of a noun, pronoun, or adjective showing its relation to other words in the sentence **in case** so as to allow for the possibility that

case[2] *n* container, protective covering ▷ *v slang* inspect (a building) with the intention of burgling it **case-hardened** *adj* having been made callous by

experience
casement *n* window that is hinged on one side
cash *n* banknotes and coins ▷*v* obtain cash for **cash in on** *v* *Informal* gain profit or advantage from **cash register** till that displays and adds the prices of the goods sold **cash-strapped** *adj* short of money
cashew *n* edible kidney-shaped nut
cashier[1] *n* person responsible for handling cash in a bank, shop, etc
cashier[2] *v* dismiss with dishonour from the armed forces
cashmere *n* fine soft wool obtained from goats
casing *n* protective case, covering
casino *n, pl* **-nos** public building or room where gambling games are played
cask *n* barrel used to hold alcoholic drink; *Aust* cubic carton containing wine, with a tap for dispensing
casket *n* small box for valuables; *US* coffin
cassava *n* starch obtained from the roots of a tropical American plant, used to make tapioca
casserole *n* covered dish in which food is cooked slowly, usu in an oven; dish cooked in this way ▷*v* cook in a casserole
cassette *n* plastic case containing a reel of film or magnetic tape
cassock *n* long tunic, usu black, worn by priests
cassowary *n, pl* **-waries** large flightless bird of Australia and New Guinea
cast *n* actors in a play or film collectively; object shaped by a mould while molten; mould used to shape such an object; rigid plaster-of-Paris casing for immobilizing broken bones while they heal; sort, kind; slight squint in the eye ▷*v* **casting, cast** select (an actor) to play a part in a play or film; give (a vote); let fall, shed; shape (molten material) in a mould; throw with force; direct (a glance) **castaway** *n* shipwrecked person **casting vote** deciding vote used by the chairperson of a meeting when the votes on each side are equal **cast-iron** *adj* made of a hard but brittle type of iron; definite, unchallengeable **cast-off** *adj, n* discarded (person or thing)
castanets *pl n* musical instrument, used by Spanish dancers, consisting of curved pieces of hollow wood clicked together in the hand
caste *n* any of the hereditary classes into which Hindu society is divided; social rank
castellated *adj* having battlements
caster sugar finely ground white sugar
castigate *v* reprimand severely **castigation** *n*
castle *n* large fortified building, often built as a ruler's residence; rook in chess
castor *n* small swivelling wheel fixed to the bottom of a piece of furniture for easy moving
castor oil *n* oil obtained from an Indian plant, used as a lubricant and purgative
castrate *v* remove the testicles of; deprive of vigour or masculinity **castration** *n*
casual *adj* careless, nonchalant; (of work or workers) occasional or not permanent; for informal wear; happening by chance **casually** *adv*
casualty *n, pl* **-ties** person killed or

injured in an accident or war; person or thing that has suffered as the result of something

casuarina [kass-yew-a-**reen**-a] *n* Australian tree with jointed green branches

casuistry *n* reasoning that is misleading or oversubtle

cat *n* small domesticated furry mammal; related wild mammal, such as the lion or tiger **catty** *adj* *Informal* spiteful **catkin** *n* drooping flower spike of certain trees **catcall** *n* derisive whistle or cry **catfish** *n* fish with whisker-like barbels round the mouth **catgut** *n* strong cord used to string musical instruments and sports rackets **catnap** *n*, *v* doze **Catseyes** *pl n* ® glass reflectors set in the road to indicate traffic lanes **cat's paw** person used by another to do unpleasant things for him or her **catwalk** *n* narrow pathway or platform

cataclysm [**kat**-a-kliz-zum] *n* violent upheaval; disaster, such as an earthquake **cataclysmic** *adj*

catacombs [**kat**-a-koomz] *pl n* underground burial place consisting of tunnels with recesses for tombs

catafalque [**kat**-a-falk] *n* raised platform on which a body lies in state before or during a funeral

catalepsy *n* trancelike state in which the body is rigid **cataleptic** *adj*

catalogue *n* book containing details of items for sale; systematic list of items ▷ *v* make a systematic list of

catalyst *n* substance that speeds up a chemical reaction without itself changing **catalyse** *v* speed up (a chemical reaction) by a catalyst **catalysis** *n* **catalytic** *adj*

catamaran *n* boat with twin parallel hulls

catapult *n* Y-shaped device with a loop of elastic, used by children for firing stones ▷ *v* shoot forwards or upwards violently

cataract *n* eye disease in which the lens becomes opaque; opaque area of an eye; large waterfall

catarrh [kat-**tar**] *n* excessive mucus in the nose and throat, during or following a cold **catarrhal** *adj*

catastrophe [kat-**ass**-trof-fee] *n* great and sudden disaster **catastrophic** *adj*

catch *v* **catching, caught** seize, capture; surprise in an act *eg two boys were caught stealing*; hit unexpectedly; be in time for (a bus, train, etc); see or hear; be infected with (an illness); entangle; understand, make out ▷ *n* device for fastening a door, window, etc; *Informal* concealed or unforeseen drawback **catch it** *Informal* be punished **catching** *adj* infectious **catchy** *adj* (of a tune) pleasant and easily remembered **catchment area** area served by a particular school or hospital; area of land draining into a river, basin, or reservoir **catch on** *v* *Informal* become popular; understand **catch out** *v* *Informal* trap (someone) in an error or lie **catch phrase** well-known phrase associated with a particular entertainer **catch 22** inescapable dilemma **catchword** *n* well-known and frequently used phrase

catechism [**kat**-ti-kiz-zum] *n* instruction on the doctrine of a Christian Church in a series of questions and answers

category *n, pl* **-ries** class, group **categorical** *adj* absolutely clear and certain **categorically** *adv* **categorize** *v* put in a category **categorization** *n*

cater *v* provide what is needed or wanted, esp food or services **caterer** *n*

caterpillar *n* wormlike larva of a moth or butterfly; ® endless track, driven by cogged wheels, used to propel a heavy vehicle

caterwaul *v* wail, yowl

catharsis [kath-**thar**-siss] *n, pl* **-ses** relief of strong suppressed emotions **cathartic** *adj*

cathedral *n* principal church of a diocese

Catherine wheel *n* rotating firework

catheter [**kath**-it-er] *n* tube inserted into a body cavity to drain fluid

cathode *n* negative electrode, by which electrons leave a circuit **cathode rays** stream of electrons from a cathode in a vacuum tube

catholic *adj* (of tastes or interests) covering a wide range ▷ *n, adj* (**C-**) (member) of the Roman Catholic Church **Catholicism** *n*

cation [**kat**-eye-on] *n* positively charged ion

cattle *pl n* domesticated cows and bulls

Caucasian *n, adj* (member) of the light-skinned racial group of humankind

caucus *n, pl* **-cuses** local committee or faction of a political party; political meeting to decide future plans

caught *v* past of **catch**

cauldron *n* large pot used for boiling

cauliflower *n* vegetable with a large head of white flower buds surrounded by green leaves

caulk *v* fill in (cracks) with paste etc

causal *adj* of or being a cause **causally** *adv* **causation, causality** *n* relationship of cause and effect

cause *n* something that produces a particular effect; (foll. by *for*) reason, motive; aim or principle supported by a person or group ▷ *v* be the cause of

cause célèbre [**kawz** sill-**leb**-ra] *n, pl* **causes célèbres** [**kawz** sill-**leb**-ra] controversial legal case or issue

causeway *n* raised path or road across water or marshland

caustic *adj* capable of burning by chemical action; bitter and sarcastic **caustically** *adv*

cauterize *v* burn (a wound) with heat or a caustic agent to prevent infection

caution *n* care, esp in the face of danger; warning ▷ *v* warn, advise **cautionary** *adj* warning **cautious** *adj* showing caution **cautiously** *adv*

cavalcade *n* procession of people on horseback or in cars

cavalier *adj* showing haughty disregard ▷ *n* (**C-**) supporter of Charles I in the English Civil War

cavalry *n, pl* **-ries** part of the army orig on horseback, but now often using fast armoured vehicles

cave *n* hollow in the side of a hill or cliff **caving** *n* sport of exploring caves **cave in** *v* collapse inwards; *Informal* yield under pressure **caveman** *n* prehistoric cave dweller

caveat [**kav**-vee-at] *n* warning

cavern *n* large cave **cavernous**

adj

caviar, caviare *n* salted sturgeon roe, regarded as a delicacy

cavil *v* **-illing, -illed** make petty objections ▷ *n* petty objection

cavity *n, pl* **-ties** hollow space; decayed area on a tooth

cavort *v* skip about

caw *n* cry of a crow, rook, or raven ▷ *v* make this cry

cayenne pepper, cayenne *n* hot red spice made from capsicum seeds

cayman *n, pl* **-mans** S American reptile similar to an alligator

CB Citizens' Band

CBE (in Britain) Commander of the Order of the British Empire

CBI Confederation of British Industry

cc cubic centimetre; carbon copy

CD compact disc

CD-ROM compact disc read-only memory

cease *v* bring or come to an end **ceaseless** *adj* **ceaselessly** *adv* **ceasefire** *n* temporary truce

cedar *n* evergreen coniferous tree; its wood

cede *v* surrender (territory or legal rights)

cedilla *n* character (¸) placed under a *c* in some languages, to show that it is pronounced *s*, not *k*

ceilidh [**kay**-lee] *n* informal social gathering for singing and dancing, esp in Scotland

ceiling *n* inner upper surface of a room; upper limit set on something

celandine *n* wild plant with yellow flowers

celebrate *v* hold festivities to mark (a happy event, anniversary, etc); perform (a religious ceremony) **celebrated** *adj* well known **celebration** *n* **celebrant** *n* person who performs a religious ceremony

celebrity *n, pl* **-rities** famous person; state of being famous

celeriac [sill-**ler**-ee-ak] *n* variety of celery with a large turnip-like root

celerity [sill-**ler**-rit-tee] *n* swiftness

celery *n* vegetable with long green crisp edible stalks

celestial *adj* heavenly, divine; of the sky

celibate *adj* unmarried or abstaining from sex, esp because of a religious vow of chastity ▷ *n* celibate person **celibacy** *n*

cell *n* smallest unit of an organism that is able to function independently; small room for a prisoner, monk, or nun; small compartment of a honeycomb etc; small group operating as the core of a larger organization; device that produces electrical energy by chemical reaction **cellular** *adj* of or consisting of cells

cellar *n* underground room for storage; stock of wine

cello [**chell**-oh] *n, pl* **-los** large low-pitched instrument of the violin family **cellist** *n*

Cellophane *n* ® thin transparent cellulose sheeting used as wrapping

celluloid *n* kind of plastic used to make toys and, formerly, photographic film

cellulose *n* main constituent of plant cell walls, used in making paper, plastics, etc

Celsius *adj* of the temperature scale in which water freezes at 0° and boils at 100°

Celt [**kelt**] *n* person from Scotland, Ireland, Wales, Cornwall, or Brittany

Celtic [**kel**-tik, **sel**-tik] *n* group of languages including Gaelic and

Welsh ▷*adj* of the Celts or the Celtic languages

cement *n* fine grey powder mixed with water and sand to make mortar or concrete; something that unites, binds, or joins; material used to fill teeth ▷*v* join, bind, or cover with cement; make (a relationship) stronger

cemetery *n, pl* **-teries** place where dead people are buried

cenotaph *n* monument honouring soldiers who died in a war

censer *n* container for burning incense

censor *n* person authorized to examine films, books, etc, to ban or cut anything considered obscene or objectionable ▷*v* ban or cut parts of (a film, book, etc) **censorship** *n* **censorious** *adj* harshly critical

censure *n* severe disapproval ▷*v* criticize severely

census *n, pl* **-suses** official count of a population

cent *n* hundredth part of a monetary unit such as the dollar or euro

centaur *n* mythical creature with the head, arms, and torso of a man, and the lower body and legs of a horse

centenary [sen-**teen**-a-ree] *n Chiefly Brit pl* **-naries** 100th anniversary or its celebration **centenarian** *n* person at least 100 years old

centennial *n* 100th anniversary or its celebration

centi- *prefix* one hundredth

centigrade *adj* same as **Celsius**

centigram, centigramme *n* one hundredth of a gram

centilitre *n* one hundredth of a litre

centimetre *n* one hundredth of a metre

centipede *n* small wormlike creature with many legs

central *adj* of, at, or forming the centre; main, principal **centrally** *adv* **centrality** *n* **centralism** *n* principle of central control of a country or organization **centralize** *v* bring under central control **centralization** *n* **central heating** system for heating a building from one central source of heat

centre *n* middle point or part; place for a specified activity; political party or group favouring moderation; *sport* player who plays in the middle of the field ▷*v* put in the centre of something **centrist** *n* person favouring political moderation **centre on** *v* have as a centre or main theme

centrifugal *adj* moving away from a centre **centrifuge** *n* machine that separates substances by centrifugal force

centripetal *adj* moving towards a centre

centurion *n* (in ancient Rome) officer commanding 100 men

century *n, pl* **-ries** period of 100 years; cricket score of 100 runs

CEO chief executive officer

cephalopod [**seff**-a-loh-pod] *n* sea mollusc with a head and tentacles, such as the octopus

ceramic *n* hard brittle material made by heating clay to a very high temperature; object made of this ▷*pl* art of producing ceramic objects ▷*adj* made of ceramic

cereal *n* grass plant with edible grain, such as oat or wheat; this grain; breakfast food made from this grain, eaten mixed with milk

cerebral [ser-rib-ral, ser-**reeb**-ral] *adj* of the brain; intellectual
cerebrum [serr-rib-rum] *n, pl* **-brums, -bra** [-bra] main part of the brain
ceremony *n, pl* **-nies** formal act or ritual; formally polite behaviour **ceremonial** *adj, n* **ceremonially** *adv* **ceremonious** *adj* excessively polite or formal **ceremoniously** *adv*
cerise [ser-**reess**] *adj* cherry-red
certain *adj* positive and confident; definite; some but not much **certainly** *adv* **certainty** *n* state of being sure *pl* **-ties** something that is inevitable
certificate *n* official document stating the details of a birth, academic course, etc
certify *v* **-fying, -fied** confirm, attest to; guarantee; declare legally insane **certifiable** *adj* considered legally insane **certification** *n*
certitude *n* confidence, certainty
cervix *n, pl* **cervixes, cervices** narrow entrance of the womb; neck **cervical** *adj*
cessation *n* ceasing
cesspit, cesspool *n* covered tank or pit for sewage
cetacean [sit-**tay**-shun] *n* fish-shaped sea mammal such as a whale or dolphin
cf compare
CFC chlorofluorocarbon
CGI computer-generated image(s)
ch. chapter; church
chafe *v* make sore or worn by rubbing; be annoyed or impatient
chaff[1] *n* grain husks
chaff[2] *v old-fashioned* tease good-naturedly
chaffinch *n* small European songbird
chagrin [**shag**-grin] *n* annoyance and disappointment **chagrined** *adj* annoyed and disappointed
chain *n* flexible length of connected metal links; series of connected facts or events; group of shops, hotels, etc owned by one firm ▷*v* restrict or fasten with or as if with a chain **chain reaction** series of events, each of which causes the next **chain-smoke** *v* smoke (cigarettes) continuously **chain smoker**
chair *n* seat with a back, for one person; official position of authority; person holding this; professorship ▷*v* preside over (a meeting) **chairlift** series of chairs suspended from a moving cable for carrying people up a slope **chairman, chairwoman** *n* person in charge of a company's board of directors or a meeting (also **chairperson**)
chaise [**shaze**] *n hist* light horse-drawn carriage
chaise longue [**long**] *n* couch with a back and a single armrest
chalcedony [kal-**sed**-don-ee] *n, pl* **-nies** variety of quartz
chalet *n* kind of Swiss wooden house with a steeply sloping roof; similar house, used as a holiday home
chalice *n* large goblet
chalk *n* soft white rock consisting of calcium carbonate; piece of chalk, often coloured, used for drawing and writing on blackboards ▷*v* draw or mark with chalk **chalky** *adj*
challenge *n* demanding or stimulating situation; call to take part in a contest or fight; questioning of a statement of fact; demand by a sentry for identification or a password ▷*v*

issue a challenge to **challenged** *adj* disabled as specified *eg physically challenged* **challenger** *n*

chamber *n* hall used for formal meetings; legislative or judicial assembly; *old-fashioned* bedroom; compartment, cavity ▷ *pl* set of rooms used as offices by a barrister **chambermaid** *n* woman employed to clean bedrooms in a hotel **chamber music** classical music to be performed by a small group of musicians **chamber pot** bowl for urine, formerly used in bedrooms

chamberlain *n hist* officer who managed the household of a king or nobleman

chameleon [kam-**meal**-yon] *n* small lizard that changes colour to blend in with its surroundings

chamfer [**cham**-fer] *v* bevel the edge of

chamois [**sham**-wah] *n, pl* **-ois** small mountain antelope [**sham**-ee] soft suede leather; piece of this, used for cleaning or polishing

chamomile [**kam**-mo-mile] *n* same as **camomile**

champ[1] *v* chew noisily **champ at the bit** *Informal* be impatient to do something

champ[2] *n* short for **champion**

champagne *n* sparkling white French wine

champion *n* overall winner of a competition; (foll. by *of*) someone who defends a person or cause ▷ *v* support ▷ *adj dialect* excellent **championship** *n*

chance *n* likelihood, probability; opportunity to do something; risk, gamble; unpredictable element that causes things to happen one way rather than another ▷ *v* risk, hazard **chancy** *adj* uncertain, risky

chancel *n* part of a church containing the altar and choir

chancellor *n* head of government in some European countries; honorary head of a university **chancellorship** *n*

Chancery *n* division of the British High Court of Justice

chandelier [shan-dill-**eer**] *n* ornamental light with branches and holders for several candles or bulbs

chandler *n* dealer, esp in ships' supplies

change *n* becoming different; variety or novelty; different set, esp of clothes; balance received when the amount paid is more than the cost of a purchase; coins of low value ▷ *v* make or become different; give and receive (something) in return; exchange (money) for its equivalent in a smaller denomination or different currency; put on other clothes; leave one vehicle and board another **changeable** *adj* changing often **changeling** *n* child believed to have been exchanged by fairies for another

channel *n* band of broadcasting frequencies; means of access or communication; broad strait connecting two areas of sea; bed or course of a river, stream, or canal; groove ▷ *v* **-nelling, -nelled** direct or convey through a channel

chant *v* utter or sing (a slogan or psalm) ▷ *n* rhythmic or repetitious slogan; psalm that has a short simple melody with several words sung on one note

chanter *n* (on bagpipes) pipe on which the melody is played

chaos *n* complete disorder or

confusion **chaotic** *adj* **chaotically** *adv*

chap *n Informal* man or boy

chapati, chapatti *n* (in Indian cookery) flat thin unleavened bread

chapel *n* place of worship with its own altar, within a church; similar place of worship in a large house or institution; Nonconformist place of worship

chaperone [**shap**-per-rone] *n* older person who accompanies and supervises a young person or young people on a social occasion ▷ *v* act as a chaperone to

chaplain *n* clergyman attached to a chapel, military body, or institution **chaplaincy** *n, pl* **-cies**

chaplet *n* garland for the head

chapped *adj* (of the skin) raw and cracked, through exposure to cold

chapter *n* division of a book; period in a life or history; branch of a society or club

char[1] *v* **charring, charred** blacken by partial burning

char[2] *Brit, Informal* ▷ *n* charwoman ▷ *v* **charring, charred** clean other people's houses as a job

char[3] *n Brit, old-fashioned slang* tea

charabanc [**shar**-rab-bang] *n old-fashioned* coach for sightseeing

character *n* combination of qualities distinguishing a person, group, or place; reputation, esp good reputation; person represented in a play, film, or story; unusual or amusing person; letter, numeral, or symbol used in writing or printing **characteristic** *n* distinguishing feature or quality ▷ *adj* typical **characteristically** *adv* **characterize** *v* be a characteristic of; (foll. by *as*) describe **characterization** *n*

charade [shar-**rahd**] *n* absurd pretence ▷ *pl* game in which one team acts out a word or phrase, which the other team has to guess

charcoal *n* black substance formed by partially burning wood

charge *v* ask as a price; enter a debit against a person's account for (a purchase); accuse formally; make a rush at or sudden attack upon; fill (a glass); fill (a battery) with electricity; command, assign ▷ *n* price charged; formal accusation; attack; command, exhortation; custody, guardianship; person or thing entrusted to someone's care; amount of electricity stored in a battery **in charge of** in control of **chargeable** *adj* **charger** *n* device for charging an accumulator; (in the Middle Ages) warhorse

chargé d'affaires [**shar**-zhay daf-**fair**] *n, pl* **chargés d'affaires** head of a diplomatic mission in the absence of an ambassador or in a small mission

chariot *n* two-wheeled horse-drawn vehicle used in ancient times in wars and races **charioteer** *n* chariot driver

charisma [kar-**rizz**-ma] *n* person's power to attract or influence people **charismatic** [kar-rizz-**mat**-ik] *adj*

charity *n, pl* **-ties** organization that gives help, such as money or food, to those in need; giving of help to those in need; help given to those in need; kindly attitude towards people **charitable** *adj* **charitably** *adv*

charlady *n Brit, Informal* same as **charwoman**

charlatan [**shar**-lat-tan] *n* person who claims expertise that he or she does not have

charleston *n* lively dance of the 1920s

charm *n* attractive quality; trinket worn on a bracelet; magic spell ▷ *v* attract, delight; influence by personal charm; protect or influence as if by magic **charmer** *n* **charming** *adj* attractive

charnel house *n hist* building or vault for the bones of the dead

chart *n* graph, table, or diagram showing information; map of the sea or stars ▷ *v* plot the course of; make a chart of **the charts** *Informal* weekly lists of the bestselling pop records

charter *n* document granting or demanding certain rights; fundamental principles of an organization; hire of transport for private use ▷ *v* hire by charter; grant a charter to **chartered** *adj* officially qualified to practise a profession

chartreuse [shar-**trerz**] *n* sweet-smelling green or yellow liqueur

charwoman *n* woman whose job is to clean other people's homes

chary [**chair**-ee] *adj* **-rier, -riest** wary, careful

chase[1] *v* run after quickly in order to catch or drive away; *Informal* rush, run; *Informal* try energetically to obtain ▷ *n* chasing, pursuit **chaser** *n* milder drink drunk after another stronger one

chase[2] *v* engrave or emboss (metal)

chasm [**kaz**-zum] *n* deep crack in the earth

chassis [**shass**-ee] *n, pl* **-sis** frame, wheels, and mechanical parts of a vehicle

chaste *adj* abstaining from sex outside marriage or altogether; (of style) simple **chastely** *adv* **chastity** *n*

chasten [**chase**-en] *v* subdue by criticism

chastise *v* scold severely; punish by beating **chastisement** *n*

chat *n* informal conversation ▷ *v* **chatting, chatted** have an informal conversation **chatty** *adj* **chatroom** *n* site on the Internet where users have group discussions by e-mail

chateau [**shat**-toe] *n, pl* **-teaux, -teaus** French castle

chatelaine [**shat**-tell-lane] *n* (formerly) mistress of a large house or castle

chattels *pl n* possessions

chatter *v* speak quickly and continuously about unimportant things; (of the teeth) rattle with cold or fear ▷ *n* idle talk **chatterbox** *n* person who chatters a lot

chauffeur *n* person employed to drive a car for someone

chauvinism [**show**-vin-iz-zum] *n* irrational belief that one's own country, race, group, or sex is superior **chauvinist** *n, adj* **chauvinistic** *adj*

cheap *adj* costing relatively little; of poor quality; not valued highly; mean, despicable **cheaply** *adv* **cheapen** *v* lower the reputation of; reduce the price of **cheapskate** *n* *Informal* miserly person

cheat *v* act dishonestly to gain profit or advantage ▷ *n* person who cheats; fraud, deception

check *v* examine, investigate; slow the growth or progress of; correspond, agree ▷ *n* test to ensure accuracy or progress; break in progress; *US* cheque; pattern of squares or crossed lines; *chess* position of a king under attack **check in** *v* register one's arrival

checkmate *n chess* winning position in which an opponent's king is under attack and unable to escape; utter defeat ▷ *v chess* place the king of (one's opponent) in checkmate; thwart, defeat **check out** *v* pay the bill and leave a hotel; examine, investigate; *Informal* have a look at **checkout** *n* counter in a supermarket, where customers pay **checkup** *n* thorough medical examination

Cheddar *n* firm orange or yellowy-white cheese

cheek *n* either side of the face below the eye; *Informal* impudence, boldness ▷ *v Brit, Aust & NZ, Informal* speak impudently to **cheeky** *adj* impudent, disrespectful **cheekily** *adv* **cheekiness** *n*

cheep *n* young bird's high-pitched cry ▷ *v* utter a cheep

cheer *v* applaud or encourage with shouts; make or become happy ▷ *n* shout of applause or encouragement **cheerful** *adj* **cheerfully** *adv* **cheerfulness** *n* **cheerless** *adj* dreary, gloomy **cheery** *adj* **cheerily** *adv*

cheerio *interj Informal* goodbye ▷ *n Aust & NZ* small red cocktail sausage

cheese *n* food made from coagulated milk curd; block of this **cheesy** *adj* **cheeseburger** *n* hamburger topped with melted cheese **cheesecake** *n* dessert with a biscuit-crumb base covered with a sweet cream-cheese mixture; *slang* photographs of naked or near-naked women **cheesecloth** *n* light cotton cloth **cheesed off** bored, annoyed

cheetah *n* large fast-running spotted African wild cat

chef *n* cook in a restaurant

chef-d'oeuvre [shay-**durv**] *n, pl* **chefs-d'oeuvre** masterpiece

chemical *n* substance used in or resulting from a reaction involving changes to atoms or molecules ▷ *adj* of chemistry or chemicals **chemically** *adv*

chemise [shem-**meez**] *n old-fashioned* woman's loose-fitting slip

chemistry *n* science of the composition, properties, and reactions of substances **chemist** *n* shop selling medicines and cosmetics; qualified dispenser of prescribed medicines; specialist in chemistry

chemotherapy *n* treatment of disease, often cancer, using chemicals

chenille [shen-**neel**] *n* (fabric of) thick tufty yarn

cheque *n* written order to one's bank to pay money from one's account **cheque card** *Brit* plastic card issued by a bank guaranteeing payment of a customer's cheques

chequer *n* piece used in Chinese chequers ▷ *pl* game of draughts

chequered *adj* marked by varied fortunes; having a pattern of squares

cherish *v* cling to (an idea or feeling); care for

cheroot [sher-**root**] *n* cigar with both ends cut flat

cherry *n, pl* **-ries** small red or black fruit with a stone; tree on which it grows ▷ *adj* deep red

cherub *n, pl* **-ubs, -ubim** angel, often represented as a winged child; sweet child **cherubic** [cher-**rew**-bik] *adj*

chervil *n* aniseed-flavoured herb

chess *n* game for two players with 16 pieces each, played on a chequered board of 64 squares **chessman** *n* piece used in chess

chest *n* front of the body, from neck to waist; large strong box **chest of drawers** piece of furniture consisting of drawers in a frame

chesterfield *n* couch with high padded sides and back

chestnut *n* reddish-brown edible nut; tree on which it grows; reddish-brown horse; *Informal* old joke ▷ *adj* (of hair or a horse) reddish-brown

chevron [**shev**-ron] *n* V-shaped pattern, esp on the sleeve of a military uniform to indicate rank

chew *v* grind (food) between the teeth **chewy** *adj* requiring a lot of chewing **chewing gum** flavoured gum to be chewed but not swallowed

chianti [kee-**ant**-ee] *n* dry red Italian wine

chiaroscuro [kee-ah-roh-**skew**-roh] *n, pl* **-ros** distribution of light and shade in a picture

chic [**sheek**] *adj* stylish, elegant ▷ *n* stylishness, elegance

chicane [shik-**kane**] *n* obstacle in a motor-racing circuit

chicanery *n* trickery, deception

chick *n* baby bird **chickpea** *n* edible yellow pealike seed **chickweed** *n* weed with small white flowers

chicken *n* domestic fowl; its flesh, used as food; *slang* coward ▷ *adj* *slang* cowardly **chicken feed** *slang* trifling amount of money **chicken out** *v* *Informal* fail to do something through cowardice **chickenpox** *n* infectious disease with an itchy rash

chicory *n, pl* **-ries** plant whose leaves are used in salads; root of this plant, used as a coffee substitute

chide *v* **chiding, chided** *or* **chid, chid** *or* **chidden** rebuke, scold

chief *n* head of a group of people ▷ *adj* most important **chiefly** *adv* especially; mainly **chieftain** *n* leader of a tribe

chiffon [**shif**-fon] *n* fine see-through fabric

chignon [**sheen**-yon] *n* knot of hair pinned up at the back of the head

chihuahua [chee-**wah**-wah] *n* tiny short-haired dog

chilblain *n* inflammation of the fingers or toes, caused by exposure to cold

child *n, pl* **children** young human being, boy or girl; son or daughter **childhood** *n* **childish** *adj* immature, silly; of or like a child **childishly** *adv* **childless** *adj* **childlike** *adj* innocent, trustful **childbirth** *n* giving birth to a child **child's play** very easy task

chill *n* feverish cold; moderate coldness ▷ *v* make (something) cool or cold; cause (someone) to feel cold or frightened ▷ *adj* unpleasantly cold **chilly** *adj* moderately cold; unfriendly **chilly-bin** *n* *NZ, Informal* insulated container for carrying food and drink **chilliness** *n* **chill (out)** *v* *Informal* relax **chill-out** *adj* *Informal* suitable for relaxation, esp after energetic activity *eg a chill-out area*

chilli, chili *n* small red or green hot-tasting capsicum pod, used in cooking; (also **chilli con carne**) hot-tasting Mexican dish of meat, onions, beans, and chilli powder

chime *n* musical ringing sound of a bell or clock ▷ *v* make a musical ringing sound; indicate (the time) by chiming; (foll. by *with*) be consistent with

chimera [kime-**meer**-a] *n* unrealistic hope or idea; fabled monster with a lion's head, goat's body, and serpent's tail

chimney *n* hollow vertical structure for carrying away smoke from a fire **chimney pot** short pipe on the top of a chimney **chimney sweep** person who cleans soot from chimneys

chimp *n Informal* short for **chimpanzee**

chimpanzee *n* intelligent black African ape

chin *n* part of the face below the mouth **chinwag** *n Brit, Aust & NZ, Informal* chat

china *n* fine earthenware or porcelain; dishes or ornaments made of this; *Brit, Aust, NZ & SAfr, Informal* friend

chinchilla *n* S American rodent bred for its soft grey fur; its fur

chine *n* cut of meat including part of the backbone

Chinese *adj* of China ▷ *n, pl* **-nese** person from China; any of the languages of China

chink¹ *n* small narrow opening

chink² *v, n* (make) a light ringing sound

chintz *n* printed cotton fabric with a glazed finish

chip *n* strip of potato, fried in deep fat; tiny wafer of semiconductor material forming an integrated circuit; counter used to represent money in gambling games; small piece removed by chopping, breaking, etc; mark left where a small piece has been broken off something ▷ *v* **chipping, chipped** break small pieces from **have a chip on one's shoulder** *Informal* bear a grudge **chip in** *v Informal* contribute (money); interrupt with a remark **chippie** *n Brit, Aust & NZ, Informal* carpenter

chipboard *n* thin board made of compressed wood particles

chipmunk *n* small squirrel-like N American rodent with a striped back

chiropodist [kir-**rop**-pod-ist] *n* person who treats minor foot complaints **chiropody** *n*

chiropractic [kire-oh-**prak**-tik] *n* system of treating bodily disorders by manipulation of the spine **chiropractor** *n*

chirp *v* (of a bird or insect) make a short high-pitched sound ▷ *n* chirping sound **chirpy** *adj Informal* lively and cheerful

chisel *n* metal tool with a sharp end for shaping wood or stone ▷ *v* **-elling, -elled** carve or form with a chisel

chit¹ *n* short official note, such as a receipt

chit² *n Brit, Aust & NZ, old-fashioned* pert or impudent girl

chitchat *n* chat, gossip

chitterlings *pl n* pig's intestines cooked as food

chivalry *n* courteous behaviour, esp by men towards women; medieval system and principles of knighthood **chivalrous** *adj*

chives *pl n* herb with a mild onion flavour

chivvy *v* **-vying, -vied** *Informal* harass, nag

chlorine *n* strong-smelling greenish-yellow gaseous element, used to disinfect water **chlorinate** *v* disinfect (water) with chlorine **chlorination** *n* **chloride** *n* compound of chlorine and another substance

chlorofluorocarbon *n* any of various gaseous compounds of carbon, hydrogen, chlorine, and fluorine, used in refrigerators and aerosol propellants, some of which break down the ozone in the atmosphere

chloroform *n* strong-smelling liquid formerly used as an anaesthetic

chlorophyll *n* green colouring matter of plants, which enables them to convert sunlight into energy

chock *n* block or wedge used to prevent a heavy object from moving **chock-full, chock-a-block** *adj* completely full

chocolate *n* sweet food made from cacao seeds; sweet or drink made from this ▷ *adj* dark brown

choice *n* choosing; opportunity or power of choosing; person or thing chosen or that may be chosen; alternative action or possibility ▷ *adj* of high quality

choir *n* organized group of singers, esp in church; part of a church occupied by the choir

choke *v* hinder or stop the breathing of (a person) by strangling or smothering; have trouble in breathing; block, clog up ▷ *n* device controlling the amount of air that is mixed with the fuel in a petrol engine **choker** *n* tight-fitting necklace **choke back** *v* suppress (tears or anger)

cholera [**kol**-ler-a] *n* serious infectious disease causing severe vomiting and diarrhoea

choleric [**kol**-ler-ik] *adj* bad-tempered

cholesterol [kol-**lest**-er-oll] *n* fatty substance found in animal tissue, an excess of which can cause heart disease

chomp *v* chew noisily

chook *n Aust & NZ* hen or chicken

choose *v* **choosing, chose, chosen** select from a number of alternatives; decide (to do something) because one wants to **choosy** *adj Informal* fussy, hard to please

chop[1] *v* **chopping, chopped** cut with a blow from an axe or knife; cut into pieces; dispense with; *boxing, karate* hit (an opponent) with a short sharp blow ▷ *n* cutting or sharp blow; slice of lamb or pork, usu with a rib **chopper** *n Informal* helicopter; small axe **choppy** *adj* (of the sea) fairly rough

chop[2] *v* **chopping, chopped chop and change** change one's mind repeatedly

chops *pl n Brit, Aust & NZ, Informal* jaws, cheeks

chopsticks *pl n* pair of thin sticks used to eat Chinese food

chop suey *n* Chinese dish of chopped meat and vegetables in a sauce

choral *adj* of a choir

chorale [kor-**rahl**] *n* slow stately hymn tune

chord[1] *n maths* straight line joining two points on a curve

chord[2] *n* simultaneous sounding of three or more musical notes

chore *n* routine task

choreography *n* composition of steps and movements for dancing **choreographer** *n* **choreographic** *adj*

chorister *n* singer in a choir

chortle *v* chuckle in amusement ▷ *n* amused chuckle

chorus *n, pl* **-ruses** large choir; part of a song repeated after each verse; something expressed by many people at once; group of singers or dancers who perform together in a show ▷ *v* **chorusing, chorused** sing or say together **in chorus** in unison

chose *v* past tense of **choose**

chosen *v* past participle of **choose**

choux pastry [**shoo**] *n* very light pastry made with eggs

chow *n* thick-coated dog with a curled tail, orig from China

chowder *n* thick soup containing clams or fish

chow mein *n* Chinese-American dish of chopped meat or vegetables fried with noodles

Christ *n* Jesus of Nazareth, regarded by Christians as the Messiah

christen *v* baptize; give a name to; *Informal* use for the first time **christening** *n*

Christendom *n* all Christian people or countries

Christian *n* person who believes in and follows Christ ▷ *adj* of Christ or Christianity; kind, good **Christianity** *n* religion based on the life and teachings of Christ **Christian name** personal name given to Christians at baptism: loosely used to mean a person's first name **Christian Science** religious system which emphasizes spiritual healing

Christmas *n* annual festival on Dec. 25 commemorating the birth of Christ; period around this time **Christmassy** *adj* **Christmas Day** Dec. 25 **Christmas Eve** Dec. 24 **Christmas tree** evergreen tree or imitation of one, decorated as part of Christmas celebrations

chromatic *adj* of colour or colours; *music* (of a scale) proceeding by semitones

chromatography *n* separation and analysis of the components of a substance by slowly passing it through an adsorbing material

chromium, chrome *n chem* grey metallic element used in steel alloys and for electroplating

chromosome *n* microscopic gene-carrying body in the nucleus of a cell

chronic *adj* (of an illness) lasting a long time; habitual *eg chronic drinking*; *Brit, Aust & NZ, Informal* of poor quality **chronically** *adv*

chronicle *n* record of events in order of occurrence ▷ *v* record in or as if in a chronicle **chronicler** *n*

chronology *n, pl* **-gies** arrangement or list of events in order of occurrence **chronological** *adj* **chronologically** *adv*

chronometer *n* timepiece designed to be accurate in all conditions

chrysalis [**kriss**-a-liss] *n* insect in the stage between larva and adult, when it is in a cocoon

chrysanthemum *n* garden flower with a large head made up of thin petals

chub *n* European freshwater fish of the carp family

chubby *adj* **-bier, -biest** plump and round

chuck[1] *v Informal* throw; *Informal* give up, reject; touch (someone) affectionately under the chin; *Aust & NZ, Informal* vomit

chuck[2] *n* cut of beef from the neck to the shoulder; device that holds a workpiece in a lathe or a tool in a drill

chuckle *v* laugh softly ▷ *n* soft laugh

chuffed *adj Informal* very pleased

chug *n* short dull sound like the

noise of an engine ▷*v* **chugging, chugged** operate or move with this sound

chukka *n* period of play in polo

chum *Informal* ▷*n* close friend ▷*v* **chumming, chummed chum up with** form a close friendship with **chummy** *adj*

chump *n Informal* stupid person; thick piece of meat

chunk *n* thick solid piece; considerable amount **chunky** *adj* (of a person) broad and heavy; (of an object) large and thick

church *n* building for public Christian worship; particular Christian denomination; (**C-**) Christians collectively; clergy **churchgoer** *n* person who attends church regularly **churchwarden** *n* member of a congregation who assists the vicar **churchyard** *n* grounds round a church, used as a graveyard

churlish *adj* surly and rude

churn *n* machine in which cream is shaken to make butter; large container for milk ▷*v* stir (cream) vigorously to make butter; move about violently **churn out** *v Informal* produce (things) rapidly in large numbers

chute[1] [**shoot**] *n* steep slope down which things may be slid

chute[2] *n Informal* short for **parachute**

chutney *n* pickle made from fruit, vinegar, spices, and sugar

CIA (in the US) Central Intelligence Agency

cicada [sik-**kah**-da] *n* large insect that makes a high-pitched drone

cicatrix [**sik**-a-trix] *n, pl* **-trices** scar

CID (in Britain) Criminal Investigation Department

cider *n* alcoholic drink made from fermented apple juice

cigar *n* roll of cured tobacco leaves for smoking

cigarette *n* thin roll of shredded tobacco in thin paper, for smoking

cinch [**sinch**] *n Informal* easy task

cinder *n* piece of material that will not burn, left after burning coal

cine camera *n* camera for taking moving pictures

cinema *n* place for showing films; films collectively **cinematic** *adj* **cinematography** *n* technique of making films **cinematographer** *n*

cineraria *n* garden plant with daisy-like flowers

cinnamon *n* spice obtained from the bark of an Asian tree

> SPELLING **Cinnamon** is a tricky word to spell. Collins Word Web shows at least 3 different ways of getting it wrong. The correct spelling has two *ns* in the middle and only one *m*

cipher [**sife**-er] *n* system of secret writing; unimportant person

circa [**sir**-ka] *prep Latin* approximately, about

circle *n* perfectly round geometric figure, line, or shape; group of people sharing an interest or activity; *theatre* section of seats above the main level of the auditorium ▷*v* move in a circle (round); enclose in a circle

circlet *n* circular ornament worn on the head

circuit *n* complete route or course, esp a circular one; complete path through which an electric current can flow; periodical journey round a district, as made by judges; motor-racing track **circuitous** [sir-**kew**-it-uss] *adj* indirect and lengthy **circuitry** [**sir**-kit-tree] *n*

electrical circuit(s)
circular *adj* in the shape of a circle; moving in a circle ▷*n* letter for general distribution **circularity** *n*
circulate *v* send, go, or pass from place to place or person to person **circulation** *n* flow of blood around the body; number of copies of a newspaper or magazine sold; sending or moving round **circulatory** *adj*
circumcise *v* remove the foreskin of **circumcision** *n*
circumference *n* boundary of a specified area or shape, esp of a circle; distance round this
circumflex *n* mark (^) over a vowel to show that it is pronounced in a particular way
circumlocution *n* indirect way of saying something
circumnavigate *v* sail right round **circumnavigation** *n*
circumscribe *v* limit, restrict; draw a line round **circumscription** *n*
circumspect *adj* cautious and careful not to take risks **circumspectly** *adv* **circumspection** *n*
circumstance *n* (usu pl) occurrence or condition that accompanies or influences a person or event **circumstantial** *adj* (of evidence) strongly suggesting something but not proving it; very detailed
circumvent *v* avoid or get round (a rule etc) **circumvention** *n*
circus *n, pl* **-cuses** (performance given by) a travelling company of acrobats, clowns, performing animals, etc
cirrhosis [sir-**roh**-siss] *n* serious liver disease, often caused by drinking too much alcohol
cirrus *n, pl* **-ri** high wispy cloud
cistern *n* water tank, esp one that holds water for flushing a toilet
citadel *n* fortress in a city
cite *v* quote, refer to; bring forward as proof **citation** *n*
citizen *n* native or naturalized member of a state or nation; inhabitant of a city or town **citizenship** *n* **Citizens' Band** range of radio frequencies for private communication by the public
citric acid *n* weak acid found in citrus fruits
citrus fruit *n* juicy sharp-tasting fruit such as an orange or lemon
city *n, pl* **-ties** large or important town **the City** *Brit* area of London as a financial centre
civet [**siv**-vit] *n* spotted catlike African mammal; musky fluid from its glands used in perfume
civic *adj* of a city or citizens **civics** *n* study of the rights and responsibilities of citizenship
civil *adj* relating to the citizens of a state as opposed to the armed forces or the Church; polite, courteous **civilly** *adv* **civility** *n* polite or courteous behaviour **civilian** *n, adj* (person) not belonging to the armed forces **civil service** service responsible for the administration of the government **civil servant** member of the civil service **civil war** war between people of the same country
civilize *v* refine or educate (a person); make (a place) more pleasant or more acceptable **civilization** *n* high level of human cultural and social development; particular society which has reached this level
civvies *pl n* *Brit, Aust & NZ, slang*

ordinary clothes that are not part of a uniform
clack *n* sound made by two hard objects striking each other ▷*v* make this sound
clad *v* a past of **clothe**
cladding *n* material used to cover the outside of a building
claim *v* assert as a fact; demand as a right; need, require ▷*n* assertion that something is true; assertion of a right; something claimed as a right **claimant** *n*
clairvoyance *n* power of perceiving things beyond the natural range of the senses **clairvoyant** *n, adj*
clam *n* edible shellfish with a hinged shell ▷*v* **clamming, clammed clam up** *Informal* stop talking, esp through nervousness
clamber *v* climb awkwardly
clammy *adj* **-mier, -miest** unpleasantly moist and sticky
clamour *n* loud protest; loud persistent noise or outcry ▷*v* make a loud noise or outcry **clamorous** *adj* **clamour for** *v* demand noisily
clamp *n* tool with movable jaws for holding things together tightly ▷*v* fasten with a clamp **clamp down on** *v* become stricter about; suppress
clan *n* group of families with a common ancestor, esp among Scottish Highlanders; close group **clannish** *adj* (of a group) tending to exclude outsiders
clandestine *adj* secret and concealed
clang *v* make a loud ringing metallic sound ▷*n* ringing metallic sound
clanger *n* *Informal* obvious mistake
clangour *n* loud continuous clanging sound
clank *n* harsh metallic sound ▷*v* make such a sound
clap[1] *v* **clapping, clapped** applaud by hitting the palms of one's hands sharply together; put quickly or forcibly ▷*n* act or sound of clapping; sudden loud noise *eg a clap of thunder* **clapped out** *slang* worn out, dilapidated
clap[2] *n slang* gonorrhoea
clapper *n* piece of metal inside a bell, which causes it to sound when struck against the side **clapperboard** *n* pair of hinged boards clapped together during filming to help in synchronizing sound and picture
claptrap *n* *Informal* foolish or pretentious talk
claret [**klar**-rit] *n* dry red wine from Bordeaux
clarify *v* **-fying, -fied** make (a matter) clear and unambiguous **clarification** *n*
clarinet *n* keyed woodwind instrument with a single reed **clarinettist** *n*
clarion *n* obsolete high-pitched trumpet; its sound **clarion call** strong encouragement to do something
clarity *n* clearness
clash *v* come into conflict; (of events) happen at the same time; (of colours) look unattractive together; (of objects) make a loud harsh sound by being hit together ▷*n* fight, argument; fact of two events happening at the same time
clasp *n* device for fastening things; firm grasp or embrace ▷*v* grasp or embrace firmly; fasten with a clasp
class *n* group of people sharing a similar social position; system of

dividing society into such groups; group of people or things sharing a common characteristic; group of pupils or students taught together; standard of quality; *Informal* elegance or excellence *eg a touch of class* ▷*v* place in a class

classic *adj* being a typical example of something; of lasting interest because of excellence; attractive because of simplicity of form ▷*n* author, artist, or work of art of recognized excellence ▷*pl* study of ancient Greek and Roman literature and culture **classical** *adj* of or in a restrained conservative style; denoting serious art music; of or influenced by ancient Greek and Roman culture **classically** *adv* **classicism** *n* artistic style showing emotional restraint and regularity of form **classicist** *n*

classify *v* **-fying, -fied** divide into groups with similar characteristics; declare (information) to be officially secret **classifiable** *adj* **classification** *n*

classy *adj* **classier, classiest** *Informal* stylish and elegant

clatter *v, n* (make) a rattling noise

clause *n* section of a legal document; part of a sentence, containing a verb

claustrophobia *n* abnormal fear of confined spaces **claustrophobic** *adj*

clavichord *n* early keyboard instrument

clavicle *n* same as **collarbone**

claw *n* sharp hooked nail of a bird or beast; similar part, such as a crab's pincer ▷*v* tear with claws or nails

clay *n* fine-grained earth, soft when moist and hardening when baked, used to make bricks and pottery **clayey** *adj* **clay pigeon** baked clay disc hurled into the air as a target for shooting

claymore *n* large two-edged sword formerly used by Scottish Highlanders

clean *adj* free from dirt or impurities; not yet used; morally acceptable, inoffensive; (of a reputation or record) free from dishonesty or corruption; complete *eg a clean break*; smooth and regular ▷*v* make (something) free from dirt ▷*adv not standard* completely *eg I clean forgot* **come clean** *Informal* reveal or admit something **cleaner** *n* **cleanly** *adv* **cleanliness** *n*

cleanse *v* make clean **cleanser** *n*

clear *adj* free from doubt or confusion; easy to see or hear; able to be seen through; free of obstruction; (of weather) free from clouds; (of skin) without blemish ▷*adv* out of the way ▷*v* make or become clear; pass by or over (something) without contact; prove (someone) innocent of a crime or mistake; make as profit **clearly** *adv* **clearance** *n* clearing; official permission **clearing** *n* treeless area in a wood **clear off** *v Brit, Aust & NZ, Informal* go away **clear out** *v* remove and sort the contents of; *Brit, Aust & NZ, Informal* go away **clear-sighted** *adj* having good judgment **clearway** *n* stretch of road on which motorists may stop in an emergency

cleat *n* wedge; piece of wood, metal, or plastic with two projecting ends round which ropes are fastened

cleave[1] *v* **cleaving, cleft, cleaved** *or* **clove, cleft, cleaved** *or* **cloven** split apart **cleavage** *n* space between a woman's breasts, as revealed by a low-cut dress; division, split

cleave² *v* cling or stick

cleaver *n* butcher's heavy knife with a square blade

clef *n music* symbol at the beginning of a stave to show the pitch

cleft *n* narrow opening or crack ▷*v* a past of **cleave¹** **in a cleft stick** in a very difficult position

clematis *n* climbing plant with large colourful flowers

clement *adj* (of weather) mild **clemency** *n* kind or lenient treatment

clementine *n* small orange citrus fruit

clench *v* close or squeeze (one's teeth or fist) tightly; grasp firmly

clerestory [**clear**-store-ee] *n, pl* **-ries** row of windows at the top of a wall above an adjoining roof

clergy *n* priests and ministers as a group **clergyman** *n*

cleric *n* member of the clergy

clerical *adj* of clerks or office work; of the clergy

clerk *n* employee in an office, bank, or court who keeps records, files, and accounts

clever *adj* intelligent, quick at learning; showing skill **cleverly** *adv* **cleverness** *n*

clianthus [klee-**anth**-us] *n* Australian or NZ plant with slender scarlet flowers

cliché [**klee**-shay] *n* expression or idea that is no longer effective because of overuse **clichéd** *adj*

click *n* short sharp sound ▷*v* make this sound; *Informal* (of two people) get on well together; *Informal* become suddenly clear; *computers* press and release (a button on a mouse); *slang* be a success

client *n* person who uses the services of a professional person or company; *computers* program or work station that requests data from a server **clientele** [klee-on-**tell**] *n* clients collectively

cliff *n* steep rock face, esp along the sea shore **cliffhanger** *n* film, game, etc, that is tense and exciting because its outcome is uncertain

climate *n* typical weather conditions of an area **climatic** *adj*

climax *n* most intense point of an experience, series of events, or story; same as **orgasm** **climactic** *adj*

climb *v* go up, ascend; rise to a higher point or intensity ▷*n* climbing; place to be climbed **climber** *n* **climb down** *v* retreat from an opinion or position

clime *n poetic* place or its climate

clinch *v* settle (an argument or agreement) decisively **clincher** *n* *Informal* something decisive

cling *v* **clinging, clung** hold tightly or stick closely **clingfilm** *n* thin polythene material for wrapping food

clinic *n* building where outpatients receive medical treatment or advice; private or specialized hospital **clinical** *adj* of a clinic; logical and unemotional **clinically** *adv*

clink¹ *v, n* (make) a light sharp metallic sound

clink² *n Brit, Aust & NZ, slang* prison

clinker *n* fused coal left over in a fire or furnace

clinker-built *adj* (of a boat) made of overlapping planks

clip¹ *v* **clipping, clipped** cut with shears or scissors; *Informal* hit sharply ▷*n* short extract of a film; *Informal* sharp blow **clippers** *pl n* tool for clipping **clipping** *n* something cut out, esp an article from a newspaper

clip² *n* device for attaching or holding things together ▷*v* **clipping, clipped** attach or hold together with a clip

clipper *n* fast commercial sailing ship

clique [**kleek**] *n* small exclusive group

clitoris [**klit**-or-iss] *n* small sexually sensitive organ at the front of the vulva **clitoral** *adj*

cloak *n* loose sleeveless outer garment ▷*v* cover or conceal **cloakroom** *n* room where coats may be left temporarily

clobber¹ *v Informal* hit; defeat utterly

clobber² *n Brit, Aust & NZ, Informal* belongings, esp clothes

cloche [**klosh**] *n* cover to protect young plants; woman's close-fitting hat

clock *n* instrument for showing the time; device with a dial for recording or measuring **clockwise** *adv, adj* in the direction in which the hands of a clock rotate **clock in** *or* **on, out off** *v* register arrival at *or* departure from work on an automatic time recorder **clock up** *v* reach (a total) **clockwork** *n* mechanism similar to the kind in a clock, used in wind-up toys

clod *n* lump of earth; *Brit, Aust & NZ* stupid person

clog *v* **clogging, clogged** obstruct ▷*n* wooden or wooden-soled shoe

cloister *n* covered pillared arcade, usu in a monastery **cloistered** *adj* sheltered

clone *n* animal or plant produced artificially from the cells of another animal or plant, and identical to the original; *Informal* person who closely resembles another ▷*v* produce as a clone

close¹ *v* [rhymes with **nose**] shut; prevent access to; end, terminate; bring or come nearer together ▷*n* end, conclusion [rhymes with **dose**] street closed at one end [rhymes with **dose**] *Brit* courtyard, quadrangle **closed shop** place of work in which all workers must belong to a particular trade union

close² *adj* [rhymes with **dose**] near; intimate; careful, thorough; compact, dense; oppressive, stifling; secretive ▷*adv* closely, tightly **closely** *adv* **closeness** *n* **close season** period when it is illegal to kill certain game or fish **close shave** *Informal* narrow escape **close-up** *n* photograph or film taken at close range

closet *n US* cupboard; small private room ▷*adj* private, secret ▷*v* **closeting, closeted** shut (oneself) away in private

closure *n* closing

clot *n* soft thick lump formed from liquid; *Brit, Aust & NZ, Informal* stupid person ▷*v* **clotting, clotted** form soft thick lumps

cloth *n* (piece of) woven fabric

clothe *v* **clothing, clothed** *or* **clad** put clothes on; provide with clothes **clothes** *pl n* articles of dress; bed coverings **clothing** *n* clothes collectively

cloud *n* mass of condensed water vapour floating in the sky; floating mass of smoke, dust, etc ▷*v* (foll. by *over*) become cloudy; confuse; make gloomy or depressed **cloudless** *adj* **cloudy** *adj* having a lot of clouds; (of liquid) not clear

cloudburst *n* heavy fall of rain
clout *Informal* ▷ *n* hard blow; power, influence ▷ *v* hit hard
clove[1] *n* dried flower bud of a tropical tree, used as a spice
clove[2] *n* segment of a bulb of garlic
clove[3] *v* a past tense of **cleave**[1]
clove hitch knot used to fasten a rope to a spar
cloven *v* a past participle of **cleave**[1]
cloven hoof divided hoof of a cow, goat, etc
clover *n* plant with three-lobed leaves **in clover** in luxury
clown *n* comic entertainer in a circus; amusing person; stupid person ▷ *v* behave foolishly; perform as a clown **clownish** *adj*
club *n* association of people with common interests; building used by such a group; thick stick used as a weapon; stick with a curved end used to hit the ball in golf; playing card with black three-leaved symbols ▷ *v* **clubbing, clubbed** hit with a club **club together** *v* combine resources for a common purpose
club foot *n* deformity of the foot causing inability to put the foot flat on the ground
cluck *n* low clicking noise made by a hen ▷ *v* make this noise
clue *n* something that helps to solve a mystery or puzzle **not have a clue** be completely baffled **clueless** *adj* stupid
clump *n* small group of things or people; dull heavy tread ▷ *v* walk heavily; form into clumps
clumsy *adj* **-sier, -siest** lacking skill or physical coordination; badly made or done **clumsily** *adv* **clumsiness** *n*
clung *v* past of **cling**
clunk *n* dull metallic sound ▷ *v* make such a sound
cluster *n* small close group ▷ *v* gather in clusters
clutch[1] *v* grasp tightly; (foll. by *at*) try to get hold of ▷ *n* device enabling two revolving shafts to be connected and disconnected, esp in a motor vehicle; tight grasp
clutch[2] *n* set of eggs laid at the same time
clutter *v* scatter objects about (a place) untidily ▷ *n* untidy mess
cm centimetre
CND Campaign for Nuclear Disarmament
CO Commanding Officer
Co. Company; County
co- *prefix* together, joint, or jointly *eg coproduction*
c/o care of; *book-keeping* carried over
coach *n* long-distance bus; railway carriage; large four-wheeled horse-drawn carriage; trainer, instructor ▷ *v* train, teach
coagulate [koh-**ag**-yew-late] *v* change from a liquid to a semisolid mass **coagulation** *n* **coagulant** *n* substance causing coagulation
coal *n* black rock consisting mainly of carbon, used as fuel **coalfield** *n* area with coal under the ground
coalesce [koh-a-**less**] *v* come together, merge **coalescence** *n*
coalition [koh-a-**lish**-un] *n* temporary alliance, esp between political parties
coarse *adj* rough in texture; unrefined, indecent **coarsely** *adv* **coarseness** *n* **coarsen** *v* **coarse fish** any freshwater fish not of the salmon family
coast *n* place where the land meets the sea ▷ *v* move by momentum, without the use of power **coastal** *adj* **coaster** *n* small mat placed

under a glass **coastguard** *n* organization that aids ships and swimmers in trouble and prevents smuggling; member of this **coastline** *n* outline of a coast

coat *n* outer garment with long sleeves; animal's fur or hair; covering layer *eg a coat of paint* ▷ *v* cover with a layer **coating** *n* covering layer **coat of arms** heraldic emblem of a family or institution

coax *v* persuade gently; obtain by persistent coaxing

coaxial [koh-**ax**-ee-al] *adj* (of a cable) transmitting by means of two concentric conductors separated by an insulator

cob *n* stalk of an ear of maize; thickset type of horse; round loaf of bread; male swan

cobalt *n chem* brittle silvery-white metallic element

cobber *n Aust & old-fashioned NZ, Informal* friend

cobble *n* cobblestone **cobblestone** *n* rounded stone used for paving **cobble together** *v* put together clumsily

cobbler *n* shoe mender

cobia [**koh**-bee-a] *n* large dark-striped game fish of tropical and subtropical seas

cobra *n* venomous hooded snake of Asia and Africa

cobweb *n* spider's web

cocaine *n* addictive drug used as a narcotic and as an anaesthetic

coccyx [**kok**-six] *n, pl* **coccyges** [kok-**sije**-eez] bone at the base of the spinal column

cochineal *n* red dye obtained from a Mexican insect, used for food colouring

cock *n* male bird, esp of domestic fowl; stopcock ▷ *v* draw back (the hammer of a gun) to firing position; lift and turn (part of the body) **cockerel** *n* young domestic cock **cock-a-hoop** *adj Brit, Aust & NZ* in high spirits **cock-and-bull story** highly improbable story

cockade *n* feather or rosette worn on a hat as a badge

cockatiel, cockateel *n* crested Australian parrot with a greyish-brown and yellow plumage

cockatoo *n* crested parrot of Australia or the East Indies

cocker spaniel *n* small spaniel

cockeyed *adj Informal* crooked, askew; foolish, absurd

cockie, cocky *n, pl* **-kies** *Aust & NZ, Informal* farmer

cockle *n* edible shellfish

Cockney *n* native of the East End of London; London dialect

cockpit *n* pilot's compartment in an aircraft; driver's compartment in a racing car

cockroach *n* beetle-like insect which is a household pest

cocksure *adj* overconfident, arrogant

cocktail *n* mixed alcoholic drink; appetizer of seafood or mixed fruits

cocky *adj* **cockier, cockiest** conceited and overconfident **cockily** *adv* **cockiness** *n*

cocoa *n* powder made from the seed of the cacao tree; drink made from this powder

coconut *n* large hard fruit of a type of palm tree; edible flesh of this fruit

cocoon *n* silky protective covering of a silkworm; protective covering ▷ *v* wrap up tightly for protection

cod *n* large food fish of the North Atlantic; any other Australian fish of the same family

COD cash on delivery

coda *n* final part of a musical

composition
coddle *v* pamper, overprotect
code *n* system of letters, symbols, or prearranged signals by which messages can be communicated secretly or briefly; set of principles or rules ▷*v* put into code **codify** *v* **-fying, -fied** organize (rules or procedures) systematically **codification** *n*
codeine [**kode**-een] *n* drug used as a painkiller
codex *n, pl* **codices** volume of manuscripts of an ancient text
codger *n Brit, Aust & NZ, Informal* old man
codicil [**kode**-iss-ill] *n* addition to a will
coeducation *n* education of boys and girls together **coeducational** *adj*
coefficient *n maths* number or constant placed before and multiplying a quantity
coelacanth [**seel**-a-kanth] *n* primitive marine fish
coeliac disease [**seel**-ee-ak] *n* disease which hampers digestion of food
coerce [koh-**urss**] *v* compel, force **coercion** *n* **coercive** *adj*
coeval [koh-**eev**-al] *adj, n* contemporary
coexist *v* exist together, esp peacefully despite differences **coexistence** *n*
C of E Church of England
coffee *n* drink made from the roasted and ground seeds of a tropical shrub; beanlike seeds of this shrub ▷*adj* medium-brown **coffee bar** café, snack bar **coffee table** small low table
coffer *n* chest for valuables ▷*pl* store of money
coffin *n* box in which a corpse is buried or cremated
cog *n* one of the teeth on the rim of a gearwheel; unimportant person in a big organization
cogent [**koh**-jent] *adj* forcefully convincing **cogency** *n*
cogitate [**koj**-it-tate] *v* think deeply about **cogitation** *n*
cognac [**kon**-yak] *n* French brandy
cognate *adj* derived from a common original form
cognition *n* act or experience of knowing or acquiring knowledge **cognitive** *adj*
cognizance *n* knowledge, understanding **cognizant** *adj*
cognoscenti [kon-yo-**shen**-tee] *pl n* connoisseurs
cohabit *v* live together as husband and wife without being married **cohabitation** *n*
cohere *v* hold or stick together; be logically connected or consistent
coherent *adj* logical and consistent; capable of intelligible speech **coherence** *n* **coherently** *adv*
cohesion *n* sticking together
cohesive *adj* sticking together to form a whole
cohort *n* band of associates; tenth part of an ancient Roman legion
coiffure *n* hairstyle **coiffeur, coiffeuse** *n* hairdresser
coil *v* wind in loops; move in a winding course ▷*n* something coiled; single loop of this; coil-shaped contraceptive device inserted in the womb
coin *n* piece of metal money; metal currency collectively ▷*v* invent (a word or phrase) **coin it in** *Informal* earn money quickly **coinage** *n* coins collectively; word or phrase coined; coining
coincide *v* happen at the same

time; agree or correspond exactly **coincidence** *n* occurrence of simultaneous or apparently connected events; coinciding **coincident** *adj* in agreement **coincidental** *adj* resulting from coincidence **coincidentally** *adv*

coir *n* coconut fibre, used for matting

coitus [koh-it-uss] **coition** [koh-**ish**-un] *n* sexual intercourse **coital** *adj*

coke[1] *n* solid fuel left after gas has been distilled from coal

coke[2] *n slang* cocaine

col *n* high mountain pass

cola *n* dark brown fizzy soft drink

colander *n* perforated bowl for straining or rinsing foods

cold *adj* lacking heat; lacking affection or enthusiasm; (of a colour) giving an impression of coldness; *slang* unconscious *eg out cold* ▷ *n* lack of heat; mild illness causing a runny nose, sneezing, and coughing **coldly** *adv* **coldness** *n* **cold-blooded** *adj* cruel, unfeeling; having a body temperature that varies according to the surrounding temperature **cold cream** creamy preparation for softening and cleansing the skin **cold feet** *slang* nervousness, fear **cold-shoulder** *v* treat with indifference **cold war** political hostility between countries without actual warfare

coleslaw *n* salad dish of shredded raw cabbage in a dressing

coley *n* codlike food fish of the N Atlantic

colic *n* severe pains in the stomach and bowels **colicky** *adj*

colitis [koh-**lie**-tiss] *n* inflammation of the colon

collaborate *v* work with another on a project; cooperate with an enemy invader **collaboration** *n* **collaborative** *adj* **collaborator** *n*

collage [kol-**lahzh**] *n* art form in which various materials or objects are glued onto a surface; picture made in this way

collapse *v* fall down suddenly; fail completely; fold compactly ▷ *n* collapsing; sudden failure or breakdown **collapsible** *adj*

collar *n* part of a garment round the neck; band put round an animal's neck; cut of meat from an animal's neck ▷ *v Brit, Aust & NZ, Informal* seize, arrest; catch in order to speak to **collarbone** *n* bone joining the shoulder blade to the breastbone

collate *v* gather together, examine, and put in order **collation** *n* collating; light meal

collateral *n* security pledged for the repayment of a loan

colleague *n* fellow worker, esp in a profession

collect[1] *v* gather together; accumulate (stamps etc) as a hobby; fetch **collected** *adj* calm and controlled **collection** *n* things collected; collecting; sum of money collected **collector** *n*

collect[2] *n* short prayer

collective *adj* of or done by a group ▷ *n* group of people working together on an enterprise and sharing the benefits from it **collectively** *adv*

colleen *n Irish* girl

college *n* place of higher education; group of people of the same profession or with special duties **collegiate** *adj*

collide *v* crash together violently; have an argument **collision** *n*

collie *n* silky-haired sheepdog

collier *n* coal miner; coal ship

colliery *n, pl* **-lieries** coal mine
collocate *v* (of words) occur together regularly **collocation** *n*
colloid *n* suspension of particles in a solution
colloquial *adj* suitable for informal speech or writing **colloquialism** *n* colloquial word or phrase
collusion *n* secret or illegal cooperation **collude** *v* act in collusion
collywobbles *pl n slang* nervousness
cologne *n* mild perfume
colon¹ *n* punctuation mark (:)
colon² *n* part of the large intestine connected to the rectum
colonel *n* senior commissioned army or air-force officer
colonnade *n* row of columns
colony *n, pl* **-nies** group of people who settle in a new country but remain under the rule of their homeland; territory occupied by a colony; group of people or animals of the same kind living together **colonial** *adj, n* (inhabitant) of a colony **colonialism** *n* policy of acquiring and maintaining colonies **colonist** *n* settler in a colony **colonize** *v* make into a colony **colonization** *n*
Colorado beetle *n* black-and-yellow beetle that is a serious pest of potatoes
coloration *n* arrangement of colours
colossal *adj* very large
colossus *n, pl* **-si, -suses** huge statue; huge or important person or thing
colostomy *n, pl* **-mies** operation to form an opening from the colon onto the surface of the body, for emptying the bowel
colour *n* appearance of things as a result of reflecting light; substance that gives colour; complexion ▷ *pl* flag of a country or regiment; *sport* badge or symbol denoting membership of a team ▷ *v* apply colour to; influence (someone's judgment); blush **coloured** *adj* having colour; (**C-**) (in S Africa) of mixed White and non-White parentage **colourful** *adj* with bright or varied colours; vivid, distinctive **colourfully** *adv* **colourless** *adj* **colour-blind** *adj* unable to distinguish between certain colours
colt *n* young male horse
columbine *n* garden flower with five petals
column *n* pillar; vertical division of a newspaper page; regular feature in a newspaper; vertical arrangement of numbers; narrow formation of troops **columnist** *n* journalist who writes a regular feature in a newspaper
coma *n* state of deep unconsciousness **comatose** *adj* in a coma; sound asleep
comb *n* toothed implement for arranging the hair; cock's crest; honeycomb ▷ *v* use a comb on; search with great care
combat *n, v* **-bating, -bated** fight, struggle **combatant** *n* **combative** *adj* **combat trousers, combats** loose casual trousers with large pockets on the legs
combine *v* join together ▷ *n* association of people or firms for a common purpose **combination** *n* combining; people or things combined; set of numbers that opens a special lock ▷ *pl Brit* old-fashioned undergarment with long sleeves and long legs

combine harvester machine that reaps and threshes grain in one process
combustion *n* process of burning **combustible** *adj* burning easily
come *v* **coming, came, come** move towards a place, arrive; occur; reach a specified point or condition; be produced; (foll. by *from*) be born in; become *eg a dream come true* **come across** *v* meet or find by accident; (often foll. by *as*) give an impression of (being) **comeback** *n Informal* return to a former position; retort **comedown** *n* decline in status; disappointment **comeuppance** *n Informal* deserved punishment
comedy *n, pl* **-dies** humorous play, film, or programme **comedian, comedienne** *n* entertainer who tells jokes; person who performs in comedy
comely *adj* **-lier, -liest** *old-fashioned* nice-looking
comestibles *pl n formal* food
comet *n* heavenly body with a long luminous tail
comfit *n old-fashioned* sugar-coated sweet
comfort *n* physical ease or wellbeing; consolation; means of consolation ▷*v* soothe, console **comfortable** *adj* giving comfort; free from pain; *Informal* well-off financially **comfortably** *adv* **comforter** *n* **comfort food** simple food that makes the eater feel better emotionally
comfrey *n* tall plant with bell-shaped flowers
comfy *adj* **-fier, -fiest** *Informal* comfortable
comic *adj* humorous, funny; of comedy ▷*n* comedian; magazine containing strip cartoons **comical** *adj* amusing **comically** *adv*
comma *n* punctuation mark (,)
command *v* order; have authority over; deserve and get; look down over ▷*n* authoritative instruction that something must be done; authority to command; knowledge; military or naval unit with a specific function **commandant** *n* officer commanding a military group **commandeer** *v* seize for military use **commandment** *n* command from God
commander *n* military officer in command of a group or operation; middle-ranking naval officer **commander-in-chief** *n, pl* **commanders-in-chief** supreme commander of a nation's armed forces
commando *n, pl* **-dos, -does** (member of) a military unit trained for swift raids in enemy territory
commemorate *v* honour the memory of **commemoration** *n* **commemorative** *adj*

> SPELLING The problem in deciding how to spell **commemorate** seems to be how many *ms* it should have. Collins Word Web shows that people often decide on four. In fact, it should have three, as in **commemoration**

commence *v* begin **commencement** *n*
commend *v* praise; recommend **commendable** *adj* **commendably** *adv* **commendation** *n*
commensurable *adj* measurable by the same standards
commensurate *adj* corresponding in degree, size, or value
comment *n* remark; talk, gossip; explanatory note ▷*v* make a

comment **commentary** *n, pl* **-taries** spoken accompaniment to a broadcast or film; explanatory notes **commentate** *v* provide a commentary **commentator** *n*

commerce *n* buying and selling, trade **commercial** *adj* of commerce; (of television or radio) paid for by advertisers; having profit as the main aim ▷ *n* television or radio advertisement **commercialize** *v* make commercial **commercialization** *n*

commiserate *v* (foll. by *with*) express sympathy (for) **commiseration** *n*

> SPELLING The most popular way to misspell **commiserate** and **commiseration** is to double the *s* as well as the *m*. There should indeed be two *m*s, but only one *s*

commissar *n* (formerly) official responsible for political education in Communist countries

commissariat *n Brit, Aust & NZ* military department in charge of food supplies

commission *n* piece of work that an artist is asked to do; duty, task; percentage paid to a salesperson for each sale made; group of people appointed to perform certain duties; committing of a crime; *mil* rank or authority officially given to an officer ▷ *v* place an order for; *mil* give a commission to; grant authority to **out of commission** not in working order **commissioner** *n* appointed official in a government department; member of a commission

commissionaire *n* uniformed doorman at a hotel, theatre, etc

commit *v* **-mitting, -mitted** perform (a crime or error); pledge (oneself) to a course of action; send (someone) to prison or hospital **committal** *n* sending someone to prison or hospital **commitment** *n* dedication to a cause; responsibility that restricts freedom of action

> SPELLING The correct spelling of **commitment** has three *m*s altogether, but only two *t*s (which are not next to each other). Although Collins Word Web has 176 examples of *committment*, with three *m*s and three *t*s, this spelling is wrong

committee *n* group of people appointed to perform a specified service or function

> SPELLING The commonest misspelling of **committee** is *commitee*, with 81 occurrences in Collins Word Web, which also has examples of *comittee*. The correct spelling is with two *m*s and two *t*s

commode *n* seat with a hinged flap concealing a chamber pot; chest of drawers

commodious *adj* roomy

commodity *n, pl* **-ities** something that can be bought or sold

commodore *n* senior commissioned officer in the navy

common *adj* occurring often; belonging to two or more people; public, general; lacking in taste or manners ▷ *n* area of grassy land belonging to a community **House of Commons, the Commons** lower chamber of the British parliament **commonly** *adv* **commoner** *n* person who does not belong to the nobility **common-law** *adj* (of a relationship) regarded as a marriage through being long-standing **Common Market** former name for **European Union** **commonplace** *adj* ordinary, everyday ▷ *n* trite remark **common sense** good practical understanding

commonwealth *n* state or nation viewed politically; (**C-**) association of independent states that used to be ruled by Britain

commotion *n* noisy disturbance

commune[1] *n* group of people who live together and share everything **communal** *adj* shared **communally** *adv*

commune[2] *v* (foll. by *with*) feel very close (to) *eg communing with nature* **communion** *n* sharing of thoughts or feelings; (**C-**) Christian ritual of sharing consecrated bread and wine; religious group with shared beliefs and practices

communicate *v* make known or share (information, thoughts, or feelings) **communicable** *adj* (of a disease) able to be passed on **communicant** *n* person who receives Communion **communicating** *adj* (of a door) joining two rooms **communication** *n* communicating; thing communicated ▷ *pl* means of travelling or sending messages **communicative** *adj* talking freely

communiqué [kom-**mune**-ik-kay] *n* official announcement

communism *n* belief that all property and means of production should be shared by the community; (**C-**) system of state control of the economy and society in some countries **communist** *n, adj*

community *n, pl* **-ties** all the people living in one district; group with shared origins or interests; the public, society **community centre** building used by a community for activities

commute *v* travel daily to and from work; reduce (a sentence) to a less severe one **commutator** *n* device used to change alternating electric current into direct current

commuter *n* person who commutes to and from work

compact[1] *adj* closely packed; neatly arranged; concise, brief ▷ *n* small flat case containing a mirror and face powder ▷ *v* pack closely together **compactly** *adv* **compactness** *n* **compact disc** small digital audio disc on which the sound is read by an optical laser system

compact[2] *n* contract, agreement

companion *n* person who associates with or accompanies someone **companionable** *adj* friendly **companionship** *n*

companionway *n* ladder linking the decks of a ship

company *n, pl* **-nies** business organization; group of actors; fact of being with someone; guest or guests

compare *v* examine (things) and point out the resemblances or differences; (foll. by *to*) declare to be (like); (foll. by *with*) be worthy of comparison **comparable** *adj* **comparability** *n* **comparative** *adj* relative; involving comparison; *grammar* denoting the form of an adjective or adverb indicating *more* ▷ *n grammar* comparative form of a word **comparatively** *adv* **comparison** *n* comparing; similarity or equivalence

compartment *n* section of a railway carriage; separate section

compass *n* instrument for showing direction, with a needle that points north; limits, range ▷*pl* hinged instrument for drawing circles
compassion *n* pity, sympathy **compassionate** *adj*
compatible *adj* able to exist, work, or be used together **compatibility** *n*
compatriot *n* fellow countryman or countrywoman
compel *v* **-pelling, -pelled** force (to be or do)
compendium *n, pl* **-diums, -dia** selection of board games in one box **compendious** *adj* brief but comprehensive
compensate *v* make amends to (someone), esp for injury or loss; (foll. by *for*) cancel out (a bad effect) **compensation** *n* payment to make up for loss or injury **compensatory** *adj*
compere *n* person who presents a stage, radio, or television show ▷*v* be the compere of
compete *v* try to win or achieve (a prize, profit, etc) **competition** *n* competing; event in which people compete; people against whom one competes **competitive** *adj* **competitor** *n*
competent *adj* having the skill or knowledge to do something well **competently** *adv* **competence** *n*
compile *v* collect and arrange (information), esp to make a book **compilation** *n* **compiler** *n*
complacent *adj* self-satisfied **complacently** *adv* **complacency** *n*
complain *v* express resentment or displeasure; (foll. by *of*) say that one is suffering from (an illness) **complaint** *n* complaining; mild illness **complainant** *n law* plaintiff
complaisant [kom-**play**-zant] *adj* willing to please **complaisance** *n*
complement *n* thing that completes something; complete amount or number; *grammar* word or words added to a verb to complete the meaning ▷*v* make complete **complementary** *adj*
complete *adj* thorough, absolute; finished; having all the necessary parts ▷*v* finish; make whole or perfect **completely** *adv* **completeness** *n* **completion** *n* finishing
complex *adj* made up of parts; complicated ▷*n* whole made up of parts; group of unconscious feelings that influences behaviour **complexity** *n*
complexion *n* skin of the face; character, nature
compliance *n* complying; tendency to do what others want **compliant** *adj*
complicate *v* make or become complex or difficult to deal with **complication** *n*
complicity *n* fact of being an accomplice in a crime
compliment *n* expression of praise ▷*pl* formal greetings ▷*v* praise **complimentary** *adj* expressing praise; free of charge
compline *n* last service of the day in the Roman Catholic Church
comply *v* **-plying, -plied** (foll. by *with*) act in accordance (with)
component *n, adj* (being) part of a whole
comport *v formal* behave (oneself) in a specified way
compose *v* put together; be the component parts of; create (a piece of music or writing); calm (oneself); arrange artistically

composer *n* person who writes music
composite *n, adj* (something) made up of separate parts
composition *n* way that something is put together or arranged; work of art, esp a musical one; essay; composing
compositor *n* person who arranges type for printing
compos mentis *adj Latin* sane
compost *n* decayed plants used as a fertilizer
composure *n* calmness
compote *n* fruit stewed with sugar
compound[1] *n, adj* (thing, esp chemical) made up of two or more combined parts or elements ▷*v* combine or make by combining; intensify, make worse
compound[2] *n* fenced enclosure containing buildings
comprehend *v* understand **comprehensible** *adj* **comprehension** *n* **comprehensive** *adj* of broad scope, fully inclusive ▷*n Brit* comprehensive school **comprehensive school** *Brit* secondary school for children of all abilities
compress *v* [kum-**press**] squeeze together; make shorter ▷*n* [**kom**-press] pad applied to stop bleeding or cool inflammation **compression** *n* **compressor** *n* machine that compresses gas or air
comprise *v* be made up of or make up
compromise [**kom**-prom-mize] *n* settlement reached by concessions on each side ▷*v* settle a dispute by making concessions; put in a dishonourable position
comptroller *n* (in titles) financial controller
compulsion *n* irresistible urge; forcing by threats or violence **compulsive** *adj* **compulsively** *adv* **compulsory** *adj* required by rules or laws
compunction *n* feeling of guilt or shame
compute *v* calculate, esp using a computer **computation** *n*
computer *n* electronic machine that stores and processes data **computerize** *v* adapt (a system) to be handled by computer; store or process in a computer **computerization** *n*
comrade *n* fellow member of a union or socialist political party; companion **comradeship** *n*
con[1] *Informal* ▷*n* short for **confidence trick** ▷*v* **conning, conned** deceive, swindle
con[2] *n* **pros and cons** see **pro[1]**
concatenation *n* series of linked events
concave *adj* curving inwards
conceal *v* cover and hide; keep secret **concealment** *n*
concede *v* admit to be true; acknowledge defeat in (a contest or argument); grant as a right
conceit *n* too high an opinion of oneself; far-fetched or clever comparison **conceited** *adj*
conceive *v* imagine, think; form in the mind; become pregnant **conceivable** *adj* imaginable, possible **conceivably** *adv*
concentrate *v* fix one's attention or efforts on something; bring or come together in large numbers in one place; make (a liquid) stronger by removing water from it ▷*n* concentrated liquid **concentration** *n* concentrating; proportion of a substance in a

mixture or solution **concentration camp** prison camp for civilian prisoners, esp in Nazi Germany

concentric *adj* having the same centre

concept *n* abstract or general idea **conceptual** *adj* of or based on concepts **conceptualize** *v* form a concept of

conception *n* general idea; becoming pregnant

concern *n* anxiety, worry; something that is of importance to someone; business, firm ▷ *v* worry (someone); involve (oneself); be relevant or important to **concerned** *adj* interested, involved; anxious, worried **concerning** *prep* about, regarding

concert *n* musical entertainment **in concert** working together; (of musicians) performing live **concerted** *adj* done together

concertina *n* small musical instrument similar to an accordion ▷ *v* **-naing, -naed** collapse or fold up like a concertina

concerto [kon-**chair**-toe] *n, pl* **-tos, -ti** large-scale composition for a solo instrument and orchestra

concession *n* grant of rights, land, or property; reduction in price for a specified category of people; conceding; thing conceded **concessionary** *adj*

conch *n* shellfish with a large spiral shell; its shell

concierge [kon-see-**airzh**] *n* (in France) caretaker in a block of flats

conciliate *v* try to end a disagreement (with) **conciliation** *n* **conciliator** *n*

conciliatory *adj* intended to end a disagreement

concise *adj* brief and to the point **concisely** *adv* **concision, conciseness** *n*

conclave *n* secret meeting; private meeting of cardinals to elect a new Pope

conclude *v* decide by reasoning; end, finish; arrange or settle finally **conclusion** *n* decision based on reasoning; ending; final arrangement or settlement **conclusive** *adj* ending doubt, convincing **conclusively** *adv*

concoct *v* make up (a story or plan); make by combining ingredients **concoction** *n*

concomitant *adj* existing along with something else

concord *n* state of peaceful agreement, harmony **concordance** *n* similarity or consistency; index of words in a book **concordant** *adj* agreeing

concourse *n* large open public place where people can gather; large crowd

concrete *n* mixture of cement, sand, stone, and water, used in building ▷ *adj* made of concrete; particular, specific; real or solid, not abstract

concubine [**kon**-kew-bine] *n hist* woman living in a man's house but not married to him and kept for his sexual pleasure

concupiscence [kon-**kew**-piss-enss] *n formal* lust

concur *v* **-curring, -curred** agree **concurrence** *n* **concurrent** *adj* happening at the same time or place **concurrently** *adv* at the same time

concussion *n* period of unconsciousness caused by a blow to the head **concussed** *adj* having concussion

condemn *v* express disapproval

of; sentence *eg he was condemned to death*; force into an unpleasant situation; declare unfit for use **condemnation** *n* **condemnatory** *adj*

condense *v* make shorter; turn from gas into liquid **condensation** *n* **condenser** *n electricity* capacitor

condescend *v* behave patronizingly towards someone; agree to do something, but as if doing someone a favour **condescension** *n*

condiment *n* seasoning for food, such as salt or pepper

condition *n* particular state of being; necessary requirement for something else to happen; restriction, qualification; state of health, physical fitness; medical problem ▷ *pl* circumstances ▷ *v* train or influence to behave in a particular way; treat with conditioner; control **on condition that** only if **conditional** *adj* depending on circumstances **conditioner** *n* thick liquid used when washing to make hair or clothes feel softer

condolence *n* sympathy ▷ *pl* expression of sympathy

condom *n* rubber sheath worn on the penis or in the vagina during sexual intercourse to prevent conception or infection

condominium *n Aust, US & Canadian* block of flats in which each flat is owned by the occupant

condone *v* overlook or forgive (wrongdoing)

condor *n* large vulture of S America

conducive *adj* (foll. by *to*) likely to lead (to)

conduct *n* management of an activity; behaviour ▷ *v* carry out (a task); behave (oneself); direct (musicians) by moving the hands or a baton; lead, guide; transmit (heat or electricity) **conduction** *n* transmission of heat or electricity **conductivity** *n* ability to transmit heat or electricity **conductive** *adj* **conductor** *n* person who conducts musicians; *fem conductress*) official on a bus who collects fares; something that conducts heat or electricity

conduit [**kon**-dew-it] *n* channel or tube for fluid or cables

cone *n* object with a circular base, tapering to a point; cone-shaped ice-cream wafer; *Brit, Aust & NZ* plastic cone used as a traffic marker on the roads; scaly fruit of a conifer tree

coney *n* same as **cony**

confab *n Informal* conversation (also **confabulation**)

confection *n* any sweet food; *old-fashioned* elaborate article of clothing

confectioner *n* maker or seller of confectionery **confectionery** *n* sweets

confederate *n* member of a confederacy; accomplice ▷ *adj* united, allied ▷ *v* unite in a confederacy **confederacy** *n, pl* **-cies** union of states or people for a common purpose **confederation** *n* alliance of political units

confer *v* **-ferring, -ferred** discuss together; grant, give **conferment** *n* granting, giving

conference *n* meeting for discussion

confess *v* admit (a fault or crime); admit to be true; declare (one's sins) to God or a priest, in hope of forgiveness **confession** *n* something confessed; confessing **confessional** *n* small stall in which a priest hears confessions **confessor** *n* priest who hears confessions

confetti *n* small pieces of coloured paper thrown at weddings

confidant *n* person confided in **confidante** *n fem*

confide *v* tell someone (a secret); entrust

confidence *n* trust; self-assurance; something confided **confidence trick** swindle involving gaining a person's trust in order to cheat him or her **in confidence** as a secret

confident *adj* sure, esp of oneself **confidently** *adv* **confidential** *adj* private, secret; entrusted with someone's secret affairs **confidentially** *adv* **confidentiality** *n*

configuration *n* arrangement of parts

confine *v* keep within bounds; restrict the free movement of **confines** *pl n* boundaries, limits **confinement** *n* being confined; period of childbirth

confirm *v* prove to be true; reaffirm, strengthen; administer the rite of confirmation to **confirmation** *n* confirming; something that confirms; *Christianity* rite that admits a baptized person to full church membership **confirmed** *adj* firmly established in a habit or condition

confiscate *v* seize (property) by authority **confiscation** *n*

conflagration *n* large destructive fire

conflate *v* combine or blend into a whole **conflation** *n*

conflict *n* disagreement; struggle or fight ▷*v* be incompatible

confluence *n* place where two rivers join

conform *v* comply with accepted standards or customs; (foll. by *to, with*) be like or in accordance with **conformist** *n, adj* (person) complying with accepted standards or customs **conformity** *n* compliance with accepted standards or customs

confound *v* astound, bewilder; confuse **confounded** *adj old-fashioned* damned

confront *v* come face to face with **confrontation** *n* serious argument

confuse *v* mix up; perplex, disconcert; make unclear **confusion** *n*

confute *v* prove wrong

conga *n* dance performed by a number of people in single file; large single-headed drum played with the hands

congeal *v* (of a liquid) become thick and sticky

congenial *adj* pleasant, agreeable; having similar interests and attitudes **congeniality** *n*

congenital *adj* (of a condition) existing from birth **congenitally** *adv*

conger *n* large sea eel

congested *adj* crowded to excess **congestion** *n*

conglomerate *n* large corporation made up of many companies; thing made up of several different elements ▷*v* form into a mass ▷*adj* made up of several different elements **conglomeration** *n*

congratulate *v* express one's pleasure to (someone) at his or her good fortune or success **congratulations** *pl n, interj* **congratulatory** *adj*

congregate *v* gather together in

a crowd **congregation** *n* people who attend a church **congregational** *adj* **Congregationalism** *n* Protestant denomination in which each church is self-governing **Congregationalist** *adj, n*

congress *n* formal meeting for discussion; (**C-**) federal parliament of the US **congressional** *adj* **Congressman, Congresswoman** *n* member of Congress

congruent *adj* similar, corresponding; *geom* identical in shape and size **congruence** *n*

conical *adj* cone-shaped

conifer *n* cone-bearing tree, such as the fir or pine **coniferous** *adj*

conjecture *n, v* guess **conjectural** *adj*

conjugal *adj* of marriage

conjugate *v* give the inflections of (a verb) **conjugation** *n* complete set of inflections of a verb

conjunction *n* combination; simultaneous occurrence of events; part of speech joining words, phrases, or clauses

conjunctivitis *n* inflammation of the membrane covering the eyeball and inner eyelid **conjunctiva** *n* this membrane

conjure *v* perform tricks that appear to be magic **conjuror** *n* **conjure up** *v* produce as if by magic

conk *n Brit, Aust & NZ, slang* nose

conker *n Informal* nut of the horse chestnut

conk out *v Informal* (of a machine) break down

connect *v* join together; associate in the mind **connection, connexion** *n* relationship, association; link or bond; opportunity to transfer from one public vehicle to another; influential acquaintance **connective** *adj*

conning tower *n* raised observation tower containing the periscope on a submarine

connive *v* (foll. by *at*) allow (wrongdoing) by ignoring it; conspire **connivance** *n*

connoisseur [kon-noss-**sir**] *n* person with special knowledge of the arts, food, or drink

connotation *n* associated idea conveyed by a word **connote** *v*

connubial *adj formal* of marriage

conquer *v* defeat; overcome (a difficulty); take (a place) by force **conqueror** *n* **conquest** *n* conquering; person or thing conquered

conscience *n* sense of right or wrong as regards thoughts and actions

conscientious *adj* painstaking **conscientiously** *adv* **conscientious objector** person who refuses to serve in the armed forces on moral or religious grounds

conscious *adj* alert and awake; aware; deliberate, intentional **consciously** *adv* **consciousness** *n*

conscript *n* person enrolled for compulsory military service ▷ *v* enrol (someone) for compulsory military service **conscription** *n*

consecrate *v* make sacred; dedicate to a specific purpose **consecration** *n*

consecutive *adj* in unbroken succession **consecutively** *adv*

consensus *n* general agreement

> SPELLING Collins Word Web has 6694 examples of the word **consensus** and another 112 of *concensus* with a *c* in the middle. The correct spelling is **consensus** and it has only one *c*

consent *n* agreement, permission ▷ *v* (foll. by *to*) permit, agree to

consequence *n* result, effect; importance **consequent** *adj* resulting **consequently** *adv* as a result, therefore **consequential** *adj* important

conservative *adj* opposing change; moderate, cautious; conventional in style; (**C-**) of the Conservative Party, the British right-wing political party which believes in private enterprise and capitalism ▷ *n* conservative person; (**C-**) supporter or member of the Conservative Party **conservatism** *n*

conservatoire [kon-**serv**-a-twahr] *n* school of music

conservatory *n, pl* **-ries** room with glass walls and a glass roof, attached to a house; *Chiefly US* conservatoire

conserve *v* protect from harm, decay, or loss; preserve (fruit) with sugar ▷ *n* jam containing large pieces of fruit **conservancy** *n* environmental conservation **conservation** *n* protection of natural resources and the environment; conserving **conservationist** *n*

consider *v* regard as; think about; be considerate of; discuss; look at **considerable** *adj* large in amount or degree **considerably** *adv* **considerate** *adj* thoughtful towards others **considerately** *adv* **consideration** *n* careful thought; fact that should be considered; thoughtfulness; payment for a service **considering** *prep* taking (a specified fact) into account

consign *v* put somewhere; send (goods) **consignment** *n* shipment of goods

consist *v* **consist of** be made up of **consist in** have as its main or only feature

consistent *adj* unchanging, constant; (foll. by *with*) in agreement **consistently** *adv* **consistency** *n, pl* **-cies** being consistent; degree of thickness or smoothness

console[1] *v* comfort in distress **consolation** *n* consoling; person or thing that consoles

console[2] *n* panel of controls for electronic equipment; cabinet for a television or audio equipment; ornamental wall bracket; part of an organ containing the pedals, stops, and keys

consolidate *v* make or become stronger or more stable; combine into a whole **consolidation** *n*

consommé [kon-**som**-may] *n* thin clear meat soup

consonant *n* speech sound made by partially or completely blocking the breath stream, such as *b* or *f*; letter representing this ▷ *adj* (foll. by *with*) agreeing (with) **consonance** *n* agreement, harmony

consort *v* (foll. by *with*) keep company (with) ▷ *n* husband or wife of a monarch

consortium *n, pl* **-tia** association of business firms

conspectus *n formal* survey or summary

conspicuous *adj* clearly visible; noteworthy, striking **conspicuously** *adv*

conspire *v* plan a crime together in secret; act together as if by design **conspiracy** *n* conspiring *pl* **-cies** plan made by conspiring **conspirator** *n* **conspiratorial** *adj*

constable *n* police officer of the lowest rank **constabulary** *n, pl* **-laries** police force of an area
constant *adj* continuous; unchanging; faithful ▷ *n* unvarying quantity; something that stays the same **constantly** *adv* **constancy** *n*
constellation *n* group of stars
consternation *n* anxiety or dismay
constipation *n* difficulty in defecating **constipated** *adj* having constipation
constituent *n* member of a constituency; component part ▷ *adj* forming part of a whole **constituency** *n, pl* **-cies** area represented by a Member of Parliament; voters in such an area
constitute *v* form, make up **constitution** *n* principles on which a state is governed; physical condition; structure **constitutional** *adj* of a constitution; in accordance with a political constitution ▷ *n* walk taken for exercise **constitutionally** *adv*
constrain *v* compel, force; limit, restrict **constraint** *n*
constrict *v* make narrower by squeezing **constriction** *n* **constrictive** *adj* **constrictor** *n* large snake that squeezes its prey to death; muscle that compresses an organ
construct *v* build or put together **construction** *n* constructing; thing constructed; interpretation; *grammar* way in which words are arranged in a sentence, clause, or phrase **constructive** *adj* (of advice, criticism, etc) useful and helpful **constructively** *adv*
construe *v* **-struing, -strued** interpret
consul *n* official representing a state in a foreign country; one of the two chief magistrates in ancient Rome **consular** *adj* **consulate** *n* workplace or position of a consul **consulship** *n*
consult *v* go to for advice or information **consultant** *n* specialist doctor with a senior position in a hospital; specialist who gives professional advice **consultancy** *n, pl* **-cies** work or position of a consultant **consultation** *n* (meeting for) consulting **consultative** *adj* giving advice
consume *v* eat or drink; use up; destroy; obsess **consumption** *n* amount consumed; consuming; *old-fashioned* tuberculosis **consumptive** *n, adj old-fashioned* (person) having tuberculosis
consumer *n* person who buys goods or uses services
consummate [**kon**-sum-mate] *v* make (a marriage) legal by sexual intercourse; complete or fulfil ▷ *adj* [kon-**sum**-mit] supremely skilled; complete, extreme **consummation** *n*
cont. continued
contact *n* communicating; touching; useful acquaintance; connection between two electrical conductors in a circuit ▷ *v* get in touch with **contact lens** lens placed on the eyeball to correct defective vision
contagion *n* passing on of disease by contact; disease spread by contact; spreading of a harmful influence **contagious** *adj* spreading by contact, catching
contain *v* hold or be capable of holding; consist of; control, restrain

container *n* object used to hold or store things in; large standard-sized box for transporting cargo by truck or ship **containment** *n* prevention of the spread of something harmful

contaminate *v* make impure, pollute; make radioactive **contaminant** *n* contaminating substance **contamination** *n*

contemplate *v* think deeply; consider as a possibility; gaze at **contemplation** *n* **contemplative** *adj*

contemporary *adj* present-day, modern; living or occurring at the same time ▷ *n, pl* **-raries** person or thing living or occurring at the same time as another **contemporaneous** *adj* happening at the same time

> SPELLING It's easy to miss a syllable out when you say **contemporary**. Collins Word Web shows that syllables get lost from spellings too - for example, *contempory* is a common mistake. But remember that the correct spelling ends in *-orary*

contempt *n* dislike and disregard; open disrespect for the authority of a court **contemptible** *adj* deserving contempt **contemptuous** *adj* showing contempt **contemptuously** *adv*

contend *v* (foll. by *with*) deal with; state, assert; compete

contender *n* competitor, esp a strong one

content[1] *n* meaning or substance of a piece of writing; amount of a substance in a mixture ▷ *pl* what something contains; list of chapters at the front of a book

content[2] *adj* satisfied with things as they are ▷ *v* make (someone) content ▷ *n* happiness and satisfaction **contented** *adj* **contentment** *n*

contention *n* disagreement or dispute; point asserted in argument **contentious** *adj* causing disagreement; quarrelsome

contest *n* competition or struggle ▷ *v* dispute, object to; fight or compete for **contestant** *n*

context *n* circumstances of an event or fact; words before and after a word or sentence that help make its meaning clear **contextual** *adj*

contiguous *adj* very near or touching

continent[1] *n* one of the earth's large masses of land **the Continent** mainland of Europe **continental** *adj* **continental breakfast** light breakfast of coffee and rolls

continent[2] *adj* able to control one's bladder and bowels; sexually restrained **continence** *n*

contingent *n* group of people that represents or is part of a larger group ▷ *adj* (foll. by *on*) dependent on (something uncertain) **contingency** *n, pl* **-cies** something that may happen

continue *v* **-tinuing, -tinued** (cause to) remain in a condition or place; carry on (doing something); resume **continual** *adj* constant; recurring frequently **continually** *adv* **continuance** *n* continuing **continuation** *n* continuing; part added **continuity** *n, pl* smooth development or sequence **continuous** *adj* continuing uninterrupted **continuously** *adv*

continuo *n, pl* **-tinuos** *music* continuous bass part, usu played on a keyboard instrument

continuum *n, pl* **-tinua, -tinuums** continuous series
contort *v* twist out of shape **contortion** *n* **contortionist** *n* performer who contorts his or her body to entertain
contour *n* outline; (also **contour line**) line on a map joining places of the same height
contra- *prefix* against or contrasting *eg contraflow*
contraband *n, adj* smuggled (goods)
contraception *n* prevention of pregnancy by artificial means **contraceptive** *n* device used or pill taken to prevent pregnancy ▷ *adj* preventing pregnancy
contract *n* (document setting out) a formal agreement ▷ *v* make a formal agreement (to do something); make or become smaller or shorter; catch (an illness) **contraction** *n* **contractor** *n* firm that supplies materials or labour **contractual** *adj*
contradict *v* declare the opposite of (a statement) to be true; be at variance with **contradiction** *n* **contradictory** *adj*
contraflow *n* flow of traffic going alongside but in an opposite direction to the usual flow
contralto *n, pl* **-tos** (singer with) the lowest female voice
contraption *n* strange-looking device
contrapuntal *adj music* of or in counterpoint
contrary *n* complete opposite ▷ *adj* opposed, completely different; perverse, obstinate ▷ *adv* in opposition **contrarily** *adv* **contrariness** *n* **contrariwise** *adv*
contrast *n* obvious difference; person or thing very different from another ▷ *v* compare in order to show differences; (foll. by *with*) be very different (from)
contravene *v* break (a rule or law) **contravention** *n*
contretemps [**kon**-tra-tahn] *n, pl* **-temps** embarrassing minor disagreement
contribute *v* give for a common purpose or fund; (foll. by *to*) be partly responsible (for) **contribution** *n* **contributor** *n* **contributory** *adj*
contrite *adj* sorry and apologetic **contritely** *adv* **contrition** *n*
contrive *v* make happen; devise or construct **contrivance** *n* device; plan; contriving **contrived** *adj* planned or artificial
control *n* power to direct something; curb or check ▷ *pl* instruments used to operate a machine ▷ *v* **-trolling, -trolled** have power over; limit, restrain; regulate, operate **controllable** *adj* **controller** *n*
controversy *n, pl* **-sies** fierce argument or debate **controversial** *adj* causing controversy
contumely [**kon**-tume-mill-ee] *n lit* scornful or insulting treatment
contusion *n formal* bruise
conundrum *n* riddle
conurbation *n* large urban area formed by the growth and merging of towns
convalesce *v* recover after an illness or operation **convalescence** *n* **convalescent** *n, adj*
convection *n* transmission of heat in liquids or gases by the circulation of currents **convector** *n* heater that gives out hot air
convene *v* gather or summon for a

formal meeting **convener, convenor** *n* person who calls a meeting

convenient *adj* suitable or opportune; easy to use; nearby **conveniently** *adv* **convenience** *n* quality of being convenient; useful object; *euphemistic* public toilet

convent *n* building where nuns live; school run by nuns

convention *n* widely accepted view of proper behaviour; assembly or meeting; formal agreement **conventional** *adj* (unthinkingly) following the accepted customs; customary; (of weapons or warfare) not nuclear **conventionally** *adv* **conventionality** *n*

converge *v* meet or join **convergence** *n*

conversant *adj* **conversant with** having knowledge or experience of

conversation *n* informal talk **conversational** *adj* **conversationalist** *n* person with a specified ability at conversation

converse[1] *v* have a conversation

converse[2] *adj, n* opposite or contrary **conversely** *adv*

convert *v* change in form, character, or function; cause to change in opinion or belief ▷*n* person who has converted to a different belief or religion **conversion** *n* (thing resulting from) converting; *rugby* score made after a try by kicking the ball over the crossbar **convertible** *adj* capable of being converted ▷*n* car with a folding or removable roof

convex *adj* curving outwards

convey *v* communicate (information); carry, transport **conveyance** *n old-fashioned* vehicle; transfer of the legal title to property **conveyancing** *n* branch of law dealing with the transfer of ownership of property **conveyor belt** continuous moving belt for transporting things, esp in a factory

convict *v* declare guilty ▷*n* person serving a prison sentence **conviction** *n* firm belief; instance of being convicted

convince *v* persuade by argument or evidence **convincing** *adj* **convincingly** *adv*

convivial *adj* sociable, lively **conviviality** *n*

convocation *n* calling together; large formal meeting **convoke** *v* call together

convoluted *adj* coiled, twisted; (of an argument or sentence) complex and hard to understand **convolution** *n*

convolvulus *n* twining plant with funnel-shaped flowers

convoy *n* group of vehicles or ships travelling together

convulse *v* (of part of the body) undergo violent spasms; *Informal* (be) overcome with laughter **convulsion** *n* violent muscular spasm ▷*pl* uncontrollable laughter **convulsive** *adj*

cony *n, pl* **conies** *Brit* rabbit; rabbit fur

coo *v* **cooing, cooed** (of a dove or pigeon) make a soft murmuring sound

cooee *interj Brit, Aust & NZ* call to attract attention

cook *v* prepare (food) by heating; (of food) be cooked ▷*n* person who cooks food **cook the books** falsify accounts **cooker** *n Chiefly Brit* apparatus for cooking heated by gas or electricity; *Chiefly Brit* apple suitable for cooking **cookery** *n* art of cooking **cookie** *n US* biscuit **cook up** *v Informal* devise (a story or scheme)

Cooktown orchid *n* purple Australian orchid

cool *adj* moderately cold; calm and unemotional; indifferent or unfriendly; *Informal* sophisticated or excellent; *Informal* (of a large sum of money) without exaggeration *eg a cool million* ▷ *v* make or become cool ▷ *n* coolness; *slang* calmness, composure **coolly** *adv* **coolness** *n* **coolant** *n* fluid used to cool machinery while it is working **cool drink** *SAfr* nonalcoholic drink **cooler** *n* container for making or keeping things cool

coolibah *n* Australian eucalypt that grows beside rivers

coolie *n old-fashioned offens* unskilled Oriental labourer

coomb, coombe *n S English* short valley or deep hollow

coon *n SAfr, offens* person of mixed race

coop¹ *n* cage or pen for poultry **coop up** *v* confine in a restricted place

coop² [**koh**-op] *n Brit, US & Aust* (shop run by) a cooperative society

cooper *n* person who makes or repairs barrels

cooperate *v* work or act together **cooperation** *n* **cooperative** *adj* willing to cooperate; (of an enterprise) owned and managed collectively ▷ *n* cooperative organization

coopt [koh-**opt**] *v* add (someone) to a group by the agreement of the existing members

coordinate *v* bring together and cause to work together efficiently ▷ *n maths* any of a set of numbers defining the location of a point ▷ *pl* clothes designed to be worn together **coordination** *n* **coordinator** *n*

coot *n* small black water bird

cop *slang* ▷ *n* policeman ▷ *v* **copping, copped** take or seize **cop it** get into trouble or be punished **cop out** *v* avoid taking responsibility or committing oneself

cope¹ *v* (often foll. by *with*) deal successfully (with)

cope² *n* large ceremonial cloak worn by some Christian priests

coping *n* sloping top row of a wall

copious [**kope**-ee-uss] *adj* abundant, plentiful **copiously** *adv*

copper¹ *n* soft reddish-brown metal; copper or bronze coin **copper-bottomed** *adj* financially reliable **copperplate** *n* fine handwriting style

copper² *n Brit, slang* policeman

coppice, copse *n* small group of trees growing close together

copra *n* dried oil-yielding kernel of the coconut

copulate *v* have sexual intercourse **copulation** *n*

copy *n, pl* **copies** thing made to look exactly like another; single specimen of a book etc; material for printing ▷ *v* **copying, copied** make a copy of; act or try to be like **copyright** *n* exclusive legal right to reproduce and control a book, work of art, etc ▷ *v* take out a copyright on ▷ *adj* protected by copyright **copywriter** *n* person who writes advertising copy

coquette *n* woman who flirts **coquettish** *adj*

coracle *n* small round boat of wicker covered with skins

coral *n* hard substance formed from the skeletons of very small sea animals ▷ *adj* orange-pink

cor anglais *n, pl* **cors anglais**

woodwind instrument similar to the oboe

cord *n* thin rope or thick string; cordlike structure in the body; corduroy ▷ *pl* corduroy trousers

cordial *adj* warm and friendly ▷ *n* drink with a fruit base **cordially** *adv* **cordiality** *n*

cordite *n* explosive used in guns and bombs

cordon *n* chain of police, soldiers, etc, guarding an area **cordon off** *v* form a cordon round

cordon bleu [**bluh**] *adj* (of cookery or cooks) of the highest standard

corduroy *n* cotton fabric with a velvety ribbed surface

core *n* central part of certain fruits, containing the seeds; central or essential part ▷ *v* remove the core from

corella *n* white Australian cockatoo

co-respondent *n Brit, Aust & NZ* person with whom someone being sued for divorce is claimed to have committed adultery

corgi *n* short-legged sturdy dog

coriander *n* plant grown for its aromatic seeds and leaves

cork *n* thick light bark of a Mediterranean oak; piece of this used as a stopper ▷ *v* seal with a cork **corkage** *n* restaurant's charge for serving wine bought elsewhere **corkscrew** *n* spiral metal tool for pulling corks from bottles

corm *n* bulblike underground stem of certain plants

cormorant *n* large dark-coloured long-necked sea bird

corn[1] *n* cereal plant such as wheat or oats; grain of such plants; *US, Canadian, Aust & NZ* maize; *slang* something unoriginal or oversentimental **corny** *adj slang* unoriginal or oversentimental

cornflakes *pl n* breakfast cereal made from toasted maize

cornflour *n Chiefly Brit* fine maize flour; *NZ* fine wheat flour

cornflower *n* plant with blue flowers

corn[2] *n* painful hard skin on the toe

cornea [**korn**-ee-a] *n, pl* **-neas, -neae** transparent membrane covering the eyeball **corneal** *adj*

corned beef *n* beef preserved in salt

corner *n* area or angle where two converging lines or surfaces meet; place where two streets meet; remote place; *sport* free kick or shot from the corner of the field ▷ *v* force into a difficult or inescapable position; (of a vehicle) turn a corner; obtain a monopoly of

cornerstone *n* indispensable part or basis

cornet *n* brass instrument similar to the trumpet; cone-shaped ice-cream wafer

cornice *n* decorative moulding round the top of a wall

corn on the cob *n* corn cooked and eaten on the cob

cornucopia [korn-yew-**kope**-ee-a] *n* great abundance; symbol of plenty, consisting of a horn overflowing with fruit and flowers

corolla *n* petals of a flower collectively

corollary *n, pl* **-laries** idea, fact, or proposition which is the natural result of something else

corona *n, pl* **-nas, -nae** ring of light round the moon or sun

coronary [**kor**-ron-a-ree] *adj* of the arteries surrounding the heart ▷ *n, pl* **-naries** coronary thrombosis

coronary thrombosis condition

in which the flow of blood to the heart is blocked by a blood clot
coronation *n* ceremony of crowning a monarch
coroner *n Brit, Aust & NZ* official responsible for the investigation of violent, sudden, or suspicious deaths
coronet *n* small crown
corpora *n* plural of **corpus**
corporal[1] *n* noncommissioned officer in an army
corporal[2] *adj* of the body **corporal punishment** physical punishment, such as caning
corporation *n* large business or company; city or town council **corporate** *adj* of business corporations; shared by a group
corporeal [kore-**pore**-ee-al] *adj* physical or tangible
corps [kore] *n, pl* **corps** military unit with a specific function; organized body of people
corpse *n* dead body
corpulent *adj* fat or plump **corpulence** *n*
corpus *n, pl* **corpora** collection of writings, esp by a single author
corpuscle *n* red or white blood cell
corral *US* ▷ *n* enclosure for cattle or horses ▷ *v* **-ralling, -ralled** put in a corral
correct *adj* free from error, true; in accordance with accepted standards ▷ *v* put right; indicate the errors in; rebuke or punish **correctly** *adv* **correctness** *n* **correction** *n* correcting; alteration correcting something **corrective** *adj* intended to put right something wrong
correlate *v* place or be placed in a mutual relationship **correlation** *n*
correspond *v* be consistent or compatible (with); be the same or similar; communicate by letter **corresponding** *adj* **correspondingly** *adv* **correspondence** *n* communication by letters; letters so exchanged; relationship or similarity **correspondent** *n* person employed by a newspaper etc to report on a special subject or from a foreign country; letter writer
corridor *n* passage in a building or train; strip of land or airspace providing access through foreign territory
corrigendum [kor-rij-**end**-um] *n, pl* **-da** error to be corrected
corroborate *v* support (a fact or opinion) by giving proof **corroboration** *n* **corroborative** *adj*
corroboree *n Aust* Aboriginal gathering or dance
corrode *v* eat or be eaten away by chemical action or rust **corrosion** *n* **corrosive** *adj*
corrugated *adj* folded into alternate grooves and ridges
corrupt *adj* open to or involving bribery; morally depraved; (of a text or data) unreliable through errors or alterations ▷ *v* make corrupt **corruptly** *adv* **corruption** *n* **corruptible** *adj*
corsage [kor-**sahzh**] *n* small bouquet worn on the bodice of a dress
corsair *n* pirate; pirate ship
corset *n* women's close-fitting undergarment worn to shape the torso
cortege [kor-**tayzh**] *n* funeral procession
cortex *n, pl* **-tices** *anat* outer layer of the brain or other internal organ **cortical** *adj*
cortisone *n* steroid hormone used

to treat various diseases

corundum *n* hard mineral used as an abrasive

coruscate *v formal* sparkle

corvette *n* lightly armed escort warship

cos *maths* cosine

cosh *n Brit* heavy blunt weapon ▷ *v* hit with a cosh

cosine [**koh**-sine] *n* (in trigonometry) ratio of the length of the adjacent side to that of the hypotenuse in a right-angled triangle

cosmetic *n* preparation used to improve the appearance of a person's skin ▷ *adj* improving the appearance only

cosmic *adj* of the whole universe **cosmic rays** electromagnetic radiation from outer space

cosmonaut *n* Russian name for an astronaut

cosmopolitan *adj* composed of people or elements from many countries; having lived and travelled in many countries ▷ *n* cosmopolitan person **cosmopolitanism** *n*

cosmos *n* the universe **cosmology** *n* study of the origin and nature of the universe **cosmological** *adj*

Cossack *n* member of a S Russian people famous as horsemen and dancers

cosset *v* **cosseting, cosseted** pamper

cost *n* amount of money, time, labour, etc, required for something ▷ *pl* expenses of a lawsuit ▷ *v* **costing, cost** have as its cost; involve the loss or sacrifice of *past* **costed** estimate the cost of **costly** *adj* expensive; involving great loss or sacrifice **costliness** *n*

costermonger *n Brit* person who sells fruit and vegetables from a street barrow

costume *n* style of dress of a particular place or time, or for a particular activity; clothes worn by an actor or performer **costumier** *n* maker or seller of costumes **costume jewellery** inexpensive artificial jewellery

cosy *adj* **-sier, -siest** warm and snug; intimate, friendly ▷ *n* cover for keeping things warm *eg a tea cosy* **cosily** *adv* **cosiness** *n*

cot *n* baby's bed with high sides; small portable bed **cot death** unexplained death of a baby while asleep

cote *n* shelter for birds or animals

coterie [**kote**-er-ee] *n* exclusive group, clique

cotoneaster [kot-tone-ee-**ass**-ter] *n* garden shrub with red berries

cottage *n* small house in the country **cottage cheese** soft mild white cheese **cottage industry** craft industry in which employees work at home **cottage pie** dish of minced meat topped with mashed potato

cotter *n* pin or wedge used to secure machine parts

cotton *n* white downy fibre covering the seeds of a tropical plant; cloth or thread made from this **cottony** *adj* **cotton on (to)** *v Informal* understand **cotton wool** fluffy cotton used for surgical dressings etc

cotyledon [kot-ill-**ee**-don] *n* first leaf of a plant embryo

couch *n* piece of upholstered furniture for seating more than one person ▷ *v* express in a particular way **couch potato** *slang* lazy person whose only hobby is

watching television
couchette [koo-**shett**] *n* bed converted from seats on a train or ship
couch grass *n* quickly spreading grassy weed
cougan *n Aust, slang* drunk and rowdy person
cougar *n* puma
cough *v* expel air from the lungs abruptly and noisily ▷*n* act or sound of coughing; illness which causes coughing
could *v* past tense of **can**[1]
couldn't could not
coulomb [**koo**-lom] *n* SI unit of electric charge
coulter *n* blade at the front of a ploughshare
council *n* group meeting for discussion or consultation; local governing body of a town or region ▷*adj* of or by a council **councillor** *n* member of a council **council tax** (in Britain) tax based on the value of property, to fund local services
counsel *n* advice or guidance; barrister or barristers ▷*v* **-selling, -selled** give guidance to; urge, recommend **counsellor** *n*
count[1] *v* say numbers in order; find the total of; be important; regard as; take into account ▷*n* counting; number reached by counting; *law* one of a number of charges **countless** *adj* too many to count **count on** *v* rely or depend on
count[2] *n* European nobleman
countdown *n* counting backwards to zero of the seconds before an event
countenance *n* (expression of) the face ▷*v* allow or tolerate
counter[1] *n* long flat surface in a bank or shop, on which business is transacted; small flat disc used in board games
counter[2] *v* oppose, retaliate against ▷*adv* in the opposite direction; in direct contrast ▷*n* opposing or retaliatory action
counter- *prefix* opposite, against *eg counterattack*; complementary, corresponding *eg counterpart*
counteract *v* act against or neutralize **counteraction** *n*
counterattack *n, v* attack in response to an attack
counterbalance *n* weight or force balancing or neutralizing another ▷*v* act as a counterbalance to
counterblast *n* aggressive response to a verbal attack
counterfeit *adj* fake, forged ▷*n* fake, forgery ▷*v* fake, forge
counterfoil *n* part of a cheque or receipt kept as a record
countermand *v* cancel (a previous order)
counterpane *n* bed covering
counterpart *n* person or thing complementary to or corresponding to another
counterpoint *n music* technique of combining melodies
counterpoise *n, v* counterbalance
counterproductive *adj* having an effect opposite to the one intended
countersign *v* sign (a document already signed by someone) as confirmation
countersink *v* drive (a screw) into a shaped hole so that its head is below the surface
countertenor *n* male alto
counterterrorism *n* measures to prevent terrorist attacks or eradicate terrorist groups
countess *n* woman holding the

rank of count or earl; wife or widow of a count or earl

country *n, pl* **-tries** nation; nation's territory; nation's people; part of the land away from cities **countrified** *adj* rustic in manner or appearance **country and western, country music** popular music based on American White folk music **countryman, countrywoman** *n* person from one's native land; *Brit, Aust & NZ* person who lives in the country **countryside** *n* land away from cities

county *n, pl* **-ties** (in some countries) division of a country

coup [koo] *n* successful action; coup d'état

coup de grâce [koo de grahss] *n* final or decisive action

coup d'état [koo day-tah] *n* sudden violent overthrow of a government

coupé [koo-pay] *n* sports car with two doors and a sloping fixed roof

couple *n* two people who are married or romantically involved; two partners in a dance or game ▷ *v* connect, associate **a couple** pair; *Informal* small number **couplet** *n* two consecutive lines of verse, usu rhyming and of the same metre **coupling** *n* device for connecting things, such as railway carriages

coupon *n* piece of paper entitling the holder to a discount or gift; detachable order form; football pools entry form

courage *n* ability to face danger or pain without fear **courageous** *adj* **courageously** *adv*

courgette *n* type of small vegetable marrow

courier *n* person employed to look after holiday-makers; person employed to deliver urgent messages

course *n* series of lessons or medical treatment; route or direction taken; area where golf is played or a race is run; any of the successive parts of a meal; mode of conduct or action; natural development of events ▷ *v* (of liquid) run swiftly **of course** as expected, naturally

court *n* body which decides legal cases; place where it meets; marked area for playing a racket game; courtyard; residence, household, or retinue of a sovereign ▷ *v* *old-fashioned* try to gain the love of; try to win the favour of; invite *eg to court disaster* **courtier** *n* attendant at a royal court **courtly** *adj* ceremoniously polite **courtliness** *n* **courtship** *n* courting of an intended spouse or mate **court martial** *n, pl* **courts martial** court for trying naval or military offences **court shoe** woman's low-cut shoe without straps or laces **courtyard** *n* paved space enclosed by buildings or walls

courtesan [kor-tiz-**zan**] *n hist* mistress or high-class prostitute

courtesy *n* politeness, good manners *pl* **-sies** courteous act **(by) courtesy of** by permission of **courteous** *adj* polite **courteously** *adv*

cousin *n* child of one's uncle or aunt

couture [koo-**toor**] *n* high-fashion designing and dressmaking **couturier** *n* person who designs women's fashion clothes

cove *n* small bay or inlet

coven [**kuv**-ven] *n* meeting of witches

covenant [**kuv**-ven-ant] *n*

contract; *Chiefly Brit* formal agreement to make an annual (charitable) payment ▷*v* agree by a covenant

Coventry *n* **send someone to Coventry** punish someone by refusing to speak to them

cover *v* place something over, to protect or conceal; extend over or lie on the surface of; travel over; insure against loss or risk; include; report (an event) for a newspaper; be enough to pay for ▷*n* anything that covers; outside of a book or magazine; insurance; shelter or protection **coverage** *n* amount or extent covered **coverlet** *n* bed cover

covert *adj* concealed, secret ▷*n* thicket giving shelter to game birds or animals **covertly** *adv*

covet *v* **coveting, coveted** long to possess (what belongs to someone else) **covetous** *adj* **covetousness** *n*

covey [**kuv**-vee] *n* small flock of grouse or partridge

cow[1] *n* mature female of cattle and of certain other mammals, such as the elephant or seal; *Informal, offens* disagreeable woman **cowboy** *n* (in the US) ranch worker who herds and tends cattle, usu on horseback; *Informal* irresponsible or unscrupulous worker

cow[2] *v* intimidate, subdue

coward *n* person who lacks courage **cowardly** *adj* **cowardice** *n* lack of courage

cower *v* cringe in fear

cowl *n* loose hood; monk's hooded robe; cover on a chimney to increase ventilation

cowling *n* cover on an engine

cowrie *n* brightly-marked sea shell

cowslip *n* small yellow wild European flower

cox *n* coxswain ▷*v* act as cox of (a boat)

coxswain [**kok**-sn] *n* person who steers a rowing boat

coy *adj* affectedly shy or modest **coyly** *adv* **coyness** *n*

coyote [koy-**ote**-ee] *n* prairie wolf of N America

coypu *n* beaver-like aquatic rodent native to S America, bred for its fur

cozen *v lit* cheat, trick

CPU *computers* central processing unit

crab *n* edible shellfish with ten legs, the first pair modified into pincers

crab apple *n* small sour apple

crabbed *adj* (of handwriting) hard to read; (also **crabby**) bad-tempered

crack *v* break or split partially; (cause to) make a sharp noise; break down or yield under strain; hit suddenly; solve (a code or problem); tell (a joke) ▷*n* sudden sharp noise; narrow gap; sharp blow; *Informal* gibe, joke; *slang* highly addictive form of cocaine ▷*adj Informal* first-rate, excellent *eg a crack shot* **cracking** *adj* very good **crackdown** *n* severe disciplinary measures **crack down on** *v* take severe measures against

cracker *n* thin dry biscuit; decorated cardboard tube, pulled apart with a bang, containing a paper hat and a joke or toy; small explosive firework; *slang* outstanding thing or person

crackers *adj slang* insane

crackle *v* make small sharp popping noises ▷*n* crackling sound **crackling** *n* crackle; crisp skin of roast pork

crackpot *n, adj Informal* eccentric

(person)

cradle *n* baby's bed on rockers; place where something originates; supporting structure ▷*v* hold gently as if in a cradle

craft *n* occupation requiring skill with the hands; skill or ability *pl* **craft** boat, ship, aircraft, or spaceship **crafty** *adj* skilled in deception **craftily** *adv* **craftiness** *n* **craftsman, craftswoman** *n* skilled worker **craftsmanship** *n*

crag *n* steep rugged rock **craggy** *adj*

cram *v* **cramming, crammed** force into too small a space; fill too full; study hard just before an examination

cramp[1] *n* painful muscular contraction; clamp for holding masonry or timber together

cramp[2] *v* confine, restrict

crampon *n* spiked plate strapped to a boot for climbing on ice

cranberry *n* sour edible red berry

crane *n* machine for lifting and moving heavy weights; large wading bird with a long neck and legs ▷*v* stretch (one's neck) to see something

crane fly *n* long-legged insect with slender wings

cranium *n, pl* **-niums, -nia** *anat* skull **cranial** *adj*

crank *n* arm projecting at right angles from a shaft, for transmitting or converting motion; *Informal* eccentric person ▷*v* start (an engine) with a crank **cranky** *adj Informal* eccentric; bad-tempered **crankshaft** *n* shaft driven by a crank

cranny *n, pl* **-nies** narrow opening

crape *n* same as **crepe**

craps *n* gambling game played with two dice

crash *n* collision involving a vehicle or vehicles; sudden loud smashing noise; financial collapse ▷*v* (cause to) collide violently with a vehicle, a stationary object, or the ground; (cause to) make a loud smashing noise; (cause to) fall with a crash; collapse or fail financially **crash course** short, very intensive course in a particular subject **crash helmet** protective helmet worn by a motorcyclist **crash-land** *v* (of an aircraft) land in an emergency, causing damage **crash-landing** *n*

crass *adj* stupid and insensitive **crassly** *adv* **crassness** *n*

crate *n* large wooden container for packing goods

crater *n* very large hole in the ground or in the surface of the moon

cravat *n* man's scarf worn like a tie

crave *v* desire intensely; beg or plead for **craving** *n*

craven *adj* cowardly

crawfish *n* same as **crayfish**

crawl *v* move on one's hands and knees; move very slowly; (foll. by *to*) flatter in order to gain some advantage; feel as if covered with crawling creatures ▷*n* crawling motion or pace; overarm swimming stroke **crawler** *n*

crayfish *n* edible shellfish like a lobster; Australian freshwater crustacean

crayon *v, n* (draw or colour with) a stick or pencil of coloured wax or clay

craze *n* short-lived fashion or enthusiasm **crazed** *adj* wild and uncontrolled; (of porcelain) having fine cracks

crazy *adj* ridiculous; (foll. by *about*) very fond (of); insane **craziness** *n*

crazy paving paving made of irregularly shaped slabs of stone

creak *v, n* (make) a harsh squeaking sound **creaky** *adj*

cream *n* fatty part of milk; food or cosmetic resembling cream in consistency; best part (of something) ▷ *adj* yellowish-white ▷ *v* beat to a creamy consistency **creamy** *adj* **cream cheese** rich soft white cheese **cream off** *v* take the best part from

crease *n* line made by folding or pressing; *cricket* line marking the bowler's and batsman's positions ▷ *v* crush or line

create *v* make, cause to exist; appoint to a new rank or position; *slang* make an angry fuss **creation** *n* **creative** *adj* imaginative or inventive **creativity** *n* **creator** *n*

creature *n* animal, person, or other being

crèche *n* place where small children are looked after while their parents are working, shopping, etc

credence *n* belief in the truth or accuracy of a statement

credentials *pl n* document giving evidence of a person's identity or qualifications

credible *adj* believable; trustworthy **credibly** *adv* **credibility** *n*

credit *n* system of allowing customers to receive goods and pay later; reputation for trustworthiness in paying debts; money at one's disposal in a bank account; side of an account book on which such sums are entered; (source or cause of) praise or approval; influence or reputation based on the good opinion of others; belief or trust ▷ *pl* list of people responsible for the production of a film, programme, or record ▷ *v* **crediting, credited** enter as a credit in an account; (foll. by *with*) attribute (to); believe **creditable** *adj* praiseworthy **creditably** *adv* **creditor** *n* person to whom money is owed **credit card** card allowing a person to buy on credit

credulous *adj* too willing to believe **credulity** *n*

creed *n* statement or system of (Christian) beliefs or principles

creek *n* narrow inlet or bay; *Aust, NZ, US & Canadian* small stream

creel *n* wicker basket used by anglers

creep *v* **creeping, crept** move quietly and cautiously; crawl with the body near to the ground; (of a plant) grow along the ground or over rocks ▷ *n slang* obnoxious or servile person **give one the creeps** *Informal* make one feel fear or disgust **creeper** *n* creeping plant **creepy** *adj Informal* causing a feeling of fear or disgust

cremate *v* burn (a corpse) to ash **cremation** *n* **crematorium** *n* building where corpses are cremated

crenellated *adj* having battlements

creole *n* language developed from a mixture of languages; **(C-)** native-born W Indian or Latin American of mixed European and African descent

creosote *n* dark oily liquid made from coal tar and used for preserving wood ▷ *v* treat with creosote

crepe [krayp] *n* fabric or rubber with a crinkled texture; very thin pancake **crepe paper** paper with a crinkled texture

crept *v* past of **creep**
crepuscular *adj lit* of or like twilight
crescendo [krish-**end**-oh] *n, pl* **-dos** gradual increase in loudness, esp in music
crescent *n* (curved shape of) the moon as seen in its first or last quarter; crescent-shaped street
cress *n* plant with strong-tasting leaves, used in salads
crest *n* top of a mountain, hill, or wave; tuft or growth on a bird's or animal's head; heraldic design used on a coat of arms and elsewhere **crested** *adj* **crestfallen** *adj* disheartened
cretin *n Informal* stupid person; *obs* person afflicted with physical and mental retardation caused by a thyroid deficiency **cretinous** *adj*
crevasse *n* deep open crack in a glacier
crevice *n* narrow crack or gap in rock
crew *n* people who work on a ship or aircraft; group of people working together; *Informal* any group of people ▷ *v* serve as a crew member (on) **crew cut** man's closely cropped haircut
crewel *n* fine worsted yarn used in embroidery
crib *n* piece of writing stolen from elsewhere; translation or list of answers used by students, often illicitly; baby's cradle; rack for fodder; short for **cribbage** ▷ *v* **cribbing, cribbed** copy (someone's work) dishonestly **crib-wall** *n NZ* retaining wall built against an earth bank
cribbage *n* card game for two to four players
crick *n* muscle spasm or cramp in the back or neck ▷ *v* cause a crick in
cricket[1] *n* outdoor game played with bats, a ball, and wickets by two teams of eleven **cricketer** *n*
cricket[2] *n* chirping insect like a grasshopper
crime *n* unlawful act; unlawful acts collectively **criminal** *n* person guilty of a crime ▷ *adj* of crime; *Informal* deplorable **criminally** *adv* **criminality** *n* **criminology** *n* study of crime **criminologist** *n*
crimp *v* fold or press into ridges
crimson *adj* deep purplish-red
cringe *v* flinch in fear; behave in a submissive or timid way
crinkle *v, n* wrinkle, crease, or fold
crinoline *n* hooped petticoat
cripple *n* person who is lame or disabled ▷ *v* make lame or disabled; damage (something)
crisis *n, pl* **-ses** crucial stage, turning point; time of extreme trouble
crisp *adj* fresh and firm; dry and brittle; clean and neat; (of weather) cold but invigorating; lively or brisk ▷ *n Brit* very thin slice of potato fried till crunchy **crisply** *adv* **crispness** *n* **crispy** *adj* hard and crunchy **crispbread** *n* thin dry biscuit
crisscross *v* move in or mark with a crosswise pattern ▷ *adj* (of lines) crossing in different directions
criterion *n, pl* **-ria** standard of judgment
critic *n* professional judge of any of the arts; person who finds fault **critical** *adj* very important or dangerous; fault-finding; able to examine and judge carefully; of a critic or criticism **critically** *adv* **criticism** *n* fault-finding; analysis of a book, work of art, etc **criticize** *v* find fault with **critique** *n* critical essay

croak *v* (of a frog or crow) give a low hoarse cry; utter or speak with a croak ▷ *n* low hoarse sound **croaky** *adj* hoarse

crochet [kroh-shay] *v* **-cheting, -cheted** make by looping and intertwining yarn with a hooked needle ▷ *n* work made in this way

crock[1] *n* earthenware pot or jar **crockery** *n* dishes

crock[2] *n Brit, Aust & NZ, Informal* old or decrepit person or thing

crocodile *n* large amphibious tropical reptile; *Brit, Aust & NZ* line of people, esp schoolchildren, walking two by two **crocodile tears** insincere show of grief

crocus *n, pl* **-cuses** small plant with yellow, white, or purple flowers in spring

croft *n* small farm worked by one family in Scotland **crofter** *n*

croissant [krwah-son] *n* rich flaky crescent-shaped roll

cromlech *n Brit* circle of prehistoric standing stones

crone *n* witchlike old woman

crony *n, pl* **-nies** close friend

crook *n Informal* criminal; bent or curved part; hooked pole ▷ *adj Aust & NZ, slang* unwell, injured **go crook** *Aust & NZ, slang* become angry **crooked** *adj* bent or twisted; set at an angle; *Informal* dishonest

croon *v* sing, hum, or speak in a soft low tone

crooner *n* male singer of sentimental ballads

crop *n* cultivated plant; season's total yield of produce; group of things appearing at one time; (handle of) a whip; pouch in a bird's gullet; very short haircut ▷ *v* **cropping, cropped** cut very short; produce or harvest as a crop; (of animals) feed on (grass) **cropper** *n* **come a cropper** *Informal* have a disastrous failure or heavy fall **crop-top** *n* short T-shirt or vest that reveals the wearer's midriff **crop up** *v Informal* happen unexpectedly

croquet [kroh-kay] *n* game played on a lawn in which balls are hit through hoops

croquette [kroh-kett] *n* fried cake of potato, meat, or fish

crosier *n* same as **crozier**

cross *v* move or go across (something); meet and pass; (with *out*) delete with a cross or lines; place (one's arms or legs) crosswise ▷ *n* structure, symbol, or mark of two intersecting lines; such a structure of wood as a means of execution; representation of the Cross as an emblem of Christianity; mixture of two things ▷ *adj* angry, annoyed **the Cross** *Christianity* the cross on which Christ was crucified **crossing** *n* place where a street may be crossed safely; place where one thing crosses another; journey across water **crossly** *adv* **crossbar** *n* horizontal bar across goalposts or on a bicycle **crossbow** *n* weapon consisting of a bow fixed across a wooden stock **crossbred** *adj* bred from two different types of animal or plant **crossbreed** *n* crossbred animal or plant **cross-check** *v* check using a different method **cross-country** *adj, adv* by way of open country or fields **cross-examine** *v law* question (a witness for the opposing side) to check his or her testimony **cross-examination** *n* **cross-eyed** *adj* with eyes looking towards each other **cross-fertilize** *v* fertilize (an animal or plant) from one of a different kind

cross-fertilization *n* **crossfire** *n* gunfire crossing another line of fire **cross-purposes** *pl n* **at cross-purposes** misunderstanding each other **cross-reference** *n* reference within a text to another part **crossroads** *n* place where roads intersect **cross section** (diagram of) a surface made by cutting across something; representative sample **crosswise** *adj, adv* across; in the shape of a cross **crossword puzzle, crossword** *n* puzzle in which words suggested by clues are written into a grid of squares

crotch *n* part of the body between the tops of the legs

crotchet *n* musical note half the length of a minim

crotchety *adj Informal* bad-tempered

crouch *v* bend low with the legs and body close ▷ *n* this position

croup[1] [kroop] *n* throat disease of children, with a cough

croup[2] [kroop] *n* hind quarters of a horse

croupier [**kroop**-ee-ay] *n* person who collects bets and pays out winnings at a gambling table in a casino

crouton *n* small piece of fried or toasted bread served in soup

crow[1] *n* large black bird with a harsh call **as the crow flies** in a straight line **crow's feet** wrinkles at the corners of the eyes **crow's nest** lookout platform at the top of a ship's mast **stone the crows!** *Brit & Aust, slang* expression of surprise, dismay, etc

crow[2] *v* (of a cock) make a shrill squawking sound; boast or gloat

crowbar *n* iron bar used as a lever

crowd *n* large group of people or things; particular group of people ▷ *v* gather together in large numbers; press together in a confined space; fill or occupy fully

crown *n* monarch's headdress of gold and jewels; wreath for the head, given as an honour; top of the head or of a hill; artificial cover for a broken or decayed tooth; former British coin worth 25 pence ▷ *v* put a crown on the head of (someone) to proclaim him or her monarch; put on or form the top of; put the finishing touch to (a series of events); *Informal* hit on the head **the Crown** power of the monarchy **crown court** local criminal court in England and Wales **crown-of-thorns** *n* starfish with a spiny outer covering that feeds on living coral **crown prince, crown princess** heir to a throne

crozier *n* bishop's hooked staff

crucial *adj* very important **crucially** *adv*

crucible *n* pot in which metals are melted

crucify *v* **-fying, -fied** put to death by fastening to a cross **crucifix** *n* model of Christ on the Cross **crucifixion** *n* crucifying **the Crucifixion** *Christianity* crucifying of Christ **cruciform** *adj* cross-shaped

crude *adj* rough and simple; tasteless, vulgar; in a natural or unrefined state **crudely** *adv* **crudity** *n*

cruel *adj* delighting in others' pain; causing pain or suffering **cruelly** *adv* **cruelty** *n*

cruet *n* small container for salt, pepper, etc, at table

cruise *n* sail for pleasure ▷ *v* sail from place to place for pleasure; (of a vehicle) travel at a moderate and economical speed **cruiser** *n* fast warship; motorboat with a cabin **cruise missile** low-flying guided missile

crumb *n* small fragment of bread or other dry food; small amount

crumble *v* break into fragments; fall apart or decay ▷ *n* pudding of stewed fruit with a crumbly topping **crumbly** *adj*

crummy *adj* **-mier, -miest** *slang* of poor quality

crumpet *n* round soft yeast cake, eaten buttered; *Brit, Aust & NZ, slang* sexually attractive women collectively

crumple *v* crush, crease; collapse, esp from shock **crumpled** *adj*

crunch *v* bite or chew with a noisy crushing sound; make a crisp or brittle sound ▷ *n* crunching sound; *Informal* critical moment **crunchy** *adj*

crupper *n* strap that passes from the back of a saddle under a horse's tail

crusade *n* medieval Christian war to recover the Holy Land from the Muslims; vigorous campaign in favour of a cause ▷ *v* take part in a crusade

crusader *n* person who took part in the medieval Christian war to recover the Holy Land from the Muslims; person who campaigns vigorously in favour of a cause

crush *v* compress so as to injure, break, or crumple; break into small pieces; defeat or humiliate utterly ▷ *n* dense crowd; *Informal* infatuation; drink made by crushing fruit

crust *n* hard outer part of something, esp bread ▷ *v* cover with or form a crust **crusty** *adj* having a crust; irritable

crustacean *n* hard-shelled, usu aquatic animal with several pairs of legs, such as the crab or lobster

crutch *n* long sticklike support with a rest for the armpit, used by a lame person; person or thing that gives support; crotch

crux *n, pl* **cruxes** crucial or decisive point

cry *v* **crying, cried** shed tears; call or utter loudly ▷ *n, pl* **cries** fit of weeping; loud utterance; urgent appeal *eg a cry for help* **crybaby** *n* person, esp a child, who cries too readily **cry off** *v Informal* withdraw from an arrangement **cry out for** *v* need urgently

cryogenics *n* branch of physics concerned with very low temperatures **cryogenic** *adj*

crypt *n* vault under a church, esp one used as a burial place

cryptic *adj* obscure in meaning, secret **cryptically** *adv* **cryptography** *n* art of writing in and deciphering codes

crystal *n* (single grain of) a symmetrically shaped solid formed naturally by some substances; very clear and brilliant glass, usu with the surface cut in many planes; tumblers, vases, etc, made of crystal ▷ *adj* bright and clear **crystalline** *adj* of or like crystal or crystals; clear **crystallize** *v* make or become definite; form into crystals **crystallization** *n*

cu. cubic

cub *n* young wild animal such as a bear or fox; **(C-)** Cub Scout ▷ *v* **cubbing, cubbed** give birth to cubs **Cub Scout** member of a junior branch of the Scout Association

cubbyhole *n* small enclosed space or room

cube *n* object with six equal square sides; number resulting from multiplying a number by itself twice ▷*v* cut into cubes; find the cube of (a number) **cubic** *adj* having three dimensions; cube-shaped **cubism** *n* style of art in which objects are represented by geometrical shapes **cubist** *adj*, *n* **cube root** number whose cube is a given number

cubicle *n* enclosed part of a large room, screened for privacy

cuckold *n* man whose wife has been unfaithful ▷*v* be unfaithful to (one's husband)

cuckoo *n* migratory bird with a characteristic two-note call, which lays its eggs in the nests of other birds ▷*adj Informal* insane or foolish

cucumber *n* long green-skinned fleshy fruit used in salads

cud *n* partially digested food which a ruminant brings back into its mouth to chew again **chew the cud** think deeply

cuddle *v*, *n* hug **cuddly** *adj*

cudgel *n* short thick stick used as a weapon

cue[1] *n* signal to an actor or musician to begin speaking or playing; signal or reminder ▷*v* **cueing, cued** give a cue to

cue[2] *n* long tapering stick used in billiards, snooker, or pool ▷*v* **cueing, cued** hit (a ball) with a cue

cuff[1] *n* end of a sleeve **off the cuff** *Informal* without preparation **cuff link** one of a pair of decorative fastenings for shirt cuffs

cuff[2] *Brit, Aust & NZ* ▷*v* hit with an open hand ▷*n* blow with an open hand

cuisine [quiz-**zeen**] *n* style of cooking

cul-de-sac *n* road with one end blocked off

culinary *adj* of kitchens or cookery

cull *v* choose, gather; remove or kill (inferior or surplus animals) from a herd ▷*n* culling

culminate *v* reach the highest point or climax **culmination** *n*

culottes *pl n* women's knee-length trousers cut to look like a skirt

culpable *adj* deserving blame **culpability** *n*

culprit *n* person guilty of an offence or misdeed

cult *n* specific system of worship; devotion to a person, idea, or activity; popular fashion

cultivate *v* prepare (land) to grow crops; grow (plants); develop or improve (something); try to develop a friendship with (someone) **cultivated** *adj* well-educated **cultivation** *n*

culture *n* ideas, customs, and art of a particular society; particular society; developed understanding of the arts; cultivation of plants or rearing of animals; growth of bacteria for study **cultural** *adj* **cultured** *adj* showing good taste or manners **cultured pearl** pearl artificially grown in an oyster shell

culvert *n* drain under a road or railway

cumbersome *adj* awkward because of size or shape

cumin, cummin *n* sweet-smelling seeds of a Mediterranean plant, used in cooking

cummerbund *n* wide sash worn round the waist

cumulative *adj* increasing steadily

cumulus [**kew**-myew-luss] *n*, *pl* **-li**

thick white or dark grey cloud

cuneiform [**kew**-nif-form] *n, adj* (written in) an ancient system of writing using wedge-shaped characters

cunjevoi *n Aust* plant of tropical Asia and Australia with small flowers, cultivated for its edible rhizome; sea squirt

cunning *adj* clever at deceiving; ingenious ▷ *n* cleverness at deceiving; ingenuity **cunningly** *adv*

cup *n* small bowl-shaped drinking container with a handle; contents of a cup; (competition with) a cup-shaped trophy given as a prize; hollow rounded shape ▷ *v* **cupping, cupped** form (one's hands) into the shape of a cup; hold in cupped hands **cupful** *n*

cupboard *n* piece of furniture or alcove with a door, for storage

cupidity [kew-**pid**-it-ee] *n* greed for money or possessions

cupola [**kew**-pol-la] *n* domed roof or ceiling

cur *n lit* mongrel dog; contemptible person

curaçao [**kew**-rah-so] *n* orange-flavoured liqueur

curare [kew-**rah**-ree] *n* poisonous resin of a S American tree, used as a muscle relaxant in medicine

curate *n* clergyman who assists a parish priest **curacy** [**kew**-rah-see] *n, pl* **-cies** work or position of a curate

curative *adj, n* (something) able to cure

curator *n* person in charge of a museum or art gallery **curatorship** *n*

curb *n* something that restrains ▷ *v* control, restrain

curd *n* coagulated milk, used to make cheese **curdle** *v* turn into curd, coagulate

cure *v* get rid of (an illness or problem); make (someone) well again; preserve by salting, smoking, or drying ▷ *n* (treatment causing) curing of an illness or person; remedy or solution **curable** *adj*

curette *n* surgical instrument for scraping tissue from body cavities ▷ *v* scrape with a curette **curettage** *n*

curfew *n* law ordering people to stay inside their homes after a specific time at night; time set as a deadline by such a law

curie *n* standard unit of radioactivity

curio *n, pl* **-rios** rare or unusual object valued as a collector's item

curious *adj* eager to learn or know; eager to find out private details; unusual or peculiar **curiously** *adv* **curiosity** *n* eagerness to know or find out *pl* **-ties** rare or unusual object

curl *n* curved piece of hair; curved spiral shape ▷ *v* make (hair) into curls or (of hair) grow in curls; make into a curved spiral shape **curly** *adj* **curling** *n* game like bowls, played with heavy stones on ice

curlew *n* long-billed wading bird

curmudgeon *n* bad-tempered person

currant *n* small dried grape; small round berry, such as a redcurrant

currajong *n* same as **kurrajong**

currawong *n* Australian songbird

current *adj* of the immediate present; most recent, up-to-date; commonly accepted ▷ *n* flow of water or air in one direction; flow of electricity; general trend **currently** *adv* **currency** *n, pl* **-cies** money in use in a particular country; general acceptance or use

curriculum *n, pl* **-la, -lums** all the courses of study offered by a school or college **curriculum vitae** [**vee**-tie] outline of someone's educational and professional history, prepared for job applications

> SPELLING You possibly read the word **curriculum** more often than you have to write it. It's easy not to notice that the only letter that is doubled is the *r* in the middle

curry[1] *n, pl* **-ries** Indian dish of meat or vegetables in a hot spicy sauce ▷ *v* **-rying, -ried** prepare (food) with curry powder **curry powder** mixture of spices for making curry

curry[2] *v* **-rying, -ried** groom (a horse) **curry favour** ingratiate oneself with an important person **curry comb** ridged comb for grooming a horse

curse *v* swear (at); ask a supernatural power to cause harm to ▷ *n* swearword; (result of) a call to a supernatural power to cause harm to someone; something causing trouble or harm **cursed** *adj*

cursive *adj, n* (handwriting) done with joined letters

cursor *n* movable point of light that shows a specific position on a visual display unit

cursory *adj* quick and superficial **cursorily** *adv*

curt *adj* brief and rather rude **curtly** *adv* **curtness** *n*

curtail *v* cut short; restrict **curtailment** *n*

curtain *n* piece of cloth hung at a window or opening as a screen; hanging cloth separating the audience and the stage in a theatre; fall or closing of the curtain at the end, or the rise or opening of the curtain at the start of a theatrical performance; something forming a barrier or screen ▷ *v* provide with curtains; (foll. by *off*) separate by a curtain

curtsy, curtsey *n, pl* **-sies, -seys** woman's gesture of respect made by bending the knees and bowing the head ▷ *v* **-sying, -sied** *or* **-seying, -seyed** make a curtsy

curve *n* continuously bending line with no straight parts ▷ *v* form or move in a curve **curvy** *adj* **curvaceous** *adj Informal* (of a woman) having a shapely body **curvature** *n* curved shape **curvilinear** *adj* consisting of or bounded by a curve

cuscus *n, pl* **-cuses** large Australian nocturnal possum

cushion *n* bag filled with soft material, to make a seat more comfortable; something that provides comfort or absorbs shock ▷ *v* lessen the effects of; protect from injury or shock

cushy *adj* **cushier, cushiest** *Informal* easy

cusp *n* pointed end, esp on a tooth; *astrol* division between houses or signs of the zodiac

cuss *Informal* ▷ *n* curse, oath; annoying person ▷ *v* swear (at) **cussed** [**kuss**-id] *adj Informal* obstinate

custard *n* sweet yellow sauce made from milk and eggs

custody *n* protective care; imprisonment prior to being tried **custodial** *adj* **custodian** *n* person in charge of a public building

custom *n* long-established activity or action; usual habit; regular use of a shop or business

▷ *pl* duty charged on imports or exports; government department which collects these; area at a port, airport, or border where baggage and freight are examined for dutiable goods **customary** *adj* usual; established by custom **customarily** *adv* **custom-built, custom-made** *adj* made to the specifications of an individual customer

customer *n* person who buys goods or services

cut *v* **cutting, cut** open up, penetrate, wound, or divide with a sharp instrument; divide; trim or shape by cutting; abridge, shorten; reduce, restrict; *Informal* hurt the feelings of; pretend not to recognize ▷ *n* stroke or incision made by cutting; piece cut off; reduction; deletion in a text, film, or play; *Informal* share, esp of profits; style in which hair or a garment is cut **cut in** *v* interrupt; obstruct another vehicle in overtaking it

cutaneous [kew-**tane**-ee-uss] *adj* of the skin

cute *adj* appealing or attractive; *Informal* clever or shrewd **cutely** *adv* **cuteness** *n*

cuticle *n* skin at the base of a fingernail or toenail

cutlass *n* curved one-edged sword formerly used by sailors

cutlery *n* knives, forks, and spoons **cutler** *n* maker of cutlery

cutlet *n* small piece of meat like a chop; flat croquette of chopped meat or fish

cutter *n* person or tool that cuts; any of various small fast boats

cut-throat *adj* fierce or relentless ▷ *n* murderer

cutting *n* article cut from a newspaper or magazine; piece cut from a plant from which to grow a new plant; passage cut through high ground for a road or railway ▷ *adj* (of a remark) hurtful

cuttlefish *n* squidlike sea mollusc

CV curriculum vitae

cwt hundredweight

cyanide *n* extremely poisonous chemical compound

cyber- *combining form* computers *eg cyberspace*

cybernetics *n* branch of science in which electronic and mechanical systems are studied and compared to biological systems

cyberspace *n* place said to contain all the data stored in computers

cyclamen [**sik**-la-men] *n* plant with red, pink, or white flowers

cycle *v* ride a bicycle ▷ *n* *Brit, Aust & NZ* bicycle; *US* motorcycle; complete series of recurring events; time taken for one such series **cyclical, cyclic** *adj* occurring in cycles **cyclist** *n* person who rides a bicycle

cyclone *n* violent wind moving round a central area

cyclotron *n* apparatus that accelerates charged particles by means of a strong vertical magnetic field

cygnet *n* young swan

cylinder *n* solid or hollow body with straight sides and circular ends; chamber within which the piston moves in an internal-combustion engine **cylindrical** *adj*

cymbal *n* percussion instrument consisting of a brass plate which is struck against another or hit with a stick

cynic [**sin**-ik] *n* person who believes that people always act

selfishly **cynical** *adj* **cynically** *adv* **cynicism** *n*
cynosure [**sin**-oh-zyure] *n* centre of attention
cypher *n* same as **cipher**
cypress *n* evergreen tree with dark green leaves
cyst [**sist**] *n* (abnormal) sac in the body containing fluid or soft matter **cystic** *adj* **cystitis** [siss-**tite**-iss] *n* inflammation of the bladder
cytology [site-**ol**-a-jee] *n* study of plant and animal cells **cytological** *adj* **cytologist** *n*
czar [zahr] *n* same as **tsar**

d

d *physics* density
D *chem* deuterium
d. *Brit* (before decimalization) penny; died
dab[1] *v* **dabbing, dabbed** pat lightly; apply with short tapping strokes ▷ *n* small amount of something soft or moist; light stroke or tap **dab hand** *Informal* person who is particularly good at something
dab[2] *n* small European flatfish with rough scales
dabble *v* be involved in something superficially; splash about **dabbler** *n*
dace *n* small European freshwater fish
dachshund *n* dog with a long body and short legs
dad *n* *Informal* father
daddy *n, pl* **-dies** *Informal* father
daddy-longlegs *n* *Brit* crane fly;

US & Canadian small web-spinning spider with long legs
dado [**day**-doe] *n, pl* **-does, -dos** lower part of an interior wall, below a rail, decorated differently from the upper part
daffodil *n* yellow trumpet-shaped flower that blooms in spring
daft *adj Informal* foolish or crazy
dag *NZ* ▷ *n* dried dung on a sheep's rear; *Informal* amusing person ▷ *pl n* **rattle one's dags** *Informal* hurry up ▷ *v* remove the dags from a sheep **daggy** *adj Informal* amusing
dagga *n SAfr, Informal* cannabis
dagger *n* short knifelike weapon with a pointed blade
daguerreotype [dag-**gair**-oh-type] *n* type of early photograph produced on chemically treated silver
dahlia [**day**-lya] *n* brightly coloured garden flower
daily *adj* occurring every day or every weekday ▷ *adv* every day ▷ *n, pl* **-lies** daily newspaper; *Brit, Informal* person who cleans other people's houses
dainty *adj* **-tier, -tiest** delicate or elegant **daintily** *adv*
daiquiri [**dak**-eer-ee] *n* iced drink containing rum, lime juice, and sugar
dairy *n, pl* **dairies** place for the processing or sale of milk and its products; *NZ* small shop selling groceries and milk often outside normal trading hours ▷ *adj* of milk or its products
dais [**day**-iss, **dayss**] *n* raised platform in a hall, used by a speaker
daisy *n, pl* **-sies** small wild flower with a yellow centre and white petals **daisy wheel** flat disc in a word processor with radiating spokes for printing letters
Dalai Lama *n* chief lama and (until 1959) ruler of Tibet
dale *n* (esp in N England) valley
dally *v* **-lying, -lied** waste time; (foll. by *with*) deal frivolously (with) **dalliance** *n* flirtation
Dalmatian *n* large dog with a white coat and black spots
dam[1] *n* barrier built across a river to create a lake; lake created by this ▷ *v* **damming, dammed** build a dam across (a river)
dam[2] *n* mother of an animal such as a sheep or horse
damage *v* harm, spoil ▷ *n* harm to a person or thing; *Informal* cost *eg what's the damage?* ▷ *pl* money awarded as compensation for injury or loss
damask *n* fabric with a pattern woven into it, used for tablecloths etc
dame *n Chiefly US & Canadian, slang* woman; (**D-**) title of a woman who has been awarded the OBE or another order of chivalry
damn *interj slang* exclamation of annoyance ▷ *adv, adj* (also **damned**) *slang* extreme(ly) ▷ *v* condemn as bad or worthless; (of God) condemn to hell **damnable** *adj* annoying **damnably** *adv* **damnation** *interj, n* **damning** *adj* proving or suggesting guilt *eg a damning report*
damp *adj* slightly wet ▷ *n* slight wetness, moisture ▷ *v* (also **dampen**) make damp; (foll. by *down*) reduce the intensity of (feelings or actions) **damply** *adv* **dampness** *n* **damper** *n* movable plate to regulate the draught in a fire; pad in a piano that deadens the vibration of each string **put a damper on** have a depressing or

inhibiting effect on

damsel *n old-fashioned* young woman

damson *n* small blue-black plumlike fruit

dance *v* move the feet and body rhythmically in time to music; perform (a particular dance); skip or leap; move rhythmically ▷ *n* series of steps and movements in time to music; social meeting arranged for dancing **dancer** *n*

D and C *n med* dilatation and curettage: a minor operation in which the neck of the womb is stretched and the lining of the womb scraped, to clear the womb or remove tissue for diagnosis

dandelion *n* yellow-flowered wild plant

dander *n* **get one's dander up** *slang* become angry

dandle *v* move (a child) up and down on one's knee

dandruff *n* loose scales of dry dead skin shed from the scalp

dandy *n, pl* **-dies** man who is overconcerned with the elegance of his appearance ▷ *adj* **-dier, -diest** *Informal* very good **dandified** *adj*

danger *n* possibility of being injured or killed; person or thing that may cause injury or harm; likelihood that something unpleasant will happen **dangerous** *adj* **dangerously** *adv*

dangle *v* hang loosely; display as an enticement

dank *adj* unpleasantly damp and chilly

dapper *adj* (of a man) neat in appearance

dappled *adj* marked with spots of a different colour **dapple-grey** *n* horse with a grey coat and darker coloured spots

dare *v* be courageous enough to try (to do something); challenge to do something risky ▷ *n* challenge to do something risky **daring** *adj* willing to take risks ▷ *n* courage to do dangerous things **daringly** *adv* **daredevil** *adj, n* recklessly bold (person).

> When *dare* is used in a question or as a negative, it does not take an *-s: He dare not come*

dark *adj* having little or no light; (of a colour) reflecting little light; (of hair or skin) brown or black; gloomy, sad; sinister, evil; secret *eg keep it dark* ▷ *n* absence of light; night **darkly** *adv* **darkness** *n* **darken** *v* **dark horse** person about whom little is known **darkroom** *n* darkened room for processing photographic film

darling *n* much-loved person; favourite ▷ *adj* much-loved

darn[1] *v* mend (a garment) with a series of interwoven stitches ▷ *n* patch of darned work

darn[2] *interj, adv, adj, v euphemistic* damn

dart *n* small narrow pointed missile that is thrown or shot, esp in the game of darts; sudden quick movement; tapered tuck made in dressmaking ▷ *pl* game in which darts are thrown at a circular numbered board ▷ *v* move or direct quickly and suddenly

Darwinism *n* theory of the origin of animal and plant species by evolution **Darwinian, Darwinist** *adj, n*

dash *v* move quickly; hurl or crash; frustrate (someone's hopes) ▷ *n* sudden quick movement; small amount; mixture of style and courage; punctuation mark (–) indicating a change of subject;

longer symbol used in Morse code **dashing** *adj* stylish and attractive **dashboard** *n* instrument panel in a vehicle

dassie *n SAfr* type of hoofed rodent-like animal (also **hyrax**)

dastardly *adj* wicked and cowardly

dasyure [**dass**-ee-your] *n* small marsupial of Australia, New Guinea, and adjacent islands

data *n* information consisting of observations, measurements, or facts; numbers, digits, etc, stored by a computer **data base** store of information that can be easily handled by a computer **data capture** process for converting information into a form that can be handled by a computer **data processing** series of operations performed on data, esp by a computer, to extract or interpret information

date[1] *n* specified day of the month; particular day or year when an event happened; *Informal* appointment, esp with a person to whom one is sexually attracted; *Informal* person with whom one has a date ▷*v* mark with the date; *Informal* go on a date (with); assign a date of occurrence to; become old-fashioned; (foll. by *from*) originate from **dated** *adj* old-fashioned

date[2] *n* dark-brown sweet-tasting fruit of the date palm **date palm** tall palm grown in tropical regions for its fruit

dative *n* (in certain languages) the form of the noun that expresses the indirect object

datum *n, pl* **data** single piece of information in the form of a fact or statistic

daub *v* smear or spread quickly or clumsily

daughter *n* female child; woman who comes from a certain place or is connected with a certain thing **daughterly** *adj* **daughter-in-law** *n, pl* **daughters-in-law** son's wife

daunting *adj* intimidating or worrying **dauntless** *adj* fearless

dauphin [**doe**-fan] *n* (formerly) eldest son of the king of France

davenport *n Chiefly Brit* small writing table with drawers; *Aust, US & Canadian* large couch

davit [**dav**-vit] *n* crane, usu one of a pair, at a ship's side, for lowering and hoisting a lifeboat

Davy lamp *n* miner's lamp designed to prevent it from igniting gas

dawdle *v* walk slowly, lag behind

dawn *n* daybreak; beginning (of something) ▷*v* begin to grow light; begin to develop or appear; (foll. by *on*) become apparent (to)

day *n* period of 24 hours; period of light between sunrise and sunset; part of a day occupied with regular activity, esp work; period or point in time; time of success **daybreak** *n* time in the morning when light first appears **daydream** *n* pleasant fantasy indulged in while awake ▷*v* indulge in idle fantasy **daydreamer** *n* **daylight** *n* light from the sun **day release** *Brit* system in which workers go to college one day a week **day-to-day** *adj* routine

daze *v* stun, by a blow or shock ▷*n* state of confusion or shock

dazzle *v* impress greatly; blind temporarily by sudden excessive light ▷*n* bright light that dazzles **dazzling** *adj* **dazzlingly** *adv*

dB, db decibel(s)

DC direct current
DD Doctor of Divinity
D-day *n* day selected for the start of some operation, orig the Allied invasion of Europe in 1944
DDT *n* kind of insecticide
de- *prefix* indicating: removal *eg dethrone;* reversal *eg declassify;* departure *eg decamp*
deacon *n Christianity* ordained minister ranking immediately below a priest; (in some Protestant churches) lay official who assists the minister
dead *adj* no longer alive; no longer in use; numb *eg my leg has gone dead;* complete, absolute *eg dead silence* *Informal* very tired; (of a place) lacking activity ▷ *n* period during which coldness or darkness is most intense *eg in the dead of night* ▷ *adv* extremely; suddenly *eg I stopped dead* **the dead** dead people **dead set** firmly decided **deadbeat** *n Informal* lazy useless person **dead beat** *Informal* exhausted **dead end** road with one end blocked off; situation in which further progress is impossible **dead heat** tie for first place between two participants in a contest **deadline** *n* time limit **deadlock** *n* point in a dispute at which no agreement can be reached **deadlocked** *adj* **deadpan** *adj, adv* showing no emotion or expression **dead reckoning** method of establishing one's position using the distance and direction travelled **dead weight** heavy weight
deaden *v* make less intense
deadly *adj* **-lier, -liest** likely to cause death; *Informal* extremely boring ▷ *adv* extremely **deadly nightshade** plant with poisonous black berries
deaf *adj* unable to hear **deaf to** refusing to listen to or take notice of **deafen** *v* make deaf, esp temporarily **deafness** *n*
deal¹ *n* agreement or transaction; kind of treatment *eg a fair deal;* large amount ▷ *v* **dealing, dealt** [delt] inflict (a blow) on; *cards* give out (cards) to the players **dealer** *n* **dealings** *pl n* transactions or business relations **deal in** *v* buy or sell (goods) **deal out** *v* distribute **deal with** *v* take action on; be concerned with
deal² *n* plank of fir or pine wood
dean *n* chief administrative official of a college or university faculty; chief administrator of a cathedral **deanery** *n, pl* **-eries** office or residence of a dean; parishes of a dean
dear *n* someone regarded with affection ▷ *adj* much-loved; costly **dearly** *adv* **dearness** *n*
dearth [dirth] *n* inadequate amount, scarcity
death *n* permanent end of life in a person or animal; instance of this; ending, destruction **deathly** *adj, adv* like death *eg a deathly silence; deathly pale* **death duty** (in Britain) former name for **inheritance tax** **death's-head** *n* human skull or a representation of one **death trap** place or vehicle considered very unsafe **deathwatch beetle** beetle that bores into wood and makes a tapping sound
deb *n Informal* debutante
debacle [day-**bah**-kl] *n* disastrous failure
debar *v* prevent, bar
debase *v* lower in value, quality, or character **debasement** *n*
debate *n* discussion ▷ *v* discuss formally; consider (a course of

action) **debatable** *adj* not absolutely certain
debauch [dib-**bawch**] *v* make (someone) bad or corrupt, esp sexually **debauched** *adj* immoral, sexually corrupt **debauchery** *n*
debenture *n* long-term bond bearing fixed interest, issued by a company or a government agency
debilitate *v* weaken, make feeble **debilitation** *n* **debility** *n* weakness, infirmity
debit *n* acknowledgment of a sum owing by entry on the left side of an account ▷ *v* **debiting, debited** charge (an account) with a debt
debonair *adj* (of a man) charming and refined
debouch *v* move out from a narrow place to a wider one
debrief *v* receive a report from (a soldier, diplomat, etc) after an event **debriefing** *n*
debris [**deb**-ree] *n* fragments of something destroyed
debt *n* something owed, esp money **in debt** owing money **debtor** *n*
debunk *v* *Informal* expose the falseness of
debut [**day**-byoo] *n* first public appearance of a performer **debutante** [**day**-byoo-tont] *n* young upper-class woman being formally presented to society
Dec. December
decade *n* period of ten years
decadence *n* deterioration in morality or culture **decadent** *adj*
decaffeinated [dee-**kaf**-fin-ate-id] *adj* (of coffee, tea, or cola) with caffeine removed
decagon *n* geometric figure with ten faces
decahedron [deck-a-**heed**-ron] *n* solid figure with ten sides
Decalogue *n* the Ten Commandments
decamp *v* depart secretly or suddenly
decant *v* pour (a liquid) from one container to another; *Chiefly Brit* rehouse (people) while their homes are being renovated
decanter *n* stoppered bottle for wine or spirits
decapitate *v* behead **decapitation** *n*
decathlon *n* athletic contest with ten events
decay *v* become weaker or more corrupt; rot ▷ *n* process of decaying; state brought about by this process
decease *n* *formal* death
deceased *adj* *formal* dead **the deceased** dead person
deceive *v* mislead by lying; be unfaithful to (one's sexual partner) **deceiver** *n* **deceit** *n* behaviour intended to deceive **deceitful** *adj*
decelerate *v* slow down **deceleration** *n*
December *n* twelfth month of the year
decent *adj* (of a person) polite and morally acceptable; fitting or proper; conforming to conventions of sexual behaviour; *Informal* kind **decently** *adv* **decency** *n*
decentralize *v* reorganize into smaller local units **decentralization** *n*
deception *n* deceiving; something that deceives, trick **deceptive** *adj* likely or designed to deceive **deceptively** *adv* **deceptiveness** *n*
deci- *combining form* one tenth
decibel *n* unit for measuring the intensity of sound
decide *v* (cause to) reach a

decision; settle (a contest or question) **decided** *adj* unmistakable; determined **decidedly** *adv*

deciduous *adj* (of a tree) shedding its leaves annually

decimal *n* fraction written in the form of a dot followed by one or more numbers ▷ *adj* relating to or using powers of ten; expressed as a decimal **decimalization** *n* **decimal currency** system of currency in which the units are parts or powers of ten **decimal point** dot between the unit and the fraction of a number in the decimal system **decimal system** number system with a base of ten, in which numbers are expressed by combinations of the digits 0 to 9

decimate *v* destroy or kill a large proportion of **decimation** *n*

decipher *v* work out the meaning of (something illegible or in code) **decipherable** *adj*

decision *n* judgment, conclusion, or resolution; act of making up one's mind; firmness of purpose **decisive** *adj* having a definite influence; having the ability to make quick decisions **decisively** *adv* **decisiveness** *n*

deck *n* area of a ship that forms a floor; similar area in a bus; platform that supports the turntable and pick-up of a record player **deck chair** folding chair made of canvas over a wooden frame **decking** *n* wooden platform in a garden **deck out** *v* decorate

declaim *v* speak loudly and dramatically; protest loudly **declamation** *n* **declamatory** *adj*

declare *v* state firmly and forcefully; announce officially; acknowledge for tax purposes **declaration** *n* **declaratory** *adj*

declension *n grammar* changes in the form of nouns, pronouns, or adjectives to show case, number, and gender

decline *v* become smaller, weaker, or less important; refuse politely to accept or do; *grammar* list the inflections of (a noun, pronoun, or adjective) ▷ *n* gradual weakening or loss

declivity *n, pl* **-ties** downward slope

declutch *v* disengage the clutch of a motor vehicle

decoct *v* extract the essence from (a substance) by boiling **decoction** *n*

decode *v* convert from code into ordinary language **decoder** *n*

décolleté [day-**kol**-tay] *adj* (of a woman's garment) low-cut

decommission *v* dismantle (a nuclear reactor, weapon, etc) which is no longer needed

decompose *v* be broken down through chemical or bacterial action **decomposition** *n*

decompress *v* free from pressure; return (a diver) to normal atmospheric pressure **decompression** *n* **decompression sickness** severe pain and difficulty in breathing, caused by a sudden change in atmospheric pressure

decongestant *n* medicine that relieves nasal congestion

decontaminate *v* make safe by removing poisons, radioactivity, etc **decontamination** *n*

decor [**day**-core] *n* style in which a room or house is decorated

decorate *v* make more attractive by adding something ornamental; paint or wallpaper; award a (military) medal to **decoration** *n*

decorative *adj* **decorator** *n*
decorous [**dek**-a-russ] *adj* polite, calm, and sensible in behaviour **decorously** *adv*
decorum [dik-**core**-um] *n* polite and socially correct behaviour
decoy *n* person or thing used to lure someone into danger; dummy bird or animal, used to lure game within shooting range ▷*v* lure away by means of a trick
decrease *v* make or become less ▷*n* lessening, reduction; amount by which something has decreased
decree *n* law made by someone in authority; court judgment ▷*v* order by decree
decrepit *adj* weakened or worn out by age or long use **decrepitude** *n*
decry *v* **-crying, -cried** express disapproval of
dedicate *v* commit (oneself or one's time) wholly to a special purpose or cause; inscribe or address (a book etc) to someone as a tribute **dedicated** *adj* devoted to a particular purpose or cause **dedication** *n*
deduce *v* reach (a conclusion) by reasoning from evidence **deducible** *adj*
deduct *v* subtract
deduction *n* deducting; something that is deducted; deducing; conclusion reached by deducing **deductive** *adj*
deed *n* something that is done; legal document
deem *v* consider, judge
deep *adj* extending or situated far down, inwards, backwards, or sideways; of a specified dimension downwards, inwards, or backwards; difficult to understand; of great intensity; (foll. by *in*) absorbed in (an activity); (of a colour) strong or dark; low in pitch **the deep** *poetic* the sea **deeply** *adv* profoundly or intensely (also **deep down**) **deepen** *v* **deep-freeze** *n* same as **freezer**
deer *n, pl* **deer** large wild animal, the male of which has antlers **deerstalker** *n* cloth hat with peaks at the back and front and earflaps
deface *v* deliberately spoil the appearance of **defacement** *n*
de facto *adv* in fact ▷*adj* existing in fact, whether legally recognized or not
defame *v* attack the good reputation of **defamation** *n* **defamatory** [dif-**fam**-a-tree] *adj*
default *n* failure to do something; *computers* instruction to a computer to select a particular option unless the user specifies otherwise ▷*v* fail to fulfil an obligation **in default of** in the absence of **defaulter** *n*
defeat *v* win a victory over; thwart, frustrate ▷*n* defeating **defeatism** *n* ready acceptance or expectation of defeat **defeatist** *adj, n*
defecate *v* discharge waste from the body through the anus **defecation** *n*
defect *n* imperfection, blemish ▷*v* desert one's cause or country to join the opposing forces **defective** *adj* imperfect, faulty **defection** *n* **defector** *n*
defence *n* resistance against attack; argument in support of something; country's military resources; defendant's case in a court of law **defenceless** *adj*
defend *v* protect from harm or danger; support in the face of criticism; represent (a defendant) in

court **defendant** *n* person accused of a crime **defensible** *adj* capable of being defended because believed to be right **defensibility** *n* **defensive** *adj* intended for defence; overanxious to protect oneself against (threatened) criticism **defensively** *adv*

defender *n* person who supports someone or something in the face of criticism; player whose chief task is to stop the opposition scoring

defer[1] *v* **-ferring, -ferred** delay (something) until a future time **deferment, deferral** *n*

defer[2] *v* **-ferring, -ferred** (foll. by *to*) comply with the wishes (of) **deference** *n* polite and respectful behaviour **deferential** *adj* **deferentially** *adv*

defiance *n* see **defy**

deficient *adj* lacking some essential thing or quality; inadequate in quality or quantity **deficiency** *n* state of being deficient; lack, shortage

deficit *n* amount by which a sum of money is too small

defile[1] *v* treat (something sacred or important) without respect **defilement** *n*

defile[2] *n* narrow valley or pass

define *v* state precisely the meaning of; show clearly the outline of **definable** *adj* **definite** *adj* firm, clear, and precise; having precise limits; known for certain **definitely** *adv* **definition** *n* statement of the meaning of a word or phrase; quality of being clear and distinct **definitive** *adj* providing an unquestionable conclusion; being the best example of something

deflate *v* (cause to) collapse through the release of air; take away the self-esteem or conceit from; *economics* cause deflation of (an economy) **deflation** *n* *economics* reduction in economic activity resulting in lower output and investment; feeling of sadness following excitement **deflationary** *adj*

deflect *v* (cause to) turn aside from a course **deflection** *n* **deflector** *n*

deflower *v* *lit* deprive (a woman) of her virginity

defoliate *v* deprive (a plant) of its leaves **defoliant** *n* **defoliation** *n*

deforestation *n* destruction of all the trees in an area

deform *v* put out of shape or spoil the appearance of **deformation** *n* **deformity** *n*

defraud *v* cheat out of money, property, etc

defray *v* provide money for (costs or expenses)

defrock *v* deprive (a priest) of priestly status

defrost *v* make or become free of ice; thaw (frozen food) by removing it from a freezer

deft *adj* quick and skilful in movement **deftly** *adv* **deftness** *n*

defunct *adj* no longer existing or operative

defuse *v* remove the fuse of (an explosive device); remove the tension from (a situation)

defy *v* **-fying, -fied** resist openly and boldly; make impossible *eg the condition of the refugees defied description* **defiance** *n* **defiant** *adj*

degenerate *adj* having deteriorated to a lower mental, moral, or physical level ▷ *n* degenerate person ▷ *v* become degenerate **degeneracy** *n* degenerate behaviour **degeneration** *n*

degrade *v* reduce to dishonour or disgrace; reduce in status or quality; *chem* decompose into smaller molecules **degradation** *n*

degree *n* stage in a scale of relative amount or intensity; academic award given by a university or college on successful completion of a course; unit of measurement for temperature, angles, or latitude and longitude

dehumanize *v* deprive of human qualities; make (an activity) mechanical or routine **dehumanization** *n*

dehydrate *v* remove water from (food) to preserve it **be dehydrated** become weak through losing too much water from the body **dehydration** *n*

de-ice *v* free of ice **de-icer** *n*

deify [day-if-fie] *v* **-fying, -fied** treat or worship as a god **deification** *n*

deign [dane] *v* agree (to do something), but as if doing someone a favour

deity [dee-it-ee, **day**-it-ee] *n, pl* **-ties** god or goddess; state of being divine

déjà vu [day-zhah **voo**] *n* feeling of having experienced before something that is actually happening now

dejected *adj* unhappy **dejectedly** *adv* **dejection** *n*

de jure *adv, adj* according to law

dekko *n Brit, Aust & NZ, slang* **have a dekko** have a look

delay *v* put off to a later time; slow up or cause to be late ▷*n* act of delaying; interval of time between events

delectable *adj* delightful, very attractive **delectation** *n formal* great pleasure

delegate *n* person chosen to represent others, esp at a meeting ▷*v* entrust (duties or powers) to someone; appoint as a delegate **delegation** *n* group chosen to represent others; delegating

delete *v* remove (something written or printed) **deletion** *n*

deleterious [del-lit-**eer**-ee-uss] *adj* harmful, injurious

deliberate *adj* planned in advance, intentional; careful and unhurried ▷*v* think something over **deliberately** *adv* **deliberation** *n* **deliberative** *adj*

delicate *adj* fine or subtle in quality or workmanship; having a fragile beauty; (of a taste etc) pleasantly subtle; easily damaged; requiring tact **delicately** *adv* **delicacy** *n* being delicate *pl* **-cies** something particularly good to eat

delicatessen *n* shop selling imported or unusual foods, often already cooked or prepared

delicious *adj* very appealing to taste or smell **deliciously** *adv*

delight *n* (source of) great pleasure ▷*v* please greatly; (foll. by *in*) take great pleasure (in) **delightful** *adj* **delightfully** *adv*

delimit *v* mark or lay down the limits of **delimitation** *n*

delineate [dill-**lin**-ee-ate] *v* show by drawing; describe in words **delineation** *n*

delinquent *n* someone, esp a young person, who repeatedly breaks the law ▷*adj* repeatedly breaking the law **delinquency** *n*

delirium *n* state of excitement and mental confusion, often with hallucinations; great excitement **delirious** *adj* **deliriously** *adv*

deliver *v* carry (goods etc) to a destination; hand over; aid in the birth of; present (a lecture or speech); release or rescue; strike (a blow) **deliverance** *n* rescue from captivity or evil **delivery** *n, pl* **-eries** delivering; something that is delivered; act of giving birth to a baby; style in public speaking

dell *n Chiefly Brit* small wooded hollow

Delphic *adj* ambiguous, like the ancient Greek oracle at Delphi

delphinium *n* large garden plant with blue flowers

delta *n* fourth letter in the Greek alphabet; flat area at the mouth of some rivers where the main stream splits up into several branches

delude *v* deceive

deluge [**del**-lyooj] *n* great flood; torrential rain; overwhelming number ▷*v* flood; overwhelm

delusion *n* mistaken idea or belief; state of being deluded **delusive** *adj*

de luxe *adj* rich or sumptuous, superior in quality

delve *v* research deeply (for information)

demagogue *n* political agitator who appeals to the prejudice and passions of the mob **demagogic** *adj* **demagogy** *n*

demand *v* request forcefully; require as just, urgent, etc; claim as a right ▷*n* forceful request; *economics* willingness and ability to purchase goods and services; something that requires special effort or sacrifice **demanding** *adj* requiring a lot of time or effort

demarcation *n formal* establishing limits or boundaries, esp between the work performed by different trade unions

demean *v* **demean oneself** do something unworthy of one's status or character

demeanour *n* way a person behaves

demented *adj* mad **dementedly** *adv* **dementia** [dim-**men**-sha] *n* state of serious mental deterioration

demerara sugar *n* brown crystallized cane sugar

demerit *n* fault, disadvantage

demesne [dim-**mane**] *n* land surrounding a house; *law* possession of one's own property or land

demi- *combining form* half

demijohn *n* large bottle with a short neck, often encased in wicker

demilitarize *v* remove the military forces from **demilitarization** *n*

demimonde *n* (esp in the 19th century) class of women considered to be outside respectable society because of promiscuity; group considered not wholly respectable

demise *n* eventual failure (of something successful); *formal* death

demo *n, pl* **demos** *Informal* demonstration, organized expression of public opinion

demob *v Brit, Aust & NZ, Informal* demobilize

demobilize *v* release from the armed forces **demobilization** *n*

democracy *n, pl* **-cies** government by the people or their elected representatives; state governed in this way **democrat** *n* advocate of democracy; (**D-**) member or supporter of the Democratic Party in the US **democratic** *adj* of democracy; upholding democracy; (**D-**) of the Democratic Party, the more liberal of the two main political parties in the US **democratically** *adv*

demography *n* study of population statistics, such as births and deaths **demographer** *n* **demographic** *adj*

demolish *v* knock down or destroy (a building); disprove (an argument) **demolition** *n*

demon *n* evil spirit; person who does something with great energy or skill **demonic** *adj* evil **demoniac, demoniacal** *adj* appearing to be possessed by a devil; frenzied **demonology** *n* study of demons

demonstrate *v* show or prove by reasoning or evidence; display and explain the workings of; reveal the existence of; show support or opposition by public parades or rallies **demonstrable** *adj* able to be proved **demonstrably** *adv* **demonstration** *n* organized expression of public opinion; explanation or display of how something works; proof **demonstrative** *adj* tending to show one's feelings unreservedly **demonstratively** *adv* **demonstrator** *n* person who demonstrates how a device or machine works; person who takes part in a public demonstration

demoralize *v* undermine the morale of **demoralization** *n*

demote *v* reduce in status or rank **demotion** *n*

demur *v* **-murring, -murred** show reluctance ▷ *n* **without demur** without objecting

demure *adj* quiet, reserved, and rather shy **demurely** *adv*

den *n* home of a wild animal; small secluded room in a home; place where people indulge in criminal or immoral activities

denationalize *v* transfer (an industry) from public to private ownership **denationalization** *n*

denature *v* change the nature of; make (alcohol) unfit to drink

denier [**den**-yer] *n* unit of weight used to measure the fineness of nylon or silk

denigrate *v* criticize unfairly **denigration** *n*

denim *n* hard-wearing cotton fabric, usu blue ▷ *pl* jeans made of denim

denizen *n* inhabitant

denominate *v* give a specific name to

denomination *n* group having a distinctive interpretation of a religious faith; unit in a system of weights, values, or measures **denominational** *adj*

denominator *n* number below the line in a fraction

denote *v* be a sign of; have as a literal meaning **denotation** *n*

denouement [day-**noo**-mon] *n* final outcome or solution in a play or book

denounce *v* speak vehemently against; give information against **denunciation** *n* open condemnation

dense *adj* closely packed; difficult to see through; stupid **densely** *adv* **density** *n, pl* **-ties** degree to which something is filled or occupied; measure of the compactness of a substance, expressed as its mass per unit volume

dent *n* hollow in the surface of something, made by hitting it ▷ *v* make a dent in

dental *adj* of teeth or dentistry **dental floss** waxed thread used to remove food particles from between the teeth **dentine** [**den**-teen] *n* hard dense tissue forming the bulk of a tooth **denture** *n* false tooth

dentist *n* person qualified to practise dentistry **dentistry** *n* branch of medicine concerned with the teeth and gums

denude *v* remove the covering or protection from

deny *v* **-nying, -nied** declare to be untrue; refuse to give or allow; refuse to acknowledge **deniable** *adj* **denial** *n* statement that something is not true; rejection of a request

deodorant *n* substance applied to the body to mask the smell of perspiration

deodorize *v* remove or disguise the smell of

depart *v* leave; differ, deviate **departed** *adj euphemistic* dead **the departed** *euphemistic* dead person **departure** *n*

department *n* specialized division of a large organization; major subdivision of the administration of a government **departmental** *adj* **department store** large shop selling many kinds of goods

depend *v* (foll. by *on*) put trust (in); be influenced or determined (by); rely (on) for income or support **dependable** *adj* **dependably** *adv* **dependability** *n* **dependant** *n* person who depends on another for financial support **dependence** *n* state of being dependent **dependency** *n, pl* **-cies** country controlled by another country; overreliance on another person or on a drug **dependent** *adj* depending on someone or something

> SPELLING The words **dependant** and **dependent** are easy to confuse. The first, ending in *-ant*, is a noun meaning a person who is *dependent* (adjective ending in *-ent*) on someone else

depict *v* produce a picture of; describe in words **depiction** *n*

depilatory [dip-**pill**-a-tree] *n, pl* **-tories,** *adj* (substance) designed to remove unwanted hair

deplete *v* use up; reduce in number **depletion** *n*

deplore *v* condemn strongly **deplorable** *adj* very bad or unpleasant

deploy *v* organize (troops or resources) into a position ready for immediate action **deployment** *n*

depopulate *v* reduce the population of **depopulation** *n*

deport *v* remove forcibly from a country **deport oneself** behave in a specified way **deportation** *n* **deportee** *n*

deportment *n* way in which a person moves or stands

depose *v* remove from an office or position of power; *law* testify on oath

deposit *v* put down; entrust for safekeeping, esp to a bank; lay down naturally ▷ *n* sum of money paid into a bank account; money given in part payment for goods or services; accumulation of sediments, minerals, etc **depositary** *n* person to whom something is entrusted for safety **depositor** *n* **depository** *n* store for furniture etc

deposition *n law* sworn statement of a witness used in court in his or her absence; deposing; depositing; something deposited

depot [**dep**-oh] *n* building where goods or vehicles are kept when not in use; *NZ & US* bus or railway station

depraved *adj* morally bad **depravity** *n*

deprecate *v* express disapproval of **deprecation** *n* **deprecatory** *adj*

depreciate *v* decline in value or price; criticize **depreciation** *n*

depredation *n* plundering

depress *v* make sad; lower (prices or wages); push down **depressing** *adj* **depressingly** *adv* **depressant** *n, adj* (drug) able to reduce nervous activity **depression** *n* mental state in which a person has feelings of gloom and inadequacy; economic condition in which there is high unemployment and low output and investment; area of low air pressure; sunken place **depressive** *adj* tending to cause depression ▷ *n* person who suffers from depression

deprive *v* (foll. by *of*) prevent from (having or enjoying) **deprivation** *n* **deprived** *adj* lacking adequate living conditions, education, etc

depth *n* distance downwards, backwards, or inwards; intensity of emotion; profundity of character or thought **depth charge** bomb used to attack submarines by exploding at a preset depth of water

depute *v* appoint (someone) to act on one's behalf **deputation** *n* body of people appointed to represent others

deputy *n, pl* **-ties** person appointed to act on behalf of another **deputize** *v* act as deputy

derail *v* cause (a train) to go off the rails **derailment** *n*

deranged *adj* insane or uncontrolled; in a state of disorder **derangement** *n*

derby [**dah**-bee] *n, pl* **-bies** sporting event between teams from the same area ▷ *n* any of various horse races

deregulate *v* remove regulations or controls from **deregulation** *n*

derelict *adj* unused and falling into ruins ▷ *n* social outcast, vagrant **dereliction** *n* state of being abandoned **dereliction of duty** failure to do one's duty

deride *v* treat with contempt or ridicule **derision** *n* **derisive** *adj* mocking, scornful **derisory** *adj* too small or inadequate to be considered seriously

de rigueur [de rig-**gur**] *adj* required by fashion

derive *v* (foll. by *from*) take or develop (from) **derivation** *n* **derivative** *adj* word, idea, etc, derived from another

dermatitis *n* inflammation of the skin

dermatology *n* branch of medicine concerned with the skin **dermatologist** *n*

derogatory [dir-**rog**-a-tree] *adj* intentionally offensive

derrick *n* simple crane; framework erected over an oil well

derv *n Brit* diesel oil, when used for road transport

dervish *n* member of a Muslim religious order noted for a frenzied whirling dance

descant *n music* tune played or sung above a basic melody

descend *v* move down (a slope etc); move to a lower level, pitch, etc; (foll. by *to*) stoop to (unworthy behaviour); (foll. by *on*) visit unexpectedly **be descended from** be connected by a blood relationship to **descendant** *n* person or animal descended from an individual, race, or species **descendent** *adj* descending **descent** *n* descending; downward slope; derivation from an ancestor

describe *v* give an account of (something or someone) in words; trace the outline of (a circle etc) **description** *n* statement that describes something or someone; sort *eg flowers of every description* **descriptive** *adj* **descriptively** *adv*

descry *v* **-scrying, -scried** catch sight of; discover by looking carefully

desecrate *v* damage or insult (something sacred) **desecration** *n*

desegregate *v* end racial segregation in **desegregation** *n*

deselect *v Brit, politics* refuse to select (an MP) for re-election **deselection** *n*

desert[1] *n* region with little or no vegetation because of low rainfall

desert[2] *v* abandon (a person or place) without intending to return; *mil* leave (a post or duty) with no intention of returning **deserter** *n* **desertion** *n*

deserts *pl n* **get one's just deserts** get the punishment one deserves

deserve *v* be entitled to or worthy of **deserved** *adj* rightfully earned **deservedly** *adv* **deserving** *adj* worthy of help, praise, or reward

deshabille [day-zab-**beel**] *n* state of being partly dressed

desiccate *v* remove most of the water from **desiccation** *n*

> SPELLING The word **desiccate** has two *cs* because it comes from the Latin word *siccus*, which means 'dry'

design *v* work out the structure or form of (something), by making a sketch or plans; plan and make artistically; intend for a specific purpose ▷ *n* preliminary drawing; arrangement or features of an artistic or decorative work; art of designing; intention *eg by design* **designedly** [dee-**zine**-id-lee] *adv* intentionally **designer** *n* person who draws up original sketches or plans from which things are made ▷ *adj* designed by a well-known designer **designing** *adj* cunning and scheming

designate [**dez**-zig-nate] *v* give a name to; select (someone) for an office or duty ▷ *adj* appointed but not yet in office **designation** *n* name

desire *v* want very much ▷ *n* wish, longing; sexual appetite; person or thing desired **desirable** *adj* worth having; arousing sexual desire **desirability** *n* **desirous of** having a desire for

desist *v* (foll. by *from*) stop (doing something)

desk *n* piece of furniture with a writing surface and drawers; service counter in a public building; section of a newspaper covering a specific subject *eg the sports desk* **desktop** *adj* (of a computer) small enough to use at a desk

desolate *adj* uninhabited and bleak; very sad ▷ *v* deprive of inhabitants; make (someone) very sad **desolation** *n*

despair *n* total loss of hope ▷ *v* lose hope

despatch *v, n* same as **dispatch**

desperado *n, pl* **-does, -dos** reckless person ready to commit any violent illegal act

desperate *adj* in despair and reckless; (of an action) undertaken as a last resort; having a strong need or desire **desperately** *adv* **desperation** *n*

> SPELLING It's often difficult to decide whether to write an *a* or an *e* when it wouldn't seem to make much difference to a word's pronunciation. An example in Collins Word Web is *desparate*, which should, of course, be spelt **desperate**

despise *v* regard with contempt **despicable** *adj* deserving contempt **despicably** *adv*

despite *prep* in spite of

despoil *v formal* plunder **despoliation** *n*

despondent *adj* unhappy **despondently** *adv* **despondency** *n*

despot *n* person in power who acts unfairly or cruelly **despotic** *adj* **despotism** *n* unfair or cruel government or behaviour

dessert *n* sweet course served at the end of a meal **dessertspoon** *n* spoon between a tablespoon and a teaspoon in size

destination *n* place to which someone or something is going

destined *adj* certain to be or to do something

destiny *n, pl* **-nies** future marked out for a person or thing; the power that predetermines the course of events

destitute *adj* having no money or possessions **destitution** *n*

destroy *v* ruin, demolish; put an end to; kill (an animal) **destroyer** *n* small heavily armed warship; person or thing that destroys

destruction *n* destroying; cause of ruin **destructive** *adj* (capable of) causing destruction **destructively** *adv*

desuetude [diss-**syoo**-it-tude] *n* condition of not being in use

desultory [**dez**-zl-tree] *adj* jumping from one thing to another, disconnected; random **desultorily** *adv*

detach *v* disengage and separate **detachable** *adj* **detached** *adj Brit, Aust & SAfr* (of a house) not joined to another house; showing no emotional involvement **detachment** *n* lack of emotional involvement; small group of soldiers

detail *n* individual piece of information; unimportant item; small individual features of something, considered collectively; *chiefly mil* (personnel assigned) a specific duty ▷ *v* list fully

detain *v* delay (someone); hold (someone) in custody **detainee** *n*

detect *v* notice; discover, find **detectable** *adj* **detection** *n* **detective** *n* policeman or private agent who investigates crime **detector** *n* instrument used to find something

detente [day-**tont**] *n* easing of tension between nations

detention *n* imprisonment; form of punishment in which a pupil is detained after school

deter *v* **-terring, -terred** discourage (someone) from doing something by instilling fear or doubt **deterrent** *n* something that deters; weapon, esp nuclear, intended to deter attack ▷ *adj* tending to deter

detergent *n* chemical substance for washing clothes or dishes

deteriorate *v* become worse **deterioration** *n*

determine *v* settle (an argument or a question) conclusively; find out the facts about; make a firm decision (to do something) **determinant** *n* factor that determines **determinate** *adj* definitely limited or fixed **determination** *n* being determined or resolute **determined** *adj* firmly decided, unable to be dissuaded **determinedly** *adv* **determiner** *n* *grammar* word that determines the object to which a noun phrase refers *eg all* **determinism** *n* theory that human choice is not free, but decided by past events **determinist** *n, adj*

detest *v* dislike intensely **detestable** *adj* **detestation** *n*

dethrone *v* remove from a throne or position of power

detonate *v* explode **detonation** *n* **detonator** *n* small amount of explosive, or a device, used to set off an explosion

detour *n* route that is not the most direct one

detract *v* (foll. by *from*) make (something) seem less good **detractor** *n*

detriment *n* disadvantage or damage **detrimental** *adj* **detrimentally** *adv*

detritus [dit-**trite**-uss] *n* loose mass of stones and silt worn away from rocks; debris

de trop [de **troh**] *adj French* unwanted, unwelcome

deuce [**dyewss**] *n tennis* score of forty all; playing card with two symbols or dice with two spots

deuterium *n* isotope of hydrogen twice as heavy as the normal atom

Deutschmark [**doytch**-mark] **Deutsche Mark** [**doytch**-a] *n* former monetary unit of Germany

devalue *v* **-valuing, -valued** reduce the exchange value of (a currency); reduce the value of (something or someone) **devaluation** *n*

devastate *v* destroy **devastated** *adj* shocked and extremely upset **devastation** *n*

develop *v* grow or bring to a later, more elaborate, or more advanced stage; come or bring into existence; build houses or factories on (an area of land); produce (photographs) by making negatives or prints from a film **developer** *n* person who develops property; chemical used to develop photographs or films **development** *n* **developing country** poor or nonindustrial country that is trying to develop its resources by industrialization

deviate *v* differ from others in belief or thought; depart from one's previous behaviour **deviation** *n* **deviant** *n, adj* (person) deviating from what is considered acceptable behaviour **deviance** *n*

device *n* machine or tool used for a specific task; scheme or plan

devil *n* evil spirit; evil person; person *eg poor devil*; daring person *eg be a devil! Informal* something difficult or annoying *eg a devil of a long time* ▷ *v* **-illing, -illed** prepare (food) with a highly flavoured spiced mixture **the Devil** *theology* chief spirit of evil and enemy of God **devilish** *adj* cruel or unpleasant ▷ *adv* (also **devilishly**) *Informal* extremely **devilment** *n* mischievous conduct **devilry** *n* mischievousness **devil-may-care** *adj* carefree and cheerful **devil's advocate** person who takes an opposing or unpopular point of view for the sake of argument

devious *adj* insincere and dishonest; indirect **deviously** *adv*

deviousness *n*
devise *v* work out (something) in one's mind
devoid *adj* (foll. by *of*) completely lacking (in)
devolve *v* (foll. by *on, to*) pass (power or duties) or (of power or duties) be passed to a successor or substitute **devolution** *n* transfer of authority from a central government to regional governments
devote *v* apply or dedicate to a particular purpose **devoted** *adj* showing loyalty or devotion **devotedly** *adv* **devotee** *n* person who is very enthusiastic about something; zealous follower of a religion **devotion** *n* strong affection for or loyalty to someone or something; religious zeal ▷ *pl* prayers **devotional** *adj*
devour *v* eat greedily; (of an emotion) engulf and destroy; read eagerly
devout *adj* deeply religious **devoutly** *adv*
dew *n* drops of water that form on the ground at night from vapour in the air **dewy** *adj*
dewlap *n* loose fold of skin hanging under the throat in dogs, cattle, etc
dexterity *n* skill in using one's hands; mental quickness **dexterous** *adj* **dexterously** *adv*
dextrose *n* glucose occurring in fruit, honey, and the blood of animals
DH (in Britain) Department of Health
DI donor insemination: method of making a woman pregnant by transferring sperm from a man other than her regular partner using artificial means
diabetes [die-a-**beet**-eez] *n* disorder in which an abnormal amount of urine containing an excess of sugar is excreted **diabetic** *n, adj*
diabolic *adj* of the Devil **diabolism** *n* witchcraft, devil worship
diabolical *adj Informal* extremely bad **diabolically** *adv*
diaconate *n* position or period of office of a deacon
diacritic *n* sign above or below a character to indicate phonetic value or stress
diadem *n old-fashioned* crown
diaeresis *n, pl* **-ses** mark (¨) placed over a vowel to show that it is pronounced separately from the preceding one, for example in *Noël*
diagnosis [die-ag-**no**-siss] *n, pl* **-ses** [-seez] discovery and identification of diseases from the examination of symptoms **diagnose** *v* **diagnostic** *adj*
diagonal *adj* from corner to corner; slanting ▷ *n* diagonal line **diagonally** *adv*
diagram *n* sketch showing the form or workings of something **diagrammatic** *adj*
dial *n* face of a clock or watch; graduated disc on a measuring instrument; control on a radio or television set used to change the station; numbered disc on the front of some telephones ▷ *v* **dialling, dialled** operate the dial or buttons on a telephone in order to contact (a number)
dialect *n* form of a language spoken in a particular area **dialectal** *adj*
dialectic *n* logical debate by question and answer to resolve differences between two views **dialectical** *adj*
dialogue *n* conversation between

two people, esp in a book, film, or play; discussion between representatives of two nations or groups **dialogue box** *n* small window that may open on a computer screen to prompt the user to enter information or select an option

dialysis [die-**al**-iss-iss] *n med* filtering of blood through a membrane to remove waste products

diamanté [die-a-**man**-tee] *adj* decorated with artificial jewels or sequins

diameter *n* (length of) a straight line through the centre of a circle or sphere **diametric, diametrical** *adj* of a diameter; completely opposed *eg the diametric opposite* **diametrically** *adv*

diamond *n* exceptionally hard, usu colourless, precious stone; *geom* figure with four sides of equal length forming two acute and two obtuse angles; playing card marked with red diamond-shaped symbols **diamond wedding** sixtieth anniversary of a wedding

diaper *n US* nappy

diaphanous [die-**af**-fan-ous] *adj* fine and almost transparent

diaphragm [**die**-a-fram] *n* muscular partition that separates the abdominal cavity and chest cavity; contraceptive device placed over the neck of the womb

diarrhoea [die-a-**ree**-a] *n* frequent discharge of abnormally liquid faeces

> SPELLING It's possibly because people don't write the word **diarrhoea** very often that there's only one example of *diarhoea*, with only one *r*, in Collins Word Web. Or is it because it's such a difficult word to spell, we always look it up to get it right?

diary *n, pl* **-ries** (book for) a record of daily events, appointments, or observations **diarist** *n*

diatribe *n* bitter critical attack

dibble *n* small hand tool used to make holes in the ground for seeds or plants

dice *n, pl* **dice** small cube each of whose sides has a different number of spots (1 to 6), used in games of chance ▷*v* cut (food) into small cubes **dice with death** take a risk **dicey** *adj Informal* dangerous or risky

dichotomy [die-**kot**-a-mee] *n, pl* **-mies** division into two opposed groups or parts

dicky[1] *n, pl* **dickies** false shirt front **dicky-bird** *n* child's word for a bird

dicky[2] *adj* **dickier, dickiest** *Informal* shaky or weak

Dictaphone *n* ® tape recorder for recording dictation for subsequent typing

dictate *v* say aloud for someone else to write down; (foll. by *to*) seek to impose one's will on (other people) ▷*n* authoritative command; guiding principle **dictation** *n* **dictator** *n* ruler who has complete power; person in power who acts unfairly or cruelly **dictatorship** *n* **dictatorial** *adj* like a dictator

diction *n* manner of pronouncing words and sounds

dictionary *n, pl* **-aries** book consisting of an alphabetical list of words with their meanings; alphabetically ordered reference book of terms relating to a particular subject

dictum *n, pl* **-tums, -ta** formal statement; popular saying

did *v* past tense of **do**

didactic *adj* intended to instruct

didactically *adv*
diddle *v Informal* swindle
didgeridoo *n* Australian musical instrument made from a long hollow piece of wood
didn't did not
die[1] *v* **dying, died** (of a person, animal, or plant) cease all biological activity permanently; (of something inanimate) cease to exist or function **be dying for, to do something** *Informal* be eager for *or* to do something **die-hard** *n* person who resists change
die[2] *n* shaped block used to cut or form metal
dieresis [die-**air**-iss-iss] *n, pl* **-ses** [-seez] same as **diaeresis**
diesel *n* diesel engine; vehicle driven by a diesel engine; diesel oil **diesel engine** internal-combustion engine in which oil is ignited by compression **diesel oil** fuel obtained from petroleum distillation
diet[1] *n* food that a person or animal regularly eats; specific range of foods, to control weight or for health reasons ▷ *v* follow a special diet so as to lose weight ▷ *adj* (of food) suitable for a weight-reduction diet **dietary** *adj* **dietary fibre** fibrous substances in fruit and vegetables that aid digestion **dieter** *n* **dietetic** *adj* prepared for special dietary requirements **dietetics** *n* study of diet and nutrition **dietician** *n* person who specializes in dietetics
diet[2] *n* parliament of some countries
differ *v* be unlike; disagree
different *adj* unlike; unusual **difference** *n* state of being unlike; disagreement; remainder left after subtraction **differently** *adv*
differential *adj* of or using a difference; *maths* involving differentials ▷ *n* factor that differentiates between two comparable things; *maths* tiny difference between values in a scale; difference between rates of pay for different types of work **differential calculus** branch of calculus concerned with derivatives and differentials **differentiate** *v* perceive or show the difference (between); make (one thing) distinct from other such things **differentiation** *n*
difficult *adj* requiring effort or skill to do or understand; not easily pleased **difficulty** *n*
diffident *adj* lacking self-confidence **diffidence** *n* **diffidently** *adv*
diffraction *n physics* deviation in the direction of a wave at the edge of an obstacle in its path; formation of light and dark fringes by the passage of light through a small aperture
diffuse *v* spread over a wide area ▷ *adj* widely spread; lacking concision **diffusion** *n*
dig *v* **digging, dug** cut into, break up, and turn over or remove (earth), esp with a spade; (foll. by *out, up*) find by effort or searching; (foll. by *in, into*) thrust or jab *n* digging; archaeological excavation; thrust or poke; spiteful remark ▷ *pl Brit, Aust & SAfr, Informal* lodgings **digger** *n* machine used for digging
digest *v* subject to a process of digestion; absorb mentally ▷ *n* shortened version of a book, report, or article **digestible** *adj* **digestion** *n* (body's system for) breaking down food into easily absorbed substances **digestive** *adj*

digestive biscuit biscuit made from wholemeal flour

digit [dij-it] *n* finger or toe; numeral from 0 to 9 **digital** *adj* displaying information as numbers rather than with hands and a dial *eg a digital clock* **digital recording** sound-recording process that converts audio or analogue signals into a series of pulses **digital television** television in which the picture is transmitted in digital form and then decoded **digitally** *adv*

digitalis *n* drug made from foxglove leaves, used as a heart stimulant

dignity *n, pl* **-ties** serious, calm, and controlled behaviour or manner; quality of being worthy of respect; sense of self-importance **dignify** *v* add distinction to **dignitary** *n* person of high official position

digress *v* depart from the main subject in speech or writing **digression** *n*

dike *n* same as **dyke**

dilapidated *adj* (of a building) having fallen into ruin **dilapidation** *n*

dilate *v* make or become wider or larger **dilation, dilatation** *n*

dilatory [dill-a-tree] *adj* tending or intended to waste time

dildo *n, pl* **-dos** object used as a substitute for an erect penis

dilemma *n* situation offering a choice between two equally undesirable alternatives

dilettante [dill-it-tan-tee] *n, pl* **-tantes, -tanti** person whose interest in a subject is superficial rather than serious **dilettantism** *n*

diligent *adj* careful and persevering in carrying out duties; carried out with care and perseverance **diligently** *adv* **diligence** *n*

dill *n* sweet-smelling herb

dilly-dally *v* **-lying, -lied** *Brit, Aust & NZ, Informal* dawdle, waste time

dilute *v* make (a liquid) less concentrated, esp by adding water; make (a quality etc) weaker in force **dilution** *n*

diluvial, diluvian *adj* of a flood, esp the great Flood described in the Old Testament

dim *adj* **dimmer, dimmest** badly lit; not clearly seen; unintelligent ▷ *v* **dimming, dimmed** make or become dim **take a dim view of** disapprove of **dimly** *adv* **dimness** *n* **dimmer** *n* device for dimming an electric light

dime *n* coin of the US and Canada, worth ten cents

dimension *n* measurement of the size of something in a particular direction; aspect, factor

diminish *v* make or become smaller, fewer, or less **diminution** *n* **diminutive** *adj* very small ▷ *n* word or affix which implies smallness or unimportance

diminuendo *n music* gradual decrease in loudness

dimple *n* small natural dent, esp in the cheeks or chin ▷ *v* produce dimples by smiling

din *n* loud unpleasant confused noise ▷ *v* **dinning, dinned** (foll. by *into*) instil (something) into someone by constant repetition

dinar [dee-nahr] *n* monetary unit of various Balkan, Middle Eastern, and North African countries

dine *v* eat dinner **diner** *n* person eating a meal; *Chiefly US* small cheap restaurant **dining car** railway coach where meals are served **dining room** room where meals are eaten

ding *n Aust dated & NZ, Informal* small dent in a vehicle

ding-dong *n* sound of a bell; *Informal* lively quarrel or fight

dinghy [**ding**-ee] *n, pl* **-ghies** small boat, powered by sails, oars, or a motor

dingo *n, pl* **-goes** Australian wild dog

dingy [**din**-jee] *adj* **-gier, -giest** *Brit, Aust & NZ* dull and drab **dinginess** *n*

dinkum *adj Aust & NZ, Informal* genuine or right

dinky *adj* **-kier, -kiest** *Brit, Aust & NZ, Informal* small and neat

dinky-di *adj Aust, Informal* typical

dinner *n* main meal of the day, eaten either in the evening or at midday **dinner jacket** man's semiformal black evening jacket

dinosaur *n* type of extinct prehistoric reptile, many of which were of gigantic size

dint *n* **by dint of** by means of

diocese [**die**-a-siss] *n* district over which a bishop has control **diocesan** *adj*

diode *n* semiconductor device for converting alternating current to direct current

dioptre [die-**op**-ter] *n* unit for measuring the refractive power of a lens

dioxide *n* oxide containing two oxygen atoms per molecule

dip *v* **dipping, dipped** plunge quickly or briefly into a liquid; slope downwards; switch (car headlights) from the main to the lower beam; lower briefly ▷ *n* dipping; brief swim; liquid chemical in which farm animals are dipped to rid them of insects; depression in a landscape; creamy mixture into which pieces of food are dipped before being eaten **dip into** *v* read passages at random from (a book or journal)

diphtheria [dif-**theer**-ya] *n* contagious disease producing fever and difficulty in breathing and swallowing

diphthong *n* union of two vowel sounds in a single compound sound

diploma *n* qualification awarded by a college on successful completion of a course

diplomacy *n* conduct of the relations between nations by peaceful means; tact or skill in dealing with people **diplomat** *n* official engaged in diplomacy **diplomatic** *adj* of diplomacy; tactful in dealing with people **diplomatically** *adv*

dipper *n* ladle used for dipping; (also **ousel, ouzel**) European songbird that lives by a river

diprotodont [die-**pro**-toe-dont] *n* marsupial with fewer than three upper incisor teeth on each side of the jaw

dipsomania *n* compulsive craving for alcohol **dipsomaniac** *n, adj*

diptych [**dip**-tik] *n* painting on two hinged panels

dire *adj* disastrous, urgent, or terrible

direct *adj* (of a route) shortest, straight; without anyone or anything intervening; likely to have an immediate effect; honest, frank ▷ *adv* in a direct manner ▷ *v* lead and organize; tell (someone) to do something; tell (someone) the way to a place; address (a letter, package, remark, etc); provide guidance to (actors, cameramen, etc) in (a play or film) **directly** *adv* in a direct manner; at once ▷ *conj* as soon as **directness** *n* **direct current** electric current that flows in one direction only

direction *n* course or line along which a person or thing moves, points, or lies; management or guidance ▷ *pl* instructions for doing something or for reaching a place **directional** *adj*

directive *n* instruction, order

director *n* person or thing that directs or controls; member of the governing board of a business etc; person responsible for the artistic and technical aspects of the making of a film etc **directorial** *adj* **directorship** *n* **directorate** *n* board of directors; position of director

directory *n, pl* **-tories** book listing names, addresses, and telephone numbers; *computers* area of a disk containing the names and locations of the files it currently holds

dirge *n* slow sad song of mourning

dirigible [dir-rij-jib-bl] *adj* able to be steered ▷ *n* airship

dirk *n* dagger, formerly worn by Scottish Highlanders

dirndl *n* full gathered skirt originating from Tyrolean peasant wear

dirt *n* unclean substance, filth; earth, soil; obscene speech or writing; *Informal* harmful gossip **dirt track** racetrack made of packed earth or cinders

dirty *adj* **dirtier, dirtiest** covered or marked with dirt; unfair or dishonest; obscene; displaying dislike or anger *eg a dirty look* ▷ *v* **dirtying, dirtied** make dirty **dirtiness** *n*

dis- *prefix* indicating: reversal *eg disconnect*; negation or lack *eg dissimilar; disgrace*; removal or release *eg disembowel*

disable *v* make ineffective, unfit, or incapable **disabled** *adj* lacking a physical power, such as the ability to walk **disablement** *n* **disability** *n, pl* **-ties** condition of being disabled; something that disables someone

disabuse *v* (foll. by *of*) rid (someone) of a mistaken idea

disadvantage *n* unfavourable or harmful circumstance **disadvantageous** *adj* **disadvantaged** *adj* socially or economically deprived

disaffected *adj* having lost loyalty to or affection for someone or something **disaffection** *n*

disagree *v* **-greeing, -greed** argue or have different opinions; be different, conflict; (foll. by *with*) cause physical discomfort (to) *eg curry disagrees with me* **disagreement** *n* **disagreeable** *adj* unpleasant; (of a person) unfriendly or unhelpful **disagreeably** *adv*

disallow *v* reject as untrue or invalid

disappear *v* cease to be visible; cease to exist **disappearance** *n*

disappoint *v* fail to meet the expectations or hopes of **disappointment** *n* feeling of being disappointed; person or thing that disappoints

> SPELLING It is a more common mistake to spell **disappointment** with no double letters at all, than to spell it with two *ss*, although *dissappointment* does occur in Collins Word Web

disapprobation *n* disapproval

disapprove *v* (foll. by *of*) consider

wrong or bad **disapproval** *n*

disarm *v* deprive of weapons; win the confidence or affection of; (of a country) decrease the size of one's armed forces **disarmament** *n* **disarming** *adj* removing hostility or suspicion **disarmingly** *adv*

disarrange *v* throw into disorder

disarray *n* confusion and lack of discipline; extreme untidiness

disaster *n* occurrence that causes great distress or destruction; project etc that fails **disastrous** *adj* **disastrously** *adv*

disavow *v* deny connection with or responsibility for **disavowal** *n*

disband *v* (cause to) cease to function as a group

disbelieve *v* reject as false; (foll. by *in*) have no faith (in) **disbelief** *n*

disburse *v* pay out **disbursement** *n*

disc *n* flat circular object; gramophone record; *anat* circular flat structure in the body, esp between the vertebrae; *computers* same as **disk** **disc jockey** person who introduces and plays pop records on a radio programme or at a disco

discard *v* get rid of (something or someone) as useless or undesirable

discern *v* see or be aware of (something) clearly **discernible** *adj* **discerning** *adj* having good judgment **discernment** *n*

discharge *v* release, allow to go; dismiss (someone) from duty or employment; fire (a gun); pour forth, send out; meet the demands of (a duty or responsibility); relieve oneself of (a debt) ▷ *n* substance that comes out from a place; discharging

disciple [diss-**sipe**-pl] *n* follower of the doctrines of a teacher, esp Jesus Christ

discipline *n* practice of imposing strict rules of behaviour; area of academic study ▷ *v* attempt to improve the behaviour of (oneself or another) by training or rules; punish **disciplined** *adj* able to behave and work in a controlled way **disciplinarian** *n* person who practises strict discipline **disciplinary** *adj*

disclaimer *n* statement denying responsibility **disclaim** *v*

disclose *v* make known; allow to be seen **disclosure** *n*

disco *n, pl* **-cos** nightclub where people dance to amplified pop records; occasion at which people dance to amplified pop records; mobile equipment for providing music for a disco

discolour *v* change in colour, fade **discoloration** *n*

discomfit *v* make uneasy or confused **discomfiture** *n*

discomfort *n* inconvenience, distress, or mild pain

discommode *v* cause inconvenience to

disconcert *v* embarrass or upset

disconnect *v* undo or break the connection between (two things); stop the supply of electricity or gas of **disconnected** *adj* (of speech or ideas) not logically connected **disconnection** *n*

disconsolate *adj* sad beyond comfort **disconsolately** *adv*

discontent *n* lack of contentment **discontented** *adj*

discontinue *v* come or bring to an end **discontinuous** *adj* characterized by interruptions **discontinuity** *n*

discord *n* lack of agreement or harmony between people; harsh

confused sounds **discordant** *adj* **discordance** *n*
discotheque *n* same as **disco**
discount *v* take no account of (something) because it is considered to be unreliable, prejudiced, or irrelevant; deduct (an amount) from the price of something ▷*n* deduction from the full price of something
discourage *v* deprive of the will to persist in something; oppose by expressing disapproval **discouragement** *n*
discourse *n* conversation; formal treatment of a subject in speech or writing ▷*v* (foll. by *on*) speak or write (about) at length
discourteous *adj* showing bad manners **discourtesy** *n*
discover *v* be the first to find or to find out about; learn about for the first time; find after study or search **discoverer** *n* **discovery** *n, pl* **-eries** discovering; person, place, or thing that has been discovered
discredit *v* damage the reputation of; cause (an idea) to be disbelieved or distrusted ▷*n* damage to someone's reputation **discreditable** *adj* bringing shame
discreet *adj* careful to avoid embarrassment, esp by keeping confidences secret; unobtrusive **discreetly** *adv*
discrepancy *n, pl* **-cies** conflict or variation between facts, figures, or claims
discrete *adj* separate, distinct
discretion *n* quality of behaving in a discreet way; freedom or authority to make judgments and decide what to do **discretionary** *adj*
discriminate *v* (foll. by *against, in favour of*) single out (a particular person or group) for worse or better treatment than others; (foll. by *between*) recognize or understand the difference (between) **discriminating** *adj* showing good taste and judgment **discrimination** *n* **discriminatory** *adj* based on prejudice
discursive *adj* passing from one topic to another
discus *n* heavy disc-shaped object thrown in sports competitions
discuss *v* consider (something) by talking it over; treat (a subject) in speech or writing **discussion** *n*
disdain *n* feeling of superiority and dislike ▷*v* refuse with disdain **disdainful** *adj* **disdainfully** *adv*
disease *n* illness, sickness **diseased** *adj*
disembark *v* get off a ship, aircraft, or bus **disembarkation** *n*
disembodied *adj* lacking a body; seeming not to be attached to or coming from anyone
disembowel *v* **-elling, -elled** remove the entrails of
disenchanted *adj* disappointed and disillusioned **disenchantment** *n*
disenfranchise *v* deprive (someone) of the right to vote or of other rights of citizenship
disengage *v* release from a connection **disengagement** *n*
disentangle *v* release from entanglement or confusion
disfavour *n* disapproval or dislike
disfigure *v* spoil the appearance of **disfigurement** *n*
disfranchise *v* same as **disenfranchise**
disgorge *v* empty out, discharge
disgrace *n* condition of shame, loss of reputation, or dishonour; shameful person or thing ▷*v* bring

shame upon (oneself or others) **disgraceful** *adj* **disgracefully** *adv*
disgruntled *adj* sulky or discontented **disgruntlement** *n*
disguise *v* change the appearance or manner in order to conceal the identity of (someone or something); misrepresent (something) in order to obscure its actual nature or meaning ▷ *n* mask, costume, or manner that disguises; state of being disguised
disgust *n* great loathing or distaste ▷ *v* sicken, fill with loathing
dish *n* shallow container used for holding or serving food; particular kind of food; short for **dish aerial** *Informal* attractive person **dish aerial** aerial consisting of a concave disc-shaped reflector, used esp for satellite television **dishcloth** *n* cloth for washing dishes **dish out** *v Informal* distribute **dish up** *v Informal* serve (food)
dishabille [diss-a-**beel**] *n* same as **deshabille**
dishearten *v* weaken or destroy the hope, courage, or enthusiasm of
dishevelled *adj* (of a person's hair, clothes, or general appearance) disordered and untidy
dishonest *adj* not honest or fair **dishonestly** *adv* **dishonesty** *n*
dishonour *v* treat with disrespect ▷ *n* lack of respect; state of shame or disgrace; something that causes a loss of honour **dishonourable** *adj* **dishonourably** *adv*
disillusion *v* destroy the illusions or false ideas of ▷ *n* (also **disillusionment**) state of being disillusioned
disincentive *n* something that acts as a deterrent
disinclined *adj* unwilling, reluctant **disinclination** *n*
disinfect *v* rid of harmful germs, chemically **disinfectant** *n* substance that destroys harmful germs **disinfection** *n*
disinformation *n* false information intended to mislead
disingenuous *adj* not sincere **disingenuously** *adv*
disinherit *v law* deprive (an heir) of inheritance **disinheritance** *n*
disintegrate *v* break up **disintegration** *n*
disinter *v* **-terring, -terred** dig up; reveal, make known
disinterested *adj* free from bias or involvement **disinterest** *n*

People sometimes use *disinterested* where they mean *uninterested*. If you want to say that someone shows a lack of interest, use *uninterested*. *Disinterested* would be used in a sentence such as *We asked him to decide because he was a disinterested observer*

disjointed *adj* having no coherence, disconnected
disk *n computers* storage device, consisting of a stack of plates coated with a magnetic layer, which rotates rapidly as a single unit
dislike *v* consider unpleasant or disagreeable ▷ *n* feeling of not liking something or someone
dislocate *v* displace (a bone or joint) from its normal position; disrupt or shift out of place **dislocation** *n*
dislodge *v* remove (something) from a previously fixed position
disloyal *adj* not loyal, deserting one's allegiance **disloyalty** *n*
dismal *adj* gloomy and depressing;

Informal of poor quality **dismally** *adv*

dismantle *v* take apart piece by piece

dismay *v* fill with alarm or depression ▷ *n* alarm mixed with sadness

dismember *v* remove the limbs of; cut to pieces **dismemberment** *n*

dismiss *v* remove (an employee) from a job; allow (someone) to leave; put out of one's mind; (of a judge) state that (a case) will not be brought to trial **dismissal** *n* **dismissive** *adj* scornful, contemptuous

dismount *v* get off a horse or bicycle

disobey *v* neglect or refuse to obey **disobedient** *adj* **disobedience** *n*

disobliging *adj* unwilling to help

disorder *n* state of untidiness and disorganization; public violence or rioting; illness **disordered** *adj* untidy **disorderly** *adj* untidy and disorganized; uncontrolled, unruly

disorganize *v* disrupt the arrangement or system of **disorganization** *n*

disorientate, disorient *v* cause (someone) to lose his or her bearings **disorientation** *n*

disown *v* deny any connection with (someone)

disparage *v* speak contemptuously of **disparagement** *n*

disparate *adj* completely different **disparity** *n*

dispassionate *adj* not influenced by emotion **dispassionately** *adv*

dispatch *v* send off to a destination or to perform a task; carry out (a duty or a task) with speed; *old-fashioned* kill ▷ *n* official communication or report, sent in haste; report sent to a newspaper by a correspondent **dispatch rider** *Brit, Aust & NZ* motorcyclist who carries dispatches

dispel *v* **-pelling, -pelled** destroy or remove

dispense *v* distribute in portions; prepare and distribute (medicine); administer (the law etc) **dispensable** *adj* not essential **dispensation** *n* dispensing; exemption from an obligation **dispenser** *n* **dispensary** *n, pl* **-saries** place where medicine is dispensed **dispense with** *v* do away with, manage without

disperse *v* scatter over a wide area; (cause to) leave a gathering **dispersal, dispersion** *n*

dispirit *v* make downhearted

displace *v* move from the usual location; remove from office **displacement** *n* **displaced person** person forced from his or her home or country, esp by war

display *v* make visible or noticeable ▷ *n* displaying; something displayed; exhibition

displease *v* annoy or upset **displeasure** *n*

disport *v* **disport oneself** indulge oneself in pleasure

dispose *v* place in a certain order **disposed** *adj* willing or eager; having an attitude as specified *eg he felt well disposed towards her* **disposable** *adj* designed to be thrown away after use; available for use *eg disposable income* **disposal** *n* getting rid of something **at one's disposal** available for use **disposition** *n* person's usual temperament; desire or tendency to do something; arrangement **dispose of** *v* throw away, get rid of;

deal with (a problem etc); kill
dispossess *v* (foll. by *of*) deprive (someone) of (a possession) **dispossession** *n*
disproportion *n* lack of proportion or equality
disproportionate *adj* out of proportion **disproportionately** *adv*
disprove *v* show (an assertion or claim) to be incorrect
dispute *n* disagreement, argument ▷ *v* argue about (something); doubt the validity of; fight over possession of
disqualify *v* stop (someone) officially from taking part in something for wrongdoing **disqualification** *n*
disquiet *n* feeling of anxiety ▷ *v* make (someone) anxious **disquietude** *n*
disregard *v* give little or no attention to ▷ *n* lack of attention or respect
disrepair *n* condition of being worn out or in poor working order
disrepute *n* loss or lack of good reputation **disreputable** *adj* having or causing a bad reputation
disrespect *n* lack of respect **disrespectful** *adj* **disrespectfully** *adv*
disrobe *v* undress
disrupt *v* interrupt the progress of **disruption** *n* **disruptive** *adj*
dissatisfied *adj* not pleased or contented **dissatisfaction** *n*
dissect *v* cut open (a corpse) to examine it; examine critically and minutely **dissection** *n*
dissemble *v* conceal one's real motives or emotions by pretence
disseminate *v* spread (information) **dissemination** *n*
dissent *v* disagree; *Christianity* reject the doctrines of an established church ▷ *n* disagreement; *Christianity* separation from an established church **dissension** *n* **dissenter** *n*
dissertation *n* written thesis, usu required for a higher university degree; long formal speech
disservice *n* harmful action
dissident *n* person who disagrees with and criticizes the government ▷ *adj* disagreeing with the government **dissidence** *n*
dissimilar *adj* not alike, different **dissimilarity** *n*
dissimulate *v* conceal one's real feelings by pretence **dissimulation** *n*
dissipate *v* waste or squander; scatter, disappear **dissipated** *adj* showing signs of overindulgence in alcohol and other physical pleasures **dissipation** *n*
dissociate *v* regard or treat as separate **dissociate oneself from** deny or break an association with **dissociation** *n*
dissolute *adj* leading an immoral life
dissolution *n* official breaking up of an organization or institution, such as Parliament; official ending of a formal agreement, such as a marriage
dissolve *v* (cause to) become liquid; break up or end officially; break down emotionally *eg she dissolved into tears*
dissonance *n* lack of agreement or harmony **dissonant** *adj*
dissuade *v* deter (someone) by persuasion from doing something **dissuasion** *n*
distaff *n* rod on which wool etc is wound for spinning **distaff side** female side of a family

distance *n* space between two points; state of being apart; remoteness in manner **the distance** most distant part of the visible scene **distance oneself from** separate oneself mentally from **distant** *adj* far apart; separated by a specified distance; remote in manner **distantly** *adv*
distaste *n* dislike, disgust **distasteful** *adj* unpleasant, offensive
distemper[1] *n* highly contagious viral disease of dogs
distemper[2] *n* paint mixed with water, glue, etc, used for painting walls
distend *v* (of part of the body) swell **distension** *n*
distil *v* **-tilling, -tilled** subject to or obtain by distillation; give off (a substance) in drops; extract the essence of **distillation** *n* process of evaporating a liquid and condensing its vapour; (also **distillate**) concentrated essence
distiller *n* person or company that makes strong alcoholic drink, esp whisky **distillery** *n, pl* **-leries** place where a strong alcoholic drink, esp whisky, is made
distinct *adj* not the same; easily sensed or understood; clear and definite **distinctly** *adv* **distinction** *n* act of distinguishing; distinguishing feature; state of being different; special honour, recognition, or fame **distinctive** *adj* easily recognizable **distinctively** *adv* **distinctiveness** *n*
distinguish *v* (usu foll. by *between*) make, show, or recognize a difference (between); be a distinctive feature of; make out by hearing, seeing, etc **distinguishable** *adj* **distinguished** *adj* dignified in appearance; highly respected
distort *v* misrepresent (the truth or facts); twist out of shape **distortion** *n*
distract *v* draw the attention of (a person) away from something; entertain **distracted** *adj* unable to concentrate, preoccupied **distraction** *n*
distrait [diss-**tray**] *adj* absent-minded or preoccupied
distraught [diss-**trawt**] *adj* extremely anxious or agitated
distress *n* extreme unhappiness; great physical pain; poverty ▷*v* upset badly **distressed** *adj* extremely upset; in financial difficulties **distressing** *adj* **distressingly** *adv*
distribute *v* hand out or deliver; share out **distribution** *n* distributing; arrangement or spread **distributor** *n* wholesaler who distributes goods to retailers in a specific area; device in a petrol engine that sends the electric current to the spark plugs **distributive** *adj*
district *n* area of land regarded as an administrative or geographical unit **district court judge** *Aust & NZ* judge presiding over a lower court
distrust *v* regard as untrustworthy ▷*n* feeling of suspicion or doubt **distrustful** *adj*
disturb *v* intrude on; worry, make anxious; change the position or shape of **disturbance** *n* **disturbing** *adj* **disturbingly** *adv* **disturbed** *adj psychiatry* emotionally upset or maladjusted
disunite *v* cause disagreement among **disunity** *n*
disuse *n* state of being no longer

used **disused** *adj*

ditch *n* narrow channel dug in the earth for drainage or irrigation ▷*v* *slang* abandon

dither *v* be uncertain or indecisive ▷*n* state of indecision or agitation **ditherer** *n* **dithery** *adj*

ditto *n, pl* **-tos** the same ▷*adv* in the same way

ditty *n, pl* **-ties** short simple poem or song

diuretic [die-yoor-**et**-ik] *n* drug that increases the flow of urine

diurnal [die-**urn**-al] *adj* happening during the day or daily

diva *n* distinguished female singer

divan *n* low backless bed; backless sofa or couch

dive *v* **diving, dived** plunge headfirst into water; (of a submarine or diver) submerge under water; fly in a steep nose-down descending path; move quickly in a specified direction; (foll. by *in, into*) start doing (something) enthusiastically *n* diving; steep nose-down descent; *slang* disreputable bar or club **diver** *n* person who works or explores underwater; person who dives for sport **dive bomber** military aircraft designed to release bombs during a dive

diverge *v* separate and go in different directions; deviate (from a prescribed course) **divergence** *n* **divergent** *adj*

divers *adj old-fashioned* various

diverse *adj* having variety, assorted; different in kind **diversity** *n, pl* **-ties** quality of being different or varied; range of difference **diversify** *v* **-fying, -fied** **diversification** *n*

divert *v* change the direction of; entertain, distract the attention of **diversion** *n* official detour used by traffic when a main route is closed; something that distracts someone's attention; diverting; amusing pastime **diversionary** *adj*

divest *v* strip (of clothes); deprive (of a role or function)

divide *v* separate into parts; share or be shared out in parts; (cause to) disagree; keep apart, be a boundary between; calculate how many times (one number) can be contained in (another) ▷*n* division, split **dividend** *n* sum of money representing part of the profit made, paid by a company to its shareholders; extra benefit **divider** *n* screen used to divide a room into separate areas ▷*pl* compasses with two pointed arms, used for measuring or dividing lines

divine *adj* of God or a god; godlike; *Informal* splendid ▷*v* discover (something) by intuition or guessing **divinely** *adv* **divination** *n* art of discovering future events, as though by supernatural powers **divinity** *n* study of religion *pl* **-ties** god; state of being divine **divining rod** forked twig said to move when held over ground in which water or metal is to be found

division *n* dividing, sharing out; one of the parts into which something is divided; mathematical operation of dividing; difference of opinion **divisional** *adj* of a division in an organization **divisible** *adj* **divisibility** *n* **divisive** *adj* tending to cause disagreement **divisor** *n* number to be divided into another number

divorce *n* legal ending of a marriage; any separation, esp a permanent one ▷ *v* legally end one's marriage (to); separate, consider separately **divorcée** *masc*, **divorcé** *n* person who is divorced

divulge *v* make known, disclose **divulgence** *n*

Dixie *n* southern states of the US (also **Dixieland**)

DIY *Brit, Aust & NZ* do-it-yourself

dizzy *adj* **-zier, -ziest** having or causing a whirling sensation; mentally confused ▷ *v* **-zying, -zied** make dizzy **dizzily** *adv* **dizziness** *n*

DJ disc jockey; *Brit* dinner jacket

DNA *n* deoxyribonucleic acid, the main constituent of the chromosomes of all living things

do *v* **does, doing, did, done** perform or complete (a deed or action); be adequate *eg that one will do*; suit or improve *eg that style does nothing for you*; find the answer to (a problem or puzzle); cause, produce *eg it does no harm to think ahead*; give, grant *eg do me a favour*; work at, as a course of study or a job; used to form questions *eg how do you know?*; used to intensify positive statements and commands *eg I do like port; do go on*; used to form negative statements and commands *eg I do not know her well; do not get up*; used to replace an earlier verb *eg he gets paid more than I do* ▷ *n, pl* **dos, do's** *Informal* party, celebration **do away with** *v* get rid of **do-it-yourself** *n* constructing and repairing things oneself **do up** *v* fasten; decorate and repair **do with** *v* find useful or benefit from *eg I could do with a rest* **do without** *v* manage without

Doberman pinscher, Doberman *n* large dog with a black-and-tan coat

dob in *v* **dobbing, dobbed** *Aust & NZ, Informal* inform against; contribute to a fund

DOC (in New Zealand) Department of Conservation

docile *adj* (of a person or animal) easily controlled **docilely** *adv* **docility** *n*

dock¹ *n* enclosed area of water where ships are loaded, unloaded, or repaired ▷ *v* bring or be brought into dock; link (two spacecraft) or (of two spacecraft) be linked together in space **docker** *n Brit* person employed to load and unload ships **dockyard** *n* place where ships are built or repaired

dock² *v* deduct money from (a person's wages); remove part of (an animal's tail) by cutting through the bone

dock³ *n* enclosed space in a court of law where the accused person sits or stands

dock⁴ *n* weed with broad leaves

docket *n* label on a package or other delivery, stating contents, delivery instructions, etc

doctor *n* person licensed to practise medicine; person who has been awarded a doctorate ▷ *v* alter in order to deceive; poison or drug (food or drink); *Informal* castrate (an animal) **doctoral** *adj* **doctorate** *n* highest academic degree in any field of knowledge

doctrine *n* body of teachings of a religious, political, or philosophical group; principle or body of principles that is taught or advocated **doctrinal** *adj* of doctrines **doctrinaire** *adj* stubbornly insistent on the application of a theory without regard to practicality

document *n* piece of paper

providing an official record of something ▷ *v* record or report (something) in detail; support (a claim) with evidence **documentation** *n*

documentary *n, pl* **-ries** film or television programme presenting the facts about a particular subject ▷ *adj* (of evidence) based on documents

docu-soap *n* television documentary series presenting the lives of the people filmed as entertainment

dodder *v* move unsteadily **doddery** *adj*

dodecagon [doe-**deck**-a-gon] *n* geometric figure with twelve sides

dodge *v* avoid (a blow, being seen, etc) by moving suddenly; evade by cleverness or trickery ▷ *n* cunning or deceitful trick **dodgy** *adj* **dodgier, dodgiest** *Informal* dangerous, risky; untrustworthy

Dodgem *n* ® small electric car driven and bumped against similar cars in a rink at a funfair

dodger *n* person who evades by a responsibility or duty

dodo *n, pl* **dodos, dodoes** large flightless extinct bird

doe *n* female deer, hare, or rabbit

does *v* third person singular of the present tense of **do**

doesn't does not

doff *v* take off or lift (one's hat) in polite greeting

dog *n* domesticated four-legged mammal of many different breeds; related wild mammal, such as the dingo or coyote; male animal of the dog family; *Informal* person *eg you lucky dog!* ▷ *v* **dogging, dogged** follow (someone) closely; trouble, plague **go to the dogs** *Informal* go to ruin physically or morally **let sleeping dogs lie** leave things undisturbed **doggy, doggie** *n, pl* **-gies** child's word for a dog **dogcart** *n* light horse-drawn two-wheeled cart **dog collar** collar for a dog; *Informal* white collar fastened at the back, worn by members of the clergy **dog-eared** *adj* (of a book) having pages folded down at the corner; shabby, worn **dogfight** *n* close-quarters combat between fighter aircraft **dogfish** *n* small shark **doghouse** *n US* kennel **in the doghouse** *Informal* in disgrace **dogleg** *n* sharp bend **dog-roll** *n NZ* sausage-shaped roll of meat processed as dog food **dog rose** wild rose with pink or white flowers **dog-tired** *adj Informal* exhausted

doge [**doje**] *n* (formerly) chief magistrate of Venice or Genoa

dogged [**dog**-gid] *adj* obstinately determined **doggedly** *adv* **doggedness** *n*

doggerel *n* poorly written poetry, usu comic

dogging *n Brit, Informal* exhibitionist sex in parked cars, often with strangers

doggo *adv* **lie doggo** *Informal* hide and keep quiet

dogma *n* doctrine or system of doctrines proclaimed by authority as true **dogmatic** *adj* habitually stating one's opinions forcefully or arrogantly **dogmatically** *adv* **dogmatism** *n*

dogsbody *n, pl* **-bodies** *Informal* person who carries out boring tasks for others

doily *n, pl* **-lies** decorative lacy paper mat, laid on a plate

doldrums *pl n* depressed state of mind; state of inactivity

dole *n Brit, Aust & NZ, Informal*

money received from the state while unemployed ▷ *v* (foll. by *out*) distribute in small quantities
doleful *adj* dreary, unhappy **dolefully** *adv*
doll *n* small model of a human being, used as a toy; *slang* pretty girl or young woman
dollar *n* standard monetary unit of many countries
dollop *n Informal* lump (of food)
dolly *n, pl* **-lies** child's word for a doll; wheeled support on which a camera may be moved
dolman sleeve *n* sleeve that is very wide at the armhole, tapering to a tight wrist
dolmen *n* prehistoric monument consisting of a horizontal stone supported by vertical stones
dolomite *n* mineral consisting of calcium magnesium carbonate
dolorous *adj* sad, mournful
dolphin *n* sea mammal of the whale family, with a beaklike snout **dolphinarium** *n* aquarium for dolphins
dolt *n* stupid person **doltish** *adj*
domain *n* field of knowledge or activity; land under one ruler or government; *computers* group of computers with the same name on the Internet; *NZ* public park
dome *n* rounded roof built on a circular base; something shaped like this **domed** *adj*
domestic *adj* of one's own country or a specific country; of the home or family; enjoying running a home; (of an animal) kept as a pet or to produce food ▷ *n* person whose job is to do housework in someone else's house **domestically** *adv* **domesticity** *n* **domesticate** *v* bring or keep (a wild animal or plant) under control or cultivation; accustom (someone) to home life **domestication** *n* **domestic science** study of household skills
domicile [**dom**-miss-ile] *n* place where one lives
dominant *adj* having authority or influence; main, chief **dominance** *n*
dominate *v* control or govern; tower above (surroundings); be very significant in **domination** *n*
domineering *adj* forceful and arrogant
Dominican *n, adj* (friar or nun) of an order founded by Saint Dominic
dominion *n* control or authority; land governed by one ruler or government; (formerly) self-governing division of the British Empire
domino *n, pl* **-noes** small rectangular block marked with dots, used in dominoes ▷ *pl* game in which dominoes with matching halves are laid together
don[1] *v* **donning, donned** put on (clothing)
don[2] *n Brit* member of the teaching staff at a university or college; Spanish gentleman or nobleman **donnish** *adj* serious and academic
donate *v* give, esp to a charity or organization **donation** *n* donating; thing donated **donor** *n med* person who gives blood or organs for use in the treatment of another person; person who makes a donation
done *v* past participle of **do**
doner kebab *n* see **kebab**
donga [**dong**-ga] *n SAfr, Aust & NZ* steep-sided gully created by soil erosion
donkey *n* long-eared member of the horse family **donkey jacket**

Brit, Aust & NZ man's long thick jacket with a waterproof panel across the shoulders **donkey's years** *Informal* long time **donkey-work** *n* tedious hard work

don't do not

doodle *v* scribble or draw aimlessly ▷ *n* shape or picture drawn aimlessly

doom *n* death or a terrible fate ▷ *v* destine or condemn to death or a terrible fate **doomsday** *n* *Christianity* day on which the Last Judgment will occur; any dreaded day

door *n* hinged or sliding panel for closing the entrance to a building, room, etc; entrance **doormat** *n* mat for wiping dirt from shoes before going indoors; *Informal* person who offers little resistance to ill-treatment **doorway** *n* opening into a building or room

dope *n* *slang* illegal drug, usu cannabis; medicine, drug; *Informal* stupid person ▷ *v* give a drug to, esp in order to improve performance in a race **dopey, dopy** *adj* half-asleep, drowsy; *slang* silly

dorba *n* *Aust, slang* stupid, inept, or clumsy person (also **dorb**)

dork *n* *slang* stupid person

dormant *adj* temporarily quiet, inactive, or not being used **dormancy** *n*

dormer, dormer window *n* window that sticks out from a sloping roof

dormitory *n, pl* **-ries** large room, esp at a school, containing several beds

dormouse *n, pl* **-mice** small mouselike rodent with a furry tail

dorp *n* *SAfr* small town

dorsal *adj* of or on the back

dory, John Dory *n, pl* **-ries** spiny-finned edible sea fish

dose *n* specific quantity of a medicine taken at one time; *Informal* something unpleasant to experience ▷ *v* give a dose to **dosage** *n* size of a dose

doss *v* **doss down** *slang* sleep in an uncomfortable place **dosshouse** *n* *Brit & SAfr, slang* cheap lodging house for homeless people

dossier [**doss**-ee-ay] *n* collection of documents about a subject or person

dot *n* small round mark; shorter symbol used in Morse code ▷ *v* **dotting, dotted** mark with a dot; scatter, spread around **on the dot** at exactly the arranged time **dotty** *adj* *slang* rather eccentric **dotcom, dot.com** *n* company that does most of its business on the Internet

dote *v* **dote on** love to an excessive degree **dotage** *n* weakness as a result of old age

double *adj* as much again in number, amount, size, etc; composed of two equal or similar parts; designed for two users *eg double room*; folded in two ▷ *adv* twice over ▷ *n* twice the number, amount, size, etc; person who looks almost exactly like another ▷ *pl* game between two pairs of players ▷ *v* make or become twice as much or as many; bend or fold (material etc); play two parts; turn sharply **at, on the double** quickly or immediately **doubly** *adv* **double agent** spy employed by two enemy countries at the same time **double bass** stringed instrument, largest and lowest member of the violin family **double chin** fold of fat under the chin **double cream** *Brit* thick cream with a high fat content **double-cross** *v* cheat or betray ▷ *n* double-crossing **double-dealing** *n* treacherous or deceitful behaviour **double-decker** *n* bus with two passenger decks one on top of the other **double Dutch** *Informal* incomprehensible talk, gibberish **double glazing** two panes of glass in a window, fitted to reduce heat loss **double talk** deceptive or ambiguous talk **double whammy** *Informal* devastating setback made up of two elements

double entendre [**doob**-bl on-**tond**-ra] *n* word or phrase that can be interpreted in two ways, one of which is rude

doublet [**dub**-lit] *n hist* man's close-fitting jacket, with or without sleeves

doubloon *n* former Spanish gold coin

doubt *n* uncertainty about the truth, facts, or existence of something; unresolved difficulty or point ▷ *v* question the truth of; distrust or be suspicious of (someone) **doubter** *n* **doubtful** *adj* unlikely; feeling doubt **doubtfully** *adv* **doubtless** *adv* probably or certainly.

> If *doubt* is followed by a clause it is connected by *whether: I doubt whether she means it*. If it is used with a negative it is followed by *that: I don't doubt that he is sincere*

douche [**doosh**] *n* (instrument for applying) a stream of water directed onto or into the body for cleansing or medical purposes ▷ *v* cleanse or treat by means of a douche

dough *n* thick mixture of flour and water or milk, used for making bread etc; *slang* money **doughnut** *n* small cake of sweetened dough fried in deep fat

doughty [**dowt**-ee] *adj* **-tier, -tiest** *old-fashioned* brave and determined

dour [**doo**-er] *adj* sullen and unfriendly **dourness** *n*

douse [rhymes with **mouse**] *v* drench with water or other liquid; put out (a light)

dove *n* bird with a heavy body, small head, and short legs; *politics* person opposed to war **dovecote, dovecot** *n* structure for housing pigeons **dovetail** *n* joint containing wedge-shaped tenons ▷ *v* fit together neatly

dowager *n* widow possessing property or a title obtained from her husband

dowdy *adj* **-dier, -diest** dull and old-fashioned **dowdiness** *n*

dowel *n* wooden or metal peg that fits into two corresponding holes to join two adjacent parts

dower *n* life interest in a part of her husband's estate allotted to a widow by law

down[1] *prep, adv* indicating movement to or position in a lower place ▷ *adv* indicating completion of an action, lessening of intensity, etc *eg calm down* ▷ *adj* depressed, unhappy ▷ *v Informal* drink quickly **have a down on** *Informal* feel hostile towards **down under** *Informal* (in or to) Australia or New Zealand **downward** *adj, adv* (descending) from a higher to a lower level, condition, or position **downwards** *adv* from a higher to a lower level, condition, or position **down-and-out** *n* person who is homeless and destitute ▷ *adj* without any means of support **down-to-earth** *adj* sensible or practical

down² *n* soft fine feathers **downy** *adj*

downbeat *adj Informal* gloomy; *Brit, Aust & NZ* relaxed

downcast *adj* sad, dejected; (of the eyes) directed downwards

downfall *n* (cause of) a sudden loss of position or reputation

downgrade *v* reduce in importance or value

downhearted *adj* sad and discouraged

downhill *adj* going or sloping down ▷ *adv* towards the bottom of a hill

download *v* transfer (data) from the memory of one computer to that of another, especially over the Internet ▷ *n* file transferred in such a way

downpour *n* heavy fall of rain

downright *adj, adv* extreme(ly)

downs *pl n* low grassy hills, esp in S England

Down's syndrome *n* genetic disorder characterized by a flat face, slanting eyes, and mental retardation

downstairs *adv* to or on a lower floor ▷ *n* lower or ground floor

downtrodden *adj* oppressed and lacking the will to resist

dowry *n, pl* **-ries** property brought by a woman to her husband at marriage

dowse [rhymes with **cows**] *v* search for underground water or minerals using a divining rod

doxology *n, pl* **-gies** short hymn of praise to God

doyen [**doy**-en] *n* senior member of a group, profession, or society **doyenne** [doy-**en**] *n fem*

doze *v* sleep lightly or briefly ▷ *n* short sleep **dozy** *adj* **dozier, doziest** feeling sleepy; *Informal* stupid **doze off** *v* fall into a light sleep

dozen *adj, n* twelve **dozenth** *adj*

DPB (in New Zealand) Domestic Purposes Benefit

DPP (in Britain) Director of Public Prosecutions

Dr Doctor; Drive

drab *adj* **drabber, drabbest** dull and dreary **drabness** *n*

drachm [**dram**] *n Brit* one eighth of a fluid ounce

drachma *n, pl* **-mas, -mae** former monetary unit of Greece

draconian *adj* severe, harsh

draft *n* plan, sketch, or drawing of something; preliminary outline of a book, speech, etc; written order for payment of money by a bank; *US & Aust* selection for compulsory military service ▷ *v* draw up an outline or plan of; send (people) from one place to another to do a specific job; *US & Aust* select for compulsory military service

drag *v* **dragging, dragged** pull with force, esp along the ground; trail on the ground; persuade or force (oneself or someone else) to go somewhere; (foll. by *on, out*) last or be prolonged tediously; search (a river) with a dragnet or hook; *computers* move (an image) on the screen by use of the mouse ▷ *n* person or thing that slows up progress; *Informal* tedious thing or person; *slang* women's clothes worn by a man **dragnet** *n* net used to scour the bottom of a pond or river to search for something **drag race** race in which specially built cars or motorcycles are timed over a measured course

dragon *n* mythical fire-breathing monster like a huge lizard; *Informal* fierce woman **dragonfly** *n* brightly coloured insect with a long slender body and two pairs of wings

dragoon *n* heavily armed cavalryman ▷ *v* coerce, force

drain *n* pipe or channel that carries off water or sewage; cause of a continuous reduction in energy or resources ▷ *v* draw off or remove liquid from; flow away or filter off; drink the entire contents of (a glass or cup); make constant demands on (energy or resources), exhaust **drainage** *n* system of drains; process or method of draining

drake *n* male duck

dram *n* small amount of a strong alcoholic drink, esp whisky; one sixteenth of an ounce

drama *n* serious play for theatre, television, or radio; writing, producing, or acting in plays; situation that is exciting or highly emotional **dramatic** *adj* of or like drama; behaving flamboyantly **dramatically** *adv* **dramatist** *n* person who writes plays **dramatize** *v* rewrite (a book) in the form of a play; express (something) in a dramatic or exaggerated way **dramatization** *n*

drank *v* past tense of **drink**

drape *v* cover with material, usu in folds; place casually ▷ *n Aust, US & Canadian* piece of cloth hung at a window or opening as a screen **drapery** *n, pl* **-peries** fabric or clothing arranged and draped; fabrics and cloth collectively

draper *n Brit* person who sells fabrics and sewing materials

drastic *adj* strong and severe

draught *n* current of cold air, esp in an enclosed space; portion of liquid to be drunk, esp medicine; gulp or swallow; one of the flat discs used in the game of draughts ▷ *pl* game for two players using a chessboard and twelve draughts each ▷ *adj* (of an animal) used for pulling heavy loads **draughty** *adj* exposed to draughts of air **draughtsman** *n* person employed to prepare detailed scale drawings of machinery, buildings, etc **draughtsmanship** *n* **draught beer** beer stored in a cask

draw *v* **drawing, drew, drawn** sketch (a figure, picture, etc) with a pencil or pen; pull (a person or thing) closer to or further away from a place; move in a specified direction *eg the car drew near*; take from a source *eg draw money from bank accounts*; attract, interest; formulate or decide *eg to draw conclusions*; (of two teams or contestants) finish a game with an equal number of points ▷ *n* raffle or lottery; contest or game ending in a tie; event, act, etc, that attracts a large audience **drawing** *n* picture or plan made by means of lines on a surface; art of making drawings **drawing pin** short tack with a broad smooth head **drawing room** *old-fashioned* room where visitors are received and entertained **drawback** *n* disadvantage **drawbridge** *n* bridge that may be raised to prevent access or to enable vessels to pass **draw out** *v* encourage (someone) to talk freely; make longer **drawstring** *n* cord run through a hem around an opening, so that when it is pulled tighter, the opening closes **draw up** *v* prepare and write out (a contract); (of a vehicle) come to a stop

drawer *n* sliding box-shaped part of a piece of furniture, used for storage ▷ *pl old-fashioned* undergarment worn on the lower part of the body

drawl *v* speak slowly, with long vowel sounds ▷ *n* drawling manner of speech

drawn *v* past participle of **draw** ▷ *adj* haggard, tired, or tense in appearance

dray *n* low cart used for carrying heavy loads

dread *v* anticipate with apprehension or fear ▷ *n* great fear **dreadful** *adj* very disagreeable or shocking; extreme **dreadfully** *adv*

dreadlocks *pl n* hair worn in the Rastafarian style of tightly twisted strands

dream *n* imagined series of events experienced in the mind while asleep; cherished hope; *Informal* wonderful person or thing ▷ *v* **dreaming, dreamed** *or* **dreamt** see imaginary pictures in the mind while asleep; (often foll. by *of*, *about*) have an image (of) or fantasy (about); (foll. by *of*) consider the possibility (of) ▷ *adj* ideal *eg a dream house* **dreamer** *n* **dreamy** *adj* vague or impractical; *Informal* wonderful **dreamily** *adv*

dreary *adj* **drearier, dreariest** dull, boring **drearily** *adv* **dreariness** *n*

dredge[1] *v* clear or search (a river bed or harbour) by removing silt or mud **dredger** *n* boat fitted with machinery for dredging

dredge[2] *v* sprinkle (food) with flour etc

dregs *pl n* solid particles that settle at the bottom of some liquids; most despised elements

drench *v* make completely wet

dress *n* one-piece garment for a woman or girl, consisting of a skirt and bodice and sometimes sleeves; complete style of clothing ▷ *v* put clothes on; put on formal clothes; apply a protective covering to (a wound); arrange or prepare **dressing** *n* sauce for salad; covering for a wound **dressing-down** *n Informal* severe scolding **dressing gown** coat-shaped garment worn over pyjamas or nightdress **dressing room** room used for changing clothes, esp backstage in a theatre **dressy** *adj* (of clothes) elegant **dress circle** first gallery in a theatre **dressmaker** *n* person who makes women's clothes **dressmaking** *n* **dress rehearsal** last rehearsal of a play or show, using costumes, lighting, etc

dressage [**dress**-ahzh] *n* training of a horse to perform manoeuvres in response to the rider's body signals

dresser[1] *n* piece of furniture with shelves and with cupboards, for storing or displaying dishes

dresser[2] *n theatre* person employed to assist actors with their costumes

drew *v* past tense of **draw**

drey *n* squirrel's nest

dribble *v* (allow to) flow in drops; allow saliva to trickle from the mouth; *sport* propel (a ball) by repeatedly tapping it with the foot, hand, or a stick ▷ *n* small quantity of liquid falling in drops **dribbler** *n*

dried *v* past of **dry**

drier[1] *adj* a comparative of **dry**

drier[2] *n* same as **dryer**

driest *adj* a superlative of **dry**

drift *v* be carried along by currents of air or water; move aimlessly from one place or activity to another ▷ *n* something piled up by the wind or current, such as a snowdrift;

general movement or development; point, meaning *eg catch my drift?* **drifter** *n* person who moves aimlessly from place to place or job to job **driftwood** *n* wood floating on or washed ashore by the sea

drill[1] *n* tool or machine for boring holes; strict and often repetitious training; *Informal* correct procedure ▷*v* bore a hole in (something) with or as if with a drill; teach by rigorous exercises or training

drill[2] *n* machine for sowing seed in rows; small furrow for seed

drill[3] *n* hard-wearing cotton cloth

drily *adv* see **dry**

drink *v* **drinking, drank, drunk** swallow (a liquid); consume alcohol, esp to excess ▷*n* (portion of) a liquid suitable for drinking; alcohol, or its habitual or excessive consumption **drinkable** *adj* **drinker** *n* **drink in** *v* pay close attention to **drink to** *v* drink a toast to

drip *v* **dripping, dripped** (let) fall in drops ▷*n* falling of drops of liquid; sound made by falling drops; *Informal* weak dull person; *med* device by which a solution is passed in small drops through a tube into a vein **drip-dry** *adj* denoting clothing that will dry free of creases if hung up when wet

dripping *n* fat that comes from meat while it is being roasted or fried

drive *v* **driving, drove, driven** guide the movement of (a vehicle); transport in a vehicle; goad into a specified state; push or propel; *sport* hit (a ball) very hard and straight ▷*n* journey by car, van, etc; (also **driveway**) path for vehicles connecting a building to a public road; united effort towards a common goal; energy and ambition; *psychol* motive or interest *eg sex drive;* means by which power is transmitted in a mechanism **drive at** *v* *Informal* intend or mean *eg what was he driving at?* **drive-in** *adj, n* (denoting) a cinema, restaurant, etc, used by people in their cars

drivel *n* foolish talk ▷*v* **-elling, -elled** speak foolishly

driver *n* person who drives a vehicle

drizzle *n* very light rain ▷*v* rain lightly **drizzly** *adj*

droll *adj* quaintly amusing **drolly** *adv* **drollery** *n*

dromedary [**drom**-mid-er-ee] *n, pl* **-daries** camel with a single hump

drone[1] *n* male bee

drone[2] *v, n* (make) a monotonous low dull sound **drone on** *v* talk for a long time in a monotonous tone

drongo *n, pl* **-gos** tropical songbird with a glossy black plumage, a forked tail, and a stout bill

drool *v* (foll. by *over*) show excessive enthusiasm (for); allow saliva to flow from the mouth

droop *v* hang downwards loosely **droopy** *adj*

drop *v* **dropping, dropped** (allow to) fall vertically; decrease in amount, strength, or value; mention (a hint or name) casually; discontinue ▷*n* small quantity of liquid forming a round shape; any small quantity of liquid; decrease in amount, strength, or value; vertical distance that something may fall ▷*pl* liquid medication applied in small drops **droplet** *n* **droppings** *pl n* faeces of certain animals, such as rabbits or birds **drop in, by** *v* pay someone a casual visit **drop off** *v Informal* fall asleep; grow smaller or less **dropout** *n* person who rejects conventional society; person who does not complete a course of study **drop out (of)** *v* abandon or withdraw from (a school, job, etc)

dropsy *n* illness in which watery fluid collects in the body

dross *n* scum formed on the surfaces of molten metals; anything worthless

drought *n* prolonged shortage of rainfall

drove[1] *v* past tense of **drive**

drove[2] *n* very large group, esp of people **drover** *n* person who drives sheep or cattle

drown *v* die or kill by immersion in liquid; forget (one's sorrows) temporarily by drinking alcohol; drench thoroughly; make (a sound) inaudible by being louder

drowse *v* be sleepy, dull, or sluggish **drowsy** *adj* **drowsily** *adv* **drowsiness** *n*

drubbing *n* utter defeat in a contest etc

drudge *n* person who works hard at uninteresting tasks **drudgery** *n*

drug *n* substance used in the treatment or prevention of disease; chemical substance, esp a narcotic, taken for the effects it produces ▷ *v* **drugging, drugged** give a drug to (a person or animal) to cause sleepiness or unconsciousness; mix a drug with (food or drink) **drugstore** *n US* pharmacy where a wide range of goods are available

Druid *n* member of an ancient order of Celtic priests **Druidic, Druidical** *adj*

drum *n* percussion instrument sounded by striking a membrane stretched across the opening of a hollow cylinder; cylindrical object or container ▷ *v* **drumming, drummed** play (music) on a drum; tap rhythmically or regularly **drum into** *v* instil into (someone) by constant repetition **drumstick** *n* stick used for playing a drum; lower joint of the leg of a cooked chicken etc **drum up** *v* obtain (support or business) by making requests or canvassing

drummer *n* person who plays a drum or drums

drunk *v* past participle of **drink** ▷ *adj* intoxicated with alcohol to the extent of losing control over normal functions; overwhelmed by a strong influence or emotion ▷ *n* person who is drunk or who frequently gets drunk **drunkard** *n* person who frequently gets drunk **drunken** *adj* drunk or frequently drunk; caused by or relating to alcoholic intoxication **drunkenly** *adv* **drunkenness** *n*

dry *adj* **drier, driest** *or* **dryer, dryest** lacking moisture; having little or no rainfall; *Informal* thirsty; (of wine) not sweet; uninteresting; (of humour) subtle and sarcastic; prohibiting the sale of alcohol *eg a dry town* ▷ *v* **drying, dried** make or become dry; preserve (food) by removing the moisture **drily, dryly** *adv* **dryness** *n* **dryer** *n* apparatus for removing moisture **dry-clean** *v* clean (clothes etc) with chemicals rather than water **dry-cleaner** *n* **dry-cleaning** *n* **dry out** *v* make or become dry; (cause to) undergo treatment for alcoholism **dry rot** crumbling and drying of timber, caused by certain fungi **dry run** *Informal* rehearsal **dry stock** *NZ* cattle raised for meat

dryad *n* wood nymph
DSS (in Britain) Department of Social Security
dual *adj* having two parts, functions, or aspects **duality** *n* **dual carriageway** *Brit, Aust & NZ* road on which traffic travelling in opposite directions is separated by a central strip of grass or concrete
dub[1] *v* **dubbing, dubbed** give (a person or place) a name or nickname
dub[2] *v* **dubbing, dubbed** provide (a film) with a new soundtrack, esp in a different language; provide (a film or tape) with a soundtrack
dubbin *n Brit* thick grease applied to leather to soften and waterproof it
dubious [**dew**-bee-uss] *adj* feeling or causing doubt **dubiously** *adv* **dubiety** [dew-**by**-it-ee] *n*
ducal [**duke**-al] *adj* of a duke
ducat [**duck**-it] *n* former European gold or silver coin
duchess *n* woman who holds the rank of duke; wife or widow of a duke
duchesse *n NZ* dressing table with a mirror
duchy *n, pl* **duchies** territory of a duke or duchess
duck[1] *n* water bird with short legs, webbed feet, and a broad blunt bill; its flesh, used as food; female of this bird; *cricket* score of nothing **duckling** *n* baby duck
duck[2] *v* move (the head or body) quickly downwards, to avoid being seen or to dodge a blow; plunge suddenly under water; *Informal* dodge (a duty or responsibility)
duct *n* tube, pipe, or channel through which liquid or gas is conveyed; bodily passage conveying secretions or excretions
ductile *adj* (of a metal) able to be shaped into sheets or wires
dud *Informal* ▷ *n* ineffectual person or thing ▷ *adj* bad or useless
dude *n US, Informal* man; *old-fashioned* dandy; any person
dudgeon *n* **in high dudgeon** angry, resentful
due *adj* expected or scheduled to be present or arrive; owed as a debt; fitting, proper ▷ *n* something that is owed or required ▷ *pl* charges for membership of a club or organization ▷ *adv* directly or exactly *eg due south* **due to** attributable to or caused by.

> The use of *due to* as a compound preposition as in *the performance has been cancelled due to bad weather* was formerly considered incorrect, but is now acceptable

duel *n* formal fight with deadly weapons between two people, to settle a quarrel ▷ *v* **duelling, duelled** fight in a duel **duellist** *n*
duet *n* piece of music for two performers
duff *adj Chiefly Brit* broken or useless **duff up** *v Brit, Informal* beat (someone) severely
duffel, duffle *n* short for **duffel coat** **duffel bag** cylindrical canvas bag fastened with a drawstring **duffel coat** wool coat with toggle fastenings, usu with a hood
duffer *n Informal* dull or incompetent person
dug[1] *v* past of **dig**
dug[2] *n* teat or udder
dugite [**doo**-gyte] *n* medium-sized Australian venomous snake
dugong *n* whalelike mammal of tropical waters
dugout *n Brit* (at a sports ground) covered bench where managers and substitutes sit; canoe made by

hollowing out a log; *mil* covered excavation to provide shelter

duke *n* nobleman of the highest rank; prince or ruler of a small principality or duchy **dukedom** *n*

dulcet [**dull**-sit] *adj* (of a sound) soothing or pleasant

dulcimer *n* tuned percussion instrument consisting of a set of strings stretched over a sounding board and struck with hammers

dull *adj* not interesting; (of an ache) not acute; (of weather) not bright or clear; lacking in spirit; not very intelligent; (of a blade) not sharp ▷*v* make or become dull **dullness** *n* **dully** *adv* **dullard** *n* dull or stupid person

duly *adv* in a proper manner; at the proper time

dumb *adj* lacking the power to speak; silent; *Informal* stupid **dumbly** *adv* **dumbness** *n* **dumbbell** *n* short bar with a heavy ball or disc at each end, used for physical exercise **dumbfounded** *adj* speechless with astonishment **dumb down** make less intellectually demanding or sophisticated **dumb show** meaningful gestures without speech

dumdum *n* soft-nosed bullet that expands on impact and causes serious wounds

dummy *n, pl* **-mies** figure representing the human form, used for displaying clothes etc; copy of an object, often lacking some essential feature of the original; rubber teat for a baby to suck; *slang* stupid person ▷*adj* imitation, substitute **dummy run** rehearsal

dump *v* drop or let fall in a careless manner; *Informal* get rid of (someone or something no longer wanted) ▷*n* place where waste materials are left; *Informal* dirty unattractive place; *mil* place where weapons or supplies are stored **down in the dumps** *Informal* depressed and miserable

dumpling *n* small ball of dough cooked and served with stew; round pastry case filled with fruit

dumpy *adj* **dumpier, dumpiest** short and plump

dun *adj* brownish-grey

dunce *n* person who is stupid or slow to learn

dunderhead *n* slow-witted person

dune *n* mound or ridge of drifted sand

dung *n* faeces from animals such as cattle

dungarees *pl n* trousers with a bib attached

dungeon *n* underground prison cell

dunk *v* dip (a biscuit or bread) in a drink or soup before eating it; put (something) in liquid

dunny *n, pl* **-nies** *Aust & old-fashioned NZ, Informal* toilet

duo *n, pl* **duos** pair of performers; *Informal* pair of closely connected people

duodenum [dew-oh-**deen**-um] *n, pl* **-na, -nums** first part of the small intestine, just below the stomach **duodenal** *adj*

dupe *v* deceive or cheat ▷*n* person who is easily deceived

duple *adj music* having two beats in a bar

duplex *n Chiefly US* apartment on two floors

duplicate *adj* copied exactly from an original ▷*n* exact copy ▷*v* make an exact copy of; do again (something that has already been

done) **duplication** *n* **duplicator** *n*
duplicity *n* deceitful behaviour
durable *adj* long-lasting **durability** *n* **durable goods, durables** *pl n* goods that require infrequent replacement
duration *n* length of time that something lasts
duress *n* compulsion by use of force or threats
during *prep* throughout or within the limit of (a period of time)
dusk *n* time just before nightfall, when it is almost dark **dusky** *adj* dark in colour; shadowy
dust *n* small dry particles of earth, sand, or dirt ▷*v* remove dust from (furniture) by wiping; sprinkle (something) with a powdery substance **duster** *n* cloth used for dusting **dusty** *adj* covered with dust **dustbin** *n* large container for household rubbish **dust bowl** dry area in which the surface soil is exposed to wind erosion **dust jacket** removable paper cover used to protect a book **dustman** *n Brit* man whose job is to collect household rubbish **dustpan** *n* short-handled shovel into which dust is swept from floors
Dutch *adj* of the Netherlands **go Dutch** *Informal* share the expenses on an outing **Dutch courage** false courage gained from drinking alcohol
duty *n, pl* **-ties** work or a task performed as part of one's job; task that a person feels morally bound to do; government tax on imports **on duty** at work **dutiable** *adj* (of goods) requiring payment of duty **dutiful** *adj* doing what is expected **dutifully** *adv*
duvet [doo-vay] *n* kind of quilt used in bed instead of a top sheet and blankets
DVD Digital Versatile (or Video) Disk
DVT deep-vein thrombosis
dwang *n NZ & SAfr* short piece of wood inserted in a timber-framed wall
dwarf *n, pl* **dwarfs, dwarves** person who is smaller than average; (in folklore) small ugly manlike creature, often possessing magical powers ▷*adj* (of an animal or plant) much smaller than the usual size for the species ▷*v* cause (someone or something) to seem small by being much larger
dwell *v* **dwelling, dwelt** *or* **dwelled** live, reside **dwelling** *n* place of residence **dwell on, upon** *v* think, speak, or write at length about
dweller *n* person who lives in a specified place *eg city dweller*
dwindle *v* grow less in size, strength, or number
dye *n* colouring substance; colour produced by dyeing ▷*v* **dyeing, dyed** colour (hair or fabric) by applying a dye **dyer** *n* **dyed-in-the-wool** *adj* uncompromising or unchanging in opinion
dying *v* present participle of **die**[1]
dyke[1] *n* wall built to prevent flooding
dyke[2] *n slang* lesbian
dynamic *adj* full of energy, ambition, and new ideas; *physics* of energy or forces that produce motion **dynamically** *adv* **dynamism** *n* great energy and enthusiasm
dynamics *n* branch of mechanics concerned with the forces that change or produce the motions of bodies ▷*pl* forces that produce

change in a system

dynamite *n* explosive made of nitroglycerine; *Informal* dangerous or exciting person or thing ▷ *v* blow (something) up with dynamite

dynamo *n, pl* **-mos** device for converting mechanical energy into electrical energy

dynasty *n, pl* **-ties** sequence of hereditary rulers **dynastic** *adj*

dysentery *n* infection of the intestine causing severe diarrhoea

dysfunction *n med* disturbance or abnormality in the function of an organ or part **dysfunctional** *adj*

dyslexia *n* disorder causing impaired ability to read **dyslexic** *adj*

dysmenorrhoea *n* painful menstruation

dyspepsia *n* indigestion **dyspeptic** *adj*

dystrophy [**diss**-trof-fee] *n* see **muscular dystrophy**

e

E East(ern) ▷ *n, pl* **Es** *or* **E's** *slang* ecstasy (the drug)

e- *prefix* electronic *eg e-mail*

each *adj, pron* every (one) taken separately

eager *adj* showing or feeling great desire, keen **eagerly** *adv* **eagerness** *n*

eagle *n* large bird of prey with keen eyesight; *golf* score of two strokes under par for a hole **eaglet** *n* young eagle

ear[1] *n* organ of hearing, esp the external part of it; sensitivity to musical or other sounds **earache** *n* pain in the ear **earbash** *v Aust & NZ, Informal* talk incessantly **earbashing** *n* **eardrum** *n* thin piece of skin inside the ear which enables one to hear sounds **earmark** *v* set (something) aside for a specific purpose **earphone** *n* receiver for a radio etc, held to or put in the ear **earring** *n* ornament for the lobe of the ear **earshot** *n* hearing range

ear² *n* head of corn

earl *n* British nobleman ranking next below a marquess **earldom** *n*

early *adj, adv* **-lier, -liest** before the expected or usual time; in the first part of a period; in a period far back in time

earn *v* obtain by work or merit; (of investments etc) gain (interest) **earnings** *pl n* money earned

earnest¹ *adj* serious and sincere **in earnest** seriously **earnestly** *adv*

earnest² *n* part payment given in advance, esp to confirm a contract

earth *n* planet that we live on; land, the ground; soil; fox's hole; wire connecting an electrical apparatus with the earth ▷ *v* connect (a circuit) to earth **earthen** *adj* made of baked clay or earth **earthenware** *n* pottery made of baked clay **earthly** *adj* conceivable or possible **earthy** *adj* coarse or crude; of or like earth **earthquake** *n* violent vibration of the earth's surface **earthwork** *n* fortification made of earth **earthworm** *n* worm which burrows in the soil

earwig *n* small insect with a pincer-like tail

ease *n* freedom from difficulty, discomfort, or worry; rest or leisure ▷ *v* give bodily or mental ease to; lessen (severity, tension, pain, etc); move carefully or gradually

easel *n* frame to support an artist's canvas or a blackboard

east *n* (direction towards) the part of the horizon where the sun rises; region lying in this direction ▷ *adj* to or in the east; (of a wind) from the east ▷ *adv* in, to, or towards the east **easterly** *adj* **eastern** *adj* **eastward** *adj, adv* **eastwards** *adv*

Easter *n* Christian spring festival commemorating the Resurrection of Jesus Christ **Easter egg** chocolate egg given at Easter

easy *adj* **easier, easiest** not needing much work or effort; free from pain, care, or anxiety; easy-going **easily** *adv* **easiness** *n* **easy chair** comfortable armchair **easy-going** *adj* relaxed in attitude, tolerant

eat *v* **eating, ate, eaten** take (food) into the mouth and swallow it; have a meal; (foll. by *away, up*) destroy **eatable** *adj* fit or suitable for eating

eau de Cologne [**oh** de kol-**lone**] *n* *French* light perfume

eaves *pl n* overhanging edges of a roof

eavesdrop *v* **-dropping, -dropped** listen secretly to a private conversation **eavesdropper** *n* **eavesdropping** *n*

ebb *v* (of tide water) flow back; fall away or decline ▷ *n* flowing back of the tide **at a low ebb** in a state of weakness

ebony *n, pl* **-onies** hard black wood ▷ *adj* deep black

ebullient *adj* full of enthusiasm or excitement **ebullience** *n*

EC European Commission; European Community: a former name for the European Union

eccentric *adj* odd or unconventional; (of circles) not having the same centre ▷ *n* eccentric person **eccentrically** *adv* **eccentricity** *n*

ecclesiastic *n* member of the clergy ▷ *adj* (also **ecclesiastical**) of the Christian Church or clergy

ECG electrocardiogram

echelon [**esh**-a-lon] *n* level of power or responsibility; *mil* formation in which units follow one another but are spaced out sideways to allow each a line of fire ahead

echidna [ik-**kid**-na] *n, pl* **-nas, -nae** [-nee] Australian spiny egg-laying mammal (also **spiny anteater**)

echo *n, pl* **-oes** repetition of sounds by reflection of sound waves off a surface; close imitation ▷ *v* **-oing, -oed** repeat or be repeated as an echo; imitate (what someone else has said) **echo sounder** sonar

éclair *n* finger-shaped pastry filled with cream and covered with chocolate

éclat [ake-**lah**] *n* brilliant success; splendour

eclectic *adj* selecting from various styles, ideas, or sources **eclecticism** *n*

eclipse *n* temporary obscuring of one star or planet by another ▷ *v* surpass or outclass **ecliptic** *n* apparent path of the sun

ecological *adj* of ecology; intended to protect the environment **ecologically** *adv* **ecology** *n* study of the relationships between living things and their environment **ecologist** *n*

e-commerce, ecommerce *n* business transactions done on the Internet

economy *n, pl* **-mies** system of interrelationship of money, industry, and employment in a country; careful use of money or resources to avoid waste **economic** *adj* of economics; profitable; *Informal* inexpensive or cheap **economics** *n* social science concerned with the production and consumption of goods and services ▷ *pl* financial aspects **economical** *adj* not wasteful, thrifty **economically** *adv* **economist** *n* specialist in economics **economize** *v* reduce expense or waste **economic migrant** person emigrating to improve his or her standard of living

ecosystem *n* system involving interactions between a community and its environment

ecru *adj* pale creamy-brown

ecstasy *n* state of intense delight; *slang* powerful drug that can produce hallucinations **ecstatic** *adj* **ecstatically** *adv*

> SPELLING People get confused about how many *cs* there are in **ecstasy**. Collins Word Web has 119 occurrences of *ecstacy*, but 3379 of the correct spelling **ecstasy**

ectoplasm *n spiritualism* substance that supposedly is emitted from the body of a medium during a trance

ecumenical *adj* of the Christian Church throughout the world, esp with regard to its unity

eczema [**ek**-sim-a] *n* skin disease causing intense itching

Edam *n* round Dutch cheese with a red waxy cover

eddy *n, pl* **eddies** circular movement of air, water, etc ▷ *v* **eddying, eddied** move with a circular motion

edelweiss [**ade**-el-vice] *n* alpine plant with white flowers

Eden *n Bible* garden in which Adam and Eve were placed at the Creation

edge *n* border or line where something ends or begins; cutting side of a blade; sharpness of tone ▷ *v* provide an edge or border for;

push (one's way) gradually **have the edge on** have an advantage over **on edge** nervous or irritable **edgeways** *adv* with the edge forwards or uppermost **edging** *n* anything placed along an edge to finish it **edgy** *adj* nervous or irritable

edible *adj* fit to be eaten **edibility** *n*

edict [**ee**-dikt] *n* order issued by an authority

edifice [**ed**-if-iss] *n* large building

edify [**ed**-if-fie] *v* **-fying, -fied** improve morally by instruction **edification** *n*

edit *v* prepare (a book, film, etc) for publication or broadcast **edition** *n* number of copies of a new publication printed at one time **editor** *n* person who edits; person in charge of one section of a newspaper or magazine **editorial** *n* newspaper article stating the opinion of the editor ▷ *adj* of editing or editors

educate *v* teach; provide schooling for **education** *n* **educational** *adj* **educationally** *adv* **educationalist** *n* expert in the theory of education **educative** *adj* educating

Edwardian *adj* of the reign of King Edward VII of Great Britain and Ireland (1901–10)

EEG electroencephalogram

eel *n* snakelike fish

eerie *adj* **eerier, eeriest** uncannily frightening or disturbing **eerily** *adv*

efface *v* remove by rubbing; make (oneself) inconspicuous **effacement** *n*

effect *n* change or result caused by someone or something; condition of being operative *eg the law comes into effect next month*; overall impression ▷ *pl* personal belongings; lighting, sounds, etc to accompany a film or a broadcast ▷ *v* cause to happen, accomplish **effective** *adj* producing a desired result; operative; impressive **effectively** *adv* **effectual** *adj* producing the intended result **effectually** *adv*

effeminate *adj* (of a man) displaying characteristics thought to be typical of a woman **effeminacy** *n*

effervescent *adj* (of a liquid) giving off bubbles of gas; (of a person) lively and enthusiastic **effervescence** *n*

effete [if-**feet**] *adj* powerless, feeble

efficacious *adj* producing the intended result **efficacy** *n*

efficient *adj* functioning effectively with little waste of effort **efficiently** *adv* **efficiency** *n*

effigy [**ef**-fij-ee] *n, pl* **-gies** image or likeness of a person

efflorescence *n* flowering

effluent *n* liquid discharged as waste

effluvium *n, pl* **-via** unpleasant smell, as of decaying matter or gaseous waste

effort *n* physical or mental exertion; attempt **effortless** *adj*

effrontery *n* brazen impudence

effusion *n* unrestrained outburst **effusive** *adj* openly emotional, demonstrative **effusively** *adv*

EFTA European Free Trade Association

eg for example

egalitarian *adj* upholding the equality of all people ▷ *n* person who holds egalitarian beliefs **egalitarianism** *n*

egg[1] *n* oval or round object laid by the females of birds and other creatures, containing a developing embryo; hen's egg used as food; (also **egg cell**) ovum **egghead** *n Informal* intellectual person **eggplant** *n US, Canadian, Aust & NZ* dark purple tropical fruit, cooked and eaten as a vegetable

egg[2] *v* **egg on** encourage or incite, esp to do wrong

ego *n, pl* **egos** the conscious mind of an individual; self-esteem **egoism, egotism** *n* excessive concern for one's own interests; excessively high opinion of oneself **egotist, egoist** *n* **egotistic, egoistic** *adj* **egocentric** *adj* self-centred

egregious [ig-**greej**-uss] *adj* outstandingly bad

egress [**ee**-gress] *n* departure; way out

egret [**ee**-grit] *n* lesser white heron

Egyptology *n* study of the culture of ancient Egypt

eider *n* Arctic duck **eiderdown** *n* quilt (orig stuffed with eider feathers)

eight *adj, n* one more than seven ▷*n* eight-oared boat; its crew **eighth** *adj, n* (of) number eight in a series **eighteen** *adj, n* eight and ten **eighteenth** *adj, n* **eighty** *adj, n* eight times ten **eightieth** *adj, n*

eisteddfod [ice-**sted**-fod] *n* Welsh festival with competitions in music and other performing arts

either *adj, pron* one or the other (of two); each of two ▷*conj* used preceding two or more possibilities joined by *or* ▷*adv* likewise *eg I don't eat meat and he doesn't either*

ejaculate *v* eject (semen); utter abruptly **ejaculation** *n*

eject *v* force out, expel **ejection** *n* **ejector** *n*

eke out *v* make (a supply) last by frugal use; make (a living) with difficulty

elaborate *adj* with a lot of fine detail ▷*v* expand upon **elaboration** *n*

élan [ale-**an**] *n* style and vigour

eland [**eel**-and] *n* large antelope of southern Africa

elapse *v* (of time) pass by

elastic *adj* resuming normal shape after distortion; adapting easily to change ▷*n* tape or fabric containing interwoven strands of flexible rubber **elasticity** *n*

elated *v* extremely happy and excited **elation** *n*

elbow *n* joint between the upper arm and the forearm ▷*v* shove or strike with the elbow **elbow grease** vigorous physical labour **elbow room** sufficient room to move freely

elder[1] *adj* older ▷*n* older person; (in certain Protestant Churches) lay officer **elderly** *adj* (fairly) old **eldest** *adj* oldest

elder[2] *n* small tree with white flowers and black berries

El Dorado [el dor-**rah**-doe] *n* fictitious country rich in gold

eldritch *adj Scot* weird, uncanny

elect *v* choose by voting; decide (to do something) ▷*adj* appointed but not yet in office *eg president elect* **election** *n* choosing of representatives by voting; act of choosing **electioneering** *n* active participation in a political campaign **elective** *adj* chosen by election; optional **elector** *n* someone who has the right to vote in an election **electoral** *adj* **electorate** *n* people who have the right to vote

electricity *n* form of energy associated with stationary or moving electrons or other charged particles; electric current or charge **electric** *adj* produced by, transmitting, or powered by electricity; exciting or tense **electrical** *adj* using or concerning electricity **electrician** *n* person trained to install and repair electrical equipment **electrics** *pl n Brit* electric appliances **electric chair** *US* chair in which criminals who have been sentenced to death are electrocuted

electrify *v* **-fying, -fied** adapt for operation by electric power; charge with electricity; startle or excite intensely **electrification** *n*

electro- *combining form* operated by or caused by electricity

electrocardiograph *n* instrument for recording the electrical activity of the heart **electrocardiogram** *n* tracing produced by this

electrocute *v* kill or injure by electricity **electrocution** *n*

electrode *n* conductor through which an electric current enters or leaves a battery, vacuum tube, etc

electrodynamics *n* branch of physics concerned with the interactions between electrical and mechanical forces

electroencephalograph [ill-lek-tro-en-**sef**-a-loh-graf] *n* instrument for recording the electrical activity of the brain **electroencephalogram** *n* tracing produced by this

electrolysis [ill-lek-**troll**-iss-iss] *n* conduction of electricity by an electrolyte, esp to induce chemical change; destruction of living tissue such as hair roots by an electric current

electrolyte *n* solution or molten substance that conducts electricity **electrolytic** *adj*

electromagnet *n* magnet containing a coil of wire through which an electric current is passed

electromagnetic *adj* of or operated by an electomagnet **electromagnetism** *n*

electron *n* elementary particle in all atoms that has a negative electrical charge **electron microscope** microscope that uses electrons, rather than light, to produce a magnified image **electronvolt** *n* unit of energy used in nuclear physics

electronic *adj* (of a device) dependent on the action of electrons; (of a process) using electronic devices **electronic mail** see **e-mail** **electronics** *n* technology concerned with the development of electronic devices and circuits

electroplate *v* coat with silver etc by electrolysis

elegant *adj* pleasing or graceful in dress, style, or design **elegance** *n*

elegy [**el**-lij-ee] *n, pl* **-egies** mournful poem, esp a lament for the dead **elegiac** *adj* mournful or plaintive

element *n* component part; substance which cannot be separated into other substances by ordinary chemical techniques; section of people within a larger group *eg the rowdy element*; heating wire in an electric kettle, stove, etc ▷ *pl* basic principles of something; weather conditions, esp wind, rain, and cold **in one's element** in a situation where one is happiest **elemental** *adj* of primitive natural forces or passions **elementary** *adj* simple and straightforward

elephant *n* huge four-footed thick-skinned animal with ivory tusks and a long trunk **elephantine** *adj* unwieldy, clumsy **elephantiasis** [el-lee-fan-**tie**-a-siss] *n* disease with hardening of the skin and enlargement of the legs etc

elevate *v* raise in rank or status; lift up **elevation** *n* raising; height above sea level; scale drawing of one side of a building **elevator** *n Aust, US & Canadian* lift for carrying people

eleven *adj, n* one more than ten ▷ *n sport* team of eleven people **eleventh** *adj, n* (of) number eleven in a series **elevenses** *n Brit & SAfr, Informal* mid-morning snack

elf *n, pl* **elves** (in folklore) small mischievous fairy **elfin** *adj* small and delicate

elicit *v* bring about (a response or reaction); find out (information) by careful questioning

elide *v* omit (a vowel or syllable) from a spoken word **elision** *n*

eligible *adj* meeting the requirements or qualifications needed; desirable as a spouse **eligibility** *n*

eliminate *v* get rid of **elimination** *n*

elite [ill-**eet**] *n* most powerful, rich, or gifted members of a group **elitism** *n* belief that society should be governed by a small group of superior people **elitist** *n, adj*

elixir [ill-**ix**-er] *n* imaginary liquid that can prolong life or turn base metals into gold

Elizabethan *adj* of the reign of Elizabeth I of England (1558–1603)

elk *n* large deer of N Europe and Asia

ellipse *n* oval shape **elliptical** *adj* oval-shaped; (of speech or writing) obscure or ambiguous

ellipsis *n, pl* **-ses** omission of letters or words in a sentence

elm *n* tree with serrated leaves

elocution *n* art of speaking clearly in public

elongate [**eel**-long-gate] *v* make or become longer **elongation** *n*

elope *v* (of two people) run away secretly to get married **elopement** *n*

eloquence *n* fluent powerful use of language **eloquent** *adj* **eloquently** *adv*

else *adv* in addition or more *eg what else can I do?*; other or different *eg it was unlike anything else that had happened* **elsewhere** *adv* in or to another place

elucidate *v* make (something difficult) clear **elucidation** *n*

elude *v* escape from by cleverness or quickness; baffle **elusive** *adj* difficult to catch or remember

elver *n* young eel

elves *n* plural of **elf**

emaciated [im-**mace**-ee-ate-id] *adj* abnormally thin **emaciation** *n*

e-mail, email *n* (also **electronic mail**) sending of messages between computer terminals ▷ *v* communicate in this way

emanate [**em**-a-nate] *v* issue, proceed from a source **emanation** *n*

emancipate *v* free from social, political, or legal restraints **emancipation** *n*

emasculate *v* deprive of power **emasculation** *n*

embalm *v* preserve (a corpse) from decay by the use of chemicals etc

embankment *n* man-made ridge that carries a road or railway or

holds back water
embargo *n, pl* **-goes** order by a government prohibiting trade with a country ▷ *v* **-going, -goed** put an embargo on
embark *v* board a ship or aircraft; (foll. by *on*) begin (a new project) **embarkation** *n*
embarrass *v* cause to feel self-conscious or ashamed **embarrassed** *adj* **embarrassing** *adj* **embarrassment** *n*

SPELLING There are 32 examples of the misspelling *embarras* in Collins Word Web and another mistake, *embarassment*, occurs 64 times. Both these words should have two *rs* and two *ss*

embassy *n, pl* **-sies** offices or official residence of an ambassador; ambassador and his staff
embattled *adj* having a lot of difficulties
embed *v* **-bedding, -bedded** fix firmly in something solid **embedded** *adj* (of a journalist) assigned to accompany an active military unit
embellish *v* decorate; embroider (a story) **embellishment** *n*
ember *n* glowing piece of wood or coal in a dying fire
embezzle *v* steal money that has been entrusted to one **embezzlement** *n* **embezzler** *n*
embittered *adj* feeling anger as a result of misfortune
emblazon *v* decorate with bright colours; proclaim or publicize
emblem *n* object or design that symbolizes a quality, type, or group **emblematic** *adj*
embody *v* **-bodying, -bodied** be an example or expression of; comprise, include **embodiment** *n*
embolden *v* encourage (someone)
embolism *n* blocking of a blood vessel by a blood clot or air bubble
embossed *adj* (of a design or pattern) standing out from a surface
embrace *v* clasp in the arms, hug; accept (an idea) eagerly; comprise ▷ *n* act of embracing
embrasure *n* door or window having splayed sides so that the opening is larger on the inside; opening like this in a fortified wall, for shooting through
embrocation *n* lotion for rubbing into the skin to relieve pain
embroider *v* decorate with needlework; make (a story) more interesting with fictitious detail **embroidery** *n*
embroil *v* involve (a person) in problems
embryo [**em**-bree-oh] *n, pl* **-bryos** unborn creature in the early stages of development; something at an undeveloped stage **embryonic** *adj* at an early stage **embryology** *n*
emend *v* remove errors from **emendation** *n*
emerald *n* bright green precious stone ▷ *adj* bright green
emerge *v* come into view; (foll. by *from*) come out of; become known **emergence** *n* **emergent** *adj*
emergency *n, pl* **-cies** sudden unforeseen occurrence needing immediate action
emeritus [im-**mer**-rit-uss] *adj* retired, but retaining an honorary title *eg emeritus professor*
emery *n* hard mineral used for smoothing and polishing **emery board** cardboard strip coated with crushed emery, for filing the nails
emetic [im-**met**-ik] *n* substance that causes vomiting ▷ *adj*

causing vomiting
emigrate *v* go and settle in another country **emigrant** *n* **emigration** *n*
émigré [em-mig-gray] *n* someone who has left his native country for political reasons
eminent *adj* distinguished, well-known **eminently** *adv* **eminence** *n* position of superiority or fame; (**E-**) title of a cardinal
emir [em-**meer**] *n* Muslim ruler **emirate** *n* his country
emissary *n, pl* **-saries** agent sent on a mission by a government
emit *v* **emitting, emitted** give out (heat, light, or a smell); utter **emission** *n*
emollient *adj* softening, soothing ▷ *n* substance which softens or soothes the skin
emolument *n formal* fees or wages from employment
emoticon [i-**mote**-i-kon] *n computers* same as **smiley**
emotion *n* strong feeling **emotional** *adj* readily affected by or appealing to the emotions **emotionally** *adv* **emotive** *adj* tending to arouse emotion
empathy *n* ability to understand someone else's feelings as if they were one's own
emperor *n* ruler of an empire **empress** *n fem*
emphasis *n, pl* **-ses** special importance or significance; stress on a word or phrase in speech **emphasize** *v* **emphatic** *adj* showing emphasis **emphatically** *adv*
emphysema [em-fiss-**see**-ma] *n* condition in which the air sacs of the lungs are grossly enlarged, causing breathlessness
empire *n* group of territories under the rule of one state or person; large organization that is directed by one person or group
empirical *adj* relying on experiment or experience, not on theory **empirically** *adv* **empiricism** *n* doctrine that all knowledge derives from experience **empiricist** *n*
emplacement *n* prepared position for a gun
employ *v* hire (a person); provide work or occupation for; use ▷ *n* **in the employ of** doing regular paid work for **employee** *n* **employment** *n* state of being employed; work done by a person to earn money
employer *n* person or organization that employs someone
emporium *n, pl* **-riums, -ria** *old-fashioned* large general shop
empower *v* enable, authorize
empress *n* see **emperor**
empty *adj* **-tier, -tiest** containing nothing; unoccupied; without purpose or value; (of words) insincere ▷ *v* **-tying, -tied** make or become empty **empties** *pl n* empty boxes, bottles, etc **emptiness** *n*
emu *n* large Australian flightless bird with long legs **emu oil** oil derived from emu fat, used as a liniment by native Australians
emulate *v* attempt to equal or surpass by imitating **emulation** *n*
emulsion *n* light-sensitive coating on photographic film; type of water-based paint ▷ *v* paint with emulsion paint **emulsify** *v* (of two liquids) join together or join (two liquids) together **emulsifier** *n*
enable *v* provide (a person) with

the means, opportunity, or authority (to do something)
enact *v* establish by law; perform (a story or play) by acting **enactment** *n*
enamel *n* glasslike coating applied to metal etc to preserve the surface; hard white coating on a tooth ▷ *v* **-elling, -elled** cover with enamel
enamoured *adj* inspired with love
en bloc *adv French* as a whole, all together
encamp *v* set up in a camp **encampment** *n*
encapsulate *v* summarize; enclose as in a capsule
encephalitis [en-sef-a-**lite**-iss] *n* inflammation of the brain
encephalogram *n* short for **electroencephalogram**
enchant *v* delight and fascinate **enchantment** *n* **enchanter** *n* **enchantress** *n fem*
encircle *v* form a circle around **encirclement** *n*
enclave *n* part of a country entirely surrounded by foreign territory
enclose *v* surround completely; include along with something else **enclosure** *n*
encomium *n, pl* **-miums, -mia** formal expression of praise
encompass *v* surround; include comprehensively
encore *interj* again, once more ▷ *n* extra performance due to enthusiastic demand
encounter *v* meet unexpectedly; be faced with ▷ *n* unexpected meeting; game or battle
encourage *v* inspire with confidence; spur on **encouragement** *n*
encroach *v* intrude gradually on a person's rights or land **encroachment** *n*
encrust *v* cover with a layer of something
encumber *v* hinder or impede **encumbrance** *n* something that impedes or is burdensome
encyclical [en-**sik**-lik-kl] *n* letter sent by the Pope to all bishops
encyclopedia, encyclopaedia *n* book or set of books containing facts about many subjects, usu in alphabetical order **encyclopedic, encyclopaedic** *adj*
end *n* furthest point or part; limit; last part of something; fragment; death or destruction; purpose; *sport* either of the two defended areas of a playing field ▷ *v* bring or come to a finish **make ends meet** have just enough money for one's needs **ending** *n* **endless** *adj* **endways** *adv* having the end forwards or upwards
endanger *v* put in danger
endear *v* cause to be liked **endearing** *adj* **endearment** *n* affectionate word or phrase
endeavour *v* try ▷ *n* effort
endemic *adj* present within a localized area or peculiar to a particular group of people
endive *n* curly-leaved plant used in salads
endocrine *adj* relating to the glands which secrete hormones directly into the bloodstream
endogenous [en-**dodge**-in-uss] *adj* originating from within
endorse *v* give approval to; sign the back of (a cheque); record a conviction on (a driving licence) **endorsement** *n*
endow *v* provide permanent income for **endowed with**

provided with **endowment** *n*

endure *v* bear (hardship) patiently; last for a long time **endurable** *adj* **endurance** *n* act or power of enduring

enema [**en**-im-a] *n* medicine injected into the rectum to empty the bowels

enemy *n, pl* **-mies** hostile person or nation, opponent

energy *n, pl* **-gies** capacity for intense activity; capacity to do work and overcome resistance; source of power, such as electricity **energetic** *adj* **energetically** *adv* **energize** *v* give vigour to **energy drink** soft drink supposed to boost the drinker's energy levels

enervate *v* deprive of strength or vitality **enervation** *n*

enfant terrible [**on**-fon ter-**reeb**-la] *n, pl* **enfants terribles** *French* clever but unconventional or indiscreet person

enfeeble *v* weaken

enfold *v* cover by wrapping something around; embrace

enforce *v* impose obedience (to a law etc); impose (a condition) **enforceable** *adj* **enforcement** *n*

enfranchise *v* grant (a person) the right to vote **enfranchisement** *n*

engage *v* take part, participate; involve (a person or his or her attention) intensely; employ (a person); begin a battle with; bring (a mechanism) into operation **engaged** *adj* pledged to be married; in use **engagement** *n* **engaging** *adj* charming

engender *v* produce, cause to occur

engine *n* any machine which converts energy into mechanical work; railway locomotive

engineer *n* person trained in any branch of engineering ▷*v* plan in a clever manner; design or construct as an engineer

engineering *n* profession of applying scientific principles to the design and construction of engines, cars, buildings, or machines

English *n* official language of Britain, Ireland, Australia, New Zealand, South Africa, Canada, the US, and several other countries ▷*adj* relating to England **the English** the people of England

engrave *v* carve (a design) onto a hard surface; fix deeply in the mind **engraver** *n* **engraving** *n* print made from an engraved plate

engross [en-**groce**] *v* occupy the attention of (a person) completely

engulf *v* cover or surround completely

enhance *v* increase in quality, value, or attractiveness **enhancement** *n*

enigma *n* puzzling thing or person **enigmatic** *adj* **enigmatically** *adv*

enjoin *v* order (someone) to do something

enjoy *v* take joy in; have the benefit of; experience **enjoyable** *adj* **enjoyment** *n*

enlarge *v* make or grow larger; (foll. by *on*) speak or write about in greater detail **enlargement** *n*

enlighten *v* give information to **enlightenment** *n*

enlist *v* enter the armed forces; obtain the support of **enlistment** *n*

enliven *v* make lively or cheerful

en masse [on **mass**] *adv French* in a group, all together

enmeshed *adj* deeply involved

enmity *n, pl* **-ties** ill will, hatred

ennoble *v* make noble, elevate

ennui [on-**nwee**] *n* boredom, dissatisfaction

enormous *adj* very big, vast **enormity** *n, pl* **-ties** great wickedness; gross offence; *Informal* great size

enough *adj* as much or as many as necessary ▷ *n* sufficient quantity ▷ *adv* sufficiently; fairly or quite *eg that's a common enough experience*

en passant [on **pass**-on] *adv French* in passing, by the way

enquire *v* same as **inquire** **enquiry** *n*

enraptured *adj* filled with delight and fascination

enrich *v* improve in quality; make wealthy or wealthier

enrol *v* **-rolling, -rolled** (cause to) become a member **enrolment** *n*

en route *adv French* on the way

ensconce *v* settle firmly or comfortably

ensemble [on-**som**-bl] *n* all the parts of something taken together; complete outfit of clothes; company of actors or musicians; *music* group of musicians playing together

enshrine *v* cherish or treasure

ensign *n* naval flag; banner; *US* naval officer

enslave *v* make a slave of (someone) **enslavement** *n*

ensnare *v* catch in or as if in a snare

ensue *v* come next, result

en suite *adv French* connected to a bedroom and entered directly from it

ensure *v* make certain or sure; make safe or protect

entail *v* bring about or impose inevitably

entangle *v* catch or involve in or as if in a tangle **entanglement** *n*

entente [on-**tont**] *n* friendly understanding between nations

enter *v* come or go in; join; become involved in, take part in; record (an item) in a journal etc; begin **entrance** *n* way into a place; act of entering; right of entering **entrant** *n* person who enters a university, contest, etc **entry** *n, pl* **-tries** entrance; entering; item entered in a journal etc

enteric [en-**ter**-ik] *adj* intestinal **enteritis** [en-ter-**rite**-iss] *n* inflammation of the intestine, causing diarrhoea

enterprise *n* company or firm; bold or difficult undertaking; boldness and energy **enterprising** *adj* full of boldness and initiative

entertain *v* amuse; receive as a guest; consider (an idea) **entertainer** *n* **entertainment** *n*

enthral [en-**thrawl**] *v* **-thralling, -thralled** hold the attention of **enthralling** *adj*

enthusiasm *n* ardent interest, eagerness **enthuse** *v* (cause to) show enthusiasm **enthusiast** *n* ardent supporter of something **enthusiastic** *adj* **enthusiastically** *adv*

entice *v* attract by exciting hope or desire, tempt **enticement** *n*

entire *adj* including every detail, part, or aspect of something **entirely** *adv* **entirety** *n*

entitle *v* give a right to; give a title to **entitlement** *n*

entity *n, pl* **-ties** separate distinct thing

entomology *n* study of insects **entomological** *adj* **entomologist** *n*

entourage [on-toor-ahzh] *n* group of people who assist an important person

entrails *pl n* intestines; innermost

parts of something
entrance¹ *n* see **enter**
entrance² *v* delight; put into a trance
entreat *v* ask earnestly **entreaty** *n, pl* **-ties** earnest request
entrée [**on**-tray] *n* dish served before a main course; main course; right of admission
entrench *v* establish firmly; establish in a fortified position with trenches **entrenchment** *n*
entrepreneur *n* business person who attempts to make a profit by risk and initiative
entropy [**en**-trop-ee] *n* lack of organization
entrust *v* put into the care or protection of
entwine *v* twist together or around
E number *n* any of a series of numbers with the prefix E indicating a specific food additive recognized by the EU
enumerate *v* name one by one **enumeration** *n*
enunciate *v* pronounce clearly; state precisely or formally **enunciation** *n*
envelop *v* **enveloping, enveloped** wrap up, enclose **envelopment** *n*
envelope *n* folded gummed paper cover for a letter
environment [en-**vire**-on-ment] *n* external conditions and surroundings in which people, animals, or plants live **environmental** *adj* **environmentalist** *n* person concerned with the protection of the natural environment

> SPELLING For every thousand correct appearances of the word **environment** in Collins Word Web, there is one *enviroment*, without the middle *n*

environs *pl n* surrounding area, esp of a town
envisage *v* conceive of as a possibility
envoy *n* messenger; diplomat ranking below an ambassador
envy *n* feeling of discontent aroused by another's good fortune ▷ *v* **-vying, -vied** grudge (another's good fortune, success, or qualities) **enviable** *adj* arousing envy, fortunate **envious** *adj* full of envy
enzyme *n* any of a group of complex proteins that act as catalysts in specific biochemical reactions
Eolithic *adj* of the early part of the Stone Age
epaulette *n* shoulder ornament on a uniform
ephemeral *adj* short-lived
epic *n* long poem, book, or film about heroic events or actions ▷ *adj* very impressive or ambitious
epicentre *n* point on the earth's surface immediately above the origin of an earthquake
epicure *n* person who enjoys good food and drink **epicurean** *adj* devoted to sensual pleasures, esp food and drink ▷ *n* epicure
epidemic *n* widespread occurrence of a disease; rapid spread of something
epidermis *n* outer layer of the skin
epidural [ep-pid-**dure**-al] *adj, n* (of) spinal anaesthetic injected to relieve pain during childbirth
epiglottis *n* thin flap that covers the opening of the larynx during swallowing
epigram *n* short witty remark or poem **epigrammatic** *adj*
epigraph *n* quotation at the start of a book; inscription
epilepsy *n* disorder of the nervous

system causing loss of consciousness and sometimes convulsions **epileptic** *adj* of or having epilepsy ▷*n* person who has epilepsy

epilogue *n* short speech or poem at the end of a literary work, esp a play

Epiphany *n* Christian festival held on January 6 commemorating the manifestation of Christ to the Magi

episcopal [ip-**piss**-kop-al] *adj* of or governed by bishops **episcopalian** *adj* advocating Church government by bishops ▷*n* advocate of such Church government

episode *n* incident in a series of incidents; section of a serialized book, television programme, etc **episodic** *adj* occurring at irregular intervals

epistemology [ip-iss-stem-**ol**-a-jee] *n* study of the source, nature, and limitations of knowledge **epistemological** *adj*

epistle *n* letter, esp of an apostle **epistolary** *adj*

epitaph *n* commemorative inscription on a tomb; commemorative speech or passage

epithet *n* descriptive word or name

epitome [ip-**pit**-a-mee] *n* typical example **epitomize** *v* be the epitome of

epoch [**ee**-pok] *n* period of notable events **epoch-making** *adj* extremely important

eponymous [ip-**pon**-im-uss] *adj* after whom a book, play, etc is named

equable [**ek**-wab-bl] *adj* even-tempered **equably** *adv*

equal *adj* identical in size, quantity, degree, etc; having identical rights or status; evenly balanced; (foll. by *to*) having the necessary ability (for) ▷*n* person or thing equal to another ▷*v* **equalling, equalled** be equal to **equally** *adv* **equality** *n* state of being equal **equalize** *v* make or become equal; reach the same score as one's opponent **equalization** *n* **equal opportunity** nondiscrimination as to sex, race, etc in employment

equanimity *n* calmness of mind

equate *v* make or regard as equivalent **equation** *n* mathematical statement that two expressions are equal; act of equating

equator *n* imaginary circle round the earth, equidistant from the poles **equatorial** *adj*

equerry [**ek**-kwer-ee] *n, pl* **-ries** *Brit* officer who acts as an attendant to a member of a royal family

equestrian *adj* of horses and riding

equidistant *adj* equally distant

equilateral *adj* having equal sides

equilibrium *n, pl* **-ria** steadiness or stability

equine *adj* of or like a horse

equinox *n* time of year when day and night are of equal length **equinoctial** *adj*

equip *v* **equipping, equipped** provide with supplies, components, etc **equipment** *n* set of tools or devices used for a particular purpose; act of equipping

equipoise *n* perfect balance

equity *n, pl* **-ties** fairness; legal system, founded on the principles of natural justice, that supplements common law ▷*pl* interest of ordinary shareholders in a company **equitable** *adj* fair and reasonable **equitably** *adv*

equivalent *adj* equal in value; having the same meaning or result ▷ *n* something that is equivalent **equivalence** *n*
equivocal *adj* ambiguous; deliberately misleading; of doubtful character or sincerity **equivocally** *adv* **equivocate** *v* use vague or ambiguous language to mislead people **equivocation** *n*
ER Queen Elizabeth
era *n* period of time considered as distinctive
eradicate *v* destroy completely **eradication** *n*
erase *v* rub out; remove sound or information from (a magnetic tape or disk) **eraser** *n* object for erasing something written **erasure** *n* erasing; place or mark where something has been erased
ere *prep, conj poetic* before
erect *v* build; found or form ▷ *adj* upright; (of the penis, clitoris, or nipples) rigid as a result of sexual excitement **erectile** *adj* capable of becoming erect from sexual excitement **erection** *n*
erg *n* unit of work or energy
ergonomics *n* study of the relationship between workers and their environment **ergonomic** *adj*
ergot *n* fungal disease of cereal; dried fungus used in medicine
ermine *n* stoat in northern regions; its white winter fur
erode *v* wear away **erosion** *n*
erogenous [ir-**roj**-in-uss] *adj* sensitive to sexual stimulation
erotic *adj* relating to sexual pleasure or desire **eroticism** *n* **erotica** *n* sexual literature or art
err *v* make a mistake **erratum** *n, pl* **-ta** error in writing or printing **erroneous** *adj* incorrect, mistaken
errand *n* short trip to do something for someone
errant *adj* behaving in a manner considered to be unacceptable
erratic *adj* irregular or unpredictable **erratically** *adv*
error *n* mistake, inaccuracy, or misjudgment
ersatz [**air**-zats] *adj* made in imitation *eg ersatz coffee*
erstwhile *adj* former
erudite *adj* having great academic knowledge **erudition** *n*
erupt *v* eject (steam, water, or volcanic material) violently; burst forth suddenly and violently; (of a blemish) appear on the skin **eruption** *n*
erysipelas [err-riss-**sip**-pel-ass] *n* acute skin infection causing purplish patches
escalate *v* increase in extent or intensity **escalation** *n*
escalator *n* moving staircase
escalope [**ess**-kal-lop] *n* thin slice of meat, esp veal
escapade *n* mischievous adventure
escape *v* get free (of); avoid *eg escape attention*; (of a gas, liquid, etc) leak gradually ▷ *n* act of escaping; means of relaxation **escapee** *n* person who has escaped **escapism** *n* taking refuge in fantasy to avoid unpleasant reality **escapologist** *n* entertainer who specializes in freeing himself from confinement **escapology** *n*
escarpment *n* steep face of a ridge or mountain
eschew [iss-**chew**] *v* abstain from, avoid
escort *n* people or vehicles accompanying another person for protection or as an honour; person who accompanies a person of the opposite sex to a social event ▷ *v*

act as an escort to
escudo [ess-**kyoo**-doe] *n, pl* **-dos** former monetary unit of Portugal
escutcheon *n* shield with a coat of arms **blot on one's escutcheon** stain on one's honour
Eskimo *n* member of the aboriginal race inhabiting N Canada, Greenland, Alaska, and E Siberia; their language
esoteric [ee-so-**ter**-rik] *adj* understood by only a small number of people with special knowledge
ESP extrasensory perception
esp especially
espadrille [**ess**-pad-drill] *n* light canvas shoe with a braided cord sole
espalier [ess-**pal**-yer] *n* shrub or fruit tree trained to grow flat; trellis for this
esparto *n, pl* **-tos** grass of S Europe and N Africa used for making rope etc
especial *adj formal* special
especially *adv* particularly
Esperanto *n* universal artificial language
espionage [**ess**-pyon-ahzh] *n* spying
esplanade *n* wide open road used as a public promenade
espouse *v* adopt or give support to (a cause etc) **espousal** *n*
espresso *n, pl* **-sos** strong coffee made by forcing steam or boiling water through ground coffee beans
esprit [ess-**pree**] *n* spirit, liveliness, or wit **esprit de corps** [de **core**] pride in and loyalty to a group
espy *v* **espying, espied** catch sight of
Esq. esquire
esquire *n* courtesy title placed after a man's name
essay *n* short literary composition; short piece of writing on a subject done as an exercise by a student ▷ *v* attempt **essayist** *n*
essence *n* most important feature of a thing which determines its identity; concentrated liquid used to flavour food **essential** *adj* vitally important; basic or fundamental ▷ *n* something fundamental or indispensable **essentially** *adv*
establish *v* set up on a permanent basis; make secure or permanent in a certain place, job, etc; prove; cause to be accepted **establishment** *n* act of establishing; commercial or other institution **the Establishment** group of people having authority within a society
estate *n* landed property; large area of property development, esp of new houses or factories; property of a deceased person **estate agent** agent concerned with the valuation, lease, and sale of property **estate car** car with a rear door and luggage space behind the rear seats
esteem *n* high regard ▷ *v* think highly of; judge or consider
ester *n chem* compound produced by the reaction between an acid and an alcohol
estimate *v* calculate roughly; form an opinion about ▷ *n* approximate calculation; statement from a workman etc of the likely charge for a job; opinion **estimable** *adj* worthy of respect **estimation** *n* considered opinion
estranged *adj* no longer living with one's spouse **estrangement** *n*
estuary *n, pl* **-aries** mouth of a

river
ETA estimated time of arrival
et al. and elsewhere
etc et cetera
et cetera [et **set**-ra] *Latin* and the rest, and others; or the like **etceteras** *pl n* miscellaneous extra things or people
etch *v* wear away or cut the surface of (metal, glass, etc) with acid; imprint vividly (on someone's mind) **etching** *n*
eternal *adj* without beginning or end; unchanging **eternally** *adv* **eternity** *n* infinite time; timeless existence after death **eternity ring** ring given as a token of lasting affection
ether *n* colourless sweet-smelling liquid used as an anaesthetic; region above the clouds **ethereal** [eth-**eer**-ee-al] *adj* extremely delicate
ethic *n* moral principle **ethical** *adj* **ethically** *adv* **ethics** *n* code of behaviour; study of morals
ethnic *adj* relating to a people or group that shares a culture, religion, or language; belonging or relating to such a group, esp one that is a minority group in a particular place **ethnic cleansing** practice, by the dominant ethnic group in an area, of removing other ethnic groups by expulsion or extermination **ethnology** *n* study of human races **ethnological** *adj* **ethnologist** *n*
ethos [**eeth**-oss] *n* distinctive spirit and attitudes of a people, culture, etc
ethyl [**eeth**-ile] *adj* of, consisting of, or containing the hydrocarbon group C_2H_5 **ethylene** *n* poisonous gas used as an anaesthetic and as fuel
etiolate [**ee**-tee-oh-late] *v* become pale and weak; *botany* whiten through lack of sunlight
etiology *n* study of the causes of diseases
etiquette *n* conventional code of conduct
étude [ay-tewd] *n* short musical composition for a solo instrument, esp intended as a technical exercise
etymology *n, pl* **-gies** study of the sources and development of words **etymological** *adj*
EU European Union
eucalyptus, eucalypt *n* tree, mainly grown in Australia, that provides timber, gum, and medicinal oil from the leaves
Eucharist [**yew**-kar-ist] *n* Christian sacrament commemorating Christ's Last Supper; consecrated elements of bread and wine **Eucharistic** *adj*
eugenics [yew-**jen**-iks] *n* study of methods of improving the human race
eulogy *n, pl* **-gies** speech or writing in praise of a person **eulogize** *v* praise (a person or thing) highly in speech or writing **eulogistic** *adj*
eunuch *n* castrated man, esp (formerly) a guard in a harem
euphemism *n* inoffensive word or phrase substituted for one considered offensive or upsetting **euphemistic** *adj* **euphemistically** *adv*
euphony *n, pl* **-nies** pleasing sound **euphonious** *adj* pleasing to the ear **euphonium** *n* brass musical instrument, tenor tuba
euphoria *n* sense of elation **euphoric** *adj*
Eurasian *adj* of Europe and Asia; of mixed European and Asian

parentage ▷*n* person of Eurasian parentage

eureka [yew-**reek**-a] *interj* exclamation of triumph at finding something

euro *n, pl* **euros** unit of the single currency of the European Union

European *n, adj* (person) from Europe **European Union** economic and political association of a number of European nations

Eustachian tube *n* passage leading from the ear to the throat

euthanasia *n* act of killing someone painlessly, esp to relieve his or her suffering

evacuate *v* send (someone) away from a place of danger; empty **evacuation** *n* **evacuee** *n*

evade *v* get away from or avoid; elude **evasion** *n* **evasive** *adj* not straightforward **evasively** *adv*

evaluate *v* find or judge the value of **evaluation** *n*

evanescent *adj* quickly fading away **evanescence** *n*

evangelical *adj* of or according to gospel teaching; of certain Protestant sects which maintain the doctrine of salvation by faith ▷*n* member of an evangelical sect **evangelicalism** *n*

evangelist *n* writer of one of the four gospels; travelling preacher **evangelism** *n* teaching and spreading of the Christian gospel **evangelize** *v* preach the gospel **evangelization** *n*

evaporate *v* change from a liquid or solid to a vapour; disappear **evaporation** *n* **evaporated milk** thick unsweetened tinned milk

eve *n* evening or day before some special event; period immediately before an event **evensong** *n* evening prayer

even *adj* flat or smooth; (foll. by *with*) on the same level (as); constant; calm; equally balanced; divisible by two ▷*adv* equally; simply; nevertheless ▷*v* make even

evening *n* end of the day or early part of the night ▷*adj* of or in the evening

event *n* anything that takes place; planned and organized occasion; contest in a sporting programme **eventful** *adj* full of exciting incidents

eventing *n Brit, Aust & NZ* riding competitions, usu involving cross-country, jumping, and dressage

eventual *adj* ultimate **eventuality** *n* possible event

eventually *adv* at the end of a situation or process

ever *adv* at any time; always **evergreen** *n, adj* (tree or shrub) having leaves throughout the year **everlasting** *adj* **evermore** *adv* for all time to come

every *adj* each without exception; all possible **everybody** *pron* every person **everyday** *adj* usual or ordinary **everyone** *pron* every person **everything** *pron* **everywhere** *adv* in all places

evict *v* legally expel (someone) from his or her home **eviction** *n*

evidence *n* ground for belief; matter produced before a law court to prove or disprove a point; sign, indication ▷*v* demonstrate, prove **in evidence** conspicuous **evident** *adj* easily seen or understood **evidently** *adv* **evidential** *adj* of, serving as, or based on evidence

evil *n* wickedness; wicked deed ▷*adj* harmful; morally bad; very unpleasant **evilly** *adv* **evildoer** *n* wicked person

evince *v* make evident

eviscerate *v* disembowel **evisceration** *n*

evoke *v* call or summon up (a memory, feeling, etc) **evocation** *n* **evocative** *adj*

evolve *v* develop gradually; (of an animal or plant species) undergo evolution **evolution** *n* gradual change in the characteristics of living things over successive generations, esp to a more complex form **evolutionary** *adj*

ewe *n* female sheep

ewer *n* large jug with a wide mouth

ex *n Informal* former wife or husband

ex- *prefix* out of, outside, from *eg exodus*; former *eg ex-wife*

exacerbate [ig-**zass**-er-bate] *v* make (pain, emotion, or a situation) worse **exacerbation** *n*

exact *adj* correct and complete in every detail; precise, as opposed to approximate ▷*v* demand (payment or obedience) **exactly** *adv* precisely, in every respect **exactness, exactitude** *n* **exacting** *adj* making rigorous or excessive demands

exaggerate *v* regard or represent as greater than is true; make greater or more noticeable **exaggeratedly** *adv* **exaggeration** *n*

> SPELLING Some apparently tricky words, like **exaggerate** for example, appear wrongly spelt relatively rarely in Collins Word Web. Similarly, there is only one occurrence of *exagerration*, instead of the correct **exaggeration**

exalt *v* praise highly; raise to a higher rank **exalted** *adj* **exaltation** *n*

exam *n* short for **examination**

examine *v* look at closely; test the knowledge of; ask questions of **examination** *n* examining; test of a candidate's knowledge or skill **examinee** *n* **examiner** *n*

example *n* specimen typical of its group; person or thing worthy of imitation; punishment regarded as a warning to others

exasperate *v* cause great irritation to **exasperation** *n*

excavate *v* unearth buried objects from (a piece of land) methodically to learn about the past; make (a hole) in solid matter by digging **excavation** *n* **excavator** *n* large machine used for digging

exceed *v* be greater than; go beyond (a limit) **exceedingly** *adv* very

excel *v* **-celling, -celled** be superior to; be outstandingly good at something

Excellency *n* title used to address a high-ranking official, such as an ambassador

excellent *adj* exceptionally good **excellence** *n*

except *prep* (sometimes foll. by *for*) other than, not including ▷*v* not include **except that** but for the fact that **excepting** *prep* except **exception** *n* excepting; thing that is excluded from or does not conform to the general rule **exceptional** *adj* not ordinary; much above the average

excerpt *n* passage taken from a book, speech, etc

excess *n* state or act of exceeding the permitted limits; immoderate amount; amount by which a thing exceeds the permitted limits **excessive** *adj* **excessively** *adv*

exchange *v* give or receive (something) in return for something else ▷ *n* act of exchanging; thing given or received in place of another; centre in which telephone lines are interconnected; *finance* place where securities or commodities are traded; transfer of sums of money of equal value between different currencies **exchangeable** *adj*

Exchequer *n Brit* government department in charge of state money

excise¹ *n* tax on goods produced for the home market

excise² *v* cut out or away **excision** *n*

excite *v* arouse to strong emotion; arouse or evoke (an emotion); arouse sexually **excitement** *n* **excitable** *adj* easily excited **excitability** *n*

exclaim *v* speak suddenly, cry out **exclamation** *n* **exclamation mark** punctuation mark (!) used after exclamations **exclamatory** *adj*

exclude *v* keep out, leave out; leave out of consideration **exclusion** *n* **exclusive** *adj* excluding everything else; not shared; catering for a privileged minority ▷ *n* story reported in only one newspaper **exclusively** *adv* **exclusivity, exclusiveness** *n*

excommunicate *v* exclude from membership and the sacraments of the Church **excommunication** *n*

excoriate *v* censure severely; strip skin from **excoriation** *n*

excrement *n* waste matter discharged from the body

excrescence *n* lump or growth on the surface of an animal or plant

excrete *v* discharge (waste matter) from the body **excretion** *n* **excreta** [ik-**skree**-ta] *n* excrement **excretory** *adj*

excruciating *adj* agonizing; hard to bear **excruciatingly** *adv*

exculpate *v* free from blame or guilt

excursion *n* short journey, esp for pleasure

excuse *n* explanation offered to justify (a fault etc) ▷ *v* put forward a reason or justification for (a fault etc); forgive (a person) or overlook (a fault etc); make allowances for; exempt; allow to leave **excusable** *adj*

ex-directory *adj* not listed in a telephone directory by request

execrable [**eks**-sik-rab-bl] *adj* of very poor quality

execute *v* put (a condemned person) to death; carry out or accomplish; produce (a work of art); render (a legal document) effective, as by signing **execution** *n* **executioner** *n*

executive *n* person or group in an administrative position; branch of government responsible for carrying out laws etc ▷ *adj* having the function of carrying out plans, orders, laws, etc

executor, executrix *n* person appointed to perform the instructions of a will

exegesis [eks-sij-**jee**-siss] *n, pl* **-ses** [-seez] explanation of a text, esp of the Bible

exemplar *n* person or thing to be copied, model; example **exemplary** *adj* being a good example; serving as a warning

exemplify *v* **-fying, -fied** show an

example of; be an example of **exemplification** *n*
exempt *adj* not subject to an obligation etc ▷*v* release from an obligation etc **exemption** *n*
exequies [**eks**-sik-wiz] *pl n* funeral rites
exercise *n* activity to train the body or mind; set of movements or tasks designed to improve or test a person's ability; performance of a function ▷*v* make use of *eg to exercise one's rights*; take exercise or perform exercises
exert *v* use (influence, authority, etc) forcefully or effectively **exert oneself** make a special effort **exertion** *n*
exeunt [**eks**-see-unt] *Latin* they go out: used as a stage direction
ex gratia [**eks gray**-sha] *adj* given as a favour where no legal obligation exists
exhale *v* breathe out **exhalation** *n*
exhaust *v* tire out; use up; discuss (a subject) thoroughly ▷*n* gases ejected from an engine as waste products; pipe through which an engine's exhaust fumes pass **exhaustion** *n* extreme tiredness; exhausting **exhaustive** *adj* comprehensive **exhaustively** *adv*
exhibit *v* display to the public; show (a quality or feeling) ▷*n* object exhibited to the public; *law* document or object produced in court as evidence **exhibitor** *n* **exhibition** *n* public display of art, skills, etc; exhibiting **exhibitionism** *n* compulsive desire to draw attention to oneself; compulsive desire to display one's genitals in public **exhibitionist** *n*
exhilarate *v* make lively and cheerful **exhilaration** *n*

> SPELLING It may surprise you that it's the vowels, not the consonants that are a problem when people try to spell **exhilarate** or **exhilaration**. They often make the mistake of writing an *e* instead of an *a* in the middle

exhort *v* urge earnestly **exhortation** *n*
exhume [ig-**zyume**] *v* dig up (something buried, esp a corpse) **exhumation** *n*
exigency *n, pl* **-cies** urgent demand or need **exigent** *adj*
exiguous *adj* scanty or meagre
exile *n* prolonged, usu enforced, absence from one's country; person banished or living away from his or her country ▷*v* expel from one's country
exist *v* have being or reality; eke out a living; live **existence** *n* **existent** *adj*

> SPELLING People often write *-ance* at the end of a word when it should be *-ence*. Collins Word Web shows this is the case for *existance* which occurs 43 times. However, the correct spelling **existence** is over 350 times commoner

existential *adj* of or relating to existence, esp human existence **existentialism** *n* philosophical movement stressing the personal experience and responsibility of the individual, who is seen as a free agent **existentialist** *adj, n*
exit *n* way out; going out; actor's going off stage ▷*v* go out; go offstage: used as a stage direction
exocrine *adj* relating to a gland, such as the sweat gland, that secretes externally through a duct
exodus [**eks**-so-duss] *n* departure

of a large number of people

ex officio [**eks** off-**fish**-ee-oh] *adv, adj Latin* by right of position or office

exonerate *v* free from blame or a criminal charge **exoneration** *n*

exorbitant *adj* (of prices, demands, etc) excessive, immoderate **exorbitantly** *adv*

exorcize *v* expel (evil spirits) by prayers and religious rites **exorcism** *n* **exorcist** *n*

exotic *adj* having a strange allure or beauty; originating in a foreign country ▷ *n* non-native plant **exotically** *adv* **exotica** *pl n* (collection of) exotic objects

expand *v* make or become larger; spread out; (foll. by *on*) enlarge (on); become more relaxed, friendly, and talkative **expansion** *n* **expanse** *n* uninterrupted wide area **expansive** *adj* wide or extensive; friendly and talkative

expat *adj, n* short for **expatriate**

expatiate [iks-**pay**-shee-ate] *v* (foll. by *on*) speak or write at great length (on)

expatriate [eks-**pat**-ree-it] *adj* living outside one's native country ▷ *n* person living outside his or her native country **expatriation** *n*

expect *v* regard as probable; look forward to, await; require as an obligation **expectancy** *n* something expected on the basis of an average *eg life expectancy*; feeling of anticipation **expectant** *adj* expecting or hopeful; pregnant **expectantly** *adv* **expectation** *n* act or state of expecting; something looked forward to; attitude of anticipation or hope

expectorant *n* medicine that helps to bring up phlegm from the respiratory passages

expectorate *v* spit out (phlegm etc) **expectoration** *n*

expedient *n* something that achieves a particular purpose ▷ *adj* suitable to the circumstances, appropriate **expediency** *n*

expedite *v* hasten the progress of **expedition** *n* organized journey, esp for exploration; people and equipment comprising an expedition; pleasure trip or excursion **expeditionary** *adj* relating to an expedition, esp a military one **expeditious** *adj* done quickly and efficiently

expel *v* **-pelling, -pelled** drive out with force; dismiss from a school etc permanently **expulsion** *n*

expend *v* spend, use up **expendable** *adj* able to be sacrificed to achieve an objective **expenditure** *n* something expended, esp money; amount expended

expense *n* cost; (cause of) spending ▷ *pl* charges, outlay incurred

expensive *adj* high-priced

experience *n* direct personal participation; particular incident, feeling, etc that a person has undergone; accumulated knowledge ▷ *v* participate in; be affected by (an emotion) **experienced** *adj* skilful from extensive participation

experiment *n* test to provide evidence to prove or disprove a theory; attempt at something new ▷ *v* carry out an experiment **experimental** *adj* **experimentally** *adv* **experimentation** *n*

expert *n* person with extensive skill or knowledge in a particular field ▷ *adj* skilful or knowledgeable

expertise [eks-per-**teez**] *n* special

skill or knowledge
expiate *v* make amends for **expiation** *n*
expire *v* finish or run out; breathe out; *lit* die **expiration** *n* **expiry** *n* end, esp of a contract period
explain *v* make clear and intelligible; account for **explanation** *n* **explanatory** *adj*
expletive *n* swearword
explicable *adj* able to be explained **explicate** *v formal* explain **explication** *n*
explicit *adj* precisely and clearly expressed; shown in realistic detail **explicitly** *adv*
explode *v* burst with great violence, blow up; react suddenly with emotion; increase rapidly; show (a theory etc) to be baseless **explosion** *n* **explosive** *adj* tending to explode ▷*n* substance that causes explosions
exploit *v* take advantage of for one's own purposes; make the best use of ▷*n* notable feat or deed **exploitation** *n* **exploiter** *n*
explore *v* investigate; travel into (unfamiliar regions), esp for scientific purposes **exploration** *n* **exploratory** *adj* **explorer** *n*
expo *n, pl* **expos** *Informal* exposition, large public exhibition
exponent *n* person who advocates an idea, cause, etc; skilful performer, esp a musician
exponential *adj Informal* very rapid **exponentially** *adv*
export *n* selling or shipping of goods to a foreign country; product shipped or sold to a foreign country ▷*v* sell or ship (goods) to a foreign country **exporter** *n*
expose *v* uncover or reveal; make vulnerable, leave unprotected; subject (a photographic film) to light **expose oneself** display one's sexual organs in public **exposure** *n* exposing; lack of shelter from the weather, esp the cold; appearance before the public, as on television
exposé [iks-**pose**-ay] *n* bringing of a crime, scandal, etc to public notice
exposition *n* see **expound**
expostulate *v* (foll. by *with*) reason (with), esp to dissuade
expound *v* explain in detail **exposition** *n* explanation; large public exhibition
express *v* put into words; show (an emotion); indicate by a symbol or formula; squeeze out (juice etc) ▷*adj* explicitly stated; (of a purpose) particular; of or for rapid transportation of people, mail, etc ▷*n* fast train or bus stopping at only a few stations ▷*adv* by express delivery **expression** *n* expressing; word or phrase; showing or communication of emotion; look on the face that indicates mood; *maths* variable, function, or some combination of these **expressionless** *adj* **expressive** *adj*
expressionism *n* early 20th-century artistic movement which sought to express emotions rather than represent the physical world **expressionist** *n, adj*
expropriate *v* deprive an owner of (property) **expropriation** *n*
expunge *v* delete, erase, blot out
expurgate *v* remove objectionable parts from (a book etc)
exquisite *adj* of extreme beauty or delicacy; intense in feeling **exquisitely** *adv*
extant *adj* still existing

extemporize *v* speak, perform, or compose without preparation

extend *v* draw out or be drawn out, stretch; last for a certain time; (foll. by *to*) include; increase in size or scope; offer *eg extend one's sympathy* **extendable** *adj* **extension** *n* room or rooms added to an existing building; additional telephone connected to the same line as another; extending **extensive** *adj* having a large extent, widespread **extensor** *n* muscle that extends a part of the body **extent** *n* range over which something extends, area

> SPELLING Lots of nouns in English end with *-tion*, but **extension** is not one of them

extenuate *v* make (an offence or fault) less blameworthy **extenuation** *n*

exterior *n* part or surface on the outside; outward appearance ▷ *adj* of, on, or coming from the outside

exterminate *v* destroy (animals or people) completely **extermination** *n* **exterminator** *n*

external *adj* of, situated on, or coming from the outside **externally** *adv*

extinct *adj* having died out; (of a volcano) no longer liable to erupt **extinction** *n*

extinguish *v* put out (a fire or light); remove or destroy entirely

extinguisher *n* device for extinguishing a fire or light

extirpate *v* destroy utterly

extol *v* **-tolling, -tolled** praise highly

extort *v* get (something) by force or threats **extortion** *n* **extortionate** *adj* (of prices) excessive

extra *adj* more than is usual, expected or needed ▷ *n* additional person or thing; something for which an additional charge is made; *films* actor hired for crowd scenes ▷ *adv* unusually or exceptionally

extra- *prefix* outside or beyond an area or scope *eg extrasensory; extraterritorial*

extract *v* pull out by force; remove; derive; copy out (an article, passage, etc) from a publication ▷ *n* something extracted, such as a passage from a book etc; preparation containing the concentrated essence of a substance *eg beef extract* **extraction** *n* **extractor** *n*

extradite *v* send (an accused person) back to his or her own country for trial **extradition** *n*

extramural *adj* connected with but outside the normal courses of a university or college

extraneous [iks-**train**-ee-uss] *adj* irrelevant

extraordinary *adj* very unusual; (of a meeting) specially arranged to deal with a particular subject **extraordinarily** *adv*

extrapolate *v* infer (something not known) from the known facts; *maths* estimate (a value of a function or measurement) beyond the known values by the extension of a curve **extrapolation** *n*

extrasensory *adj* **extrasensory perception** supposed ability to obtain information other than through the normal senses

extravagant *adj* spending money excessively; going beyond reasonable limits **extravagance** *n* **extravaganza** *n* elaborate and lavish entertainment, display, etc

> SPELLING Make sure that **extravagant** ends in *-ant*, even though *-ent* sounds like a possibility

extreme *adj* of a high or the highest degree or intensity; severe; immoderate; farthest or outermost ▷ *n* either of the two limits of a scale or range **extremely** *adv* **extreme sport** sport with a high risk of injury or death **extremist** *n* person who favours immoderate methods ▷ *adj* holding extreme opinions **extremity** *n, pl* **-ties** farthest point; extreme condition, as of misfortune ▷ *pl* hands and feet

extricate *v* free from complication or difficulty **extrication** *n*

extrovert *adj* lively and outgoing; concerned more with external reality than inner feelings ▷ *n* extrovert person

extrude *v* squeeze or force out **extrusion** *n*

exuberant *adj* high-spirited; growing luxuriantly **exuberance** *n*

exude *v* (of a liquid or smell) seep or flow out slowly and steadily; make apparent by mood or behaviour *eg exude confidence*

exult *v* be joyful or jubilant **exultation** *n* **exultant** *adj*

eye *n* organ of sight; ability to judge or appreciate *eg a good eye for detail;* one end of a sewing needle; dark spot on a potato from which a stem grows ▷ *v* **eyeing** *or* **eying, eyed** look at carefully or warily **eyeless** *adj* **eyelet** *n* small hole for a lace or cord to be passed through; ring that strengthens this **eyeball** *n* ball-shaped part of the eye **eyebrow** *n* line of hair on the bony ridge above the eye **eyeglass** *n* lens for aiding defective vision **eyelash** *n* short hair that grows out from the eyelid **eyelid** *n* fold of skin that covers the eye when it is closed **eyeliner** *n* cosmetic used to outline the eyes **eye-opener** *n* *Informal* something startling or revealing **eye shadow** coloured cosmetic worn on the upper eyelids **eyesight** *n* ability to see **eyesore** *n* ugly object **eye tooth** canine tooth **eyewitness** *n* person who was present at an event and can describe what happened

eyrie *n* nest of an eagle; high isolated place

f

f *music* forte
F Fahrenheit; farad
FA Football Association (of England)
fable *n* story with a moral; false or fictitious account; legend **fabled** *adj* made famous in legend
fabric *n* knitted or woven cloth; framework or structure
fabricate *v* make up (a story or lie); make or build **fabrication** *n*
fabulous *adj Informal* excellent; astounding; told of in fables **fabulously** *adv*
facade [fas-**sahd**] *n* front of a building; (false) outward appearance
face *n* front of the head; facial expression; distorted expression; outward appearance; front or main side; dial of a clock; dignity, self-respect ▷*v* look or turn towards; be opposite; be confronted by; provide with a surface **faceless** *adj* impersonal, anonymous **face-lift** *n* operation to tighten facial skin, to remove wrinkles **face-saving** *adj* maintaining dignity or self-respect **face up to** *v* accept (an unpleasant fact or reality) **face value** apparent worth or meaning
facet *n* aspect; surface of a cut gem
facetious [fas-**see**-shuss] *adj* funny or trying to be funny, esp at inappropriate times
facia *n, pl* **-ciae** same as **fascia**
facial *adj* of the face ▷*n* beauty treatment for the face
facile [**fas**-sile] *adj* (of a remark, argument, etc) superficial and showing lack of real thought
facilitate *v* make easy **facilitation** *n*
facility *n, pl* **-ties** skill; easiness ▷*pl* means or equipment for an activity
facing *n* lining or covering for decoration or reinforcement ▷*pl* contrasting collar and cuffs on a jacket
facsimile [fak-**sim**-ill-ee] *n* exact copy
fact *n* event or thing known to have happened or existed; provable truth **facts of life** details of sex and reproduction **factual** *adj*
faction *n* (dissenting) minority group within a larger body; dissension **factious** *adj* of or producing factions
factitious *adj* artificial
factor *n* element contributing to a result; *maths* one of the integers multiplied together to give a given number; *Scot* property manager **factorial** *n* product of all the integers from one to a given number **factorize** *v* calculate the factors of (a number)

factory *n, pl* **-ries** building where goods are manufactured
factotum *n* person employed to do all sorts of work
faculty *n, pl* **-ties** physical or mental ability; department in a university or college
fad *n* short-lived fashion; whim **faddy, faddish** *adj*
fade *v* (cause to) lose brightness, colour, or strength; vanish slowly
faeces [**fee**-seez] *pl n* waste matter discharged from the anus **faecal** [**fee**-kl] *adj*
fag[1] *n Informal* boring task; *Brit* young public schoolboy who does menial chores for a senior boy ▷ *v Brit* do menial chores in a public school
fag[2] *n Brit, slang* cigarette **fag end** last and worst part; *slang* cigarette stub
faggot[1] *n Brit, Aust & NZ* ball of chopped liver, herbs, and bread; bundle of sticks for fuel
faggot[2] *n offens* male homosexual
Fahrenheit [**far**-ren-hite] *adj* of a temperature scale with the freezing point of water at 32° and the boiling point at 212°
faïence [**fie**-ence] *n* tin-glazed earthenware
fail *v* be unsuccessful; stop operating; be or judge to be below the required standard in a test; disappoint or be useless to (someone); neglect or be unable to do (something); go bankrupt ▷ *n* instance of not passing an exam or test **without fail** regularly; definitely **failing** *n* weak point ▷ *prep* in the absence of **failure** *n* act or instance of failing; unsuccessful person or thing
fain *adv obs* gladly
faint *adj* lacking clarity, brightness, or volume; feeling dizzy or weak; lacking conviction or force ▷ *v* lose consciousness temporarily ▷ *n* temporary loss of consciousness
fair[1] *adj* unbiased and reasonable; light in colour; beautiful; quite good *eg a fair attempt*; quite large *eg a fair amount of money*; (of weather) fine ▷ *adv* fairly **fairly** *adv* moderately; to a great degree or extent; as deserved, reasonably **fairness** *n* **fairway** *n golf* smooth area between the tee and the green
fair[2] *n* travelling entertainment with sideshows, rides, and amusements; exhibition of commercial or industrial products **fairground** *n* open space used for a fair
Fair Isle *n* intricate multicoloured knitted pattern
fairy *n, pl* **fairies** imaginary small creature with magic powers; *offens* male homosexual **fairy godmother** person who helps in time of trouble **fairyland** *n* **fairy lights** small coloured electric bulbs used as decoration **fairy penguin** small penguin with a bluish head and back, found on the Australian coast **fairy tale, story** story about fairies or magic; unbelievable story or explanation
fait accompli [**fate** ak-**kom**-plee] *n French* something already done that cannot be altered
faith *n* strong belief, esp without proof; religion; complete confidence or trust; allegiance to a person or cause **faithful** *adj* loyal; consistently reliable; accurate in detail **faithfully** *adv* **faithless** *adj* disloyal or dishonest **faith school** *Brit* school that provides a general education within a framework of a

specific religious belief

fake *v* cause something not genuine to appear real or more valuable by fraud; pretend to have (an illness, emotion, etc) ▷ *n* person, thing, or act that is not genuine ▷ *adj* not genuine

fakir [fay-keer] *n* Muslim who spurns worldly possessions; Hindu holy man

falcon *n* small bird of prey **falconry** *n* art of training falcons; sport of hunting with falcons **falconer** *n*

fall *v* **falling, fell, fallen** drop from a higher to a lower place through the force of gravity; collapse to the ground; decrease in number or quality; pass into a specified condition; occur ▷ *n* falling; thing or amount that falls; decrease in value or number; decline in power or influence; *US* autumn ▷ *pl* waterfall **fall for** *v Informal* fall in love with; be deceived by (a lie or trick) **fall guy** *Informal* victim of a confidence trick; scapegoat **fallout** *n* radioactive particles spread as a result of a nuclear explosion

fallacy *n, pl* **-cies** false belief; unsound reasoning **fallacious** *adj*

fallible *adj* (of a person) liable to make mistakes **fallibility** *n*

Fallopian tube *n* either of a pair of tubes through which egg cells pass from the ovary to the womb

fallow *adj* (of land) ploughed but left unseeded to regain fertility

false *adj* not true or correct; artificial, fake; deceptive *eg false promises* **falsely** *adv* **falseness** *n* **falsity** *n* **falsehood** *n* quality of being untrue; lie

falsetto *n, pl* **-tos** voice pitched higher than one's natural range

falsify *v* **-fying, -fied** alter fraudulently **falsification** *n*

falter *v* be hesitant, weak, or unsure; lose power momentarily; utter hesitantly; move unsteadily

fame *n* state of being widely known or recognized **famed** *adj* famous

familiar *adj* well-known; intimate, friendly; too friendly ▷ *n* demon supposed to attend a witch; friend **familiarly** *adv* **familiarity** *n* **familiarize** *v* acquaint fully with a particular subject **familiarization** *n*

family *n, pl* **-lies** group of parents and their children; one's spouse and children; group descended from a common ancestor; group of related objects or beings ▷ *adj* suitable for parents and children together **familial** *adj* **family planning** control of the number of children in a family by the use of contraception

famine *n* severe shortage of food

famished *adj* very hungry

famous *adj* very well-known **famously** *adv Informal* excellently

fan[1] *n* hand-held or mechanical object used to create a current of air for ventilation or cooling ▷ *v* **fanning, fanned** blow or cool with a fan; spread out like a fan **fanbase** *n* body of admirers of a particular pop singer, sports team, etc **fan belt** belt that drives a cooling fan in a car engine **fantail** *n* small New Zealand bird with a tail like a fan

fan[2] *n Informal* devotee of a pop star, sport, or hobby

fanatic *n* person who is excessively enthusiastic about something **fanatical** *adj* **fanatically** *adv* **fanaticism** *n*

fancy *adj* **-cier, -ciest** elaborate, not plain; (of prices) higher than usual ▷*n, pl* **-cies** sudden irrational liking or desire; uncontrolled imagination ▷*v* **-cying, -cied** *Informal* be sexually attracted to; *Informal* have a wish for; picture in the imagination; suppose **fancy oneself** *Informal* have a high opinion of oneself **fanciful** *adj* not based on fact; excessively elaborate **fancifully** *adv* **fancy dress** party costume representing a historical figure, animal, etc **fancy-free** *adj* not in love

fandango *n, pl* **-gos** lively Spanish dance

fanfare *n* short loud tune played on brass instruments

fang *n* snake's tooth which injects poison; long pointed tooth

fantasia *n* musical composition of an improvised nature

fantastic *adj Informal* very good; unrealistic or absurd; strange or difficult to believe **fantastically** *adv*

fantasy *n, pl* **-sies** far-fetched notion; imagination unrestricted by reality; daydream; fiction with a large fantasy content **fantasize** *v* indulge in daydreams

FAQ *computers* frequently asked question *or* questions

far *adv* **farther** *or* **further, farthest** *or* **furthest** at, to, or from a great distance; at or to a remote time; very much ▷*adj* remote in space or time **Far East** East Asia **far-fetched** *adj* hard to believe

farad *n* unit of electrical capacitance

farce *n* boisterous comedy; ludicrous situation **farcical** *adj* ludicrous **farcically** *adv*

fare *n* charge for a passenger's journey; passenger; food provided ▷*v* get on (as specified) *eg we fared badly*

farewell *interj* goodbye ▷*n* act of saying goodbye and leaving ▷*v NZ* say goodbye

farinaceous *adj* containing starch or having a starchy texture

farm *n* area of land for growing crops or rearing livestock; area of land or water for growing or rearing a specified animal or plant *eg fish farm* ▷*v* cultivate (land); rear (stock) **farmhouse** *n* **farm out** *v* send (work) to be done by others **farmstead** *n* farm and its buildings **farmyard** *n*

farmer *n* person who owns or runs a farm

farrago [far-**rah**-go] *n, pl* **-gos, -goes** jumbled mixture of things

farrier *n* person who shoes horses

farrow *n* litter of piglets ▷*v* (of a sow) give birth

fart *vulgar slang* ▷*n* emission of gas from the anus ▷*v* emit gas from the anus

farther, farthest *adv, adj* see **far**

farthing *n* former British coin equivalent to a quarter of a penny

fascia [**fay**-shya] *n, pl* **-ciae, -cias** outer surface of a dashboard; flat surface above a shop window

fascinate *v* attract and interest strongly; make motionless from fear or awe **fascinating** *adj* **fascination** *n*

> SPELLING Remember that there is a silent *c* after the *s* in **fascinate**, **fascinated**, and **fascinating**

fascism [**fash**-iz-zum] *n* right-wing totalitarian political system characterized by state control and extreme nationalism **fascist** *adj, n*

fashion *n* style in clothes, hairstyle, etc, popular at a particular time; way something happens or is done ▷*v* form or make into a particular shape **fashionable** *adj* currently popular **fashionably** *adv*

fast[1] *adj* (capable of) acting or moving quickly; done in or lasting a short time; adapted to or allowing rapid movement; (of a clock or watch) showing a time later than the correct time; dissipated; firmly fixed, fastened, or shut ▷*adv* quickly; soundly, deeply *eg fast asleep*; tightly and firmly **fast food** food, such as hamburgers, prepared and served very quickly **fast-track** *adj* taking the quickest but most competitive route to success *eg fast-track executives* ▷*v* speed up the progress of (a project or person)

fast[2] *v* go without food, esp for religious reasons ▷*n* period of fasting

fasten *v* make or become firmly fixed or joined; close by fixing in place or locking; (foll by *on*) direct (one's attention) towards **fastener, fastening** *n* device that fastens

fastidious *adj* very fussy about details; excessively concerned with cleanliness **fastidiously** *adv* **fastidiousness** *n*

fastness *n* fortress, safe place

fat *adj* **fatter, fattest** having excess flesh on the body; (of meat) containing a lot of fat; thick; profitable ▷*n* extra flesh on the body; oily substance obtained from animals or plants **fatness** *n* **fatten** *v* (cause to) become fat **fatty** *adj* containing fat **fathead** *n Informal* stupid person **fat-headed** *adj*

fatal *adj* causing death or ruin **fatally** *adv* **fatality** *n, pl* **-ties** death caused by an accident or disaster

fatalism *n* belief that all events are predetermined and people are powerless to change their destinies **fatalist** *n* **fatalistic** *adj*

fate *n* power supposed to predetermine events; inevitable fortune that befalls a person or thing **fated** *adj* destined; doomed to death or destruction **fateful** *adj* having important, usu disastrous, consequences

father *n* male parent; person who founds a line or family; man who starts, creates, or invents something; (**F-**) God; (**F-**) title of some priests ▷*v* be the father of (offspring) **fatherhood** *n* **fatherless** *adj* **fatherly** *adj* **father-in-law** *n, pl* **fathers-in-law** father of one's husband or wife **fatherland** *n* one's native country

fathom *n* unit of length, used in navigation, equal to six feet (1.83 metres) ▷*v* understand **fathomable** *adj* **fathomless** *adj* too deep or difficult to fathom

fatigue [fat-**eeg**] *n* extreme physical or mental tiredness; weakening of a material due to stress; soldier's nonmilitary duty ▷*v* tire out

fatuous *adj* foolish **fatuously** *adv* **fatuity** *n*

faucet [**faw**-set] *n US* tap

fault *n* responsibility for something wrong; defect or flaw; mistake or error; *geology* break in layers of rock; *tennis, squash, etc* invalid serve ▷*v* criticize or blame **at fault** guilty of error **find fault with** seek out minor imperfections in **to a fault** excessively **faulty** *adj* **faultless** *adj* **faultlessly** *adv*

faun *n* (in Roman legend) creature

with a human face and torso and a goat's horns and legs

fauna *n, pl* **-nas, -nae** animals of a given place or time

faux pas [**foe pah**] *n, pl* **faux pas** social blunder

favour *n* approving attitude; act of goodwill or generosity; partiality ▷ *v* prefer; regard or treat with especial kindness; support or advocate

favourable *adj* encouraging or advantageous; giving consent; useful or beneficial **favourably** *adv*

favourite *adj* most liked ▷ *n* preferred person or thing; *sport* competitor expected to win **favouritism** *n* practice of giving special treatment to a person or group

fawn[1] *n* young deer ▷ *adj* light yellowish-brown

fawn[2] *v* (foll by *on*) seek attention from (someone) by insincere flattery; (of a dog) try to please by a show of extreme affection

fax *n* electronic system for sending facsimiles of documents by telephone; document sent by this system ▷ *v* send (a document) by this system

FBI *US* Federal Bureau of Investigation

FC (in Britain) Football Club

Fe *chem* iron

fealty *n* (in feudal society) subordinate's loyalty to his ruler or lord

fear *n* distress or alarm caused by impending danger or pain; something that causes distress ▷ *v* be afraid of (something or someone) **fear for** feel anxiety about something **fearful** *adj* feeling fear; causing fear; *Informal* very unpleasant **fearfully** *adv* **fearless** *adj* **fearlessly** *adv* **fearsome** *adj* terrifying

feasible *adj* able to be done, possible **feasibly** *adv* **feasibility** *n*

feast *n* lavish meal; something extremely pleasing; annual religious celebration ▷ *v* eat a feast; give a feast to; (foll by *on*) eat a large amount of

feat *n* remarkable, skilful, or daring action

feather *n* one of the barbed shafts forming the plumage of birds ▷ *v* fit or cover with feathers; turn (an oar) edgeways **feather in one's cap** achievement one can be pleased with **feather one's nest** make one's life comfortable **feathered** *adj* **feathery** *adj* **featherweight** *n* boxer weighing up to 126lb (professional) or 57kg (amateur); insignificant person or thing

feature *n* part of the face, such as the eyes; prominent or distinctive part; special article in a newspaper or magazine; main film in a cinema programme ▷ *v* have as a feature or be a feature in; give prominence to **featureless** *adj*

Feb. February

febrile [**fee**-brile] *adj* feverish

February *n* second month of the year

feckless *adj* ineffectual or irresponsible

fecund *adj* fertile **fecundity** *n*

fed *v* past of **feed** **fed up** *Informal* bored, dissatisfied

federal *adj* of a system in which power is divided between one central government and several regional governments; of the central government of a federation **federalism** *n* **federalist** *n* **federate** *v* unite in a federation

federation *n* union of several states, provinces, etc; association
fedora [fid-**or**-a] *n* man's soft hat with a brim
fee *n* charge paid to be allowed to do something; payment for professional services
feeble *adj* lacking physical or mental power; unconvincing **feebleness** *n* **feebly** *adv* **feeble-minded** *adj* unable to think or understand effectively
feed *v* **feeding, fed** give food to; give (something) as food; eat; supply or prepare food for; supply (what is needed) ▷ *n* act of feeding; food, esp for babies or animals; *Informal* meal **feeder** *n* road or railway line linking outlying areas to the main traffic network **feedback** *n* information received in response to something done; return of part of the output of an electrical circuit or loudspeaker to its source
feel *v* **feeling, felt** have a physical or emotional sensation of; become aware of or examine by touch; believe ▷ *n* act of feeling; impression; way something feels; sense of touch; instinctive aptitude **feeler** *n* organ of touch in some animals; remark made to test others' opinion **feeling** *n* emotional reaction; intuitive understanding; opinion; sympathy, understanding; ability to experience physical sensations; sensation experienced ▷ *pl* emotional sensitivities **feel like** wish for, want
feet *n* plural of **foot**
feign [fane] *v* pretend
feint[1] [faint] *n* sham attack or blow meant to distract an opponent ▷ *v* make a feint
feint[2] [faint] *n* narrow lines on ruled paper
feldspar *n* hard mineral that is the main constituent of igneous rocks
felicity *n* happiness *pl* **-ties** appropriate expression or style **felicitations** *pl n* congratulations **felicitous** *adj*
feline *adj* of cats; catlike ▷ *n* member of the cat family
fell[1] *v* past tense of **fall**
fell[2] *v* cut down (a tree); knock down
fell[3] *adj* **in one fell swoop** in a single action or occurrence
fell[4] *n Scot & N English* mountain, hill, or moor
felloe *n* (segment of) the rim of a wheel
fellow *n* man or boy; comrade or associate; person in the same group or condition; member of a learned society or the governing body of a college ▷ *adj* in the same group or condition **fellowship** *n* sharing of aims or interests; group with shared aims or interests; feeling of friendliness; paid research post in a college or university
felon *n criminal law* (formerly) person guilty of a felony **felony** *n, pl* **-nies** serious crime **felonious** *adj*
felspar *n* same as **feldspar**
felt[1] *v* past of **feel**
felt[2] *n* matted fabric made by bonding fibres by pressure **felt-tip pen** pen with a writing point made from pressed fibres
fem. feminine
female *adj* of the sex which bears offspring; (of plants) producing fruits ▷ *n* female person or animal
feminine *adj* having qualities traditionally regarded as suitable for, or typical of, women; of women;

belonging to a particular class of grammatical inflection in some languages **femininity** *n*
feminism *n* advocacy of equal rights for women **feminist** *n, adj*

femme fatale [**fam** fat-**tahl**] *n, pl* **femmes fatales** alluring woman who leads men into dangerous situations by her charm

femur [**fee**-mer] *n* thighbone **femoral** *adj* of the thigh

fen *n Brit* low-lying flat marshy land

fence *n* barrier of posts linked by wire or wood, enclosing an area; *slang* dealer in stolen property ▷ *v* enclose with or as if with a fence; fight with swords as a sport; avoid a question **fencing** *n* sport of fighting with swords; material for making fences **fencer** *n*

fend *v* **fend for oneself** provide for oneself **fend off** *v* defend oneself against (verbal or physical attack)

fender *n* low metal frame in front of a fireplace; soft but solid object hung over a ship's side to prevent damage when docking; *Chiefly US* wing of a car

feng shui [fung **shway**] *n* Chinese art of deciding the best design of a building, etc, in order to bring good luck

fennel *n* fragrant plant whose seeds, leaves, and root are used in cookery

fenugreek *n* Mediterranean plant grown for its heavily scented seeds

feral *adj* wild

ferment *n* commotion, unrest ▷ *v* undergo or cause to undergo fermentation **fermentation** *n* reaction in which an organic molecule splits into simpler substances, esp the conversion of sugar to alcohol

fern *n* flowerless plant with fine fronds

ferocious *adj* savagely fierce or cruel **ferocity** *n*

ferret *n* tamed polecat used to catch rabbits or rats ▷ *v* **ferreting, ferreted** hunt with ferrets; search around **ferret out** *v* find by searching

ferric, ferrous *adj* of or containing iron

Ferris wheel *n* large vertical fairground wheel with hanging seats for riding in

ferry *n, pl* **-ries** boat for transporting people and vehicles ▷ *v* **-rying, -ried** carry by ferry; convey (goods or people) **ferryman** *n*

fertile *adj* capable of producing young, crops, or vegetation; highly productive *eg a fertile mind* **fertility** *n* **fertilize** *v* provide (an animal or plant) with sperm or pollen to bring about fertilization; supply (soil) with nutrients **fertilization** *n*

fertilizer *n* substance added to the soil to increase its productivity

fervent, fervid *adj* intensely passionate and sincere **fervently** *adv* **fervour** *n* intensity of feeling

fescue *n* pasture and lawn grass with stiff narrow leaves

fester *v* grow worse and increasingly hostile; (of a wound) form pus; rot and decay

festival *n* organized series of special events or performances; day or period of celebration **festive** *adj* of or like a celebration **festivity** *n, pl* **-ties** happy celebration ▷ *pl* celebrations

festoon *v* hang decorations in loops

feta *n* white salty Greek cheese

fetch *v* go after and bring back; be sold for; *Informal* deal (a blow) **fetching** *adj* attractive **fetch up** *v* *Informal* arrive or end up

fete [fate] *n* gala, bazaar, etc, usu held outdoors ▷ *v* honour or entertain regally

fetid *adj* stinking

fetish *n* form of behaviour in which sexual pleasure is derived from looking at or handling an inanimate object; thing with which one is excessively concerned; object believed to have magical powers **fetishism** *n* **fetishist** *n*

fetlock *n* projection behind and above a horse's hoof

fetter *n* chain or shackle for the foot ▷ *pl* restrictions ▷ *v* restrict; bind in fetters

fettle *n* state of health or spirits

fetus [**fee**-tuss] *n, pl* **-tuses** embryo of a mammal in the later stages of development **fetal** *adj*

feu *n* (in Scotland) right of use of land in return for a fixed annual payment

feud *n* long bitter hostility between two people or groups ▷ *v* carry on a feud

feudalism *n* medieval system in which people held land from a lord, and in return worked and fought for him **feudal** *adj* of or like feudalism

fever *n* (illness causing) high body temperature; nervous excitement **fevered** *adj* **feverish** *adj* suffering from fever; in a state of nervous excitement **feverishly** *adv*

few *adj* not many **a few** small number **quite a few, a good few** several.

> *Few(er)* is used of things that can be counted: *Fewer than five visits.* Compare *less*, which is used for quantity: *It uses less sugar.*

fey *adj* whimsically strange; having the ability to look into the future

fez *n, pl* **fezzes** brimless tasselled cap, orig from Turkey

ff *music* fortissimo

fiancé [fee-**on**-say] *n* man engaged to be married **fiancée** *n fem*

fiasco *n, pl* **-cos, -coes** ridiculous or humiliating failure

fiat [**fee**-at] *n* arbitrary order; official permission

fib *n* trivial lie ▷ *v* **fibbing, fibbed** tell a lie **fibber** *n*

fibre *n* thread that can be spun into yarn; threadlike animal or plant tissue; fibrous material in food; strength of character; essential substance or nature **fibrous** *adj* **fibreglass** *n* material made of fine glass fibres **fibre optics** transmission of information by light along very thin flexible fibres of glass

fibro *n Aust* mixture of cement and asbestos fibre, used in sheets for building (also **fibrocement**)

fibroid [**fibe**-royd] *n* benign tumour composed of fibrous connective tissue **fibrositis** [fibe-roh-**site**-iss] *n* inflammation of the tissues of muscle sheaths

fibula *n, pl* **-lae, -las** slender outer bone of the lower leg

fiche [**feesh**] *n* sheet of film for storing publications in miniaturized form

fickle *adj* changeable, inconstant **fickleness** *n*

fiction *n* literary works of the imagination, such as novels; invented story **fictional** *adj* **fictionalize** *v* turn into fiction **fictitious** *adj* not genuine; of or in fiction

fiddle *n* violin; *Informal* dishonest action or scheme ▷ *v* play the violin; falsify (accounts); move or touch something restlessly **fiddling** *adj* trivial **fiddly** *adj* awkward to do or use **fiddlesticks** *interj* expression of annoyance or disagreement

fidelity *n* faithfulness; accuracy in detail; quality of sound reproduction

fidget *v* move about restlessly ▷ *n* person who fidgets ▷ *pl* restlessness **fidgety** *adj*

fiduciary [fid-**yew**-she-er-ee] *law* ▷ *n, pl* **-aries** person bound to act for someone else's benefit, as a trustee ▷ *adj* of a trust or trustee

fief [**feef**] *n hist* land granted by a lord in return for war service

field *n* enclosed piece of agricultural land; marked off area for sports; area rich in a specified natural resource; sphere of knowledge or activity; place away from the laboratory or classroom where practical work is done ▷ *v sport* catch and return (a ball); deal with (a question) successfully **fielder** *n sport* player whose task is to field the ball **field day** day or time of exciting activity **field events** throwing and jumping events in athletics **fieldfare** *n* type of large Old World thrush **field glasses** binoculars **field marshal** army officer of the highest rank **field sports** hunting, shooting, and fishing **fieldwork** *n* investigation made in the field as opposed to the classroom or the laboratory

fiend [**feend**] *n* evil spirit; cruel or wicked person; *Informal* person devoted to something *eg fitness fiend* **fiendish** *adj* **fiendishly** *adv*

fierce *adj* wild or aggressive; intense or strong **fiercely** *adv* **fierceness** *n*

fiery *adj* **fierier, fieriest** consisting of or like fire; easily angered; (of food) very spicy

fiesta *n* religious festival, carnival

fife *n* small high-pitched flute

fifteen *adj, n* five and ten **fifteenth** *adj, n*

fifth *adj, n* (of) number five in a series **fifth column** group secretly helping the enemy

fifty *adj, n, pl* **-ties** five times ten **fiftieth** *adj, n*

fig *n* soft pear-shaped fruit; tree bearing it

fight *v* **fighting, fought** struggle (against) in battle or physical combat; struggle to overcome someone or obtain something; carry on (a battle or contest); make (one's way) somewhere with difficulty ▷ *n* aggressive conflict between two (groups of) people; quarrel or contest; resistance; boxing match **fighter** *n* boxer; determined person; aircraft designed to destroy other aircraft **fight off** *v* drive away (an attacker); struggle to avoid

figment *n* **figment of one's imagination** imaginary thing

figure *n* numerical symbol; amount expressed in numbers; bodily shape; well-known person; representation in painting or sculpture of a human form; *maths* any combination of lines, planes, points, or curves ▷ *v* consider, conclude; (usu foll by *in*) be included (in) **figure of speech** expression in which words do not have their literal meaning **figurative** *adj* (of language) abstract, imaginative, or symbolic **figuratively** *adv* **figurine** *n* statuette **figurehead** *n* nominal leader; carved bust at the bow of a ship **figure out** *v* solve or understand

filament *n* fine wire in a light bulb that gives out light; fine thread

filbert *n* hazelnut

filch *v* steal (small amounts)

file[1] *n* box or folder used to keep documents in order; documents in a file; information about a person or subject; line of people one behind the other; *computers* organized collection of related material ▷ *v* place (a document) in a file; place (a legal document) on official record; bring a lawsuit, esp for divorce; walk or march in a line

file[2] *n* tool with a roughened blade for smoothing or shaping ▷ *v* shape or smooth with a file **filings** *pl n* shavings removed by a file

filial *adj* of or befitting a son or daughter

filibuster *n* obstruction of legislation by making long speeches; person who filibusters ▷ *v* obstruct (legislation) with such delaying tactics

filigree *n* delicate ornamental work of gold or silver wire ▷ *adj* made of filigree

fill *v* make or become full; occupy completely; plug (a gap); satisfy (a need); hold and perform the duties of (a position); appoint to (a job or position) **one's fill** sufficient for one's needs or wants **filler** *n* substance that fills a gap or increases bulk **filling** *n* substance that fills a gap or cavity, esp in a tooth ▷ *adj* (of food) substantial and satisfying **filling station** *Chiefly Brit* garage selling petrol, oil, etc

fillet *n* boneless piece of meat or fish ▷ *v* **filleting, filleted** remove the bones from

fillip *n* something that adds stimulation or enjoyment

filly *n, pl* **-lies** young female horse

film *n* sequence of images projected on a screen, creating the illusion of movement; story told in such a sequence of images; thin strip of light-sensitive cellulose used to make photographic negatives and transparencies; thin sheet or layer ▷ *v* photograph with a movie or video camera; make a film of (a scene, story, etc); cover or become covered with a thin layer ▷ *adj* connected with films or the cinema **filmy** *adj* very thin, delicate **film strip** set of pictures on a strip of film, projected separately as slides

filter *n* material or device permitting fluid to pass but retaining solid particles; device that blocks certain frequencies of sound or light; *Brit* traffic signal that allows vehicles to turn either left or right while the main signals are at red ▷ *v* remove impurities from (a substance) with a filter; pass slowly or faintly

filth *n* disgusting dirt; offensive material or language **filthy** *adj* **filthiness** *n*

filtrate *n* filtered gas or liquid ▷ *v* remove impurities with a filter **filtration** *n*

fin *n* projection from a fish's body enabling it to balance and swim; vertical tailplane of an aircraft

finagle [fin-**nay**-gl] *v* get or achieve by craftiness or trickery

final *adj* at the end; having no possibility of further change, action, or discussion ▷ *n* deciding contest between winners of previous rounds in a competition ▷ *pl Brit & SAfr* last examinations in an educational course **finally** *adv* **finality** *n* **finalist** *n* competitor in a final **finalize** *v* put into final form **finale** [fin-**nah**-lee] *n* concluding part of a dramatic performance or musical work

finance *v* provide or obtain funds for ▷ *n* management of money, loans, or credits; (provision of) funds ▷ *pl* money resources **financial** *adj* **financially** *adv* **financier** *n* person involved in large-scale financial business **financial year** twelve-month period used for financial calculations

finch *n, pl* **finches** small songbird with a short strong beak

find *v* **finding, found** discover by chance; discover by search or effort; become aware of; consider to have a particular quality; experience (a particular feeling); *law* pronounce (the defendant) guilty or not guilty; provide, esp with difficulty ▷ *n* person or thing found, esp when valuable **finder** *n* **finding** *n* conclusion from an investigation **find out** *v* gain knowledge of; detect (a crime, deception, etc)

fine¹ *adj* very good; (of weather) clear and dry; in good health; satisfactory; of delicate workmanship; thin or slender; subtle or abstruse *eg a fine distinction* **finely** *adv* **fineness** *n* **finery** *n* showy clothing **fine art** art produced to appeal to the sense of beauty **fine-tune** *v* make small adjustments to (something) so that it works really well

fine² *n* payment imposed as a penalty ▷ *v* impose a fine on

finesse [fin-**ness**] *n* delicate skill; subtlety and tact

finger *n* one of the four long jointed parts of the hand; part of a glove that covers a finger; quantity of liquid in a glass as deep as a finger is wide ▷ *v* touch or handle with the fingers **fingering** *n* technique of using the fingers in playing a musical instrument **fingerboard** *n* part of a stringed instrument against which the strings are pressed **fingerprint** *n* impression of the ridges on the tip of the finger ▷ *v* take the fingerprints of (someone) **finger stall** cover to protect an injured finger

finicky *adj* excessively particular, fussy; overelaborate

finish *v* bring to an end, stop; use up; bring to a desired or completed condition; put a surface texture on (wood, cloth, or metal); defeat or destroy ▷ *n* end, last part; death or defeat; surface texture

finite *adj* having limits in space, time, or size

fiord *n* same as **fjord**

fir *n* pyramid-shaped tree with needle-like leaves and erect cones

fire *n* state of combustion producing heat, flames, and smoke; *Brit* burning coal or wood, or a gas or electric device, used to heat a room; uncontrolled destructive burning; shooting of guns; intense passion, ardour ▷ *v* operate (a weapon) so that a bullet or missile is released; *Informal* dismiss from employment; bake (ceramics etc) in a kiln; excite **firearm** *n* rifle, pistol, or shotgun **firebrand** *n* person who causes unrest **firebreak** *n* strip of cleared land to stop the advance of a fire **fire brigade** organized body of people whose job is to put out fires **firedamp** *n* explosive gas, composed mainly of methane, formed in mines **fire**

drill rehearsal of procedures for escape from a fire **fire engine** vehicle with apparatus for extinguishing fires **fire escape** metal staircase or ladder down the outside of a building for escape in the event of fire **firefighter** *n* member of a fire brigade **firefly** *n, pl* **-flies** beetle that glows in the dark **fireguard** *n* protective grating in front of a fire **fire irons** tongs, poker, and shovel for tending a domestic fire **fireplace** *n* recess in a room for a fire **fire power** *mil* amount a weapon or unit can fire **fire station** building where firefighters are stationed **firewall** *n computers* computer that prevents unauthorized access to a computer network from the Internet **firework** *n* device containing chemicals that is ignited to produce spectacular explosions and coloured sparks ▷ *pl* show of fireworks; *Informal* outburst of temper **firing squad** group of soldiers ordered to execute an offender by shooting

firm[1] *adj* not soft or yielding; securely in position; definite; having determination or strength ▷ *adv* in an unyielding manner *eg hold firm* ▷ *v* make or become firm **firmly** *adv* **firmness** *n*

firm[2] *n* business company

firmament *n lit* sky or the heavens

first *adj* earliest in time or order; graded or ranked above all others ▷ *n* person or thing coming before all others; outset or beginning; first-class honours degree at university; lowest forward gear in a motor vehicle ▷ *adv* before anything else; for the first time **firstly** *adv* **first aid** immediate medical assistance given in an emergency **first-class** *adj* of the highest class or grade; excellent **first-hand** *adj, adv* (obtained) directly from the original source **first mate** officer of a merchant ship second in command to the captain **first person** *grammar* category of verbs and pronouns used by a speaker to refer to himself or herself **first-rate** *adj* excellent **first-strike** *adj* (of a nuclear missile) for use in an opening attack to destroy enemy weapons

firth *n* narrow inlet of the sea, esp in Scotland

fiscal *adj* of government finances, esp taxes

fish *n, pl* **fish, fishes** cold-blooded vertebrate with gills, that lives in water; its flesh as food ▷ *v* try to catch fish; fish in (a particular area of water); (foll by *for*) grope for and find with difficulty; (foll by *for*) seek indirectly **fisherman** *n* person who catches fish for a living or for pleasure **fishery** *n, pl* **-eries** area of the sea used for fishing **fishy** *adj* of or like fish; *Informal* suspicious or questionable **fishfinger** *n* oblong piece of fish covered in breadcrumbs **fishmeal** dried ground fish used as animal feed or fertilizer **fishmonger** *n* seller of fish **fishnet** *n* open mesh fabric resembling netting **fishwife** *n, pl* **-wives** coarse scolding woman

fishplate *n* metal plate holding rails together

fission *n* splitting; *biol* asexual reproduction involving a division into two or more equal parts; splitting of an atomic nucleus with the release of a large amount of energy **fissionable** *adj* **fissile** *adj* capable of undergoing nuclear fission; tending to split

fissure [**fish**-er] *n* long narrow cleft or crack

fist *n* clenched hand **fisticuffs** *pl n* fighting with the fists

fit[1] *v* **fitting, fitted** be appropriate or suitable for; be of the correct size or shape (for); adjust so as to make appropriate; try (clothes) on and note any adjustments needed; make competent or ready; correspond with the facts or circumstances ▷ *adj* appropriate; in good health; worthy or deserving ▷ *n* way in which something fits **fitness** *n* **fitter** *n* person skilled in the installation and adjustment of machinery; person who fits garments **fitting** *adj* appropriate, suitable ▷ *n* accessory or part; trying on of clothes for size ▷ *pl* furnishings and accessories in a building **fitment** *n* detachable part of the furnishings of a room **fit in** *v* give a place or time to; belong or conform **fit out** *v* provide with the necessary equipment

fit[2] *n* sudden attack or convulsion, such as an epileptic seizure; sudden short burst or spell

fitful *adj* occurring in irregular spells **fitfully** *adv*

five *adj, n* one more than four **fiver** *n Informal* five-pound note **fives** *n* ball game resembling squash but played with bats or the hands

fix *v* make or become firm, stable, or secure; repair; place permanently; settle definitely; direct (the eyes etc) steadily; *Informal* unfairly influence the outcome of ▷ *n Informal* difficult situation; ascertaining of the position of a ship by radar etc; *slang* injection of a narcotic drug **fixed** *adj* **fixedly** *adv* steadily **fixer** *n* solution used to make a photographic image permanent; *slang* person who arranges things **fix up** *v* arrange; provide (with)

fixation *n* obsessive interest in something **fixated** *adj* obsessed

fixative *n* liquid used to preserve or hold things in place

fixture *n* permanently fitted piece of household equipment; person whose presence seems permanent; sports match or the date fixed for it

fizz *v* make a hissing or bubbling noise; give off small bubbles ▷ *n* hissing or bubbling noise; releasing of small bubbles of gas by a liquid; effervescent drink **fizzy** *adj*

fizzle *v* make a weak hissing or bubbling sound **fizzle out** *v Informal* come to nothing, fail

fjord [fee-**ord**] *n* long narrow inlet of the sea between cliffs, esp in Norway

flab *n Informal* unsightly body fat

flabbergasted *adj* completely astonished

flabby *adj* **-bier, -biest** having flabby flesh; loose or limp

flaccid [**flas**-sid] *adj* soft and limp **flaccidity** *n*

flag[1] *n* piece of cloth attached to a pole as an emblem or signal ▷ *v* **flagging, flagged** mark with a flag or sticker; (often foll by *down*) signal (a vehicle) to stop by waving the arm **flag day** *Brit* day on which small stickers are sold in the streets for charity **flagpole, flagstaff** *n* pole for a flag **flagship** *n* admiral's ship; most important product of an organization

flag[2] *v* **flagging, flagged** lose enthusiasm or vigour

flag[3], **flagstone** *n* flat paving-stone **flagged** *adj* paved

with flagstones
flagellate [**flaj**-a-late] *v* whip, esp in religious penance or for sexual pleasure **flagellation** *n* **flagellant** *n* person who whips himself or herself
flageolet [flaj-a-**let**] *n* small instrument like a recorder
flagon *n* wide bottle for wine or cider; narrow-necked jug for liquid
flagrant [**flayg**-rant] *adj* openly outrageous **flagrantly** *adv*
flail *v* wave about wildly; beat or thrash ▷ *n* tool formerly used for threshing grain by hand
flair *n* natural ability; stylishness
flak *n* anti-aircraft fire; *Informal* severe criticism
flake[1] *n* small thin piece, esp chipped off something; *Aust & NZ, Informal* unreliable person ▷ *v* peel off in flakes **flaky** *adj* **flake out** *v Informal* collapse or fall asleep from exhaustion
flake[2] *n* (in Australia) the commercial name for the meat of the gummy shark
flambé [**flahm**-bay] *v* **flambéing, flambéed** cook or serve (food) in flaming brandy
flamboyant *adj* behaving in a very noticeable, extravagant way; very bright and showy **flamboyance** *n*
flame *n* luminous burning gas coming from burning material ▷ *v* burn brightly; become bright red **old flame** *Informal* former sweetheart
flamenco *n, pl* **-cos** rhythmical Spanish dance accompanied by a guitar and vocalist; music for this dance
flamingo *n, pl* **-gos, -goes** large pink wading bird with a long neck and legs
flammable *adj* easily set on fire **flammability** *n*

> This now replaces *inflammable* in labelling and packaging because *inflammable* was often mistaken to mean 'not flammable'

flan *n* open sweet or savoury tart
flange *n* projecting rim or collar
flank *n* part of the side between the hips and ribs; side of a body of troops ▷ *v* be at or move along the side of
flannel *n Brit* small piece of cloth for washing the face; soft woollen fabric for clothing; *Informal* evasive talk ▷ *pl* trousers made of flannel ▷ *v* **-nelling, -nelled** *Informal* talk evasively **flannelette** *n* cotton imitation of flannel
flap *v* **flapping, flapped** move back and forwards or up and down ▷ *n* action or sound of flapping; piece of something attached by one edge only; *Informal* state of excitement or panic
flapjack *n* chewy biscuit made with oats
flare *v* blaze with a sudden unsteady flame; *Informal* (of temper, violence, or trouble) break out suddenly; (of a skirt or trousers) become wider towards the hem ▷ *n* sudden unsteady flame; signal light ▷ *pl* flared trousers **flared** *adj* (of a skirt or trousers) becoming wider towards the hem
flash *n* sudden burst of light or flame; sudden occurrence (of intuition or emotion); very short time; brief unscheduled news announcement; *photog* small bulb that produces an intense flash of light ▷ *adj* (also **flashy**) vulgarly showy ▷ *v* (cause to) burst into flame; (cause to) emit light suddenly or intermittently; move

very fast; come rapidly (to mind or view); *Informal* display ostentatiously; *slang* expose oneself indecently **flasher** *n slang* man who exposes himself indecently **flashback** *n* scene in a book, play, or film, that shows earlier events **flash flood** sudden short-lived flood **flashlight** *n US* torch **flash point** critical point beyond which a situation will inevitably erupt into violence; lowest temperature at which vapour given off by a liquid can ignite

flashing *n* watertight material used to cover joins in a roof

flask *n* same as **vacuum flask:** flat bottle for carrying alcoholic drink in the pocket; narrow-necked bottle

flat[1] *adj* **flatter, flattest** level and horizontal; even and smooth; (of a tyre) deflated; outright; fixed; without variation or emotion; (of a drink) no longer fizzy; (of a battery) with no electrical charge; *music* below the true pitch ▷ *adv* in or into a flat position; completely or absolutely; exactly; *music* too low in pitch ▷ *n music* symbol lowering the pitch of a note by a semitone; mud bank exposed at low tide **flat out** with maximum speed or effort **flatly** *adv* **flatness** *n* **flatten** *v* **flatfish** *n* sea fish, such as the sole, which has a flat body **flat-pack** *adj* (of furniture, etc) supplied in pieces in a flat box for assembly by the buyer **flat racing** horse racing over level ground with no jumps

flat[2] *n* set of rooms for living in which are part of a larger building ▷ *v* **flatting, flatted** *Aust & NZ* live in a flat **flatlet** *n Brit, Aust & SAfr* small flat **flatmate** *n* person with whom one shares a flat

flatter *v* praise insincerely; show to advantage; make (a person) appear more attractive in a picture than in reality **flatterer** *n* **flattery** *n*

flattie *n NZ & SAfr, Informal* flat tyre

flatulent *adj* suffering from or caused by too much gas in the intestines **flatulence** *n*

flaunt *v* display (oneself or one's possessions) arrogantly.

> Be careful not to confuse this with *flout* meaning 'disobey'

flautist *n* flute player

flavour *n* distinctive taste; distinctive characteristic or quality ▷ *v* give flavour to **flavouring** *n* substance used to flavour food **flavourless** *adj*

flaw *n* imperfection or blemish; mistake that makes a plan or argument invalid **flawed** *adj* **flawless** *adj*

flax *n* plant grown for its stem fibres and seeds; its fibres, spun into linen thread **flaxen** *adj* (of hair) pale yellow

flay *v* strip the skin off; criticize severely

flea *n* small wingless jumping bloodsucking insect **flea market** market for cheap goods **fleapit** *n Informal* shabby cinema or theatre

fleck *n* small mark, streak, or speck ▷ *v* speckle

fled *v* past of **flee**

fledged *adj* (of young birds) able to fly; (of people) fully trained **fledgling, fledgeling** *n* young bird ▷ *adj* new or inexperienced

flee *v* **fleeing, fled** run away (from)

fleece *n* sheep's coat of wool; sheepskin used as a lining for coats etc; warm polyester fabric; *Brit* jacket or top made of this fabric ▷ *v* defraud or overcharge **fleecy** *adj*

made of or like fleece
fleet[1] *n* number of warships organized as a unit; number of vehicles under the same ownership
fleet[2] *adj* swift in movement **fleeting** *adj* rapid and soon passing **fleetingly** *adv*
flesh *n* soft part of a human or animal body; *Informal* excess fat; meat of animals as opposed to fish or fowl; thick soft part of a fruit or vegetable; human body as opposed to the soul **in the flesh** in person, actually present **one's own flesh and blood** one's family **flesh-coloured** *adj* yellowish-pink **fleshly** *adj* carnal; worldly **fleshy** *adj* plump; like flesh **flesh wound** wound affecting only superficial tissue
fleur-de-lys, fleur-de-lis [flur-de-**lee**] *n, pl* **fleurs-de-lys, fleurs-de-lis** heraldic lily with three petals
flew *v* past tense of **fly**[1]
flex *n* flexible insulated electric cable ▷*v* bend **flexible** *adj* easily bent; adaptable **flexibly** *adv* **flexibility** *n* **flexitime, flextime** *n* system permitting variation in starting and finishing times of work
flick *v* touch or move with the finger or hand in a quick movement; move with a short sudden movement, often repeatedly ▷*n* tap or quick stroke ▷*pl slang* the cinema **flick knife** knife with a spring-loaded blade which shoots out when a button is pressed **flick through** *v* look at (a book or magazine) quickly or idly
flicker *v* shine unsteadily or intermittently; move quickly to and fro ▷*n* unsteady brief light; brief faint indication
flier *n* see **fly**[1]
flight[1] *n* journey by air; act or manner of flying through the air; group of birds or aircraft flying together; aircraft flying on a scheduled journey; set of stairs between two landings; stabilizing feathers or plastic fins on an arrow or dart **flightless** *adj* (of certain birds or insects) unable to fly **flight attendant** person who looks after passengers on an aircraft **flight deck** crew compartment in an airliner; runway deck on an aircraft carrier **flight recorder** electronic device in an aircraft storing information about its flight
flight[2] *n* act of running away
flighty *adj* **flightier, flightiest** frivolous and fickle
flimsy *adj* **-sier, -siest** not strong or substantial; thin; not very convincing **flimsily** *adv* **flimsiness** *n*
flinch *v* draw back or wince, as from pain **flinch from** *v* shrink from or avoid
fling *v* **flinging, flung** throw, send, or move forcefully or hurriedly ▷*n* spell of self-indulgent enjoyment; brief romantic or sexual relationship **fling oneself into** (start to) do with great vigour
flint *n* hard grey stone; piece of this; small piece of an iron alloy, used in cigarette lighters **flinty** *adj* cruel; of or like flint
flip *v* **flipping, flipped** throw (something small or light) carelessly; turn (something) over; (also **flip one's lid**) *slang* fly into an emotional state ▷*n* snap or tap ▷*adj Informal* flippant **flipper** *n* limb of a sea animal adapted for swimming; one of a pair of paddle-like rubber devices worn on

the feet to help in swimming **flip-flop** *n Brit & SAfr* rubber-soled sandal held on by a thong between the big toe and the next toe **flip through** *v* look at (a book or magazine) quickly or idly

flippant *adj* treating serious things lightly **flippancy** *n*

flirt *v* behave as if sexually attracted to someone; consider lightly, toy (with) ▷ *n* person who flirts **flirtation** *n* **flirtatious** *adj*

flit *v* **flitting, flitted** move lightly and rapidly; *Scot* move house; *Informal* depart hurriedly and secretly ▷ *n* act of flitting

float *v* rest on the surface of a liquid; move lightly and freely; move about aimlessly; launch (a company); offer for sale on the stock market; allow (a currency) to fluctuate against other currencies ▷ *n* light object used to help someone or something float; indicator on a fishing line that moves when a fish bites; decorated truck in a procession; *Brit* small delivery vehicle; sum of money used for minor expenses or to provide change **floating** *adj* moving about, changing *eg floating population;* (of a voter) not committed to one party

flock[1] *n* number of animals of one kind together; large group of people; *Christianity* congregation ▷ *v* gather in a crowd

flock[2] *n* wool or cotton waste used as stuffing ▷ *adj* (of wallpaper) with a velvety raised pattern

floe *n* sheet of floating ice

flog *v* **flogging, flogged** beat with a whip or stick; (sometimes foll by *off*) *Brit, NZ & SAfr, Informal* sell; *NZ, Informal* steal **flogging** *n*

flood *n* overflow of water onto a normally dry area; large amount of water; rising of the tide ▷ *v* cover or become covered with water; fill to overflowing; come in large numbers or quantities **floodgate** *n* gate used to control the flow of water **floodlight** *n* lamp that casts a broad intense beam of light ▷ *v* **-lighting, -lit** illuminate by floodlight

floor *n* lower surface of a room; level of a building; flat bottom surface; (right to speak in) a legislative hall ▷ *v* knock down; *Informal* disconcert or defeat **floored** *adj* covered with a floor **flooring** *n* material for floors **floor show** entertainment in a nightclub

floozy *n, pl* **-zies** *old-fashioned slang* disreputable woman

flop *v* **flopping, flopped** bend, fall, or collapse loosely or carelessly; *Informal* fail ▷ *n Informal* failure; flopping movement **floppy** *adj* hanging downwards, loose **floppy disk** *computers* flexible magnetic disk that stores information

flora *n* plants of a given place or time

floral *adj* consisting of or decorated with flowers

floret *n* small flower forming part of a composite flower head

floribunda *n* type of rose whose flowers grow in large clusters

florid *adj* with a red or flushed complexion; ornate

florin *n* former British and Australian coin

florist *n* seller of flowers

floss *n* fine silky fibres

flotation *n* launching or financing of a business enterprise

flotilla *n* small fleet or fleet of small ships

flotsam *n* floating wreckage **flotsam and jetsam** odds and ends; *Brit* homeless or vagrant people

flounce[1] *v* go with emphatic movements ▷ *n* flouncing movement

flounce[2] *n* ornamental frill on a garment

flounder[1] *v* move with difficulty, as in mud; behave or speak in a bungling or hesitating manner

flounder[2] *n* edible flatfish

flour *n* powder made by grinding grain, esp wheat ▷ *v* sprinkle with flour **floury** *adj*

flourish *v* be active, successful, or widespread; be at the peak of development; wave (something) dramatically ▷ *n* dramatic waving motion; ornamental curly line in writing **flourishing** *adj*

flout *v* deliberately disobey (a rule, law, etc).

> Be careful not to confuse this with *flaunt* meaning 'display'

flow *v* (of liquid) move in a stream; (of blood or electricity) circulate; proceed smoothly; hang loosely; be abundant ▷ *n* act, rate, or manner of flowing; continuous stream or discharge **flow chart** diagram showing a sequence of operations in a process

flower *n* part of a plant that produces seeds; plant grown for its colourful flowers; best or finest part ▷ *v* produce flowers, bloom; reach full growth or maturity **in flower** with flowers open **flowered** *adj* decorated with a floral design **flowery** *adj* decorated with a floral design; (of language or style) elaborate **flowerbed** *n* piece of ground for growing flowers

flown *v* past participle of **fly**[1]

fl. oz. fluid ounce(s)

flu *n* short for **influenza**

fluctuate *v* change frequently and erratically **fluctuation** *n*

flue *n* passage or pipe for smoke or hot air

fluent *adj* able to speak or write with ease; spoken or written with ease **fluently** *adv* **fluency** *n*

fluff *n* soft fibres; *Brit, Aust & NZ, Informal* mistake ▷ *v* make or become soft and puffy; *Informal* make a mistake **fluffy** *adj*

fluid *n* substance able to flow and change its shape; a liquid or a gas ▷ *adj* able to flow or change shape easily **fluidity** *n* **fluid ounce** *Brit* one twentieth of a pint (28.4 ml)

fluke[1] *n* accidental stroke of luck

fluke[2] *n* flat triangular point of an anchor; lobe of a whale's tail

fluke[3] *n* parasitic worm

flume *n* narrow sloping channel for water; enclosed water slide at a swimming pool

flummox *v* puzzle or confuse

flung *v* past of **fling**

flunk *v US, Aust, NZ & S Afr, Informal* fail

flunky, flunkey *n, pl* **flunkies, flunkeys** servile person; manservant who wears a livery

fluorescence *n* emission of light from a substance bombarded by particles, such as electrons, or by radiation **fluoresce** *v* exhibit fluorescence

fluorescent *adj* of or resembling fluorescence

fluoride *n* compound containing fluorine **fluoridate** *v* add fluoride to (water) as protection against tooth decay **fluoridation** *n*

fluorine *n chem* toxic yellow gas, most reactive of all the elements

flurry *n, pl* **-ries** sudden

commotion; gust of rain or wind or fall of snow ▷ *v* **-rying, -ried** confuse

flush[1] *v* blush or cause to blush; send water through (a toilet or pipe) so as to clean it; elate ▷ *n* blush; rush of water; excitement or elation

flush[2] *adj* level with the surrounding surface; *Informal* having plenty of money

flush[3] *v* drive out of a hiding place

flush[4] *n* (in card games) hand all of one suit

fluster *v* make nervous or upset ▷ *n* nervous or upset state

flute *n* wind instrument consisting of a tube with sound holes and a mouth hole in the side; tall narrow wineglass **fluted** *adj* having decorative grooves

flutter *v* wave rapidly; flap the wings; move quickly and irregularly; (of the heart) beat abnormally quickly ▷ *n* flapping movement; nervous agitation; *Informal* small bet; abnormally fast heartbeat

fluvial *adj* of rivers

flux *n* constant change or instability; flow or discharge; substance mixed with metal to assist in fusion

fly[1] *v* **flying, flew, flown** move through the air on wings or in an aircraft; control the flight of; float, flutter, display, or be displayed in the air; transport or be transported by air; move quickly or suddenly; (of time) pass rapidly; flee ▷ *n, pl* **flies** (often pl) *Brit* fastening at the front of trousers; flap forming the entrance to a tent ▷ *pl* space above a stage, used for storage **flyer, flier** *n* small advertising leaflet; aviator **flying fox** *Aust & NZ* platform suspended from an overhead cable, used for transporting people or materials **flying phalanger** phalanger with black-striped greyish fur, which moves with gliding leaps **flyleaf** *n* blank leaf at the beginning or end of a book **flyover** *n* road passing over another by a bridge **flywheel** *n* heavy wheel regulating the speed of a machine

fly[2] *n, pl* **flies** two-winged insect **flycatcher** *n* small insect-eating songbird **fly-fishing** *n* fishing with an artificial fly as a lure **flypaper** *n* paper with a sticky poisonous coating, used to kill flies **flyweight** *n* boxer weighing up to 112lb (professional) or 51kg (amateur)

fly[3] *adj slang* sharp and cunning

flying *adj* hurried and brief **flying boat** aircraft fitted with floats instead of landing wheels **flying colours** conspicuous success **flying fish** fish with winglike fins used for gliding above the water **flying fox** large fruit-eating bat **flying saucer** unidentified disc-shaped flying object, supposedly from outer space **flying squad** small group of police, soldiers, etc, ready to act quickly **flying start** very good start

FM frequency modulation

foal *n* young of a horse or related animal ▷ *v* give birth to a foal

foam *n* mass of small bubbles on a liquid; frothy saliva; light spongelike solid used for insulation, packing, etc ▷ *v* produce foam **foamy** *adj*

fob *n* short watch chain; small pocket in a waistcoat

fob off *v* **fobbing, fobbed** pretend to satisfy (a person) with lies or excuses; sell or pass off (inferior

goods) as valuable
fo'c's'le *n* same as **forecastle**
focus *n, pl* **-cuses, -ci** [-sye] point at which light or sound waves converge; state of an optical image when it is clearly defined; state of an instrument producing such an image; centre of interest or activity ▷ *v* **-cusing, -cused** *or* **-cussing, -cussed** bring or come into focus; concentrate (on) **focal** *adj* of or at a focus **focus group** group of people gathered by a market-research company to discuss and assess a product or service
fodder *n* feed for livestock
foe *n* enemy, opponent
foetid *adj* same as **fetid**
foetus *n, pl* **-tuses** same as **fetus**
fog *n* mass of condensed water vapour in the lower air, often greatly reducing visibility ▷ *v* **fogging, fogged** cover with steam **foggy** *adj* **foghorn** *n* large horn sounded to warn ships in fog
fogey, fogy *n, pl* **-geys, -gies** old-fashioned person
foible *n* minor weakness or slight peculiarity
foil[1] *v* ruin (someone's plan)
foil[2] *n* metal in a thin sheet, esp for wrapping food; anything which sets off another thing to advantage
foil[3] *n* light slender flexible sword tipped with a button
foist *v* (foll by *on, upon*) force or impose on
fold[1] *v* bend so that one part covers another; interlace (the arms); clasp (in the arms); *cooking* mix gently; *Informal* fail or go bankrupt ▷ *n* folded piece or part; mark, crease, or hollow made by folding **folder** *n* piece of folded cardboard for holding loose papers
fold[2] *n Brit, Aust & SAfr* enclosure for sheep; church or its members
foliage *n* leaves **foliation** *n* process of producing leaves
folio *n, pl* **-lios** sheet of paper folded in half to make two leaves of a book; book made up of such sheets; page number
folk *n* people in general; race of people ▷ *pl* relatives **folksy** *adj* simple and unpretentious **folk dance** traditional country dance **folklore** *n* traditional beliefs and stories of a people **folk song** song handed down among the common people; modern song like this **folk singer**
follicle *n* small cavity in the body, esp one from which a hair grows
follow *v* go or come after; be a logical or natural consequence of; keep to the course or track of; act in accordance with; accept the ideas or beliefs of; understand; have a keen interest in **follower** *n* disciple or supporter **following** *adj* about to be mentioned; next in time ▷ *n* group of supporters ▷ *prep* as a result of **follow up** *v* investigate; do a second, often similar, thing after (a first) **follow-up** *n* something done to reinforce an initial action
folly *n, pl* **-lies** foolishness; foolish action or idea; useless extravagant building
foment [foam-**ent**] *v* encourage or stir up (trouble)
fond *adj* tender, loving; unlikely to be realized *eg a fond hope* **fond of** having a liking for **fondly** *adv* **fondness** *n*
fondant *n* (sweet made from) flavoured paste of sugar and water
fondle *v* caress
fondue *n* Swiss dish of a hot

melted cheese sauce into which pieces of bread are dipped

font¹ *n* bowl in a church for baptismal water

font² *n* set of printing type of one style and size

fontanelle *n* soft membranous gap between the bones of a baby's skull

food *n* what one eats, solid nourishment **foodie** *n Informal* gourmet **foodstuff** *n* substance used as food

fool¹ *n* person lacking sense or judgment; person made to appear ridiculous; *hist* jester, clown ▷ *v* deceive (someone) **foolish** *adj* unwise, silly, or absurd **foolishly** *adv* **foolishness** *n* **foolery** *n* foolish behaviour **fool around** *v* act or play irresponsibly or aimlessly **foolproof** *adj* unable to fail

fool² *n* dessert of puréed fruit mixed with cream

foolhardy *adj* recklessly adventurous **foolhardiness** *n*

foolscap *n* size of paper, 34.3 x 43.2 centimetres

foot *n, pl* **feet** part of the leg below the ankle; unit of length of twelve inches (0.3048 metre); lowest part of anything; unit of poetic rhythm **foot it** *Informal* walk **foot the bill** pay the entire cost **footage** *n* amount of film used **foot-and-mouth disease** infectious viral disease of sheep, cattle, etc **footbridge** *n* bridge for pedestrians **footfall** *n* sound of a footstep **foothills** *pl n* hills at the foot of a mountain **foothold** *n* secure position from which progress may be made; small place giving a secure grip for the foot **footlights** *pl n* lights across the front of a stage **footloose** *adj* free from ties **footman** *n* male servant in uniform **footnote** *n* note printed at the foot of a page **footpath** *n* narrow path for walkers only; *Aust* raised space alongside a road, for pedestrians **footplate** *n* platform in the cab of a locomotive for the driver **footprint** *n* mark left by a foot **footstep** *n* step in walking; sound made by walking **footstool** *n* low stool used to rest the feet on while sitting **footwear** *n* anything worn to cover the feet **footwork** *n* skilful use of the feet, as in sport or dancing

football *n* game played by two teams of eleven players kicking a ball in an attempt to score goals; any of various similar games, such as rugby; ball used for this **footballer** *n* **football pools** form of gambling on the results of soccer matches

footing *n* basis or foundation; relationship between people; secure grip by or for the feet

footling *adj Chiefly Brit, Informal* trivial

footsie *n Informal* flirtation involving the touching together of feet

fop *n* man excessively concerned with fashion **foppery** *n* **foppish** *adj*

for *prep* indicating a person intended to benefit from or receive something, span of time or distance, person or thing represented by someone, etc *eg a gift for you; for five miles; playing for his country* ▷ *conj* because **for it** *Informal* liable for punishment or blame

forage *v* search about (for) ▷ *n* food for cattle or horses

foray *n* brief raid or attack; first attempt or new undertaking
forbear *v* cease or refrain (from doing something) **forbearance** *n* tolerance, patience
forbid *v* prohibit, refuse to allow **forbidden** *adj* **forbidding** *adj* severe, threatening
force *n* strength or power; compulsion; *physics* influence tending to produce a change in a physical system; mental or moral strength; person or thing with strength or influence; vehemence or intensity; group of people organized for a particular task or duty ▷*v* compel, make (someone) do something; acquire or produce through effort, strength, etc; propel or drive; break open; impose or inflict; cause to grow at an increased rate **in force** having legal validity; in great numbers **forced** *adj* compulsory; false or unnatural; due to an emergency **forceful** *adj* emphatic and confident; effective **forcefully** *adv* **forcible** *adj* involving physical force or violence; strong and emphatic **forcibly** *adv*
forceps *pl n* surgical pincers
ford *n* shallow place where a river may be crossed ▷*v* cross (a river) at a ford
fore *adj* in, at, or towards the front ▷*n* front part **to the fore** in a conspicuous position
fore- *prefix* before in time or rank *eg forefather*; at the front *eg forecourt*
fore-and-aft *adj* located at both ends of a ship
forearm[1] *n* arm from the wrist to the elbow
forearm[2] *v* prepare beforehand
forebear *n* ancestor
foreboding *n* feeling that something bad is about to happen
forecast *v* **-casting, -cast** *or* **-casted** predict (weather, events, etc) ▷*n* prediction
forecastle [**foke**-sl] *n* raised front part of a ship
foreclose *v* take possession of (property bought with borrowed money which has not been repaid) **foreclosure** *n*
forecourt *n* courtyard or open space in front of a building
forefather *n* ancestor
forefinger *n* finger next to the thumb
forefront *n* most active or prominent position; very front
foregather *v* meet together or assemble
forego *v* same as **forgo**
foregoing *adj* going before, preceding **foregone conclusion** inevitable result
foreground *n* part of a view, esp in a picture, nearest the observer
forehand *n tennis etc* stroke played with the palm of the hand facing forward
forehead *n* part of the face above the eyebrows
foreign *adj* not of, or in, one's own country; relating to or connected with other countries; unfamiliar, strange; in an abnormal place or position *eg foreign matter* **foreigner** *n*
foreleg *n* either of the front legs of an animal
forelock *n* lock of hair over the forehead
foreman *n* person in charge of a group of workers; leader of a jury
foremast *n* mast nearest the bow of a ship
foremost *adj, adv* first in time, place, or importance

forename *n* first name
forenoon *n Chiefly US & Canadian* morning
forensic *adj* used in or connected with courts of law **forensic medicine** use of medical knowledge for the purposes of the law
foreplay *n* sexual stimulation before intercourse
forerunner *n* person or thing that goes before, precursor
foresail *n* main sail on the foremast of a ship
foresee *v* see or know beforehand **foreseeable** *adj*

> SPELLING There are 665 occurrences of the word **unforeseen** in Collins Word Web. The misspelling *unforseen* occurs 50 times

foreshadow *v* show or indicate beforehand
foreshore *n* part of the shore between high- and low-tide marks
foreshorten *v* represent (an object) in a picture as shorter than it really is, in accordance with perspective
foresight *n* ability to anticipate and provide for future needs
foreskin *n* fold of skin covering the tip of the penis
forest *n* large area with a thick growth of trees **forested** *adj* **forestry** *n* science of planting and caring for trees; management of forests **forester** *n* person skilled in forestry
forestall *v* prevent or guard against in advance
foretaste *n* early limited experience of something to come
foretell *v* tell or indicate beforehand
forethought *n* thoughtful planning for future events
forever, for ever *adv* without end; at all times; *Informal* for a long time
forewarn *v* warn beforehand
foreword *n* introduction to a book
forfeit [**for**-fit] *n* thing lost or given up as a penalty for a fault or mistake ▷*v* lose as a forfeit ▷*adj* lost as a forfeit **forfeiture** *n*
forge[1] *n* place where metal is worked, smithy; furnace for melting metal ▷*v* make a fraudulent imitation of (something); shape (metal) by heating and hammering it; create (an alliance etc)
forge[2] *v* advance steadily **forge ahead** increase speed or take the lead
forger *n* person who makes an illegal copy of something
forgery *n, pl* **-ries** illegal copy of something; crime of making an illegal copy
forget *v* **-getting, -got, -gotten** fail to remember; neglect; leave behind by mistake **forgetful** *adj* tending to forget **forgetfulness** *n* **forget-me-not** *n* plant with clusters of small blue flowers
forgive *v* **-giving, -gave, -given** cease to blame or hold resentment against, pardon **forgiveness** *n*
forgo *v* do without or give up
forgot *v* past tense of **forget** **forgotten** *v* past participle of **forget**
fork *n* tool for eating food, with prongs and a handle; large similarly-shaped tool for digging or lifting; point where a road, river, etc divides into branches; one of the branches ▷*v* pick up, dig, etc with a fork; branch; take one or other branch at a fork in the road **forked** *adj* **fork-lift truck** vehicle with a

forklike device at the front which can be raised or lowered to move loads **fork out** *v Informal* pay

forlorn *adj* lonely and unhappy **forlorn hope** hopeless enterprise **forlornly** *adv*

form *n* shape or appearance; mode in which something appears; type or kind; printed document with spaces for details; physical or mental condition; previous record of an athlete, racehorse, etc; class in school ▷ *v* give a (particular) shape to or take a (particular) shape; come or bring into existence; make or be made; train; acquire or develop **formless** *adj*

formal *adj* of or characterized by established conventions of ceremony and behaviour; of or for formal occasions; stiff in manner; organized; symmetrical **formally** *adv* **formality** *n, pl* **-ties** requirement of custom or etiquette; necessary procedure without real importance **formalize** *v* make official or formal

formaldehyde [for-**mal**-de-hide] *n* colourless pungent gas used to make formalin **formalin** *n* solution of formaldehyde in water, used as a disinfectant or a preservative for biological specimens

format *n* style in which something is arranged ▷ *v* **-matting, -matted** arrange in a format

formation *n* forming; thing formed; structure or shape; arrangement of people or things acting as a unit

formative *adj* of or relating to development; shaping

former *adj* of an earlier time, previous **the former** first mentioned of two **formerly** *adv*

Formica *n* ® kind of laminated sheet used to make heat-resistant surfaces

formic acid *n* acid derived from ants

formidable *adj* frightening because difficult to overcome or manage; extremely impressive **formidably** *adv*

formula *n, pl* **-las, -lae** group of numbers, letters, or symbols expressing a scientific or mathematical rule; method or rule for doing or producing something; set form of words used in religion, law, etc; specific category of car in motor racing **formulaic** *adj* **formulate** *v* plan or describe precisely and clearly **formulation** *n*

fornicate *v* have sexual intercourse without being married **fornication** *n* **fornicator** *n*

forsake *v* **-saking, -sook, -saken** withdraw support or friendship from; give up, renounce

forsooth *adv obs* indeed

forswear *v* **-swearing, -swore, -sworn** renounce or reject

forsythia [for-**syth**-ee-a] *n* shrub with yellow flowers in spring

fort *n* fortified building or place **hold the fort** *Informal* keep things going during someone's absence

forte¹ [**for**-tay] *n* thing at which a person excels

forte² [**for**-tay] *adv music* loudly

forth *adv* forwards, out, or away

forthcoming *adj* about to appear or happen; available; (of a person) communicative

forthright *adj* direct and outspoken

forthwith *adv* at once

fortieth *adj, n* see **forty**

fortify *v* **-fying, -fied** make (a

place) defensible, as by building walls; strengthen; add vitamins etc to (food); add alcohol to (wine) to make sherry or port **fortification** *n*

fortissimo *adv music* very loudly

fortitude *n* courage in adversity or pain

fortnight *n* two weeks **fortnightly** *adv, adj*

FORTRAN *n computers* programming language for mathematical and scientific purposes

fortress *n* large fort or fortified town

fortuitous [for-**tyew**-it-uss] *adj* happening by (lucky) chance **fortuitously** *adv*

fortunate *adj* having good luck; occurring by good luck **fortunately** *adv*

fortune *n* luck, esp when favourable; power regarded as influencing human destiny; wealth, large sum of money ▷ *pl* person's destiny **fortune-teller** *n* person who claims to predict the future of others

forty *adj, n, pl* **-ties** four times ten **fortieth** *adj, n*

forum *n* meeting or medium for open discussion or debate

forward *adj* directed or moving ahead; in, at, or near the front; presumptuous; well developed or advanced; relating to the future ▷ *n* attacking player in various team games, such as soccer or hockey ▷ *adv* forwards ▷ *v* send (a letter etc) on to an ultimate destination; advance or promote **forwards** *adv* towards or at a place further ahead in space or time; towards the front

fossick *v Aust & NZ* search, esp for gold or precious stones

fossil *n* hardened remains of a prehistoric animal or plant preserved in rock **fossilize** *v* turn into a fossil; become out-of-date or inflexible

foster *v* promote the growth or development of; bring up (a child not one's own) ▷ *adj* of or involved in fostering a child *eg foster parents*

fought *v* past of **fight**

foul *adj* loathsome or offensive; stinking or dirty; (of language) obscene or vulgar; unfair ▷ *n sport* violation of the rules ▷ *v* make dirty or polluted; make or become entangled or clogged; *sport* commit a foul against (an opponent) **fall foul of** come into conflict with **foul-mouthed** *adj* habitually using foul language **foul play** unfair conduct, esp involving violence

found[1] *v* past of **find**

found[2] *v* establish or bring into being; lay the foundation of; (foll by *on, upon*) have a basis (in) **founder** *n*

found[3] *v* cast (metal or glass) by melting and setting in a mould; make (articles) by this method

foundation *n* basis or base; part of a building or wall below the ground; act of founding; institution supported by an endowment; cosmetic used as a base for make-up

founder *v* break down or fail; (of a ship) sink; stumble or fall

foundling *n Chiefly Brit* abandoned baby

foundry *n, pl* **-ries** place where metal is melted and cast

fount[1] *n lit* fountain; source

fount[2] *n* set of printing type of one style and size

fountain *n* jet of water; structure from which such a jet spurts; source

fountainhead *n* original source **fountain pen** pen supplied with ink from a container inside it
four *adj, n* one more than three ▷*n* (crew of) four-oared rowing boat **on all fours** on hands and knees **four-letter word** short obscene word referring to sex or excrement **four-poster** *n* bed with four posts supporting a canopy **foursome** *n* group of four people
fourteen *adj, n* four and ten **fourteenth** *adj, n*
fourth *adj, n* (of) number four in a series ▷*n* quarter **fourth dimension** time **fourth estate** the press
fowl *n* domestic cock or hen; any bird used for food or hunted as game
fox *n* reddish-brown bushy-tailed animal of the dog family; its fur; cunning person ▷*v Informal* perplex or deceive **foxy** *adj* of or like a fox, esp in craftiness **foxglove** *n* tall plant with purple or white flowers **foxhole** *n mil* small pit dug for protection **foxhound** *n* dog bred for hunting foxes **fox terrier** small short-haired terrier **foxtrot** *n* ballroom dance with slow and quick steps; music for this
foyer [foy-ay] *n* entrance hall in a theatre, cinema, or hotel
fracas [frak-ah] *n, pl* **-cas** noisy quarrel
fraction *n* numerical quantity that is not a whole number; fragment, piece; *chem* substance separated by distillation **fractional** *adj* **fractionally** *adv*
fractious *adj* easily upset and angered
fracture *n* breaking, esp of a bone ▷*v* break
fragile *adj* easily broken or damaged; in a weakened physical state **fragility** *n*
fragment *n* piece broken off; incomplete piece ▷*v* break into pieces **fragmentary** *adj* **fragmentation** *n*
fragrant *adj* sweet-smelling **fragrance** *n* pleasant smell; perfume, scent
frail *adj* physically weak; easily damaged **frailty** *n, pl* **-ties** physical or moral weakness
frame *n* structure giving shape or support; enclosing case or border, as round a picture; person's build; individual exposure on a strip of film; individual game of snooker in a match ▷*v* put together, construct; put into words; put into a frame; *slang* incriminate (a person) on a false charge **frame of mind** mood or attitude **frame-up** *n slang* false incrimination **framework** *n* supporting structure
franc *n* monetary unit of Switzerland, various African countries, and formerly of France and Belgium
franchise *n* right to vote; authorization to sell a company's goods
Franciscan *n, adj* (friar or nun) of the order founded by St. Francis of Assisi
francium *n chem* radioactive metallic element
Franco- *combining form* of France or the French
frangipani [fran-jee-**pah**-nee] *n* Australian evergreen tree with large yellow fragrant flowers; tropical shrub with fragrant white or pink flowers
frank *adj* honest and straightforward in speech or attitude ▷*n* official mark on a

letter permitting delivery ▷*v* put such a mark on (a letter) **frankly** *adv* **frankness** *n*

frankfurter *n* smoked sausage

frankincense *n* aromatic gum resin burned as incense

frantic *adj* distracted with rage, grief, joy, etc; hurried and disorganized **frantically** *adv*

fraternal *adj* of a brother, brotherly **fraternally** *adv* **fraternity** *n* group of people with shared interests, aims, etc; brotherhood; *US* male social club at college **fraternize** *v* associate on friendly terms **fraternization** *n* **fratricide** *n* crime of killing one's brother; person who does this

Frau [rhymes with **how**] *n, pl* **Fraus, Frauen** German title, equivalent to *Mrs* **Fräulein** [**froy**-line] *n, pl* **-leins, -lein** German title, equivalent to *Miss*

fraud *n* (criminal) deception, swindle; person who acts in a deceitful way **fraudulent** *adj* **fraudulence** *n*

fraught [**frawt**] *adj* tense or anxious **fraught with** involving, filled with

fray[1] *n Brit, Aust & NZ* noisy quarrel or conflict

fray[2] *v* make or become ragged at the edge; become strained

frazzle *n Informal* exhausted state

freak *n* abnormal person or thing; person who is excessively enthusiastic about something ▷*adj* abnormal **freakish** *adj* **freak out** *v Informal* (cause to) be in a heightened emotional state

freckle *n* small brown spot on the skin **freckled** *adj* marked with freckles

free *adj* **freer, freest** able to act at will, not compelled or restrained; not subject (to); provided without charge; not in use; (of a person) not busy; not fixed or joined ▷*v* **freeing, freed** release, liberate; remove (obstacles, pain, etc) from; make available or usable **a free hand** unrestricted freedom to act **freely** *adv* **free fall** part of a parachute descent before the parachute opens **free-for-all** *n Informal* brawl **freehand** *adj* drawn without guiding instruments **freehold** *n* tenure of land for life without restrictions **freeholder** *n* **free house** *Brit* public house not bound to sell only one brewer's products **freelance** *adj, n* (of) a self-employed person doing specific pieces of work for various employers **freeloader** *n slang* habitual scrounger **free-range** *adj* kept or produced in natural conditions **freeway** *n US & Aust* motorway **freewheel** *v* travel downhill on a bicycle without pedalling

-free *combining form* without *eg a trouble-free journey*

freedom *n* being free; right or privilege of unlimited access *eg the freedom of the city*

Freemason *n* member of a secret fraternity pledged to help each other

freesia *n* plant with fragrant tubular flowers

freeze *v* **freezing, froze, frozen** change from a liquid to a solid by the reduction of temperature, as water to ice; preserve (food etc) by extreme cold; (cause to) be very cold; become motionless with fear, shock, etc; fix (prices or wages) at a particular level; ban the exchange or collection of (loans, assets, etc) ▷*n* period of very cold weather;

freezing of prices or wages **freezer** *n* insulated cabinet for cold-storage of perishable foods **freeze-dry** *v* preserve (food) by rapid freezing and drying in a vacuum **freezing** *adj Informal* very cold

freight [frate] *n* commercial transport of goods; cargo transported; cost of this ▷*v* send by freight **freighter** *n* ship or aircraft for transporting goods

French *n* language of France, also spoken in parts of Belgium, Canada, and Switzerland ▷*adj* of France, its people, or their language **French bread** white bread in a long thin crusty loaf **French dressing** salad dressing of oil and vinegar **French fries** potato chips **French horn** brass wind instrument with a coiled tube **French letter** *slang* condom **French polish** shellac varnish for wood **French window** window extending to floor level, used as a door

frenetic [frin-net-ik] *adj* uncontrolled, excited **frenetically** *adv*

frenzy *n, pl* **-zies** violent mental derangement; wild excitement **frenzied** *adj* **frenziedly** *adv*

frequent *adj* happening often; habitual ▷*v* visit habitually **frequently** *adv* **frequency** *n, pl* **-cies** rate of occurrence; *physics* number of times a wave repeats itself in a given time

fresco *n, pl* **-coes, -cos** watercolour painting done on wet plaster on a wall

fresh *adj* newly made, acquired, etc; novel, original; further, additional; (of food) not preserved; (of water) not salty; (of weather) brisk or invigorating; not tired **freshly** *adv* **freshness** *n* **freshen** *v* make or become fresh or fresher **fresher, freshman** *n Brit & US* first-year student

fret[1] *v* **fretting, fretted** be worried **fretful** *adj* irritable

fret[2] *n* small bar on the fingerboard of a guitar etc

fretwork *n* decorative carving in wood **fretsaw** *n* fine saw with a narrow blade, used for fretwork

Freudian [froy-dee-an] *adj* of or relating to the psychoanalyst Sigmund Freud or his theories

friable *adj* easily crumbled

friar *n* member of a male Roman Catholic religious order **friary** *n, pl* **-ries** house of friars

fricassee *n* stewed meat served in a thick white sauce

friction *n* resistance met with by a body moving over another; rubbing; clash of wills or personalities **frictional** *adj*

Friday *n* sixth day of the week **Good Friday** Friday before Easter

fridge *n* apparatus in which food and drinks are kept cool

fried *v* past of **fry**[1]

friend *n* person whom one knows well and likes; supporter or ally; **(F-)** Quaker **friendly** *adj* showing or expressing liking; not hostile, on the same side ▷*n, pl* **-lies** *sport* match played for its own sake and not as part of a competition **-friendly** *combining form* good or easy for the person or thing specified *eg user-friendly* **friendly society** (in Britain) association of people who pay regular dues in return for pensions, sickness benefits, etc **friendliness** *n* **friendless** *adj* **friendship** *n*

Friesian [free-zhan] *n* breed of black-and-white dairy cattle

frieze [**freeze**] *n* ornamental band on a wall
frigate [**frig**-it] *n* medium-sized fast warship
fright *n* sudden fear or alarm; sudden alarming shock **frightful** *adj* horrifying; *Informal* very great **frightfully** *adv*
frighten *v* scare or terrify; force (someone) to do something from fear **frightening** *adj*
frigid [**frij**-id] *adj* (of a woman) sexually unresponsive; very cold; excessively formal **frigidity** *n*
frill *n* gathered strip of fabric attached at one edge ▷ *pl* superfluous decorations or details **frilled** *adj* **frilled lizard** large tree-living Australian lizard with an erectile fold of skin round the neck **frilly** *adj*
fringe *n* hair cut short and hanging over the forehead; ornamental edge of hanging threads, tassels, etc; outer edge; less important parts of an activity or group ▷ *v* decorate with a fringe ▷ *adj* (of theatre) unofficial or unconventional **fringed** *adj* **fringe benefit** benefit given in addition to a regular salary
frippery *n, pl* **-peries** useless ornamentation; trivia
frisk *v* move or leap playfully; *Informal* search (a person) for concealed weapons etc **frisky** *adj* lively or high-spirited
frisson [**frees**-sonn] *n* shiver of fear or excitement
fritter *n* piece of food fried in batter
fritter away *v* waste
frivolous *adj* not serious or sensible; enjoyable but trivial **frivolity** *n*
frizz *v* form (hair) into stiff wiry curls **frizzy** *adj*
frizzle *v* cook or heat until crisp and shrivelled
frock *n* dress **frock coat** man's skirted coat as worn in the 19th century
frog *n* smooth-skinned tailless amphibian with long back legs used for jumping **frog in one's throat** phlegm on the vocal cords, hindering speech **frogman** *n* swimmer with a rubber suit and breathing equipment for working underwater **frogspawn** *n* jelly-like substance containing frog's eggs
frolic *v* **-icking, -icked** run and play in a lively way ▷ *n* lively and merry behaviour **frolicsome** *adj* playful
from *prep* indicating the point of departure, source, distance, cause, change of state, etc.

> The use of *off* to mean *from* is very informal: *They bought milk from* (rather than *off*) *a farmer*

frond *n* long leaf or leaflike part of a fern, palm, or seaweed
front *n* fore part; position directly before or ahead; battle line or area; *meteorol* dividing line between two different air masses; outward appearance; *Informal* cover for another, usu criminal, activity; particular field of activity *eg on the economic front* ▷ *adj* of or at the front ▷ *v* face (onto); be the presenter of (a television show) **frontal** *adj* **frontage** *n* facade of a building **front bench** (in Britain) parliamentary leaders of the government or opposition **front-bencher** *n* **frontrunner** *n* *Informal* person regarded as most likely to win a race, election, etc
frontier *n* area of a country bordering on another
frontispiece *n* illustration facing

the title page of a book

frost *n* white frozen dew or mist; atmospheric temperature below freezing point ▷*v* become covered with frost **frosted** *adj* (of glass) having a rough surface to make it opaque **frosting** *n Chiefly US* sugar icing **frosty** *adj* characterized or covered by frost; unfriendly **frostily** *adv* **frostiness** *n* **frostbite** *n* destruction of tissue, esp of the fingers or ears, by cold **frostbitten** *adj*

froth *n* mass of small bubbles ▷*v* foam **frothy** *adj*

frown *v* wrinkle one's brows in worry, anger, or thought; look disapprovingly (on) ▷*n* frowning expression

frowsty *adj Brit* stale or musty

frowzy, frowsy *adj* **-zier, -ziest** *or* **-sier, -siest** dirty or unkempt

froze *v* past tense of **freeze** **frozen** *v* past participle of **freeze**

frugal *adj* thrifty, sparing; meagre and inexpensive **frugally** *adv* **frugality** *n*

fruit *n* part of a plant containing seeds, esp if edible; any plant product useful to humans; (often pl) result of an action or effort ▷*v* bear fruit **fruiterer** *n* person who sells fruit **fruit fly** small fly that feeds on and lays its eggs in plant tissues; similar fly that feeds on plant sap, decaying fruit, etc, and is widely used in genetics experiments **fruitful** *adj* useful or productive **fruitfully** *adv* **fruitless** *adj* useless or unproductive **fruitlessly** *adv* **fruity** *adj* of or like fruit; (of a voice) mellow; *Brit, Informal* mildly bawdy **fruit machine** coin-operated gambling machine

fruition [froo-**ish**-on] *n* fulfilment of something worked for or desired

frump *n* dowdy woman **frumpy** *adj*

frustrate *v* upset or anger; hinder or prevent **frustrated** *adj* **frustrating** *adj* **frustration** *n*

fry[1] *v* **frying, fried** cook or be cooked in fat or oil ▷*n, pl* **fries** (also **fry-up**) dish of fried food ▷*pl* potato chips

fry[2] *pl n* young fishes **small fry** young or insignificant people

ft. foot; feet

fuchsia [**fyew**-sha] *n* ornamental shrub with hanging flowers

fuddle *v* cause to be intoxicated or confused **fuddled** *adj*

fuddy-duddy *adj, n, pl* **-dies** *Informal* old-fashioned (person)

fudge[1] *n* soft caramel-like sweet

fudge[2] *v* avoid making a firm statement or decision

fuel *n* substance burned or treated to produce heat or power; something that intensifies (a feeling etc) ▷*v* **fuelling, fuelled** provide with fuel

fug *n* hot stale atmosphere **fuggy** *adj*

fugitive [**fyew**-jit-iv] *n* person who flees, esp from arrest or pursuit ▷*adj* fleeing; transient

fugue [**fyewg**] *n* musical composition in which a theme is repeated in different parts

fulcrum *n, pl* **-crums, -cra** pivot about which a lever turns

fulfil *v* **-filling, -filled** bring about the achievement of (a desire or promise); carry out (a request or order); do what is required **fulfilment** *n* **fulfil oneself** *v* achieve one's potential

full *adj* containing as much or as many as possible; abundant in supply; having had enough to eat; plump; complete, whole; (of a garment) of ample cut; (of a sound or flavour) rich and strong ▷ *adv* completely; directly; very **fully** *adv* **fullness** *n* **in full** without shortening **full-blooded** *adj* vigorous or enthusiastic **full-blown** *adj* fully developed **full moon** phase of the moon when it is visible as a fully illuminated disc **full-scale** *adj* (of a plan) of actual size; using all resources **full stop** punctuation mark (.) at the end of a sentence and after abbreviations

fulmar *n* Arctic sea bird

fulminate *v* (foll by *against*) criticize or denounce angrily

fulsome *adj* distastefully excessive or insincere

fumble *v* handle awkwardly; say awkwardly ▷ *n* act of fumbling

fume *v* be very angry; give out smoke or vapour ▷ *pl n* pungent smoke or vapour

fumigate [**fyew**-mig-gate] *v* disinfect with fumes **fumigation** *n*

fun *n* enjoyment or amusement **make fun of** mock or tease **funny** *adj* comical, humorous; odd **funny bone** part of the elbow where the nerve is near the surface **funnily** *adv*

function *n* purpose something exists for; way something works; large or formal social event; *maths* quantity whose value depends on the varying value of another; sequence of operations performed by a computer at a key stroke ▷ *v* operate or work; (foll by *as*) fill the role of **functional** *adj* of or as a function; practical rather than decorative; in working order **functionally** *adv* **functionary** *n, pl* **-aries** official

fund *n* stock of money for a special purpose; supply or store ▷ *pl* money resources ▷ *v* provide money to **funding** *n*

fundamental *adj* essential or primary; basic ▷ *n* basic rule or fact **fundamentally** *adv* **fundamentalism** *n* literal or strict interpretation of a religion **fundamentalist** *n, adj*

fundi *n SAfr* expert or boffin

funeral *n* ceremony of burying or cremating a dead person

funerary *adj* of or for a funeral

funereal [fyew-**neer**-ee-al] *adj* gloomy or sombre

funfair *n* entertainment with machines to ride on and stalls

fungus *n, pl* **-gi, -guses** plant without leaves, flowers, or roots, such as a mushroom or mould **fungal, fungous** *adj* **fungicide** *n* substance that destroys fungi

funicular *n* cable railway on a mountainside or cliff

funk[1] *n* style of dance music with a strong beat **funky** *adj* (of music) having a strong beat

funk[2] *Informal* ▷ *n* nervous or fearful state ▷ *v* avoid (doing something) through fear

funnel *n* cone-shaped tube for pouring liquids into a narrow opening; chimney of a ship or locomotive ▷ *v* **-nelling, -nelled** (cause to) move through or as if through a funnel **funnel-web** *n* large poisonous black spider that builds funnel-shaped webs

fur *n* soft hair of a mammal; animal skin with the fur left on; garment made of this; whitish coating on the tongue or inside a kettle ▷ *v* cover or become covered with fur **furry** *adj* **furrier** *n* dealer in furs

furbish *v* smarten up

furious *adj* very angry; violent or unrestrained **furiously** *adv*

furl *v* roll up and fasten (a sail, umbrella, or flag)
furlong *n* unit of length equal to 220 yards (201.168 metres)
furlough [**fur**-loh] *n* leave of absence
furnace *n* enclosed chamber containing a very hot fire
furnish *v* provide (a house or room) with furniture; supply, provide **furnishings** *pl n* furniture, carpets, and fittings **furniture** *n* large movable articles such as chairs and wardrobes
furore [fyew-**ror**-ee] *n* very excited or angry reaction
furrow *n* trench made by a plough; groove, esp a wrinkle on the forehead ▷ *v* make or become wrinkled; make furrows in
further *adv* in addition; to a greater distance or extent ▷ *adj* additional; more distant ▷ *v* assist the progress of **further education** *Brit* education beyond school other than at a university **furthest** *adv* to the greatest distance or extent ▷ *adj* most distant **furtherance** *n* **furthermore** *adv* besides **furthermost** *adj* most distant
furtive *adj* sly and secretive **furtively** *adv*
fury *n, pl* **-ries** wild anger; uncontrolled violence
furze *n* gorse
fuse[1] *n* cord containing an explosive for detonating a bomb
fuse[2] *n* safety device for electric circuits, containing a wire that melts and breaks the connection when the circuit is overloaded ▷ *v* (cause to) fail as a result of a blown fuse; join or combine; unite by melting; melt with heat
fuselage [**fyew**-zill-lahzh] *n* body of an aircraft
fusilier [fyew-zill-**leer**] *n* soldier of certain regiments
fusillade [fyew-zill-**lade**] *n* continuous discharge of firearms; outburst of criticism, questions, etc
fusion *n* melting; product of fusing; combination of the nucleus of two atoms with the release of energy; something new created by a mixture of qualities, ideas, or things; popular music blending styles, esp jazz and funk ▷ *adj* of a style of cooking that combines traditional Western techniques and ingredients with those used in Eastern cuisine
fuss *n* needless activity or worry; complaint or objection; great display of attention ▷ *v* make a fuss **fussy** *adj* inclined to fuss; overparticular; overelaborate **fussily** *adv* **fussiness** *n*
fusty *adj* **-tier, -tiest** stale-smelling; behind the times **fustiness** *n*
futile *adj* unsuccessful or useless **futility** *n*
futon [**foo**-tonn] *n* Japanese-style bed
future *n* time to come; what will happen; prospects ▷ *adj* yet to come or be; of or relating to time to come; (of a verb tense) indicating that the action specified has not yet taken place **futuristic** *adj* of a design appearing to belong to some future time
fuzz[1] *n* mass of fine or curly hairs or fibres **fuzzy** *adj* of, like, or covered with fuzz; blurred or indistinct; (of hair) tightly curled **fuzzily** *adv* **fuzziness** *n*
fuzz[2] *n slang* police

g

g gram(s); (acceleration due to) gravity
gab *n, v* **gabbing, gabbed** *Informal* talk or chatter **gift of the gab** eloquence **gabby** *adj* **-bier, -biest** *Informal* talkative
gabardine, gaberdine *n* strong twill cloth used esp for raincoats
gabble *v* speak rapidly and indistinctly ▷ *n* rapid indistinct speech
gable *n* triangular upper part of a wall between sloping roofs **gabled** *adj*
gad *v* **gadding, gadded gad about, around** go around in search of pleasure **gadabout** *n* pleasure-seeker
gadfly *n* fly that bites cattle; constantly annoying person
gadget *n* small mechanical device or appliance **gadgetry** *n* gadgets
Gael [gayl] *n* speaker of Gaelic **Gaelic** [gay-lik, gal-lik] *n* any of the Celtic languages of Ireland and the Scottish Highlands ▷ *adj* of the Gaels or their language
gaff[1] *n* stick with an iron hook for landing large fish
gaff[2] *n* **blow the gaff** *slang* divulge a secret
gaffe *n* social blunder
gaffer *n Brit, Informal* foreman or boss; *Informal* old man; senior electrician on a TV or film set
gag[1] *v* **gagging, gagged** choke or retch; stop up the mouth of (a person) with cloth etc; deprive of free speech ▷ *n* cloth etc put into or tied across the mouth
gag[2] *n Informal* joke
gaga [gah-gah] *adj slang* senile
gaggle *n Informal* disorderly crowd; flock of geese
gaiety *n* cheerfulness; merrymaking **gaily** *adv* merrily; colourfully
gain *v* acquire or obtain; increase or improve; reach; (of a watch or clock) be or become too fast ▷ *n* profit or advantage; increase or improvement **gainful** *adj* useful or profitable **gainfully** *adv* **gain on, upon** *v* get nearer to or catch up with
gainsay *v* **-saying, -said** deny or contradict
gait *n* manner of walking
gaiter *n* cloth or leather covering for the lower leg
gala [gah-la] *n* festival; competitive sporting event
galaxy *n, pl* **-axies** system of stars; gathering of famous people **galactic** *adj*
gale *n* strong wind; *Informal* loud outburst
gall[1] [gawl] *n Informal* impudence;

bitter feeling **gall bladder** sac attached to the liver, storing bile **gallstone** *n* hard mass formed in the gall bladder or its ducts

gall² [**gawl**] *v* annoy; make sore by rubbing

gall³ [**gawl**] *n* abnormal outgrowth on a tree or plant

gallant *adj* brave and noble; (of a man) attentive to women **gallantly** *adv* **gallantry** *n* showy, attentive treatment of women; bravery

galleon *n* large three-masted sailing ship of the 15th–17th centuries

gallery *n, pl* **-ries** room or building for displaying works of art; balcony in a church, theatre, etc; passage in a mine; long narrow room for a specific purpose *eg shooting gallery*

galley *n* kitchen of a ship or aircraft; *hist* ship propelled by oars, usu rowed by slaves **galley slave** *hist* slave forced to row in a galley; *Informal* drudge

Gallic *adj* French; of ancient Gaul

gallium *n chem* soft grey metallic element used in semiconductors

gallivant *v* go about in search of pleasure

gallon *n* liquid measure of eight pints, equal to 4.55 litres

gallop *n* horse's fastest pace; galloping ▷ *v* **galloping, galloped** go or ride at a gallop; move or progress rapidly

> SPELLING Although **gallop** has two *l*s, remember that **galloping** and **galloped** have only one *p*

gallows *n* wooden structure used for hanging criminals

Gallup poll *n* public opinion poll carried out by questioning a cross section of the population

galore *adv* in abundance

galoshes *pl n Brit, Aust & NZ* waterproof overshoes

galumph *v Brit, Aust & NZ, Informal* leap or move about clumsily

galvanic *adj* of or producing an electric current generated by chemical means; *Informal* stimulating or startling **galvanize** *v* stimulate into action; coat (metal) with zinc

gambit *n* opening line or move intended to secure an advantage; *chess* opening move involving the sacrifice of a pawn

gamble *v* play games of chance to win money; act on the expectation of something ▷ *n* risky undertaking; bet or wager **gambler** *n* **gambling** *n*

gamboge [gam-**boje**] *n* gum resin used as a yellow pigment and purgative

gambol *v* **-bolling, -bolled** jump about playfully, frolic ▷ *n* frolic

> SPELLING Although the pronunciation is the same as *gamble*, both the verb and the noun **gambol** must always contain an *o*

game¹ *n* amusement or pastime; contest for amusement; single period of play in a contest; animals or birds hunted for sport or food; their flesh; scheme or trick ▷ *v* gamble ▷ *adj* brave; willing **gamely** *adv* **gaming** *n* gambling **gamekeeper** *n Brit, Aust & SAfr* person employed to breed game and prevent poaching **gamer** *n* person who plays computer games **gamesmanship** *n* art of winning by cunning practices without actually cheating

game² *adj Brit, Aust & NZ* lame, crippled

gamete *n biol* reproductive cell

gamine [**gam**-een] *n* slim boyish young woman
gamma *n* third letter of the Greek alphabet **gamma ray** electromagnetic ray of shorter wavelength and higher energy than an x-ray
gammon *n* cured or smoked ham
gammy *adj* **-mier, -miest** same as game²
gamut *n* whole range or scale (of music, emotions, etc)
gander *n* male goose; *Informal* quick look
gang *n* (criminal) group; organized group of workmen **gangland** *n* criminal underworld **gang up** *v* form an alliance (against)
gangling *adj* lanky and awkward
ganglion *n* group of nerve cells; small harmless tumour
gangplank *n* portable bridge for boarding or leaving a ship
gangrene *n* decay of body tissue as a result of disease or injury **gangrenous** *adj*
gangsta rap *n* style of music portraying life in Black ghettos in the US
gangster *n* member of a criminal gang
gangway *n* passage between rows of seats; gangplank
gannet *n* large sea bird; *Brit, slang* greedy person
gantry *n, pl* **-tries** structure supporting something such as a crane or rocket
gaol [**jayl**] *n* same as **jail**
gap *n* break or opening; interruption or interval; divergence or difference **gappy** *adj*
gape *v* stare in wonder; open the mouth wide; be or become wide open **gaping** *adj*
garage *n* building used to house cars; place for the refuelling, sale, and repair of cars ▷ *v* put or keep a car in a garage
garb *n* clothes ▷ *v* clothe
garbage *n* rubbish
garbled *adj* (of a story etc) jumbled and confused
garden *n* piece of land for growing flowers, fruit, or vegetables ▷ *pl* ornamental park ▷ *v* cultivate a garden **gardener** *n* **gardening** *n* **garden centre** place selling plants and gardening equipment
gardenia [gar-**deen**-ya] *n* large fragrant white waxy flower; shrub bearing this
garfish *n* freshwater fish with a long body and very long toothed jaws; sea fish with similar characteristics
gargantuan *adj* huge
gargle *v* wash the throat with (a liquid) by breathing out slowly through the liquid ▷ *n* liquid used for gargling
gargoyle *n* waterspout carved in the form of a grotesque face, esp on a church
garish *adj* crudely bright or colourful **garishly** *adv* **garishness** *n*
garland *n* wreath of flowers worn or hung as a decoration ▷ *v* decorate with garlands
garlic *n* pungent bulb of a plant of the onion family, used in cooking
garment *n* article of clothing ▷ *pl* clothes
garner *v* collect or store
garnet *n* red semiprecious stone
garnish *v* decorate (food) ▷ *n* decoration for food
garret *n* attic in a house
garrison *n* troops stationed in a town or fort; fortified place ▷ *v* station troops in

garrotte, garotte *n* Spanish method of execution by strangling; cord or wire used for this ▷*v* kill by this method

garrulous *adj* talkative

garter *n* band worn round the leg to hold up a sock or stocking

gas *n, pl* **gases, gasses** airlike substance that is not liquid or solid; fossil fuel in the form of a gas, used for heating; gaseous anaesthetic; *Chiefly US* petrol ▷*v* **gassing, gassed** poison or render unconscious with gas; *Informal* talk idly or boastfully **gassy** *adj* filled with gas **gaseous** *adj* of or like gas **gasbag** *n Informal* person who talks too much **gas chamber** airtight room which is filled with poison gas to kill people or animals **gasholder, gasometer** [gas-**som**-it-er] *n* large tank for storing gas **gas mask** mask with a chemical filter to protect the wearer against poison gas

gash *v* make a long deep cut in ▷*n* long deep cut

gasket *n* piece of rubber etc placed between the faces of a metal joint to act as a seal

gasoline *n US* petrol

gasp *v* draw in breath sharply or with difficulty; utter breathlessly ▷*n* convulsive intake of breath

gastric *adj* of the stomach **gastritis** *n* inflammation of the stomach lining

gastroenteritis *n* inflammation of the stomach and intestines

gastronomy *n* art of good eating **gastronomic** *adj*

gastropod *n* mollusc, such as a snail, with a single flattened muscular foot

gate *n* movable barrier, usu hinged, in a wall or fence; opening with a gate; any entrance or way in; (entrance money paid by) those attending a sporting event **gate-crash** *v* enter (a party) uninvited **gatehouse** *n* building at or above a gateway **gateway** *n* entrance with a gate; means of access *eg London's gateway to Scotland*

gâteau [gat-toe] *n, pl* **-teaux** [-toes] rich elaborate cake

gather *v* assemble; collect gradually; increase gradually; learn from information given; pick or harvest; draw (material) into small tucks or folds **gathers** *pl n* gathered folds in material **gathering** *n* assembly

gauche [gohsh] *adj* socially awkward **gaucheness** *n*

gaucho [gow-choh] *n, pl* **-chos** S American cowboy

gaudy *adj* **gaudier, gaudiest** vulgarly bright or colourful **gaudily** *adv* **gaudiness** *n*

gauge [gayj] *v* estimate or judge; measure the amount or condition of ▷*n* measuring instrument; scale or standard of measurement; distance between the rails of a railway track

> SPELLING The vowels in **gauge** are often confused so that the misspelling *guage* is common in Collins Word Web

gaunt *adj* lean and haggard **gauntness** *n*

gauntlet¹ *n* heavy glove with a long cuff **throw down the gauntlet** offer a challenge

gauntlet² *n* **run the gauntlet** be exposed to criticism or unpleasant treatment

gauze *n* transparent loosely-woven fabric, often used for surgical dressings **gauzy** *adj*

gave *v* past tense of **give**

gavel [**gav**-el] *n* small hammer banged on a table by a judge, auctioneer, or chairman to call for attention

gavotte *n* old formal dance; music for this

gawk *v* stare stupidly **gawky** *adj* clumsy or awkward **gawkiness** *n*

gawp *v* *slang* stare stupidly

gay *adj* homosexual; carefree and merry; colourful ▷ *n* homosexual **gayness** *n* homosexuality

gaze *v* look fixedly ▷ *n* fixed look

gazebo [gaz-**zee**-boh] *n, pl* **-bos, -boes** summerhouse with a good view

gazelle *n* small graceful antelope

gazette *n* official publication containing announcements **gazetteer** *n* (part of) a book that lists and describes places

gazillion *n* *Informal* extremely large, unspecified amount **gazillionaire** *n* *Informal* enormously rich person

gazump *v* *Brit & Aust* raise the price of a property after verbally agreeing it with (a prospective buyer)

GB Great Britain

GBH (in Britain) grievous bodily harm

GCE (in Britain) General Certificate of Education

GCSE (in Britain) General Certificate of Secondary Education

gear *n* set of toothed wheels connecting with another or with a rack to change the direction or speed of transmitted motion; mechanism for transmitting motion by gears; setting of a gear to suit engine speed *eg first gear;* clothing or belongings; equipment ▷ *v* prepare or organize for something **in, out of gear** with the gear mechanism engaged *or* disengaged **gearbox** *n* case enclosing a set of gears in a motor vehicle **gear up** *v* prepare for an activity

gecko *n, pl* **geckos, geckoes** small tropical lizard

geebung [**gee**-bung] *n* Australian tree or shrub with an edible but tasteless fruit; fruit of this tree

geek *n* *Informal* boring, unattractive person; person highly knowledgeable in computing **geeky** *adj*

geelbek *n* *SAfr* edible marine fish

geese *n* plural of **goose**

geezer *n* *Brit, Aust & NZ, Informal* man

Geiger counter [**guy**-ger] *n* instrument for detecting and measuring radiation

geisha [**gay**-sha] *n, pl* **-sha, -shas** (in Japan) professional female companion for men

gel [**jell**] *n* jelly-like substance, esp one used to secure a hairstyle ▷ *v* **gelling, gelled** form a gel; *Informal* take on a definite form

gelatine [**jel**-at-teen] **gelatin** *n* substance made by boiling animal bones; edible jelly made of this **gelatinous** [jel-**at**-in-uss] *adj* of or like jelly

geld *v* castrate

gelding *n* castrated horse

gelignite *n* type of dynamite used for blasting

gem *n* precious stone or jewel; highly valued person or thing **gemfish** *n* Australian food fish with a delicate flavour

gen *n* *Informal* information **gen up on** *v* **genning, genned** *Brit, Informal* make or become fully informed about

gendarme [**zhohn**-darm] *n*

member of the French police force

gender *n* state of being male or female; *grammar* classification of nouns in certain languages as masculine, feminine, or neuter

gene [jean] *n* part of a cell which determines inherited characteristics

genealogy [jean-ee-**al**-a-gee] *n, pl* **-gies** (study of) the history and descent of a family or families **genealogical** *adj* **genealogist** *n*

genera [**jen**-er-a] *n* plural of **genus**

general *adj* common or widespread; of or affecting all or most; not specific; including or dealing with various or miscellaneous items; highest in authority or rank *eg general manager* ▷ *n* very senior army officer **in general** mostly or usually **generally** *adv* **generality** *n, pl* **-ties** general principle; state of being general **generalize** *v* draw general conclusions; speak in generalities; make widely known or used **generalization** *n* **general election** election in which representatives are chosen for every constituency **general practitioner** nonspecialist doctor serving a local area

generate *v* produce or bring into being **generative** *adj* capable of producing **generator** *n* machine for converting mechanical energy into electrical energy

generation *n* all the people born about the same time; average time between two generations (about 30 years); generating

generic [jin-**ner**-ik] *adj* of a class, group, or genus **generically** *adv*

generous *adj* free in giving; free from pettiness; plentiful **generously** *adv* **generosity** *n*

genesis [**jen**-iss-iss] *n, pl* **-eses** [-iss-eez] beginning or origin

genetic [jin-**net**-tik] *adj* of genes or genetics **genetics** *n* study of heredity and variation in organisms **geneticist** *n* **genetic engineering** alteration of the genetic structure of an organism for a particular purpose **genetic fingerprinting** use of a person's unique DNA pattern as a means of identification

genial [**jean**-ee-al] *adj* cheerful and friendly **genially** *adv* **geniality** *n*

genie [**jean**-ee] *n* (in fairy tales) servant who appears by magic and grants wishes

genital *adj* of the sexual organs or reproduction **genitals, genitalia** [jen-it-**ail**-ya] *pl n* external sexual organs

genitive *n* grammatical case indicating possession or association

genius [**jean**-yuss] *n* (person with) exceptional ability in a particular field

genocide [**jen**-no-side] *n* murder of a race of people

genre [**zhohn**-ra] *n* style of literary, musical, or artistic work

gent *n Brit, Aust & NZ, Informal* gentleman **gents** *n* men's public toilet

genteel *adj* affectedly proper and polite **genteelly** *adv*

gentian [**jen**-shun] *n* mountain plant with deep blue flowers

gentile *adj, n* non-Jewish (person)

gentle *adj* mild or kindly; not rough or severe; gradual; easily controlled, tame **gentleness** *n* **gently** *adv* **gentleman** *n* polite well-bred man; man of high social position; polite name for a man **gentlemanly** *adj* **gentlewoman** *n fem*

gentry *n* people just below the nobility in social rank **gentrification** *n* taking-over of a traditionally working-class area by middle-class incomers **gentrify** *v*

genuflect *v* bend the knee as a sign of reverence or deference **genuflection, genuflexion** *n*

genuine *adj* not fake, authentic; sincere **genuinely** *adv* **genuineness** *n*

genus [jean-uss] *n, pl* **genera** group into which a family of animals or plants is divided; kind, type

geocentric *adj* having the earth as a centre; measured as from the earth's centre

geography *n* study of the earth's physical features, climate, population, etc **geographer** *n* **geographical, geographic** *adj* **geographically** *adv*

geology *n* study of the earth's origin, structure, and composition **geological** *adj* **geologically** *adv* **geologist** *n*

geometry *n* branch of mathematics dealing with points, lines, curves, and surfaces **geometric, geometrical** *adj* **geometrically** *adv*

Geordie *n* person from, or dialect of, Tyneside, an area of NE England

Georgian *adj* of the time of any of the four kings of Britain called George, esp 1714–1830

geostationary *adj* (of a satellite) orbiting so as to remain over the same point of the earth's surface

geothermal *adj* of or using the heat in the earth's interior

geranium *n* cultivated plant with red, pink, or white flowers

gerbil [jer-bill] *n* burrowing desert rodent of Asia and Africa

geriatrics *n* branch of medicine dealing with old age and its diseases **geriatric** *adj, n* old (person)

germ *n* microbe, esp one causing disease; beginning from which something may develop; simple structure that can develop into a complete organism

German *n* language of Germany, Austria, and part of Switzerland; person from Germany ▷ *adj* of Germany or its language **Germanic** *adj* **German measles** contagious disease accompanied by a cough, sore throat, and red spots **German shepherd dog** Alsatian

germane *adj* **germane to** relevant to

germanium *n chem* brittle grey element that is a semiconductor

germinate *v* (cause to) sprout or begin to grow **germination** *n* **germinal** *adj* of or in the earliest stage of development

gerrymandering *n* alteration of voting constituencies in order to give an unfair advantage to one party

gerund [jer-rund] *n* noun formed from a verb, such as *living*

Gestapo *n* secret state police of Nazi Germany

gestation *n* (period of) carrying of young in the womb between conception and birth; developing of a plan or idea in the mind

gesticulate *v* make expressive movements with the hands and arms **gesticulation** *n*

gesture *n* movement to convey meaning; thing said or done to show one's feelings ▷ *v* gesticulate

get *v* **getting, got** obtain or receive; bring or fetch; contract (an illness); (cause to) become as specified *eg get wet*; understand; (often foll by *to*) come (to) or arrive (at); go on board (a plane, bus, etc); persuade; *Informal* annoy **get across** *v* (cause to) be understood **get at** *v* gain access to; imply or mean; criticize **getaway** *adj, n* (used in) escape **get by** *v* manage in spite of difficulties **get off** *v* (cause to) avoid the consequences of, or punishment for, an action **get off with** *v Informal* start a romantic or sexual relationship with **get over** *v* recover from **get through** *v* (cause to) succeed; use up (money or supplies) **get through to** *v* make (a person) understand; contact by telephone **get-up** *n Informal* costume **get up to** *v* be involved in

geyser [geez-er] *n* spring that discharges steam and hot water; *Brit & SAfr* domestic gas water heater

ghastly *adj* **-lier, -liest** *Informal* unpleasant; deathly pale; *Informal* unwell; *Informal* horrible **ghastliness** *n*

ghat *n* (in India) steps leading down to a river; mountain pass

ghee [gee] *n* (in Indian cookery) clarified butter

gherkin *n* small pickled cucumber

ghetto *n, pl* **-tos, -toes** slum area inhabited by a deprived minority **ghetto-blaster** *n Informal* large portable cassette recorder or CD player

ghillie *n* same as **gillie**

ghost *n* disembodied spirit of a dead person; faint trace ▷*v* ghostwrite **ghost gum** *Aust* eucalyptus with white trunk and branches **ghostly** *adj* **ghost town** deserted town **ghostwriter** *n* writer of a book or article on behalf of another person who is credited as the author

ghoul [gool] *n* person with morbid interests; demon that eats corpses **ghoulish** *adj*

GI *n Informal* US soldier

giant *n* mythical being of superhuman size; very large person or thing ▷*adj* huge

gibber[1] [jib-ber] *v* speak or utter rapidly and unintelligibly **gibberish** *n* rapid unintelligible talk

gibber[2] [gib-ber] *n Aust* boulder; barren land covered with stones

gibbet [jib-bit] *n* gallows for displaying executed criminals

gibbon [gib-bon] *n* agile tree-dwelling ape of S Asia

gibbous *adj* (of the moon) more than half but less than fully illuminated

gibe [jibe] *v, n* same as **jibe**[1]

giblets [jib-lets] *pl n* gizzard, liver, heart, and neck of a fowl

gidday, g'day *interj Aust & NZ* expression of greeting

giddy *adj* **-dier, -diest** having or causing a feeling of dizziness **giddily** *adv* **giddiness** *n*

gift *n* present; natural talent ▷*v* make a present of **gifted** *adj* talented

gig[1] *n* single performance by pop or jazz musicians ▷*v* **gigging, gigged** play a gig or gigs

gig[2] *n* light two-wheeled horse-drawn carriage

gigantic *adj* enormous

giggle *v* laugh nervously or foolishly ▷*n* such a laugh **giggly** *adj*

gigolo [jig-a-lo] *n, pl* **-los** man paid by an older woman to be her escort or lover

gigot *n Chiefly Brit* leg of lamb or mutton
gild *v* **gilding, gilded** *or* **gilt** put a thin layer of gold on; make falsely attractive
gill [jill] *n* liquid measure of quarter of a pint, equal to 0.142 litres
gillie *n* (in Scotland) attendant for hunting or fishing
gills [gillz] *pl n* breathing organs in fish and other water creatures
gilt *adj* covered with a thin layer of gold ▷*n* thin layer of gold used as decoration **gilt-edged** *adj* denoting government stocks on which interest payments and final repayments are guaranteed
gimbals *pl n* set of pivoted rings which allow nautical instruments to remain horizontal at sea
gimcrack [jim-krak] *adj* showy but cheap; shoddy
gimlet [gim-let] *n* small tool with a screwlike tip for boring holes in wood **gimlet-eyed** *adj* having a piercing glance
gimmick *n* something designed to attract attention or publicity **gimmickry** *n* **gimmicky** *adj*
gin¹ *n* spirit flavoured with juniper berries
gin² *n* wire noose used to trap small animals; machine for separating seeds from raw cotton
gin³ *n Aust, offens* Aboriginal woman
ginger *n* root of a tropical plant, used as a spice; light orange-brown colour **gingery** *adj* **ginger ale, beer** fizzy ginger-flavoured soft drink **gingerbread** *n* moist cake flavoured with ginger **ginger group** *Brit, Aust & NZ* group within a larger group that agitates for a more active policy **ginger nut, snap** crisp ginger-flavoured biscuit
gingerly *adv* cautiously
gingham *n* cotton cloth, usu checked or striped
gingivitis [jin-jiv-**vite**-iss] *n* inflammation of the gums
ginkgo [gink-go] *n, pl* **-goes** ornamental Chinese tree
ginseng [jin-seng] *n* (root of) a plant believed to have tonic and energy-giving properties
Gipsy *n, pl* **-sies** same as **Gypsy**
giraffe *n* African ruminant mammal with a spotted yellow skin and long neck and legs
gird *v* **girding, girded** *or* **girt** put a belt round; secure with or as if with a belt; surround **gird (up) one's loins** prepare for action
girder *n* large metal beam
girdle¹ *n* woman's elastic corset; belt; *anat* encircling structure or part ▷*v* surround or encircle
girdle² *n Scot* griddle
girl *n* female child; young woman; girlfriend; *Informal* any woman **girlhood** *n* **girlish** *adj* **girlie, girly** *adj Informal* featuring photographs of naked or scantily clad women **girlfriend** *n* girl or woman with whom a person is romantically or sexually involved; female friend
giro [jire-oh] *n, pl* **-ros** (in some countries) system of transferring money within a post office or bank directly from one account to another; *Brit, Informal* social security payment by giro cheque
girt *v* a past of **gird**
girth *n* measurement round something; band round a horse to hold the saddle in position
gist [jist] *n* substance or main point of a matter
give *v* **giving, gave, given** present (something) to another person;

impart; administer; utter or emit; sacrifice or devote; organize or host; yield or break under pressure ▷ *n* resilience or elasticity **give away** *v* donate as a gift; reveal **giveaway** *n* something that reveals hidden feelings or intentions ▷ *adj* very cheap or free **give in** *v* admit defeat **give off** *v* emit **give out** *v* distribute; emit; come to an end or fail **give over** *v* set aside for a specific purpose; *Informal* cease **give up** *v* abandon; acknowledge defeat

gizzard *n* part of a bird's stomach

glacé [**glass**-say] *adj* preserved in a thick sugary syrup

glacier *n* slow-moving mass of ice formed by accumulated snow **glacial** *adj* of ice or glaciers; very cold; unfriendly **glaciated** *adj* covered with or affected by glaciers **glaciation** *n*

glad *adj* **gladder, gladdest** pleased and happy; causing happiness **glad to** very willing to (do something) **the glad eye** *Chiefly Brit, Informal* inviting or seductive glance **gladly** *adv* **gladness** *n* **gladden** *v* make glad **glad rags** *Informal* best clothes

glade *n* open space in a forest

gladiator *n* (in ancient Rome) man trained to fight in arenas to provide entertainment

gladiolus *n, pl* **-lus, -li, -luses** garden plant with sword-shaped leaves

gladwrap *Aust, NZ & S Afr* ▷ *n* ® thin polythene material for wrapping food ▷ *v* wrap in gladwrap

glamour *n* alluring charm or fascination **glamorous** *adj* alluring **glamorize** *v*

SPELLING People often forget to drop the *u* in **glamour** when they add *ous*. That's why there are 124 occurrences of *glamourous* in Collins Word Web. But the correct spelling is **glamorous**

glance *v* look rapidly or briefly; glint or gleam ▷ *n* brief look **glancing** *adj* hitting at an oblique angle **glance off** *v* strike and be deflected off (an object) at an oblique angle

gland *n* organ that produces and secretes substances in the body **glandular** *adj*

glare *v* stare angrily; be unpleasantly bright ▷ *n* angry stare; unpleasant brightness **glaring** *adj* conspicuous; unpleasantly bright **glaringly** *adv*

glass *n* hard brittle, usu transparent substance consisting of metal silicates or similar compounds; tumbler; its contents; objects made of glass; mirror; barometer ▷ *pl* spectacles **glassy** *adj* like glass; expressionless **glasshouse** *n* greenhouse; *Brit, Informal* army prison

glaucoma *n* eye disease

glaze *v* fit or cover with glass; cover with a protective shiny coating ▷ *n* transparent coating; substance used for this **glazier** *n* person who fits windows with glass

gleam *n* small beam or glow of light; brief or faint indication ▷ *v* emit a gleam **gleaming** *adj*

glean *v* gather (facts etc) bit by bit; gather (the useful remnants of a crop) after harvesting **gleaner** *n*

glee *n* triumph and delight **gleeful** *adj* **gleefully** *adv*

glen *n* deep narrow valley, esp in Scotland

glib *adj* **glibber, glibbest** fluent but

insincere or superficial **glibly** *adv* **glibness** *n*

glide *v* move easily and smoothly; (of an aircraft) move without the use of engines ▷*n* smooth easy movement **glider** *n Aust* flying phalanger **gliding** *n* sport of flying gliders

glimmer *v* shine faintly, flicker ▷*n* faint gleam; faint indication

glimpse *n* brief or incomplete view ▷*v* catch a glimpse of

glint *v* gleam brightly ▷*n* bright gleam

glissando *n music* slide between two notes in which all intermediate notes are played

glisten *v* gleam by reflecting light

glitch *n* small problem that stops something from working properly

glitter *v* shine with bright flashes; be showy ▷*n* sparkle or brilliance; tiny pieces of shiny decorative material

gloaming *n Scot, poetic* twilight

gloat *v* (often foll by *over*) regard one's own good fortune or the misfortune of others with smug or malicious pleasure

glob *n* rounded mass of thick fluid

globe *n* sphere with a map of the earth on it; spherical object; *SAfr* light bulb **the globe** the earth **global** *adj* worldwide; total or comprehensive **globalization** *n* process by which a company, etc, expands to operate internationally **global warming** increase in the overall temperature worldwide believed to be caused by the greenhouse effect **globally** *adv* **globetrotter** *n* habitual worldwide traveller **globetrotting** *n, adj*

globule *n* small round drop **globular** *adj*

glockenspiel *n* percussion instrument consisting of small metal bars played with hammers

gloom *n* melancholy or depression; darkness **gloomy** *adj* **gloomier, gloomiest** **gloomily** *adv*

glory *n, pl* **-ries** praise or honour; splendour; praiseworthy thing ▷*v* **-rying, -ried** (foll by *in*) triumph or exalt **glorify** *v* make (something) seem more worthy than it is; praise **glorification** *n* **glorious** *adj* brilliantly beautiful; delightful; full of or conferring glory **gloriously** *adv* **glory hole** *Informal* untidy cupboard or storeroom

gloss[1] *n* surface shine or lustre; paint or cosmetic giving a shiny finish **glossy** *adj* **-sier, -siest** smooth and shiny; (of a magazine) printed on shiny paper **glossily** *adv* **glossiness** *n* **gloss over** *v* (try to) cover up or pass over (a fault or error)

gloss[2] *n* explanatory comment added to the text of a book ▷*v* add glosses to

glossary *n, pl* **-ries** list of special or technical words with definitions

glottal *adj* of the glottis

glottis *n, pl* **-tises, -tides** vocal cords and the space between them

glove *n* covering for the hand with individual sheaths for each finger and the thumb **gloved** *adj* covered by a glove or gloves **glove compartment** *or* **box** small storage area in the dashboard of a car

glow *v* emit light and heat without flames; shine; have a feeling of wellbeing or satisfaction; (of a colour) look warm; be hot ▷*n* glowing light; warmth of colour; feeling of wellbeing **glow-worm** *n*

insect giving out a green light
glower [rhymes with **power**] *v, n* scowl
gloxinia *n* tropical plant with large bell-shaped flowers
glucose *n* kind of sugar found in fruit
glue *n* natural or synthetic sticky substance used as an adhesive ▷ *v* **gluing** *or* **glueing, glued** fasten with glue; (foll by *to*) pay full attention to *eg her eyes were glued to the TV* **gluey** *adj* **glue-sniffing** *n* inhaling of glue fumes for intoxicating or hallucinatory effects
glum *adj* **glummer, glummest** sullen or gloomy **glumly** *adv*
glut *n* excessive supply ▷ *v* **glutting, glutted** oversupply
gluten [**gloo**-ten] *n* protein found in cereal grain
glutinous [**gloo**-tin-uss] *adj* sticky or gluey
glutton *n* greedy person; person with a great capacity for something **gluttonous** *adj* **gluttony** *n*
glycerine, glycerin *n* colourless sweet liquid used widely in chemistry and industry
glycerol [**gliss**-ser-ol] *n* technical name for **glycerine**
gm gram
GM genetically modified
GMO genetically modified organism
GMT Greenwich Mean Time
gnarled *adj* rough, twisted, and knobbly
gnash *v* grind (the teeth) together in anger or pain
gnat *n* small biting two-winged fly
gnaw *v* **gnawing, gnawed, gnawed** *or* **gnawn** bite or chew steadily; (foll by *at*) cause constant distress (to)
gneiss *n* coarse-grained metamorphic rock
gnome *n* imaginary creature like a little old man
gnomic [**no**-mik] *adj* of pithy sayings
Gnosticism *n* religious movement believing in intuitive spiritual knowledge **Gnostic** *n, adj*
gnu [noo] *n* oxlike S African antelope
go *v* **going, went, gone** move to or from a place; be in regular attendance at; depart; be, do, or become as specified; be allotted to a specific purpose or recipient; blend or harmonize; fail or break down; elapse; be got rid of; attend; be acceptable ▷ *n* attempt; verbal attack; turn **make a go of** be successful at **go back on** *v* break (a promise etc) **go-between** *n* intermediary **go for** *v Informal* choose; attack; apply to equally **go-getter** *n* energetically ambitious person **go-go dancer** scantily dressed erotic dancer **go off** *v* explode; ring or sound; *Informal* become stale or rotten; *Informal* stop liking **go out** *v* go to entertainments or social functions; be romantically involved (with); be extinguished **go over** *v* examine or check **go-slow** *n* deliberate slowing of work-rate as an industrial protest **go through** *v* suffer or undergo; examine or search
goad *v* provoke (someone) to take some kind of action, usu in anger ▷ *n* spur or provocation; spiked stick for driving cattle
goal *n sport* posts through which the ball or puck has to be propelled to score; score made in this way; aim or purpose **goalie** *n Informal*

goalkeeper **goalkeeper** *n* player whose task is to stop shots entering the goal **goalpost** *n* one of the two posts marking the limit of a goal **move the goalposts** change the aims of an activity to ensure the desired result

goanna *n* large Australian lizard

goat *n* sure-footed ruminant animal with horns **get someone's goat** *slang* annoy someone **goatee** *n* pointed tuftlike beard

gob *n* lump of a soft substance; *Brit, Aust & NZ, slang* mouth

gobbet *n* lump, esp of food

gobble¹ *v* eat hastily and greedily

gobble² *n* rapid gurgling cry of the male turkey ▷ *v* make this noise

gobbledegook, gobbledygook *n* unintelligible (official) language or jargon

goblet *n* drinking cup without handles

goblin *n* (in folklore) small malevolent creature

goby *n, pl* **-by, -bies** small spiny-finned fish

god *n* spirit or being worshipped as having supernatural power; object of worship, idol; (**G-**) (in monotheistic religions) the Supreme Being, creator and ruler of the universe **the gods** top balcony in a theatre **goddess** *n fem* **godlike** *adj* **godly** *adj* devout or pious **godliness** *n* **god-fearing** *adj* pious and devout **godforsaken** *adj* desolate or dismal **godsend** *n* something unexpected but welcome

godetia *n* plant with showy flowers

godparent *n* person who promises at a child's baptism to bring the child up as a Christian **godchild** *n* child for whom a person stands as godparent **goddaughter** *n* **godfather** *n* male godparent; head of a criminal, esp Mafia, organization **godmother** *n* **godson** *n*

gogga *n SAfr, Informal* any small insect

goggle *v* (of the eyes) bulge; stare **goggles** *pl n* protective spectacles

going *n* condition of the ground for walking or riding over; speed or progress; departure ▷ *adj* thriving; current or accepted **going-over** *n, pl* **goings-over** *Informal* investigation or examination; scolding or thrashing **goings-on** *pl n* mysterious or unacceptable events

goitre [goy-ter] *n* swelling of the thyroid gland in the neck

go-kart *n* small low-powered racing car

gold *n* yellow precious metal; coins or articles made of this; colour of gold ▷ *adj* made of gold; gold-coloured **goldcrest** *n* small bird with a yellow crown **gold-digger** *n Informal* woman who uses her sexual attractions to get money from a man **goldfinch** *n* kind of finch, the male of which has yellow-and-black wings **goldfish** *n* orange fish kept in ponds or aquariums **gold leaf** thin gold sheet used for gilding **gold medal** medal given to the winner of a competition or race

golden *adj* made of gold; gold-coloured; very successful or promising **golden eagle** large mountain eagle of the N hemisphere **golden handshake** *Informal* payment to a departing employee **golden rule** important principle **golden wattle** Australian plant with yellow flowers that yields a useful gum and bark **golden wedding** fiftieth wedding anniversary

golf *n* outdoor game in which a ball is struck with clubs into a series of holes ▷*v* play golf **golfer** *n*

golliwog *n* soft black-faced doll

gonad *n* organ producing reproductive cells, such as a testicle or ovary

gondola *n* long narrow boat used in Venice; suspended cabin of a cable car, airship, etc **gondolier** *n* person who propels a gondola

gone *v* past participle of **go** **goner** *n Informal* person or thing beyond help or recovery

gong *n* rimmed metal disc that produces a note when struck; *slang* medal

gonorrhoea [gon-or-**ree**-a] *n* venereal disease with a discharge from the genitals

good *adj* **better, best** giving pleasure; morally excellent; beneficial; kindly; talented; well-behaved; valid; reliable; complete or full ▷*n* benefit; positive moral qualities ▷*pl* merchandise; property **as good as** virtually **for good** permanently **goodness** *n* **goodly** *adj* considerable **goody** *n Informal* hero in a book or film; enjoyable thing **goody-goody** *adj, n* smugly virtuous (person) **good-for-nothing** *adj, n* irresponsible or worthless (person) **Good Samaritan** person who helps another in distress **goodwill** *n* kindly feeling; value of a business in reputation etc over and above its tangible assets

goodbye *interj, n* expression used on parting

gooey *adj* **gooier, gooiest** *Informal* sticky and soft

goof *Informal* ▷*n* mistake ▷*v* make a mistake

googly *n, pl* **-lies** *cricket* ball that spins unexpectedly from off to leg on the bounce

goon *n Informal* stupid person; *Chiefly US* hired thug

goose *n, pl* **geese** web-footed bird like a large duck; female of this bird **goose flesh, pimples** bumpy condition of the skin and bristling of the hair due to cold or fright **goose step** march step in which the leg is raised rigidly

gooseberry *n* edible yellowy-green berry; *Brit, Informal* unwanted third person accompanying a couple

gopher [**go**-fer] *n* American burrowing rodent

gore[1] *n* blood from a wound

gore[2] *v* pierce with horns

gorge *n* deep narrow valley ▷*v* eat greedily **make one's gorge rise** cause feelings of disgust or nausea

gorgeous *adj* strikingly beautiful or attractive; *Informal* very pleasant **gorgeously** *adv*

gorgon *n* terrifying or repulsive woman

Gorgonzola *n* sharp-flavoured blue-veined Italian cheese

gorilla *n* largest of the apes, found in Africa

gormless *adj Informal* stupid

gorse *n* prickly yellow-flowered shrub

gory *adj* **gorier, goriest** horrific or bloodthirsty; involving bloodshed

goshawk *n* large hawk

gosling *n* young goose

gospel *n* (**G-**) any of the first four books of the New Testament; unquestionable truth; Black religious music originating in the churches of the Southern US

gossamer *n* very fine fabric; filmy cobweb

gossip *n* idle talk, esp about other people; person who engages in gossip ▷ *v* **gossiping, gossiped** engage in gossip **gossipy** *adj*

got *v* past of **get** **have got** possess **have got to** need or be required to

Gothic *adj* (of architecture) of or in the style common in Europe from the 12th–16th centuries, with pointed arches; of or in an 18th-century literary style characterized by gloom and the supernatural; (of print) using a heavy ornate typeface

gouache *n* (painting using) watercolours mixed with glue

Gouda *n* mild-flavoured Dutch cheese

gouge [**gowj**] *v* scoop or force out; cut (a hole or groove) in (something) ▷ *n* hole or groove; chisel with a curved cutting edge

goulash [**goo**-lash] *n* rich stew seasoned with paprika

gourd [**goord**] *n* fleshy fruit of a climbing plant; its dried shell, used as a container

gourmand [**goor**-mand] *n* person who is very keen on food and drink

gourmet [**goor**-may] *n* connoisseur of food and drink

gout [**gowt**] *n* disease causing inflammation of the joints

govern *v* rule, direct, or control; exercise restraint over (temper etc) **governable** *adj* **governance** *n* governing **governess** *n* woman teacher in a private household **governor** *n* official governing a province or state; senior administrator of a society, institution, or prison **governor general** representative of the Crown in a Commonwealth country

government *n* executive policy-making body of a state; exercise of political authority over a country or state; system by which a country or state is ruled **governmental** *adj*

> SPELLING In Collins Word Web, there are hundreds of examples of *goverment* without its middle *n*. Remember it has two *n*s: **government**

gown *n* woman's long formal dress; surgeon's overall; official robe worn by judges, clergymen, etc

goy *n, pl* **goyim, goys** *slang* Jewish word for a non-Jew

GP general practitioner

GPS Global Positioning System: a satellite-based navigation system

grab *v* **grabbing, grabbed** grasp suddenly, snatch ▷ *n* sudden snatch; mechanical device for gripping

grace *n* beauty and elegance; polite, kind behaviour; goodwill or favour; delay granted; short prayer of thanks for a meal; (**G-**) title of a duke, duchess, or archbishop ▷ *v* add grace to **graceful** *adj* **gracefully** *adv* **graceless** *adj* **gracious** *adj* kind and courteous; condescendingly polite; elegant **graciously** *adv* **grace note** *music* note ornamenting a melody

grade *n* place on a scale of quality, rank, or size; mark or rating; *US, Aust & SAfr* class in school ▷ *v* arrange in grades; assign a grade to **make the grade** succeed **gradation** *n* (stage in) a series of degrees or steps; arrangement in stages

gradient *n* (degree of) slope

gradual *adj* occurring, developing, or moving in small

stages **gradually** *adv*

graduate *v* receive a degree or diploma; group by type or quality; mark (a container etc) with units of measurement ▷ *n* holder of a degree **graduation** *n*

graffiti [graf-**fee**-tee] *pl n* words or drawings scribbled or sprayed on walls etc

> SPELLING People get confused about the number of *f*s and *t*s in **graffiti**. The favourite misspelling in Collins Word Web is *grafitti*. The correct spelling has two *f*s and only one *t*

graft[1] *n* surgical transplant of skin or tissue; shoot of a plant set in the stalk of another ▷ *v* transplant (living tissue) surgically; insert (a plant shoot) in another stalk

graft[2] *Brit, Informal* ▷ *n* hard work; obtaining of money by misusing one's position ▷ *v* work hard **grafter** *n*

grail *n* same as **Holy Grail**

grain *n* seedlike fruit of a cereal plant; cereal plants in general; small hard particle; very small amount; arrangement of fibres, as in wood; texture or pattern resulting from this **go against the grain** be contrary to one's natural inclination **grainy** *adj*

gram, gramme *n* metric unit of mass equal to one thousandth of a kilogram

grammar *n* branch of linguistics dealing with the form, function, and order of words; use of words; book on the rules of grammar **grammarian** *n* **grammatical** *adj* according to the rules of grammar **grammatically** *adv* **grammar school** *Brit* esp formerly, a secondary school providing an education with a strong academic bias

gramophone *n* old-fashioned type of record player

grampus *n, pl* **-puses** dolphin-like mammal

gran *n Brit, Aust & NZ, Informal* grandmother

granary *n, pl* **-ries** storehouse for grain

grand *adj* large or impressive, imposing; dignified or haughty; *Informal* excellent; (of a total) final ▷ *n slang* thousand pounds or dollars; grand piano **grandchild** *n* child of one's child **granddaughter** *n* female grandchild **grandfather** *n* male grandparent **grandfather clock** tall standing clock with a pendulum and wooden case **grandmother** *n* female grandparent **grandparent** *n* parent of one's parent **grand piano** large harp-shaped piano with the strings set horizontally **grand slam** winning of all the games or major tournaments in a sport in one season **grandson** *n* male grandchild **grandstand** *n* terraced block of seats giving the best view at a sports ground

grandee *n* person of high station

grandeur *n* magnificence; nobility or dignity

grandiloquent *adj* using pompous language **grandiloquence** *n*

grandiose *adj* imposing; pretentiously grand **grandiosity** *n*

grange *n Brit* country house with farm buildings

granite [**gran**-nit] *n* very hard igneous rock often used in building

granny, grannie *n, pl* **-nies** *Informal* grandmother **granny flat** flat in or added to a house, suitable for an elderly parent

grant *v* consent to fulfil (a request); give formally; admit ▷ *n* sum of money provided by a government for a specific purpose, such as education **take for granted** accept as true without proof; take advantage of without due appreciation

granule *n* small grain **granular** *adj* of or like grains **granulated** *adj* (of sugar) in the form of coarse grains

grape *n* small juicy green or purple berry, eaten raw or used to produce wine, raisins, currants, or sultanas **grapevine** *n* grape-bearing vine; *Informal* unofficial way of spreading news

grapefruit *n* large round yellow citrus fruit

graph *n* drawing showing the relation of different numbers or quantities plotted against a set of axes

graphic *adj* vividly descriptive; of or using drawing, painting, etc **graphics** *pl n* diagrams, graphs, etc, esp as used on a television programme or computer screen **graphically** *adv*

graphite *n* soft black form of carbon, used in pencil leads

graphology *n* study of handwriting **graphologist** *n*

grapnel *n* device with several hooks, used to grasp or secure things

grapple *v* try to cope with (something difficult); come to grips with (a person) **grappling iron** grapnel

grasp *v* grip something firmly; understand; try to seize ▷ *n* grip or clasp; understanding; total rule or possession **grasping** *adj* greedy or avaricious

grass *n* common type of plant with jointed stems and long narrow leaves, including cereals and bamboo; lawn; pasture land; *slang* marijuana; *Brit, slang* person who informs, esp on criminals ▷ *v* cover with grass; (often foll by *on*) *Brit, slang* inform on **grassy** *adj* **-sier, -siest** **grasshopper** *n* jumping insect with long hind legs **grass roots** ordinary members of a group, as distinct from its leaders; essentials **grassroots** *adj* **grass tree** Australian plant with stiff grasslike leaves and small white flowers

grate[1] *v* rub into small bits on a rough surface; scrape with a harsh rasping noise; annoy **grater** *n* **grating** *adj* harsh or rasping; annoying

grate[2] *n* framework of metal bars for holding fuel in a fireplace **grating** *n* framework of metal bars covering an opening

grateful *adj* feeling or showing gratitude **gratefully** *adv*

gratify *v* **-fying, -fied** satisfy or please; indulge (a desire or whim) **gratification** *n*

gratis *adv, adj* free, for nothing

gratitude *n* feeling of being thankful for a favour or gift

gratuitous *adj* unjustified *eg gratuitous violence*; given free **gratuitously** *adv*

gratuity *n, pl* **-ties** money given for services rendered, tip

grave[1] *n* hole for burying a corpse **gravestone** *n* stone marking a grave **graveyard** *n* cemetery

grave[2] *adj* causing concern; serious and solemn **gravely** *adv*

grave[3] [rhymes with **halve**] *n* accent (`) over a vowel to indicate a special pronunciation

gravel *n* mixture of small stones and coarse sand **gravelled** *adj* covered with gravel **gravelly** *adj* covered with gravel; rough-sounding
graven *adj* carved or engraved
gravid [grav-id] *adj med* pregnant
gravitate *v* be influenced or drawn towards; *physics* move by gravity **gravitation** *n* **gravitational** *adj*
gravity *n, pl* **-ties** force of attraction of one object for another, esp of objects to the earth; seriousness or importance; solemnity
gravy *n, pl* **-vies** juices from meat in cooking; sauce made from these
gray *adj Chiefly US* grey
grayling *n* fish of the salmon family
graze[1] *v* feed on grass
graze[2] *v* scratch or scrape the skin; touch lightly in passing ▷ *n* slight scratch or scrape
grease *n* soft melted animal fat; any thick oily substance ▷ *v* apply grease to **greasy** *adj* **greasier, greasiest** covered with or containing grease **greasiness** *n* **greasepaint** *n* theatrical make-up
great *adj* large in size or number; important; pre-eminent; *Informal* excellent **great-** *prefix* one generation older or younger than *eg great-grandfather* **greatly** *adv* **greatness** *n* **greatcoat** *n* heavy overcoat **Great Dane** very large dog with short smooth hair
greave *n* piece of armour for the shin
grebe *n* diving water bird
Grecian [gree-shan] *adj* of ancient Greece
greed *n* excessive desire for food, wealth, etc **greedy** *adj* **greedily** *adv* **greediness** *n*
Greek *n* language of Greece; person from Greece ▷ *adj* of Greece, the Greeks, or the Greek language
green *adj* of a colour between blue and yellow; characterized by green plants or foliage; (**G-**) of or concerned with environmental issues; unripe; envious or jealous; immature or gullible ▷ *n* colour between blue and yellow; area of grass kept for a special purpose; (**G-**) person concerned with environmental issues ▷ *pl* green vegetables ▷ *v* make or become green **greenness** *n* **greenish, greeny** *adj* **greenery** *n* vegetation **green belt** protected area of open country around a town **greenfinch** *n* European finch with dull green plumage in the male **green fingers** skill in gardening **greenfly** *n* green aphid, a common garden pest **greengage** *n* sweet green plum **greengrocer** *n Brit* shopkeeper selling vegetables and fruit **greenhorn** *n Chiefly US* novice **greenhouse** *n* glass building for rearing plants **greenhouse effect** rise in the temperature of the earth caused by heat absorbed from the sun being unable to leave the atmosphere **green light** signal to go; permission to proceed with something **greenshank** *n* large European sandpiper **greenstone** *n NZ* type of green jade used for Maori ornaments
greet *v* meet with expressions of welcome; receive in a specified manner; be immediately noticeable to **greeting** *n*
gregarious *adj* fond of company; (of animals) living in flocks or herds

gremlin *n* imaginary being blamed for mechanical malfunctions
grenade *n* small bomb thrown by hand or fired from a rifle **grenadier** *n* soldier of a regiment formerly trained to throw grenades
grenadine [gren-a-**deen**] *n* syrup made from pomegranates
grevillea *n* any of various Australian evergreen trees and shrubs
grew *v* past tense of **grow**
grey *adj* of a colour between black and white; (of hair) partly turned white; dismal or dark; dull or boring ▷*n* grey colour; grey or white horse **greying** *adj* (of hair) turning grey **greyish** *adj* **greyness** *n* **grey matter** *Informal* brains
greyhound *n* swift slender dog used in racing
grid *n* network of horizontal and vertical lines, bars, etc; national network of electricity supply cables
griddle *n* flat iron plate for cooking
gridiron *n* frame of metal bars for grilling food; American football pitch
gridlock *n* situation where traffic is not moving; point in a dispute at which no agreement can be reached **gridlocked** *adj*
grief *n* deep sadness **grieve** *v* (cause to) feel grief **grievance** *n* real or imaginary cause for complaint **grievous** *adj* very severe or painful; very serious
griffin *n* mythical monster with an eagle's head and wings and a lion's body
grill *n* device on a cooker that radiates heat downwards; grilled food; gridiron ▷*v* cook under a grill; question relentlessly **grilling** *n* relentless questioning
grille, grill *n* grating over an opening
grilse [**grillss**] *n* salmon on its first return from the sea to fresh water
grim *adj* **grimmer, grimmest** stern; harsh or forbidding; very unpleasant **grimly** *adv* **grimness** *n*
grimace *n* ugly or distorted facial expression of pain, disgust, etc ▷*v* make a grimace
grime *n* ingrained dirt ▷*v* make very dirty **grimy** *adj*
grin *v* **grinning, grinned** smile broadly, showing the teeth ▷*n* broad smile
grind *v* **grinding, ground** crush or rub to a powder; smooth or sharpen by friction; scrape together with a harsh noise; oppress ▷*n* *Informal* hard work; act or sound of grinding **grind out** *v* produce in a routine or uninspired manner **grindstone** *n* stone used for grinding
grip *n* firm hold or grasp; way in which something is grasped; mastery or understanding; *US* travelling bag; handle ▷*v* **gripping, gripped** grasp or hold tightly; hold the interest or attention of **gripping** *adj*
gripe *v* *Informal* complain persistently ▷*n* *Informal* complaint; sudden intense bowel pain
grisly *adj* **-lier, -liest** horrifying or ghastly
grist *n* grain for grinding **grist to one's mill** something which can be turned to advantage
gristle *n* tough stringy animal tissue found in meat **gristly** *adj*
grit *n* rough particles of sand; courage ▷*pl* coarsely ground grain ▷*v* **gritting, gritted** spread grit on (an icy road etc); clench or grind (the

teeth) **gritty** *adj* **-tier, -tiest** **grittiness** *n*

grizzle *v Brit, Aust & NZ, Informal* whine or complain

grizzled *adj* grey-haired

grizzly *n, pl* **-zlies** large American bear (also **grizzly bear**)

groan *n* deep sound of grief or pain; *Informal* complaint ▷*v* utter a groan; *Informal* complain

groat *n hist* fourpenny piece

grocer *n* shopkeeper selling foodstuffs **grocery** *n, pl* **-ceries** business or premises of a grocer ▷*pl* goods sold by a grocer

grog *n Brit, Aust & NZ* spirit, usu rum, and water

groggy *adj* **-gier, -giest** *Informal* faint, shaky, or dizzy

groin *n* place where the legs join the abdomen

grommet *n* ring or eyelet; *med* tube inserted in the ear to drain fluid from the middle ear

groom *n* person who looks after horses; bridegroom; officer in a royal household ▷*v* make or keep one's clothes and appearance neat and tidy; brush or clean a horse; train (someone) for a future role

groove *n* long narrow channel in a surface

grope *v* feel about or search uncertainly; *slang* fondle (someone) in a rough sexual way **groping** *n*

gross *adj* flagrant; vulgar; *slang* disgusting or repulsive; repulsively fat; total, without deductions ▷*n* twelve dozen ▷*v* make as total revenue before deductions **grossly** *adv* **grossness** *n*

grotesque [grow-**tesk**] *adj* strangely distorted; absurd ▷*n* grotesque person or thing; artistic style mixing distorted human, animal, and plant forms **grotesquely** *adv*

grotto *n, pl* **-toes, -tos** small picturesque cave

grotty *adj* **-tier, -tiest** *Informal* nasty or in bad condition

grouch *Informal* ▷*v* grumble or complain ▷*n* person who is always complaining; persistent complaint **grouchy** *adj*

ground[1] *n* surface of the earth; soil; area used for a specific purpose *eg rugby ground*; position in an argument or controversy ▷*pl* enclosed land round a house; reason or motive; coffee dregs ▷*v* base or establish; instruct in the basics; ban an aircraft or pilot from flying; run (a ship) aground **groundless** *adj* without reason **grounding** *n* basic knowledge of a subject **ground-breaking** *adj* innovative **ground floor** floor of a building level with the ground **groundnut** *n Brit* peanut **groundsheet** *n* waterproof sheet put on the ground under a tent **groundsman** *n* person employed to maintain a sports ground or park **groundswell** *n* rapidly developing general feeling or opinion **groundwork** *n* preliminary work

ground[2] *v* past of **grind**

group *n* number of people or things regarded as a unit; small band of musicians or singers ▷*v* place or form into a group

grouse[1] *n* stocky game bird; its flesh

grouse[2] *v* grumble or complain ▷*n* complaint

grout *n* thin mortar ▷*v* fill up with grout

grove *n* small group of trees

grovel [**grov**-el] *v* **-elling, -elled** behave humbly in order to win a superior's favour; crawl on the floor

grow *v* **growing, grew, grown** develop physically; (of a plant) exist; cultivate (plants); increase in size or degree; originate; become gradually *eg it was growing dark* **growth** *n* growing; increase; something grown or growing; tumour **grown-up** *adj, n* adult **grow up** *v* mature

growl *v* make a low rumbling sound; utter with a growl ▷ *n* growling sound

groyne *n* wall built out from the shore to control erosion

grub *n* legless insect larva; *slang* food ▷ *v* **grubbing, grubbed** search carefully for something by digging or by moving things about; dig up the surface of (soil)

grubby *adj* **-bier, -biest** dirty **grubbiness** *n*

grudge *v* be unwilling to give or allow ▷ *n* resentment

gruel *n* thin porridge

gruelling *adj* exhausting or severe

gruesome *adj* causing horror and disgust

gruff *adj* rough or surly in manner or voice **gruffly** *adv* **gruffness** *n*

grumble *v* complain; rumble ▷ *n* complaint; rumble **grumbler** *n* **grumbling** *adj, n*

grumpy *adj* **grumpier, grumpiest** bad-tempered **grumpily** *adv* **grumpiness** *n*

grunge *n* style of rock music with a fuzzy guitar sound; deliberately untidy and uncoordinated fashion style

grunt *v* make a low short gruff sound, like a pig ▷ *n* pig's sound; gruff noise

Gruyère [**grew**-yair] *n* hard yellow Swiss cheese with holes

gryphon *n* same as **griffin**

GST (in Australia, New Zealand, and Canada) Goods and Services Tax

G-string *n* small strip of cloth covering the genitals and attached to a waistband

GT gran turismo, used of a sports car

guano [**gwah**-no] *n* dried sea-bird manure, used as fertilizer

guarantee *n* formal assurance, esp in writing, that a product will meet certain standards; something that makes a specified condition or outcome certain ▷ *v* **-teeing, -teed** give a guarantee; secure against risk etc; ensure **guarantor** *n* person who gives or is bound by a guarantee

guard *v* watch over to protect or to prevent escape ▷ *n* person or group that guards; official in charge of a train; protection; screen for enclosing anything dangerous; posture of defence in sports such as boxing or fencing ▷ *pl* (**G-**) regiment with ceremonial duties **guarded** *adj* cautious or noncommittal **guardedly** *adv* **guard against** *v* take precautions against **guardsman** *n* member of the Guards

guardian *n* keeper or protector; person legally responsible for a child, mentally ill person, etc **guardianship** *n*

guava [**gwah**-va] *n* yellow-skinned tropical American fruit

gudgeon *n* small freshwater fish

Guernsey [**gurn**-zee] *n* breed of dairy cattle

guerrilla, guerilla *n* member of an unofficial armed force fighting regular forces

guess *v* estimate or draw a conclusion without proper knowledge; estimate correctly by guessing; suppose ▷ *n* estimate or conclusion reached by guessing **guesswork** *n* process or results of guessing

guest *n* person entertained at another's house or at another's expense; invited performer or speaker; customer at a hotel or restaurant ▷ *v* appear as a visiting player or performer **guesthouse** *n* boarding house

guff *n Brit, Aust & NZ, slang* nonsense

guffaw *n* crude noisy laugh ▷ *v* laugh in this way

guide *n* person who conducts tour expeditions; person who shows the way; book of instruction or information; model for behaviour; something used to gauge something or to help in planning one's actions; (**G-**) member of an organization for girls equivalent to the Scouts ▷ *v* act as a guide for; control, supervise, or influence **guidance** *n* leadership, instruction, or advice **guided missile** missile whose flight is controlled electronically **guide dog** dog trained to lead a blind person **guideline** *n* set principle for doing something

guild *n* organization or club; *hist* society of men in the same trade or craft

guilder *n* former monetary unit of the Netherlands

guile [gile] *n* cunning or deceit **guileful** *adj* **guileless** *adj*

guillemot [gil-lee-mot] *n* black-and-white diving sea bird of N hemisphere

guillotine *n* machine for beheading people; device for cutting paper or sheet metal; method of preventing lengthy debate in parliament by fixing a time for taking the vote ▷ *v* behead by guillotine; limit debate by the guillotine

guilt *n* fact or state of having done wrong; remorse for wrongdoing **guiltless** *adj* innocent **guilty** *adj* responsible for an offence or misdeed; feeling or showing guilt **guiltily** *adv*

guinea *n* former British monetary unit worth 21 shillings (1.05 pounds); former gold coin of this value **guinea fowl** wild bird related to the pheasant **guinea pig** tailless S American rodent, commonly kept as a pet; *Informal* person used for experimentation

guise [rhymes with **size**] *n* false appearance; external appearance

guitar *n* stringed instrument with a flat back and a long neck, played by plucking or strumming **guitarist** *n*

gulch *n US* deep narrow valley

gulf *n* large deep bay; chasm; large difference in opinion or understanding

gull *n* long-winged sea bird

gullet *n* muscular tube through which food passes from the mouth to the stomach

gullible *adj* easily tricked **gullibility** *n*

gully *n, pl* **-lies** channel cut by running water

gulp *v* swallow hastily; gasp ▷ *n* gulping; thing gulped

gum[1] *n* firm flesh in which the teeth are set **gummy** *adj* **-mier, -miest** toothless

gum[2] *n* sticky substance obtained from certain trees; adhesive; chewing gum; gumdrop; gum tree ▷ *v* **gumming, gummed** stick with gum **gummy** *adj* **-mier, -miest** **gumboots** *pl n Chiefly Brit*

Wellington boots **gumdrop** *n* hard jelly-like sweet **gum tree** eucalypt tree

gumption *n Informal* resourcefulness; courage

gun *n* weapon with a metal tube from which missiles are fired by explosion; device from which a substance is ejected under pressure ▷ *v* **gunning, gunned** cause (an engine) to run at high speed **jump the gun** act prematurely **gunner** *n* artillery soldier **gunnery** *n* use or science of large guns **gunboat** *n* small warship **gun dog** dog used to retrieve game **gun down** *v* shoot (a person) **gun for** *v* seek or pursue vigorously **gunman** *n* armed criminal **gunmetal** *n* alloy of copper, tin, and zinc ▷ *adj* dark grey **gunpowder** *n* explosive mixture of potassium nitrate, sulphur, and charcoal **gunrunning** *n* smuggling of guns and ammunition **gunrunner** *n* **gunshot** *n* shot or range of a gun

gunge *n Informal* sticky unpleasant substance **gungy** *adj* **-gier, -giest**

gunny *n* strong coarse fabric used for sacks

gunwale, gunnel [gun-nel] *n* top of a ship's side

gunyah *n Aust* hut or shelter in the bush

guppy *n, pl* **-pies** small colourful aquarium fish

gurgle *v, n* (make) a bubbling noise

Gurkha *n* person, esp a soldier, belonging to a Hindu people of Nepal

guru *n* Hindu or Sikh religious teacher or leader; leader, adviser, or expert

gush *v* flow out suddenly and profusely; express admiration effusively ▷ *n* sudden copious flow; sudden surge of strong feeling **gusher** *n* spurting oil well

gusset *n* piece of material sewn into a garment to strengthen it

gust *n* sudden blast of wind ▷ *v* blow in gusts **gusty** *adj*

gusto *n* enjoyment or zest

gut *n* intestine; *Informal* fat stomach; short for **catgut** ▷ *pl* internal organs; *Informal* courage ▷ *v* **gutting, gutted** remove the guts from; (of a fire) destroy the inside of (a building) ▷ *adj* basic or instinctive *eg a gut reaction* **gutsy** *adj* **-sier, -siest** *Informal* courageous; vigorous or robust *eg a gutsy performance* **gutted** *adj Brit, Aust & NZ, Informal* disappointed and upset

gutta-percha *n* whitish rubbery substance obtained from an Asian tree

gutter *n* shallow channel for carrying away water from a roof or roadside ▷ *v* (of a candle) burn unsteadily, with wax running down the sides **the gutter** degraded or criminal environment **guttering** *n* material for gutters **gutter press** newspapers that rely on sensationalism **guttersnipe** *n Brit* neglected slum child

guttural *adj* (of a sound) produced at the back of the throat; (of a voice) harsh-sounding

guy[1] *n Informal* man or boy; effigy of Guy Fawkes burnt on Nov. 5th (**Guy Fawkes Day**)

guy[2] *n* rope or chain to steady or secure something **guy rope**

guzzle *v* eat or drink greedily

gybe [jibe] *v* (of a fore-and-aft sail) swing suddenly from one side to the other; (of a boat) change course by letting the sail gybe

gym *n* gymnasium; gymnastics

gymkhana [jim-**kah**-na] *n* horse-riding competition

gymnasium *n* large room with equipment for physical training **gymnast** *n* expert in gymnastics **gymnastic** *adj* **gymnastics** *pl n* exercises to develop strength and agility

gynaecology [guy-nee-**kol**-la-jee] *n* branch of medicine dealing with diseases and conditions specific to women **gynaecological** *adj* **gynaecologist** *n*

gypsophila *n* garden plant with small white flowers

gypsum *n* chalklike mineral used to make plaster of Paris

Gypsy *n, pl* **-sies** member of a travelling people found throughout Europe

gyrate [jire-**rate**] *v* rotate or spiral about a point or axis **gyration** *n* **gyratory** *adj* gyrating

gyrocompass *n* compass using a gyroscope

gyroscope [**jire**-oh-skohp] *n* disc rotating on an axis that can turn in any direction, so the disc maintains the same position regardless of the movement of the surrounding structure **gyroscopic** *adj*

h

H *chem* hydrogen

habeas corpus [**hay**-bee-ass **kor**-puss] *n* writ ordering a prisoner to be brought before a court

haberdasher *n Brit, Aust & NZ* dealer in small articles used for sewing **haberdashery** *n*

habit *n* established way of behaving; addiction to a drug; costume of a monk or nun

habitable *adj* fit to be lived in **habitation** *n* (occupation of) a dwelling place

habitat *n* natural home of an animal or plant

habitual *adj* done regularly and repeatedly **habitually** *adv*

habituate *v* accustom **habituation** *n* **habitué** [hab-**it**-yew-ay] *n* frequent visitor to a place

hacienda [hass-ee-**end**-a] *n* ranch

or large estate in Latin America

hack[1] *v* cut or chop violently; *Brit & NZ, Informal* tolerate

hack[2] *n* (inferior) writer or journalist; horse kept for riding

hacker *n slang* computer enthusiast, esp one who breaks into the computer system of a company or government

hackles *pl n* **make one's hackles rise** make one feel angry or hostile

hackney *n Brit* taxi

hackneyed *adj* (of a word or phrase) unoriginal and overused

hacksaw *n* small saw for cutting metal

had *v* past of **have**

haddock *n* edible sea fish of N Atlantic

Hades [hay-deez] *n Greek myth* underworld home of the dead

hadj *n* same as **hajj**

haematology *n* study of blood and its diseases

haemoglobin [hee-moh-**globe**-in] *n* protein found in red blood cells which carries oxygen

haemophilia [hee-moh-**fill**-lee-a] *n* hereditary illness in which the blood does not clot **haemophiliac** *n*

haemorrhage [**hem**-or-ij] *n* heavy bleeding ▷*v* bleed heavily

> SPELLING Collins Word Web shows that the most usual mistake in spelling **haemorrhage** is to miss out the second *h*, which is silent

haemorrhoids [**hem**-or-oydz] *pl n* swollen veins in the anus (also **piles**)

hafnium *n chem* metallic element found in zirconium ores

haft *n* handle of an axe, knife, or dagger

hag *n* ugly old woman **hag-ridden** *adj* distressed or worried

haggard *adj* looking tired and ill

haggis *n* Scottish dish made from sheep's offal, oatmeal, suet, and seasonings, boiled in a bag made from the sheep's stomach

haggle *v* bargain or wrangle over a price

hagiography *n, pl* **-phies** writing about the lives of the saints

hail[1] *n* (shower of) small pellets of ice; large number of insults, missiles, blows, etc ▷*v* fall as or like hail **hailstone** *n*

hail[2] *v* call out to, greet; stop (a taxi) by waving; acknowledge publicly **hail from** *v* come originally from

hair *n* threadlike growth on the skin; such growths collectively, esp on the head **hairy** *adj* covered with hair; *slang* dangerous or exciting **hairiness** *n* **hairclip** *n* small bent metal hairpin **hairdo** *n Informal* hairstyle **hairdresser** *n* person who cuts and styles hair **hairgrip** *n Brit* same as **hairclip** **hairline** *n* edge of hair at the top of the forehead ▷*adj* very fine or narrow **hairpin** *n* U-shaped wire used to hold the hair in place **hairpin bend** very sharp bend in a road **hair-raising** *adj* frightening or exciting **hair-splitting** *n, adj* making petty distinctions **hairstyle** *n* cut and arrangement of a person's hair

hajj *n* pilgrimage a Muslim makes to Mecca

haka *n NZ* ceremonial Maori dance with chanting; similar dance performed by a sports team before a match

hake *n* edible sea fish of N hemisphere; *Aust* same as **barracouta**

hakea [**hah**-kee-a] *n* Australian tree or shrub with hard woody fruit
halal *n* meat from animals slaughtered according to Muslim law
halberd *n hist* spear with an axe blade
halcyon [**hal**-see-on] *adj* peaceful and happy **halcyon days** time of peace and happiness
hale *adj* healthy, robust
half *n, pl* **halves** either of two equal parts; *Informal* half-pint of beer etc; half-price ticket ▷ *adj* denoting one of two equal parts ▷ *adv* to the extent of half; partially **half-baked** *adj Informal* not properly thought out **half-brother, half-sister** *n* brother *or* sister related through one parent only **half-caste** *n offens* person with parents of different races **half-cocked** *adj* **go off half-cocked, (at) half-cock** fail because of inadequate preparation **half-hearted** *adj* unenthusiastic **half-life** *n* time taken for half the atoms in radioactive material to decay **half-nelson** *n* wrestling hold in which one wrestler's arm is pinned behind his back by his opponent **half-pie** *adj NZ, Informal* incomplete **half-pipe** large U-shaped ramp used for skateboarding, snowboarding, etc **half-timbered** *adj* (of a house) having an exposed wooden frame filled in with plaster **half-time** *n sport* short rest period between two halves of a game **halftone** *n* illustration showing lights and shadows by means of very small dots **halfway** *adv, adj* at or to half the distance **halfwit** *n* foolish or stupid person
halfpenny [**hayp**-nee] *n* former British coin worth half an old penny
halibut *n* large edible flatfish of N Atlantic
halitosis *n* unpleasant-smelling breath
hall *n* (also **hallway**) entrance passage; large room or building for public meetings, dances, etc; *Brit* large country house
hallelujah [hal-ee-**loo**-ya] *interj* exclamation of praise to God
hallmark *n* typical feature; mark indicating the standard of tested gold and silver ▷ *v* stamp with a hallmark
hallo *interj* same as **hello**
hallowed *adj* regarded as holy
Halloween, Hallowe'en *n* October 31, celebrated by children by dressing up as ghosts, witches, etc
hallucinate *v* seem to see something that is not really there **hallucination** *n* **hallucinatory** *adj* **hallucinogen** *n* drug that causes hallucinations **hallucinogenic** *adj*
halo [**hay**-loh] *n, pl* **-loes, -los** ring of light round the head of a sacred figure; circle of refracted light round the sun or moon
halogen [**hal**-oh-jen] *n chem* any of a group of nonmetallic elements including chlorine and iodine
halt *v* come or bring to a stop ▷ *n* temporary stop; minor railway station without a building **halting** *adj* hesitant, uncertain
halter *n* strap round a horse's head with a rope to lead it with **halterneck** *n* woman's top or dress with a strap fastened at the back of the neck
halve *v* divide in half; reduce by half
halves *n* plural of **half**
halyard *n* rope for raising a ship's sail or flag
ham[1] *n* smoked or salted meat from a pig's thigh **ham-fisted** *adj*

clumsy

ham² *Informal* ▷*n* amateur radio operator; actor who overacts ▷*v* **hamming, hammed ham it up** overact

hamburger *n* minced beef shaped into a flat disc, cooked and usu served in a bread roll

hamlet *n* small village

hammer *n* tool with a heavy metal head and a wooden handle, used to drive in nails etc; part of a gun which causes the bullet to be fired; heavy metal ball on a wire, thrown as a sport; auctioneer's mallet; striking mechanism in a piano ▷*v* hit (as if) with a hammer; *Informal* punish or defeat utterly **go at it hammer and tongs** do something, esp argue, very vigorously **hammerhead** *n* shark with a wide flattened head **hammer toe** condition in which a toe is permanently bent at the joint

hammock *n* hanging bed made of canvas or net

hamper¹ *v* make it difficult for (someone or something) to move or progress

hamper² *n* large basket with a lid; selection of food and drink packed as a gift

hamster *n* small rodent with a short tail and cheek pouches

> SPELLING The word **hamster** appears 750 times in Collins Word Web. The misspelling *hampster*, with a *p*, appears 13 times

hamstring *n* tendon at the back of the knee ▷*v* make it difficult for (someone) to take any action

hand *n* part of the body at the end of the arm, consisting of a palm, four fingers, and a thumb; style of handwriting; round of applause; manual worker; pointer on a dial, esp on a clock; cards dealt to a player in a card game; unit of length of four inches (10.16 centimetres) used to measure horses ▷*v* pass, give **have a hand in** be involved in **lend a hand** help **out of hand** beyond control; definitely and finally **to hand, at hand, on hand** nearby **win hands down** win easily **handbag** *n* woman's small bag for carrying personal articles in **handbill** *n* small printed notice **handbook** *n* small reference or instruction book **handcuff** *n* one of a linked pair of metal rings designed to be locked round a prisoner's wrists by the police ▷*v* put handcuffs on **hand-held** *adj* (of a film camera) held rather than mounted, as in close-up action shots; (of a computer) able to be held in the hand ▷*n* computer that can be held in the hand **hand-out** *n* clothing, food, or money given to a needy person; written information given out at a talk etc **hands-free** *adj, n* (of) a device allowing the user to make and receive phonecalls without holding the handset **hands-on** *adj* involving practical experience of equipment **handstand** *n* act of supporting the body on the hands in an upside-down position **handwriting** *n* (style of) writing by hand

handful *n* amount that can be held in the hand; small number; *Informal* person or animal that is difficult to control

handicap *n* physical or mental disability; something that makes progress difficult; contest in which the competitors are given advantages or disadvantages in an attempt to equalize their chances; advantage or disadvantage given ▷*v* make it difficult for (someone) to do something

handicraft *n* objects made by hand

handiwork *n* result of someone's work or activity

handkerchief *n* small square of fabric used to wipe the nose

> SPELLING People often forget to write a *d* in **handkerchief**, probably because they don't say or hear it

handle *n* part of an object that is held so that it can be used ▷*v* hold, feel, or move with the hands; control or deal with **handler** *n* person who controls an animal **handlebars** *pl n* curved metal bar used to steer a cycle

handsome *adj* (esp of a man) good-looking; large or generous *eg a handsome profit*

handy *adj* **handier, handiest** convenient, useful; good at manual work **handily** *adv* **handyman** *n* man who is good at making or repairing things

hang *v* **hanging, hung** attach or be attached at the top with the lower part free *past* **hanged** suspend or be suspended by the neck until dead; fasten to a wall **get the hang of** *Informal* begin to understand **hanger** *n* curved piece of wood, wire, or plastic, with a hook, for hanging up clothes (also **coat hanger**) **hang back** *v* hesitate, be reluctant **hangman** *n* man who executes people by hanging **hangover** *n* headache and nausea as a result of drinking too much alcohol **hang-up** *n* *Informal* emotional or psychological problem

hangar *n* large shed for storing aircraft

hangdog *adj* guilty, ashamed *eg a hangdog look*

hang-glider *n* glider with a light framework from which the pilot hangs in a harness **hang-gliding** *n*

hangi *n, pl* **-gi, -gis** *NZ* Maori oven consisting of a hole in the ground filled with hot stones

hank *n* coil, esp of yarn

hanker *v* (foll by *after, for*) desire intensely

hanky, hankie *n, pl* **hankies** *Informal* handkerchief

hanky-panky *n* *Informal* illicit sexual relations

hansom cab *n* (formerly) two-wheeled horse-drawn carriage for hire

haphazard *adj* not organized or planned **haphazardly** *adv*

hapless *adj* unlucky

happen *v* take place, occur; chance (to be or do something) **happening** *n* event, occurrence

happy *adj* **-pier, -piest** feeling or causing joy; lucky, fortunate **happily** *adv* **happiness** *n* **happy-go-lucky** *adj* carefree and cheerful

hara-kiri *n* (formerly, in Japan) ritual suicide by disembowelling

harangue *v* address angrily or forcefully ▷*n* angry or forceful speech

harass *v* annoy or trouble constantly **harassed** *adj* **harassment** *n*

> SPELLING The commonest misspelling of **harass** is *harrass*. There should be only one *r*, but it's obviously difficult to remember: there are 232 instances of *harrassment* in Collins Word Web and 10 of *harrasment*. The correct spelling is **harassment**

harbinger [**har**-binj-a] *n* someone or something that announces the approach of something

harbour *n* sheltered port ▷ *v* maintain secretly in the mind; give shelter or protection to

hard *adj* firm, solid, or rigid; difficult; requiring a lot of effort; unkind, unfeeling; causing pain, sorrow, or hardship; (of water) containing calcium salts which stop soap lathering freely; (of a drug) strong and addictive ▷ *adv* with great energy or effort; with great intensity **hard of hearing** unable to hear properly **hard up** *Informal* short of money **harden** *v* **hardness** *n* **hardship** *n* suffering; difficult circumstances **hard-bitten** *adj* tough and determined **hard-boiled** *adj* (of an egg) boiled until solid; *Informal* tough, unemotional **hard copy** computer output printed on paper **hardfill** *n NZ & SAfr* stone waste material used for landscaping **hard-headed** *adj* shrewd, practical **hardhearted** *adj* unsympathetic, uncaring **hard sell** aggressive sales technique **hard shoulder** surfaced verge at the edge of a motorway for emergency stops

hardboard *n* thin stiff board made of compressed sawdust and wood chips

hardly *adv* scarcely or not at all; with difficulty

hardware *n* metal tools or implements; machinery used in a computer system; heavy military equipment, such as tanks and missiles

hardwood *n* wood of a broadleaved tree such as oak or ash

hardy *adj* **hardier, hardiest** able to stand difficult conditions **hardiness** *n*

hare *n* animal like a large rabbit, with longer ears and legs ▷ *v* (usu foll by *off*) run (away) quickly **harebell** *n* blue bell-shaped flower **harebrained** *adj* foolish or impractical **harelip** *n* slight split in the upper lip

harem *n* (apartments of) a Muslim man's wives and concubines

haricot bean [**har**-rik-oh] *n* small pale edible bean, usu sold dried

hark *v old-fashioned* listen **hark back** *v* return (to an earlier subject)

harlequin *n* stock comic character with a diamond-patterned costume and mask ▷ *adj* in many colours

harlot *n lit* prostitute

harm *v* injure physically, mentally, or morally ▷ *n* physical, mental, or moral injury **harmful** *adj* **harmless** *adj*

harmonica *n* small wind instrument played by sucking and blowing

harmonium *n* keyboard instrument like a small organ

harmony *n, pl* **-nies** peaceful agreement and cooperation; pleasant combination of notes sounded at the same time **harmonious** *adj* **harmoniously** *adv* **harmonic** *adj* of harmony **harmonics** *n* science of musical sounds **harmonize** *v* blend well together **harmonization** *n*

harness *n* arrangement of straps for attaching a horse to a cart or plough; set of straps fastened round someone's body to attach something *eg a safety harness* ▷ *v* put a harness on; control (something) in order to make use of it

harp *n* large triangular stringed

instrument played with the fingers **harpist** *n* **harp on about** *v* talk about continuously

harpoon *n* barbed spear attached to a rope used for hunting whales ▷*v* spear with a harpoon

harpsichord *n* stringed keyboard instrument

harpy *n, pl* **-pies** nasty or bad-tempered woman

harridan *n* nagging or vicious woman

harrier *n* cross-country runner

harrow *n* implement used to break up lumps of soil ▷*v* draw a harrow over

harrowing *adj* very distressing

harry *v* **-rying, -ried** keep asking (someone) to do something, pester

harsh *adj* severe and difficult to cope with; unkind, unsympathetic; extremely hard, bright, or rough **harshly** *adv* **harshness** *n*

hart *n* adult male deer

harum-scarum *adj* reckless

harvest *n* (season for) the gathering of crops; crops gathered ▷*v* gather (a ripened crop) **harvester** *n*

has *v* third person singular of the present tense of **have** **has-been** *n* *Informal* person who is no longer popular or successful

hash[1] *n* dish of diced cooked meat and vegetables reheated **make a hash of** *Informal* spoil, do badly

hash[2] *n* *Informal* hashish

hashish [**hash**-eesh] *n* drug made from the cannabis plant, smoked for its intoxicating effects

hasp *n* clasp that fits over a staple and is secured by a bolt or padlock, used as a fastening

hassle *Informal* ▷*n* trouble, bother ▷*v* bother or annoy

hassock *n* cushion for kneeling on in church

haste *n* (excessive) quickness **make haste** hurry, rush **hasten** *v* (cause to) hurry **hasty** *adj* (too) quick **hastily** *adv*

hat *n* covering for the head, often with a brim, usu worn to give protection from the weather **keep something under one's hat** keep something secret **hat trick** any three successive achievements, esp in sport

hatch[1] *v* (cause to) emerge from an egg; devise (a plot)

hatch[2] *n* hinged door covering an opening in a floor or wall; opening in the wall between a kitchen and a dining area; door in an aircraft or spacecraft **hatchback** *n* car with a lifting door at the back **hatchway** *n* opening in the deck of a ship

hatchet *n* small axe **bury the hatchet** become reconciled **hatchet job** malicious verbal or written attack **hatchet man** *Informal* person carrying out unpleasant tasks for an employer

hate *v* dislike intensely; be unwilling (to do something) ▷*n* intense dislike; person or thing hated **hateful** *adj* causing or deserving hate **hater** *n* **hatred** *n* intense dislike

haughty *adj* **-tier, -tiest** proud, arrogant **haughtily** *adv* **haughtiness** *n*

haul *v* pull or drag with effort ▷*n* amount gained by effort or theft **long haul** something that takes a lot of time and effort **haulage** *n* (charge for) transporting goods **haulier** *n* firm or person that transports goods by road

haunch *n* human hip or fleshy hindquarter of an animal

haunt *v* visit in the form of a ghost;

remain in the memory or thoughts of ▷*n* place visited frequently **haunted** *adj* frequented by ghosts; worried **haunting** *adj* memorably beautiful or sad

haute couture [**oat** koo-**ture**] *n* *French* high fashion

hauteur [oat-**ur**] *n* haughtiness

have *v* **has, having, had** possess, hold; receive, take, or obtain; experience or be affected by; (foll by *to*) be obliged, must *eg I had to go*; cause to be done; give birth to; used to form past tenses (with a past participle) *eg we have looked; she had done enough* **have it out** *Informal* settle a matter by argument **have on** *v* wear; *Informal* tease or trick **have up** *v* bring to trial

haven *n* place of safety

haversack *n* canvas bag carried on the back or shoulder

havoc *n* disorder and confusion

haw *n* hawthorn berry

hawk[1] *n* bird of prey with a short hooked bill and very good eyesight; *politics* supporter or advocate of warlike policies **hawkish, hawklike** *adj* **hawk-eyed** *adj* having very good eyesight

hawk[2] *v* offer (goods) for sale in the street or door-to-door **hawker** *n*

hawk[3] *v* cough noisily

hawser *n* large rope used on a ship

hawthorn *n* thorny shrub or tree

hay *n* grass cut and dried as fodder **hay fever** allergy to pollen, causing sneezing and watery eyes **haystack** *n* large pile of stored hay **haywire** *adj* **go haywire** *Informal* not function properly

hazard *n* something that could be dangerous ▷*v* put in danger; make (a guess) **hazardous** *adj*

haze *n* mist, often caused by heat **hazy** *adj* not clear, misty; confused or vague

hazel *n* small tree producing edible nuts ▷*adj* (of eyes) greenish-brown **hazelnut** *n*

H-bomb *n* hydrogen bomb

he *pron* refers to: male person or animal ▷*n* male person or animal: *a he-goat*

head *n* upper or front part of the body, containing the sense organs and the brain; mind and mental abilities; upper or most forward part of anything; person in charge of a group, organization, or school; pus-filled tip of a spot or boil; white froth on beer *pl* **head** person or animal considered as a unit ▷*adj* chief, principal ▷*v* be at the top or front of; be in charge of; move (in a particular direction); hit (a ball) with the head; provide with a heading **go to one's head** make one drunk or conceited **head over heels (in love)** very much in love **not make head nor tail of** not understand **off one's head** *slang* foolish or insane **heads** *adv* *Informal* with the side of a coin which has a portrait of a head on it uppermost **header** *n* striking a ball with the head; headlong fall **heading** *n* title written or printed at the top of a page **heady** *adj* intoxicating or exciting **headache** *n* continuous pain in the head; cause of worry or annoyance **headboard** *n* vertical board at the top end of a bed **headdress** *n* decorative head covering **head-hunt** *v* (of a company) approach and offer a job to (a person working for a rival company) **head-hunter** *n* **headland** *n* area of land jutting out into the sea **headlight** *n* powerful light on the front of a vehicle **headline** *n* title at the top of a newspaper article, esp on the front page ▷ *pl* main points of a news broadcast **headlong** *adv, adj* with the head first; hastily **headphones** *pl n* two small loudspeakers held against the ears **headquarters** *pl n* centre from which operations are directed **head start** advantage in a competition **headstone** *n* memorial stone on a grave **headstrong** *adj* self-willed, obstinate **headway** *n* progress **headwind** *n* wind blowing against the course of an aircraft or ship

heal *v* make or become well **healer** *n*

health *n* normal (good) condition of someone's body **health food** natural food, organically grown and free from additives **healthy** *adj* having good health; of or producing good health; functioning well, sound **healthily** *adv*

heap *n* pile of things one on top of another; (also **heaps**) large number or quantity ▷ *v* gather into a pile; (foll by *on*) give liberally (to)

hear *v* **hearing, heard** perceive (a sound) by ear; listen to; learn or be informed; *law* try (a case) **hear! hear!** exclamation of approval or agreement **hearer** *n* **hearing** *n* ability to hear; trial of a case **within hearing** close enough to be heard

hearsay *n* gossip, rumour

hearse *n* funeral car used to carry a coffin

heart *n* organ that pumps blood round the body; centre of emotions, esp love; courage, spirit; central or most important part; figure representing a heart; playing card with red heart heart-shaped symbols **break someone's heart** cause someone great grief **by heart** from memory **set one's heart on something** greatly desire something **take something to heart** be upset about something **hearten** *v* encourage, make cheerful **heartless** *adj* cruel, unkind **hearty** *adj* substantial, nourishing; friendly, enthusiastic **heartily** *adv* **heart attack** sudden severe malfunction of the heart **heart failure** sudden stopping of the heartbeat **heart-rending** *adj* causing great sorrow **heart-throb** *n slang* very attractive man, esp a film or pop star

heartache *n* intense anguish

heartbeat *n* one complete pulsation of the heart

heartbreak *n* intense grief

heartburn *n* burning sensation in the chest caused by indigestion

heartfelt *adj* felt sincerely or strongly

hearth *n* floor of a fireplace

heat *v* make or become hot ▷ *n* state of being hot; energy transferred as a result of a difference in temperature; hot weather; intensity of feeling; preliminary eliminating contest in a competition **on, in heat** (of some female animals) ready for mating **heated** *adj* angry and excited **heatedly** *adv* **heater** *n*

heath *n Brit* area of open uncultivated land

heathen *adj, n* (of) a person who does not believe in an established religion

heather *n* low-growing plant with small purple, pinkish, or white flowers, growing on heaths and mountains

heave *v* lift with effort; throw

(something heavy); utter (a sigh); rise and fall; vomit ▷*n* heaving

heaven *n* place believed to be the home of God, where good people go when they die; place or state of bliss **the heavens** sky **heavenly** *adj* of or like heaven; of or occurring in space; wonderful or beautiful

heavy *adj* **heavier, heaviest** of great weight; having a high density; great in degree or amount; *Informal* (of a situation) serious **heavily** *adv* **heaviness** *n* **heavy industry** large-scale production of raw material or machinery **heavy metal** very loud rock music featuring guitar riffs **heavyweight** *n* boxer weighing over 175lb (professional) or 81kg (amateur)

Hebrew *n* member of an ancient Semitic people; ancient language of the Hebrews; its modern form, used in Israel ▷*adj* of the Hebrews

heckle *v* interrupt (a public speaker) with comments, questions, or taunts **heckler** *n*

hectare *n* one hundred ares or 10 000 square metres (2.471 acres)

hectic *adj* rushed or busy

hector *v* bully

hedge *n* row of bushes forming a barrier or boundary ▷*v* be evasive or noncommittal; (foll by *against*) protect oneself (from) **hedgerow** *n* bushes forming a hedge

hedgehog *n* small mammal with a protective covering of spines

hedonism *n* doctrine that pleasure is the most important thing in life **hedonist** *n* **hedonistic** *adj*

heed *n* careful attention ▷*v* pay careful attention to **heedless** *adj* **heedless of** taking no notice of

heel[1] *n* back part of the foot; part of a shoe supporting the heel; *old-fashioned* contemptible person ▷*v* repair the heel of (a shoe) **heeler** *n Aust & NZ* dog that herds cattle by biting at their heels

heel[2] *v* (foll by *over*) lean to one side

hefty *adj* **heftier, heftiest** large, heavy, or strong

hegemony [hig-**em**-on-ee] *n* political domination

Hegira *n* Mohammed's flight from Mecca to Medina in 622 AD

heifer [**hef**-fer] *n* young cow

height *n* distance from base to top; distance above sea level; highest degree or topmost point **heighten** *v* make or become higher or more intense

heinous *adj* evil and shocking

heir *n* person entitled to inherit property or rank **heiress** *n fem* **heirloom** *n* object that has belonged to a family for generations

held *v* past of **hold**[1]

helical *adj* spiral

helicopter *n* aircraft lifted and propelled by rotating overhead blades **heliport** *n* airport for helicopters

heliotrope *n* plant with purple flowers ▷*adj* light purple

helium [**heel**-ee-um] *n chem* very light colourless odourless gas

helix [**heel**-iks] *n, pl* **helices, helixes** spiral

hell *n* place believed to be where wicked people go when they die; place or state of wickedness, suffering, or punishment **hell for leather** at great speed **hellish** *adj* **hellbent** *adj* (foll by *on*) intent

Hellenic *adj* of the (ancient) Greeks or their language

hello *interj* expression of greeting or surprise

helm *n* tiller or wheel for steering a ship

helmet *n* hard hat worn for protection

help *v* make something easier, better, or quicker for (someone); improve (a situation); refrain from *eg I can't help smiling* ▷ *n* assistance or support **help oneself** take something, esp food or drink, without being served; *Informal* steal something **helper** *n* **helpful** *adj* **helping** *n* single portion of food **helpless** *adj* weak or incapable **helplessly** *adv* **helpline** *n* telephone line set aside for callers to contact an organization for help with a problem **helpmate** *n* companion and helper, esp a husband or wife

helter-skelter *adj* haphazard and careless ▷ *adv* in a haphazard and careless manner ▷ *n* high spiral slide at a fairground

hem *n* bottom edge of a garment, folded under and stitched down ▷ *v* **hemming, hemmed** provide with a hem **hem in** *v* surround and prevent from moving **hemline** *n* level to which the hem of a skirt hangs

hemisphere *n* half of a sphere, esp the earth **hemispherical** *adj*

hemlock *n* poison made from a plant with spotted stems and small white flowers

hemp *n* (also **cannabis**) Asian plant with tough fibres; its fibre, used to make canvas and rope; narcotic drug obtained from hemp

hen *n* female domestic fowl; female of any bird **hen night, party** party for women only **henpecked** *adj* (of a man) dominated by his wife

hence *conj* for this reason ▷ *adv* from this time **henceforth** *adv* from now on

henchman *n* person employed by someone powerful to carry out orders

henna *n* reddish dye made from a shrub or tree ▷ *v* dye (the hair) with henna

henry *n, pl* **-ry, -ries, -rys** unit of electrical inductance

hepatitis *n* inflammation of the liver

heptagon *n* geometric figure with seven sides

heptathlon *n* athletic contest for women, involving seven events

her *pron* refers to a female person or animal or anything personified as feminine when the object of a sentence or clause ▷ *adj* belonging to her

herald *n* person who announces important news; forerunner ▷ *v* signal the approach of **heraldry** *n* study of coats of arms and family trees **heraldic** *adj*

herb *n* plant used for flavouring in cookery, and in medicine **herbal** *adj* **herbalist** *n* person who grows or specializes in the use of medicinal herbs **herbaceous** *adj* (of a plant) soft-stemmed **herbicide** *n* chemical used to destroy plants, esp weeds **herbivore** *n* animal that eats only plants **herbivorous** [her-**biv**-or-uss] *adj*

herculean [her-kew-**lee**-an] *adj* requiring great strength or effort

herd *n* group of animals feeding and living together; large crowd of people ▷ *v* collect into a herd **herdsman** *n* man who looks after a herd of animals

here *adv* in, at, or to this place or point **hereabouts** *adv* near here

hereafter *adv* after this point or time **the hereafter** life after death **hereby** *adv* by means of or as a result of this **herein** *adv* in this place, matter, or document **herewith** *adv* with this

heredity [hir-**red**-it-ee] *n* passing on of characteristics from one generation to another **hereditary** *adj* passed on genetically from one generation to another; passed on by inheritance

> SPELLING There are several ways to misspell **hereditary**. The problems always come after the *t*, where there should be three more letters: *-ary*

heresy [**herr**-iss-ee] *n, pl* **-sies** opinion contrary to accepted opinion or belief **heretic** [**herr**-it-ik] *n* person who holds unorthodox opinions **heretical** [hir-**ret**-ik-al] *adj*

heritage *n* something inherited; anything from the past, considered as the inheritance of present-day society

hermaphrodite [her-**maf**-roe-dite] *n* animal, plant, or person with both male and female reproductive organs

hermetic *adj* sealed so as to be airtight **hermetically** *adv*

hermit *n* person living in solitude, esp for religious reasons **hermitage** *n* home of a hermit

hernia *n* protrusion of an organ or part through the lining of the surrounding body cavity

hero *n, pl* **heroes** principal character in a film, book, etc; man greatly admired for his exceptional qualities or achievements **heroine** *n fem* **heroic** *adj* courageous; of or like a hero **heroics** *pl n* extravagant behaviour **heroically** *adv* **heroism** [**herr**-oh-izz-um] *n*

heroin *n* highly addictive drug derived from morphine

heron *n* long-legged wading bird

herpes [**her**-peez] *n* any of several inflammatory skin diseases, including shingles and cold sores

Herr [**hair**] *n, pl* **Herren** German term of address equivalent to *Mr*

herring *n* important food fish of northern seas **herringbone** *n* pattern of zigzag lines

hertz *n, pl* **hertz** *physics* unit of frequency

hesitate *v* be slow or uncertain in doing something; be reluctant (to do something) **hesitation** *n* **hesitant** *adj* undecided or wavering **hesitantly** *adv* **hesitancy** *n*

hessian *n* coarse jute fabric

heterodox *adj* differing from accepted doctrines or beliefs **heterodoxy** *n*

heterogeneous [het-er-oh-**jean**-ee-uss] *adj* composed of diverse elements **heterogeneity** *n*

heterosexual *n, adj* (person) sexually attracted to members of the opposite sex **heterosexuality** *n*

heuristic [hew-**rist**-ik] *adj* involving learning by investigation

hew *v* **hewing, hewed, hewed** *or* **hewn** cut with an axe; carve from a substance

hexagon *n* geometrical figure with six sides **hexagonal** *adj*

hey *interj* expression of surprise or for catching attention

heyday *n* time of greatest success, prime

hiatus [hie-**ay**-tuss] *n, pl* **-tuses, -tus** pause or interruption in continuity

hibernate *v* (of an animal) pass the winter as if in a deep sleep **hibernation** *n*
Hibernian *adj poetic* Irish
hibiscus *n, pl* **-cuses** tropical plant with large brightly coloured flowers
hiccup, hiccough *n* spasm of the breathing organs with a sharp coughlike sound; *Informal* small problem, hitch ▷ *v* make a hiccup
hick *n US, Aust & NZ, Informal* unsophisticated country person
hickory *n, pl* **-ries** N American nut-bearing tree; its wood
hide[1] *v* **hiding, hid, hidden** put (oneself or an object) somewhere difficult to see or find; keep secret ▷ *n* place of concealment, esp for a bird-watcher **hiding** *n* state of concealment *eg in hiding* **hide-out** *n* place to hide in
hide[2] *n* skin of an animal **hiding** *n slang* severe beating **hidebound** *adj* unwilling to accept new ideas
hideous [**hid**-ee-uss] *adj* ugly, revolting **hideously** *adv*
hierarchy [**hire**-ark-ee] *n, pl* **-chies** system of people or things arranged in a graded order **hierarchical** *adj*
hieroglyphic [hire-oh-**gliff**-ik] *adj* of a form of writing using picture symbols, as used in ancient Egypt ▷ *n* symbol that is difficult to decipher; (also **hieroglyph**) symbol representing an object, idea, or sound
hi-fi *n* set of high-quality sound-reproducing equipment ▷ *adj* high fidelity
higgledy-piggledy *adv, adj* in a muddle
high *adj* of a great height; far above ground or sea level; being at its peak; greater than usual in intensity or amount; (of a sound) acute in pitch; of great importance, quality, or rank; *Informal* under the influence of alcohol or drugs ▷ *adv* at or to a high level **highly** *adv* **highly strung** nervous and easily upset **Highness** *n* title used to address or refer to a royal person **High-Church** *adj* belonging to a section within the Church of England stressing the importance of ceremony and ritual **higher education** education at colleges and universities **high-fidelity** *adj* able to reproduce sound with little or no distortion **high-flown** *adj* (of language) extravagant or pretentious **high-handed** *adj* excessively forceful **high-rise** *adj* (of a building) having many storeys **high tea** early evening meal consisting of a cooked dish, bread, cakes, and tea **high time** latest possible time
highbrow *adj, n* intellectual and serious (person)
highlands *pl n* area of high ground
highlight *n* outstanding part or feature; light-toned area in a painting or photograph; lightened streak in the hair ▷ *v* give emphasis to
highway *n US, Aust & NZ* main road **Highway Code** regulations and recommendations applying to all road users **highwayman** *n* (formerly) robber, usu on horseback, who robbed travellers at gunpoint
hijack *v* seize control of (an aircraft or other vehicle) while travelling **hijacker** *n*
hike *n* long walk in the country, esp for pleasure ▷ *v* go for a long walk; (foll by *up*) pull (up) or raise **hiker** *n*
hilarious *adj* very funny **hilariously** *adv* **hilarity** *n*
hill *n* raised part of the earth's

surface, less high than a mountain **hilly** *adj* **hillock** *n* small hill **hillbilly** *n* *US* unsophisticated country person

hilt *n* handle of a sword or knife

him *pron* refers to a male person or animal when the object of a sentence or clause

hind[1] *adj* **hinder, hindmost** situated at the back

hind[2] *n* female deer

hinder *v* get in the way of **hindrance** *n*

Hindu *n* person who practises Hinduism ▷ *adj* of Hinduism **Hindi** *n* language of N central India **Hinduism** *n* dominant religion of India, which involves the worship of many gods and a belief in reincarnation

hinge *n* device for holding together two parts so that one can swing freely ▷ *v* (foll by *on*) depend (on); fit a hinge to

hint *n* indirect suggestion; piece of advice; small amount ▷ *v* suggest indirectly

hinterland *n* land lying behind a coast or near a city, esp a port

hip[1] *n* either side of the body between the pelvis and the thigh

hip[2] *n* rosehip

hip-hop *n* pop-culture movement originating in the 1980s, comprising rap music, graffiti, and break dancing

hippie *adj, n* same as **hippy**

hippo *n, pl* **-pos** *Informal* hippopotamus

hippodrome *n* music hall, variety theatre, or circus

hippopotamus *n, pl* **-muses, -mi** large African mammal with thick wrinkled skin, living near rivers

hippy *adj, n, pl* **-pies** (esp in the 1960s) (of) a person whose behaviour and dress imply a rejection of conventional values

hire *v* pay to have temporary use of; employ for wages ▷ *n* hiring **for hire** available to be hired **hireling** *n* person who works only for wages **hire-purchase** *n* system of purchase by which the buyer pays for goods by instalments

hirsute [**her**-suit] *adj* hairy

his *pron, adj* (something) belonging to him

Hispanic *adj* Spanish or Latin-American

hiss *n* sound like that of a long *s* (as an expression of contempt) ▷ *v* utter a hiss; show derision or anger towards

histamine [**hiss**-ta-meen] *n* substance released by the body tissues in allergic reactions

histogram *n* statistical graph in which the frequency of values is represented by vertical bars of varying heights and widths

histology *n* study of the tissues of an animal or plant

history *n, pl* **-ries** (record or account of) past events and developments; study of these; record of someone's past **historian** *n* writer of history **historic** *adj* famous or significant in history **historical** *adj* occurring in the past; based on history **historically** *adv*

histrionic *adj* excessively dramatic **histrionics** *pl n* excessively dramatic behaviour

hit *v* **hitting, hit** strike, touch forcefully; come into violent contact with; affect badly; reach (a point or place) ▷ *n* hitting; successful record, film, etc; *computers* single visit to a website **hit it off** *Informal* get on well together **hit the road** *Informal*

start a journey **hit-and-miss** *adj* sometimes successful and sometimes not **hit man** hired assassin **hit on** *v* think of (an idea)
hitch *n* minor problem ▷ *v* *Informal* obtain (a lift) by hitchhiking; fasten with a knot or tie; (foll by *up*) pull up with a jerk **hitchhike** *v* travel by obtaining free lifts **hitchhiker** *n*
hi-tech *adj* using sophisticated technology
hither *adv old-fashioned* to or towards this place
hitherto *adv* until this time
HIV human immunodeficiency virus, the cause of AIDS
hive *n* same as **beehive** **hive of activity** place where people are very busy **hive off** *v* separate from a larger group
hives *n* allergic reaction in which itchy red or whitish patches appear on the skin
HM (in Britain) Her (or His) Majesty
HMS (in Britain) Her (or His) Majesty's Ship
HNC (in Britain) Higher National Certificate
HND (in Britain) Higher National Diploma
hoard *n* store hidden away for future use ▷ *v* save or store **hoarder** *n*
hoarding *n* large board for displaying advertisements
hoarfrost *n* white ground frost
hoarse *adj* (of a voice) rough and unclear; having a rough and unclear voice **hoarsely** *adv* **hoarseness** *n*
hoary *adj* **hoarier, hoariest** grey or white(-haired); very old
hoax *n* deception or trick ▷ *v* deceive or play a trick upon **hoaxer** *n*
hob *n Brit* flat top part of a cooker, or a separate flat surface, containing gas or electric rings for cooking on
hobble *v* walk lamely; tie the legs of (a horse) together
hobby *n, pl* **-bies** activity pursued in one's spare time **hobbyhorse** *n* favourite topic; toy horse
hobgoblin *n* mischievous goblin
hobnail boots *pl n* heavy boots with short nails in the soles
hobnob *v* **-nobbing, -nobbed** (foll by *with*) be on friendly terms (with)
hobo *n, pl* **-bos** *US, Aust & NZ* tramp or vagrant
hock[1] *n* joint in the back leg of an animal such as a horse that corresponds to the human ankle
hock[2] *n* white German wine
hock[3] *v Informal* pawn **in hock** *Informal* in debt
hockey *n* team game played on a field with a ball and curved sticks; *US* ice hockey
hocus-pocus *n* trickery
hod *n* open wooden box attached to a pole, for carrying bricks or mortar
hoe *n* long-handled tool used for loosening soil or weeding ▷ *v* scrape or weed with a hoe
hog *n* castrated male pig; *Informal* greedy person ▷ *v* **hogging, hogged** *Informal* take more than one's share of **hogshead** *n* large cask **hogwash** *n Informal* nonsense
Hogmanay *n* (in Scotland) New Year's Eve
hoick *v* raise abruptly and sharply
hoi polloi *n* the ordinary people
hoist *v* raise or lift up ▷ *n* device for lifting things
hoity-toity *adj Informal* arrogant or haughty
hokey-pokey *n NZ* brittle toffee

sold in lumps

hold[1] *v* **holding, held** keep or support in or with the hands or arms; arrange for (a meeting, party, etc) to take place; consider to be as specified *eg who are you holding responsible?;* maintain in a specified position or state; have the capacity for; *Informal* wait, esp on the telephone; restrain or keep back; own, possess ▷ *n* act or way of holding; controlling influence **holder** *n* **holding** *n* property, such as land or stocks and shares **holdall** *n* large strong travelling bag **hold-up** *n* armed robbery; delay

hold[2] *n* cargo compartment in a ship or aircraft

hole *n* area hollowed out in a solid; opening or hollow; animal's burrow; *Informal* unattractive place; *Informal* difficult situation ▷ *v* make holes in; hit (a golf ball) into the target hole

holiday *n* time spent away from home for rest or recreation; day or other period of rest from work or studies

holiness *n* state of being holy; (**H-**) title used to address or refer to the Pope

holistic *adj* considering the complete person, physically and mentally, in the treatment of an illness **holism** *n*

hollow *adj* having a hole or space inside; (of a sound) as if echoing in a hollow place; without any real value or worth ▷ *n* cavity or space; dip in the land ▷ *v* form a hollow in

holly *n* evergreen tree with prickly leaves and red berries

hollyhock *n* tall garden plant with spikes of colourful flowers

holocaust *n* destruction or loss of life on a massive scale

hologram *n* three-dimensional photographic image

holograph *n* document handwritten by the author

holster *n* leather case for a pistol, hung from a belt

holy *adj* **-lier, -liest** of God or a god; devout or virtuous **holier-than-thou** *adj* self-righteous **Holy Communion** *Christianity* service in which people take bread and wine in remembrance of the death and resurrection of Jesus Christ **Holy Grail** (in medieval legend) the bowl used by Jesus Christ at the Last Supper **Holy Spirit, Ghost** *Christianity* one of the three aspects of God **Holy Week** *Christianity* week before Easter

homage *n* show of respect or honour towards someone or something

home *n* place where one lives; institution for the care of the elderly, orphans, etc ▷ *adj* of one's home, birthplace, or native country; *sport* played on one's own ground ▷ *adv* to or at home ▷ *v* (foll by *in, in on*) direct towards (a point or target) **at home** at ease **bring home to** make clear to **home and dry** *Informal* safe or successful **homeless** *adj* having nowhere to live ▷ *pl n* people who have nowhere to live **homelessness** *n* **homely** *adj* simple, ordinary, and comfortable; *US* unattractive **homeward** *adj, adv* **homewards** *adv* **home-brew** *n* beer made at home **home-made** *adj* made at home or on the premises **home page** *computers* introductory information about a website with links to the information or services provided **home truths** unpleasant facts told to a person about himself or herself

homeland *n* country from which a person's ancestors came

homeopathy [home-ee-**op**-ath-ee] *n* treatment of disease by small doses of a drug that produces symptoms of the disease in healthy people **homeopath** *n* person who practises homeopathy **homeopathic** *adj*

homesick *adj* sad because missing one's home and family **homesickness** *n*

homework *n* school work done at home

homicide *n* killing of a human being; person who kills someone **homicidal** *adj*

homily *n, pl* **-lies** speech telling people how they should behave

hominid *n* man or any extinct forerunner of man

homo- *combining form* same, like *eg homosexual*

homogeneous [home-oh-**jean**-ee-uss] *adj* formed of similar parts **homogeneity** *n* **homogenize** *v* break up fat globules in (milk or cream) to distribute them evenly; make homogeneous

homograph *n* word spelt the same as another, but with a different meaning

homologous [hom-**ol**-log-uss] *adj* having a related or similar position or structure

homonym *n* word spelt or pronounced the same as another, but with a different meaning

homophobia *n* hatred or fear of homosexuals **homophobic** *adj*

homophone *n* word pronounced the same as another, but with a different meaning or spelling

Homo sapiens [**hoe**-moh **sap**-ee-enz] *n* human beings as a species

homosexual *n, adj* (person) sexually attracted to members of the same sex **homosexuality** *n*

hone *v* sharpen

honest *adj* truthful and moral; open and sincere **honestly** *adv* **honesty** *n* quality of being honest; plant with silvery seed pods

honey *n* sweet edible sticky substance made by bees from nectar; term of endearment **honeycomb** *n* waxy structure of six-sided cells in which honey is stored by bees in a beehive **honeydew melon** melon with a yellow skin and sweet pale flesh **honeymoon** *n* holiday taken by a newly married couple **honeysuckle** *n* climbing shrub with sweet-smelling flowers; Australian tree or shrub with nectar-rich flowers

hongi [**hong**-jee] *n NZ* Maori greeting in which people touch noses

honk *n* sound made by a car horn; sound made by a goose ▷ *v* (cause to) make this sound

honour *n* sense of honesty and fairness; (award given out of) respect; pleasure or privilege ▷ *pl* university degree of a higher standard than an ordinary degree ▷ *v* give praise and attention to; give an award to (someone) out of respect; accept or pay (a cheque or bill); keep (a promise) **do the honours** act as host or hostess by pouring drinks or giving out food **honourable** *adj* worthy of respect or esteem **honourably** *adv* **honorary** *adj* held or given only as an honour; unpaid **honorific** *adj* showing respect

hood[1] *n* head covering, often attached to a coat or jacket; folding roof of a convertible car or a pram; *US & Aust* car bonnet **hooded** *adj* (of a garment) having a hood; (of eyes) having heavy eyelids that appear to be half-closed

hood[2] *n Chiefly US, slang* hoodlum

hoodlum *n slang* violent criminal, gangster

hoodoo *n, pl* **-doos** (cause of) bad luck

hoodwink *v* trick, deceive

hoof *n, pl* **hooves, hoofs** horny covering of the foot of a horse, deer, etc **hoof it** *slang* walk

hoo-ha *n* fuss or commotion

hook *n* curved piece of metal, plastic, etc, used to hang, hold, or pull something; short swinging punch ▷*v* fasten or catch (as if) with a hook **hooked** *adj* bent like a hook; (foll by *on*) *slang* addicted (to) or obsessed (with) **hooker** *n Chiefly US, slang* prostitute; *rugby* player who uses his feet to get the ball in a scrum **hook-up** *n* linking of radio or television stations **hookworm** *n* blood-sucking worm with hooked mouthparts

hookah *n* oriental pipe in which smoke is drawn through water and a long tube

hooligan *n* rowdy young person **hooliganism** *n*

hoon *n Aust & NZ, slang* loutish youth who drives irresponsibly

hoop *n* rigid circular band, used esp as a child's toy or for animals to jump through in the circus **jump, be put through the hoops** go through an ordeal or test **hoop pine** Australian tree or shrub with flowers in dense spikes

hoopla *n* fairground game in which hoops are thrown over objects in an attempt to win them

hooray *interj* same as **hurrah**

hoot *n* sound of a car horn; cry of an owl; cry of derision; *Informal* amusing person or thing ▷*v* sound (a car horn); jeer or yell contemptuously (at someone) **hooter** *n* device that hoots; *Chiefly Brit, slang* nose

Hoover *n* ® vacuum cleaner ▷*v* (**h-**) clean with a vacuum cleaner

hooves *n* a plural of **hoof**

hop[1] *v* **hopping, hopped** jump on one foot; move in short jumps; *Informal* move quickly ▷*n* instance of hopping; *Informal* dance; short journey, esp by air **catch someone on the hop** *Informal* catch someone unprepared

hop[2] *n* (often pl) climbing plant, the dried flowers of which are used to make beer

hope *v* want (something) to happen or be true ▷*n* expectation of something desired; thing that gives cause for hope or is desired **hopeful** *adj* having, expressing, or inspiring hope ▷*n* person considered to be on the brink of success **hopefully** *adv* in a hopeful manner; it is hoped **hopeless** *adj*

hopper *n* container for storing substances such as grain or sand

hopscotch *n* children's game of hopping in a pattern drawn on the ground

horde *n* large crowd

horizon *n* apparent line that divides the earth and the sky ▷*pl* limits of scope, interest, or knowledge

horizontal *adj* parallel to the horizon, level, flat **horizontally** *adv*

hormone *n* substance secreted by certain glands which stimulates certain organs of the body; synthetic substance with the same effect **hormonal** *adj*

horn *n* one of a pair of bony growths sticking out of the heads of cattle, sheep, etc; substance of which horns are made; musical instrument with a tube or pipe of brass fitted with a mouthpiece; device on a vehicle sounded as a warning **horned** *adj* **horny** *adj* of or like horn; *slang* (easily) sexually aroused **hornbeam** *n* tree with smooth grey bark **hornbill** *n* bird with a bony growth on its large beak **hornpipe** *n* (music for) a solo dance, traditionally performed by sailors

hornblende *n* mineral containing aluminium, calcium, sodium, magnesium, and iron

hornet *n* large wasp with a severe sting

horoscope *n* prediction of a person's future based on the positions of the planets, sun, and moon at his or her birth

horrendous *adj* very unpleasant and shocking

horrible *adj* disagreeable, unpleasant; causing horror **horribly** *adv*

horrid *adj* disagreeable, unpleasant; *Informal* nasty

horrify *v* **-fying, -fied** cause to feel horror or shock **horrific** *adj* causing horror

horror *n* (thing or person causing) terror or hatred

hors d'oeuvre [**or durv**] *n* appetizer served before a main meal

horse *n* large animal with hooves, a mane, and a tail, used for riding and pulling carts etc; piece of gymnastic equipment used for vaulting over **(straight) from the horse's mouth** from the original source **horsey, horsy** *adj* very keen on horses; of or like a horse **horse around** *v Informal* play roughly or boisterously **horse chestnut** tree with broad leaves and inedible large brown shiny nuts in spiky cases **horsefly** *n* large bloodsucking fly **horsehair** *n* hair from the tail or mane of a horse **horse laugh** loud coarse laugh **horseman, horsewoman** *n* person riding a horse **horseplay** *n* rough or rowdy play **horsepower** *n* unit of power (equivalent to 745.7 watts), used to measure the power of an engine **horseradish** *n* strong-tasting root of a plant, usu made into a sauce **horseshoe** *n* protective U-shaped piece of iron nailed to a horse's hoof, regarded as a symbol of good luck

horticulture *n* art or science of cultivating gardens **horticultural** *adj* **horticulturalist, horticulturist** *n*

hosanna *interj* exclamation of praise to God

hose[1] *n* flexible pipe for conveying liquid ▷*v* water with a hose

hose[2] *n* stockings, socks, and tights **hosiery** *n* stockings, socks, and tights collectively

hospice [**hoss**-piss] *n* nursing home for the terminally ill

hospital *n* place where people who are ill are looked after and treated **hospitalize** *v* send or admit to hospital **hospitalization** *n*

hospitality *n* kindness in

welcoming strangers or guests **hospitable** *adj* welcoming to strangers or guests

host[1] *n fem* **hostess** person who entertains guests, esp in his own home; place or country providing the facilities for an event; compere of a show; animal or plant on which a parasite lives ▷*v* be the host of

host[2] *n* large number

Host *n Christianity* bread used in Holy Communion

hostage *n* person who is illegally held prisoner until certain demands are met by other people

hostel *n* building providing accommodation at a low cost for a specific group of people such as students, travellers, homeless people, etc

hostelry *n, pl* **-ries** *old-fashioned or facetious* inn, pub

hostile *adj* unfriendly; (foll by *to*) opposed (to); of an enemy **hostility** *n, pl* **-ties** unfriendly and aggressive feelings or behaviour ▷*pl* acts of warfare

hot *adj* **hotter, hottest** having a high temperature; strong, spicy; (of news) very recent; (of a contest) fiercely fought; (of a temper) quick to rouse; liked very much *eg a hot favourite*; *slang* stolen **in hot water** *Informal* in trouble **hotly** *adv* **hot air** *Informal* empty talk **hot-blooded** *adj* passionate or excitable **hot dog** long roll split lengthways with a hot frankfurter inside **hot-headed** *adj* rash, having a hot temper **hotline** *n* direct telephone link for emergency use **hot pool** *NZ* geothermally heated pool

hotbed *n* any place encouraging a particular activity *eg hotbeds of unrest*

hotchpotch *n* jumbled mixture

hotel *n* commercial establishment providing lodging and meals **hotelier** *n* owner or manager of a hotel

hotfoot *adv Informal* quickly and eagerly **hotfoot it** *Informal* go quickly and eagerly

hothouse *n* greenhouse

hotplate *n* heated metal surface on an electric cooker; portable device for keeping food warm

hound *n* hunting dog ▷*v* pursue relentlessly

hour *n* twenty-fourth part of a day, sixty minutes; time of day ▷*pl* period regularly appointed for work or business **hourly** *adj, adv* (happening) every hour; frequent(ly) **hourglass** *n* device with two glass compartments, containing a quantity of sand that takes an hour to trickle from the top section to the bottom one

houri *n islam* any of the nymphs of paradise

house *n* building used as a home; building used for some specific purpose *eg the opera house*; business firm; law-making body or the hall where it meets; family or dynasty; theatre or cinema audience ▷*v* give accommodation to; contain or cover **get on like a house on fire** *Informal* get on very well together **on the house** *Informal* provided free by the management **housing** *n* (providing of) houses; protective case or covering of a machine **house arrest** confinement to one's home rather than in prison **houseboat** *n* stationary boat used as a home **housebreaker** *n* burglar **housecoat** *n* woman's long loose coat-shaped garment for wearing at home **household** *n* all the people living in a house **householder** *n* person who owns or rents a house **housekeeper** *n* person employed to run someone else's household **housekeeping** *n* (money for) running a household **housemaid** *n* female servant employed to do housework **house-train** *v* train (a pet) to urinate and defecate outside **house-warming** *n* party to celebrate moving into a new home **housewife** *n* woman who runs her own household and does not have a job **housework** *n* work of running a home, such as cleaning, cooking, and shopping

House music, House *n* electronic funk-based disco music with samples of other recordings edited in

hovea *n* Australian plant with purple flowers

hovel *n* small dirty house or hut

hover *v* (of a bird etc) remain suspended in one place in the air; loiter; be in a state of indecision **hovercraft** *n* vehicle which can travel over both land and sea on a cushion of air

how *adv* in what way, by what means; to what degree *eg I know how hard it is* **however** *adv* nevertheless; by whatever means; no matter how *eg however much it hurt, he could do it*

howdah *n* canopied seat on an elephant's back

howitzer *n* large gun firing shells at a steep angle

howl *n* loud wailing cry; loud burst of laughter ▷*v* utter a howl **howler** *n Informal* stupid mistake

hoyden *n old-fashioned* wild or boisterous girl

HP, h.p. hire-purchase; horsepower

HQ headquarters

HRH Her (or His) Royal Highness

HRT hormone replacement therapy

HTML hypertext markup language: text description language used on the Internet

hub *n* centre of a wheel, through which the axle passes; central point of activity

hubbub *n* confused noise of many voices

hubby *n, pl* **-bies** *Informal* husband

hubris [**hew**-briss] *n formal* pride, arrogance

huckster *n* person using aggressive methods of selling

huddle *v* hunch (oneself) through cold or fear; crowd closely together ▷*n* small group; *Informal* impromptu conference

hue *n* colour, shade

hue and cry *n* public outcry

huff *n* passing mood of anger or resentment ▷*v* blow or puff heavily **huffy** *adj* **huffily** *adv*

hug *v* **hugging, hugged** clasp tightly in the arms, usu with affection; keep close to (the ground, kerb, etc) ▷*n* tight or fond embrace

huge *adj* very big **hugely** *adv*

huh *interj* exclamation of derision, bewilderment, or inquiry

hui [**hoo**-ee] *n NZ* meeting of Maori people; meeting to discuss Maori matters

hula *n* swaying Hawaiian dance **Hula Hoop** ® plastic hoop twirled round the body by gyrating the hips

hulk *n* body of an abandoned ship; *offens* large heavy person or thing **hulking** *adj* bulky, unwieldy

hull *n* main body of a boat; leaves round the stem of a strawberry, raspberry, etc ▷*v* remove the hulls from

hullabaloo *n, pl* **-loos** loud confused noise or clamour

hum *v* **humming, hummed** make a low continuous vibrating sound; sing with the lips closed; *slang* (of a place) be very busy ▷ *n* humming sound **hummingbird** *n* very small American bird whose powerful wings make a humming noise as they vibrate

human *adj* of or typical of people ▷ *n* human being **humanly** *adv* by human powers or means **human being** man, woman, or child

humane *adj* kind or merciful **humanely** *adv*

humanism *n* belief in human effort rather than religion **humanist** *n*

humanitarian *n, adj* (person) having the interests of humankind at heart

humanity *n, pl* **-ties** human race; the quality of being human; kindness or mercy ▷ *pl* study of literature, philosophy, and the arts

humanize *v* make human or humane

humankind *n.* human race

humble *adj* conscious of one's failings; modest, unpretentious; unimportant ▷ *v* cause to feel humble, humiliate **humbly** *adv*

humbug *n Brit* hard striped peppermint sweet; nonsense; dishonest person

humdinger *n slang* excellent person or thing

humdrum *adj* ordinary, dull

humerus [hew-mer-uss] *n, pl* **-meri** [-mer-rye] bone from the shoulder to the elbow

humid *adj* damp and hot **humidity** *n* **humidify** *v* **-fying, -fied** **humidifier** *n* device for increasing the amount of water vapour in the air in a room

humiliate *v* lower the dignity or hurt the pride of **humiliating** *adj* **humiliation** *n*

humility *n* quality of being humble

hummock *n* very small hill

humour *n* ability to say or perceive things that are amusing; amusing quality in a situation, film, etc; state of mind, mood; *old-fashioned* fluid in the body ▷ *v* be kind and indulgent to **humorous** *adj* **humorously** *adv* **humorist** *n* writer or entertainer who uses humour in his or her work

> SPELLING A lot of people simply add *-ous* to the noun **humour** to make *humourous*, but this is a mistake; you have to drop the second *u* when you write **humorous** or **humorist**

hump *n* raised piece of ground; large lump on the back of an animal or person ▷ *v slang* carry or heave **get, take the hump** *Informal* be annoyed, sulk **hump-back, humpbacked bridge** road bridge with a sharp slope on each side

humus [hew-muss] *n* decomposing vegetable and animal mould in the soil

hunch *n* feeling or suspicion not based on facts ▷ *v* draw (one's shoulders) up or together **hunchback** *n offens* person with an abnormal curvature of the spine

hundred *adj, n* ten times ten ▷ *n* (often pl) large but unspecified number **hundredth** *adj, n* **hundredweight** *n Brit* unit of weight of 112 pounds (50.8 kilograms)

hung *v* past of **hang** ▷ *adj* (of a parliament or jury) with no side having a clear majority **hung over** *Informal* suffering the effects of a hangover

hunger *n* discomfort or weakness from lack of food; desire or craving ▷ *v* (foll by *for*) want very much **hunger strike** refusal of all food, as a means of protest

hungry *adj* **hungrier, hungriest** desiring food; (foll by *for*) having a desire or craving (for) **hungrily** *adv*

hunk *n* large piece; *slang* sexually attractive man

hunt *v* seek out and kill (wild animals) for food or sport; (foll by *for*) search (for) ▷ *n* hunting; (party organized for) hunting wild animals for sport **huntaway** *n NZ* sheepdog trained to drive sheep by barking **huntsman** *n* man who hunts wild animals, esp foxes

hunter *n* person or animal that hunts wild animals for food or sport

hurdle *n sport* light barrier for jumping over in some races; problem or difficulty ▷ *pl* race involving hurdles ▷ *v* jump over (something) **hurdler** *n*

hurdy-gurdy *n, pl* **-dies** mechanical musical instrument, such as a barrel organ

hurl *v* throw or utter forcefully

hurling, hurley *n* Irish game like hockey

hurly-burly *n* loud confusion

hurrah, hurray *interj* exclamation of joy or applause

hurricane *n* very strong, often destructive, wind or storm **hurricane lamp** paraffin lamp with a glass covering

hurry *v* **-rying, -ried** (cause to) move or act very quickly ▷ *n* doing something quickly or the need to do something quickly **hurriedly** *adv*

hurt *v* **hurting, hurt** cause physical or mental pain to; be painful; *Informal* feel pain ▷ *n* physical or mental pain **hurtful** *adj* unkind

hurtle *v* move quickly or violently

husband *n* woman's partner in marriage ▷ *v* use economically **husbandry** *n* farming; management of resources

hush *v* make or be silent ▷ *n* stillness or silence **hush-hush** *adj Informal* secret **hush up** *v* suppress information about

husk *n* outer covering of certain seeds and fruits ▷ *v* remove the husk from

husky[1] *adj* **huskier, huskiest** slightly hoarse; *Informal* big and strong **huskily** *adv*

husky[2] *n, pl* **huskies** Arctic sledge dog with thick hair and a curled tail

hussar [hoo-**zar**] *n hist* lightly armed cavalry soldier

hussy *n, pl* **-sies** immodest or promiscuous woman

hustings *pl n* political campaigns and speeches before an election

hustle *v* push about, jostle ▷ *n* lively activity or bustle

hut *n* small house, shelter, or shed

hutch *n* cage for pet rabbits etc

hyacinth *n* sweet-smelling spring flower that grows from a bulb

hyaena *n* same as **hyena**

hybrid *n* offspring of two plants or animals of different species; anything of mixed origin ▷ *adj* of mixed origin

hydra *n* mythical many-headed water serpent

hydrangea *n* ornamental shrub with clusters of pink, blue, or white flowers

hydrant *n* outlet from a water main with a nozzle for a hose

hydrate *n* chemical compound of

water with another substance

hydraulic *adj* operated by pressure forced through a pipe by a liquid such as water or oil **hydraulics** *n* study of the mechanical properties of fluids as they apply to practical engineering **hydraulically** *adv*

hydro¹ *n, pl* **hydros** hotel offering facilities for hydropathy

hydro² *adj* short for **hydroelectric**

hydro- *combining form* water *eg hydroelectric*; hydrogen *eg hydrochloric acid*

hydrocarbon *n* compound of hydrogen and carbon

hydrochloric acid *n* strong colourless acid used in many industrial and laboratory processes

hydroelectric *adj* of the generation of electricity by water pressure

hydrofoil *n* fast light boat with its hull raised out of the water on one or more pairs of fins

hydrogen *n chem* light flammable colourless gas that combines with oxygen to form water **hydrogen bomb** extremely powerful bomb in which energy is released by fusion of hydrogen nuclei to give helium nuclei **hydrogen peroxide** colourless liquid used as a hair bleach and as an antiseptic

hydrolysis [hie-**drol**-iss-iss] *n* decomposition of a chemical compound reacting with water

hydrometer [hie-**drom**-it-er] *n* instrument for measuring the density of a liquid

hydropathy *n* method of treating disease by the use of large quantities of water both internally and externally

hydrophobia *n* rabies; fear of water

hydroplane *n* light motorboat that skims the water

hydroponics *n* method of growing plants in water rather than soil

hydrotherapy *n med* treatment of certain diseases by exercise in water

hyena *n* scavenging doglike mammal of Africa and S Asia

hygiene *n* principles and practice of health and cleanliness **hygienic** *adj* **hygienically** *adv*

hymen *n* membrane partly covering the opening of a girl's vagina, which breaks before puberty or at the first occurrence of sexual intercourse

hymn *n* Christian song of praise sung to God or a saint **hymnal** *n* book of hymns (also **hymn book**)

hype *n* intensive or exaggerated publicity or sales promotion ▷*v* promote (a product) using intensive or exaggerated publicity

hyper *adj Informal* overactive or overexcited

hyper- *prefix* over, above, excessively *eg hyperactive*

hyperbola [hie-**per**-bol-a] *n geom* curve produced when a cone is cut by a plane at a steeper angle to its base than its side

hyperbole [hie-**per**-bol-ee] *n* deliberate exaggeration for effect **hyperbolic** *adj*

hyperlink *computers* ▷*n* link from a hypertext file that gives users instant access to related material in another file ▷*v* link (files) in this way

hypermarket *n* huge self-service store

hypersensitive *adj* extremely sensitive to certain drugs, extremes of temperature, etc; very easily upset

hypersonic *adj* having a speed of at least five times the speed of sound

hypertension *n* very high blood pressure

hypertext *n* computer software and hardware that allows users to store and view text and move between related items easily

hyphen *n* punctuation mark (-) indicating that two words or syllables are connected **hyphenated** *adj* (of two words or syllables) having a hyphen between them **hyphenation** *n*

hypnosis *n* artificially induced state of relaxation in which the mind is more than usually receptive to suggestion **hypnotic** *adj* of or (as if) producing hypnosis **hypnotism** *n* inducing hypnosis in someone **hypnotist** *n* **hypnotize** *v*

hypo- *prefix* beneath, less than *eg hypothermia*

hypoallergenic *adj* (of cosmetics) not likely to cause an allergic reaction

hypochondria *n* undue preoccupation with one's health **hypochondriac** *n*

hypocrisy [hip-**ok**-rass-ee] *n, pl* **-sies** (instance of) pretence of having standards or beliefs that are contrary to one's real character or actual behaviour **hypocrite** [**hip**-oh-krit] *n* person who pretends to be what he or she is not **hypocritical** *adj* **hypocritically** *adv*

hypodermic *adj, n* (denoting) a syringe or needle used to inject a drug beneath the skin

hypotension *n* very low blood pressure

hypotenuse [hie-**pot**-a-news] *n* side of a right-angled triangle opposite the right angle

hypothermia *n* condition in which a person's body temperature is dangerously low as a result of prolonged exposure to severe cold

hypothesis [hie-**poth**-iss-iss] *n, pl* **-ses** [-seez] suggested but unproved explanation of something **hypothetical** *adj* based on assumption rather than fact or reality **hypothetically** *adv*

hyrax *n, pl* **-raxes** *or* **-races** type of hoofed rodent-like animal of Africa and Asia

hysterectomy *n, pl* **-mies** surgical removal of the womb

hysteria *n* state of uncontrolled excitement, anger, or panic **hysterical** *adj* **hysterically** *adv* **hysterics** *pl n* attack of hysteria; *Informal* uncontrollable laughter

Hz hertz

I

I *pron* used by a speaker or writer to refer to himself or herself as the subject of a verb
Iberian *adj* of Iberia, the peninsula comprising Spain and Portugal
ibex [**ibe**-eks] *n* wild goat of N with large backward-curving horns
ibid. (referring to a book, page, or passage already mentioned) in the same place
ibis [**ibe**-iss] *n* large wading bird with long legs
ice *n* frozen water; *Chiefly Brit* portion of ice cream **the Ice** *NZ, Informal* Antarctica ▷ *v* (foll by *up, over*) become covered with ice; cover with icing **break the ice** create a relaxed atmosphere, esp between people meeting for the first time **iced** *adj* covered with icing; (of a drink) containing ice **icy** *adj* **icier, iciest** very cold; covered with ice; aloof and unfriendly **icily** *adv* **iciness** *n* **Ice Age** period when much of the earth's surface was covered in glaciers **iceberg** *n* large floating mass of ice **icebox** *n US* refrigerator **icecap** *n* mass of ice permanently covering an area **ice cream** sweet creamy frozen food **ice cube** small square block of ice added to a drink to cool it **ice floe** sheet of ice floating in the sea **ice hockey** team game like hockey played on ice with a puck **ice lolly** flavoured ice on a stick **ice pick** pointed tool for breaking ice **ice skate** boot with a steel blade fixed to the sole, to enable the wearer to glide over ice **ice-skate** *v* **ice-skater** *n*
ichthyology [ik-thi-**ol**-a-jee] *n* scientific study of fish
icicle *n* tapering spike of ice hanging where water has dripped
icing *n* mixture of sugar and water etc, used to cover and decorate cakes **icing sugar** finely ground sugar for making icing
icon *n* picture of Christ or another religious figure, regarded as holy in the Orthodox Church; picture on a computer screen representing a function that can be activated by moving the cursor over it
iconoclast *n* person who attacks established ideas or principles **iconoclastic** *adj*
id *n psychoanalysis* the mind's instinctive unconscious energies
idea *n* plan or thought formed in the mind; thought of something; belief or opinion
ideal *adj* most suitable; perfect ▷ *n* conception of something that is perfect; perfect person or thing **ideally** *adv* **idealism** *n* tendency to seek perfection in everything

idealist *n* **idealistic** *adj* **idealize** *v* regard or portray as perfect or nearly perfect **idealization** *n*
idem *pron, adj Latin* the same: used to refer to an article, chapter, or book already quoted
identical *adj* exactly the same **identically** *adv*
identify *v* **-fying, -fied** prove or recognize as being a certain person or thing; (foll by *with*) understand and sympathize with (a person or group that one regards as being similar or similarly situated); treat as being the same **identifiable** *adj* **identification** *n*
Identikit *n* ® composite picture, assembled from descriptions given, of a person wanted by the police
identity *n, pl* **-ties** state of being a specified person or thing; individuality or personality; state of being the same
ideology *n, pl* **-gies** body of ideas and beliefs of a group, nation, etc **ideological** *adj* **ideologist** *n*
idiocy *n* utter stupidity
idiom *n* group of words which when used together have a different meaning from the words individually *eg raining cats and dogs*; way of expression natural or peculiar to a language or group **idiomatic** *adj* **idiomatically** *adv*
idiosyncrasy *n, pl* **-sies** personal peculiarity of mind, habit, or behaviour
idiot *n* foolish or stupid person; *offens* mentally retarded person **idiotic** *adj* **idiotically** *adv*
idle *adj* not doing anything; not willing to work, lazy; not being used; useless or meaningless *eg an idle threat* ▷ *v* (usu foll by *away*) spend (time) doing very little; (of an engine) run slowly with the gears disengaged **idleness** *n* **idler** *n* **idly** *adv*
idol *n* object of excessive devotion; image of a god as an object of worship **idolatry** *n* worship of idols **idolatrous** *adj* **idolize** *v* love or admire excessively
idyll [**id**-ill] *n* scene or time of great peace and happiness **idyllic** *adj* **idyllically** *adv*
i.e. that is to say
if *conj* on the condition or supposition that; whether; even though ▷ *n* uncertainty or doubt *eg no ifs, ands, or buts* **iffy** *adj Informal* doubtful, uncertain
igloo *n, pl* **-loos** dome-shaped Inuit house made of snow and ice
igneous [**ig**-nee-uss] *adj* (of rock) formed as molten rock cools and hardens
ignite *v* catch fire or set fire to
ignition *n* system that ignites the fuel-and-air mixture to start an engine; igniting
ignoble *adj* dishonourable
ignominy [**ig**-nom-in-ee] *n* humiliating disgrace **ignominious** *adj* **ignominiously** *adv*
ignoramus *n, pl* **-muses** ignorant person
ignorant *adj* lacking knowledge; rude through lack of knowledge of good manners **ignorance** *n*
ignore *v* refuse to notice, disregard deliberately
iguana *n* large tropical American lizard
ileum *n* lowest part of the small intestine
ilk *n* type *eg others of his ilk*
ill *adj* not in good health; harmful or unpleasant *eg ill effects* ▷ *n* evil, harm ▷ *adv* badly; hardly, with difficulty *eg I can ill afford to lose him*

ill at ease uncomfortable, unable to relax **illness** *n* **ill-advised** *adj* badly thought out; unwise **ill-disposed** *adj* (often foll by *towards*) unfriendly, unsympathetic **ill-fated** *adj* doomed to end unhappily **ill-gotten** *adj* obtained dishonestly **ill-health** *n* condition of being unwell **ill-mannered** *adj* having bad manners **ill-treat** *v* treat cruelly **ill will** unkind feeling, hostility

illegal *adj* against the law **illegally** *adv* **illegality** *n, pl* **-ties**

illegible *adj* unable to be read or deciphered

illegitimate *adj* born of parents not married to each other; not lawful **illegitimacy** *n*

illicit *adj* illegal; forbidden or disapproved of by society

illiterate *n, adj* (person) unable to read or write **illiteracy** *n*

illogical *adj* unreasonable; not logical **illogicality** *n*

illuminate *v* light up; make clear, explain; decorate with lights; *hist* decorate (a manuscript) with designs of gold and bright colours **illumination** *n* **illuminating** *adj*

illusion *n* deceptive appearance or belief **illusionist** *n* conjuror **illusory** *adj* seeming to be true, but actually false

illustrate *v* explain by use of examples; provide (a book or text) with pictures; be an example of **illustration** *n* picture or diagram; example **illustrative** *adj* **illustrator** *n*

illustrious *adj* famous and distinguished

image *n* mental picture of someone or something; impression people have of a person, organization, etc; representation of a person or thing in a work of art; optical reproduction of someone or something, for example in a mirror; person or thing that looks almost exactly like another; figure of speech, esp a metaphor or simile **imagery** *n* images collectively, esp in the arts

imagine *v* form a mental image of; think, believe, or guess **imaginable** *adj* **imaginary** *adj* existing only in the imagination **imagination** *n* ability to make mental images of things that may not exist in real life; creative mental ability **imaginative** *adj* having or showing a lot of creative mental ability **imaginatively** *adv*

> SPELLING Remembering that an *e* changes to an *a* to form **imagination** is a good way of getting **imaginary** right, because it has an *a* instead of an *e* too

imago [im-**may**-go] *n, pl* **imagoes, imagines** [im-**maj**-in-ees] sexually mature adult insect

imam *n* leader of prayers in a mosque; title of some Islamic leaders

IMAX [**eye**-max] *n* ® film projection process which produces an image ten times larger than standard

imbalance *n* lack of balance or proportion

imbecile [**imb**-ess-eel] *n* stupid person ▷ *adj* (also **imbecilic**) stupid or senseless **imbecility** *n*

imbibe *v* drink (alcoholic drinks); *lit* absorb (ideas etc)

imbroglio [imb-**role**-ee-oh] *n, pl* **-ios** confusing and complicated situation

imbue *v* **-buing, -bued** (usu foll by *with*) fill or inspire with (ideals or

principles)
IMF International Monetary Fund
imitate *v* take as a model; copy the voice and mannerisms of, esp for entertainment **imitation** *n* copy of an original; imitating **imitative** *adj* **imitator** *n*
immaculate *adj* completely clean or tidy; completely flawless **immaculately** *adv*
immanent *adj* present within and throughout something **immanence** *n*
immaterial *adj* not important, not relevant
immature *adj* not fully developed; lacking wisdom or stability because of youth **immaturity** *n*
immediate *adj* occurring at once; next or nearest in time, space, or relationship **immediately** *adv* **immediacy** *n*
immemorial *adj* **since, from time immemorial** longer than anyone can remember
immense *adj* extremely large **immensely** *adv* to a very great degree **immensity** *n*
immerse *v* involve deeply, engross; plunge (something or someone) into liquid **immersion** *n* **immersion heater** electrical device in a domestic hot-water tank for heating water
immigration *n* coming to a foreign country in order to settle there **immigrant** *n*
imminent *adj* about to happen **imminently** *adv* **imminence** *n*
immobile *adj* not moving; unable to move **immobility** *n* **immobilize** *v* make unable to move or work
immoderate *adj* excessive or unreasonable
immolate *v* kill as a sacrifice **immolation** *n*
immoral *adj* morally wrong, corrupt; sexually depraved or promiscuous **immorality** *n*

> Do not confuse **immoral** with *amoral*, which means 'having no moral standards'

immortal *adj* living forever; famous for all time ▷ *n* person whose fame will last for all time; immortal being **immortality** *n* **immortalize** *v*
immune *adj* protected against a specific disease; (foll by *to*) secure (against); (foll by *from*) exempt (from) **immunity** *n, pl* **-ties** ability to resist disease; freedom from prosecution, tax, etc **immunize** *v* make immune to a disease **immunization** *n*
immunodeficiency *n* deficiency in or breakdown of a person's ability to fight diseases
immunology *n* branch of medicine concerned with the study of immunity **immunological** *adj* **immunologist** *n*
immutable [im-**mute**-a-bl] *adj* unchangeable **immutability** *n*
imp *n* (in folklore) mischievous small creature with magical powers; mischievous child
impact *n* strong effect; (force of) a collision ▷ *v* press firmly into something
impair *v* weaken or damage **impairment** *n*
impala [imp-**ah**-la] *n* southern African antelope
impale *v* pierce with a sharp object
impalpable *adj* difficult to define or understand
impart *v* communicate (information); give
impartial *adj* not favouring one

side or the other **impartially** *adv* **impartiality** *n*

impassable *adj* (of a road etc) impossible to travel through or over

impasse [am-pass] *n* situation in which progress is impossible

impassioned *adj* full of emotion

impassive *adj* showing no emotion, calm

impatient *adj* irritable at any delay or difficulty; restless (to have or do something) **impatiently** *adv* **impatience** *n*

impeach *v* charge with a serious crime against the state **impeachment** *n*

impeccable *adj* without fault, excellent **impeccably** *adv*

impecunious *adj* penniless, poor

impedance [imp-**eed**-anss] *n* *electricity* measure of the opposition to the flow of an alternating current

impede *v* hinder in action or progress **impediment** *n* something that makes action, speech, or progress difficult **impedimenta** *pl n* objects impeding progress, esp baggage or equipment

impel *v* **-pelling, -pelled** push or force (someone) to do something

impending *adj* (esp of something bad) about to happen

impenetrable *adj* impossible to get through; impossible to understand

imperative *adj* extremely urgent, vital; *grammar* denoting a mood of verbs used in commands ▷ *n* *grammar* imperative mood

imperceptible *adj* too slight or gradual to be noticed **imperceptibly** *adv*

imperfect *adj* having faults or mistakes; not complete; *grammar* denoting a tense of verbs describing continuous, incomplete, or repeated past actions ▷ *n* *grammar* imperfect tense **imperfection** *n*

imperial *adj* of or like an empire or emperor; denoting a system of weights and measures formerly used in Britain **imperialism** *n* rule by one country over many others **imperialist** *adj, n*

imperil *v* **-illing, -illed** put in danger

imperious *adj* proud and domineering

impersonal *adj* not relating to any particular person, objective; lacking human warmth or sympathy; *grammar* (of a verb) without a personal subject *eg it is snowing* **impersonality** *n*

impersonate *v* pretend to be (another person); copy the voice and mannerisms of, esp for entertainment **impersonation** *n* **impersonator** *n*

impertinent *adj* disrespectful or rude **impertinently** *adv* **impertinence** *n*

imperturbable *adj* calm, not excitable

impervious *adj* (foll by *to*) not letting (water etc) through; not influenced by (a feeling, argument, etc)

impetigo [imp-it-**tie**-go] *n* contagious skin disease

impetuous *adj* done or acting without thought, rash **impetuously** *adv* **impetuosity** *n*

impetus [imp-it-uss] *n, pl* **-tuses** incentive, impulse; force that starts a body moving

impinge *v* (foll by *on*) affect or restrict

impious [imp-ee-uss] *adj* showing a lack of respect or reverence

impish *adj* mischievous
implacable *adj* not prepared to be appeased, unyielding **implacably** *adv* **implacability** *n*
implant *n med* something put into someone's body, usu by surgical operation ▷*v* put (something) into someone's body, usu by surgical operation; fix firmly in someone's mind **implantation** *n*
implement *v* carry out (instructions etc) ▷*n* tool, instrument **implementation** *n*
implicate *v* show to be involved, esp in a crime **implication** *n* something implied
implicit *adj* expressed indirectly; absolute and unquestioning *eg implicit support* **implicitly** *adv*
implore *v* beg earnestly
imply *v* **-plying, -plied** indicate by hinting, suggest; involve as a necessary consequence
impolitic *adj* unwise or inadvisable
imponderable *n, adj* (something) impossible to assess
import *v* bring in (goods) from another country ▷*n* something imported; importance; meaning **importation** *n* **importer** *n*
important *adj* of great significance or value; having influence or power **importance** *n*
importunate *adj* persistent or demanding **importune** *v* harass with persistent requests **importunity** *n, pl* **-ties**
impose *v* force the acceptance of; (foll by *on*) take unfair advantage (of) **imposing** *adj* grand, impressive **imposition** *n* unreasonable demand
impossible *adj* not able to be done or to happen; absurd or unreasonable **impossibly** *adv* **impossibility** *n, pl* **-ties**
imposter, impostor *n* person who cheats or swindles by pretending to be someone else
impotent [**imp**-a-tent] *adj* powerless; (of a man) incapable of sexual intercourse **impotence** *n* **impotently** *adv*
impound *v* take legal possession of, confiscate
impoverish *v* make poor or weak **impoverishment** *n*
impracticable *adj* incapable of being put into practice
impractical *adj* not sensible
imprecation *n* curse
impregnable *adj* impossible to break into **impregnability** *n*
impregnate *v* saturate, spread all through; make pregnant **impregnation** *n*
impresario *n, pl* **-ios** person who runs theatre performances, concerts, etc

> SPELLING Don't be fooled into spelling **impresario** as *impressario*, which occurs 33 times in Collins Word Web. The correct spelling has only one *s*

impress *v* affect strongly, usu favourably; stress, emphasize; imprint, stamp **impression** *n* effect, esp a strong or favourable one; vague idea; impersonation for entertainment; mark made by pressing **impressionable** *adj* easily impressed or influenced
Impressionism *n* art style that gives a general effect or mood rather than form or structure **Impressionist** *n* **Impressionistic** *adj*
impressive *adj* making a strong impression, esp through size, importance, or quality
imprimatur [imp-rim-**ah**-ter] *n*

official approval to print a book
imprint *n* mark made by printing or stamping; publisher's name and address on a book ▷*v* produce (a mark) by printing or stamping
imprison *v* put in prison **imprisonment** *n*
improbable *adj* not likely to be true or to happen **improbability** *n, pl* **-ties**
impromptu *adj* without planning or preparation
improper *adj* indecent; incorrect or irregular **improper fraction** fraction in which the numerator is larger than the denominator, as in ⁵⁄₃
impropriety [imp-roe-**pry**-a-tee] *n, pl* **-ties** unsuitable or slightly improper behaviour
improve *v* make or become better **improvement** *n*
improvident *adj* not planning for future needs **improvidence** *n*
improvise *v* make use of whatever materials are available; make up (a piece of music, speech, etc) as one goes along **improvisation** *n*
impudent *adj* cheeky, disrespectful **impudently** *adv* **impudence** *n*
impugn [imp-**yoon**] *v* challenge the truth or validity of
impulse *n* sudden urge to do something; short electrical signal passing along a wire or nerve or through the air **on impulse** suddenly and without planning **impulsive** *adj* acting or done without careful consideration **impulsively** *adv*
impunity [imp-**yoon**-it-ee] *n* **with impunity** without punishment
impure *adj* having dirty or unwanted substances mixed in; immoral, obscene **impurity** *n*
impute *v* attribute responsibility to **imputation** *n*
in *prep* indicating position inside, state or situation, etc *eg in the net; in tears* ▷*adv* indicating position inside, entry into, etc *eg she stayed in; come in* ▷*adj* fashionable **inward** *adj* directed towards the middle; situated within; spiritual or mental ▷*adv* (also **inwards**) towards the inside or middle **inwardly** *adv*
inability *n* lack of means or skill to do something
inaccurate *adj* not correct **inaccuracy** *n, pl* **-cies**
inadequate *adj* not enough; not good enough **inadequacy** *n*
inadvertent *adj* unintentional **inadvertently** *adv*
inalienable *adj* not able to be taken away *eg an inalienable right*
inane *adj* senseless, silly **inanity** *n*
inanimate *adj* not living
inappropriate *adj* not suitable
inarticulate *adj* unable to express oneself clearly or well
inasmuch as *conj* because or in so far as
inaugurate *v* open or begin the use of, esp with ceremony; formally establish (a new leader) in office **inaugural** *adj* **inauguration** *n*
inauspicious *adj* unlucky, likely to have an unfavourable outcome
inboard *adj* (of a boat's engine) inside the hull
inborn *adj* existing from birth, natural
inbred *adj* produced as a result of inbreeding; inborn or ingrained
inbreeding *n* breeding of animals or people that are closely related
inbuilt *adj* present from the start
Inc. *US & Aust* (of a company) incorporated

incalculable *adj* too great to be estimated
in camera *adv* see **camera**
incandescent *adj* glowing with heat **incandescence** *n*
incantation *n* ritual chanting of magic words or sounds
incapable *adj* (foll by *of*) unable (to do something); incompetent
incapacitate *v* deprive of strength or ability **incapacity** *n*
incarcerate *v* imprison **incarceration** *n*
incarnate *adj* in human form **incarnation** *n* **Incarnation** *n* *Christianity* God's coming to earth in human form as Jesus Christ
incendiary [in-**send**-ya-ree] *adj* (of a bomb, attack, etc) designed to cause fires ▷ *n, pl* **-aries** bomb designed to cause fires
incense¹ *v* make very angry
incense² *n* substance that gives off a sweet perfume when burned
incentive *n* something that encourages effort or action
inception *n* beginning
incessant *adj* never stopping **incessantly** *adv*
incest *n* sexual intercourse between two people too closely related to marry **incestuous** *adj*
inch *n* unit of length equal to one twelfth of a foot or 2.54 centimetres ▷ *v* move slowly and gradually
inchoate [in-**koe**-ate] *adj* just begun and not yet properly developed
incidence *n* extent or frequency of occurrence
incident *n* something that happens; event involving violence
incidental *adj* occurring in connection with or resulting from something more important **incidentally** *adv* **incidental music** background music for a film or play
incinerate *v* burn to ashes **incineration** *n* **incinerator** *n* furnace for burning rubbish
incipient *adj* just starting to appear or happen
incise *v* cut into with a sharp tool **incision** *n* **incisor** *n* front tooth, used for biting into food
incisive *adj* direct and forceful
incite *v* stir up, provoke **incitement** *n*
incivility *n, pl* **-ties** rudeness or a rude remark
inclement *adj* (of weather) stormy or severe
incline *v* lean, slope; (cause to) have a certain disposition or tendency ▷ *n* slope **inclination** *n* liking, tendency, or preference; slope
include *v* have as part of the whole; put in as part of a set or group **inclusion** *n* **inclusive** *adj* including everything (specified) **inclusively** *adv*
incognito [in-kog-**nee**-toe] *adj, adv* having adopted a false identity ▷ *n, pl* **-tos** false identity
incoherent *adj* unclear and impossible to understand **incoherence** *n* **incoherently** *adv*
income *n* amount of money earned from work, investments, etc **income support** (in New Zealand) allowance paid by the government to people with a very low income **income tax** personal tax levied on annual income
incoming *adj* coming in; about to come into office
incommode *v* cause inconvenience to
incommunicado *adj, adv* deprived of communication with other people
incomparable *adj* beyond comparison, unequalled

incomparably *adv*
incompatible *adj* inconsistent or conflicting **incompatibility** *n*
incompetent *adj* not having the necessary ability or skill to do something **incompetence** *n*
inconceivable *adj* extremely unlikely, unimaginable
inconclusive *adj* not giving a final decision or result
incongruous *adj* inappropriate or out of place **incongruously** *adv* **incongruity** *n, pl* **-ties**
inconsequential *adj* unimportant, insignificant
inconsiderable *adj* **not inconsiderable** fairly large
inconstant *adj* liable to change one's loyalties or opinions
incontinent *adj* unable to control one's bladder or bowels **incontinence** *n*
incontrovertible *adj* impossible to deny or disprove
inconvenience *n* trouble or difficulty ▷ *v* cause trouble or difficulty to **inconvenient** *adj*
incorporate *v* include or be included as part of a larger unit
incorporeal *adj* without material form
incorrigible *adj* beyond correction or reform
incorruptible *adj* too honest to be bribed or corrupted; not subject to decay
increase *v* make or become greater in size, number, etc ▷ *n* rise in number, size, etc; amount by which something increases **increasingly** *adv*
incredible *adj* hard to believe or imagine; *Informal* marvellous, amazing **incredibly** *adv*
incredulous *adj* not willing to believe something **incredulity** *n*
increment *n* increase in money or value, esp a regular salary increase **incremental** *adj*
incriminate *v* make (someone) seem guilty of a crime **incriminating** *adj*
incubate [in-cube-ate] *v* (of a bird) hatch (eggs) by sitting on them; grow (bacteria); (of bacteria) remain inactive in an animal or person before causing disease **incubation** *n* **incubator** *n* heated enclosed apparatus for rearing premature babies; apparatus for artificially hatching birds' eggs
incubus [in-cube-uss] *n, pl* **-bi, -buses** (in folklore) demon believed to have sex with sleeping women; nightmarish burden or worry
inculcate *v* fix in someone's mind by constant repetition **inculcation** *n*
incumbent *n* person holding a particular office or position ▷ *adj* **it is incumbent on** it is the duty of **incumbency** *n, pl* **-cies**
incur *v* **-curring, -curred** cause (something unpleasant) to happen
incurable *adj* not able to be cured **incurably** *adv*
incurious *adj* showing no curiosity or interest
incursion *n* sudden brief invasion
indebted *adj* owing gratitude for help or favours; owing money **indebtedness** *n*
indecent *adj* morally or sexually offensive; unsuitable or unseemly *eg indecent haste* **indecently** *adv* **indecency** *n* **indecent assault** sexual attack which does not include rape **indecent exposure** showing of one's genitals in public
indecipherable *adj* impossible to read
indeed *adv* really, certainly ▷ *interj*

expression of indignation or surprise

indefatigable *adj* never getting tired **indefatigably** *adv*

indefensible *adj* unable to be justified; impossible to defend

indefinite *adj* without exact limits *eg for an indefinite period;* vague, unclear **indefinite article** *grammar* the word *a* or *an* **indefinitely** *adv*

indelible *adj* impossible to erase or remove; making indelible marks **indelibly** *adv*

indelicate *adj* offensive or embarrassing

indemnify *v* **-ifying, -ified** secure against loss, damage, or liability; compensate for loss or damage

indemnity *n, pl* **-ties** insurance against loss or damage; compensation for loss or damage

indent *v* start (a line of writing) further from the margin than the other lines; order (goods) using a special order form **indentation** *n* dent in a surface or edge

indenture *n* contract, esp one binding an apprentice to his or her employer

independent *adj* free from the control or influence of others; separate; financially self-reliant; capable of acting for oneself or on one's own ▷ *n* politician who does not represent any political party **independently** *adv* **independence** *n*

> SPELLING People often get confused about how to spell **independent**. It is spelt *independant* 44 times in Collins Word Web. It should be spelt with an *e* at the end in the same way as the noun it is related to: **independent** and **independence**

in-depth *adj* detailed, thorough

indescribable *adj* too intense or extreme for words **indescribably** *adv*

indeterminate *adj* uncertain in extent, amount, or nature **indeterminacy** *n*

index *n, pl* **indices** [**in**-diss-eez] alphabetical list of names or subjects dealt with in a book; file or catalogue used to find things ▷ *v* provide (a book) with an index; enter in an index; make index-linked **index finger** finger next to the thumb **index-linked** *adj* (of pensions, wages, etc) rising or falling in line with the cost of living

Indian *n, adj* (person) from India; Native American **Indian summer** period of warm sunny weather in autumn

indicate *v* be a sign or symptom of; point out; state briefly; (of a measuring instrument) show a reading of **indication** *n* **indicative** *adj* (foll by *of*) suggesting; *grammar* denoting a mood of verbs used to make a statement ▷ *n grammar* indicative mood **indicator** *n* something acting as a sign or indication; flashing light on a vehicle showing the driver's intention to turn; dial or gauge

indict [in-**dite**] *v* formally charge with a crime **indictable** *adj* **indictment** *n*

indie *adj Informal* (of rock music) released by an independent record company

indifferent *adj* showing no interest or concern; of poor quality **indifference** *n* **indifferently** *adv*

indigenous [in-**dij**-in-uss] *adj* born in or natural to a country

indigent *adj* extremely poor **indigence** *n*
indigestion *n* (discomfort or pain caused by) difficulty in digesting food **indigestible** *adj*
indignation *n* anger at something unfair or wrong **indignant** *adj* feeling or showing indignation **indignantly** *adv*
indignity *n, pl* **-ties** embarrassing or humiliating treatment
indigo *adj* deep violet-blue ▷*n* dye of this colour
indirect *adj* done or caused by someone or something else; not by a straight route **indirect object** *grammar* person or thing indirectly affected by the action of a verb, eg *Amy* in *I bought Amy a bag* **indirect tax** tax added to the price of something
indiscreet *adj* incautious or tactless in revealing secrets **indiscreetly** *adv* **indiscretion** *n*
indiscriminate *adj* showing lack of careful thought
indispensable *adj* absolutely essential

> SPELLING For every twenty examples of the word **indispensable** in Collins Word Web, there is one example of the misspelling *indispensible*. So remember that it ends in *-able*

indisposed *adj* unwell, ill **indisposition** *n*
indisputable *adj* beyond doubt **indisputably** *adv*
indissoluble *adj* permanent
indium *n chem* soft silvery-white metallic element
individual *adj* characteristic of or meant for a single person or thing; separate, distinct; distinctive, unusual ▷*n* single person or thing **individually** *adv* **individuality** *n* **individualism** *n* principle of living one's life in one's own way **individualist** *n* **individualistic** *adj*
indoctrinate *v* teach (someone) to accept a doctrine or belief uncritically **indoctrination** *n*
Indo-European *adj, n* (of) a family of languages spoken in most of Europe and much of Asia, including English, Russian, and Hindi
indolent *adj* lazy **indolence** *n*
indomitable *adj* too strong to be defeated or discouraged **indomitably** *adv*
indoor *adj* inside a building **indoors** *adv*
indubitable *adj* beyond doubt, certain **indubitably** *adv*
induce *v* persuade or influence; cause; *med* cause (a woman) to go into labour or bring on (labour) by the use of drugs etc **inducement** *n* something used to persuade someone to do something
induct *v* formally install (someone, esp a clergyman) in office
inductance *n* property of an electric circuit creating voltage by a change of current
induction *n* reasoning process by which general conclusions are drawn from particular instances; process by which electrical or magnetic properties are produced by the proximity of an electrified or magnetic object; formal introduction into an office or position **inductive** *adj* **induction coil** transformer for producing a high voltage from a low voltage **induction course** training course to help familiarize someone with a new job
indulge *v* allow oneself pleasure;

allow (someone) to have or do everything he or she wants **indulgence** *n* something allowed because it gives pleasure; act of indulging oneself or someone else; liberal or tolerant treatment **indulgent** *adj* **indulgently** *adv*

industrial *adj* of, used in, or employed in industry **industrialize** *v* develop large-scale industry in (a country or region) **industrialization** *n* **industrial action** ways in which workers can protest about their conditions, eg by striking or working to rule **industrial estate** area of land set aside for factories and warehouses **industrial relations** relations between management and workers

industry *n, pl* **-tries** manufacture of goods; branch of this *eg the music industry*; quality of working hard **industrious** *adj* hard-working

inebriate *n, adj* (person who is) habitually drunk **inebriated** *adj* drunk **inebriation** *n*

inedible *adj* not fit to be eaten

ineffable *adj* too great for words **ineffably** *adv*

ineffectual *adj* having very little effect

ineligible *adj* not qualified for or entitled to something

ineluctable *adj* impossible to avoid

inept *adj* clumsy, lacking skill **ineptitude** *n*

inequitable *adj* unfair

ineradicable *adj* impossible to remove

inert *adj* without the power of motion or resistance; chemically unreactive **inertness** *n*

inertia *n* feeling of unwillingness to do anything; *physics* tendency of a body to remain still or continue moving unless a force is applied to it

inescapable *adj* unavoidable

inestimable *adj* too great to be estimated **inestimably** *adv*

inevitable *adj* unavoidable, sure to happen **the inevitable** something that cannot be prevented **inevitably** *adv* **inevitability** *n*

inexorable *adj* unable to be prevented from continuing or progressing **inexorably** *adv*

inexpert *adj* lacking skill

inexplicable *adj* impossible to explain **inexplicably** *adv*

in extremis *adv Latin* in great difficulty; on the point of death

inextricable *adj* impossible to escape from; impossible to disentangle or separate

infallible *adj* never wrong **infallibly** *adv* **infallibility** *n*

infamous [in-fam-uss] *adj* well-known for something bad **infamously** *adv* **infamy** *n*

infant *n* very young child **infancy** *n* early childhood; early stage of development **infantile** *adj* childish

infanticide *n* murder of an infant; person guilty of this

infantry *n* soldiers who fight on foot

infatuated *adj* feeling intense unreasoning passion

infatuation *n* intense unreasoning passion

infect *v* affect with a disease; affect with a feeling **infection** *n* **infectious** *adj* (of a disease) spreading without actual contact; spreading from person to person *eg infectious enthusiasm*

infer *v* **-ferring, -ferred** work out from evidence **inference** *n*

> Someone *infers* something by 'reading between the lines' of a remark. Do not confuse with *imply*, which means 'to hint'

inferior *adj* lower in quality, position, or status ▷ *n* person of lower position or status **inferiority** *n*
infernal *adj* of hell; *Informal* irritating **infernally** *adv*
inferno *n, pl* **-nos** intense raging fire
infertile *adj* unable to produce offspring; (of soil) barren, not productive **infertility** *n*
infest *v* inhabit or overrun in unpleasantly large numbers **infestation** *n*
infidel *n* person with no religion; person who rejects a particular religion, esp Christianity or Islam
infidelity *n, pl* **-ties** (act of) sexual unfaithfulness to one's husband, wife, or lover
infighting *n* quarrelling within a group
infiltrate *v* enter gradually and secretly **infiltration** *n* **infiltrator** *n*
infinite [**in**-fin-it] *adj* without any limit or end **infinitely** *adv*
infinitesimal *adj* extremely small
infinitive *n grammar* form of a verb not showing tense, person, or number *eg to sleep*
infinity *n* endless space, time, or number
infirm *adj* physically or mentally weak **infirmity** *n, pl* **-ties**
infirmary *n, pl* **-ries** hospital
inflame *v* make angry or excited **inflamed** *adj* (of part of the body) red, swollen, and painful because of infection **inflammation** *n*
inflammable *adj* easily set on fire.

> SPELLING **Inflammable** means the same as *flammable* but is falling out of general use as it was often mistaken to mean 'not flammable'.

inflammatory *adj* likely to provoke anger
inflate *v* expand by filling with air or gas; cause economic inflation in **inflatable** *adj* able to be inflated ▷ *n* plastic or rubber object which can be inflated
inflation *n* inflating; increase in prices and fall in the value of money **inflationary** *adj*
inflection, inflexion *n* change in the pitch of the voice; *grammar* change in the form of a word to show grammatical use
inflexible *adj* unwilling to be persuaded, obstinate; (of a policy etc) firmly fixed, unalterable **inflexibly** *adv* **inflexibility** *n*
inflict *v* impose (something unpleasant) on **infliction** *n*
inflorescence *n botany* arrangement of flowers on a stem
influence *n* effect of one person or thing on another; (person with) the power to have such an effect ▷ *v* have an effect on **influential** *adj*
influenza *n* contagious viral disease causing headaches, muscle pains, and fever
influx *n* arrival or entry of many people or things
info *n Informal* information
inform *v* tell; give incriminating information to the police **informant** *n* person who gives information **information** *n* knowledge or facts **informative** *adj* giving useful information **information superhighway** worldwide network of computers transferring information at high

speed **information technology** use of computers and electronic technology to store and communicate information **informer** *n* person who informs to the police

informal *adj* relaxed and friendly; appropriate for everyday life or use **informally** *adv* **informality** *n*

infra dig *adj Informal* beneath one's dignity

infrared *adj* of or using rays below the red end of the visible spectrum

infrastructure *n* basic facilities, services, and equipment needed for a country or organization to function properly

infringe *v* break (a law or agreement) **infringement** *n*

infuriate *v* make very angry

infuse *v* fill (with an emotion or quality); soak to extract flavour **infusion** *n* infusing; liquid obtained by infusing

ingenious [in-**jean**-ee-uss] *adj* showing cleverness and originality **ingeniously** *adv* **ingenuity** [in-jen-**new**-it-ee] *n*

ingénue [**an**-jay-new] *n* naive young woman, esp as a role played by an actress

ingenuous [in-**jen**-new-uss] *adj* unsophisticated and trusting **ingenuously** *adv*

ingest *v* take (food or liquid) into the body **ingestion** *n*

inglorious *adj* dishonourable, shameful

ingot *n* oblong block of cast metal

ingrained *adj* firmly fixed

ingratiate *v* try to make (oneself) popular with someone **ingratiating** *adj* **ingratiatingly** *adv*

ingredient *n* component of a mixture or compound

ingress *n* act or right of entering

ingrowing *adj* (of a toenail) growing abnormally into the flesh

inhabit *v* **-habiting, -habited** live in **inhabitable** *adj* **inhabitant** *n*

inhale *v* breathe in (air, smoke, etc) **inhalation** *n* **inhalant** *n* medical preparation inhaled to help breathing problems **inhaler** *n* container for an inhalant

inherent *adj* existing as an inseparable part **inherently** *adv*

inherit *v* **-heriting, -herited** receive (money etc) from someone who has died; receive (a characteristic) from an earlier generation; receive from a predecessor **inheritance** *n* **inheritance tax** tax paid on property left at death **inheritor** *n*

inhibit *v* **-hibiting, -hibited** restrain (an impulse or desire); hinder or prevent (action) **inhibited** *adj* **inhibition** *n* feeling of fear or embarrassment that stops one from behaving naturally

inhospitable *adj* not welcoming, unfriendly; difficult to live in, harsh

inhuman *adj* cruel or brutal; not human

inhumane *adj* cruel or brutal **inhumanity** *n*

inimical *adj* unfavourable or hostile

inimitable *adj* impossible to imitate, unique

iniquity *n, pl* **-ties** injustice or wickedness; wicked act **iniquitous** *adj*

initial *adj* first, at the beginning ▷ *n* first letter, esp of a person's name ▷ *v* **-tialling, -tialled** sign with one's initials **initially** *adv*

initiate *v* begin or set going; admit (someone) into a closed group; instruct in the basics of something ▷ *n* recently initiated person

initiation *n* **initiator** *n*
initiative *n* first step, commencing move; ability to act independently
inject *v* put (a fluid) into the body with a syringe; introduce (a new element) *eg try to inject a bit of humour* **injection** *n*
injudicious *adj* showing poor judgment, unwise
injunction *n* court order not to do something
injure *v* hurt physically or mentally **injury** *n, pl* **-ries** **injury time** *sport* playing time added at the end of a match to compensate for time spent treating injured players **injurious** *adj*
injustice *n* unfairness; unfair action
ink *n* coloured liquid used for writing or printing ▷ *v* (foll by *in*) mark in ink (something already marked in pencil) **inky** *adj* dark or black; covered in ink
inkling *n* slight idea or suspicion
inlaid *adj* set in another material so that the surface is smooth; made like this *eg an inlaid table*
inland *adj, adv* in or towards the interior of a country, away from the sea **Inland Revenue** (in Britain) government department that collects taxes
in-laws *pl n* one's husband's or wife's family
inlay *n* inlaid substance or pattern
inlet *n* narrow strip of water extending from the sea into the land; valve etc through which liquid or gas enters
in loco parentis *Latin* in place of a parent
inmate *n* person living in an institution such as a prison
inmost *adj* innermost
inn *n* pub or small hotel, esp in the country **innkeeper** *n*
innards *pl n Informal* internal organs; working parts of a machine
innate *adj* being part of someone's nature, inborn
inner *adj* happening or located inside; relating to private feelings *eg the inner self* **innermost** *adj* furthest inside **inner city** parts of a city near the centre, esp having severe social and economic problems
innings *n sport* player's or side's turn of batting; period of opportunity
innocent *adj* not guilty of a crime; without experience of evil; without malicious intent ▷ *n* innocent person, esp a child **innocently** *adv* **innocence** *n*
innocuous *adj* not harmful **innocuously** *adv*

> SPELLING Always make sure there are two *n*s in **innocuous**. It is more common to miss out an *n* than to double the *c* by mistake

innovation *n* new idea or method; introduction of new ideas or methods **innovate** *v* **innovative** *adj* **innovator** *n*
innuendo *n, pl* **-does** (remark making) an indirect reference to something rude or unpleasant
innumerable *adj* too many to be counted
innumerate *adj* having no understanding of mathematics or science **innumeracy** *n*
inoculate *v* protect against disease by injecting with a vaccine **inoculation** *n*

> SPELLING The verb **inoculate** has only one *n* and one *c*. There are 235 occurrences of the correct spelling of the noun **inoculation** in Collins Word Web, with lots of different misspellings. The most popular one, *innoculation*, occurs 31 times

inoperable *adj* (of a tumour or cancer) unable to be surgically removed
inopportune *adj* badly timed, unsuitable
inordinate *adj* excessive
inorganic *adj* not having the characteristics of living organisms; of chemical substances that do not contain carbon
inpatient *n* patient who stays in a hospital for treatment
input *n* resources put into a project etc; data fed into a computer. ▷ *v* **-putting, -put** enter (data) in a computer
inquest *n* official inquiry into a sudden death
inquire *v* seek information or ask (about) **inquirer** *n*
inquiry *n, pl* **-ries** question; investigation
inquisition *n* thorough investigation; (**I-**) *hist* organization within the Catholic Church for suppressing heresy **inquisitor** *n* **inquisitorial** *adj*
inquisitive *adj* excessively curious about other people's affairs **inquisitively** *adv*
inquorate *adj* without enough people present to make a quorum
inroads *pl n* **make inroads into** start affecting or reducing
insalubrious *adj* unpleasant, unhealthy, or sordid
insane *adj* mentally ill; stupidly irresponsible **insanely** *adv* **insanity** *n*
insanitary *adj* dirty or unhealthy
insatiable [in-**saysh**-a-bl] *adj* unable to be satisfied
inscribe *v* write or carve words on **inscription** *n* words inscribed
inscrutable *adj* mysterious, enigmatic **inscrutably** *adv*
insect *n* small animal with six legs and usu wings, such as an ant or fly **insecticide** *n* substance for killing insects **insectivorous** *adj* insect-eating
insecure *adj* anxious, not confident; not safe or well-protected
insemination *n* putting semen into a woman's or female animal's body to try to make her pregnant **inseminate** *v*
insensate *adj* without sensation, unconscious; unfeeling
insensible *adj* unconscious, without feeling; (foll by *to, of*) not aware (of) or affected (by)
insensitive *adj* unaware of or ignoring other people's feelings **insensitivity** *n*
inseparable *adj* (of two people) spending most of the time together; (of two things) impossible to separate

> SPELLING The word **inseparable** occurs in Collins Word Web 914 times. The misspelling *inseperable*, with an *e* instead of an *a* in the middle, appears 6 times

insert *v* put inside or include ▷ *n* something inserted **insertion** *n*
inset *n* small picture inserted within a larger one
inshore *adj* close to the shore ▷ *adj, adv* towards the shore
inside *prep* in or to the interior of ▷ *adj* on or of the inside; by or from someone within an organization *eg inside information* ▷ *adv* on, in, or to the inside, indoors; *Brit, Aust & NZ, slang* in(to) prison ▷ *n* inner side, surface, or part ▷ *pl Informal* stomach and bowels **inside out** with the inside facing outwards **know inside out** know thoroughly

insider *n* member of a group who has privileged knowledge about it.

> Avoid using the expression *inside of*, as the second preposition *of* is superfluous

insidious *adj* subtle or unseen but dangerous **insidiously** *adv*
insight *n* deep understanding
insignia *n, pl* **-nias, -nia** badge or emblem of honour or office
insignificant *adj* not important **insignificance** *n*
insincere *adj* showing false feelings, not genuine **insincerely** *adv* **insincerity** *n, pl* **-ties**
insinuate *v* suggest indirectly; work (oneself) into a position by gradual manoeuvres **insinuation** *n*
insipid *adj* lacking interest, spirit, or flavour
insist *v* demand or state firmly **insistent** *adj* making persistent demands; demanding attention **insistently** *adv* **insistence** *n*
in situ *adv, adj Latin* in its original position
in so far as, insofar as *prep* to the extent that
insole *n* inner sole of a shoe or boot
insolent *adj* rude and disrespectful **insolence** *n* **insolently** *adv*
insoluble *adj* incapable of being solved; incapable of being dissolved
insolvent *adj* unable to pay one's debts **insolvency** *n*
insomnia *n* inability to sleep **insomniac** *n*
insouciant *adj* carefree and unconcerned **insouciance** *n*
inspect *v* check closely or officially **inspection** *n* **inspector** *n* person who inspects; high-ranking police officer
inspire *v* fill with enthusiasm, stimulate; arouse (an emotion) **inspiration** *n* creative influence or stimulus; brilliant idea **inspirational** *adj*
instability *n* lack of steadiness or reliability
install *v* put in and prepare (equipment) for use; place (a person) formally in a position or rank **installation** *n* installing; equipment installed; place containing equipment for a particular purpose *eg oil installations*
instalment *n* any of the portions of a thing presented or a debt paid in successive parts
instance *n* particular example ▷ *v* mention as an example **for instance** as an example
instant *n* very brief time; particular moment ▷ *adj* happening at once; (of foods) requiring little preparation **instantly** *adv*
instantaneous *adj* happening at once **instantaneously** *adv*
instead *adv* as a replacement or substitute
instep *n* part of the foot forming the arch between the ankle and toes; part of a shoe or boot covering this
instigate *v* cause to happen **instigation** *n* **instigator** *n*
instil *v* **-stilling, -stilled** introduce (an idea etc) gradually into someone's mind
instinct *n* inborn tendency to behave in a certain way **instinctive** *adj* **instinctively** *adv*
institute *n* organization set up for a specific purpose, esp research or teaching ▷ *v* start or establish
institution *n* large important organization such as a university or bank; hospital etc for people with

special needs; long-established custom **institutional** *adj* **institutionalize** *v*
instruct *v* order to do something; teach (someone) how to do something **instruction** *n* order to do something; teaching ▷ *pl* information on how to do or use something **instructive** *adj* informative or helpful **instructor** *n*
instrument *n* tool used for particular work; object played to produce a musical sound; measuring device to show height, speed, etc; *Informal* someone or something used to achieve an aim **instrumental** *adj* (foll by *in*) having an important function (in); played by or composed for musical instruments **instrumentalist** *n* player of a musical instrument **instrumentation** *n* set of instruments in a car etc; arrangement of music for instruments
insubordinate *adj* not submissive to authority **insubordination** *n*
insufferable *adj* unbearable
insular *adj* not open to new ideas, narrow-minded **insularity** *n*
insulate *v* prevent or reduce the transfer of electricity, heat, or sound by surrounding or lining with a nonconducting material; isolate or set apart **insulation** *n* **insulator** *n*
insulin *n* hormone produced in the pancreas that controls the amount of sugar in the blood
insult *v* behave rudely to, offend ▷ *n* insulting remark or action **insulting** *adj*
insuperable *adj* impossible to overcome
insupportable *adj* impossible to tolerate; impossible to justify
insurance *n* agreement by which one makes regular payments to a company who pay an agreed sum if damage, loss, or death occurs; money paid to or by an insurance company; means of protection **insure** *v* protect by insurance **insurance policy** contract of insurance
insurgent *n, adj* (person) in revolt against an established authority
insurrection *n* rebellion
intact *adj* not changed or damaged in any way
intaglio [in-**tah**-lee-oh] *n, pl* **-lios** (gem carved with) an engraved design
intake *n* amount or number taken in
integer *n* positive or negative whole number or zero
integral *adj* being an essential part of a whole ▷ *n maths* sum of a large number of very small quantities
integrate *v* combine into a whole; amalgamate (a religious or racial group) into a community **integration** *n* **integrated circuit** tiny electronic circuit on a chip of semiconducting material
integrity *n* quality of having high moral principles; quality of being united
intellect *n* power of thinking and reasoning
intellectual *adj* of or appealing to the intellect; clever, intelligent ▷ *n* intellectual person **intellectually** *adv*
intelligent *adj* able to understand, learn, and think things out quickly; (of a computerized device) able to initiate or modify action in the light of ongoing events **intelligence** *n* quality of

being intelligent; secret government or military information; people or department collecting such information **intelligently** *adv*

intelligentsia *n* intellectual or cultured people in a society

intelligible *adj* able to be understood **intelligibility** *n*

intemperate *adj* unrestrained, uncontrolled; drinking alcohol to excess **intemperance** *n*

intend *v* propose or plan (to do something); have as one's purpose

intense *adj* of great strength or degree; deeply emotional **intensity** *n* **intensify** *v* **-fying, -fied** make or become more intense **intensification** *n*

intensive *adj* using or needing concentrated effort or resources **intensively** *adv*

intent *n* intention ▷*adj* paying close attention **intently** *adv* **intentness** *n* **intent on doing something** determined to do something

intention *n* something intended **intentional** *adj* planned in advance, deliberate **intentionally** *adv*

inter [in-ter] *v* **-terring, -terred** bury (a corpse) **interment** *n*

inter- *prefix* between or among *eg international*

interact *v* act on or in close relation with each other **interaction** *n* **interactive** *adj*

interbreed *v* breed within a related group

intercede *v* try to end a dispute between two people or groups **intercession** *n*

intercept *v* seize or stop in transit **interception** *n*

interchange *v* (cause to) exchange places ▷*n* motorway junction **interchangeable** *adj*

Intercity *adj* ® (in Britain) denoting a fast train (service) travelling between cities

intercom *n* internal communication system with loudspeakers

intercontinental *adj* travelling between or linking continents

intercourse *n* sexual intercourse; communication or dealings between people or groups

interdiction, interdict *n* formal order forbidding something

interdisciplinary *adj* involving more than one branch of learning

interest *n* desire to know or hear more about something; something in which one is interested; (often pl) advantage, benefit; sum paid for the use of borrowed money; (often pl) right or share ▷*v* arouse the interest of **interested** *adj* feeling or showing interest; involved in or affected by something **interesting** *adj* **interestingly** *adv*

interface *n* area where two things interact or link; circuit linking a computer and another device

interfere *v* try to influence other people's affairs where one is not involved or wanted; (foll by *with*) clash (with); (foll by *with*) *Brit, Aust & NZ, euphemistic* abuse (a child) sexually **interfering** *adj* **interference** *n* interfering; *radio* interruption of reception by atmospherics or unwanted signals

interferon *n* protein that stops the development of an invading virus

interim *adj* temporary or provisional

interior *n* inside; inland region ▷*adj* inside, inner; mental or

spiritual
interject *v* make (a remark) suddenly or as an interruption **interjection** *n*
interlace *v* join together as if by weaving
interlink *v* connect together
interlock *v* join firmly together
interlocutor [in-ter-**lok**-yew-ter] *n* person who takes part in a conversation
interloper [**in**-ter-lope-er] *n* person in a place or situation where he or she has no right to be
interlude *n* short rest or break in an activity or event
intermarry *v* (of families, races, or religions) become linked by marriage **intermarriage** *n*
intermediary *n, pl* **-ries** person trying to create agreement between others
intermediate *adj* coming between two points or extremes
intermezzo [in-ter-**met**-so] *n, pl* **-zos** short piece of music, esp one performed between the acts of an opera
interminable *adj* seemingly endless because boring **interminably** *adv*
intermingle *v* mix together
intermission *n* interval between parts of a play, film, etc
intermittent *adj* occurring at intervals **intermittently** *adv*
intern *v* imprison, esp during a war ▷ *n* trainee doctor in a hospital **internment** *n* **internee** *n* person who is interned
internal *adj* of or on the inside; within a country or organization; spiritual or mental **internally** *adv* **internal-combustion engine** engine powered by the explosion of a fuel-and-air mixture within the cylinders
international *adj* of or involving two or more countries ▷ *n* game or match between teams of different countries; player in such a match **internationally** *adv*
internecine *adj* mutually destructive
Internet, internet *n* large international computer network
interplanetary *adj* of or linking planets
interplay *n* action and reaction of two things upon each other
interpolate [in-**ter**-pole-ate] *v* insert (a comment or passage) into (a conversation or text) **interpolation** *n*
interpose *v* insert between or among things; say as an interruption
interpret *v* explain the meaning of; translate orally from one language into another; convey the meaning of (a poem, song, etc) in performance **interpretation** *n*
interpreter *n* person who translates orally from one language into another
interregnum *n, pl* **-nums, -na** interval between reigns
interrogate *v* question closely **interrogation** *n* **interrogative** *adj* questioning ▷ *n* word used in asking a question, such as *how* or *why* **interrogator** *n*
interrupt *v* break into (a conversation etc); stop (a process or activity) temporarily **interruption** *n*
intersect *v* (of roads) meet and cross; divide by passing across or through **intersection** *n*
interspersed *adj* scattered (among, between, or on)
interstellar *adj* between or

among stars

interstice [in-**ter**-stiss] *n* small crack or gap between things

intertwine *v* twist together

interval *n* time between two particular moments or events; break between parts of a play, concert, etc; difference in pitch between musical notes **at intervals** repeatedly; with spaces left between

intervene *v* involve oneself in a situation, esp to prevent conflict; happen so as to stop something **intervention** *n*

interview *n* formal discussion, esp between a job-seeker and an employer; questioning of a well-known person about his or her career, views, etc, by a reporter ▷ *v* conduct an interview with **interviewee** *n* **interviewer** *n*

interweave *v* weave together

intestate *adj* not having made a will **intestacy** *n*

intestine *n* (often pl) lower part of the alimentary canal between the stomach and the anus **intestinal** *adj* **intestinally** *adv*

intimate[1] *adj* having a close personal relationship; personal or private; (of knowledge) extensive and detailed; (foll by *with*) *euphemistic* having a sexual relationship (with); having a friendly quiet atmosphere ▷ *n* close friend **intimately** *adv* **intimacy** *n*

intimate[2] *v* hint at or suggest; announce **intimation** *n*

intimidate *v* subdue or influence by fear **intimidating** *adj* **intimidation** *n*

into *prep* indicating motion towards the centre, result of a change, division, etc *eg into the valley; turned into a madman; cut into pieces*; *Informal* interested in

intolerable *adj* more than can be endured **intolerably** *adv*

intolerant *adj* refusing to accept practices and beliefs different from one's own **intolerance** *n*

intonation *n* sound pattern produced by variations in the voice

intone *v* speak or recite in an unvarying tone of voice

intoxicate *v* make drunk; excite to excess **intoxicant** *n* intoxicating drink

intoxication *n* state of being drunk; overexcited state

intractable *adj* (of a person) difficult to control; (of a problem or issue) difficult to deal with

intranet *n computers* internal network that makes use of Internet technology

intransigent *adj* refusing to change one's attitude **intransigence** *n*

intransitive *adj* (of a verb) not taking a direct object

intrauterine *adj* within the womb

intravenous [in-tra-**vee**-nuss] *adj* into a vein **intravenously** *adv*

intrepid *adj* fearless, bold **intrepidity** *n*

intricate *adj* involved or complicated; full of fine detail **intricately** *adv* **intricacy** *n, pl* **-cies**

intrigue *v* make interested or curious; plot secretly ▷ *n* secret plotting; secret love affair **intriguing** *adj*

intrinsic *adj* essential to the basic nature of something **intrinsically** *adv*

introduce *v* present (someone) by name (to another person); present (a radio or television programme);

bring forward for discussion; bring into use; insert **introduction** *n* presentation of one person to another; preliminary part or treatment **introductory** *adj*

introspection *n* examination of one's own thoughts and feelings **introspective** *adj*

introvert *n* person concerned more with his or her thoughts and feelings than with the outside world **introverted** *adj* **introversion** *n*

intrude *v* come in or join in without being invited **intrusion** *n* **intrusive** *adj*

intruder *n* person who enters a place without permission

intuition *n* instinctive knowledge or insight without conscious reasoning **intuitive** *adj* **intuitively** *adv*

Inuit *n* indigenous inhabitant of North America or Greenland

inundate *v* flood; overwhelm **inundation** *n*

inured *adj* accustomed, esp to hardship or danger

invade *v* enter (a country) by military force; enter in large numbers; disturb (someone's privacy) **invader** *n*

invalid[1] *adj, n* disabled or chronically ill (person) ▷ *v* (often foll by *out*) dismiss from active service because of illness or injury **invalidity** *n*

invalid[2] *adj* having no legal force; (of an argument etc) not valid because based on a mistake **invalidate** *v* make or show to be invalid

invaluable *adj* of very great value or worth

invasion *n* invading; intrusion *eg an invasion of privacy*

invective *n* abusive speech or writing

inveigh [in-**vay**] *v* (foll by *against*) criticize strongly

inveigle *v* coax by cunning or trickery

invent *v* think up or create (something new); make up (a story, excuse, etc) **invention** *n* something invented; ability to invent **inventive** *adj* creative and resourceful **inventiveness** *n* **inventor** *n*

inventory *n, pl* **-tories** detailed list of goods or furnishings

inverse *adj* reversed in effect, sequence, direction, etc; *maths* linking two variables in such a way that one increases as the other decreases **inversely** *adv*

invert *v* turn upside down or inside out **inversion** *n* **inverted commas** quotation marks

invertebrate *n* animal with no backbone

invest *v* spend (money, time, etc) on something with the expectation of profit; (foll by *with*) give (power or rights) to **investment** *n* money invested; something invested in **investor** *n* **invest in** *v* buy

investigate *v* inquire into, examine **investigation** *n* **investigative** *adj* **investigator** *n*

investiture *n* formal installation of a person in an office or rank

inveterate *adj* firmly established in a habit or condition

invidious *adj* likely to cause resentment

invigilate *v* supervise people sitting an examination **invigilator** *n*

invigorate *v* give energy to, refresh

invincible *adj* impossible to

defeat **invincibility** *n*
inviolable *adj* unable to be broken or violated
inviolate *adj* unharmed, unaffected
invisible *adj* not able to be seen **invisibly** *adv* **invisibility** *n*
invite *v* request the company of; ask politely for; encourage or provoke *eg the two works inevitably invite comparison* ▷ *n Informal* invitation **inviting** *adj* tempting, attractive **invitation** *n*
in-vitro *adj* happening outside the body in an artificial environment
invoice *v, n* (present with) a bill for goods or services supplied
invoke *v* put (a law or penalty) into operation; prompt or cause (a certain feeling); call on (a god or spirit) for help, inspiration, etc **invocation** *n*
involuntary *adj* not done consciously, unintentional **involuntarily** *adv*
involve *v* include as a necessary part; affect, concern; implicate (a person) **involved** *adj* complicated; concerned, taking part **involvement** *n*
invulnerable *adj* not able to be wounded or harmed
inward *adj, adv* see **in**
iodine *n chem* bluish-black element used in medicine and photography **iodize** *v* treat with iodine
ion *n* electrically charged atom **ionic** *adj* **ionize** *v* change into ions **ionization** *n* **ionosphere** *n* region of ionized air in the upper atmosphere that reflects radio waves
iota *n* very small amount
IOU *n* signed paper acknowledging debt
IPA International Phonetic Alphabet
ipso facto *adv Latin* by that very fact
IQ intelligence quotient
IRA Irish Republican Army
irascible *adj* easily angered **irascibility** *n*
irate *adj* very angry
ire *n lit* anger
iridescent *adj* having shimmering changing colours like a rainbow **iridescence** *n*
iridium *n chem* very hard corrosion-resistant metal
iris *n* coloured circular membrane of the eye containing the pupil; tall plant with purple, yellow, or white flowers
Irish *adj* of Ireland
irk *v* irritate, annoy **irksome** *adj* irritating, annoying
iron *n* strong silvery-white metallic element, widely used for structural and engineering purposes; appliance used, when heated, to press clothes; metal-headed golf club ▷ *pl* chains, restraints ▷ *adj* made of iron; strong, inflexible *eg iron will* ▷ *v* smooth (clothes or fabric) with an iron **ironbark** *n* Australian eucalyptus with hard rough bark **ironing** *n* clothes to be ironed **ironing board** long cloth-covered board with folding legs, for ironing clothes on **Iron Age** era when iron tools were used **iron out** *v* settle (a problem) through discussion
ironic, ironical *adj* using irony; odd or amusing because the opposite of what one would expect **ironically** *adv*
ironmonger *n* shopkeeper or shop dealing in hardware **ironmongery** *n*

ironstone *n* rock consisting mainly of iron ore
irony *n, pl* **-nies** mildly sarcastic use of words to imply the opposite of what is said; aspect of a situation that is odd or amusing because the opposite of what one would expect
irradiate *v* subject to or treat with radiation **irradiation** *n*
irrational *adj* not based on or not using logical reasoning
irredeemable *adj* not able to be reformed or corrected
irreducible *adj* impossible to put in a simpler form
irrefutable *adj* impossible to deny or disprove
irregular *adj* not regular or even; not conforming to accepted practice; (of a word) not following the typical pattern of formation in a language **irregularly** *adv* **irregularity** *n, pl* **-ties**
irrelevant *adj* not connected with the matter in hand **irrelevantly** *adv* **irrelevance** *n*
irreparable *adj* not able to be repaired or put right **irreparably** *adv*
irreplaceable *adj* impossible to replace
irreproachable *adj* blameless, faultless
irresistible *adj* too attractive or strong to resist **irresistibly** *adv*
irrespective of *prep* without taking account of
irresponsible *adj* not showing or not done with due care for the consequences of one's actions or attitudes; not capable of accepting responsibility **irresponsibility** *n*
irreverent *adj* not showing due respect **irreverence** *n*
irreversible *adj* not able to be reversed or put right again *eg irreversible change* **irreversibly** *adv*
irrevocable *adj* not possible to change or undo **irrevocably** *adv*
irrigate *v* supply (land) with water by artificial channels or pipes **irrigation** *n*
irritate *v* annoy, anger; cause (a body part) to itch or become inflamed **irritable** *adj* easily annoyed **irritably** *adv* **irritant** *n, adj* (person or thing) causing irritation **irritation** *n*
is *v* third person singular present tense of **be**
ISA (in Britain) Individual Savings Account
isinglass [**ize**-ing-glass] *n* kind of gelatine obtained from some freshwater fish
Islam *n* Muslim religion teaching that there is one God and that Mohammed is his prophet; Muslim countries and civilization **Islamic** *adj*
island *n* piece of land surrounded by water **islander** *n* person who lives on an island; (**I-**) *NZ* Pacific Islander
isle *n poetic* island **islet** *n* small island
isobar [**ice**-oh-bar] *n* line on a map connecting places of equal atmospheric pressure
isolate *v* place apart or alone; *chem* obtain (a substance) in uncombined form **isolation** *n* **isolationism** *n* policy of not participating in international affairs **isolationist** *n, adj*
isomer [**ice**-oh-mer] *n* substance whose molecules contain the same atoms as another but in a different arrangement
isometric *adj* relating to muscular contraction without shortening of the muscle **isometrics** *pl n*

isometric exercises

isosceles triangle [ice-**soss**-ill-eez] *n* triangle with two sides of equal length

isotherm [**ice**-oh-therm] *n* line on a map connecting points of equal temperature

isotope [**ice**-oh-tope] *n* one of two or more atoms with the same number of protons in the nucleus but a different number of neutrons

ISP Internet service provider

issue *n* topic of interest or discussion; reason for quarrelling; particular edition of a magazine or newspaper; outcome or result; *law* child or children ▷ *v* make (a statement etc) publicly; supply officially (with); produce and make available **take issue with** disagree with

isthmus [**iss**-muss] *n, pl* **-muses** narrow strip of land connecting two areas of land

it *pron* refers to a nonhuman, animal, plant, or inanimate object; refers to a thing mentioned or being discussed; used as the subject of impersonal verbs *eg it's windy*; *Informal* crucial or ultimate point **its** *adj, pron* belonging to it **it's** it is; it has **itself** *pron* emphatic form of **it**

> SPELLING Many people find **its** and **it's** confusing. But it's quite simple really. **It's** only needs an apostrophe when it is used as the informal short form of 'it is' or 'it has'

IT information technology

italic *adj* (of printing type) sloping to the right **italics** *pl n* this type, used for emphasis **italicize** *v* put in italics

itch *n* skin irritation causing a desire to scratch; restless desire ▷ *v* have an itch **itchy** *adj*

item *n* single thing in a list or collection; piece of information **itemize** *v* make a list of

iterate *v* repeat **iteration** *n*

itinerant *adj* travelling from place to place

itinerary *n, pl* **-aries** detailed plan of a journey

ITV (in Britain) Independent Television

IUD intrauterine device: a coil-shaped contraceptive fitted into the womb

IVF in-vitro fertilization

ivory *n* hard white bony substance forming the tusks of elephants ▷ *adj* yellowish-white **ivory tower** remoteness from the realities of everyday life

ivy *n, pl* **ivies** evergreen climbing plant

iwi [**ee**-wee] *n NZ* Maori tribe

J

jab *v* **jabbing, jabbed** poke sharply ▷ *n* quick punch or poke; *Informal* injection
jabber *v* talk rapidly or incoherently
jabiru *n* large white-and-black Australian stork
jacaranda *n* tropical tree with sweet-smelling wood
jack *n* device for raising a motor vehicle or other heavy object; playing card with a picture of a pageboy; *bowls* small white bowl aimed at by the players; socket in electrical equipment into which a plug fits; flag flown at the bow of a ship, showing nationality **jack-up** *n NZ, Informal* something achieved dishonestly **jack up** *v* raise with a jack; *NZ, Informal* organize by dishonest means
jackal *n* doglike wild animal of Africa and Asia
jackaroo, jackeroo *n, pl* **-roos** *Aust* trainee on a sheep station
jackass *n* fool; male of the ass **laughing jackass** same as **kookaburra**
jackboot *n* high military boot
jackdaw *n* black-and-grey Eurasian bird of the crow family
jacket *n* short coat; skin of a baked potato; outer paper cover on a hardback book
jackknife *v* (of an articulated truck) go out of control so that the trailer swings round at a sharp angle to the cab ▷ *n* large clasp knife
jackpot *n* largest prize that may be won in a game **hit the jackpot** be very successful through luck
Jacobean [jak-a-**bee**-an] *adj* of the reign of James I of England
Jacobite *n* supporter of James II of England and his descendants
Jacquard [**jak**-ard] *n* fabric in which the design is incorporated into the weave
Jacuzzi [jak-**oo**-zee] *n* ® circular bath with a device that swirls the water
jade *n* ornamental semiprecious stone, usu dark green ▷ *adj* bluish-green
jaded *adj* tired and unenthusiastic
jagged [**jag**-gid] *adj* having an uneven edge with sharp points
jaguar *n* large S American spotted cat
jail *n* prison ▷ *v* send to prison **jailer** *n* **jailbird** *n Informal* person who has often been in prison
jalopy [jal-**lop**-ee] *n, pl* **-lopies** *Informal* old car
jam[1] *v* **jamming, jammed** pack tightly into a place; crowd or congest; make or become stuck; *radio* block (another station) with

impulses of equal wavelength ▷ *n* hold-up of traffic; *Informal* awkward situation **jam on the brakes** apply brakes fiercely **jam-packed** *adj* filled to capacity **jam session** informal rock or jazz performance

jam² *n* food made from fruit boiled with sugar

jamb *n* side post of a door or window frame

jamboree *n* large gathering or celebration

Jan. January

jandal *n NZ* sandal with a strap between the toes

jangle *v* (cause to) make a harsh ringing noise; (of nerves) be upset or irritated

janitor *n* caretaker of a school or other building

January *n* first month of the year

japan *n* very hard varnish, usu black ▷ *v* **-panning, -panned** cover with this varnish

jape *n old-fashioned* joke or prank

japonica *n* shrub with red flowers

jar¹ *n* wide-mouthed container, usu round and made of glass

jar² *v* **jarring, jarred** have a disturbing or unpleasant effect; jolt or bump ▷ *n* jolt or shock

jargon *n* specialized technical language of a particular subject

jarrah *n* Australian eucalypt yielding valuable timber

jasmine *n* shrub with sweet-smelling yellow or white flowers

jasper *n* red, yellow, dark green, or brown variety of quartz

jaundice *n* disease marked by yellowness of the skin **jaundiced** *adj* (of an attitude or opinion) bitter or cynical; having jaundice

jaunt *n* short journey for pleasure

jaunty *adj* **-tier, -tiest** sprightly and cheerful; smart **jauntily** *adv*

javelin *n* light spear thrown in sports competitions

jaw *n* one of the bones in which the teeth are set ▷ *pl* mouth; gripping part of a tool; narrow opening of a gorge or valley ▷ *v slang* talk lengthily

jay *n* bird with a pinkish body and blue-and-black wings

jaywalker *n* person who crosses the road in a careless or dangerous manner **jaywalking** *n*

jazz *n* kind of music with an exciting rhythm, usu involving improvisation **jazzy** *adj* flashy or showy **jazz up** *v* make more lively

JCB *n* ®, *Brit* construction machine with a shovel at the front and an excavator at the rear

jealous *adj* fearful of losing a partner or possession to a rival; envious; suspiciously watchful **jealously** *adv* **jealousy** *n, pl* **-sies**

jeans *pl n* casual denim trousers

Jeep *n* ® four-wheel-drive motor vehicle

jeer *v* scoff or deride ▷ *n* cry of derision

Jehovah *n* God

jejune *adj* simple or naive; dull or boring

jell *v* form into a jelly-like substance; take on a definite form

jelly *n, pl* **-lies** soft food made of liquid set with gelatine; jam made from fruit juice and sugar **jellied** *adj* prepared in a jelly

jellyfish *n* small jelly-like sea animal

jemmy *n, pl* **-mies** short steel crowbar used by burglars

jenny *n, pl* **-nies** female ass or wren

jeopardy *n* danger **jeopardize** *v* place in danger

jerboa *n* small mouselike rodent with long hind legs
jerk *v* move or throw abruptly ▷*n* sharp or abruptly stopped movement; *slang* contemptible person **jerky** *adj* sudden or abrupt **jerkily** *adv* **jerkiness** *n*
jerkin *n* sleeveless jacket
jerry-built *adj* built badly using flimsy materials
jerry can *n* flat-sided can for carrying petrol etc
jersey *n* knitted jumper; machine-knitted fabric; (**J-**) breed of cow
Jerusalem artichoke *n* small yellowish-white root vegetable
jest *n*, *v* joke
jester *n hist* professional clown at court
Jesuit [**jezz**-yoo-it] *n* member of the Society of Jesus, a Roman Catholic order
jet[1] *n* aircraft driven by jet propulsion; stream of liquid or gas, esp one forced from a small hole; nozzle from which gas or liquid is forced ▷*v* **jetting, jetted** fly by jet aircraft **jetboat** *n* motorboat propelled by a jet of water **jet lag** fatigue caused by crossing time zones in an aircraft **jet propulsion** propulsion by thrust provided by a jet of gas or liquid **jet-propelled** *adj* **jet set** rich and fashionable people who travel the world for pleasure
jet[2] *n* hard black mineral **jet-black** *adj* glossy black
jetsam *n* goods thrown overboard to lighten a ship
jettison *v* **-soning, -soned** abandon; throw overboard
jetty *n*, *pl* **-ties** small pier
Jew *n* person whose religion is Judaism; descendant of the ancient Hebrews **Jewish** *adj* **Jewry** *n* Jews collectively **jew's-harp** *n* musical instrument held between the teeth and played by plucking a metal strip with one's finger
jewel *n* precious stone; special person or thing **jeweller** *n* dealer in jewels **jewellery** *n* objects decorated with precious stones
jewfish *n Aust* freshwater catfish
jib[1] *n* triangular sail set in front of a mast
jib[2] *v* **jibbing, jibbed** (of a horse, person, etc) stop and refuse to go on **jib at** *v* object to (a proposal etc)
jib[3] *n* projecting arm of a crane or derrick
jibe[1] *n*, *v* taunt or jeer
jibe[2] *v* same as **gybe**
jiffy *n*, *pl* **-fies** *Informal* very short period of time
jig *n* type of lively dance; music for it; device that holds a component in place for cutting etc ▷*v* **jigging, jigged** make jerky up-and-down movements
jiggery-pokery *n Informal* trickery or mischief
jiggle *v* move up and down with short jerky movements
jigsaw *n* (also **jigsaw puzzle**) picture cut into interlocking pieces, which the user tries to fit together again; mechanical saw for cutting along curved lines
jihad *n* Islamic holy war against unbelievers
jilt *v* leave or reject (one's lover)
jingle *n* catchy verse or song used in a radio or television advert; gentle ringing noise ▷*v* (cause to) make a gentle ringing sound
jingoism *n* aggressive nationalism **jingoistic** *adj*
jinks *pl n* **high jinks** boisterous merrymaking

jinni *n, pl* **jinn** spirit in Muslim mythology
jinx *n* person or thing bringing bad luck ▷ *v* be or put a jinx on
jitters *pl n* worried nervousness **jittery** *adj* nervous
jive *n* lively dance of the 1940s and '50s ▷ *v* dance the jive
job *n* occupation or paid employment; task to be done; *Informal* difficult task; *Brit, Aust & NZ, Informal* crime, esp robbery **jobbing** *adj* doing individual jobs for payment **jobless** *adj, pl n* unemployed (people) **job lot** assortment sold together **job sharing** splitting of one post between two people working part-time
jockey *n* (professional) rider of racehorses ▷ *v* **jockey for position** manoeuvre to obtain an advantage
jockstrap *n* belt with a pouch to support the genitals, worn by male athletes
jocose [joke-**kohss**] *adj* playful or humorous
jocular *adj* fond of joking; meant as a joke **jocularity** *n* **jocularly** *adv*
jocund [**jok**-kund] *adj lit* merry or cheerful
jodhpurs *pl n* riding trousers, loose-fitting above the knee but tight below
joey *n Aust* young kangaroo
jog *v* **jogging, jogged** run at a gentle pace, esp for exercise; nudge slightly ▷ *n* slow run **jogger** *n* **jogging** *n*
joggle *v* shake or move jerkily
joie de vivre [jwah de **veev**-ra] *n French* enjoyment of life
join *v* become a member (of); come into someone's company; take part (in); come or bring together ▷ *n* place where two things are joined **join up** *v* enlist in the armed services **joined-up** *adj* integrated by an overall strategy: *joined-up government*
joiner *n* maker of finished woodwork **joinery** *n* joiner's work
joint *adj* shared by two or more ▷ *n* place where bones meet but can move; junction of two or more parts or objects; piece of meat for roasting; *slang* house or place, esp a disreputable bar or nightclub; *slang* marijuana cigarette ▷ *v* divide meat into joints **out of joint** disorganized; dislocated **jointed** *adj* **jointly** *adv*
joist *n* horizontal beam that helps support a floor or ceiling
jojoba [hoe-**hoe**-ba] *n* shrub of SW North America whose seeds yield oil used in cosmetics
joke *n* thing said or done to cause laughter; amusing or ridiculous person or thing ▷ *v* make jokes **jokey** *adj* **jokingly** *adv* **joker** *n* person who jokes; *slang* fellow; extra card in a pack, counted as any other in some games
jolly *adj* **-lier, -liest** (of a person) happy and cheerful; (of an occasion) merry and festive ▷ *v* **-lying, -lied** **jolly along** try to keep (someone) cheerful by flattery or coaxing **jollity** *n* **jollification** *n* merrymaking
jolt *n* unpleasant surprise or shock; sudden jerk or bump ▷ *v* surprise or shock; move or shake with a jerk
jonquil *n* fragrant narcissus
josh *v Chiefly US, slang* tease
joss stick *n* stick of incense giving off a sweet smell when burnt
jostle *v* knock or push against
jot *v* **jotting, jotted** write briefly

▷*n* very small amount **jotter** *n* notebook **jottings** *pl n* notes jotted down

joule [jool] *n physics* unit of work or energy

journal *n* daily newspaper or magazine; daily record of events **journalese** *n* superficial style of writing, found in some newspapers **journalism** *n* writing in or editing of newspapers and magazines **journalist** *n* **journalistic** *adj*

journey *n* act or process of travelling from one place to another ▷*v* travel

journeyman *n* qualified craftsman employed by another

joust *hist* ▷*n* combat with lances between two mounted knights ▷*v* fight on horseback using lances

jovial *adj* happy and cheerful **jovially** *adv* **joviality** *n*

jowl[1] *n* lower jaw ▷*pl* cheeks

jowl[2] *n* fatty flesh hanging from the lower jaw

joy *n* feeling of great delight or pleasure; cause of this feeling **joyful** *adj* **joyless** *adj* **joyous** *adj* extremely happy and enthusiastic **joyriding** *n* driving for pleasure, esp in a stolen car **joyride** *n* **joyrider** *n* **joystick** *n* control device for an aircraft or computer

JP (in Britain) Justice of the Peace

JPEG [jay-peg] *computing* standard compressed file format used for pictures; picture held in this file format

Jr Junior

JSA jobseeker's allowance: in Britain, a payment made to unemployed people

jubilant *adj* feeling or expressing great joy **jubilantly** *adv* **jubilation** *n*

jubilee *n* special anniversary, esp 25th (**silver jubilee**) or 50th (**golden jubilee**)

Judaism *n* religion of the Jews, based on the Old Testament and the Talmud **Judaic** *adj*

judder *v* vibrate violently ▷*n* violent vibration **judder bar** *NZ* raised strip across a road designed to slow down vehicles

judge *n* public official who tries cases and passes sentence in a court of law; person who decides the outcome of a contest ▷*v* act as a judge; appraise critically; consider something to be the case **judgment, judgement** *n* opinion reached after careful thought; verdict of a judge; ability to appraise critically **judgmental, judgemental** *adj*

> The alternative spellings **judgment** and **judgement** with or without an 'e' between 'g' and 'm' are equally acceptable

judicial *adj* of or by a court or judge; showing or using judgment **judicially** *adv*

judiciary *n* system of courts and judges

judicious *adj* well-judged and sensible **judiciously** *adv*

judo *n* sport in which two opponents try to throw each other to the ground

jug *n* container for liquids, with a handle and small spout **jugged hare** hare stewed in an earthenware pot

juggernaut *n Brit* large heavy truck; any irresistible destructive force

juggle *v* throw and catch (several objects) so that most are in the air at the same time; manipulate (figures, situations, etc) to suit one's purposes **juggler** *n*

jugular, jugular vein *n* one of three large veins of the neck that return blood from the head to the heart
juice *n* liquid part of vegetables, fruit, or meat; *Brit, Aust & NZ, Informal* petrol ▷*pl* fluids secreted by an organ of the body **juicy** *adj* full of juice; interesting
jujitsu *n* Japanese art of wrestling and self-defence
juju *n* W African magic charm or fetish
jukebox *n* coin-operated machine on which records, CDs, or videos can be played
Jul. July
julep *n* sweet alcoholic drink
July *n* seventh month of the year
jumble *n* confused heap or state; articles for a jumble sale ▷*v* mix in a disordered way **jumble sale** sale of miscellaneous second-hand items
jumbo *adj Informal* very large ▷*n* (also **jumbo jet**) large jet airliner
jumbuck *n Aust, old-fashioned slang* sheep
jump *v* leap or spring into the air using the leg muscles; move quickly and suddenly; jerk with surprise; increase suddenly; change the subject abruptly; *Informal* attack without warning; pass over or miss out (intervening material) ▷*n* act of jumping; sudden rise; break in continuity **jump the gun** act prematurely **jump the queue** not wait one's turn **jumpy** *adj* nervous **jump at** *v* accept (a chance etc) gladly **jumped-up** *adj* arrogant because of recent promotion **jump jet** fixed-wing jet that can take off and land vertically **jump leads** electric cables to connect a flat car battery to an external battery to aid starting an engine **jump on** *v* attack suddenly and forcefully **jump suit** one-piece garment of trousers and top
jumper *n* sweater or pullover
Jun. June; Junior
junction *n* place where routes, railway lines, or roads meet
juncture *n* point in time, esp a critical one
June *n* sixth month of the year
jungle *n* tropical forest of dense tangled vegetation; confusion or mess; place of intense struggle for survival
junior *adj* of lower standing; younger ▷*n* junior person
juniper *n* evergreen shrub with purple berries
junk[1] *n* discarded or useless objects; *Informal* rubbish; *slang* narcotic drug, esp heroin **junkie, junky** *n, pl* **junkies** *slang* drug addict **junk food** snack food of low nutritional value **junk mail** unwanted mail advertising goods or services
junk[2] *n* flat-bottomed Chinese sailing boat
junket *n* excursion by public officials paid for from public funds; sweetened milk set with rennet
junta *n* group of military officers holding power in a country, esp after a coup
Jupiter *n* king of the Roman gods; largest of the planets
juridical *adj* of law or the administration of justice
jurisdiction *n* right or power to administer justice and apply laws; extent of this right or power
jurisprudence *n* science or philosophy of law
jurist *n* expert in law
jury *n, pl* **-ries** group of people

sworn to deliver a verdict in a court of law **juror** *n* member of a jury

just *adv* very recently; at this instant; merely, only; exactly; barely; really ▷ *adj* fair or impartial in action or judgment; proper or right **justly** *adv* **justness** *n*

justice *n* quality of being just; judicial proceedings; judge or magistrate **justice of the peace** (in Britain) person who is authorized to act as a judge in a local court of law

justify *v* **-fying, -fied** prove right or reasonable; explain the reasons for an action; align (text) so the margins are straight **justifiable** *adj* **justifiably** *adv* **justification** *n*

jut *v* **jutting, jutted** project or stick out

jute *n* plant fibre, used for rope, canvas, etc

juvenile *adj* young; of or suitable for young people; immature and rather silly ▷ *n* young person or child **juvenilia** *pl n* works produced in an author's youth **juvenile delinquent** young person guilty of a crime

juxtapose *v* put side by side **juxtaposition** *n*

k

K *Informal* thousand(s)

Kaffir [**kaf**-fer] *n SAfr, taboo* Black African

kaftan *n* long loose Eastern garment; woman's dress resembling this

kaiser [**kize**-er] *n hist* German or Austro-Hungarian emperor

kak *n SAfr, slang* faeces; rubbish

Kalashnikov *n* Russian-made automatic rifle

kale *n* cabbage with crinkled leaves

kaleidoscope *n* tube-shaped toy containing loose coloured pieces reflected by mirrors so that intricate patterns form when the tube is twisted **kaleidoscopic** *adj*

kamikaze [kam-mee-**kah**-zee] *n* (in World War II) Japanese pilot who performed a suicide mission ▷ *adj* (of an action) undertaken in the knowledge that it will kill or injure the person performing it

kangaroo *n, pl* **-roos** Australian marsupial which moves by jumping with its powerful hind legs **kangaroo court** unofficial court set up by a group to discipline its members **kangaroo paw** Australian plant with green-and-red flowers

kaolin *n* fine white clay used to make porcelain and in some medicines

kapok *n* fluffy fibre from a tropical tree, used to stuff cushions etc

kaput [kap-**poot**] *adj Informal* ruined or broken

karaoke *n* form of entertainment in which people sing over a prerecorded backing tape

karate *n* Japanese system of unarmed combat using blows with the feet, hands, elbows, and legs

karma *n Buddhism, Hinduism* person's actions affecting his or her fate in the next reincarnation

karri *n, pl* **-ris** Australian eucalypt; its wood, used for building

katipo *n* small poisonous New Zealand spider

kayak *n* Inuit canoe made of sealskins stretched over a frame; fibreglass or canvas-covered canoe of this design

kbyte *computers* kilobyte

kebab *n* dish of small pieces of meat grilled on skewers; (also **doner kebab**) grilled minced lamb served in a split slice of unleavened bread

kedgeree *n* dish of fish with rice and eggs

keel *n* main lengthways timber or steel support along the base of a ship **keel over** *v* turn upside down; *Informal* collapse suddenly

keen[1] *adj* eager or enthusiastic; intense or strong; intellectually acute; (of the senses) capable of recognizing small distinctions; sharp; cold and penetrating; competitive **keenly** *adv* **keenness** *n*

keen[2] *v* wail over the dead

keep *v* **keeping, kept** have or retain possession of; store; stay or cause to stay (in, on, or at a place or position); continue or persist; detain (someone); look after or maintain ▷ *n* cost of food and everyday expenses **keeper** *n* person who looks after animals in a zoo; person in charge of a museum or collection; short for **goalkeeper** **keeping** *n* care or charge **in, out of keeping with** appropriate *or* inappropriate for **keep fit** exercises designed to promote physical fitness **keepsake** *n* gift treasured for the sake of the giver **keep up** *v* maintain at the current level **keep up with** *v* maintain a pace set by (someone)

keg *n* small metal beer barrel

kelp *n* large brown seaweed

kelpie *n* Australian sheepdog with a smooth coat and upright ears

kelvin *n* SI unit of temperature **Kelvin scale** temperature scale starting at absolute zero (-273.15° Celsius)

ken *v* **kenning, kenned** *or* **kent** *Scot* know **beyond one's ken** beyond one's range of knowledge

kendo *n* Japanese sport of fencing using wooden staves

kennel *n* hutlike shelter for a dog ▷ *pl* place for breeding, boarding, or training dogs

kept *v* past of **keep**

keratin *n* fibrous protein found in the hair and nails

kerb *n* edging to a footpath **kerb crawling** *Brit* act of driving slowly

beside a pavement to pick up a prostitute
kerchief *n* piece of cloth worn over the head or round the neck
kerfuffle *n Informal* commotion or disorder
kernel *n* seed of a nut, cereal, or fruit stone; central and essential part of something
kerosene *n US, Canadian, Aust & NZ* liquid mixture distilled from petroleum and used as a fuel or solvent
kestrel *n* type of small falcon
ketch *n* two-masted sailing ship
ketchup *n* thick cold sauce, usu made of tomatoes
kettle *n* container with a spout and handle used for boiling water **kettledrum** *n* large bowl-shaped metal drum
key *n* device for operating a lock by moving a bolt; device turned to wind a clock, operate a machine, etc; any of a set of levers or buttons pressed to operate a typewriter, computer, or musical keyboard instrument; *music* set of related notes; something crucial in providing an explanation or interpretation; means of achieving a desired end; list of explanations of codes, symbols, etc ▷*adj* of great importance ▷*v* (also **key in**) enter (text) using a keyboard **keyed up** very excited or nervous
keyboard *n* set of keys on a piano, computer, etc; musical instrument played using a keyboard ▷*v* enter (text) using a keyboard
keyhole *n* opening for inserting a key into a lock
keynote *n* dominant idea of a speech etc; basic note of a musical key
keystone *n* most important part of a process, organization, etc; central stone of an arch which locks the others in position
kg kilogram(s)
KGB *n* (formerly) Soviet secret police
khaki *adj* dull yellowish-brown ▷*n* hard-wearing fabric of this colour used for military uniforms
kHz kilohertz
kia ora [kee-a **aw**-ra] *interj NZ* Maori greeting
kibbutz *n, pl* **kibbutzim** communal farm or factory in Israel
kibosh *n* **put the kibosh on** *slang* put a stop to
kick *v* drive, push, or strike with the foot; (of a gun) recoil when fired; *Informal* object or resist; *Informal* free oneself of (an addiction); *rugby* score with a kick ▷*n* thrust or blow with the foot; recoil of a gun; *Informal* excitement or thrill **kickback** *n* money paid illegally for favours done **kick off** *v* start a game of soccer; *Informal* begin **kick out** *v* dismiss or expel forcibly **kick-start** *v* start (a motorcycle) by kicking a pedal **kick up** *v Informal* create (a fuss)
kid¹ *n Informal* child; young goat; leather made from the skin of a young goat
kid² *v* **kidding, kidded** *Informal* tease or deceive (someone)
kidnap *v* **-napping, -napped** seize and hold (a person) to ransom **kidnapper** *n*
kidney *n* either of the pair of organs that filter waste products from the blood to produce urine; animal kidney used as food **kidney bean** reddish-brown kidney-shaped bean, edible when cooked
kill *v* cause the death of; *Informal*

cause (someone) pain or discomfort; put an end to; pass (time) ▷ *n* act of killing; animals or birds killed in a hunt **killer** *n* **killing** *Informal* ▷ *adj* very tiring; very funny ▷ *n* sudden financial success **killjoy** *n* person who spoils others' pleasure

kiln *n* oven for baking, drying, or processing pottery, bricks, etc

kilo *n* short for **kilogram**

kilo- *combining form* one thousand *eg kilometre*

kilobyte *n computers* 1024 units of information

kilogram, kilogramme *n* one thousand grams

kilohertz *n* one thousand hertz

kilometre *n* one thousand metres

kilowatt *n electricity* one thousand watts

kilt *n* knee-length pleated tartan skirt worn orig by Scottish Highlanders **kilted** *adj*

kimono *n, pl* **-nos** loose wide-sleeved Japanese robe, fastened with a sash; European dressing gown resembling this

kin, kinsfolk *n* person's relatives collectively **kinship** *n*

kind¹ *adj* considerate, friendly, and helpful **kindness** *n* **kindly** *adj* having a warm-hearted nature; pleasant or agreeable ▷ *adv* in a considerate way; please *eg will you kindly be quiet!* **kindliness** *n* **kind-hearted** *adj*

kind² *n* class or group with common characteristics; essential nature or character **in kind** (of payment) in goods rather than money; with something similar **kind of** to a certain extent

kindergarten *n* class or school for children under six years old

kindle *v* set (a fire) alight; (of a fire) start to burn; arouse or be aroused **kindling** *n* dry wood or straw for starting fires

kindred *adj* having similar qualities; related by blood or marriage ▷ *n* same as **kin**

kindy, kindie *n, pl* **-dies** *Aust & NZ, Informal* kindergarten

kinetic [kin-**net**-ik] *adj* relating to or caused by motion

king *n* male ruler of a monarchy; ruler or chief; best or most important of its kind; piece in chess that must be defended; playing card with a picture of a king on it **kingdom** *n* state ruled by a king or queen; division of the natural world **king prawn** large prawn, fished commercially in Australian waters **kingship** *n* **king-size, king-sized** *adj* larger than standard size

kingfisher *n* small bird, often with a bright-coloured plumage, that dives for fish

kingpin *n* most important person in an organization

kink *n* twist or bend in rope, wire, hair, etc; *Informal* quirk in someone's personality **kinky** *adj slang* given to unusual sexual practices; full of kinks

kiosk *n* small booth selling drinks, cigarettes, newspapers, etc; public telephone box

kip *n, v* **kipping, kipped** *Informal* sleep

kipper *n* cleaned, salted, and smoked herring

kirk *n Scot* church

Kirsch *n* brandy made from cherries

kismet *n* fate or destiny

kiss *v* touch with the lips in affection or greeting; join lips with a person in love or desire ▷ *n* touch with the lips **kisser** *n slang* mouth or face **kissagram** *n* greetings service in which a messenger kisses the person celebrating **kissing crust** *NZ & SAfr* soft end of a loaf of bread where two loaves have been separated **kiss of life** mouth-to-mouth resuscitation

kist *n SAfr* large wooden chest

kit *n* outfit or equipment for a specific purpose; set of pieces of equipment sold ready to be assembled; *NZ* flax basket **kitbag** *n* bag for a soldier's or traveller's belongings **kit out** *v* **kitting, kitted** provide with clothes or equipment needed for a particular activity **kitset** *n NZ* unassembled pieces for constructing a piece of furniture

kitchen *n* room used for cooking **kitchenette** *n* small kitchen **kitchen garden** garden for growing vegetables, herbs, etc

kite *n* light frame covered with a thin material flown on a string in the wind; large hawk with a forked tail **Kite mark** *Brit* official mark on articles approved by the British Standards Institution

kith *n* **kith and kin** friends and relatives

kitsch *n* art or literature with popular sentimental appeal

kitten *n* young cat **kittenish** *adj* lively and flirtatious

kittiwake *n* type of seagull

kitty *n, pl* **-ties** communal fund; total amount wagered in certain gambling games

kiwi *n* New Zealand flightless bird with a long beak and no tail; *Informal* New Zealander **kiwi fruit** edible fruit with a fuzzy brownish skin and green flesh

klaxon *n* loud horn used on emergency vehicles as a warning signal

kleptomania *n* compulsive tendency to steal **kleptomaniac** *n*

kloof *n SAfr* mountain pass or gorge

km kilometre(s)

knack *n* skilful way of doing something; innate ability

knacker *n Brit* buyer of old horses for killing

knackered *adj slang* extremely tired; no longer functioning

knapsack *n* soldier's or traveller's bag worn strapped on the back

knave *n* jack at cards; *obs* dishonest man

knead *v* work (dough) into a smooth mixture with the hands; squeeze or press with the hands

knee *n* joint between thigh and lower leg; lap; part of a garment covering the knee ▷ *v* **kneeing, kneed** strike or push with the knee **kneecap** *n* bone in front of the knee ▷ *v* shoot in the kneecap **kneejerk** *adj* (of a reply or reaction) automatic and predictable **knees-up** *n Brit, Informal* party

kneel *v* **kneeling, kneeled** *or* **knelt** fall or rest on one's knees

knell *n* sound of a bell, esp at a funeral or death; portent of doom

knew *v* past tense of **know**

knickerbockers *pl n* loose-fitting short trousers gathered in at the knee

knickers *pl n* woman's or girl's undergarment covering the lower trunk and having legs or legholes

knick-knack *n* trifle or trinket

knife *n, pl* **knives** cutting tool or weapon consisting of a sharp-edged blade with a handle ▷ *v* cut or stab with a knife

knight *n* man who has been given a knighthood; *hist* man who served his lord as a mounted armoured soldier; chess piece shaped like a horse's head ▷*v* award a knighthood to **knighthood** *n* honorary title given to a man by the British sovereign **knightly** *adj*

knit *v* **knitting, knitted** *or* **knit** make (a garment) by interlocking a series of loops in wool or other yarn; join closely together; draw (one's eyebrows) together **knitting** *n* **knitwear** *n* knitted clothes, such as sweaters

knob *n* rounded projection, such as a switch on a radio; rounded handle on a door or drawer; small amount of butter **knobbly** *adj* covered with small bumps

knobkerrie *n SAfr* club with a rounded end

knock *v* give a blow or push to; rap audibly with the knuckles; make or drive by striking; *Informal* criticize adversely; (of an engine) make a regular banging noise as a result of a fault ▷*n* blow or rap; knocking sound **knocker** *n* metal fitting for knocking on a door **knock about, around** *v* wander or spend time aimlessly; hit or kick brutally **knockabout** *adj* (of comedy) boisterous **knock back** *v Informal* drink quickly; cost; reject or refuse **knock down** *v* demolish; reduce the price of **knockdown** *adj* (of a price) very low **knock-knees** *pl n* legs that curve in at the knees **knock off** *v Informal* cease work; *Informal* make or do (something) hurriedly or easily; take (a specified amount) off a price; *Brit, Aust & NZ, Informal* steal **knock out** *v* render (someone) unconscious; *Informal* overwhelm or amaze; defeat in a knockout competition **knockout** *n* blow that renders an opponent unconscious; competition from which competitors are progressively eliminated; *Informal* overwhelmingly attractive person or thing **knock up** *v Informal* assemble (something) quickly; *Informal* waken **knock-up** *n* practice session at tennis, squash, or badminton

knoll *n* small rounded hill

knot *n* fastening made by looping and pulling tight strands of string, cord, or rope; tangle (of hair); small cluster or huddled group; round lump or spot in timber; feeling of tightness, caused by tension or nervousness; unit of speed used by ships, equal to one nautical mile (1.85 kilometres) per hour ▷*v* **knotting, knotted** tie with or into a knot **knotty** *adj* full of knots; puzzling or difficult

know *v* **knowing, knew, known** be or feel certain of the truth of (information etc); be acquainted with; have a grasp of or understand (a skill or language); be aware of **in the know** *Informal* informed or aware **knowable** *adj* **knowing** *adj* suggesting secret knowledge **knowingly** *adv* deliberately; in a way that suggests secret knowledge **know-all** *n offens* person who acts as if knowing more than other people **know-how** *n Informal* ingenuity, aptitude, or skill

knowledge *n* facts or experiences known by a person; state of knowing; specific information on a subject **knowledgeable, knowledgable** *adj* intelligent or well-informed

knuckle *n* bone at the finger joint; knee joint of a calf or pig **near the knuckle** *Informal* rather rude or offensive **knuckle-duster** *n* metal appliance worn on the knuckles to add force to a blow **knuckle under** *v* yield or submit

KO knockout

koala *n* tree-dwelling Australian marsupial with dense grey fur

kohanga reo, kohanga *n NZ* infant class where children are taught in Maori

kohl *n* cosmetic powder used to darken the edges of the eyelids

kookaburra *n* large Australian kingfisher with a cackling cry

koori *n, pl* **-ris** Australian Aborigine

kopje, koppie *n SAfr* small hill

Koran *n* sacred book of Islam

kosher [**koh**-sher] *adj* conforming to Jewish religious law, esp (of food) to Jewish dietary law; *Informal* legitimate or authentic ▷*n* kosher food

kowhai *n* New Zealand tree with clusters of yellow flowers

kowtow *v* be servile (towards)

kph kilometres per hour

kraal *n* S African village surrounded by a strong fence

Kremlin *n* central government of Russia and, formerly, the Soviet Union

krill *n, pl* **krill** small shrimplike sea creature

krypton *n chem* colourless gas present in the atmosphere and used in fluorescent lights

kudos *n* fame or credit

kugel [**koog**-el] *n SAfr* rich, fashion-conscious, materialistic young woman

kumara *n NZ* tropical root vegetable with yellow flesh

kumquat [**kumm**-kwott] *n* citrus fruit resembling a tiny orange

kung fu *n* Chinese martial art combining hand, foot, and weapon techniques

kura kaupapa Maori *n NZ* primary school where the teaching is done in Maori

kurrajong *n* Australian tree or shrub with tough fibrous bark

kW kilowatt

kWh kilowatt-hour

l

l litre
L large; learner (driver)
lab *n Informal* short for **laboratory**
label *n* piece of card or other material fixed to an object to show its ownership, destination, etc ▷*v* **-elling, -elled** give a label to
labia *pl n, sing* **labium** four liplike folds of skin forming part of the female genitals **labial** [**lay**-bee-al] *adj* of the lips
labor *n US & Aust* same as **labour** **Labor Day** (in the US and Canada) public holiday in honour of labour, held on the first Monday in September; (in Australia) public holiday observed on different days in different states
laboratory *n, pl* **-ries** building or room designed for scientific research or for the teaching of practical science
laborious *adj* involving great prolonged effort **laboriously** *adv*
Labor Party *n* main left-wing political party in Australia
labour *US & Aust* **labor** *n* physical work or exertion; workers in industry; final stage of pregnancy, leading to childbirth ▷*v* work hard; stress to excess or too persistently; be at a disadvantage because of a mistake or false belief **laboured** *adj* uttered or done with difficulty **labourer** *n* person who labours, esp someone doing manual work for wages **Labour Day** (in Britain) a public holiday in honour of work, held on May 1; (in New Zealand) a public holiday commemorating the introduction of the eight-hour day, held on the 4th Monday in October **Labour Party** main left-wing political party in a number of countries including Britain and New Zealand
labrador *n* large retriever dog with a usu gold or black coat
laburnum *n* ornamental tree with yellow hanging flowers
labyrinth [**lab**-er-inth] *n* complicated network of passages; interconnecting cavities in the internal ear **labyrinthine** *adj*
lace *n* delicate decorative fabric made from threads woven into an open weblike pattern; cord drawn through eyelets and tied ▷*v* fasten with laces; thread a cord or string through holes in something; add a small amount of alcohol, a drug, etc to (food or drink) **lacy** *adj* fine, like lace **lace-ups** *pl n* shoes which fasten with laces
lacerate [**lass**-er-rate] *v* tear (flesh) **laceration** *n*
lachrymose *adj* tearful; sad
lack *n* shortage or absence of something needed or wanted ▷*v*

need or be short of (something)
lackadaisical *adj* lazy and careless in a dreamy way
lackey *n* servile follower; uniformed male servant
lacklustre *adj* lacking brilliance or vitality
laconic *adj* using only a few words, terse **laconically** *adv*
lacquer *n* hard varnish for wood or metal; clear sticky substance sprayed onto the hair to hold it in place
lacrimal *adj* of tears or the glands which produce them
lacrosse *n* sport in which teams catch and throw a ball using long sticks with a pouched net at the end, in an attempt to score goals
lactation *n* secretion of milk by female mammals to feed young **lactic** *adj* of or derived from milk **lactose** *n* white crystalline sugar found in milk
lacuna [lak-**kew**-na] *n, pl* **-nae** gap or missing part, esp in a document or series
lad *n* boy or young man
ladder *n* frame of two poles connected by horizontal steps used for climbing; line of stitches that have come undone in tights or stockings ▷*v* have or cause to have such a line of undone stitches
laden *adj* loaded; burdened
la-di-da, lah-di-dah *adj Informal* affected or pretentious
ladle *n* spoon with a long handle and a large bowl, used for serving soup etc ▷*v* serve out
lady *n, pl* **-dies** woman regarded as having characteristics of good breeding or high rank; polite term of address for a woman; (**L-**) title of some female members of the British nobility **Our Lady** the Virgin Mary **lady-in-waiting** *n, pl* **ladies-in-waiting** female servant of a queen or princess **ladykiller** *n Informal* man who is or thinks he is irresistible to women **ladylike** *adj* polite and dignified
ladybird *n* small red beetle with black spots
lag[1] *v* **lagging, lagged** go too slowly, fall behind ▷*n* delay between events **laggard** *n* person who lags behind
lag[2] *v* **lagging, lagged** wrap (a boiler, pipes, etc) with insulating material **lagging** *n* insulating material
lag[3] *n* **old lag** *Brit, Aust & NZ, slang* convict
lager *n* light-bodied beer
lagoon *n* body of water cut off from the open sea by coral reefs or sand bars
laid *v* past of **lay**[1] **laid-back** *adj Informal* relaxed
lain *v* past participle of **lie**[2]
lair *n* resting place of an animal
laird *n* Scottish landowner
laissez-faire [less-ay-**fair**] *n* principle of nonintervention, esp by a government in commercial affairs
laity [**lay**-it-ee] *n* people who are not members of the clergy
lake[1] *n* expanse of water entirely surrounded by land **lakeside** *n*
lake[2] *n* red pigment
lama *n* Buddhist priest in Tibet or Mongolia
lamb *n* young sheep; its meat ▷*v* (of sheep) give birth to a lamb or lambs **lamb's fry** *Aust & NZ* lamb's liver for cooking **lambskin** *n* **lambswool** *n*
lambast, lambaste *v* beat or thrash; reprimand severely
lambent *adj lit* (of a flame) flickering softly

lame *adj* having an injured or disabled leg or foot; (of an excuse) unconvincing ▷ *v* make lame **lamely** *adv* **lameness** *n* **lame duck** person or thing unable to cope without help

lamé [**lah**-may] *n, adj* (fabric) interwoven with gold or silver thread

lament *v* feel or express sorrow (for) ▷ *n* passionate expression of grief **lamentable** *adj* very disappointing **lamentation** *n* **lamented** *adj* grieved for

laminate *v* make (a sheet of material) by sticking together thin sheets; cover with a thin sheet of material ▷ *n* laminated sheet **laminated** *adj*

lamington *n Aust & NZ* sponge cake coated with a sweet coating

Lammas *n* August 1, formerly a harvest festival

lamp *n* device which produces light from electricity, oil, or gas **lamppost** *n* post supporting a lamp in the street **lampshade** *n*

lampoon *n* humorous satire ridiculing someone ▷ *v* satirize or ridicule

lamprey *n* eel-like fish with a round sucking mouth

lance *n* long spear used by a mounted soldier ▷ *v* pierce (a boil or abscess) with a lancet **lancer** *n* formerly, cavalry soldier armed with a lance **lance corporal** noncommissioned army officer of the lowest rank

lancet *n* pointed two-edged surgical knife; narrow window in the shape of a pointed arch

land *n* solid part of the earth's surface; ground, esp with reference to its type or use; rural or agricultural area; property consisting of land; country or region ▷ *v* come or bring to earth after a flight, jump, or fall; go or take from a ship at the end of a voyage; come to or touch shore; come or bring to some point or condition; *Informal* obtain; take (a hooked fish) from the water; *Informal* deliver (a punch) **landed** *adj* possessing or consisting of lands **landless** *adj* **landward** *adj* nearest to or facing the land ▷ *adv* (also **landwards**) towards land **landfall** *n* ship's first landing after a voyage **landlocked** *adj* completely surrounded by land **land up** *v* arrive at a final point or condition

landau [**lan**-daw] *n* four-wheeled carriage with two folding hoods

landing *n* floor area at the top of a flight of stairs; bringing or coming to land; (also **landing stage**) place where people or goods go onto or come off a boat

landlord, landlady *n* person who rents out land, houses, etc; owner or manager of a pub or boarding house

landlubber *n* person who is not experienced at sea

landmark *n* prominent object in or feature of a landscape; event, decision, etc considered as an important development

landscape *n* extensive piece of inland scenery seen from one place; picture of it ▷ *v* improve natural features of (a piece of land)

landslide *n* (also **landslip**) falling of soil, rock, etc down the side of a mountain; overwhelming electoral victory

lane *n* narrow road; area of road for one stream of traffic; specified route followed by ships or aircraft;

strip of a running track or swimming pool for use by one competitor

language *n* system of sounds, symbols, etc for communicating thought; particular system used by a nation or people; system of words and symbols for computer programming

languid *adj* lacking energy or enthusiasm **languidly** *adv*

languish *v* suffer neglect or hardship; lose or diminish in strength or vigour; pine (for)

languor [**lang**-ger] *n* state of dreamy relaxation; laziness or weariness **languorous** *adj*

lank *adj* (of hair) straight and limp; thin or gaunt **lanky** *adj* ungracefully tall and thin

lanolin *n* grease from sheep's wool used in ointments etc

lantana [lan-**tay**-na] *n* shrub with orange or yellow flowers, considered a weed in Australia

lantern *n* light in a transparent protective case **lantern jaw** long thin jaw **lantern-jawed** *adj*

lanthanum *n chem* silvery-white metallic element **lanthanide series** class of 15 elements chemically related to lanthanum

lanyard *n* cord worn round the neck to hold a knife or whistle; *naut* short rope

lap[1] *n* part between the waist and knees of a person when sitting **laptop** *adj* (of a computer) small enough to fit on a user's lap ▷ *n* computer small enough to fit on a user's lap

lap[2] *n* single circuit of a racecourse or track; stage of a journey ▷ *v* **lapping, lapped** overtake an opponent so as to be one or more circuits ahead

lap[3] *v* **lapping, lapped** (of waves) beat softly against (a shore etc) **lap up** *v* drink by scooping up with the tongue; accept (information or attention) eagerly

lapel [lap-**pel**] *n* part of the front of a coat or jacket folded back towards the shoulders

lapidary *adj* of or relating to stones

lapis lazuli [**lap**-iss **lazz**-yoo-lie] *n* bright blue gemstone

lapse *n* temporary drop in a standard, esp through forgetfulness or carelessness; instance of bad behaviour by someone usually well-behaved; break in occurrence or usage ▷ *v* drop in standard; end or become invalid, esp through disuse; abandon religious faith; (of time) slip away **lapsed** *adj*

lapwing *n* plover with a tuft of feathers on the head

larboard *adj, n old-fashioned* port (side of a ship)

larceny *n, pl* **-nies** *law* theft

larch *n* deciduous coniferous tree

lard *n* soft white fat obtained from a pig ▷ *v* insert strips of bacon in (meat) before cooking; decorate (speech or writing) with strange words unnecessarily

larder *n* storeroom for food

large *adj* great in size, number, or extent **at large** in general; free, not confined; fully **largely** *adv* **largish** *adj* **large-scale** *adj* wide-ranging or extensive

largesse, largess [lar-**jess**] *n* generous giving, esp of money

largo *n, pl* **-gos,** *adv music* (piece to be played) in a slow and dignified manner

lariat *n* lasso

lark[1] *n* small brown songbird, skylark

lark² *n Informal* harmless piece of mischief or fun; unnecessary activity or job **lark about** *v* play pranks

larkspur *n* plant with spikes of blue, pink, or white flowers with spurs

larrikin *n Aust & NZ, old-fashioned slang* mischievous or unruly person

larva *n, pl* **-vae** insect in an immature stage, often resembling a worm **larval** *adj*

larynx *n, pl* **larynges** part of the throat containing the vocal cords **laryngeal** *adj* **laryngitis** *n* inflammation of the larynx

lasagne, lasagna [laz-**zan**-ya] *n* pasta in wide flat sheets; dish made from layers of lasagne, meat, and cheese

lascivious [lass-**iv**-ee-uss] *adj* showing or producing sexual desire **lasciviously** *adv*

laser [**lay**-zer] *n* device that produces a very narrow intense beam of light, used for cutting very hard materials and in surgery etc

lash¹ *n* eyelash; sharp blow with a whip ▷ *v* hit with a whip; (of rain or waves) beat forcefully against; attack verbally, scold; flick or wave sharply to and fro **lash out** *v* make a sudden physical or verbal attack; *Informal* spend (money) extravagantly

lash² *v* fasten or bind tightly with cord etc

lashings *pl n old-fashioned* large amounts

lass, lassie *n Scot & N English* girl

lassitude *n* physical or mental weariness

lasso [lass-**oo**] *n, pl* **-sos, -soes** rope with a noose for catching cattle and horses ▷ *v* **-soing, -soed** catch with a lasso

last¹ *adj, adv* coming at the end or after all others; most recent(ly) ▷ *adj* only remaining ▷ *n* last person or thing **lastly** *adv* **last-ditch** *adj* done as a final resort **last post** army bugle-call played at sunset or funerals **last straw** small irritation or setback that, coming after others, is too much to bear **last word** final comment in an argument; most recent or best example of something

last² *v* continue; be sufficient for (a specified amount of time); remain fresh, uninjured, or unaltered **lasting** *adj*

last³ *n* model of a foot on which shoes and boots are made or repaired

latch *n* fastening for a door with a bar and lever; lock which can only be opened from the outside with a key ▷ *v* fasten with a latch **latch onto** *v* become attached to (a person or idea)

late *adj* after the normal or expected time; towards the end of a period; being at an advanced time; recently dead; recent; former ▷ *adv* after the normal or expected time; at a relatively advanced age; recently **lately** *adv* in recent times **lateness** *n*

latent *adj* hidden and not yet developed **latency** *n*

lateral [**lat**-ter-al] *adj* of or relating to the side or sides **laterally** *adv*

latex *n* milky fluid found in some plants, esp the rubber tree, used in making rubber

lath *n* thin strip of wood used to support plaster, tiles, etc

lathe *n* machine for turning wood or metal while it is being shaped

lather *n* froth of soap and water; frothy sweat; *Informal* state of

agitation ▷*v* make frothy; rub with soap until lather appears
Latin *n* language of the ancient Romans ▷*adj* of or in Latin; of a people whose language derives from Latin **Latin America** parts of South and Central America whose official language is Spanish or Portuguese **Latin American** *n, adj*
latitude *n* angular distance measured in degrees N or S of the equator; scope for freedom of action or thought ▷*pl* regions considered in relation to their distance from the equator
latrine *n* toilet in a barracks or camp
latter *adj* second of two; later; recent **latterly** *adv* **latter-day** *adj* modern
lattice [**lat**-iss] *n* framework of intersecting strips of wood, metal, etc; gate, screen, etc formed of such a framework **latticed** *adj*
laud *v* praise or glorify **laudable** *adj* praiseworthy **laudably** *adv* **laudatory** *adj* praising or glorifying
laudanum [**lawd**-a-num] *n* opium-based sedative
laugh *v* make inarticulate sounds with the voice expressing amusement, merriment, or scorn; utter or express with laughter ▷*n* act or instance of laughing; *Informal* person or thing causing amusement **laughable** *adj* ridiculously inadequate **laughter** *n* sound or action of laughing **laughing gas** nitrous oxide as an anaesthetic **laughing stock** object of general derision **laugh off** *v* treat (something serious or difficult) lightly
launch¹ *v* put (a ship or boat) into the water, esp for the first time; begin (a campaign, project, etc); put a new product on the market; send (a missile or spacecraft) into space or the air ▷*n* launching **launcher** *n* **launch into** *v* start doing something enthusiastically **launch out** *v* start doing something new
launch² *n* open motorboat
launder *v* wash and iron (clothes and linen); make (illegally obtained money) seem legal by passing it through foreign banks or legitimate businesses **laundry** *n, pl* **-dries** clothes etc for washing or which have recently been washed; place for washing clothes and linen **Launderette** *n* ® shop with coin-operated washing and drying machines
laureate [**lor**-ee-at] *adj* see **poet laureate**
laurel *n* glossy-leaved shrub, bay tree ▷*pl* wreath of laurel, an emblem of victory or merit
lava *n* molten rock thrown out by volcanoes, which hardens as it cools
lavatory *n, pl* **-ries** toilet
lavender *n* shrub with fragrant flowers ▷*adj* bluish-purple **lavender water** light perfume made from lavender
lavish *adj* great in quantity or richness; giving or spending generously; extravagant ▷*v* give or spend generously **lavishly** *adv*
law *n* rule binding on a community; system of such rules; *Informal* police; invariable sequence of events in nature; general principle deduced from facts **lawful** *adj* allowed by law **lawfully** *adv* **lawless** *adj* breaking the law, esp in a violent way **lawlessness** *n* **law-abiding** *adj* obeying the laws **law-breaker** *n* **lawsuit** *n* court

case brought by one person or group against another

lawn[1] *n* area of tended and mown grass **lawn mower** machine for cutting grass **lawn tennis** tennis, esp when played on a grass court

lawn[2] *n* fine linen or cotton fabric

lawyer *n* professionally qualified legal expert

lax *adj* not strict **laxity** *n*

laxative *n, adj* (medicine) inducing the emptying of the bowels

lay[1] *v* **laying, laid** cause to lie; devise or prepare; set in a particular place or position; attribute (blame); put forward (a plan, argument, etc); (of a bird or reptile) produce eggs; arrange (a table) for a meal **lay waste** devastate **lay-by** *n* stopping place for traffic beside a road **lay off** *v* dismiss staff during a slack period **lay-off** *n* **lay on** *v* provide or supply **lay out** *v* arrange or spread out; prepare (a corpse) for burial; *Informal* spend money, esp lavishly; *Informal* knock unconscious **layout** *n* arrangement, esp of matter for printing or of a building

lay[2] *v* past tense of **lie[2]** **layabout** *n* lazy person

lay[3] *adj* of or involving people who are not clergymen; nonspecialist **layman** *n* person who is not a member of the clergy; person without specialist knowledge

lay[4] *n* short narrative poem designed to be sung

layer *n* single thickness of some substance, as a cover or coating on a surface; laying hen; shoot of a plant pegged down or partly covered with earth to encourage root growth ▷ *v* form a layer; propagate plants by layers **layered** *adj*

layette *n* clothes for a newborn baby

laze *v* be idle or lazy ▷ *n* time spent lazing

lazy *adj* **lazier, laziest** not inclined to work or exert oneself; done in a relaxed manner without much effort; (of movement) slow and gentle **lazily** *adv* **laziness** *n*

lb pound (weight)

lbw *cricket* leg before wicket

lea *n poetic* meadow

leach *v* remove or be removed from a substance by a liquid passing through it

lead[1] *v* **leading, led** guide or conduct; cause to feel, think, or behave in a certain way; be, go, or play first; (of a road, path, etc) go towards; control or direct; (foll by *to*) result in; pass or spend (one's life) ▷ *n* first or most prominent place; amount by which a person or group is ahead of another; clue; length of leather or chain attached to a dog's collar to control it; principal role or actor in a film, play, etc; cable bringing current to an electrical device ▷ *adj* acting as a leader or lead **leading** *adj* principal; in the first position **leading question** question worded to prompt the answer desired **lead-in** *n* introduction to a subject

lead[2] *n* soft heavy grey metal; (in a pencil) graphite; lead weight on a line, used for sounding depths of water **leaded** *adj* (of windows) made from many small panes of glass held together by lead strips **leaden** *adj* heavy or sluggish; dull grey; made from lead

leader *n* person who leads; article in a newspaper expressing editorial views **leadership** *n*

leaf *n, pl* **leaves** flat usu green

blade attached to the stem of a plant; single sheet of paper in a book; very thin sheet of metal; extending flap on a table **leafy** *adj* **leafless** *adj* **leaf mould** rich soil composed of decayed leaves **leaf through** *v* turn pages without reading them

leaflet *n* sheet of printed matter for distribution; small leaf

league[1] *n* association promoting the interests of its members; association of sports clubs organizing competitions between its members; *Informal* class or level

league[2] *n obs* measure of distance, about three miles

leak *n* hole or defect that allows the escape or entrance of liquid, gas, radiation, etc; liquid etc that escapes or enters; disclosure of secrets ▷*v* let liquid etc in or out; (of liquid etc) find its way through a leak; disclose secret information **leakage** *n* act or instance of leaking **leaky** *adj*

lean[1] *v* **leaning, leaned** *or* **leant** rest against; bend or slope from an upright position; tend (towards) **leaning** *n* tendency **lean on** *v* *Informal* threaten or intimidate; depend on for help or advice **lean-to** *n* shed built against an existing wall

lean[2] *adj* thin but healthy-looking; (of meat) lacking fat; unproductive ▷*n* lean part of meat **leanness** *n*

leap *v* **leaping, leapt** *or* **leaped** make a sudden powerful jump ▷*n* sudden powerful jump; abrupt increase, as in costs or prices **leapfrog** *n* game in which a player vaults over another bending down **leap year** year with February 29th as an extra day

learn *v* **learning, learned** *or* **learnt** gain skill or knowledge by study, practice, or teaching; memorize (something); find out or discover **learned** *adj* erudite, deeply read; showing much learning **learner** *n* **learning** *n* knowledge got by study

lease *n* contract by which land or property is rented for a stated time by the owner to a tenant ▷*v* let or rent by lease **leasehold** *n, adj* (land or property) held on lease **leaseholder** *n*

leash *n* lead for a dog

least *adj* superlative of **little**: smallest ▷*n* smallest one ▷*adv* in the smallest degree

leather *n* material made from specially treated animal skins ▷*adj* made of leather ▷*v* beat or thrash **leathery** *adj* like leather, tough

leave[1] *v* **leaving, left** go away from; allow to remain, accidentally or deliberately; cause to be or remain in a specified state; discontinue membership of; permit; entrust; bequeath **leave out** *v* exclude or omit

leave[2] *n* permission to be absent from work or duty; period of such absence; permission to do something; formal parting

leaven [**lev**-ven] *n* substance that causes dough to rise; influence that produces a gradual change ▷*v* raise with leaven; spread through and influence (something)

lecher *n* man who has or shows excessive sexual desire **lechery** *n*

lecherous [**letch**-er-uss] *adj* (of a man) having or showing excessive sexual desire

lectern *n* sloping reading desk, esp in a church

lecture *n* informative talk to an audience on a subject; lengthy rebuke or scolding ▷*v* give a talk;

scold
lecturer *n* person who lectures, esp in a university or college **lectureship** *n* appointment as a lecturer
ledge *n* narrow shelf sticking out from a wall; shelflike projection from a cliff etc
ledger *n* book of debit and credit accounts of a firm
lee *n* sheltered part or side **leeward** *adj*, *n* (on) the lee side ▷ *adv* towards this side **leeway** *n* room for free movement within limits
leech *n* species of bloodsucking worm; person who lives off others
leek *n* vegetable of the onion family with a long bulb and thick stem
leer *v* look or grin at in a sneering or suggestive manner ▷ *n* sneering or suggestive look or grin
leery *adj Informal* suspicious or wary (of)
lees *pl n* sediment of wine
left[1] *adj* of the side that faces west when the front faces north ▷ *adv* on or towards the left ▷ *n* left hand or part; *politics* people supporting socialism rather than capitalism **leftist** *n*, *adj* (person) of the political left **left-handed** *adj* more adept with the left hand than with the right **left-wing** *adj* socialist; belonging to the more radical part of a political party
left[2] *v* past of **leave**[1]
leftover *n* unused portion of food or material
leg *n* one of the limbs on which a person or animal walks, runs, or stands; part of a garment covering the leg; structure that supports, such as one of the legs of a table; stage of a journey; *sport* (part of) one game or race in a series **pull someone's leg** tease someone **leggy** *adj* having long legs **legless** *adj* without legs; *slang* very drunk **leggings** *pl n* covering of leather or other material for the legs; close-fitting trousers for women or children
legacy *n*, *pl* **-cies** thing left in a will; thing handed down to a successor
legal *adj* established or permitted by law; relating to law or lawyers **legally** *adv* **legality** *n* **legalize** *v* make legal **legalization** *n*
legate *n* messenger or representative, esp from the Pope **legation** *n* diplomatic minister and his staff; official residence of a diplomatic minister
legatee *n* recipient of a legacy
legato [leg-**ah**-toe] *n*, *pl* **-tos,** *adv music* (piece to be played) smoothly
legend *n* traditional story or myth; traditional literature; famous person or event; stories about such a person or event; inscription **legendary** *adj* famous; of or in legend
legerdemain [lej-er-de-**main**] *n* sleight of hand; cunning deception
legible *adj* easily read **legibility** *n* **legibly** *adv*
legion *n* large military force; large number; association of veterans; infantry unit in the Roman army **legionary** *adj*, *n* **legionnaire** *n* member of a legion **legionnaire's disease** serious bacterial disease similar to pneumonia
legislate *v* make laws **legislative** *adj* **legislator** *n* maker of laws **legislature** *n* body of people that makes, amends, or repeals laws
legislation *n* legislating; laws made

legitimate *adj* authorized by or in accordance with law; fairly deduced; born to parents married to each other ▷*v* make legitimate **legitimacy** *n* **legitimately** *adv* **legitimize** *v* make legitimate, legalize **legitimization** *n*

Lego *n* ® construction toy of plastic bricks fitted together by studs

leguaan [leg-oo-ahn] *n* large S African lizard

legume *n* pod of a plant of the pea or bean family ▷*pl* peas or beans **leguminous** *adj* (of plants) pod-bearing

lei *n* (in Hawaii) garland of flowers

leisure *n* time for relaxation or hobbies **at one's leisure** when one has time **leisurely** *adj* deliberate, unhurried ▷*adv* slowly **leisured** *adj* with plenty of spare time **leisure centre** building with facilities such as a swimming pool, gymnasium, and café

leitmotif [lite-mote-eef] *n music* recurring theme associated with a person, situation, or thought

lekker *adj S Afr, slang* attractive or nice; tasty

lemming *n* rodent of arctic regions, reputed to run into the sea and drown during mass migrations

lemon *n* yellow oval fruit that grows on trees; *slang* useless or defective person or thing ▷*adj* pale-yellow **lemonade** *n* lemon-flavoured soft drink, often fizzy **lemon curd** creamy spread made of lemons, butter, etc **lemon sole** edible flatfish

lemur *n* nocturnal animal like a small monkey, found in Madagascar

lend *v* **lending, lent** give the temporary use of; provide (money) temporarily, often for interest; add (a quality or effect) *eg her presence lent beauty to the scene* **lend itself to** be suitable for **lender** *n*

length *n* extent or measurement from end to end; period of time for which something happens; quality of being long; piece of something narrow and long **at length** at last; in full detail **lengthy** *adj* very long or tiresome **lengthily** *adv* **lengthen** *v* make or become longer **lengthways, lengthwise** *adj, adv*

lenient [lee-nee-ent] *adj* tolerant, not strict or severe **leniency** *n* **leniently** *adv*

lens *n, pl* **lenses** piece of glass or similar material with one or both sides curved, used to bring together or spread light rays in cameras, spectacles, telescopes, etc; transparent structure in the eye that focuses light

lent *v* past of **lend**

Lent *n* period from Ash Wednesday to Easter Saturday **Lenten** *adj* of, in, or suitable to Lent

lentil *n* edible seed of a leguminous Asian plant

lento *n, pl* **-tos,** *adv music* (piece to be played) slowly

leonine *adj* like a lion

leopard *n* large spotted carnivorous animal of the cat family

leotard *n* tight-fitting garment covering the upper body, worn for dancing or exercise

leper *n* person suffering from leprosy; ignored or despised person

lepidoptera *pl n* order of insects with four wings covered with fine gossamer scales, as moths and butterflies **lepidopterist** *n* person who studies or collects butterflies or moths

leprechaun *n* mischievous elf of

Irish folklore

leprosy *n* disease attacking the nerves and skin, resulting in loss of feeling in the affected parts **leprous** *adj*

lesbian *n* homosexual woman ▷ *adj* of homosexual women **lesbianism** *n*

lese-majesty [lezz-**maj**-est-ee] *n* treason; taking of liberties against people in authority

lesion *n* structural change in an organ of the body caused by illness or injury; injury or wound

less *adj* smaller in extent, degree, or duration; not so much; comparative of **little** ▷ *pron* smaller part or quantity ▷ *adv* to a smaller extent or degree ▷ *prep* after deducting, minus **lessen** *v* make or become smaller or not as much **lesser** *adj* not as great in quantity, size, or worth

lessee *n* person to whom a lease is granted

lesson *n* single period of instruction in a subject; content of this; experience that teaches; portion of Scripture read in church

lest *conj* so as to prevent any possibility that; for fear that

let¹ *v* **letting, let** allow, enable, or cause; used as an auxiliary to express a proposal, command, threat, or assumption; grant use of for rent, lease; allow to escape **let alone** not to mention **let down** *v* disappoint; lower; deflate **letdown** *n* disappointment **let off** *v* excuse from (a duty or punishment); fire or explode (a weapon); emit (gas, steam, etc) **let on** *v* *Informal* reveal (a secret) **let out** *v* emit; release **let up** *v* diminish or stop **let-up** *n* lessening

let² *n tennis* minor infringement or obstruction of the ball requiring a replay of the point; hindrance

lethal *adj* deadly

lethargy *n* sluggishness or dullness; abnormal lack of energy **lethargic** *adj* **lethargically** *adv*

letter *n* written message, usu sent by post; alphabetical symbol; strict meaning (of a law etc) ▷ *pl* literary knowledge or ability **lettered** *adj* learned **lettering** *n* **letter bomb** explosive device in a parcel or letter that explodes on opening **letter box** slot in a door through which letters are delivered; box in a street or post office where letters are posted **letterhead** *n* printed heading on stationery giving the sender's name and address

lettuce *n* plant with large green leaves used in salads

leucocyte [**loo**-koh-site] *n* white blood cell

leukaemia [loo-**kee**-mee-a] *n* disease caused by uncontrolled overproduction of white blood cells

levee *n US* natural or artificial river embankment

level *adj* horizontal; having an even surface; of the same height as something else; equal to or even with (someone or something else); not going above the top edge of (a spoon etc) ▷ *v* **-elling, -elled** make even or horizontal; make equal in position or status; direct (a gun, accusation, etc) at; raze to the ground ▷ *n* horizontal line or surface; device for showing or testing if something is horizontal; position on a scale; standard or grade; flat area of land **on the level** *Informal* honest or trustworthy **level crossing** point where a railway line and road cross **level-headed** *adj* not apt to be carried away by emotion

lever *n* handle used to operate machinery; bar used to move a heavy object or to open something; rigid bar pivoted about a fulcrum to transfer a force to a load; means of exerting pressure to achieve an aim ▷ *v* prise or move with a lever **leverage** *n* action or power of a lever; influence or strategic advantage

leveret [**lev**-ver-it] *n* young hare

leviathan [lev-**vie**-ath-an] *n* sea monster; anything huge or formidable

Levis *pl n* ® denim jeans

levitation *n* raising of a solid body into the air supernaturally **levitate** *v* rise or cause to rise into the air

levity *n, pl* **-ties** inclination to make a joke of serious matters

levy [**lev**-vee] *v* **levying, levied** impose and collect (a tax); raise (troops) ▷ *n, pl* **levies** imposition or collection of taxes; money levied

lewd *adj* lustful or indecent **lewdly** *adv* **lewdness** *n*

lexicon *n* dictionary; vocabulary of a language **lexical** *adj* relating to the vocabulary of a language **lexicographer** *n* writer of dictionaries **lexicography** *n*

liable *adj* legally obliged or responsible; given to or at risk from a condition **liability** *n* hindrance or disadvantage; state of being liable; financial obligation

liaise *v* establish and maintain communication (with) **liaison** *n* communication and contact between groups; secret or adulterous relationship

> SPELLING A lot of people forget to include a second *i* in **liaise**. They make the same mistake when they write *liason*, which occurs 58 times in Collins Word Web and which should, of course, be **liaison**

liana *n* climbing plant in tropical forests

liar *n* person who tells lies

lib *n Informal* short for **liberation**

libation [lie-**bay**-shun] *n* drink poured as an offering to the gods

libel *n* published statement falsely damaging a person's reputation ▷ *v* **-belling, -belled** falsely damage the reputation of (someone) **libellous** *adj*

liberal *adj* having social and political views that favour progress and reform; generous in behaviour or temperament; tolerant; abundant; (of education) designed to develop general cultural interests ▷ *n* person who has liberal ideas or opinions **liberally** *adv* **liberalism** *n* belief in democratic reforms and individual freedom **liberality** *n* generosity **liberalize** *v* make (laws, a country, etc) less restrictive **liberalization** *n* **Liberal Democrat, Lib Dem** member of the Liberal Democrats, a British political party favouring a mixed economy and individual freedom **Liberal Party** main right-wing political party in Australia

liberate *v* set free **liberation** *n* **liberator** *n*

libertarian *n* believer in freedom of thought and action ▷ *adj* having such a belief

libertine [**lib**-er-teen] *n* morally dissolute person

liberty *n, pl* **-ties** freedom; act or comment regarded as forward or socially unacceptable **at liberty** free; having the right **take liberties** be presumptuous

libido [lib-**ee**-doe] *n, pl* **-dos** psychic energy; emotional drive, esp of sexual origin **libidinous** *adj* lustful

library *n, pl* **-braries** room or building where books are kept; collection of books, records, etc for consultation or borrowing **librarian** *n* keeper of or worker in a library **librarianship** *n*

libretto *n, pl* **-tos, -ti** words of an opera **librettist** *n*

lice *n* a plural of **louse**

licence *n* document giving official permission to do something; formal permission; disregard of conventions for effect *eg poetic licence*; excessive liberty **license** *v* grant a licence to **licensed** *adj* **licensee** *n* holder of a licence, esp to sell alcohol

licentiate *n* person licensed as competent to practise a profession

licentious *adj* sexually unrestrained or promiscuous

lichen *n* small flowerless plant forming a crust on rocks, trees, etc

licit *adj* lawful, permitted

lick *v* pass the tongue over; touch lightly or flicker round; *slang* defeat ▷ *n* licking; small amount (of paint etc); *Informal* fast pace

licorice *n* same as **liquorice**

lid *n* movable cover; short for **eyelid**

lido [**lee**-doe] *n, pl* **-dos** open-air centre for swimming and water sports

lie[1] *v* **lying, lied** make a deliberately false statement ▷ *n* deliberate falsehood **white lie** see **white**

lie[2] *v* **lying, lay, lain** place oneself or be in a horizontal position; be situated; be or remain in a certain state or position; exist or be found ▷ *n* way something lies **lie-down** *n* rest **lie in** *v* remain in bed late into the morning **lie-in** *n* long stay in bed in the morning

lied [leed] *n, pl* **lieder** *music* setting for voice and piano of a romantic poem

liege [leej] *adj* bound to give or receive feudal service ▷ *n* lord

lien *n law* right to hold another's property until a debt is paid

lieu [lyew] *n* **in lieu of** instead of

lieutenant [lef-**ten**-ant] *n* junior officer in the army or navy; main assistant

life *n, pl* **lives** state of living beings, characterized by growth, reproduction, and response to stimuli; period between birth and death or between birth and the present time; way of living; amount of time something is active or functions; biography; liveliness or high spirits; living beings collectively **lifeless** *adj* dead; not lively or exciting; unconscious **lifelike** *adj* **lifelong** *adj* lasting all of a person's life **life belt, jacket** buoyant device to keep afloat a person in danger of drowning **lifeboat** *n* boat used for rescuing people at sea **life cycle** series of changes undergone by each generation of an animal or plant **lifeline** *n* means of contact or support; rope used in rescuing a person in danger **life science** any science concerned with living organisms, such as biology, botany, or zoology **lifestyle** *n* particular attitudes, habits, etc **life-support** *adj* (of equipment or treatment) necessary to keep a person alive **lifetime** *n* length of time a person is alive

lift *v* move upwards in position, status, volume, etc; revoke or cancel; take (plants) out of the ground for harvesting; (of fog, etc) disappear; make or become more cheerful ▷ *n* cage raised and lowered in a vertical shaft to transport people or goods; ride in a car etc as a passenger; *Informal* feeling of cheerfulness; lifting **liftoff** *n* moment a rocket leaves the ground

ligament *n* band of tissue joining bones

ligature *n* link, bond, or tie

light¹ *n* electromagnetic radiation by which things are visible; source of this, lamp; anything that lets in light, such as a window; aspect or view; mental vision; means of setting fire to ▷ *pl* traffic lights ▷ *adj* bright; (of a colour) pale ▷ *v* **lighting, lighted** *or* **lit** ignite; illuminate or cause to illuminate **lighten** *v* make less dark **lighting** *n* apparatus for and use of artificial light in theatres, films, etc **light bulb** glass part of an electric lamp **lighthouse** *n* tower with a light to guide ships **light year** *astronomy* distance light travels in one year, about six million million miles

light² *adj* not heavy, weighing relatively little; relatively low in strength, amount, density, etc; not clumsy; not serious or profound; easily digested ▷ *adv* with little equipment or luggage ▷ *v* **lighting, lighted, lit** (esp of birds) settle after flight; come (upon) by chance **lightly** *adv* **lightness** *n* **lighten** *v* make less heavy or burdensome; make more cheerful or lively **light-fingered** *adj* skilful at stealing **light-headed** *adj* feeling faint, dizzy **light-hearted** *adj* carefree **lightweight** *n, adj* (person) of little importance ▷ *n* boxer weighing up to 135lb (professional) or 60kg (amateur)

lighter¹ *n* device for lighting cigarettes etc

lighter² *n* flat-bottomed boat for unloading ships

lightning *n* visible discharge of electricity in the atmosphere ▷ *adj* fast and sudden

> SPELLING Do not confuse this noun with the verb 'lighten', which has the form 'lightening'. Collins Word Web shows that people often make the mistake of writing *lightening*, when they mean the noun **lightning**, which doesn't have an *e* in the middle

lights *pl n* lungs of animals as animal food

ligneous *adj* of or like wood

lignite [**lig**-nite] *n* woody textured rock used as fuel

like¹ *prep, conj, adj, pron* indicating similarity, comparison, etc **liken** *v* compare **likeness** *n* resemblance; portrait **likewise** *adv* similarly

like² *v* find enjoyable; be fond of; prefer, choose, or wish **likeable, likable** *adj* **liking** *n* fondness; preference

likely *adj* tending or inclined; probable; hopeful, promising ▷ *adv* probably **not likely** *Informal* definitely not **likelihood** *n* probability

lilac *n* shrub with pale mauve or white flowers ▷ *adj* light-purple

Lilliputian [lil-lip-**pew**-shun] *adj* tiny

Lilo *n, pl* **-los** ® inflatable rubber mattress

lilt *n* pleasing musical quality in speaking; jaunty rhythm; graceful rhythmic motion **lilting** *adj*

lily *n, pl* **lilies** plant which grows from a bulb and has large, often white, flowers

limb *n* arm, leg, or wing; main branch of a tree

limber *v* (foll by *up*) loosen stiff muscles by exercising ▷ *adj* pliant or supple

limbo¹ *n* **in limbo** not knowing the result or next stage of something and powerless to influence it

limbo² *n, pl* **-bos** West Indian dance in which dancers lean backwards to pass under a bar

lime¹ *n* calcium compound used as a fertilizer or in making cement **limelight** *n* glare of publicity **limestone** *n* sedimentary rock used in building

lime² *n* small green citrus fruit **lime-green** *adj* greenish-yellow

lime³ *n* deciduous tree with heart-shaped leaves and fragrant flowers

limerick [**lim**-mer-ik] *n* humorous verse of five lines

limey *n US, slang* British person

limit *n* ultimate extent, degree, or amount of something; boundary or edge ▷ *v* **-iting, -ited** restrict or confine **limitation** *n* **limitless** *adj* **limited company** company whose shareholders' liability for debts is restricted

limousine *n* large luxurious car

limp¹ *v* walk with an uneven step ▷ *n* limping walk

limp² *adj* without firmness or stiffness **limply** *adv*

limpet *n* shellfish which sticks tightly to rocks

limpid *adj* clear or transparent; easy to understand **limpidity** *n*

linchpin, lynchpin *n* pin to hold a wheel on its axle; essential person or thing

linctus *n, pl* **-tuses** syrupy cough medicine

linden *n* same as **lime³**

line¹ *n* long narrow mark; indented mark or wrinkle; boundary or limit; edge or contour of a shape; string or wire for a particular use; telephone connection; wire or cable for transmitting electricity; shipping company; railway track; course or direction of movement; prescribed way of thinking; field of interest or activity; row or queue of people; class of goods; row of words ▷ *pl* words of a theatrical part; school punishment of writing out a sentence a specified number of times ▷ *v* mark with lines; be or form a border or edge **in line for** likely to receive **in line with** in accordance with **line dancing** form of dancing performed by rows of people to country and western music **line-up** *n* people or things assembled for a particular purpose

line² *v* give a lining to; cover the inside of

lineage [**lin**-ee-ij] *n* descent from an ancestor

lineament *n* facial feature

linear [**lin**-ee-er] *adj* of or in lines

linen *n* cloth or thread made from flax; sheets, tablecloths, etc

liner¹ *n* large passenger ship or aircraft

liner² *n* something used as a lining

linesman *n* (in some sports) an official who helps the referee or umpire; person who maintains railway, electricity, or telephone lines

ling¹ *n* slender food fish

ling² *n* heather

linger *v* delay or prolong

departure; continue in a weakened state for a long time before dying or disappearing; spend a long time doing something
lingerie [**lan**-zher-ee] *n* women's underwear or nightwear
lingo *n, pl* **-goes** *Informal* foreign or unfamiliar language or jargon
lingua franca *n* language used for communication between people of different mother tongues
lingual *adj* of the tongue
linguist *n* person skilled in foreign languages; person who studies linguistics **linguistic** *adj* of languages **linguistics** *n* scientific study of language
liniment *n* medicated liquid rubbed on the skin to relieve pain or stiffness
lining *n* layer of cloth attached to the inside of a garment etc; inner covering of anything
link *n* any of the rings forming a chain; person or thing forming a connection; type of communications connection *eg a radio link* ▷ *v* connect with or as if with links; connect by association **linkage** *n* **link-up** *n* joining together of two systems or groups
links *pl n* golf course, esp one by the sea
linnet *n* songbird of the finch family
lino *n* short for **linoleum**
linoleum *n* floor covering of hessian or jute with a smooth decorative coating of powdered cork
Linotype *n* ® typesetting machine which casts lines of words in one piece
linseed *n* seed of the flax plant
lint *n* soft material for dressing a wound
lintel *n* horizontal beam at the top of a door or window
lion *n* large animal of the cat family, the male of which has a shaggy mane **lioness** *n fem* **the lion's share** the biggest part
lion-hearted *adj* brave
lip *n* either of the fleshy edges of the mouth; rim of a jug etc; *slang* impudence **lip-reading** *n* method of understanding speech by interpreting lip movements **lip service** insincere tribute or respect
lipstick *n* cosmetic in stick form, for colouring the lips
liquefy *v* **-fying, -fied** make or become liquid **liquefaction** *n*
liqueur [lik-**cure**] *n* flavoured and sweetened alcoholic spirit
liquid *n* substance in a physical state which can change shape but not size ▷ *adj* of or being a liquid; flowing smoothly; (of assets) in the form of money or easily converted into money **liquidize** *v* make or become liquid **liquidizer** *n* kitchen appliance that liquidizes food **liquidity** *n* state of being able to meet financial obligations
liquidate *v* pay (a debt); dissolve a company and share its assets among creditors; wipe out or kill **liquidation** *n* **liquidator** *n* official appointed to liquidate a business
liquor *n* alcoholic drink, esp spirits; liquid in which food has been cooked
liquorice [**lik**-ker-iss] *n* black substance used in medicine and as a sweet
lira *n, pl* **-re, -ras** monetary unit of Turkey and formerly of Italy
lisle [rhymes with **mile**] *n* strong fine cotton thread or fabric
lisp *n* speech defect in which *s* and *z* are pronounced *th* ▷ *v* speak or

utter with a lisp

lissom, lissome *adj* supple, agile

list[1] *n* item-by-item record of names or things, usu written one below another ▷*v* make a list of; include in a list

list[2] *v* (of a ship) lean to one side ▷*n* leaning to one side

listen *v* concentrate on hearing something; heed or pay attention to **listener** *n* **listen in** *v* listen secretly, eavesdrop

listeriosis *n* dangerous form of food poisoning

listless *adj* lacking interest or energy **listlessly** *adv*

lit *v* past of **light**[1] or [2]

litany *n, pl* **-nies** prayer with responses from the congregation; any tedious recital

literacy *n* ability to read and write

literal *adj* according to the explicit meaning of a word or text, not figurative; (of a translation) word for word; actual, true **literally** *adv*

literary *adj* of or knowledgeable about literature; (of a word) formal, not colloquial

literate *adj* able to read and write; educated **literati** *pl n* literary people

literature *n* written works such as novels, plays, and poetry; books and writings of a country, period, or subject

lithe *adj* flexible or supple, pliant

lithium *n chem* chemical element, the lightest known metal

litho *n, pl* **-thos** short for **lithograph** ▷*adj* short for **lithographic**

lithography [lith-**og**-ra-fee] *n* method of printing from a metal or stone surface in which the printing areas are made receptive to ink **lithograph** *n* print made by lithography ▷*v* reproduce by lithography **lithographer** *n* **lithographic** *adj*

litigant *n* person involved in a lawsuit

litigation *n* legal action **litigate** *v* bring or contest a law suit; engage in legal action **litigious** [lit-**ij**-uss] *adj* frequently going to law

litmus *n* blue dye turned red by acids and restored to blue by alkalis **litmus test** something which is regarded as a simple and accurate test of a particular thing

litotes [lie-**toe**-teez] *n* ironical understatement used for effect

litre *n* unit of liquid measure equal to 1000 cubic centimetres or 1.76 pints

litter *n* untidy rubbish dropped in public places; group of young animals produced at one birth; straw etc as bedding for an animal; dry material to absorb a cat's excrement; bed or seat on parallel sticks for carrying people ▷*v* strew with litter; scatter or be scattered about untidily; give birth to young

little *adj* small or smaller than average; young ▷*adv* not a lot; hardly; not much or often ▷*n* small amount, extent, or duration

littoral *adj* of or by the seashore ▷*n* coastal district

liturgy *n, pl* **-gies** prescribed form of public worship **liturgical** *adj*

live[1] *v* be alive; remain in life or existence; exist in a specified way *eg we live well*; reside; continue or last; subsist; enjoy life to the full **liver** *n* person who lives in a specified way **live down** *v* wait till people forget a past mistake or misdeed **live-in** *adj* resident **live together** *v* (of an unmarried couple) share a house and have a sexual relationship **live up to** *v* meet (expectations) **live with** *v* tolerate

live² *adj* living, alive; (of a broadcast) transmitted during the actual performance; (of a performance) done in front of an audience; (of a wire, circuit, etc) carrying an electric current; causing interest or controversy; capable of exploding; glowing or burning ▷ *adv* in the form of a live performance **lively** *adj* full of life or vigour; animated; vivid **liveliness** *n* **liven up** *v* make (more) lively

livelihood *n* occupation or employment

liver *n* organ secreting bile; animal liver as food **liverish** *adj* having a disorder of the liver; touchy or irritable

livery *n, pl* **-eries** distinctive dress, esp of a servant or servants; distinctive design or colours of a company **liveried** *adj* **livery stable** stable where horses are kept at a charge or hired out

livestock *n* farm animals

livid *adj Informal* angry or furious; bluish-grey

living *adj* possessing life, not dead or inanimate; currently in use or existing; of everyday life *eg living conditions* ▷ *n* condition of being alive; manner of life; financial means **living room** room in a house used for relaxation and entertainment

lizard *n* four-footed reptile with a long body and tail

llama *n* woolly animal of the camel family used as a beast of burden in S America

LLB Bachelor of Laws

loach *n* carplike freshwater fish

load *n* burden or weight; amount carried; source of worry; amount of electrical energy drawn from a source ▷ *pl Informal* lots ▷ *v* put a load on or into; burden or oppress; cause to be biased; put ammunition into (a weapon); put film into (a camera); transfer (a program) into computer memory **loaded** *adj* (of a question) containing a hidden trap or implication; (of dice) dishonestly weighted; *slang* wealthy

loaf¹ *n, pl* **loaves** shaped mass of baked bread; shaped mass of food; *slang* head, esp as the source of common sense *eg use your loaf*

loaf² *v* idle, loiter **loafer** *n*

loam *n* fertile soil

loan *n* money lent at interest; lending; thing lent ▷ *v* lend **loan shark** person who lends money at an extremely high interest rate

loath, loth [rhymes with **both**] *adj* unwilling or reluctant (to).

> Distinguish between **loath** 'reluctant' and *loathe* 'be disgusted by'

loathe *v* hate, be disgusted by **loathing** *n* **loathsome** *adj*

lob *sport* ▷ *n* ball struck or thrown in a high arc ▷ *v* **lobbing, lobbed** strike or throw (a ball) in a high arc

lobby *n, pl* **-bies** corridor into which rooms open; group which tries to influence legislators; hall in a legislative building to which the public has access ▷ *v* try to influence (legislators) in the formulation of policy **lobbyist** *n*

lobe *n* rounded projection; soft hanging part of the ear; subdivision of a body organ **lobed** *adj*

lobelia *n* garden plant with blue, red, or white flowers

lobola [law-**bawl**-a] *n SAfr* (in

African custom) price paid by a bridegroom's family to his bride's family

lobotomy *n, pl* **-mies** surgical incision into a lobe of the brain to treat mental disorders

lobster *n* shellfish with a long tail and claws, which turns red when boiled; *Aust, Informal* $20 note

local *adj* of or existing in a particular place; confined to a particular place ▷*n* person belonging to a particular district; *Informal* pub close to one's home **locally** *adv* **locality** *n* neighbourhood or area **localize** *v* restrict to a particular place **locale** [loh-**kahl**] *n* scene of an event **local anaesthetic** anaesthetic which produces loss of feeling in one part of the body **local authority** governing body of a county, district, or region **local government** government of towns, counties, and districts by locally elected political bodies

locate *v* discover the whereabouts of; situate or place **location** *n* site or position; act of discovering where something is; site of a film production away from the studio; *SAfr* Black African or coloured township

loch *n Scot* lake; long narrow bay

lock[1] *n* appliance for fastening a door, case, etc; section of a canal shut off by gates between which the water level can be altered to aid boats moving from one level to another; extent to which a vehicle's front wheels will turn; interlocking of parts; mechanism for firing a gun; wrestling hold ▷*v* fasten or become fastened securely; become or cause to become fixed or united; become or cause to become immovable; embrace closely **lockout** *n* closing of a workplace by an employer to force workers to accept terms **locksmith** *n* person who makes and mends locks **lockup** *n* prison; garage or storage place away from the main premises

lock[2] *n* strand of hair

locker *n* small cupboard with a lock

locket *n* small hinged pendant for a portrait etc

lockjaw *n* tetanus

locomotive *n* self-propelled engine for pulling trains ▷*adj* of locomotion **locomotion** *n* action or power of moving

locum *n* temporary stand-in for a doctor or clergyman

locus [loh-kuss] *n, pl* **loci** [**loh**-sigh] area or place where something happens; *maths* set of points or lines satisfying one or more specified conditions

locust *n* destructive African insect that flies in swarms and eats crops

lode *n* vein of ore **lodestar** *n* star used in navigation or astronomy as a point of reference **lodestone** *n* magnetic iron ore

lodge *n Chiefly Brit* gatekeeper's house; house or cabin used occasionally by hunters, skiers, etc; porters' room in a university or college; local branch of some societies ▷*v* live in another's house at a fixed charge; stick or become stuck (in a place); make (a complaint etc) formally **lodger** *n* **lodging** *n* temporary residence ▷*pl* rented room or rooms in another person's house

loft *n* space between the top storey and roof of a building; gallery in a church etc ▷*v sport* strike, throw, or kick (a ball) high into the air

lofty *adj* **loftier, loftiest** of great height; exalted or noble; haughty **loftily** *adv* haughtily

log[1] *n* portion of a felled tree stripped of branches; detailed record of a journey of a ship, aircraft, etc ▷ *v* **logging, logged** saw logs from a tree; record in a log **logging** *n* work of cutting and transporting logs **logbook** *n* book recording the details about a car or a ship's journeys **log in, out** *v* gain entrance to *or* leave a computer system by keying in a special command

log[2] *n* short for **logarithm**

loganberry *n* purplish-red fruit, similar to a raspberry

logarithm *n* one of a series of arithmetical functions used to make certain calculations easier

loggerheads *pl n* **at loggerheads** quarrelling, disputing

loggia [**loj**-ya] *n* covered gallery at the side of a building

logic *n* philosophy of reasoning; reasoned thought or argument **logical** *adj* of logic; capable of or using clear valid reasoning; reasonable **logically** *adv* **logician** *n*

logistics *n* detailed planning and organization of a large, esp military, operation **logistical, logistic** *adj*

logo [**loh**-go] *n, pl* **-os** emblem used by a company or other organization

loin *n* part of the body between the ribs and the hips; cut of meat from this part of an animal ▷ *pl* hips and inner thighs **loincloth** *n* piece of cloth covering the loins only

loiter *v* stand or wait aimlessly or idly

loll *v* lounge lazily; hang loosely

lollipop *n* boiled sweet on a small wooden stick **lollipop man, lady** *Brit, Informal* person holding a circular sign on a pole, who controls traffic so that children may cross the road safely

lolly *n, pl* **-ies** *Informal* lollipop or ice lolly; *Aust & NZ, Informal* sweet; *slang* money **lolly scramble** *NZ* sweets scattered on the ground for children to collect

lone *adj* solitary **lonely** *adj* sad because alone; resulting from being alone; unfrequented **loneliness** *n* **loner** *n Informal* person who prefers to be alone **lonesome** *adj* lonely

long[1] *adj* having length, esp great length, in space or time ▷ *adv* for an extensive period **long-distance** *adj* going between places far apart **long face** glum expression **longhand** *n* ordinary writing, not shorthand or typing **long johns** *Informal* long underpants **long-life** *adj* (of milk, batteries, etc) lasting longer than the regular kind **long-lived** *adj* living or lasting for a long time **long-range** *adj* extending into the future; (of vehicles, weapons, etc) designed to cover great distances **long shot** competitor, undertaking, or bet with little chance of success **long-sighted** *adj* able to see distant objects in focus but not nearby ones **long-standing** *adj* existing for a long time **long-suffering** *adj* enduring trouble or unhappiness without complaint **long-term** *adj* lasting or effective for a long time **long wave** radio wave with a wavelength of over 1000 metres **long-winded** *adj* speaking or writing at tedious length

long[2] *v* have a strong desire (for)

longing *n* yearning **longingly** *adv*

longevity [lon-**jev**-it-ee] *n* long life

longitude *n* distance east or west from a standard meridian **longitudinal** *adj* of length or longitude; lengthways

longshoreman *n US* docker

loo *n Informal* toilet

loofah *n* sponge made from the dried pod of a gourd

look *v* direct the eyes or attention (towards); have the appearance of being; face in a particular direction; search (for); hope (for) ▷ *n* instance of looking; (often pl) appearance **look after** *v* take care of **lookalike** *n* person who is the double of another **look down on** *v* treat as inferior or unimportant **look forward to** *v* anticipate with pleasure **look on** *v* be a spectator; consider or regard **lookout** *n* guard; place for watching; *Informal* worry or concern; chances or prospect **look out** *v* be careful **look up** *v* discover or confirm by checking in a book; improve; visit **look up to** *v* respect

loom[1] *n* machine for weaving cloth

loom[2] *v* appear dimly; seem ominously close

loony *slang* ▷ *adj* **loonier, looniest** foolish or insane ▷ *n, pl* **loonies** foolish or insane person

loop *n* rounded shape made by a curved line or rope crossing itself ▷ *v* form or fasten with a loop **loop the loop** fly or be flown in a complete vertical circle **loophole** *n* means of evading a rule without breaking it

loose *adj* not tight, fastened, fixed, or tense; vague; dissolute or promiscuous ▷ *adv* in a loose manner ▷ *v* free; unfasten; slacken; let fly (an arrow, bullet, etc) **at a loose end** bored, with nothing to do **loosely** *adv* **looseness** *n* **loosen** *v* make loose **loosen up** *v* relax, stop worrying **loose-leaf** *adj* allowing the addition or removal of pages

loot *n, v* plunder ▷ *n Informal* money **looter** *n* **looting** *n*

lop *v* **lopping, lopped** cut away twigs and branches; chop off

lope *v* run with long easy strides

lop-eared *adj* having drooping ears

lopsided *adj* greater in height, weight, or size on one side

loquacious *adj* talkative **loquacity** *n*

lord *n* person with power over others, such as a monarch or master; male member of the British nobility; *hist* feudal superior; (**L-**) God or Jesus; (**L-**) (in Britain) title given to certain male officials and peers **House of Lords** unelected upper chamber of the British parliament **lord it over** act in a superior manner towards **the Lord's Prayer** prayer taught by Christ to his disciples **lordly** *adj* imperious, proud **Lordship** *n* (in Britain) title of some male officials and peers

lore *n* body of traditions on a subject

lorgnette [lor-**nyet**] *n* pair of spectacles mounted on a long handle

lorikeet *n* small brightly coloured Australian parrot

lorry *n, pl* **-ries** *Brit & SAfr* large vehicle for transporting loads by road

lose *v* **losing, lost** come to be without, esp by accident or carelessness; fail to keep or maintain; be deprived of; fail to get or make use of; be defeated in a competition etc; be or become engrossed *eg lost in thought* **loser** *n* person or thing that loses; *Informal* person who seems destined to fail

> SPELLING The verb **lose** (*I don't want to lose my hair*) should not be confused with *loose*, which, although existing as a verb, is more often used as an adjective (*a loose tooth*) or adverb (*to work loose*)

loss *n* losing; that which is lost; damage resulting from losing **at a loss** confused or bewildered; not earning enough to cover costs **loss leader** item sold at a loss to attract customers

lost *v* past of **lose** ▷ *adj* unable to find one's way; unable to be found

lot *pron* great number ▷ *n* collection of people or things; fate or destiny; one of a set of objects drawn at random to make a selection or choice; item at auction ▷ *pl Informal* great numbers or quantities **a lot** *Informal* great deal

loth *adj* same as **loath**

lotion *n* medical or cosmetic liquid for use on the skin

lottery *n, pl* **-teries** method of raising money by selling tickets that win prizes by chance; gamble

lotto *n* game of chance like bingo; (**L-**) national lottery

lotus *n* legendary plant whose fruit induces forgetfulness; Egyptian water lily

loud *adj* relatively great in volume; capable of making much noise; insistent and emphatic; unpleasantly patterned or colourful **loudly** *adv* **loudness** *n* **loudspeaker** *n* instrument for converting electrical signals into sound

lough *n Irish* loch

lounge *n* living room in a private house; more expensive bar in a pub; area for waiting in an airport ▷ *v* sit, lie, or stand in a relaxed manner **lounge suit** man's suit for daytime wear

lour *v* same as **lower²**

louse *n, pl* **lice** wingless parasitic insect; *pl* **louses** unpleasant person **lousy** *adj slang* mean or unpleasant; bad, inferior; unwell

lout *n* crude, oafish, or aggressive person **loutish** *adj*

louvre [**loo**-ver] *n* one of a set of parallel slats slanted to admit air but not rain **louvred** *adj*

love *v* have a great affection for; feel sexual passion for; enjoy (something) very much ▷ *n* great affection; sexual passion; wholehearted liking for something; beloved person; *tennis, squash, etc* score of nothing **fall in love** become in love **in love (with)** feeling a strong emotional (and sexual) attraction (for) **make love (to)** have sexual intercourse (with) **lovable, loveable** *adj* **loveless** *adj* **lovely** *adj* **-lier, -liest** very attractive; highly enjoyable **lover** *n* person having a sexual relationship outside marriage; person in love; someone who loves a specified person or thing **loving** *adj* affectionate, tender **lovingly** *adv* **love affair** romantic or sexual relationship between two people who are not married to each other **lovebird** *n* small parrot **love child** *euphemistic* child of an unmarried couple **love life** person's romantic or sexual relationships **lovelorn** *adj* miserable because of unhappiness in love **lovemaking** *n*

low[1] *adj* not tall, high, or elevated; of little or less than the usual amount, degree, quality, or cost; coarse or vulgar; dejected; not loud; deep in pitch ▷ *adv* in or to a low position, level, or degree ▷ *n* low position, level, or degree; area of low atmospheric pressure, depression **lowly** *adj* modest, humble **lowliness** *n* **lowbrow** *n, adj* (person) with nonintellectual tastes and interests **Low Church** section of the Anglican Church stressing evangelical beliefs and practices **lowdown** *n Informal* inside information **low-down** *adj Informal* mean, underhand, or dishonest **low-key** *adj* subdued, restrained, not intense **lowland** *n* low-lying country ▷ *pl* (**L-**) less mountainous parts of Scotland **low profile** position or attitude avoiding prominence or publicity **low-spirited** *adj* depressed

low[2] *n* cry of cattle, moo ▷ *v* moo

lower[1] *adj* below one or more other things; smaller or reduced in amount or value ▷ *v* cause or allow to move down; lessen **lower case** small, as distinct from capital, letters

lower[2]**, lour** *v* (of the sky or weather) look gloomy or threatening **lowering** *adj*

loyal *adj* faithful to one's friends, country, or government **loyally** *adv* **loyalty** *n* **loyalty card** swipe card issued by a supermarket or chain store to a customer, used to record credit points awarded for money spent in the store **loyalist** *n*

lozenge *n* medicated tablet held in the mouth until it dissolves; four-sided diamond-shaped figure

LP *n* record playing approximately 20–25 minutes each side

L-plate *n Brit & Aust* sign on a car being driven by a learner driver

LSD lysergic acid diethylamide, a hallucinogenic drug

Lt Lieutenant

Ltd *Brit* Limited (Liability)

lubricate [loo-brik-ate] *v* oil or grease to lessen friction **lubricant** *n* lubricating substance, such as oil **lubrication** *n*

lubricious *adj lit* lewd

lucerne *n* fodder plant like clover, alfalfa

lucid *adj* clear and easily understood; able to think clearly; bright and clear **lucidly** *adv* **lucidity** *n*

Lucifer *n* Satan

luck *n* fortune, good or bad; good fortune **lucky** *adj* having or bringing good luck **lucky dip** game in which prizes are picked from a tub at random **luckily** *adv* fortunately **luckless** *adj* having bad luck

lucrative *adj* very profitable

lucre [loo-ker] *n* **filthy lucre** *facetious* money

Luddite *n* person opposed to change in industrial methods

luderick *n* Australian fish, usu black or dark brown in colour

ludicrous *adj* absurd or ridiculous **ludicrously** *adv*

ludo *n* game played with dice and counters on a board

lug[1] *v* **lugging, lugged** carry or drag with great effort

lug[2] *n* projection serving as a handle; *Brit, Informal* ear

luggage *n* traveller's cases, bags, etc

lugubrious *adj* mournful, gloomy **lugubriously** *adv*

lugworm *n* large worm used as

bait
lukewarm *adj* moderately warm, tepid; indifferent or half-hearted
lull *v* soothe (someone) by soft sounds or motions; calm (fears or suspicions) by deception ▷*n* brief time of quiet in a storm etc
lullaby *n, pl* **-bies** quiet song to send a child to sleep
lumbago [lum-**bay**-go] *n* pain in the lower back **lumbar** *adj* relating to the lower back
lumber[1] *n Brit* unwanted disused household articles; *Chiefly US* sawn timber ▷*v Informal* burden with something unpleasant **lumberjack** *n US* man who fells trees and prepares logs for transport
lumber[2] *v* move heavily and awkwardly **lumbering** *adj*
luminous *adj* reflecting or giving off light **luminosity** *n* **luminary** *n* famous person; *lit* heavenly body giving off light **luminescence** *n* emission of light at low temperatures by any process other than burning **luminescent** *adj*
lump[1] *n* shapeless piece or mass; swelling; *Informal* awkward or stupid person ▷*v* consider as a single group **lump in one's throat** tight dry feeling in one's throat, usu caused by great emotion **lumpy** *adj* **lump sum** relatively large sum of money paid at one time
lump[2] *v* **lump it** *Informal* tolerate or put up with it
lunar *adj* relating to the moon
lunatic *adj* foolish and irresponsible ▷*n* foolish or annoying person; *old-fashioned* insane person **lunacy** *n*
lunch *n* meal taken in the middle of the day ▷*v* eat lunch **luncheon** *n* formal lunch **luncheon meat** tinned ground mixture of meat and cereal **luncheon voucher** *Brit* voucher for a certain amount, given to an employee and accepted by some restaurants as payment for a meal
lung *n* organ that allows an animal or bird to breathe air: humans have two lungs in the chest **lungfish** *n* freshwater bony fish with an air-breathing lung of South America and Australia
lunge *n* sudden forward motion; thrust with a sword ▷*v* move with or make a lunge
lupin *n* garden plant with tall spikes of flowers
lupine *adj* like a wolf
lurch[1] *v* tilt or lean suddenly to one side; stagger ▷*n* lurching movement
lurch[2] *n* **leave someone in the lurch** abandon someone in difficulties
lurcher *n* crossbred dog trained to hunt silently
lure *v* tempt or attract by the promise of reward ▷*n* person or thing that lures; brightly-coloured artificial angling bait
lurid *adj* vivid in shocking detail, sensational; glaring in colour **luridly** *adv*
lurk *v* lie hidden or move stealthily, esp for sinister purposes; be latent
luscious [**lush**-uss] *adj* extremely pleasurable to taste or smell; very attractive
lush[1] *adj* (of grass etc) growing thickly and healthily; opulent
lush[2] *n slang* alcoholic
lust *n* strong sexual desire; any strong desire ▷*v* have passionate desire (for) **lustful** *adj* **lusty** *adj* vigorous, healthy **lustily** *adv*
lustre *n* gloss, sheen; splendour or

glory; metallic pottery glaze **lustrous** *adj* shining, luminous

lute *n* ancient guitar-like musical instrument with a body shaped like a half pear

Lutheran *adj* of Martin Luther (1483–1546), German Reformation leader, his doctrines, or a Church following these doctrines

luxuriant *adj* rich and abundant; very elaborate **luxuriance** *n* **luxuriantly** *adv*

luxuriate *v* take self-indulgent pleasure (in); flourish

luxury *n, pl* **-ries** enjoyment of rich, very comfortable living; enjoyable but not essential thing ▷ *adj* of or providing luxury **luxurious** *adj* full of luxury, sumptuous **luxuriously** *adv*

lychee [lie-**chee**] *n* Chinese fruit with a whitish juicy pulp

lych gate *n* roofed gate to a churchyard

Lycra *n* ® elastic fabric used for tight-fitting garments, such as swimsuits

lye *n* caustic solution obtained by leaching wood ash

lying *v* present participle of **lie**[1] or [2]

lymph *n* colourless bodily fluid consisting mainly of white blood cells **lymphatic** *adj*

lymphocyte *n* type of white blood cell

lynch *v* put to death without a trial

lynx *n* animal of the cat family with tufted ears and a short tail

lyre *n* ancient musical instrument like a U-shaped harp

lyric *adj* (of poetry) expressing personal emotion in songlike style; like a song ▷ *n* short poem in a songlike style ▷ *pl* words of a popular song **lyrical** *adj* lyric; enthusiastic **lyricist** *n* person who writes the words of songs or musicals

m

m metre(s); mile(s); minute(s)
M Motorway; Monsieur
m. male; married; masculine; meridian; month
ma *n Informal* mother
MA Master of Arts
ma'am *n* madam
mac *n Brit, Informal* mackintosh
macabre [mak-**kahb**-ra] *adj* strange and horrible, gruesome
macadam *n* road surface of pressed layers of small broken stones
macadamia *n* Australian tree with edible nuts
macaroni *n* pasta in short tube shapes
macaroon *n* small biscuit or cake made with ground almonds
macaw *n* large tropical American parrot
mace¹ *n* ceremonial staff of office; medieval weapon with a spiked metal head
mace² *n* spice made from the dried husk of the nutmeg
macerate [**mass**-er-ate] *v* soften by soaking **maceration** *n*
machete [mash-**ett**-ee] *n* broad heavy knife used for cutting or as a weapon
Machiavellian [mak-ee-a-**vel**-yan] *adj* unprincipled, crafty, and opportunist
machinations [mak-in-**nay**-shunz] *pl n* cunning plots and ploys
machine *n* apparatus, usu powered by electricity, designed to perform a particular task; vehicle, such as a car or aircraft; controlling system of an organization ▷ *v* make or produce by machine **machinery** *n* machines or machine parts collectively **machinist** *n* person who operates a machine **machine gun** automatic gun that fires rapidly and continuously **machine-gun** *v* fire at with such a gun **machine-readable** *adj* (of data) in a form suitable for processing by a computer
machismo [mak-**izz**-moh] *n* exaggerated or strong masculinity
Mach number [**mak**] *n* ratio of the speed of a body in a particular medium to the speed of sound in that medium
macho [**match**-oh] *adj* strongly or exaggeratedly masculine
mackerel *n* edible sea fish
mackintosh *n* waterproof raincoat of rubberized cloth
macramé [mak-**rah**-mee] *n* ornamental work of knotted cord
macrobiotics *n* dietary system advocating whole grains and vegetables grown without chemical additives **macrobiotic**

adj

macrocosm *n* the universe; any large complete system

mad *adj* **madder, maddest** mentally deranged, insane; very foolish; *Informal* angry; frantic; (foll by *about, on*) very enthusiastic (about) **like mad** *Informal* with great energy, enthusiasm, or haste **madly** *adv* **madness** *n* **madden** *v* infuriate or irritate **maddening** *adj* **madman, madwoman** *n*

madam *n* polite form of address to a woman; *Informal* precocious or conceited girl

madame [mad-**dam**] *n, pl* **mesdames** [may-**dam**] French title equivalent to *Mrs*

madcap *adj* foolish or reckless

madder *n* climbing plant; red dye made from its root

made *v* past of **make**

Madeira [mad-**deer**-a] *n* fortified white wine **Madeira cake** rich sponge cake

mademoiselle [mad-mwah-**zel**] *n, pl* **mesdemoiselles** [maid-mwah-**zel**] French title equivalent to *Miss*

Madonna *n* the Virgin Mary; picture or statue of her

madrigal *n* 16th–17th-century part song for unaccompanied voices

maelstrom [**male**-strom] *n* great whirlpool; turmoil

maestro [**my**-stroh] *n, pl* **-tri, -tros** outstanding musician or conductor; any master of an art

Mafia *n* international secret criminal organization founded in Sicily **mafioso** *n, pl* **-sos, -si** member of the Mafia

magazine *n* periodical publication with articles by different writers; television or radio programme made up of short nonfictional items; appliance for automatically supplying cartridges to a gun or slides to a projector; storehouse for explosives or arms

magenta [maj-**jen**-ta] *adj* deep purplish-red

maggot *n* larva of an insect **maggoty** *adj*

Magi [**maje**-eye] *pl n* wise men from the East who came to worship the infant Jesus

magic *n* supposed art of invoking supernatural powers to influence events; mysterious quality or power ▷ *adj* (also **magical**) of, using, or like magic; *Informal* wonderful, marvellous **magically** *adv* **magician** *n* conjuror; person with magic powers

magistrate *n* public officer administering the law; *Brit* justice of the peace; *Aust & NZ* former name for **district court judge** **magisterial** *adj* commanding or authoritative; of a magistrate

magma *n* molten rock inside the earth's crust

magnanimous *adj* noble and generous **magnanimously** *adv* **magnanimity** *n*

magnate *n* influential or wealthy person, esp in industry

magnesia *n* white tasteless substance used as an antacid and a laxative; magnesium oxide

magnesium *n chem* silvery-white metallic element

magnet *n* piece of iron or steel capable of attracting iron and pointing north when suspended **magnetic** *adj* having the properties of a magnet; powerfully attractive **magnetically** *adv* **magnetism** *n* magnetic property; powerful personal charm; science of magnetic properties

magnetize *v* make into a magnet; attract strongly **magnetic tape** plastic strip coated with a magnetic substance for recording sound or video signals
magneto [mag-**nee**-toe] *n, pl* **-tos** apparatus for ignition in an internal-combustion engine
magnificent *adj* splendid or impressive; excellent **magnificently** *adv* **magnificence** *n*
magnify *v* **-fying, -fied** increase in apparent size, as with a lens; exaggerate **magnification** *n*
magnitude *n* relative importance or size
magnolia *n* shrub or tree with showy white or pink flowers
magnum *n* large wine bottle holding about 1.5 litres
magpie *n* black-and-white bird; any of various similar Australian birds, eg the butcherbird
maharajah *n* former title of some Indian princes **maharani** *n fem*
mah jong, mah-jongg *n* Chinese table game for four, played with tiles bearing different designs
mahogany *n* hard reddish-brown wood of several tropical trees
mahout [ma-**howt**] *n* (in India and the East Indies) elephant driver or keeper
maid *n* (also **maidservant**) female servant; *lit* young unmarried woman
maiden *n lit* young unmarried woman ▷ *adj* unmarried; first *eg maiden voyage* **maidenly** *adj* modest **maidenhair** *n* fern with delicate fronds **maidenhead** *n* virginity **maiden name** woman's surname before marriage **maiden over** *cricket* over in which no runs are scored
mail[1] *n* letters and packages transported and delivered by the post office; postal system; single collection or delivery of mail; train, ship, or aircraft carrying mail; same as **e-mail** ▷ *v* send by mail **mailbox** *n US, Canadian & Aust* box into which letters and parcels are delivered **mail order** system of buying goods by post **mailshot** *n Brit* posting of advertising material to many selected people at once
mail[2] *n* flexible armour of interlaced rings or links
maim *v* cripple or mutilate
main *adj* chief or principal ▷ *n* principal pipe or line carrying water, gas, or electricity ▷ *pl* main distribution network for water, gas, or electricity **in the main** on the whole **mainly** *adv* for the most part, Chiefly **mainframe** *n, adj computers* (denoting) a high-speed general-purpose computer **mainland** *n* stretch of land which forms the main part of a country **mainmast** *n* chief mast of a ship **mainsail** *n* largest sail on a mainmast **mainspring** *n* chief cause or motive; chief spring of a watch or clock **mainstay** *n* chief support; rope securing a mainmast **mainstream** *adj* (of) a prevailing cultural trend
maintain *v* continue or keep in existence; keep up or preserve; support financially; assert **maintenance** *n* maintaining; upkeep of a building, car, etc; provision of money for a separated or divorced spouse
maisonette *n Brit* flat with more than one floor
maître d'hôtel [met-ra dote-**tell**] *n French* head waiter
maize *n* type of corn with spikes of

yellow grains

majesty *n, pl* **-ties** stateliness or grandeur; supreme power **majestic** *adj* **majestically** *adv*

major *adj* greater in number, quality, or extent; significant or serious ▷ *n* middle-ranking army officer; scale in music; *US, Canadian, SAfr, Aust & NZ* principal field of study at a university etc ▷ *v* (foll by *in*) *US, Canadian, SAfr, Aust & NZ* do one's principal study in (a particular subject) **major-domo** *n, pl* **-domos** chief steward of a great household

majority *n, pl* **-ties** greater number; number by which the votes on one side exceed those on the other; largest party voting together; state of being legally an adult

make *v* **making, made** create, construct, or establish; cause to do or be; bring about or produce; perform (an action); serve as or become; amount to; earn ▷ *n* brand, type, or style **make do** manage with an inferior alternative **make it** *Informal* be successful **on the make** *Informal* out for profit or conquest **maker** *n* **making** *n* creation or production ▷ *pl* necessary requirements or qualities **make-believe** *n* fantasy or pretence **make for** *v* head towards **make off with** *v* steal or abduct **makeshift** *adj* serving as a temporary substitute **make up** *v* form or constitute; prepare; invent; supply what is lacking, complete; (foll by *for*) compensate (for); settle a quarrel; apply cosmetics **make-up** *n* cosmetics; way something is made; mental or physical constitution **makeweight** *n* something unimportant added to make up a lack

mal- *combining form* bad or badly *eg malformation*

malachite [**mal**-a-kite] *n* green mineral

maladjusted *adj psychol* unable to meet the demands of society **maladjustment** *n*

maladministration *n* inefficient or dishonest administration

maladroit *adj* clumsy or awkward

malady *n, pl* **-dies** disease or illness

malaise [mal-**laze**] *n* vague feeling of unease, illness, or depression

malapropism *n* comical misuse of a word by confusion with one which sounds similar, eg *I am not under the affluence of alcohol*

malaria *n* infectious disease caused by the bite of some mosquitoes **malarial** *adj*

Malay *n* member of a people of Malaysia or Indonesia; language of this people **Malayan** *adj, n*

malcontent *n* discontented person

male *adj* of the sex which can fertilize female reproductive cells ▷ *n* male person or animal

malediction [mal-lid-**dik**-shun] *n* curse

malefactor [**mal**-if-act-or] *n* criminal or wrongdoer

malevolent [mal-**lev**-a-lent] *adj* wishing evil to others **malevolently** *adv* **malevolence** *n*

malfeasance [mal-**fee**-zanss] *n* misconduct, esp by a public official

malformed *adj* misshapen or deformed **malformation** *n*

malfunction *v* function imperfectly or fail to function ▷ *n* defective functioning or failure to function

malice [**mal**-iss] *n* desire to cause

harm to others **malicious** *adj* **maliciously** *adv*
malign [mal-**line**] *v* slander or defame ▷ *adj* evil in influence or effect **malignity** *n* evil disposition
malignant [mal-**lig**-nant] *adj* seeking to harm others; (of a tumour) harmful and uncontrollable **malignancy** *n*
malinger *v* feign illness to avoid work **malingerer** *n*
mall [**mawl**] *n* street or shopping area closed to vehicles
mallard *n* wild duck
malleable [**mal**-lee-a-bl] *adj* capable of being hammered or pressed into shape; easily influenced **malleability** *n*
mallee *n Aust* low-growing eucalypt in dry regions
mallet *n* (wooden) hammer; stick with a head like a hammer, used in croquet or polo
mallow *n* plant with pink or purple flowers
malnutrition *n* inadequate nutrition
malodorous [mal-**lode**-or-uss] *adj* bad-smelling
malpractice *n* immoral, illegal, or unethical professional conduct
malt *n* grain, such as barley, prepared for use in making beer or whisky
maltreat *v* treat badly **maltreatment** *n*
mama *n old-fashioned* mother
mamba *n* deadly S African snake
mamma *n* same as **mama**
mammal *n* animal of the type that suckles its young **mammalian** *adj*
mammary *adj* of the breasts or milk-producing glands
mammon *n* wealth regarded as a source of evil
mammoth *n* extinct elephant-like mammal ▷ *adj* colossal
man *n, pl* **men** adult male; human being or person; mankind; manservant; piece used in chess etc ▷ *v* **manning, manned** supply with sufficient people for operation or defence **manhood** *n* **mankind** *n* human beings collectively **manly** *adj* (possessing qualities) appropriate to a man **manliness** *n* **mannish** *adj* (of a woman) like a man **man-hour** *n* work done by one person in one hour **man-made** *adj* made artificially
mana *n NZ* authority, influence
manacle [**man**-a-kl] *n, v* handcuff or fetter
manage *v* succeed in doing; be in charge of, administer; handle or control; cope with (financial) difficulties **manageable** *adj* **management** *n* managers collectively; administration or organization
manager, manageress *n* person in charge of a business, institution, actor, sports team, etc **managerial** *adj*
manatee *n* large tropical plant-eating aquatic mammal
mandarin *n* high-ranking government official; kind of small orange
mandate *n* official or authoritative command; authorization or instruction from an electorate to its representative or government ▷ *v* give authority to **mandatory** *adj* compulsory
mandible *n* lower jawbone or jawlike part
mandolin *n* musical instrument with four pairs of strings
mandrake *n* plant with a forked root, formerly used as a narcotic

mandrel *n* shaft on which work is held in a lathe
mandrill *n* large blue-faced baboon
mane *n* long hair on the neck of a horse, lion, etc
manful *adj* determined and brave **manfully** *adv*
manganese *n chem* brittle greyish-white metallic element
mange *n* skin disease of domestic animals
mangelwurzel *n* variety of beet used as cattle food
manger *n* eating trough in a stable or barn
mangetout [mawnzh-too] *n* variety of pea with an edible pod
mangle[1] *v* destroy by crushing and twisting; spoil
mangle[2] *n* machine with rollers for squeezing water from washed clothes ▷ *v* put through a mangle
mango *n, pl* **-goes, -gos** tropical fruit with sweet juicy yellow flesh
mangrove *n* tropical tree with exposed roots, which grows beside water
mangy *adj* **mangier, mangiest** having mange; scruffy or shabby
manhandle *v* treat roughly
manhole *n* hole with a cover, through which a person can enter a drain or sewer
mania *n* extreme enthusiasm; madness **maniac** *n* mad person; *Informal* person who has an extreme enthusiasm for something **maniacal** [man-**eye**-a-kl] *adj*
manic *adj* affected by mania
manicure *n* cosmetic care of the fingernails and hands ▷ *v* care for (the fingernails and hands) in this way **manicurist** *n*
manifest *adj* easily noticed, obvious ▷ *v* show plainly; be evidence of ▷ *n* list of cargo or passengers for customs **manifestation** *n*
manifesto *n, pl* **-tos, -toes** declaration of policy as issued by a political party
manifold *adj* numerous and varied ▷ *n* pipe with several outlets, esp in an internal-combustion engine
manikin *n* little man or dwarf; model of the human body
manila, manilla *n* strong brown paper used for envelopes
manipulate *v* handle skilfully; control cleverly or deviously **manipulation** *n* **manipulative** *adj* **manipulator** *n*
manna *n Bible* miraculous food which sustained the Israelites in the wilderness; windfall
mannequin *n* woman who models clothes at a fashion show; life-size dummy of the human body used to fit or display clothes
manner *n* way a thing happens or is done; person's bearing or behaviour; type or kind; custom or style ▷ *pl* (polite) social behaviour **mannered** *adj* affected **mannerism** *n* person's distinctive habit or trait
mannikin *n* same as **manikin**
manoeuvre [man-**noo**-ver] *n* skilful movement; contrived, complicated, and possibly deceptive plan or action ▷ *pl* military or naval exercises ▷ *v* manipulate or contrive skilfully or cunningly; perform manoeuvres **manoeuvrable** *adj*
manor *n Brit* large country house and its lands **manorial** *adj*
manpower *n* available number of workers
manqué [mong-kay] *adj* would-be

eg an actor manqué
mansard roof *n* roof with a break in its slope, the lower part being steeper than the upper
manse *n* house provided for a minister in some religious denominations
manservant *n, pl* **menservants** male servant, esp a valet
mansion *n* large house
manslaughter *n* unlawful but unintentional killing of a person
mantel *n* structure round a fireplace **mantelpiece, mantel shelf** *n* shelf above a fireplace
mantilla *n* (in Spain) a lace scarf covering a woman's head and shoulders
mantis *n, pl* **-tises, -tes** carnivorous insect like a grasshopper
mantle *n* loose cloak; covering; responsibilities and duties which go with a particular job or position
mantra *n Hinduism, Buddhism* any sacred word or syllable used as an object of concentration
manual *adj* of or done with the hands; by human labour rather than automatic means ▷ *n* handbook; organ keyboard **manually** *adv*
manufacture *v* process or make (goods) on a large scale using machinery; invent or concoct (an excuse etc) ▷ *n* process of manufacturing goods
manufacturer *n* company that manufactures goods
manure *n* animal excrement used as a fertilizer
manuscript *n* book or document, orig one written by hand; copy for printing
Manx *adj* of the Isle of Man or its inhabitants ▷ *n* almost extinct language of the Isle of Man **Manx cat** tailless breed of cat
many *adj* **more, most** numerous ▷ *n* large number
Maoism *n* form of Marxism advanced by Mao Tse-tung in China **Maoist** *n, adj*
Maori *n, pl* **-ri, -ris** member of the indigenous race of New Zealand; language of the Maoris ▷ *adj* of the Maoris or their language
map *n* representation of the earth's surface or some part of it, showing geographical features ▷ *v* **mapping, mapped** make a map of **map out** *v* plan
maple *n* tree with broad leaves, a variety of which (**sugar maple**) yields sugar
mar *v* **marring, marred** spoil or impair
Mar. March
marabou *n* large black-and-white African stork; its soft white down, used to trim hats etc
maraca [mar-**rak**-a] *n* shaken percussion instrument made from a gourd containing dried seeds etc
marae *n NZ* enclosed space in front of a Maori meeting house; Maori meeting house and its buildings
maraschino cherry [mar-rass-**kee**-no] *n* cherry preserved in a cherry liqueur with a taste like bitter almonds
marathon *n* long-distance race of 26 miles 385 yards (42.195 kilometres); long or arduous task
marauding *adj* wandering or raiding in search of plunder **marauder** *n*
marble *n* kind of limestone with a mottled appearance, which can be highly polished; slab of or sculpture in this; small glass ball used in playing marbles ▷ *pl* game of

rolling these at one another **marbled** *adj* having a mottled appearance like marble

march¹ *v* walk with a military step; make (a person or group) proceed; progress steadily ▷*n* action of marching; steady progress; distance covered by marching; piece of music, as for a march **marcher** *n* **marching girl** *Aust & NZ* girl who does team formation marching as a sport

march² *n* border or frontier

March *n* third month of the year

marchioness [marsh-on-**ness**] *n* woman holding the rank of marquis; wife or widow of a marquis

mare *n* female horse or zebra **mare's nest** discovery which proves worthless

margarine *n* butter substitute made from animal or vegetable fats

marge *n Informal* margarine

margin *n* edge or border; blank space round a printed page; additional amount or one greater than necessary; limit **marginal** *adj* insignificant, unimportant; near a limit; *politics* (of a constituency) won by only a small margin ▷*n politics* marginal constituency **marginalize** *v* make or treat as insignificant **marginally** *adv*

marguerite *n* large daisy

marigold *n* plant with yellow or orange flowers

marijuana [mar-ree-**wah**-na] *n* dried flowers and leaves of the cannabis plant, used as a drug, esp in cigarettes

marina *n* harbour for yachts and other pleasure boats

marinade *n* seasoned liquid in which fish or meat is soaked before cooking ▷*v* same as **marinate** **marinate** *v* soak in marinade

marine *adj* of the sea or shipping ▷*n* (esp in Britain and the US) soldier trained for land and sea combat; country's shipping or fleet **mariner** *n* sailor

marionette *n* puppet worked with strings

marital *adj* relating to marriage

maritime *adj* relating to shipping; of, near, or living in the sea

marjoram *n* aromatic herb used for seasoning food and in salads

mark¹ *n* line, dot, scar, etc visible on a surface; distinguishing sign or symbol; written or printed symbol; letter or number used to grade academic work; indication of position; indication of some quality; target or goal ▷*v* make a mark on; characterize or distinguish; indicate; pay attention to; notice or watch; grade (academic work); stay close to (a sporting opponent) to hamper his or her play **marked** *adj* noticeable **markedly** *adv* **marker** *n*

mark² *n* same as **Deutschmark**

market *n* assembly or place for buying and selling; demand for goods ▷*v* **-keting, -keted** offer or produce for sale **on the market** for sale **marketable** *adj* **marketing** *n* part of a business that controls the way that goods or services are sold **market garden** place where fruit and vegetables are grown for sale **market maker** (in London Stock Exchange) person who uses a firm's money to create a market for a stock **marketplace** *n* market; commercial world **market research** research into consumers' needs and purchases

marksman *n* person skilled at shooting **marksmanship** *n*

marl *n* soil formed of clay and lime, used as fertilizer
marlin *n* large food and game fish of warm and tropical seas, with a very long upper jaw
marlinespike, marlinspike *n* pointed hook used to separate strands of rope
marmalade *n* jam made from citrus fruits
marmoreal *adj* of or like marble
marmoset *n* small bushy-tailed monkey
marmot *n* burrowing rodent
maroon¹ *adj* reddish-purple
maroon² *v* abandon ashore, esp on an island; isolate without resources
marquee *n* large tent used for a party or exhibition
marquess [mar-kwiss] *n Brit* nobleman of the rank below a duke
marquetry *n* ornamental inlaid work of wood
marquis *n* (in some European countries) nobleman of the rank above a count
marram grass *n* grass that grows on sandy shores
marrow *n* fatty substance inside bones; long thick striped green vegetable with whitish flesh
marry *v* **-rying, -ried** take as a husband or wife; join or give in marriage; unite closely **marriage** *n* state of being married; wedding **marriageable** *adj*
Mars *n* Roman god of war; fourth planet from the sun
Marsala [mar-**sah**-la] *n* dark sweet wine
marsh *n* low-lying wet land **marshy** *adj*
marshal *n* officer of the highest rank; official who organizes ceremonies or events; *US* law officer ▷ *v* **-shalling, -shalled** arrange in order; assemble; conduct with ceremony **marshalling yard** railway depot for goods trains
marshmallow *n* spongy pink or white sweet
marsupial [mar-**soop**-ee-al] *n* animal that carries its young in a pouch, such as a kangaroo
mart *n* market
Martello tower *n* round tower for coastal defence, formerly used in Europe
marten *n* weasel-like animal
martial *adj* of war, warlike **martial art** any of various philosophies and techniques of self-defence, orig Eastern, such as karate **martial law** law enforced by military authorities in times of danger or emergency
Martian [**marsh**-an] *adj* of Mars ▷ *n* supposed inhabitant of Mars
martin *n* bird with a slightly forked tail
martinet *n* person who maintains strict discipline
martini *n* cocktail of vermouth and gin
martyr *n* person who dies or suffers for his or her beliefs ▷ *v* make a martyr of **be a martyr to** be constantly suffering from **martyrdom** *n*
marvel *v* **-velling, -velled** be filled with wonder ▷ *n* wonderful thing **marvellous** *adj* amazing; wonderful
Marxism *n* political philosophy of Karl Marx **Marxist** *n, adj*
marzipan *n* paste of ground almonds, sugar, and egg whites
masc. masculine
mascara *n* cosmetic for darkening the eyelashes
mascot *n* person, animal, or thing

supposed to bring good luck
masculine *adj* relating to males; manly; *grammar* of the gender of nouns that includes some male animate things **masculinity** *n*
mash *n Informal* mashed potatoes; bran or meal mixed with warm water as food for horses etc ▷*v* crush into a soft mass
mask *n* covering for the face, as a disguise or protection; behaviour that hides one's true feelings ▷*v* cover with a mask; hide or disguise
masochism [**mass**-oh-kiz-zum] *n* condition in which (sexual) pleasure is obtained from feeling pain or from being humiliated **masochist** *n* **masochistic** *adj*
mason *n* person who works with stone; (**M-**) Freemason **Masonic** *adj* of Freemasonry **masonry** *n* stonework; (**M-**) Freemasonry
masque [mask] *n hist* 16th–17th-century form of dramatic entertainment
masquerade [mask-er-**aid**] *n* deceptive show or pretence; party at which masks and costumes are worn ▷*v* pretend to be someone or something else
mass *n* coherent body of matter; large quantity or number; *physics* amount of matter in a body ▷*adj* large-scale; involving many people ▷*v* form into a mass **the masses** ordinary people **massive** *adj* large and heavy **mass-market** *adj* for or appealing to a large number of people **mass media** means of communication to many people, such as television and newspapers **mass-produce** *v* manufacture (standardized goods) in large quantities
Mass *n* service of the Eucharist, esp in the RC Church
massacre [**mass**-a-ker] *n* indiscriminate killing of large numbers of people ▷*v* kill in large numbers
massage [**mass**-ahzh] *n* rubbing and kneading of parts of the body to reduce pain or stiffness ▷*v* give a massage to **masseur**, *fem* **masseuse** *n* person who gives massages
massif [**mass**-seef] *n* connected group of mountains
mast[1] *n* tall pole for supporting something, esp a ship's sails
mast[2] *n* fruit of the beech, oak, etc, used as pig fodder
mastectomy [mass-**tek**-tom-ee] *n, pl* **-mies** surgical removal of a breast
master *n* person in control, such as an employer or an owner of slaves or animals; expert; great artist; original thing from which copies are made; male teacher ▷*adj* overall or controlling; main or principal ▷*v* acquire knowledge of or skill in; overcome **masterful** *adj* domineering; showing great skill **masterly** *adj* showing great skill **mastery** *n* expertise; control or command **master key** key that opens all the locks of a set **mastermind** *v* plan and direct (a complex task) ▷*n* person who plans and directs a complex task **masterpiece** *n* outstanding work of art
mastic *n* gum obtained from certain trees; putty-like substance used as a filler, adhesive, or seal
masticate *v* chew **mastication** *n*
mastiff *n* large dog
mastitis *n* inflammation of a breast or udder
mastodon *n* extinct elephant-like

mammal
mastoid *n* projection of the bone behind the ear
masturbate *v* fondle the genitals (of) **masturbation** *n*
mat *n* piece of fabric used as a floor covering or to protect a surface; thick tangled mass ▷ *v* **matting, matted** tangle or become tangled into a dense mass
matador *n* man who kills the bull in bullfights
match[1] *n* contest in a game or sport; person or thing exactly like, equal to, or in harmony with another; marriage ▷ *v* be exactly like, equal to, or in harmony with; put in competition (with); find a match for; join (in marriage) **matchless** *adj* unequalled **matchmaker** *n* person who schemes to bring about a marriage **matchmaking** *n, adj*
match[2] *n* small stick with a tip which ignites when scraped on a rough surface **matchbox** *n* **matchstick** *n* wooden part of a match ▷ *adj* (of drawn figures) thin and straight **matchwood** *n* small splinters
mate[1] *n Informal* friend; associate or colleague *eg team-mate*; sexual partner of an animal; officer in a merchant ship; tradesman's assistant ▷ *v* pair (animals) or (of animals) be paired for reproduction
mate[2] *n, v chess* checkmate
material *n* substance of which a thing is made; cloth; information on which a piece of work may be based ▷ *pl* things needed for an activity ▷ *adj* of matter or substance; not spiritual; affecting physical wellbeing; relevant **materially** *adv* considerably **materialism** *n* excessive interest in or desire for money and possessions; belief that only the material world exists **materialist** *adj, n* **materialistic** *adj* **materialize** *v* actually happen; come into existence or view **materialization** *n*
maternal *adj* of a mother; related through one's mother **maternity** *n* motherhood ▷ *adj* of or for pregnant women
matey *adj Brit, Informal* friendly or intimate
mathematics *n* science of number, quantity, shape, and space **mathematical** *adj* **mathematically** *adv* **mathematician** *n*
maths *n Informal* mathematics
Matilda *n Aust hist* swagman's bundle of belongings **waltz Matilda** *Aust* travel about carrying one's bundle of belongings
matinée [mat-in-nay] *n* afternoon performance in a theatre or cinema
matins *pl n* early morning service in various Christian Churches
matriarch [mate-ree-ark] *n* female head of a tribe or family **matriarchal** *adj* **matriarchy** *n* society governed by a female, in which descent is traced through the female line
matricide *n* crime of killing one's mother; person who does this
matriculate *v* enrol or be enrolled in a college or university **matriculation** *n*
matrimony *n* marriage **matrimonial** *adj*
matrix [may-trix] *n, pl* **matrices** substance or situation in which something originates, takes form, or is enclosed; mould for casting; *maths* rectangular array of numbers or elements

matron *n* staid or dignified married woman; woman who supervises the domestic or medical arrangements of an institution; former name for **nursing officer** **matronly** *adj*

matt *adj* dull, not shiny

matter *n* substance of which something is made; physical substance; event, situation, or subject; written material in general; pus ▷*v* be of importance **what's the matter?** what is wrong?

mattock *n* large pick with one of its blade ends flattened for loosening soil

mattress *n* large stuffed flat case, often with springs, used on or as a bed

mature *adj* fully developed or grown-up; ripe ▷*v* make or become mature; (of a bill or bond) become due for payment **maturity** *n* state of being mature **maturation** *n*

maudlin *adj* foolishly or tearfully sentimental

maul *v* handle roughly; beat or tear

maunder *v* talk or act aimlessly or idly

mausoleum [maw-so-**lee**-um] *n* stately tomb

mauve *adj* pale purple

maverick *n, adj* independent and unorthodox (person)

maw *n* animal's mouth, throat, or stomach

mawkish *adj* foolishly sentimental

maxim *n* general truth or principle

maximum *adj, n, pl* **-mums, -ma** greatest possible (amount or number) **maximal** *adj* **maximize** *v* increase to a maximum

may *v, past tense* **might** used as an auxiliary to express possibility, permission, opportunity, etc

May *n* fifth month of the year; **(m-)** same as **hawthorn** **mayfly** *n* short-lived aquatic insect **maypole** *n* pole set up for dancing round on the first day of May to celebrate spring

maybe *adv* perhaps, possibly

Mayday *n* international radio distress signal

mayhem *n* violent destruction or confusion

mayonnaise *n* creamy sauce of egg yolks, oil, and vinegar

> SPELLING There are two *n*s to remember in the middle of **mayonnaise** - possibly a good reason for the increasing use of the abbreviation 'mayo'

mayor *n* head of a municipality **mayoress** *n* mayor's wife; female mayor **mayoralty** *n* (term of) office of a mayor

maze *n* complex network of paths or lines designed to puzzle; any confusing network or system

mazurka *n* lively Polish dance; music for this

MB Bachelor of Medicine

MBE (in Britain) Member of the Order of the British Empire

MC Master of Ceremonies

MD Doctor of Medicine

me *pron* objective form of **I**

ME myalgic encephalomyelitis: painful muscles and general weakness sometimes persisting long after a viral illness

mead *n* alcoholic drink made from honey

meadow *n* piece of grassland **meadowsweet** *n* plant with dense heads of small fragrant flowers

meagre *adj* scanty or insufficient

meal[1] *n* occasion when food is

served and eaten; the food itself
meal² *n* grain ground to powder **mealy** *adj* **mealy-mouthed** *adj* not outspoken enough
mealie *n SAfr* maize
mean¹ *v* **meaning, meant** intend to convey or express; signify, denote, or portend; intend; have importance as specified **meaning** *n* sense, significance **meaningful** *adj* **meaningless** *adj*
mean² *adj* miserly, ungenerous, or petty; despicable or callous; *Chiefly US, Informal* bad-tempered **meanly** *adv* **meanness** *n*
mean³ *n* middle point between two extremes; average ▷ *pl* method by which something is done; money ▷ *adj* intermediate in size or quantity; average **by all means** certainly **by no means** in no way **means test** inquiry into a person's means to decide on eligibility for financial aid
meander [mee-**and**-er] *v* follow a winding course; wander aimlessly ▷ *n* winding course
meantime *n* intervening period ▷ *adv* meanwhile
meanwhile *adv* during the intervening period; at the same time
measles *n* infectious disease producing red spots **measly** *adj Informal* meagre
measure *n* size or quantity; graduated scale etc for measuring size or quantity; unit of size or quantity; extent; action taken; law; poetical rhythm ▷ *v* determine the size or quantity of; be (a specified amount) in size or quantity **measurable** *adj* **measured** *adj* slow and steady; carefully considered **measurement** *n* measuring; size **measure up to** *v* fulfil (expectations or requirements)
meat *n* animal flesh as food **meaty** *adj* (tasting) of or like meat; brawny; full of significance or interest
Mecca *n* holy city of Islam; place that attracts visitors
mechanic *n* person skilled in repairing or operating machinery **mechanics** *n* scientific study of motion and force **mechanical** *adj* of or done by machines; (of an action) without thought or feeling **mechanically** *adv*
mechanism *n* way a machine works; piece of machinery; process or technique *eg defence mechanism* **mechanize** *v* equip with machinery; make mechanical or automatic; *mil* equip (an army) with armoured vehicles **mechanization** *n*
med. medical; medicine; medieval; medium
medal *n* piece of metal with an inscription etc, given as a reward or memento **medallion** *n* disc-shaped ornament worn on a chain round the neck; large medal; circular decorative device in architecture **medallist** *n* winner of a medal
meddle *v* interfere annoyingly **meddler** *n* **meddlesome** *adj*
media *n* a plural of **medium:** the mass media collectively
mediaeval *adj* same as **medieval**
medial *adj* of or in the middle
median *adj, n* middle (point or line)
mediate *v* intervene in a dispute to bring about agreement **mediation** *n* **mediator** *n*
medic *n Informal* doctor or medical student

medical *adj* of the science of medicine ▷*n Informal* medical examination **medically** *adv* **medicate** *v* treat with a medicinal substance **medication** *n* (treatment with) a medicinal substance

medicine *n* substance used to treat disease; science of preventing, diagnosing, or curing disease **medicinal** [med-**diss**-in-al] *adj* having therapeutic properties **medicine man** witch doctor

medieval [med-ee-**eve**-al] *adj* of the Middle Ages

mediocre [mee-dee-**oak**-er] *adj* average in quality; second-rate **mediocrity** [mee-dee-**ok**-rit-ee] *n*

meditate *v* reflect deeply, esp on spiritual matters; think about or plan **meditation** *n* **meditative** *adj* **meditatively** *adv* **meditator** *n*

medium *adj* midway between extremes, average ▷*n, pl* **-dia, -diums** middle state, degree, or condition; intervening substance producing an effect; means of communicating news or information to the public, such as radio or newspapers; person who can supposedly communicate with the dead; surroundings or environment; category of art according to the material used **medium wave** radio wave with a wavelength between 100 and 1000 metres

medlar *n* apple-like fruit of a small tree, eaten when it begins to decay

medley *n* miscellaneous mixture; musical sequence of different tunes

medulla [mid-**dull**-la] *n, pl* **-las, -lae** marrow, pith, or inner tissue

meek *adj* submissive or humble **meekly** *adv* **meekness** *n*

meerkat *n* S African mongoose

meerschaum [**meer**-shum] *n* white substance like clay; tobacco pipe with a bowl made of this

meet[1] *v* **meeting, met** come together (with); come into contact (with); be at the place of arrival of; make the acquaintance of; satisfy (a need etc); experience ▷*n* meeting, esp a sports meeting; assembly of a hunt **meeting** *n* coming together; assembly

meet[2] *adj obs* fit or suitable

mega- *combining form* denoting one million *eg megawatt*; very great *eg megastar*

megabyte *n computers* 2^{20} or 1 048 576 bytes

megahertz *n, pl* **-hertz** one million hertz

megalith *n* great stone, esp as part of a prehistoric monument **megalithic** *adj*

megalomania *n* craving for or mental delusions of power **megalomaniac** *adj, n*

megaphone *n* cone-shaped instrument used to amplify the voice

megapode *n* bird of Australia, New Guinea, and adjacent islands

megaton *n* explosive power equal to that of one million tons of TNT

melaleuca [mel-a-**loo**-ka] *n* Australian shrub or tree with a white trunk and black branches

melancholy [**mel**-an-kol-lee] *n* sadness or gloom ▷*adj* sad or gloomy **melancholia** [mel-an-**kole**-lee-a] *n* state of depression **melancholic** *adj, n*

melange [may-**lahnzh**] *n* mixture

melanin *n* dark pigment found in the hair, skin, and eyes of humans and animals

mêlée [**mel**-lay] *n* noisy confused fight or crowd

mellifluous [mel-**lif**-flew-uss] *adj* (of sound) smooth and sweet
mellow *adj* soft, not harsh; kind-hearted, esp through maturity; (of fruit) ripe ▷ *v* make or become mellow
melodrama *n* play full of extravagant action and emotion; overdramatic behaviour or emotion **melodramatic** *adj*
melody *n, pl* **-dies** series of musical notes which make a tune; sweet sound **melodic** [mel-**lod**-ik] *adj* of melody; melodious **melodious** [mel-**lode**-ee-uss] *adj* pleasing to the ear; tuneful
melon *n* large round juicy fruit with a hard rind
melt *v* (cause to) become liquid by heat; dissolve; disappear; blend (into); soften through emotion **meltdown** *n* (in a nuclear reactor) melting of the fuel rods, with the possible release of radiation
member *n* individual making up a body or society; limb **membership** *n* **Member of Parliament** person elected to parliament
membrane *n* thin flexible tissue in a plant or animal body **membranous** *adj*
memento *n, pl* **-tos, -toes** thing serving to remind, souvenir
memo *n, pl* **memos** short for **memorandum**
memoir [**mem**-wahr] *n* biography or historical account based on personal knowledge ▷ *pl* collection of these; autobiography
memorable *adj* worth remembering, noteworthy **memorably** *adv*
memorandum *n, pl* **-dums, -da** written record or communication within a business; note of things to be remembered
memory *n, pl* **-ries** ability to remember; sum of things remembered; particular recollection; length of time one can remember; commemoration; part of a computer which stores information **memorize** *v* commit to memory **memorial** *n* something serving to commemorate a person or thing ▷ *adj* serving as a memorial
men *n* plural of **man**
menace *n* threat; *Informal* nuisance ▷ *v* threaten, endanger **menacing** *adj*
ménage [may-**nahzh**] *n* household
menagerie [min-**naj**-er-ee] *n* collection of wild animals for exhibition
mend *v* repair or patch; recover or heal; make or become better ▷ *n* mended area **on the mend** regaining health
mendacity *n* (tendency to) untruthfulness **mendacious** *adj*
mendicant *adj* begging ▷ *n* beggar
menhir [**men**-hear] *n* single upright prehistoric stone
menial [**mean**-nee-al] *adj* involving boring work of low status ▷ *n* person with a menial job
meningitis [men-in-**jite**-iss] *n* inflammation of the membranes of the brain
meniscus *n* curved surface of a liquid; crescent-shaped lens
menopause *n* time when a woman's menstrual cycle ceases **menopausal** *adj*
menstruation *n* approximately monthly discharge of blood and cellular debris from the womb of a nonpregnant woman **menstruate** *v* **menstrual** *adj*

mensuration *n* measuring, esp in geometry
mental *adj* of, in, or done by the mind; of or for mental illness; *Informal* insane **mentally** *adv* **mentality** *n* way of thinking
menthol *n* organic compound found in peppermint, used medicinally
mention *v* refer to briefly; acknowledge ▷ *n* brief reference to a person or thing; acknowledgment
mentor *n* adviser or guide
menu *n* list of dishes to be served, or from which to order; *computers* list of options displayed on a screen
MEP Member of the European Parliament
mercantile *adj* of trade or traders
mercenary *adj* influenced by greed; working merely for reward ▷ *n, pl* **-aries** hired soldier
merchandise *n* commodities
merchant *n* person engaged in trade, wholesale trader **merchant bank** bank dealing mainly with businesses and investment **merchantman** *n* trading ship **merchant navy** ships or crew engaged in a nation's commercial shipping
mercury *n chem* silvery liquid metal; (**M-**) *Roman myth* messenger of the gods; (**M-**) planet nearest the sun **mercurial** *adj* lively, changeable
mercy *n, pl* **-cies** compassionate treatment of an offender or enemy who is in one's power; merciful act **merciful** *adj* compassionate; giving relief **merciless** *adj*
mere[1] *adj* nothing more than *eg mere chance* **merely** *adv*
mere[2] *n Brit, obs* lake
meretricious *adj* superficially or garishly attractive but of no real value
merganser [mer-**gan**-ser] *n* large crested diving duck
merge *v* combine or blend
merger *n* combination of business firms into one
meridian *n* imaginary circle of the earth passing through both poles
meringue [mer-**rang**] *n* baked mixture of egg whites and sugar; small cake of this
merino *n, pl* **-nos** breed of sheep with fine soft wool; this wool
merit *n* excellence or worth ▷ *pl* admirable qualities ▷ *v* **-iting, -ited** deserve **meritorious** *adj* deserving praise **meritocracy** [mer-it-**tok**-rass-ee] *n* rule by people of superior talent or intellect
merlin *n* small falcon
mermaid *n* imaginary sea creature with the upper part of a woman and the lower part of a fish
merry *adj* **-rier, -riest** cheerful or jolly; *Informal* slightly drunk **merrily** *adv* **merriment** *n* **merry-go-round** *n* roundabout **merrymaking** *n* noisy, cheerful celebrations or fun
mesdames *n* plural of **madame**
mesdemoiselles *n* plural of **mademoiselle**
mesh *n* network or net; (open space between) strands forming a network ▷ *v* (of gear teeth) engage
mesmerize *v* hold spellbound; *obs* hypnotize
meson [**mee**-zon] *n* elementary atomic particle
mess *n* untidy or dirty confusion; trouble or difficulty; place where servicemen eat; group of servicemen who regularly eat together ▷ *v* muddle or dirty; (foll by *about*) potter about; (foll by *with*) interfere with; *Brit, Aust & NZ* (of

servicemen) eat in a group
message *n* communication sent; meaning or moral **messaging** *n* sending and receiving of textual communications by mobile phone **messenger** *n* bearer of a message
Messiah *n* Jews' promised deliverer; Christ **Messianic** *adj*
messieurs *n* plural of **monsieur**
Messrs [mess-erz] *n* plural of **Mr**
messy *adj* **messier, messiest** dirty, confused, or untidy **messily** *adv*
met *v* past of **meet**[1]
metabolism [met-**tab**-oh-liz-zum] *n* chemical processes of a living body **metabolic** *adj* **metabolize** *v* produce or be produced by metabolism
metal *n* chemical element, such as iron or copper, that is malleable and capable of conducting heat and electricity **metallic** *adj* **metallurgy** *n* scientific study of the structure, properties, extraction, and refining of metals **metallurgical** *adj* **metallurgist** *n* **metal road** *NZ* unsealed road covered in gravel
metamorphosis [met-a-**more**-foss-is] *n, pl* **-phoses** [-foss-eez] change of form or character **metamorphic** *adj* (of rocks) changed in texture or structure by heat and pressure **metamorphose** *v* transform
metaphor *n* figure of speech in which a term is applied to something it does not literally denote in order to imply a resemblance *eg he is a lion in battle* **metaphorical** *adj* **metaphorically** *adv*
metaphysics *n* branch of philosophy concerned with being and knowing **metaphysical** *adj*
mete *v* (usu with *out*) deal out as punishment
meteor *n* small fast-moving heavenly body, visible as a streak of incandescence if it enters the earth's atmosphere **meteoric** [meet-ee-**or**-rik] *adj* of a meteor; brilliant and very rapid **meteorite** *n* meteor that has fallen to earth
meteorology *n* study of the earth's atmosphere, esp for weather forecasting **meteorological** *adj* **meteorologist** *n*
meter *n* instrument for measuring and recording something, such as the consumption of gas or electricity ▷ *v* measure by meter
methane *n* colourless inflammable gas
methanol *n* colourless poisonous liquid used as a solvent and fuel (also **methyl alcohol**)
methinks *v, past tense* **methought** *obs* it seems to me
method *n* way or manner; technique; orderliness **methodical** *adj* orderly **methodically** *adv* **methodology** *n* particular method or procedure
Methodist *n* member of any of the Protestant churches originated by John Wesley and his followers ▷ *adj* of Methodists or their Church **Methodism** *n*
meths *n Informal* methylated spirits
methyl *n* (compound containing) a saturated hydrocarbon group of atoms **methylated spirits** alcohol with methanol added, used as a solvent and for heating
meticulous *adj* very careful about details **meticulously** *adv*
métier [met-ee-ay] *n* profession or trade; one's strong point
metonymy [mit-**on**-im-ee] *n*

figure of speech in which one thing is replaced by another associated with it, such as 'the Crown' for 'the queen'

metre *n* basic unit of length equal to about 1.094 yards (100 centimetres); rhythm of poetry **metric** *adj* of the decimal system of weights and measures based on the metre **metrical** *adj* of measurement; of poetic metre **metrication** *n* conversion to the metric system

metronome *n* instrument which marks musical time by means of a ticking pendulum

metropolis [mit-**trop**-oh-liss] *n* chief city of a country or region

metropolitan *adj* of a metropolis

metrosexual *adj, n Aust* (of) a heterosexual man who is preoccupied with his appearance

mettle *n* courage or spirit

mew *n* cry of a cat ▷*v* utter this cry

mews *n* yard or street orig of stables, now often converted into houses

mezzanine [**mez**-zan-een] *n* intermediate storey, esp between the ground and first floor

mezzo-soprano [**met**-so-] *n* voice or singer between a soprano and contralto (also **mezzo**)

mezzotint [**met**-so-tint] *n* method of engraving by scraping the roughened surface of a metal plate; print so made

mg milligram(s)

MHz megahertz

miaow [mee-**ow**] *n, v* same as **mew**

miasma [mee-**azz**-ma] *n* unwholesome or foreboding atmosphere

mica [**my**-ka] *n* glasslike mineral used as an electrical insulator

mice *n* plural of **mouse**

Michaelmas [**mik**-kl-mass] *n* Sept. 29th, feast of St Michael the archangel **Michaelmas daisy** garden plant with small daisy-shaped flowers

mickey *n* **take the mickey (out of)** *Informal* tease

micro *n, pl* **-cros** short for **microcomputer** or

microbe *n* minute organism, esp one causing disease **microbial** *adj*

microchip *n* small wafer of silicon containing electronic circuits

microcomputer *n* computer with a central processing unit contained in one or more silicon chips

microcosm *n* miniature representation of something

microfiche [**my**-kroh-feesh] *n* microfilm in sheet form

microfilm *n* miniaturized recording of books or documents on a roll of film

microlight *n* very small light private aircraft with large wings

micrometer [my-**krom**-it-er] *n* instrument for measuring very small distances or angles

micron [**my**-kron] *n* one millionth of a metre

microorganism *n* organism of microscopic size

microphone *n* instrument for amplifying or transmitting sounds

microprocessor *n* integrated circuit acting as the central processing unit in a small computer

microscope *n* instrument with lens(es) which produces a magnified image of a very small object **microscopic** *adj* too small to be seen except with a microscope; very small; of a

microscope **microscopically** *adv* **microscopy** *n* use of a microscope
microsurgery *n* intricate surgery using a special microscope and miniature precision instruments
microwave *n* electromagnetic wave with a wavelength of a few centimetres, used in radar and cooking; microwave oven ▷ *v* cook in a microwave oven **microwave oven** oven using microwaves to cook food quickly
mid *adj* intermediate, middle
midday *n* noon
midden *n Brit & Aust* dunghill or rubbish heap
middle *adj* equidistant from two extremes; medium, intermediate ▷ *n* middle point or part **middle age** period of life between youth and old age **middle-aged** *adj* **Middle Ages** period from about 1000AD to the 15th century **middle class** social class of business and professional people **middle-class** *adj* **Middle East** area around the eastern Mediterranean up to and including Iran **middleman** *n* trader who buys from the producer and sells to the consumer **middle-of-the-road** *adj* politically moderate; (of music) generally popular **middleweight** *n* boxer weighing up to 160lb (professional) or 75kg (amateur)
middling *adj* mediocre; moderate
midge *n* small mosquito-like insect
midget *n* very small person or thing
midland *n Brit, Aust & US* middle part of a country ▷ *pl* (**M-**) central England
midnight *n* twelve o'clock at night
midriff *n* middle part of the body
midshipman *n* naval officer of the lowest commissioned rank
midst *n* **in the midst of** surrounded by; at a point during
midsummer *n* middle of summer; summer solstice **Midsummer's Day, Midsummer Day** (in Britain and Ireland) June 24th
midway *adj, adv* halfway
midwife *n* trained person who assists at childbirth **midwifery** *n*
midwinter *n* middle or depth of winter; winter solstice
mien [mean] *n lit* person's bearing, demeanour, or appearance
miffed *adj Informal* offended or upset
might[1] *v* past tense of **may**
might[2] *n* power or strength **with might and main** energetically or forcefully **mighty** *adj* powerful; important ▷ *adv US & Aust, Informal* very **mightily** *adv*
migraine [**mee**-grain] *n* severe headache, often with nausea and visual disturbances
migrate *v* move from one place to settle in another; (of animals) journey between different habitats at specific seasons **migration** *n* **migrant** *n* person or animal that moves from one place to another ▷ *adj* moving from one place to another **migratory** *adj* (of an animal) migrating every year
mike *n Informal* microphone
milch *adj Chiefly Brit* (of a cow) giving milk
mild *adj* not strongly flavoured; gentle; calm or temperate **mildly** *adv* **mildness** *n*
mildew *n* destructive fungus on plants or things exposed to damp **mildewed** *adj*
mile *n* unit of length equal to 1760 yards or 1.609 kilometres **mileage**

n distance travelled in miles; miles travelled by a motor vehicle per gallon of petrol; *Informal* usefulness of something **mileometer** *n Brit* device that records the number of miles a vehicle has travelled **milestone** *n* significant event; stone marker showing the distance to a certain place

milieu [meal-**yer**] *n, pl* **milieux, milieus** [meal-**yerz**] environment or surroundings

militant *adj* aggressive or vigorous in support of a cause **militancy** *n*

military *adj* of or for soldiers, armies, or war ▷ *n* armed services **militarism** *n* belief in the use of military force and methods **militarist** *n* **militarized** *adj*

militate *v* (usu with *against, for*) have a strong influence or effect

militia [mill-**ish**-a] *n* military force of trained citizens for use in emergency only

milk *n* white fluid produced by female mammals to feed their young; milk of cows, goats, etc, used by humans as food; fluid in some plants ▷ *v* draw milk from; exploit (a person or situation) **milky** *adj* **Milky Way** luminous band of stars stretching across the night sky **milk float** *Brit* small electrically powered vehicle used to deliver milk to houses **milkmaid** *n* (esp in former times) woman who milks cows **milkman** *n Brit, Aust & NZ* man who delivers milk to people's houses **milkshake** *n* frothy flavoured cold milk drink **milksop** *n* feeble man **milk teeth** first set of teeth in young children

mill *n* factory; machine for grinding, processing, or rolling ▷ *v* grind, press, or process in or as if in a mill; cut fine grooves across the edges of (coins); (of a crowd) move in a confused manner

millennium *n, pl* **-nia, -niums** period of a thousand years; future period of peace and happiness **millennium bug** computer problem caused by the date change at the beginning of the 21st century

> SPELLING If you spell **millennium** with only one *n*, you are not alone: there are 338 occurrences of this in Collins Word Web. The correct spelling has two *l*s and two *n*s

miller *n* person who works in a mill

millet *n* type of cereal grass

milli- *combining form* denoting a thousandth part *eg millisecond*

millibar *n* unit of atmospheric pressure

millimetre *n* thousandth part of a metre

milliner *n* maker or seller of women's hats **millinery** *n*

million *n* one thousand thousands **millionth** *adj, n* **millionaire** *n* person who owns at least a million pounds, dollars, etc

> SPELLING Lots of people find it difficult to decide how many *l*s and *n*s to put in **millionaire**. They usually get the double *l* right, but remembering the single *n* is trickier

millipede *n* small animal with a jointed body and many pairs of legs

millstone *n* flat circular stone for grinding corn

millwheel *n* waterwheel that drives a mill

milometer *n Brit* same as **mileometer**

milt *n* sperm of fish

mime *n* acting without the use of words; performer who does this ▷ *v*

act in mime
mimic *v* **-icking, -icked** imitate (a person or manner), esp for satirical effect ▷*n* person or animal that is good at mimicking **mimicry** *n*
min. minimum; minute(s)
minaret *n* tall slender tower of a mosque
mince *v* cut or grind into very small pieces; walk or speak in an affected manner; soften or moderate (one's words) ▷*n* minced meat **mincer** *n* machine for mincing meat **mincing** *adj* affected in manner **mincemeat** *n* sweet mixture of dried fruit and spices **mince pie** pie containing mincemeat
mind *n* thinking faculties; memory or attention; intention; sanity ▷*v* take offence at; pay attention to; take care of; be cautious or careful about (something) **minded** *adj* having an inclination as specified *eg politically minded* **minder** *n Informal* aide or bodyguard **mindful** *adj* heedful; keeping aware **mindless** *adj* stupid; requiring no thought; careless
mine¹ *pron* belonging to me
mine² *n* deep hole for digging out coal, ores, etc; bomb placed under the ground or in water; profitable source ▷*v* dig for minerals; dig (minerals) from a mine; place explosive mines in or on **miner** *n* person who works in a mine **minefield** *n* area of land or water containing mines **minesweeper** *n* ship for clearing away mines
mineral *n* naturally occurring inorganic substance, such as metal ▷*adj* of, containing, or like minerals **mineralogy** [min-er-**al**-a-jee] *n* study of minerals **mineral water** water containing dissolved mineral salts or gases
minestrone [min-ness-**strone**-ee] *n* soup containing vegetables and pasta
minger *n Brit, Informal* unattractive person **minging** *adj Brit, Informal* unattractive or unpleasant
mingle *v* mix or blend; come into association (with)
mingy *adj* **-gier, -giest** *Informal* miserly
mini *n, adj* (something) small or miniature; short (skirt)
miniature *n* small portrait, model, or copy ▷*adj* small-scale **miniaturist** *n* **miniaturize** *v* make to a very small scale
minibar *n* selection of drinks and confectionery provided in a hotel room
minibus *n* small bus
minicab *n Brit* ordinary car used as a taxi
minicomputer *n* computer smaller than a mainframe but more powerful than a microcomputer
minidisc *n* small recordable compact disc
minim *n music* note half the length of a semibreve
minimum *adj, n, pl* **-mums, -ma** least possible (amount or number) **minimal** *adj* minimum **minimize** *v* reduce to a minimum; belittle
minion *n* servile assistant
miniseries *n* TV programme shown in several parts, often on consecutive days
minister *n* head of a government department; diplomatic representative; (in nonconformist churches) member of the clergy ▷*v* (foll by *to*) attend to the needs of **ministerial** *adj* **ministration** *n* giving of help **ministry** *n, pl* **-tries** profession or duties of a clergyman;

ministers collectively; government department

mink *n* stoatlike animal; its highly valued fur

minnow *n* small freshwater fish

minor *adj* lesser; *music* (of a scale) having a semitone between the second and third notes ▷*n* person regarded legally as a child; *music* minor scale **minority** *n* lesser number; smaller party voting together; group in a minority in any state

minster *n Brit* cathedral or large church

minstrel *n* medieval singer or musician

mint[1] *n* plant with aromatic leaves used for seasoning and flavouring; sweet flavoured with this

mint[2] *n* place where money is coined ▷*v* make (coins)

minuet [min-new-**wet**] *n* stately dance; music for this

minus *prep, adj* indicating subtraction ▷*adj* less than zero ▷*n* sign (-) denoting subtraction or a number less than zero

minuscule [**min**-niss-skyool] *adj* very small

> SPELLING The pronunciation of **minuscule** often influences the way people spell it. It's spelt *miniscule* 121 times in Collins Word Web, but it should only have one *i* and two *u*s

minute[1] [**min**-it] *n* 60th part of an hour or degree; moment ▷*pl* record of the proceedings of a meeting ▷*v* record in the minutes

minute[2] [my-**newt**] *adj* very small; precise **minutely** *adv* **minutiae** [my-**new**-shee-eye] *pl n* trifling or precise details

minx *n* bold or flirtatious girl

miracle *n* wonderful supernatural event; marvel **miraculous** *adj* **miraculously** *adv* **miracle play** medieval play based on a sacred subject

mirage [mir-**rahzh**] *n* optical illusion, esp one caused by hot air

mire *n* swampy ground; mud

mirror *n* coated glass surface for reflecting images ▷*v* reflect in or as if in a mirror

mirth *n* laughter, merriment, or gaiety **mirthful** *adj* **mirthless** *adj*

mis- *prefix* wrong(ly), bad(ly)

misadventure *n* unlucky chance

misanthrope [**miz**-zan-thrope] *n* person who dislikes people in general **misanthropic** [miz-zan-**throp**-ik] *adj* **misanthropy** [miz-**zan**-throp-ee] *n*

misapprehend *v* misunderstand **misapprehension** *n*

misappropriate *v* take and use (money) dishonestly **misappropriation** *n*

miscarriage *n* spontaneous premature expulsion of a fetus from the womb; failure *eg a miscarriage of justice* **miscarry** *v* have a miscarriage; fail

miscast *v* **-casting, -cast** cast (a role or actor) in (a play or film) inappropriately

miscegenation [miss-ij-in-**nay**-shun] *n* interbreeding of races

miscellaneous [miss-sell-**lane**-ee-uss] *adj* mixed or assorted **miscellany** [miss-**sell**-a-nee] *n* mixed assortment

mischance *n* unlucky event

mischief *n* annoying but not malicious behaviour; inclination to tease; harm **mischievous** *adj* full of mischief; intended to cause harm

mischievously *adv*
miscible [miss-sib-bl] *adj* able to be mixed
misconception *n* wrong idea or belief
misconduct *n* immoral or unethical behaviour
miscreant [miss-kree-ant] *n* wrongdoer
misdeed *n* wrongful act
misdemeanour *n* minor wrongdoing
miser *n* person who hoards money and hates spending it **miserly** *adj*
miserable *adj* very unhappy, wretched; causing misery; squalid; mean **misery** *n, pl* **-eries** great unhappiness; *Informal* complaining person
misfire *v* (of a firearm or engine) fail to fire correctly; (of a plan) fail to turn out as intended
misfit *n* person not suited to his or her social environment
misfortune *n* (piece of) bad luck
misgiving *n* feeling of fear or doubt
misguided *adj* mistaken or unwise
mishandle *v* handle badly or inefficiently
mishap *n* minor accident
misinform *v* give incorrect information to **misinformation** *n*
misjudge *v* judge wrongly or unfairly **misjudgment, misjudgement** *n*
mislay *v* lose (something) temporarily
mislead *v* give false or confusing information to **misleading** *adj*
mismanage *v* organize or run (something) badly **mismanagement** *n*
misnomer [miss-**no**-mer] *n* incorrect or unsuitable name; use of this
misogyny [miss-**oj**-in-ee] *n* hatred of women **misogynist** *n*
misplace *v* mislay; put in the wrong place; give (trust or affection) inappropriately
misprint *n* printing error
misrepresent *v* represent wrongly or inaccurately
miss *v* fail to notice, hear, hit, reach, find, or catch; not be in time for; notice or regret the absence of; avoid; (of an engine) misfire ▷ *n* fact or instance of missing **missing** *adj* lost or absent
Miss *n* title of a girl or unmarried woman
missal *n* book containing the prayers and rites of the Mass
misshapen *adj* badly shaped, deformed
missile *n* object or weapon thrown, shot, or launched at a target
mission *n* specific task or duty; group of people sent on a mission; building in which missionaries work; *SAfr* long and difficult process **missionary** *n, pl* **-aries** person sent abroad to do religious and social work
missive *n* letter
misspent *adj* wasted or misused
mist *n* thin fog; fine spray of liquid **misty** *adj* full of mist; dim or obscure
mistake *n* error or blunder ▷ *v* **-taking, -took, -taken** misunderstand; confuse (a person or thing) with another
Mister *n* polite form of address to a man
mistletoe *n* evergreen plant with white berries growing as a parasite on trees
mistral *n* strong dry northerly

wind of S France

mistress *n* woman who has a continuing sexual relationship with a married man; woman in control of people or animals; female teacher

mistrial *n law* trial made void because of some error

mistrust *v* have doubts or suspicions about ▷*n* lack of trust **mistrustful** *adj*

misunderstand *v* fail to understand properly **misunderstanding** *n*

misuse *n* incorrect, improper, or careless use ▷*v* use wrongly; treat badly

mite *n* very small spider-like animal; very small thing or amount

mitigate *v* make less severe **mitigation** *n*

mitre [my-ter] *n* bishop's pointed headdress; joint between two pieces of wood bevelled to meet at right angles ▷*v* join with a mitre joint

mitt *n* short for **mitten:** baseball catcher's glove

mitten *n* glove with one section for the thumb and one for the four fingers together

mix *v* combine or blend into one mass; form (something) by mixing; be sociable ▷*n* mixture **mixed** *adj* **mix up** *v* confuse; make into a mixture **mixed up** *adj* **mix-up** *n* **mixer** *n* **mixture** *n* something mixed; combination

mizzenmast *n* (on a vessel with three or more masts) third mast from the bow

mm millimetre(s)

mnemonic [nim-**on**-ik] *n, adj* (something, such as a rhyme) intended to help the memory

mo *n, pl* **mos** *Informal* short for moment

MO Medical Officer

moa *n* large extinct flightless New Zealand bird

moan *n* low cry of pain; *Informal* grumble ▷*v* make or utter with a moan; *Informal* grumble

moat *n* deep wide ditch, esp round a castle

mob *n* disorderly crowd; *slang* gang ▷*v* **mobbing, mobbed** surround in a mob to acclaim or attack

mobile *adj* able to move ▷*n* same as **mobile phone:** hanging structure designed to move in air currents **mobile phone** cordless phone powered by batteries **mobility** *n*

mobilize *v* (of the armed services) prepare for active service; organize for a purpose **mobilization** *n*

moccasin *n* soft leather shoe

> SPELLING **Moccasin** has a double *c*, but only one *s*. The plural is spelt **moccasins**

mocha [**mock**-a] *n* kind of strong dark coffee; flavouring made from coffee and chocolate

mock *v* make fun of; mimic ▷*adj* sham or imitation **mocks** *pl n* *Informal* (in England and Wales) practice exams taken before public exams **put the mockers on** *Brit, Aust & NZ, Informal* ruin the chances of success of **mockery** *n* derision; inadequate or worthless attempt **mockingbird** *n* N American bird which imitates other birds' songs **mock orange** shrub with white fragrant flowers **mock-up** *n* full-scale model for test or study

mod. moderate; modern

mode *n* method or manner; current fashion

model *n* (miniature) representation; pattern; person or thing worthy of imitation; person who poses for an artist or photographer; person who wears clothes to display them to prospective buyers ▷ *v* **-elling, -elled** make a model of; mould; display (clothing) as a model

modem [**mode**-em] *n* device for connecting two computers by a telephone line

moderate *adj* not extreme; self-restrained; average ▷ *n* person of moderate views ▷ *v* make or become less violent or extreme **moderately** *adv* **moderation** *n* **moderator** *n* (Presbyterian Church) minister appointed to preside over a Church court, general assembly, etc; person who presides over a public or legislative assembly

modern *adj* of present or recent times; up-to-date **modernity** *n* **modernism** *n* (support of) modern tendencies, thoughts, or styles **modernist** *adj, n* **modernize** *v* bring up to date **modernization** *n*

modest *adj* not vain or boastful; not excessive; not showy; shy **modestly** *adv* **modesty** *n*

modicum *n* small quantity

modify *v* **-fying, -fied** change slightly; tone down; (of a word) qualify (another word) **modifier** *n* word that qualifies the sense of another **modification** *n*

modish [**mode**-ish] *adj* in fashion

modulate *v* vary in tone; adjust; change the key of (music) **modulation** *n* **modulator** *n*

module *n* self-contained unit, section, or component with a specific function

modus operandi [**mode**-uss op-er-**an**-die] *n Latin* method of operating

mogul [**moh**-gl] *n* important or powerful person

mohair *n* fine hair of the Angora goat; yarn or fabric made from this

mohican *n* punk hairstyle with shaved sides and a stiff central strip of hair, often brightly coloured

moiety [**moy**-it-ee] *n, pl* **-ties** half

moist *adj* slightly wet **moisten** *v* make or become moist **moisture** *n* liquid diffused as vapour or condensed in drops **moisturize** *v* add moisture to (the skin etc)

molar *n* large back tooth used for grinding

molasses *n* dark syrup, a by-product of sugar refining

mole[1] *n* small dark raised spot on the skin

mole[2] *n* small burrowing mammal; *Informal* spy who has infiltrated and become a trusted member of an organization

mole[3] *n* unit of amount of substance

mole[4] *n* breakwater; harbour protected by this

molecule [**mol**-lik-kyool] *n* simplest freely existing chemical unit, composed of two or more atoms; very small particle **molecular** [mol-**lek**-yew-lar] *adj*

molest *v* interfere with sexually; annoy or injure **molester** *n* **molestation** *n*

moll *n slang* gangster's female accomplice

mollify *v* **-fying, -fied** pacify or soothe

mollusc *n* soft-bodied, usu hard-shelled, animal, such as a snail or oyster

mollycoddle *v* pamper

Molotov cocktail *n* petrol bomb

molten *adj* liquefied or melted

molybdenum [mol-**lib**-din-um] *n chem* hard silvery-white metallic element

moment *n* short space of time; (present) point in time **momentary** *adj* lasting only a moment **momentarily** *adv*

momentous [moh-**men**-tuss] *adj* of great significance

momentum *n* impetus of a moving body; product of a body's mass and velocity

monarch *n* sovereign ruler of a state **monarchical** *adj* **monarchist** *n* supporter of monarchy **monarchy** *n* government by or a state ruled by a sovereign

monastery *n, pl* **-teries** residence of a community of monks **monastic** *adj* of monks, nuns, or monasteries; simple and austere **monasticism** *n*

Monday *n* second day of the week

monetary *adj* of money or currency **monetarism** *n* theory that inflation is caused by an increase in the money supply **monetarist** *n, adj*

money *n* medium of exchange, coins or banknotes **moneyed, monied** *adj* rich

mongol *n, adj offens* (person) affected by Down's syndrome **mongolism** *n*

mongoose *n, pl* **-gooses** stoatlike mammal of Asia and Africa that kills snakes

mongrel *n* animal, esp a dog, of mixed breed; something arising from a variety of sources ▷ *adj* of mixed breed or origin

monitor *n* person or device that checks, controls, warns, or keeps a record of something; *Brit, Aust & NZ* pupil assisting a teacher with duties; television set used in a studio to check what is being transmitted; large lizard of Africa, Asia, and Australia ▷ *v* watch and check on

monk *n* member of an all-male religious community bound by vows **monkish** *adj*

monkey *n* long-tailed primate; mischievous child ▷ *v* (usu foll by *about, around*) meddle or fool **monkey nut** *Brit* peanut **monkey puzzle** coniferous tree with sharp stiff leaves **monkey wrench** wrench with adjustable jaws

mono- *combining form* single *eg monosyllable*

monochrome *adj photog* black-and-white; in only one colour

monocle *n* eyeglass for one eye only

monogamy *n* custom of being married to one person at a time

monogram *n* design of combined letters, esp a person's initials

monograph *n* book or paper on a single subject

monolith *n* large upright block of stone **monolithic** *adj*

monologue *n* long speech by one person; dramatic piece for one performer

monomania *n* obsession with one thing **monomaniac** *n, adj*

monoplane *n* aeroplane with one pair of wings

monopoly *n, pl* **-lies** exclusive possession of or right to do something; **(M-)**® board game for four to six players who deal in 'property' as they move around the board **monopolize** *v* have or take exclusive possession of

monorail *n* single-rail railway

monotheism *n* belief in only one God **monotheistic** *adj*

monotone *n* unvaried pitch in speech or sound **monotonous** *adj* tedious due to lack of variety **monotonously** *adv* **monotony** *n*

Monseigneur [mon-sen-**nyur**] *n, pl* **Messeigneurs** [may-sen-**nyur**] title of French prelates

monsieur [muss-**syur**] *n, pl* **messieurs** [may-**syur**] French title of address equivalent to *sir* or *Mr*

Monsignor *n RC church* title attached to certain offices

monsoon *n* seasonal wind of SE Asia; rainy season accompanying this

monster *n* imaginary, usu frightening, beast; huge person, animal, or thing; very wicked person ▷ *adj* huge **monstrosity** *n* large ugly thing **monstrous** *adj* unnatural or ugly; outrageous or shocking; huge **monstrously** *adv*

monstrance *n RC church* container in which the consecrated Host is exposed for adoration

montage [**mon**-tahzh] *n* (making of) a picture composed from pieces of others; method of film editing incorporating several shots to form a single image

month *n* one of the twelve divisions of the calendar year; period of four weeks **monthly** *adj* happening or payable once a month ▷ *adv* once a month ▷ *n* monthly magazine

monument *n* something, esp a building or statue, that commemorates something **monumental** *adj* large, impressive, or lasting; of or being a monument; *Informal* extreme **monumentally** *adv*

moo *n* long deep cry of a cow ▷ *v* make this noise

mooch *v slang* loiter about aimlessly

mood[1] *n* temporary (gloomy) state of mind **moody** *adj* sullen or gloomy; changeable in mood **moodily** *adv*

mood[2] *n grammar* form of a verb indicating whether it expresses a fact, wish, supposition, or command

moon *n* natural satellite of the earth; natural satellite of any planet ▷ *v* (foll by *about, around*) be idle in a listless or dreamy way **moonlight** *n* light from the moon ▷ *v Informal* work at a secondary job, esp illegally **moonshine** *n US & Canad* illicitly distilled whisky; nonsense **moonstone** *n* translucent semiprecious stone **moonstruck** *adj* slightly mad or odd

moor[1] *n Brit* tract of open uncultivated ground covered with grass and heather **moorhen** *n* small black water bird

moor[2] *v* secure (a ship) with ropes etc **mooring** *n* place for mooring a ship ▷ *pl* ropes etc used in mooring a ship

Moor *n* member of a Muslim people of NW Africa who ruled Spain between the 8th and 15th centuries **Moorish** *adj*

moose *n* large N American deer

moot *adj* debatable *eg a moot point* ▷ *v* bring up for discussion

mop *n* long stick with twists of cotton or a sponge on the end, used for cleaning; thick mass of hair ▷ *v* **mopping, mopped** clean or soak up with or as if with a mop

mope *v* be gloomy and apathetic

moped *n* light motorized cycle

mopoke *n* small spotted owl of Australia and New Zealand

moraine *n* accumulated mass of debris deposited by a glacier

moral *adj* concerned with right and wrong conduct; based on a sense of right and wrong; (of support or a victory) psychological rather than practical ▷*n* lesson to be obtained from a story or event ▷*pl* principles of behaviour with respect to right and wrong **morally** *adv* **moralist** *n* person with a strong sense of right and wrong **morality** *n* good moral conduct; moral goodness or badness **morality play** medieval play with a moral lesson **moralize** *v* make moral pronouncements

morale [mor-**rahl**] *n* degree of confidence or hope of a person or group

morass *n* marsh; mess

moratorium *n, pl* **-ria, -riums** legally authorized ban or delay

moray *n* large voracious eel

morbid *adj* unduly interested in death or unpleasant events; gruesome

mordant *adj* sarcastic or scathing ▷*n* substance used to fix dyes

more *adj* greater in amount or degree; comparative of **much** or additional or further ▷*adv* to a greater extent; in addition ▷*pron* greater or additional amount or number **moreover** *adv* in addition to what has already been said

mores [**more**-rayz] *pl n* customs and conventions embodying the fundamental values of a community

Moreton Bay bug *n* Australian flattish edible shellfish

morganatic marriage *n* marriage of a person of high rank to a lower-ranking person whose status remains unchanged

morgue *n* mortuary

moribund *adj* without force or vitality

Mormon *n* member of a religious sect founded in the USA

morn *n poetic* morning

morning *n* part of the day before noon **morning-glory** *n* plant with trumpet-shaped flowers which close in the late afternoon

morocco *n* goatskin leather

moron *n Informal* foolish or stupid person; (formerly) person with a low intelligence quotient **moronic** *adj*

morose [mor-**rohss**] *adj* sullen or moody

morphine, morphia *n* drug extracted from opium, used as an anaesthetic and sedative

morphology *n* science of forms and structures of organisms or words **morphological** *adj*

morris dance *n* traditional English folk dance

morrow *n poetic* next day

Morse *n* former system of signalling in which letters of the alphabet are represented by combinations of short and long signals

morsel *n* small piece, esp of food

mortal *adj* subject to death; causing death ▷*n* human being **mortally** *adv* **mortality** *n* state of being mortal; great loss of life; death rate **mortal sin** *RC church* sin meriting damnation

mortar *n* small cannon with a short range; mixture of lime, sand, and water for holding bricks and stones together; bowl in which substances are pounded **mortarboard** *n* black square academic cap

mortgage *n* conditional pledging of property, esp a house, as security for the repayment of a loan; the loan itself ▷*v* pledge (property) as security thus **mortgagee** *n* creditor in a mortgage **mortgagor** *n* debtor in a mortgage

mortice, mortise [more-tiss] *n* hole in a piece of wood or stone shaped to receive a matching projection on another piece **mortice lock** lock set into a door

mortify *v* **-fying, -fied** humiliate; subdue by self-denial; (of flesh) become gangrenous **mortification** *n*

mortuary *n, pl* **-aries** building where corpses are kept before burial or cremation

mosaic [mow-**zay**-ik] *n* design or decoration using small pieces of coloured stone or glass

Mosaic *adj* of Moses

Moselle *n* light white German wine

Moslem *n, adj* same as **Muslim**

mosque *n* Muslim temple

mosquito *n, pl* **-toes, -tos** blood-sucking flying insect

moss *n* small flowerless plant growing in masses on moist surfaces **mossy** *adj*

most *n* greatest number or degree ▷*adj* greatest in number or degree; superlative of **much** or **many** ▷*adv* in the greatest degree **mostly** *adv* for the most part, generally

MOT, MOT test *n* (in Britain) compulsory annual test of the roadworthiness of vehicles over a certain age

motel *n* roadside hotel for motorists

motet *n* short sacred choral song

moth *n* nocturnal insect like a butterfly **mothball** *n* small ball of camphor or naphthalene used to repel moths from stored clothes ▷*v* store (something operational) for future use; postpone (a project etc) **moth-eaten** *adj* decayed or scruffy; eaten or damaged by moth larvae

mother *n* female parent; head of a female religious community ▷*adj* native or inborn *eg mother wit* ▷*v* look after as a mother **motherhood** *n* **motherly** *adj* **motherless** *adj* **mother-in-law** *n* mother of one's husband or wife **mother of pearl** iridescent lining of certain shells **mother tongue** one's native language

motif [moh-**teef**] *n* (recurring) theme or design

motion *n* process, action, or way of moving; proposal in a meeting; evacuation of the bowels ▷*v* direct (someone) by gesture **motionless** *adj* not moving **motion picture** cinema film

motive *n* reason for a course of action ▷*adj* causing motion **motivate** *v* give incentive to **motivation** *n*

motley *adj* miscellaneous; multicoloured

motocross *n* motorcycle race over a rough course

motor *n* engine, esp of a vehicle; machine that converts electrical energy into mechanical energy; *Chiefly Brit* car ▷*v* travel by car **motorist** *n* driver of a car **motorized** *adj* equipped with a motor or motor transport **motorbike** *n* **motorboat** *n* **motorcar** *n* **motorcycle** *n* **motorcyclist** *n* **motor scooter** light motorcycle with small wheels and an enclosed engine **motorway** *n* main road for fast-moving traffic

mottled *adj* marked with blotches

motto *n, pl* **-toes, -tos** saying expressing an ideal or rule of conduct; verse or maxim in a paper cracker

mould[1] *n* hollow container in which metal etc is cast; shape, form, or pattern; nature or character ▷*v* shape; influence or direct **moulding** *n* moulded ornamental edging

mould[2] *n* fungal growth caused by dampness **mouldy** *adj* stale or musty; dull or boring

mould[3] *n* loose soil **moulder** *v* decay into dust

moult *v* shed feathers, hair, or skin to make way for new growth ▷*n* process of moulting

mound *n* heap, esp of earth or stones; small hill

mount *v* climb or ascend; get up on (a horse etc); increase or accumulate; fix on a support or backing; organize *eg mount a campaign* ▷*n* backing or support on which something is fixed; horse for riding; hill

mountain *n* hill of great size; large heap **mountainous** *adj* full of mountains; huge **mountaineer** *n* person who climbs mountains **mountaineering** *n* **mountain bike** bicycle with straight handlebars and heavy-duty tyres, for cycling over rough terrain **mountain oyster** *NZ, Informal* sheep's testicle eaten as food

mountebank *n* charlatan or fake

Mountie *n Informal* member of the Royal Canadian Mounted Police

mourn *v* feel or express sorrow for (a dead person or lost thing) **mournful** *adj* sad or dismal **mournfully** *adv* **mourning** *n* grieving; conventional symbols of grief for death, such as the wearing of black

mourner *n* person attending a funeral

mouse *n, pl* **mice** small long-tailed rodent; timid person; *computers* hand-held device for moving the cursor without keying **mouser** *n* cat used to catch mice **mousy** *adj* like a mouse, esp in hair colour; meek and shy

mousse *n* dish of flavoured cream whipped and set

moustache *n* hair on the upper lip

mouth *n* opening in the head for eating and issuing sounds; entrance; point where a river enters the sea; opening ▷*v* form (words) with the lips without speaking; speak or utter insincerely, esp in public **mouthful** *n* amount of food or drink put into the mouth at any one time when eating or drinking **mouth organ** same as **harmonica** **mouthpiece** *n* part of a telephone into which a person speaks; part of a wind instrument into which the player blows; spokesperson

move *v* change in place or position; change (one's house etc); take action; stir the emotions of; incite; suggest (a proposal) formally ▷*n* moving; action towards some goal **movable, moveable** *adj* **movement** *n* action or process of moving; group with a common aim; division of a piece of music; moving parts of a machine

movie *n Informal* cinema film

mow *v* **mowing, mowed, mowed** *or* **mown** cut (grass or crops) **mow down** *v* kill in large numbers

mower *n* machine for cutting grass

mozzarella [mot-sa-**rel**-la] *n* moist white cheese originally made in Italy from buffalo milk

MP Member of Parliament; Military

Police(man)

MP3 *computing* Motion Picture Expert Group-1, Audio Layer-3: a digital compression format used to compress audio files to a fraction of their original size without loss of sound quality

MPEG [**em**-peg] *computing* Motion Picture Expert Group: standard compressed file format used for audio and video files; file in this format

mpg miles per gallon

mph miles per hour

Mr Mister

Mrs *n* title of a married woman

Ms [**mizz**] *n* title used instead of Miss or Mrs

MS manuscript; multiple sclerosis

MSc Master of Science

MSP (in Britain) Member of the Scottish Parliament

MSS manuscripts

Mt Mount

much *adj* **more, most** large amount or degree of ▷ *n* large amount or degree ▷ *adv* **more, most** to a great degree; nearly

mucilage [**mew**-sill-ij] *n* gum or glue

muck *n* dirt, filth; manure **mucky** *adj*

mucus [**mew**-kuss] *n* slimy secretion of the mucous membranes **mucous membrane** tissue lining body cavities or passages

mud *n* wet soft earth **muddy** *adj* **mudguard** *n* cover over a wheel to prevent mud or water being thrown up by it **mud pack** cosmetic paste to improve the complexion

muddle *v* (often foll by *up*) confuse; mix up ▷ *n* state of confusion

muesli [**mewz**-lee] *n* mixture of grain, nuts, and dried fruit, eaten with milk

muezzin [moo-**ezz**-in] *n* official who summons Muslims to prayer

muff[1] *n* tube-shaped covering to keep the hands warm

muff[2] *v* bungle (an action)

muffin *n* light round flat yeast cake

muffle *v* wrap up for warmth or to deaden sound **muffler** *n Brit* scarf; device to reduce the noise of an engine exhaust

mufti *n* civilian clothes worn by a person who usually wears a uniform

mug[1] *n* large drinking cup

mug[2] *n slang* face; *slang* gullible person ▷ *v* **mugging, mugged** *Informal* attack in order to rob **mugger** *n*

mug[3] *v* **mugging, mugged** (foll by *up*) *Informal* study hard

muggins *n Informal* stupid or gullible person

muggy *adj* **-gier, -giest** (of weather) damp and stifling

mulatto [mew-**lat**-toe] *n, pl* **-tos, -toes** child of one Black and one White parent

mulberry *n* tree whose leaves are used to feed silkworms; purple fruit of this tree

mulch *n* mixture of wet straw, leaves, etc, used to protect the roots of plants ▷ *v* cover (land) with mulch

mule[1] *n* offspring of a horse and a donkey **mulish** *adj* obstinate

mule[2] *n* backless shoe or slipper

mulga *n* Australian acacia shrub growing in desert regions; *Aust* the outback

mull *v* think (over) or ponder **mulled** *adj* (of wine or ale) flavoured with sugar and spices and served hot

mullah *n* Muslim scholar, teacher, or religious leader

mullet[1] *n* edible sea fish
mullet[2] *n* haircut in which the hair is short at the top and sides and long at the back
mulligatawny *n* soup made with curry powder
mullion *n* vertical dividing bar in a window **mullioned** *adj*
mulloway *n* large Australian sea fish, valued for sport and food
multi- *combining form* many *eg multicultural; multistorey*
multifarious [mull-tee-**fare**-ee-uss] *adj* having many various parts
multiple *adj* having many parts ▷*n* quantity which contains another an exact number of times
multiplex *n* purpose-built complex containing several cinemas and usu restaurants and bars ▷*adj* having many elements, complex
multiplicity *n, pl* **-ties** large number or great variety
multiply *v* **-plying, -plied** (cause to) increase in number, quantity, or degree; add (a number or quantity) to itself a given number of times; increase in number by reproduction **multiplication** *n* **multiplicand** *n maths* number to be multiplied
multipurpose *adj* having many uses *eg a multipurpose tool* **multipurpose vehicle** large vanlike car designed to carry up to eight passengers
multitude *n* great number; great crowd **multitudinous** *adj* very numerous
mum[1] *n Informal* mother
mum[2] *adj* **keep mum** remain silent
mumble *v* speak indistinctly, mutter
mumbo jumbo *n* meaningless language; foolish religious ritual or incantation
mummer *n* actor in a traditional English folk play or mime
mummy[1] *n, pl* **-mies** body embalmed and wrapped for burial in ancient Egypt **mummified** *adj* (of a body) preserved as a mummy
mummy[2] *n, pl* **-mies** child's word for **mother**
mumps *n* infectious disease with swelling in the glands of the neck
munch *v* chew noisily and steadily
mundane *adj* everyday; earthly
municipal *adj* relating to a city or town **municipality** *n* city or town with local self-government; governing body of this
munificent [mew-**niff**-fiss-sent] *adj* very generous **munificence** *n*
muniments *pl n* title deeds or similar documents
munitions *pl n* military stores
munted *adj NZ, slang* destroyed or ruined; abnormal or peculiar
mural *n* painting on a wall
murder *n* unlawful intentional killing of a human being ▷*v* kill in this way **murderer, murderess** *n* **murderous** *adj*
murky *adj* dark or gloomy **murk** *n* thick darkness
murmur *v* **-muring, -mured** speak or say in a quiet indistinct way; complain ▷*n* continuous low indistinct sound
muscle *n* tissue in the body which produces movement by contracting; strength or power **muscular** *adj* with well-developed muscles; of muscles **muscular dystrophy** disease with wasting of the muscles **muscle in** *v Informal* force one's way in
muse *v* ponder quietly
Muse *n Greek myth* one of nine

goddesses, each of whom inspired an art or science; (**m-**) force that inspires a creative artist
museum *n* building where natural, artistic, historical, or scientific objects are exhibited and preserved
mush *n* soft pulpy mass; *Informal* cloying sentimentality **mushy** *adj*
mushroom *n* edible fungus with a stem and cap ▷*v* grow rapidly
music *n* art form using a melodious and harmonious combination of notes; written or printed form of this **musical** *adj* of or like music; talented in or fond of music; pleasant-sounding ▷*n* play or film with songs and dancing **musically** *adv* **musician** *n* **musicology** *n* scientific study of music **musicologist** *n* **music centre** *Brit* combined record or CD player, radio, and cassette player **music hall** variety theatre
musk *n* scent obtained from a gland of the musk deer or produced synthetically **musky** *adj* **muskrat** *n* N American beaver-like rodent; its fur
musket *n hist* long-barrelled gun **musketeer** *n* **musketry** *n* (use of) muskets
Muslim *n* follower of the religion of Islam ▷*adj* of or relating to Islam
muslin *n* fine cotton fabric
mussel *n* edible shellfish with a dark hinged shell
must[1] *v* used as an auxiliary to express obligation, certainty, or resolution ▷*n* essential or necessary thing
must[2] *n* newly pressed grape juice
mustang *n* wild horse of SW USA
mustard *n* paste made from the powdered seeds of a plant, used as a condiment; the plant **mustard gas** poisonous gas causing blistering burns and blindness
muster *v* assemble ▷*n* assembly of military personnel
musty *adj* **mustier, mustiest** smelling mouldy and stale **mustiness** *n*
mutable [**mew**-tab-bl] *adj* liable to change **mutability** *n*
mutation *n* (genetic) change **mutate** *v* (cause to) undergo mutation **mutant** *n* mutated animal, plant, etc
mute *adj* silent; unable to speak ▷*n* person who is unable to speak; *music* device to soften the tone of an instrument **muted** *adj* (of sound or colour) softened; (of a reaction) subdued **mutely** *adv*
muti [**moo**-ti] *n SAfr, Informal* medicine, esp herbal medicine
mutilate [**mew**-till-ate] *v* deprive of a limb or other part; damage (a book or text) **mutilation** *n*
mutiny [**mew**-tin-ee] *n, pl* **-nies** rebellion against authority, esp by soldiers or sailors ▷*v* **-nying, -nied** commit mutiny **mutineer** *n* **mutinous** *adj*
mutt *n slang* mongrel dog; stupid person
mutter *v* utter or speak indistinctly; grumble ▷*n* muttered sound or grumble
mutton *n* flesh of sheep, used as food **mutton bird** *Aust* sea bird with dark plumage; *NZ* any of a number of migratory sea birds, the young of which are a Maori delicacy
mutual [**mew**-chew-al] *adj* felt or expressed by each of two people about the other; common to both or all **mutually** *adv*
Muzak *n* ® recorded light music played in shops etc
muzzle *n* animal's mouth and

nose; cover for these to prevent biting; open end of a gun ▷ *v* prevent from being heard or noticed; put a muzzle on

muzzy *adj* **-zier, -ziest** confused or muddled; blurred or hazy

mW milliwatt(s)

MW megawatt(s)

my *adj* belonging to me

myall *n* Australian acacia with hard scented wood

mycology *n* study of fungi

myna, mynah, mina *n* Asian bird which can mimic human speech

myopia [my-**oh**-pee-a] *n* short-sightedness **myopic** [my-**op**-ik] *adj*

myriad [**mir**-ree-ad] *adj* innumerable ▷ *n* large indefinite number

myrrh [**mur**] *n* aromatic gum used in perfume, incense, and medicine

myrtle [**mur**-tl] *n* flowering evergreen shrub

myself *pron* emphatic or reflexive form of **I** or

mystery *n, pl* **-teries** strange or inexplicable event or phenomenon; obscure or secret thing; story or film that arouses suspense **mysterious** *adj* **mysteriously** *adv*

mystic *n* person who seeks spiritual knowledge ▷ *adj* mystical **mystical** *adj* having a spiritual or religious significance beyond human understanding **mysticism** *n*

mystify *v* **-fying, -fied** bewilder or puzzle **mystification** *n*

mystique [miss-**steek**] *n* aura of mystery or power

myth *n* tale with supernatural characters, usu of how the world and mankind began; untrue idea or explanation; imaginary person or object **mythical, mythic** *adj* **mythology** *n* myths collectively; study of myths **mythological** *adj*

myxomatosis [mix-a-mat-**oh**-siss] *n* contagious fatal viral disease of rabbits

n

N *chem* nitrogen; *physics* newton(s); North(ern)
n. neuter; noun; number
Na *chem* sodium
Naafi *n Brit* canteen or shop for military personnel
naan *n* same as **nan bread**
naartjie [**nahr**-chee] *n SAfr* tangerine
nab *v* **nabbing, nabbed** *Informal* arrest (someone); catch (someone) in wrongdoing
nadir *n* point in the sky opposite the zenith; lowest point
naevus [**nee**-vuss] *n, pl* **-vi** birthmark or mole
naff *adj Brit, slang* lacking quality or taste
nag¹ *v* **nagging, nagged** scold or find fault constantly; be a constant source of discomfort or worry to ▷ *n* person who nags **nagging** *adj, n*
nag² *n Informal* old horse
naiad [**nye**-ad] *n Greek myth* nymph living in a lake or river
nail *n* pointed piece of metal with a head, hit with a hammer to join two objects together; hard covering of the upper tips of the fingers and toes ▷ *v* attach (something) with nails; *Informal* catch or arrest **hit the nail on the head** say something exactly correct **nail file** small metal file used to smooth or shape the finger or toe nails **nail varnish, polish** cosmetic lacquer applied to the finger or toe nails
naive [nye-**eev**] *adj* innocent and gullible; simple and lacking sophistication **naively** *adv* **naivety, naäveté** [nye-**eev**-tee] *n*
naked *adj* without clothes; without any covering **the naked eye** the eye unassisted by any optical instrument **nakedness** *n*
namby-pamby *adj Brit, Aust & NZ* sentimental or insipid
name *n* word by which a person or thing is known; reputation, esp a good one ▷ *v* give a name to; refer to by name; fix or specify **call someone names, a name** insult someone by using rude words to describe him or her **nameless** *adj* without a name; unspecified; too horrible to be mentioned **namely** *adv* that is to say **namesake** *n* person with the same name as another
nan bread *n* slightly leavened Indian bread in a large flat leaf shape
nanny *n, pl* **-nies** woman whose job is looking after young children **nanny goat** female goat
nap¹ *n* short sleep ▷ *v* **napping, napped** have a short sleep
nap² *n* raised fibres of velvet or

similar cloth
nap[3] *n* card game similar to whist
napalm *n* highly inflammable jellied petrol, used in bombs
nape *n* back of the neck
naphtha *n* liquid mixture distilled from coal tar or petroleum, used as a solvent and in petrol **naphthalene** *n* white crystalline product distilled from coal tar or petroleum, used in disinfectants, mothballs, and explosives
napkin *n* piece of cloth or paper for wiping the mouth or protecting the clothes while eating
nappy *n, pl* **-pies** piece of absorbent material fastened round a baby's lower torso to absorb urine and faeces
narcissism *n* exceptional interest in or admiration for oneself **narcissistic** *adj*
narcissus *n, pl* **-cissi** yellow, orange, or white flower related to the daffodil
narcotic *n, adj* (of) a drug, such as morphine or opium, which produces numbness and drowsiness, used medicinally but addictive **narcosis** *n* effect of a narcotic
nark *slang* ▷*v* annoy ▷*n* informer or spy; *Brit* someone who complains in an irritating manner **narky** *adj slang* irritable or complaining
narrate *v* tell (a story); speak the words accompanying and telling what is happening in a film or TV programme **narration** *n* **narrator** *n*
narrative *n* account, story
narrow *adj* small in breadth in comparison to length; limited in range, extent, or outlook; with little margin *eg a narrow escape* ▷*v* make or become narrow; (often foll by *down*) limit or restrict **narrows** *pl n* narrow part of a strait, river, or current **narrowly** *adv* **narrowness** *n* **narrow boat** *Brit* long bargelike canal boat **narrow-minded** *adj* intolerant or bigoted
narwhal *n* arctic whale with a long spiral tusk
NASA *US* National Aeronautics and Space Administration
nasal *adj* of the nose; (of a sound) pronounced with air passing through the nose **nasally** *adv*
nascent *adj* starting to grow or develop
nasturtium *n* plant with yellow, red, or orange trumpet-shaped flowers
nasty *adj* **-tier, -tiest** unpleasant; (of an injury) dangerous or painful; spiteful or unkind **nastily** *adv* **nastiness** *n*
natal *adj* of or relating to birth
nation *n* people of one or more cultures or races organized as a single state
national *adj* characteristic of a particular nation ▷*n* citizen of a nation **nationally** *adv* **National Curriculum** curriculum of subjects taught in state schools in England and Wales since 1989 **National Health Service** (in Britain) system of national medical services financed mainly by taxation **national insurance** (in Britain) state insurance scheme providing payments to the unemployed, sick, and retired **national park** area of countryside protected by a government for its natural or environmental importance **national service** compulsory military service

nationalism *n* policy of national independence; patriotism, sometimes to an excessive degree **nationalist** *n, adj*

nationality *n, pl* **-ities** fact of being a citizen of a particular nation; group of people of the same race

nationalize *v* put (an industry or a company) under state control **nationalization** *n*

native *adj* relating to a place where a person was born; born in a specified place; (foll by *to*) originating (in); inborn ▷ *n* person born in a specified place; indigenous animal or plant; member of the original race of a country **Native American** (person) descended from the original inhabitants of the American continent **native bear** *Aust* same as **koala** **native companion** *Aust* same as **brolga** **native dog** *Aust* dingo

Nativity *n Christianity* birth of Jesus Christ

NATO North Atlantic Treaty Organization

natter *Informal* ▷ *v* talk idly or chatter ▷ *n* long idle chat

natty *adj* **-tier, -tiest** *Informal* smart and spruce

natural *adj* normal or to be expected; genuine or spontaneous; of, according to, existing in, or produced by nature; not created by human beings; not synthetic ▷ *n* person with an inborn talent or skill **naturally** *adv* of course; in a natural or normal way; instinctively **natural gas** gas found below the ground, used mainly as a fuel **natural history** study of animals and plants in the wild **natural selection** process by which only creatures and plants well adapted to their environment survive

naturalism *n* movement in art and literature advocating detailed realism **naturalistic** *adj*

naturalist *n* student of natural history

naturalize *v* give citizenship to (a person born in another country) **naturalization** *n*

nature *n* whole system of the existence, forces, and events of the physical world that are not controlled by human beings; fundamental or essential qualities; kind or sort

naturism *n* nudism **naturist** *n*

naught *n lit* nothing

naughty *adj* **-tier, -tiest** disobedient or mischievous; mildly indecent **naughtily** *adv* **naughtiness** *n*

nausea [naw-zee-a] *n* feeling of being about to vomit **nauseate** *v* make (someone) feel sick; disgust **nauseous** *adj* as if about to vomit; sickening

nautical *adj* of the sea or ships **nautical mile** 1852 metres (6076.12 feet)

nautilus *n, pl* **-luses, -li** shellfish with many tentacles

naval *adj* see **navy**

nave *n* long central part of a church

navel *n* hollow in the middle of the abdomen where the umbilical cord was attached

navigate *v* direct or plot the path or position of a ship, aircraft, or car; travel over or through **navigation** *n* **navigator** *n* **navigable** *adj* wide, deep, or safe enough to be sailed through; able to be steered

navvy *n, pl* **-vies** *Brit* labourer employed on a road or a building site

navy *n, pl* **-vies** branch of a country's armed services comprising warships with their crews and organization; warships of a nation ▷ *adj* navy-blue **naval** *adj* of or relating to a navy or ships **navy-blue** *adj* very dark blue

nay *interj obs* no

Nazi *n* member of the fascist National Socialist Party, which came to power in Germany in 1933 under Adolf Hitler ▷ *adj* of or relating to the Nazis **Nazism** *n*

NB note well

NCO *mil* noncommissioned officer

NE northeast(ern)

Neanderthal [nee-**ann**-der-tahl] *adj* of a type of primitive man that lived in Europe before 12 000 BC

neap tide *n* tide at the first and last quarters of the moon when there is the smallest rise and fall in tidal level

near *prep, adv, adj* indicating a place or time not far away ▷ *adj* almost being the thing specified *eg a near disaster* ▷ *v* draw close (to) **nearly** *adv* almost **nearness** *n* **nearby** *adj* not far away **nearside** *n* side of a vehicle that is nearer the kerb

neat *adj* tidy and clean; smoothly or competently done; undiluted **neatly** *adv* **neatness** *n*

nebula *n, pl* **-lae** *astronomy* hazy cloud of particles and gases **nebulous** *adj* vague and unclear *eg a nebulous concept*

necessary *adj* needed to obtain the desired result *eg the necessary skills*; certain or unavoidable *eg the necessary consequences* **necessarily** *adv* **necessitate** *v* compel or require **necessity** *n* circumstances that inevitably require a certain result; something needed

SPELLING There are 41 examples of the misspelling *neccessary* in Collins Word Web; *necesary* is also popular. The correct spelling, **necessary**, has one *c* and two *s*s. When you add *un-* at the beginning, you end up with a double *n* too: **unnecessary**

neck *n* part of the body joining the head to the shoulders; part of a garment round the neck; long narrow part of a bottle or violin ▷ *v slang* kiss and cuddle **neck and neck** absolutely level in a race or competition **neckerchief** *n* piece of cloth worn tied round the neck **necklace** *n* decorative piece of jewellery worn around the neck; *SAfr* burning petrol-filled tyre placed round someone's neck to kill him or her

necromancy *n* communication with the dead; sorcery

necropolis [neck-**rop**-pol-liss] *n* cemetery

nectar *n* sweet liquid collected from flowers by bees; drink of the gods

nectarine *n* smooth-skinned peach

née [nay] *prep* indicating the maiden name of a married woman

need *v* require or be in want of; be obliged (to do something) ▷ *n* condition of lacking something; requirement or necessity; poverty **needs** *adv* (preceded or foll by *must*) necessarily **needy** *adj* poor, in need of financial support **needful** *adj* necessary or required **needless** *adj* unnecessary

needle *n* thin pointed piece of metal with an eye through which thread is passed for sewing; long pointed rod used in knitting; pointed part of a hypodermic syringe; small pointed part in a record player that touches the record and picks up the sound signals, stylus; pointer on a measuring instrument or compass; long narrow stiff leaf ▷ *v Informal* goad or provoke **needlework** *n* sewing and embroidery

ne'er *adv lit* never **ne'er-do-well** *n* useless or lazy person

nefarious [nif-**fair**-ee-uss] *adj* wicked

negate *v* invalidate; deny the existence of **negation** *n*

negative *adj* expressing a denial or refusal; lacking positive qualities; (of an electrical charge) having the same electrical charge as an electron ▷ *n* negative word or statement; *photog* image with a reversal of tones or colours from which positive prints are made

neglect *v* take no care of; fail (to do something) through carelessness; disregard ▷ *n* neglecting or being neglected **neglectful** *adj*

negligee [**neg**-lee-zhay] *n* woman's lightweight usu lace-trimmed dressing gown

negligence *n* neglect or carelessness **negligent** *adj* **negligently** *adv*

negligible *adj* so small or unimportant as to be not worth considering

negotiate *v* discuss in order to reach (an agreement); succeed in passing round or over (a place or problem) **negotiation** *n* **negotiator** *n* **negotiable** *adj*

Negro *n, pl* **-groes** *old-fashioned* member of any of the Black peoples originating in Africa **Negroid** *adj* of or relating to the Negro race

neigh *n* loud high-pitched sound made by a horse ▷ *v* make this sound

neighbour *n* person who lives or is situated near another **neighbouring** *adj* situated nearby **neighbourhood** *n* district; surroundings; people of a district **neighbourly** *adj* kind, friendly, and helpful

neither *adj, pron* not one nor the other ▷ *conj* not

nemesis [**nem**-miss-iss] *n, pl* **-ses** retribution or vengeance

neo- *combining form* new, recent, or a modern form of *eg neoclassicism*

neo-conservatism *n* (in the US) a right-wing tendency that originated amongst supporters of the political left **neo-conservative** *adj*

Neolithic *adj* of the later Stone Age

neologism [nee-**ol**-a-jiz-zum] *n* newly-coined word or an established word used in a new sense

neon *n chem* colourless odourless gaseous element used in illuminated signs and lights

neophyte *n* beginner or novice; new convert

nephew *n* son of one's sister or brother

nephritis [nif-**frite**-tiss] *n* inflammation of a kidney

nepotism [**nep**-a-tiz-zum] *n* favouritism in business shown to relatives and friends

Neptune *n* Roman god of the sea; eighth planet from the sun

nerd *n slang* boring person obsessed with a particular subject; stupid and feeble person

nerve *n* cordlike bundle of fibres that conducts impulses between the brain and other parts of the body; bravery and determination;

impudence ▷ *pl* anxiety or tension; ability or inability to remain calm in a difficult situation **get on someone's nerves** irritate someone **nerve oneself** prepare oneself (to do something difficult or unpleasant) **nerveless** *adj* numb, without feeling; fearless **nervy** *adj* excitable or nervous **nerve centre** place from which a system or organization is controlled **nerve-racking** *adj* very distressing or harrowing

nervous *adj* apprehensive or worried; of or relating to the nerves **nervously** *adv* **nervousness** *n* **nervous breakdown** mental illness in which the sufferer ceases to function properly

nest *n* place or structure in which birds or certain animals lay eggs or give birth to young; secluded place; set of things of graduated sizes designed to fit together ▷ *v* make or inhabit a nest **nest egg** fund of money kept in reserve

nestle *v* snuggle; be in a sheltered position

nestling *n* bird too young to leave the nest

net[1] *n* fabric of meshes of string, thread, or wire with many openings; piece of net used to protect or hold things or to trap animals ▷ *v* **netting, netted** catch (a fish or animal) in a net **netting** *n* material made of net **netball** *n* team game in which a ball has to be thrown through a net hanging from a ring at the top of a pole

net[2]**, nett** *adj* left after all deductions; (of weight) excluding the wrapping or container ▷ *v* **netting, netted** yield or earn as a clear profit

nether *adj* lower

nettle *n* plant with stinging hairs on the leaves **nettled** *adj* irritated or annoyed

network *n* system of intersecting lines, roads, etc; interconnecting group or system; (in broadcasting) group of stations that all transmit the same programmes simultaneously

neural *adj* of a nerve or the nervous system

neuralgia *n* severe pain along a nerve

neuritis [nyoor-**rite**-tiss] *n* inflammation of a nerve or nerves

neurology *n* scientific study of the nervous system **neurologist** *n*

neurosis *n, pl* **-ses** mental disorder producing hysteria, anxiety, depression, or obsessive behaviour **neurotic** *adj* emotionally unstable; suffering from neurosis ▷ *n* neurotic person

neuter *adj* belonging to a particular class of grammatical inflections in some languages ▷ *v* castrate (an animal)

neutral *adj* taking neither side in a war or dispute; of or belonging to a neutral party or country; (of a colour) not definite or striking ▷ *n* neutral person or nation; neutral gear **neutrality** *n* **neutralize** *v* make ineffective or neutral **neutral gear** position of the controls of a gearbox that leaves the gears unconnected to the engine

neutrino [new-**tree**-no] *n, pl* **-nos** elementary particle with no mass or electrical charge

neutron *n* electrically neutral elementary particle of about the same mass as a proton **neutron bomb** nuclear bomb designed to kill people and animals while leaving buildings virtually undamaged

never *adv* at no time **nevertheless** *adv* in spite of that

never-never *n Informal* hire-purchase

new *adj* not existing before; recently acquired; having lately come into some state; additional; (foll by *to*) unfamiliar ▷ *adv* recently **newness** *n* **New Age** philosophy, originating in the late 1980s, characterized by a belief in alternative medicine and spiritualism **newbie** *n Informal* person new to a job, club, etc **newborn** *adj* recently or just born **newcomer** *n* recent arrival or participant **newfangled** *adj* objectionably or unnecessarily modern **newlyweds** *pl n* recently married couple **new moon** moon when it appears as a narrow crescent at the beginning of its cycle

newel *n* post at the top or bottom of a flight of stairs that supports the handrail

news *n* important or interesting new happenings; information about such events reported in the mass media **newsy** *adj* full of news **newsagent** *n Brit* shopkeeper who sells newspapers and magazines **newsflash** *n* brief important news item, which interrupts a radio or television programme **newsletter** *n* bulletin issued periodically to members of a group **newspaper** *n* weekly or daily publication containing news **newsprint** *n* inexpensive paper used for newspapers **newsreader, newscaster** *n* person who reads the news on the television or radio **newsreel** *n* short film giving news **newsroom** *n* room where news is received and prepared for publication or broadcasting **newsworthy** *adj* sufficiently interesting to be reported as news

newt *n* small amphibious creature with a long slender body and tail

newton *n* unit of force

next *adj, adv* immediately following; nearest **next-of-kin** *n* closest relative

nexus *n, pl* **nexus** connection or link

NHS (in Britain) National Health Service

nib *n* writing point of a pen

nibble *v* take little bites (of) ▷ *n* little bite

nibs *n* **his, her nibs** *slang* mock title of respect

nice *adj* pleasant; kind; good or satisfactory; subtle *eg a nice distinction* **nicely** *adv* **niceness** *n*

nicety *n, pl* **-ties** subtle point; refinement or delicacy

niche [**neesh**] *n* hollow area in a wall; suitable position for a particular person

nick *v* make a small cut in; *Chiefly Brit, slang* steal; *Chiefly Brit, slang* arrest ▷ *n* small cut; *slang* prison or police station **in good nick** *Informal* in good condition **in the nick of time** just in time

nickel *n chem* silvery-white metal often used in alloys; US coin worth five cents

nickelodeon *n US* early type of jukebox

nickname *n* familiar name given to a person or place ▷ *v* call by a nickname

nicotine *n* poisonous substance found in tobacco

niece *n* daughter of one's sister or brother

nifty *adj* **-tier, -tiest** *Informal* neat

or smart
niggardly *adj* stingy **niggard** *n* stingy person
nigger *n offens* Black person
niggle *v* worry slightly; continually find fault (with) ▷ *n* small worry or doubt
nigh *adv, prep lit* near
night *n* time of darkness between sunset and sunrise **nightly** *adj, adv* (happening) each night **nightcap** *n* drink taken just before bedtime; soft cap formerly worn in bed **nightclub** *n* establishment for dancing, music, etc, open late at night **nightdress** *n* woman's loose dress worn in bed **nightfall** *n* approach of darkness **nightie** *n Informal* nightdress **nightingale** *n* small bird with a musical song usu heard at night **nightjar** *n* nocturnal bird with a harsh cry **nightlife** *n* entertainment and social activities available at night in a town or city **nightmare** *n* very bad dream; very unpleasant experience **night school** place where adults can attend educational courses in the evenings **nightshade** *n* plant with bell-shaped flowers which are often poisonous **nightshirt** *n* long loose shirt worn in bed **night-time** *n* time from sunset to sunrise
nihilism [nye-ill-liz-zum] *n* rejection of all established authority and institutions **nihilist** *n* **nihilistic** *adj*
nil *n* nothing, zero
nimble *adj* agile and quick; mentally alert or acute **nimbly** *adv*
nimbus *n, pl* **-bi, -buses** dark grey rain cloud
nincompoop *n Informal* stupid person
nine *adj, n* one more than eight **ninth** *adj, n* (of) number nine in a series **ninepins** *n* game of skittles
nineteen *adj, n* ten and nine **nineteenth** *adj, n*
ninety *adj, n* ten times nine **ninetieth** *adj, n*
niobium *n chem* white superconductive metallic element
nip¹ *v* **nipping, nipped** *Informal* hurry; pinch or squeeze; bite lightly ▷ *n* pinch or light bite; sharp coldness **nipper** *n Brit, Aust & NZ, Informal* small child **nippy** *adj* frosty or chilly; *Informal* quick or nimble
nip² *n* small alcoholic drink
nipple *n* projection in the centre of a breast
nirvana [near-**vah**-na] *n Buddhism, Hinduism* absolute spiritual enlightenment and bliss
nit *n* egg or larva of a louse; *Informal* short for **nitwit** **nit-picking** *adj Informal* overconcerned with insignificant detail, esp to find fault **nitwit** *n Informal* stupid person
nitrogen [**nite**-roj-jen] *n chem* colourless odourless gas that forms four fifths of the air **nitric, nitrous, nitrogenous** *adj* of or containing nitrogen **nitrate** *n* compound of nitric acid, used as a fertilizer **nitroglycerine, nitroglycerin** *n* explosive liquid
nitty-gritty *n Informal* basic facts
no *interj* expresses denial, disagreement, or refusal ▷ *adj* not any, not a ▷ *adv* not at all ▷ *n, pl* **noes, nos** answer or vote of 'no'; person who answers or votes 'no' **no-go area** district barricaded off so that the police or army can enter only by force **no-man's-land** *n* land between boundaries, esp contested land between two opposing forces **no-one, no one**

pron nobody

no. number

nob *n Chiefly Brit, slang* person of wealth or social distinction

nobble *v Brit, slang* attract the attention of (someone) in order to talk to him or her; bribe or threaten

nobelium *n chem* artificially-produced radioactive element

Nobel Prize *n* prize awarded annually for outstanding achievement in various fields

noble *adj* showing or having high moral qualities; of the nobility; impressive and magnificent ▷ *n* member of the nobility **nobility** *n* quality of being noble; class of people holding titles and high social rank **nobly** *adv* **nobleman, noblewoman** *n*

nobody *pron* no person ▷ *n, pl* **-bodies** person of no importance

nocturnal *adj* of the night; active at night

nocturne *n* short dreamy piece of music

nod *v* **nodding, nodded** lower and raise (one's head) briefly in agreement or greeting; let one's head fall forward with sleep ▷ *n* act of nodding **nod off** *v Informal* fall asleep

noddle *n Chiefly Brit, Informal* the head

node *n* point on a plant stem from which leaves grow; point at which a curve crosses itself

nodule *n* small knot or lump; rounded mineral growth on the root of a plant

Noel *n* Christmas

noggin *n Informal* head; small quantity of an alcoholic drink

noise *n* sound, usu a loud or disturbing one **noisy** *adj* making a lot of noise; full of noise **noisily** *adv* **noiseless** *adj*

noisome *adj* (of smells) offensive; harmful or poisonous

nomad *n* member of a tribe with no fixed dwelling place, wanderer **nomadic** *adj*

nom de plume *n, pl* **noms de plume** pen name

nomenclature *n* system of names used in a particular subject

nominal *adj* in name only; very small in comparison with real worth **nominally** *adv*

nominate *v* suggest as a candidate; appoint to an office or position **nomination** *n* **nominee** *n* candidate **nominative** *n* form of a noun indicating the subject of a verb

non- *prefix* indicating: negation *eg nonexistent*; refusal or failure *eg noncooperation*; exclusion from a specified class *eg nonfiction*; lack or absence *eg nonevent*

nonagenarian *n* person aged between ninety and ninety-nine

nonaggression *n* policy of not attacking other countries

nonagon *n* geometric figure with nine sides

nonalcoholic *adj* containing no alcohol

nonaligned *adj* (of a country) not part of a major alliance or power bloc

nonce *n* **for the nonce** for the present

nonchalant *adj* casually unconcerned or indifferent **nonchalantly** *adv* **nonchalance** *n*

noncombatant *n* member of the armed forces whose duties do not include fighting

noncommissioned officer *n* (in the armed forces) a subordinate officer, risen from the ranks

noncommittal *adj* not committing oneself to any particular opinion

non compos mentis *adj* of unsound mind

nonconductor *n* substance that is a poor conductor of heat, electricity, or sound

nonconformist *n* person who does not conform to generally accepted patterns of behaviour or thought; (**N-**) member of a Protestant group separated from the Church of England ▷ *adj* (of behaviour or ideas) not conforming to accepted patterns **nonconformity** *n*

noncontributory *adj Brit* denoting a pension scheme for employees, the premiums of which are paid entirely by the employer

nondescript *adj* lacking outstanding features

none *pron* not any; no-one **nonetheless** *adv* despite that, however

nonentity [non-**enn**-tit-tee] *n, pl* **-ties** insignificant person or thing

nonevent *n* disappointing or insignificant occurrence

nonflammable *adj* not easily set on fire

nonintervention *n* refusal to intervene in the affairs of others

nonpareil [non-par-**rail**] *n* person or thing that is unsurpassed

nonpayment *n* failure to pay money owed

nonplussed *adj* perplexed

nonsense *n* something that has or makes no sense; absurd language; foolish behaviour **nonsensical** *adj*

non sequitur [**sek**-wit-tur] *n* statement with little or no relation to what preceded it

nonstandard *adj* denoting language that is not regarded as correct by educated native speakers

nonstarter *n* person or idea that has little chance of success

nonstick *adj* coated with a substance that food will not stick to when cooked

nonstop *adj, adv* without a stop

nontoxic *adj* not poisonous

noodles *pl n* long thin strips of pasta

nook *n* sheltered place

noon *n* twelve o'clock midday **noonday** *adj* happening at noon

noose *n* loop in the end of a rope, tied with a slipknot

nor *conj* and not

Nordic *adj* of Scandinavia or its typically tall blond and blue-eyed people

norm *n* standard that is regarded as normal

normal *adj* usual, regular, or typical; free from mental or physical disorder **normally** *adv* **normality** *n* **normalize** *v*

Norse *n, adj* (language) of ancient and medieval Norway

north *n* direction towards the North Pole, opposite south; area lying in or towards the north ▷ *adj* to or in the north; (of a wind) from the north ▷ *adv* in, to, or towards the north **northerly** *adj* **northern** *adj* **northerner** *n* person from the north of a country or area **northward** *adj, adv* **northwards** *adv* **North Pole** northernmost point on the earth's axis

nos. numbers

nose *n* organ of smell, used also in breathing; front part of a vehicle ▷ *v* move forward slowly and carefully; pry or snoop **nose dive** sudden drop **nosegay** *n* small bunch of flowers **nosey, nosy** *adj Informal* prying or inquisitive **nosiness** *n*

nosh *Brit, Aust & NZ, slang* ▷*n* food ▷*v* eat

nostalgia *n* sentimental longing for the past **nostalgic** *adj*

nostril *n* one of the two openings at the end of the nose

nostrum *n* quack medicine; favourite remedy

not *adv* expressing negation, refusal, or denial

notable *adj* worthy of being noted, remarkable ▷*n* person of distinction **notably** *adv* **notability** *n*

notary *n, pl* **-ries** person authorized to witness the signing of legal documents

notation *n* representation of numbers or quantities in a system by a series of symbols; set of such symbols

notch *n* V-shaped cut; *Informal* step or level ▷*v* make a notch in; (foll by *up*) score or achieve

note *n* short letter; brief comment or record; banknote; (symbol for) a musical sound; hint or mood ▷*v* notice, pay attention to; record in writing; remark upon **noted** *adj* well-known **notebook** *n* book for writing in **noteworthy** *adj* worth noting, remarkable

nothing *pron* not anything; matter of no importance; figure 0 ▷*adv* not at all **nothingness** *n* nonexistence; insignificance.

> SPELLING *Nothing* is usually followed by a singular verb but, if it comes before a plural noun, this can sound odd: *Nothing but books was/were on the shelf.* A solution is to rephrase the sentence: *Only books were …*

notice *n* observation or attention; sign giving warning or an announcement; advance notification of intention to end a contract of employment ▷*v* observe, become aware of; point out or remark upon **noticeable** *adj* easily seen or detected, appreciable

notify *v* **-fying, -fied** inform **notification** *n* **notifiable** *adj* having to be reported to the authorities

notion *n* idea or opinion; whim **notional** *adj* speculative, imaginary, or unreal

notorious *adj* well known for something bad **notoriously** *adv* **notoriety** *n*

notwithstanding *prep* in spite of

nougat *n* chewy sweet containing nuts and fruit

nought *n* figure 0; nothing **noughties** *pl n Informal* decade from 2000 to 2009

noun *n* word that refers to a person, place, or thing

nourish *v* feed; encourage or foster (an idea or feeling) **nourishment** *n* **nourishing** *adj* providing the food necessary for life and growth

nouvelle cuisine [noo-vell kwee-**zeen**] *n* style of preparing and presenting food with light sauces and unusual combinations of flavours

Nov. November

nova *n, pl* **-vae, -vas** star that suddenly becomes brighter and then gradually decreases to its original brightness

novel[1] *n* long fictitious story in book form **novelist** *n* writer of novels **novella** *n, pl* **-las, -lae** short novel

novel[2] *adj* fresh, new, or original **novelty** *n* newness; something

new or unusual
November *n* eleventh month of the year
novena [no-**vee**-na] *n, pl* **-nas** *RC church* set of prayers or services on nine consecutive days
novice *n* beginner; person who has entered a religious order but has not yet taken vows
now *adv* at or for the present time; immediately ▷ *conj* seeing that, since **just now** very recently **now and again, then** occasionally **nowadays** *adv* in these times
nowhere *adv* not anywhere
noxious *adj* poisonous or harmful; extremely unpleasant
nozzle *n* projecting spout through which fluid is discharged
NSPCC (in Britain) National Society for the Prevention of Cruelty to Children
NSW New South Wales
NT (in Britain) National Trust; New Testament; Northern Territory
nuance [**new**-ahnss] *n* subtle difference in colour, meaning, or tone
nub *n* point or gist (of a story etc)
nubile [**new**-bile] *adj* (of a young woman) sexually attractive; old enough to get married
nuclear *adj* of nuclear weapons or energy; of a nucleus, esp the nucleus of an atom **nuclear energy** energy released as a result of nuclear fission or fusion **nuclear fission** splitting of an atomic nucleus **nuclear fusion** combination of two nuclei to form a heavier nucleus with the release of energy **nuclear power** power produced by a nuclear reactor **nuclear reaction** change in structure and energy content of an atomic nucleus by interaction with another nucleus or particle **nuclear reactor** device in which a nuclear reaction is maintained and controlled to produce nuclear energy **nuclear weapon** weapon whose force is due to uncontrolled nuclear fusion or fission **nuclear winter** theoretical period of low temperatures and little light after a nuclear war
nucleic acid *n* complex compound, such as DNA or RNA, found in all living cells
nucleus *n, pl* **-clei** centre, esp of an atom or cell; central thing around which others are grouped
nude *adj* naked ▷ *n* naked figure in painting, sculpture, or photography **nudity** *n* **nudism** *n* practice of not wearing clothes **nudist** *n*
nudge *v* push gently, esp with the elbow ▷ *n* gentle push or touch
nugatory [**new**-gat-tree] *adj* of little value; not valid
nugget *n* small lump of gold in its natural state; something small but valuable ▷ *v NZ & SAfr* polish footwear
nuisance *n* something or someone that causes annoyance or bother
nuke *slang* ▷ *v* attack with nuclear weapons ▷ *n* nuclear weapon
null *adj* **null and void** not legally valid **nullity** *n* **nullify** *v* make ineffective; cancel
nulla-nulla *n* wooden club used by Australian Aborigines
numb *adj* without feeling, as through cold, shock, or fear ▷ *v* make numb **numbly** *adv* **numbness** *n* **numbskull** *n* stupid person
numbat *n* small Australian marsupial with a long snout and

tongue

number *n* sum or quantity; word or symbol used to express a sum or quantity, numeral; numeral or string of numerals used to identify a person or thing; one of a series, such as a copy of a magazine; song or piece of music; group of people; *grammar* classification of words depending on how many persons or things are referred to ▷ *v* count; give a number to; amount to; include in a group **numberless** *adj* too many to be counted **number crunching** *computers* large-scale processing of numerical data **number one** *n Informal* oneself; bestselling pop record in any one week ▷ *adj* first in importance or quality **numberplate** *n* plate on a car showing the registration number

numeral *n* word or symbol used to express a sum or quantity

numerate *adj* able to do basic arithmetic **numeracy** *n*

numeration *n* act or process of numbering or counting

numerator *n maths* number above the line in a fraction

numerical *adj* measured or expressed in numbers **numerically** *adv*

numerous *adj* existing or happening in large numbers

numismatist *n* coin collector

numskull *n* same as **numbskull**

nun *n* female member of a religious order **nunnery** *n* convent

nuncio *n RC church* Pope's ambassador

nuptial *adj* relating to marriage **nuptials** *pl n* wedding

nurse *n* person employed to look after sick people, usu in a hospital; woman employed to look after children ▷ *v* look after (a sick person); breast-feed (a baby); try to cure (an ailment); harbour or foster (a feeling) **nursing home** private hospital or home for old people **nursing officer** (in Britain) administrative head of the nursing staff of a hospital

nursery *n, pl* **-ries** room where children sleep or play; place where children are taken care of while their parents are at work; place where plants are grown for sale **nurseryman** *n* person who raises plants for sale **nursery school** school for children from 3 to 5 years old **nursery slopes** gentle ski slopes for beginners

nurture *n* act or process of promoting the development of a child or young plant ▷ *v* promote or encourage the development of

nut *n* fruit consisting of a hard shell and a kernel; small piece of metal that screws onto a bolt; (also **nutcase**) *slang* insane or eccentric person; *slang* head **nutter** *n Brit, slang* insane person **nutty** *adj* containing or resembling nuts; *slang* insane or eccentric **nutcracker** *n* device for cracking the shells of nuts **nuthatch** *n* small songbird **nutmeg** *n* spice made from the seed of a tropical tree

nutria *n* fur of the coypu

nutrient *n* substance that provides nourishment

nutriment *n* food or nourishment required by all living things to grow and stay healthy

nutrition *n* process of taking in and absorbing nutrients; process of being nourished **nutritional** *adj* **nutritious, nutritive** *adj* nourishing

nuzzle *v* push or rub gently with the nose or snout
NW northwest(ern)
nylon *n* synthetic material used for clothing etc ▷ *pl* stockings made of nylon
nymph *n* mythical spirit of nature, represented as a beautiful young woman; larva of certain insects, resembling the adult form
nymphet *n* sexually precocious young girl
nymphomaniac *n* woman with an abnormally intense sexual desire
NZ New Zealand
NZE New Zealand English
NZRFU New Zealand Rugby Football Union
NZSE40 Index New Zealand Share Price 40 Index

O

O *chem* oxygen
oaf *n* stupid or clumsy person **oafish** *adj*
oak *n* deciduous forest tree; its wood, used for furniture **oaken** *adj* **oak apple** brownish lump found on oak trees
oakum *n* fibre obtained by unravelling old rope
OAP (in Britain) old-age pensioner
oar *n* pole with a broad blade, used for rowing a boat
oasis *n, pl* **-ses** fertile area in a desert
oast *n Chiefly Brit* oven for drying hops
oat *n* hard cereal grown as food ▷ *pl* grain of this cereal **sow one's wild oats** have many sexual relationships when young **oatmeal** *adj* pale brownish-cream
oath *n* solemn promise, esp to be truthful in court; swearword

obbligato [ob-lig-**gah**-toe] *n, pl* **-tos** *music* essential part or accompaniment

obdurate *adj* hardhearted or stubborn **obduracy** *n*

OBE (in Britain) Officer of the Order of the British Empire

obedient *adj* obeying or willing to obey **obedience** *n* **obediently** *adv*

obeisance [oh-**bay**-sanss] *n* attitude of respect; bow or curtsy

obelisk [**ob**-bill-isk] *n* four-sided stone column tapering to a pyramid at the top

obese [oh-**beess**] *adj* very fat **obesity** *n*

obey *v* carry out instructions or orders

obfuscate *v* make (something) confusing

obituary *n, pl* **-aries** announcement of someone's death, esp in a newspaper **obituarist** *n*

object[1] *n* physical thing; focus of thoughts or action; aim or purpose; *grammar* word that a verb or preposition affects **no object** not a hindrance

object[2] *v* express disapproval **objection** *n* **objectionable** *adj* unpleasant **objector** *n*

objective *n* aim or purpose ▷ *adj* not biased; existing in the real world outside the human mind **objectively** *adv* **objectivity** *n*

objet d'art [**ob**-zhay **dahr**] *n, pl* **objets d'art** small object of artistic value

oblation *n* religious offering

oblige *v* compel (someone) morally or by law to do something; do a favour for (someone) **obliging** *adj* ready to help other people **obligingly** *adv* **obligated** *adj* obliged to do something **obligation** *n* duty **obligatory** *adj* required by a rule or law

oblique [oh-**bleak**] *adj* slanting; indirect ▷ *n* the symbol (/) **obliquely** *adv* **oblique angle** angle that is not a right angle

obliterate *v* wipe out, destroy **obliteration** *n*

oblivious *adj* unaware **oblivion** *n* state of being forgotten; state of being unaware or unconscious

oblong *adj* having two long sides, two short sides, and four right angles ▷ *n* oblong figure

obloquy [**ob**-lock-wee] *n, pl* **-quies** verbal abuse; discredit

obnoxious *adj* offensive

oboe *n* double-reeded woodwind instrument **oboist** *n*

obscene *adj* portraying sex offensively; disgusting **obscenity** *n*

obscure *adj* not well known; hard to understand; indistinct ▷ *v* make (something) obscure **obscurity** *n*

obsequies [**ob**-sick-weez] *pl n* funeral rites

obsequious [ob-**seek**-wee-uss] *adj* overattentive in order to gain favour **obsequiousness** *n*

observe *v* see or notice; watch (someone or something) carefully; remark; act according to (a law or custom) **observation** *n* action or habit of observing; remark **observable** *adj* **observance** *n* observing of a custom **observant** *adj* quick to notice things **observatory** *n* building equipped for studying the weather and the stars

observer *n* person who observes, esp one who watches someone or something carefully

obsess *v* preoccupy (someone) compulsively **obsessed** *adj*

obsessive *adj* **obsession** *n*

> SPELLING Some people get carried away with doubling ss and write *obssession* instead of **obsession**

obsidian *n* dark glassy volcanic rock

obsolete *adj* no longer in use **obsolescent** *adj* becoming obsolete **obsolescence** *n*

obstacle *n* something that makes progress difficult

obstetrics *n* branch of medicine concerned with pregnancy and childbirth **obstetric** *adj* **obstetrician** *n*

obstinate *adj* stubborn; difficult to remove or change **obstinately** *adv* **obstinacy** *n*

obstreperous *adj* unruly, noisy

obstruct *v* block with an obstacle **obstruction** *n* **obstructive** *adj*

obtain *v* acquire intentionally; be customary **obtainable** *adj*

obtrude *v* push oneself or one's ideas on others **obtrusive** *adj* unpleasantly noticeable **obtrusively** *adv*

obtuse *adj* mentally slow; *maths* (of an angle) between 90° and 180°; not pointed **obtuseness** *n*

obverse *n* opposite way of looking at an idea; main side of a coin or medal

obviate *v* make unnecessary

obvious *adj* easy to see or understand, evident **obviously** *adv*

ocarina *n* small oval wind instrument

occasion *n* time at which a particular thing happens; reason *eg no occasion for complaint*; special event ▷*v* cause **occasional** *adj* happening sometimes **occasionally** *adv*

> SPELLING The commonest misspelling of **occasion** is *occassion*, with 44 occurrences in Collins Word Web. As you might expect, there are also examples of *ocasion* and *ocassion*. The correct spelling has two *c*s and one *s*

Occident *n lit* the West **Occidental** *adj*

occiput [ox-sip-put] *n* back of the head

occlude *v* obstruct; close off **occlusion** *n* **occluded front** *meteorol* front formed when a cold front overtakes a warm front and warm air rises

occult *adj* relating to the supernatural **the occult** knowledge or study of the supernatural

occupant *n* person occupying a specified place **occupancy** *n* (length of) a person's stay in a specified place

occupation *n* profession; activity that occupies one's time; control of a country by a foreign military power; being occupied **occupational** *adj* **occupational therapy** purposeful activities, designed to aid recovery from illness etc

occupy *v* **-pying, -pied** live or work in (a building); take up the attention of (someone); take up (space or time); take possession of (a place) by force **occupier** *n*

occur *v* **-curring, -curred** happen; exist **occur to** come to the mind of **occurrence** *n* something that occurs; fact of occurring

> SPELLING Rather surprisingly, there are no examples in Collins Word Web where **occurrence** has been spelt with only one *c*. However, there are 85 examples of *occurence*, with only one *r*, as

opposed to 2013 instances where the word is spelt correctly: **occurrence**

ocean *n* vast area of sea between continents **oceanic** *adj* **oceanography** *n* scientific study of the oceans **ocean-going** *adj* able to sail on the open sea

ocelot [oss-ill-lot] *n* American wild cat with a spotted coat

oche [ok-kee] *n darts* mark on the floor behind which a player must stand

ochre [oak-er] *adj, n* brownish-yellow (earth)

o'clock *adv* used after a number to specify an hour

Oct. October

octagon *n* geometric figure with eight sides **octagonal** *adj*

octahedron [ok-ta-heed-ron] *n, pl* **-drons, -dra** three-dimensional geometric figure with eight faces

octane *n* hydrocarbon found in petrol **octane rating** measure of petrol quality

octave *n music* (interval between the first and) eighth note of a scale

octet *n* group of eight performers; music for such a group

October *n* tenth month of the year

octogenarian *n* person aged between eighty and eighty-nine

octopus *n, pl* **-puses** sea creature with a soft body and eight tentacles

ocular *adj* relating to the eyes or sight

OD *Informal* ▷ *n* overdose ▷ *v* **OD'ing, OD'd** take an overdose

odd *adj* unusual; occasional; not divisible by two; not part of a set **odds** *pl n* (ratio showing) the probability of something happening **at odds** in conflict **odds and ends** small miscellaneous items **oddity** *n* odd person or thing **oddness** *n* quality of being odd **oddments** *pl n* things left over

ode *n* lyric poem, usu addressed to a particular subject

odium [oh-dee-um] *n* widespread dislike **odious** *adj* offensive

odour *n* particular smell **odorous** *adj* **odourless** *adj*

odyssey [odd-iss-ee] *n* long eventful journey

OE *NZ, Informal* overseas experience *eg he's away on his OE.*

OECD Organization for Economic Cooperation and Development

oedema [id-deem-a] *n, pl* **-mata** *med* abnormal swelling

oesophagus [ee-soff-a-guss] *n, pl* **-gi** passage between the mouth and stomach

oestrogen [ee-stra-jen] *n* female hormone that controls the reproductive cycle

of *prep* belonging to; consisting of; connected with; characteristic of

off *prep* away from ▷ *adv* away ▷ *adj* not operating; cancelled; (of food) gone bad ▷ *n cricket* side of the field to which the batsman's feet point **off colour** slightly ill **off-line** *adj* (of a computer) not directly controlled by a central processor **off-message** *adj* (esp of a politician) not following the official Party line **off-road** *adj* (of a motor vehicle) designed for use away from public roads

offal *n* edible organs of an animal, such as liver or kidneys **offal pit, offal hole** *NZ* place on a farm for the disposal of animal offal

offcut *n* piece remaining after the required parts have been cut out

offend *v* hurt the feelings of, insult; commit a crime **offence** *n* (cause of) hurt feelings or annoyance; illegal act **offensive** *adj* disagreeable; insulting; aggressive ▷ *n* position or action of attack

offender *n* person who commits a crime

offer *v* present (something) for acceptance or rejection; provide; be willing (to do something); propose as payment ▷ *n* instance of offering something **offering** *n* thing offered **offertory** *n* *Christianity* offering of the bread and wine for Communion

offhand *adj* casual, curt ▷ *adv* without preparation

office *n* room or building where people work at desks; department of a commercial organization; formal position of responsibility; place where tickets or information can be obtained

officer *n* person in authority in the armed services; member of the police force; person with special responsibility in an organization

official *adj* of a position of authority; approved or arranged by someone in authority ▷ *n* person who holds a position of authority **officially** *adv* **officialdom** *n* officials collectively **Official Receiver** *Brit* person who deals with the affairs of a bankrupt company

officiate *v* act in an official role

officious *adj* interfering unnecessarily

offing *n* area of the sea visible from the shore **in the offing** *Brit, Aust & NZ* likely to happen soon

off-licence *n Brit* shop licensed to sell alcohol for drinking elsewhere

offset *v* cancel out, compensate for

offshoot *n* something developed from something else

offside *adj, adv sport* (positioned) illegally ahead of the ball

offspring *n, pl* **offspring** child

often *adv* frequently, much of the time **oft** *adv poetic* often

ogle *v* stare at (someone) lustfully

ogre *n* giant that eats human flesh; monstrous or cruel person

oh *interj* exclamation of surprise, pain, etc

ohm *n* unit of electrical resistance

OHMS *Brit* On Her *or* His Majesty's Service

oil *n* viscous liquid, insoluble in water and usu flammable; same as **petroleum**; petroleum derivative, used as a fuel or lubricant ▷ *pl* oil-based paints used in art ▷ *v* lubricate (a machine) with oil **oily** *adj* **oilfield** *n* area containing oil reserves **oil rig** platform constructed for drilling oil wells **oilskin** *n* (garment made from) waterproof material

ointment *n* greasy substance used for healing skin or as a cosmetic

O.K., okay *Informal* ▷ *interj* expression of approval ▷ *v* approve (something) ▷ *n* approval

okapi [ok-**kah**-pee] *n* African animal related to the giraffe but with a shorter neck

okra *n* tropical plant with edible green pods

old *adj* having lived or existed for a long time; of a specified age *eg two years old*; former **olden** *adj* old *eg in the olden days* **oldie** *n Informal* old but popular song or film **old-fashioned** *adj* no longer commonly used or valued **old guard** group of people in an organization who have traditional values **old hat** boring because so familiar **old maid** elderly unmarried woman **old master** European painter or painting from the period 1500–1800 **Old Nick** *Brit, Aust & NZ, Informal* the Devil **old school tie** system of mutual help between former pupils of public schools **Old Testament** part of the Bible recording Hebrew history **Old World** world as it was known before the discovery of the Americas

oleaginous [ol-lee-**aj**-in-uss] *adj* oily, producing oil

oleander [ol-lee-**ann**-der] *n* Mediterranean flowering evergreen shrub

olfactory *adj* relating to the sense of smell

oligarchy [**ol**-lee-gark-ee] *n, pl* **-chies** government by a small group of people; state governed this way **oligarchic, oligarchical** *adj*

olive *n* small green or black fruit used as food or pressed for its oil; tree on which this fruit grows ▷ *adj* greyish-green **olive branch** peace offering

Olympic Games *pl n* four-yearly international sports competition

ombudsman *n* official who investigates complaints against government organizations

omelette *n* dish of eggs beaten and fried

> SPELLING You don't hear it in the pronunciation, but there is an *e* after the *m* in **omelette**

omen *n* happening or object thought to foretell success or misfortune **ominous** *adj* worrying, seeming to foretell misfortune

omit *v* **omitting, omitted** leave out; neglect (to do something) **omission** *n*

omnibus *n* several books or TV or radio programmes made into one; *old-fashioned* bus

omnipotent *adj* having unlimited power **omnipotence** *n*

omnipresent *adj* present everywhere **omnipresence** *n*

omniscient [om-**niss**-ee-ent] *adj* knowing everything **omniscience** *n*

omnivorous [om-**niv**-vor-uss] *adj* eating food obtained from both animals and plants **omnivore** *n* omnivorous animal

on *prep* indicating position above, attachment, closeness, etc *eg lying on the ground; a puppet on a string; on the coast* ▷ *adv* in operation; continuing; forwards ▷ *adj* operating; taking place ▷ *n cricket* side of the field on which the batsman stands **on line, online** *adj* (of a computer) directly controlled by a central processor; relating to the Internet *eg online shopping* **on-message** *adj* (esp of a politician) following the official Party line

once *adv* on one occasion; formerly ▷ *conj* as soon as **at once** immediately; simultaneously **once-over** *n Informal* quick examination

oncogene [**on**-koh-jean] *n* gene that can cause cancer when abnormally activated

oncoming *adj* approaching from the front

one *adj* single, lone ▷ *n* number or figure 1; single unit ▷ *pron* any person **oneness** *n* unity **oneself** *pron* reflexive form of **one** **one-armed bandit** fruit machine operated by a lever on one side **one-liner** *n* witty remark **one-night stand** sexual encounter lasting one night **one-sided** *adj* considering only one point of view **one-way** *adj* allowing movement in one direction only

onerous [own-er-uss] *adj* (of a task) difficult to carry out

ongoing *adj* in progress, continuing

onion *n* strongly flavoured edible bulb

onlooker *n* person who watches without taking part

only *adj* alone of its kind ▷ *adv* exclusively; merely; no more than ▷ *conj* but

onomatopoeia [on-a-mat-a-**pee**-a] *n* use of a word which imitates the sound it represents, such as *hiss* **onomatopoeic** *adj*

onset *n* beginning

onslaught *n* violent attack

onto *prep* to a position on; aware of *eg she's onto us*

ontology *n* branch of philosophy concerned with existence **ontological** *adj*

onus [own-uss] *n, pl* **onuses** responsibility or burden

onward *adj* directed or moving forward ▷ *adv* (also **onwards**) ahead, forward

onyx *n* type of quartz with coloured layers

oodles *pl n Informal* great quantities

ooze[1] *v* flow slowly ▷ *n* sluggish flow **oozy** *adj*

ooze[2] *n* soft mud at the bottom of a lake or river

opal *n* iridescent precious stone **opalescent** *adj* iridescent like an opal

opaque *adj* not able to be seen through, not transparent **opacity** *n*

op. cit. [op sit] in the work cited

OPEC Organization of Petroleum-Exporting Countries

open *adj* not closed; not covered; unfolded; ready for business; free from obstruction, accessible; frank ▷ *v* (cause to) become open; begin ▷ *n sport* competition which all may enter **in the open** outdoors **openly** *adv* without concealment **opening** *n* opportunity; hole ▷ *adj* first **opencast mining** mining at the surface and not underground **open day** day on which a school or college is open to the public **open-handed** *adj* generous **open-hearted** *adj* generous; frank **open-heart surgery** surgery on the heart during which the blood circulation is maintained by machine **open house** hospitality to visitors at any time **open letter** letter to an individual that the writer makes public in a newspaper or magazine **open-minded** *adj* receptive to new ideas **open-plan** *adj* (of a house or office) having few interior walls **open prison** prison with minimal security **open verdict** coroner's verdict not stating the cause of death

opera[1] *n* drama in which the text is sung to an orchestral accompaniment **operatic** *adj* **operetta** *n* light-hearted comic opera

opera[2] *n* a plural of **opus**

operate *v* (cause to) work; direct; perform an operation **operator** *n* **operation** *n* method or procedure of working; medical procedure in which the body is worked on to repair a damaged part **operational** *adj* in working order; relating to an operation **operative** *adj* working ▷ *n* worker with a

special skill
ophthalmic *adj* relating to the eye **ophthalmology** *n* study of the eye and its diseases **ophthalmologist** *n*
opiate *n* narcotic drug containing opium
opinion *n* personal belief or judgment **opinionated** *adj* having strong opinions **opine** *v old-fashioned* express an opinion **opinion poll** see **poll**
opium *n* addictive narcotic drug made from poppy seeds
opossum *n* small marsupial of America or Australasia
opponent *n* person one is working against in a contest, battle, or argument
opportunity *n, pl* **-ties** favourable time or condition; good chance **opportunity shop** *Aust & NZ* shop selling second-hand clothes, sometimes for charity (also **op-shop**) **opportune** *adj* happening at a suitable time **opportunist** *n, adj* (person) doing whatever is advantageous without regard for principles **opportunism** *n*

> SPELLING Lots of people forget that **opportunity**, which is a very common word, has two *ps*

oppose *v* work against **be opposed to** disagree with or disapprove of **opposition** *n* obstruction or hostility; group opposing another; political party not in power
opposite *adj* situated on the other side; facing; completely different ▷ *n* person or thing that is opposite ▷ *prep* facing ▷ *adv* on the other side
oppress *v* control by cruelty or force; depress **oppression** *n* **oppressor** *n* **oppressive** *adj* tyrannical; (of weather) hot and humid **oppressively** *adv*
opprobrium [op-**probe**-ree-um] *n* state of being criticized severely for wrong one has done
opt *v* show a preference, choose **opt out** *v* choose not to be part (of)
optic *adj* relating to the eyes or sight **optics** *n* science of sight and light **optical** *adj* **optical character reader** device that electronically reads and stores text **optical fibre** fine glass-fibre tube used to transmit information
optician *n* (also **ophthalmic optician**) person qualified to prescribe glasses; (also **dispensing optician**) person who supplies and fits glasses
optimism *n* tendency to take the most hopeful view **optimist** *n* **optimistic** *adj* **optimistically** *adv*
optimum *n, pl* **-ma, -mums** best possible conditions ▷ *adj* most favourable **optimal** *adj* **optimize** *v* make the most of
option *n* choice; thing chosen; right to buy or sell something at a specified price within a given time **optional** *adj* possible but not compulsory
optometrist *n* person qualified to prescribe glasses **optometry** *n*
opulent [**op**-pew-lent] *adj* having or indicating wealth **opulence** *n*
opus *n, pl* **opuses, opera** artistic creation, esp a musical work
or *conj* used to join alternatives *eg tea or coffee*
oracle *n* shrine of an ancient god; prophecy, often obscure, revealed at a shrine; person believed to make infallible predictions **oracular** *adj*
oral *adj* spoken; (of a drug) to be taken by mouth ▷ *n* spoken

examination **orally** *adv*

orange *n* reddish-yellow citrus fruit ▷ *adj* reddish-yellow **orangeade** *n Brit* orange-flavoured, usu fizzy drink **orangery** *n* greenhouse for growing orange trees

orang-utan, orang-utang *n* large reddish-brown ape with long arms

orator [**or**-rat-tor] *n* skilful public speaker **oration** *n* formal speech

oratorio [or-rat-**tor**-ee-oh] *n, pl* **-rios** musical composition for choir and orchestra, usu with a religious theme

oratory[1] [**or**-rat-tree] *n* art of making speeches **oratorical** *adj*

oratory[2] *n, pl* **-ries** small private chapel

orb *n* ceremonial decorated sphere with a cross on top, carried by a monarch

orbit *n* curved path of a planet, satellite, or spacecraft around another body; sphere of influence ▷ *v* **orbiting, orbited** move in an orbit around; put (a satellite or spacecraft) into orbit **orbital** *adj*

orchard *n* area where fruit trees are grown

orchestra *n* large group of musicians, esp playing a variety of instruments; (also **orchestra pit**) area of a theatre in front of the stage, reserved for the musicians **orchestral** *adj* **orchestrate** *v* arrange (music) for orchestra; organize (something) to produce a particular result **orchestration** *n*

orchid *n* plant with flowers that have unusual lip-shaped petals

ordain *v* make (someone) a member of the clergy; order or establish with authority

ordeal *n* painful or difficult experience

order *n* instruction to be carried out; methodical arrangement or sequence; established social system; condition of a law-abiding society; request for goods to be supplied; kind, sort; religious society of monks or nuns ▷ *v* give an instruction to; request (something) to be supplied **in order** so that it is possible **orderly** *adj* well-organized; well-behaved ▷ *n, pl* **-lies** male hospital attendant **orderliness** *n*

ordinal number *n* number showing a position in a series *eg first; second*

ordinance *n* official rule or order

ordinary *adj* usual or normal; dull or commonplace **ordinarily** *adv*

ordination *n* act of making someone a member of the clergy

ordnance *n* weapons and military supplies **Ordnance Survey** official organization making maps of Britain

ordure *n* excrement

ore *n* (rock containing) a mineral which yields metal

oregano [or-rig-**gah**-no] *n* sweet-smelling herb used in cooking

organ *n* part of an animal or plant that has a particular function, such as the heart or lungs; musical keyboard instrument in which notes are produced by forcing air through pipes; means of conveying information, esp a newspaper **organist** *n* organ player

organdie *n* fine cotton fabric

organic *adj* of or produced from animals or plants; grown without artificial fertilizers or pesticides; *chem* relating to compounds of carbon; organized systematically

organically *adv* **organism** *n* any living animal or plant
organize *v* make arrangements for; arrange systematically **organization** *n* group of people working together; act of organizing **organizational** *adj* **organizer** *n*
orgasm *n* most intense point of sexual pleasure **orgasmic** *adj*
orgy *n, pl* **-gies** party involving promiscuous sexual activity; unrestrained indulgence *eg an orgy of destruction* **orgiastic** *adj*
oriel window *n* upper window built out from a wall
orient, orientate *v* position (oneself) according to one's surroundings; position (a map) in relation to the points of the compass **orientation** *n* **orienteering** *n* sport in which competitors hike over a course using a compass and map
Orient *n* **the Orient** *lit* East Asia **Oriental** *adj* **Orientalist** *n* specialist in the languages and history of the Far East
orifice [**or**-rif-fiss] *n* opening or hole
origami [or-rig-**gah**-mee] *n* Japanese decorative art of paper folding
origin *n* point from which something develops; ancestry **original** *adj* first or earliest; new, not copied or based on something else; able to think up new ideas ▷ *n* first version, from which others are copied **original sin** human imperfection and mortality as a result of Adam's disobedience **originality** *n* **originally** *adv* **originate** *v* come or bring into existence **origination** *n* **originator** *n*
oriole *n* tropical or American songbird
ormolu *n* gold-coloured alloy used for decoration
ornament *n* decorative object ▷ *v* decorate **ornamental** *adj* **ornamentation** *n*
ornate *adj* highly decorated, elaborate
ornithology *n* study of birds **ornithological** *adj* **ornithologist** *n*
orphan *n* child whose parents are dead **orphanage** *n* children's home for orphans **orphaned** *adj* having no living parents
orrery *n, pl* **-ries** mechanical model of the solar system
orris *n* kind of iris; (also **orris root**) fragrant root used for perfume
orthodontics *n* branch of dentistry concerned with correcting irregular teeth **orthodontist** *n*
orthodox *adj* conforming to established views **orthodoxy** *n* **Orthodox Church** dominant Christian Church in Eastern Europe
orthography *n* correct spelling
orthopaedics *n* branch of medicine concerned with disorders of the bones or joints **orthopaedic** *adj*
oryx *n* large African antelope
Oscar *n* award in the form of a statuette given for achievements in films
oscillate [**oss**-ill-late] *v* swing back and forth **oscillation** *n* **oscillator** *n* **oscilloscope** [oss-**sill**-oh-scope] *n* instrument that shows the shape of a wave on a cathode-ray tube
osier [**oh**-zee-er] *n* willow tree
osmium *n chem* heaviest known metallic element
osmosis *n* movement of a liquid through a membrane from a lower

to a higher concentration; process of subtle influence **osmotic** *adj*
osprey *n* large fish-eating bird of prey
ossify *v* **-fying, -fied** (cause to) become bone, harden; become inflexible **ossification** *n*
ostensible *adj* apparent, seeming **ostensibly** *adv*
ostentation *n* pretentious display **ostentatious** *adj* **ostentatiously** *adv*
osteopathy *n* medical treatment involving manipulation of the joints **osteopath** *n*
osteoporosis *n* brittleness of the bones, caused by lack of calcium
ostracize *v* exclude (a person) from a group **ostracism** *n*
ostrich *n* large African bird that runs fast but cannot fly
OT Old Testament
other *adj* remaining in a group of which one or some have been specified; different from the ones specified or understood; additional ▷ *n* other person or thing **otherwise** *conj* or else, if not ▷ *adv* differently, in another way **otherworldly** *adj* concerned with spiritual rather than practical matters
otiose [**oh**-tee-oze] *adj* not useful *eg otiose language*
otter *n* small brown freshwater mammal that eats fish
ottoman *n, pl* **-mans** storage chest with a padded lid for use as a seat **Ottoman** *n, adj hist* (member) of the former Turkish empire
oubliette [oo-blee-**ett**] *n* dungeon entered only by a trapdoor
ouch *interj* exclamation of sudden pain
ought *v* used to express: obligation *eg you ought to pay;* advisability *eg you ought to diet;* probability *eg you ought to know by then*
Ouija board *n* ® lettered board on which supposed messages from the dead are spelt out
ounce *n* unit of weight equal to one sixteenth of a pound (28.4 grams)
our *adj* belonging to us **ours** *pron* thing(s) belonging to us **ourselves** *pron* emphatic and reflexive form of **we** or
ousel *n* see **dipper**
oust *v* force (someone) out, expel
out *adv, adj* denoting movement or distance away from, a state of being used up or extinguished, public availability, etc *eg oil was pouring out; turn the light out; her new book is out* ▷ *v Informal* name (a public figure) as being homosexual **out of** at or to a point outside **out-of-date** *adj* old-fashioned **outer** *adj* on the outside **outermost** *adj* furthest out **outer space** space beyond the earth's atmosphere **outing** *n* leisure trip **outward** *adj* apparent ▷ *adv* (also **outwards**) away from somewhere **outwardly** *adv*
out- *prefix* surpassing *eg outlive; outdistance*
outback *n* remote bush country of Australia
outbid *v* offer a higher price than
outboard motor *n* engine externally attached to the stern of a boat
outbreak *n* sudden occurrence (of something unpleasant)
outburst *n* sudden expression of emotion
outcast *n* person rejected by a particular group
outclass *v* surpass in quality

outcome *n* result
outcrop *n* part of a rock formation that sticks out of the earth
outcry *n, pl* **-cries** vehement or widespread protest
outdo *v* surpass in performance
outdoors *adv* in(to) the open air ▷*n* the open air **outdoor** *adj*
outface *v* subdue or disconcert (someone) by staring
outfield *n cricket* area far from the pitch
outfit *n* matching set of clothes; *Informal* group of people working together **outfitter** *n* supplier of men's clothes
outflank *v* get round the side of (an enemy army); outdo (someone)
outgoing *adj* leaving; sociable **outgoings** *pl n* expenses
outgrow *v* become too large or too old for **outgrowth** *n* natural development
outhouse *n* building near a main building
outlandish *adj* extremely unconventional
outlaw *n hist* criminal deprived of legal protection, bandit ▷*v* make illegal; *hist* make (someone) an outlaw
outlay *n* expenditure
outlet *n* means of expressing emotion; market for a product; place where a product is sold; opening or way out
outline *n* short general explanation; line defining the shape of something ▷*v* summarize; show the general shape of
outlook *n* attitude; probable outcome
outlying *adj* distant from the main area
outmanoeuvre *v* get an advantage over
outmoded *adj* no longer fashionable or accepted
outnumber *v* exceed in number
outpatient *n* patient who does not stay in hospital overnight
outpost *n* outlying settlement
outpouring *n* passionate outburst
output *n* amount produced; power, voltage, or current delivered by an electrical circuit; *computers* data produced ▷*v computers* produce (data) at the end of a process
outrage *n* great moral indignation; gross violation of morality ▷*v* offend morally **outrageous** *adj* shocking; offensive **outrageously** *adv*
outré [oo-tray] *adj* shockingly eccentric
outrider *n* motorcyclist acting as an escort
outrigger *n* stabilizing frame projecting from a boat
outright *adj, adv* absolute(ly); open(ly) and direct(ly)
outrun *v* run faster than; exceed
outset *n* beginning
outshine *v* surpass (someone) in excellence
outside *prep, adj, adv* indicating movement to or position on the exterior ▷*adj* unlikely *eg an outside chance*; coming from outside ▷*n* external area or surface **outsider** *n* person outside a specific group; contestant thought unlikely to win
outsize, outsized *adj* larger than normal
outskirts *pl n* outer areas, esp of a town
outsmart *v Informal* outwit
outspan *v SAfr* relax
outspoken *adj* tending to say what one thinks; said openly

outstanding *adj* excellent; still to be dealt with or paid
outstrip *v* surpass; go faster than
outtake *n* unreleased take from a recording session, film, or TV programme
outweigh *v* be more important, significant, or influential than
outwit *v* **-witting, -witted** get the better of (someone) by cunning
ouzel [ooze-el] *n* see **dipper**
ova *n* plural of **ovum**
oval *adj* egg-shaped ▷*n* anything that is oval in shape
ovary *n, pl* **-ries** female egg-producing organ **ovarian** *adj*
ovation *n* enthusiastic round of applause
oven *n* heated compartment or container for cooking or for drying or firing ceramics
over *prep, adv* indicating position on the top of, movement to the other side of, amount greater than, etc *eg a room over the garage; climbing over the fence; over fifty pounds* ▷*adj* finished ▷*n cricket* series of six balls bowled from one end **overly** *adv* excessively
over- *prefix* too much *eg overeat;* above *eg overlord;* on top *eg overshoe*
overall *adj, adv* in total ▷*n* coat-shaped protective garment ▷*pl* protective garment consisting of trousers with a jacket or bib and braces attached
overarm *adj, adv* (thrown) with the arm above the shoulder
overawe *v* affect (someone) with an overpowering sense of awe
overbalance *v* lose balance
overbearing *adj* unpleasantly forceful
overblown *adj* excessive
overboard *adv* from a boat into the water **go overboard** go to extremes, esp in enthusiasm
overcast *adj* (of the sky) covered by clouds
overcoat *n* heavy coat
overcome *v* gain control over after an effort; (of an emotion) affect strongly
overcrowded *adj* containing more people or things than is desirable
overdo *v* do to excess; exaggerate (something) **overdo it** do something to a greater degree than is advisable
overdose *n* excessive dose of a drug ▷*v* take an overdose
overdraft *n* overdrawing; amount overdrawn
overdraw *v* withdraw more money than is in (one's bank account)
overdrawn *adj* having overdrawn one's account; (of an account) in debit
overdrive *n* very high gear in a motor vehicle
overdue *adj* still due after the time allowed
overgrown *adj* thickly covered with plants and weeds
overhaul *v* examine and repair ▷*n* examination and repair
overhead *adv, adj* above one's head **overheads** *pl n* general cost of maintaining a business
overhear *v* hear (a speaker or remark) unintentionally or without the speaker's knowledge
overjoyed *adj* extremely pleased
overkill *n* treatment that is greater than required
overland *adj, adv* by land
overlap *v* share part of the same space or period of time (as) ▷*n* area overlapping
overleaf *adv* on the back of the

current page

overlook *v* fail to notice; ignore; look at from above

overnight *adj, adv* (taking place) during one night; (happening) very quickly

overpower *v* subdue or overcome (someone)

overreach *v* **overreach oneself** fail by trying to be too clever

override *v* overrule; replace

overrule *v* reverse the decision of (a person with less power); reverse (someone else's decision)

overrun *v* spread over (a place) rapidly; extend beyond a set limit

overseas *adv, adj* to, of, or from a distant country

oversee *v* watch over from a position of authority **overseer** *n*

overshadow *v* reduce the significance of (a person or thing) by comparison; sadden the atmosphere of

oversight *n* mistake caused by not noticing something

overspill *n Brit* rehousing of people from crowded cities in smaller towns

overstay *v* **overstay one's welcome** stay longer than one's host or hostess would like **overstayer** *n NZ* person who remains in New Zealand after their permit has expired

overt *adj* open, not hidden **overtly** *adv*

overtake *v* move past (a vehicle or person) travelling in the same direction

overthrow *v* defeat and replace ▷ *n* downfall, destruction

overtime *n, adv* (paid work done) in addition to one's normal working hours

overtone *n* additional meaning

overture *n music* orchestral introduction ▷ *pl* opening moves in a new relationship

overturn *v* turn upside down; overrule (a legal decision); overthrow (a government)

overweight *adj* weighing more than is healthy

overwhelm *v* overpower, esp emotionally; defeat by force **overwhelming** *adj* **overwhelmingly** *adv*

overwrought *adj* nervous and agitated

ovoid [**oh**-void] *adj* egg-shaped

ovulate [**ov**-yew-late] *v* produce or release an egg cell from an ovary **ovulation** *n*

ovum [**oh**-vum] *n, pl* **ova** unfertilized egg cell

owe *v* be obliged to pay (a sum of money) to (a person) **owing to** as a result of

owl *n* night bird of prey **owlish** *adj*

own *adj* used to emphasize possession *eg my own idea* ▷ *v* possess **owner** *n* **ownership** *n* **own up** *v* confess

ox *n, pl* **oxen** castrated bull

Oxfam Oxford Committee for Famine Relief

oxide *n* compound of oxygen and one other element **oxidize** *v* combine chemically with oxygen, as in burning or rusting

oxygen *n chem* gaseous element essential to life and combustion **oxygenate** *v* add oxygen to

oxymoron [ox-see-**more**-on] *n* figure of speech that combines two apparently contradictory ideas *eg cruel kindness*

oyez *interj hist* shouted three times by a public crier, listen

oyster *n* edible shellfish **oystercatcher** *n* wading bird with

black-and-white feathers
Oz *n slang* Australia
oz. ounce
ozone *n* strong-smelling form of oxygen **ozone layer** layer of ozone in the upper atmosphere that filters out ultraviolet radiation

p

p *Brit, Aust & NZ* penny; *Brit* pence
P parking
p. *pl* **pp** page
pa *n NZ* (formerly) a fortified Maori settlement
PA personal assistant; public-address system
p.a. each year
pace *n* single step in walking; length of a step; rate of progress ▷ *v* walk up and down, esp in anxiety; (foll by *out*) cross or measure with steps **pacemaker** *n* electronic device surgically implanted in a person with heart disease to regulate the heartbeat; person who, by taking the lead early in a race, sets the pace for the rest of the competitors
pachyderm [**pak**-ee-durm] *n* thick-skinned animal such as an elephant
pacifist *n* person who refuses on

principle to take part in war **pacifism** *n*

pacify *v* **-fying, -fied** soothe, calm **pacification** *n*

pack *v* put (clothes etc) together in a suitcase or bag; put (goods) into containers or parcels; fill with people or things ▷ *n* bag carried on a person's or animal's back; *Chiefly US* same as **packet:** set of playing cards; group of dogs or wolves that hunt together **pack ice** mass of floating ice in the sea **pack in** *v Informal* stop doing **pack off** *v* send away

package *n* small parcel; (also **package deal**) deal in which separate items are presented together as a unit ▷ *v* put into a package **packaging** *n* **package holiday** holiday in which everything is arranged by one company for a fixed price

packet *n* small container (and contents); small parcel; *slang* large sum of money

packhorse *n* horse used for carrying goods

pact *n* formal agreement

pad *n* piece of soft material used for protection, support, absorption of liquid, etc; number of sheets of paper fastened at the edge; fleshy underpart of an animal's paw; place for launching rockets; *slang* home ▷ *v* **padding, padded** protect or fill with soft material; walk with soft steps **padding** *n* soft material used to pad something; unnecessary words put into a speech or written work to make it longer

paddle¹ *n* short oar with a broad blade at one or each end ▷ *v* move (a canoe etc) with a paddle **paddle steamer** ship propelled by paddle wheels **paddle wheel** wheel with crosswise blades that strike the water successively to propel a ship

paddle² *v* walk barefoot in shallow water

paddock *n* small field or enclosure for horses

paddy *n Brit, Informal* fit of temper

paddy field *n* field where rice is grown (also **paddy**)

pademelon, paddymelon [**pad**-ee-mel-an] *n* small Australian wallaby

padlock *n* detachable lock with a hinged hoop fastened over a ring on the object to be secured

padre [**pah**-dray] *n* chaplain to the armed forces

paean [**pee**-an] *n* song of triumph or thanksgiving

paediatrics *n* branch of medicine concerned with diseases of children **paediatrician** *n*

paedophilia *n* condition of being sexually attracted to children **paedophile** *n* person who is sexually attracted to children

paella [pie-**ell**-a] *n* Spanish dish of rice, chicken, shellfish, and vegetables

pagan *n, adj* (person) not belonging to one of the world's main religions

page¹ *n* (one side of) a sheet of paper forming a book etc; screenful of information from a website or teletext service

page² *n* (also **pageboy**) small boy who attends a bride at her wedding; *hist* boy in training for knighthood ▷ *v* summon (someone) by bleeper or loudspeaker, in order to pass on a message

pageant *n* parade or display of people in costume, usu illustrating a scene from history **pageantry** *n*

pagination *n* numbering of the pages of a book etc
pagoda *n* pyramid-shaped Asian temple or tower
paid *v* past of **pay** **put paid to** *Informal* end or destroy
pail *n* (contents of) a bucket
pain *n* physical or mental suffering ▷ *pl* trouble, effort **on pain of** subject to the penalty of **painful** *adj* **painfully** *adv* **painless** *adj* **painlessly** *adv* **painkiller** *n* drug that relieves pain
painstaking *adj* extremely thorough and careful
paint *n* coloured substance, spread on a surface with a brush or roller ▷ *v* colour or coat with paint; use paint to make a picture of **painter** *n* **painting** *n*
painter *n* rope at the front of a boat, for tying it up
pair *n* set of two things matched for use together ▷ *v* group or be grouped in twos
paisley pattern *n* pattern of small curving shapes, used in fabric
Pakeha [pah-kee-ha] *n NZ* New Zealander who is not of Maori descent
pal *n Informal, old-fashioned in NZ* friend
palace *n* residence of a king, bishop, etc; large grand building
palaeography [pal-ee-**og**-ra-fee] *n* study of ancient manuscripts
Palaeolithic [pal-ee-oh-**lith**-ik] *adj* of the Old Stone Age
palaeontology [pal-ee-on-**tol**-a-jee] *n* study of past geological periods and fossils
Palagi [pa-**lang**-gee] *n, pl* **-gis** *NZ* Samoan name for a Pakeha
palatable *adj* pleasant to taste
palate *n* roof of the mouth; sense of taste
palatial *adj* like a palace, magnificent
palaver [pal-**lah**-ver] *n* time-wasting fuss
pale[1] *adj* light, whitish; whitish in the face, esp through illness or shock ▷ *v* become pale
pale[2] *n* wooden or metal post used in fences **beyond the pale** outside the limits of social convention
palette *n* artist's flat board for mixing colours on
palindrome *n* word or phrase that reads the same backwards as forwards
paling *n* wooden or metal post used in fences
palisade *n* fence made of wooden posts driven into the ground
pall[1] *n* cloth spread over a coffin; dark cloud (of smoke); depressing oppressive atmosphere **pallbearer** *n* person who helps to carry the coffin at a funeral
pall[2] *v* become boring
palladium *n chem* silvery-white element of the platinum metal group
pallet[1] *n* portable platform for storing and moving goods
pallet[2] *n* straw-filled mattress or bed
palliate *v* lessen the severity of (something) without curing it
palliative *adj* giving temporary or partial relief ▷ *n* something, for example a drug, that palliates
pallid *adj* pale, esp because ill or weak **pallor** *n*
pally *adj* **-lier, -liest** *Informal* on friendly terms
palm[1] *n* inner surface of the hand **palm off** *v* get rid of (an unwanted thing or person), esp by deceit
palm[2] *n* tropical tree with long

pointed leaves growing out of the top of a straight trunk **Palm Sunday** Sunday before Easter

palmistry *n* fortune-telling from lines on the palm of the hand **palmist** *n*

palmtop *adj* (of a computer) small enough to be held in the hand ▷ *n* computer small enough to be held in the hand

palomino *n, pl* **-nos** gold-coloured horse with a white mane and tail

palpable *adj* obvious *eg a palpable hit*; so intense as to seem capable of being touched *eg the tension is almost palpable* **palpably** *adv*

palpate *v med* examine (an area of the body) by touching

palpitate *v* (of the heart) beat rapidly; flutter or tremble **palpitation** *n*

palsy [**pawl**-zee] *n* paralysis **palsied** *adj* affected with palsy

paltry *adj* **-trier, -triest** insignificant

pampas *pl n* vast grassy plains in S America **pampas grass** tall grass with feathery ornamental flower branches

pamper *v* treat (someone) with great indulgence, spoil

pamphlet *n* thin paper-covered booklet **pamphleteer** *n* writer of pamphlets

pan¹ *n* wide long-handled metal container used in cooking; bowl of a toilet ▷ *v* **panning, panned** sift gravel from (a river) in a pan to search for gold; *Informal* criticize harshly **pan out** *v* result

pan² *v* **panning, panned** (of a film camera) be moved slowly so as to cover a whole scene or follow a moving object

pan- *combining form* all *eg pan-American*

panacea [pan-a-**see**-a] *n* remedy for all diseases or problems

panache [pan-**ash**] *n* confident elegant style

panama hat *n* straw hat

panatella *n* long slender cigar

pancake *n* thin flat circle of fried batter

panchromatic *adj photog* sensitive to light of all colours

pancreas [**pang**-kree-ass] *n* large gland behind the stomach that produces insulin and helps digestion **pancreatic** *adj*

panda *n* large black-and-white bearlike mammal from China **panda car** *Brit* police patrol car

pandemic *adj* (of a disease) occurring over a wide area

pandemonium *n* wild confusion, uproar

pander¹ *v* (foll by *to*) indulge (a person his or her desires)

pander² *n old-fashioned* person who procures a sexual partner for someone

p&p postage and packing

pane *n* sheet of glass in a window or door

panegyric [pan-ee-**jire**-ik] *n* formal speech or piece of writing in praise of someone or something

panel *n* flat distinct section of a larger surface, for example in a door; group of people as a team in a quiz etc; list of jurors, doctors, etc; board or surface containing switches and controls to operate equipment ▷ *v* **-elling, -elled** cover or decorate with panels **panelling** *n* panels collectively, esp on a wall **panellist** *n* member of a panel **panel beater** person who repairs damage to car bodies

pang *n* sudden sharp feeling of pain or sadness

pangolin *n* animal of tropical countries with a scaly body and a long snout for eating ants and termites (also **scaly anteater**)
panic *n* sudden overwhelming fear, often affecting a whole group of people ▷*v* **-icking, -icked** feel or cause to feel panic **panicky** *adj* **panic-stricken** *adj*
pannier *n* bag fixed on the back of a cycle; basket carried by a beast of burden
panoply *n* magnificent array
panorama *n* wide unbroken view of a scene **panoramic** *adj*
pansy *n, pl* **-sies** small garden flower with velvety purple, yellow, or white petals; *offens* effeminate or homosexual man
pant *v* breathe quickly and noisily during or after exertion
pantaloons *pl n* baggy trousers gathered at the ankles
pantechnicon *n* large van for furniture removals
pantheism *n* belief that God is present in everything **pantheist** *n* **pantheistic** *adj*
pantheon *n* (in ancient Greece and Rome) temple built to honour all the gods
panther *n* leopard, esp a black one
panties *pl n* women's underpants
pantile *n* roofing tile with an S-shaped cross section
pantomime *n* play based on a fairy tale, performed at Christmas time
pantry *n, pl* **-tries** small room or cupboard for storing food
pants *pl n* undergarment for the lower part of the body; *US, Canadian, Aust & NZ* trousers
pap *n* soft food for babies or invalids; worthless entertainment or information
papacy [pay-pa-see] *n, pl* **-cies** position or term of office of a Pope **papal** *adj* of the Pope
paparazzo [pap-a-**rat**-so] *n, pl* **-razzi** photographer specializing in candid photographs of famous people
papaya [pa-**pie**-ya] *n* large sweet West Indian fruit
paper *n* material made in sheets from wood pulp or other fibres; printed sheet of this; newspaper; set of examination questions; article or essay ▷*pl* personal documents ▷*v* cover (walls) with wallpaper **paperback** *n* book with covers made of flexible card **paperweight** *n* heavy decorative object placed on top of loose papers **paperwork** *n* clerical work, such as writing reports and letters
papier-mâché [pap-yay **mash**-ay] *n* material made from paper mixed with paste and moulded when moist
papist *n, adj offens* Roman Catholic
papoose *n* Native American child
paprika *n* mild powdered seasoning made from red peppers
papyrus [pap-**ire**-uss] *n, pl* **-ri, -ruses** tall water plant; (manuscript written on) a kind of paper made from this plant
par *n* usual or average condition *eg feeling under par*; *golf* expected standard score; face value of stocks and shares **on a par with** equal to
parable *n* story that illustrates a religious teaching
parabola [par-**ab**-bol-a] *n* regular curve resembling the course of an object thrown forward and up **parabolic** *adj*
paracetamol *n* mild pain-relieving drug

parachute *n* large fabric canopy that slows the descent of a person or object from an aircraft ▷*v* land or drop by parachute **parachutist** *n*
parade *n* procession or march; street or promenade ▷*v* display or flaunt; march in procession
paradigm [par-a-dime] *n* example or model
paradise *n* heaven; place or situation that is near-perfect
paradox *n* statement that seems self-contradictory but may be true **paradoxical** *adj* **paradoxically** *adv*
paraffin *n Brit & SAfr* liquid mixture distilled from petroleum and used as a fuel or solvent

> SPELLING People have trouble remembering whether the *r* or the *f* is doubled in **paraffin**, but according to Collins Word Web, the most popular mistake is to decide on neither, as in *parafin*

paragliding *n* cross-country gliding wearing a parachute shaped like wings
paragon *n* model of perfection
paragraph *n* section of a piece of writing starting on a new line
parakeet *n* small long-tailed parrot
parallax *n* apparent change in an object's position due to a change in the observer's position
parallel *adj* separated by an equal distance at every point; exactly corresponding ▷*n* line separated from another by an equal distance at every point; thing with similar features to another; line of latitude ▷*v* correspond to
parallelogram *n* four-sided geometric figure with opposite sides parallel
paralysis *n* inability to move or feel, because of damage to the nervous system **paralyse** *v* affect with paralysis; make temporarily unable to move or take action **paralytic** *n, adj* (person) affected with paralysis
paramedic *n* person working in support of the medical profession **paramedical** *adj*
parameter [par-**am**-it-er] *n* limiting factor, boundary
paramilitary *adj* organized on military lines
paramount *adj* of the greatest importance
paramour *n old-fashioned* lover, esp of a person married to someone else
paranoia *n* mental illness causing delusions of grandeur or persecution; *Informal* intense fear or suspicion **paranoid, paranoiac** *adj, n*
paranormal *adj* beyond scientific explanation
parapet *n* low wall or railing along the edge of a balcony or roof
paraphernalia *n* personal belongings or bits of equipment
paraphrase *v* put (a statement or text) into other words
paraplegia [par-a-**pleej**-ya] *n* paralysis of the lower half of the body **paraplegic** *adj, n*
parapsychology *n* study of mental phenomena such as telepathy
Paraquat *n* ® extremely poisonous weedkiller
parasite *n* animal or plant living in or on another; person who lives at the expense of others **parasitic** *adj*
parasol *n* umbrella-like sunshade
paratrooper *n* soldier trained to be dropped by parachute into a battle area **paratroops** *pl n*

parboil *v* boil until partly cooked
parcel *n* something wrapped up, package ▷ *v* **-celling, -celled** (often foll by *up*) wrap up **parcel out** *v* divide into parts
parch *v* make very hot and dry; make thirsty
parchment *n* thick smooth writing material made from animal skin
pardon *v* forgive, excuse ▷ *n* forgiveness; official release from punishment for a crime **pardonable** *adj*
pare *v* cut off the skin or top layer of; (often foll by *down*) reduce in size or amount **paring** *n* piece pared off
parent *n* father or mother **parental** *adj* **parenthood** *n*
parentage *n* ancestry or family
parenting *n* activity of bringing up children
parenthesis [par-**en**-thiss-iss] *n*, *pl* **-ses** word or sentence inserted into a passage, marked off by brackets or dashes ▷ *pl* round brackets, ( ) **parenthetical** *adj*
pariah [par-**rye**-a] *n* social outcast
parietal [par-**rye**-it-al] *adj* of the walls of a body cavity such as the skull
parish *n* area that has its own church and a priest or pastor **parishioner** *n* inhabitant of a parish
parity *n* equality or equivalence
park *n* area of open land for recreational use by the public; area containing a number of related enterprises *eg a business park*; *Brit* area of private land around a large country house ▷ *v* stop and leave (a vehicle) temporarily
parka *n* large waterproof jacket with a hood
parky *adj* **parkier, parkiest** *Brit, Informal* (of the weather) chilly
parlance *n* particular way of speaking, idiom
parley *n* meeting between leaders or representatives of opposing forces to discuss terms ▷ *v* have a parley
parliament *n* law-making assembly of a country **parliamentary** *adj*
parlour *n* *old-fashioned* living room for receiving visitors
parlous *adj* *old-fashioned* dire; dangerously bad
Parmesan *n* hard strong-flavoured Italian cheese, used grated on pasta dishes and soups
parochial *adj* narrow in outlook; of a parish **parochialism** *n*
parody *n*, *pl* **-dies** exaggerated and amusing imitation of someone else's style ▷ *v* **-dying, -died** make a parody of
parole *n* early freeing of a prisoner on condition that he or she behaves well ▷ *v* put on parole **on parole** (of a prisoner) released on condition that he or she behaves well
paroxysm *n* uncontrollable outburst of rage, delight, etc; spasm or convulsion of coughing, pain, etc
parquet [**par**-kay] *n* floor covering made of wooden blocks arranged in a geometric pattern **parquetry** *n*
parricide *n* crime of killing either of one's parents; person who does this
parrot *n* tropical bird with a short hooked beak and an ability to imitate human speech ▷ *v* **-roting, -roted** repeat (someone else's words) without thinking
parry *v* **-rying, -ried** ward off (an attack); cleverly avoid (an awkward

question)

parse [**parz**] *v* analyse (a sentence) in terms of grammar

parsimony *n* extreme caution in spending money **parsimonious** *adj*

parsley *n* herb used for seasoning and decorating food

parsnip *n* long tapering cream-coloured root vegetable

parson *n* Anglican parish priest; any member of the clergy **parsonage** *n* parson's house

part *n* one of the pieces that make up a whole; one of several equal divisions; actor's role; (often pl) region, area; component of a vehicle or machine ▷*v* divide or separate; (of people) leave each other **take someone's part** support someone in an argument etc **take (something) in good part** respond to (teasing or criticism) with good humour **parting** *n* occasion when one person leaves another; line of scalp between sections of hair combed in opposite directions; dividing or separating **partly** *adv* not completely **part of speech** particular grammatical class of words, such as noun or verb **part-time** *adj* occupying or working less than the full working week **part with** *v* give away, hand over

partake *v* **-taking, -took, -taken** (foll by *of*) take (food or drink); (foll by *in*) take part in

partial *adj* not complete; prejudiced **partial to** having a liking for **partiality** *n* **partially** *adv*

participate *v* become actively involved **participant** *n* **participation** *n*

participle *n* form of a verb used in compound tenses or as an adjective *eg worried; worrying*

particle *n* extremely small piece or amount; *physics* minute piece of matter, such as a proton or electron

particular *adj* relating to one person or thing, not general; exceptional or special; very exact; difficult to please, fastidious ▷*n* item of information, detail **particularly** *adv* **particularize** *v* give details about

partisan *n* strong supporter of a party or group; guerrilla, member of a resistance movement ▷*adj* prejudiced or one-sided

partition *n* screen or thin wall that divides a room; division of a country into independent parts ▷*v* divide with a partition

partner *n* either member of a couple in a relationship or activity; member of a business partnership ▷*v* be the partner of **partnership** *n* joint business venture between two or more people

partridge *n* game bird of the grouse family

parturition *n* act of giving birth

party *n, pl* **-ties** social gathering for pleasure; group of people travelling or working together; group of people with a common political aim; person or people forming one side in a lawsuit or dispute **party line** official view of a political party; telephone line shared by two or more subscribers **party wall** common wall separating adjoining buildings

parvenu [**par**-ven-new] *n* person newly risen to a position of power or wealth

pascal *n* unit of pressure

paspalum [pass-**pale**-um] *n Aust &*

NZ type of grass with wide leaves

pass *v* go by, past, or through; be successful in (a test or examination); spend (time) or (of time) go by; give, hand; be inherited by; *sport* hit, kick, or throw (the ball) to another player; (of a law-making body) agree to (a law); exceed ▷*n* successful result in a test or examination; permit or licence **make a pass at** *Informal* make sexual advances to **passable** *adj* (just) acceptable; (of a road) capable of being travelled along **passing** *adj* brief or transitory; cursory or casual **pass away** *v* die **pass out** *v Informal* faint **pass up** *v Informal* fail to take advantage of (something)

passage *n* channel or opening providing a way through; hall or corridor; section of a book etc; journey by sea; right or freedom to pass **passageway** *n* passage or corridor

passbook *n* book issued by a bank or building society for keeping a record of deposits and withdrawals; *SAfr* formerly, an official identity document

passé [pas-say] *adj* out-of-date

passenger *n* person travelling in a vehicle driven by someone else; member of a team who does not pull his or her weight

passer-by *n, pl* **passers-by** person who is walking past something or someone

passim *adv Latin* everywhere, throughout

passion *n* intense sexual love; any strong emotion; great enthusiasm; **(P-)** *Christianity* the suffering of Christ **passionate** *adj* **passionflower** *n* tropical American plant **passion fruit** edible fruit of the passionflower **Passion play** play about Christ's suffering

passive *adj* not playing an active part; submissive and receptive to outside forces; *grammar* (of a verb) in a form indicating that the subject receives the action, eg *was jeered* in *he was jeered by the crowd* **passivity** *n* **passive resistance** resistance to a government, law, etc by nonviolent acts **passive smoking** inhalation of smoke from others' cigarettes by a nonsmoker

Passover *n* Jewish festival commemorating the sparing of the Jews in Egypt

passport *n* official document of nationality granting permission to travel abroad

password *n* secret word or phrase that ensures admission

past *adj* of the time before the present; ended, gone by; *grammar* (of a verb tense) indicating that the action specified took place earlier ▷*n* period of time before the present; person's earlier life, esp a disreputable period; *grammar* past tense ▷*adv* by, along ▷*prep* beyond **past it** *Informal* unable to do the things one could do when younger **past master** person with great talent or experience in a particular subject

pasta *n* type of food, such as spaghetti, that is made in different shapes from flour and water

paste *n* moist soft mixture, such as toothpaste; adhesive, esp for paper; *Brit* pastry dough; shiny glass used to make imitation jewellery ▷*v* fasten with paste **pasting** *n* *Informal* heavy defeat; strong criticism **pasteboard** *n* stiff thick paper

pastel *n* coloured chalk crayon for

drawing; picture drawn in pastels; pale delicate colour ▷ *adj* pale and delicate in colour

pasteurize *v* sterilize by heating **pasteurization** *n*

pastiche [pass-**teesh**] *n* work of art that mixes styles or copies the style of another artist

pastille *n* small fruit-flavoured and sometimes medicated sweet

pastime *n* activity that makes time pass pleasantly

pastor *n* member of the clergy in charge of a congregation **pastoral** *adj* of or depicting country life; of a clergyman or his duties

pastrami *n* highly seasoned smoked beef

pastry *n, pl* **-ries** baking dough made of flour, fat, and water; cake or pie

pasture *n* grassy land for farm animals to graze on

pasty[1] [**pay**-stee] *adj* **pastier, pastiest** (of a complexion) pale and unhealthy

pasty[2] [**pass**-tee] *n, pl* **pasties** round of pastry folded over a savoury filling

pat[1] *v* **patting, patted** tap lightly ▷ *n* gentle tap or stroke; small shaped mass of butter etc

pat[2] *adj* quick, ready, or glib **off pat** learned thoroughly

patch *n* piece of material sewn on a garment; small contrasting section; plot of ground; protective pad for the eye ▷ *v* mend with a patch **patchy** *adj* of uneven quality or intensity **patch up** *v* repair clumsily; make up (a quarrel) **patchwork** *n* needlework made of pieces of different materials sewn together

pate *n old-fashioned* head

pâté [**pat**-ay] *n* spread of finely minced liver etc

patella *n, pl* **-lae** kneecap

patent *n* document giving the exclusive right to make or sell an invention ▷ *adj* open to public inspection *eg letters patent*; obvious; protected by a patent ▷ *v* obtain a patent for **patently** *adv* obviously **patent leather** leather processed to give a hard glossy surface

paternal *adj* fatherly; related through one's father **paternity** *n* fact or state of being a father

paternalism *n* authority exercised in a way that limits individual responsibility **paternalistic** *adj*

path *n* surfaced walk or track; course of action **pathname** *n computers* file name listing the sequence of directories leading to a particular file or directory

pathetic *adj* causing feelings of pity or sadness; distressingly inadequate **pathetically** *adv*

pathogen *n* thing that causes disease **pathogenic** *adj*

pathology *n* scientific study of diseases **pathological** *adj* of pathology; *Informal* compulsively motivated **pathologist** *n*

pathos *n* power of arousing pity or sadness

patient *adj* enduring difficulties or delays calmly ▷ *n* person receiving medical treatment **patience** *n* quality of being patient; card game for one

patina *n* fine layer on a surface; sheen of age on woodwork

patio *n, pl* **-tios** paved area adjoining a house

patois [**pat**-wah] *n, pl* **patois** [**pat**-wahz] regional dialect, esp of French

patriarch *n* male head of a family or tribe; highest-ranking bishop in

Orthodox Churches **patriarchal** *adj* **patriarchy** *n, pl* **-chies** society in which men have most of the power

patrician *n* member of the nobility ▷*adj* of noble birth

patricide *n* crime of killing one's father; person who does this

patrimony *n, pl* **-nies** property inherited from ancestors

patriot *n* person who loves his or her country and supports its interests **patriotic** *adj* **patriotism** *n*

patrol *n* regular circuit by a guard; person or small group patrolling; unit of Scouts or Guides ▷*v* **-trolling, -trolled** go round on guard, or reconnoitring

patron *n* person who gives financial support to charities, artists, etc; regular customer of a shop, pub, etc **patronage** *n* support given by a patron **patronize** *v* treat in a condescending way; be a patron of **patron saint** saint regarded as the guardian of a country or group

patronymic *n* name derived from one's father or a male ancestor

patter[1] *v* make repeated soft tapping sounds ▷*n* quick succession of taps

patter[2] *n* glib rapid speech

pattern *n* arrangement of repeated parts or decorative designs; regular way that something is done; diagram or shape used as a guide to make something **patterned** *adj* decorated with a pattern

patty *n, pl* **-ties** small flattened cake of minced food

paucity *n* scarcity; smallness of amount or number

paunch *n* protruding belly

pauper *n* very poor person

pause *v* stop for a time ▷*n* stop or rest in speech or action

pave *v* form (a surface) with stone or brick **pavement** *n* paved path for pedestrians

pavilion *n* building on a playing field etc; building for housing an exhibition etc

paw *n* animal's foot with claws and pads ▷*v* scrape with the paw or hoof; *Informal* touch in a rough or overfamiliar way

pawn[1] *v* deposit (an article) as security for money borrowed **in pawn** deposited as security with a pawnbroker **pawnbroker** *n* lender of money on goods deposited

pawn[2] *n* chessman of the lowest value; person manipulated by someone else

pay *v* **paying, paid** give money etc in return for goods or services; settle a debt or obligation; compensate (for); give; be profitable to ▷*n* wages or salary **payment** *n* act of paying; money paid **payable** *adj* due to be paid **payee** *n* person to whom money is paid or due **paying guest** lodger or boarder **pay off** *v* pay (debt) in full; turn out successfully **pay out** *v* spend; release (a rope) bit by bit

PAYE pay as you earn: system by which income tax is paid by an employer straight to the government

payload *n* passengers or cargo of an aircraft; explosive power of a missile etc

payola *n* *Chiefly US, Informal* bribe to get special treatment, esp to promote a commercial product

pc per cent

PC personal computer; (in Britain)

Police Constable; politically correct; (in Britain) Privy Councillor

PDA personal digital assistant

PDF *computers* portable document format: a format in which documents may be viewed

PE physical education

pea *n* climbing plant with seeds growing in pods; its seed, eaten as a vegetable

peace *n* calm, quietness; absence of anxiety; freedom from war; harmony between people **peaceable** *adj* inclined towards peace **peaceably** *adv* **peaceful** *adj* **peacefully** *adv*

peach *n* soft juicy fruit with a stone and a downy skin; *Informal* very pleasing person or thing ▷ *adj* pinkish-orange

peacock *n* large male bird with a brilliantly coloured fanlike tail **peahen** *n fem*

peak *n* pointed top, esp of a mountain; point of greatest development etc; projecting piece on the front of a cap ▷ *v* form or reach a peak ▷ *adj* of or at the point of greatest demand **peaked** *adj* **peaky** *adj* pale and sickly

peal *n* long loud echoing sound, esp of bells or thunder ▷ *v* sound with a peal or peals

peanut *n* pea-shaped nut that ripens underground ▷ *pl Informal* trifling amount of money

pear *n* sweet juicy fruit with a narrow top and rounded base

pearl *n* hard round shiny object found inside some oyster shells and used as a jewel **pearly** *adj*

peasant *n* person working on the land, esp in poorer countries or in the past **peasantry** *n* peasants collectively

peat *n* decayed vegetable material found in bogs, used as fertilizer or fuel

pebble *n* small roundish stone **pebbly** *adj* **pebble dash** coating for exterior walls consisting of small stones set in plaster

pecan [pee-kan] *n* edible nut of a N American tree

peccadillo *n, pl* **-loes, -los** trivial misdeed

peck *v* strike or pick up with the beak; *Informal* kiss quickly ▷ *n* pecking movement **peckish** *adj Informal* slightly hungry **peck at** *v* nibble, eat reluctantly

pecs *pl n Informal* pectoral muscles

pectin *n* substance in fruit that makes jam set

pectoral *adj* of the chest or thorax ▷ *n* pectoral muscle or fin

peculiar *adj* strange; distinct, special; belonging exclusively to **peculiarity** *n, pl* **-ties** oddity, eccentricity; distinguishing trait

pecuniary *adj* relating to, or consisting of, money

pedagogue *n* schoolteacher, esp a pedantic one

pedal *n* foot-operated lever used to control a vehicle or machine, or to modify the tone of a musical instrument ▷ *v* **-alling, -alled** propel (a bicycle) by using its pedals

pedant *n* person who is excessively concerned with details and rules, esp in academic work **pedantic** *adj* **pedantry** *n*

peddle *v* sell (goods) from door to door

peddler *n* person who sells illegal drugs

pederast *n* man who has homosexual relations with boys **pederasty** *n*

pedestal *n* base supporting a column, statue, etc

pedestrian *n* person who walks ▷*adj* dull, uninspiring **pedestrian crossing** place marked where pedestrians may cross a road **pedestrian precinct** *Brit* (shopping) area for pedestrians only

pedicure *n* medical or cosmetic treatment of the feet

pedigree *n* register of ancestors, esp of a purebred animal

pediment *n* triangular part over a door etc

pedlar *n* person who sells goods from door to door

pee *Informal* ▷*v* **peeing, peed** urinate ▷*n* act of urinating

peek *v, n* peep or glance

peel *v* remove the skin or rind of (a vegetable or fruit); (of skin or a surface) come off in flakes ▷*n* rind or skin **peelings** *pl n*

peep[1] *v* look slyly or quickly ▷*n* peeping look **Peeping Tom** man who furtively watches women undressing

peep[2] *v* make a small shrill noise ▷*n* small shrill noise

peer[1] *n, fem* **peeress** (in Britain) member of the nobility; person of the same status, age, etc **peerage** *n Brit* whole body of peers; rank of a peer **peerless** *adj* unequalled, unsurpassed **peer group** group of people of similar age, status, etc

peer[2] *v* look closely and intently

peeved *adj Informal* annoyed

peevish *adj* fretful or irritable **peevishly** *adv*

peewee *n* black-and-white Australian bird

peewit *n* same as **lapwing**

peg *n* pin or clip for joining, fastening, marking, etc; hook or knob for hanging things on ▷*v* **pegging, pegged** fasten with pegs; stabilize (prices) **off the peg** (of clothes) ready-to-wear, not tailor-made

peggy square *n NZ* small hand-knitted square

peignoir [**pay**-nwahr] *n* woman's light dressing gown

pejorative [pij-**jor**-a-tiv] *adj* (of words etc) with an insulting or critical meaning

Pekingese, Pekinese *n, pl* **-ese** small dog with a short wrinkled muzzle

pelargonium *n* plant with red, white, purple, or pink flowers

pelican *n* large water bird with a pouch beneath its bill for storing fish **pelican crossing** (in Britain) road crossing with pedestrian-operated traffic lights

pellagra *n* disease caused by lack of vitamin B

pellet *n* small ball of something

pell-mell *adv* in utter confusion, headlong

pellucid *adj* very clear

pelmet *n* ornamental drapery or board, concealing a curtain rail

pelt[1] *v* throw missiles at; run fast, rush; rain heavily **at full pelt** at top speed

pelt[2] *n* skin of a fur-bearing animal

pelvis *n* framework of bones at the base of the spine, to which the hips are attached **pelvic** *adj*

pen[1] *n* instrument for writing in ink ▷*v* **penning, penned** write or compose **pen friend** friend with whom a person corresponds without meeting **penknife** *n* small knife with blade(s) that fold into the handle **pen name** name used by a writer instead of his or her real name

pen[2] *n* small enclosure for domestic animals ▷*v* **penning,**

penned put or keep in a pen
pen[3] *n* female swan
penal [**pee**-nal] *adj* of or used in punishment **penalize** *v* impose a penalty on; handicap, hinder
penalty *n, pl* **-ties** punishment for a crime or offence; *sport* handicap or disadvantage imposed for breaking a rule
penance *n* voluntary self-punishment to make amends for wrongdoing
pence *n Brit* a plural of **penny**
penchant [**pon**-shon] *n* inclination or liking
pencil *n* thin cylindrical instrument containing graphite, for writing or drawing ▷ *v* **-cilling, -cilled** draw, write, or mark with a pencil
pendant *n* ornament worn on a chain round the neck
pendent *adj* hanging
pending *prep* while waiting for ▷ *adj* not yet decided or settled
pendulous *adj* hanging, swinging
pendulum *n* suspended weight swinging to and fro, esp as a regulator for a clock
penetrate *v* find or force a way into or through; arrive at the meaning of **penetrable** *adj* capable of being penetrated **penetrating** *adj* (of a sound) loud and unpleasant; quick to understand **penetration** *n*
penguin *n* flightless black-and-white sea bird of the southern hemisphere
penicillin *n* antibiotic drug effective against a wide range of diseases and infections
peninsula *n* strip of land nearly surrounded by water **peninsular** *adj*
penis *n* organ of copulation and urination in male mammals
penitent *adj* feeling sorry for having done wrong ▷ *n* someone who is penitent **penitence** *n* **penitentiary** *n, pl* **-ries** *US* prison ▷ *adj* (also **penitential**) relating to penance
pennant *n* long narrow flag
penny *n, pl* **pence, pennies** British bronze coin worth one hundredth of a pound; former British and Australian coin worth one twelfth of a shilling **penniless** *adj* very poor
pension[1] *n* regular payment to people above a certain age, retired employees, widows, etc **pensionable** *adj* **pensioner** *n* person receiving a pension **pension off** *v* force (someone) to retire from a job and pay him or her a pension
pension[2] [**pon**-syon] *n* boarding house in Europe
pensive *adj* deeply thoughtful, often with a tinge of sadness
pentagon *n* geometric figure with five sides; (**P-**) headquarters of the US military **pentagonal** *adj*
pentameter [pen-**tam**-it-er] *n* line of poetry with five metrical feet
Pentateuch [**pent**-a-tyuke] *n* first five books of the Old Testament
Pentecost *n* Christian festival celebrating the descent of the Holy Spirit to the apostles, Whitsuntide
penthouse *n* flat built on the roof or top floor of a building
pent-up *adj* (of an emotion) not released, repressed
penultimate *adj* second last
penumbra *n, pl* **-brae, -bras** (in an eclipse) the partially shadowed region which surrounds the full shadow; partial shadow
penury *n* extreme poverty

penurious *adj*
peony *n, pl* **-nies** garden plant with showy red, pink, or white flowers
people *pl n* persons generally; the community; one's family ▷*n* race or nation ▷*v* provide with inhabitants **people mover** *Brit, Aust & NZ* same as **multipurpose vehicle**
pep *n Informal* high spirits, energy, or enthusiasm **pep talk** *Informal* talk designed to increase confidence and enthusiasm **pep up** *v* **pepping, pepped** stimulate, invigorate
pepper *n* sharp hot condiment made from the fruit of an East Indian climbing plant; colourful tropical fruit used as a vegetable, capsicum ▷*v* season with pepper; sprinkle, dot; pelt with missiles **peppery** *adj* tasting of pepper; irritable **peppercorn** *n* dried berry of the pepper plant **peppercorn rent** *Chiefly Brit* low or nominal rent
peppermint *n* plant that yields an oil with a strong sharp flavour; sweet flavoured with this
peptic *adj* relating to digestion or the digestive juices
per *prep* for each **as per** in accordance with
perambulate *v old-fashioned* walk through or about (a place) **perambulation** *n* **perambulator** *n* pram
per annum *adv Latin* in each year
per capita *adj, adv Latin* of or for each person
perceive *v* become aware of (something) through the senses; understand
per cent in each hundred **percentage** *n* proportion or rate per hundred
perceptible *adj* discernible, recognizable
perception *n* act of perceiving; intuitive judgment **perceptive** *adj*
perch[1] *n* resting place for a bird ▷*v* alight, rest, or place on or as if on a perch
perch[2] *n* any of various edible fishes
perchance *adv old-fashioned* perhaps
percipient *adj* quick to notice things, observant
percolate *v* pass or filter through small holes; spread gradually; make (coffee) or (of coffee) be made in a percolator **percolation** *n* **percolator** *n* coffeepot in which boiling water is forced through a tube and filters down through coffee
percussion *n* striking of one thing against another **percussion instrument** musical instrument played by being struck, such as drums or cymbals
perdition *n Christianity* spiritual ruin
peregrination *n obs* travels, roaming
peregrine falcon *n* falcon with dark upper parts and a light underside
peremptory *adj* authoritative, imperious
perennial *adj* lasting through many years ▷*n* plant lasting more than two years **perennially** *adv*
perfect *adj* having all the essential elements; faultless; correct, precise; utter or absolute; excellent ▷*n grammar* perfect tense ▷*v* improve; make fully correct **perfectly** *adv* **perfection** *n* state of being perfect **perfectionist** *n* person who demands the highest

standards of excellence
perfectionism *n*

perfidious *adj lit* treacherous, disloyal **perfidy** *n*

perforate *v* make holes in **perforation** *n*

perforce *adv* of necessity

perform *v* carry out (an action); act, sing, or present a play before an audience; fulfil (a request etc) **performance** *n* **performer** *n*

perfume *n* liquid cosmetic worn for its pleasant smell; fragrance ▷ *v* give a pleasant smell to **perfumery** *n* perfumes in general

perfunctory *adj* done only as a matter of routine, superficial **perfunctorily** *adv*

pergola *n* arch or framework of trellis supporting climbing plants

perhaps *adv* possibly, maybe

pericardium *n, pl* **-dia** membrane enclosing the heart

perihelion *n, pl* **-lia** point in the orbit of a planet or comet that is nearest to the sun

peril *n* great danger **perilous** *adj* **perilously** *adv*

perimeter [per-**rim**-it-er] *n* (length of) the outer edge of an area

perinatal *adj* of or in the weeks shortly before or after birth

period *n* particular portion of time; single occurrence of menstruation; division of time at school etc when a particular subject is taught; *US* full stop ▷ *adj* (of furniture, dress, a play, etc) dating from or in the style of an earlier time **periodic** *adj* recurring at intervals **periodic table** *chem* chart of the elements, arranged to show their relationship to each other **periodical** *n* magazine issued at regular intervals ▷ *adj* periodic

peripatetic [per-rip-a-**tet**-ik] *adj* travelling about from place to place

periphery [per-**if**-er-ee] *n, pl* **-eries** boundary or edge; fringes of a field of activity **peripheral** [per-**if**-er-al] *adj* unimportant, not central; of or on the periphery

periscope *n* instrument used, esp in submarines, to give a view of objects on a different level

perish *v* be destroyed or die; decay, rot **perishable** *adj* liable to rot quickly **perishing** *adj Informal* very cold

peritoneum [per-rit-toe-**nee**-um] *n, pl* **-nea, -neums** membrane lining the internal surface of the abdomen **peritonitis** [per-rit-tone-**ite**-iss] *n* inflammation of the peritoneum

periwinkle[1] *n* small edible shellfish, the winkle

periwinkle[2] *n* plant with trailing stems and blue flowers

perjury *n, pl* **-juries** act or crime of lying while under oath in a court **perjure oneself** commit perjury

perk *n Informal* incidental benefit gained from a job, such as a company car

perk up *v* cheer up **perky** *adj* lively or cheerful

perlemoen *n SAfr* edible sea creature with a shell lined with mother of pearl

perm *n* long-lasting curly hairstyle produced by treating the hair with chemicals ▷ *v* give (hair) a perm

permafrost *n* permanently frozen ground

permanent *adj* lasting forever **permanence** *n* **permanently** *adv*

permeate *v* pervade or pass through the whole of (something) **permeable** *adj* able to be permeated, esp by liquid

permit *v* **-mitting, -mitted** give

permission, allow ▷*n* document giving permission to do something **permission** *n* authorization to do something **permissible** *adj* **permissive** *adj* (excessively) tolerant, esp in sexual matters

permutation *n* any of the ways a number of things can be arranged or combined

pernicious *adj* wicked; extremely harmful, deadly

pernickety *adj Informal* (excessively) fussy about details

peroration *n* concluding part of a speech, usu summing up the main points

peroxide *n* hydrogen peroxide used as a hair bleach; oxide containing a high proportion of oxygen

perpendicular *adj* at right angles to a line or surface; upright or vertical ▷*n* line or plane at right angles to another

perpetrate *v* commit or be responsible for (a wrongdoing) **perpetration** *n* **perpetrator** *n*

perpetual *adj* lasting forever; continually repeated **perpetually** *adv* **perpetuate** *v* cause to continue or be remembered **perpetuation** *n* **in perpetuity** forever

perplex *v* puzzle, bewilder **perplexity** *n, pl* **-ties**

perquisite *n formal* same as **perk**

perry *n, pl* **-ries** alcoholic drink made from fermented pears

per se [per **say**] *adv Latin* in itself

persecute *v* treat cruelly because of race, religion, etc; subject to persistent harassment **persecution** *n* **persecutor** *n*

persevere *v* keep making an effort despite difficulties **perseverance** *n*

persimmon *n* sweet red tropical fruit

persist *v* continue to be or happen, last; continue in spite of obstacles or objections **persistent** *adj* **persistently** *adv* **persistence** *n*

person *n* human being; body of a human being; *grammar* form of pronouns and verbs that shows if a person is speaking, spoken to, or spoken of **in person** actually present

persona [per-**soh**-na] *n, pl* **-nae** [-nee] someone's personality as presented to others

personable *adj* pleasant in appearance and personality

personage *n* important person

personal *adj* individual or private; of the body *eg personal hygiene*; (of a remark etc) offensive **personally** *adv* directly, not by delegation to others; in one's own opinion **personal computer** small computer used for word processing or computer games **personal pronoun** pronoun like *I* or *she* that stands for a definite person **personal stereo** very small portable cassette player with headphones

personality *n, pl* **-ties** person's distinctive characteristics; celebrity ▷*pl* personal remarks *eg the discussion degenerated into personalities*

personify *v* **-fying, -fied** give human characteristics to; be an example of, typify **personification** *n*

personnel *n* people employed in an organization; department in an organization that appoints or keeps records of employees

perspective *n* view of the relative importance of situations or facts;

method of drawing that gives the effect of solidity and relative distances and sizes

Perspex *n* ® transparent acrylic substitute for glass

perspicacious *adj* having quick mental insight **perspicacity** *n*

perspire *v* sweat **perspiration** *n*

persuade *v* make (someone) do something by argument, charm, etc; convince **persuasion** *n* act of persuading; way of thinking or belief **persuasive** *adj*

pert *adj* saucy and cheeky

pertain *v* belong or be relevant (to)

pertinacious *adj formal* very persistent and determined **pertinacity** *n*

pertinent *adj* relevant **pertinence** *n*

perturb *v* disturb greatly **perturbation** *n*

peruse *v* read in a careful or leisurely manner **perusal** *n*

pervade *v* spread right through (something) **pervasive** *adj*

perverse *adj* deliberately doing something different from what is thought normal or proper **perversely** *adv* **perversity** *n*

pervert *v* use or alter for a wrong purpose; lead into abnormal (sexual) behaviour ▷ *n* person who practises sexual perversion **perversion** *n* sexual act or desire considered abnormal; act of perverting

pervious *adj* able to be penetrated, permeable

peseta [pa-**say**-ta] *n* former monetary unit of Spain

pessary *n, pl* **-ries** appliance worn in the vagina, either to prevent conception or to support the womb; vaginal suppository

pessimism *n* tendency to expect the worst in all things **pessimist** *n* **pessimistic** *adj* **pessimistically** *adv*

pest *n* annoying person; insect or animal that damages crops **pesticide** *n* chemical for killing insect pests

pester *v* annoy or nag continually

pestilence *n* deadly epidemic disease **pestilent** *adj* annoying, troublesome; deadly **pestilential** *adj*

pestle *n* club-shaped implement for grinding things to powder in a mortar

pet *n* animal kept for pleasure and companionship; person favoured or indulged ▷ *adj* particularly cherished ▷ *v* **petting, petted** treat as a pet; pat or stroke affectionately; *old-fashioned* kiss and caress erotically

petal *n* one of the brightly coloured outer parts of a flower **petalled** *adj*

petard *n* **hoist with one's own petard** being the victim of one's own schemes

peter out *v* gradually come to an end

petite *adj* (of a woman) small and dainty

petition *n* formal request, esp one signed by many people and presented to parliament ▷ *v* present a petition to **petitioner** *n*

petrel *n* sea bird with a hooked bill and tubular nostrils

petrify *v* **-fying, -fied** frighten severely; turn to stone **petrification** *n*

petrochemical *n* substance, such as acetone, obtained from petroleum

petrol *n* flammable liquid obtained from petroleum, used as fuel in internal-combustion engines **petrol bomb** home-made incendiary device consisting of a bottle filled with petrol

petroleum *n* thick dark oil found underground

petticoat *n* woman's skirt-shaped undergarment

pettifogging *adj* excessively concerned with unimportant detail

petty *adj* **-tier, -tiest** unimportant, trivial; small-minded; on a small scale *eg petty crime* **pettiness** *n* **petty cash** cash kept by a firm to pay minor expenses **petty officer** noncommissioned officer in the navy

petulant *adj* childishly irritable or peevish **petulance** *n* **petulantly** *adv*

petunia *n* garden plant with funnel-shaped flowers

pew *n* fixed benchlike seat in a church; *Informal* chair, seat

pewter *n* greyish metal made of tin and lead

pH *chem* measure of the acidity of a solution

phalanger *n* long-tailed Australian tree-dwelling marsupial

phalanx *n, pl* **phalanxes** closely grouped mass of people

phallus *n, pl* **-luses, -li** penis, esp as a symbol of reproductive power in primitive rites **phallic** *adj*

phantasm *n* unreal vision, illusion **phantasmal** *adj*

phantasmagoria *n* shifting medley of dreamlike figures

phantom *n* ghost; unreal vision

Pharaoh [**fare**-oh] *n* title of the ancient Egyptian kings

pharmaceutical *adj* of pharmacy

pharmacology *n* study of drugs **pharmacological** *adj* **pharmacologist** *n*

pharmacopoeia [far-ma-koh-**pee**-a] *n* book with a list of and directions for the use of drugs

pharmacy *n, pl* **-cies** preparation and dispensing of drugs and medicines; pharmacist's shop **pharmacist** *n* person qualified to prepare and sell drugs and medicines

pharynx [**far**-rinks] *n, pl* **pharynges, pharynxes** cavity forming the back part of the mouth **pharyngitis** [far-rin-**jite**-iss] *n* inflammation of the pharynx

phase *n* any distinct or characteristic stage in a development or chain of events ▷ *v* arrange or carry out in stages or to coincide with something else **phase in, out** *v* introduce *or* discontinue gradually

PhD Doctor of Philosophy

pheasant *n* game bird with bright plumage

phenobarbitone *n* drug inducing sleep or relaxation

phenol *n* chemical used in disinfectants and antiseptics

phenomenon *n, pl* **-ena** anything appearing or observed; remarkable person or thing **phenomenal** *adj* extraordinary, outstanding **phenomenally** *adv*

phial *n* small bottle for medicine etc

philadelphus *n* shrub with sweet-scented flowers

philanderer *n* man who flirts or has many casual love affairs **philandering** *adj, n*

philanthropy *n* practice of helping people less well-off than oneself **philanthropic** *adj* **philanthropist** *n*

philately [fill-**lat**-a-lee] *n* stamp collecting **philatelist** *n*
philharmonic *adj* (in names of orchestras etc) music-loving
philistine *adj, n* boorishly uncultivated (person) **philistinism** *n*
philology *n* science of the structure and development of languages **philological** *adj* **philologist** *n*
philosopher *n* person who studies philosophy
philosophy *n, pl* **-phies** study of the meaning of life, knowledge, thought, etc; theory or set of ideas held by a particular philosopher; person's outlook on life **philosophical, philosophic** *adj* of philosophy; calm in the face of difficulties or disappointments **philosophically** *adv* **philosophize** *v* discuss in a philosophical manner
philtre *n* magic drink supposed to arouse love in the person who drinks it
phlebitis [fleb-**bite**-iss] *n* inflammation of a vein
phlegm [**flem**] *n* thick yellowish substance formed in the nose and throat during a cold
phlegmatic [fleg-**mat**-ik] *adj* not easily excited, unemotional **phlegmatically** *adv*
phlox *n, pl* **phlox, phloxes** flowering garden plant
phobia *n* intense and unreasoning fear or dislike
phoenix *n* legendary bird said to set fire to itself and rise anew from its ashes
phone *n, v Informal* telephone **phonecard** *n* card used to operate certain public telephones **phone-in** *n Brit, Aust & SAfr* broadcast in which telephone comments or questions from the public are transmitted live
phonetic *adj* of speech sounds; (of spelling) written as it is sounded **phonetics** *n* science of speech sounds **phonetically** *adv*
phoney, phony *Informal* ▷ *adj* **phonier, phoniest** not genuine; insincere ▷ *n, pl* **phoneys, phonies** phoney person or thing
phonograph *n US, old-fashioned* record player
phosphorescence *n* faint glow in the dark **phosphorescent** *adj*
phosphorus *n chem* toxic flammable nonmetallic element which appears luminous in the dark **phosphate** *n* compound of phosphorus; fertilizer containing phosphorus
photo *n, pl* **photos** short for photograph **photo finish** finish of a race in which the contestants are so close that a photograph is needed to decide the result
photocopy *n, pl* **-copies** photographic reproduction ▷ *v* **-copying, -copied** make a photocopy of **photocopier** *n*
photoelectric *adj* using or worked by electricity produced by the action of light
photogenic *adj* always looking attractive in photographs
photograph *n* picture made by the chemical action of light on sensitive film ▷ *v* take a photograph of **photographic** *adj* **photography** *n* art of taking photographs
photographer *n* person who takes photographs, esp professionally
photostat *n* copy made by photocopying machine
photosynthesis *n* process by

which a green plant uses sunlight to build up carbohydrate reserves

phrase *n* group of words forming a unit of meaning, esp within a sentence; short effective expression ▷*v* express in words **phrasal verb** phrase consisting of a verb and an adverb or preposition, with a meaning different from the parts, such as *take in* meaning *deceive*

phraseology *n, pl* **-gies** way in which words are used

physical *adj* of the body, as contrasted with the mind or spirit; of material things or nature; of physics **physically** *adv* **physical education** training and practice in sports and gymnastics

physician *n* doctor of medicine

physics *n* science of the properties of matter and energy **physicist** *n* person skilled in or studying physics

physiognomy [fiz-ee-**on**-om-ee] *n* face

physiology *n* science of the normal function of living things **physiological** *adj* **physiologist** *n*

physiotherapy *n* treatment of disease or injury by physical means such as massage, rather than by drugs **physiotherapist** *n*

physique *n* person's bodily build and muscular development

pi *n maths* ratio of the circumference of a circle to its diameter

pianissimo *adv music* very quietly

piano[1] *n, pl* **pianos** musical instrument with strings which are struck by hammers worked by a keyboard (also **pianoforte**) **pianist** *n* **Pianola** *n* ® mechanically played piano

piano[2] *adv music* quietly

piazza *n* square or marketplace, esp in Italy

pic *n, pl* **pics, pix** *Informal* photograph or illustration

picador *n* mounted bullfighter with a lance

picaresque *adj* denoting a type of fiction in which the hero, a rogue, has a series of adventures

piccalilli *n* pickle of vegetables in mustard sauce

piccolo *n, pl* **-los** small flute

pick[1] *v* choose; remove (flowers or fruit) from a plant; take hold of and move with the fingers; provoke (a fight etc) deliberately; open (a lock) by means other than a key ▷*n* choice; best part **pick-me-up** *n* *Informal* stimulating drink, tonic **pick on** *v* continually treat unfairly **pick out** *v* recognize, distinguish **pick up** *v* raise, lift; collect; improve, get better; become acquainted with for a sexual purpose **pick-up** *n* small truck; casual acquaintance made for a sexual purpose; device for conversion of vibrations into electrical signals, as in a record player

pick[2] *n* tool with a curved iron crossbar and wooden shaft, for breaking up hard ground or rocks

pickaxe *n* large pick

picket *n* person or group standing outside a workplace to deter would-be workers during a strike; sentry or sentries posted to give warning of an attack; pointed stick used as part of a fence ▷*v* form a picket outside (a workplace) **picket line** line of people acting as pickets

pickings *pl n* money easily acquired

pickle *n* food preserved in vinegar or salt water; *Informal* awkward situation ▷*v* preserve in vinegar or

salt water **pickled** *adj* (of food) preserved; *Informal* drunk
pickpocket *n* thief who steals from someone's pocket
picnic *n* informal meal out of doors ▷ *v* **-nicking, -nicked** have a picnic
Pict *n* member of an ancient race of N Britain **Pictish** *adj*
pictorial *adj* of or in painting or pictures
picture *n* drawing or painting; photograph; mental image; beautiful or picturesque object; image on a TV screen ▷ *pl* cinema ▷ *v* visualize, imagine; represent in a picture **picturesque** *adj* (of a place or view) pleasant to look at; (of language) forceful, vivid **picture window** large window made of a single sheet of glass
piddle *v Informal* urinate
pidgin *n* language, not a mother tongue, made up of elements of two or more other languages
pie *n* dish of meat, fruit, etc baked in pastry **pie chart** circular diagram with sectors representing quantities
piebald *n, adj* (horse) with irregular black-and-white markings
piece *n* separate bit or part; instance *eg a piece of luck*; example, specimen; literary or musical composition; coin; small object used in draughts, chess, etc **piece together** *v* make or assemble bit by bit
pièce de résistance [pyess de ray-**ziss**-tonss] *n French* most impressive item
piecemeal *adv* bit by bit
piecework *n* work paid for according to the quantity produced
pied *adj* having markings of two or more colours
pied-à-terre [pyay da **tair**] *n, pl* **pieds-à-terre** [pyay da **tair**] small flat or house for occasional use
pier *n* platform on stilts sticking out into the sea; pillar, esp one supporting a bridge
pierce *v* make a hole in or through with a sharp instrument; make a way through **piercing** *adj* (of a sound) shrill and high-pitched
Pierrot [**pier**-roe] *n* pantomime clown with a whitened face
piety *n, pl* **-ties** deep devotion to God and religion
piffle *n Informal* nonsense
pig *n* animal kept and killed for pork, ham, and bacon; *Informal* greedy, dirty, or rude person; *offens slang* policeman **piggish, piggy** *adj Informal* dirty; greedy; stubborn **piggery** *n, pl* **-geries** place for keeping and breeding pigs **pig-headed** *adj* obstinate **pig iron** crude iron produced in a blast furnace
pigeon[1] *n* bird with a heavy body and short legs, sometimes trained to carry messages **pigeonhole** *n* compartment for papers in a desk etc ▷ *v* classify; put aside and do nothing about **pigeon-toed** *adj* with the feet or toes turned inwards
pigeon[2] *n Informal* concern or responsibility
piggyback *n* ride on someone's shoulders ▷ *adv* carried on someone's shoulders
pigment *n* colouring matter, paint or dye **pigmentation** *n*
Pigmy *n, pl* **-mies** same as **Pygmy**
pigtail *n* plait of hair hanging from the back or either side of the head
pike[1] *n* large predatory freshwater fish
pike[2] *n hist* long-handled spear
pikelet *n Aust & NZ* small thick

pancake
piker *n Aust & NZ, slang* shirker
pilaster *n* square column, usu set in a wall
pilau, pilaf, pilaff *n* Middle Eastern dish of meat, fish, or poultry boiled with rice, spices, etc
pilchard *n* small edible sea fish of the herring family
pile¹ *n* number of things lying on top of each other; *Informal* large amount; large building ▷*v* collect into a pile; (foll by *in, out*) move in a group **pile-up** *n Informal* traffic accident involving several vehicles
pile² *n* beam driven into the ground, esp as a foundation for building
pile³ *n* fibres of a carpet or a fabric, esp velvet, that stand up from the weave
piles *pl n* swollen veins in the rectum, haemorrhoids
pilfer *v* steal in small quantities
pilgrim *n* person who journeys to a holy place **pilgrimage** *n*
pill *n* small ball of medicine swallowed whole **the pill** pill taken by a woman to prevent pregnancy
pillage *v* steal property by violence in war ▷*n* violent seizure of goods, esp in war
pillar *n* upright post, usu supporting a roof; strong supporter **pillar box** (in Britain) red pillar-shaped letter box in the street
pillion *n* seat for a passenger behind the rider of a motorcycle
pillory *n, pl* **-ries** *hist* frame with holes for the head and hands in which an offender was locked and exposed to public abuse ▷*v* **-rying, -ried** ridicule publicly
pillow *n* stuffed cloth bag for supporting the head in bed ▷*v* rest as if on a pillow **pillowcase, pillowslip** *n* removable cover for a pillow
pilot *n* person qualified to fly an aircraft or spacecraft; person employed to steer a ship entering or leaving a harbour ▷*adj* experimental and preliminary ▷*v* act as the pilot of; guide, steer **pilot light** small flame lighting the main one in a gas appliance
pimento *n, pl* **-tos** mild-tasting red pepper
pimp *n* man who gets customers for a prostitute in return for a share of his or her earnings ▷*v* act as a pimp
pimpernel *n* wild plant with small star-shaped flowers
pimple *n* small pus-filled spot on the skin **pimply** *adj*
pin *n* short thin piece of stiff wire with a point and head, for fastening things; wooden or metal peg or stake ▷*v* **pinning, pinned** fasten with a pin; seize and hold fast **pin down** *v* force (someone) to make a decision, take action, etc; define clearly **pin money** small amount earned to buy small luxuries **pin-up** *n* picture of a sexually attractive person, esp (partly) naked
pinafore *n* apron; dress with a bib top
pinball *n* electrically operated table game in which a small ball is shot through various hazards
pince-nez [panss-**nay**] *n, pl* **pince-nez** glasses kept in place only by a clip on the bridge of the nose
pincers *pl n* tool consisting of two hinged arms, for gripping; claws of a lobster etc
pinch *v* squeeze between finger

and thumb; cause pain by being too tight; *Informal* steal ▷*n* act of pinching; as much as can be taken up between the finger and thumb **at a pinch** if absolutely necessary **feel the pinch** have to economize

pinchbeck *n* alloy of zinc and copper, used as imitation gold

pine[1] *n* evergreen coniferous tree; its wood **pine cone** woody seed case of the pine tree **pine marten** wild mammal of the coniferous forests of Europe and Asia

pine[2] *v* (foll by *for*) feel great longing (for); become thin and ill through grief etc

pineal gland *n* small cone-shaped gland at the base of the brain

pineapple *n* large tropical fruit with juicy yellow flesh and a hard skin

ping *v, n* (make) a short high-pitched sound

Ping-Pong *n*® table tennis

pinion[1] *n* bird's wing ▷*v* immobilize (someone) by tying or holding his or her arms

pinion[2] *n* small cogwheel

pink *n* pale reddish colour; fragrant garden plant ▷*adj* of the colour pink ▷*v* (of an engine) make a metallic noise because not working properly, knock **in the pink** in good health

pinking shears *pl n* scissors with a serrated edge that give a wavy edge to material to prevent fraying

pinnacle *n* highest point of fame or success; mountain peak; small slender spire

pinotage [**pin**-no-tajj] *n* blended red wine of S Africa

pinpoint *v* locate or identify exactly

pinstripe *n* very narrow stripe in fabric; the fabric itself

pint *n* liquid measure, 1/8 gallon (.568 litre)

pioneer *n* explorer or early settler of a new country; originator or developer of something new ▷*v* be the pioneer or leader of

pious *adj* deeply religious, devout

pip[1] *n* small seed in a fruit

pip[2] *n* high-pitched sound used as a time signal on radio; *Informal* star on a junior army officer's shoulder showing rank

pip[3] *n* **give someone the pip** *Brit, NZ & SAfr, slang* annoy

pipe *n* tube for conveying liquid or gas; tube with a small bowl at the end for smoking tobacco; tubular musical instrument ▷*pl* bagpipes ▷*v* play on a pipe; utter in a shrill tone; convey by pipe; decorate with piping **piper** *n* player on a pipe or bagpipes **piping** *n* system of pipes; decoration of icing on a cake etc; fancy edging on clothes etc **piped music** recorded music played as background music in public places **pipe down** *v Informal* stop talking **pipe dream** fanciful impossible plan **pipeline** *n* long pipe for transporting oil, water, etc; means of communication **in the pipeline** in preparation **pipe up** *v* speak suddenly or shrilly

pipette *n* slender glass tube used to transfer or measure fluids

pipi *n Aust* mollusc often used as bait; *NZ* edible shellfish

pipit *n* small brownish songbird

pippin *n* type of eating apple

piquant [**pee**-kant] *adj* having a pleasant spicy taste; mentally stimulating **piquancy** *n*

pique [**peek**] *n* feeling of hurt pride, baffled curiosity, or resentment ▷*v* hurt the pride of;

arouse (curiosity)
piqué [**pee**-kay] *n* stiff ribbed cotton fabric
piquet [pik-**ket**] *n* card game for two
piranha *n* small fierce freshwater fish of tropical America
pirate *n* sea robber; person who illegally publishes or sells work owned by someone else; person or company that broadcasts illegally ▷ *v* sell or reproduce (artistic work etc) illegally **piracy** *n* **piratical** *adj*
pirouette *v, n* (make) a spinning turn balanced on the toes of one foot
piss *vulgar slang* ▷ *v* urinate ▷ *n* act of urinating; urine
pistachio *n, pl* **-chios** edible nut of a Mediterranean tree
piste [**peest**] *n* ski slope
pistil *n* seed-bearing part of a flower
pistol *n* short-barrelled handgun
piston *n* cylindrical part in an engine that slides to and fro in a cylinder
pit *n* deep hole in the ground; coal mine; dent or depression; servicing and refuelling area on a motor-racing track; same as **orchestra pit** ▷ *v* **pitting, pitted** mark with small dents or scars **pit one's wits against** compete against in a test or contest **pit bull terrier** strong muscular terrier with a short coat
pitch¹ *v* throw, hurl; set up (a tent); fall headlong; (of a ship or plane) move with the front and back going up and down alternately; set the level or tone of ▷ *n* area marked out for playing sport; degree or angle of slope; degree of highness or lowness of a (musical) sound; place where a street or market trader regularly sells; *Informal* persuasive sales talk **pitch in** *v* join in enthusiastically **pitch into** *v* *Informal* attack
pitch² *n* dark sticky substance obtained from tar **pitch-black, pitch-dark** *adj* very dark
pitchblende *n* mineral composed largely of uranium oxide, yielding radium
pitcher *n* large jug with a narrow neck
pitchfork *n* large long-handled fork for lifting hay ▷ *v* thrust abruptly or violently
pitfall *n* hidden difficulty or danger
pith *n* soft white lining of the rind of oranges etc; essential part; soft tissue in the stems of certain plants **pithy** *adj* short and full of meaning
piton [**peet**-on] *n* metal spike used in climbing to secure a rope
pittance *n* very small amount of money
pituitary *n, pl* **-taries** gland at the base of the brain, that helps to control growth (also **pituitary gland**)
pity *n, pl* **pities** sympathy or sorrow for others' suffering; regrettable fact ▷ *v* **pitying, pitied** feel pity for **piteous, pitiable** *adj* arousing pity **pitiful** *adj* arousing pity; woeful, contemptible **pitifully** *adv* **pitiless** *adj* feeling no pity or mercy **pitilessly** *adv*
pivot *n* central shaft on which something turns ▷ *v* provide with or turn on a pivot **pivotal** *adj* of crucial importance
pix *n* *Informal* a plural of **pic**
pixie *n* (in folklore) fairy
pizza *n* flat disc of dough covered with a wide variety of savoury toppings and baked
pizzazz *n* *Informal* attractive

combination of energy and style
pizzicato [pit-see-**kah**-toe] *adj music* played by plucking the string of a violin etc with the finger
placard *n* notice that is carried or displayed in public
placate *v* make (someone) stop feeling angry or upset **placatory** *adj*
place *n* particular part of an area or space; particular town, building, etc; position or point reached; seat or space; duty or right; position of employment; usual position ▷ *v* put in a particular place; identify, put in context; make (an order, bet, etc) **be placed** (of a competitor in a race) be among the first three **take place** happen, occur
placebo [plas-**see**-bo] *n, pl* **-bos, -boes** sugar pill etc given to an unsuspecting patient instead of an active drug
placenta [plass-**ent**-a] *n, pl* **-tas, -tae** organ formed in the womb during pregnancy, providing nutrients for the fetus **placental** *adj*
placid *adj* not easily excited or upset, calm **placidity** *n*
plagiarize [**play**-jer-ize] *v* steal ideas, passages, etc from (someone else's work) and present them as one's own **plagiarism** *n*
plague *n* fast-spreading fatal disease; *hist* bubonic plague; widespread infestation ▷ *v* **plaguing, plagued** trouble or annoy continually
plaice *n* edible European flatfish
plaid *n* long piece of tartan cloth worn as part of Highland dress; tartan cloth or pattern
plain *adj* easy to see or understand; expressed honestly and clearly; without decoration or pattern; not beautiful; simple, ordinary ▷ *n* large stretch of level country **plainly** *adv* **plainness** *n* **plain clothes** ordinary clothes, as opposed to uniform **plain sailing** easy progress **plain speaking** saying exactly what one thinks
plainsong *n* unaccompanied singing, esp in a medieval church
plaintiff *n* person who sues in a court of law
plaintive *adj* sad, mournful **plaintively** *adv*
plait [platt] *n* intertwined length of hair ▷ *v* intertwine separate strands in a pattern
plan *n* way thought out to do or achieve something; diagram showing the layout or design of something ▷ *v* **planning, planned** arrange beforehand; make a diagram of **planner** *n*
plane[1] *n* aeroplane; *maths* flat surface; level of attainment etc ▷ *adj* perfectly flat or level ▷ *v* glide or skim
plane[2] *n* tool for smoothing wood ▷ *v* smooth (wood) with a plane
plane[3] *n* tree with broad leaves
planet *n* large body in space that revolves round the sun or another star **planetary** *adj*
planetarium *n, pl* **-iums, -ia** building where the movements of the stars, planets, etc are shown by projecting lights on the inside of a dome
plangent *adj* (of sounds) mournful and resounding
plank *n* long flat piece of sawn timber
plankton *n* minute animals and plants floating in the surface water of a sea or lake
plant *n* living organism that grows in the ground and has no power to

move; equipment or machinery used in industrial processes; factory or other industrial premises ▷*v* put in the ground to grow; place firmly in position; *Informal* put (a person) secretly in an organization to spy; *Informal* hide (stolen goods etc) on a person to make him or her seem guilty **planter** *n* owner of a plantation

plantain[1] *n* low-growing wild plant with broad leaves

plantain[2] *n* tropical fruit like a green banana

plantation *n* estate for the cultivation of tea, tobacco, etc; wood of cultivated trees

plaque *n* inscribed commemorative stone or metal plate; filmy deposit on teeth that causes decay

plasma *n* clear liquid part of blood

plaster *n* mixture of lime, sand, etc for coating walls; adhesive strip of material for dressing cuts etc ▷*v* cover with plaster; coat thickly **plastered** *adj slang* drunk **plaster of Paris** white powder which dries to form a hard solid when mixed with water, used for sculptures and casts for broken limbs

plastic *n* synthetic material that can be moulded when soft but sets in a hard long-lasting shape; credit cards etc as opposed to cash ▷*adj* made of plastic; easily moulded, pliant **plasticity** *n* ability to be moulded **plastic bullet** solid PVC cylinder fired by police in riot control **plastic surgery** repair or reconstruction of missing or malformed parts of the body

Plasticine *n* ® soft coloured modelling material used esp by children

plate *n* shallow dish for holding food; flat thin sheet of metal, glass, etc; thin coating of metal on another metal; dishes or cutlery made of gold or silver; illustration, usu on fine quality paper, in a book; *Informal* set of false teeth ▷*v* cover with a thin coating of gold, silver, or other metal **plateful** *n* **plate glass** glass in thin sheets, used for mirrors and windows **plate tectonics** study of the structure of the earth's crust, esp the movement of layers of rocks

plateau *n, pl* **-teaus, -teaux** area of level high land; stage when there is no change or development

platen *n* roller of a typewriter, against which the paper is held

platform *n* raised floor; raised area in a station from which passengers board trains; structure in the sea which holds machinery, stores, etc for drilling an oil well; programme of a political party

platinum *n chem* valuable silvery-white metal **platinum blonde** woman with silvery-blonde hair

platitude *n* remark that is true but not interesting or original **platitudinous** *adj*

platonic *adj* (of a relationship) friendly or affectionate but not sexual

platoon *n* smaller unit within a company of soldiers

platteland *n SAfr* rural district

platter *n* large dish

platypus *n* Australian egg-laying amphibious mammal, with dense fur, webbed feet, and a ducklike bill (also **duck-billed platypus**)

plaudits *pl n* expressions of approval

plausible *adj* apparently true or reasonable; persuasive but insincere **plausibly** *adv* **plausibility** *n*

play *v* occupy oneself in (a game or recreation); compete against in a game or sport; behave carelessly; act (a part) on the stage; perform on (a musical instrument); cause (a radio, record player, etc) to give out sound; move lightly or irregularly, flicker ▷ *n* story performed on stage or broadcast; activities children take part in for amusement; playing of a game; conduct *eg fair play*; (scope for) freedom of movement **playful** *adj* lively **play back** *v* listen to or watch (something recorded) **playcentre** *n* *NZ & SAfr* centre for preschool children run by parents **play down** *v* minimize the importance of **playgroup** *n* regular meeting of very young children for supervised play **playhouse** *n* theatre **playing card** one of a set of 52 cards used in card games **playing field** extensive piece of ground for sport **play-lunch** *n* *Aust & NZ* child's mid-morning snack at school **play off** *v* set (two people) against each other for one's own ends **play on** *v* exploit or encourage (someone's sympathy or weakness) **playschool** *n* nursery group for young children **plaything** *n* toy; person regarded or treated as a toy **play up** *v* give prominence to; cause trouble **playwright** *n* author of plays

playboy *n* rich man who lives only for pleasure

player *n* person who plays a game or sport; actor or actress; person who plays a musical instrument

plaza *n* open space or square; modern shopping complex

PLC, plc (in Britain) Public Limited Company

plea *n* serious or urgent request, entreaty; statement of a prisoner or defendant; excuse

plead *v* ask urgently or with deep feeling; give as an excuse; *law* declare oneself to be guilty or innocent of a charge made against one

pleasant *adj* pleasing, enjoyable **pleasantly** *adv* **pleasantry** *n, pl* **-tries** polite or joking remark

please *v* give pleasure or satisfaction to ▷ *adv* polite word of request **please oneself** do as one likes **pleased** *adj* **pleasing** *adj*

pleasure *n* feeling of happiness and satisfaction; something that causes this **pleasurable** *adj* giving pleasure **pleasurably** *adv*

pleat *n* fold made by doubling material back on itself ▷ *v* arrange (material) in pleats

plebeian [pleb-**ee**-an] *adj* of the lower social classes; vulgar or rough ▷ *n* (also **pleb**) member of the lower social classes

plebiscite [**pleb**-iss-ite] *n* decision by direct voting of the people of a country

plectrum *n, pl* **-trums, -tra** small implement for plucking the strings of a guitar etc

pledge *n* solemn promise; something valuable given as a guarantee that a promise will be kept or a debt paid ▷ *v* promise solemnly; bind by or as if by a pledge

plenary *adj* (of a meeting) attended by all members

plenipotentiary *adj* having full powers ▷ *n, pl* **-aries** diplomat or representative having full powers

plenitude *n* completeness, abundance

plenteous *adj* plentiful
plenty *n* large amount or number; quite enough **plentiful** *adj* existing in large amounts or numbers **plentifully** *adv*
pleonasm *n* use of more words than necessary
plethora *n* excess
pleurisy *n* inflammation of the membrane covering the lungs
pliable *adj* easily bent; easily influenced **pliability** *n*
pliant *adj* pliable **pliancy** *n*
pliers *pl n* tool with hinged arms and jaws for gripping
plight¹ *n* difficult or dangerous situation
plight² *v* **plight one's troth** *old-fashioned* promise to marry
Plimsoll line *n* mark on a ship showing the level water should reach when the ship is fully loaded
plimsolls *pl n Brit* rubber-soled canvas shoes
plinth *n* slab forming the base of a statue, column, etc
PLO Palestine Liberation Organization
plod *v* **plodding, plodded** walk with slow heavy steps; work slowly but determinedly **plodder** *n*
plonk¹ *v* put (something) down heavily and carelessly
plonk² *n Informal* cheap inferior wine
plop *n* sound of an object falling into water without a splash ▷ *v* **plopping, plopped** make this sound
plot¹ *n* secret plan to do something illegal or wrong; story of a film, novel, etc ▷ *v* **plotting, plotted** plan secretly, conspire; mark the position or course of (a ship or aircraft) on a map; mark and join up (points on a graph)
plot² *n* small piece of land
plough *n* agricultural tool for turning over soil ▷ *v* turn over (earth) with a plough; move or work through slowly and laboriously **ploughman** *n* **ploughshare** *n* blade of a plough
plover *n* shore bird with a straight bill and long pointed wings
ploy *n* manoeuvre designed to gain an advantage
pluck *v* pull or pick off; pull out the feathers of (a bird for cooking); sound the strings of (a guitar etc) with the fingers or a plectrum ▷ *n* courage **plucky** *adj* brave **pluckily** *adv* **pluck up** *v* summon up (courage)
plug *n* thing fitting into and filling a hole; device connecting an appliance to an electricity supply; *Informal* favourable mention of a product etc, to encourage people to buy it ▷ *v* **plugging, plugged** block or seal (a hole or gap) with a plug; *Informal* advertise (a product etc) by constant repetition **plug away** *v Informal* work steadily **plug in** *v* connect (an electrical appliance) to a power source by pushing a plug into a socket
plum *n* oval usu dark red fruit with a stone in the middle ▷ *adj* dark purplish-red; very desirable
plumage *n* bird's feathers
plumb *v* understand (something obscure); test with a plumb line ▷ *adv* exactly **plumb the depths of** experience the worst extremes of (an unpleasant quality or emotion) **plumbing** *n* pipes and fixtures used in water and drainage systems **plumb in** *v* connect (an appliance such as a washing machine) to a water supply **plumb line** string with a weight at the

end, used to test the depth of water or to test whether something is vertical

plumber *n* person who fits and repairs pipes and fixtures for water and drainage systems

plume *n* feather, esp one worn as an ornament

plummet *v* **-meting, -meted** plunge downward

plump¹ *adj* moderately or attractively fat **plumpness** *n* **plump up** *v* make (a pillow) fuller or rounded

plump² *v* sit or fall heavily and suddenly **plump for** *v* choose, vote for

plunder *v* take by force, esp in time of war ▷*n* things plundered, spoils

plunge *v* put or throw forcibly or suddenly (into); descend steeply ▷*n* plunging, dive **take the plunge** *Informal* embark on a risky enterprise **plunger** *n* rubber suction cup used to clear blocked pipes **plunge into** *v* become deeply involved in

plunket baby *n NZ* baby brought up on the diet recommended by the Plunket Society **plunket nurse** *NZ* nurse working for the Plunket Society

pluperfect *n, adj grammar* (tense) expressing an action completed before a past time, eg *had gone* in *his wife had gone already*

plural *adj* of or consisting of more than one ▷*n* word indicating more than one

pluralism *n* existence and toleration of a variety of peoples, opinions, etc in a society **pluralist** *n* **pluralistic** *adj*

plus *prep, adj* indicating addition ▷*adj* more than zero; positive; advantageous ▷*n* sign (+) denoting addition; advantage

plus fours *pl n* trousers gathered in just below the knee

plush *n* fabric with long velvety pile ▷*adj* (also **plushy**) luxurious

Pluto *n* Greek god of the underworld; farthest planet from the sun

plutocrat *n* person who is powerful because of being very rich **plutocratic** *adj*

plutonium *n chem* radioactive metallic element used esp in nuclear reactors and weapons

ply¹ *v* **plying, plied** work at (a job or trade); use (a tool); (of a ship) travel regularly along or between **ply with** *v* supply with or subject to persistently

ply² *n* thickness of wool, fabric, etc

plywood *n* board made of thin layers of wood glued together

PM prime minister

p.m. after noon; postmortem

PMT premenstrual tension

pneumatic *adj* worked by or inflated with wind or air

pneumonia *n* inflammation of the lungs

PO *Brit* postal order; Post Office

poach¹ *v* catch (animals) illegally on someone else's land; encroach on or steal something belonging to someone else

poach² *v* simmer (food) gently in liquid

poacher *n* person who catches animals illegally on someone else's land

pocket *n* small bag sewn into clothing for carrying things; pouchlike container, esp for catching balls at the edge of a snooker table; isolated or distinct group or area ▷*v* **pocketing, pocketed** put into one's pocket;

take secretly or dishonestly ▷ *adj* small **out of pocket** having made a loss **pocket money** small regular allowance given to children by parents; money for small personal expenses

pockmarked *adj* (of the skin) marked with hollow scars where diseased spots have been

pod *n* long narrow seed case of peas, beans, etc

podgy *adj* **podgier, podgiest** short and fat

podium *n, pl* **-diums, -dia** small raised platform for a conductor or speaker

poem *n* imaginative piece of writing in rhythmic lines

poep *n SAfr, slang* emission of gas from the anus

poesy *n obs* poetry

poet *n* writer of poems **poetry** *n* poems; art of writing poems; beautiful or pleasing quality **poetic, poetical** *adj* of or like poetry **poetically** *adv* **poetic justice** suitable reward or punishment for someone's past actions **poet laureate** poet appointed by the British sovereign to write poems on important occasions

pogrom *n* organized persecution and massacre

poignant *adj* sharply painful to the feelings **poignancy** *n*

poinsettia *n* Central American shrub widely grown for its clusters of scarlet leaves, which resemble petals

point *n* main idea in a discussion, argument, etc; aim or purpose; detail or item; characteristic; particular position, stage, or time; dot indicating decimals; sharp end; unit for recording a value or score; one of the direction marks of a compass; electrical socket ▷ *v* show the direction or position of something or draw attention to it by extending a finger or other pointed object towards it; direct or face towards **on the point of** very shortly going to **pointed** *adj* having a sharp end; (of a remark) obviously directed at a particular person **pointedly** *adv* **pointer** *n* helpful hint; indicator on a measuring instrument; breed of gun dog **pointless** *adj* meaningless, irrelevant **point-blank** *adj* fired at a very close target; (of a remark or question) direct, blunt ▷ *adv* directly or bluntly **point duty** control of traffic by a policeman at a road junction **point of view** way of considering something **point-to-point** *n Brit* horse race across open country

poise *n* calm dignified manner **poised** *adj* absolutely ready; behaving with or showing poise

poison *n* substance that kills or injures when swallowed or absorbed ▷ *v* give poison to; have a harmful or evil effect on, spoil **poisoner** *n* **poisonous** *adj* **poison-pen letter** malicious anonymous letter

poke *v* jab or prod with one's finger, a stick, etc; thrust forward or out ▷ *n* poking **poky** *adj* small and cramped

poker[1] *n* metal rod for stirring a fire

poker[2] *n* card game in which players bet on the hands dealt **poker-faced** *adj* expressionless

polar *adj* of or near either of the earth's poles **polar bear** white bear that lives in the regions around the North Pole

polarize *v* form or cause to form into groups with directly opposite views; *physics* restrict (light waves) to certain directions of vibration **polarization** *n*

Polaroid *n* ® plastic which polarizes light and so reduces glare; camera that develops a print very quickly inside itself

polder *n* land reclaimed from the sea, esp in the Netherlands

pole[1] *n* long rounded piece of wood etc

pole[2] *n* point furthest north or south on the earth's axis of rotation; either of the opposite ends of a magnet or electric cell **Pole Star** star nearest to the North Pole in the northern hemisphere

poleaxe *v* hit or stun with a heavy blow

polecat *n* small animal of the weasel family

polemic [pol-**em**-ik] *n* fierce attack on or defence of a particular opinion, belief, etc **polemical** *adj*

police *n* organized force in a state which keeps law and order ▷ *v* control or watch over with police or a similar body **policeman, policewoman** *n* member of a police force

policy[1] *n, pl* **-cies** plan of action adopted by a person, group, or state

policy[2] *n, pl* **-cies** document containing an insurance contract

polio *n* disease affecting the spinal cord, which often causes paralysis (also **poliomyelitis**)

polish *v* make smooth and shiny by rubbing; make more nearly perfect ▷ *n* substance used for polishing; pleasing elegant style **polished** *adj* accomplished; done or performed well or professionally **polish off** *v* finish completely, dispose of

polite *adj* showing consideration for others in one's manners, speech, etc; socially correct or refined **politely** *adv* **politeness** *n*

politic *adj* wise and likely to prove advantageous

politics *n* winning and using of power to govern society; (study of) the art of government; person's beliefs about how a country should be governed **political** *adj* of the state, government, or public administration **politically** *adv* **politically correct** (of language) intended to avoid any implied prejudice **political prisoner** person imprisoned because of his or her political beliefs **politician** *n* person actively engaged in politics, esp a member of parliament

polka *n* lively 19th-century dance; music for this **polka dots** pattern of bold spots on fabric

poll *n* (also **opinion poll**) questioning of a random sample of people to find out general opinion; voting; number of votes recorded ▷ *v* receive (votes); question in an opinion poll **pollster** *n* person who conducts opinion polls **polling station** building where people vote in an election

pollarded *adj* (of a tree) growing very bushy because its top branches have been cut short

pollen *n* fine dust produced by flowers to fertilize other flowers **pollinate** *v* fertilize with pollen **pollen count** measure of the amount of pollen in the air, esp as a warning to people with hay fever

pollute *v* contaminate with something poisonous or harmful **pollution** *n* **pollutant** *n* something that pollutes

polo *n* game like hockey played by

teams of players on horseback **polo neck** sweater with tight turned-over collar
polonaise *n* old stately dance; music for this
polonium *n chem* radioactive element that occurs in trace amounts in uranium ores
poltergeist *n* spirit believed to move furniture and throw objects around
poltroon *n obs* utter coward
poly- *combining form* many, much
polyandry *n* practice of having more than one husband at the same time
polyanthus *n* garden primrose
polychromatic *adj* many-coloured
polyester *n* synthetic material used to make plastics and textile fibres
polygamy [pol-**ig**-a-mee] *n* practice of having more than one husband or wife at the same time **polygamous** *adj* **polygamist** *n*
polyglot *n, adj* (person) able to speak or write several languages
polygon *n* geometrical figure with three or more angles and sides **polygonal** *adj*
polyhedron *n, pl* **-drons, -dra** solid figure with four or more sides
polymer *n* chemical compound with large molecules made of simple molecules of the same kind **polymerize** *v* form into polymers **polymerization** *n*
polyp *n* small simple sea creature with a hollow cylindrical body; small growth on a mucous membrane
polyphonic *adj music* consisting of several melodies played simultaneously
polystyrene *n* synthetic material used esp as white rigid foam for packing and insulation
polytechnic *n* (in New Zealand and formerly in Britain) college offering courses in many subjects at and below degree level
polytheism *n* belief in many gods **polytheistic** *adj*
polythene *n* light plastic used for bags etc
polyunsaturated *adj* of a group of fats that do not form cholesterol in the blood
polyurethane *n* synthetic material used esp in paints
pom *n Aust & NZ, slang* person from England (also **pommy**)
pomander *n* (container for) a mixture of sweet-smelling petals, herbs, etc
pomegranate *n* round tropical fruit with a thick rind containing many seeds in a red pulp
Pomeranian *n* small dog with long straight hair
pommel *n* raised part on the front of a saddle; knob at the top of a sword hilt
pomp *n* stately display or ceremony
pompom *n* decorative ball of tufted wool, silk, etc
pompous *adj* foolishly serious and grand, self-important **pompously** *adv* **pomposity** *n*
ponce *n offens* effeminate man; pimp **ponce around** *v Brit, Aust & NZ* behave in a ridiculous or posturing way
poncho *n, pl* **-chos** loose circular cloak with a hole for the head
pond *n* small area of still water
ponder *v* think thoroughly or deeply (about)
ponderous *adj* serious and dull; heavy and unwieldy; (of movement)

slow and clumsy **ponderously** *adv*

pong *v, n Informal* (give off) a strong unpleasant smell

pontiff *n* the Pope **pontificate** *v* state one's opinions as if they were the only possible correct ones ▷ *n* period of office of a Pope

pontoon¹ *n* floating platform supporting a temporary bridge

pontoon² *n* gambling card game

pony *n, pl* **ponies** small horse **ponytail** *n* long hair tied in one bunch at the back of the head

poodle *n* dog with curly hair often clipped fancifully

poof, poofter *n Brit, Aust & NZ, offens* homosexual man

pool¹ *n* small body of still water; puddle of spilt liquid; swimming pool

pool² *n* shared fund or group of workers or resources; game like snooker ▷ *pl Brit* short for **football pools** ▷ *v* put in a common fund

poop *n* raised part at the back of a sailing ship

poor *adj* having little money and few possessions; less, smaller, or weaker than is needed or expected; inferior; unlucky, pitiable **poorly** *adv* in a poor manner ▷ *adj* not in good health

pop¹ *v* **popping, popped** make or cause to make a small explosive sound; *Informal* go, put, or come unexpectedly or suddenly ▷ *n* small explosive sound; *Brit* nonalcoholic fizzy drink **popcorn** *n* grains of maize heated until they puff up and burst

pop² *n* music of general appeal, esp to young people

pop³ *n Informal* father

Pope *n* head of the Roman Catholic Church **popish** *adj offens* Roman Catholic

poplar *n* tall slender tree

poplin *n* ribbed cotton material

poppadom *n* thin round crisp Indian bread

poppy *n, pl* **-pies** plant with a large red flower

populace *n* the ordinary people

popular *adj* widely liked and admired; of or for the public in general **popularly** *adv* **popularity** *n* **popularize** *v* make popular; make (something technical or specialist) easily understood

populate *v* live in, inhabit; fill with inhabitants **populous** *adj* densely populated

population *n* all the people who live in a particular place; the number of people living in a particular place

porbeagle *n* kind of shark

porcelain *n* fine china; objects made of it

porch *n* covered approach to the entrance of a building

porcine *adj* of or like a pig

porcupine *n* animal covered with long pointed quills

pore *n* tiny opening in the skin or in the surface of a plant

pork *n* pig meat **porker** *n* pig raised for food

porn, porno *n, adj Informal* short for **pornography** or

pornography *n* writing, films, or pictures designed to be sexually exciting **pornographer** *n* producer of pornography **pornographic** *adj*

porous *adj* allowing liquid to pass through gradually **porosity** *n*

porphyry [**por**-fir-ee] *n* reddish rock with large crystals in it

porpoise *n* fishlike sea mammal

porridge *n* breakfast food made of

oatmeal cooked in water or milk; *Chiefly Brit, slang* term in prison
port[1] *n* (town with) a harbour
port[2] *n* left side of a ship or aircraft when facing the front of it
port[3] *n* strong sweet wine, usu red
port[4] *n* opening in the side of a ship; porthole
portable *adj* easily carried **portability** *n*
portal *n* large imposing doorway or gate
portcullis *n* grating suspended above a castle gateway, that can be lowered to block the entrance
portend *v* be a sign of
portent *n* sign of a future event **portentous** *adj* of great or ominous significance; pompous, self-important
porter[1] *n* man who carries luggage; hospital worker who transfers patients between rooms etc
porter[2] *n* doorman or gatekeeper of a building
portfolio *n, pl* **-os** (flat case for carrying) examples of an artist's work; area of responsibility of a government minister; list of investments held by an investor
porthole *n* small round window in a ship or aircraft
portico *n, pl* **-coes, -cos** porch or covered walkway with columns supporting the roof
portion *n* part or share; helping of food for one person; destiny or fate **portion out** *v* divide into shares
portly *adj* **-lier, -liest** rather fat
portmanteau *n, pl* **-teaus, -teaux** *old-fashioned* large suitcase that opens into two compartments ▷ *adj* combining aspects of different things
portrait *n* picture of a person; lifelike description
portray *v* describe or represent by artistic means, as in writing or film **portrayal** *n*
Portuguese *adj* of Portugal, its people, or their language ▷ *n* person from Portugal; language of Portugal and Brazil **Portuguese man-of-war** sea creature resembling a jellyfish, with stinging tentacles
pose *v* place in or take up a particular position to be photographed or drawn; raise (a problem); ask (a question) ▷ *n* position while posing; behaviour adopted for effect **pose as** pretend to be **poser** *n* puzzling question; poseur **poseur** *n* person who behaves in an affected way to impress others
posh *adj Informal* smart, luxurious; affectedly upper-class
posit [pozz-it] *v* lay down as a basis for argument
position *n* place; usual or expected place; way in which something is placed or arranged; attitude, point of view; social standing; job ▷ *v* place
positive *adj* feeling no doubts, certain; confident, hopeful; helpful, providing encouragement; absolute, downright; *maths* greater than zero; (of an electrical charge) having a deficiency of electrons **positively** *adv* **positive discrimination** provision of special opportunities for a disadvantaged group
positron *n physics* particle with same mass as electron but positive charge
posse [poss-ee] *n US* group of men organized to maintain law and order; *Brit & Aust, Informal* group of

friends or associates

possess *v* have as one's property; (of a feeling, belief, etc) have complete control of, dominate **possessor** *n* **possession** *n* state of possessing, ownership ▷ *pl* things a person possesses **possessive** *adj* wanting all the attention or love of another person; (of a word) indicating the person or thing that something belongs to **possessiveness** *n*

possible *adj* able to exist, happen, or be done; worthy of consideration ▷ *n* person or thing that might be suitable or chosen **possibility** *n, pl* **-ties** **possibly** *adv* perhaps, not necessarily

possum *n* same as **opossum**; *Aust & NZ* same as **phalanger** **play possum** pretend to be dead or asleep to deceive an opponent

post[1] *n* official system of delivering letters and parcels; (single collection or delivery of) letters and parcels sent by this system ▷ *v* send by post **keep someone posted** supply someone regularly with the latest information **postage** *n* charge for sending a letter or parcel by post **postal** *adj* **postal order** *Brit* written money order sent by post and cashed at a post office by the person who receives it **postbag** *n* postman's bag; post received by a magazine, famous person, etc **postcode** *n* system of letters and numbers used to aid the sorting of mail **postie** *n* *Scot, Aust & NZ, Informal* postman **postman, postwoman** *n* person who collects and delivers post **postmark** *n* official mark stamped on letters showing place and date of posting **postmaster, postmistress** *n* (in some countries) official in charge of a post office **post office** place where postal business is conducted **post shop** *NZ* shop providing postal services

post[2] *n* length of wood, concrete, etc fixed upright to support or mark something ▷ *v* put up (a notice) in a public place

post[3] *n* job; position to which someone, esp a soldier, is assigned for duty; military establishment ▷ *v* send (a person) to a new place to work; put (a guard etc) on duty

post- *prefix* after, later than *eg postwar*

postcard *n* card for sending a message by post without an envelope

postdate *v* write a date on (a cheque) that is later than the actual date

poster *n* large picture or notice stuck on a wall

posterior *n* buttocks ▷ *adj* behind, at the back of

posterity *n* future generations, descendants

postern *n* small back door or gate

postgraduate *n* person with a degree who is studying for a more advanced qualification

posthaste *adv* with great speed

posthumous [**poss**-tume-uss] *adj* occurring after one's death **posthumously** *adv*

postilion, postillion *n hist* person riding one of a pair of horses drawing a carriage

postmortem *n* medical examination of a body to establish the cause of death

postnatal *adj* occurring after childbirth

postpone *v* put off to a later time **postponement** *n*

postscript *n* passage added at the end of a letter

postulant *n* candidate for admission to a religious order

postulate *v* assume to be true as the basis of an argument or theory

posture *n* position or way in which someone stands, walks, etc ▷*v* behave in an exaggerated way to get attention

posy *n, pl* **-sies** small bunch of flowers

pot[1] *n* round deep container; teapot ▷*pl Informal* large amount ▷*v* **potting, potted** plant in a pot; *snooker* hit (a ball) into a pocket **potted** *adj* grown in a pot; (of meat or fish) cooked or preserved in a pot; *Informal* abridged **pot shot** shot taken without aiming carefully **potting shed** shed where plants are potted

pot[2] *n slang* cannabis

potable [pote-a-bl] *adj* drinkable

potash *n* white powdery substance obtained from ashes and used as fertilizer

potassium *n chem* silvery metallic element

potato *n, pl* **-toes** roundish starchy vegetable that grows underground

poteen *n* (in Ireland) illegally made alcoholic drink

potent *adj* having great power or influence; (of a male) capable of having sexual intercourse **potency** *n*

potentate *n* ruler or monarch

potential *adj* possible but not yet actual ▷*n* ability or talent not yet fully used; *electricity* level of electric pressure **potentially** *adv* **potentiality** *n, pl* **-ties**

pothole *n* hole in the surface of a road; deep hole in a limestone area **potholing** *n* sport of exploring underground caves **potholer** *n*

potion *n* dose of medicine or poison

potluck *n* **take potluck** accept whatever happens to be available

potoroo *n, pl* **-roos** Australian leaping rodent

potpourri [po-**poor**-ee] *n* fragrant mixture of dried flower petals; assortment or medley

pottage *n old-fashioned* thick soup or stew

potter[1] *n* person who makes pottery

potter[2] *v* be busy in a pleasant but aimless way

pottery *n, pl* **-ries** articles made from baked clay; place where they are made

potty[1] *adj* **-tier, -tiest** *Informal* crazy or silly

potty[2] *n, pl* **-ties** bowl used by a small child as a toilet

pouch *n* small bag; baglike pocket of skin on an animal

pouf, pouffe [**poof**] *n* large solid cushion used as a seat

poulterer *n Brit* person who sells poultry

poultice [**pole**-tiss] *n* moist dressing, often heated, applied to inflamed skin

poultry *n* domestic fowls

pounce *v* spring upon suddenly to attack or capture ▷*n* pouncing

pound[1] *n* monetary unit of Britain and some other countries; unit of weight equal to 0.454 kg

pound[2] *v* hit heavily and repeatedly; crush to pieces or powder; (of the heart) throb heavily; run heavily

pound[3] *n* enclosure for stray animals or officially removed vehicles

pour *v* flow or cause to flow out in a stream; rain heavily; come or go in large numbers

pout *v* thrust out one's lips, look sulky ▷ *n* pouting look

poverty *n* state of being without enough food or money; lack of, scarcity

POW prisoner of war

powder *n* substance in the form of tiny loose particles; medicine or cosmetic in this form ▷ *v* apply powder to **powdered** *adj* in the form of a powder *eg powdered milk* **powdery** *adj* **powder room** ladies' toilet

power *n* ability to do or act; strength; position of authority or control; *maths* product from continuous multiplication of a number by itself; *physics* rate at which work is done; electricity supply; particular form of energy *eg nuclear power* **powered** *adj* having or operated by mechanical or electrical power **powerful** *adj* **powerless** *adj* **power cut** temporary interruption in the supply of electricity **power point** socket on a wall for plugging in electrical appliances **power station** installation for generating and distributing electric power

powwow *n Informal* talk or conference

pox *n* disease in which skin pustules form; *Informal* syphilis

pp (in signing a document) for and on behalf of

pp. pages

PPTA (in New Zealand) Post Primary Teachers Association

PR proportional representation; public relations

practicable *adj* capable of being done successfully; usable **practicability** *n*

practical *adj* involving experience or actual use rather than theory; sensible, useful, and effective; good at making or doing things; in effect though not in name ▷ *n* examination in which something has to be done or made **practically** *adv* **practical joke** trick intended to make someone look foolish

practice *n* something done regularly or habitually; repetition of something so as to gain skill; doctor's or lawyer's place of work **in practice** what actually happens as distinct from what is supposed to happen **put into practice** carry out, do

> SPELLING It is extremely common for people to confuse the noun, **practice**, which has a *c* at the end, and the verb **practise**, which has an *s*

practise *v* do repeatedly so as to gain skill; take part in, follow (a religion etc); work at *eg practise medicine*; do habitually

practitioner *n* person who practises a profession

pragmatic *adj* concerned with practical consequences rather than theory **pragmatism** *n* **pragmatist** *n*

prairie *n* large treeless area of grassland, esp in N America and Canada **prairie dog** rodent that lives in burrows in the N American prairies

praise *v* express approval or admiration of (someone or something); express honour and thanks to (one's God) ▷ *n* something said or written to show approval or admiration **sing someone's praises** praise someone highly **praiseworthy** *adj*

praline [**prah**-leen] *n* sweet made of nuts and caramelized sugar
pram *n* four-wheeled carriage for a baby, pushed by hand
prance *v* walk with exaggerated bouncing steps
prang *v, n slang* (have) a crash in a car or aircraft
prank *n* mischievous trick
prat *n Brit, Aust & NZ, Informal* stupid person
prattle *v* chatter in a childish or foolish way ▷*n* childish or foolish talk
prawn *n* edible shellfish like a large shrimp
praxis *n* practice as opposed to theory
pray *v* say prayers; ask earnestly, entreat
prayer *n* thanks or appeal addressed to one's God; set form of words used in praying; earnest request
pre- *prefix* before, beforehand *eg prenatal; prerecorded; preshrunk*
preach *v* give a talk on a religious theme as part of a church service; speak in support of (an idea, principle, etc)
preacher *n* person who preaches, esp in church
preamble *n* introductory part to something said or written
prearranged *adj* arranged beforehand
prebendary *n, pl* **-daries** clergyman who is a member of the chapter of a cathedral
precarious *adj* insecure, unsafe, likely to fall or collapse **precariously** *adv*
precaution *n* action taken in advance to prevent something bad happening **precautionary** *adj*
precede *v* go or be before
precedence [**press**-ee-denss] *n* formal order of rank or position **take precedence over** be more important than **precedent** *n* previous case or occurrence regarded as an example to be followed
precentor *n* person who leads the singing in a church
precept *n* rule of behaviour **preceptive** *adj*
precinct *n Brit, Aust & SAfr* area in a town closed to traffic; *Brit, Aust & SAfr* enclosed area round a building; *US* administrative area of a city ▷*pl* surrounding region
precious *adj* of great value and importance; loved and treasured; (of behaviour) affected, unnatural **precious metal** gold, silver, or platinum **precious stone** rare mineral, such as a ruby, valued as a gem
precipice *n* very steep face of cliff or rockface **precipitous** *adj* sheer
precipitate *v* cause to happen suddenly; *chem* cause to be deposited in solid form from a solution; throw headlong ▷*adj* done rashly or hastily ▷*n chem* substance precipitated from a solution **precipitately** *adv* **precipitation** *n* precipitating; rain, snow, etc
précis [**pray**-see] *n, pl* **précis** short written summary of a longer piece ▷*v* make a précis of
precise *adj* exact, accurate in every detail; strict in observing rules or standards **precisely** *adv* **precision** *n*
preclude *v* make impossible to happen
precocious *adj* having developed or matured early or too soon **precocity** *n*

precognition *n* alleged ability to foretell the future
preconceived *adj* (of an idea) formed without real experience or reliable information **preconception** *n*
precondition *n* something that must happen or exist before something else can
precursor *n* something that precedes and is a signal of something else, forerunner; predecessor
predate *v* occur at an earlier date than; write a date on (a document) that is earlier than the actual date
predatory [**pred**-a-tree] *adj* habitually hunting and killing other animals for food **predator** *n* predatory animal
predecease *v* die before (someone else)
predecessor *n* person who precedes another in an office or position; ancestor
predestination *n theology* belief that future events have already been decided by God or fate **predestined** *adj*
predetermined *adj* decided in advance
predicament *n* embarrassing or difficult situation
predicate *n grammar* part of a sentence in which something is said about the subject, eg *went home* in *I went home* ▷*v* declare or assert
predict *v* tell about in advance, prophesy **predictable** *adj* **prediction** *n* **predictive** *adj* relating to or able to make predictions; (of a word processer) able to complete words after only part of a word has been keyed
predilection *n formal* preference or liking
predispose *v* influence (someone) in favour of something; make (someone) susceptible to something **predisposition** *n*
predominate *v* be the main or controlling element **predominance** *n* **predominant** *adj* **predominantly** *adv*
pre-eminent *adj* excelling all others, outstanding **pre-eminence** *n*
pre-empt *v* prevent an action by doing something which makes it pointless or impossible **pre-emption** *n* **pre-emptive** *adj*
preen *v* (of a bird) clean or trim (feathers) with the beak **preen oneself** smarten oneself; show self-satisfaction
prefab *n* prefabricated house
prefabricated *adj* (of a building) manufactured in shaped sections for rapid assembly on site
preface [**pref**-iss] *n* introduction to a book ▷*v* serve as an introduction to (a book, speech, etc) **prefatory** *adj*
prefect *n* senior pupil in a school, with limited power over others; senior administrative officer in some countries **prefecture** *n* office or area of authority of a prefect
prefer *v* **-ferring, -ferred** like better; *law* bring (charges) before a court **preferable** *adj* more desirable **preferably** *adv* **preference** *n* **preferential** *adj* showing preference **preferment** *n* promotion or advancement
prefigure *v* represent or suggest in advance
prefix *n* letter or group of letters put at the beginning of a word to make a new word, such as *un-* in *unhappy* ▷*v* put as an introduction

or prefix (to)

pregnant *adj* carrying a fetus in the womb; full of meaning or significance *eg a pregnant pause* **pregnancy** *n, pl* **-cies**

prehensile *adj* capable of grasping

prehistoric *adj* of the period before written history begins **prehistory** *n*

prejudice *n* unreasonable or unfair dislike or preference ▷ *v* cause (someone) to have a prejudice; harm, cause disadvantage to **prejudicial** *adj* disadvantageous, harmful

SPELLING There are examples in Collins Word Web of **prejudice** being misspelt as *predjudice*, with an extra *d*. Although *d* often combines with *g* in English, it is not necessary before *j*

prelate [**prel**-it] *n* bishop or other churchman of high rank

preliminary *adj* happening before and in preparation, introductory ▷ *n, pl* **-naries** preliminary remark, contest, etc

prelude *n* introductory movement in music; event preceding and introducing something else

premarital *adj* occurring before marriage

premature *adj* happening or done before the normal or expected time; (of a baby) born before the end of the normal period of pregnancy **prematurely** *adv*

premeditated *adj* planned in advance **premeditation** *n*

premenstrual *adj* occurring or experienced before a menstrual period *eg premenstrual tension*

premier *n* prime minister ▷ *adj* chief, leading **premiership** *n*

première *n* first performance of a play, film, etc

premise, premiss *n* statement assumed to be true and used as the basis of reasoning

premises *pl n* house or other building and its land

premium *n* additional sum of money, as on a wage or charge; (regular) sum paid for insurance **at a premium** in great demand because scarce **premium bonds** (in Britain) savings certificates issued by the government, on which no interest is paid but cash prizes can be won

premonition *n* feeling that something unpleasant is going to happen; foreboding **premonitory** *adj*

prenatal *adj* before birth, during pregnancy

preoccupy *v* **-pying, -pied** fill the thoughts or attention of (someone) to the exclusion of other things **preoccupation** *n*

preordained *adj* decreed or determined in advance

prep. preparatory; preposition

prepacked *adj* sold already wrapped

prepaid *adj* paid for in advance

prepare *v* make or get ready **prepared** *adj* willing; ready **preparation** *n* preparing; something done in readiness for something else; mixture prepared for use as a cosmetic, medicine, etc **preparatory** [prip-**par**-a-tree] *adj* preparing for **preparatory school** *Brit & SAfr* private school for children between 7 and 13

preponderance *n* greater force, amount, or influence **preponderant** *adj*

preposition *n* word used before a noun or pronoun to show its relationship with other words, such as *by* in *go by bus* **prepositional** *adj*

prepossessing *adj* making a favourable impression, attractive

preposterous *adj* utterly absurd

prep school *n* short for **preparatory school**

prepuce [**pree**-pyewss] *n* retractable fold of skin covering the tip of the penis, foreskin

prerecorded *adj* recorded in advance to be played or broadcast later

prerequisite *n, adj* (something) required before something else is possible

prerogative *n* special power or privilege

> SPELLING The way **prerogative** is often pronounced is presumably the reason why *perogative* is a common way of misspelling it

presage [**press**-ij] *v* be a sign or warning of

Presbyterian *n, adj* (member) of a Protestant church governed by lay elders **Presbyterianism** *n*

presbytery *n, pl* **-teries** *Presbyterian church* local church court; *RC church* priest's house

prescience [**press**-ee-enss] *n* knowledge of events before they happen **prescient** *adj*

prescribe *v* recommend the use of (a medicine); lay down as a rule **prescription** *n* written instructions from a doctor for the making up and use of a medicine **prescriptive** *adj* laying down rules

presence *n* fact of being in a specified place; impressive dignified appearance **presence of mind** ability to act sensibly in a crisis

present[1] *adj* being in a specified place; existing or happening now; *grammar* (of a verb tense) indicating that the action specified is taking place now ▷ *n* present time or tense **presently** *adv* soon; *US & Scot* now

present[2] *n* something given to bring pleasure to another person ▷ *v* introduce formally or publicly; introduce and compere (a TV or radio show); cause *eg present a difficulty*; give, award **presentation** *n* **presentable** *adj* attractive, neat, fit for people to see **presenter** *n* person introducing a TV or radio show

presentiment [priz-**zen**-tim-ent] *n* sense of something unpleasant about to happen

preserve *v* keep from being damaged, changed, or ended; treat (food) to prevent it decaying ▷ *n* area of interest restricted to a particular person or group; fruit preserved by cooking in sugar; area where game is kept for private hunting or fishing **preservation** *n* **preservative** *n* chemical that prevents decay

preshrunk *adj* (of fabric or a garment) having been shrunk during manufacture so that further shrinkage will not occur when washed

preside *v* be in charge, esp of a meeting

president *n* head of state in many countries; head of a society, institution, etc **presidential** *adj* **presidency** *n, pl* **-cies**

press[1] *v* apply force or weight to; squeeze; smooth by applying pressure or heat; urge insistently; crowd, push ▷ *n* printing machine **pressed for** short of **pressing** *adj* urgent **press box** room at a sports ground reserved for reporters

press conference interview for reporters given by a celebrity
press² *v* **press into service** force to be involved or used **press gang** *hist* group of men used to capture men and boys and force them to join the navy
pressure *n* force produced by pressing; urgent claims or demands; *physics* force applied to a surface per unit of area **pressure cooker** airtight pot which cooks food quickly by steam under pressure **pressure group** group that tries to influence policies, public opinion, etc
prestidigitation *n* skilful quickness with the hands, conjuring
prestige *n* high status or respect resulting from success or achievements **prestigious** *adj*
presto *adv music* very quickly
prestressed *adj* (of concrete) containing stretched steel wires to strengthen it
presume *v* suppose to be the case; dare (to) **presumably** *adv* one supposes (that) **presumption** *n* bold insolent behaviour; strong probability **presumptive** *adj* assumed to be true or valid until the contrary is proved **presumptuous** *adj* doing things one has no right to do
presuppose *v* need as a previous condition in order to be true **presupposition** *n*
pretend *v* claim or give the appearance of (something untrue) to deceive or in play **pretender** *n* person who makes a false or disputed claim to a position of power **pretence** *n* behaviour intended to deceive, pretending **pretentious** *adj* making (unjustified) claims to special merit or importance **pretension** *n*
preternatural *adj* beyond what is natural, supernatural
pretext *n* false reason given to hide the real one
pretty *adj* **-tier, -tiest** pleasing to look at ▷ *adv* fairly, moderately *eg I'm pretty certain* **prettily** *adv* **prettiness** *n*
pretzel *n* brittle salted biscuit
prevail *v* gain mastery; be generally established **prevailing** *adj* widespread; predominant **prevalence** *n* **prevalent** *adj* widespread, common
prevaricate *v* avoid giving a direct or truthful answer **prevarication** *n*
prevent *v* keep from happening or doing **preventable** *adj* **prevention** *n* **preventive** *adj, n*
preview *n* advance showing of a film or exhibition before it is shown to the public
previous *adj* coming or happening before **previously** *adv*
prey *n* animal hunted and killed for food by another animal; victim **bird of prey** bird that kills and eats other birds or animals **prey on** *v* hunt and kill for food; worry, obsess
price *n* amount of money for which a thing is bought or sold; unpleasant thing that must be endured to get something desirable ▷ *v* fix or ask the price of **priceless** *adj* very valuable; *Informal* very funny **pricey** *adj* **pricier, priciest** *Informal* expensive
prick *v* pierce lightly with a sharp point; cause to feel mental pain; (of an animal) make (the ears) stand erect ▷ *n* sudden sharp pain caused by pricking; mark made by pricking; remorse **prick up one's**

ears listen intently

prickle *n* thorn or spike on a plant ▷*v* have a tingling or pricking sensation **prickly** *adj* **prickly heat** itchy rash occurring in hot moist weather

pride *n* feeling of pleasure and satisfaction when one has done well; too high an opinion of oneself; sense of dignity and self-respect; something that causes one to feel pride; group of lions **pride of place** most important position **pride oneself on** feel pride about

priest *n* (in the Christian church) a person who can administer the sacraments and preach; (in some other religions) an official who performs religious ceremonies **priestess** *n fem* **priesthood** *n* **priestly** *adj*

prig *n* self-righteous person who acts as if superior to others **priggish** *adj* **priggishness** *n*

prim *adj* **primmer, primmest** formal, proper, and rather prudish **primly** *adv*

prima ballerina *n* leading female ballet dancer

primacy *n, pl* **-cies** state of being first in rank, grade, etc; office of an archbishop

prima donna *n* leading female opera singer; *Informal* temperamental person

primaeval *adj* same as **primeval**

prima facie [**prime**-a **fay**-shee] *adv Latin* as it seems at first

primal *adj* of basic causes or origins

primary *adj* chief, most important; being the first stage, elementary **primarily** *adv* **primary colours** (in physics) red, green, and blue or (in art) red, yellow, and blue, from which all other colours can be produced by mixing **primary school** school for children from five to eleven years or (in New Zealand) between five to thirteen years

primate[1] *n* member of an order of mammals including monkeys and humans

primate[2] *n* archbishop

prime *adj* main, most important; of the highest quality ▷*n* time when someone is at his or her best or most vigorous ▷*v* give (someone) information in advance to prepare them for something; prepare (a surface) for painting; prepare (a gun, pump, etc) for use **primer** *n* special paint applied to bare wood etc before the main paint **Prime Minister** leader of a government **prime number** number that can be divided exactly only by itself and one

primer *n* beginners' school book or manual

primeval [prime-**ee**-val] *adj* of the earliest age of the world

primitive *adj* of an early simple stage of development; basic, crude

primogeniture *n* system under which the eldest son inherits all his parents' property

primordial *adj* existing at or from the beginning

primrose *n* pale yellow spring flower

primula *n* type of primrose with brightly coloured flowers

Primus *n* ® portable cooking stove used esp by campers

prince *n* male member of a royal family, esp the son of the king or queen; male ruler of a small country **princely** *adj* of or like a prince; generous, lavish, or magnificent **prince consort** husband of a reigning queen **Prince of Wales** eldest son of the British sovereign **princess** *n* female member of a royal family, esp the daughter of the king or queen **Princess Royal** title sometimes given to the eldest daughter of the British sovereign

principal *adj* main, most important ▷*n* head of a school or college; person taking a leading part in something; sum of money lent on which interest is paid **principally** *adv* **principal boy** *Brit* leading male role in pantomime, played by a woman

principality *n, pl* **-ties** territory ruled by a prince

principle *n* moral rule guiding behaviour; general or basic truth; scientific law concerning the working of something **in principle** in theory but not always in practice **on principle** because of one's beliefs

print *v* reproduce (a newspaper, book, etc) in large quantities by mechanical or electronic means; reproduce (text or pictures) by pressing ink onto paper etc; write in letters that are not joined up; stamp (fabric) with a design; *photog* produce (pictures) from negatives ▷*n* printed words etc; printed copy of a painting; printed lettering; photograph; printed fabric; mark left on a surface by something that has pressed against it **out of print** no longer available from a publisher **printer** *n* person or company engaged in printing; machine that prints **printing** *n* **printed circuit** electronic circuit with wiring printed on an insulating base **print-out** *n* printed information from a computer

prior[1] *adj* earlier **prior to** before

prior[2] *n* head monk in a priory **prioress** *n* deputy head nun in a convent **priory** *n, pl* **-ries** place where certain orders of monks or nuns live

priority *n, pl* **-ties** most important thing that must be dealt with first; right to be or go before others

prise *v* force open by levering

prism *n* transparent block usu with triangular ends and rectangular sides, used to disperse light into a spectrum or refract it in optical instruments **prismatic** *adj* of or shaped like a prism; (of colour) as if produced by refraction through a prism, rainbow-like

prison *n* building where criminals and accused people are held

prisoner *n* person held captive **prisoner of war** serviceman captured by an enemy in wartime

prissy *adj* **-sier, -siest** prim, correct, and easily shocked **prissily** *adv*

pristine *adj* clean, new, and unused

private *adj* for the use of one person or group only; secret; personal, unconnected with one's work; owned or paid for by individuals rather than by the government; quiet, not likely to be disturbed ▷*n* soldier of the lowest rank **privately** *adv* **privacy** *n*

privateer *n hist* privately owned armed vessel authorized by the government to take part in a war; captain of such a ship

privation *n* loss or lack of the necessities of life

privatize *v* sell (a publicly owned company) to individuals or a private company **privatization** *n*

privet *n* bushy evergreen shrub used for hedges

privilege *n* advantage or favour that only some people have **privileged** *adj* enjoying a special right or immunity

> SPELLING Although Collins Word Web shows that people find it difficult to decide whether to use *il* or *el* when spelling **privilege**, the commonest mistake is to insert an extra *d* to make *priviledge*. The adjective, **privileged**, should not have a *d* in the middle either

privy *adj* sharing knowledge of something secret ▷ *n, pl* **privies** *obs* toilet, esp an outside one **Privy Council** private council of the British monarch

prize[1] *n* reward given for success in a competition etc ▷ *adj* winning or likely to win a prize **prizefighter** *n* boxer who fights for money

prize[2] *v* value highly

prize[3] *v* same as **prise**

pro[1] *adv, prep* in favour of **pros and cons** arguments for and against

pro[2] *n, pl* **pros** *Informal* professional; prostitute

pro- *prefix* in favour of *eg pro-Russian*; instead of *eg pronoun*

probable *adj* likely to happen or be true **probability** *n, pl* **-ties**

probably *adv* in all likelihood

probate *n* process of proving the validity of a will; certificate stating that a will is genuine

probation *n* system of dealing with law-breakers, esp juvenile ones, by placing them under supervision; period when someone is assessed for suitability for a job etc **probationer** *n* person on probation

probe *v* search into or examine closely ▷ *n* surgical instrument used to examine a wound, cavity, etc

probiotic *adj, n* (of) a bacterium that protects the body from harmful bacteria: *probiotic yogurts*

probity *n* honesty, integrity

problem *n* something difficult to deal with or solve; question or puzzle set for solution **problematic, problematical** *adj*

proboscis [pro-**boss**-iss] *n* long trunk or snout; elongated mouth of some insects

procedure *n* way of doing something, esp the correct or usual one **procedural** *adj*

proceed *v* start or continue doing; *formal* walk, go; start a legal action; arise from **proceeds** *pl n* money obtained from an event or activity **proceedings** *pl n* organized or related series of events; minutes of a meeting; legal action

process *n* series of actions or changes; method of doing or producing something ▷ *v* handle or prepare by a special method of manufacture **processed** *adj* (of food) treated to prevent it decaying **processor** *n*

procession *n* line of people or vehicles moving forward together in order

proclaim *v* declare publicly **proclamation** *n*

proclivity *n, pl* **-ties** inclination, tendency

procrastinate *v* put off taking action, delay **procrastination** *n*

procreate *v formal* produce offspring **procreation** *n*

procurator fiscal *n* (in Scotland) law officer who acts as public prosecutor and coroner

procure *v* get, provide; obtain (people) to act as prostitutes

procurement *n* **procurer, procuress** *n* person who obtains people to act as prostitutes

prod *v* **prodding, prodded** poke with something pointed; goad (someone) to take action ▷ *n* prodding

prodigal *adj* recklessly extravagant, wasteful **prodigality** *n*

prodigy *n, pl* **-gies** person with some marvellous talent; wonderful thing **prodigious** *adj* very large, immense; wonderful **prodigiously** *adv*

produce *v* bring into existence; present to view, show; make, manufacture; present on stage, film, or television ▷ *n* food grown for sale **producer** *n* person with control over the making of a film, record, etc; person or company that produces something

product *n* something produced; number resulting from multiplication **production** *n* producing; things produced; presentation of a play, opera, etc **productive** *adj* producing large quantities; useful, profitable **productivity** *n*

profane *adj* showing disrespect for religion or holy things; (of language) coarse, blasphemous ▷ *v* treat (something sacred) irreverently, desecrate **profanation** *n* act of profaning **profanity** *n, pl* **-ties** profane talk or behaviour, blasphemy

profess *v* state or claim (something as true), sometimes falsely; have as one's belief or religion **professed** *adj* supposed

profession *n* type of work, such as being a doctor, that needs special training; all the people employed in a profession *eg the legal profession*; declaration of a belief or feeling **professional** *adj* working in a profession; taking part in an activity, such as sport or music, for money; very competent ▷ *n* person who works in a profession; person paid to take part in sport, music, etc **professionally** *adv* **professionalism** *n*

professor *n* teacher of the highest rank in a university **professorial** *adj* **professorship** *n*

proffer *v* offer

proficient *adj* skilled, expert **proficiency** *n*

profile *n* outline, esp of the face, as seen from the side; brief biographical sketch

profit *n* money gained; benefit obtained ▷ *v* gain or benefit **profitable** *adj* making profit **profitably** *adv* **profitability** *n* **profiteer** *n* person who makes excessive profits at the expense of the public **profiteering** *n*

profligate *adj* recklessly extravagant; shamelessly immoral ▷ *n* profligate person **profligacy** *n*

pro forma *adj Latin* prescribing a set form

profound *adj* showing or needing great knowledge; strongly felt, intense **profundity** *n, pl* **-ties**

profuse *adj* plentiful **profusion** *n*

progeny [proj-in-ee] *n, pl* **-nies** children **progenitor** [pro-**jen**-it-er] *n* ancestor

progesterone *n* hormone which prepares the womb for pregnancy and prevents further ovulation

prognosis *n, pl* **-noses** doctor's forecast about the progress of an illness; any forecast

prognostication *n* forecast or prediction

program *n* sequence of coded instructions for a computer ▷*v* **-gramming, -grammed** arrange (data) so that it can be processed by a computer; feed a program into (a computer) **programmer** *n* **programmable** *adj*

programme *n* planned series of events; broadcast on radio or television; list of items or performers in an entertainment

progress *n* improvement, development; movement forward ▷*v* become more advanced or skilful; move forward **in progress** taking place **progression** *n* **progressive** *adj* favouring political or social reform; happening gradually **progressively** *adv*

prohibit *v* forbid or prevent from happening **prohibition** *n* act of forbidding; ban on the sale or drinking of alcohol **prohibitive** *adj* (of prices) too high to be affordable **prohibitively** *adv*

project *n* planned scheme to do or examine something over a period ▷*v* make a forecast based on known data; make (a film or slide) appear on a screen; communicate (an impression); stick out beyond a surface or edge **projector** *n* apparatus for projecting photographic images, films, or slides on a screen **projection** *n* **projectionist** *n* person who operates a projector

projectile *n* object thrown as a weapon or fired from a gun

prolapse *n* slipping down of an internal organ of the body from its normal position

prole *adj, n Chiefly Brit, slang* proletarian

proletariat [pro-lit-**air**-ee-at] *n* working class **proletarian** *adj, n*

proliferate *v* grow or reproduce rapidly **proliferation** *n*

prolific *adj* very productive **prolifically** *adv*

prolix *adj* (of speech or a piece of writing) overlong and boring

prologue *n* introduction to a play or book

prolong *v* make (something) last longer **prolongation** *n*

prom *n* short for **promenade** or

promenade *n Chiefly Brit* paved walkway along the seafront at a holiday resort ▷*v, n old-fashioned* (take) a leisurely walk **promenade concert** *Brit* concert at which part of the audience stands rather than sits

prominent *adj* very noticeable; famous, widely known **prominently** *adv* **prominence** *n*

promiscuous *adj* having many casual sexual relationships **promiscuity** *n*

promise *v* say that one will definitely do or not do something; show signs of, seem likely ▷*n* undertaking to do or not to do something; indication of future success **promising** *adj* likely to succeed or turn out well

promo *n, pl* **-mos** *Informal* short film to promote a product

promontory *n, pl* **-ries** point of high land jutting out into the sea

promote *v* help to make (something) happen or increase; raise to a higher rank or position; encourage the sale of by advertising **promoter** *n* person who organizes or finances an event etc **promotion** *n* **promotional** *adj*

prompt *v* cause (an action); remind (an actor or speaker) of words that he or she has forgotten ▷*adj* done without delay ▷*adv* exactly *eg six o'clock prompt* **promptly** *adv* immediately, without delay **promptness** *n* **prompter, prompt** *n* person offstage who prompts actors

promulgate *v* put (a law etc) into effect by announcing it officially; make widely known **promulgation** *n*

prone *adj* (foll by *to*) likely to do or be affected by (something); lying face downwards

prong *n* one spike of a fork or similar instrument **pronged** *adj*

pronoun *n* word, such as *she* or *it*, used to replace a noun

pronounce *v* form the sounds of (words or letters), esp clearly or in a particular way; declare formally or officially **pronounceable** *adj* **pronounced** *adj* very noticeable **pronouncement** *n* formal announcement **pronunciation** *n* way in which a word or language is pronounced

SPELLING The noun **pronunciation**, which appears in Collins Word Web 823 times, is spelt *pronounciation* 21 times, probably because of the way **pronounce** is spelt. Remember, there is no *o* between the *n* and the *u*

pronto *adv Informal* at once

proof *n* evidence that shows that something is true or has happened; copy of something printed, such as the pages of a book, for checking before final production ▷ *adj* able to withstand *eg proof against criticism*; denoting the strength of an alcoholic drink *eg seventy proof* **proofread** *v* read and correct (printer's proofs) **proofreader** *n*

prop¹ *v* **propping, propped** support (something) so that it stays upright or in place ▷ *n* pole, beam, etc used as a support

prop² *n* movable object used on the set of a film or play

prop³ *n Informal* propeller

propaganda *n* (organized promotion of) information to assist or damage the cause of a government or movement **propagandist** *n*

propagate *v* spread (information and ideas); reproduce, breed, or grow **propagation** *n*

propane *n* flammable gas found in petroleum and used as a fuel

propel *v* **-pelling, -pelled** cause to move forward **propellant** *n* something that provides or causes propulsion; gas used in an aerosol spray **propulsion** *n* method by which something is propelled; act of propelling or state of being propelled

propeller *n* revolving shaft with blades for driving a ship or aircraft

propensity *n, pl* **-ties** natural tendency

proper *adj* real or genuine; suited to a particular purpose; correct in behaviour; excessively moral; *Brit, Aust & NZ, Informal* complete **properly** *adv*

property *n, pl* **-ties** something owned; possessions collectively; land or buildings owned by somebody; quality or attribute

prophet *n* person supposedly chosen by God to spread His word; person who predicts the future **prophetic** *adj* **prophetically** *adv* **prophecy** *n, pl* **-cies** prediction; message revealing God's will **prophesy** *v* **-sying, -sied** foretell

prophylactic *n, adj* (drug) used to prevent disease

propitiate *v* appease, win the

favour of **propitiation** *n*
propitious *adj* favourable or auspicious
proponent *n* person who argues in favour of something
proportion *n* relative size or extent; correct relation between connected parts; part considered with respect to the whole ▷*pl* dimensions or size ▷*v* adjust in relative amount or size **in proportion** comparable in size, rate of increase, etc; without exaggerating **proportional, proportionate** *adj* being in proportion **proportionally, proportionately** *adv*
propose *v* put forward for consideration; nominate; intend or plan (to do); make an offer of marriage **proposal** *n* **proposition** *n* offer; statement or assertion; *maths* theorem; *Informal* thing to be dealt with ▷*v* *Informal* ask (someone) to have sexual intercourse
propound *v* put forward for consideration
proprietor *n* owner of a business establishment **proprietress** *n fem* **proprietary** *adj* made and distributed under a trade name; denoting or suggesting ownership
propriety *n, pl* **-ties** correct conduct
propulsion *n* see **propel**
pro rata *adv, adj Latin* in proportion
prorogue *v* suspend (parliament) without dissolving it **prorogation** *n*
prosaic [pro-**zay**-ik] *adj* lacking imagination, dull **prosaically** *adv*
proscenium *n, pl* **-nia, -niums** arch in a theatre separating the stage from the auditorium
proscribe *v* prohibit, outlaw **proscription** *n* **proscriptive** *adj*
prose *n* ordinary speech or writing in contrast to poetry
prosecute *v* bring a criminal charge against; continue to do **prosecution** *n* **prosecutor** *n*
proselyte [**pross**-ill-ite] *n* recent convert
proselytize [**pross**-ill-it-ize] *v* attempt to convert
prospect *n* something anticipated; *old-fashioned* view from a place ▷*pl* probability of future success ▷*v* explore, esp for gold **prospective** *adj* future; expected **prospector** *n* **prospectus** *n* booklet giving details of a university, company, etc
prosper *v* be successful **prosperity** *n* success and wealth **prosperous** *adj*
prostate *n* gland in male mammals that surrounds the neck of the bladder
prosthesis [pross-**theess**-iss] *n, pl* **-ses** [-seez] artificial body part, such as a limb or breast **prosthetic** *adj*
prostitute *n* person who offers sexual intercourse in return for payment ▷*v* make a prostitute of; offer (oneself or one's talents) for unworthy purposes **prostitution** *n*
prostrate *adj* lying face downwards; physically or emotionally exhausted ▷*v* lie face downwards; exhaust physically or emotionally **prostration** *n*
protagonist *n* supporter of a cause; leading character in a play or a story
protea [**pro**-tee-a] *n* African shrub with showy flowers
protean [pro-**tee**-an] *adj*

constantly changing

protect *v* defend from trouble, harm, or loss **protection** *n* **protectionism** *n* policy of protecting industries by taxing competing imports **protectionist** *n, adj* **protective** *adj* giving protection *eg protective clothing;* tending or wishing to protect someone **protector** *n* person or thing that protects; regent **protectorate** *n* territory largely controlled by a stronger state; (period of) rule of a regent

protégé, *fem* **protégée** [**pro**-ti-zhay] *n* person who is protected and helped by another

protein *n* any of a group of complex organic compounds that are essential for life

pro tempore *adv, adj* for the time being (also **pro tem**)

protest *n* declaration or demonstration of objection ▷*v* object, disagree; assert formally **protestation** *n* strong declaration

Protestant *n* follower of any of the Christian churches that split from the Roman Catholic Church in the sixteenth century ▷*adj* of or relating to such a church **Protestantism** *n*

proto- *combining form* first *eg protohuman*

protocol *n* rules of behaviour for formal occasions

proton *n* positively charged particle in the nucleus of an atom

protoplasm *n* substance forming the living contents of a cell

prototype *n* original or model to be copied or developed

protozoan [pro-toe-**zoe**-an] *n, pl* **-zoa** microscopic one-celled creature

protracted *adj* lengthened or extended

protractor *n* instrument for measuring angles

protrude *v* stick out, project **protrusion** *n*

protuberant *adj* swelling out, bulging **protuberance** *n*

proud *adj* feeling pleasure and satisfaction; feeling honoured; thinking oneself superior to other people; dignified **proudly** *adv*

prove *v* **proving, proved, proved** *or* **proven** establish the validity of; demonstrate, test; be found to be **proven** *adj* known from experience to work

provenance [**prov**-in-anss] *n* place of origin

provender *n old-fashioned* fodder

proverb *n* short saying that expresses a truth or gives a warning **proverbial** *adj*

provide *v* make available **provider** *n* **provided that, providing** on condition that **provide for** *v* take precautions (against); support financially

providence *n* God or nature seen as a protective force that arranges people's lives **provident** *adj* thrifty; showing foresight **providential** *adj* lucky

province *n* area governed as a unit of a country or empire; area of learning, activity, etc ▷*pl* parts of a country outside the capital **provincial** *adj* of a province or the provinces; unsophisticated and narrow-minded ▷*n* unsophisticated person; person from a province or the provinces **provincialism** *n* narrow-mindedness and lack of sophistication

provision *n* act of supplying something; something supplied;

law condition incorporated in a document ▷ *pl* food ▷ *v* supply with food **provisional** *adj* temporary or conditional **provisionally** *adv*

proviso [pro-**vize**-oh] *n, pl* **-sos, -soes** condition, stipulation

provoke *v* deliberately anger; cause (an adverse reaction) **provocation** *n* **provocative** *adj*

provost *n* head of certain university colleges in Britain; chief councillor of a Scottish town

prow *n* bow of a vessel

prowess *n* superior skill or ability; bravery, fearlessness

prowl *v* move stealthily around a place as if in search of prey or plunder ▷ *n* prowling

prowler *n* person who moves stealthily around a place as if in search of prey or plunder

proximity *n* nearness in space or time; nearness or closeness in a series **proximate** *adj*

proxy *n, pl* **proxies** person authorized to act on behalf of someone else; authority to act on behalf of someone else

prude *n* person who is excessively modest, prim, or proper **prudish** *adj* **prudery** *n*

prudent *adj* cautious, discreet, and sensible **prudence** *n* **prudential** *adj old-fashioned* prudent

prune[1] *n* dried plum

prune[2] *v* cut off dead parts or excessive branches from (a tree or plant); shorten, reduce

prurient *adj* excessively interested in sexual matters **prurience** *n*

pry *v* **prying, pried** make an impertinent or uninvited inquiry into a private matter

PS postscript

PSA (in New Zealand) Public Service Association

psalm *n* sacred song **psalmist** *n* writer of psalms

Psalter *n* book containing (a version of) psalms from the Bible **psaltery** *n, pl* **-ries** ancient instrument played by plucking strings

PSBR (in Britain) public sector borrowing requirement

psephology [sef-**fol**-a-jee] *n* statistical study of elections

pseud *n Informal* pretentious person

pseudo- *combining form* false, pretending, or unauthentic *eg pseudoclassical*

pseudonym *n* fictitious name adopted esp by an author **pseudonymous** *adj*

psittacosis *n* disease of parrots that can be transmitted to humans

psyche [**sye**-kee] *n* human mind or soul

psychedelic *adj* denoting a drug that causes hallucinations; having vivid colours and complex patterns similar to those experienced during hallucinations

> SPELLING The main problem with **psychedelic** is which vowel follows the *ch*; it should be *e* of course

psychiatry *n* branch of medicine concerned with mental disorders **psychiatric** *adj* **psychiatrist** *n*

psychic *adj* (also **psychical**) having mental powers which cannot be explained by natural laws; relating to the mind ▷ *n* person with psychic powers

psycho *n, pl* **-chos** *Informal* psychopath

psychoanalysis *n* method of

treating mental and emotional disorders by discussion and analysis of one's thoughts and feelings **psychoanalyse** *v* **psychoanalyst** *n*

psychology *n, pl* **-gies** study of human and animal behaviour; *Informal* person's mental make-up **psychologist** *n* **psychological** *adj* of or affecting the mind; of psychology **psychologically** *adv*

psychopath *n* person afflicted with a personality disorder causing him or her to commit antisocial or violent acts **psychopathic** *adj*

psychosis *n, pl* **-ses** severe mental disorder in which the sufferer's contact with reality becomes distorted **psychotic** *adj*

psychosomatic *adj* (of a physical disorder) thought to have psychological causes

psychotherapy *n* treatment of nervous disorders by psychological methods **psychotherapeutic** *adj* **psychotherapist** *n*

psych up *v* prepare (oneself) mentally for a contest or task

pt part; point

PT *old-fashioned* physical training

pt. pint

PTA Parent-Teacher Association

ptarmigan [**tar**-mig-an] *n* bird of the grouse family which turns white in winter

pterodactyl [terr-roe-**dak**-til] *n* extinct flying reptile with batlike wings

PTO please turn over

ptomaine [**toe**-main] *n* any of a group of poisonous alkaloids found in decaying matter

Pty *Aust, NZ & SAfr* Proprietary

pub *n* building with a bar licensed to sell alcoholic drinks

puberty *n* beginning of sexual maturity **pubertal** *adj*

pubic *adj* of the lower abdomen *eg pubic hair*

public *adj* of or concerning the people as a whole; for use by everyone; well-known; performed or made openly ▷ *n* the community, people in general **publicly** *adv* **public house** pub **public relations** promotion of a favourable opinion towards an organization among the public **public school** private fee-paying school in Britain **public-spirited** *adj* having or showing an active interest in the good of the community

publican *n* *Brit, Aust & NZ* person who owns or runs a pub

publicity *n* process or information used to arouse public attention; public interest so aroused **publicist** *n* person, esp a press agent or journalist, who publicizes something **publicize** *v* bring to public attention

publish *v* produce and issue (printed matter) for sale; announce formally or in public **publication** *n* **publisher** *n*

puce *adj* purplish-brown

puck[1] *n* small rubber disc used in ice hockey

puck[2] *n* mischievous or evil spirit **puckish** *adj*

pucker *v* gather into wrinkles ▷ *n* wrinkle or crease

pudding *n* dessert, esp a cooked one served hot; savoury dish with pastry or batter *eg steak-and-kidney pudding*; sausage-like mass of meat *eg black pudding*

puddle *n* small pool of water, esp of rain

puerile *adj* silly and childish

puerperal [pew-**er**-per-al] *adj*

concerning the period following childbirth

puff *n* (sound of) a short blast of breath, wind, etc; act of inhaling cigarette smoke ▷*v* blow or breathe in short quick draughts; take draws at (a cigarette); send out in small clouds; swell **out of puff** out of breath **puffy** *adj* **puffball** *n* ball-shaped fungus **puff pastry** light flaky pastry

puffin *n* black-and-white sea bird with a brightly-coloured beak

pug *n* small snub-nosed dog **pug nose** short stubby upturned nose

pugilist [**pew**-jil-ist] *n* boxer **pugilism** *n* **pugilistic** *adj*

pugnacious *adj* ready and eager to fight **pugnacity** *n*

puissance [**pwee**-sonce] *n* showjumping competition that tests a horse's ability to jump large obstacles

puke *slang* ▷*v* vomit ▷*n* act of vomiting; vomited matter

pulchritude *n lit* beauty

pull *v* exert force on (an object) to move it towards the source of the force; strain or stretch; remove or extract; attract ▷*n* act of pulling; force used in pulling; act of taking in drink or smoke; *Informal* power, influence **pull in** *v* (of a vehicle or driver) draw in to the side of the road or stop; reach a destination; attract in large numbers; *Brit, Aust & NZ, slang* arrest **pull off** *v Informal* succeed in performing **pull out** *v* (of a vehicle or driver) move away from the side of the road or move out to overtake; (of a train) depart; withdraw; remove by pulling **pull up** *v* (of a vehicle or driver) stop; remove by the roots; reprimand

pullet *n* young hen

pulley *n* wheel with a grooved rim in which a belt, chain, or piece of rope runs in order to lift weights by a downward pull

Pullman *n, pl* **-mans** luxurious railway coach

pullover *n* sweater that is pulled on over the head

pulmonary *adj* of the lungs

pulp *n* soft wet substance made from crushed or beaten matter; flesh of a fruit; poor-quality books and magazines ▷*v* reduce to pulp

pulpit *n* raised platform for a preacher

pulsar *n* small dense star which emits regular bursts of radio waves

pulse¹ *n* regular beating of blood through the arteries at each heartbeat; any regular beat or vibration **pulsate** *v* throb, quiver **pulsation** *n*

pulse² *n* edible seed of a pod-bearing plant such as a bean or pea

pulverize *v* reduce to fine pieces; destroy completely

puma *n* large American wild cat with a greyish-brown coat

pumice [**pumm**-iss] *n* light porous stone used for scouring

pummel *v* **-melling, -melled** strike repeatedly with or as if with the fists

pump¹ *n* machine used to force a liquid or gas to move in a particular direction ▷*v* raise or drive with a pump; supply in large amounts; operate or work in the manner of a pump; extract information from

pump² *n* light flat-soled shoe

pumpkin *n* large round fruit with an orange rind, soft flesh, and many seeds

pun *n* use of words to exploit double meanings for humorous effect ▷*v* **punning, punned** make puns

punch[1] *v* strike at with a clenched fist ▷*n* blow with a clenched fist; *Informal* effectiveness or vigour **punchy** *adj* forceful **punch-drunk** *adj* dazed by or as if by repeated blows to the head

punch[2] *n* tool or machine for shaping, piercing, or engraving ▷*v* pierce, cut, stamp, shape, or drive with a punch

punch[3] *n* drink made from a mixture of wine, spirits, fruit, sugar, and spices

punctilious *adj* paying great attention to correctness in etiquette; careful about small details

punctual *adj* arriving or taking place at the correct time **punctuality** *n* **punctually** *adv*

punctuate *v* put punctuation marks in; interrupt at frequent intervals **punctuation** *n* (use of) marks such as commas, colons, etc in writing, to assist in making the sense clear

puncture *n* small hole made by a sharp object, esp in a tyre ▷*v* pierce a hole in

pundit *n* expert who speaks publicly on a subject

pungent *adj* having a strong sharp bitter flavour **pungency** *n*

punish *v* cause (someone) to suffer or undergo a penalty for some wrongdoing **punishing** *adj* harsh or difficult **punishment** *n* **punitive** [**pew**-nit-tiv] *adj* relating to punishment

punk *n* anti-Establishment youth movement and style of rock music of the late 1970s; follower of this music; worthless person

punnet *n* small basket for fruit

punt[1] *n* open flat-bottomed boat propelled by a pole ▷*v* travel in a punt

punt[2] *sport* ▷*n* kick of a ball before it touches the ground when dropped from the hands ▷*v* kick (a ball) in this way

punt[3] *n* former monetary unit of the Irish Republic

punter *n* person who bets; *Brit, Aust & NZ* any member of the public

puny *adj* **-nier, -niest** small and feeble

pup *n* young of certain animals, such as dogs and seals

pupa *n, pl* **-pae, -pas** insect at the stage of development between a larva and an adult

pupil[1] *n* person who is taught by a teacher

pupil[2] *n* round dark opening in the centre of the eye

puppet *n* small doll or figure moved by strings or by the operator's hand; person or country controlled by another **puppeteer** *n*

puppy *n, pl* **-pies** young dog

purchase *v* obtain by payment ▷*n* thing that is bought; act of buying; leverage, grip **purchaser** *n*

purdah *n* Muslim and Hindu custom of keeping women in seclusion, with clothing that conceals them completely when they go out

pure *adj* unmixed, untainted; innocent; complete *eg pure delight*; concerned with theory only *eg pure mathematics* **purely** *adv* **purity** *n* **purify** *v* **-fying, -fied** make or become pure **purification** *n* **purist** *n* person concerned with strict obedience to the traditions of a subject

purée [**pure**-ray] *n* pulp of cooked food ▷*v* **-réeing, -réed** make into a purée

purgatory *n* place or state of temporary suffering; (**P-**) *RC church* place where souls of the dead undergo punishment for their sins before being admitted to Heaven **purgatorial** *adj*

purge *v* rid (a thing or place) of (unwanted things or people) ▷ *n* purging **purgative** *n, adj* (medicine) designed to cause defecation

Puritan *n hist* member of the English Protestant group who wanted simpler church ceremonies; (**p-**) person with strict moral and religious principles **puritanical** *adj* **puritanism** *n*

purl *n* stitch made by knitting a plain stitch backwards ▷ *v* knit in purl

purlieus [**per**-lyooz] *pl n lit* outskirts

purloin *v* steal

purple *adj, n* (of) a colour between red and blue

purport *v* claim (to be or do something) ▷ *n* apparent meaning, significance

purpose *n* reason for which something is done or exists; determination; practical advantage or use *eg use the time to good purpose* **purposely** *adv* intentionally (also **on purpose**)

purr *v* (of cats) make low vibrant sound, usu when pleased ▷ *n* this sound

purse *n* small bag for money; *US & NZ* handbag; financial resources; prize money ▷ *v* draw (one's lips) together into a small round shape **purser** *n* ship's officer who keeps the accounts

pursue *v* chase; follow (a goal); engage in; continue to discuss or ask about (something) **pursuer** *n*

pursuit *n* pursuing; occupation or pastime

> SPELLING The misspelling *persue* is very common, occurring in Collins Word Web 52 times. It should, of course, be spelt with a *u* in each half of the word, as in **pursuing** and **pursued**

purulent [**pure**-yoo-lent] *adj* of or containing pus

purvey *v* supply (provisions) **purveyor** *n*

purview *n* scope or range of activity or outlook

pus *n* yellowish matter produced by infected tissue

push *v* move or try to move by steady force; drive or spur (oneself or another person) to do something; *Informal* sell (drugs) illegally ▷ *n* act of pushing; special effort **the push** *slang* dismissal from a job or relationship **pusher** *n* person who sells illegal drugs **pushy** *adj* too assertive or ambitious **pushchair** *n Brit* folding chair on wheels for a baby

pusillanimous *adj* timid and cowardly **pusillanimity** *n*

puss, pussy *n, pl* **pusses, pussies** *Informal* cat

pussyfoot *v Informal* behave too cautiously

pustule *n* pimple containing pus

put *v* **putting, put** cause to be (in a position, state, or place); express; throw (the shot) in the shot put ▷ *n* throw in putting the shot **put across** *v* express successfully **put off** *v* postpone; disconcert; repel **put up** *v* erect; accommodate; nominate **put-upon** *adj* taken advantage of

putative *adj* reputed, supposed

putrid *adj* rotten and foul-smelling **putrefy** *v* **-fying, -fied** rot and produce an offensive smell **putrefaction** *n* **putrescent** *adj* rotting

putsch *n* sudden violent attempt to remove a government from power

putt *golf* ▷*n* stroke on the putting green to roll the ball into or near the hole ▷*v* strike (the ball) in this way **putter** *n* golf club for putting

putty *n* adhesive used to fix glass into frames and fill cracks in woodwork

puzzle *v* perplex and confuse or be perplexed or confused ▷*n* problem that cannot be easily solved; toy, game, or question that requires skill or ingenuity to solve **puzzlement** *n* **puzzling** *adj*

PVC polyvinyl chloride: plastic material used in clothes etc

Pygmy *n, pl* **-mies** member of one of the very short peoples of Equatorial Africa ▷*adj* (**p-**) very small

pyjamas *pl n* loose-fitting trousers and top worn in bed

pylon *n* steel tower-like structure supporting electrical cables

pyramid *n* solid figure with a flat base and triangular sides sloping upwards to a point; building of this shape, esp an ancient Egyptian one **pyramidal** *adj*

pyre *n* pile of wood for burning a corpse on

Pyrex *n* ® heat-resistant glassware

pyromania *n* uncontrollable urge to set things on fire **pyromaniac** *n*

pyrotechnics *n* art of making fireworks; firework display **pyrotechnic** *adj*

Pyrrhic victory [pir-ik] *n* victory in which the victor's losses are as great as those of the defeated

python *n* large nonpoisonous snake that crushes its prey

q

QC Queen's Counsel
QED which was to be shown or proved
Qld Queensland
QM Quartermaster
qr. quarter; quire
qt. quart
qua [**kwah**] *prep* in the capacity of
quack[1] *v* (of a duck) utter a harsh guttural sound ▷*n* sound made by a duck
quack[2] *n* unqualified person who claims medical knowledge
quad *n* see **quadrangle**; *Informal* quadruplet ▷*adj* short for **quadraphonic** **quad bike, quad** vehicle like a small motorcycle with four large wheels, designed for agricultural and sporting uses
quadrangle *n* (also **quad**) rectangular courtyard with buildings on all four sides; geometric figure consisting of four points connected by four lines **quadrangular** *adj*
quadrant *n* quarter of a circle; quarter of a circle's circumference; instrument for measuring the altitude of the stars
quadraphonic *adj* using four independent channels to reproduce or record sound
quadratic *maths* ▷*n* equation in which the variable is raised to the power of two, but nowhere raised to a higher power ▷*adj* of the second power
quadrennial *adj* occurring every four years; lasting four years
quadri- *combining form* four *eg quadrilateral*
quadrilateral *adj* having four sides ▷*n* polygon with four sides
quadrille *n* square dance for four couples
quadriplegia *n* paralysis of all four limbs
quadruped [**kwod**-roo-ped] *n* any animal with four legs
quadruple *v* multiply by four ▷*adj* four times as much or as many; consisting of four parts
quadruplet *n* one of four offspring born at one birth
quaff [**kwoff**] *v* drink heartily or in one draught
quagmire [**kwog**-mire] *n* soft wet area of land
quail[1] *n* small game bird of the partridge family
quail[2] *v* shrink back with fear
quaint *adj* attractively unusual, esp in an old-fashioned style **quaintly** *adv*
quake *v* shake or tremble with or as if with fear ▷*n Informal* earthquake
Quaker *n* member of a Christian sect, the Society of Friends

Quakerism *n*

qualify *v* **-fying, -fied** provide or be provided with the abilities necessary for a task, office, or duty; moderate or restrict (a statement) **qualified** *adj* **qualification** *n* official record of achievement in a course or examination; quality or skill needed for a particular activity; condition that modifies or limits; act of qualifying

quality *n, pl* **-ties** degree or standard of excellence; distinguishing characteristic or attribute; basic character or nature of something ▷ *adj* excellent or superior **qualitative** *adj* of or relating to quality

qualm [kwahm] *n* pang of conscience; sudden sensation of misgiving

quandary *n, pl* **-ries** difficult situation or dilemma

quandong [kwon-dong] *n* small Australian tree with edible fruit and nuts used in preserves; Australian tree with pale timber

quango *n, pl* **-gos** *Chiefly Brit* quasi-autonomous nongovernmental organization: any partly independent official body set up by a government

quanta *n* plural of **quantum**

quantify *v* **-fying, -fied** discover or express the quantity of **quantifiable** *adj* **quantification** *n*

quantity *n, pl* **-ties** specified or definite amount or number; aspect of anything that can be measured, weighed, or counted **quantitative** *adj* of or relating to quantity **quantity surveyor** person who estimates the cost of the materials and labour necessary for a construction job

quantum *n, pl* **-ta** desired or required amount, esp a very small one **quantum leap, jump** *Informal* sudden large change, increase, or advance **quantum theory** physics theory based on the idea that energy of electrons is discharged in discrete quanta

quarantine *n* period of isolation of people or animals to prevent the spread of disease ▷ *v* isolate in or as if in quarantine

quark *n physics* subatomic particle thought to be the fundamental unit of matter

quarrel *n* angry disagreement; cause of dispute ▷ *v* **-relling, -relled** have a disagreement or dispute **quarrelsome** *adj*

quarry¹ *n, pl* **-ries** place where stone is dug from the surface of the earth ▷ *v* **-rying, -ried** extract (stone) from a quarry

quarry² *n, pl* **-ries** person or animal that is being hunted

quart *n* unit of liquid measure equal to two pints (1.136 litres)

quarter *n* one of four equal parts of something; fourth part of a year; *Informal* unit of weight equal to 4 ounces; region or district of a town or city; *US* 25-cent piece; mercy or pity, as shown towards a defeated opponent ▷ *pl* lodgings ▷ *v* divide into four equal parts; billet or be billeted in lodgings **quarterly** *adj* occurring, due, or issued at intervals of three months ▷ *n* magazine issued every three months ▷ *adv* once every three months **quarter day** *Brit* any of the four days in the year when certain payments become due **quarterdeck** *n naut* rear part of the upper deck of a ship **quarterfinal** *n* round before the semifinal in a competition **quartermaster** *n* military officer responsible for accommodation, food, and equipment

quartet *n* group of four performers; music for such a group

quarto *n, pl* **-tos** book size in which the sheets are folded into four leaves

quartz *n* hard glossy mineral

quasar [**kway**-zar] *n* extremely distant starlike object that emits powerful radio waves

quash *v* annul or make void; subdue forcefully and completely

quasi- [**kway**-zie] *combining form* almost but not really *eg quasi-religious; a quasi-scholar*

quatrain *n* stanza or poem of four lines

quaver *v* (of a voice) quiver or tremble ▷ *n music* note half the length of a crotchet; tremulous sound or note

quay [**kee**] *n* wharf built parallel to the shore

queasy *adj* **-sier, -siest** having the feeling that one is about to vomit; feeling or causing uneasiness **queasiness** *n*

queen *n* female sovereign who is the official ruler or head of state; wife of a king; woman, place, or thing considered to be the best of her or its kind; *slang* effeminate male homosexual; only fertile female in a colony of bees, wasps, or ants; the most powerful piece in chess **queenly** *adj* **Queen's Counsel** barrister or advocate appointed Counsel to the Crown

queer *adj* not normal or usual; *Brit* faint, giddy, or queasy; *offens* homosexual ▷ *n offens* homosexual **queer someone's pitch** *Informal* spoil someone's chances of something.

> Although the term *queer* meaning homosexual is still considered derogatory when used by non-homosexuals, it is used by homosexuals of themselves as a positive term: *queer politics, queer cinema*

quell *v* suppress; overcome

quench *v* satisfy (one's thirst); put out or extinguish

quern *n* stone hand mill for grinding corn

querulous [**kwer**-yoo-luss] *adj* complaining or whining **querulously** *adv*

query *n, pl* **-ries** question, esp one raising doubt; question mark ▷ *v* **-rying, -ried** express uncertainty, doubt, or an objection concerning (something)

quest *n* long and difficult search ▷ *v* (foll by *for, after*) go in search of

question *n* form of words addressed to a person in order to obtain an answer; point at issue; difficulty or uncertainty ▷ *v* put a question or questions to (a person); express uncertainty about **in question** under discussion **out of the question** impossible **questionable** *adj* of disputable value or authority **questionably** *adv* **questionnaire** *n* set of questions on a form, used to collect information from people **question mark** punctuation mark (?) written at the end of questions

> SPELLING There are 28 occurrences of the misspelling *questionaire* (with only one *n*), in Collins Word Web. The correct spelling, **questionnaire**, has two *n*s, and appears in Collins Word Web over 3000 times

queue *n* line of people or vehicles waiting for something ▷ *v* **queuing**

or **queueing, queued** (often foll by *up*) form or remain in a line while waiting

quibble *v* make trivial objections ▷ *n* trivial objection

quiche [**keesh**] *n* savoury flan with an egg custard filling to which vegetables etc are added

quick *adj* speedy, fast; lasting or taking a short time; alert and responsive; easily excited or aroused ▷ *n* area of sensitive flesh under a nail ▷ *adv Informal* in a rapid manner **cut someone to the quick** hurt someone's feelings deeply **quickly** *adv* **quicken** *v* make or become faster; make or become more lively **quicklime** *n* white solid used in the manufacture of glass and steel **quicksand** *n* deep mass of loose wet sand that sucks anything on top of it into it **quicksilver** *n* mercury **quickstep** *n* fast modern ballroom dance

quid *n, pl* **quid** *Brit, slang* pound (sterling)

quid pro quo *n, pl* **quid pro quos** one thing, esp an advantage or object, given in exchange for another

quiescent [kwee-**ess**-ent] *adj* quiet, inactive, or dormant **quiescence** *n*

quiet *adj* with little noise; calm or tranquil; untroubled ▷ *n* quietness ▷ *v* make or become quiet **on the quiet** without other people knowing, secretly **quietly** *adv* **quietness** *n* **quieten** *v* (often foll by *down*) make or become quiet **quietude** *n* quietness, peace, or tranquillity

quietism *n* passivity and calmness of mind towards external events

quiff *n* tuft of hair brushed up above the forehead

quill *n* pen made from the feather of a bird's wing or tail; stiff hollow spine of a hedgehog or porcupine

quilt *n* padded covering for a bed **quilted** *adj* consisting of two layers of fabric with a layer of soft material between them

quin *n* short for **quintuplet**

quince *n* acid-tasting pear-shaped fruit

quinine *n* bitter drug used as a tonic and formerly to treat malaria

quinquennial *adj* occurring every five years; lasting five years

quinsy *n* inflammation of the throat or tonsils

quintessence *n* most perfect representation of a quality or state **quintessential** *adj*

quintet *n* group of five performers; music for such a group

quintuplet *n* one of five offspring born at one birth

quip *n* witty saying ▷ *v* **quipping, quipped** make a quip

quire *n* set of 24 or 25 sheets of paper

quirk *n* peculiarity of character; unexpected twist or turn *eg a quirk of fate* **quirky** *adj*

quisling *n* traitor who aids an occupying enemy force

quit *v* **quitting, quit** stop (doing something); give up (a job); depart from **quitter** *n* person who lacks perseverance **quits** *adj Informal* on an equal footing

quite *adv* somewhat *eg she's quite pretty;* absolutely *eg you're quite right;* in actuality, truly ▷ *interj* expression of agreement.

> Note that because *quite* can mean 'extremely': *quite amazing;* or can express a reservation: *quite friendly,* it should be used carefully.

quiver¹ *v* shake with a tremulous movement ▷ *n* shaking or trembling
quiver² *n* case for arrows
quixotic [kwik-**sot**-ik] *adj* romantic and unrealistic
quixotically *adv*
quiz *n, pl* **quizzes** entertainment in which the knowledge of the players is tested by a series of questions ▷ *v* **quizzing, quizzed** investigate by close questioning
quizzical *adj* questioning and mocking *eg a quizzical look*
quizzically *adv*
quod *n Brit, slang* jail
quoit *n* large ring used in the game of quoits ▷ *pl* game in which quoits are tossed at a stake in the ground in attempts to encircle it
quokka *n* small Australian wallaby
quorum *n* minimum number of people required to be present at a meeting before any transactions can take place
quota *n* share that is due from, due to, or allocated to a group or person; prescribed number or quantity allowed, required, or admitted
quote *v* repeat (words) exactly from (an earlier work, speech, or conversation); state (a price) for goods or a job of work ▷ *n Informal* quotation **quotable** *adj*
quotation *n* written or spoken passage repeated exactly in a later work, speech, or conversation; act of quoting; estimate of costs submitted by a contractor to a prospective client **quotation marks** raised commas used in writing to mark the beginning and end of a quotation or passage of speech
quoth *v obs* said
quotidian *adj* daily; commonplace
quotient *n* result of the division of one number or quantity by another
q.v. which see: used to refer a reader to another item in the same book

r

r radius; ratio; right
R Queen; King; River
RA (in Britain) Royal Academy; (in Britain) Royal Artillery
RAAF Royal Australian Air Force
rabbi [**rab**-bye] *n, pl* **-bis** Jewish spiritual leader **rabbinical** *adj*
rabbit *n* small burrowing mammal with long ears **rabbit on** *v* **rabbiting, rabbited** *Brit, Informal* talk too much
rabble *n* disorderly crowd of noisy people
rabid *adj* fanatical; having rabies **rabidly** *adv*
rabies [**ray**-beez] *n* usu fatal viral disease transmitted by dogs and certain other animals
RAC (in Britain) Royal Automobile Club
raccoon *n* small N American mammal with a long striped tail
race[1] *n* contest of speed ▷ *pl* meeting for horse racing ▷ *v* compete with in a race; run swiftly; (of an engine) run faster than normal **racer** *n* **racecourse** *n* **racehorse** *n* **racetrack** *n*
race[2] *n* group of people of common ancestry with distinguishing physical features, such as skin colour **racial** *adj* **racism, racialism** *n* hostile attitude or behaviour to members of other races, based on a belief in the innate superiority of one's own race **racist, racialist** *adj, n*
raceme [rass-**eem**] *n* cluster of flowers along a central stem, as in the foxglove
rack[1] *n* framework for holding particular articles, such as coats or luggage; *hist* instrument of torture that stretched the victim's body ▷ *v* cause great suffering to **rack one's brains** try very hard to remember
rack[2] *n* **go to rack and ruin** be destroyed
racket[1] *n* noisy disturbance; occupation by which money is made illegally
racket[2]**, racquet** *n* bat with strings stretched in an oval frame, used in tennis etc **rackets** *n* ball game played in a paved walled court
racketeer *n* person making illegal profits
raconteur [rak-on-**tur**] *n* skilled storyteller
racy *adj* **racier, raciest** slightly shocking; spirited or lively
radar *n* device for tracking distant objects by bouncing high-frequency radio pulses off them
radial *adj* spreading out from a common central point; of a radius; (also **radial-ply**) (of a tyre) having flexible sides strengthened with

radial cords

radiant *adj* looking happy; shining; emitting radiation **radiance** *n*

radiate *v* spread out from a centre; emit or be emitted as radiation **radiator** *n* *Brit* arrangement of pipes containing hot water or steam to heat a room; tubes containing water as cooling apparatus for a car engine; *Aust & NZ* electric fire

radiation *n* transmission of energy from one body to another; particles or waves emitted in nuclear decay; process of radiating

radical *adj* fundamental; thorough; advocating fundamental change ▷*n* person advocating fundamental (political) change; number expressed as the root of another **radically** *adv* **radicalism** *n*

radicle *n* small or developing root

radii *n* a plural of **radius**

radio *n, pl* **-dios** use of electromagnetic waves for broadcasting, communication, etc; device for receiving and amplifying radio signals; sound broadcasting ▷*v* transmit (a message) by radio

radio- *combining form* of radio, radiation, or radioactivity

radioactive *adj* emitting radiation as a result of nuclear decay **radioactivity** *n*

radiography [ray-dee-**og**-ra-fee] *n* production of an image on a film or plate by radiation **radiographer** *n*

radiology [ray-dee-**ol**-a-jee] *n* science of using x-rays in medicine **radiologist** *n*

radiotherapy *n* treatment of disease, esp cancer, by radiation **radiotherapist** *n*

radish *n* small hot-flavoured root vegetable eaten raw in salads

radium *n chem* radioactive metallic element

radius *n, pl* **radii, radiuses** (length of) a straight line from the centre to the circumference of a circle; outer of two bones in the forearm

radon [**ray**-don] *n chem* radioactive gaseous element

RAF (in Britain) Royal Air Force

raffia *n* prepared palm fibre for weaving mats etc

raffish *adj* slightly disreputable

raffle *n* lottery with goods as prizes ▷*v* offer as a prize in a raffle

raft *n* floating platform of logs, planks, etc

rafter *n* one of the main beams of a roof

rag[1] *n* fragment of cloth; *Brit, Aust & NZ, Informal* newspaper ▷*pl* tattered clothing **ragged** [**rag**-gid] *adj* dressed in shabby or torn clothes; torn; lacking smoothness

rag[2] *Brit* ▷*v* **ragging, ragged** tease ▷*adj, n* (of) events organized by students to raise money for charities

ragamuffin *n* ragged dirty child

rage *n* violent anger or passion ▷*v* speak or act with fury; proceed violently and without check **all the rage** very popular

raglan *adj* (of a sleeve) joined to a garment by diagonal seams from the neck to the underarm

ragout [rag-**goo**] *n* richly seasoned stew of meat and vegetables

ragtime *n* style of jazz piano music

raid *n* sudden surprise attack or search ▷*v* make a raid on **raider** *n*

rail[1] *n* horizontal bar, esp as part of a fence or track; railway **railing** *n* fence made of rails supported by posts **railway** *n* track of iron rails

on which trains run; company operating a railway
rail² *v* (foll by *at, against*) complain bitterly or loudly **raillery** *n* teasing or joking
rail³ *n* small marsh bird
raiment *n obs* clothing
rain *n* water falling in drops from the clouds ▷ *v* fall or pour down as rain; fall rapidly and in large quantities **rainy** *adj* **rainbow** *n* arch of colours in the sky **rainbow nation** South African nation **raincoat** *n* water-resistant overcoat **rainfall** *n* amount of rain **rainforest** *n* dense forest in tropical and temperate areas
raise *v* lift up; set upright; increase in amount or intensity; collect or levy; bring up (a family); put forward for consideration
raisin *n* dried grape
raison d'être [ray-zon **det**-ra] *n, pl* **raisons d'être** *French* reason or justification for existence
Raj *n* **the Raj** former British rule in India
raja, rajah *n hist* Indian prince or ruler
rake¹ *n* tool with a long handle and a crosspiece with teeth, used for smoothing earth or gathering leaves, hay, etc ▷ *v* gather or smooth with a rake; search (through); sweep (with gunfire) **rake it in** *Informal* make a large amount of money **rake-off** *n slang* share of profits, esp illegal **rake up** *v* revive memories of (a forgotten unpleasant event)
rake² *n* dissolute or immoral man **rakish** *adj*
rakish *adj* dashing or jaunty
rally *n, pl* **-lies** large gathering of people for a meeting; marked recovery of strength; *tennis etc* lively exchange of strokes; car-driving competition on public roads ▷ *v* **-lying, -lied** bring or come together after dispersal or for a common cause; regain health or strength, revive
ram *n* male sheep; hydraulic machine ▷ *v* **ramming, rammed** strike against with force; force or drive; cram or stuff
RAM *computers* random access memory
Ramadan *n* 9th Muslim month; strict fasting from dawn to dusk observed during this time
ramble *v* walk without a definite route; talk incoherently ▷ *n* walk, esp in the country
rambler *n* person who rambles; climbing rose
ramekin [**ram**-ik-in] *n* small ovenproof dish for a single serving of food
ramifications *pl n* consequences resulting from an action
ramp *n* slope joining two level surfaces
rampage *v* dash about violently **on the rampage** behaving violently or destructively
rampant *adj* growing or spreading uncontrollably; (of a heraldic beast) on its hind legs
rampart *n* mound or wall for defence
ramshackle *adj* tumbledown, rickety, or makeshift
ran *v* past tense of **run**
ranch *n* large cattle farm in the American West **rancher** *n*
rancid *adj* (of butter, bacon, etc) stale and having an offensive smell **rancidity** *n*
rancour *n* deep bitter hate **rancorous** *adj*
rand *n* monetary unit of S Africa

random *adj* made or done by chance or without plan **at random** haphazard(ly)

randy *adj* **randier, randiest** *Informal* sexually aroused

rang *v* past tense of **ring**[1]

range *n* limits of effectiveness or variation; distance that a missile or plane can travel; distance of a mark shot at; whole set of related things; chain of mountains; place for shooting practice or rocket testing; kitchen stove ▷*v* vary between one point and another; cover or extend over; roam **ranger** *n* official in charge of a nature reserve etc; (**R-**) member of the senior branch of Guides **rangefinder** *n* instrument for finding how far away an object is

rangy [**rain**-jee] *adj* **rangier, rangiest** having long slender limbs

rank[1] *n* relative place or position; status; social class; row or line ▷*v* have a specific rank or position; arrange in rows or lines **rank and file** ordinary people or members **the ranks** common soldiers

rank[2] *adj* complete or absolute *eg rank favouritism*; smelling offensively strong; growing too thickly

rankle *v* continue to cause resentment or bitterness

ransack *v* search thoroughly; pillage, plunder

ransom *n* money demanded in return for the release of someone who has been kidnapped

rant *v* talk in a loud and excited way **ranter** *n*

rap *v* **rapping, rapped** hit with a sharp quick blow; utter (a command) abruptly; perform a rhythmic monologue with musical backing ▷*n* quick sharp blow; rhythmic monologue performed to music **take the rap** *slang* suffer punishment for something whether guilty or not **rapper** *n*

rapacious *adj* greedy or grasping **rapacity** *n*

rape[1] *v* force to submit to sexual intercourse ▷*n* act of raping; any violation or abuse **rapist** *n*

rape[2] *n* plant with oil-yielding seeds, also used as fodder

rapid *adj* quick, swift **rapids** *pl n* part of a river with a fast turbulent current **rapidly** *adv* **rapidity** *n*

rapier [**ray**-pyer] *n* fine-bladed sword

rapport [rap-**pore**] *n* harmony or agreement

rapprochement [rap-**prosh**-mong] *n* re-establishment of friendly relations, esp between nations

rapt *adj* engrossed or spellbound **rapture** *n* ecstasy **rapturous** *adj*

rare[1] *adj* uncommon; infrequent; of uncommonly high quality; (of air at high altitudes) having low density, thin **rarely** *adv* seldom **rarity** *n*

rare[2] *adj* (of meat) lightly cooked

rarebit *n* see **Welsh rarebit**

rarefied [**rare**-if-ide] *adj* highly specialized, exalted; (of air) thin

raring *adj* **raring to** enthusiastic, willing, or ready to

rascal *n* rogue; naughty (young) person **rascally** *adj*

rash[1] *adj* hasty, reckless, or incautious **rashly** *adv*

rash[2] *n* eruption of spots or patches on the skin; outbreak of (unpleasant) occurrences

rasher *n* thin slice of bacon

rasp *n* harsh grating noise; coarse file ▷*v* speak in a grating voice; make a scraping noise

raspberry *n* red juicy edible berry; *Informal* spluttering noise made with the tongue and lips, to show contempt

Rastafarian *n, adj* (member) of a religion originating in Jamaica and regarding Haile Selassie as God (also **Rasta**)

rat *n* small rodent; *Informal* contemptible person, esp a deserter or informer ▷ *v* **ratting, ratted** *Informal* inform (on); hunt rats **ratty** *adj Brit & NZ, Informal* bad-tempered, irritable **rat race** continual hectic competitive activity

ratafia [rat-a-**fee**-a] *n* liqueur made from fruit

ratatouille [rat-a-**twee**] *n* vegetable casserole of tomatoes, aubergines, etc

ratchet *n* set of teeth on a bar or wheel allowing motion in one direction only

rate *n* degree of speed or progress; proportion between two things; charge ▷ *pl* local tax on business ▷ *v* consider or value; estimate the value of **at any rate** in any case **rateable** *adj* able to be rated; (of property) liable to payment of rates **ratepayer** *n*

rather *adv* to some extent; more truly or appropriately; more willingly

ratify *v* **-fying, -fied** give formal approval to **ratification** *n*

rating *n* valuation or assessment; classification; noncommissioned sailor ▷ *pl* size of the audience for a TV programme

ratio *n, pl* **-tios** relationship between two numbers or amounts expressed as a proportion

ration *n* fixed allowance of food etc ▷ *v* limit to a certain amount per person

rational *adj* reasonable, sensible; capable of reasoning **rationally** *adv* **rationality** *n* **rationale** [rash-a-**nahl**] *n* reason for an action or decision **rationalism** *n* philosophy that regards reason as the only basis for beliefs or actions **rationalist** *n* **rationalize** *v* justify by plausible reasoning; reorganize to improve efficiency or profitability **rationalization** *n*

rattan *n* climbing palm with jointed stems used for canes

rattle *v* give out a succession of short sharp sounds; shake briskly causing sharp sounds; *Informal* confuse or fluster ▷ *n* short sharp sound; instrument for making such a sound **rattlesnake** *n* poisonous snake with loose horny segments on the tail that make a rattling sound

raucous *adj* hoarse or harsh

raunchy *adj* **-chier, -chiest** *slang* earthy, sexy

ravage *v* cause extensive damage to **ravages** *pl n* damaging effects

rave *v* talk wildly or with enthusiasm ▷ *n slang* large-scale party with electronic dance music **raving** *adj* delirious; *Informal* exceptional *eg a raving beauty*

ravel *v* **-elling, -elled** tangle or become entangled

raven *n* black bird like a large crow ▷ *adj* (of hair) shiny black

ravenous *adj* very hungry

ravine [rav-**veen**] *n* narrow steep-sided valley worn by a stream

ravioli *pl n* small squares of pasta with a savoury filling

ravish *v* enrapture; *lit* rape **ravishing** *adj* lovely or entrancing

raw *adj* uncooked; not manufactured or refined; inexperienced; chilly **raw deal** unfair or dishonest treatment

rawhide *n* untanned hide
ray¹ *n* single line or narrow beam of light
ray² *n* large sea fish with a flat body and a whiplike tail
rayon *n* (fabric made of) a synthetic fibre
raze *v* destroy (buildings or a town) completely
razor *n* sharp instrument for shaving **razorbill** *n* sea bird of the North Atlantic with a stout sideways flattened bill
razzle-dazzle, razzmatazz *n* *slang* showy activity
RC Roman Catholic; Red Cross
Rd Road
re *prep* with reference to, concerning
RE (in Britain) religious education
re- *prefix* again *eg re-enter; retrial*
reach *v* arrive at; make a movement in order to grasp or touch; succeed in touching; make contact or communication with; extend as far as ▷ *n* distance that one can reach; range of influence ▷ *pl* stretch of a river **reachable** *adj*
react *v* act in response (to); (foll by *against*) act in an opposing or contrary manner **reaction** *n* physical or emotional response to a stimulus; any action resisting another; opposition to change; chemical or nuclear change, combination, or decomposition **reactionary** *n, adj* (person) opposed to change, esp in politics **reactance** *n electricity* resistance to the flow of an alternating current caused by the inductance or capacitance of the circuit **reactive** *adj* chemically active **reactor** *n* apparatus in which a nuclear reaction is maintained and controlled to produce nuclear energy
read *v* **reading, read** look at and understand or take in (written or printed matter); look at and say aloud; interpret the significance or meaning of; (of an instrument) register; study ▷ *n* matter suitable for reading *eg a good read* **readable** *adj* enjoyable to read; legible **reading** *n*
reader *n* person who reads; textbook; *Chiefly Brit* senior university lecturer **readership** *n* readers of a publication collectively
readjust *v* adapt to a new situation **readjustment** *n*
ready *adj* **readier, readiest** prepared for use or action; willing, prompt **readily** *adv* **readiness** *n* **ready-made** *adj* for immediate use by any customer
reagent [ree-**age**-ent] *n* chemical substance that reacts with another, used to detect the presence of the other
real *adj* existing in fact; actual; genuine **really** *adv* very; truly ▷ *interj* exclamation of dismay, doubt, or surprise **reality** *n* state of things as they are **reality TV** television programmes focusing on members of the public living in conditions created especially by the programme makers **real ale** *Chiefly Brit* beer allowed to ferment in the barrel **real estate** property consisting of land and houses
realistic *adj* seeing and accepting things as they really are, practical **realistically** *adv* **realism** *n* **realist** *n*
realize *v* become aware or grasp the significance of; achieve (a plan, hopes, etc); convert into money **realization** *n*
realm *n* kingdom; sphere of

interest

ream *n* twenty quires of paper, generally 500 sheets ▷ *pl Informal* large quantity (of written matter)

reap *v* cut and gather (a harvest); receive as the result of a previous activity **reaper** *n*

reappear *v* appear again **reappearance** *n*

rear[1] *n* back part; part of an army, procession, etc behind the others **bring up the rear** come last **rearmost** *adj* **rear admiral** high-ranking naval officer **rearguard** *n* troops protecting the rear of an army

rear[2] *v* care for and educate (children); breed (animals); (of a horse) rise on its hind feet

rearrange *v* organize differently, alter **rearrangement** *n*

reason *n* cause or motive; faculty of rational thought; sanity ▷ *v* think logically in forming conclusions **reason with** persuade by logical argument into doing something **reasonable** *adj* sensible; not excessive; logical **reasonably** *adv*

reassess *v* reconsider the value or importance of

reassure *v* restore confidence to **reassurance** *n*

rebate *n* discount or refund

rebel *v* **-belling, -belled** revolt against the ruling power; reject accepted conventions ▷ *n* person who rebels **rebellion** *n* organized open resistance to authority; rejection of conventions **rebellious** *adj*

rebore, reboring *n* boring of a cylinder to restore its true shape

rebound *v* spring back; misfire so as to hurt the perpetrator of a plan or deed **on the rebound** *Informal* while recovering from rejection

rebuff *v* reject or snub ▷ *n* blunt refusal, snub

rebuke *v* scold sternly ▷ *n* stern scolding

rebus *n, pl* **-buses** puzzle consisting of pictures and symbols representing words or syllables

rebut *v* **-butting, -butted** prove that (a claim) is untrue **rebuttal** *n*

recalcitrant *adj* wilfully disobedient **recalcitrance** *n*

recall *v* recollect or remember; order to return; annul or cancel ▷ *n* ability to remember; order to return

recant *v* withdraw (a statement or belief) publicly **recantation** *n*

recap *Informal* ▷ *v* **-capping, -capped** recapitulate ▷ *n* recapitulation

recapitulate *v* state again briefly, repeat **recapitulation** *n*

recapture *v* experience again; capture again

recce *Chiefly Brit, slang* ▷ *v* **-ceing, -ced** *or* **-ceed** reconnoitre ▷ *n* reconnaissance

recede *v* move to a more distant place; (of the hair) stop growing at the front

receipt *n* written acknowledgment of money or goods received; receiving or being received

receive *v* take, accept, or get; experience; greet (guests) **received** *adj* generally accepted **receiver** *n* part of telephone that is held to the ear; equipment in a telephone, radio, or television that converts electrical signals into sound; person appointed by a court to manage the property of a bankrupt **receivership** *n* state of being administered by a receiver

recent *adj* having happened lately;

new **recently** *adv*
receptacle *n* object used to contain something
reception *n* area for receiving guests, clients, etc; formal party; manner of receiving; welcome; (in broadcasting) quality of signals received **receptionist** *n* person who receives guests, clients, etc
receptive *adj* willing to accept new ideas, suggestions, etc **receptivity** *n*
recess *n* niche or alcove; holiday between sessions of work; secret hidden place **recessed** *adj* hidden or placed in a recess
recession *n* period of economic difficulty when little is being bought or sold **recessive** *adj* receding
recherché [rish-**air**-shay] *adj* refined or elegant; known only to experts
recidivism *n* habitual relapse into crime **recidivist** *n*
recipe *n* directions for cooking a dish; method for achieving something
recipient *n* person who receives something
reciprocal [ris-**sip**-pro-kl] *adj* mutual; given or done in return **reciprocally** *adv* **reciprocate** *v* give or feel in return; (of a machine part) move backwards and forwards **reciprocation** *n* **reciprocity** *n*
recite *v* repeat (a poem etc) aloud to an audience **recital** *n* musical performance by a soloist or soloists; act of reciting **recitation** *n* recital, usu from memory, of poetry or prose **recitative** [ress-it-a-**teev**] *n* speechlike style of singing, used esp for narrative passages in opera
reckless *adj* heedless of danger **recklessly** *adv* **recklessness** *n*
reckon *v* consider or think; make calculations, count; expect **reckoning** *n*
reclaim *v* regain possession of; make fit for cultivation **reclamation** *n*
recline *v* rest in a leaning position **reclining** *adj*
recluse *n* person who avoids other people **reclusive** *adj*
recognize *v* identify as (a person or thing) already known; accept as true or existing; treat as valid; notice, show appreciation of **recognition** *n* **recognizable** *adj* **recognizance** [rik-**og**-nizz-anss] *n* undertaking before a court to observe some condition
recoil *v* jerk or spring back; draw back in horror; (of an action) go wrong so as to hurt the doer ▷ *n* backward jerk; recoiling
recollect *v* call back to mind, remember **recollection** *n*
recommend *v* advise or counsel; praise or commend; make acceptable **recommendation** *n*

> SPELLING If you wonder how many *c*s and *m*s to put in **recommend**, you are not alone. Most people who make the wrong decision go for single letters throughout (*recomend* and *recomendation*); they should, of course, double the *m*, as in **recommendation**

recompense *v* pay or reward; compensate or make up for ▷ *n* compensation; reward or remuneration
reconcile *v* harmonize (conflicting beliefs etc); bring back into friendship; accept or cause to accept (an unpleasant situation) **reconciliation** *n*
recondite *adj* difficult to

understand

recondition *v* restore to good condition or working order

reconnaissance [rik-**kon**-iss-anss] *n* survey for military or engineering purposes

SPELLING Collins Word Web shows that the most common way to misspell **reconnaissance** is to miss out an *s*, although there are examples where an *n* has been missed out instead. Remember, there are two *ns* in the middle and two *ss*

reconnoitre [rek-a-**noy**-ter] *v* make a reconnaissance of

reconsider *v* think about again, consider changing

reconstitute *v* reorganize; restore (dried food) to its former state by adding water **reconstitution** *n*

reconstruct *v* rebuild; use evidence to re-create **reconstruction** *n*

record *n* [**rek**-ord] document or other thing that preserves information; disc with indentations which a record player transforms into sound; best recorded achievement; known facts about a person's past ▷ *v* [rik-**kord**] put in writing; preserve (sound, TV programmes, etc) on plastic disc, magnetic tape, etc, for reproduction on a playback device; show or register **off the record** not for publication **recorder** *n* person or machine that records, esp a video, cassette, or tape recorder; type of flute, held vertically; judge in certain courts **recording** *n* **record player** instrument for reproducing sound on records

recount *v* tell in detail

re-count *v* count again ▷ *n* second or further count, esp of votes

recoup [rik-**koop**] *v* regain or make good (a loss); recompense or compensate

recourse *n* source of help **have recourse to** turn to a source of help or course of action

recover *v* become healthy again; regain a former condition; find again; get back (a loss or expense) **recovery** *n* **recoverable** *adj*

re-create *v* make happen or exist again

recreation *n* agreeable or refreshing occupation, relaxation, or amusement **recreational** *adj*

recrimination *n* mutual blame **recriminatory** *adj*

recruit *v* enlist (new soldiers, members, etc) ▷ *n* newly enlisted soldier; new member or supporter **recruitment** *n*

rectangle *n* oblong four-sided figure with four right angles **rectangular** *adj*

rectify *v* **-fying, -fied** put right, correct; *chem* purify by distillation; *electricity* convert (alternating current) into direct current **rectification** *n* **rectifier** *n*

rectilinear *adj* in a straight line; characterized by straight lines

rectitude *n* moral correctness

recto *n, pl* **-tos** right-hand page of a book

rector *n* clergyman in charge of a parish; head of certain academic institutions **rectory** *n* rector's house

rectum *n, pl* **-tums, -ta** final section of the large intestine

recumbent *adj* lying down

recuperate *v* recover from illness **recuperation** *n* **recuperative** *adj*

recur *v* **-curring, -curred** happen

again **recurrence** *n* repetition **recurrent** *adj*

recycle *v* reprocess (used materials) for further use **recyclable** *adj*

red *adj* **redder, reddest** of a colour varying from crimson to orange and seen in blood, fire, etc; flushed in the face from anger, shame, etc ▷ *n* red colour; (**R-**) *Informal* communist **in the red** *Informal* in debt **see red** *Informal* be angry **redness** *n* **redden** *v* make or become red **reddish** *adj* **redback spider** small venomous Australian spider with a red stripe on the back of the abdomen **red-blooded** *adj* *Informal* vigorous or virile **redbrick** *adj* (of a university in Britain) founded in the late 19th or early 20th century **red card** *soccer* piece of red pasteboard shown by a referee to indicate that a player has been sent off **red carpet** very special welcome for an important guest **redcoat** *n hist* British soldier **Red Cross** international organization providing help for victims of war or natural disasters **redcurrant** *n* small round edible red berry **red-handed** *adj* *Informal* (caught) in the act of doing something wrong or illegal **red herring** something which diverts attention from the main issue **red-hot** *adj* glowing red; extremely hot; very keen **Red Indian** *offens* Native American **red light** traffic signal to stop; danger signal **red meat** dark meat, esp beef or lamb **red tape** excessive adherence to official rules

redeem *v* make up for; reinstate (oneself) in someone's good opinion; free from sin; buy back; pay off (a loan or debt) **the Redeemer** Jesus Christ **redeemable** *adj* **redemption** *n* **redemptive** *adj*

redeploy *v* assign to a new position or task **redeployment** *n*

redevelop *v* rebuild or renovate (an area or building) **redevelopment** *n*

redolent *adj* reminiscent (of); smelling strongly (of)

redouble *v* increase, multiply, or intensify

redoubt *n* small fort defending a hilltop or pass

redoubtable *adj* formidable

redound *v* cause advantage or disadvantage (to)

redox *n* chemical reaction in which one substance is reduced and the other is oxidized

redress *v* make amends for ▷ *n* compensation or amends

reduce *v* bring down, lower; lessen, weaken; bring by force or necessity to some state or action; slim; simplify; make (a sauce) more concentrated **reducible** *adj* **reduction** *n*

redundant *adj* (of a worker) no longer needed; superfluous **redundancy** *n*

reed *n* tall grass that grows in swamps and shallow water; tall straight stem of this plant; *music* vibrating cane or metal strip in certain wind instruments **reedy** *adj* harsh and thin in tone

reef[1] *n* ridge of rock or coral near the surface of the sea; vein of ore

reef[2] *n* part of a sail which can be rolled up to reduce its area ▷ *v* take in a reef of **reefer** *n* short thick jacket worn esp by sailors; *old-fashioned slang* hand-rolled cigarette containing cannabis **reef knot** two simple knots turned opposite ways

reek *v* smell strongly ▷*n* strong unpleasant smell **reek of** give a strong suggestion of

reel[1] *n* cylindrical object on which film, tape, thread, or wire is wound; winding apparatus, as of a fishing rod **reel in** *v* draw in by means of a reel **reel off** *v* recite or write fluently or quickly

reel[2] *v* stagger, sway, or whirl

reel[3] *n* lively Scottish dance

ref *n Informal* referee in sport

refectory *n, pl* **-tories** room for meals in a college etc

refer *v* **-ferring, -ferred** (foll by *to*) allude (to); be relevant (to); send (to) for information; submit (to) for decision **referral** *n* **reference** *n* act of referring; citation or direction in a book; written testimonial regarding character or capabilities **with reference to** concerning.

> Do not confuse a *reference* with a *testimonial* which is an open letter of recommendation about someone

referee *n* umpire in sports, esp soccer or boxing; person willing to testify to someone's character etc; arbitrator ▷*v* **-eeing, -eed** act as referee of

referendum *n, pl* **-dums, -da** direct vote of the electorate on an important question

refill *v* fill again ▷*n* second or subsequent filling; replacement supply of something in a permanent container

refine *v* purify; improve **refined** *adj* cultured or polite; purified **refinement** *n* improvement or elaboration; fineness of taste or manners; subtlety **refinery** *n* place where sugar, oil, etc is refined

reflation *n* increase in the supply of money and credit designed to encourage economic activity **reflate** *v* **reflationary** *adj*

reflect *v* throw back, esp rays of light, heat, etc; form an image of; show; consider at length; bring credit or discredit upon **reflection** *n* act of reflecting; return of rays of heat, light, etc from a surface; image of an object given back by a mirror etc; conscious thought or meditation; attribution of discredit or blame **reflective** *adj* quiet, contemplative; capable of reflecting images **reflector** *n* polished surface for reflecting light etc

reflex *n* involuntary response to a stimulus or situation ▷*adj* (of a muscular action) involuntary; reflected; (of an angle) more than 180° **reflexive** *adj grammar* denoting a verb whose subject is the same as its object *eg dress oneself*

reflexology *n* foot massage as a therapy in alternative medicine

reform *n* improvement ▷*v* improve; abandon evil practices **reformer** *n* **reformation** *n* act or instance of something being reformed; (**R-**) religious movement in 16th-century Europe that resulted in the establishment of the Protestant Churches **reformatory** *n* (formerly) institution for reforming young offenders

refract *v* change the course of (light etc) passing from one medium to another **refraction** *n* **refractive** *adj* **refractor** *n*

refractory *adj* unmanageable or rebellious; *med* resistant to treatment; resistant to heat

refrain[1] *v* **refrain from** keep oneself from doing

refrain[2] *n* frequently repeated part

of a song

refresh *v* revive or reinvigorate, as through food, drink, or rest; stimulate (the memory) **refresher** *n* **refreshing** *adj* having a reviving effect; pleasantly different or new **refreshment** *n* something that refreshes, esp food or drink

refrigerate *v* cool or freeze in order to preserve **refrigeration** *n* **refrigerator** *n* full name for **fridge**

refuge *n* (source of) shelter or protection **refugee** *n* person who seeks refuge, esp in a foreign country

refulgent *adj* shining, radiant

refund *v* pay back ▷ *n* return of money; amount returned

refurbish *v* renovate and brighten up

refuse[1] *v* decline, deny, or reject **refusal** *n* denial of anything demanded or offered

refuse[2] *n* rubbish or useless matter

refute *v* disprove **refutation** *n*

regain *v* get back or recover; reach again

regal *adj* of or like a king or queen **regally** *adv* **regalia** *pl n* ceremonial emblems of royalty or high office

regale *v* entertain (someone) with stories etc

regard *v* consider; look at; heed ▷ *n* respect or esteem; attention; look ▷ *pl* expression of goodwill **as regards, regarding** in respect of, concerning **regardless** *adj* heedless ▷ *adv* in spite of everything

regatta *n* meeting for yacht or boat races

regenerate *v* (cause to) undergo spiritual, moral, or physical renewal; reproduce or re-create **regeneration** *n* **regenerative** *adj*

regent *n* ruler of a kingdom during the absence, childhood, or illness of its monarch ▷ *adj* ruling as a regent *eg prince regent* **regency** *n* status or period of office of a regent

reggae *n* style of Jamaican popular music with a strong beat

regicide *n* killing of a king; person who kills a king

regime [ray-**zheem**] *n* system of government; particular administration

regimen *n* prescribed system of diet etc

regiment *n* organized body of troops as a unit of the army **regimental** *adj* **regimentation** *n* **regimented** *adj* very strictly controlled

region *n* administrative division of a country; area considered as a unit but with no definite boundaries; part of the body **regional** *adj*

register *n* (book containing) an official list or record of things; range of a voice or instrument ▷ *v* enter in a register or set down in writing; show or be shown on a meter or the face **registration** *n* **registration number** numbers and letters displayed on a vehicle to identify it **registrar** *n* keeper of official records; senior hospital doctor, junior to a consultant **register office, registry office** place where births, marriages, and deaths are recorded

Regius professor [**reej**-yuss] *n* (in Britain) professor appointed by the Crown to a university chair founded by a royal patron

regress *v* revert to a former worse condition **regression** *n* act of regressing; *psychol* use of an earlier (inappropriate) mode of behaviour **regressive** *adj*

regret *v* **-gretting, -gretted** feel sorry about; express apology or distress ▷ *n* feeling of repentance, guilt, or sorrow **regretful** *adj* **regrettable** *adj*

regular *adj* normal, customary, or usual; symmetrical or even; done or occurring according to a rule; periodical; employed continuously in the armed forces ▷ *n* regular soldier; *Informal* frequent customer **regularity** *n* **regularize** *v* **regularly** *adv*

regulate *v* control, esp by rules; adjust slightly **regulation** *n* rule; regulating **regulator** *n* device that automatically controls pressure, temperature, etc

regurgitate *v* vomit; (of some birds and animals) bring back (partly digested food) into the mouth; reproduce (ideas, facts, etc) without understanding them **regurgitation** *n*

rehabilitate *v* help (a person) to readjust to society after illness, imprisonment, etc; restore to a former position or rank; restore the good reputation of **rehabilitation** *n*

rehash *v* rework or reuse ▷ *n* old ideas presented in a new form

rehearse *v* practise (a play, concert, etc); repeat aloud **rehearsal** *n*

rehouse *v* provide with a new (and better) home

reign *n* period of a sovereign's rule ▷ *v* rule (a country); be supreme

reimburse *v* refund, pay back **reimbursement** *n*

rein *v* check or manage with reins; control or limit **reins** *pl n* narrow straps attached to a bit to guide a horse; means of control

reincarnation *n* rebirth of a soul in successive bodies; one of a series of such transmigrations **reincarnate** *v*

reindeer *n, pl* **-deer, -deers** deer of arctic regions with large branched antlers

reinforce *v* strengthen with new support, material, or force; strengthen with additional troops, ships, etc **reinforcement** *n* **reinforced concrete** concrete strengthened by having steel mesh or bars embedded in it

reinstate *v* restore to a former position **reinstatement** *n*

reiterate *v* repeat again and again **reiteration** *n*

reject *v* refuse to accept or believe; rebuff (a person); discard as useless ▷ *n* person or thing rejected as not up to standard **rejection** *n*

rejig *v* **-jigging, -jigged** re-equip (a factory or plant); rearrange

rejoice *v* feel or express great happiness

rejoin[1] *v* join again

rejoin[2] *v* reply **rejoinder** *n* answer, retort

rejuvenate *v* restore youth or vitality to **rejuvenation** *n*

relapse *v* fall back into bad habits, illness, etc ▷ *n* return of bad habits, illness, etc

relate *v* establish a relation between; have reference or relation to; have an understanding (of people or ideas); tell (a story) or describe (an event) **related** *adj*

relation *n* connection between things; relative; connection by blood or marriage; act of relating (a story) ▷ *pl* social or political dealings; family **relationship** *n* dealings and feelings between

people or countries; emotional or sexual affair; connection between two things; association by blood or marriage, kinship
relative *adj* dependent on relation to something else, not absolute; having reference or relation (to); *grammar* referring to a word or clause earlier in the sentence ▷ *n* person connected by blood or marriage **relatively** *adv* **relativity** *n* subject of two theories of Albert Einstein, dealing with relationships of space, time, and motion, and acceleration and gravity; state of being relative
relax *v* make or become looser, less tense, or less rigid; ease up from effort or attention, rest; be less strict about; become more friendly **relaxing** *adj* **relaxation** *n*
relay *n* fresh set of people or animals relieving others; *electricity* device for making or breaking a local circuit; broadcasting station receiving and retransmitting programmes ▷ *v* **-laying, -layed** pass on (a message) **relay race** race between teams in which each runner races part of the distance
release *v* set free; let go or fall; issue (a record, film, etc) for sale or public showing; emit heat, energy, etc ▷ *n* setting free; statement to the press; act of issuing for sale or publication; newly issued film, record, etc
relegate *v* put in a less important position; demote (a sports team) to a lower league **relegation** *n*
relent *v* give up a harsh intention, become less severe **relentless** *adj* unremitting; merciless
relevant *adj* to do with the matter in hand **relevance** *n*

SPELLING A common word in English, **relevant** is not always spelt correctly. The final syllable is the problem and sometimes appears incorrectly in Collins Word Web as *-ent*

reliable *adj* able to be trusted, dependable **reliably** *adv* **reliability** *n*
reliance *n* dependence, confidence, or trust **reliant** *adj*
relic *n* something that has survived from the past; body or possession of a saint, regarded as holy ▷ *pl* remains or traces **relict** *n obs* widow
relief *n* gladness at the end or removal of pain, distress, etc; release from monotony or duty; money or food given to victims of disaster, poverty, etc; freeing of a besieged city etc; person who replaces another; projection of a carved design from the surface; any vivid effect resulting from contrast *eg comic relief* **relieve** *v* bring relief to **relieve oneself** urinate or defecate **relief map** map showing the shape and height of land by shading
religion *n* system of belief in and worship of a supernatural power or god **religious** *adj* of religion; pious or devout; scrupulous or conscientious **religiously** *adv*
relinquish *v* give up or abandon
reliquary *n, pl* **-quaries** case or shrine for holy relics
relish *v* enjoy, like very much ▷ *n* liking or enjoyment; appetizing savoury food, such as pickle; zestful quality or flavour
relocate *v* move to a new place to live or work **relocation** *n*
reluctant *adj* unwilling or disinclined **reluctantly** *adv*

reluctance *n*
rely *v* **-lying, -lied** depend (on); trust
remain *v* continue; stay, be left behind; be left (over); be left to be done, said, etc **remains** *pl n* relics, esp of ancient buildings; dead body **remainder** *n* part which is left; amount left over after subtraction or division ▷ *v* offer (copies of a poorly selling book) at reduced prices
remand *v* send back into custody or put on bail before trial **on remand** in custody or on bail before trial **remand centre** (in Britain) place where accused people are detained awaiting trial
remark *v* make a casual comment (on); say; observe or notice ▷ *n* observation or comment **remarkable** *adj* worthy of note or attention; striking or unusual **remarkably** *adv*
remedy *n, pl* **-edies** means of curing pain or disease; means of solving a problem ▷ *v* **-edying, -edied** put right **remedial** *adj* intended to correct a specific disability, handicap, etc
remember *v* retain in or recall to one's memory; keep in mind **remembrance** *n* memory; token or souvenir; honouring of the memory of a person or event
remind *v* cause to remember; put in mind (of) **reminder** *n* something that recalls the past; note to remind a person of something not done
reminisce *v* talk or write of past times, experiences, etc **reminiscence** *n* remembering; thing recollected ▷ *pl* memoirs **reminiscent** *adj* reminding or suggestive (of)
remiss *adj* negligent or careless
remission *n* reduction in the length of a prison term; easing of intensity, as of an illness
remit *v* [rim-**mitt**] **-mitting, -mitted** send (money) for goods, services, etc, esp by post; cancel (a punishment or debt); refer (a decision) to a higher authority or later date ▷ *n* [**ree**-mitt] area of competence or authority **remittance** *n* money sent as payment
remnant *n* small piece, esp of fabric, left over; surviving trace
remonstrate *v* argue in protest **remonstrance** *n*
remorse *n* feeling of sorrow and regret for something one did **remorseful** *adj* **remorseless** *adj* pitiless; persistent **remorselessly** *adv*
remote *adj* far away, distant; aloof; slight or faint **remotely** *adv* **remote control** control of an apparatus from a distance by an electrical device
remould *v Brit* renovate (a worn tyre) ▷ *n Brit* renovated tyre
remove *v* take away or off; get rid of; dismiss from office ▷ *n* degree of difference **removable** *adj* **removal** *n* removing, esp changing residence
remunerate *v* reward or pay **remunerative** *adj*
remuneration *n* reward or payment
renaissance *n* revival or rebirth; (**R-**) revival of learning in the 14th–16th centuries
renal [**ree**-nal] *adj* of the kidneys
renascent *adj* becoming active or vigorous again
rend *v* **rending, rent** tear or wrench apart; (of a sound) break

(the silence) violently
render *v* cause to become; give or provide (aid, a service, etc); submit or present (a bill); portray or represent; cover with plaster; melt down (fat)
rendezvous [ron-day-voo] *n, pl* **-vous** appointment; meeting place ▷*v* meet as arranged
rendition *n* performance; translation
renegade *n* person who deserts a cause
renege [rin-**nayg**] *v* go back (on a promise etc)
renew *v* begin again; make valid again; grow again; restore to a former state; replace (a worn part); restate or reaffirm **renewable** *adj* **renewal** *n*
rennet *n* substance for curdling milk to make cheese
renounce *v* give up (a belief, habit, etc) voluntarily; give up (a title or claim) formally **renunciation** *n*
renovate *v* restore to good condition **renovation** *n*
renown *n* widespread good reputation
renowned *adj* famous
rent[1] *v* give or have use of in return for regular payments ▷*n* regular payment for use of land, a building, machine, etc **rental** *n* sum payable as rent
rent[2] *n* tear or fissure ▷*v* past of **rend**
renunciation *n* see **renounce**
reorganize *v* organize in a new and more efficient way **reorganization** *n*
rep[1] *n* short for **repertory company**
rep[2] *n* short for **representative**
repair[1] *v* restore to good condition, mend ▷*n* act of repairing; repaired part; state or condition *eg in good repair* **reparation** *n* something done or given as compensation
repair[2] *v* go (to)
repartee *n* interchange of witty retorts; witty retort
repast *n* meal
repatriate *v* send (someone) back to his or her own country **repatriation** *n*
repay *v* **repaying, repaid** pay back, refund; do something in return for *eg repay hospitality* **repayable** *adj* **repayment** *n*
repeal *v* cancel (a law) officially ▷*n* act of repealing
repeat *v* say or do again; happen again, recur ▷*n* act or instance of repeating; programme broadcast again **repeatedly** *adv* **repeater** *n* firearm that may be discharged many times without reloading
repel *v* **-pelling, -pelled** be disgusting to; drive back, ward off; resist **repellent** *adj* distasteful; resisting water etc ▷*n* something that repels, esp a chemical to repel insects
repent *v* feel regret for (a deed or omission) **repentance** *n* **repentant** *adj*
repercussions *pl n* indirect effects, often unpleasant
repertoire *n* stock of plays, songs, etc that a player or company can give
repertory *n, pl* **-ries** repertoire **repertory company** permanent theatre company producing a succession of plays
repetition *n* act of repeating; thing repeated **repetitive, repetitious** *adj* full of repetition
rephrase *v* express in different words
repine *v* fret or complain

replace *v* substitute for; put back **replacement** *n*

replay *n* (also **action replay**) immediate reshowing on TV of an incident in sport, esp in slow motion; second sports match, esp one following an earlier draw ▷ *v* play (a match, recording, etc) again

replenish *v* fill up again, resupply **replenishment** *n*

replete *adj* filled or gorged

replica *n* exact copy **replicate** *v* make or be a copy of

reply *v* **-plying, -plied** answer or respond ▷ *n, pl* **-plies** answer or response

report *v* give an account of; make a report (on); make a formal complaint about; present oneself (to); be responsible (to) ▷ *n* account or statement; rumour; written statement of a child's progress at school; bang **reportedly** *adv* according to rumour **reporter** *n* person who gathers news for a newspaper, TV, etc

repose *n* peace; composure; sleep ▷ *v* lie or lay at rest

repository *n, pl* **-ries** place where valuables are deposited for safekeeping, store

repossess *v* (of a lender) take back property from a customer who is behind with payments **repossession** *n*

reprehensible *adj* open to criticism, unworthy

represent *v* act as a delegate or substitute for; stand for; symbolize; make out to be; portray, as in art **representation** *n* **representative** *n* person chosen to stand for a group; (travelling) salesperson ▷ *adj* typical

repress *v* keep (feelings) in check; restrict the freedom of **repression** *n* **repressive** *adj*

reprieve *v* postpone the execution of (a condemned person); give temporary relief to ▷ *n* (document granting) postponement or cancellation of a punishment; temporary relief

reprimand *v* blame (someone) officially for a fault ▷ *n* official blame

reprint *v* print further copies of (a book) ▷ *n* reprinted copy

reprisal *n* retaliation

reproach *n, v* blame, rebuke **reproachful** *adj* **reproachfully** *adv*

reprobate *adj, n* depraved or disreputable (person)

reproduce *v* produce a copy of; bring new individuals into existence; re-create **reproducible** *adj* **reproduction** *n* process of reproducing; facsimile, as of a painting etc; quality of sound from an audio system **reproductive** *adj*

reprove *v* speak severely to (someone) about a fault **reproof** *n* severe blaming of someone for a fault

reptile *n* cold-blooded egg-laying vertebrate with horny scales or plates, such as a snake or tortoise **reptilian** *adj*

republic *n* form of government in which the people or their elected representatives possess the supreme power; country in which a president is the head of state **Republican** *n, adj* (member or supporter) of the Republican Party, the more conservative of the two main political parties in the US **Republicanism** *n*

repudiate [rip-**pew**-dee-ate] *v* reject the authority or validity of; disown **repudiation** *n*

repugnant *adj* offensive or distasteful **repugnance** *n*
repulse *v* be disgusting to; drive (an army) back; rebuff or reject ▷ *n* driving back; rejection or rebuff **repulsion** *n* distaste or aversion; *physics* force separating two objects **repulsive** *adj* loathsome, disgusting
reputation *n* estimation in which a person is held **reputable** *adj* of good reputation, respectable **repute** *n* reputation **reputed** *adj* supposed **reputedly** *adv*
request *v* ask ▷ *n* asking; thing asked for
Requiem [**rek**-wee-em] *n* Mass for the dead; music for this
require *v* want or need; demand **requirement** *n* essential condition; specific need or want.

> *Require* suggests a demand imposed by some regulation. *Need* is usually something that comes from a person

requisite [**rek**-wizz-it] *adj* necessary, essential ▷ *n* essential thing
requisition *v* demand (supplies) ▷ *n* formal demand, such as for materials or supplies
requite *v* return to someone (the same treatment or feeling as received)
reredos [**rear**-doss] *n* ornamental screen behind an altar
rescind *v* annul or repeal
rescue *v* **-cuing, -cued** deliver from danger or trouble, save ▷ *n* rescuing **rescuer** *n*
research *n* systematic investigation to discover facts or collect information ▷ *v* carry out investigations **researcher** *n*
resemble *v* be or look like **resemblance** *n*
resent *v* feel bitter about **resentful** *adj* **resentment** *n*
reservation *n* doubt; exception or limitation; seat, room, etc that has been reserved; area of land reserved for use by a particular group; (also **central reservation**) *Brit* strip of ground separating the two carriageways of a dual carriageway or motorway
reserve *v* set aside, keep for future use; obtain by arranging beforehand, book; retain ▷ *n* something, esp money or troops, kept for emergencies; area of land reserved for a particular purpose; *sport* substitute; concealment of feelings or friendliness **reserved** *adj* not showing one's feelings, lacking friendliness; set aside for use by a particular person **reservist** *n* member of a military reserve
reservoir *n* natural or artificial lake storing water for community supplies; store or supply of something
reshuffle *n* reorganization ▷ *v* reorganize
reside *v* dwell permanently
resident *n* person who lives in a place ▷ *adj* living in a place **residence** *n* home or house **residential** *adj* (of part of a town) consisting mainly of houses; providing living accommodation
residue *n* what is left, remainder **residual** *adj*
resign *v* give up office, a job, etc; reconcile (oneself) to **resigned** *adj* content to endure **resignation** *n* resigning; passive endurance of difficulties
resilient *adj* (of a person) recovering quickly from a shock etc;

able to return to normal shape after stretching etc **resilience** *n*

resin [**rezz**-in] *n* sticky substance from plants, esp pines; similar synthetic substance **resinous** *adj*

resist *v* withstand or oppose; refrain from despite temptation; be proof against **resistance** *n* act of resisting; capacity to withstand something; *electricity* opposition offered by a circuit to the passage of a current through it **resistant** *adj* **resistible** *adj* **resistor** *n* component of an electrical circuit producing resistance

resit *v* take (an exam) again ▷ *n* exam that has to be taken again

resolute *adj* firm in purpose **resolutely** *adv*

resolution *n* firmness of conduct or character; thing resolved upon; decision of a court or vote of an assembly; act of resolving

resolve *v* decide with an effort of will; form (a resolution) by a vote; separate the component parts of; make clear, settle **resolved** *adj* determined

resonance *n* echoing, esp with a deep sound; sound produced in one object by sound waves coming from another object **resonant** *adj* **resonate** *v*

resort *v* have recourse (to) for help etc ▷ *n* place for holidays; recourse

resound [riz-**zownd**] *v* echo or ring with sound **resounding** *adj* echoing; clear and emphatic

resource *n* thing resorted to for support; ingenuity; means of achieving something ▷ *pl* sources of economic wealth; stock that can be drawn on, funds **resourceful** *adj* **resourcefulness** *n*

respect *n* consideration; deference or esteem; point or aspect; reference or relation *eg with respect to* ▷ *v* treat with esteem; show consideration for **respecter** *n* **respectful** *adj* **respecting** *prep* concerning

respectable *adj* worthy of respect; fairly good **respectably** *adv* **respectability** *n*

respective *adj* relating separately to each of those in question **respectively** *adv*

respiration [ress-per-**ray**-shun] *n* breathing **respirator** *n* apparatus worn over the mouth and breathed through as protection against dust, poison gas, etc, or to provide artificial respiration **respiratory** *adj* **respire** *v* breathe

respite *n* pause, interval of rest; delay

resplendent *adj* brilliant or splendid; shining **resplendence** *n*

respond *v* answer; act in answer to any stimulus; react favourably **respondent** *n law* defendant **response** *n* answer; reaction to a stimulus **responsive** *adj* readily reacting to some influence **responsiveness** *n*

responsible *adj* having control and authority; reporting or accountable (to); sensible and dependable; involving responsibility **responsibly** *adv* **responsibility** *n, pl* **-ties** state of being responsible; person or thing for which one is responsible

rest[1] *n* freedom from exertion etc; repose; pause, esp in music; object used for support ▷ *v* take a rest; give a rest (to); be supported; place on a support **restful** *adj* **restless** *adj*

rest[2] *n* what is left; others ▷ *v* remain, continue to be

restaurant *n* commercial

establishment serving meals **restaurateur** [rest-er-a-**tur**] *n* person who owns or runs a restaurant

restitution *n* giving back; reparation or compensation

restive *adj* restless or impatient

restore *v* return (a building, painting, etc) to its original condition; cause to recover health or spirits; give back, return; re-establish **restoration** *n* **restorative** *adj* restoring ▷ *n* food or medicine to strengthen etc **restorer** *n*

restrain *v* hold (someone) back from action; control or restrict **restrained** *adj* not displaying emotion **restraint** *n* control, esp self-control; restraining **restraining order** *Aust, NZ, Canadian & US* temporary court order imposing restrictions on a company or a person

restrict *v* confine to certain limits **restriction** *n* **restrictive** *adj*

restructure *v* organize in a different way

result *n* outcome or consequence; score; number obtained from a calculation; exam mark or grade ▷ *v* (foll by *from*) be the outcome or consequence (of); (foll by *in*) end (in) **resultant** *adj*

resume *v* begin again; occupy or take again **resumption** *n*

résumé [rezz-yew-may] *n* summary

resurgence *n* rising again to vigour **resurgent** *adj*

resurrect *v* restore to life; use once more (something discarded etc), revive **resurrection** *n* rising again (esp from the dead); revival

resuscitate [ris-**suss**-it-tate] *v* restore to consciousness **resuscitation** *n*

> SPELLING There is a silent *c* in **resuscitate**, but only one: it comes after the second *s*, not after the first one

retail *n* selling of goods individually or in small amounts to the public ▷ *adv* by retail ▷ *v* sell or be sold retail; recount in detail

retailer *n* person or company that sells goods to the public

retain *v* keep in one's possession; engage the services of **retainer** *n* fee to retain someone's services; old-established servant of a family

retaliate *v* repay an injury or wrong in kind **retaliation** *n* **retaliatory** *adj*

retard *v* delay or slow (progress or development) **retarded** *adj* underdeveloped, esp mentally **retardation** *n*

retch *v* try to vomit

rethink *v* consider again, esp with a view to changing one's tactics

reticent *adj* uncommunicative, reserved **reticence** *n*

retina *n, pl* **-nas, -nae** light-sensitive membrane at the back of the eye

retinue *n* band of attendants

retire *v* (cause to) give up office or work, esp through age; go away or withdraw; go to bed **retired** *adj* having retired from work etc **retirement** *n* **retiring** *adj* shy

retort[1] *v* reply quickly, wittily, or angrily ▷ *n* quick, witty, or angry reply

retort[2] *n* glass container with a bent neck used for distilling

retouch *v* restore or improve by new touches, esp of paint

retrace *v* go back over (a route etc) again

retract *v* withdraw (a statement

etc); draw in or back **retractable, retractile** *adj* able to be retracted **retraction** *n*

retread *v, n* same as **remould**

retreat *v* move back from a position, withdraw ▷*n* act of or military signal for retiring or withdrawal; place to which anyone retires, refuge

retrench *v* reduce expenditure, cut back **retrenchment** *n*

retrial *n* second trial of a case or defendant in a court of law

retribution *n* punishment or vengeance for evil deeds **retributive** *adj*

retrieve *v* fetch back again; restore to a better state; recover (information) from a computer **retrievable** *adj* **retrieval** *n* **retriever** *n* dog trained to retrieve shot game

retroactive *adj* effective from a date in the past

retrograde *adj* tending towards an earlier worse condition

retrogressive *adj* going back to an earlier worse condition **retrogression** *n*

retrorocket *n* small rocket engine used to slow a spacecraft

retrospect *n* **in retrospect** when looking back on the past **retrospective** *adj* looking back in time; applying from a date in the past ▷*n* exhibition of an artist's life's work

retroussé [rit-**troo**-say] *adj* (of a nose) turned upwards

retsina *n* Greek wine flavoured with resin

return *v* go or come back; give, put, or send back; reply; elect ▷*n* returning; (thing) being returned; profit; official report, as of taxable income; return ticket **returnable** *adj* **returning officer** person in charge of an election **return ticket** ticket allowing a passenger to travel to a place and back

reunion *n* meeting of people who have been apart **reunite** *v* bring or come together again after a separation

reuse *v* use again **reusable** *adj*

rev *Informal* ▷*n* revolution (of an engine) ▷*v* **revving, revved** (foll by *up*) increase the speed of revolution of (an engine)

Rev., Revd. Reverend

revalue *v* adjust the exchange value of (a currency) upwards **revaluation** *n*

revamp *v* renovate or restore

reveal *v* make known; expose or show **revelation** *n*

reveille [riv-**val**-ee] *n* morning bugle call to waken soldiers

revel *v* **-elling, -elled** take pleasure (in); make merry **revels** *pl n* merrymaking **reveller** *n* **revelry** *n* festivity

revenge *n* retaliation for wrong done ▷*v* make retaliation for; avenge (oneself or another) **revengeful** *adj*

revenue *n* income, esp of a state

reverberate *v* echo or resound **reverberation** *n*

revere *v* be in awe of and respect greatly **reverence** *n* awe mingled with respect and esteem **Reverend** *adj* title of respect for a clergyman **reverent** *adj* showing reverence **reverently** *adv* **reverential** *adj* marked by reverence

reverie *n* absent-minded daydream

revers [riv-**veer**] *n* turned back part of a garment, such as the lapel

reverse *v* turn upside down or the

other way round; change completely; move (a vehicle) backwards ▷ *n* opposite; back side; change for the worse; reverse gear ▷ *adj* opposite or contrary **reversal** *n* **reversible** *adj* **reverse gear** mechanism enabling a vehicle to move backwards

revert *v* return to a former state; come back to a subject; (of property) return to its former owner **reversion** *n*

review *n* critical assessment of a book, concert, etc; publication with critical articles; general survey; formal inspection ▷ *v* hold or write a review of; examine, reconsider, or look back on; inspect formally **reviewer** *n* writer of reviews

revile *v* be abusively scornful of

revise *v* change or alter; restudy (work) in preparation for an examination **revision** *n*

revive *v* bring or come back to life, vigour, use, etc **revival** *n* reviving or renewal; movement seeking to restore religious faith **revivalism** *n* **revivalist** *n*

revoke *v* cancel (a will, agreement, etc) **revocation** *n*

revolt *n* uprising against authority ▷ *v* rise in rebellion; cause to feel disgust **revolting** *adj* disgusting, horrible

revolution *n* overthrow of a government by the governed; great change; spinning round; complete rotation **revolutionary** *adj* advocating or engaged in revolution; radically new or different ▷ *n, pl* **-aries** person advocating or engaged in revolution **revolutionize** *v* change considerably

revolve *v* turn round, rotate **revolve around** be centred on

revolver *n* repeating pistol

revue *n* theatrical entertainment with topical sketches and songs

revulsion *n* strong disgust

reward *n* something given in return for a service; sum of money offered for finding a criminal or missing property ▷ *v* pay or give something to (someone) for a service, information, etc **rewarding** *adj* giving personal satisfaction, worthwhile

rewind *v* run (a tape or film) back to an earlier point in order to replay

rewire *v* provide (a house, engine, etc) with new wiring

rewrite *v* write again in a different way ▷ *n* something rewritten

rhapsody *n, pl* **-dies** freely structured emotional piece of music; expression of ecstatic enthusiasm **rhapsodic** *adj* **rhapsodize** *v* speak or write with extravagant enthusiasm

rhea [**ree**-a] *n* S American three-toed ostrich

rhenium *n chem* silvery-white metallic element with a high melting point

rheostat *n* instrument for varying the resistance of an electrical circuit

rhesus [**ree**-suss] *n* small long-tailed monkey of S Asia **rhesus factor, Rh factor** antigen commonly found in human blood

rhetoric *n* art of effective speaking or writing; artificial or exaggerated language **rhetorical** *adj* (of a question) not requiring an answer **rhetorically** *adv*

rheumatism *n* painful inflammation of joints or muscles **rheumatic** *n, adj* (person) affected by rheumatism **rheumatoid** *adj* of or like rheumatism

Rh factor *n* see **rhesus**
rhinestone *n* imitation diamond
rhino *n* short for **rhinoceros**
rhinoceros *n, pl* **-oses, -os** large thick-skinned animal with one or two horns on its nose

> SPELLING The pronunciation of **rhinoceros** probably misleads some people into making the mistake of adding a *u* before the final *s* (*rhinocerous*)

rhizome *n* thick underground stem producing new plants
rhodium *n chem* hard metallic element
rhododendron *n* evergreen flowering shrub
rhombus *n, pl* **-buses, -bi** parallelogram with sides of equal length but no right angles, diamond-shaped figure **rhomboid** *n* parallelogram with adjacent sides of unequal length
rhubarb *n* garden plant of which the fleshy stalks are cooked as fruit
rhyme *n* sameness of the final sounds at the ends of lines of verse, or in words; word identical in sound to another in its final sounds; verse marked by rhyme ▷ *v* make a rhyme
rhythm *n* any regular movement or beat; arrangement of the durations of and stress on the notes of a piece of music, usu grouped into a regular pattern; (in poetry) arrangement of words to form a regular pattern of stresses **rhythmic, rhythmical** *adj* **rhythmically** *adv* **rhythm and blues** popular music, orig Black American, influenced by the blues

> SPELLING The second letter of **rhythm** is a silent *h*, which people often forget in writing

rib¹ *n* one of the curved bones forming the framework of the upper part of the body; cut of meat including the rib(s); curved supporting part, as in the hull of a boat; raised series of rows in knitting ▷ *v* **ribbing, ribbed** provide or mark with ribs; knit to form a rib pattern **ribbed** *adj* **ribbing** *n* **ribcage** *n* bony structure of ribs enclosing the lungs
rib² *v* **ribbing, ribbed** *Informal* tease or ridicule **ribbing** *n*
ribald *adj* humorously or mockingly rude or obscene **ribaldry** *n*
ribbon *n* narrow band of fabric used for trimming, tying, etc; any long strip, for example of inked tape in a typewriter
riboflavin [rye-boe-**flay**-vin] *n* form of vitamin B
rice *n* cereal plant grown on wet ground in warm countries; its seeds as food
rich *adj* owning a lot of money or property, wealthy; abounding; fertile; (of food) containing much fat or sugar; mellow; amusing **riches** *pl n* wealth **richly** *adv* elaborately; fully **richness** *n*
rick¹ *n* stack of hay etc
rick² *v, n* sprain or wrench
rickets *n* disease of children marked by softening of the bones, bow legs, etc, caused by vitamin D deficiency
rickety *adj* shaky or unstable
rickshaw *n* light two-wheeled man-drawn Asian vehicle
ricochet [**rik**-osh-ay] *v* (of a bullet) rebound from a solid surface ▷ *n* such a rebound
rid *v* **ridding, rid** clear or relieve (of) **get rid of** free oneself of (something undesirable) **good riddance** relief at getting rid of

something or someone

ridden *v* past participle of **ride** ▷ *adj* afflicted or affected by the thing specified *eg disease-ridden*

riddle¹ *n* question made puzzling to test one's ingenuity; puzzling person or thing

riddle² *v* pierce with many holes ▷ *n* coarse sieve for gravel etc **riddled with** full of

ride *v* **riding, rode, ridden** sit on and control or propel (a horse, bicycle, etc); go on horseback or in a vehicle; travel over; be carried on or across; lie at anchor ▷ *n* journey on a horse etc, or in a vehicle; type of movement experienced in a vehicle **ride up** *v* (of a garment) move up from the proper position

rider *n* person who rides; supplementary clause added to a document

ridge *n* long narrow hill; long narrow raised part on a surface; line where two sloping surfaces meet; *meteorol* elongated area of high pressure **ridged** *adj*

ridiculous *adj* deserving to be laughed at, absurd **ridicule** *n* treatment of a person or thing as ridiculous ▷ *v* laugh at, make fun of

Riding *n* former administrative district of Yorkshire

riesling *n* type of white wine

rife *adj* widespread or common **rife with** full of

riff *n jazz, rock* short repeated melodic figure

riffle *v* flick through (pages etc) quickly

riffraff *n* rabble, disreputable people

rifle¹ *n* firearm with a long barrel

rifle² *v* search and rob; steal

rift *n* break in friendly relations; crack, split, or cleft **rift valley** long narrow valley resulting from subsidence between faults

rig *v* **rigging, rigged** arrange in a dishonest way; equip, esp a ship ▷ *n* apparatus for drilling for oil and gas; way a ship's masts and sails are arranged; *Informal* outfit of clothes **rigging** *n* ship's spars and ropes **rig up** *v* set up or build temporarily

right *adj* just; true or correct; proper; in a satisfactory condition; of the side that faces east when the front is turned to the north; of the outer side of a fabric ▷ *adv* properly; straight or directly; on or to the right side ▷ *n* claim, title, etc allowed or due; what is just or due; (**R-**) conservative political party or group ▷ *v* bring or come back to a normal or correct state; bring or come back to a vertical position **in the right** morally or legally correct **right away** immediately **rightly** *adv* **rightful** *adj* **rightfully** *adv* **rightist** *n, adj* (person) on the political right **right angle** angle of 90° **right-handed** *adj* using or for the right hand **right-hand man** person's most valuable assistant **right of way** right of one vehicle to go before another; legal right to pass over someone's land **right-wing** *adj* conservative or reactionary; belonging to the more conservative part of a political party

righteous [**rye**-chuss] *adj* upright, godly, or virtuous; morally justified **righteousness** *n*

rigid *adj* inflexible or strict; unyielding or stiff **rigidly** *adv* **rigidity** *n*

rigmarole *n* long complicated procedure

rigor mortis *n* stiffening of the body after death

rigour *n* harshness, severity, or strictness; hardship **rigorous** *adj* harsh, severe, or stern
rile *v* anger or annoy
rill *n* small stream
rim *n* edge or border; outer ring of a wheel **rimmed** *adj*
rime *n lit* hoarfrost
rimu *n NZ* New Zealand tree whose wood is used for building and furniture
rind *n* tough outer coating of fruits, cheese, or bacon
ring[1] *v* **ringing, rang, rung** give out a clear resonant sound, as a bell; cause (a bell) to sound; telephone; resound ▷ *n* ringing; telephone call **ring off** *v* end a telephone call **ringtone** *n* tune played by a mobile phone when it receives a call **ring up** *v* telephone; record on a cash register.

> The simple past is *rang*: *He rang the bell*. Avoid the use of the past participle *rung* for the simple past

ring[2] *n* circle of gold etc, esp for a finger; any circular band, coil, or rim; circle of people; enclosed area, esp a circle for a circus or a roped-in square for boxing; group operating (illegal) control of a market ▷ *v* put a ring round; mark (a bird) with a ring; kill (a tree) by cutting the bark round the trunk **ringer** *n Brit, Aust & NZ, slang* person or thing apparently identical to another (also **dead ringer**) **ringlet** *n* curly lock of hair **ringleader** *n* instigator of a mutiny, riot, etc **ring road** *Brit, Aust & SAfr* main road that bypasses a town (centre) **ringside** *n* row of seats nearest a boxing or circus ring **ringtail** *n Aust* possum with a curling tail used to grip branches while climbing **ringworm** *n* fungal skin disease in circular patches
rink *n* sheet of ice for skating or curling; floor for roller-skating
rinse *v* remove soap from (washed clothes, hair, etc) by applying clean water; wash lightly ▷ *n* rinsing; liquid to tint hair
riot *n* disorderly unruly disturbance; *Brit, Aust & NZ* loud revelry; profusion; *slang* very amusing person or thing ▷ *v* take part in a riot **read the riot act** reprimand severely **run riot** behave without restraint; grow profusely **riotous** *adj* unrestrained; unruly or rebellious
rip *v* **ripping, ripped** tear violently; tear away; *Informal* rush ▷ *n* split or tear **let rip** act or speak without restraint **ripcord** *n* cord pulled to open a parachute **rip off** *v slang* cheat by overcharging **rip-off** *n slang* cheat or swindle **rip-roaring** *adj Informal* boisterous and exciting
RIP rest in peace
riparian [rip-**pair**-ee-an] *adj* of or on the banks of a river
ripe *adj* ready to be reaped, eaten, etc; matured; ready or suitable **ripen** *v* grow ripe; mature
riposte [rip-**posst**] *n* verbal retort; counterattack, esp in fencing ▷ *v* make a riposte
ripple *n* slight wave or ruffling of a surface; sound like ripples of water ▷ *v* flow or form into little waves (on); (of sounds) rise and fall gently
rise *v* **rising, rose, risen** get up from a lying, sitting, or kneeling position; move upwards; (of the sun or moon) appear above the horizon; reach a higher level; (of an amount or price) increase; rebel; (of a court) adjourn ▷ *n* rising; upward slope;

increase, esp of wages **give rise to** cause **riser** *n* person who rises, esp from bed; vertical part of a step **rising** *n* revolt ▷ *adj* increasing in rank or maturity

risible [**riz**-zib-bl] *adj* causing laughter, ridiculous

risk *n* chance of disaster or loss; person or thing considered as a potential hazard ▷ *v* act in spite of the possibility of (injury or loss); expose to danger or loss **risky** *adj* full of risk, dangerous

risotto *n, pl* **-tos** dish of rice cooked in stock with vegetables, meat, etc

risqué [**risk**-ay] *adj* bordering on indecency

rissole *n* cake of minced meat, coated with breadcrumbs and fried

rite *n* formal practice or custom, esp religious

ritual *n* prescribed order of rites; regular repeated action or behaviour ▷ *adj* concerning rites **ritually** *adv* **ritualistic** *adj* like a ritual

ritzy *adj* **ritzier, ritziest** *slang* luxurious or elegant

rival *n* person or thing that competes with or equals another for favour, success, etc ▷ *adj* in the position of a rival ▷ *v* **-valling, -valled** (try to) equal **rivalry** *n* keen competition

riven *adj* split apart

river *n* large natural stream of water; plentiful flow

rivet [**riv**-vit] *n* bolt for fastening metal plates, the end being put through holes and then beaten flat ▷ *v* **riveting, riveted** fasten with rivets; cause to be fixed, as in fascination **riveting** *adj* very interesting and exciting

rivulet *n* small stream

RN (in Britain) Royal Navy

RNA ribonucleic acid: substance in living cells essential for the synthesis of protein

RNZ Radio New Zealand

RNZAF Royal New Zealand Air Force

RNZN Royal New Zealand Navy

roach *n* Eurasian freshwater fish

road *n* way prepared for passengers, vehicles, etc; route in a town or city with houses along it; way or course *eg the road to fame* **on the road** travelling **roadie** *n Brit, Aust & NZ, Informal* person who transports and sets up equipment for a band **roadblock** *n* barricade across a road to stop traffic for inspection etc **road hog** *Informal* selfish aggressive driver **roadhouse** *n Brit, Aust & SAfr* pub or restaurant on a country road **road map** map for drivers; plan or guide for future actions **roadside** *n, adj* **road test** test of a vehicle etc in actual use **roadway** *n* the part of a road used by vehicles **roadworks** *pl n* repairs to a road, esp blocking part of the road **roadworthy** *adj* (of a vehicle) mechanically sound

roam *v* wander about

roan *adj* (of a horse) having a brown or black coat sprinkled with white hairs ▷ *n* roan horse

roar *v* make or utter a loud deep hoarse sound like that of a lion; shout (something) as in anger; laugh loudly ▷ *n* such a sound **a roaring trade** *Informal* brisk and profitable business **roaring drunk** noisily drunk

roast *v* cook by dry heat, as in an oven; make or be very hot ▷ *n* roasted joint of meat ▷ *adj* roasted **roasting** *Informal* ▷ *adj* extremely hot ▷*n* severe criticism or scolding

rob *v* **robbing, robbed** steal from; deprive **robber** *n* **robbery** *n*

robe *n* long loose outer garment ▷*v* put a robe on

robin *n* small brown bird with a red breast

robot *n* automated machine, esp one performing functions in a human manner; person of machine-like efficiency; *SAfr* set of coloured lights at a junction to control the traffic flow **robotic** *adj* **robotics** *n* science of designing and using robots

robust *adj* very strong and healthy **robustly** *adv* **robustness** *n*

roc *n* monstrous bird of Arabian mythology

rock[1] *n* hard mineral substance that makes up part of the earth's crust, stone; large rugged mass of stone; *Brit* hard sweet in sticks **on the rocks** (of a marriage) about to end; (of an alcoholic drink) served with ice **rocky** *adj* having many rocks **rockery** *n* mound of stones in a garden for rock plants **rock bottom** lowest possible level **rock cake** small fruit cake with a rough surface

rock[2] *v* (cause to) sway to and fro; *NZ, slang* be very good ▷*n* (also **rock music**) style of pop music with a heavy beat **rocky** *adj* shaky or unstable **rock and roll, rock'n'roll** style of pop music blending rhythm and blues and country music **rocking chair** chair allowing the sitter to rock backwards and forwards

rocker *n* rocking chair; curved piece of wood etc on which something may rock **off one's rocker** *Informal* insane

rocket *n* self-propelling device powered by the burning of explosive contents (used as a firework, weapon, etc); vehicle propelled by a rocket engine, as a weapon or carrying a spacecraft ▷*v* **-eting, -eted** move fast, esp upwards, like a rocket

rock melon *n US, Aust & NZ* kind of melon with sweet orange flesh

rococo [rok-**koe**-koe] *adj* (of furniture, architecture, etc) having much elaborate decoration in an early 18th-century style

rod *n* slender straight bar, stick; cane

rode *v* past tense of **ride**

rodent *n* animal with teeth specialized for gnawing, such as a rat, mouse, or squirrel

rodeo *n, pl* **-deos** display of skill by cowboys, such as bareback riding

roe[1] *n* mass of eggs in a fish, sometimes eaten as food

roe[2] *n* small species of deer

roentgen [**ront**-gan] *n* unit measuring a radiation dose

rogue *n* dishonest or unprincipled person; mischief-loving person ▷*adj* (of a wild beast) having a savage temper and living apart from the herd **roguish** *adj*

roister *v* make merry noisily or boisterously

role, rôle *n* task or function; actor's part

roll *v* move by turning over and over; move or sweep along; wind round; undulate; smooth out with a roller; (of a ship or aircraft) turn from side to side about a line from nose to tail ▷*n* act of rolling over or from side to side; piece of paper etc rolled up; small round individually baked piece of bread; list or register; continuous sound, as of drums, thunder, etc; swaying unsteady movement or gait **roll call** calling out of a list of names, as in a school or the army, to check who is present **rolled gold** metal coated with a thin layer of gold **rolling pin** cylindrical roller for flattening pastry **rolling stock** locomotives and coaches of a railway **rolling stone** restless wandering person **roll-on/roll-off** *adj Brit, Aust & NZ* denoting a ship allowing vehicles to be driven straight on and off **roll-top** *adj* (of a desk) having a flexible lid sliding in grooves **roll up** *v Informal* appear or arrive **roll-up** *n Brit, Informal* cigarette made by the smoker from loose tobacco and cigarette paper

roller *n* rotating cylinder used for smoothing or supporting a thing to be moved, spreading paint, etc; long wave of the sea **Rollerblade** *n* ® roller skate with the wheels set in one straight line **roller coaster** (at a funfair) narrow railway with steep slopes **roller skate** skate with wheels

rollicking *adj* boisterously carefree

roly-poly *adj* round or plump

ROM *computers* read only memory

Roman *adj* of Rome or the Roman Catholic Church **Roman Catholic** (member) of that section of the Christian Church that acknowledges the supremacy of the Pope **Roman numerals** the letters I, V, X, L, C, D, M, used to represent numbers **roman type** plain upright letters in printing

romance *n* love affair; mysterious or exciting quality; novel or film dealing with love, esp sentimentally; story with scenes remote from ordinary life

Romance *adj* (of a language) developed from Latin, such as French or Spanish

romantic *adj* of or dealing with love; idealistic but impractical; (of literature, music, etc) displaying passion and imagination rather than order and form ▷ *n* romantic person or artist **romantically** *adv* **romanticism** *n* **romanticize** *v* describe or regard in an idealized and unrealistic way

Romany *n, pl* **-nies,** *adj* Gypsy

romp *v* play wildly and joyfully ▷ *n* boisterous activity **romp home** win easily **rompers** *pl n* child's overalls

rondo *n, pl* **-dos** piece of music with a leading theme continually returned to

roo *n Aust, Informal* kangaroo

rood *n Christianity* the Cross; crucifix **rood screen** (in a church) screen separating the nave from the choir

roof *n, pl* **roofs** outside upper covering of a building, car, etc ▷ *v* put a roof on

rooibos [roy-boss] *n SAfr* tea prepared from the dried leaves of an African plant

rook[1] *n* Eurasian bird of the crow family **rookery** *n, pl* **-eries** colony of rooks, penguins, or seals

rook[2] *n* chess piece shaped like a castle

rookie *n Informal* new recruit

room *n* enclosed area in a building; unoccupied space; scope or opportunity ▷ *pl* lodgings **roomy** *adj* spacious

roost *n* perch for fowls ▷ *v* perch

rooster *n* domestic cock

root[1] *n* part of a plant that grows down into the earth obtaining nourishment; plant with an edible root, such as a carrot; part of a tooth, hair, etc below the skin; source or origin; form of a word from which other words and forms are derived; *maths* factor of a quantity which, when multiplied by itself the number of times indicated, gives the quantity ▷ *pl* person's sense of belonging ▷ *v* establish a root and start to grow **rootless** *adj* having no sense of belonging **root for** *v Informal* cheer on **root out** *v* get rid of completely

root² *v* dig or burrow

rope *n* thick cord **know the ropes** be thoroughly familiar with an activity **rope in** *v* persuade to join in

ropey, ropy *adj* **ropier, ropiest** *Brit, Informal* inferior or inadequate; not well

rorqual *n* toothless whale with a dorsal fin

rort *Aust, Informal* ▷ *n* dishonest scheme ▷ *v* take unfair advantage of something

rosary *n, pl* **-saries** series of prayers; string of beads for counting these prayers

rose¹ *n* shrub or climbing plant with prickly stems and fragrant flowers; flower of this plant; perforated flat nozzle for a hose; pink colour ▷ *adj* pink **roseate** [**roe**-zee-ate] *adj* rose-coloured **rose window** circular window with spokes branching from the centre **rosewood** *n* fragrant wood used to make furniture

rose² *v* past tense of **rise**

rosé [**roe**-zay] *n* pink wine

rosehip *n* berry-like fruit of a rose plant

rosella *n* type of Australian parrot

rosemary *n* fragrant flowering shrub; its leaves as a herb

rosette *n* rose-shaped ornament, esp a circular bunch of ribbons

rosin [**rozz**-in] *n* resin used for treating the bows of violins etc

roster *n* list of people and their turns of duty

rostrum *n, pl* **-trums, -tra** platform or stage

rosy *adj* **rosier, rosiest** pink-coloured; hopeful or promising

rot *v* **rotting, rotted** decompose or decay; slowly deteriorate physically or mentally ▷ *n* decay; *Informal* nonsense

rota *n* list of people who take it in turn to do a particular task

rotary *adj* revolving; operated by rotation

rotate *v* (cause to) move round a centre or on a pivot; (cause to) follow a set sequence **rotation** *n*

rote *n* mechanical repetition **by rote** by memory

rotisserie *n* rotating spit for cooking meat

rotor *n* revolving portion of a dynamo, motor, or turbine; rotating device with long blades that provides thrust to lift a helicopter

rotten *adj* decaying; *Informal* very bad; corrupt

rotter *n Chiefly Brit, slang* despicable person

Rottweiler [**rot**-vile-er] *n* large sturdy dog with a smooth black and tan coat and usu a docked tail

rotund [roe-**tund**] *adj* round and plump; sonorous **rotundity** *n*

rotunda *n* circular building or room, esp with a dome

rouble [**roo**-bl] *n* monetary unit of Russia, Belarus, and Tajikistan

roué [**roo**-ay] *n* man given to immoral living

rouge *n* red cosmetic used to

colour the cheeks

rough *adj* uneven or irregular; not careful or gentle; difficult or unpleasant; approximate; violent, stormy, or boisterous; in preliminary form; lacking refinement ▷ *v* make rough ▷ *n* rough state or area **rough it** live without the usual comforts etc **roughen** *v* **roughly** *adv* **roughness** *n* **roughage** *n* indigestible constituents of food which aid digestion **rough-and-ready** *adj* hastily prepared but adequate **rough-and-tumble** *n* playful fight **rough-hewn** *adj* roughly shaped **roughhouse** *n Chiefly US, slang* fight **rough out** *v* prepare (a sketch or report) in preliminary form

roughcast *n* mixture of plaster and small stones for outside walls ▷ *v* coat with this

roughshod *adv* **ride roughshod over** act with total disregard for

roulette *n* gambling game played with a revolving wheel and a ball

round *adj* spherical, cylindrical, circular, or curved ▷ *adv, prep* indicating an encircling movement, presence on all sides, etc *eg tied round the waist; books scattered round the room* ▷ *v* move round ▷ *n* customary course, as of a milkman; game (of golf); stage in a competition; one of several periods in a boxing match etc; number of drinks bought at one time; bullet or shell for a gun **roundly** *adv* thoroughly **rounders** *n* bat-and-ball team game **round robin** petition signed with names in a circle to conceal the order; tournament in which each player plays against every other player **round-the-clock** *adj* throughout the day and night **round trip** journey out and back again **round up** *v* gather (people or animals) together **roundup** *n*

roundabout *n* road junction at which traffic passes round a central island; revolving circular platform on which people ride for amusement ▷ *adj* not straightforward

roundel *n* small disc **roundelay** *n* simple song with a refrain

Roundhead *n hist* supporter of Parliament against Charles I in the English Civil War

rouse[1] [rhymes with **cows**] *v* wake up; provoke or excite **rousing** *adj* lively, vigorous

rouse[2] [rhymes with **mouse**] *v* (foll by *on*) *Aust* scold or rebuke

rouseabout *n Aust & NZ* labourer in a shearing shed

roustabout *n* labourer on an oil rig

rout *n* overwhelming defeat; disorderly retreat ▷ *v* defeat and put to flight

route *n* roads taken to reach a destination; chosen way **route march** long military training march

routine *n* usual or regular method of procedure; set sequence ▷ *adj* ordinary or regular

roux [roo] *n* fat and flour cooked together as a basis for sauces

rove *v* wander

rover *n* wanderer, traveller

row[1] [rhymes with **go**] *n* straight line of people or things **in a row** in succession

row[2] [rhymes with **go**] *v* propel (a boat) by oars ▷ *n* spell of rowing **rowing boat** boat propelled by oars

row[3] [rhymes with **now**] *Informal* ▷*n* dispute; disturbance; reprimand ▷*v* quarrel noisily

rowan *n* tree producing bright red berries, mountain ash

rowdy *adj* **-dier, -diest** disorderly, noisy, and rough ▷*n, pl* **-dies** person like this

rowel [rhymes with **towel**] *n* small spiked wheel on a spur

rowlock [**rol**-luk] *n* device on a boat that holds an oar in place

royal *adj* of, befitting, or supported by a king or queen; splendid ▷*n* *Informal* member of a royal family **royally** *adv* **royalist** *n* supporter of monarchy **royalty** *n* royal people; rank or power of a monarch *pl* **-ties** payment to an author, musician, inventor, etc **royal blue** deep blue

RPI (in Britain) retail price index: measure of change in the average level of prices

rpm revolutions per minute

RSA Republic of South Africa; (in New Zealand) Returned Services Association

RSI repetitive strain injury

RSPCA (in Britain) Royal Society for the Prevention of Cruelty to Animals

RSVP please reply

rub *v* **rubbing, rubbed** apply pressure and friction to (something) with a circular or backwards-and-forwards movement; clean, polish, or dry by rubbing; chafe or fray through rubbing ▷*n* act of rubbing **rub it in** emphasize an unpleasant fact **rub out** *v* remove with a rubber

rubato *adv, n music* (with) expressive flexibility of tempo

rubber[1] *n* strong waterproof elastic material, orig made from the dried sap of a tropical tree, now usu synthetic; piece of rubber used for erasing writing ▷*adj* made of or producing rubber **rubbery** *adj* **rubberneck** *v* stare with unthinking curiosity **rubber stamp** device for imprinting the date, a name, etc; automatic authorization

rubber[2] *n* match consisting of three games of bridge, whist, etc; series of matches

rubbish *n* waste matter; anything worthless; nonsense **rubbishy** *adj*

rubble *n* fragments of broken stone, brick, etc

rubella *n* same as **German measles**

rubicund *adj* ruddy

rubidium *n chem* soft highly reactive radioactive element

rubric *n* heading or explanation inserted in a text

ruby *n, pl* **-bies** red precious gemstone ▷*adj* deep red

ruck[1] *n* rough crowd of common people; *rugby* loose scrummage

ruck[2] *n, v* wrinkle or crease

rucksack *n Brit, Aust & SAfr* large pack carried on the back

ructions *pl n Informal* noisy uproar

rudder *n* vertical hinged piece at the stern of a boat or at the rear of an aircraft, for steering

ruddy *adj* **-dier, -diest** of a fresh healthy red colour

rude *adj* impolite or insulting; coarse, vulgar, or obscene; unexpected and unpleasant; roughly made; robust **rudely** *adv* **rudeness** *n*

rudiments *pl n* simplest and most basic stages of a subject **rudimentary** *adj* basic, elementary

rue[1] *v* **ruing, rued** feel regret for **rueful** *adj* regretful or sorry **ruefully** *adv*

rue[2] *n* plant with evergreen bitter

leaves

ruff *n* starched and frilled collar; natural collar of feathers, fur, etc on certain birds and animals

ruffian *n* violent lawless person

ruffle *v* disturb the calm of; annoy, irritate ▷*n* frill or pleat

rug *n* small carpet; thick woollen blanket

rugby *n* form of football played with an oval ball which may be handled by the players

rugged [**rug**-gid] *adj* rocky or steep; uneven and jagged; strong-featured; tough and sturdy

rugger *n Chiefly Brit, Informal* rugby

ruin *v* destroy or spoil completely; impoverish ▷*n* destruction or decay; loss of wealth, position, etc; broken-down unused building **ruination** *n* act of ruining; state of being ruined; cause of ruin **ruinous** *adj* causing ruin; more expensive than can be afforded **ruinously** *adv*

rule *n* statement of what is allowed, for example in a game or procedure; what is usual; government, authority, or control; measuring device with a straight edge ▷*v* govern; be pre-eminent; give a formal decision; mark with straight line(s); restrain **as a rule** usually **ruler** *n* person who governs; measuring device with a straight edge **ruling** *n* formal decision **rule of thumb** practical but imprecise approach **rule out** *v* dismiss from consideration

rum *n* alcoholic drink distilled from sugar cane

rumba *n* lively ballroom dance of Cuban origin

rumble *v* make a low continuous noise; *Brit, Informal* discover the (disreputable) truth about ▷*n* deep resonant sound

rumbustious *adj* boisterous or unruly

ruminate *v* chew the cud; ponder or meditate **ruminant** *adj*, *n* cud-chewing (animal, such as a cow, sheep, or deer) **rumination** *n* quiet meditation and reflection **ruminative** *adj*

rummage *v* search untidily and at length ▷*n* untidy search through a collection of things

rummy *n* card game in which players try to collect sets or sequences

rumour *n* unproved statement; gossip or common talk **rumoured** *adj* suggested by rumour

rump *n* buttocks; rear of an animal

rumple *v* make untidy, crumpled, or dishevelled

rumpus *n, pl* **-puses** noisy commotion

run *v* **running, ran, run** move with a more rapid gait than walking; compete in a race, election, etc; travel according to schedule; function; manage; continue in a particular direction or for a specified period; expose oneself to (a risk); flow; spread; (of stitches) unravel ▷*n* act or spell of running; ride in a car; continuous period; series of unravelled stitches, ladder **run away** *v* make one's escape, flee **run down** *v* be rude about; reduce in number or size; stop working **rundown** *n* **run-down** *adj* exhausted **run into** *v* meet **run-of-the-mill** *adj* ordinary **run out** *v* be completely used up **run over** *v* knock down (a person) with a moving vehicle **run up** *v* incur (a debt)

rune *n* any character of the earliest

Germanic alphabet **runic** *adj*
rung[1] *n* crossbar on a ladder
rung[2] *v* past participle of **ring**[1]
runnel *n* small brook
runner *n* competitor in a race; messenger; part underneath an ice skate etc, on which it slides; slender horizontal stem of a plant, such as a strawberry, running along the ground and forming new roots at intervals; long strip of carpet or decorative cloth **runner-up** *n* person who comes second in a competition
running *adj* continuous; consecutive; (of water) flowing ▷*n* act of moving or flowing quickly; management of a business etc **in, out of the running** having *or* not having a good chance in a competition
runny *adj* **-nier, -niest** tending to flow; exuding moisture
runt *n* smallest animal in a litter; undersized person
runway *n* hard level roadway where aircraft take off and land
rupee *n* monetary unit of India and Pakistan
rupture *n* breaking, breach; hernia ▷*v* break, burst, or sever
rural *adj* in or of the countryside
ruse [rooz] *n* stratagem or trick
rush[1] *v* move or do very quickly; force (someone) to act hastily; make a sudden attack upon (a person or place) ▷*n* sudden quick or violent movement ▷*pl* first unedited prints of a scene for a film ▷*adj* done with speed, hasty **rush hour** period at the beginning and end of the working day, when many people are travelling to or from work
rush[2] *n* marsh plant with a slender pithy stem **rushy** *adj* full of rushes
rusk *n* hard brown crisp biscuit, used esp for feeding babies
russet *adj* reddish-brown ▷*n* apple with rough reddish-brown skin
rust *n* reddish-brown coating formed on iron etc that has been exposed to moisture; disease of plants which produces rust-coloured spots ▷*adj* reddish-brown ▷*v* become coated with rust **rusty** *adj* coated with rust; of a rust colour; out of practice
rustic *adj* of or resembling country people; rural; crude, awkward, or uncouth; (of furniture) made of untrimmed branches ▷*n* person from the country
rustle[1] *v, n* (make) a low whispering sound
rustle[2] *v US* steal (cattle) **rustler** *n US* cattle thief **rustle up** *v* prepare at short notice
rut[1] *n* furrow made by wheels; dull settled habits or way of living
rut[2] *n* recurrent period of sexual excitability in male deer ▷*v* **rutting, rutted** be in a period of sexual excitability
ruthenium *n chem* rare hard brittle white element
ruthless *adj* pitiless, merciless **ruthlessly** *adv* **ruthlessness** *n*
rye *n* kind of grain used for fodder and bread; *US* whiskey made from rye
rye-grass *n* any of several grasses cultivated for fodder

S

s second(s)
S South(ern)
SA Salvation Army; South Africa; South Australia
SAA South African Airways
Sabbath *n* day of worship and rest: Saturday for Jews, Sunday for Christians **sabbatical** *adj, n* (denoting) leave for study
SABC South African Broadcasting Corporation
sable *n* dark fur from a small weasel-like Arctic animal ▷ *adj* black
sabot [**sab**-oh] *n* wooden shoe traditionally worn by peasants in France
sabotage *n* intentional damage done to machinery, systems, etc ▷ *v* damage intentionally **saboteur** *n* person who commits sabotage
sabre *n* curved cavalry sword
sac *n* pouchlike structure in an animal or plant
saccharin *n* artificial sweetener
saccharine *adj* excessively sweet
sacerdotal *adj* of priests
sachet *n* small envelope or bag containing a single portion
sack[1] *n* large bag made of coarse material; *Informal* dismissal; *slang* bed ▷ *v* *Informal* dismiss
sackcloth *n* coarse fabric used for sacks, formerly worn as a penance
sack[2] *n* plundering of a captured town ▷ *v* plunder (a captured town)
sacrament *n* ceremony of the Christian Church, esp Communion
sacramental *adj*
sacred *adj* holy; connected with religion; set apart, reserved
sacrifice *n* giving something up; thing given up; making of an offering to a god; thing offered ▷ *v* offer as a sacrifice; give (something) up **sacrificial** *adj*
sacrilege *n* misuse or desecration of something sacred **sacrilegious** *adj*

> SPELLING It may sound as if **sacrilegious** has something to do with the word 'religious', which might explain why the most common misspelling of the word in Collins Word Web is *sacreligious*. But it should be spelt **sacrilegious**

sacristan *n* person in charge of the contents of a church **sacristy** *n, pl* **-ties** room in a church where sacred objects are kept
sacrosanct *adj* regarded as sacred, inviolable
sacrum [**say**-krum] *n, pl* **-cra** wedge-shaped bone at the base of the spine
sad *adj* **sadder, saddest** sorrowful, unhappy; deplorably bad **sadden** *v*

make sad

saddo *n, pl* **-dos, -does** *Brit, Informal* socially inadequate or pathetic person **sadly** *adv* **sadness** *n*

saddle *n* rider's seat on a horse or bicycle; joint of meat ▷ *v* put a saddle on (a horse); burden (with a responsibility) **saddler** *n* maker or seller of saddles

sadism [**say**-dizz-um] *n* gaining of (sexual) pleasure from inflicting pain **sadist** *n* **sadistic** *adj* **sadistically** *adv*

sadomasochism *n* combination of sadism and masochism **sadomasochist** *n*

s.a.e. *Brit, Aust & NZ* stamped addressed envelope

safari *n, pl* **-ris** expedition to hunt or observe wild animals, esp in Africa **safari park** park where lions, elephants, etc are kept uncaged so that people can see them from cars

safe *adj* secure, protected; uninjured, out of danger; not involving risk ▷ *n* strong lockable container **safely** *adv* **safe-conduct** *n* permit allowing travel through a dangerous area **safekeeping** *n* protection

safeguard *v* protect ▷ *n* protection

safety *n, pl* **-ties** state of being safe **safety net** net to catch performers on a trapeze or high wire if they fall **safety pin** pin with a spring fastening and a guard over the point when closed **safety valve** valve that allows steam etc to escape if pressure becomes excessive

saffron *n* orange-coloured flavouring obtained from a crocus ▷ *adj* orange

sag *v* **sagging, sagged** sink in the middle; tire; (of clothes) hang loosely ▷ *n* droop

saga [**sah**-ga] *n* legend of Norse heroes; any long story or series of events

sagacious *adj* wise **sagacity** *n*

sage[1] *n* very wise man ▷ *adj lit* wise **sagely** *adv*

sage[2] *n* aromatic herb with grey-green leaves

sago *n* starchy cereal from the powdered pith of the sago palm tree

said *v* past of **say**

sail *n* sheet of fabric stretched to catch the wind for propelling a sailing boat; arm of a windmill ▷ *v* travel by water; begin a voyage; move smoothly **sailor** *n* member of a ship's crew **sailboard** *n* board with a mast and single sail, used for windsurfing

saint *n Christianity* person venerated after death as specially holy; exceptionally good person **saintly** *adj* **saintliness** *n*

sake[1] *n* benefit; purpose **for the sake of** for the purpose of; to please or benefit (someone)

sake[2], **saki** [**sah**-kee] *n* Japanese alcoholic drink made from fermented rice

salaam [sal-**ahm**] *n* low bow of greeting among Muslims

salacious *adj* excessively concerned with sex

salad *n* dish of raw vegetables, eaten as a meal or part of a meal

salamander *n* amphibian which looks like a lizard

salami *n* highly spiced sausage

salary *n, pl* **-ries** fixed regular payment, usu monthly, to an employee **salaried** *adj*

sale *n* exchange of goods for money; selling of goods at unusually low prices; auction

saleable *adj* fit or likely to be sold **salesman, saleswoman, salesperson** *n* person who sells goods **salesmanship** *n* skill in selling

salient [**say**-lee-ent] *adj* prominent, noticeable ▷ *n mil* projecting part of a front line

saline [**say**-line] *adj* containing salt **salinity** *n*

saliva *n* liquid that forms in the mouth, spittle **salivary** *adj* **salivate** *v* produce saliva

sallee *n Aust* (also **snow gum**) SE Australian eucalyptus with a pale grey bark; acacia tree

sallow *adj* of an unhealthy pale or yellowish colour

sally *n, pl* **-lies** witty remark; sudden brief attack by troops ▷ *v* **-lying, -lied** (foll by *forth*) rush out; go out

salmon *n* large fish with orange-pink flesh valued as food ▷ *adj* orange-pink

salmonella *n, pl* **-lae** bacterium causing food poisoning

salon *n* commercial premises of a hairdresser, beautician, etc; elegant reception room for guests

saloon *n* two-door or four-door car with body closed off from rear luggage area; large public room, as on a ship; *US* bar serving alcoholic drinks **saloon bar** more expensive bar in a pub

salt *n* white crystalline substance used to season food; chemical compound of acid and metal ▷ *v* season or preserve with salt **old salt** experienced sailor **with a pinch of salt** allowing for exaggeration **worth one's salt** efficient **salty** *adj* **saltbush** *n* shrub that grows in alkaline desert regions **salt cellar** small container for salt at table

saltire *n heraldry* diagonal cross on a shield

saltpetre *n* compound used in gunpowder and as a preservative

salubrious *adj* favourable to health

Saluki *n* tall hound with a silky coat

salutary *adj* producing a beneficial result

salute *n* motion of the arm as a formal military sign of respect; firing of guns as a military greeting of honour ▷ *v* greet with a salute; make a salute; acknowledge with praise **salutation** *n* greeting by words or actions

salvage *n* saving of a ship or other property from destruction; property so saved ▷ *v* save from destruction or waste

salvation *n* fact or state of being saved from harm or the consequences of sin

salve *n* healing or soothing ointment ▷ *v* soothe or appease

salver *n* (silver) tray on which something is presented

salvia *n* plant with blue or red flowers

salvo *n, pl* **-vos, -voes** simultaneous discharge of guns etc; burst of applause or questions

sal volatile [sal vol-**at**-ill-ee] *n* preparation of ammonia, used to revive a person who feels faint

SAM surface-to-air missile

Samaritan *n* person who helps people in distress

samba *n* lively Brazilian dance

same *adj* identical, not different, unchanged; just mentioned **sameness** *n*

samovar *n* Russian tea urn

Samoyed *n* dog with a thick white

coat and tightly curled tail

sampan *n* small boat with oars used in China

samphire *n* plant found on rocks by the seashore

sample *n* part taken as representative of a whole; *music* short extract from an existing recording mixed into a backing track to produce a new recording ▷*v* take and test a sample of; *music* take a short extract from (one recording) and mix it into a backing track; record (a sound) and feed it into a computerized synthesizer so that it can be reproduced at any pitch **sampler** *n* piece of embroidery showing the embroiderer's skill; *music* piece of electronic equipment used for sampling **sampling** *n*

samurai *n, pl* **-rai** member of an ancient Japanese warrior caste

sanatorium *n, pl* **-riums, -ria** institution for invalids or convalescents; room for sick pupils at a boarding school

sanctify *v* **-fying, -fied** make holy

sanctimonious *adj* pretending to be religious and virtuous

sanction *n* permission, authorization; coercive measure or penalty ▷*v* allow, authorize

sanctity *n* sacredness, inviolability

sanctuary *n, pl* **-aries** holy place; part of a church nearest the altar; place of safety for a fugitive; place where animals or birds can live undisturbed

sanctum *n, pl* **-tums, -ta** sacred place; person's private room

sand *n* substance consisting of small grains of rock, esp on a beach or in a desert ▷*pl* stretches of sand forming a beach or desert ▷*v* smooth with sandpaper **sandy** *adj* covered with sand; (of hair) reddish-fair **sandbag** *n* bag filled with sand, used as protection against gunfire or flood water **sandblast** *v, n* (clean with) a jet of sand blown from a nozzle under pressure **sandpaper** *n* paper coated with sand for smoothing a surface **sandpiper** *n* shore bird with a long bill and slender legs **sandstone** *n* rock composed of sand **sandstorm** *n* desert wind that whips up clouds of sand

sandal *n* light shoe consisting of a sole attached by straps

sandalwood *n* sweet-scented wood

sander *n* power tool for smoothing surfaces

sandwich *n* two slices of bread with a layer of food between ▷*v* insert between two other things **sandwich board** pair of boards hung over a person's shoulders to display advertisements in front and behind

sane *adj* of sound mind; sensible, rational **sanity** *n*

sang *v* past tense of **sing**

sang-froid [sahng-**frwah**] *n* composure and calmness in a difficult situation

sangoma *n SAfr* witch doctor or herbalist

sanguinary *adj* accompanied by bloodshed; bloodthirsty

sanguine *adj* cheerful, optimistic

sanitary *adj* promoting health by getting rid of dirt and germs **sanitation** *n* sanitary measures, esp drainage or sewerage

sank *v* past tense of **sink**

Sanskrit *n* ancient language of India

sap[1] *n* moisture that circulates in

plants; *Informal* gullible person
sap² *v* **sapping, sapped** undermine; weaken **sapper** *n* soldier in an engineering unit
sapient [say-pee-ent] *adj lit* wise, shrewd
sapling *n* young tree
sapphire *n* blue precious stone ▷ *adj* deep blue
sarabande, saraband *n* slow stately Spanish dance
Saracen *n hist* Arab or Muslim who opposed the Crusades
sarcasm *n* (use of) bitter or wounding ironic language **sarcastic** *adj* **sarcastically** *adv*
sarcophagus *n, pl* **-gi, -guses** stone coffin
sardine *n* small fish of the herring family, usu preserved tightly packed in tins
sardonic *adj* mocking or scornful **sardonically** *adv*
sargassum, sargasso *n* type of floating seaweed
sari, saree *n* long piece of cloth draped around the body and over one shoulder, worn by Hindu women
sarmie *n SAfr, slang* sandwich
sarong *n* long piece of cloth tucked around the waist or under the armpits, worn esp in Malaysia
sarsaparilla *n* soft drink, orig made from the root of a tropical American plant
sartorial *adj* of men's clothes or tailoring
SAS (in Britain) Special Air Service
sash¹ *n* decorative strip of cloth worn round the waist or over one shoulder
sash² *n* wooden frame containing the panes of a window **sash window** window consisting of two sashes that can be opened by sliding one over the other
sassafras *n* American tree with aromatic bark used medicinally
Sassenach *n Scot* English person
sat *v* past of **sit**
Satan *n* the Devil **satanic** *adj* of Satan; supremely evil **Satanism** *n* worship of Satan **Great Satan** radical Islamic term for the United States
satay, saté [sat-ay] *n* Indonesian and Malaysian dish consisting of pieces of chicken, pork, etc, grilled on skewers and served with peanut sauce
satchel *n* bag, usu with a shoulder strap, for carrying books
sate *v* satisfy (a desire or appetite) fully
satellite *n* man-made device orbiting in space; heavenly body that orbits another; country that is dependent on a more powerful one ▷ *adj* of or used in the transmission of television signals from a satellite to the home
satiate [say-she-ate] *v* provide with more than enough, so as to disgust **satiety** [sat-tie-a-tee] *n* feeling of having had too much
satin *n* silky fabric with a glossy surface on one side **satiny** *adj* of or like satin **satinwood** *n* tropical tree yielding hard wood
satire *n* use of ridicule to expose vice or folly; poem or other work that does this **satirical** *adj* **satirist** *n* **satirize** *v* ridicule by means of satire
satisfy *v* **-fying, -fied** please, content; provide amply for (a need or desire); convince, persuade **satisfaction** *n* **satisfactory** *adj*
satnav *n motoring, Informal* satellite navigation
satsuma *n* kind of small orange

saturate *v* soak thoroughly; cause to absorb the maximum amount of something **saturation** *n*

Saturday *n* seventh day of the week

Saturn *n* Roman god of agriculture; sixth planet from the sun **saturnine** *adj* gloomy in temperament or appearance **saturnalia** *n* wild party or orgy

satyr *n* woodland god, part man, part goat; lustful man

sauce *n* liquid added to food to enhance flavour; *Chiefly Brit, Informal* impudence **saucy** *adj* impudent; pert, jaunty **saucily** *adv* **saucepan** *n* cooking pot with a long handle

saucer *n* small round dish put under a cup

sauerkraut *n* shredded cabbage fermented in brine

sauna *n* Finnish-style steam bath

saunter *v* walk in a leisurely manner, stroll ▷ *n* leisurely walk

sausage *n* minced meat in an edible tube-shaped skin **sausage roll** skinless sausage covered in pastry

sauté [so-tay] *v* **-téing** *or* **-téeing, -téed** fry quickly in a little fat

savage *adj* wild, untamed; cruel and violent; uncivilized, primitive ▷ *n* uncivilized person ▷ *v* attack ferociously **savagely** *adv* **savagery** *n*

savannah, savanna *n* extensive open grassy plain in Africa

savant *n* learned person

save *v* rescue or preserve from harm, protect; keep for the future; set aside (money); *sport* prevent the scoring of (a goal) ▷ *n sport* act of preventing a goal **saver** *n* **saving** *n* economy ▷ *pl* money put by for future use

saveloy *n Brit, Aust & NZ* spicy smoked sausage

saviour *n* person who rescues another; (**S-**) Christ

savoir-faire [sav-wahr-**fair**] *n French* ability to do and say the right thing in any situation

savory *n* aromatic herb used in cooking

savour *v* enjoy, relish; (foll by *of*) have a flavour or suggestion of ▷ *n* characteristic taste or odour; slight but distinctive quality **savoury** *adj* salty or spicy ▷ *n, pl* **-vouries** savoury dish served before or after a meal

savoy *n* variety of cabbage

savvy *slang* ▷ *v* **-vying, -vied** understand ▷ *n* understanding, intelligence

saw[1] *n* cutting tool with a toothed metal blade ▷ *v* **sawing, sawed, sawed** *or* **sawn** cut with a saw; move (something) back and forth **sawyer** *n* person who saws timber for a living **sawdust** *n* fine wood fragments made in sawing **sawfish** *n* fish with a long toothed snout **sawmill** *n* mill where timber is sawn into planks

saw[2] *v* past tense of **see**[1]

saw[3] *n* wise saying, proverb

sax *n Informal* short for **saxophone**

saxifrage *n* alpine rock plant with small flowers

Saxon *n* member of the W Germanic people who settled widely in Europe in the early Middle Ages ▷ *adj* of the Saxons

saxophone *n* brass wind instrument with keys and a curved body **saxophonist** *n*

say *v* **saying, said** speak or utter; express (an idea) in words; give as one's opinion; suppose as an example or possibility ▷ *n* right or

chance to speak; share in a decision **saying** *n* maxim, proverb
scab *n* crust formed over a wound; *offens* blackleg **scabby** *adj* covered with scabs; *Informal* despicable
scabbard *n* sheath for a sword or dagger
scabies [**skay**-beez] *n* itchy skin disease
scabrous [**skay**-bruss] *adj* rough and scaly; indecent
scaffold *n* temporary platform for workmen; gallows **scaffolding** *n* (materials for building) scaffolds
scalar *n, adj* (variable quantity) having magnitude but no direction
scald *v* burn with hot liquid or steam; sterilize with boiling water; heat (liquid) almost to boiling point ▷*n* injury by scalding
scale¹ *n* one of the thin overlapping plates covering fishes and reptiles; thin flake; coating which forms in kettles etc due to hard water; tartar formed on the teeth ▷*v* remove scales from; come off in scales **scaly** *adj*
scale² *n* (often pl) weighing instrument
scale³ *n* graduated table or sequence of marks at regular intervals, used as a reference in making measurements; ratio of size between a thing and a representation of it; relative degree or extent; fixed series of notes in music ▷*v* climb **scale up, down** *v* increase *or* decrease proportionately in size
scalene *adj* (of a triangle) with three unequal sides
scallop *n* edible shellfish with two fan-shaped shells; one of a series of small curves along an edge **scalloped** *adj* decorated with small curves along the edge
scallywag *n Informal* scamp, rascal
scalp *n* skin and hair on top of the head ▷*v* cut off the scalp of
scalpel *n* small surgical knife
scam *n Informal* dishonest scheme
scamp *n* mischievous child
scamper *v* run about hurriedly or in play ▷*n* scampering
scampi *pl n* large prawns
scan *v* **scanning, scanned** scrutinize carefully; glance over quickly; examine or search (an area) by passing a radar or sonar beam over it; (of verse) conform to metrical rules ▷*n* scanning **scanner** *n* electronic device used for scanning **scansion** *n* metrical scanning of verse
scandal *n* disgraceful action or event; malicious gossip **scandalize** *v* shock by scandal **scandalous** *adj*
scandium *n chem* rare silvery-white metallic element
scant *adj* barely sufficient, meagre
scanty *adj* **scantier, scantiest** barely sufficient or not sufficient **scantily** *adv*
scapegoat *n* person made to bear the blame for others
scapula *n, pl* **-lae, -las** shoulder blade **scapular** *adj*
scar *n* mark left by a healed wound; permanent emotional damage left by an unpleasant experience ▷*v* **scarring, scarred** mark or become marked with a scar
scarab *n* sacred beetle of ancient Egypt
scarce *adj* insufficient to meet demand; not common, rarely found **make oneself scarce** *Informal* go away **scarcely** *adv* hardly at all; definitely or probably not **scarcity** *n*

scare *v* frighten or be frightened ▷ *n* fright, sudden panic **scary** *adj Informal* frightening **scarecrow** *n* figure dressed in old clothes, set up to scare birds away from crops; raggedly dressed person **scaremonger** *n* person who spreads alarming rumours

scarf[1] *n, pl* **scarves, scarfs** piece of material worn round the neck, head, or shoulders

scarf[2] *n* joint between two pieces of timber made by notching the ends and fastening them together ▷ *v* join in this way

scarify *v* **-fying, -fied** scratch or cut slightly all over; break up and loosen (topsoil); criticize mercilessly **scarification** *n*

scarlatina *n* scarlet fever

scarlet *adj, n* brilliant red **scarlet fever** infectious fever with a scarlet rash

scarp *n* steep slope

scarper *v Brit, slang* run away

scat[1] *v* **scatting, scatted** *Informal* go away

scat[2] *n* jazz singing using improvised vocal sounds instead of words

scathing *adj* harshly critical

scatological *adj* preoccupied with obscenity, esp with references to excrement **scatology** *n*

scatter *v* throw about in various directions; disperse **scatterbrain** *n* empty-headed person

scatty *adj* **-tier, -tiest** *Informal* empty-headed

scavenge *v* search for (anything usable) among discarded material

scavenger *n* person who scavenges; animal that feeds on decaying matter

scenario *n, pl* **-rios** summary of the plot of a play or film; imagined sequence of future events

scene *n* place of action of a real or imaginary event; subdivision of a play or film in which the action is continuous; view of a place; display of emotion; *Informal* specific activity or interest *eg the fashion scene* **behind the scenes** backstage; in secret **scenery** *n* natural features of a landscape; painted backcloths or screens used on stage to represent the scene of action **scenic** *adj* picturesque

scent *n* pleasant smell; smell left in passing, by which an animal can be traced; series of clues; perfume ▷ *v* detect by smell; suspect; fill with fragrance

sceptic [**skep**-tik] *n* person who habitually doubts generally accepted beliefs **sceptical** *adj* **sceptically** *adv* **scepticism** *n*

sceptre *n* ornamental rod symbolizing royal power

schedule *n* plan of procedure for a project; list; timetable ▷ *v* plan to occur at a certain time

schema *n, pl* **-mata** overall plan or diagram **schematic** *adj* presented as a plan or diagram

scheme *n* systematic plan; secret plot ▷ *v* plan in an underhand manner **scheming** *adj, n*

scherzo [**skairt**-so] *n, pl* **-zos, -zi** brisk lively piece of music

schism [**skizz**-um] *n* (group resulting from) division in an organization **schismatic** *adj, n*

schist [**skist**] *n* crystalline rock which splits into layers

schizoid *adj* abnormally introverted; *Informal* contradictory ▷ *n* schizoid person

schizophrenia *n* mental disorder involving deterioration of or confusion about the personality;

Informal contradictory behaviour or attitudes **schizophrenic** *adj, n*

schmaltz *n* excessive sentimentality **schmaltzy** *adj*

schnapps *n* strong alcoholic spirit

schnitzel *n* thin slice of meat, esp veal

scholar *n* learned person; student receiving a scholarship; pupil **scholarly** *adj* learned **scholarship** *n* learning; financial aid given to a student because of academic merit **scholastic** *adj* of schools or scholars

school[1] *n* place where children are taught or instruction is given in a subject; group of artists, thinkers, etc with shared principles or methods ▷ *v* educate or train **schoolie** *Aust* schoolteacher or high-school student

school[2] *n* shoal of fish, whales, etc

schooner *n* sailing ship rigged fore-and-aft; large glass

sciatica *n* severe pain in the large nerve in the back of the leg **sciatic** *adj* of the hip; of or afflicted with sciatica

science *n* systematic study and knowledge of natural or physical phenomena **scientific** *adj* of science; systematic **scientifically** *adv* **scientist** *n* person who studies or practises a science **science fiction** stories making imaginative use of scientific knowledge **science park** area where scientific research and commercial development are carried on in cooperation

sci-fi *n* short for **science fiction**

scimitar *n* curved oriental sword

scintillate *v* give off sparks

scintillating *adj* very lively and amusing

scion [**sy**-on] *n* descendant or heir; shoot of a plant for grafting

scissors *pl n* cutting instrument with two crossed pivoted blades

sclerosis *n, pl* **-ses** abnormal hardening of body tissues

scoff[1] *v* express derision

scoff[2] *v Informal* eat rapidly

scold *v* find fault with, reprimand ▷ *n* person who scolds **scolding** *n*

sconce *n* bracket on a wall for holding candles or lights

scone *n* small plain cake baked in an oven or on a griddle

scoop *n* shovel-like tool for ladling or hollowing out; news story reported in one newspaper before all its rivals ▷ *v* take up or hollow out with or as if with a scoop; beat (rival newspapers) in reporting a news item

scoot *v slang* leave or move quickly

scooter *n* child's vehicle propelled by pushing on the ground with one foot; light motorcycle

scope *n* opportunity for using abilities; range of activity

scorch *v* burn on the surface; parch or shrivel from heat ▷ *n* slight burn **scorcher** *n Informal* very hot day

score *n* points gained in a game or competition; twenty; written version of a piece of music showing parts for each musician; mark or cut; grievance *eg settle old scores* ▷ *pl* lots ▷ *v* gain (points) in a game; keep a record of points; mark or cut; (foll by *out*) cross out; arrange music (for); achieve a success

scorn *n* open contempt ▷ *v* despise; reject with contempt **scornful** *adj* **scornfully** *adv*

scorpion *n* small lobster-shaped animal with a sting at the end of a jointed tail

Scot *n* person from Scotland

Scottish *adj* of Scotland, its people, or their languages **Scotch** *n* whisky distilled in Scotland **Scots** *adj* Scottish **Scotsman, Scotswoman** *n*

scotch *v* put an end to

scot-free *adj* without harm or punishment

scoundrel *n old-fashioned* cheat or deceiver

scour[1] *v* clean or polish by rubbing with something rough; clear or flush out **scourer** *n* small rough nylon pad used for cleaning pots and pans

scour[2] *v* search thoroughly and energetically

scourge *n* person or thing causing severe suffering; whip ▷ *v* cause severe suffering to; whip

scout *n* person sent out to reconnoitre; (**S-**) member of the Scout Association, an organization for young people which aims to develop character and promotes outdoor activities ▷ *v* act as a scout; reconnoitre

scowl *v, n* (have) an angry or sullen expression

scrabble *v* scrape at with the hands, feet, or claws

scrag *n* thin end of a neck of mutton **scraggy** *adj* thin, bony

scram *v* **scramming, scrammed** *Informal* go away quickly

scramble *v* climb or crawl hastily or awkwardly; struggle with others (for); mix up; cook (eggs beaten up with milk); (of an aircraft or aircrew) take off hurriedly in an emergency; make (transmitted speech) unintelligible by the use of an electronic device ▷ *n* scrambling; rough climb; disorderly struggle; motorcycle race over rough ground **scrambler** *n* electronic device that makes transmitted speech unintelligible

scrap[1] *n* small piece; waste metal collected for reprocessing ▷ *pl* leftover food ▷ *v* **scrapping, scrapped** discard as useless **scrappy** *adj* fragmentary, disjointed **scrapbook** *n* book with blank pages in which newspaper cuttings or pictures are stuck

scrap[2] *n, v* **scrapping, scrapped** *Informal* fight or quarrel

scrape *v* rub with something rough or sharp; clean or smooth thus; rub with a harsh noise; economize ▷ *n* act or sound of scraping; mark or wound caused by scraping; *Informal* awkward situation **scraper** *n* **scrape through** *v* succeed in or obtain with difficulty

scratch *v* mark or cut with claws, nails, or anything rough or sharp; scrape (skin) with nails or claws to relieve itching; withdraw from a race or competition ▷ *n* wound, mark, or sound made by scratching ▷ *adj* put together at short notice **from scratch** from the very beginning **up to scratch** up to standard **scratchy** *adj* **scratchcard** *n* ticket that reveals whether or not the holder has won a prize when the surface is removed by scratching

scrawl *v* write carelessly or hastily ▷ *n* scribbled writing

scrawny *adj* **scrawnier, scrawniest** thin and bony

scream *v* utter a piercing cry, esp of fear or pain; utter with a scream ▷ *n* shrill piercing cry; *Informal* very funny person or thing

scree *n* slope of loose shifting stones

screech *v*, *n* (utter) a shrill cry
screed *n* long tedious piece of writing
screen *n* surface of a television set, VDU, etc, on which an image is formed; white surface on which films or slides are projected; movable structure used to shelter, divide, or conceal something ▷*v* shelter or conceal with or as if with a screen; examine (a person or group) to determine suitability for a task or to detect the presence of disease or weapons; show (a film) **the screen** cinema generally **screen saver** *computers* software that produces changing images on a monitor when the computer is operative but idle
screw *n* metal pin with a spiral ridge along its length, twisted into materials to fasten them together; *slang* prison guard ▷*v* turn (a screw); twist; fasten with screw(s); *Informal* extort **screwy** *adj* *Informal* crazy or eccentric **screwdriver** *n* tool for turning screws **screw up** *v* *Informal* bungle; distort
scribble *v* write hastily or illegibly; make meaningless or illegible marks ▷*n* something scribbled
scribe *n* person who copied manuscripts before the invention of printing; *bible* scholar of the Jewish Law
scrimmage *n* rough or disorderly struggle
scrimp *v* be very economical
scrip *n* certificate representing a claim to stocks or shares
script *n* text of a film, play, or TV programme; particular system of writing *eg Arabic script*; handwriting
scripture *n* sacred writings of a religion **scriptural** *adj*
scrofula *n* tuberculosis of the lymphatic glands **scrofulous** *adj*
scroggin *n* *NZ* mixture of nuts and dried fruits
scroll *n* roll of parchment or paper; ornamental carving shaped like a scroll ▷*v* move (text) up or down on a VDU screen
scrotum *n, pl* **-ta, -tums** pouch of skin containing the testicles
scrounge *v* *Informal* get by cadging or begging **scrounger** *n*
scrub[1] *v* **scrubbing, scrubbed** clean by rubbing, often with a hard brush and water; *Informal* delete or cancel ▷*n* scrubbing
scrub[2] *n* stunted trees; area of land covered with scrub **scrubby** *adj* covered with scrub; stunted; *Informal* shabby
scruff[1] *n* nape (of the neck)
scruff[2] *n* *Informal* untidy person **scruffy** *adj* unkempt or shabby
scrum, scrummage *n rugby* restarting of play in which opposing packs of forwards push against each other to gain possession of the ball; disorderly struggle
scrumptious *adj* *Informal* delicious
scrunch *v* crumple or crunch or be crumpled or crunched ▷*n* act or sound of scrunching
scruple *n* doubt produced by one's conscience or morals ▷*v* have doubts on moral grounds **scrupulous** *adj* very conscientious; very careful or precise **scrupulously** *adv*
scrutiny *n, pl* **-nies** close examination **scrutinize** *v* examine closely
scuba diving *n* sport of swimming under water using cylinders containing compressed

air attached to breathing apparatus

scud *v* **scudding, scudded** move along swiftly

scuff *v* drag (the feet) while walking; scrape (one's shoes) by doing so ▷*n* mark caused by scuffing

scuffle *v* fight in a disorderly manner ▷*n* disorderly struggle; scuffling sound

scull *n* small oar ▷*v* row (a boat) using sculls

scullery *n, pl* **-leries** small room where washing-up and other kitchen work is done

sculpture *n* art of making figures or designs in wood, stone, etc; product of this art ▷*v* (also **sculpt**) represent in sculpture **sculptor, sculptress** *n* **sculptural** *adj*

scum *n* impure or waste matter on the surface of a liquid; worthless people **scummy** *adj*

scungy *adj* **-ier, -iest** *Aust & NZ, Informal* sordid or dirty

scupper *v Informal* defeat or ruin

scurf *n* flaky skin on the scalp

scurrilous *adj* untrue and defamatory

scurry *v* **-rying, -ried** move hastily ▷*n* act or sound of scurrying

scurvy *n* disease caused by lack of vitamin C

scut *n* short tail of the hare, rabbit, or deer

scuttle[1] *n* fireside container for coal

scuttle[2] *v* run with short quick steps ▷*n* hurried run

scuttle[3] *v* make a hole in (a ship) to sink it

scythe *n* long-handled tool with a curved blade for cutting grass ▷*v* cut with a scythe

SE southeast(ern)

sea *n* mass of salt water covering three quarters of the earth's surface; particular area of this; vast expanse **at sea** in a ship on the ocean; confused or bewildered **sea anemone** sea animal with suckers like petals **seaboard** *n* coast **sea dog** experienced sailor **seafaring** *adj* working or travelling by sea **seafood** *n* edible saltwater fish or shellfish **seagull** *n* gull **sea horse** small sea fish with a plated body and horselike head **sea level** average level of the sea's surface in relation to the land **sea lion** kind of large seal **seaman** *n* sailor **seaplane** *n* aircraft designed to take off from and land on water **seasick** *adj* suffering from nausea caused by the motion of a ship **seasickness** *n* **seaside** *n* area, esp a holiday resort, on the coast **sea urchin** sea animal with a round spiky shell **seaweed** *n* plant growing in the sea **seaworthy** *adj* (of a ship) in fit condition for a sea voyage

seal[1] *n* piece of wax, lead, etc with a special design impressed upon it, attached to a letter or document as a mark of authentication; device or material used to close an opening tightly ▷*v* close with or as if with a seal; make airtight or watertight; affix a seal to or stamp with a seal; decide (one's fate) irrevocably **sealant** *n* any substance used for sealing **seal off** *v* enclose or isolate (a place) completely

seal[2] *n* amphibious mammal with flippers as limbs **sealskin** *n*

seam *n* line where two edges are joined, as by stitching; thin layer of coal or ore ▷*v* mark with furrows or wrinkles **seamless** *adj* **seamy** *adj* sordid

seamstress *n* woman who sews,

esp professionally

seance [say-anss] *n* meeting at which spiritualists attempt to communicate with the dead

sear *v* scorch, burn the surface of **searing** *adj* (of pain) very sharp; highly critical

search *v* examine closely in order to find something ▷*n* searching **searching** *adj* keen or thorough **search engine** *computers* Internet service enabling users to search for items of interest **searchlight** *n* powerful light with a beam that can be shone in any direction

season *n* one of four divisions of the year, each of which has characteristic weather conditions; period during which a thing happens or is plentiful; fitting or proper time ▷*v* flavour with salt, herbs, etc; dry (timber) till ready for use **seasonable** *adj* appropriate for the season; timely or opportune **seasonal** *adj* depending on or varying with the seasons **seasoned** *adj* experienced **seasoning** *n* salt, herbs, etc added to food to enhance flavour **season ticket** ticket for a series of journeys or events within a specified period

seat *n* thing designed or used for sitting on; place to sit in a theatre, esp one that requires a ticket; buttocks; *Brit* country house; membership of a legislative or administrative body ▷*v* cause to sit; provide seating for **seat belt** belt worn in a car or aircraft to prevent a person being thrown forward in a crash

sebaceous *adj* of, like, or secreting fat or oil

secateurs *pl n* small pruning shears

secede *v* withdraw formally from a political alliance or federation **secession** *n*

seclude *v* keep (a person) from contact with others **secluded** *adj* private, sheltered **seclusion** *n*

second[1] *adj* coming directly after the first; alternate, additional; inferior ▷*n* person or thing coming second; attendant in a duel or boxing match ▷*pl* inferior goods ▷*v* express formal support for (a motion proposed in a meeting) **secondly** *adv* **second-class** *adj* inferior; cheaper, slower, or less comfortable than first-class **second-hand** *adj* bought after use by another **second nature** something so habitual that it seems part of one's character **second sight** supposed ability to predict events **second thoughts** revised opinion on a matter already considered **second wind** renewed ability to continue effort

second[2] *n* sixtieth part of a minute of an angle or time; moment

second[3] [si-**kond**] *v* transfer (a person) temporarily to another job **secondment** *n*

secondary *adj* of less importance; coming after or derived from what is primary or first; relating to the education of people between the ages of 11 and 18 or, in New Zealand, between 13 and 18

secret *adj* kept from the knowledge of others ▷*n* something kept secret; mystery; underlying explanation *eg the secret of my success* **in secret** without other people knowing **secretly** *adv* **secrecy** *n* **secretive** *adj* inclined to keep things secret **secretiveness** *n*

secretariat *n* administrative

office or staff of a legislative body

secretary *n, pl* **-ries** person who deals with correspondence and general clerical work; (**S-**) head of a state department *eg Home Secretary* **secretarial** *adj* **Secretary of State** head of a major government department

secrete[1] *v* (of an organ, gland, etc) produce and release (a substance) **secretion** *n* **secretory** [sek-**reet**-or-ee] *adj*

secrete[2] *v* hide or conceal

sect *n* subdivision of a religious or political group, esp one with extreme beliefs **sectarian** *adj* of a sect; narrow-minded

section *n* part cut off; part or subdivision of something; distinct part of a country or community; cutting; drawing of something as if cut through ▷*v* cut or divide into sections **sectional** *adj*

sector *n* part or subdivision; part of a circle enclosed by two radii and the arc which they cut off

secular *adj* worldly, as opposed to sacred; not connected with religion or the church

secure *adj* free from danger; free from anxiety; firmly fixed; reliable ▷*v* obtain; make safe; make firm; guarantee payment of (a loan) by giving something as security **securely** *adv* **security** *n, pl* **-ties** precautions against theft, espionage, or other danger; state of being secure; certificate of ownership of a share, stock, or bond; something given or pledged to guarantee payment of a loan

sedan *n US, Aust & NZ* two-door or four-door car with the body closed off from the rear luggage area **sedan chair** *hist* enclosed chair for one person, carried on poles by two bearers

sedate[1] *adj* calm and dignified; slow or unhurried **sedately** *adv*

sedate[2] *v* give a sedative drug to **sedation** *n* **sedative** *adj* having a soothing or calming effect ▷*n* sedative drug

sedentary *adj* done sitting down, involving little exercise

sedge *n* coarse grasslike plant growing on wet ground

sediment *n* matter which settles to the bottom of a liquid; material deposited by water, ice, or wind **sedimentary** *adj*

sedition *n* speech or action encouraging rebellion against the government **seditious** *adj*

seduce *v* persuade into sexual intercourse; tempt into wrongdoing **seducer, seductress** *n* **seduction** *n* **seductive** *adj*

sedulous *adj* diligent or persevering **sedulously** *adv*

see[1] *v* **seeing, saw, seen** perceive with the eyes or mind; understand; watch; find out; make sure (of something); consider or decide; have experience of; meet or visit; accompany **seeing** *conj* in view of the fact that

see[2] *n* diocese of a bishop

seed *n* mature fertilized grain of a plant; such grains used for sowing; origin; *obs* offspring; *sport* player ranked according to his or her ability ▷*v* sow with seed; remove seeds from; arrange (the draw of a sports tournament) so that the outstanding competitors will not meet in the early rounds **go, run to seed** (of plants) produce or shed seeds after flowering; lose vigour or usefulness **seedling** *n* young plant raised from a seed **seedy** *adj* shabby

seek *v* **seeking, sought** try to find or obtain; try (to do something)
seem *v* appear to be **seeming** *adj* apparent but not real **seemingly** *adv*
seemly *adj* proper or fitting
seen *v* past participle of **see**[1]
seep *v* trickle through slowly, ooze **seepage** *n*
seer *n* prophet
seersucker *n* light cotton fabric with a slightly crinkled surface
seesaw *n* plank balanced in the middle so that two people seated on either end ride up and down alternately ▷ *v* move up and down
seethe *v* **seething, seethed** be very agitated; (of a liquid) boil or foam
segment *n* one of several sections into which something may be divided ▷ *v* divide into segments **segmentation** *n*
segregate *v* set apart **segregation** *n*
seine [sane] *n* large fishing net that hangs vertically from floats
seismic *adj* relating to earthquakes **seismology** *n* study of earthquakes **seismological** *adj* **seismologist** *n* **seismograph, seismometer** *n* instrument that records the strength of earthquakes
seize *v* take hold of forcibly or quickly; take immediate advantage of; (usu foll by *up*) (of mechanical parts) stick tightly through overheating **seizure** *n* sudden violent attack of an illness; seizing or being seized
seldom *adv* not often, rarely
select *v* pick out or choose ▷ *adj* chosen in preference to others; restricted to a particular group, exclusive **selection** *n* selecting; things that have been selected; range from which something may be selected **selective** *adj* chosen or choosing carefully **selectively** *adv* **selectivity** *n* **selector** *n*
selenium *n chem* nonmetallic element with photoelectric properties
self *n, pl* **selves** distinct individuality or identity of a person or thing; one's basic nature; one's own welfare or interests **selfish** *adj* caring too much about oneself and not enough about others **selfishly** *adv* **selfishness** *n* **selfless** *adj* unselfish
self- *prefix* used with many main words to mean: of oneself or itself; by, to, in, due to, for, or from the self; automatic(ally) **self-assured** *adj* confident **self-catering** *adj* (of accommodation) for people who provide their own food **self-coloured** *adj* having only a single colour **self-conscious** *adj* embarrassed at being the object of others' attention **self-contained** *adj* containing everything needed, complete; (of a flat) having its own facilities **self-determination** *n* the right of a nation to decide its own form of government **self-evident** *adj* obvious without proof **self-help** *n* use of one's own abilities to solve problems; practice of solving one's problems within a group of people with similar problems **self-interest** *n* one's own advantage **self-made** *adj* having achieved wealth or status by one's own efforts **self-possessed** *adj* having control of one's emotions, calm **self-raising** *adj* (of flour) containing a raising agent **self-righteous** *adj* thinking oneself more virtuous than others **selfsame** *adj* the very same

self-seeking *adj, n* seeking to promote only one's own interests **self-service** *adj* denoting a shop, café, or garage where customers serve themselves and then pay a cashier **self-styled** *adj* using a title or name that one has taken without right **self-sufficient** *adj* able to provide for oneself without help **self-willed** *adj* stubbornly determined to get one's own way

sell *v* **selling, sold** exchange (something) for money; stock, deal in; (of goods) be sold; (foll by *for*) have a specified price; *Informal* persuade (someone) to accept (something) ▷*n* manner of selling **seller** *n* **sell-by date** *Brit* date on packaged food after which it should not be sold **sell out** *v* dispose of (something) completely by selling; *Informal* betray **sellout** *n* performance of a show etc for which all the tickets are sold; *Informal* betrayal

Sellotape *n* ® type of adhesive tape ▷*v* stick with Sellotape

selvage, selvedge *n* edge of cloth, woven so as to prevent unravelling

selves *n* plural of **self**

semantic *adj* relating to the meaning of words **semantics** *n* study of linguistic meaning

semaphore *n* system of signalling by holding two flags in different positions to represent letters of the alphabet

semblance *n* outward or superficial appearance

semen *n* sperm-carrying fluid produced by male animals

semester *n* either of two divisions of the academic year

semi *n Brit & SAfr, Informal* semidetached house

semi- *prefix* used with many main words to mean: half *eg semicircle*; partly or almost *eg semiprofessional*

semibreve *n* musical note four beats long

semicolon *n* the punctuation mark (;)

semiconductor *n* substance with an electrical conductivity that increases with temperature

semidetached *adj* (of a house) joined to another on one side

semifinal *n* match or round before the final **semifinalist** *n*

seminal *adj* original and influential; capable of developing; of semen or seed

seminar *n* meeting of a group of students for discussion

seminary *n, pl* **-ries** college for priests

semiprecious *adj* (of gemstones) having less value than precious stones

semiquaver *n* musical note half the length of a quaver

Semite *n* member of the group of peoples including Jews and Arabs

Semitic *adj* of the group of peoples including Jews and Arabs

semitone *n* smallest interval between two notes in Western music

semitrailer *n Aust* large truck in two separate sections joined by a pivoted bar (also **semi**)

semolina *n* hard grains of wheat left after the milling of flour, used to make puddings and pasta

Senate *n* upper house of some parliaments; governing body of some universities **senator** *n* member of a Senate **senatorial** *adj*

send *v* **sending, sent** cause (a person or thing) to go to or be taken or transmitted to a place; bring into a specified state or condition **sendoff** *n* demonstration of good wishes at a person's departure **send up** *v Informal* make fun of by imitating **send-up** *n Informal* imitation

senile *adj* mentally or physically weak because of old age **senility** *n*

senior *adj* superior in rank or standing; older; of or for older pupils ▷ *n* senior person **seniority** *n*

senna *n* tropical plant; its dried leaves or pods used as a laxative

señor [sen-**nyor**] *n, pl* **-ores** Spanish term of address equivalent to *sir* or *Mr* **señora** [sen-**nyor**-a] *n* Spanish term of address equivalent to *madam* or *Mrs* **señorita** [sen-nyor-**ee**-ta] *n* Spanish term of address equivalent to *madam* or *Miss*

sensation *n* ability to feel things physically; physical feeling; general feeling or awareness; state of excitement; exciting person or thing **sensational** *adj* causing intense shock, anger, or excitement; *Informal* very good **sensationalism** *n* deliberate use of sensational language or subject matter **sensationalist** *adj, n*

sense *n* any of the faculties of perception or feeling (sight, hearing, touch, taste, or smell); ability to perceive; feeling perceived through one of the senses; awareness; (sometimes pl) sound practical judgment or intelligence; specific meaning ▷ *v* perceive **senseless** *adj*

sensible *adj* having or showing good sense; practical *eg sensible shoes* (foll by *of*) aware **sensibly** *adv* **sensibility** *n* ability to experience deep feelings

sensitive *adj* easily hurt or offended; responsive to external stimuli; (of a subject) liable to arouse controversy or strong feelings; (of an instrument) responsive to slight changes **sensitively** *adv* **sensitivity** *n* **sensitize** *v* make sensitive

sensor *n* device that detects or measures the presence of something, such as radiation

sensory *adj* of the senses or sensation

sensual *adj* giving pleasure to the body and senses rather than the mind; having a strong liking for physical pleasures **sensually** *adv* **sensuality** *n* **sensualist** *n*

sensuous *adj* pleasing to the senses **sensuously** *adv*

sent *v* past of **send**

sentence *n* sequence of words capable of standing alone as a statement, question, or command; punishment passed on a criminal ▷ *v* pass sentence on (a convicted person)

sententious *adj* trying to sound wise; pompously moralizing

sentient [**sen**-tee-ent] *adj* capable of feeling **sentience** *n*

sentiment *n* thought, opinion, or attitude; feeling expressed in words; exaggerated or mawkish emotion **sentimental** *adj* excessively romantic or nostalgic **sentimentalism** *n* **sentimentality** *n* **sentimentalize** *v* make sentimental

sentinel *n* sentry

sentry *n, pl* **-tries** soldier on watch

sepal *n* leaflike division of the calyx of a flower

separate *v* act as a barrier between; distinguish between; divide up into parts; (of a couple) stop living together ▷ *adj* not the same, different; set apart; not shared, individual **separately** *adv* **separation** *n* separating or being separated; *law* living apart of a married couple without divorce **separable** *adj* **separatist** *n* person who advocates the separation of a group from an organization or country **separatism** *n*

SPELLING There are 101 examples of *seperate* in Collins Word Web, which makes it the most popular misspelling of **separate**

sepia *adj, n* reddish-brown (pigment)

sepsis *n* poisoning caused by pus-forming bacteria

Sept. September

September *n* ninth month of the year

septet *n* group of seven performers; music for such a group

septic *adj* (of a wound) infected; of or caused by harmful bacteria **septic tank** tank in which sewage is decomposed by the action of bacteria

septicaemia [sep-tis-**see**-mee-a] *n* infection of the blood

septuagenarian *n* person aged between seventy and seventy-nine

sepulchre [**sep**-pull-ker] *n* tomb or burial vault **sepulchral** [sip-**pulk**-ral] *adj* gloomy

sequel *n* novel, play, or film that continues the story of an earlier one; consequence

sequence *n* arrangement of two or more things in successive order; the successive order of two or more things; section of a film showing a single uninterrupted episode **sequential** *adj*

sequester *v* seclude; sequestrate

sequestrate *v* confiscate (property) until its owner's debts are paid or a court order is complied with **sequestration** *n*

sequin *n* small ornamental metal disc on a garment **sequined** *adj*

sequoia *n* giant Californian coniferous tree

seraglio [sir-**ah**-lee-oh] *n, pl* **-raglios** harem of a Muslim palace; Turkish sultan's palace

seraph *n, pl* **-aphs, -aphim** member of the highest order of angels **seraphic** *adj*

Serbian, Serb *adj* of Serbia ▷ *n* person from Serbia **Serbo-Croat, Serbo-Croatian** *adj, n* (of) the chief official language of Serbia and Croatia

serenade *n* music played or sung to a woman by a lover ▷ *v* sing or play a serenade to (someone)

serendipity *n* gift of making fortunate discoveries by accident

serene *adj* calm, peaceful **serenely** *adv* **serenity** *n*

serf *n* medieval farm labourer who could not leave the land he worked on **serfdom** *n*

serge *n* strong woollen fabric

sergeant *n* noncommissioned officer in the army; police officer ranking between constable and inspector **sergeant at arms** parliamentary or court officer with ceremonial duties **sergeant major** highest rank of noncommissioned officer in the army

serial *n* story or play produced in successive instalments ▷ *adj* of or forming a series; published or presented as a serial **serialize** *v* publish or present as a serial **serial killer** person who commits a series of murders

series *n, pl* **-ries** group or succession of related things, usu arranged in order; set of radio or TV programmes about the same subject or characters

serious *adj* giving cause for concern; concerned with important matters; not cheerful, grave; sincere, not joking **seriously** *adv* **seriousness** *n*

sermon *n* speech on a religious or moral subject by a clergyman in a church service; long moralizing speech **sermonize** *v* make a long moralizing speech

serpent *n lit* snake **serpentine** *adj* twisting like a snake

serrated *adj* having a notched or sawlike edge

serried *adj* in close formation

serum [**seer**-um] *n* watery fluid left after blood has clotted; this fluid from the blood of immunized animals used for inoculation or vaccination

servant *n* person employed to do household work for another

serve *v* work for (a person, community, or cause); perform official duties; attend to (customers); provide (someone) with (food or drink); provide with a service; be a member of the armed forces; spend (time) in prison; be useful or suitable; *tennis etc* put (the ball) into play ▷ *n tennis etc* act of serving the ball

server *n* player who serves in racket games; *computers* computer or program that supplies data to other machines on a network

service *n* system that provides something needed by the public; department of public employment and its employees; availability for use; overhaul of a machine or vehicle; formal religious ceremony; *tennis etc* act, manner, or right of serving the ball ▷ *pl* armed forces ▷ *v* overhaul (a machine or vehicle) **serviceable** *adj* useful or helpful; able or ready to be used **service area** area beside a motorway with garage, restaurant, and toilet facilities **serviceman, servicewoman** *n* member of the armed forces **service road** narrow road giving access to houses and shops **service station** garage selling fuel for motor vehicles

serviette *n* table napkin

servile *adj* too eager to obey people, fawning; suitable for a slave **servility** *n*

servitude *n* bondage or slavery

sesame [**sess**-am-ee] *n* plant cultivated for its seeds and oil, which are used in cooking

session *n* period spent in an activity; meeting of a court, parliament, or council; series or period of such meetings; academic term or year

set[1] *v* **setting, set** put in a specified position or state; make ready; make or become firm or rigid; establish, arrange; prescribe, assign; (of the sun) go down ▷ *n* scenery used in a play or film ▷ *adj* fixed or established beforehand; rigid or inflexible; determined (to do something) **setback** *n* anything that delays progress **set square** flat right-angled triangular instrument used for drawing angles **set-top box** device which enables digital television broadcasts to be viewed on a standard television set **set up** *v* arrange or establish **setup** *n* way in which anything is organized or arranged

set[2] *n* number of things or people grouped or belonging together; *maths* group of numbers or objects that satisfy a given condition or share a property; television or radio receiver; *sport* group of games in a match

sett, set *n* badger's burrow

settee *n* couch

setter *n* long-haired gun dog

setting *n* background or surroundings; time and place where a film, book, etc is supposed to have taken place; music written for the words of a text; decorative metalwork in which a gem is set; plates and cutlery for a single place at table; position or level to which the controls of a machine can be adjusted

settle[1] *v* arrange or put in order; come to rest; establish or become established as a resident; make quiet, calm, or stable; pay (a bill); bestow (property) legally **settlement** *n* act of settling; place newly colonized; subsidence (of a building); property bestowed legally **settler** *n* colonist

settle[2] *n* long wooden bench with high back and arms

seven *adj, n* one more than six **seventh** *adj, n* (of) number seven in a series **seventeen** *adj, n* ten and seven **seventeenth** *adj, n* **seventy** *adj, n* ten times seven **seventieth** *adj, n*

sever *v* cut through or off; break off (a relationship) **severance** *n* **severance pay** compensation paid by a firm to an employee who leaves because the job he or she was appointed to do no longer exists

several *adj* some, a few; various, separate **severally** *adv* separately

severe *adj* strict or harsh; very intense or unpleasant; strictly restrained in appearance **severely** *adv* **severity** *n*

sew *v* **sewing, sewed, sewn** *or* **sewed** join with thread repeatedly passed through with a needle; make or fasten by sewing

sewage *n* waste matter or excrement carried away in sewers

sewer *n* drain to remove waste water and sewage **sewerage** *n* system of sewers

sewn *v* a past participle of **sew**

sex *n* state of being male or female; male or female category; sexual intercourse; sexual feelings or behaviour ▷ *v* find out the sex of **sexy** *adj* sexually exciting or attractive; *Informal* exciting or trendy **sexism** *n* discrimination on the basis of a person's sex **sexist** *adj, n* **sexual** *adj* **sexually** *adv* **sexuality** *n* **sexual intercourse** sexual act in which the male's penis is inserted into the female's vagina **sex up** *vb Informal* make (something) more exciting

sexagenarian *n* person aged between sixty and sixty-nine

sextant *n* navigator's instrument for measuring angles, as between the sun and horizon, to calculate one's position

sextet *n* group of six performers; music for such a group

sexton *n* official in charge of a church and churchyard

SF science fiction

shabby *adj* **-bier, -biest** worn or dilapidated in appearance; mean or unworthy *eg shabby treatment* **shabbily** *adv* **shabbiness** *n*

shack *n* rough hut **shack up with** *v slang* live with (one's lover)

shackle *n* one of a pair of metal rings joined by a chain, for securing a person's wrists or ankles ▷ *v* fasten with shackles

shad *n* herring-like fish

shade *n* relative darkness; place sheltered from sun; screen or cover used to protect from a direct source of light; depth of colour; slight amount; *lit* ghost ▷ *pl slang* sunglasses ▷ *v* screen from light; darken; represent (darker areas) in drawing; change slightly or by degrees **shady** *adj* situated in or giving shade; of doubtful honesty or legality

shadow *n* dark shape cast on a surface when something stands between a light and the surface; patch of shade; slight trace; threatening influence; inseparable companion ▷ *v* cast a shadow over; follow secretly **shadowy** *adj* **shadow-boxing** *n* boxing against an imaginary opponent for practice **Shadow Cabinet** members of the main opposition party in Parliament who would be ministers if their party were in power

shaft *n* long narrow straight handle of a tool or weapon; ray of light; revolving rod that transmits power in a machine; vertical passageway, as for a lift or a mine; one of the bars between which an animal is harnessed to a vehicle

shag[1] *n* coarse shredded tobacco ▷ *adj* (of a carpet) having a long pile **shaggy** *adj* covered with rough hair or wool; tousled, unkempt **shaggy-dog story** long anecdote with a humorous twist at the end

shag[2] *n* kind of cormorant

shagreen *n* sharkskin; rough grainy untanned leather

shah *n* formerly, ruler of Iran

shake *v* **shaking, shook, shaken** move quickly up and down or back and forth; make unsteady; tremble; grasp (someone's hand) in greeting or agreement; shock or upset ▷ *n* shaking; vibration; *Informal* short period of time **shaky** *adj* unsteady; uncertain or questionable **shakily** *adv*

shale *n* flaky sedimentary rock

shall *v, past tense* **should** used as an auxiliary to make the future tense or to indicate intention, obligation, or inevitability

shallot *n* kind of small onion

shallow *adj* not deep; lacking depth of character or intellect **shallows** *pl n* area of shallow water **shallowness** *n*

sham *n* thing or person that is not genuine ▷ *adj* not genuine ▷ *v* **shamming, shammed** fake, feign

shamble *v* walk in a shuffling awkward way

shambles *n* disorderly event or place

shame *n* painful emotion caused by awareness of having done something dishonourable or foolish; capacity to feel shame; cause of shame; cause for regret ▷ *v* cause to feel shame; disgrace; compel by shame ▷ *interj SAfr, Informal* exclamation of sympathy or endearment **shameful** *adj* causing or deserving shame **shamefully** *adv* **shameless** *adj* with no sense of shame **shamefaced** *adj* looking ashamed

shammy *n, pl* **-mies** *Informal* piece of chamois leather

shampoo *n* liquid soap for washing hair, carpets, or upholstery; process of shampooing ▷ *v* wash with shampoo

shamrock *n* clover leaf, esp as the Irish emblem

shandy *n, pl* **-dies** drink made of beer and lemonade

shanghai *v* **-haiing, -haied** force or trick (someone) into doing

something ▷*n Aust & NZ* catapult
shank *n* lower leg; shaft or stem
shan't shall not
shantung *n* soft Chinese silk with a knobbly surface
shanty[1] *n, pl* **-ties** shack or crude dwelling **shantytown** *n* slum consisting of shanties
shanty[2] *n, pl* **-ties** sailor's traditional song
shape *n* outward form of an object; way in which something is organized; pattern or mould; condition or state ▷*v* form or mould; devise or develop **shapeless** *adj* **shapely** *adj* having an attractive shape
shard *n* broken piece of pottery or glass
share[1] *n* part of something that belongs to or is contributed by a person; one of the equal parts into which the capital stock of a public company is divided ▷*v* give or take a share of (something); join with others in doing or using (something) **shareholder** *n* **sharemilker** *NZ* person who works on a dairy farm belonging to someone else
share[2] *n* blade of a plough
shark *n* large usu predatory sea fish; person who cheats others
sharkskin *n* stiff glossy fabric
sharp *adj* having a keen cutting edge or fine point; not gradual; clearly defined; mentally acute; shrill; bitter or sour in taste; *music* above the true pitch ▷*adv* promptly; *music* too high in pitch ▷*n music* symbol raising a note one semitone above natural pitch **sharply** *adv* **sharpness** *n* **sharpen** *v* make or become sharp or sharper **sharpener** *n* **sharpshooter** *n* marksman
shatter *v* break into pieces; destroy completely **shattered** *adj Informal* completely exhausted; badly upset
shave *v* **shaving, shaved, shaved** *or* **shaven** remove (hair) from (the face, head, or body) with a razor or shaver; pare away; touch lightly in passing ▷*n* shaving **close shave** *Informal* narrow escape **shaver** *n* electric razor **shavings** *pl n* parings
shawl *n* piece of cloth worn over a woman's head or shoulders or wrapped around a baby
she *pron* refers to: female person or animal previously mentioned; something regarded as female, such as a car, ship, or nation
sheaf *n, pl* **sheaves** bundle of papers; tied bundle of reaped corn
shear *v* **shearing, sheared, sheared** *or* **shorn** clip hair or wool from; cut through **shears** *pl n* large scissors or a cutting tool shaped like these **shearer** *n* **shearing shed** *Aust & NZ* farm building with equipment for shearing sheep
shearwater *n* medium-sized sea bird
sheath *n* close-fitting cover, esp for a knife or sword; *Brit, Aust & NZ* condom **sheathe** *v* put into a sheath
shebeen *n Scot, Irish & SAfr* place where alcohol is sold illegally
shed[1] *n* building used for storage or shelter or as a workshop
shed[2] *v* **shedding, shed** pour forth (tears); cast off (skin, hair, or leaves)
sheen *n* glistening brightness on the surface of something
sheep *n, pl* **sheep** ruminant animal bred for wool and meat **sheep-dip** *n* liquid disinfectant in

which sheep are immersed **sheepdog** *n* dog used for herding sheep **sheepskin** *n* skin of a sheep with the fleece still on, used for clothing or rugs

sheepish *adj* embarrassed because of feeling foolish **sheepishly** *adv*

sheer¹ *adj* absolute, complete *eg sheer folly*; perpendicular, steep; (of material) so fine as to be transparent

sheer² *v* change course suddenly

sheet¹ *n* large piece of cloth used as an inner bed cover; broad thin piece of any material; large expanse

sheet² *n* rope for controlling the position of a sail **sheet anchor** strong anchor for use in an emergency; person or thing relied on

sheikh, sheik [shake] *n* Arab chief **sheikhdom, sheikdom** *n*

sheila *n Aust & NZ, slang* girl or woman

shekel *n* monetary unit of Israel ▷ *pl Informal* money

shelf *n, pl* **shelves** board fixed horizontally for holding things; ledge **shelf life** time a packaged product will remain fresh

shell *n* hard outer covering of an egg, nut, or certain animals; external frame of something; explosive projectile fired from a large gun ▷ *v* take the shell from; fire at with artillery shells **shellfish** *n* sea-living animal, esp one that can be eaten, with a shell **shell out** *v Informal* pay out or hand over (money) **shell shock** nervous disorder caused by exposure to battle conditions **shell suit** *Brit* lightweight tracksuit made of a waterproof nylon layer over a cotton layer

shellac *n* resin used in varnishes ▷ *v* **-lacking, -lacked** coat with shellac

shelter *n* structure providing protection from danger or the weather; protection ▷ *v* give shelter to; take shelter

shelve¹ *v* put aside or postpone; provide with shelves **shelving** *n* (material for) shelves

shelve² *v* slope

shenanigans *pl n Informal* mischief or nonsense; trickery

shepherd *n* person who tends sheep ▷ *v* guide or watch over (people) **shepherdess** *n fem* **shepherd's pie** baked dish of mince covered with mashed potato

sherbet *n Brit, Aust & NZ* fruit-flavoured fizzy powder; *US, Canadian & SAfr* flavoured water ice

sheriff *n* (in the US) chief law enforcement officer of a county; (in England and Wales) chief executive officer of the Crown in a county; (in Scotland) chief judge of a district; (in Australia) officer of the Supreme Court

Sherpa *n* member of a people of Tibet and Nepal

sherry *n, pl* **-ries** pale or dark brown fortified wine

shibboleth *n* slogan or principle, usu considered outworn, characteristic of a particular group

shield *n* piece of armour carried on the arm to protect the body from blows or missiles; anything that protects; sports trophy in the shape of a shield ▷ *v* protect

shift *v* move; transfer (blame or responsibility); remove or be removed ▷ *n* shifting; group of workers who work during a specified period; period of time during which they work;

loose-fitting straight underskirt or dress **shiftless** *adj* lacking in ambition or initiative **shifty** *adj* evasive or untrustworthy **shiftiness** *n*

shillelagh [shil-lay-lee] *n* (in Ireland) a cudgel

shilling *n* former British coin, replaced by the 5p piece; former Australian coin, worth one twentieth of a pound

shillyshally *v* **-lying, -lied** *Informal* be indecisive

shimmer *v, n* (shine with) a faint unsteady light

shin *n* front of the lower leg ▷ *v* **shinning, shinned** climb by using the hands or arms and legs **shinbone** *n* tibia

shindig *n Informal* noisy party; brawl

shine *v* **shining, shone** give out or reflect light; aim (a light); polish; excel ▷ *n* brightness or lustre **shiny** *adj* **take a shine to** *Informal* take a liking to (someone) **shiner** *n Informal* black eye

shingle¹ *n* wooden roof tile ▷ *v* cover (a roof) with shingles

shingle² *n* coarse gravel found on beaches **shingle slide** *NZ* loose stones on a steep slope

shingles *n* disease causing a rash of small blisters along a nerve

Shinto *n* Japanese religion in which ancestors and nature spirits are worshipped **Shintoism** *n*

shinty *n* game like hockey

ship *n* large seagoing vessel ▷ *v* **shipping, shipped** send or transport by carrier, esp a ship; bring or go aboard a ship **shipment** *n* act of shipping cargo; consignment of goods shipped **shipping** *n* freight transport business; ships collectively **shipshape** *adj* orderly or neat **shipwreck** *n* destruction of a ship through storm or collision ▷ *v* cause to undergo shipwreck **shipyard** *n* place where ships are built

shire *n Brit* county; *Aust* rural area with an elected council

shire horse *n* large powerful breed of horse

shirk *v* avoid (duty or work) **shirker** *n*

shirt *n* garment for the upper part of the body

shirty *adj* **-tier, -tiest** *Chiefly Brit, slang* bad-tempered or annoyed

shish kebab *n* meat and vegetable dish cooked on a skewer

shiver¹ *v* tremble, as from cold or fear ▷ *n* shivering

shiver² *v* splinter into pieces

shoal¹ *n* large number of fish swimming together

shoal² *n* stretch of shallow water; sandbank

shock¹ *v* horrify, disgust, or astonish ▷ *n* sudden violent emotional disturbance; sudden violent blow or impact; something causing this; state of bodily collapse caused by physical or mental shock; pain and muscular spasm caused by an electric current passing through the body **shocker** *n* **shocking** *adj* causing horror, disgust, or astonishment; *Informal* very bad

shock² *n* bushy mass (of hair)

shod *v* past of **shoe**

shoddy *adj* **-dier, -diest** made or done badly

shoe *n* outer covering for the foot, ending below the ankle; horseshoe ▷ *v* **shoeing, shod** fit with a shoe or shoes **shoehorn** *n* smooth curved implement inserted at the heel of a shoe to ease the foot into it

shoestring *n* **on a shoestring** using a very small amount of money
shone *v* past of **shine**
shonky *adj* **-kier, -kiest** *Aust & NZ, Informal* unreliable or unsound
shoo *interj* go away! ▷ *v* drive away as by saying 'shoo'
shook *v* past tense of **shake**
shoot *v* **shooting, shot** hit, wound, or kill with a missile fired from a weapon; fire (a missile from) a weapon; hunt; send out or move rapidly; (of a plant) sprout; photograph or film; *sport* take a shot at goal ▷ *n* new branch or sprout of a plant; hunting expedition **shooting star** meteor **shooting stick** stick with a spike at one end and a folding seat at the other
shop *n* place for sale of goods and services; workshop ▷ *v* **shopping, shopped** visit a shop or shops to buy goods; *Brit, Aust & NZ, slang* inform against (someone) **talk shop** discuss one's work, esp on a social occasion **shop around** *v* visit various shops to compare goods and prices **shop floor** production area of a factory; workers in a factory **shoplifter** *n* person who steals from a shop **shop-soiled** *adj* soiled or faded from being displayed in a shop **shop steward** (in some countries) trade-union official elected to represent his or her fellow workers
shore¹ *n* edge of a sea or lake
shore² *v* (foll by *up*) prop or support
shorn *v* a past participle of **shear**
short *adj* not long; not tall; not lasting long, brief; deficient *eg short of cash*; abrupt, rude; (of a drink) consisting chiefly of a spirit; (of pastry) crumbly ▷ *adv* abruptly ▷ *n* drink of spirits; short film; *Informal* short circuit ▷ *pl* short trousers **shortage** *n* deficiency **shorten** *v* make or become shorter **shortly** *adv* soon; rudely **shortbread, shortcake** *n* crumbly biscuit made with butter **short-change** *v* give (someone) less than the correct amount of change; *slang* swindle **short circuit** faulty or accidental connection in a circuit, which deflects current through a path of low resistance **shortcoming** *n* failing or defect **short cut** quicker route or method **shortfall** *n* deficit **shorthand** *n* system of rapid writing using symbols to represent words **short-handed** *adj* not having enough workers **short list** selected list of candidates for a job or prize, from which the final choice will be made **short-list** *v* put on a short list **short shrift** brief and unsympathetic treatment **short-sighted** *adj* unable to see distant things clearly; lacking in foresight **short wave** radio wave with a wavelength of less than 60 metres
shot¹ *n* shooting; small lead pellets used in a shotgun; person with specified skill in shooting; *slang* attempt; *sport* act or instance of hitting, kicking, or throwing the ball; photograph; uninterrupted film sequence; *Informal* injection **shotgun** *n* gun for firing a charge of shot at short range
shot² *v* past of **shoot** ▷ *adj* woven to show changing colours
shot put *n* athletic event in which contestants hurl a heavy metal ball as far as possible **shot-putter** *n*
should *v* past tense of **shall** used as an auxiliary to make the subjunctive mood or to indicate obligation or possibility

shoulder *n* part of the body to which an arm, foreleg, or wing is attached; cut of meat including the upper foreleg; side of a road ▷ *v* bear (a burden or responsibility); push with one's shoulder; put on one's shoulder **shoulder blade** large flat triangular bone at the shoulder

shouldn't should not

shout *n* loud cry; *Informal* person's turn to buy a round of drinks ▷ *v* cry out loudly; *Aust & NZ, Informal* treat (someone) to (something, such as a drink) **shout down** *v* silence (someone) by shouting

shove *v* push roughly; *Informal* put ▷ *n* rough push **shove off** *v* *Informal* go away

shovel *n* tool for lifting or moving loose material ▷ *v* **-elling, -elled** lift or move as with a shovel

show *v* **showing, showed, shown** *or* **showed** make, be, or become noticeable or visible; exhibit or display; indicate; instruct by demonstration; prove; guide; reveal or display (an emotion) ▷ *n* public exhibition; theatrical or other entertainment; mere display or pretence **showy** *adj* gaudy; ostentatious **showily** *adv* **show business** the entertainment industry **showcase** *n* situation in which something is displayed to best advantage; glass case used to display objects **showdown** *n* confrontation that settles a dispute **showjumping** *n* competitive sport of riding horses to demonstrate skill in jumping **showman** *n* man skilled at presenting anything spectacularly **showmanship** *n* **show off** *v* exhibit to invite admiration; *Informal* behave flamboyantly in order to attract attention **show-off** *n* *Informal* person who shows off **showpiece** *n* excellent specimen shown for display or as an example **showroom** *n* room in which goods for sale are on display **show up** *v* reveal or be revealed clearly; expose the faults or defects of; *Informal* embarrass; *Informal* arrive

shower *n* kind of bath in which a person stands while being sprayed with water; wash in this; short period of rain, hail, or snow; sudden abundant fall of objects ▷ *v* wash in a shower; bestow (things) or present (someone) with things liberally **showery** *adj*

shown *v* a past participle of **show**

shrank *v* a past tense of **shrink**

shrapnel *n* artillery shell filled with pellets which scatter on explosion; fragments from this

shred *n* long narrow strip torn from something; small amount ▷ *v* **shredding, shredded** *or* **shred** tear to shreds

shrew *n* small mouselike animal; bad-tempered nagging woman **shrewish** *adj*

shrewd *adj* clever and perceptive **shrewdly** *adv* **shrewdness** *n*

shriek *n* shrill cry ▷ *v* utter (with) a shriek

shrike *n* songbird with a heavy hooked bill

shrill *adj* (of a sound) sharp and high-pitched **shrillness** *n* **shrilly** *adv*

shrimp *n* small edible shellfish; *Informal* small person **shrimping** *n* fishing for shrimps

shrine *n* place of worship associated with a sacred person or object

shrink *v* **shrinking, shrank** *or* **shrunk, shrunk** *or* **shrunken**

become or make smaller; recoil or withdraw ▷*n* *slang* psychiatrist **shrinkage** *n* decrease in size, value, or weight

shrivel *v* **-elling, -elled** shrink and wither

shroud *n* piece of cloth used to wrap a dead body; anything which conceals ▷*v* conceal

Shrove Tuesday *n* day before Ash Wednesday

shrub *n* woody plant smaller than a tree **shrubbery** *n, pl* **-beries** area planted with shrubs

shrug *v* **shrugging, shrugged** raise and then drop (the shoulders) as a sign of indifference, ignorance, or doubt ▷*n* shrugging **shrug off** *v* dismiss as unimportant

shrunk *v* a past of **shrink**

shrunken *v* a past participle of **shrink**

shudder *v* shake or tremble violently, esp with horror ▷*n* shaking or trembling

shuffle *v* walk without lifting the feet; jumble together; rearrange ▷*n* shuffling; rearrangement

shun *v* **shunning, shunned** avoid

shunt *v* move (objects or people) to a different position; move (a train) from one track to another

shush *interj* be quiet!

shut *v* **shutting, shut** bring together or fold, close; prevent access to; (of a shop etc) stop operating for the day **shutter** *n* hinged doorlike cover for closing off a window; device in a camera letting in the light required to expose a film **shut down** *v* close or stop (a factory, machine, or business) **shutdown** *n*

shuttle *n* vehicle going to and fro over a short distance; instrument which passes the weft thread between the warp threads in weaving ▷*v* travel by or as if by shuttle

shuttlecock *n* small light cone with feathers stuck in one end, struck to and fro in badminton

shy[1] *adj* not at ease in company; timid; (foll by *of*) cautious or wary ▷*v* **shying, shied** start back in fear; (foll by *away from*) avoid (doing something) through fear or lack of confidence **shyly** *adv* **shyness** *n*

shy[2] *v* **shying, shied** throw ▷*n, pl* **shies** throw

SI *French* Système International (d'Unités), international metric system of units of measurement

Siamese *adj* of Siam, former name of Thailand **Siamese cat** breed of cat with cream fur, dark ears and face, and blue eyes **Siamese twins** twins born joined to each other at some part of the body

sibilant *adj* hissing ▷*n* consonant pronounced with a hissing sound

sibling *n* brother or sister

sibyl *n* (in ancient Greece and Rome) prophetess

sic *Latin* thus: used to indicate that an odd spelling or reading is in fact accurate

sick *adj* vomiting or likely to vomit; physically or mentally unwell; *Informal* amused or fascinated by something sadistic or morbid; (foll by *of*) *Informal* disgusted (by) or weary (of) **sickness** *n* **sicken** *v* make nauseated or disgusted; become ill **sickly** *adj* unhealthy, weak; causing revulsion or nausea **sick bay** place for sick people, such as that on a ship

sickle *n* tool with a curved blade for cutting grass or grain

side *n* line or surface that borders

anything; either of two halves into which something can be divided; either surface of a flat object; area immediately next to a person or thing; aspect or part; one of two opposing groups or teams ▷ *adj* at or on the side; subordinate **on the side** as an extra; unofficially **siding** *n* short stretch of railway track on which trains or wagons are shunted from the main line **sideboard** *n* piece of furniture for holding plates, cutlery, etc in a dining room **sideburns, sideboards** *pl n* man's side whiskers **side effect** additional undesirable effect **sidekick** *n Informal* close friend or associate **sidelight** *n* either of two small lights on the front of a vehicle **sideline** *n* subsidiary interest or source of income; *sport* line marking the boundary of a playing area **sidelong** *adj* sideways ▷ *adv* obliquely **side-saddle** *n* saddle designed to allow a woman rider to sit with both legs on the same side of the horse **sidestep** *v* dodge (an issue); avoid by stepping sideways **sidetrack** *v* divert from the main topic **sidewalk** *n US* paved path for pedestrians, at the side of a road **sideways** *adv* to or from the side; obliquely **side with** *v* support (one side in a dispute)

sidereal [side-**eer**-ee-al] *adj* of or determined with reference to the stars

sidle *v* walk in a furtive manner

SIDS sudden infant death syndrome, cot death

siege *n* surrounding and blockading of a place

sienna *n* reddish- or yellowish-brown pigment made from natural earth

sierra *n* range of mountains in Spain or America with jagged peaks

siesta *n* afternoon nap, taken in hot countries

sieve [**siv**] *n* utensil with mesh through which a substance is sifted or strained ▷ *v* sift or strain through a sieve

sift *v* remove the coarser particles from a substance with a sieve; examine (information or evidence) to select what is important

sigh *n* long audible breath expressing sadness, tiredness, relief, or longing ▷ *v* utter a sigh

sight *n* ability to see; instance of seeing; range of vision; device for guiding the eye while using a gun or optical instrument; thing worth seeing; *Informal* a lot ▷ *v* catch sight of **sightless** *adj* blind **sight-read** *v* play or sing printed music without previous preparation **sightseeing** *n* visiting places of interest **sightseer** *n*

sign *n* indication of something not immediately or outwardly observable; gesture, mark, or symbol conveying a meaning; notice displayed to advertise, inform, or warn; omen ▷ *v* write (one's name) on (a document or letter) to show its authenticity or one's agreement; communicate using sign language; make a sign or gesture **sign language** system of communication by gestures, as used by deaf people (also **signing**) **sign on** *v* register as unemployed; sign a document committing oneself to a job, course, etc **signpost** *n* post bearing a sign that shows the way

signal *n* sign or gesture to convey information; sequence of electrical impulses or radio waves transmitted or received ▷ *adj formal* very important ▷ *v* **-nalling, -nalled** convey (information) by signal **signally** *adv* **signal box** building from which railway signals are operated **signalman** *n* railwayman in charge of signals and points

signatory *n, pl* **-ries** one of the parties who sign a document

signature *n* person's name written by himself or herself in signing something; sign at the start of a piece of music to show the key or tempo **signature tune** tune used to introduce a particular television or radio programme

signet *n* small seal used to authenticate documents **signet ring** finger ring bearing a signet

significant *adj* important; having or expressing a meaning **significantly** *adv* **significance** *n*

signify *v* **-fying, -fied** indicate or suggest; be a symbol or sign for; be important **signification** *n*

signor [see-**nyor**] *n* Italian term of address equivalent to *sir* or *Mr* **signora** [see-**nyor**-a] *n* Italian term of address equivalent to *madam* or *Mrs* **signorina** [see-nyor-**ee**-na] *n* Italian term of address equivalent to *madam* or *Miss*

Sikh [**seek**] *n* member of an Indian religion having only one God

silage [**sile**-ij] *n* fodder crop harvested while green and partially fermented in a silo or plastic bags

silence *n* absence of noise or speech ▷ *v* make silent; put a stop to **silent** *adj* **silently** *adv* **silencer** *n* device to reduce the noise of an engine exhaust or gun

silhouette *n* outline of a dark shape seen against a light background ▷ *v* show in silhouette

silica *n* hard glossy mineral found as quartz and in sandstone **silicosis** *n* lung disease caused by inhaling silica dust

silicon *n chem* brittle nonmetallic element widely used in chemistry and industry **silicone** *n* tough synthetic substance made from silicon and used in lubricants, paints, and resins **silicon chip** tiny wafer of silicon processed to form an integrated circuit

silk *n* fibre made by the larva (**silkworm**) of a certain moth; thread or fabric made from this **silky, silken** *adj* of or like silk

sill *n* ledge at the bottom of a window or door

silly *adj* **-lier, -liest** foolish **silliness** *n*

silo *n, pl* **-los** pit or airtight tower for storing silage or grains; underground structure in which nuclear missiles are kept ready for launching

silt *n* mud deposited by moving water ▷ *v* (foll by *up*) fill or be choked with silt

silvan *adj* same as **sylvan**

silver *n* white precious metal; coins or articles made of silver ▷ *adj* made of or of the colour of silver **silverbeet** *n Aust & NZ* leafy green vegetable with white stalks **silver birch** tree with silvery-white bark **silver fern NZ** sporting symbol of New Zealand **silverfish** *n* small wingless silver-coloured insect **silverside** *n* cut of beef from below the rump and above the leg **silver wedding** twenty-fifth wedding anniversary

sim *n* computer game that simulates an activity such as flying or playing a sport

simian *adj, n* (of or like) a monkey or ape
similar *adj* alike but not identical **similarity** *n* **similarly** *adv*
simile [**sim**-ill-ee] *n* figure of speech comparing one thing to another, using 'as' or 'like' *eg as blind as a bat*
similitude *n* similarity, likeness
simmer *v* cook gently at just below boiling point; be in a state of suppressed rage **simmer down** *v Informal* calm down
simnel cake *n Brit* fruit cake covered with marzipan
simper *v* smile in a silly or affected way; utter (something) with a simper ▷ *n* simpering smile
simple *adj* easy to understand or do; plain or unpretentious; not combined or complex; sincere or frank; feeble-minded **simply** *adv* **simplicity** *n* **simplify** *v* make less complicated **simplification** *n* **simplistic** *adj* too simple or naive **simpleton** *n* foolish or half-witted person
simulate *v* make a pretence of; imitate the conditions of (a particular situation); have the appearance of **simulation** *n* **simulator** *n*
simultaneous *adj* occurring at the same time **simultaneously** *adv*
sin¹ *n* breaking of a religious or moral law; offence against a principle or standard ▷ *v* **sinning, sinned** commit a sin **sinful** *adj* guilty of sin; being a sin **sinfully** *adv* **sinner** *n*
sin² *maths* sine
since *prep* during the period of time after ▷ *conj* from the time when; for the reason that ▷ *adv* from that time
sincere *adj* without pretence or deceit **sincerely** *adv* **sincerity** *n*
sine *n* (in trigonometry) ratio of the length of the opposite side to that of the hypotenuse in a right-angled triangle
sinecure [**sin**-ee-cure] *n* paid job with minimal duties
sine die [**sin**-ay **dee**-ay] *adv Latin* with no date fixed for future action
sine qua non [**sin**-ay kwah **non**] *n Latin* essential requirement
sinew *n* tough fibrous tissue joining muscle to bone; muscles or strength **sinewy** *adj*
sing *v* **singing, sang, sung** make musical sounds with the voice; perform (a song); make a humming or whistling sound **singing telegram** service in which a messenger presents greetings to a person by singing **singsong** *n* informal singing session ▷ *adj* (of the voice) repeatedly rising and falling in pitch
singe *v* **singeing, singed** burn the surface of ▷ *n* superficial burn
singer *n* person who sings, esp professionally
single *adj* one only; distinct from others of the same kind; unmarried; designed for one user; formed of only one part; (of a ticket) valid for an outward journey only ▷ *n* single thing; thing intended for one person; record with one short song or tune on each side; single ticket ▷ *pl* game between two players ▷ *v* (foll by *out*) pick out from others **singly** *adv* **single file** (of people or things) arranged in one line **single-handed** *adj* without assistance **single-minded** *adj* having one aim only
singlet *n* sleeveless vest
singular *adj* (of a word or form)

denoting one person or thing; remarkable, unusual ▷*n* singular form of a word **singularity** *n* **singularly** *adv*

sinister *adj* threatening or suggesting evil or harm

sink *v* **sinking, sank, sunk** *or* **sunken** submerge (in liquid); descend or cause to descend; decline in value or amount; become weaker in health; dig or drill (a hole or shaft); invest (money); *golf, snooker* hit (a ball) into a hole or pocket ▷*n* fixed basin with a water supply and drainage pipe **sinker** *n* weight for a fishing line **sink in** *v* penetrate the mind **sinking fund** money set aside regularly to repay a long-term debt

Sino- *combining form* Chinese

sinuous *adj* curving; lithe **sinuously** *adv*

sinus [**sine**-uss] *n* hollow space in a bone, esp an air passage opening into the nose

sip *v* **sipping, sipped** drink in small mouthfuls ▷*n* amount sipped

siphon *n* bent tube which uses air pressure to draw liquid from a container ▷*v* draw off thus; redirect (resources)

sir *n* polite term of address for a man; (**S-**) title of a knight or baronet

sire *n* male parent of a horse or other domestic animal; respectful term of address to a king ▷*v* father

siren *n* device making a loud wailing noise as a warning; dangerously alluring woman

sirloin *n* prime cut of loin of beef

sirocco *n, pl* **-cos** hot wind blowing from N Africa into S Europe

sis *interj SAfr, Informal* exclamation of disgust

sisal [**size**-al] *n* (fibre of) plant used in making ropes

siskin *n* yellow-and-black finch

sissy *adj, n, pl* **-sies** weak or cowardly (person)

sister *n* girl or woman with the same parents as another person; female fellow-member of a group; senior nurse; nun ▷*adj* closely related, similar **sisterhood** *n* state of being a sister; group of women united by common aims or beliefs **sisterly** *adj* **sister-in-law** *n, pl* **sisters-in-law** sister of one's husband or wife; one's brother's wife

sit *v* **sitting, sat** rest one's body upright on the buttocks; cause to sit; perch; occupy an official position; (of an official body) hold a session; take (an examination) **sitting room** room in a house where people sit and relax **sit-in** *n* protest in which demonstrators occupy a place and refuse to move

sitar *n* Indian stringed musical instrument

sitcom *n Informal* situation comedy

site *n* place where something is, was, or is intended to be located; same as **website** ▷*v* provide with a site

situate *v* place

situation *n* state of affairs; location and surroundings; position of employment **situation comedy** radio or television series involving the same characters in various situations

six *adj, n* one more than five **sixth** *adj, n* (of) number six in a series **sixteen** *adj, n* six and ten **sixteenth** *adj, n* **sixty** *adj, n* six times ten **sixtieth** *adj, n*

size[1] *n* dimensions, bigness; one of a series of standard measurements of goods ▷*v* arrange according to size **sizeable, sizable** *adj* quite large **size up** *v Informal* assess

size² *n* gluey substance used as a protective coating

sizzle *v* make a hissing sound like frying fat

skanky *adj slang* dirty or unattractive; promiscuous

skate¹ *n* boot with a steel blade or sets of wheels attached to the sole for gliding over ice or a hard surface ▷*v* glide on or as if on skates **skateboard** *n* board mounted on small wheels for riding on while standing up **skateboarding** *n* **skate over, round** *v* avoid discussing or dealing with (a matter) fully

skate² *n* large marine flatfish

skedaddle *v Informal* run off

skein *n* yarn wound in a loose coil; flock of geese in flight

skeleton *n* framework of bones inside a person's or animal's body; essential framework of a structure ▷*adj* reduced to a minimum **skeletal** *adj* **skeleton key** key which can open many different locks

sketch *n* rough drawing; brief description; short humorous play ▷*v* make a sketch (of) **sketchy** *adj* incomplete or inadequate

skew *v* make slanting or crooked ▷*adj* slanting or crooked **skew-whiff** *adj Brit, Informal* slanting or crooked

skewer *n* pin to hold meat together during cooking ▷*v* fasten with a skewer

ski *n* one of a pair of long runners fastened to boots for gliding over snow or water ▷*v* **skiing, skied** *or* **ski'd** travel on skis **skier** *n*

skid *v* **skidding, skidded** (of a moving vehicle) slide sideways uncontrollably ▷*n* skidding

skiff *n* small boat

skill *n* special ability or expertise; something requiring special training or expertise **skilful** *adj* having or showing skill **skilfully** *adv* **skilled** *adj*

> SPELLING When you make an adjective from **skill**, you should drop an *l* to make **skilful**. This is not the case in American English, and this is probably why there are over 100 examples of *skillful* in Collins Word Web

skillet *n* small frying pan or shallow cooking pot

skim *v* **skimming, skimmed** remove floating matter from the surface of (a liquid); glide smoothly over; read quickly **skimmed, skim milk** milk from which the cream has been removed

skimp *v* not invest enough time, money, material, etc **skimpy** *adj* scanty or insufficient

skin *n* outer covering of the body; complexion; outer layer or covering; film on a liquid; animal skin used as a material or container ▷*v* **skinning, skinned** remove the skin of **skinless** *adj* **skinny** *adj* thin **skin-deep** *adj* superficial **skin diving** underwater swimming using flippers and light breathing apparatus **skin-diver** *n* **skinflint** *n* miser **skinhead** *n* youth with very short hair

skint *adj Brit, slang* having no money

skip¹ *v* **skipping, skipped** leap lightly from one foot to the other; jump over a rope as it is swung under one; *Informal* pass over, omit ▷*n* skipping

skip² *n* large open container for

builders' rubbish

skipper *n, v* captain

skirl *n* sound of bagpipes

skirmish *n* brief or minor fight or argument ▷*v* take part in a skirmish

skirt *n* woman's garment hanging from the waist; part of a dress or coat below the waist; cut of beef from the flank ▷*v* border; go round; avoid dealing with (an issue) **skirting board** narrow board round the bottom of an interior wall

skit *n* brief satirical sketch

skite *v, n Aust & NZ* boast

skittish *adj* playful or lively

skittle *n* bottle-shaped object used as a target in some games ▷*pl* game in which players try to knock over skittles by rolling a ball at them

skive *v Brit, Informal* evade work or responsibility

skivvy *n, pl* **-vies** *Brit* female servant who does menial work

skua *n* large predatory gull

skulduggery *n Informal* trickery

skulk *v* move stealthily; lurk

skull *n* bony framework of the head **skullcap** *n* close-fitting brimless cap

skunk *n* small black-and-white N American mammal which emits a foul-smelling fluid when attacked; *slang* despicable person

sky *n, pl* **skies** upper atmosphere as seen from the earth **skydiving** *n* sport of jumping from an aircraft and performing manoeuvres before opening one's parachute **skylark** *n* lark that sings while soaring at a great height **skylight** *n* window in a roof or ceiling **skyscraper** *n* very tall building

slab *n* broad flat piece

slack *adj* not tight; negligent; not busy ▷*n* slack part ▷*pl* informal trousers ▷*v* neglect one's work or duty **slackness** *n* **slacken** *v* make or become slack **slacker** *n*

slag *n* waste left after metal is smelted ▷*v* **slagging, slagged** (foll by *off*) *Brit, Aust & NZ, slang* criticize

slain *v* past participle of **slay**

slake *v* satisfy (thirst or desire); combine (quicklime) with water

slalom *n* skiing or canoeing race over a winding course

slam *v* **slamming, slammed** shut, put down, or hit violently and noisily; *Informal* criticize harshly ▷*n* act or sound of slamming **grand slam** see **grand**

slander *n* false and malicious statement about a person; crime of making such a statement ▷*v* utter slander about **slanderous** *adj*

slang *n* very informal language **slangy** *adj* **slanging match** abusive argument

slant *v* lean at an angle, slope; present (information) in a biased way ▷*n* slope; point of view, esp a biased one **slanting** *adj*

slap *n* blow with the open hand or a flat object ▷*v* **slapping, slapped** strike with the open hand or a flat object; *Informal* place forcefully or carelessly **slapdash** *adj* careless and hasty **slap-happy** *adj Informal* cheerfully careless **slapstick** *n* boisterous knockabout comedy **slap-up** *adj* (of a meal) large and luxurious

slash *v* cut with a sweeping stroke; gash; reduce drastically ▷*n* sweeping stroke; gash

slat *n* narrow strip of wood or metal

slate[1] *n* rock which splits easily into thin layers; piece of this for covering a roof or, formerly, for writing on

slate² *v Informal* criticize harshly
slattern *n old-fashioned* slovenly woman **slatternly** *adj*
slaughter *v* kill (animals) for food; kill (people) savagely or indiscriminately ▷ *n* slaughtering **slaughterhouse** *n* place where animals are killed for food
Slav *n* member of any of the peoples of E Europe or the former Soviet Union who speak a Slavonic language **Slavonic** *n* language group including Russian, Polish, and Czech ▷ *adj* of this language group
slave *n* person owned by another for whom he or she has to work; person dominated by another or by a habit; drudge ▷ *v* work like a slave **slaver** *n* person or ship engaged in the slave trade **slavery** *n* state or condition of being a slave; practice of owning slaves **slavish** *adj* of or like a slave; imitative **slave-driver** *n* person who makes others work very hard
slaver [**slav**-ver] *v* dribble saliva from the mouth
slay *v* **slaying, slew, slain** kill
sleazy *adj* **-zier, -ziest** run-down or sordid **sleaze** *n*
sledge¹, sled *n* carriage on runners for sliding on snow; light wooden frame for sliding over snow ▷ *v* travel by sledge
sledge², sledgehammer *n* heavy hammer with a long handle
sleek *adj* glossy, smooth, and shiny
sleep *n* state of rest characterized by unconsciousness; period of this ▷ *v* **sleeping, slept** be in or as if in a state of sleep; have sleeping accommodation for (a specified number) **sleeper** *n* railway car fitted for sleeping in; beam supporting the rails of a railway; ring worn in a pierced ear to stop the hole from closing up; person who sleeps **sleepy** *adj* **sleepily** *adv* **sleepiness** *n* **sleepless** *adj* **sleeping bag** padded bag for sleeping in **sleeping sickness** African disease spread by the tsetse fly **sleepout** *n NZ* small building for sleeping in **sleepover** *n* occasion when a person stays overnight at a friend's house **sleep with, together** *v* have sexual intercourse (with)
sleet *n* rain and snow or hail falling together
sleeve *n* part of a garment which covers the arm; tubelike cover; gramophone record cover **up one's sleeve** secretly ready **sleeveless** *adj*
sleigh *n, v* sledge
sleight of hand [**slite**] *n* skilful use of the hands when performing conjuring tricks
slender *adj* slim; small in amount
slept *v* past of **sleep**
sleuth [**slooth**] *n* detective
slew¹ *v* past tense of **slay**
slew² *v* twist or swing round
slice *n* thin flat piece cut from something; share; kitchen tool with a broad flat blade; *sport* hitting of a ball so that it travels obliquely ▷ *v* cut into slices; *sport* hit (a ball) with a slice
slick *adj* persuasive and glib; skilfully devised or carried out; well-made and attractive, but superficial ▷ *n* patch of oil on water ▷ *v* make smooth or sleek
slide *v* **sliding, slid** slip smoothly along (a surface); pass unobtrusively ▷ *n* sliding; piece of glass holding an object to be viewed under a microscope; photographic transparency; surface or structure

for sliding on or down; ornamental hair clip **slide rule** mathematical instrument formerly used for rapid calculations **sliding scale** variable scale according to which things such as wages alter in response to changes in other factors

slight *adj* small in quantity or extent; not important; slim and delicate ▷*v*, *n* snub **slightly** *adv*

slim *adj* **slimmer, slimmest** not heavy or stout, thin; slight ▷*v* **slimming, slimmed** make or become slim by diet and exercise **slimmer** *n*

slime *n* unpleasant thick slippery substance **slimy** *adj* of, like, or covered with slime; ingratiating

sling[1] *n* bandage hung from the neck to support an injured hand or arm; rope or strap for lifting something; strap with a string at each end for throwing a stone ▷*v* **slinging, slung** throw; carry, hang, or throw with or as if with a sling

sling[2] *n* sweetened drink with a spirit base *eg gin sling*

slink *v* **slinking, slunk** move furtively or guiltily **slinky** *adj* (of clothes) figure-hugging

slip[1] *v* **slipping, slipped** lose balance by sliding; move smoothly, easily, or quietly; (foll by *on, off*) put on or take off easily or quickly; pass out of (the mind) ▷*n* slipping; mistake; petticoat **give someone the slip** escape from someone **slippy** *adj Informal* slippery **slipknot** *n* knot tied so that it will slip along the rope round which it is made **slipped disc** painful condition in which one of the discs connecting the bones of the spine becomes displaced **slip road** narrow road giving access to a motorway **slipshod** *adj* (of an action) careless **slipstream** *n* stream of air forced backwards by a fast-moving object **slip up** *v* make a mistake **slipway** *n* launching slope on which ships are built or repaired

slip[2] *n* small piece (of paper)

slip[3] *n* clay mixed with water used for decorating pottery

slipper *n* light shoe for indoor wear

slippery *adj* so smooth or wet as to cause slipping or be difficult to hold; (of a person) untrustworthy

slit *n* long narrow cut or opening ▷*v* **slitting, slit** make a long straight cut in

slither *v* slide unsteadily

sliver [sliv-ver] *n* small thin piece

slob *n Informal* lazy and untidy person **slobbish** *adj*

slobber *v* dribble or drool **slobbery** *adj*

sloe *n* sour blue-black fruit

slog *v* **slogging, slogged** work hard and steadily; make one's way with difficulty; hit hard ▷*n* long and exhausting work or walk

slogan *n* catchword or phrase used in politics or advertising

sloop *n* small single-masted ship

slop *v* **slopping, slopped** splash or spill ▷*n* spilt liquid; liquid food ▷*pl* liquid refuse and waste food used to feed animals **sloppy** *adj* careless or untidy; gushingly sentimental

slope *v* slant ▷*n* sloping surface; degree of inclination ▷*pl* hills **slope off** *v Informal* go furtively

slosh *v* splash carelessly; *slang* hit hard ▷*n* splashing sound **sloshed** *adj slang* drunk

slot *n* narrow opening for inserting something; *Informal* place in a series or scheme ▷ *v* **slotting, slotted** make a slot or slots in; fit into a slot **slot machine** automatic machine worked by placing a coin in a slot

sloth [rhymes with **both**] *n* slow-moving animal of tropical America; laziness **slothful** *adj* lazy or idle

slouch *v* sit, stand, or move with a drooping posture ▷ *n* drooping posture **be no slouch** *Informal* be very good or talented

slough¹ [rhymes with **now**] *n* bog

slough² [**sluff**] *v* (of a snake) shed (its skin) or (of a skin) be shed **slough off** *v* get rid of (something unwanted or unnecessary)

sloven *n* habitually dirty or untidy person **slovenly** *adj* dirty or untidy; careless

slow *adj* taking a longer time than is usual or expected; not fast; (of a clock or watch) showing a time earlier than the correct one; stupid ▷ *v* reduce the speed (of) **slowly** *adv* **slowness** *n* **slowcoach** *n* *Informal* person who moves or works slowly

slowworm *n* small legless lizard

sludge *n* thick mud; sewage

slug¹ *n* land snail with no shell **sluggish** *adj* slow-moving, lacking energy **sluggishly** *adv* **sluggishness** *n* **sluggard** *n* lazy person

slug² *n* bullet; *Informal* mouthful of an alcoholic drink

slug³ *v* **slugging, slugged** hit hard ▷ *n* heavy blow

sluice *n* channel carrying off water; sliding gate used to control the flow of water in this; water controlled by a sluice ▷ *v* pour a stream of water over or through

slum *n* squalid overcrowded house or area ▷ *v* **slumming, slummed** temporarily and deliberately experience poorer places or conditions than usual

slumber *v, n lit* sleep

slump *v* (of prices or demand) decline suddenly; sink or fall heavily ▷ *n* sudden decline in prices or demand; time of substantial unemployment

slung *v* past of **sling¹**

slunk *v* past of **slink**

slur *v* **slurring, slurred** pronounce or utter (words) indistinctly; *music* sing or play (notes) smoothly without a break ▷ *n* slurring of words; remark intended to discredit someone; *music* slurring of notes; curved line indicating notes to be slurred

slurp *Informal* ▷ *v* eat or drink noisily ▷ *n* slurping sound

slurry *n, pl* **-ries** muddy liquid mixture

slush *n* watery muddy substance; sloppy sentimental talk or writing **slushy** *adj* **slush fund** fund for financing bribery or corruption

slut *n offens* dirty or immoral woman **sluttish** *adj*

sly *adj* **slyer, slyest** *or* **slier, sliest** crafty; secretive and cunning; roguish **on the sly** secretly **slyly** *adv* **slyness** *n*

smack¹ *v* slap sharply; open and close (the lips) loudly in enjoyment or anticipation ▷ *n* sharp slap; loud kiss; slapping sound ▷ *adv Informal* squarely or directly *eg smack in the middle* **smacker** *n slang* loud kiss

smack² *n* slight flavour or trace; *slang* heroin ▷ *v* have a slight flavour or trace (of)

smack³ *n* small single-masted fishing boat

small *adj* not large in size, number,

or amount; unimportant; mean or petty ▷ *n* narrow part of the lower back ▷ *pl Informal* underwear **smallness** *n* **smallholding** *n* small area of farming land **small hours** hours just after midnight **small-minded** *adj* intolerant, petty **smallpox** *n* contagious disease with blisters that leave scars **small talk** light social conversation **small-time** *adj* insignificant or minor

smarmy *adj* **smarmier, smarmiest** *Informal* unpleasantly suave or flattering

smart *adj* well-kept and neat; astute; witty; fashionable; brisk ▷ *v* feel or cause stinging pain ▷ *n* stinging pain **smartly** *adv* **smartness** *n* **smart aleck** *Informal* irritatingly clever person **smart card** plastic card used for storing and processing computer data **smarten** *v* make or become smart

smash *v* break violently and noisily; throw (against) violently; collide forcefully; destroy ▷ *n* act or sound of smashing; violent collision of vehicles; *Informal* popular success; *sport* powerful overhead shot **smasher** *n Informal* attractive person or thing **smashing** *adj Informal* excellent

smattering *n* slight knowledge

smear *v* spread with a greasy or sticky substance; rub so as to produce a dirty mark or smudge; slander ▷ *n* dirty mark or smudge; slander; *med* sample of a secretion smeared on to a slide for examination under a microscope

smell *v* **smelling, smelt** *or* **smelled** perceive (a scent or odour) by means of the nose; have or give off a smell; have an unpleasant smell; detect by instinct ▷ *n* ability to perceive odours by the nose; odour or scent; smelling **smelly** *adj* having a nasty smell **smelling salts** preparation of ammonia used to revive a person who feels faint

smelt[1] *v* extract (a metal) from (an ore) by heating

smelt[2] *n* small fish of the salmon family

smelt[3] *v* a past of **smell**

smelter *n* industrial plant where smelting is carried out

smile *n* turning up of the corners of the mouth to show pleasure, amusement, or friendliness ▷ *v* give a smile **smiley** *n* symbol depicting a smile or other facial expression, used in e-mail **smile on, upon** *v* regard favourably

smirch *v, n* stain

smirk *n* smug smile ▷ *v* give a smirk

smite *v* **smiting, smote, smitten** *old-fashioned* strike hard; affect severely

smith *n* worker in metal **smithy** *n* blacksmith's workshop

smithereens *pl n* shattered fragments

smitten *v* past participle of **smite**

smock *n* loose overall; woman's loose blouselike garment ▷ *v* gather (material) by sewing in a honeycomb pattern **smocking** *n*

smog *n* mixture of smoke and fog

smoke *n* cloudy mass that rises from something burning; act of smoking tobacco ▷ *v* give off smoke; inhale and expel smoke of (a cigar, cigarette, or pipe); do this habitually; cure (meat, fish, or cheese) by treating with smoke **smokeless** *adj* **smoker** *n* **smoky** *adj* **smoke screen** something said or done to hide the truth

smooch *Informal* ▷*v* kiss and cuddle ▷*n* smooching
smooth *adj* even in surface, texture, or consistency; without obstructions or difficulties; charming and polite but possibly insincere; free from jolts; not harsh in taste ▷*v* make smooth; calm **smoothie** *n Informal* charming but possibly insincere man; thick drink made from puréed fresh fruit **smoothly** *adv*
smorgasbord *n* buffet meal of assorted dishes
smote *v* past tense of **smite**
smother *v* suffocate or stifle; suppress; cover thickly
smoulder *v* burn slowly with smoke but no flame; (of feelings) exist in a suppressed state
SMS short message system: used for sending data to mobile phones
smudge *v* make or become smeared or soiled ▷*n* dirty mark; blurred form **smudgy** *adj*
smug *adj* **smugger, smuggest** self-satisfied **smugly** *adv* **smugness** *n*
smuggle *v* import or export (goods) secretly and illegally; take somewhere secretly **smuggler** *n*
smut *n* obscene jokes, pictures, etc; speck of soot or dark mark left by soot **smutty** *adj*
snack *n* light quick meal **snack bar** place where snacks are sold
snaffle *n* jointed bit for a horse ▷*v Brit, Aust & NZ, slang* steal
snag *n* difficulty or disadvantage; sharp projecting point; hole in fabric caused by a sharp object ▷*v* **snagging, snagged** catch or tear on a point
snail *n* slow-moving mollusc with a spiral shell **snail mail** *Informal* conventional post, as opposed to e-mail **snail's pace** very slow speed
snake *n* long thin scaly limbless reptile ▷*v* move in a winding course like a snake **snake in the grass** treacherous person **snaky** *adj* twisted or winding
snap *v* **snapping, snapped** break suddenly; (cause to) make a sharp cracking sound; move suddenly; bite (at) suddenly; speak sharply and angrily; take a snapshot of ▷*n* act or sound of snapping; *Informal* snapshot; sudden brief spell of cold weather; card game in which the word 'snap' is called when two similar cards are put down ▷*adj* made on the spur of the moment **snappy** *adj* (also **snappish**) irritable; *slang* quick; *slang* smart and fashionable **snapdragon** *n* plant with flowers that can open and shut like a mouth **snapper** *n* food fish of Australia and New Zealand with a pinkish body covered with blue spots **snapshot** *n* informal photograph **snap up** *v* take eagerly and quickly
snare *n* trap with a noose ▷*v* catch in or as if in a snare
snarl[1] *v* (of an animal) growl with bared teeth; speak or utter fiercely ▷*n* act or sound of snarling
snarl[2] *n* tangled mess ▷*v* make tangled **snarl-up** *n Informal* confused situation such as a traffic jam
snatch *v* seize or try to seize suddenly; take (food, rest, etc) hurriedly ▷*n* snatching; fragment
snazzy *adj* **-zier, -ziest** *Informal* stylish and flashy
sneak *v* move furtively; bring, take, or put furtively; *Informal* tell tales ▷*n* cowardly or underhand person **sneaking** *adj* slight but

persistent; secret **sneaky** *adj*
sneakers *pl n* canvas shoes with rubber soles
sneer *n* contemptuous expression or remark ▷ *v* show contempt by a sneer
sneeze *v* expel air from the nose suddenly, involuntarily, and noisily ▷ *n* act or sound of sneezing
snicker *n, v* same as **snigger**
snide *adj* critical in an unfair and nasty way
sniff *v* inhale through the nose in short audible breaths; smell by sniffing ▷ *n* act or sound of sniffing **sniffle** *v* sniff repeatedly, as when suffering from a cold ▷ *n* slight cold **sniff at** *v* express contempt for **sniffer dog** police dog trained to detect drugs or explosives by smell
snifter *n Informal* small quantity of alcoholic drink
snigger *n* sly disrespectful laugh, esp one partly stifled ▷ *v* utter a snigger
snip *v* **snipping, snipped** cut in small quick strokes with scissors or shears ▷ *n Informal* bargain; act or sound of snipping **snippet** *n* small piece
snipe *n* wading bird with a long straight bill ▷ *v* (foll by *at*) shoot at (a person) from cover; make critical remarks about
sniper *n* person who shoots at someone from cover
snitch *Informal* ▷ *v* act as an informer; steal ▷ *n* informer
snivel *v* **-elling, -elled** cry in a whining way
snob *n* person who judges others by social rank; person who feels smugly superior in his or her tastes or interests **snobbery** *n* **snobbish** *adj*
snoek *n SAfr* edible marine fish
snood *n* pouch, often of net, loosely holding a woman's hair at the back
snook *n* **cock a snook at** show contempt for
snooker *n* game played on a billiard table ▷ *v* leave (a snooker opponent) in a position such that another ball blocks the target ball; *Informal* put (someone) in a position where he or she can do nothing
snoop *Informal* ▷ *v* pry ▷ *n* snooping **snooper** *n*
snooty *adj* **snootier, snootiest** *Informal* haughty
snooze *Informal* ▷ *v* take a brief light sleep ▷ *n* brief light sleep
snore *v* make snorting sounds while sleeping ▷ *n* sound of snoring
snorkel *n* tube allowing a swimmer to breathe while face down on the surface of the water ▷ *v* **-kelling, -kelled** swim using a snorkel
snort *v* exhale noisily through the nostrils; express contempt or anger by snorting ▷ *n* act or sound of snorting
snot *n slang* mucus from the nose
snout *n* animal's projecting nose and jaws
snow *n* frozen vapour falling from the sky in flakes; *slang* cocaine ▷ *v* fall as or like snow **be snowed under** be overwhelmed, esp with paperwork **snowy** *adj* **snowball** *n* snow pressed into a ball for throwing ▷ *v* increase rapidly **snowboard** *n* board on which a person stands to slide across the snow **snowboarding** *n* **snowdrift** *n* bank of deep snow **snowdrop** *n* small white bell-shaped spring flower

snowflake *n* single crystal of snow **snow gum** same as **sallee** **snow line** (on a mountain) height above which there is permanent snow **snowman** *n* figure shaped out of snow **snowplough** *n* vehicle for clearing away snow **snowshoes** *pl n* racket-shaped shoes for travelling on snow

snub *v* **snubbing, snubbed** insult deliberately ▷ *n* deliberate insult ▷ *adj* (of a nose) short and blunt **snub-nosed** *adj*

snuff[1] *n* powdered tobacco for sniffing up the nostrils

snuff[2] *v* extinguish (a candle) **snuff it** *Informal* die

snuffle *v* breathe noisily or with difficulty

snug *adj* **snugger, snuggest** warm and comfortable; comfortably close-fitting ▷ *n* (in Britain and Ireland) small room in a pub **snugly** *adv*

snuggle *v* nestle into a person or thing for warmth or from affection

so *adv* to such an extent; in such a manner; very; also; thereupon ▷ *conj* in order that; with the result that; therefore ▷ *interj* exclamation of surprise, triumph, or realization **so-and-so** *n* *Informal* person whose name is not specified; unpleasant person or thing **so-called** *adj* called (in the speaker's opinion, wrongly) by that name **so long** goodbye **so that** in order that

soak *v* make wet; put or lie in liquid so as to become thoroughly wet; (of liquid) penetrate ▷ *n* soaking; *slang* drunkard **soaking** *n, adj* **soak up** *v* absorb

soap *n* compound of alkali and fat, used with water as a cleaning agent; *Informal* soap opera ▷ *v* apply soap to **soapy** *adj* **soap opera** radio or television serial dealing with domestic themes

soar *v* rise or fly upwards; increase suddenly

sob *v* **sobbing, sobbed** weep with convulsive gasps; utter with sobs ▷ *n* act or sound of sobbing **sob story** tale of personal distress told to arouse sympathy

sober *adj* not drunk; serious; (of colours) plain and dull ▷ *v* make or become sober **soberly** *adv* **sobriety** *n* state of being sober

sobriquet [**so**-brik-ay] *n* nickname

soccer *n* football played by two teams of eleven kicking a spherical ball

sociable *adj* friendly or companionable; (of an occasion) providing companionship **sociability** *n* **sociably** *adv*

social *adj* living in a community; of society or its organization; sociable ▷ *n* informal gathering **socially** *adv* **socialite** *n* member of fashionable society **socialize** *v* meet others socially **social security** state provision for the unemployed, elderly, or sick **social services** welfare services provided by local authorities or the state **social work** work which involves helping or advising people with serious financial or family problems

socialism *n* political system which advocates public ownership of industries, resources, and transport **socialist** *n, adj*

society *n, pl* **-ties** human beings considered as a group; organized community; structure and institutions of such a community; organized group with common aims and interests; upper-class or

fashionable people collectively; companionship
sociology *n* study of human societies **sociological** *adj* **sociologist** *n*
sock[1] *n* knitted covering for the foot
sock[2] *slang* ▷*v* hit hard ▷*n* hard blow
socket *n* hole or recess into which something fits
sod[1] *n* (piece of) turf
sod[2] *n slang* obnoxious person
soda *n* compound of sodium; soda water **soda water** fizzy drink made from water charged with carbon dioxide
sodden *adj* soaked
sodium *n chem* silvery-white metallic element **sodium bicarbonate** white soluble compound used in baking powder
sodomy *n* anal intercourse **sodomite** *n* person who practises sodomy
sofa *n* couch
soft *adj* easy to shape or cut; not hard, rough, or harsh; (of a breeze or climate) mild; (too) lenient; easily influenced or imposed upon; (of drugs) not liable to cause addiction **softly** *adv* **soften** *v* make or become soft or softer **soft drink** nonalcoholic drink **soft furnishings** curtains, rugs, lampshades, and furniture covers **soft option** easiest alternative **soft-pedal** *v* deliberately avoid emphasizing something **soft-soap** *v Informal* flatter **software** *n* computer programs **softwood** *n* wood of a coniferous tree
soggy *adj* **-gier, -giest** soaked; moist and heavy **sogginess** *n*
soigné, *fem* **soignée** [**swah**-nyay] *adj* well-groomed, elegant
soil[1] *n* top layer of earth; country or territory
soil[2] *v* make or become dirty; disgrace
soiree [**swah**-ray] *n* evening party or gathering
sojourn [**soj**-urn] *n* temporary stay ▷*v* stay temporarily
solace [**sol**-iss] *n, v* comfort in distress
solar *adj* of the sun; using the energy of the sun **solar plexus** network of nerves at the pit of the stomach; this part of the stomach **solar system** the sun and the heavenly bodies that go round it
solarium *n, pl* **-lariums, -laria** place with beds and ultraviolet lights used for acquiring an artificial suntan
sold *v* past of **sell**
solder *n* soft alloy used to join two metal surfaces ▷*v* join with solder **soldering iron** tool for melting and applying solder
soldier *n* member of an army ▷*v* serve in an army **soldierly** *adj* **soldier on** *v* persist doggedly
sole[1] *adj* one and only; not shared, exclusive **solely** *adv* only, completely; alone **sole charge school** *NZ* country school with only one teacher
sole[2] *n* underside of the foot; underside of a shoe ▷*v* provide (a shoe) with a sole
sole[3] *n* small edible flatfish
solecism [**sol**-iss-izz-um] *n* minor grammatical mistake; breach of etiquette
solemn *adj* serious, deeply sincere; formal **solemnly** *adv* **solemnity** *n*
solenoid [**sole**-in-oid] *n* coil of wire magnetized by passing a current through it

sol-fa *n* system of syllables used as names for the notes of a scale

solicit *v* **-iting, -ited** request; (of a prostitute) offer (a person) sex for money **solicitation** *n*

solicitor *n Brit, Aust & NZ* lawyer who advises clients and prepares documents and cases

solicitous *adj* anxious about someone's welfare **solicitude** *n*

solid *adj* (of a substance) keeping its shape; not liquid or gas; not hollow; of the same substance throughout; strong or substantial; sound or reliable; having three dimensions ▷ *n* three-dimensional shape; solid substance **solidly** *adv* **solidify** *v* make or become solid or firm **solidity** *n*

solidarity *n* agreement in aims or interests, total unity

soliloquy *n, pl* **-quies** speech made by a person while alone, esp in a play

solipsism *n* doctrine that the self is the only thing known to exist **solipsist** *n*

solitaire *n* game for one person played with pegs set in a board; gem set by itself

solitary *adj* alone, single; (of a place) lonely **solitude** *n* state of being alone

solo *n, pl* **-los** music for one performer; any act done without assistance ▷ *adj* done alone ▷ *adv* by oneself, alone **soloist** *n* **solo parent** *NZ* parent bringing up a child or children alone

solstice *n* either the shortest (in winter) or longest (in summer) day of the year

soluble *adj* able to be dissolved; able to be solved **solubility** *n*

solution *n* answer to a problem; act of solving a problem; liquid with something dissolved in it; process of dissolving

solve *v* find the answer to (a problem) **solvable** *adj*

solvent *adj* having enough money to pay one's debts ▷ *n* liquid capable of dissolving other substances **solvency** *n* **solvent abuse** deliberate inhaling of intoxicating fumes from certain solvents

sombre *adj* dark, gloomy

sombrero *n, pl* **-ros** wide-brimmed Mexican hat

some *adj* unknown or unspecified; unknown or unspecified quantity or number of; considerable number or amount of; *Informal* remarkable ▷ *pron* certain unknown or unspecified people or things; unknown or unspecified number or quantity **somebody** *pron* some person ▷ *n* important person **somehow** *adv* in some unspecified way **someone** *pron* somebody **something** *pron* unknown or unspecified thing or amount; impressive or important thing **sometime** *adv* at some unspecified time ▷ *adj* former **sometimes** *adv* from time to time, now and then **somewhat** *adv* to some extent, rather **somewhere** *adv* in, to, or at some unspecified or unknown place

somersault *n* leap or roll in which the trunk and legs are turned over the head ▷ *v* perform a somersault

somnambulist *n* person who walks in his or her sleep **somnambulism** *n*

somnolent *adj* drowsy

son *n* male offspring **son-in-law** *n, pl* **sons-in-law** daughter's husband

sonar *n* device for detecting underwater objects by the reflection of sound waves
sonata *n* piece of music in several movements for one instrument with or without piano
son et lumière [**sawn** eh **loo**-mee-er] *n French* night-time entertainment with lighting and sound effects, telling the story of the place where it is staged
song *n* music for the voice; tuneful sound made by certain birds; singing **for a song** very cheaply **songster, songstress** *n* singer **songbird** *n* any bird with a musical call
sonic *adj* of or producing sound **sonic boom** loud bang caused by an aircraft flying faster than sound
sonnet *n* fourteen-line poem with a fixed rhyme scheme
sonorous *adj* (of sound) deep or resonant **sonorously** *adv* **sonority** *n*
soon *adv* in a short time
sooner *adv* rather *eg I'd sooner go alone* **sooner or later** eventually
soot *n* black powder formed by the incomplete burning of an organic substance **sooty** *adj*
soothe *v* make calm; relieve (pain etc)
soothsayer *n* seer or prophet
sop *n* concession to pacify someone ▷ *v* **sopping, sopped** mop up or absorb (liquid) **sopping** *adj* completely soaked **soppy** *adj Informal* oversentimental
sophist *n* person who uses clever but invalid arguments
sophisticate *v* make less natural or innocent; make more complex or refined ▷ *n* sophisticated person
sophisticated *adj* having or appealing to refined or cultured tastes and habits; complex and refined **sophistication** *n*
sophistry, sophism *n* clever but invalid argument
sophomore *n US* student in second year at college
soporific *adj* causing sleep ▷ *n* drug that causes sleep
soprano *n, pl* **-pranos** (singer with) the highest female or boy's voice; highest pitched of a family of instruments
sorbet *n* flavoured water ice
sorcerer *n* magician **sorceress** *n fem* **sorcery** *n* witchcraft or magic
sordid *adj* dirty, squalid; base, vile; selfish and grasping **sordidly** *adv* **sordidness** *n*
sore *adj* painful; causing annoyance; resentful; (of need) urgent ▷ *n* painful area on the body ▷ *adv obs* greatly **sorely** *adv* greatly **soreness** *n*
sorghum *n* kind of grass cultivated for grain
sorrel *n* bitter-tasting plant
sorrow *n* grief or sadness; cause of sorrow ▷ *v* grieve **sorrowful** *adj* **sorrowfully** *adv*
sorry *adj* **-rier, -riest** feeling pity or regret; pitiful or wretched
sort *n* group all sharing certain qualities or characteristics; *Informal* type of character ▷ *v* arrange according to kind; mend or fix **out of sorts** slightly unwell or bad-tempered
sortie *n* relatively short return trip; operational flight made by military aircraft
SOS *n* international code signal of distress; call for help
so-so *adj Informal* mediocre
sot *n* habitual drunkard
sotto voce [**sot**-toe **voe**-chay] *adv* in an undertone

soubriquet [so-brik-ay] *n* same as sobriquet
soufflé [soo-flay] *n* light fluffy dish made with beaten egg whites and other ingredients
sough [rhymes with **now**] *v* (of the wind) make a sighing sound
sought [sawt] *v* past of **seek**
souk [sook] *n* marketplace in Muslim countries, often open-air
soul *n* spiritual and immortal part of a human being; essential part or fundamental nature; deep and sincere feelings; person regarded as typifying some quality; person; type of Black music combining blues, pop, and gospel **soulful** *adj* full of emotion **soulless** *adj* lacking human qualities, mechanical; (of a person) lacking sensitivity
sound[1] *n* something heard, noise ▷*v* make or cause to make a sound; seem to be as specified; pronounce **sound barrier** *Informal* sudden increase in air resistance against an object as it approaches the speed of sound **sound bite** short pithy sentence or phrase extracted from a longer speech, esp by a politician, for use on television or radio **soundproof** *adj* not penetrable by sound ▷*v* make soundproof **soundtrack** *n* recorded sound accompaniment to a film
sound[2] *adj* in good condition; firm, substantial; financially reliable; showing good judgment; ethically correct; (of sleep) deep; thorough **soundly** *adv*
sound[3] *v* find the depth of (water etc); examine (the body) by tapping or with a stethoscope; ascertain the views of **soundings** *pl n* measurements of depth taken by sounding **sounding board** person or group used to test a new idea
sound[4] *n* channel or strait
soup *n* liquid food made from meat, vegetables, etc **soupy** *adj* **soup kitchen** place where food and drink is served to needy people **souped-up** *adj* (of an engine) adjusted so as to be more powerful than normal
soupçon [soop-sonn] *n* small amount
sour *adj* sharp-tasting; (of milk) gone bad; (of a person's temperament) sullen ▷*v* make or become sour **sourly** *adv* **sourness** *n*
source *n* origin or starting point; person, book, etc providing information; spring where a river or stream begins
souse *v* plunge (something) into liquid; drench; pickle
soutane [soo-**tan**] *n* Roman Catholic priest's cassock
south *n* direction towards the South Pole, opposite north; area lying in or towards the south ▷*adj* to or in the south; (of a wind) from the south ▷*adv* in, to, or towards the south **southerly** *adj* **southern** *adj* **southerner** *n* person from the south of a country or area **southward** *adj, adv* **southwards** *adv* **southpaw** *n* *Informal* left-handed person, esp a boxer **South Pole** southernmost point on the earth's axis
souvenir *n* keepsake, memento
sou'wester *n* seaman's waterproof hat covering the head and back of the neck
sovereign *n* king or queen; former British gold coin worth one pound ▷*adj* (of a state) independent; supreme in rank or authority; excellent **sovereignty** *n*

soviet *n* formerly, elected council at various levels of government in the USSR ▷ *adj* (**S-**) of the former USSR

sow[1] [rhymes with **know**] *v* **sowing, sowed, sown** *or* **sowed** scatter or plant (seed) in or on (the ground); implant or introduce

sow[2] [rhymes with **cow**] *n* female adult pig

soya *n* plant whose edible bean (**soya bean**) is used for food and as a source of oil **soy sauce** sauce made from fermented soya beans, used in Chinese and Japanese cookery

sozzled *adj Brit, Aust & NZ, slang* drunk

spa *n* resort with a mineral-water spring

space *n* unlimited expanse in which all objects exist and move; interval; blank portion; unoccupied area; the universe beyond the earth's atmosphere ▷ *v* place at intervals **spacious** *adj* having a large capacity or area **spacecraft, spaceship** *n* vehicle for travel beyond the earth's atmosphere **space shuttle** manned reusable vehicle for repeated space flights **spacesuit** *n* sealed pressurized suit worn by an astronaut

spade[1] *n* tool for digging **spadework** *n* hard preparatory work

spade[2] *n* playing card of the suit marked with black leaf-shaped symbols

spaghetti *n* pasta in the form of long strings

span *n* space between two points; complete extent; distance from thumb to little finger of the expanded hand ▷ *v* **spanning, spanned** stretch or extend across

spangle *n* small shiny metallic ornament ▷ *v* decorate with spangles

spaniel *n* dog with long ears and silky hair

spank *v* slap with the open hand, on the buttocks or legs ▷ *n* such a slap **spanking** *n*

spanking *adj Informal* outstandingly fine or smart; quick

spanner *n* tool for gripping and turning a nut or bolt

spar[1] *n* pole used as a ship's mast, boom, or yard

spar[2] *v* **sparring, sparred** box or fight using light blows for practice; argue (with someone)

spare *adj* extra; in reserve; (of a person) thin ▷ *n* duplicate kept in case of damage or loss ▷ *v* refrain from punishing or harming; protect (someone) from (something unpleasant); afford to give **to spare** in addition to what is needed **sparing** *adj* economical **spare ribs** pork ribs with most of the meat trimmed off

spark *n* fiery particle thrown out from a fire or caused by friction; flash of light produced by an electrical discharge; trace or hint (of a particular quality) ▷ *v* give off sparks; initiate **sparkie** *n NZ, Informal* electrician **spark plug** device in an engine that ignites the fuel by producing an electric spark

sparkle *v* glitter with many points of light; be vivacious or witty ▷ *n* sparkling points of light; vivacity or wit **sparkler** *n* hand-held firework that emits sparks **sparkling** *adj* (of wine or mineral water) slightly fizzy

sparrow *n* small brownish bird **sparrowhawk** *n* small hawk

sparse *adj* thinly scattered **sparsely** *adv* **sparseness** *n*

spartan *adj* strict and austere
spasm *n* involuntary muscular contraction; sudden burst of activity or feeling **spasmodic** *adj* occurring in spasms **spasmodically** *adv*
spastic *n* person with cerebral palsy ▷ *adj* suffering from cerebral palsy; affected by spasms
spat[1] *n* slight quarrel
spat[2] *v* past of **spit**[1]
spate *n* large number of things happening within a period of time; sudden outpouring or flood
spatial *adj* of or in space
spats *pl n* coverings formerly worn over the ankle and instep
spatter *v* scatter or be scattered in drops over (something) ▷ *n* spattering sound; something spattered
spatula *n* utensil with a broad flat blade for spreading or stirring
spawn *n* jelly-like mass of eggs of fish, frogs, or molluscs ▷ *v* (of fish, frogs, or molluscs) lay eggs; generate
spay *v* remove the ovaries from (a female animal)
speak *v* **speaking, spoke, spoken** say words, talk; communicate or express in words; give a speech or lecture; know how to talk in (a specified language) **speaker** *n* person who speaks, esp at a formal occasion; loudspeaker; (**S-**) official chairman of a body
spear[1] *n* weapon consisting of a long shaft with a sharp point ▷ *v* pierce with or as if with a spear **spearhead** *v* lead (an attack or campaign) ▷ *n* leading force in an attack or campaign
spear[2] *n* slender shoot
spearmint *n* type of mint
spec *n* **on spec** *Informal* as a risk or gamble
special *adj* distinguished from others of its kind; for a specific purpose; exceptional; particular **specially** *adv* **specialist** *n* expert in a particular activity or subject **speciality** *n* special interest or skill; product specialized in **specialize** *v* be a specialist **specialization** *n*
specie *n* coins as distinct from paper money
species *n, pl* **-cies** group of plants or animals that are related closely enough to interbreed naturally
specific *adj* particular, definite ▷ *n* drug used to treat a particular disease ▷ *pl* particular details **specifically** *adv* **specification** *n* detailed description of something to be made or done **specify** *v* refer to or state specifically **specific gravity** ratio of the density of a substance to that of water
specimen *n* individual or part typifying a whole; sample of blood etc taken for analysis
specious [**spee**-shuss] *adj* apparently true, but actually false
speck *n* small spot or particle **speckle** *n* small spot ▷ *v* mark with speckles
specs *pl n* *Informal* short for **spectacles**
spectacle *n* strange, interesting, or ridiculous sight; impressive public show ▷ *pl* pair of glasses for correcting faulty vision **spectacular** *adj* impressive ▷ *n* spectacular public show **spectacularly** *adv*
spectator *n* person viewing anything, onlooker **spectate** *v* watch
spectre *n* ghost; menacing mental image **spectral** *adj*
spectrum *n, pl* **-tra** range of

different colours, radio waves, etc in order of their wavelengths; entire range of anything **spectroscope** *n* instrument for producing or examining spectra

speculate *v* guess, conjecture; buy property, shares, etc in the hope of selling them at a profit **speculation** *n* **speculative** *adj* **speculator** *n*

sped *v* a past of **speed**

speech *n* act, power, or manner of speaking; talk given to an audience; language or dialect **speechless** *adj* unable to speak because of great emotion

speed *n* swiftness; rate at which something moves or acts; *slang* amphetamine ▷ *v* **speeding, sped** *or* **speeded** go quickly; drive faster than the legal limit **speedy** *adj* prompt; rapid **speedily** *adv* **speedboat** *n* light fast motorboat **speed camera** *Brit, Aust & NZ* camera for photographing vehicles breaking the speed limit **speed dating** dating method in which each participant engages in a timed chat with all the others in turn **speedometer** *n* instrument to show the speed of a vehicle **speed up** *v* accelerate **speedway** *n* track for motorcycle racing; *US, Canadian & NZ* track for motor racing **speedwell** *n* plant with small blue flowers

speleology *n* study and exploration of caves

spell[1] *v* **spelling, spelt** *or* **spelled** give in correct order the letters that form (a word); (of letters) make up (a word); indicate **spelling** *n* way a word is spelt; person's ability to spell **spellchecker** *n computing* program that highlights wrongly spelled words in a word-processed document **spell out** *v* make explicit

spell[2] *n* formula of words supposed to have magic power; effect of a spell; fascination **spellbound** *adj* entranced

spell[3] *n* period of time of weather or activity; *Scot, Aust & NZ* period of rest

spelt *v* a past of **spell**[1]

spend *v* **spending, spent** pay out (money); use or pass (time); use up completely **spendthrift** *n* person who spends money wastefully

sperm *n, pl* **sperms** *or* **sperm** male reproductive cell; semen **spermicide** *n* substance that kills sperm **sperm whale** large toothed whale

spermaceti [sper-ma-**set**-ee] *n* waxy solid obtained from the sperm whale

spermatozoon [sper-ma-toe-**zoe**-on] *n, pl* **-zoa** sperm

spew *v* vomit; send out in a stream

sphagnum *n* moss found in bogs

sphere *n* perfectly round solid object; field of activity **spherical** *adj*

sphincter *n* ring of muscle which controls the opening and closing of a hollow organ

Sphinx *n* statue in Egypt with a lion's body and human head; (**s-**) enigmatic person

spice *n* aromatic substance used as flavouring; something that adds zest or interest ▷ *v* flavour with spices **spicy** *adj* flavoured with spices; *Informal* slightly scandalous

spick-and-span *adj* neat and clean

spider *n* small eight-legged creature which spins a web to catch insects for food **spidery** *adj*

spiel *n* speech made to persuade someone to do something

spigot *n* stopper for, or tap fitted to, a cask

spike *n* sharp point; sharp pointed metal object ▷*pl* sports shoes with spikes for greater grip ▷*v* put spikes on; pierce or fasten with a spike; add alcohol to (a drink) **spike someone's guns** thwart someone **spiky** *adj*

spill[1] *v* **spilling, spilt** *or* **spilled** pour from or as if from a container ▷*n* fall; amount spilt **spill the beans** *Informal* give away a secret **spillage** *n*

spill[2] *n* thin strip of wood or paper for lighting pipes or fires

spin *v* **spinning, spun** revolve or cause to revolve rapidly; draw out and twist (fibres) into thread; *Informal* present information in a way that creates a favourable impression ▷*n* revolving motion; continuous spiral descent of an aircraft; *Informal* short drive for pleasure; *Informal* presenting of information in a way that creates a favourable impression **spin a yarn** tell an improbable story **spinner** *n* **spin doctor** *Informal* person who provides a favourable slant to a news item or policy on behalf of a politician or a political party **spin-dry** *v* dry (clothes) in a spin-dryer **spin-dryer** *n* machine in which washed clothes are spun in a perforated drum to remove excess water **spin-off** *n* incidental benefit **spin out** *v* prolong

spina bifida *n* condition in which part of the spinal cord protrudes through a gap in the backbone, often causing paralysis

spinach *n* dark green leafy vegetable

spindle *n* rotating rod that acts as an axle; weighted rod rotated for spinning thread by hand **spindly** *adj* long, slender, and frail

spindrift *n* spray blown up from the sea

spine *n* backbone; edge of a book on which the title is printed; sharp point on an animal or plant **spinal** *adj* of the spine **spineless** *adj* lacking courage **spiny** *adj* covered with spines

spinet *n* small harpsichord

spinifex *n* coarse spiny Australian grass

spinnaker *n* large sail on a racing yacht

spinney *n* *Chiefly Brit* small wood

spinster *n* unmarried woman

spiral *n* continuous curve formed by a point winding about a central axis at an ever-increasing distance from it; steadily accelerating increase or decrease ▷*v* **-ralling, -ralled** move in a spiral; increase or decrease with steady acceleration ▷*adj* having the form of a spiral

spire *n* pointed part of a steeple

spirit[1] *n* nonphysical aspect of a person concerned with profound thoughts; nonphysical part of a person believed to live on after death; courage and liveliness; essential meaning as opposed to literal interpretation; ghost ▷*pl* emotional state ▷*v* **-iting, -ited** carry away mysteriously **spirited** *adj* lively

spirit[2] *n* liquid obtained by distillation **spirit level** glass tube containing a bubble in liquid, used to check whether a surface is level

spiritual *adj* relating to the spirit; relating to sacred things ▷*n* type of religious folk song originating among Black slaves in America

spiritually *adv* **spirituality** *n*
spiritualism *n* belief that the spirits of the dead can communicate with the living **spiritualist** *n*
spit¹ *v* **spitting, spat** eject (saliva or food) from the mouth; throw out particles explosively; rain slightly; utter (words) in a violent manner ▷ *n* saliva **spitting image** *Informal* person who looks very like another **spittle** *n* fluid produced in the mouth, saliva **spittoon** *n* bowl to spit into
spit² *n* sharp rod on which meat is skewered for roasting; long narrow strip of land jutting out into the sea
spite *n* deliberate nastiness ▷ *v* annoy or hurt from spite **in spite of** in defiance of **spiteful** *adj* **spitefully** *adv*
spitfire *n* person with a fiery temper
spiv *n* *Brit, Aust & NZ, slang* smartly dressed man who makes a living by shady dealings
splash *v* scatter liquid on (something); scatter (liquid) or (of liquid) be scattered in drops; print (a story or photograph) prominently in a newspaper ▷ *n* splashing sound; patch (of colour or light); extravagant display; small amount of liquid added to a drink **splash out** *v* *Informal* spend extravagantly
splatter *v, n* splash
splay *v* spread out, with ends spreading in different directions
spleen *n* abdominal organ which filters bacteria from the blood; bad temper **splenetic** *adj* spiteful or irritable
splendid *adj* excellent; brilliant in appearance **splendidly** *adv* **splendour** *n*
splice *v* join by interweaving or overlapping ends **get spliced** *slang* get married
splint *n* rigid support for a broken bone
splinter *n* thin sharp piece broken off, esp from wood ▷ *v* break into fragments **splinter group** group that has broken away from an organization
split *v* **splitting, split** break into separate pieces; separate; share ▷ *n* crack or division caused by splitting ▷ *pl* act of sitting with the legs outstretched in opposite directions **split second** very short period of time
splotch, splodge *n, v* splash, daub
splurge *v* spend money extravagantly ▷ *n* bout of extravagance
splutter *v* utter with spitting or choking sounds; make hissing spitting sounds ▷ *n* spluttering
spoil *v* **spoiling, spoilt** *or* **spoiled** damage; harm the character of (a child) by giving it all it wants; rot, go bad **spoils** *pl n* booty **spoiling for** eager for **spoilsport** *n* person who spoils the enjoyment of others
spoke¹ *v* past tense of **speak**
spoke² *n* bar joining the hub of a wheel to the rim
spoken *v* past participle of **speak**
spokesman, spokeswoman, spokesperson *n* person chosen to speak on behalf of a group
spoliation *n* plundering
sponge *n* sea animal with a porous absorbent skeleton; skeleton of a sponge, or a substance like it, used for cleaning; type of light cake ▷ *v* wipe with a sponge; live at the expense of others **sponger** *n* *slang* person who sponges on others **spongy** *adj*

sponsor *n* person who promotes something; person who agrees to give money to a charity on completion of a specified activity by another; godparent ▷*v* act as a sponsor for **sponsorship** *n*

spontaneous *adj* not planned or arranged; occurring through natural processes without outside influence **spontaneously** *adv* **spontaneity** *n*

spoof *n* mildly satirical parody

spook *n Informal* ghost **spooky** *adj*

spool *n* cylinder round which something can be wound

spoon *n* shallow bowl attached to a handle for eating, stirring, or serving food ▷*v* lift with a spoon **spoonful** *n* **spoonbill** *n* wading bird of warm regions with a long flat bill **spoon-feed** *v* feed with a spoon; give (someone) too much help

spoonerism *n* accidental changing over of the initial sounds of a pair of words, such as *half-warmed fish* for *half-formed wish*

spoor *n* trail of an animal

sporadic *adj* intermittent, scattered **sporadically** *adv*

spore *n* minute reproductive body of some plants

sporran *n* pouch worn in front of a kilt

sport *n* activity for pleasure, competition, or exercise; such activities collectively; enjoyment; playful joking; person who reacts cheerfully ▷*v* wear proudly **sporting** *adj* of sport; behaving in a fair and decent way **sporting chance** reasonable chance of success **sporty** *adj* **sportive** *adj* playful **sports car** fast low-built car, usu open-topped **sports jacket** man's casual jacket **sportsman, sportswoman** *n* person who plays sports; person who plays fair and is good-humoured when losing **sportsmanlike** *adj* **sportsmanship** *n*

spot *n* small mark on a surface; pimple; location; *Informal* small quantity; *Informal* awkward situation ▷*v* **spotting, spotted** notice; mark with spots; watch for and take note of **on the spot** at the place in question; immediately; in an awkward predicament **spotless** *adj* absolutely clean **spotlessly** *adv* **spotty** *adj* with spots **spot check** random examination **spotlight** *n* powerful light illuminating a small area; centre of attention **spot-on** *adj Informal* absolutely accurate

spouse *n* husband or wife

spout *v* pour out in a stream or jet; *slang* utter (a stream of words) lengthily ▷*n* projecting tube or lip for pouring liquids; stream or jet of liquid

sprain *v* injure (a joint) by a sudden twist ▷*n* such an injury

sprang *v* a past tense of **spring**

sprat *n* small sea fish

sprawl *v* lie or sit with the limbs spread out; spread out in a straggling manner ▷*n* part of a city that has spread untidily over a large area

spray[1] *n* (device for producing) fine drops of liquid ▷*v* scatter in fine drops; cover with a spray **spray gun** device for spraying paint etc

spray[2] *n* branch with buds, leaves, flowers, or berries; ornament like this

spread *v* **spreading, spread** open out or be displayed to the fullest extent; extend over a larger expanse; apply as a coating; send or be sent in all directions ▷*n* spreading; extent; *Informal* large meal; soft food which can be spread **spread-eagled** *adj* with arms and legs outstretched **spreadsheet** *n* computer program for manipulating figures

spree *n* session of overindulgence, usu in drinking or spending money

sprig *n* twig or shoot; *NZ* stud on the sole of a soccer or rugby boot

sprightly *adj* **-lier, -liest** lively and brisk **sprightliness** *n*

spring *v* **springing, sprang** *or* **sprung, sprung** move suddenly upwards or forwards in a single motion, jump; develop unexpectedly; originate (from); *Informal* arrange the escape of (someone) from prison ▷*n* season between winter and summer; jump; coil which can be compressed, stretched, or bent and returns to its original shape when released; natural pool forming the source of a stream; elasticity **springy** *adj* elastic **springboard** *n* flexible board used to gain height or momentum in diving or gymnastics **spring-clean** *v* clean (a house) thoroughly **spring tide** high tide at new or full moon

springbok *n* S African antelope

springer *n* small spaniel

sprinkle *v* scatter (liquid or powder) in tiny drops or particles over (something) **sprinkler** *n* **sprinkling** *n* small quantity or number

sprint *n* short race run at top speed; fast run ▷*v* run a short distance at top speed **sprinter** *n*

sprite *n* elf

sprocket *n* wheel with teeth on the rim, that drives or is driven by a chain

sprout *v* put forth shoots; begin to grow or develop ▷*n* shoot; short for **Brussels sprout**

spruce[1] *n* kind of fir

spruce[2] *adj* neat and smart **spruce up** *v* make neat and smart

sprung *v* a past of **spring**

spry *adj* **spryer, spryest** *or* **sprier, spriest** active or nimble

spud *n Informal* potato

spume *n, v* froth

spun *v* past of **spin**

spunk *n Informal* courage, spirit **spunky** *adj*

spur *n* stimulus or incentive; spiked wheel on the heel of a rider's boot used to urge on a horse; projection ▷*v* **spurring, spurred** urge on, incite (someone) **on the spur of the moment** on impulse

spurge *n* plant with milky sap

spurious *adj* not genuine

spurn *v* reject with scorn

spurt *v* gush or cause to gush out in a jet ▷*n* short sudden burst of activity or speed; sudden gush

sputnik *n* early Soviet artificial satellite

sputter *v, n* splutter

sputum *n, pl* **-ta** spittle, usu mixed with mucus

spy *n, pl* **spies** person employed to obtain secret information; person who secretly watches others ▷*v* **spying, spied** act as a spy; catch sight of

Sq. Square

squabble *v, n* (engage in) a petty or noisy quarrel

squad *n* small group of people working or training together

squadron *n* division of an air force, fleet, or cavalry regiment

squalid *adj* dirty and unpleasant;

morally sordid **squalor** *n* disgusting dirt and filth
squall[1] *n* sudden strong wind
squall[2] *v* cry noisily, yell ▷ *n* harsh cry
squander *v* waste (money or resources)
square *n* geometric figure with four equal sides and four right angles; open area in a town in this shape; product of a number multiplied by itself ▷ *adj* square in shape; denoting a measure of area; straight or level; fair and honest; with all accounts or debts settled ▷ *v* multiply (a number) by itself; make square; be or cause to be consistent ▷ *adv* squarely, directly **squarely** *adv* in a direct way; in an honest and frank manner **square dance** formation dance in which the couples form squares **square meal** substantial meal **square root** number of which a given number is the square **square up to** *v* prepare to confront (a person or problem)
squash[1] *v* crush flat; suppress; push into a confined space; humiliate with a crushing retort ▷ *n* sweet fruit drink diluted with water; crowd of people in a confined space; game played in an enclosed court with a rubber ball and long-handled rackets **squashy** *adj*
squash[2] *n* marrow-like vegetable
squat *v* **squatting, squatted** crouch with the knees bent and the weight on the feet; occupy unused premises to which one has no legal right ▷ *n* place where squatters live ▷ *adj* short and broad
squatter *n* illegal occupier of unused premises
squaw *n offens* Native American woman
squawk *n* loud harsh cry ▷ *v* utter a squawk
squeak *n* short shrill cry or sound ▷ *v* make or utter a squeak **squeaky** *adj*
squeal *n* long shrill cry or sound ▷ *v* make or utter a squeal; *slang* inform on someone to the police
squeamish *adj* easily sickened or shocked
squeegee *n* tool with a rubber blade for clearing water from a surface
squeeze *v* grip or press firmly; crush or press to extract liquid; push into a confined space; hug; obtain (something) by force or great effort ▷ *n* squeezing; amount extracted by squeezing; hug; crush of people in a confined space; restriction on borrowing
squelch *v* make a wet sucking sound, as by walking through mud ▷ *n* squelching sound
squib *n* small firework that hisses before exploding
squid *n* sea creature with a long soft body and ten tentacles
squiggle *n* wavy line **squiggly** *adj*
squint *v* have eyes which face in different directions; glance sideways ▷ *n* squinting condition of the eye; *Informal* glance ▷ *adj* crooked
squire *n* country gentleman, usu the main landowner in a community; *hist* knight's apprentice
squirm *v* wriggle, writhe; feel embarrassed ▷ *n* wriggling movement
squirrel *n* small bushy-tailed tree-living animal
squirt *v* force (a liquid) or (of a liquid) be forced out of a narrow opening; squirt liquid at ▷ *n* jet of

liquid; *Informal* small or insignificant person

squish *v, n* (make) a soft squelching sound **squishy** *adj*

Sr Senior; Señor

SS Schutzstaffel: Nazi paramilitary security force; steamship

St Saint; Street

st. stone (weight)

stab *v* **stabbing, stabbed** pierce with something pointed; jab (at) ▷ *n* stabbing; sudden unpleasant sensation; *Informal* attempt

stabilize *v* make or become stable **stabilization** *n* **stabilizer** *n* device for stabilizing a child's bicycle, an aircraft, or a ship

stable[1] *n* building in which horses are kept; establishment that breeds and trains racehorses; establishment that manages or trains several entertainers or athletes ▷ *v* put or keep (a horse) in a stable

stable[2] *adj* firmly fixed or established; firm in character; *science* not subject to decay or decomposition **stability** *n*

staccato [stak-**ah**-toe] *adj, adv music* with the notes sharply separated ▷ *adj* consisting of short abrupt sounds

stack *n* ordered pile; large amount; chimney ▷ *v* pile in a stack; control (aircraft waiting to land) so that they fly at different altitudes

stadium *n, pl* **-diums, -dia** sports arena with tiered seats for spectators

staff[1] *n* people employed in an organization; stick used as a weapon, support, etc ▷ *v* supply with personnel

staff[2] *n, pl* **staves** set of five horizontal lines on which music is written

stag *n* adult male deer **stag beetle** beetle with large branched jaws **stag night, party** party for men only

stage *n* step or period of development; platform in a theatre where actors perform; portion of a journey ▷ *v* put (a play) on stage; organize and carry out (an event) **the stage** theatre as a profession **stagey** *adj* overtheatrical **stagecoach** *n* large horse-drawn vehicle formerly used to carry passengers and mail **stage fright** nervousness felt by a person about to face an audience **stage whisper** loud whisper intended to be heard by an audience

stagger *v* walk unsteadily; astound; set apart to avoid congestion ▷ *n* staggering

stagnant *adj* (of water or air) stale from not moving; not growing or developing **stagnate** *v* be stagnant **stagnation** *n*

staid *adj* sedate, serious, and rather dull

stain *v* discolour, mark; colour with a penetrating pigment ▷ *n* discoloration or mark; moral blemish or slur; penetrating liquid used to colour things **stainless** *adj* **stainless steel** steel alloy that does not rust

stairs *pl n* flight of steps between floors, usu indoors **staircase, stairway** *n* flight of stairs with a handrail or banisters

stake[1] *n* pointed stick or post driven into the ground as a support or marker ▷ *v* support or mark out with stakes **stake a claim to** claim a right to **stake out** *v slang* (of police) keep (a place) under surveillance

stake[2] *n* money wagered; interest,

usu financial, held in something ▷*v* wager, risk; support financially **at stake** being risked **stakeholder** *n* person who has a concern or interest in something, esp a business

stalactite *n* lime deposit hanging from the roof of a cave

stalagmite *n* lime deposit sticking up from the floor of a cave

stale *adj* not fresh; lacking energy or ideas through overwork or monotony; uninteresting from overuse **staleness** *n*

stalemate *n chess* position in which any of a player's moves would put his king in check, resulting in a draw; deadlock, impasse

stalk[1] *n* plant's stem

stalk[2] *v* follow or approach stealthily; pursue persistently and, sometimes, attack (a person with whom one is obsessed); walk in a stiff or haughty manner **stalker** *n* person who follows or stealthily approaches a person or an animal; person who persistently pursues and, sometimes, attacks someone with whom he or she is obsessed **stalking-horse** *n* pretext

stall[1] *n* small stand for the display and sale of goods; compartment in a stable; small room or compartment ▷*pl* ground-floor seats in a theatre or cinema; row of seats in a church for the choir or clergy ▷*v* stop (a motor vehicle or engine) or (of a motor vehicle or engine) stop accidentally

stall[2] *v* employ delaying tactics

stallion *n* uncastrated male horse

stalwart [**stawl**-wart] *adj* strong and sturdy; dependable ▷*n* stalwart person

stamen *n* pollen-producing part of a flower

stamina *n* enduring energy and strength

stammer *v* speak or say with involuntary pauses or repetition of syllables ▷*n* tendency to stammer

stamp *n* (also **postage stamp**) piece of gummed paper stuck to an envelope or parcel to show that the postage has been paid; act of stamping; instrument for stamping a pattern or mark; pattern or mark stamped; characteristic feature ▷*v* bring (one's foot) down forcefully; walk with heavy footsteps; characterize; impress (a pattern or mark) on; stick a postage stamp on **stamping ground** favourite meeting place **stamp out** *v* suppress by force

stampede *n* sudden rush of frightened animals or of a crowd ▷*v* (cause to) take part in a stampede

stance *n* attitude; manner of standing

stanch [**stahnch**] *v* same as **staunch**[2]

stanchion *n* upright bar used as a support

stand *v* **standing, stood** be in, rise to, or place in an upright position; be situated; be in a specified state or position; remain unchanged or valid; tolerate; offer oneself as a candidate; *Informal* treat to ▷*n* stall for the sale of goods; structure for spectators at a sports ground; firmly held opinion; *US & Aust* witness box; rack or piece of furniture on which things may be placed **standing** *adj* permanent, lasting ▷*n* reputation or status; duration **stand for** *v* represent or mean; *Informal* tolerate **stand in** *v* act as a substitute **stand-in** *n* substitute **standoffish** *adj* reserved or haughty **stand up for** *v* support or defend

standard *n* level of quality; example against which others are judged or measured; moral principle; distinctive flag; upright pole ▷ *adj* usual, regular, or average; of recognized authority; accepted as correct **standardize** *v* cause to conform to a standard **standardization** *n* **standard lamp** lamp attached to an upright pole on a base

standpipe *n* tap attached to a water main to provide a public water supply

standpoint *n* point of view

standstill *n* complete halt

stank *v* a past tense of **stink**

stanza *n* verse of a poem

staple[1] *n* U-shaped piece of metal used to fasten papers or secure things ▷ *v* fasten with staples **stapler** *n* small device for fastening papers together

staple[2] *adj* of prime importance, principal ▷ *n* main constituent of anything

star *n* hot gaseous mass in space, visible in the night sky as a point of light; star-shaped mark used to indicate excellence; asterisk; celebrity in the entertainment or sports world ▷ *pl* astrological forecast, horoscope ▷ *v* **starring, starred** feature or be featured as a star; mark with a star or stars ▷ *adj* leading, famous **stardom** *n* status of a star in the entertainment or sports world **starry** *adj* full of or like stars **starry-eyed** *adj* full of naive optimism **starfish** *n* star-shaped sea creature

starboard *n* right-hand side of a ship, when facing forward ▷ *adj* of or on this side

starch *n* carbohydrate forming the main food element in bread, potatoes, etc, and used mixed with water for stiffening fabric ▷ *v* stiffen (fabric) with starch **starchy** *adj* containing starch; stiff and formal

stare *v* look or gaze fixedly (at) ▷ *n* fixed gaze

stark *adj* harsh, unpleasant, and plain; desolate, bare; absolute ▷ *adv* completely

starling *n* songbird with glossy black speckled feathers

start *v* take the first step, begin; set or be set in motion; make a sudden involuntary movement from fright; establish or set up ▷ *n* first part of something; place or time of starting; advantage or lead in a competitive activity; sudden movement made from fright **starter** *n* first course of a meal; device for starting a car's engine; person who signals the start of a race **start-up** *n* recently launched project or business enterprise ▷ *adj* recently launched *eg start-up grants*

startle *v* slightly surprise or frighten

starve *v* die or suffer or cause to die or suffer from hunger; deprive of something needed **starvation** *n*

stash *Informal* ▷ *v* store in a secret place ▷ *n* secret store

state *n* condition of a person or thing; sovereign political power or its territory; (**S-**) the government; *Informal* excited or agitated condition; pomp ▷ *adj* of or concerning the State; involving ceremony ▷ *v* express in words **stately** *adj* dignified or grand **statehouse** *n* *NZ* publicly-owned house rented to a low-income tenant **statement** *n* something stated; printed financial account **stateroom** *n* private cabin on a ship; large room in a palace, used for ceremonial occasions **statesman, stateswoman** *n* experienced and respected political leader **statesmanship** *n*

static *adj* stationary or inactive; (of a force) acting but producing no movement ▷ *n* crackling sound or speckled picture caused by interference in radio or television reception; (also **static electricity**) electric sparks produced by friction

station *n* place where trains stop for passengers; headquarters or local offices of the police or a fire brigade; building with special equipment for a particular purpose *eg power station*; television or radio channel; position in society; large Australian sheep or cattle property ▷ *v* assign (someone) to a particular place **station wagon** *US & Aust* car with a rear door and luggage space behind the rear seats

stationary *adj* not moving

> SPELLING The words **stationary** and **stationery** are completely different in meaning and should not be confused

stationery *n* writing materials such as paper and pens **stationer** *n* dealer in stationery

statistic *n* numerical fact collected and classified systematically **statistics** *n* science of classifying and interpreting numerical information **statistical** *adj* **statistically** *adv* **statistician** *n* person who compiles and studies statistics

statue *n* large sculpture of a human or animal figure **statuary** *n* statues collectively **statuesque** *adj* (of a woman) tall and well-proportioned **statuette** *n* small statue

stature *n* person's height; reputation of a person or their achievements

status *n* social position; prestige; person's legal standing **status quo** existing state of affairs

statute *n* written law **statutory** *adj* required or authorized by law

staunch[1] *adj* loyal, firm

staunch[2]**, stanch** *v* stop (a flow of blood)

stave *n* one of the strips of wood forming a barrel; *music* same as **staff**[2] **stave in** *v* **staving, stove** burst a hole in **stave off** *v* **staving, staved** ward off

stay[1] *v* remain in a place or condition; reside temporarily; endure; *Scot & SAfr* live permanently *eg where do you stay?* ▷ *n* period of staying in a place; postponement **staying power** stamina

stay[2] *n* prop or buttress ▷ *pl* corset

stay[3] *n* rope or wire supporting a ship's mast

STD sexually transmitted disease; *Brit, Aust & SAfr* subscriber trunk dialling; *NZ* subscriber toll dialling

stead *n* **in someone's stead** in someone's place **stand someone in good stead** be useful to someone

steadfast *adj* firm, determined **steadfastly** *adv*

steady *adj* **steadier, steadiest** not shaky or wavering; regular or continuous; sensible and dependable ▷ *v* **steadying, steadied** make steady ▷ *adv* in a steady manner **steadily** *adv* **steadiness** *n*

steak *n* thick slice of meat, esp beef; slice of fish
steal *v* **stealing, stole, stolen** take unlawfully or without permission; move stealthily
stealth *n* secret or underhand behaviour ▷ *adj* (of technology) able to render an aircraft almost invisible to radar; disguised or hidden *stealth taxes* **stealthy** *adj* **stealthily** *adv*
steam *n* vapour into which water changes when boiled; power, energy, or speed ▷ *v* give off steam; (of a vehicle) move by steam power; cook or treat with steam **steamer** *n* steam-propelled ship; container used to cook food in steam **steam engine** engine worked by steam **steamroller** *n* steam-powered vehicle with heavy rollers, used to level road surfaces ▷ *v* use overpowering force to make (someone) do what one wants
steed *n lit* horse
steel *n* hard malleable alloy of iron and carbon; steel rod used for sharpening knives; hardness of character or attitude ▷ *v* prepare (oneself) for something unpleasant **steely** *adj*
steep[1] *adj* sloping sharply; *Informal* (of a price) unreasonably high **steeply** *adv* **steepness** *n*
steep[2] *v* soak or be soaked in liquid **steeped in** filled with
steeple *n* church tower with a spire **steeplejack** *n* person who repairs steeples and chimneys
steeplechase *n* horse race with obstacles to jump; track race with hurdles and a water jump
steer[1] *v* direct the course of (a vehicle or ship); direct (one's course) **steerage** *n* cheapest accommodation on a passenger ship **steering wheel** wheel turned by the driver of a vehicle in order to steer it
steer[2] *n* castrated male ox
stein [stine] *n* earthenware beer mug
stellar *adj* of stars
stem[1] *n* long thin central part of a plant; long slender part, as of a wineglass; part of a word to which inflections are added ▷ *v* **stemming, stemmed stem from** originate from
stem[2] *v* **stemming, stemmed** stop (the flow of something)
stench *n* foul smell
stencil *n* thin sheet with cut-out pattern through which ink or paint passes to form the pattern on the surface below; pattern made thus ▷ *v* **-cilling, -cilled** make (a pattern) with a stencil
stenographer *n* shorthand typist
stent *n* surgical implant used to keep an artery open
stentorian *adj* (of a voice) very loud
step *v* **stepping, stepped** move and set down the foot, as when walking; walk a short distance ▷ *n* stepping; distance covered by a step; sound made by stepping; foot movement in a dance; one of a sequence of actions taken in order to achieve a goal; degree in a series or scale; flat surface for placing the foot on when going up or down ▷ *pl* stepladder **step in** *v* intervene **stepladder** *n* folding portable ladder with supporting frame **stepping stone** one of a series of stones for stepping on in crossing a stream; means of progress towards a goal **step up** *v* increase (something) by stages

step- *prefix* denoting a relationship created by the remarriage of a parent *eg stepmother*

steppes *pl n* wide grassy treeless plains in Russia and Ukraine

stereo *adj* short for **stereophonic** ▷ *n* stereophonic record player; stereophonic sound

stereophonic *adj* using two separate loudspeakers to give the effect of naturally distributed sound

stereotype *n* standardized idea of a type of person or thing ▷ *v* form a stereotype of

sterile *adj* free from germs; unable to produce offspring or seeds; lacking inspiration or vitality **sterility** *n* **sterilize** *v* make sterile **sterilization** *n*

sterling *n* British money system ▷ *adj* genuine and reliable

stern[1] *adj* severe, strict **sternly** *adv* **sternness** *n*

stern[2] *n* rear part of a ship

sternum *n, pl* **-na, -nums** same as **breastbone**

steroid *n* organic compound containing a carbon ring system, such as many hormones

stethoscope *n* medical instrument for listening to sounds made inside the body

Stetson *n* ® tall broad-brimmed hat, worn mainly by cowboys

stevedore *n* person who loads and unloads ships

stew *n* food cooked slowly in a closed pot; *Informal* troubled or worried state ▷ *v* cook slowly in a closed pot

steward *n* person who looks after passengers on a ship or aircraft; official who helps at a public event such as a race; person who administers another's property **stewardess** *n fem*

stick[1] *n* long thin piece of wood; such a piece of wood shaped for a special purpose *eg hockey stick;* something like a stick *eg stick of celery*; *slang* verbal abuse, criticism

stick[2] *v* **sticking, stuck** push (a pointed object) into (something); fasten or be fastened by or as if by pins or glue; (foll by *out*) extend beyond something else, protrude; *Informal* put; remain for a long time **sticker** *n* adhesive label or sign **sticky** *adj* covered with an adhesive substance; *Informal* difficult, unpleasant; (of weather) warm and humid **stick-in-the-mud** *n* person who does not like anything new **stick-up** *n slang* robbery at gunpoint **stick up for** *v Informal* support or defend

stickleback *n* small fish with sharp spines on its back

stickler *n* person who insists on something *eg stickler for detail*

stiff *adj* not easily bent or moved; severe *eg stiff punishment*; unrelaxed or awkward; firm in consistency; strong *eg a stiff drink* ▷ *n slang* corpse **stiffly** *adv* **stiffness** *n* **stiffen** *v* make or become stiff **stiff-necked** *adj* haughtily stubborn

stifle *v* suppress; suffocate

stigma *n, pl* **-mas, -mata** mark of social disgrace; part of a plant that receives pollen **stigmata** *pl n* marks resembling the wounds of the crucified Christ **stigmatize** *v* mark as being shameful

stile *n* set of steps allowing people to climb a fence

stiletto *n, pl* **-tos** high narrow heel on a woman's shoe; small slender dagger

still[1] *adv* now or in the future as before; up to this or that time; even or yet *eg still more insults*; quietly or without movement ▷ *adj* motionless; silent and calm, undisturbed; (of a drink) not fizzy ▷ *n* photograph from a film scene ▷ *v* make still **stillness** *n* **stillborn** *adj* born dead **still life** painting of inanimate objects

still² *n* apparatus for distilling alcoholic drinks

stilted *adj* stiff and formal in manner

stilts *pl n* pair of poles with footrests for walking raised from the ground; long posts supporting a building above ground level

stimulus *n, pl* **-li** something that rouses a person or thing to activity **stimulant** *n* something, such as a drug, that acts as a stimulus **stimulate** *v* act as a stimulus (on) **stimulation** *n*

sting *v* **stinging, stung** (of certain animals or plants) wound by injecting with poison; feel or cause to feel sharp physical or mental pain; *slang* cheat (someone) by overcharging ▷ *n* wound or pain caused by or as if by stinging; mental pain; sharp pointed organ of certain animals or plants by which poison can be injected

stingy *adj* **-gier, -giest** mean or miserly **stinginess** *n*

stink *n* strong unpleasant smell; *slang* unpleasant fuss ▷ *v* **stinking, stank** *or* **stunk, stunk** give off a strong unpleasant smell; *slang* be very unpleasant

stint *v* (foll by *on*) be miserly with (something) ▷ *n* allotted amount of work

stipend [sty-pend] *n* regular allowance or salary, esp that paid to a clergyman **stipendiary** *adj* receiving a stipend

stipple *v* paint, draw, or engrave using dots

stipulate *v* specify as a condition of an agreement **stipulation** *n*

stir *v* **stirring, stirred** mix up (a liquid) by moving a spoon etc around in it; move; excite or stimulate (a person) emotionally ▷ *n* a stirring; strong reaction, usu of excitement **stir-fry** *v* **-fries, -frying, -fried** cook (food) quickly by stirring it in a pan over a high heat ▷ *n, pl* **-fries** dish cooked in this way

stirrup *n* metal loop attached to a saddle for supporting a rider's foot

stitch *n* link made by drawing thread through material with a needle; loop of yarn formed round a needle or hook in knitting or crochet; sharp pain in the side ▷ *v* sew **in stitches** *Informal* laughing uncontrollably **not a stitch** *Informal* no clothes at all

stoat *n* small mammal of the weasel family, with brown fur that turns white in winter

stock *n* total amount of goods available for sale in a shop; supply stored for future use; financial shares in, or capital of, a company; liquid produced by boiling meat, fish, bones, or vegetables ▷ *pl hist* instrument of punishment consisting of a wooden frame with holes into which the hands and feet of the victim were locked ▷ *adj* kept in stock, standard; hackneyed ▷ *v* keep for sale or future use; supply (a farm) with livestock or (a lake etc) with fish **stockist** *n* dealer who stocks a particular product **stocky** *adj* (of a person) broad and sturdy **stockbroker** *n* person who buys and sells stocks and shares for customers **stock**

car car modified for a form of racing in which the cars often collide **stock exchange, market** institution for the buying and selling of shares **stockpile** *v* store a large quantity of (something) for future use ▷ *n* accumulated store **stock-still** *adj* motionless **stocktaking** *n* counting and valuing of the goods in a shop

stockade *n* enclosure or barrier made of stakes

stocking *n* close-fitting covering for the foot and leg

stodgy *adj* **stodgier, stodgiest** (of food) heavy and starchy; (of a person) serious and boring **stodge** *n Brit, Aust & NZ* heavy starchy food

stoep [stoop] *n SAfr* verandah

stoic [stow-ik] *n* person who suffers hardship without showing his or her feelings ▷ *adj* (also **stoical**) suffering hardship without showing one's feelings **stoically** *adv* **stoicism** [stow-iss-izz-um] *n*

stoke *v* feed and tend (a fire or furnace) **stoker** *n*

stole[1] *v* past tense of **steal**

stole[2] *n* long scarf or shawl

stolen *v* past participle of **steal**

stolid *adj* showing little emotion or interest **stolidly** *adv*

stomach *n* organ in the body which digests food; front of the body around the waist; desire or inclination ▷ *v* put up with

stomp *v Informal* tread heavily

stone *n* material of which rocks are made; piece of this; gem; hard central part of a fruit; unit of weight equal to 14 pounds or 6.350 kilograms; hard deposit formed in the kidney or bladder ▷ *v* throw stones at; remove stones from (a fruit) **stoned** *adj slang* under the influence of alcohol or drugs **stony** *adj* of or like stone; unfeeling or hard **stony-broke** *adj slang* completely penniless **stonily** *adv* **Stone Age** prehistoric period when tools were made of stone **stone-cold** *adj* completely cold **stone-deaf** *adj* completely deaf **stonewall** *v* obstruct or hinder discussion **stoneware** *n* hard kind of pottery fired at a very high temperature

stood *v* past of **stand**

stooge *n* actor who feeds lines to a comedian or acts as the butt of his jokes; *slang* person taken advantage of by a superior

stool *n* chair without arms or back; piece of excrement

stool pigeon *n* informer for the police

stoop *v* bend (the body) forward and downward; carry oneself habitually in this way; degrade oneself ▷ *n* stooping posture

stop *v* **stopping, stopped** cease or cause to cease from doing (something); bring to or come to a halt; prevent or restrain; withhold; block or plug; stay or rest ▷ *n* stopping or being stopped; place where something stops; full stop; knob on an organ that is pulled out to allow a set of pipes to sound **stoppage** *n* **stoppage time** same as **injury time** **stopper** *n* plug for closing a bottle etc **stopcock** *n* valve to control or stop the flow of fluid in a pipe **stopgap** *n* temporary substitute **stopover** *n* short break in a journey **stop press** news item put into a newspaper after printing has been started **stopwatch** *n* watch which can be stopped instantly for exact timing of a sporting event

store *v* collect and keep (things) for

future use; put (furniture etc) in a warehouse for safekeeping; stock (goods); *computers* enter or retain (data) ▷*n* shop; supply kept for future use; storage place, such as a warehouse ▷*pl* stock of provisions **in store** about to happen **set great store by** value greatly **storage** *n* storing; space for storing **storage heater** electric device that can accumulate and radiate heat generated by off-peak electricity

storey *n* floor or level of a building

stork *n* large wading bird

storm *n* violent weather with wind, rain, or snow; strongly expressed reaction ▷*v* attack or capture (a place) suddenly; shout angrily; rush violently or angrily **stormy** *adj* characterized by storms; involving violent emotions

story *n, pl* **-ries** description of a series of events told or written for entertainment; plot of a book or film; news report; *Informal* lie

stoup [**stoop**] *n* small basin for holy water

stout *adj* fat; thick and strong; brave and resolute ▷*n* strong dark beer **stoutly** *adv*

stove[1] *n* apparatus for cooking or heating

stove[2] *v* a past of **stave**

stow *v* pack or store **stowaway** *n* person who hides on a ship or aircraft in order to travel free **stow away** *v* hide as a stowaway

straddle *v* have one leg or part on each side of (something)

strafe *v* attack (an enemy) with machine guns from the air

straggle *v* go or spread in a rambling or irregular way **straggler** *n* **straggly** *adj*

straight *adj* not curved or crooked; level or upright; honest or frank; (of spirits) undiluted; *slang* heterosexual ▷*adv* in a straight line; immediately; in a level or upright position ▷*n* straight part, esp of a racetrack; *slang* heterosexual person **go straight** *Informal* reform after being a criminal **straighten** *v* **straightaway** *adv* immediately **straight face** serious facial expression concealing a desire to laugh **straightforward** *adj* honest, frank; (of a task) easy

strain[1] *v* cause (something) to be used or tested beyond its limits; make an intense effort; injure by overexertion; sieve ▷*n* tension or tiredness; force exerted by straining; injury from overexertion; great demand on strength or resources; melody or theme **strained** *adj* not natural, forced; not relaxed, tense **strainer** *n* sieve

strain[2] *n* breed or race; trace or streak

strait *n* narrow channel connecting two areas of sea ▷*pl* position of acute difficulty **straitjacket** *n* strong jacket with long sleeves used to bind the arms of a violent person **strait-laced, straight-laced** *adj* prudish or puritanical

straitened *adj* **in straitened circumstances** not having much money

strand[1] *v* run aground; leave in difficulties ▷*n* *poetic* shore

strand[2] *n* single thread of string, wire, etc

strange *adj* odd or unusual; not familiar; inexperienced (in) or unaccustomed (to) **strangely** *adv* **strangeness** *n*

stranger *n* person who is not

known or is new to a place or experience

strangle *v* kill by squeezing the throat; prevent the development of **strangler** *n* **strangulation** *n* strangling **stranglehold** *n* strangling grip in wrestling; powerful control

strap *n* strip of flexible material for lifting, fastening, or holding in place ▷ *v* **strapping, strapped** fasten with a strap or straps **strapping** *adj* tall and sturdy

strata *n* plural of **stratum**

stratagem *n* clever plan, trick

strategy *n, pl* **-gies** overall plan; art of planning in war **strategic** [strat-**ee**-jik] *adj* advantageous; (of weapons) aimed at an enemy's homeland **strategically** *adv* **strategist** *n*

strathspey *n* Scottish dance with gliding steps

stratosphere *n* atmospheric layer between about 15 and 50 kilometres above the earth

stratum [**strah**-tum] *n, pl* **strata** layer, esp of rock; social class **stratified** *adj* divided into strata **stratification** *n*

straw *n* dried stalks of grain; single stalk of straw; long thin tube used to suck up liquid into the mouth **straw poll** unofficial poll taken to determine general opinion

strawberry *n* sweet fleshy red fruit with small seeds on the outside **strawberry mark** red birthmark

stray *v* wander; digress; deviate from certain moral standards ▷ *adj* having strayed; scattered, random ▷ *n* stray animal

streak *n* long band of contrasting colour or substance; quality or characteristic; short stretch (of good or bad luck) ▷ *v* mark with streaks; move rapidly; *Informal* run naked in public **streaker** *n* **streaky** *adj*

stream *n* small river; steady flow, as of liquid, speech, or people; schoolchildren grouped together because of similar ability ▷ *v* flow steadily; move in unbroken succession; float in the air; group (pupils) in streams **streamer** *n* strip of coloured paper that unrolls when tossed; long narrow flag

streamline *v* make more efficient by simplifying; give (a car, plane, etc) a smooth even shape to offer least resistance to the flow of air or water

street *n* public road, usu lined with buildings **streetcar** *n US* tram **streetwise** *adj* knowing how to survive in big cities

strength *n* quality of being strong; quality or ability considered an advantage; degree of intensity; total number of people in a group **on the strength of** on the basis of **strengthen** *v*

strenuous *adj* requiring great energy or effort **strenuously** *adv*

streptococcus [strep-toe-**kok**-uss] *n, pl* **-cocci** bacterium occurring in chains, many species of which cause disease

stress *n* tension or strain; emphasis; stronger sound in saying a word or syllable; *physics* force producing strain ▷ *v* emphasize; put stress on (a word or syllable) **stressed-out** *adj Informal* suffering from tension

stretch *v* extend or be extended; be able to be stretched; extend the limbs or body; strain (resources or abilities) to the utmost ▷ *n* stretching; continuous expanse; period; *Informal* term of imprisonment **stretchy** *adj*

stretcher *n* frame covered with canvas, on which an injured person is carried

strew *v* **strewing, strewed, strewed** *or* **strewn** scatter (things) over a surface

striated *adj* having a pattern of scratches or grooves

stricken *adj* seriously affected by disease, grief, pain, etc

strict *adj* stern or severe; adhering closely to specified rules; complete, absolute **strictly** *adv* **strictness** *n*

stricture *n* severe criticism

stride *v* **striding, strode, stridden** walk with long steps ▷ *n* long step; regular pace ▷ *pl* progress

strident *adj* loud and harsh **stridently** *adv* **stridency** *n*

strife *n* conflict, quarrelling

strike *v* **striking, struck** cease work as a protest; hit; attack suddenly; ignite (a match) by friction; (of a clock) indicate (a time) by sounding a bell; enter the mind of; afflict; discover (gold, oil, etc); agree (a bargain) ▷ *n* stoppage of work as a protest **striking** *adj* impressive; noteworthy **strike camp** dismantle and pack up tents **strike home** have the desired effect **strike off, out** *v* cross out **strike up** *v* begin (a conversation or friendship); begin to play music

striker *n* striking worker; attacking player at soccer

string *n* thin cord used for tying; set of objects threaded on a string; series of things or events; stretched wire or cord on a musical instrument that produces sound when vibrated ▷ *pl* restrictions or conditions; section of an orchestra consisting of stringed instruments ▷ *v* **stringing, strung** provide with a string or strings; thread on a string **stringed** *adj* (of a musical instrument) having strings that are plucked or played with a bow **stringy** *adj* like string; (of meat) fibrous **pull strings** use one's influence **string along** *v* deceive over a period of time **string up** *v* *Informal* kill by hanging **stringy-bark** *n* Australian eucalyptus with a fibrous bark

stringent [strin-jent] *adj* strictly controlled or enforced **stringently** *adv* **stringency** *n*

strip¹ *v* **stripping, stripped** take (the covering or clothes) off; take a title or possession away from (someone); dismantle (an engine) **stripper** *n* person who performs a striptease **striptease** *n* entertainment in which a performer undresses to music

strip² *n* long narrow piece; *Brit, Aust & NZ* clothes a sports team plays in **strip cartoon** sequence of drawings telling a story

stripe *n* long narrow band of contrasting colour or substance; chevron or band worn on a uniform to indicate rank **striped, stripy, stripey** *adj*

stripling *n* youth

strive *v* **striving, strove, striven** make a great effort

strobe *n* short for **stroboscope**

stroboscope *n* instrument producing a very bright flashing light

strode *v* past tense of **stride**

stroke *v* touch or caress lightly with the hand ▷ *n* light touch or caress with the hand; rupture of a blood vessel in the brain; blow; action or occurrence of the kind specified *eg a stroke of luck*; chime of a clock; mark made by a pen or paintbrush; style or method of swimming

stroll *v* walk in a leisurely manner ▷*n* leisurely walk

strong *adj* having physical power; not easily broken; great in degree or intensity; having moral force; having a specified number *eg twenty strong* **strongly** *adv* **stronghold** *n* area of predominance of a particular belief; fortress **strongroom** *n* room designed for the safekeeping of valuables

strontium *n chem* silvery-white metallic element

strop *n* leather strap for sharpening razors

stroppy *adj* **-pier, -piest** *slang* angry or awkward

strove *v* past tense of **strive**

struck *v* past of **strike**

structure *n* complex construction; manner or basis of construction or organization ▷*v* give a structure to **structural** *adj* **structuralism** *n* approach to literature, social sciences, etc, which sees changes in the subject as caused and organized by a hidden set of universal rules **structuralist** *n, adj*

strudel *n* thin sheet of filled dough rolled up and baked, usu with an apple filling

struggle *v* work, strive, or make one's way with difficulty; move about violently in an attempt to get free; fight (with someone) ▷*n* striving; fight

strum *v* **strumming, strummed** play (a guitar or banjo) by sweeping the thumb or a plectrum across the strings

strumpet *n old-fashioned* prostitute

strung *v* past of **string**

strut *v* **strutting, strutted** walk pompously, swagger ▷*n* bar supporting a structure

strychnine [**strik**-neen] *n* very poisonous drug used in small quantities as a stimulant

stub *n* short piece left after use; counterfoil of a cheque or ticket ▷*v* **stubbing, stubbed** strike (the toe) painfully against an object; put out (a cigarette) by pressing the end against a surface **stubby** *adj* short and broad

stubble *n* short stalks of grain left in a field after reaping; short growth of hair on the chin of a man who has not shaved recently **stubbly** *adj*

stubborn *adj* refusing to agree or give in; difficult to deal with **stubbornly** *adv* **stubbornness** *n*

stucco *n* plaster used for coating or decorating walls

stuck *v* past of **stick²** **stuck-up** *adj Informal* conceited or snobbish

stud¹ *n* small piece of metal attached to a surface for decoration; disc-like removable fastener for clothes; one of several small round objects fixed to the sole of a football boot to give better grip ▷*v* **studding, studded** set with studs

stud² *n* male animal, esp a stallion, kept for breeding; (also **stud farm**) place where horses are bred; *slang* virile or sexually active man

student *n* person who studies a subject, esp at university

studio *n, pl* **-dios** workroom of an artist or photographer; room or building in which television or radio programmes, records, or films are made **studio flat** *Brit* one-room flat with a small kitchen and bathroom

study *v* **studying, studied** be engaged in learning (a subject); investigate by observation and research; scrutinize ▷ *n, pl* **studies** act or process of studying; room for studying in; book or paper produced as a result of study; sketch done as practice or preparation; musical composition designed to improve playing technique **studied** *adj* carefully practised or planned **studious** *adj* fond of study; careful and deliberate **studiously** *adv*

stuff *n* substance or material; collection of unnamed things ▷ *v* pack, cram, or fill completely; fill (food) with a seasoned mixture; fill (an animal's skin) with material to restore the shape of the live animal **stuffing** *n* seasoned mixture with which food is stuffed; padding

stuffy *adj* **stuffier, stuffiest** lacking fresh air; *Informal* dull or conventional

stultifying *adj* very boring and repetitive

stumble *v* trip and nearly fall; walk in an unsure way; make frequent mistakes in speech ▷ *n* stumbling **stumble across** *v* discover accidentally **stumbling block** obstacle or difficulty

stump *n* base of a tree left when the main trunk has been cut away; part of a thing left after a larger part has been removed; *cricket* one of the three upright sticks forming the wicket ▷ *v* baffle; *cricket* dismiss (a batsman) by breaking his wicket with the ball; walk with heavy steps **stumpy** *adj* short and thick **stump up** *v* *Informal* give (the money required)

stun *v* **stunning, stunned** shock or overwhelm; knock senseless **stunning** *adj* very attractive or impressive

stung *v* past of **sting**

stunk *v* a past of **stink**

stunt¹ *v* prevent or impede the growth of **stunted** *adj*

stunt² *n* acrobatic or dangerous action; anything spectacular done to gain publicity

stupefy *v* **-fying, -fied** make insensitive or lethargic; astound **stupefaction** *n*

stupendous *adj* very large or impressive **stupendously** *adv*

stupid *adj* lacking intelligence; silly; in a stupor **stupidity** *n* **stupidly** *adv*

stupor *n* dazed or unconscious state

sturdy *adj* **-dier, -diest** healthy and robust; strongly built **sturdily** *adv*

sturgeon *n* fish from which caviar is obtained

stutter *v* speak with repetition of initial consonants ▷ *n* tendency to stutter

sty *n, pl* **sties** pen for pigs

stye, sty *n, pl* **styes, sties** inflammation at the base of an eyelash

style *n* shape or design; manner of writing, speaking, or doing something; elegance, refinement; prevailing fashion ▷ *v* shape or design; name or call **stylish** *adj* smart, elegant, and fashionable **stylishly** *adv* **stylist** *n* hairdresser; person who writes or performs with great attention to style **stylistic** *adj* of literary or artistic style **stylize** *v* cause to conform to an established stylistic form

stylus *n* needle-like device on a record player that rests in the groove of the record and picks up the sound signals

stymie *v* **-mieing, -mied** hinder or thwart

styptic *n, adj* (drug) used to stop bleeding

suave [swahv] *adj* smooth and sophisticated in manner **suavely** *adv*

sub *n* subeditor; submarine; subscription; substitute; *Brit, Informal* advance payment of wages or salary ▷ *v* **subbing, subbed** act as a substitute; grant advance payment to

sub- *prefix* used with many main words to mean: under or beneath *eg submarine*; subordinate *eg sublieutenant*; falling short of *eg subnormal*; forming a subdivision *eg subheading*

subaltern *n* British army officer below the rank of captain

subatomic *adj* of or being one of the particles which make up an atom

subcommittee *n* small committee formed from some members of a larger committee

subconscious *adj* happening or existing without one's awareness ▷ *n psychoanalysis* that part of the mind of which one is not aware but which can influence one's behaviour **subconsciously** *adv*

subcontinent *n* large land mass that is a distinct part of a continent

subcontract *n* secondary contract by which the main contractor for a job puts work out to others ▷ *v* put out (work) on a subcontract **subcontractor** *n*

subcutaneous [sub-cute-**ayn**-ee-uss] *adj* under the skin

subdivide *v* divide (a part of something) into smaller parts **subdivision** *n*

subdue *v* **-duing, -dued** overcome; make less intense

subeditor *n* person who checks and edits text for a newspaper or magazine

subject *n* person or thing being dealt with or studied; *grammar* word or phrase that represents the person or thing performing the action of the verb in a sentence; person under the rule of a monarch or government ▷ *adj* being under the rule of a monarch or government ▷ *v* (foll by *to*) cause to undergo **subject to** liable to; conditional upon **subjection** *n* **subjective** *adj* based on personal feelings or prejudices **subjectively** *adv*

sub judice [sub **joo**-diss-ee] *adj Latin* before a court of law and therefore prohibited from public discussion

subjugate *v* bring (a group of people) under one's control **subjugation** *n*

subjunctive *grammar* ▷ *n* mood of verbs used when the content of the clause is doubted, supposed, or wished ▷ *adj* in or of that mood

sublet *v* **-letting, -let** rent out (property rented from someone else)

sublimate *v psychol* direct the energy of (a strong desire, esp a sexual one) into socially acceptable activities **sublimation** *n*

sublime *adj* of high moral, intellectual, or spiritual value; unparalleled, supreme ▷ *v chem* change from a solid to a vapour without first melting **sublimely** *adv*

subliminal *adj* relating to mental processes of which the individual is

not aware
sub-machine-gun *n* portable machine gun with a short barrel
submarine *n* vessel which can operate below the surface of the sea ▷ *adj* below the surface of the sea
submerge *v* put or go below the surface of water or other liquid **submersion** *n*
submit *v* **-mitting, -mitted** surrender; put forward for consideration; be (voluntarily) subjected to a process or treatment **submission** *n* submitting; something submitted for consideration; state of being submissive **submissive** *adj* meek and obedient
subordinate *adj* of lesser rank or importance ▷ *n* subordinate person or thing ▷ *v* make or treat as subordinate **subordination** *n*
suborn *v formal* bribe or incite (a person) to commit a wrongful act
subpoena [sub-**pee**-na] *n* writ requiring a person to appear before a lawcourt ▷ *v* summon (someone) with a subpoena
subscribe *v* pay (a subscription); give support or approval (to) **subscriber** *n* **subscription** *n* payment for issues of a publication over a period; money contributed to a charity etc; membership fees paid to a society
subsection *n* division of a section
subsequent *adj* occurring after, succeeding **subsequently** *adv*
subservient *adj* submissive, servile **subservience** *n*
subside *v* become less intense; sink to a lower level **subsidence** *n* act or process of subsiding
subsidiary *adj* of lesser importance ▷ *n, pl* **-aries** subsidiary person or thing
subsidize *v* help financially **subsidy** *n, pl* **-dies** financial aid
subsist *v* manage to live **subsistence** *n*
subsonic *adj* moving at a speed less than that of sound
substance *n* physical composition of something; solid, powder, liquid, or paste; essential meaning of something; solid or meaningful quality; wealth **substantial** *adj* of considerable size or value; (of food or a meal) sufficient and nourishing; solid or strong; real **substantially** *adv* **substantiate** *v* support (a story) with evidence **substantiation** *n* **substantive** *n* noun ▷ *adj* of or being the essential element of a thing
substitute *v* take the place of or put in place of another ▷ *n* person or thing taking the place of (another) **substitution** *n*
subsume *v* include (an idea, case, etc) under a larger classification or group
subterfuge *n* trick used to achieve an objective
subterranean *adj* underground
subtitle *n* secondary title of a book ▷ *pl* printed translation at the bottom of the picture in a film with foreign dialogue ▷ *v* provide with a subtitle or subtitles
subtle *adj* not immediately obvious; having or requiring ingenuity **subtly** *adv* **subtlety** *n*
subtract *v* take (one number or quantity) from another **subtraction** *n*
subtropical *adj* of the regions bordering on the tropics
suburb *n* residential area on the outskirts of a city **suburban** *adj* of or inhabiting a suburb; narrow or

unadventurous in outlook **suburbia** *n* suburbs and their inhabitants

subvention *n formal* subsidy

subvert *v* overthrow the authority of **subversion** *n* **subversive** *adj, n*

subway *n* passage under a road or railway; underground railway

succeed *v* accomplish an aim; turn out satisfactorily; come next in order after (something); take over a position from (someone) **success** *n* achievement of something attempted; attainment of wealth, fame, or position; successful person or thing **successful** *adj* having success **successfully** *adv* **succession** *n* series of people or things following one another in order; act or right by which one person succeeds another in a position **successive** *adj* consecutive **successively** *adv* **successor** *n* person who succeeds someone in a position

> SPELLING Collins Word Web evidence shows that people are able to remember the double *s* at the end of **success** more easily than the double *c* in the middle

succinct *adj* brief and clear **succinctly** *adv*

succour *v, n* help in distress

succulent *adj* juicy and delicious; (of a plant) having thick fleshy leaves ▷*n* succulent plant **succulence** *n*

succumb *v* (foll by *to*) give way (to something overpowering); die of (an illness)

such *adj* of the kind specified; so great, so much ▷*pron* such things **such-and-such** *adj* specific, but not known or named **suchlike** *pron* such or similar things

suck *v* draw (liquid or air) into the mouth; take (something) into the mouth and moisten, dissolve, or roll it around with the tongue; (foll by *in*) draw in by irresistible force ▷*n* sucking **sucker** *n slang* person who is easily deceived or swindled; organ or device which adheres by suction; shoot coming from a plant's root or the base of its main stem **suck up to** *v Informal* flatter (someone) for one's own profit

suckle *v* feed at the breast **suckling** *n* unweaned baby or young animal

sucrose [**soo**-kroze] *n* chemical name for sugar

suction *n* sucking; force produced by drawing air out of a space to make a vacuum that will suck in a substance from another space

sudden *adj* done or occurring quickly and unexpectedly **all of a sudden** quickly and unexpectedly **suddenly** *adv* **suddenness** *n* **sudden death** *sport* period of extra time in which the first competitor to score wins

sudorific [syoo-dor-**if**-ik] *n, adj* (drug) causing sweating

suds *pl n* froth of soap and water, lather

sue *v* **suing, sued** start legal proceedings against

suede *n* leather with a velvety finish on one side

suet *n* hard fat obtained from sheep and cattle, used in cooking

suffer *v* undergo or be subjected to; tolerate **sufferer** *n* **suffering** *n* **sufferance** *n* **on sufferance** tolerated with reluctance

suffice [suf-**fice**] *v* be enough for a purpose

sufficient *adj* enough, adequate **sufficiency** *n* adequate amount

sufficiently *adv*
suffix *n* letter or letters added to the end of a word to form another word, such as *-s* and *-ness* in *dogs* and *softness*
suffocate *v* kill or be killed by deprivation of oxygen; feel uncomfortable from heat and lack of air **suffocation** *n*
suffragan *n* bishop appointed to assist an archbishop
suffrage *n* right to vote in public elections **suffragette** *n* (in Britain in the early 20th century) a woman who campaigned militantly for the right to vote
suffuse *v* spread through or over (something) **suffusion** *n*
sugar *n* sweet crystalline carbohydrate found in many plants and used to sweeten food and drinks ▷*v* sweeten or cover with sugar **sugary** *adj* **sugar beet** beet grown for the sugar obtained from its roots **sugar cane** tropical grass grown for the sugar obtained from its canes **sugar daddy** *slang* elderly man who gives a young woman money and gifts in return for sexual favours **sugar glider** common Australian phalanger that glides from tree to tree feeding on insects and nectar
suggest *v* put forward (an idea) for consideration; bring to mind by the association of ideas; give a hint of **suggestible** *adj* easily influenced **suggestion** *n* thing suggested; hint or indication **suggestive** *adj* suggesting something indecent; conveying a hint (of) **suggestively** *adv*
suicide *n* killing oneself intentionally; person who kills himself intentionally; self-inflicted ruin of one's own prospects or interests **suicidal** *adj* liable to commit suicide **suicidally** *adv*
suit *n* set of clothes designed to be worn together; outfit worn for a specific purpose; one of the four sets into which a pack of cards is divided; lawsuit ▷*v* be appropriate for; be acceptable to **suitable** *adj* appropriate or proper **suitably** *adv* **suitability** *n* **suitcase** *n* portable travelling case for clothing
suite *n* set of connected rooms in a hotel; matching set of furniture; set of musical pieces in the same key
suitor *n* *old-fashioned* man who is courting a woman
sulk *v* be silent and sullen because of resentment or bad temper ▷*n* resentful or sullen mood **sulky** *adj* **sulkily** *adv*
sullen *adj* unwilling to talk or be sociable **sullenly** *adv* **sullenness** *n*
sully *v* **-lying, -lied** ruin (someone's reputation); make dirty
sulphate *n* salt or ester of sulphuric acid
sulphide *n* compound of sulphur with another element
sulphite *n* salt or ester of sulphurous acid
sulphonamide [sulf-**on**-a-mide] *n* any of a class of drugs that prevent the growth of bacteria
sulphur *n chem* pale yellow nonmetallic element **sulphuric, sulphurous** *adj* of or containing sulphur
sultan *n* sovereign of a Muslim country **sultana** *n* kind of raisin; sultan's wife, mother, or daughter **sultanate** *n* territory of a sultan
sultry *adj* **-trier, -triest** (of weather or climate) hot and humid; passionate, sensual
sum *n* result of addition, total;

problem in arithmetic; quantity of money **sum total** complete or final total **sum up** *v* **summing, summed** summarize; form a quick opinion of

summary *n, pl* **-ries** brief account giving the main points of something ▷ *adj* done quickly, without formalities **summarily** *adv* **summarize** *v* make or be a summary of (something) **summation** *n* summary; adding up

summer *n* warmest season of the year, between spring and autumn **summery** *adj* **summerhouse** *n* small building in a garden **summertime** *n* period or season of summer

summit *n* top of a mountain or hill; highest point; conference between heads of state or other high officials

summon *v* order (someone) to come; call upon (someone) to do something; gather (one's courage, strength, etc) **summons** *n* command summoning someone; order requiring someone to appear in court ▷ *v* order (someone) to appear in court

sumo *n* Japanese style of wrestling

sump *n* container in an internal-combustion engine into which oil can drain; hollow into which liquid drains

sumptuous *adj* lavish, magnificent **sumptuously** *adv*

sun *n* star around which the earth and other planets revolve; any star around which planets revolve; heat and light from the sun ▷ *v* **sunning, sunned** expose (oneself) to the sun's rays **sunless** *adj* **sunny** *adj* full of or exposed to sunlight; cheerful **sunbathe** *v* lie in the sunshine in order to get a suntan **sunbeam** *n* ray of sun **sunburn** *n* painful reddening of the skin caused by overexposure to the sun **sunburnt, sunburned** *adj* **sundial** *n* device showing the time by means of a pointer that casts a shadow on a marked dial **sundown** *n* sunset **sunflower** *n* tall plant with large golden flowers **sunrise** *n* daily appearance of the sun above the horizon; time of this **sunset** *n* daily disappearance of the sun below the horizon; time of this **sunshine** *n* light and warmth from the sun **sunspot** *n* dark patch appearing temporarily on the sun's surface; *Aust* small area of skin damage caused by exposure to the sun **sunstroke** *n* illness caused by prolonged exposure to intensely hot sunlight **suntan** *n* browning of the skin caused by exposure to the sun

sundae *n* ice cream topped with fruit etc

Sunday *n* first day of the week and the Christian day of worship **Sunday school** school for teaching children about Christianity

sundry *adj* several, various **sundries** *pl n* several things of various sorts **all and sundry** everybody

sung *v* past participle of **sing**

sunk *v* a past participle of **sink**

sunken *v* a past participle of **sink**

sup *v* **supping, supped** take (liquid) by sips ▷ *n* sip

super *adj Informal* excellent

super- *prefix* used with many main words to mean: above or over *eg superimpose*; outstanding *eg superstar*; of greater size or extent *eg supermarket*

superannuation *n* regular payment by an employee into a pension fund; pension paid from this **superannuated** *adj* discharged with a pension, owing to old age or illness

superb *adj* excellent, impressive, or splendid **superbly** *adv*

superbug *n Informal* bacterium resistant to antibiotics

supercharged *adj* (of an engine) having a supercharger **supercharger** *n* device that increases the power of an internal-combustion engine by forcing extra air into it

supercilious *adj* showing arrogant pride or scorn

superconductor *n* substance which has almost no electrical resistance at very low temperatures **superconductivity** *n*

superficial *adj* not careful or thorough; (of a person) without depth of character, shallow; of or on the surface **superficially** *adv* **superficiality** *n*

superfluous [soo-**per**-flew-uss] *adj* more than is needed **superfluity** *n*

superhuman *adj* beyond normal human ability or experience

superimpose *v* place (something) on or over something else

superintendent *n* senior police officer; supervisor **superintend** *v* supervise (a person or activity)

superior *adj* greater in quality, quantity, or merit; higher in position or rank; believing oneself to be better than others ▷ *n* person of greater rank or status **superiority** *n*

superlative [soo-**per**-lat-iv] *adj* of outstanding quality; *grammar* denoting the form of an adjective or adverb indicating *most* ▷ *n grammar* superlative form of a word

superman *n* man with great physical or mental powers

supermarket *n* large self-service store selling food and household goods

supermodel *n* famous and highly-paid fashion model

supernatural *adj* of or relating to things beyond the laws of nature **the supernatural** supernatural forces, occurrences, and beings collectively

supernova *n, pl* **-vae, -vas** star that explodes and briefly becomes exceptionally bright

supernumerary *adj* exceeding the required or regular number ▷ *n, pl* **-ries** supernumerary person or thing

superpower *n* extremely powerful nation

superscript *n, adj* (character) printed above the line

supersede *v* replace, supplant

> SPELLING Although there is a word 'cede', spelt with a *c*, the word **supersede** must have an *s* in the middle

supersonic *adj* of or travelling at a speed greater than the speed of sound

superstition *n* belief in omens, ghosts, etc; idea or practice based on this **superstitious** *adj*

superstore *n* large supermarket

superstructure *n* structure erected on something else; part of a ship above the main deck

supervene *v* occur as an unexpected development

supervise *v* watch over to direct or check **supervision** *n* **supervisor** *n* **supervisory** *adj*

supine *adj* lying flat on one's back

supper *n* light evening meal

supplant *v* take the place of, oust
supple *adj* (of a person) moving and bending easily and gracefully; bending easily without damage **suppleness** *n*
supplement *n* thing added to complete something or make up for a lack; magazine inserted into a newspaper; section added to a publication to supply further information ▷ *v* provide or be a supplement to (something) **supplementary** *adj*
supplication *n* humble request **supplicant** *n* person who makes a humble request
supply *v* **-plying, -plied** provide with something required ▷ *n, pl* **-plies** supplying; amount available; *economics* willingness and ability to provide goods and services ▷ *pl* food or equipment **supplier** *n*
support *v* bear the weight of; provide the necessities of life for; give practical or emotional help to; take an active interest in (a sports team, political principle, etc); help to prove (a theory etc); speak in favour of ▷ *n* supporting; means of support **supporter** *n* person who supports a team, principle, etc **supportive** *adj*
suppose *v* presume to be true; consider as a proposal for the sake of discussion **supposed** *adj* presumed to be true without proof, doubtful **supposed to** expected or required to *eg you were supposed to phone me*; permitted to *eg we're not supposed to swim here* **supposedly** *adv* **supposition** *n* supposing; something supposed
suppository *n, pl* **-ries** solid medication inserted into the rectum or vagina and left to melt
suppress *v* put an end to; prevent publication of (information); restrain (an emotion or response) **suppression** *n*
suppurate *v* (of a wound etc) produce pus
supreme *adj* highest in authority, rank, or degree **supremely** *adv* extremely **supremacy** *n* supreme power; state of being supreme **supremo** *n* *Informal* person in overall authority
surcharge *n* additional charge
surd *n maths* number that cannot be expressed in whole numbers
sure *adj* free from uncertainty or doubt; reliable; inevitable ▷ *adv, interj* *Informal* certainly **surely** *adv* it must be true that **sure-footed** *adj* unlikely to slip or stumble
surety *n, pl* **-ties** person who takes responsibility, or thing given as a guarantee, for the fulfilment of another's obligation
surf *n* foam caused by waves breaking on the shore ▷ *v* take part in surfing; move quickly through a medium such as the Internet **surfing** *n* sport of riding towards the shore on a surfboard on the crest of a wave **surfer** *n* **surfboard** *n* long smooth board used in surfing
surface *n* outside or top of an object; material covering the surface of an object; superficial appearance ▷ *v* rise to the surface; put a surface on
surfeit *n* excessive amount
surge *n* sudden powerful increase; strong rolling movement, esp of the sea ▷ *v* increase suddenly; move forward strongly
surgeon *n* doctor who specializes in surgery **surgery** *n* treatment in which the patient's body is cut open in order to treat the affected part *pl*

-geries place where, or time when, a doctor, dentist, etc can be consulted; *Brit* occasion when an elected politician can be consulted **surgical** *adj* **surgically** *adv*

surly *adj* **-lier, -liest** ill-tempered and rude **surliness** *n*

surmise *v, n* guess, conjecture

surmount *v* overcome (a problem); be on top of (something) **surmountable** *adj*

surname *n* family name

surpass *v* be greater than or superior to

surplice *n* loose white robe worn by clergymen and choristers

surplus *n* amount left over in excess of what is required

surprise *n* unexpected event; amazement and wonder ▷ *v* cause to feel amazement or wonder; come upon, attack, or catch suddenly and unexpectedly

surrealism *n* movement in art and literature involving the combination of incongruous images, as in a dream **surreal** *adj* bizarre **surrealist** *n, adj* **surrealistic** *adj*

surrender *v* give oneself up; give (something) up to another; yield (to a temptation or influence) ▷ *n* surrendering

surreptitious *adj* done secretly or stealthily **surreptitiously** *adv*

surrogate *n* substitute **surrogate mother** woman who gives birth to a child on behalf of a couple who cannot have children

surround *v* be, come, or place all around (a person or thing) ▷ *n* border or edging **surroundings** *pl n* area or environment around a person, place, or thing

surveillance *n* close observation

survey *v* view or consider in a general way; make a map of (an area); inspect (a building) to assess its condition and value; find out the incomes, opinions, etc of (a group of people) ▷ *n* surveying; report produced by a survey **surveyor** *n*

survive *v* continue to live or exist after (a difficult experience); live after the death of (another) **survival** *n* condition of having survived **survivor** *n*

susceptible *adj* liable to be influenced or affected by **susceptibility** *n*

sushi [**soo**-shee] *n* Japanese dish of small cakes of cold rice with a topping of raw fish

suspect *v* believe (someone) to be guilty without having any proof; think (something) to be false or questionable; believe (something) to be the case ▷ *adj* not to be trusted ▷ *n* person who is suspected

suspend *v* hang from a high place; cause to remain floating or hanging; cause to cease temporarily; remove (someone) temporarily from a job or team **suspenders** *pl n* straps for holding up stockings; *US* braces

suspense *n* state of uncertainty while awaiting news, an event, etc

suspension *n* suspending or being suspended; system of springs and shock absorbers supporting the body of a vehicle; mixture of fine particles of a solid in a fluid **suspension bridge** bridge hanging from cables attached to towers at each end

suspicion *n* feeling of not trusting a person or thing; belief that something is true without definite proof; slight trace **suspicious** *adj* feeling or causing suspicion

suspiciously *adv*
suss out *v slang* work out using one's intuition
sustain *v* maintain or prolong; keep up the vitality or strength of; suffer (an injury or loss); support **sustenance** *n* food
suture [soo-cher] *n* stitch joining the edges of a wound
suzerain *n* state or sovereign with limited authority over another self-governing state **suzerainty** *n*
svelte *adj* attractively or gracefully slim
SW southwest(ern)
swab *n* small piece of cotton wool used to apply medication, clean a wound, etc ▷*v* **swabbing, swabbed** clean (a wound) with a swab; clean (the deck of a ship) with a mop
swaddle *v* wrap (a baby) in swaddling clothes **swaddling clothes** long strips of cloth formerly wrapped round a newborn baby
swag *n slang* stolen property **swagman** *n Aust hist* tramp who carries his belongings in a bundle on his back
swagger *v* walk or behave arrogantly ▷*n* arrogant walk or manner
swain *n poetic* suitor; country youth
swallow[1] *v* cause to pass down one's throat; make a gulping movement in the throat, as when nervous; *Informal* believe (something) gullibly; refrain from showing (a feeling); engulf or absorb ▷*n* swallowing; amount swallowed
swallow[2] *n* small migratory bird with long pointed wings and a forked tail
swam *v* past tense of **swim**
swamp *n* watery area of land, bog ▷*v* cause (a boat) to fill with water and sink; overwhelm **swampy** *adj*
swan *n* large usu white water bird with a long graceful neck ▷*v* **swanning, swanned** *Informal* wander about idly **swan song** person's last performance before retirement or death
swank *slang* ▷*v* show off or boast ▷*n* showing off or boasting **swanky** *adj slang* expensive and showy, stylish
swanndri [swan-dry] *n* ®, *NZ* weatherproof woollen shirt or jacket (also **swannie**)
swap *v* **swapping, swapped** exchange (something) for something else ▷*n* exchange
sward *n* stretch of short grass
swarm[1] *n* large group of bees or other insects; large crowd ▷*v* move in a swarm; (of a place) be crowded or overrun
swarm[2] *v* (foll by *up*) climb (a ladder or rope) by gripping with the hands and feet
swarthy *adj* **-thier, -thiest** dark-complexioned
swashbuckling *adj* having the exciting behaviour of pirates, esp those depicted in films **swashbuckler** *n*
swastika *n* symbol in the shape of a cross with the arms bent at right angles, used as the emblem of Nazi Germany
swat *v* **swatting, swatted** hit sharply ▷*n* sharp blow
swatch *n* sample of cloth
swath [swawth] *n* see **swathe**
swathe *v* wrap in bandages or layers of cloth ▷*n* long strip of cloth wrapped around something; (also **swath**) the width of one

sweep of a scythe or mower

sway *v* swing to and fro or from side to side; waver or cause to waver in opinion ▷ *n* power or influence; swaying motion

swear *v* **swearing, swore, sworn** use obscene or blasphemous language; state or promise on oath; state earnestly **swear by** *v* have complete confidence in **swear in** *v* cause to take an oath **swearword** *n* word considered obscene or blasphemous

sweat *n* salty liquid given off through the pores of the skin; *slang* drudgery or hard labour ▷ *v* have sweat coming through the pores; be anxious **sweaty** *adj* **sweatband** *n* strip of cloth tied around the forehead or wrist to absorb sweat **sweatshirt** *n* long-sleeved cotton jersey **sweatshop** *n* place where employees work long hours in poor conditions for low pay

sweater *n* (woollen) garment for the upper part of the body

swede *n* kind of turnip

sweep *v* **sweeping, swept** remove dirt from (a floor) with a broom; move smoothly and quickly; spread rapidly; move majestically; carry away suddenly or forcefully; stretch in a long wide curve ▷ *n* sweeping; sweeping motion; wide expanse; sweepstake; chimney sweep **sweeping** *adj* wide-ranging; indiscriminate **sweepstake** *n* lottery in which the stakes of the participants make up the prize

sweet *adj* tasting of or like sugar; kind and charming; agreeable to the senses or mind; (of wine) with a high sugar content ▷ *n* shaped piece of food consisting mainly of sugar; dessert **sweetly** *adv* **sweetness** *n* **sweeten** *v* **sweetener** *n* sweetening agent that does not contain sugar; *Brit, Aust & NZ, slang* bribe **sweetbread** *n* animal's pancreas used as food **sweet corn** type of maize with sweet yellow kernels, eaten as a vegetable **sweetheart** *n* lover **sweetmeat** *n* *old-fashioned* sweet delicacy such as a small cake **sweet pea** climbing plant with bright fragrant flowers **sweet potato** tropical root vegetable with yellow flesh **sweet-talk** *v* *Informal* coax or flatter **sweet tooth** strong liking for sweet foods

swell *v* **swelling, swelled, swollen** *or* **swelled** expand or increase; (of a sound) become gradually louder ▷ *n* swelling or being swollen; movement of waves in the sea; *old-fashioned slang* fashionable person ▷ *adj US, slang* excellent or fine **swelling** *n* enlargement of part of the body, caused by injury or infection

swelter *v* feel uncomfortably hot

sweltering *adj* uncomfortably hot

swept *v* past of **sweep**

swerve *v* turn aside from a course sharply or suddenly ▷ *n* swerving

swift *adj* moving or able to move quickly ▷ *n* fast-flying bird with pointed wings **swiftly** *adv* **swiftness** *n*

swig *n* large mouthful of drink ▷ *v* **swigging, swigged** drink in large mouthfuls

swill *v* drink greedily; rinse (something) in large amounts of water ▷ *n* sloppy mixture containing waste food, fed to pigs; deep drink

swim *v* **swimming, swam, swum** move along in water by movements of the limbs; be covered or flooded with liquid; reel *eg her head was swimming* ▷ *n* act or period of swimming **swimmer** *n* **swimmingly** *adv* successfully and effortlessly **swimming pool** (building containing) an artificial pond for swimming in

swindle *v* cheat (someone) out of money ▷ *n* instance of swindling **swindler** *n*

swine *n* contemptible person; pig

swing *v* **swinging, swung** move to and fro, sway; move in a curve; (of an opinion or mood) change sharply; hit out with a sweeping motion; *slang* be hanged ▷ *n* swinging; suspended seat on which a child can swing to and fro; sudden or extreme change

swingeing [**swin**-jing] *adj* punishing, severe

swipe *v* strike (at) with a sweeping blow; *slang* steal; pass (a credit card or debit card) through a machine that electronically reads information stored in the card ▷ *n* hard blow **swipe card** credit card or debit card that is passed through a machine that electronically reads information stored in the card

swirl *v* turn with a whirling motion ▷ *n* whirling motion; twisting shape

swish *v* move with a whistling or hissing sound ▷ *n* whistling or hissing sound ▷ *adj Informal* fashionable, smart

Swiss *adj* of Switzerland or its people ▷ *n, pl* **Swiss** person from Switzerland **swiss roll** sponge cake spread with jam or cream and rolled up

switch *n* device for opening and closing an electric circuit; abrupt change; exchange or swap; flexible rod or twig ▷ *v* change abruptly; exchange or swap **switchback** *n* road or railway with many sharp hills or bends **switchboard** *n* installation in a telephone exchange or office where telephone calls are connected **switch on, off** *v* turn (a device) on *or* off by means of a switch

swivel *v* **-elling, -elled** turn on a central point ▷ *n* coupling device that allows an attached object to turn freely

swizzle stick *n* small stick used to stir cocktails

swollen *v* a past participle of **swell**

swoon *v, n* faint

swoop *v* sweep down or pounce on suddenly ▷ *n* swooping

swop *v* **swopping, swopped,** *n* same as **swap**

sword *n* weapon with a long sharp blade **swordfish** *n* large fish with a very long upper jaw **swordsman** *n* person skilled in the use of a sword

swore *v* past tense of **swear**

sworn *v* past participle of **swear** ▷ *adj* bound by or as if by an oath *eg sworn enemies*

swot *Informal* ▷ *v* **swotting, swotted** study hard ▷ *n* person who studies hard

swum *v* past participle of **swim**

swung *v* past of **swing**

sybarite [**sib**-bar-ite] *n* lover of luxury **sybaritic** *adj*

sycamore *n* tree with five-pointed leaves and two-winged fruits

sycophant *n* person who uses flattery to win favour from people with power or influence **sycophantic** *adj* **sycophancy** *n*

syllable *n* part of a word pronounced as a unit **syllabic** *adj*

syllabub *n* dessert of beaten

cream, sugar, and wine
syllabus *n, pl* **-buses, -bi** list of subjects for a course of study
syllogism *n* form of logical reasoning consisting of two premises and a conclusion
sylph *n* slender graceful girl or woman; imaginary being supposed to inhabit the air **sylphlike** *adj*
sylvan *adj lit* relating to woods and trees
symbiosis *n* close association of two species living together to their mutual benefit **symbiotic** *adj*
symbol *n* sign or thing that stands for something else **symbolic** *adj* **symbolically** *adv* **symbolism** *n* representation of something by symbols; movement in art and literature using symbols to express abstract and mystical ideas **symbolist** *n, adj* **symbolize** *v* be a symbol of; represent with a symbol
symmetry *n* state of having two halves that are mirror images of each other **symmetrical** *adj* **symmetrically** *adv*
sympathy *n, pl* **-thies** compassion for someone's pain or distress; agreement with someone's feelings or interests **sympathetic** *adj* feeling or showing sympathy; likeable or appealing **sympathetically** *adv* **sympathize** *v* feel or express sympathy **sympathizer** *n*
symphony *n, pl* **-nies** composition for orchestra, with several movements **symphonic** *adj*
symposium *n, pl* **-siums, -sia** conference for discussion of a particular topic
symptom *n* sign indicating the presence of an illness; sign that something is wrong **symptomatic** *adj*
synagogue *n* Jewish place of worship and religious instruction
sync, synch *Informal* ▷ *n* synchronization ▷ *v* synchronize
synchromesh *adj* (of a gearbox) having a device that synchronizes the speeds of gears before they engage
synchronize *v* (of two or more people) perform (an action) at the same time; set (watches) to show the same time; match (the soundtrack and action of a film) precisely **synchronization** *n* **synchronous** *adj* happening or existing at the same time
syncopate *v music* stress the weak beats in (a rhythm) instead of the strong ones **syncopation** *n*
syncope [**sing**-kop-ee] *n med* a faint
syndicate *n* group of people or firms undertaking a joint business project; agency that sells material to several newspapers; association of individuals who control organized crime ▷ *v* publish (material) in several newspapers; form a syndicate **syndication** *n*
syndrome *n* combination of symptoms indicating a particular disease; set of characteristics indicating a particular problem
synergy *n* potential ability for people or groups to be more successful working together than on their own
synod *n* church council
synonym *n* word with the same meaning as another **synonymous** *adj*
synopsis *n, pl* **-ses** summary or outline
syntax *n grammar* way in which words are arranged to form phrases

and sentences **syntactic** *adj*

synthesis *n, pl* **-ses** combination of objects or ideas into a whole; artificial production of a substance **synthesize** *v* produce by synthesis **synthesizer** *n* electronic musical instrument producing a range of sounds **synthetic** *adj* (of a substance) made artificially; not genuine, insincere **synthetically** *adv*

syphilis *n* serious sexually transmitted disease **syphilitic** *adj*

syphon *n, v* same as **siphon**

syringe *n* device for withdrawing or injecting fluids, consisting of a hollow cylinder, a piston, and a hollow needle ▷ *v* wash out or inject with a syringe

syrup *n* solution of sugar in water; thick sweet liquid **syrupy** *adj*

system *n* method or set of methods; scheme of classification or arrangement; network or assembly of parts that form a whole **systematic** *adj* **systematically** *adv* **systematize** *v* organize using a system **systematization** *n* **systemic** *adj* affecting the entire animal or body

systole [siss-tol-ee] *n* regular contraction of the heart as it pumps blood **systolic** *adj*

t

t tonne

T *n* **to a T** in every detail; perfectly

t. ton

ta *interj Informal* thank you

TA (in Britain) Territorial Army

tab *n* small flap or projecting label **keep tabs on** *Informal* watch closely

TAB (in New Zealand) Totalisator Agency Board

tabard *n* short sleeveless tunic decorated with a coat of arms, worn in medieval times

Tabasco *n* ® very hot red pepper sauce

tabby *n, pl* **-bies,** *adj* (cat) with dark stripes on a lighter background

tabernacle *n* portable shrine of the Israelites; Christian place of worship not called a church; *RC church* receptacle for the consecrated Host

tabla *n, pl* **-bla, -blas** one of a pair

of Indian drums played with the hands

table *n* piece of furniture with a flat top supported by legs; arrangement of information in columns ▷*v* submit (a motion) for discussion by a meeting; *US* suspend discussion of (a proposal) **tableland** *n* high plateau **tablespoon** *n* large spoon for serving food **table tennis** game like tennis played on a table with small bats and a light ball

tableau [tab-loh] *n, pl* **-leaux** silent motionless group arranged to represent some scene

table d'hôte [tah-bla **dote**] *n, pl* **tables d'hôte,** *adj* (meal) having a set number of dishes at a fixed price

tablet *n* pill of compressed medicinal substance; inscribed slab of stone etc

tabloid *n* small-sized newspaper with many photographs and a concise, usu sensational style

taboo *n, pl* **-boos** prohibition resulting from religious or social conventions ▷*adj* forbidden by a taboo

tabular *adj* arranged in a table **tabulate** *v* arrange (information) in a table **tabulation** *n*

tachograph *n* device for recording the speed and distance travelled by a motor vehicle

tachometer *n* device for measuring speed, esp that of a revolving shaft

tacit [tass-it] *adj* implied but not spoken **tacitly** *adv*

taciturn [tass-it-turn] *adj* habitually uncommunicative **taciturnity** *n*

tack[1] *n* short nail with a large head; long loose stitch ▷*v* fasten with tacks; stitch with tacks **tack on** *v* append

tack[2] *n* course of a ship sailing obliquely into the wind; course of action ▷*v* sail into the wind on a zigzag course

tack[3] *n* riding harness for horses

tackies, takkies *pl n, sing* **tacky** *S Afr, Informal* tennis shoes or plimsolls

tackle *v* deal with (a task); confront (an opponent); *sport* attempt to get the ball from (an opposing player) ▷*n sport* act of tackling an opposing player; equipment for a particular activity; set of ropes and pulleys for lifting heavy weights

tacky[1] *adj* **tackier, tackiest** slightly sticky

tacky[2] *adj* **tackier, tackiest** *Informal* vulgar and tasteless; shabby

taco [tah-koh] *n, pl* **tacos** *Mexican cookery* tortilla fried until crisp, served with a filling

tact *n* skill in avoiding giving offence **tactful** *adj* **tactfully** *adv* **tactless** *adj* **tactlessly** *adv*

tactics *n* art of directing military forces in battle **tactic** *n* method or plan to achieve an end **tactical** *adj* **tactician** *n*

tactile *adj* of or having the sense of touch

tadpole *n* limbless tailed larva of a frog or toad

TAFE *Aust* Technical and Further Education

taffeta *n* shiny silk or rayon fabric

tag[1] *n* label bearing information; pointed end of a cord or lace; trite quotation ▷*v* **tagging, tagged** attach a tag to **tag along** *v* accompany someone, esp if uninvited

tag[2] *n* children's game where the

person being chased becomes the chaser upon being touched ▷ *v* **tagging, tagged** touch and catch in this game

tagliatelle *n* pasta in long narrow strips

tail *n* rear part of an animal's body, usu forming a flexible appendage; rear or last part or parts of something; *Informal* person employed to follow and spy on another ▷ *pl Informal* tail coat ▷ *adj* at the rear ▷ *v Informal* follow (someone) secretly **turn tail** run away **tailless** *adj* **tails** *adv* with the side of a coin uppermost that does not have a portrait of a head on it **tailback** *n Brit* queue of traffic stretching back from an obstruction **tailboard** *n* removable or hinged rear board on a truck etc **tail coat** man's coat with a long back split into two below the waist **tail off, away** *v* diminish gradually **tailplane** *n* small stabilizing wing at the rear of an aircraft **tailspin** *n* uncontrolled spinning dive of an aircraft **tailwind** *n* wind coming from the rear

tailor *n* person who makes men's clothes ▷ *v* adapt to suit a purpose **tailor-made** *adj* made by a tailor; perfect for a purpose

taint *v* spoil with a small amount of decay, contamination, or other bad quality ▷ *n* something that taints

taipan *n* large poisonous Australian snake

take *v* **taking, took, taken** remove from a place; carry or accompany; use; get possession of, esp dishonestly; capture; require (time, resources, or ability); assume; accept ▷ *n* one of a series of recordings from which the best will be used **take place** happen **taking** *adj* charming **takings** *pl n* money received by a shop **take after** *v* look or behave like (a parent etc) **take away** *v* remove or subtract **takeaway** *n* shop or restaurant selling meals for eating elsewhere; meal bought at a takeaway **take in** *v* understand; deceive or swindle; make (clothing) smaller **take off** *v* (of an aircraft) leave the ground; *Informal* depart; *Informal* parody **takeoff** *n* **takeover** *n* act of taking control of a company by buying a large number of its shares **take up** *v* occupy or fill (space or time); adopt the study or activity of; shorten (a garment); accept (an offer)

talc *n* talcum powder; soft mineral of magnesium silicate **talcum powder** powder, usu scented, used to dry or perfume the body

tale *n* story; malicious piece of gossip

talent *n* natural ability; ancient unit of weight or money **talented** *adj*

talisman *n, pl* **-mans** object believed to have magic power **talismanic** *adj*

talk *v* express ideas or feelings by means of speech; utter; discuss *eg let's talk business*; reveal information; (be able to) speak in a specified language ▷ *n* speech or lecture **talker** *n* **talkative** *adj* fond of talking **talk back** *v* answer impudently **talkback** *n NZ* broadcast in which telephone comments or questions from the public are transmitted live **talking-to** *n Informal* telling-off

tall *adj* higher than average; of a specified height **tall order**

difficult task **tall story** unlikely and probably untrue tale
tallboy *n* high chest of drawers
tallow *n* hard animal fat used to make candles
tally *v* **-lying, -lied** (of two things) correspond ▷ *n, pl* **-lies** record of a debt or score
tally-ho *interj* huntsman's cry when the quarry is sighted
Talmud *n* body of Jewish law **Talmudic** *adj*
talon *n* bird's hooked claw
tamarind *n* tropical tree; its acid fruit
tamarisk *n* evergreen shrub with slender branches and feathery flower clusters
tambourine *n* percussion instrument like a small drum with jingling metal discs attached
tame *adj* (of animals) brought under human control; (of animals) not afraid of people; meek or submissive; uninteresting ▷ *v* make tame **tamely** *adv*
tamer *n* person who tames wild animals
Tamil *n* member of a people of Sri Lanka and S India; their language
tam-o'-shanter *n* brimless wool cap with a bobble in the centre
tamp *v* pack down by repeated taps
tamper *v* (foll by *with*) interfere
tampon *n* absorbent plug of cotton wool inserted into the vagina during menstruation
tan *n* brown coloration of the skin from exposure to sunlight ▷ *v* **tanning, tanned** (of skin) go brown from exposure to sunlight; convert (a hide) into leather ▷ *adj* yellowish-brown **tannery** *n* place where hides are tanned
tandem *n* bicycle for two riders, one behind the other **in tandem** together
tandoori *adj* (of food) cooked in an Indian clay oven
tang *n* strong taste or smell; trace or hint **tangy** *adj*
tangata whenua [**tang**-ah-tah **fen**-noo-ah] *pl n NZ* original Polynesian settlers in New Zealand
tangent *n* line that touches a curve without intersecting it; (in trigonometry) ratio of the length of the opposite side to that of the adjacent side of a right-angled triangle **go off at a tangent** suddenly take a completely different line of thought or action **tangential** *adj* of superficial relevance only; of a tangent **tangentially** *adv*
tangerine *n* small orange-like fruit of an Asian citrus tree
tangible *adj* able to be touched; clear and definite **tangibly** *adv*
tangle *n* confused mass or situation ▷ *v* twist together in a tangle; (often foll by *with*) come into conflict
tango *n, pl* **-gos** S American dance ▷ *v* dance a tango
taniwha [**tun**-ee-fah] *n NZ* mythical Maori monster that lives in water
tank *n* container for liquids or gases; armoured fighting vehicle moving on tracks **tanker** *n* ship or truck for carrying liquid in bulk
tankard *n* large beer-mug, often with a hinged lid
tannin, tannic acid *n* vegetable substance used in tanning
Tannoy *n* ®, *Brit* type of public-address system
tansy *n, pl* **-sies** yellow-flowered plant
tantalize *v* torment by showing

but withholding something desired **tantalizing** *adj* **tantalizingly** *adv*

tantalum *n chem* hard greyish-white metallic element

tantamount *adj* **tantamount to** equivalent in effect to

tantrum *n* childish outburst of temper

tap[1] *v* **tapping, tapped** knock lightly and usu repeatedly ▷ *n* light knock **tap dancing** style of dancing in which the feet beat out an elaborate rhythm

tap[2] *n* valve to control the flow of liquid from a pipe or cask ▷ *v* **tapping, tapped** listen in on (a telephone call) secretly by making an illegal connection; draw off with or as if with a tap **on tap** *Informal* readily available; (of beer etc) drawn from a cask

tape *n* narrow long strip of material; (recording made on) a cassette containing magnetic tape; string stretched across a race track to mark the finish ▷ *v* record on magnetic tape; bind or fasten with tape **tape measure** tape marked off in centimetres or inches for measuring **tape recorder** device for recording and reproducing sound on magnetic tape **tapeworm** *n* long flat parasitic worm living in the intestines of vertebrates

taper *v* become narrower towards one end ▷ *n* long thin candle **taper off** *v* become gradually less

tapestry *n, pl* **-tries** fabric decorated with coloured woven designs

tapioca *n* beadlike starch made from cassava root, used in puddings

tapir [tape-er] *n* piglike mammal of tropical America and SE Asia, with a long snout

tappet *n* short steel rod in an engine, transferring motion from one part to another

taproot *n* main root of a plant, growing straight down

tar *n* thick black liquid distilled from coal etc ▷ *v* **tarring, tarred** coat with tar **tar-seal** *n NZ* tarred road surface

taramasalata *n* creamy pink pâté made from fish roe

tarantella *n* lively Italian dance; music for this

tarantula *n* large hairy spider with a poisonous bite

tardy *adj* **tardier, tardiest** slow or late **tardily** *adv* **tardiness** *n*

tare *n* type of vetch plant; *bible* weed

target *n* object or person a missile is aimed at; goal or objective; object of criticism ▷ *v* **-geting, -geted** aim or direct

> SPELLING Lots of people put an extra *t* to make *targetting* and *targetted*, but they are wrong: the correct spellings are **targeting** and **targeted**

tariff *n* tax levied on imports; list of fixed prices

Tarmac *n* ® mixture of tar, bitumen, and crushed stones used for roads etc; **(t-)** airport runway

tarn *n* small mountain lake

tarnish *v* make or become stained or less bright; damage or taint ▷ *n* discoloration or blemish

tarot [tarr-oh] *n* special pack of cards used mainly in fortune-telling **tarot card** card in a tarot pack

tarpaulin *n* (sheet of) heavy waterproof fabric

tarragon *n* aromatic herb

tarry *v* **-rying, -ried** *old-fashioned* linger or delay; stay briefly

tarsus *n, pl* **-si** bones of the heel

and ankle collectively
tart¹ *n* pie or flan with a sweet filling
tart² *adj* sharp or bitter **tartly** *adv* **tartness** *n*
tart³ *n Informal* sexually provocative or promiscuous woman **tart up** *v Informal* dress or decorate in a smart or flashy way
tartan *n* design of straight lines crossing at right angles, esp one associated with a Scottish clan; cloth with such a pattern
tartar¹ *n* hard deposit on the teeth; deposit formed during the fermentation of wine
tartar² *n* fearsome or formidable person
tartare sauce *n* mayonnaise sauce mixed with chopped herbs and capers, served with seafood
tartrazine [tar-traz-zeen] *n* artificial yellow dye used in food etc
TAS Tasmania
task *n* (difficult or unpleasant) piece of work to be done **take to task** criticize or scold **task force** (military) group formed to carry out a specific task **taskmaster** *n* person who enforces hard work
Tasmanian *n, adj* (person) from Tasmania **Tasmanian devil** small carnivorous Tasmanian marsupial **Tasmanian tiger** same as **thylacine**
tassel *n* decorative fringed knot of threads
taste *n* sense by which the flavour of a substance is distinguished in the mouth; distinctive flavour; small amount tasted; brief experience of something; liking; ability to appreciate what is beautiful or excellent ▷*v* distinguish the taste of (a substance); take a small amount of (something) into the mouth; have a specific taste; experience briefly **tasteful** *adj* having or showing good taste **tastefully** *adv* **tasteless** *adj* bland or insipid; showing bad taste **tastelessly** *adv* **tasty** *adj* pleasantly flavoured **taste bud** small organ on the tongue which perceives flavours
tat *n Brit* tatty or tasteless article(s)
tattered *adj* ragged or torn **in tatters** in ragged pieces
tattle *v, n Brit, Aust & NZ* gossip or chatter
tattoo¹ *n* pattern made on the body by pricking the skin and staining it with indelible inks ▷*v* **-tooing, -tooed** make such a pattern on the skin **tattooist** *n*
tattoo² *n* military display or pageant; drumming or tapping
tatty *adj* **-tier, -tiest** shabby or worn out
taught *v* past of **teach**
taunt *v* tease with jeers ▷*n* jeering remark
taupe *adj* brownish-grey
taut *adj* drawn tight; showing nervous strain **tauten** *v* make or become taut
tautology *n, pl* **-gies** use of words which merely repeat something already stated **tautological** *adj*
tavern *n old-fashioned* pub
tawdry *adj* **-drier, -driest** cheap, showy, and of poor quality
tawny *adj* **-nier, -niest** yellowish-brown
tax *n* compulsory payment levied by a government on income, property, etc to raise revenue ▷*v* levy a tax on; make heavy demands on **taxable** *adj* **taxation** *n* levying of taxes **tax-free** *adj* (of goods, services and income) not taxed **taxpayer** *n* **tax relief**

reduction in the amount of tax a person or company has to pay **tax return** statement of personal income for tax purposes

taxi *n* (also **taxicab**) car with a driver that may be hired to take people to any specified destination ▷ *v* **taxiing, taxied** (of an aircraft) run along the ground before taking off or after landing **taxi meter** meter in a taxi that registers the fare **taxi rank** place where taxis wait to be hired

taxidermy *n* art of stuffing and mounting animal skins to give them a lifelike appearance **taxidermist** *n*

taxonomy *n* classification of plants and animals into groups **taxonomic** *adj* **taxonomist** *n*

TB tuberculosis

tbs., tbsp. tablespoon(ful)

tea *n* drink made from infusing the dried leaves of an Asian bush in boiling water; leaves used to make this drink; *Brit, Aust & NZ* main evening meal; *Chiefly Brit* light afternoon meal of tea, cakes, etc; drink like tea, made from other plants **tea bag** small porous bag of tea leaves **tea cosy** covering for a teapot to keep the tea warm **teapot** *n* container with a lid, spout, and handle for making and serving tea **teaspoon** *n* small spoon for stirring tea **tea towel, tea cloth** towel for drying dishes **tea tree** tree of Australia and New Zealand that yields an oil used as an antiseptic

teach *v* **teaching, taught** tell or show (someone) how to do something; give lessons in (a subject); cause to learn or understand **teaching** *n*

teacher *n* person who teaches, esp in a school

teak *n* very hard wood of an E Indian tree

teal *n* kind of small duck

team *n* group of people forming one side in a game; group of people or animals working together **teamster** *n* *US* commercial vehicle driver **team up** *v* make or join a team **teamwork** *n* cooperative work by a team

tear[1], teardrop *n* drop of fluid appearing in and falling from the eye **in tears** weeping **tearful** *adj* weeping or about to weep **tear gas** gas that stings the eyes and causes temporary blindness **tear-jerker** *n* *Informal* excessively sentimental film or book

tear[2] *v* **tearing, tore, torn** rip a hole in; rip apart; rush ▷ *n* hole or split **tearaway** *n* wild or unruly person

tease *v* make fun of (someone) in a provoking or playful way ▷ *n* person who teases **teasing** *adj*, *n* **tease out** *v* remove tangles from (hair etc) by combing

teasel, teazel, teazle *n* plant with prickly leaves and flowers

teat *n* nipple of a breast or udder; rubber nipple of a feeding bottle

tech *n* *Informal* technical college

techie *Informal* ▷ *n* person who is skilled in the use of technology ▷ *adj* relating to or skilled in the use of technology

technetium [tek-**neesh**-ee-um] *n* *chem* artificially produced silvery-grey metallic element

technical *adj* of or specializing in industrial, practical, or mechanical arts and applied sciences; skilled in technical subjects; relating to a particular field; according to the letter of the law; showing technique *eg technical brilliance* **technically** *adv* **technicality** *n* petty point based on a strict application of rules **technician** *n* person skilled in a particular technical field **technical college** higher educational institution with courses in art and technical subjects

Technicolor *n* ® system of colour photography used for the cinema

technique *n* method or skill used for a particular task; technical proficiency

techno *n* type of electronic dance music with a very fast beat

technocracy *n, pl* **-cies** government by technical experts **technocrat** *n*

technology *n* application of practical or mechanical sciences to industry or commerce; scientific methods used in a particular field **technological** *adj* **technologist** *n*

tectonics *n* study of the earth's crust and the forces affecting it

teddy *n, pl* **-dies** teddy bear; combined camisole and knickers **teddy bear** soft toy bear

tedious *adj* causing fatigue or boredom **tediously** *adv* **tedium** *n* monotony

tee *n* small peg from which a golf ball can be played at the start of each hole; area of a golf course from which the first stroke of a hole is made **tee off** *v* make the first stroke of a hole in golf

teem[1] *v* be full of

teem[2] *v* rain heavily

teenager *n* person aged between 13 and 19 **teenage** *adj*

teens *pl n* period of being a teenager

teepee *n* same as **tepee**

tee-shirt *n* same as **T-shirt**

teeter *v* wobble or move unsteadily

teeth *n* plural of **tooth**

teethe *v* (of a baby) grow his or her first teeth **teething troubles** problems during the early stages of something

teetotal *adj* drinking no alcohol **teetotaller** *n*

TEFL Teaching of English as a Foreign Language

Teflon *n* ® substance used for nonstick coatings on saucepans etc

tele- *combining form* distance *eg telecommunications*; telephone or television *eg teleconference*

telecommunications *n* communications using telephone, radio, television, etc

telegram *n* formerly, a message sent by telegraph

telegraph *n* formerly, a system for sending messages over a distance along a cable ▷ *v* communicate by telegraph **telegraphic** *adj* **telegraphist** *n* **telegraphy** *n* science or use of a telegraph

telekinesis *n* movement of objects by thought or willpower

telemetry *n* use of electronic devices to record or measure a distant event and transmit the data to a receiver

teleology *n* belief that all things have a predetermined purpose **teleological** *adj*

telepathy *n* direct communication between minds **telepathic** *adj* **telepathically** *adv*

telephone *n* device for transmitting sound over a distance along wires ▷ *v* call or talk to (a person) by telephone **telephony** *n* **telephonic** *adj* **telephonist** *n* person operating a telephone switchboard

telephoto lens *n* camera lens producing a magnified image of a distant object
teleprinter *n Brit* apparatus like a typewriter for sending and receiving typed messages by wire
telesales *n* selling of a product or service by telephone
telescope *n* optical instrument for magnifying distant objects ▷*v* shorten **telescopic** *adj*
Teletext *n* ® system which shows information and news on television screens
television *n* system of producing a moving image and accompanying sound on a distant screen; device for receiving broadcast signals and converting them into sound and pictures; content of television programmes **televise** *v* broadcast on television **televisual** *adj*
telex *n* international communication service using teleprinters; message sent by telex ▷*v* transmit by telex
tell *v* **telling, told** make known in words; order or instruct; give an account of; discern or distinguish; have an effect; *Informal* reveal secrets **teller** *n* narrator; bank cashier; person who counts votes **telling** *adj* having a marked effect **tell off** *v* reprimand **telling-off** *n* **telltale** *n* person who reveals secrets ▷*adj* revealing
tellurium *n chem* brittle silvery-white nonmetallic element
telly *n, pl* **-lies** *Informal* television
temerity [tim-**merr**-it-tee] *n* boldness or audacity
temp *Brit, Informal* ▷*n* temporary employee, esp a secretary ▷*v* work as a temp
temp. temperature; temporary
temper *n* outburst of anger; tendency to become angry; calm mental condition *eg I lost my temper;* frame of mind ▷*v* make less extreme; strengthen or toughen (metal)
tempera *n* painting medium for powdered pigments
temperament *n* person's character or disposition **temperamental** *adj* having changeable moods; *Informal* erratic and unreliable **temperamentally** *adv*
temperate *adj* (of climate) not extreme; self-restrained or moderate **temperance** *n* moderation; abstinence from alcohol
temperature *n* degree of heat or cold; *Informal* abnormally high body temperature
tempest *n* violent storm **tempestuous** *adj* violent or stormy
template *n* pattern used to cut out shapes accurately
temple[1] *n* building for worship
temple[2] *n* region on either side of the forehead **temporal** *adj*
tempo *n, pl* **-pi, -pos** rate or pace; speed of a piece of music
temporal *adj* of time; worldly rather than spiritual
temporary *adj* lasting only for a short time **temporarily** *adv*
temporize *v* gain time by negotiation or evasiveness; adapt to circumstances
tempt *v* entice (a person) to do something wrong **tempt fate** take foolish or unnecessary risks **tempter, temptress** *n* **temptation** *n* tempting; tempting thing **tempting** *adj* attractive or inviting
ten *adj, n* one more than nine **tenth** *adj, n* (of) number ten in a

series

tenable *adj* able to be upheld or maintained

tenacious *adj* holding fast; stubborn **tenaciously** *adv* **tenacity** *n*

tenant *n* person who rents land or a building **tenancy** *n*

tench *n, pl* **tench** freshwater game fish of the carp family

tend[1] *v* be inclined; go in the direction of **tendency** *n* inclination to act in a certain way **tendentious** *adj* biased, not impartial

tend[2] *v* take care of

tender[1] *adj* not tough; gentle and affectionate; vulnerable or sensitive **tenderly** *adv* **tenderness** *n* **tenderize** *v* soften (meat) by pounding or treatment with a special substance

tender[2] *v* offer; make a formal offer to supply goods or services at a stated cost ▷ *n* such an offer **legal tender** currency that must, by law, be accepted as payment

tender[3] *n* small boat that brings supplies to a larger ship in a port; carriage for fuel and water attached to a steam locomotive

tendon *n* strong tissue attaching a muscle to a bone

tendril *n* slender stem by which a climbing plant clings

tenement *n* (esp in Scotland or the US) building divided into several flats

tenet [ten-nit] *n* doctrine or belief

tenner *n Brit, Informal* ten-pound note

tennis *n* game in which players use rackets to hit a ball back and forth over a net

tenon *n* projecting end on a piece of wood fitting into a slot in another

tenor *n* (singer with) the second highest male voice; general meaning ▷ *adj* (of a voice or instrument) between alto and baritone

tenpin bowling *n* game in which players try to knock over ten skittles by rolling a ball at them

tense[1] *adj* emotionally strained; stretched tight ▷ *v* make or become tense

tense[2] *n grammar* form of a verb showing the time of action

tensile *adj* of tension

tension *n* hostility or suspense; emotional strain; degree of stretching

tent *n* portable canvas shelter

tentacle *n* flexible organ of many invertebrates, used for grasping, feeding, etc

tentative *adj* provisional or experimental; cautious or hesitant **tentatively** *adv*

tenterhooks *pl n* **on tenterhooks** in anxious suspense

tenuous *adj* slight or flimsy **tenuously** *adv*

tenure *n* (period of) the holding of an office or position

tepee [tee-pee] *n* cone-shaped tent, formerly used by Native Americans

tepid *adj* slightly warm; half-hearted

tequila *n* Mexican alcoholic drink

tercentenary *adj, n, pl* **-naries** (of) a three hundredth anniversary

term *n* word or expression; fixed period; period of the year when a school etc is open or a lawcourt holds sessions ▷ *pl* conditions; mutual relationship ▷ *v* name or designate

terminal *adj* (of an illness) ending in death; at or being an end ▷ *n*

place where people or vehicles begin or end a journey; point where current enters or leaves an electrical device; keyboard and VDU having input and output links with a computer **terminally** *adv*
terminate *v* bring or come to an end **termination** *n*
terminology *n* technical terms relating to a subject
terminus *n, pl* **-ni, -nuses** railway or bus station at the end of a line
termite *n* white antlike insect that destroys timber
tern *n* gull-like sea bird with a forked tail and pointed wings
ternary *adj* consisting of three parts
Terpsichorean *adj* of dancing
terrace *n* row of houses built as one block; paved area next to a building; level tier cut out of a hill ▷ *pl* (also **terracing**) tiered area in a stadium where spectators stand ▷ *v* form into or provide with a terrace
terracotta *adj, n* (made of) brownish-red unglazed pottery ▷ *adj* brownish-red
terra firma *n Latin* dry land or solid ground
terrain *n* area of ground, esp with reference to its physical character
terrapin *n* small turtle-like reptile
terrarium *n, pl* **-raria, -rariums** enclosed container for small plants or animals
terrazzo *n, pl* **-zos** floor of marble chips set in mortar and polished
terrestrial *adj* of the earth; of or living on land
terrible *adj* very serious; *Informal* very bad; causing fear **terribly** *adv*
terrier *n* any of various breeds of small active dog
terrific *adj* great or intense; *Informal* excellent
terrify *v* **-fying, -fied** fill with fear **terrified** *adj* **terrifying** *adj*
terrine [terr-**reen**] *n* earthenware dish with a lid; pâté or similar food
territory *n, pl* **-ries** district; area under the control of a particular government; area inhabited and defended by an animal; area of knowledge **territorial** *adj* **Territorial Army** (in Britain) reserve army
terror *n* great fear; terrifying person or thing; *Brit, Aust & NZ, Informal* troublesome person or thing **terrorism** *n* use of violence and intimidation to achieve political ends **terrorist** *n, adj* **terrorize** *v* force or oppress by fear or violence
terry *n* fabric with small loops covering both sides, used esp for making towels
terse *adj* neat and concise; curt **tersely** *adv*
tertiary [**tur**-shar-ee] *adj* third in degree, order, etc
Terylene *n* ® synthetic polyester yarn or fabric
tessellated *adj* paved or inlaid with a mosaic of small tiles
test *v* try out to ascertain the worth, capability, or endurance of; carry out an examination on ▷ *n* critical examination; Test match **testing** *adj* **test case** lawsuit that establishes a precedent **Test match** one of a series of international cricket or rugby matches **test tube** narrow round-bottomed glass tube used in scientific experiments **test-tube baby** baby conceived outside the mother's body
testament *n* proof or tribute; *law* will; **(T-)** one of the two main

divisions of the Bible

testator [test-**tay**-tor], *fem* **testatrix** [test-**tay**-triks] *n* maker of a will

testicle *n* either of the two male reproductive glands

testify *v* **-fying, -fied** give evidence under oath **testify to** be evidence of

testimony *n, pl* **-nies** declaration of truth or fact; evidence given under oath **testimonial** *n* recommendation of the worth of a person or thing; tribute for services or achievement

testis *n, pl* **-tes** testicle

testosterone *n* male sex hormone secreted by the testes

testy *adj* **-tier, -tiest** irritable or touchy **testily** *adv* **testiness** *n*

tetanus *n* acute infectious disease producing muscular spasms and convulsions

tête-à-tête *n, pl* **-têtes, -tête** private conversation

tether *n* rope or chain for tying an animal to a spot ▷ *v* tie up with rope **at the end of one's tether** at the limit of one's endurance

tetrahedron [tet-ra-**heed**-ron] *n, pl* **-drons, -dra** solid figure with four faces

tetralogy *n, pl* **-gies** series of four related works

Teutonic [tew-**tonn**-ik] *adj* of or like the (ancient) Germans

text *n* main body of a book as distinct from illustrations etc; passage of the Bible as the subject of a sermon; novel or play studied for a course; text message ▷ *v* send a text message to (someone) **textual** *adj* **textbook** *n* standard book on a particular subject ▷ *adj* perfect *eg a textbook landing* **text message** message sent in text form, esp by means of a mobile phone

textile *n* fabric or cloth, esp woven

texture *n* structure, feel, or consistency **textured** *adj* **textural** *adj*

thalidomide [thal-**lid**-oh-mide] *n* drug formerly used as a sedative, but found to cause abnormalities in developing fetuses

thallium *n chem* highly toxic metallic element

than *conj, prep* used to introduce the second element of a comparison

thane *n hist* Anglo-Saxon or medieval Scottish nobleman

thank *v* express gratitude to; hold responsible **thanks** *pl n* words of gratitude ▷ *interj* (also **thank you**) polite expression of gratitude **thanks to** because of **thankful** *adj* grateful **thankless** *adj* unrewarding or unappreciated **Thanksgiving Day** autumn public holiday in Canada and the US

that *adj, pron* used to refer to something already mentioned or familiar, or further away ▷ *conj* used to introduce a clause ▷ *pron* used to introduce a relative clause

thatch *n* roofing material of reeds or straw ▷ *v* roof (a house) with reeds or straw

thaw *v* make or become unfrozen; become more relaxed or friendly ▷ *n* thawing; weather causing snow or ice to melt

the *adj* the definite article, used before a noun

theatre *n* place where plays etc are performed; hospital operating room; drama and acting in general **theatrical** *adj* of the theatre; exaggerated or affected **theatricals** *pl n* (amateur) dramatic performances **theatrically** *adv* **theatricality** *n*

thee *pron obs* objective form of thou

theft *n* act or an instance of stealing

their *adj* of or associated with them **theirs** *pron* (thing or person) belonging to them

> SPELLING Do not confuse **their** and **theirs**, which do not have apostrophes, with **they're** and **there's**, which do because letters have been missed out where two words have been joined together

theism [thee-iz-zum] *n* belief in a God or gods **theist** *n, adj* **theistic** *adj*

them *pron* refers to people or things other than the speaker or those addressed **themselves** *pron* emphatic and reflexive form of **they** or

theme *n* main idea or subject being discussed; recurring melodic figure in music **thematic** *adj* **theme park** leisure area in which all the activities and displays are based on a single theme

then *adv* at that time; after that; that being so

thence *adv* from that place or time; therefore

theocracy *n, pl* **-cies** government by a god or priests **theocratic** *adj*

theodolite [thee-**odd**-oh-lite] *n* surveying instrument for measuring angles

theology *n, pl* **-gies** study of religions and religious beliefs **theologian** *n* **theological** *adj* **theologically** *adv*

theorem *n* proposition that can be proved by reasoning

theory *n, pl* **-ries** set of ideas to explain something; abstract knowledge or reasoning; idea or opinion **in theory** in an ideal or hypothetical situation **theoretical** *adj* based on theory rather than practice or fact **theoretically** *adv* **theorist** *n* **theorize** *v* form theories, speculate

theosophy *n* religious or philosophical system claiming to be based on intuitive insight into the divine nature **theosophical** *adj*

therapy *n, pl* **-pies** curing treatment **therapist** *n* **therapeutic** [ther-rap-**pew**-tik] *adj* curing **therapeutics** *n* art of curing

there *adv* in or to that place; in that respect **thereby** *adv* by that means **therefore** *adv* consequently, that being so **thereupon** *adv* immediately after that

> SPELLING Do not confuse **there**, which is closely connected in meaning and in spelling with 'here', and **their**, which means 'belonging to them'

therm *n* unit of measurement of heat

thermal *adj* of heat; hot or warm; (of clothing) retaining heat ▷ *n* rising current of warm air

thermodynamics *n* scientific study of the relationship between heat and other forms of energy

thermometer *n* instrument for measuring temperature

thermonuclear *adj* involving nuclear fusion

thermoplastic *adj* (of a plastic) softening when heated and resetting on cooling

Thermos *n* ® vacuum flask

thermosetting *adj* (of a plastic) remaining hard when heated

thermostat *n* device for automatically regulating temperature **thermostatic** *adj* **thermostatically** *adv*

thesaurus [thiss-**sore**-uss] *n, pl* **-ruses** book containing lists of synonyms and related words

these *adj, pron* plural of **this**

thesis *n, pl* **theses** written work submitted for a degree; opinion supported by reasoned argument

Thespian *n* actor or actress ▷ *adj* of the theatre

they *pron* refers to: people or things other than the speaker or people addressed; people in general; *Informal* he or she

thiamine *n* vitamin found in the outer coat of rice and other grains

thick *adj* of great or specified extent from one side to the other; having a dense consistency; *Informal* stupid or insensitive; *Brit, Aust & NZ, Informal* friendly **a bit thick** *Informal* unfair or unreasonable **the thick** busiest or most intense part **thick with** full of **thicken** *v* make or become thick or thicker **thickly** *adv* **thickness** *n* state of being thick; dimension through an object; layer **thickset** *adj* stocky in build

thicket *n* dense growth of small trees

thief *n, pl* **thieves** person who steals **thieve** *v* steal **thieving** *adj*

thigh *n* upper part of the human leg

thimble *n* cap protecting the end of the finger when sewing

thin *adj* **thinner, thinnest** not thick; slim or lean; sparse or meagre; of low density; poor or unconvincing ▷ *v* **thinning, thinned** make or become thin **thinly** *adv* **thinness** *n*

thine *pron, adj obs* (something) of or associated with you (thou)

thing *n* material object; object, fact, or idea considered as a separate entity; *Informal* obsession ▷ *pl* possessions, clothes, etc

think *v* **thinking, thought** consider, judge, or believe; make use of the mind; be considerate enough or remember to do something **thinker** *n* **thinking** *adj, n* **think-tank** *n* group of experts studying specific problems **think up** *v* invent or devise

third *adj* of number three in a series; rated or graded below the second level ▷ *n* one of three equal parts **third degree** violent interrogation **third party** (applying to) a person involved by chance or only incidentally in legal proceedings, an accident, etc **Third World** developing countries of Africa, Asia, and Latin America

thirst *n* desire to drink; craving or yearning ▷ *v* feel thirst **thirsty** *adj* **thirstily** *adv*

thirteen *adj, n* three plus ten **thirteenth** *adj, n*

thirty *adj, n* three times ten **thirtieth** *adj, n*

this *adj, pron* used to refer to a thing or person nearby, just mentioned, or about to be mentioned ▷ *adj* used to refer to the present time *eg this morning*

thistle *n* prickly plant with dense flower heads

thither *adv obs* to or towards that place

thong *n* thin strip of leather etc; skimpy article of underwear or beachwear that covers the genitals while leaving the buttocks bare

thorax *n, pl* **thoraxes, thoraces** part of the body between the neck and the abdomen **thoracic** *adj*

thorn *n* prickle on a plant; bush with thorns **thorn in one's side, flesh** source of irritation **thorny** *adj*

thorough *adj* complete; careful or methodical **thoroughly** *adv* **thoroughness** *n* **thoroughbred** *n, adj* (animal) of pure breed **thoroughfare** *n* way through from one place to another

those *adj, pron* plural of **that**

thou *pron obs* singular form of **you**

though *conj* despite the fact that ▷ *adv* nevertheless

thought *v* past of **think** ▷ *n* thinking; concept or idea; ideas typical of a time or place; consideration; intention or expectation **thoughtful** *adj* considerate; showing careful thought; pensive or reflective **thoughtless** *adj* inconsiderate

thousand *adj, n* ten hundred; large but unspecified number **thousandth** *adj, n* (of) number one thousand in a series

thrall *n* state of being in the power of another person

thrash *v* beat, esp with a stick or whip; defeat soundly; move about wildly; thresh **thrashing** *n* severe beating **thrash out** *v* solve by thorough argument

thread *n* fine strand or yarn; unifying theme; spiral ridge on a screw, nut, or bolt ▷ *v* pass thread through; pick (one's way etc) **threadbare** *adj* (of fabric) with the nap worn off; hackneyed; shabby

threat *n* declaration of intent to harm; dangerous person or thing **threaten** *v* make or be a threat to; be a menacing indication of

three *adj, n* one more than two **threesome** *n* group of three **three-dimensional, 3-D** *adj* having three dimensions

threnody *n, pl* **-dies** lament for the dead

thresh *v* beat (wheat etc) to separate the grain from the husks and straw **thresh about** move about wildly

threshold *n* bar forming the bottom of a doorway; entrance; starting point; point at which something begins to take effect

threw *v* past tense of **throw**

thrice *adv lit* three times

thrift *n* wisdom and caution with money; low-growing plant with pink flowers **thrifty** *adj*

thrill *n* sudden feeling of excitement ▷ *v* (cause to) feel a thrill **thrilling** *adj*

thriller *n* book, film, etc with an atmosphere of mystery or suspense

thrive *v* **thriving, thrived** *or* **throve, thrived** *or* **thriven** flourish or prosper; grow well

throat *n* passage from the mouth and nose to the stomach and lungs; front of the neck **throaty** *adj* (of the voice) hoarse

throb *v* **throbbing, throbbed** pulsate repeatedly; vibrate rhythmically ▷ *n* throbbing

throes *pl n* violent pangs or pains **in the throes of** struggling to cope with

thrombosis *n, pl* **-ses** forming of a clot in a blood vessel or the heart

throne *n* ceremonial seat of a monarch or bishop; sovereign power

throng *n, v* crowd

throstle *n* song thrush

throttle *n* device controlling the amount of fuel entering an engine ▷ *v* strangle

through *prep* from end to end or

side to side of; because of; during ▷ *adj* finished; (of transport) going directly to a place **through and through** completely **throughout** *prep, adv* in every part (of) **throughput** *n* amount of material processed

throve *v* a past tense of **thrive**

throw *v* **throwing, threw, thrown** hurl through the air; move or put suddenly or carelessly; bring into a specified state, esp suddenly; give (a party); *Informal* baffle or disconcert ▷ *n* throwing; distance thrown **throwaway** *adj* done or said casually; designed to be discarded after use **throwback** *n* person or thing that reverts to an earlier type **throw up** *v* vomit

thrush[1] *n* brown songbird

thrush[2] *n* fungal disease of the mouth or vagina

thrust *v* **thrusting, thrust** push forcefully ▷ *n* forceful stab; force or power; intellectual or emotional drive

thud *n* dull heavy sound ▷ *v* **thudding, thudded** make such a sound

thug *n* violent man, esp a criminal **thuggery** *n* **thuggish** *adj*

thumb *n* short thick finger set apart from the others ▷ *v* touch or handle with the thumb; signal with the thumb for a lift in a vehicle **thumb through** flick through (a book or magazine)

thump *n* (sound of) a dull heavy blow ▷ *v* strike heavily

thunder *n* loud noise accompanying lightning ▷ *v* rumble with thunder; shout; move fast, heavily, and noisily **thunderous** *adj* **thundery** *adj* **thunderbolt** *n* lightning flash; something sudden and unexpected **thunderclap** *n* peal of thunder **thunderstruck** *adj* amazed

Thursday *n* fifth day of the week

thus *adv* therefore; in this way

thwack *v, n* whack

thwart *v* foil or frustrate ▷ *n* seat across a boat

thy *adj obs* of or associated with you (thou) **thyself** *pron obs* emphatic form of **thou**

thylacine *n* extinct doglike Tasmanian marsupial

thyme [**time**] *n* aromatic herb

thymus *n, pl* **-muses, -mi** small gland at the base of the neck

thyroid *adj, n* (of) a gland in the neck controlling body growth

tiara *n* semicircular jewelled headdress

tibia *n, pl* **tibiae, tibias** inner bone of the lower leg **tibial** *adj*

tic *n* spasmodic muscular twitch

tick[1] *n* mark (✓) used to check off or indicate the correctness of something; recurrent tapping sound, as of a clock; *Informal* moment ▷ *v* mark with a tick; make a ticking sound **tick off** *v* mark with a tick; reprimand **tick over** *v* (of an engine) idle; function smoothly **ticktack** *n Brit* bookmakers' sign language

tick[2] *n* tiny bloodsucking parasitic animal

tick[3] *n Informal* credit or account

ticket *n* card or paper entitling the holder to admission, travel, etc; label, esp showing price; official notification of a parking or traffic offence; *Chiefly US & NZ* declared policy of a political party ▷ *v* **-eting, -eted** attach or issue a ticket to

ticking *n* strong material for mattress covers

tickle *v* touch or stroke (a person) to produce laughter; itch or tingle;

please or amuse ▷*n* tickling **ticklish** *adj* sensitive to tickling; requiring care or tact

tiddler *n Informal* very small fish

tiddly[1] *adj* **-dlier, -dliest** tiny

tiddly[2] *adj* **-dlier, -dliest** *Informal* slightly drunk

tiddlywinks *n* game in which players try to flip small plastic discs into a cup

tide *n* rise and fall of the sea caused by the gravitational pull of the sun and moon; current caused by this; widespread feeling or tendency **tidal** *adj* **tidal wave** large destructive wave **tide over** *v* help (someone) temporarily

tidings *pl n* news

tidy *adj* **-dier, -diest** neat and orderly; *Brit, Aust & NZ, Informal* considerable ▷*v* **-dying, -died** put in order **tidily** *adv* **tidiness** *n*

tie *v* **tying, tied** fasten or be fastened with string, rope, etc; make (a knot or bow) in (something); restrict or limit; score the same as another competitor ▷*n* long narrow piece of material worn knotted round the neck; bond or fastening; drawn game or contest **tied** *adj Brit* (of a cottage etc) rented to the tenant only as long as he or she is employed by the owner

tier *n* one of a set of rows placed one above and behind the other

tiff *n* petty quarrel

tiger *n* large yellow-and-black striped Asian cat **tiger snake** *n* highly venomous brown-and-yellow Australian snake **tigress** *n* female tiger; *Informal* fierce woman

tight *adj* stretched or drawn taut; closely fitting; secure or firm; cramped; *Brit, Aust & NZ, Informal* not generous; (of a match or game) very close; *Informal* drunk **tights** *pl n* one-piece clinging garment covering the body from the waist to the feet **tightly** *adv* **tighten** *v* make or become tight or tighter **tightrope** *n* rope stretched taut on which acrobats perform

tiki *n NZ* small carving of a grotesque person worn as a pendant

tikka *adj indian cookery* marinated in spices and dry-roasted

tilde *n* mark (~) used in Spanish to indicate that the letter 'n' is to be pronounced in a particular way

tile *n* flat piece of ceramic, plastic, etc used to cover a roof, floor, or wall ▷*v* cover with tiles **tiled** *adj* **tiling** *n* tiles collectively

till[1] *conj, prep* until

till[2] *v* cultivate (land) **tillage** *n*

till[3] *n* drawer for money, usu in a cash register

tiller *n* lever to move a rudder of a boat

tilt *v* slant at an angle; *hist* compete against in a jousting contest ▷*n* slope; *hist* jousting contest; attempt **at full tilt** at full speed or force

timber *n* wood as a building material; trees collectively; wooden beam in the frame of a house, boat, etc **timbered** *adj* **timber line** limit beyond which trees will not grow

timbre [**tam**-bra] *n* distinctive quality of sound of a voice or instrument

time *n* past, present, and future as a continuous whole; specific point in time; unspecified interval; instance or occasion; period with specific features; musical tempo; *Brit, Aust & NZ, slang* imprisonment

▷*v* note the time taken by; choose a time for **timeless** *adj* unaffected by time; eternal **timely** *adj* at the appropriate time **time-honoured** *adj* sanctioned by custom **time-lag** *n* period between cause and effect **timepiece** *n* watch or clock **time-poor** *adj* having little free time **timeserver** *n* person who changes his or her views to gain support or favour **time sharing** system of part ownership of a holiday property for a specified period each year **timetable** *n* plan showing the times when something takes place, the departure and arrival times of trains or buses, etc

timid *adj* easily frightened; shy, not bold **timidly** *adv* **timidity** *n* **timorous** *adj* timid

timpani [**tim**-pan-ee] *pl n* set of kettledrums **timpanist** *n*

tin *n* soft metallic element; (airtight) metal container **tinned** *adj* (of food) preserved by being sealed in a tin **tinny** *adj* (of sound) thin and metallic **tinpot** *adj* *Informal* worthless or unimportant

tincture *n* medicinal extract in a solution of alcohol

tinder *n* dry easily-burning material used to start a fire **tinderbox** *n*

tine *n* prong of a fork or antler

ting *n* high metallic sound, as of a small bell

tinge *n* slight tint; trace ▷*v* **tingeing, tinged** give a slight tint or trace to

tingle *v, n* (feel) a prickling or stinging sensation

tinker *n* travelling mender of pots and pans; *Scot & Irish* Gypsy ▷*v* fiddle with (an engine etc) in an attempt to repair it

tinkle *v* ring with a high tinny sound like a small bell ▷*n* this sound or action

tinsel *n* decorative metallic strips or threads

tint *n* (pale) shade of a colour; dye for the hair ▷*v* give a tint to

tiny *adj* **tinier, tiniest** very small

tip[1] *n* narrow or pointed end of anything; small piece forming an end ▷*v* **tipping, tipped** put a tip on

tip[2] *n* money given in return for service; helpful hint or warning; piece of inside information ▷*v* **tipping, tipped** give a tip to **tipster** *n* person who sells tips about races

tip[3] *v* **tipping, tipped** tilt or overturn; dump (rubbish) ▷*n* rubbish dump **tipping point** moment or event that marks a decisive change

tipple *v* drink alcohol habitually, esp in small quantities ▷*n* alcoholic drink **tippler** *n*

tipsy *adj* **-sier, -siest** slightly drunk

tiptoe *v* **-toeing, -toed** walk quietly with the heels off the ground

tiptop *adj* of the highest quality or condition

tirade *n* long angry speech

tire *v* reduce the energy of, as by exertion; weary or bore **tired** *adj* exhausted; hackneyed or stale **tiring** *adj* **tireless** *adj* energetic and determined **tiresome** *adj* boring and irritating

tissue *n* substance of an animal body or plant; piece of thin soft paper used as a handkerchief etc; interwoven series

tit[1] *n* any of various small songbirds

tit[2] *n slang* female breast

titanic *adj* huge or very important

titanium *n chem* strong light metallic element used to make alloys
titbit *n* tasty piece of food; pleasing scrap of scandal
tit-for-tat *adj* done in retaliation
tithe *n* esp formerly, one tenth of one's income or produce paid to the church as a tax
Titian [**tish**-an] *adj* (of hair) reddish-gold
titillate *v* excite or stimulate pleasurably **titillating** *adj* **titillation** *n*
titivate *v* smarten up
title *n* name of a book, film, etc; name signifying rank or position; formal designation, such as *Mrs*; *sport* championship; *law* legal right of possession **titled** *adj* aristocratic **title deed** legal document of ownership
titter *v* laugh in a suppressed way ▷ *n* suppressed laugh
tittle-tattle *n*, *v* gossip
titular *adj* in name only; of a title
tizzy *n, pl* **-zies** *Informal* confused or agitated state
TNT *n* trinitrotoluene, a powerful explosive
to *prep* indicating movement towards, equality or comparison, etc *eg walking to school; forty miles to the gallon*; used to mark the indirect object or infinitive of a verb ▷ *adv* to a closed position *eg pull the door to* **to and fro** back and forth
toad *n* animal like a large frog
toad-in-the-hole *n Brit* sausages baked in batter
toadstool *n* poisonous fungus like a mushroom
toady *n, pl* **toadies** ingratiating person ▷ *v* **toadying, toadied** be ingratiating
toast¹ *n* sliced bread browned by heat ▷ *v* brown (bread) by heat; warm or be warmed **toaster** *n* electrical device for toasting bread
toast² *n* tribute or proposal of health or success marked by people raising glasses and drinking together; person or thing so honoured ▷ *v* drink a toast to
tobacco *n, pl* **-cos, -coes** plant with large leaves dried for smoking **tobacconist** *n* person or shop selling tobacco, cigarettes, etc
toboggan *n* narrow sledge for sliding over snow ▷ *v* **-ganing, -ganed** ride a toboggan
toby jug *n Chiefly Brit* mug in the form of a stout seated man
toccata [tok-**kah**-ta] *n* rapid piece of music for a keyboard instrument
today *n* this day; the present age ▷ *adv* on this day; nowadays
toddler *n* child beginning to walk **toddle** *v* walk with short unsteady steps
toddy *n, pl* **-dies** sweetened drink of spirits and hot water
to-do *n, pl* **-dos** *Brit, Aust & NZ* fuss or commotion
toe *n* digit of the foot; part of a shoe or sock covering the toes ▷ *v* **toeing, toed** touch or kick with the toe **toe the line** conform
toff *n Brit, slang* well-dressed or upper-class person
toffee *n* chewy sweet made of boiled sugar
tofu *n* soft food made from soya-bean curd
tog *n* unit for measuring the insulating power of duvets
toga [**toe**-ga] *n* garment worn by citizens of ancient Rome
together *adv* in company; simultaneously ▷ *adj Informal* organized
toggle *n* small bar-shaped button

inserted through a loop for fastening; switch used to turn a machine or computer function on or off

toil *n* hard work ▷*v* work hard; progress with difficulty

toilet *n* (room with) a bowl connected to a drain for receiving and disposing of urine and faeces; washing and dressing **toiletry** *n, pl* **-ries** object or cosmetic used to clean or groom oneself **toilet water** light perfume

token *n* sign or symbol; voucher exchangeable for goods of a specified value; disc used as money in a slot machine ▷*adj* nominal or slight **tokenism** *n* policy of making only a token effort, esp to comply with a law

told *v* past of **tell**

tolerate *v* allow to exist or happen; endure patiently **tolerable** *adj* bearable; *Informal* quite good **tolerably** *adv* **tolerance** *n* acceptance of other people's rights to their own opinions or actions; ability to endure something **tolerant** *adj* **tolerantly** *adv* **toleration** *n*

toll[1] *v* ring (a bell) slowly and regularly, esp to announce a death ▷*n* tolling

toll[2] *n* charge for the use of a bridge or road; total loss or damage from a disaster

tom *n* male cat

tomahawk *n* fighting axe of the Native Americans

tomato *n, pl* **-toes** red fruit used in salads and as a vegetable

tomb *n* grave; monument over a grave **tombstone** *n* gravestone

tombola *n* lottery with tickets drawn from a revolving drum

tomboy *n* girl who acts or dresses like a boy

tome *n* large heavy book

tomfoolery *n* foolish behaviour

Tommy gun *n* light sub-machine-gun

tomorrow *adv, n* (on) the day after today; (in) the future

tom-tom *n* drum beaten with the hands

ton *n* unit of weight equal to 2240 pounds or 1016 kilograms (**long ton**) or, in the US, 2000 pounds or 907 kilograms (**short ton**) **tonnage** *n* weight capacity of a ship

tone *n* sound with reference to its pitch, volume, etc; *US* musical note; *music* (also **whole tone**) interval of two semitones; quality of a sound or colour; general character; healthy bodily condition ▷*v* harmonize (with); give tone to **tonal** *adj music* written in a key **tonality** *n* **toneless** *adj* **tone-deaf** *adj* unable to perceive subtle differences in pitch **tone down** *v* make or become more moderate

tongs *pl n* large pincers for grasping and lifting

tongue *n* muscular organ in the mouth, used in speaking and tasting; language; animal tongue as food; thin projecting strip; flap of leather on a shoe

tonic *n* medicine to improve body tone ▷*adj* invigorating **tonic water** mineral water containing quinine

tonight *adv, n* (in or during) the night or evening of this day

tonne [tunn] *n* unit of weight equal to 1000 kilograms

tonsil *n* small gland in the throat **tonsillectomy** *n* surgical removal of the tonsils **tonsillitis** *n* inflammation of the tonsils

tonsure *n* shaving of all or the top of the head as a religious or monastic practice; shaved part of the head **tonsured** *adj*

too *adv* also, as well; to excess; extremely

took *v* past tense of **take**

tool *n* implement used by hand; person used by another to perform unpleasant or dishonourable tasks

toot *n* short hooting sound ▷ *v* (cause to) make such a sound

tooth *n, pl* **teeth** bonelike projection in the jaws of most vertebrates for biting and chewing; toothlike prong or point **sweet tooth** strong liking for sweet food **toothless** *adj* **toothpaste** *n* paste used to clean the teeth **toothpick** *n* small stick for removing scraps of food from between the teeth

top[1] *n* highest point or part; lid or cap; highest rank; garment for the upper part of the body ▷ *adj* at or of the top ▷ *v* **topping, topped** form a top on; be at the top of; exceed or surpass **topping** *n* sauce or garnish for food **topless** *adj* (of a costume or woman) with no covering for the breasts **topmost** *adj* highest or best **top brass** most important officers or leaders **top hat** man's tall cylindrical hat **top-heavy** *adj* unstable through being overloaded at the top **top-notch** *adj* excellent, first-class **topsoil** *n* surface layer of soil

top[2] *n* toy which spins on a pointed base

topaz [**toe**-pazz] *n* semiprecious stone in various colours

topee, topi [**toe**-pee] *n* lightweight hat worn in tropical countries

topiary [**tope**-yar-ee] *n* art of trimming trees and bushes into decorative shapes

topic *n* subject of a conversation, book, etc **topical** *adj* relating to current events **topicality** *n*

topography *n, pl* **-phies** (science of describing) the surface features of a place **topographer** *n* **topographical** *adj*

topology *n* geometry of the properties of a shape which are unaffected by continuous distortion **topological** *adj*

topple *v* (cause to) fall over; overthrow (a government etc)

topsy-turvy *adj* upside down; in confusion

toque [**toke**] *n* small round hat

tor *n* high rocky hill

Torah *n* body of traditional Jewish teaching

torch *n* small portable battery-powered lamp; wooden shaft dipped in wax and set alight ▷ *v* *Informal* deliberately set (a building) on fire

tore *v* past tense of **tear[2]**

toreador [**torr**-ee-a-dor] *n* bullfighter

torment *v* cause (someone) great suffering; tease cruelly ▷ *n* great suffering; source of suffering **tormentor** *n*

torn *v* past participle of **tear[2]**

tornado *n, pl* **-dos, -does** violent whirlwind

torpedo *n, pl* **-does** self-propelled underwater missile ▷ *v* **-doing, -doed** attack or destroy with or as if with torpedoes

torpid *adj* sluggish and inactive **torpor** *n* torpid state

torque [**tork**] *n* force causing rotation; Celtic necklace or armband of twisted metal

torrent *n* rushing stream; rapid flow of questions, abuse, etc

torrential *adj* (of rain) very heavy
torrid *adj* very hot and dry; highly emotional
torsion *n* twisting of a part by equal forces being applied at both ends but in opposite directions
torso *n, pl* **-sos** trunk of the human body; statue of a nude human trunk
tort *n law* civil wrong or injury for which damages may be claimed
tortilla *n* thin Mexican pancake
tortoise *n* slow-moving land reptile with a dome-shaped shell **tortoiseshell** *n* mottled brown shell of a turtle, used for making ornaments ▷ *adj* having brown, orange, and black markings
tortuous *adj* winding or twisting; not straightforward
torture *v* cause (someone) severe pain or mental anguish ▷ *n* severe physical or mental pain; torturing **torturer** *n*
Tory *n, pl* **Tories** member of the Conservative Party in Great Britain or Canada ▷ *adj* of Tories **Toryism** *n*
toss *v* throw lightly; fling or be flung about; coat (food) by gentle stirring or mixing; (of a horse) throw (its rider); throw up (a coin) to decide between alternatives by guessing which side will land uppermost ▷ *n* tossing **toss up** *v* toss a coin **toss-up** *n* even chance or risk
tot[1] *n* small child; small drink of spirits
tot[2] *v* **totting, totted tot up** add (numbers) together
total *n* whole, esp a sum of parts ▷ *adj* complete; of or being a total ▷ *v* **-talling, -talled** amount to; add up **totally** *adv* **totality** *n*
totalitarian *adj* of a dictatorial one-party government **totalitarianism** *n*
tote[1] *v* carry (a gun etc)
tote[2] *n* short for **totalizator**
totem *n* tribal badge or emblem **totem pole** post carved or painted with totems by Native Americans
totter *v* move unsteadily; be about to fall
toucan *n* tropical American bird with a large bill
touch *v* come into contact with; tap, feel, or stroke; affect; move emotionally; eat or drink; equal or match; *Brit, Aust & NZ, slang* ask for money ▷ *n* sense by which an object's qualities are perceived when they come into contact with part of the body; gentle tap, push, or caress; small amount; characteristic style; detail ▷ *adj* of a non-contact version of particular sport *eg touch rugby* **touch and go** risky or critical **touched** *adj* emotionally moved; slightly mad **touching** *adj* emotionally moving **touchy** *adj* easily offended **touch down** *v* (of an aircraft) land **touchline** *n* side line of the pitch in some games **touch on** *v* refer to in passing **touch-type** *v* type without looking at the keyboard
touché [too-shay] *interj* acknowledgment of the striking home of a remark or witty reply
touchstone *n* standard by which a judgment is made
tough *adj* strong or resilient; difficult to chew or cut; firm and determined; rough and violent; difficult; *Informal* unlucky or unfair ▷ *n Informal* rough violent person **toughness** *n* **toughen** *v* make or become tough or tougher
toupee [too-pay] *n* small wig
tour *n* journey visiting places of interest along the way; trip to

perform or play in different places ▷*v* make a tour (of) **tourism** *n* tourist travel as an industry **tourist** *n* person travelling for pleasure **touristy** *adj Informal, often derogatory* full of tourists or tourist attractions

tour de force *n, pl* **tours de force** *French* brilliant stroke or achievement

tournament *n* sporting competition with several stages to decide the overall winner; *hist* contest between knights on horseback

tourniquet [**tour**-nick-kay] *n* something twisted round a limb to stop bleeding

tousled *adj* ruffled and untidy

tout [rhymes with **shout**] *v* seek business in a persistent manner; recommend (a person or thing) ▷*n* person who sells tickets for a popular event at inflated prices

tow[1] *v* drag, esp by means of a rope ▷*n* towing **in tow** following closely behind **on tow** being towed **towbar** *n* metal bar on a car for towing vehicles **towpath** *n* path beside a canal or river, originally for horses towing boats

tow[2] *n* fibre of hemp or flax

towards, toward *prep* in the direction of; with regard to; as a contribution to

towel *n* cloth for drying things **towelling** *n* material used for making towels

tower *n* tall structure, often forming part of a larger building **tower of strength** person who supports or comforts **tower over** *v* be much taller than

town *n* group of buildings larger than a village; central part of this; people of a town **township** *n* small town; (in S Africa) urban settlement of Black or Coloured people **town hall** large building used for council meetings, concerts, etc

toxaemia [tox-**seem**-ya] *n* blood poisoning; high blood pressure in pregnancy

toxic *adj* poisonous; caused by poison **toxicity** *n* **toxicology** *n* study of poisons **toxin** *n* poison of bacterial origin

toy *n* something designed to be played with ▷*adj* (of a dog) of a variety much smaller than is normal for that breed **toy with** *v* play or fiddle with

toy-toy *SAfr* ▷*n* dance of political protest ▷*v* perform this dance

trace *v* track down and find; follow the course of; copy exactly by drawing on a thin sheet of transparent paper set on top of the original ▷*n* track left by something; minute quantity; indication **traceable** *adj* **tracer** *n* projectile which leaves a visible trail **tracery** *n* pattern of interlacing lines **tracing** *n* traced copy **trace element** chemical element occurring in very small amounts in soil etc

traces *pl n* strap by which a horse pulls a vehicle **kick over the traces** escape or defy control

trachea [track-**kee**-a] *n, pl* **tracheae** windpipe **tracheotomy** [track-ee-**ot**-a-mee] *n* surgical incision into the trachea

track *n* rough road or path; mark or trail left by the passage of anything; railway line; course for racing; separate section on a record, tape, or CD; course of action or thought; endless band round the wheels of a tank, bulldozer, etc ▷*v* follow the trail or path of **track down** *v* hunt for and find **track event** athletic sport held on a running track **track record** past accomplishments of a person or organization **tracksuit** *n* warm loose-fitting suit worn by athletes etc, esp during training

tract[1] *n* wide area; *anat* system of organs with a particular function

tract[2] *n* pamphlet, esp a religious one

tractable *adj* easy to manage or control

traction *n* pulling, esp by engine power; *med* application of a steady pull on an injured limb by weights and pulleys; grip of the wheels of a vehicle on the ground **traction engine** old-fashioned steam-powered vehicle for pulling heavy loads

tractor *n* motor vehicle with large rear wheels for pulling farm machinery

trade *n* buying, selling, or exchange of goods; person's job or craft; (people engaged in) a particular industry or business ▷*v* buy and sell; exchange; engage in trade **trader** *n* **trading** *n* **trade-in** *n* used article given in part payment for a new one **trademark** *n* (legally registered) name or symbol used by a firm to distinguish its goods **trade-off** *n* exchange made as a compromise **tradesman** *n* skilled worker; shopkeeper **trade union** society of workers formed to protect their interests **trade wind** wind blowing steadily towards the equator

tradition *n* body of beliefs, customs, etc handed down from generation to generation; custom or practice of long standing **traditional** *adj* **traditionally** *adv*

traduce *v* slander

traffic *n* vehicles coming and going on a road; (illicit) trade ▷*v* **-ficking, -ficked** trade, usu illicitly **trafficker** *n* **traffic lights** set of coloured lights at a junction to control the traffic flow **traffic warden** *Brit* person employed to control the movement and parking of traffic

tragedy *n, pl* **-dies** shocking or sad event; serious play, film, etc in which the hero is destroyed by a personal failing in adverse circumstances **tragedian** [traj-**jee**-dee-an], **tragedienne** [traj-jee-dee-**enn**] *n* person who acts in or writes tragedies **tragic** *adj* of or like a tragedy **tragically** *adv* **tragicomedy** *n* play with both tragic and comic elements

trail *n* path, track, or road; tracks left by a person, animal, or object ▷*v* drag along the ground; lag behind; follow the tracks of

trailer *n* vehicle designed to be towed by another vehicle; extract from a film or programme used to advertise it

train *v* instruct in a skill; learn the skills needed to do a particular job or activity; prepare for a sports event etc; aim (a gun etc); cause (an animal) to perform or (a plant) to grow in a particular way ▷*n* line of railway coaches or wagons drawn by an engine; sequence or series; long trailing back section of a dress **trainer** *n* person who trains an athlete or sportsman; sports shoe **trainee** *n* person being trained

traipse *v Informal* walk wearily

trait *n* characteristic feature

traitor *n* person guilty of treason or treachery **traitorous** *adj*

trajectory *n, pl* **-ries** line of flight, esp of a projectile

tram *n* public transport vehicle powered by an overhead wire and running on rails laid in the road **tramlines** *pl n* track for trams

tramp *v* travel on foot, hike; walk heavily ▷*n* homeless person who travels on foot; hike; sound of tramping; cargo ship available for hire; *US, Aust & NZ, slang* promiscuous woman

trample *v* tread on and crush

trampoline *n* tough canvas sheet attached to a frame by springs, used by acrobats etc ▷*v* bounce on a trampoline

trance *n* unconscious or dazed state

tranche *n* portion of something large, esp a sum of money

tranquil *adj* calm and quiet **tranquilly** *adv* **tranquillity** *n*

tranquillize *v* make calm **tranquillizer** *n* drug which reduces anxiety or tension

trans- *prefix* across, through, or beyond

transact *v* conduct or negotiate (a business deal)

transaction *n* business deal transacted

transatlantic *adj* on, from, or to the other side of the Atlantic

transceiver *n* transmitter and receiver of radio or electronic signals

transcend *v* rise above; be superior to **transcendence** *n* **transcendent** *adj* **transcendental** *adj* based on intuition rather than experience; supernatural or mystical **transcendentalism** *n*

transcribe *v* write down (something said); record for a later broadcast; arrange (music) for a different instrument **transcript** *n* copy

transducer *n* device that converts one form of energy to another

transept *n* either of the two shorter wings of a cross-shaped church

transfer *v* **-ferring, -ferred** move or send from one person or place to another ▷*n* transferring; design which can be transferred from one surface to another **transferable** *adj* **transference** *n* transferring **transfer station** *NZ* depot where rubbish is sorted for recycling

transfigure *v* change in appearance **transfiguration** *n*

transfix *v* astound or stun; pierce through

transform *v* change the shape or character of **transformation** *n* **transformer** *n* device for changing the voltage of an alternating current

transfusion *n* injection of blood into the blood vessels of a patient **transfuse** *v* give a transfusion to; permeate or infuse

transgress *v* break (a moral law) **transgression** *n* **transgressor** *n*

transient *adj* lasting only for a short time **transience** *n*

transistor *n* semiconducting device used to amplify electric currents; portable radio using transistors

transit *n* movement from one place to another **transition** *n* change from one state to another **transitional** *adj* **transitive** *adj* *grammar* (of a verb) requiring a direct object **transitory** *adj* not lasting long

translate *v* turn from one language into another

translation *n* **translator** *n*

transliterate *v* convert to the letters of a different alphabet **transliteration** *n*

translucent *adj* letting light pass through, but not transparent **translucency, translucence** *n*

transmigrate *v* (of a soul) pass into another body **transmigration** *n*

transmit *v* **-mitting, -mitted** pass (something) from one person or place to another; send out (signals) by radio waves; broadcast (a radio or television programme) **transmission** *n* transmitting; shafts and gears through which power passes from a vehicle's engine to its wheels **transmittable** *adj* **transmitter** *n*

transmogrify *v* **-fying, -fied** *Informal* change completely

transmute *v* change the form or nature of **transmutation** *n*

transom *n* horizontal bar across a window; bar separating a door from the window over it

transparent *adj* able to be seen through, clear; easily understood or recognized **transparently** *adv* **transparency** *n* transparent quality; colour photograph on transparent film that can be viewed by means of a projector

transpire *v* become known; *Informal* happen; give off water vapour through pores **transpiration** *n*

transplant *v* transfer (an organ or tissue) surgically from one part or body to another; remove and transfer (a plant) to another place ▷ *n* surgical transplanting; thing transplanted **transplantation** *n*

transport *v* convey from one place to another; *hist* exile (a criminal) to a penal colony; enrapture ▷ *n* business or system of transporting; vehicle used in transport; ecstasy or rapture **transportation** *n* **transporter** *n* large goods vehicle

transpose *v* interchange two things; put (music) into a different key **transposition** *n*

transsexual, transexual *n* person of one sex who believes his or her true identity is of the opposite sex

transubstantiation *n* *Christianity* doctrine that the bread and wine consecrated in Communion changes into the substance of Christ's body and blood

transuranic [tranz-yoor-**ran**-ik] *adj* (of an element) having an atomic number greater than that of uranium

transverse *adj* crossing from side to side

transvestite *n* person who seeks sexual pleasure by wearing the clothes of the opposite sex **transvestism** *n*

trap *n* device for catching animals; plan for tricking or catching a person; bend in a pipe containing liquid to prevent the escape of gas; stall in which greyhounds are enclosed before a race; two-wheeled carriage; *Brit, Aust & NZ, slang* mouth ▷ *v* **trapping, trapped** catch; trick **trapper** *n* person who traps animals for their fur **trapdoor** *n* door in floor or roof **trap-door spider** spider that builds a silk-lined hole in the ground closed by a hinged door of earth and silk

trapeze *n* horizontal bar suspended from two ropes, used by

circus acrobats
trapezium *n, pl* **-ziums, -zia** quadrilateral with two parallel sides of unequal length **trapezoid** [**trap**-piz-zoid] *n* quadrilateral with no sides parallel; *Chiefly US* trapezium
trappings *pl n* accessories that symbolize an office or position
Trappist *n* member of an order of Christian monks who observe strict silence
trash *n* anything worthless; *US & S Afr* rubbish **trashy** *adj*
trauma [**traw**-ma] *n* emotional shock; injury or wound **traumatic** *adj* **traumatize** *v*
travail *n lit* labour or toil
travel *v* **-elling, -elled** go from one place to another, through an area, or for a specified distance ▷ *n* travelling, esp as a tourist ▷ *pl* (account of) travelling **traveller** *n* **travelogue** *n* film or talk about someone's travels
traverse *v* move over or back and forth over
travesty *n, pl* **-ties** grotesque imitation or mockery
trawl *n* net dragged at deep levels behind a fishing boat ▷ *v* fish with such a net
trawler *n* trawling boat
tray *n* flat board, usu with a rim, for carrying things; open receptacle for office correspondence
treachery *n, pl* **-eries** wilful betrayal **treacherous** *adj* disloyal; unreliable or dangerous **treacherously** *adv*
treacle *n* thick dark syrup produced when sugar is refined **treacly** *adj*
tread *v* **treading, trod, trodden** *or* **trod** set one's foot on; crush by walking on ▷ *n* way of walking or dancing; upper surface of a step; part of a tyre or shoe that touches the ground **treadmill** *n hist* cylinder turned by treading on steps projecting from it; dreary routine
treadle [**tred**-dl] *n* lever worked by the foot to turn a wheel
treason *n* betrayal of one's sovereign or country; treachery or disloyalty **treasonable** *adj*
treasure *n* collection of wealth, esp gold or jewels; valued person or thing ▷ *v* prize or cherish **treasury** *n* storage place for treasure; (**T-**) government department in charge of finance **treasure-trove** *n* treasure found with no evidence of ownership
treasurer *n* official in charge of funds
treat *v* deal with or regard in a certain manner; give medical treatment to; subject to a chemical or industrial process; provide (someone) with (something) as a treat ▷ *n* pleasure, entertainment, etc given or paid for by someone else **treatment** *n* medical care; way of treating a person or thing
treatise [**treat**-izz] *n* formal piece of writing on a particular subject
treaty *n, pl* **-ties** signed contract between states
treble *adj* triple; *music* high-pitched ▷ *n* (singer with or part for) a soprano voice ▷ *v* increase three times **trebly** *adv*
tree *n* large perennial plant with a woody trunk **treeless** *adj* **tree kangaroo** tree-living kangaroo of New Guinea and N Australia **tree surgery** repair of damaged trees **tree surgeon**
trefoil [**tref**-foil] *n* plant, such as clover, with a three-lobed leaf; carved ornament like this

trek *n* long difficult journey, esp on foot; *SAfr* migration by ox wagon ▷*v* **trekking, trekked** make such a journey
trellis *n* framework of horizontal and vertical strips of wood
tremble *v* shake or quiver; feel fear or anxiety ▷*n* trembling **trembling** *adj*
tremendous *adj* huge; *Informal* great in quality or amount **tremendously** *adv*
tremolo *n, pl* **-los** *music* quivering effect in singing or playing
tremor *n* involuntary shaking; minor earthquake
tremulous *adj* trembling, as from fear or excitement
trench *n* long narrow ditch, esp one used as a shelter in war **trench coat** double-breasted waterproof coat
trenchant *adj* incisive; effective
trencher *n hist* wooden plate for serving food **trencherman** *n* hearty eater
trend *n* general tendency or direction; fashion **trendy** *adj, n Informal* consciously fashionable (person) **trendiness** *n*
trepidation *n* fear or anxiety
trespass *v* go onto another's property without permission ▷*n* trespassing; *old-fashioned* sin or wrongdoing **trespasser** *n* **trespass on** *v* take unfair advantage of (someone's friendship, patience, etc)
tresses *pl n* long flowing hair
trestle *n* board fixed on pairs of spreading legs, used as a support
trevally *n, pl* **-lies** *Aust & NZ* any of various food and game fishes
trews *pl n* close-fitting tartan trousers
tri- *combining form* three
triad *n* group of three; **(T-)** Chinese criminal secret society
trial *n law* investigation of a case before a judge; trying or testing; thing or person straining endurance or patience ▷*pl* sporting competition for individuals
triangle *n* geometric figure with three sides; triangular percussion instrument; situation involving three people **triangular** *adj*
tribe *n* group of clans or families believed to have a common ancestor **tribal** *adj* **tribalism** *n* loyalty to a tribe
tribulation *n* great distress
tribunal *n* board appointed to inquire into a specific matter; lawcourt
tribune *n* people's representative, esp in ancient Rome
tributary *n, pl* **-taries** stream or river flowing into a larger one ▷*adj* (of a stream or river) flowing into a larger one
tribute *n* sign of respect or admiration; tax paid by one state to another
trice *n* **in a trice** instantly
triceps *n* muscle at the back of the upper arm
trichology [trick-**ol**-a-jee] *n* study and treatment of hair and its diseases **trichologist** *n*
trick *n* deceitful or cunning action or plan; joke or prank; feat of skill or cunning; mannerism; cards played in one round ▷*v* cheat or deceive **trickery** *n* **trickster** *n* **tricky** *adj* difficult, needing careful handling; crafty
trickle *v* (cause to) flow in a thin stream or drops; move gradually ▷*n* gradual flow
tricolour [**trick**-kol-lor] *n*

three-coloured striped flag
tricycle *n* three-wheeled cycle
trident *n* three-pronged spear
triennial *adj* happening every three years
trifle *n* insignificant thing or amount; dessert of sponge cake, fruit, custard, and cream **trifling** *adj* insignificant **trifle with** *v* toy with
trigger *n* small lever releasing a catch on a gun or machine; action that sets off a course of events ▷ *v* (usu foll by *off*) set (an action or process) in motion **trigger-happy** *adj* too quick to use guns
trigonometry *n* branch of mathematics dealing with relations of the sides and angles of triangles
trike *n Informal* tricycle
trilateral *adj* having three sides
trilby *n, pl* **-bies** man's soft felt hat
trill *n music* rapid alternation between two notes; shrill warbling sound made by some birds ▷ *v* play or sing a trill
trillion *n* one million million, 10^{12}; (formerly) one million million million, 10^{18}
trilobite [**trile**-oh-bite] *n* small prehistoric sea animal
trilogy *n, pl* **-gies** series of three related books, plays, etc
trim *adj* **trimmer, trimmest** neat and smart; slender ▷ *v* **trimming, trimmed** cut or prune into good shape; decorate with lace, ribbons, etc; adjust the balance of (a ship or aircraft) by shifting the cargo etc ▷ *n* decoration; upholstery and decorative facings in a car; trim state; haircut that neatens the existing style **trimming** *n* decoration ▷ *pl* usual accompaniments
trimaran [**trime**-a-ran] *n* three-hulled boat
trinitrotoluene *n* full name for TNT
trinity *n, pl* **-ties** group of three; (T-) *Christianity* union of three persons, Father, Son, and Holy Spirit, in one God
trinket *n* small or worthless ornament or piece of jewellery
trio *n, pl* **trios** group of three; piece of music for three performers
trip *n* journey to a place and back, esp for pleasure; stumble; *Informal* hallucinogenic drug experience; switch on a mechanism ▷ *v* **tripping, tripped** (cause to) stumble; (often foll by *up*) catch (someone) in a mistake; move or tread lightly; *Informal* experience the hallucinogenic effects of a drug **tripper** *n* tourist
tripe *n* stomach of a cow used as food; *Brit, Aust & NZ, Informal* nonsense
triple *adj* having three parts; three times as great or as many ▷ *v* increase three times **triplet** *n* one of three babies born at one birth **triple jump** athletic event in which competitors make a hop, a step, and a jump as a continuous movement
triplicate *adj* triple **in triplicate** in three copies
tripod [**tripe**-pod] *n* three-legged stand, stool, etc
tripos [**tripe**-poss] *n* final examinations for an honours degree at Cambridge University
triptych [**trip**-tick] *n* painting or carving on three hinged panels, often forming an altarpiece
trite *adj* (of a remark or idea) commonplace and unoriginal
tritium *n* radioactive isotope of hydrogen

triumph *n* (happiness caused by) victory or success ▷*v* be victorious or successful; rejoice over a victory **triumphal** *adj* celebrating a triumph **triumphant** *adj* feeling or showing triumph

triumvirate [try-**umm**-vir-rit] *n* group of three people in joint control

trivet [**triv**-vit] *n* metal stand for a pot or kettle

trivial *adj* of little importance **trivially** *adv* **trivia** *pl n* trivial things or details **triviality** *n* **trivialize** *v* make (something) seem less important or complex than it is

trod *v* past tense and a past participle of **tread**

trodden *v* a past participle of **tread**

troglodyte *n* cave dweller

troika *n* Russian vehicle drawn by three horses abreast; group of three people in authority

troll *n* giant or dwarf in Scandinavian folklore

trolley *n* small wheeled table for food and drink; wheeled cart for moving goods **trolley bus** bus powered by electricity from an overhead wire but not running on rails

trollop *n old-fashioned* promiscuous or slovenly woman

trombone *n* brass musical instrument with a sliding tube **trombonist** *n*

troop *n* large group; artillery or cavalry unit; Scout company ▷*pl* soldiers ▷*v* move in a crowd **trooper** *n* cavalry soldier

trope *n* figure of speech

trophy *n, pl* **-phies** cup, shield, etc given as a prize; memento of success

tropic *n* either of two lines of latitude at 23½°N (**tropic of Cancer**) or 23½°S (**tropic of Capricorn**) ▷*pl* part of the earth's surface between these lines

tropical *adj* of or in the tropics; (of climate) very hot

trot *v* **trotting, trotted** (of a horse) move at a medium pace, lifting the feet in diagonal pairs; (of a person) move at a steady brisk pace ▷*n* trotting **trotter** *n* pig's foot **trot out** *v* repeat (old ideas etc) without fresh thought

troth [rhymes with **growth**] *n obs* pledge of devotion, esp a betrothal

troubadour [**troo**-bad-oor] *n* medieval travelling poet and singer

trouble *n* (cause of) distress or anxiety; disease or malfunctioning; state of disorder or unrest; care or effort ▷*v* (cause to) worry; exert oneself; cause inconvenience to **troubled** *adj* **troublesome** *adj* **troubleshooter** *n* person employed to locate and deal with faults or problems

trough [**troff**] *n* long open container, esp for animals' food or water; narrow channel between two waves or ridges; *meteorol* area of low pressure

trounce *v* defeat utterly

troupe [**troop**] *n* company of performers **trouper** *n*

trousers *pl n* two-legged outer garment with legs reaching usu to the ankles **trouser** *adj* of trousers

trousseau [**troo**-so] *n, pl* **-seaux, -seaus** bride's collection of clothing etc for her marriage

trout *n* game fish related to the salmon

trowel *n* hand tool with a wide blade for spreading mortar, lifting plants, etc

troy weight, troy *n* system of

weights used for gold, silver, and jewels

truant *n* pupil who stays away from school without permission **play truant** stay away from school without permission **truancy** *n*

truce *n* temporary agreement to stop fighting

truck[1] *n* railway goods wagon; large vehicle for transporting loads by road **trucker** *n* truck driver

truck[2] *n* **have no truck with** refuse to be involved with

truculent [truck-yew-lent] *adj* aggressively defiant **truculence** *n*

trudge *v* walk heavily or wearily ▷ *n* long tiring walk

true *adj* **truer, truest** in accordance with facts; genuine; faithful; exact **truly** *adv* **truism** *n* self-evident truth **truth** *n* state of being true; something true **truthful** *adj* honest; exact **truthfully** *adv*

truffle *n* edible underground fungus; sweet flavoured with chocolate

trug *n Brit* long shallow basket used by gardeners

trump[1] *n, adj* (card) of the suit outranking the others ▷ *v* play a trump card on (another card) ▷ *pl n* suit outranking the others **turn up trumps** achieve an unexpected success **trumped up** invented or concocted

trump[2] *n lit* (sound of) a trumpet

trumpet *n* valved brass instrument with a flared tube ▷ *v* **-peting, -peted** proclaim loudly; (of an elephant) cry loudly **trumpeter** *n*

truncate *v* cut short

truncheon *n* club carried by a policeman

trundle *v* move heavily on wheels

trunk *n* main stem of a tree; large case or box for clothes etc; person's body excluding the head and limbs; elephant's long nose; *US* car boot ▷ *pl* man's swimming shorts **trunk call** *Chiefly Brit* long-distance telephone call **trunk road** main road

truss *v* tie or bind up ▷ *n* device for holding a hernia in place; framework supporting a roof, bridge, etc

trust *v* believe in and rely on; consign to someone's care; expect or hope ▷ *n* confidence in the truth, reliability, etc of a person or thing; obligation arising from responsibility; arrangement in which one person administers property, money, etc on another's behalf; property held for another; *Brit* self-governing hospital or group of hospitals within the National Health Service; group of companies joined to control a market **trustee** *n* person holding property on another's behalf **trustful, trusting** *adj* inclined to trust others **trustworthy** *adj* reliable or honest **trusty** *adj* faithful or reliable

truth *n* see **true**

try *v* **trying, tried** make an effort or attempt; test or sample; put strain on *eg he tries my patience;* investigate (a case); examine (a person) in a lawcourt ▷ *n, pl* **tries** attempt or effort; *rugby* score gained by touching the ball down over the opponent's goal line **try it on** *Informal* try to deceive or fool someone **trying** *adj Informal* difficult or annoying

tryst *n* arrangement to meet

tsar, czar [zahr] *n hist* Russian emperor

tsetse fly [tset-see] *n* bloodsucking African fly whose bite transmits disease, esp sleeping sickness
T-shirt *n* short-sleeved casual shirt or top
tsp. teaspoon
T-square *n* T-shaped ruler
tsunami *n, pl* **-mis, -mi** tidal wave, usu caused by an earthquake under the sea
TT teetotal
tuatara *n* large lizard-like New Zealand reptile
tub *n* open, usu round container; bath **tubby** *adj* (of a person) short and fat
tuba [**tube**-a] *n* valved low-pitched brass instrument
tube *n* hollow cylinder; flexible cylinder with a cap to hold pastes **the tube** underground railway, esp the one in London **tubing** *n* length of tube; system of tubes **tubular** [**tube**-yew-lar] *adj* of or shaped like a tube
tuber [**tube**-er] *n* fleshy underground root of a plant such as a potato **tuberous** *adj*
tubercle [**tube**-er-kl] *n* small rounded swelling
tuberculosis [tube-berk-yew-**lohss**-iss] *n* infectious disease causing tubercles, esp in the lungs **tubercular** *adj* **tuberculin** *n* extract from a bacillus used to test for tuberculosis
TUC (in Britain and S Africa) Trades Union Congress
tuck *v* push or fold into a small space; stitch in folds ▷ *n* stitched fold; *Brit, Informal* food **tuck away** *v* eat (a large amount of food)
tucker *n Aust & NZ, Informal* food
Tudor *adj* of the English royal house ruling from 1485–1603
Tuesday *n* third day of the week
tufa [**tew**-fa] *n* porous rock formed as a deposit from springs
tuffet *n* small mound or seat
tuft *n* bunch of feathers, grass, hair, etc held or growing together at the base
tug *v* **tugging, tugged** pull hard ▷ *n* hard pull; (also **tugboat**) small ship used to tow other vessels **tug of war** contest in which two teams pull against one another on a rope
tuition *n* instruction, esp received individually or in a small group
tulip *n* plant with bright cup-shaped flowers
tulle [**tewl**] *n* fine net fabric of silk etc
tumble *v* (cause to) fall, esp awkwardly or violently; roll or twist, esp in play; rumple ▷ *n* fall; somersault **tumbler** *n* stemless drinking glass; acrobat; spring catch in a lock **tumbledown** *adj* dilapidated **tumble dryer, drier** machine that dries laundry by rotating it in warm air **tumble to** *v Informal* realize, understand
tumbril, tumbrel *n* farm cart used during the French Revolution to take prisoners to the guillotine
tumescent [tew-**mess**-ent] *adj* swollen or becoming swollen
tummy *n, pl* **-mies** *Informal* stomach
tumour [**tew**-mer] *n* abnormal growth in or on the body
tumult *n* uproar or commotion **tumultuous** [tew-**mull**-tew-uss] *adj*
tumulus *n, pl* **-li** burial mound
tun *n* large beer cask
tuna *n* large marine food fish
tundra *n* vast treeless Arctic region with permanently frozen

subsoil

tune *n* (pleasing) sequence of musical notes; correct musical pitch *eg she sang out of tune* ▷ *v* adjust (a musical instrument) so that it is in tune; adjust (a machine) to obtain the desired performance **tuneful** *adj* **tunefully** *adv* **tuneless** *adj* **tuner** *n* **tune in** *v* adjust (a radio or television) to receive (a station or programme)

tungsten *n chem* greyish-white metal

tunic *n* close-fitting jacket forming part of some uniforms; loose knee-length garment

tunnel *n* underground passage ▷ *v* **-nelling, -nelled** make a tunnel (through)

tunny *n, pl* **-nies, -ny** same as **tuna**

tup *n* male sheep

turban *n* Muslim, Hindu, or Sikh man's head covering, made by winding cloth round the head

turbid *adj* muddy, not clear

turbine *n* machine or generator driven by gas, water, etc turning blades

turbot *n* large European edible flatfish

turbulence *n* confusion, movement, or agitation; atmospheric instability causing gusty air currents **turbulent** *adj*

tureen *n* serving dish for soup

turf *n, pl* **turfs, turves** short thick even grass; square of this with roots and soil attached ▷ *v* cover with turf **the turf** racecourse; horse racing **turf accountant** bookmaker **turf out** *v Informal* throw out

turgid [tur-jid] *adj* (of language) pompous; swollen and thick

turkey *n* large bird bred for food

Turkish *adj* of Turkey, its people, or their language ▷ *n* Turkish language **Turkish bath** steam bath **Turkish delight** jelly-like sweet coated with icing sugar

turmeric *n* yellow spice obtained from the root of an Asian plant

turmoil *n* agitation or confusion

turn *v* change the position or direction (of); move around an axis, rotate; (usu foll by *into*) change in nature or character; reach or pass in age, time, etc *eg she has just turned twenty*; shape on a lathe; become sour ▷ *n* turning; opportunity to do something as part of an agreed succession; direction or drift; period or spell; short theatrical performance **good, bad turn** helpful *or* unhelpful act **turner** *n* **turning** *n* road or path leading off a main route **turncoat** *n* person who deserts one party or cause to join another **turn down** *v* reduce the volume or brightness (of); refuse or reject **turn in** *v* go to bed; hand in **turning point** moment when a decisive change occurs **turn off** *v* stop (something) working by using a knob etc **turn on** *v* start (something) working by using a knob etc; become aggressive towards; *Informal* excite, esp sexually **turnout** *n* number of people appearing at a gathering **turnover** *n* total sales made by a business over a certain period; small pastry; rate at which staff leave and are replaced **turnpike** *n Brit* road where a toll is collected at barriers **turnstile** *n* revolving gate for admitting one person at a time **turntable** *n* revolving platform **turn up** *v* arrive or appear; find or be found; increase the volume or brightness (of) **turn-up** *n* turned-up fold at

the bottom of a trouser leg; *Informal* unexpected event
turnip *n* root vegetable with orange or white flesh
turpentine *n* (oil made from) the resin of certain trees **turps** *n* turpentine oil
turpitude *n* wickedness
turquoise *adj* blue-green ▷*n* blue-green precious stone
turret *n* small tower; revolving gun tower on a warship or tank
turtle *n* sea tortoise **turn turtle** capsize **turtledove** *n* small wild dove **turtleneck** *n* (sweater with) a round high close-fitting neck
tusk *n* long pointed tooth of an elephant, walrus, etc
tussle *n, v* fight or scuffle
tussock *n* tuft of grass
tutelage [**tew**-till-lij] *n* instruction or guidance, esp by a tutor; state of being supervised by a guardian or tutor **tutelary** [**tew**-till-lar-ee] *adj*
tutor *n* person teaching individuals or small groups ▷*v* act as a tutor to **tutorial** *n* period of instruction with a tutor
tutu *n* short stiff skirt worn by ballerinas
tuxedo *n, pl* **-dos** *US & Aust* dinner jacket
TV television
twaddle *n* silly or pretentious talk or writing
twain *n obs* two
twang *n* sharp ringing sound; nasal speech ▷*v* (cause to) make a twang
tweak *v* pinch or twist sharply ▷*n* tweaking
twee *adj Informal* too sentimental, sweet, or pretty
tweed *n* thick woollen cloth ▷*pl* suit of tweed **tweedy** *adj*
tweet *n, v* chirp
tweeter *n* loudspeaker reproducing high-frequency sounds
tweezers *pl n* small pincer-like tool
twelve *adj, n* two more than ten **twelfth** *adj, n* (of) number twelve in a series
twenty *adj, n* two times ten **twentieth** *adj, n*
twenty-four-seven, 24/7 *adv Informal* all the time
twerp *n Informal* silly person
twice *adv* two times
twiddle *v* fiddle or twirl in an idle way **twiddle one's thumbs** be bored, have nothing to do
twig[1] *n* small branch or shoot
twig[2] *v* **twigging, twigged** *Informal* realize or understand
twilight *n* soft dim light just after sunset
twill *n* fabric woven to produce parallel ridges
twin *n* one of a pair, esp of two children born at one birth ▷*v* **twinning, twinned** pair or be paired
twine *n* string or cord ▷*v* twist or coil round
twinge *n* sudden sharp pain or emotional pang
twinkle *v* shine brightly but intermittently ▷*n* flickering brightness
twirl *v* turn or spin around quickly; twist or wind, esp idly
twist *v* turn out of the natural position; distort or pervert; wind or twine ▷*n* twisting; twisted thing; unexpected development in the plot of a film, book, etc; bend or curve; distortion **twisted** *adj* (of a person) cruel or perverted **twister** *n Brit, Informal* swindler

twit[1] *v* **twitting, twitted** poke fun at (someone)
twit[2] *n Informal* foolish person
twitch *v* move spasmodically; pull sharply ▷*n* nervous muscular spasm; sharp pull
twitter *v* (of birds) utter chirping sounds ▷*n* act or sound of twittering
two *adj, n* one more than one **two-edged** *adj* (of a remark) having both a favourable and an unfavourable interpretation **two-faced** *adj* deceitful, hypocritical **two-time** *v Informal* deceive (a lover) by having an affair with someone else
tycoon *n* powerful wealthy businessman
tyke *n Brit, Aust & NZ, Informal* small cheeky child
type *n* class or category; *Informal* person, esp of a specified kind; block with a raised character used for printing; printed text ▷*v* print with a typewriter or word processor; typify; classify **typist** *n* person who types with a typewriter or word processor **typecast** *v* continually cast (an actor or actress) in similar roles **typewriter** *n* machine which prints a character when the appropriate key is pressed
typhoid fever *n* acute infectious feverish disease
typhoon *n* violent tropical storm
typhus *n* infectious feverish disease
typical *adj* true to type, characteristic **typically** *adv* **typify** *v* **-fying, -fied** be typical of
typography *n* art or style of printing **typographical** *adj* **typographer** *n*
tyrannosaurus [tirr-ran-oh-**sore**-uss] *n* large two-footed flesh-eating dinosaur
tyrant *n* oppressive or cruel ruler; person who exercises authority oppressively **tyrannical** *adj* like a tyrant, oppressive **tyrannize** *v* exert power (over) oppressively or cruelly **tyrannous** *adj* **tyranny** *n* tyrannical rule
tyre *n* rubber ring, usu inflated, over the rim of a vehicle's wheel to grip the road
tyro *n, pl* **-ros** novice or beginner

U

ubiquitous [yew-**bik**-wit-uss] *adj* being or seeming to be everywhere at once **ubiquity** *n*
udder *n* large baglike milk-producing gland of cows, sheep, or goats
UFO unidentified flying object
ugly *adj* **uglier, ugliest** of unpleasant appearance; ominous or menacing **ugliness** *n*
UHF ultrahigh frequency
UHT (of milk or cream) ultra-heat-treated
UK United Kingdom
ukulele, ukelele [yew-kal-**lay**-lee] *n* small guitar with four strings
ulcer *n* open sore on the surface of the skin or mucous membrane. **ulcerated** *adj* made or becoming ulcerous **ulceration** *n* **ulcerous** *adj* of, like, or characterized by ulcers
ulna *n, pl* **-nae, -nas** inner and longer of the two bones of the human forearm
ulterior *adj* (of an aim, reason, etc) concealed or hidden
ultimate *adj* final in a series or process; highest or supreme **ultimately** *adv*
ultimatum [ult-im-**may**-tum] *n* final warning stating that action will be taken unless certain conditions are met
ultra- *prefix* beyond a specified extent, range, or limit *eg ultrasonic;* extremely *eg ultramodern*
ultrahigh frequency *n* radio frequency between 3000 and 300 megahertz
ultramarine *adj* vivid blue
ultrasonic *adj* of or producing sound waves with a higher frequency than the human ear can hear
ultraviolet *adj, n* (of) light beyond the limit of visibility at the violet end of the spectrum
ululate [**yewl**-yew-late] *v* howl or wail **ululation** *n*
umber *adj* dark brown to reddish-brown
umbilical *adj* of the navel **umbilical cord** long flexible tube of blood vessels that connects a fetus with the placenta
umbrage *n* **take umbrage** feel offended or upset
umbrella *n* portable device used for protection against rain, consisting of a folding frame covered in material attached to a central rod; single organization, idea, etc that contains or covers many different organizations, ideas, etc
umpire *n* official who rules on the playing of a game ▷*v* act as umpire in (a game)

umpteen *adj Informal* very many **umpteenth** *n, adj*

UN United Nations

un- *prefix* not *eg unidentified*; denoting reversal of an action *eg untie*; denoting removal from *eg unthrone*

unable *adj* **unable to** lacking the necessary power, ability, or authority to (do something)

unaccountable *adj* unable to be explained; (foll by *to*) not answerable to **unaccountably** *adv*

unadulterated *adj* with nothing added, pure

unanimous [yew-**nan**-im-uss] *adj* in complete agreement; agreed by all **unanimity** *n*

unarmed *adj* without weapons

unassuming *adj* modest or unpretentious

unaware *adj* not aware or conscious **unawares** *adv* by surprise *eg caught unawares*; without knowing.

> SPELLING Note the difference between the adjective *unaware*, usually followed by *of* or *that*, and the adverb *unawares*.

unbalanced *adj* biased or one-sided; mentally deranged

unbearable *adj* not able to be endured **unbearably** *adv*

unbeknown *adv* **unbeknown to** without the knowledge of (a person)

unbend *v Informal* become less strict or more informal in one's attitudes or behaviour **unbending** *adj*

unbidden *adj* not ordered or asked

unborn *adj* not yet born

unbosom *v* relieve (oneself) of (secrets or feelings) by telling someone

unbridled *adj* (of feelings or behaviour) not controlled in any way

unburden *v* relieve (one's mind or oneself) of a worry by confiding in someone

uncalled-for *adj* not fair or justified

uncanny *adj* weird or mysterious **uncannily** *adv*

unceremonious *adj* relaxed and informal; abrupt or rude **unceremoniously** *adv*

uncertain *adj* not able to be accurately known or predicted; not able to be depended upon; changeable **uncertainty** *n*

un-Christian *adj* not in accordance with Christian principles

uncle *n* brother of one's father or mother; husband of one's aunt

unclean *adj* lacking moral, spiritual, or physical cleanliness

uncomfortable *adj* not physically relaxed; anxious or uneasy

uncommon *adj* not happening or encountered often; in excess of what is normal **uncommonly** *adv*

uncompromising *adj* not prepared to compromise

unconcerned *adj* lacking in concern or involvement **unconcernedly** *adv*

unconditional *adj* without conditions or limitations

unconscionable *adj* having no principles, unscrupulous; excessive in amount or degree

unconscious *adj* lacking normal awareness through the senses; not aware of one's actions or behaviour ▷ *n* part of the mind containing instincts and ideas that exist without one's awareness **unconsciously** *adv*

unconsciousness *n*
uncooperative *adj* not willing to help other people with what they are doing
uncouth *adj* lacking in good manners, refinement, or grace
uncover *v* reveal or disclose; remove the cover, top, etc, from
unction *n* act of anointing with oil in sacramental ceremonies
unctuous *adj* pretending to be kind and concerned
undecided *adj* not having made up one's mind; (of an issue or problem) not agreed or decided upon
undeniable *adj* unquestionably true **undeniably** *adv*
under *prep, adv* indicating movement to or position beneath the underside or base ▷ *prep* less than; subject to
under- *prefix* below *eg underground;* insufficient or insufficiently *eg underrate*
underage *adj* below the required or standard age
underarm *adj sport* denoting a style of throwing, bowling, or serving in which the hand is swung below shoulder level ▷ *adv sport* in an underarm style
undercarriage *n* landing gear of an aircraft; framework supporting the body of a vehicle
underclass *n* class consisting of the most disadvantaged people, such as the long-term unemployed
undercoat *n* coat of paint applied before the final coat
undercover *adj* done or acting in secret
undercurrent *n* current that is not apparent at the surface; underlying opinion or emotion
undercut *v* charge less than (a competitor) to obtain trade
underdog *n* person or team in a weak or underprivileged position
underdone *adj* not cooked enough
underestimate *v* make too low an estimate of; not realize the full potential of
underfoot *adv* under the feet
undergarment *n* any piece of underwear
undergo *v* experience, endure, or sustain
undergraduate *n* person studying in a university for a first degree
underground *adj* occurring, situated, used, or going below ground level; secret ▷ *n* electric passenger railway operated in underground tunnels; movement dedicated to overthrowing a government or occupation forces
undergrowth *n* small trees and bushes growing beneath taller trees in a wood or forest
underhand *adj* sly, deceitful, and secretive
underlie *v* lie or be placed under; be the foundation, cause, or basis of **underlying** *adj* fundamental or basic
underline *v* draw a line under; state forcibly, emphasize
underling *n* subordinate
undermine *v* weaken gradually
underneath *prep, adv* under or beneath ▷ *adj, n* lower (part or surface)
underpants *pl n* man's undergarment for the lower part of the body
underpass *n* section of a road that passes under another road or a railway line
underpin *v* give strength or

support to

underprivileged *adj* lacking the rights and advantages of other members of society

underrate *v* not realize the full potential of **underrated** *adj*

underseal *n Chiefly Brit* coating of tar etc applied to the underside of a motor vehicle to prevent corrosion

underside *n* bottom or lower surface

understand *v* know and comprehend the nature or meaning of; realize or grasp (something); assume, infer, or believe **understandable** *adj* **understandably** *adv* **understanding** *n* ability to learn, judge, or make decisions; personal interpretation of a subject; mutual agreement, usu an informal or private one ▷ *adj* kind and sympathetic

understate *v* describe or represent (something) in restrained terms; state that (something, such as a number) is less than it is **understatement** *n*

understudy *n* actor who studies a part in order to be able to replace the usual actor if necessary ▷ *v* act as an understudy for

undertake *v* agree or commit oneself to (something) or to do (something); promise **undertaking** *n* task or enterprise; agreement to do something

undertaker *n* person whose job is to prepare corpses for burial or cremation and organize funerals

undertone *n* quiet tone of voice; underlying quality or feeling

undertow *n* strong undercurrent flowing in a different direction from the surface current

underwear *n* clothing worn under the outer garments and next to the skin

underworld *n* criminals and their associates; *Greek & Roman myth* regions below the earth's surface regarded as the abode of the dead

underwrite *v* accept financial responsibility for (a commercial project); sign and issue (an insurance policy), thus accepting liability

underwriter *n* person who underwrites (esp an insurance policy)

undesirable *adj* not desirable or pleasant, objectionable ▷ *n* objectionable person

undo *v* open, unwrap; reverse the effects of; cause the downfall of **undone** *adj* **undoing** *n* cause of someone's downfall

undoubted *adj* certain or indisputable **undoubtedly** *adv*

undue *adj* greater than is reasonable, excessive **unduly** *adv*

undulate *v* move in waves **undulation** *n*

undying *adj* never ending, eternal

unearth *v* reveal or discover by searching; dig up out of the earth

unearthly *adj* ghostly or eerie; ridiculous or unreasonable

uneasy *adj* (of a person) anxious or apprehensive; (of a condition) precarious or uncomfortable **uneasily** *adv* **uneasiness** *n* **unease** *n* feeling of anxiety; state of dissatisfaction

unemployed *adj* out of work **unemployment** *n*

unequivocal *adj* completely clear in meaning **unequivocally** *adv*

unerring *adj* never mistaken, consistently accurate

unexceptionable *adj* beyond criticism or objection

unfailing *adj* continuous or reliable **unfailingly** *adv*
unfair *adj* not right, fair, or just **unfairly** *adv* **unfairness** *n*
unfaithful *adj* having sex with someone other than one's regular partner; not true to a promise or vow **unfaithfulness** *n*
unfeeling *adj* without sympathy
unfit *adj* unqualified or unsuitable; in poor physical condition
unflappable *adj Informal* not easily upset **unflappability** *n*
unfold *v* open or spread out from a folded state; reveal or be revealed
unforgettable *adj* impossible to forget, memorable
unfortunate *adj* unlucky, unsuccessful, or unhappy; regrettable or unsuitable **unfortunately** *adv*
unfrock *v* deprive (a priest in holy orders) of his or her priesthood
ungainly *adj* **-lier, -liest** lacking grace when moving
ungodly *adj Informal* unreasonable or outrageous *eg an ungodly hour*; wicked or sinful
ungrateful *adj* not grateful or thankful
unguarded *adj* not protected; incautious or careless
unguent [ung-gwent] *n lit* ointment
unhand *v old-fashioned or lit* release from one's grasp
unhappy *adj* sad or depressed; unfortunate or wretched **unhappily** *adv* **unhappiness** *n*
unhealthy *adj* likely to cause poor health; not fit or well; morbid, unnatural
unhinge *v* derange or unbalance (a person or his or her mind)
uni *n Informal* short for **university**
uni- *combining form* of, consisting of, or having only one *eg unicellular*
unicorn *n* imaginary horselike creature with one horn growing from its forehead
uniform *n* special identifying set of clothes for the members of an organization, such as soldiers ▷ *adj* regular and even throughout, unvarying; alike or like **uniformly** *adv* **uniformity** *n*
unify *v* **-fying, -fied** make or become one **unification** *n*
unilateral *adj* made or done by only one person or group **unilaterally** *adv*
unimpeachable *adj* completely honest and reliable
uninterested *adj* having or showing no interest in someone or something
union *n* uniting or being united; short for **trade union**: association or confederation of individuals or groups for a common purpose **unionist** *n* member or supporter of a trade union **unionize** *v* organize (workers) into a trade union **unionization** *n* **Union Jack, Flag** national flag of the United Kingdom
unique [yoo-**neek**] *adj* being the only one of a particular type; without equal or like **uniquely** *adv*

> Because of its meaning, avoid using *unique* with modifiers like *very* and *rather*.

unisex *adj* designed for use by both sexes
unison *n* complete agreement; *music* singing or playing of the same notes together at the same time
unit *n* single undivided entity or whole; group or individual regarded as a basic element of a larger whole; fixed quantity etc, used as a standard of measurement; piece of

furniture designed to be fitted with other similar pieces **unit trust** investment trust that issues units for public sale and invests the money in many different businesses

Unitarian *n* person who believes that God is one being and rejects the Trinity **Unitarianism** *n*

unitary *adj* consisting of a single undivided whole; of a unit or units

unite *v* make or become an integrated whole; (cause to) enter into an association or alliance

unity *n* state of being one; mutual agreement

universe *n* whole of all existing matter, energy, and space; the world **universal** *adj* of or typical of the whole of mankind or of nature; existing everywhere **universally** *adv* **universality** *n*

university *n, pl* **-ties** institution of higher education with the authority to award degrees

unkempt *adj* (of the hair) not combed; slovenly or untidy

unknown *adj* not known; not famous ▷ *n* unknown person, quantity, or thing

unleaded *adj* (of petrol) containing less tetraethyl lead, in order to reduce environmental pollution

unless *conj* except under the circumstances that

unlike *adj* dissimilar or different ▷ *prep* not like or typical of

unlikely *adj* improbable

unload *v* remove (cargo) from (a ship, truck, or plane); remove the ammunition from (a firearm)

unmask *v* remove the mask or disguise from; (cause to) appear in true character

unmentionable *adj* unsuitable as a topic of conversation

unmistakable, unmistakeable *adj* not ambiguous, clear **unmistakably, unmistakeably** *adv*

unmitigated *adj* not reduced or lessened in severity etc; total and complete

unmoved *adj* not affected by emotion, indifferent

unnatural *adj* strange and frightening because not usual; not in accordance with accepted standards of behaviour

unnerve *v* cause to lose courage, confidence, or self-control

unnumbered *adj* countless; not counted or given a number

unorthodox *adj* (of ideas, methods, etc) unconventional and not generally accepted; (of a person) having unusual opinions or methods

unpack *v* remove the contents of (a suitcase, trunk, etc); take (something) out of a packed container

unparalleled *adj* not equalled, supreme

unpick *v* undo (the stitches) of (a piece of sewing)

unpleasant *adj* not pleasant or agreeable **unpleasantly** *adv* **unpleasantness** *n*

unprintable *adj* unsuitable for printing for reasons of obscenity or libel

unprofessional *adj* contrary to the accepted code of a profession **unprofessionally** *adv*

unqualified *adj* lacking the necessary qualifications; total or complete

unravel *v* **-elling, -elled** reduce (something knitted or woven) to separate strands; become unravelled; explain or solve

unremitting *adj* never slackening or stopping
unrequited *adj* not returned *eg unrequited love*
unrest *n* rebellious state of discontent
unrivalled *adj* having no equal
unroll *v* open out or unwind (something rolled or coiled) or (of something rolled or coiled) become opened out or unwound
unruly *adj* **-lier, -liest** difficult to control or organize
unsavoury *adj* distasteful or objectionable
unscathed *adj* not harmed or injured
unscrupulous *adj* prepared to act dishonestly, unprincipled
unseat *v* throw or displace from a seat or saddle; depose from an office or position
unsettled *adj* lacking order or stability; disturbed and restless; constantly changing or moving from place to place
unsightly *adj* unpleasant to look at
unsocial *adj* (also **unsociable**) avoiding the company of other people; falling outside the normal working day *eg unsocial hours*
unsound *adj* unhealthy or unstable; not based on truth or fact
unstable *adj* lacking stability or firmness; having abrupt changes of mood or behaviour
unsuitable *adj* not right or appropriate for a particular purpose **unsuitably** *adv*
unsuited *adj* not appropriate for a particular task or situation
unswerving *adj* firm, constant, not changing
unthinkable *adj* out of the question, inconceivable
untidy *adj* messy and disordered **untidily** *adv* **untidiness** *n*
untie *v* open or free (something that is tied); free from constraint
until *conj* up to the time that ▷ *prep* in or throughout the period before **not until** not before (a time or event)
untimely *adj* occurring before the expected or normal time; inappropriate to the occasion or time
unto *prep old-fashioned* to
untold *adj* incapable of description; incalculably great in number or quantity
untouchable *adj* above reproach or suspicion; unable to be touched ▷ *n* member of the lowest Hindu caste in India
untoward *adj* causing misfortune or annoyance
untrue *adj* incorrect or false; disloyal or unfaithful **untruth** *n* statement that is not true, lie
unusual *adj* uncommon or extraordinary **unusually** *adv*
unutterable *adj* incapable of being expressed in words **unutterably** *adv*
unvarnished *adj* not elaborated upon *eg the unvarnished truth*
unwieldy *adj* too heavy, large, or awkward to be easily handled
unwind *v* relax after a busy or tense time; slacken, undo, or unravel
unwitting *adj* not intentional; not knowing or conscious **unwittingly** *adv*
unwonted *adj* out of the ordinary
unworthy *adj* not deserving or worthy; lacking merit or value **unworthy of** beneath the level considered befitting (to)
unwrap *v* remove the wrapping

from (something)

unwritten *adj* not printed or in writing; operating only through custom

up *prep, adv* indicating movement to or position at a higher place ▷ *adv* indicating readiness, intensity or completeness, etc *eg warm up; drink up* ▷ *adj* of a high or higher position; out of bed ▷ *v* **upping, upped** increase or raise **up against** having to cope with **up and** *Informal* do something suddenly *eg he upped and left* **ups and downs** alternating periods of good and bad luck **what's up?** *Informal* what is wrong? **upward** *adj* directed or moving towards a higher place or level ▷ *adv* (also **upwards**) from a lower to a higher place, level, or condition

upbeat *adj Informal* cheerful and optimistic ▷ *n music* unaccented beat

upbraid *v* scold or reproach

upbringing *n* education of a person during the formative years

update *v* bring up to date

upend *v* turn or set (something) on its end

upfront *adj* open and frank ▷ *adv, adj* (of money) paid out at the beginning of a business arrangement

upgrade *v* promote (a person or job) to a higher rank

upheaval *n* strong, sudden, or violent disturbance

uphill *adj* sloping or leading upwards; requiring a great deal of effort ▷ *adv* up a slope ▷ *n SAfr* difficulty

uphold *v* maintain or defend against opposition; give moral support to **upholder** *n*

upholster *v* fit (a chair or sofa) with padding, springs, and covering **upholsterer** *n*

upholstery *n* soft covering on a chair or sofa

upkeep *n* act, process, or cost of keeping something in good repair

upland *adj* of or in an area of high or relatively high ground **uplands** *pl n* area of high or relatively high ground

uplift *v* raise or lift up; raise morally or spiritually ▷ *n* act or process of improving moral, social, or cultural conditions **uplifting** *adj*

upload *v* transfer (data or a program) from one's own computer into the memory of another computer

upon *prep* on; up and on

upper *adj* higher or highest in physical position, wealth, rank, or status ▷ *n* part of a shoe above the sole **uppermost** *adj* highest in position, power, or importance ▷ *adv* in or into the highest place or position **upper class** highest social class **upper-class** *adj* **upper crust** *Brit, Aust & NZ, Informal* upper class **upper hand** position of control

uppish, uppity *adj Brit, Informal* snobbish, arrogant, or presumptuous

upright *adj* vertical or erect; honest or just ▷ *adv* vertically or in an erect position ▷ *n* vertical support, such as a post **uprightness** *n*

uprising *n* rebellion or revolt

uproar *n* disturbance characterized by loud noise and confusion **uproarious** *adj* very funny; (of laughter) loud and boisterous **uproariously** *adv*

uproot *v* pull up by or as if by the roots; displace (a person or people)

from their native or usual surroundings
upset *adj* emotionally or physically disturbed or distressed ▷*v* tip over; disturb the normal state or stability of; disturb mentally or emotionally; make physically ill ▷*n* unexpected defeat or reversal; disturbance or disorder of the emotions, mind, or body **upsetting** *adj*
upshot *n* final result or conclusion
upside down *adj* turned over completely; *Informal* confused or jumbled ▷*adv* in an inverted fashion; in a chaotic manner
upstage *adj* at the back half of the stage ▷*v Informal* draw attention to oneself from (someone else)
upstairs *adv* to or on an upper floor of a building ▷*n* upper floor ▷*adj* situated on an upper floor
upstanding *adj* of good character
upstart *n* person who has risen suddenly to a position of power and behaves arrogantly
upstream *adv, adj* in or towards the higher part of a stream
upsurge *n* rapid rise or swell
uptake *n* **quick, slow on the uptake** *Informal* quick *or* slow to understand or learn
uptight *adj Informal* nervously tense, irritable, or angry
up-to-date *adj* modern or fashionable
upturn *n* upward trend or improvement **upturned** *adj* facing upwards
uranium *n chem* radioactive silvery-white metallic element, used chiefly as a source of nuclear energy
Uranus *n Greek myth* god of the sky; seventh planet from the sun
urban *adj* of or living in a city or town; denoting modern pop music of African-American origin, such as hip-hop **urbanize** *v* make (a rural area) more industrialized and urban **urbanization** *n*
urbane *adj* characterized by courtesy, elegance, and sophistication **urbanity** *n*
urchin *n* mischievous child
urethra [yew-**reeth**-ra] *n* canal that carries urine from the bladder out of the body
urge *n* strong impulse, inner drive, or yearning ▷*v* plead with or press (a person to do something); advocate earnestly; force or drive onwards
urgent *adj* requiring speedy action or attention **urgency** *n* **urgently** *adv*
urine *n* pale yellow fluid excreted by the kidneys to the bladder and passed as waste from the body **urinary** *adj* **urinate** *v* discharge urine **urination** *n* **urinal** *n* sanitary fitting used by men for urination
URL uniform resource locator: a standardized address of a location on the Internet
urn *n* vase used as a container for the ashes of the dead; large metal container with a tap, used for making and holding tea or coffee
ursine *adj* of or like a bear
us *pron* objective case of **we**
US, USA United States (of America)
use *v* put into service or action; take advantage of, exploit; consume or expend ▷*n* using or being used; ability or permission to use; usefulness or advantage; purpose for which something is used **user** *n* **user-friendly** *adj* easy to familiarize oneself with, understand, and use **username** *n*

computers name entered into a computer for identification purposes **usable** *adj* able to be used **usage** *n* regular or constant use; way in which a word is used in a language **use-by date** *Aust, NZ & S Afr* date on packaged food after which it should not be sold **used** *adj* second-hand **used to** *adj* accustomed to ▷*v* used as an auxiliary to express past habitual or accustomed actions *eg I used to live there* **useful** *adj* **usefully** *adv* **usefulness** *n* **useless** *adj* **uselessly** *adv* **uselessness** *n*

usher *n* official who shows people to their seats, as in a church ▷*v* conduct or escort **usherette** *n* female assistant in a cinema who shows people to their seats

USSR (formerly) Union of Soviet Socialist Republics

usual *adj* of the most normal, frequent, or regular type **usually** *adv* most often, in most cases

> SPELLING Collins Word Web shows that it's very common to write *usualy*, forgetting the double *l* of **usually**

usurp [yewz-**zurp**] *v* seize (a position or power) without authority **usurpation** *n* **usurper** *n*

usury *n* practice of lending money at an extremely high rate of interest **usurer** [**yewz**-yoor-er] *n*

ute [yoot] *n Aust & NZ, Informal* utility truck

utensil *n* tool or container for practical use *eg cooking utensils*

uterus [**yew**-ter-russ] *n* womb **uterine** *adj*

utilitarian *adj* useful rather than beautiful; of utilitarianism **utilitarianism** *n ethics* doctrine that the right action is the one that brings about the greatest good for the greatest number of people

utility *n* usefulness *pl* **-ties** public service, such as electricity ▷*adj* designed for use rather than beauty **utility room** room used for large domestic appliances and equipment **utility truck** *Aust & NZ* small truck with an open body and low sides

utilize *v* make practical use of **utilization** *n*

utmost *adj, n* (of) the greatest possible degree or amount *eg the utmost point; I was doing my utmost to comply*

Utopia [yew-**tope**-ee-a] *n* any real or imaginary society, place, or state considered to be perfect or ideal **Utopian** *adj*

utter[1] *v* express (something) in sounds or words **utterance** *n* something uttered; act or power of uttering

utter[2] *adj* total or absolute **utterly** *adv*

uttermost *adj, n* same as **utmost**

U-turn *n* turn, made by a vehicle, in the shape of a U, resulting in a reversal of direction; complete change in policy *eg a humiliating U-turn by the Prime Minister*

UV ultraviolet

uvula [**yew**-view-la] *n* small fleshy part of the soft palate that hangs in the back of the throat **uvular** *adj*

uxorious [ux-**or**-ee-uss] *adj* excessively fond of or dependent on one's wife

V

V volt

v. versus; very

vacant *adj* (of a toilet, room, etc) unoccupied; without interest or understanding **vacantly** *adv* **vacancy** *n, pl* **-cies** unfilled job; unoccupied room in a guesthouse; state of being unoccupied

vacate *v* cause (something) to be empty by leaving; give up (a job or position) **vacation** *n* time when universities and law courts are closed; *Chiefly US* holiday

vaccinate *v* inject with a vaccine **vaccination** *n* **vaccine** *n* substance designed to cause a mild form of a disease to make a person immune to the disease itself

vacillate [vass-ill-late] *v* keep changing one's mind or opinions **vacillation** *n*

vacuous *adj* not expressing intelligent thought **vacuity** *n*

vacuum *n, pl* **vacuums, vacua** empty space from which all or most air or gas has been removed ▷ *v* clean with a vacuum cleaner **vacuum cleaner** electrical appliance which sucks up dust and dirt from carpets and upholstery **vacuum flask** double-walled flask with a vacuum between the walls that keeps drinks hot or cold **vacuum-packed** *adj* contained in packaging from which the air has been removed

vagabond *n* person with no fixed home, esp a beggar

vagary [vaig-a-ree] *n, pl* **-garies** unpredictable change

vagina [vaj-**jine**-a] *n* (in female mammals) passage from the womb to the external genitals **vaginal** *adj*

vagrant [vaig-rant] *n* person with no settled home ▷ *adj* wandering **vagrancy** *n*

vague *adj* not clearly explained; unable to be seen or heard clearly; absent-minded **vaguely** *adv*

vain *adj* excessively proud, esp of one's appearance; bound to fail, futile **in vain** unsuccessfully

vainglorious *adj lit* boastful

valance [val-lenss] *n* piece of drapery round the edge of a bed

vale *n lit* valley

valedictory [val-lid-**dik**-tree] *adj* (of a speech, performance, etc) intended as a farewell **valediction** *n* farewell speech

valence [**vale**-ence] *n* molecular bonding between atoms

valency *n, pl* **-cies** power of an atom to make molecular bonds

valentine *n* (person to whom one sends) a romantic card on Saint Valentine's Day, 14th February

valerian *n* herb used as a sedative

valet *n* man's personal male

servant

valetudinarian [val-lit-yew-din-**air**-ee-an] *n* person with a long-term illness; person overconcerned about his or her health

valiant *adj* brave or courageous

valid *adj* soundly reasoned; having legal force **validate** *v* make valid **validation** *n* **validity** *n*

valise [val-**leez**] *n old-fashioned* small suitcase

Valium *n* ® drug used as a tranquillizer

valley *n* low area between hills, often with a river running through it

valour *n lit* bravery

value *n* importance, usefulness; monetary worth ▷ *pl* moral principles ▷ *v* **valuing, valued** assess the worth or desirability of; have a high regard for **valuable** *adj* having great worth **valuables** *pl n* valuable personal property **valuation** *n* assessment of worth **valueless** *adj* **valuer** *n* **value-added tax** *Brit & SAfr* see **VAT** **value judgment** opinion based on personal belief

valve *n* device to control the movement of fluid through a pipe; *anat* flap in a part of the body allowing blood to flow in one direction only; *physics* tube containing a vacuum, allowing current to flow from a cathode to an anode **valvular** *adj*

vamp[1] *n Informal* sexually attractive woman who seduces men

vamp[2] *v* **vamp up** make (a story, piece of music, etc) seem new by inventing additional parts

vampire *n* (in folklore) corpse that rises at night to drink the blood of the living **vampire bat** tropical bat that feeds on blood

van[1] *n* motor vehicle for transporting goods; railway carriage for goods, luggage, or mail

van[2] *n* short for **vanguard**

vanadium *n chem* metallic element, used in steel

vandal *n* person who deliberately damages property **vandalism** *n* **vandalize** *v*

vane *n* flat blade on a rotary device such as a weathercock or propeller

vanguard *n* unit of soldiers leading an army; most advanced group or position in a movement or activity

vanilla *n* seed pod of a tropical climbing orchid, used for flavouring

vanish *v* disappear suddenly or mysteriously; cease to exist

vanity *n, pl* **-ties** (display of) excessive pride

vanquish *v lit* defeat (someone) utterly

vantage *n* **vantage point** position that gives one an overall view

vapid *adj* lacking character, dull

vapour *n* moisture suspended in air as steam or mist; gaseous form of something that is liquid or solid at room temperature **vaporize** *v* **vaporizer** *n* **vaporous** *adj*

variable *adj* not always the same, changeable ▷ *n maths* expression with a range of values **variability** *n*

variant *adj* differing from a standard or type ▷ *n* something that differs from a standard or type **at variance** in disagreement

variation *n* something presented in a slightly different form; difference in level, amount, or quantity; *music* repetition in different forms of a basic theme

varicose veins *pl n* knotted and swollen veins, esp in the legs
variegated *adj* having patches or streaks of different colours **variegation** *n*
variety *n, pl* **-ties** state of being diverse or various; different things of the same kind; particular sort or kind; light entertainment composed of unrelated acts
various *adj* of several kinds **variously** *adv*
varnish *n* solution of oil and resin, put on a surface to make it hard and glossy ▷*v* apply varnish to
vary *v* **varying, varied** change; cause differences in **varied** *adj*
vascular *adj biol* relating to vessels
vas deferens *n, pl* **vasa deferentia** *anat* sperm-carrying duct in each testicle
vase *n* ornamental jar, esp for flowers
vasectomy *n, pl* **-mies** surgical removal of part of the vas deferens, as a contraceptive method
Vaseline *n* ® thick oily cream made from petroleum, used in skin care
vassal *n hist* man given land by a lord in return for military service; subordinate person or nation **vassalage** *n*
vast *adj* extremely large **vastly** *adv* **vastness** *n*
vat *n* large container for liquids
VAT *Brit & SAfr* value-added tax: tax on the difference between the cost of materials and the selling price
Vatican *n* the Pope's palace
vaudeville *n* variety entertainment of songs and comic turns
vault[1] *n* secure room for storing valuables; underground burial chamber **vaulted** *adj* having an arched roof
vault[2] *v* jump over (something) by resting one's hand(s) on it. ▷*n* such a jump
vaunt *v* describe or display (success or possessions) boastfully **vaunted** *adj*
VC Vice Chancellor; Victoria Cross
VCR video cassette recorder
VD venereal disease
VDU visual display unit
veal *n* calf meat
vector *n maths* quantity that has size and direction, such as force; animal, usu an insect, that carries disease
veer *v* change direction suddenly
vegan [**vee**-gan] *n* person who eats no meat, fish, eggs, or dairy products ▷*adj* suitable for a vegan **veganism** *n*
vegetable *n* edible plant; *Informal* severely brain-damaged person ▷*adj* of or like plants or vegetables
vegetarian *n* person who eats no meat or fish ▷*adj* suitable for a vegetarian **vegetarianism** *n*
vegetate *v* live a dull boring life with no mental stimulation
vegetation *n* plant life of a given place
vehement *adj* expressing strong feelings **vehemence** *n* **vehemently** *adv*
vehicle *n* machine, esp with an engine and wheels, for carrying people or objects; something used to achieve a particular purpose or as a means of expression **vehicular** *adj*
veil *n* piece of thin cloth covering the head or face; something that masks the truth *eg a veil of secrecy* ▷*v* cover with or as if with a veil **take the veil** become a nun **veiled** *adj*

disguised
vein *n* tube that takes blood to the heart; line in a leaf or an insect's wing; layer of ore or mineral in rock; streak in marble, wood, or cheese; feature of someone's writing or speech *eg a vein of humour*; mood or style *eg in a lighter vein* **veined** *adj*
Velcro *n* ® fastening consisting of one piece of fabric with tiny hooked threads and another with a coarse surface that sticks to it
veld, veldt *n* high grassland in southern Africa **veldskoen, velskoen** *n SAfr* leather ankle boot
vellum *n* fine calfskin parchment; type of strong good-quality paper
velocity *n, pl* **-ties** speed of movement in a given direction
velour, velours [vel-**loor**] *n* fabric similar to velvet
velvet *n* fabric with a thick soft pile **velvety** *adj* soft and smooth **velveteen** *n* cotton velvet
venal *adj* easily bribed; characterized by bribery
vend *v* sell **vendor** *n* **vending machine** machine that dispenses goods when coins are inserted
vendetta *n* prolonged quarrel between families, esp one involving revenge killings
veneer *n* thin layer of wood etc covering a cheaper material; superficial appearance *eg a veneer of sophistication*
venerable *adj* worthy of deep respect **venerate** *v* hold (a person) in deep respect **veneration** *n*
venereal disease [ven-**ear**-ee-al] *n* disease transmitted sexually
Venetian *adj* of Venice, port in NE Italy **Venetian blind** window blind made of thin horizontal slats that turn to let in more or less light
vengeance *n* revenge **vengeful** *adj* wanting revenge
venial [**veen**-ee-al] *adj* (of a sin or fault) easily forgiven
venison *n* deer meat
venom *n* malice or spite; poison produced by snakes etc **venomous** *adj*
venous *adj anat* of veins
vent[1] *n* outlet releasing fumes or fluid ▷ *v* express (an emotion) freely **give vent to** release (an emotion) in an outburst
vent[2] *n* vertical slit in a jacket
ventilate *v* let fresh air into; discuss (ideas or feelings) openly **ventilation** *n* **ventilator** *n*
ventral *adj* relating to the front of the body
ventricle *n anat* one of the four cavities of the heart or brain
ventriloquist *n* entertainer who can speak without moving his or her lips, so that a voice seems to come from elsewhere **ventriloquism** *n*
venture *n* risky undertaking, esp in business ▷ *v* do something risky; dare to express (an opinion); go to an unknown place **venturesome** *adj* daring
venue *n* place where an organized gathering is held
Venus *n* planet second nearest to the sun; Roman goddess of love **Venus flytrap** plant that traps and digests insects between hinged leaves
veracity *n* habitual truthfulness **veracious** *adj*
verandah, veranda *n* open porch attached to a house
verb *n* word that expresses the idea of action, happening, or being **verbal** *adj* spoken; of a verb **verbally** *adv* **verbalize** *v* express

(something) in words
verbatim [verb-**bait**-im] *adv, adj* word for word
verbena *n* plant with sweet-smelling flowers
verbiage *n* excessive use of words
verbose [verb-**bohss**] *adj* speaking at tedious length **verbosity** *n*
verdant *adj lit* covered in green vegetation
verdict *n* decision of a jury; opinion formed after examining the facts
verdigris [**ver**-dig-riss] *n* green film on copper, brass, or bronze
verdure *n lit* flourishing green vegetation
verge *n* grass border along a road **on the verge of** having almost reached (a point or condition) **verge on** *v* be near to (a condition)
verger *n C of E* church caretaker
verify *v* **-ifying, -ified** check the truth or accuracy of **verifiable** *adj* **verification** *n*
verily *adv obs* in truth
verisimilitude *n* appearance of being real or true
veritable *adj* rightly called, without exaggeration *eg a veritable feast* **veritably** *adv*
verity *n, pl* **-ties** true statement or principle
vermicelli [ver-me-**chell**-ee] *n* fine strands of pasta
vermiform *adj* shaped like a worm **vermiform appendix** *anat* same as **appendix**
vermilion *adj* orange-red
vermin *pl n* animals, esp insects and rodents, that spread disease or cause damage **verminous** *adj*
vermouth [**ver**-muth] *n* wine flavoured with herbs
vernacular [ver-**nak**-yew-lar] *n* most widely spoken language of a particular people or place
vernal *adj* occurring in spring
vernier [**ver**-nee-er] *n* movable scale on a graduated measuring instrument for taking readings in fractions
veronica *n* plant with small blue, pink, or white flowers
verruca [ver-**roo**-ka] *n* wart, usu on the foot
versatile *adj* having many skills or uses **versatility** *n*
verse *n* group of lines forming part of a song or poem; poetry as distinct from prose; subdivision of a chapter of the Bible **versed in** knowledgeable about
versification *n* writing in verse
version *n* form of something, such as a piece of writing, with some differences from other forms; account of an incident from a particular point of view
verso *n, pl* **-sos** left-hand page of a book
versus *prep* in opposition to or in contrast with; *sport, law* against
vertebra *n, pl* **vertebrae** one of the bones that form the spine **vertebral** *adj* **vertebrate** *n, adj* (animal) having a spine
vertex *n, pl* **-texes, -tices** *maths* point on a geometric figure where the sides form an angle; highest point of a triangle
vertical *adj* straight up and down ▷ *n* vertical direction
vertigo *n* dizziness, usu when looking down from a high place **vertiginous** *adj*
vervain *n* plant with spikes of blue, purple, or white flowers
verve *n* enthusiasm or liveliness
very *adv* more than usually, extremely ▷ *adj* absolute, exact *eg the very top; the very man*

vesicle *n biol* sac or small cavity, esp one containing fluid
vespers *pl n RC church* (service of) evening prayer
vessel *n* ship; *lit* container, esp for liquids; *biol* tubular structure in animals and plants that carries body fluids, such as blood or sap
vest *n* undergarment worn on the top half of the body; *US & Aust* waistcoat ▷ *v* (foll by *in, with*) give (authority) to (someone) **vested interest** interest someone has in a matter because he or she might benefit from it
vestibule *n* small entrance hall
vestige [**vest**-ij] *n* small amount or trace **vestigial** *adj*
vestments *pl n* priest's robes
vestry *n, pl* **-tries** room in a church used as an office by the priest or minister
vet[1] *n* short for **veterinary surgeon** ▷ *v* **vetting, vetted** check the suitability of
vet[2] *n US, Aust & NZ* military veteran
vetch *n* climbing plant with a beanlike fruit used as fodder
veteran *n* person with long experience in a particular activity, esp military service ▷ *adj* long-serving
veterinary *adj* concerning animal health **veterinary surgeon** medical specialist who treats sick animals
veto *n, pl* **-toes** official power to cancel a proposal ▷ *v* **-toing, -toed** enforce a veto against
vex *v* frustrate, annoy **vexation** *n* something annoying; being annoyed **vexatious** *adj* **vexed question** much debated subject
VHF very high frequency: radio frequency band between 30 and 300 MHz
VHS ® Video Home System: format for recording on video
via *prep* by way of
viable *adj* able to be put into practice; *biol* able to live and grow independently **viability** *n*
viaduct *n* bridge over a valley
Viagra [vie-**ag**-ra] *n* ® drug used to treat impotence in men
vial *n* same as **phial**
viands *pl n obs* food
vibes *pl n Informal* emotional reactions between people; atmosphere of a place; short for **vibraphone**
vibrant [**vibe**-rant] *adj* vigorous in appearance, energetic; (of a voice) resonant; (of a colour) strong and bright
vibraphone *n* musical instrument with metal bars that resonate electronically when hit
vibrate *v* move back and forth rapidly; (cause to) resonate **vibration** *n* **vibrator** *n* device that produces vibratory motion, used for massage or as a sex aid **vibratory** *adj*
vibrato *n, pl* **-tos** *music* rapid fluctuation in the pitch of a note
Vic Victoria
vicar *n C of E* member of the clergy in charge of a parish **vicarage** *n* vicar's house
vicarious [vick-**air**-ee-uss] *adj* felt indirectly by imagining what another person experiences; delegated **vicariously** *adv*
vice[1] *n* immoral or evil habit or action; habit regarded as a weakness in someone's character; criminal immorality, esp involving sex
vice[2] *n* tool with a pair of jaws for holding an object while working on

it

vice[3] *adj* serving in place of

vice chancellor *n* chief executive of a university

viceroy *n* governor of a colony who represents the monarch **viceregal** *adj*

vice versa [vie-see **ver**-sa] *adv Latin* conversely, the other way round

vicinity [viss-**in**-it-ee] *n* surrounding area

vicious *adj* cruel and violent **viciously** *adv* **vicious circle, cycle** situation in which an attempt to resolve one problem creates new problems that recreate the original one

vicissitudes [viss-**iss**-it-yewds] *pl n* changes in fortune

victim *n* person or thing harmed or killed **victimize** *v* punish unfairly; discriminate against **victimization** *n*

victor *n* person who has defeated an opponent, esp in war or in sport

Victoria Cross *n Brit* highest award for bravery in battle

Victorian *adj* of or in the reign of Queen Victoria (1837–1901); characterized by prudery or hypocrisy; of or relating to the Australian state of Victoria

victory *n* winning of a battle or contest **victorious** *adj*

victuals [**vit**-tals] *pl n old-fashioned* food and drink

vicuña [vik-**koo**-nya] *n* S American animal like the llama; fine cloth made from its wool

video *n, pl* **-os** short for **video cassette (recorder)** ▷ *v* **videoing, videoed** record (a TV programme or event) on video ▷ *adj* relating to or used in producing television images **video nasty** horrific or pornographic film, usu made for video **videotext** *n* means of representing on a TV screen information that is held in a computer

video cassette *n* cassette containing video tape **video cassette recorder** tape recorder for recording and playing back TV programmes and films

video tape *n* magnetic tape used to record video-frequency signals in TV production; magnetic tape used to record programmes when they are broadcast **videotape** *v* record (a TV programme) on video tape **video tape recorder** tape recorder for vision signals, used in TV production

vie *v* **vying, vied** compete (with someone)

view *n* opinion or belief; everything that can be seen from a given place; picture of this ▷ *v* think of (something) in a particular way **in view of** taking into consideration **on view** exhibited to the public **viewer** *n* person who watches television; hand-held device for looking at photographic slides **viewfinder** *n* window on a camera showing what will appear in a photograph

Viewdata *n* ® videotext service linking users to a computer by telephone

vigil [**vij**-ill] *n* night-time period of staying awake to look after a sick person, pray, etc **vigilant** *adj* watchful in case of danger **vigilance** *n*

vigilante [vij-ill-**ant**-ee] *n* person, esp as one of a group, who takes it upon himself or herself to enforce the law

vignette [vin-**yet**] *n* concise

description of the typical features of something; small decorative illustration in a book

vigour *n* physical or mental energy **vigorous** *adj* **vigorously** *adv*

Viking *n hist* seafaring raider and settler from Scandinavia

vile *adj* very wicked; disgusting **vilely** *adv* **vileness** *n*

vilify *v* **-ifying, -ified** attack the character of **vilification** *n*

villa *n* large house with gardens; holiday home, usu in the Mediterranean

village *n* small group of houses in a country area; rural community **villager** *n*

villain *n* wicked person; main wicked character in a play **villainous** *adj* **villainy** *n*

villein [**vill**-an] *n hist* peasant bound in service to his lord

vinaigrette *n* salad dressing of oil and vinegar

vindicate *v* clear (someone) of guilt; provide justification for **vindication** *n*

vindictive *adj* maliciously seeking revenge **vindictiveness** *n* **vindictively** *adv*

vine *n* climbing plant, esp one producing grapes **vineyard** [**vinn**-yard] *n* plantation of grape vines, esp for making wine

vinegar *n* acid liquid made from wine, beer, or cider **vinegary** *adj*

vino [**vee**-noh] *n Informal* wine

vintage *n* wine from a particular harvest of grapes ▷ *adj* best and most typical **vintage car** car built between 1919 and 1930

vintner *n* dealer in wine

vinyl [**vine**-ill] *n* type of plastic, used in mock leather and records

viol [**vie**-oll] *n* early stringed instrument preceding the violin

viola[1] [vee-**oh**-la] *n* stringed instrument lower in pitch than a violin

viola[2] [**vie**-ol-la] *n* variety of pansy

violate *v* break (a law or agreement); disturb (someone's privacy); treat (a sacred place) disrespectfully; rape **violation** *n* **violator** *n*

violence *n* use of physical force, usu intended to cause injury or destruction; great force or strength in action, feeling, or expression **violent** *adj* **violently** *adv*

violet *n* plant with bluish-purple flowers ▷ *adj* bluish-purple

violin *n* small four-stringed musical instrument played with a bow. **violinist** *n*

VIP very important person

viper *n* poisonous snake

virago [vir-**rah**-go] *n, pl* **-goes, -gos** aggressive woman

viral *adj* of or caused by a virus

virgin *n* person, esp a woman, who has not had sexual intercourse ▷ *adj* not having had sexual intercourse; not yet exploited or explored **virginal** *adj* like a virgin ▷ *n* early keyboard instrument like a small harpsichord **virginity** *n*

virile *adj* having the traditional male characteristics of physical strength and a high sex drive **virility** *n*

virology *n* study of viruses

virtual *adj* having the effect but not the form of; of or relating to virtual reality **virtual reality** computer-generated environment that seems real to the user **virtually** *adv* practically, almost

virtue *n* moral goodness; positive moral quality; merit **by virtue of** by reason of **virtuous** *adj* morally good **virtuously** *adv*

virtuoso *n, pl* **-sos, -si** person with impressive esp musical skill **virtuosity** *n*

virulent [**vir**-yew-lent] *adj* very infectious; violently harmful

virus *n* microorganism that causes disease in humans, animals, and plants; *computers* program that propagates itself, via disks and electronic networks, to cause disruption

visa *n* permission to enter a country, granted by its government and shown by a stamp on one's passport

visage [**viz**-zij] *n lit* face

vis-à-vis [veez-ah-**vee**] *prep* in relation to, regarding

viscera [**viss**-er-a] *pl n* large abdominal organs

visceral [**viss**-er-al] *adj* instinctive; of or relating to the viscera

viscid [**viss**-id] *adj* sticky

viscose *n* synthetic fabric made from cellulose

viscount [**vie**-count] *n* British nobleman ranking between an earl and a baron

viscountess [**vie**-count-iss] *n* woman holding the rank of viscount in her own right; wife or widow of a viscount

viscous *adj* thick and sticky **viscosity** *n*

visible *adj* able to be seen; able to be perceived by the mind. **visibly** *adv* **visibility** *n* range or clarity of vision

vision *n* ability to see; mental image of something; foresight; hallucination **visionary** *adj* showing foresight; idealistic but impractical ▷ *n* visionary person

visit *v* **-iting, -ited** go or come to see; stay temporarily with; (foll by *upon*) *lit* afflict ▷ *n* instance of visiting; official call **visitor** *n* **visitation** *n* formal visit or inspection; catastrophe seen as divine punishment

visor [**vize**-or] *n* transparent part of a helmet that pulls down over the face; eyeshade, esp in a car; peak on a cap

vista *n* (beautiful) extensive view

visual *adj* done by or used in seeing; designed to be looked at **visualize** *v* form a mental image of **visualization** *n* **visual display unit** device with a screen for displaying data held in a computer

vital *adj* essential or highly important; lively; necessary to maintain life **vitals** *pl n* bodily organs necessary to maintain life **vitally** *adv* **vitality** *n* physical or mental energy **vital statistics** statistics of births, deaths, and marriages; *Informal* woman's bust, waist, and hip measurements

vitamin *n* one of a group of substances that are essential in the diet for specific body processes

vitiate [**vish**-ee-ate] *v* spoil the effectiveness of

viticulture *n* cultivation of grapevines

vitreous *adj* like or made from glass

vitriol *n* language expressing bitterness and hatred; sulphuric acid **vitriolic** *adj*

vituperative [vite-**tyew**-pra-tiv] *adj* bitterly abusive **vituperation** *n*

viva[1] *interj* long live (a person or thing)

viva[2] *n Brit* examination in the form of an interview

vivace [viv-**vah**-chee] *adv music* in a lively manner

vivacious *adj* full of energy and

enthusiasm **vivacity** *n*
viva voce [vive-a **voh**-chee] *adv* by word of mouth ▷ *n* same as **viva²**
vivid *adj* very bright; conveying images that are true to life **vividly** *adv* **vividness** *n*
vivisection *n* performing surgical experiments on living animals **vivisectionist** *n*
vixen *n* female fox; *Brit, Aust & NZ, Informal* spiteful woman
viz. (introducing specified items) namely
vizier [viz-**zeer**] *n* high official in certain Muslim countries
vizor *n* same as **visor**
vocabulary *n, pl* **-aries** all the words that a person knows; all the words in a language; specialist terms used in a given subject; list of words in another language with their translation
vocal *adj* relating to the voice; outspoken **vocals** *pl n* singing part of a piece of pop music **vocally** *adv* **vocalist** *n* singer **vocalize** *v* express with or use the voice **vocalization** *n* **vocal cords** membranes in the larynx that vibrate to produce sound
vocation *n* profession or trade; occupation that someone feels called to **vocational** *adj* directed towards a particular profession or trade
vociferous *adj* shouting, noisy
vodka *n* (Russian) spirit distilled from potatoes or grain
voetsek *interj SAfr, offens* expression of rejection
vogue *n* popular style; period of popularity
voice *n* (quality of) sound made when speaking or singing; expression of opinion by a person or group; property of verbs that makes them active or passive ▷ *v* express verbally **voiceless** *adj* **voice mail** electronic system for the transfer and storage of telephone messages, which can be dealt with by the user at a later time **voice-over** *n* film commentary spoken by someone off-camera
void *adj* not legally binding; empty ▷ *n* empty space ▷ *v* make invalid; empty
voile [**voyl**] *n* light semitransparent fabric
vol. volume
volatile *adj* liable to sudden change, esp in behaviour; evaporating quickly **volatility** *n*
vol-au-vent [**voll**-oh-von] *n* small puff-pastry case with a savoury filling
volcano *n, pl* **-noes, -nos** mountain with a vent through which lava is ejected **volcanic** *adj*
vole *n* small rodent
volition *n* ability to decide things for oneself **of one's own volition** through one's own choice
volley *n* simultaneous discharge of ammunition; burst of questions or critical comments; *sport* stroke or kick at a moving ball before it hits the ground ▷ *v* discharge (ammunition) in a volley; hit or kick (a ball) in a volley **volleyball** *n* team game where a ball is hit with the hands over a high net
volt *n* unit of electric potential **voltage** *n* electric potential difference expressed in volts **voltmeter** *n* instrument for measuring voltage
volte-face [volt-**fass**] *n* reversal of opinion
voluble *adj* talking easily and at length **volubility** *n* **volubly** *adv*
volume *n* size of the space

occupied by something; amount; loudness of sound; book, esp one of a series **voluminous** *adj* (of clothes) large and roomy; (of writings) extensive **volumetric** *adj* relating to measurement by volume

voluntary *adj* done by choice; done or maintained without payment; (of muscles) controlled by the will ▷ *n, pl* **-taries** organ solo in a church service **voluntarily** *adv*

volunteer *n* person who offers voluntarily to do something; person who voluntarily undertakes military service ▷ *v* offer one's services; give (information) willingly; offer the services of (another person)

voluptuous *adj* (of a woman) sexually alluring through fullness of figure; sensually pleasurable **voluptuary** *n* person devoted to sensual pleasures

volute *n* spiral or twisting turn, form, or object

vomit *v* **-iting, -ited** eject (the contents of the stomach) through the mouth ▷ *n* matter vomited

voodoo *n* religion involving ancestor worship and witchcraft, practised by Black people in the West Indies, esp in Haiti.

voracious *adj* craving great quantities of food; insatiably eager **voraciously** *adv* **voracity** *n*

vortex *n, pl* **-texes, -tices** whirlpool

vote *n* choice made by a participant in a shared decision, esp in electing a candidate; right to this choice; total number of votes cast; collective voting power of a given group *eg the Black vote* ▷ *v* make a choice by a vote; authorize (something) by vote **voter** *n*

votive *adj* done or given to fulfil a vow

vouch *v* **vouch for** give one's personal assurance about; provide evidence for

voucher *n* ticket used instead of money to buy specified goods; record of a financial transaction, receipt

vouchsafe *v old-fashioned* give, entrust

vow *n* solemn and binding promise ▷ *pl* formal promises made when marrying or entering a religious order ▷ *v* promise solemnly

vowel *n* speech sound made without obstructing the flow of breath; letter representing this

vox pop *n Brit* interviews with members of the public on TV or radio

vox populi *n* public opinion

voyage *n* long journey by sea or in space ▷ *v* make a voyage **voyager** *n*

voyeur *n* person who obtains pleasure from watching people undressing or having sex **voyeurism** *n*

vs versus

V-sign *n* offensive gesture made by sticking up the index and middle fingers with the palm inwards; similar gesture, with the palm outwards, meaning victory or peace

VSO (in Britain) Voluntary Service Overseas

VSOP (of brandy or port) very superior old pale

VTOL vertical takeoff and landing

VTR video tape recorder

vulcanize *v* strengthen (rubber) by treating it with sulphur

vulgar *adj* showing lack of good taste, decency, or refinement

vulgarly *adv* **vulgarity** *n*
vulgarian *n* vulgar (rich) person
vulgar fraction simple fraction
Vulgate *n* fourth-century Latin version of the Bible
vulnerable *adj* liable to be physically or emotionally hurt; exposed to attack **vulnerability** *n*
vulpine *adj* of or like a fox
vulture *n* large bird that feeds on the flesh of dead animals
vulva *n* woman's external genitals
vying *v* present participle of **vie**

W

W watt; West(ern)
WA Western Australia
wacky *adj* **wackier, wackiest** *Informal* eccentric or funny **wackiness** *n*
wad *n* small mass of soft material; roll or bundle, esp of banknotes **wadding** *n* soft material used for padding or stuffing
waddle *v* walk with short swaying steps ▷ *n* swaying walk
waddy *n, pl* **-dies** heavy wooden club used by Australian Aborigines
wade *v* walk with difficulty through water or mud; proceed with difficulty **wader** *n* long-legged water bird ▷ *pl* angler's long waterproof boots
wadi [**wod**-dee] *n, pl* **-dies** (in N Africa and Arabia) river which is dry except in the wet season
wafer *n* thin crisp biscuit; thin disc of unleavened bread used at

Communion; thin slice

waffle[1] *Informal* ▷ *v* speak or write in a vague wordy way ▷ *n* vague wordy talk or writing

waffle[2] *n* square crisp pancake with a gridlike pattern

waft *v* drift or carry gently through the air ▷ *n* something wafted

wag *v* **wagging, wagged** move rapidly from side to side ▷ *n* wagging movement; *old-fashioned* humorous witty person **wagtail** *n* small long-tailed bird

wage *n* (often pl) payment for work done, esp when paid weekly ▷ *v* engage in (an activity)

wager *n, v* bet on the outcome of something

waggle *v* move with a rapid shaking or wobbling motion

wagon, waggon *n* four-wheeled vehicle for heavy loads; railway freight truck

wahoo *n* food and game fish of tropical seas

waif *n* young person who is, or seems, homeless or neglected

wail *v* cry out in pain or misery ▷ *n* mournful cry

wain *n poetic* farm wagon

wainscot, wainscoting *n* wooden lining of the lower part of the walls of a room

waist *n* part of the body between the ribs and hips; narrow middle part **waistband** *n* band of material sewn on to the waist of a garment to strengthen it **waistcoat** *n* sleeveless garment which buttons up the front, usu worn over a shirt and under a jacket **waistline** *n* (size of) the waist of a person or garment

wait *v* remain inactive in expectation (of something); be ready (for something); delay or be delayed; serve in a restaurant etc ▷ *n* act or period of waiting **waiter** *n* man who serves in a restaurant etc **waitress** *n fem*

Waitangi Day *n* February 6th, the national day of New Zealand commemorating the Treaty Of Waitangi in 1840

waive *v* refrain from enforcing (a law, right, etc)

waiver *n* act or instance of voluntarily giving up a claim, right, etc

waka *n NZ* Maori canoe

wake[1] *v* **waking, woke, woken** rouse from sleep or inactivity ▷ *n* vigil beside a corpse the night before the funeral **waken** *v* wake **wakeful** *adj*

wake[2] *n* track left by a moving ship **in the wake of** following, often as a result

walk *v* move on foot with at least one foot always on the ground; pass through or over on foot; escort or accompany on foot ▷ *n* act or instance of walking; distance walked; manner of walking; place or route for walking **walk of life** social position or profession **walker** *n* **walkabout** *n* informal walk among the public by royalty etc **walkie-talkie** *n* portable radio transmitter and receiver **walking stick** stick used as a support when walking **walk into** *v* meet with unwittingly **Walkman** *n* ® small portable cassette player with headphones **walkout** *n* strike; act of leaving as a protest **walkover** *n* easy victory

wall *n* structure of brick, stone, etc used to enclose, divide, or support; something having the function or effect of a wall ▷ *v* enclose or seal with a wall or walls **wallflower** *n* fragrant garden plant; (at a dance) woman who remains seated because she has no partner **wallpaper** *n* decorative paper to cover interior walls

wallaby *n, pl* **-bies** marsupial like a small kangaroo

wallaroo *n* large stocky Australian kangaroo of rocky regions

wallet *n* small folding case for paper money, documents, etc

walleye *n* fish with large staring eyes (also **dory**)

wallop *Informal* ▷ *v* **-loping, -loped** hit hard ▷ *n* hard blow **walloping** *Informal* ▷ *n* thrashing ▷ *adj* large or great

wallow *v* revel in an emotion; roll in liquid or mud ▷ *n* act or instance of wallowing

wally *n, pl* **-lies** *Brit, slang* stupid person

walnut *n* edible nut with a wrinkled shell; tree it grows on; its wood, used for making furniture

walrus *n, pl* **-ruses, -rus** large sea mammal with long tusks

waltz *n* ballroom dance; music for this ▷ *v* dance a waltz; *Informal* move in a relaxed confident way

wampum [**wom**-pum] *n* shells woven together, formerly used by Native Americans for money and ornament

wan [rhymes with **swan**] *adj* **wanner, wannest** pale and sickly looking

wand *n* thin rod, esp one used in performing magic tricks

wander *v* move about without a definite destination or aim; go astray, deviate ▷ *n* act or instance of wandering **wanderer** *n* **wanderlust** *n* great desire to travel

wane *v* decrease gradually in size or strength; (of the moon) decrease in size **on the wane** decreasing in size, strength, or power

wangle *v Informal* get by devious methods

want *v* need or long for; desire or wish ▷ *n* act or instance of wanting; thing wanted; lack or absence; state of being in need, poverty **wanted** *adj* sought by the police **wanting** *adj* lacking; not good enough

wanton *adj* without motive, provocation, or justification; *old-fashioned* (of a woman) sexually unrestrained or immodest

WAP Wireless Application Protocol: a system that allows mobile phone users to access the Internet and other information services

war *n* fighting between nations; conflict or contest ▷ *adj* of, like, or caused by war ▷ *v* **warring, warred** conduct a war **warring** *adj* **warlike** *adj* of or relating to war; hostile and eager to have a war **war crime** crime, such as killing, committed during a war in violation of accepted conventions **war criminal** person who has committed war crimes **warfare** *n* fighting or hostilities **warhead** *n* explosive front part of a missile **warmonger** *n* person who encourages war **warship** *n* ship designed and equipped for naval combat

waratah *n* Australian shrub with crimson flowers

warble *v* sing in a trilling voice

warbler *n* any of various small songbirds

ward *n* room in a hospital for patients needing a similar kind of care; electoral division of a town; child under the care of a guardian or court **warder** *n* prison officer

wardress *n fem* **ward off** *v* avert or repel **wardroom** *n* officers' quarters on a warship

warden *n* person in charge of a building and its occupants; official responsible for the enforcement of regulations

wardrobe *n* cupboard for hanging clothes in; person's collection of clothes; costumes of a theatrical company

ware *n* articles of a specified type or material *eg silverware* ▷ *pl* goods for sale **warehouse** *n* building for storing goods prior to sale or distribution

warlock *n* man who practises black magic

warm *adj* moderately hot; providing warmth; (of a colour) predominantly yellow or red; affectionate; enthusiastic ▷ *v* make or become warm **warmly** *adv* **warmth** *n* mild heat; cordiality; intensity of emotion **warm up** *v* make or become warmer; do preliminary exercises before a race or more strenuous exercise; make or become more lively **warm-up** *n*

warn *v* make aware of possible danger or harm; caution or scold; inform (someone) in advance **warning** *n* something that warns; scolding or caution **warn off** *v* advise (someone) not to become involved with

warp *v* twist out of shape; pervert ▷ *n* state of being warped; lengthwise threads on a loom

warrant *n* (document giving) official authorization ▷ *v* make necessary; guarantee **warranty** *n, pl* **-ties** (document giving) a guarantee **warrant officer** officer in certain armed services with a rank between a commissioned and noncommissioned officer

warren *n* series of burrows in which rabbits live; overcrowded building or part of a town

warrigal *Aust* ▷ *n* dingo ▷ *adj* wild

warrior *n* person who fights in a war

wart *n* small hard growth on the skin **wart hog** kind of African wild pig

wary [**ware**-ree] *adj* **warier, wariest** watchful or cautious **warily** *adv* **wariness** *n*

was *v* first and third person singular past tense of **be**

wash *v* clean (oneself, clothes, etc) with water and usu soap; be washable; flow or sweep over or against; *Informal* be believable or acceptable *eg that excuse won't wash* ▷ *n* act or process of washing; clothes washed at one time; thin coat of paint; disturbance in the water after a ship has passed by **washable** *adj* **washer** *n* ring put under a nut or bolt or in a tap as a seal **washing** *n* clothes to be washed **washing-up** *n* (washing of) dishes and cutlery needing to be cleaned after a meal **wash away** *v* carry or be carried off by moving water **washout** *n* *Informal* complete failure **wash up** *v* wash dishes and cutlery after a meal

wasp *n* stinging insect with a slender black-and-yellow striped body **waspish** *adj* bad-tempered

waste *v* use pointlessly or thoughtlessly; fail to take advantage of ▷ *n* act of wasting or state of being wasted; anything wasted; rubbish ▷ *pl* desert ▷ *adj* rejected as worthless or surplus to requirements; not cultivated or inhabited **waste away** (cause to) decline in health or strength **wastage** *n* loss by wear or waste; reduction in size of a workforce by not filling vacancies **wasteful** *adj* extravagant **wastefully** *adv* **waster, wastrel** *n* layabout **wastepaper basket** container for discarded paper

watch *v* look at closely; guard or supervise ▷*n* portable timepiece for the wrist or pocket; (period of) watching; sailor's spell of duty **watchable** *adj* **watcher** *n* **watchful** *adj* vigilant or alert **watchfully** *adv* **watchdog** *n* dog kept to guard property; person or group guarding against inefficiency or illegality **watch for** *v* be keenly alert to or cautious about **watchman** *n* man employed to guard a building or property **watchword** *n* word or phrase that sums up the attitude of a particular group

water *n* clear colourless tasteless liquid that falls as rain and forms rivers etc; body of water, such as a sea or lake; level of the tide; urine ▷*v* put water on or into; (of the eyes) fill with tears; (of the mouth) salivate **watery** *adj* **water buffalo** oxlike Asian animal **water closet** *old-fashioned* (room containing) a toilet flushed by water **watercolour** *n* paint thinned with water; painting done in this **watercourse** *n* bed of a stream or river **watercress** *n* edible plant growing in clear ponds and streams **water down** *v* dilute, make less strong **waterfall** *n* place where the waters of a river drop vertically **waterfront** *n* part of a town alongside a body of water **water lily** water plant with large floating leaves **watermark** *n* faint translucent design in a sheet of paper **watermelon** *n* melon with green skin and red flesh **water polo** team game played by swimmers with a ball **waterproof** *adj* not letting water through ▷*n* waterproof garment ▷*v* make waterproof **watershed** *n* important period or factor serving as a dividing line; line separating two river systems **watersider** *n* NZ person employed to load and unload ships **water-skiing** *n* sport of riding over water on skis towed by a speedboat **watertight** *adj* not letting water through; with no loopholes or weak points **water wheel** large wheel which is turned by flowing water to drive machinery

watt [wott] *n* unit of power **wattage** *n* electrical power expressed in watts

wattle [wott-tl] *n* branches woven over sticks to make a fence; Australian acacia with flexible branches formerly used for making fences

wave *v* move the hand to and fro as a greeting or signal; move or flap to and fro ▷*n* moving ridge on water; curve(s) in the hair; prolonged spell of something; gesture of waving; vibration carrying energy through a medium **wavy** *adj* **wavelength** *n* distance between the same points of two successive waves

waver *v* hesitate or be irresolute; be or become unsteady **waverer** *n*

wax[1] *n* solid shiny fatty or oily substance used for sealing, making candles, etc; similar substance made by bees; waxy secretion of the ear ▷*v* coat or polish with wax **waxen** *adj* made of or like wax

waxy *adj* **waxwork** *n* lifelike wax model of a (famous) person ▷ *pl* place exhibiting these

wax² *v* increase in size or strength; (of the moon) get gradually larger

way *n* manner or method; characteristic manner; route or direction; track or path; distance; room for movement or activity *eg you're in the way;* passage or journey **wayfarer** *n lit* traveller **waylay** *v* lie in wait for and accost or attack **wayside** *adj, n* (situated by) the side of a road

wayward *adj* erratic, selfish, or stubborn **waywardness** *n*

WC water closet

we *pron* (used as the subject of a verb) the speaker or writer and one or more others; people in general; formal word for 'I' used by editors and monarchs

weak *adj* lacking strength; liable to give way; unconvincing; lacking flavour **weaken** *v* make or become weak **weakling** *n* feeble person or animal **weakly** *adv* feebly **weakness** *n* being weak; failing; self-indulgent liking

weal *n* raised mark left on the skin by a blow

wealth *n* state of being rich; large amount of money and valuables; great amount or number **wealthy** *adj*

wean *v* accustom (a baby or young mammal) to food other than mother's milk; coax (someone) away from former habits

weapon *n* object used in fighting; anything used to get the better of an opponent **weaponry** *n* weapons collectively

wear *v* **wearing, wore, worn** have on the body as clothing or ornament; show as one's expression; (cause to) deteriorate by constant use or action; endure constant use ▷ *n* clothes suitable for a particular time or purpose *eg beach wear;* damage caused by use; ability to endure constant use **wearer** *n* **wear off** *v* gradually decrease in intensity **wear on** *v* (of time) pass slowly

weary *adj* **-rier, -riest** tired or exhausted; tiring ▷ *v* **-rying, -ried** make or become weary **wearily** *adv* **weariness** *n* **wearisome** *adj* tedious

weasel *n* small carnivorous mammal with a long body and short legs

weather *n* day-to-day atmospheric conditions of a place ▷ *v* (cause to) be affected by the weather; come safely through **under the weather** *Informal* slightly ill **weather-beaten** *adj* worn, damaged, or (of skin) tanned by exposure to the weather **weathercock, weathervane** *n* device that revolves to show the direction of the wind

weave *v* **weaving, wove** *or* **weaved, woven** *or* **weaved** make (fabric) by interlacing (yarn) on a loom; compose (a story); move from side to side while going forwards **weaver** *n*

web *n* net spun by a spider; anything intricate or complex *eg web of deceit;* skin between the toes of a duck, frog, etc **the Web** short for **World Wide Web** **webbed** *adj* **webbing** *n* strong fabric woven in strips **webcam** *n* camera that transmits images over the Internet **webcast** *n* broadcast of an event over the Internet **weblog** *n* person's online journal (also **blog**) **website** *n* group of connected pages on the World Wide Web

wed *v* **wedding, wedded** *or* **wed** marry; unite closely **wedding** *n* act or ceremony of marriage **wedlock** *n* marriage

wedge *n* piece of material thick at one end and thin at the other ▷ *v* fasten or split with a wedge; squeeze into a narrow space **wedge-tailed eagle** large brown Australian eagle with a wedge-shaped tail

Wednesday *n* fourth day of the week

wee *adj Brit, Aust & NZ, Informal* small or short

weed *n* plant growing where undesired; *Informal* thin ineffectual person ▷ *v* clear of weeds **weedy** *adj Informal* (of a person) thin and weak **weed out** *v* remove or eliminate (what is unwanted)

weeds *pl n obs* widow's mourning clothes

week *n* period of seven days, esp one beginning on a Sunday; hours or days of work in a week **weekly** *adj, adv* happening, done, etc once a week ▷ *n, pl* **-lies** newspaper or magazine published once a week **weekday** *n* any day of the week except Saturday or Sunday **weekend** *n* Saturday and Sunday

weep *v* **weeping, wept** shed tears; ooze liquid **weepy** *adj* liable to cry **weeping willow** willow with drooping branches

weevil *n* small beetle which eats grain etc

weft *n* cross threads in weaving

weigh *v* have a specified weight; measure the weight of; consider carefully; be influential; be burdensome **weigh anchor** raise a ship's anchor or (of a ship) have its anchor raised **weighbridge** *n* machine for weighing vehicles by means of a metal plate set into the road

weight *n* heaviness of an object; unit of measurement of weight; object of known mass used for weighing; heavy object; importance or influence ▷ *v* add weight to; slant (a system) so that it favours one side rather than another **weightless** *adj* **weightlessness** *n*

weighting *n Brit* extra allowance paid in special circumstances

weighty *adj* **weightier, weightiest** important or serious; very heavy **weightily** *adv*

weir *n* river dam

weird *adj* strange or bizarre; unearthly or eerie

> SPELLING The pronunciation of **weird** possibly leads people to spell it with the vowels the wrong way round. Collins Word Web shows that *wierd* is a common misspelling

weirdo *n, pl* **-dos** *Informal* peculiar person

welch *v* same as **welsh**

welcome *v* **-coming, -comed** greet with pleasure; receive gladly ▷ *n* kindly greeting ▷ *adj* received gladly; freely permitted

weld *v* join (pieces of metal or plastic) by softening with heat; unite closely ▷ *n* welded joint **welder** *n*

welfare *n* wellbeing; help given to people in need **welfare state** system in which the government takes responsibility for the wellbeing of its citizens

well[1] *adv* **better, best** satisfactorily; skilfully; completely; intimately; considerably; very likely ▷ *adj* in good health ▷ *interj* exclamation of surprise, interrogation, etc

well² *n* hole sunk into the earth to reach water, oil, or gas; deep open shaft ▷ *v* flow upwards or outwards

wellbeing *n* state of being well, happy, or prosperous

well-disposed *adj* inclined to be friendly or sympathetic

wellies *pl n Brit & Aust, Informal* wellingtons

wellingtons *pl n Brit & Aust* high waterproof rubber boots

well-meaning *adj* having good intentions

well-spoken *adj* speaking in a polite or articulate way

well-worn *adj* (of a word or phrase) stale from overuse; so much used as to be affected by wear

welsh *v* fail to pay a debt or fulfil an obligation

Welsh *adj* of Wales ▷ *n* language or people of Wales **Welsh rarebit, rabbit** dish of melted cheese on toast

welt *n* raised mark on the skin produced by a blow; raised or strengthened seam

welter *n* jumbled mass

welterweight *n* boxer weighing up to 147lb (professional) or 67kg (amateur)

wen *n* cyst on the scalp

wench *n facetious* young woman

wend *v* go or travel

went *v* past tense of **go**

wept *v* past of **weep**

were *v* form of the past tense of **be** used after *we, you, they*, or a plural noun; subjunctive of **be**

we're we are

weren't were not

werewolf *n* (in folklore) person who can turn into a wolf

west *n* (direction towards) the part of the horizon where the sun sets; region lying in this direction; **(W-)** western Europe and the US ▷ *adj* to or in the west; (of a wind) from the west ▷ *adv* in, to, or towards the west **westerly** *adj* **western** *adj* of or in the west ▷ *n* film or story about cowboys in the western US **westernize** *v* adapt to the customs and culture of the West **westward** *adj, adv* **westwards** *adv*

wet *adj* **wetter, wettest** covered or soaked with water or another liquid; not yet dry; rainy; *Brit, Informal* (of a person) feeble or foolish ▷ *n* moisture or rain; *Brit, Informal* feeble or foolish person ▷ *v* **wetting, wet** *or* **wetted** make wet **wet blanket** *Informal* person who has a depressing effect on others **wetland** *n* area of marshy land **wet nurse** woman employed to breast-feed another's child **wet suit** close-fitting rubber suit worn by divers etc

whack *v* strike with a resounding blow ▷ *n* such a blow; *Informal* share; *Informal* attempt **whacked** *adj* exhausted **whacking** *adj Informal* huge

whale *n* large fish-shaped sea mammal **have a whale of a time** *Informal* enjoy oneself very much **whaler** *n* ship or person involved in whaling **whaling** *n* hunting of whales for food and oil

wharf *n, pl* **wharves, wharfs** platform at a harbour for loading and unloading ships **wharfie** *n Aust* person employed to load and unload ships

what *pron* which thing; that which; request for a statement to be repeated ▷ *interj* exclamation of anger, surprise, etc ▷ *adv* in which way, how much *eg what do you care?* **what for?** why? **whatever** *pron* everything or anything that; no matter what **whatnot** *n Informal* similar unspecified things **whatsoever** *adj* at all

wheat *n* grain used in making flour, bread, and pasta; plant producing this **wheaten** *adj* **wheatear** *n* small songbird

wheedle *v* coax or cajole

wheel *n* disc that revolves on an axle; pivoting movement ▷*v* push or pull (something with wheels); turn as if on an axis; turn round suddenly **wheeling and dealing** use of shrewd and sometimes unscrupulous methods to achieve success **wheeler-dealer** *n* **wheelbarrow** *n* shallow box for carrying loads, with a wheel at the front and two handles **wheelbase** *n* distance between a vehicle's front and back axles **wheelchair** *n* chair mounted on wheels for use by people who cannot walk **wheel clamp** immobilizing device fixed to one wheel of an illegally parked car

wheeze *v* breathe with a hoarse whistling noise ▷*n* wheezing sound; *Informal* trick or plan **wheezy** *adj*

whelk *n* edible snail-like shellfish

whelp *n* pup or cub; *offens* youth ▷*v* (of an animal) give birth

when *adv* at what time? ▷*conj* at the time that; although; considering the fact that ▷*pron* at which time **whenever** *adv, conj* at whatever time

whence *adv, conj obs* from what place or source

where *adv* in, at, or to what place? ▷*pron* in, at, or to which place ▷*conj* in the place at which **whereabouts** *n* present position ▷*adv* at what place **whereas** *conj* but on the other hand **whereby** *pron* by which **wherefore** *obs* ▷*adv* why ▷*conj* consequently **whereupon** *conj* at which point **wherever** *conj, adv* at whatever place **wherewithal** *n* necessary funds, resources, etc

whet *v* **whetting, whetted** sharpen (a tool) **whet someone's appetite** increase someone's desire **whetstone** *n* stone for sharpening tools

whether *conj* used to introduce an indirect question or a clause expressing doubt or choice

whey [way] *n* watery liquid that separates from the curd when milk is clotted

which *adj, pron* used to request or refer to a choice from different possibilities ▷*pron* used to refer to a thing already mentioned **whichever** *adj, pron* any out of several; no matter which

whiff *n* puff of air or odour; trace or hint

Whig *n* member of a British political party of the 18th–19th centuries that sought limited reform

while *conj* at the same time that; whereas ▷*n* period of time **whilst** *conj* while **while away** *v* pass (time) idly but pleasantly

whim *n* sudden fancy **whimsy** *n* capricious idea; light or fanciful humour **whimsical** *adj* unusual, playful, and fanciful

whimper *v* cry in a soft whining way ▷*n* soft plaintive whine

whin *n Brit* gorse

whine *n* high-pitched plaintive cry; peevish complaint ▷*v* make such a sound **whining** *n, adj*

whinge *Brit, Aust & NZ, Informal* ▷ *v* complain ▷ *n* complaint

whinny *v* **-nying, -nied** neigh softly ▷ *n, pl* **-nies** soft neigh

whip *n* cord attached to a handle, used for beating animals or people; politician responsible for organizing and disciplining fellow party or caucus members; call made on members of Parliament to attend for important votes; dessert made from beaten cream or egg whites ▷ *v* **whipping, whipped** strike with a whip, strap, or cane; *Informal* pull, remove, or move quickly; beat (esp eggs or cream) to a froth; rouse into a particular condition; *Informal* steal **whip bird** *Aust* bird with a whistle ending in a whipcrack note **whiplash injury** neck injury caused by a sudden jerk to the head, as in a car crash **whip-round** *n Informal* collection of money

whippet *n* racing dog like a small greyhound

whirl *v* spin or revolve; be dizzy or confused ▷ *n* whirling movement; bustling activity; confusion or giddiness **whirlpool** *n* strong circular current of water **whirlwind** *n* column of air whirling violently upwards in a spiral ▷ *adj* much quicker than normal

whirr, whir *n* prolonged soft buzz ▷ *v* **whirring, whirred** (cause to) make a whirr

whisk *v* move or remove quickly; beat (esp eggs or cream) to a froth ▷ *n* egg-beating utensil

whisker *n* any of the long stiff hairs on the face of a cat or other mammal ▷ *pl* hair growing on a man's face **by a whisker** *Informal* only just

whisky *n, pl* **-kies** spirit distilled from fermented cereals **whiskey** *n, pl* **-keys** Irish or American whisky

whisper *v* speak softly, without vibration of the vocal cords; rustle ▷ *n* soft voice; *Informal* rumour; rustling sound

whist *n* card game in which one pair of players tries to win more tricks than another pair

whistle *v* produce a shrill sound, esp by forcing the breath through pursed lips; signal by a whistle ▷ *n* whistling sound; instrument blown to make a whistling sound **blow the whistle on** *Informal* inform on or put a stop to **whistling** *n, adj*

whit *n* **not a whit** not the slightest amount

white *adj* of the colour of snow; pale; light in colour; (of coffee) served with milk ▷ *n* colour of snow; clear fluid round the yolk of an egg; white part, esp of the eyeball; **(W-)** member of the race of people with light-coloured skin **whiten** *v* make or become white or whiter **whiteness** *n* **whitish** *adj* **white-collar** *adj* denoting professional and clerical workers **white elephant** useless or unwanted possession **white flag** signal of surrender or truce **white goods** large household appliances such as cookers and fridges **white-hot** *adj* very hot **white lie** minor unimportant lie **white paper** report by the government, outlining its policy on a matter

whitebait *n* small edible fish

whitewash *n* substance for whitening walls ▷ *v* cover with whitewash; conceal or gloss over unpleasant facts

whither *adv obs* to what place

whiting *n* edible sea fish

Whitsun *n* Christian festival

celebrating the descent of the Holy Spirit to the apostles

whittle *v* cut or carve (wood) with a knife **whittle down, away** *v* reduce or wear away gradually

whizz, whiz *v* **whizzing, whizzed** make a loud buzzing sound; *Informal* move quickly ▷ *n, pl* **whizzes** loud buzzing sound; *Informal* person skilful at something **whizz kid, whiz kid** *Informal* person who is outstandingly able for his or her age

who *pron* which person; used to refer to a person or people already mentioned **whoever** *pron* any person who; no matter who

whodunnit, whodunit [hoo-**dun**-nit] *n Informal* detective story, play, or film

whole *adj* containing all the elements or parts; uninjured or undamaged ▷ *n* complete thing or system **on the whole** taking everything into consideration **wholly** *adv* **wholefood** *n* food that has been processed as little as possible **wholehearted** *adj* sincere or enthusiastic **wholemeal** *adj* (of flour) made from the whole wheat grain; made from wholemeal flour **whole number** number that does not contain a fraction

wholesale *adj, adv* dealing by selling goods in large quantities to retailers; on a large scale **wholesaler** *n*

wholesome *adj* physically or morally beneficial

whom *pron* objective form of **who**

whoop *v, n* shout or cry to express excitement

whoopee *interj Informal* cry of joy

whooping cough *n* infectious disease marked by convulsive coughing and noisy breathing

whopper *n Informal* anything unusually large; huge lie **whopping** *adj*

whore [hore] *n* prostitute

whorl *n* ring of leaves or petals; one turn of a spiral

whose *pron* of whom or of which

why *adv* for what reason ▷ *pron* because of which

wick *n* cord through a lamp or candle which carries fuel to the flame

wicked *adj* morally bad; mischievous **wickedly** *adv* **wickedness** *n*

wicker *adj* made of woven cane **wickerwork** *n*

wicket *n* set of three cricket stumps and two bails; ground between the two wickets on a cricket pitch

wide *adj* large from side to side; having a specified width; spacious or extensive; far from the target; opened fully ▷ *adv* to the full extent; over an extensive area; far from the target **widely** *adv* **widen** *v* make or become wider **widespread** *adj* affecting a wide area or a large number of people

widgeon *n* same as **wigeon**

widow *n* woman whose husband is dead and who has not remarried **widowed** *adj* **widowhood** *n* **widower** *n* man whose wife is dead and who has not remarried

width *n* distance from side to side; quality of being wide

wield *v* hold and use (a weapon); have and use (power)

wife *n, pl* **wives** woman to whom a man is married

wig *n* artificial head of hair

wigeon *n* duck found in marshland

wiggle *v* move jerkily from side to

side ▷*n* wiggling movement

wigwam *n* Native American's tent

wild *adj* (of animals) not tamed or domesticated; (of plants) not cultivated; lacking restraint or control; violent or stormy; *Informal* excited; *Informal* furious; random **wilds** *pl n* desolate or uninhabited place **wildly** *adv* **wildness** *n* **wild-goose chase** search that has little chance of success

wildcat *n* European wild animal like a large domestic cat **wildcat strike** sudden unofficial strike

wildebeest *n* gnu

wilderness *n* uninhabited uncultivated region

wildfire *n* **spread like wildfire** spread quickly and uncontrollably

wildlife *n* wild animals and plants collectively

wiles *pl n* tricks or ploys **wily** *adj* crafty or sly

wilful *adj* headstrong or obstinate; intentional **wilfully** *adv*

will[1] *v, past* **would** used as an auxiliary to form the future tense or to indicate intention, ability, or expectation

will[2] *n* strong determination; desire or wish; directions written for disposal of one's property after death ▷*v* use one's will in an attempt to do (something); wish or desire; leave (property) by a will **willing** *adj* ready or inclined (to do something); keen and obliging **willingly** *adv* **willingness** *n* **willpower** *n* ability to control oneself and one's actions

will-o'-the-wisp *n* elusive person or thing; pale light sometimes seen over marshes at night

willow *n* tree with thin flexible branches; its wood, used for making cricket bats **willowy** *adj* slender and graceful

willy-nilly *adv* whether desired or not

willy wagtail *n Aust* black-and-white flycatcher

willy-willy *n Aust* small tropical dust storm

wilt *v* (cause to) become limp or lose strength

wimp *n Informal* feeble ineffectual person

wimple *n* garment framing the face, worn by medieval women and now by nuns

win *v* **winning, won** come first in (a competition, fight, etc); gain (a prize) in a competition; get by effort ▷*n* victory, esp in a game **winner** *n* **winning** *adj* gaining victory; charming **winnings** *pl n* sum won, esp in gambling **win over** *v* gain the support or consent of (someone)

wince *v* draw back, as if in pain ▷*n* wincing

winch *n* machine for lifting or hauling using a cable or chain wound round a drum ▷*v* lift or haul using a winch

wind[1] *n* current of air; hint or suggestion; breath; flatulence; idle talk ▷*v* render short of breath **windy** *adj* **windward** *adj, n* (of or in) the direction from which the wind is blowing **windfall** *n* unexpected good luck; fallen fruit **wind instrument** musical instrument played by blowing **windmill** *n* machine for grinding or pumping driven by sails turned by the wind **windpipe** *n* tube linking the throat and the lungs **windscreen** *n* front window of a motor vehicle **windscreen wiper** device that wipes rain etc from a windscreen **windsock** *n* cloth cone on a mast at an airfield to indicate wind direction **windsurfing** *n* sport of riding on water using a surfboard propelled and steered by a sail

wind² *v* **winding, wound** coil or wrap around; tighten the spring of (a clock or watch); move in a twisting course **wind up** *v* bring to or reach an end; tighten the spring of (a clock or watch); *Informal* make tense or agitated; *slang* tease

windlass *n* winch worked by a crank

window *n* opening in a wall to let in light or air; glass pane or panes fitted in such an opening; display area behind the window of a shop; area on a computer screen that can be manipulated separately from the rest of the display area; period of unbooked time in a diary or schedule **window-dressing** *n* arrangement of goods in a shop window; attempt to make something more attractive than it really is **window-shopping** *n* looking at goods in shop windows without intending to buy

wine *n* alcoholic drink made from fermented grapes; similar drink made from other fruits **wine and dine** entertain or be entertained with fine food and drink

wing *n* one of the limbs or organs of a bird, insect, or bat that are used for flying; one of the winglike supporting parts of an aircraft; projecting side part of a building; faction of a political party; part of a car body surrounding the wheels; *sport* (player on) either side of the pitch ▷ *pl* sides of a stage ▷ *v* fly; wound slightly in the wing or arm **winged** *adj* **winger** *n sport* player positioned on a wing

wink *v* close and open (an eye) quickly as a signal; twinkle ▷ *n* winking; smallest amount of sleep

winkle *n* shellfish with a spiral shell **winkle out** *v Informal* extract or prise out

winnow *v* separate (chaff) from (grain); examine to select desirable elements

winsome *adj* charming or winning

winter *n* coldest season ▷ *v* spend the winter **wintry** *adj* of or like winter; cold or unfriendly **winter sports** open-air sports held on snow or ice

wipe *v* clean or dry by rubbing; erase (a tape) ▷ *n* wiping **wipe out** *v* destroy completely

wire *n* thin flexible strand of metal; length of this used to carry electric current; *obs* telegram ▷ *v* equip with wires **wiring** *n* system of wires **wiry** *adj* lean and tough; like wire **wire-haired** *adj* (of a dog) having a stiff wiry coat

wireless *n old-fashioned* same as **radio**

wireless *adj* (of a computer network) connected by radio rather than by cables or fibre optics ▷ *n old-fashioned* same as **radio**

wisdom *n* good sense and judgment; accumulated knowledge **wisdom tooth** any of the four large molar teeth that come through usu after the age of twenty

wise¹ *adj* having wisdom **wisely** *adv* **wiseacre** *n* person who wishes to seem wise

wise² *n obs* manner

wisecrack *Informal* ▷ *n* clever, sometimes unkind, remark ▷ *v* make a wisecrack

wish *v* want or desire; feel or express a hope about someone's wellbeing, success, etc ▷*n* expression of a desire; thing desired **wishful** *adj* too optimistic **wishbone** *n* V-shaped bone above the breastbone of a fowl

wishy-washy *adj Informal* insipid or bland

wisp *n* light delicate streak; twisted bundle or tuft **wispy** *adj*

wisteria *n* climbing shrub with blue or purple flowers

wistful *adj* sadly longing **wistfully** *adv*

wit *n* ability to use words or ideas in a clever and amusing way; person with this ability; (sometimes pl) practical intelligence **witless** *adj* foolish

witch *n* person, usu female, who practises (black) magic; ugly or wicked woman **witchcraft** *n* use of magic **witch doctor** (in certain societies) a man appearing to cure or cause injury or disease by magic **witch-hunt** *n* campaign against people with unpopular views

witchetty grub *n* wood-boring edible Australian caterpillar

with *prep* indicating presence alongside, possession, means of performance, characteristic manner, etc *eg walking with his dog; a man with two cars; hit with a hammer; playing with skill* **within** *prep, adv* in or inside **without** *prep* not accompanied by, using, or having

withdraw *v* **-drawing, -drew, -drawn** take or move out or away **withdrawal** *n* **withdrawn** *adj* unsociable

wither *v* wilt or dry up **withering** *adj* (of a look or remark) scornful

withers *pl n* ridge between a horse's shoulder blades

withhold *v* **-holding, -held** refrain from giving

withstand *v* **-standing, -stood** oppose or resist successfully

witness *n* person who has seen something happen; person giving evidence in court; evidence or testimony ▷*v* see at first hand; sign (a document) to certify that it is genuine

witter *v Chiefly Brit* chatter pointlessly or at unnecessary length

wittingly *adv* intentionally

witty *adj* **wittier, wittiest** clever and amusing **wittily** *adv* **witticism** *n* witty remark

wives *n* plural of **wife**

wizard *n* magician; person with outstanding skill in a particular field **wizardry** *n*

wizened [**wiz**-zend] *adj* shrivelled or wrinkled

WMD weapon(s) of mass destruction

woad *n* blue dye obtained from a plant, used by the ancient Britons as a body dye

wobbegong *n* Australian shark with brown-and-white skin

wobble *v* move unsteadily; shake ▷*n* wobbling movement or sound **wobbly** *adj*

wodge *n Informal* thick lump or chunk

woe *n* grief **woeful** *adj* extremely sad; pitiful **woefully** *adv* **woebegone** *adj* looking miserable

wok *n* bowl-shaped Chinese cooking pan, used for stir-frying

woke *v* past tense of **wake**[1] **woken** *v* past participle of **wake**[1]

wold *n* high open country

wolf *n, pl* **wolves** wild predatory canine mammal ▷*v* eat ravenously **cry wolf** raise a false alarm **wolf whistle** whistle by a man indicating that he thinks a woman is attractive

wolverine *n* carnivorous mammal of Arctic regions

woman *n, pl* **women** adult human female; women collectively **womanhood** *n* **womanish** *adj* effeminate **womanly** *adj* having qualities traditionally associated with a woman **womanizing** *n* practice of indulging in casual affairs with women **womanizer** *n* **Women's Liberation** movement for the removal of inequalities between women and men (also **women's lib**)

womb *n* hollow organ in female mammals where babies are conceived and develop

wombat *n* small heavily-built burrowing Australian marsupial

won *v* past of **win**

wonder *v* be curious about; be amazed ▷ *n* wonderful thing; emotion caused by an amazing or unusual thing ▷ *adj* spectacularly successful *eg a wonder drug* **wonderful** *adj* very fine; remarkable **wonderfully** *adv* **wonderment** *n* **wondrous** *adj* *old-fashioned* wonderful

wonky *adj* **-kier, -kiest** *Brit, Aust & NZ, Informal* shaky or unsteady

wont [rhymes with **don't**] *adj* accustomed ▷ *n* custom

won't will not

woo *v* try to persuade; *old-fashioned* try to gain the love of

wood *n* substance trees are made of, used in carpentry and as fuel; area where trees grow; long-shafted golf club, usu with wooden head **wooded** *adj* covered with trees **wooden** *adj* made of wood; without expression **woody** *adj* **woodbine** *n* honeysuckle **woodcock** *n* game bird **woodcut** *n* (print made from) an engraved block of wood **woodland** *n* forest **woodlouse** *n* small insect-like creature with many legs **woodpecker** *n* bird which searches tree trunks for insects **woodwind** *adj, n* (of) a type of wind instrument made of wood **woodworm** *n* insect larva that bores into wood

woof[1] *n* cross threads in weaving

woof[2] *n* barking noise made by a dog **woofer** *n* loudspeaker reproducing low-frequency sounds

wool *n* soft hair of sheep, goats, etc; yarn spun from this **woollen** *adj* **woolly** *adj* of or like wool; vague or muddled ▷ *n* knitted woollen garment

woomera *n* notched stick used by Australian Aborigines to aid the propulsion of a spear

woozy *adj* **woozier, wooziest** *Informal* weak, dizzy, and confused

wop-wops *pl n NZ, Informal* remote rural areas

word *n* smallest single meaningful unit of speech or writing; chat or discussion; brief remark; message; promise; command ▷ *v* express in words **wordy** *adj* using too many words **wording** *n* choice and arrangement of words **word processor** keyboard, microprocessor, and VDU for electronic organization and storage of text **word processing**

wore *v* past tense of **wear**

work *n* physical or mental effort directed to making or doing something; paid employment; duty or task; something made or done ▷ *pl* factory; total of a writer's or artist's achievements; *Informal* full treatment; mechanism of a machine ▷*adj* of or for work ▷*v* (cause to) do work; be employed; (cause to) operate; (of a plan etc) be successful; cultivate (land); manipulate, shape, or process; (cause to) reach a specified condition **work-to-rule** *n* protest in which workers keep strictly to all regulations to reduce the rate of work **workable** *adj* **worker** *n* **workaholic** *n* person obsessed with work **workhorse** *n* person or thing that does a lot of dull or routine work **workhouse** *n* (in England, formerly) institution where the poor were given food and lodgings in return for work **working class** social class consisting of wage earners, esp manual workers **working-class** *adj* **working party** committee investigating a specific problem **workman** *n* manual worker **workmanship** *n* skill with which an object is made **workshop** *n* room or building for a manufacturing process **worktop** *n* surface in a kitchen, used for food preparation

world *n* the planet earth; mankind; society of a particular area or period; sphere of existence ▷*adj* of the whole world **worldly** *adj* not spiritual; concerned with material things; wise in the ways of the world **world-weary** *adj* no longer finding pleasure in life **World Wide Web** global network of linked computer files

worm *n* small limbless invertebrate animal; *Informal* wretched or spineless person; shaft with a spiral thread forming part of a gear system; *computers* type of virus ▷*pl* illness caused by parasitic worms in the intestines ▷*v* rid of worms **worm one's way** crawl; insinuate (oneself) **wormy** *adj* **worm-eaten** *adj* eaten into by worms **worm out** *v* extract (information) craftily

wormwood *n* bitter plant

worn *v* past participle of **wear**

worry *v* **-rying, -ried** (cause to) be anxious or uneasy; annoy or bother; (of a dog) chase and try to bite (sheep etc) ▷*n, pl* **-ries** (cause of) anxiety or concern **worried** *adj* **worrying** *adj, n*

worse *adj, adv* comparative of **bad** or **worst** ▷*adj, adv* superlative of **bad** or **badly** ▷*n* worst thing **worsen** *v* make or grow worse

worship *v* **-shipping, -shipped** show religious devotion to; love and admire ▷*n* act or instance of worshipping; (**W-**) title for a mayor or magistrate **worshipper** *n* **worshipful** *adj* worshipping

worsted [**wooss**-tid] *n* type of woollen yarn or fabric

worth *prep* having a value of; meriting or justifying ▷*n* value or price; excellence; amount to be had for a given sum **worthless** *adj* **worthy** *adj* deserving admiration or respect ▷*n Informal* notable person **worthily** *adv* **worthiness** *n* **worthwhile** *adj* worth the time or effort involved

would *v* used as an auxiliary to express a request, describe a habitual past action, or form the past tense or subjunctive mood of **will**[1] **would-be** *adj* wishing or pretending to be

wouldn't would not

wound[1] *n* injury caused by violence; injury to the feelings ▷*v* inflict a wound on

wound[2] *v* past of **wind**[2]

wove *v* a past tense of **weave**

woven *v* a past participle of **weave**
wow *interj* exclamation of astonishment ▷ *n Informal* astonishing person or thing
wowser *n Aust & NZ, slang* puritanical person; teetotaller
wpm words per minute
wrack *n* seaweed
wraith *n* ghost
wrangle *v* argue noisily ▷ *n* noisy argument
wrap *v* **wrapping, wrapped** fold (something) round (a person or thing) so as to cover ▷ *n* garment wrapped round the shoulders; sandwich made by wrapping a filling in a tortilla **wrapper** *n* cover for a product **wrapping** *n* material used to wrap **wrap up** *v* fold paper round; put warm clothes on; *Informal* finish or settle (a matter)
wrasse *n* colourful sea fish
wrath [roth] *n* intense anger **wrathful** *adj*
wreak *v* **wreak havoc** cause chaos **wreak vengeance on** take revenge on
wreath *n* twisted ring or band of flowers or leaves used as a memorial or tribute **wreathed** *adj* surrounded or encircled
wreck *v* destroy ▷ *n* remains of something that has been destroyed or badly damaged, esp a ship; person in very poor condition **wrecker** *n* **wreckage** *n* wrecked remains
wren *n* small brown songbird; Australian warbler
Wren *n Informal* (in Britain) member of the former Women's Royal Naval Service
wrench *v* twist or pull violently; sprain (a joint) ▷ *n* violent twist or pull; sprain; difficult or painful parting; adjustable spanner
wrest *v* twist violently; take by force
wrestle *v* fight, esp as a sport, by grappling with and trying to throw down an opponent; struggle hard with **wrestler** *n* **wrestling** *n*
wretch *n* despicable person; pitiful person
wretched [retch-id] *adj* miserable or unhappy; worthless **wretchedly** *adv* **wretchedness** *n*
wrier *adj* a comparative of **wry**
wriest *adj* a superlative of **wry**
wriggle *v* move with a twisting action; manoeuvre oneself by devious means ▷ *n* wriggling movement
wright *n* maker *eg wheelwright*
wring *v* **wringing, wrung** twist, esp to squeeze liquid out of; clasp and twist (the hands); obtain by forceful means
wrinkle *n* slight crease, esp one in the skin due to age ▷ *v* make or become slightly creased **wrinkly** *adj*
wrist *n* joint between the hand and the arm **wristwatch** *n* watch worn on the wrist
writ *n* written legal command
write *v* **writing, wrote, written** mark paper etc with symbols or words; set down in words; communicate by letter; be the author or composer of **writing** *n* **writer** *n* author; person who has written something specified **write-off** *n Informal* something damaged beyond repair **write-up** *n* published account of something
writhe *v* twist or squirm in or as if in pain
wrong *adj* incorrect or mistaken; immoral or bad; not intended or suitable; not working properly

▷*adv* in a wrong manner ▷*n* something immoral or unjust ▷*v* treat unjustly; malign **wrongly** *adv* **wrongful** *adj* **wrongfully** *adv* **wrongdoing** *n* immoral or illegal behaviour **wrongdoer** *n*

wrote *v* past tense of **write**

wrought [rawt] *v lit* past of **work** ▷*adj* (of metals) shaped by hammering or beating **wrought iron** pure form of iron used for decorative work

wrung *v* past of **wring**

wry *adj* **wrier, wriest** *or* **wryer, wryest** drily humorous; (of a facial expression) contorted **wryly** *adv*

wt. weight

WWW World Wide Web

wych-elm *n* elm with large rough leaves

X

X indicating an error, a choice, or a kiss; indicating an unknown, unspecified, or variable factor, number, person, or thing

xenon *n chem* colourless odourless gas found in very small quantities in the air

xenophobia [zen-oh-**fobe**-ee-a] *n* fear or hatred of people from other countries

Xerox [**zeer**-ox] *n* ® machine for copying printed material; ® copy made by a Xerox machine ▷*v* copy (a document) using such a machine

Xmas [**eks**-mass] *n Informal* Christmas

X-ray, x-ray *n* stream of radiation that can pass through some solid materials; picture made by sending X-rays through someone's body to examine internal organs ▷*v* photograph, treat, or examine using X-rays

xylem [**zy**-lem] *n* plant tissue that conducts water and minerals from the roots to all other parts

xylophone [**zile**-oh-fone] *n* musical instrument made of a row of wooden bars played with hammers

Y

Y2K *n Informal* name for the year 2000 AD (esp referring to the millennium bug)

ya *interj SAfr* yes

yabby *n, pl* **-bies** *Aust* small freshwater crayfish; marine prawn used as bait

yacht [yott] *n* large boat with sails or an engine, used for racing or pleasure cruising **yachting** *n* **yachtsman, yachtswoman** *n*

yak¹ *n* Tibetan ox with long shaggy hair

yak² *v* **yakking, yakked** *slang* talk continuously about unimportant matters

yakka *n Aust & NZ, Informal* work

yam *n* tropical root vegetable

yank *v* pull or jerk suddenly ▷ *n* sudden pull or jerk

Yankee, Yank *n slang* person from the United States

yap *v* **yapping, yapped** bark with

a high-pitched sound; *Informal* talk continuously ▷*n* high-pitched bark

yard[1] *n* unit of length equal to 36 inches or about 91.4 centimetres **yardstick** *n* standard against which to judge other people or things

yard[2] *n* enclosed area, usu next to a building and often used for a particular purpose *eg builder's yard*

yarmulke [**yar**-mull-ka] *n* skullcap worn by Jewish men

yarn *n* thread used for knitting or making cloth; *Informal* long involved story

yashmak *n* veil worn by a Muslim woman to cover her face in public

yaw *v* (of an aircraft or ship) turn to one side or from side to side while moving

yawl *n* two-masted sailing boat

yawn *v* open the mouth wide and take in air deeply, often when sleepy or bored; (of an opening) be large and wide ▷*n* act of yawning **yawning** *adj*

yd yard

ye [**yee**] *pron obs* you

year *n* time taken for the earth to make one revolution around the sun, about 365 days; twelve months from January 1 to December 31 **yearly** *adj, adv* (happening) every year or once a year **yearling** *n* animal between one and two years old

yearn *v* want (something) very much **yearning** *n, adj*

yeast *n* fungus used to make bread rise and to ferment alcoholic drinks **yeasty** *adj*

yebo *interj SAfr, Informal* yes

yell *v* shout or scream in a loud or piercing way ▷*n* loud cry of pain, anger, or fear

yellow *n* the colour of gold, a lemon, etc ▷*adj* of this colour; *Informal* cowardly ▷*v* make or become yellow **yellow belly** *Aust* freshwater food fish with yellow underparts **yellow fever** serious infectious tropical disease **yellowhammer** *n* European songbird with a yellow head and body **Yellow Pages** ® telephone directory which lists businesses under the headings of the type of service they provide

yelp *v, n* (give) a short sudden cry

yen[1] *n, pl* **yen** monetary unit of Japan

yen[2] *n Informal* longing or desire

yeoman [**yo**-man] *n, pl* **-men** *hist* farmer owning and farming his own land **yeoman of the guard** member of the ceremonial bodyguard of the British monarchy

yes *interj* expresses consent, agreement, or approval; used to answer when one is addressed **yes man** person who always agrees with their superior

yesterday *adv, n* (on) the day before today; (in) the recent past

yet *conj* nevertheless, still ▷*adv* up until then or now; still; now

yeti *n* same as **abominable snowman**

yew *n* evergreen tree with needle-like leaves and red berries

Yiddish *adj, n* (of or in) a language of German origin spoken by many Jews in Europe and elsewhere

yield *v* produce or bear; give up control of, surrender; give in ▷*n* amount produced **yielding** *adj* submissive; soft or flexible

YMCA Young Men's Christian Association

yob, yobbo *n slang* bad-mannered aggressive youth

yodel *v* **-delling, -delled** sing with abrupt changes between a normal and a falsetto voice

yoga *n* Hindu method of exercise and discipline aiming at spiritual, mental, and physical wellbeing **yogi** *n* person who practises yoga

yogurt, yoghurt *n* slightly sour custard-like food made from milk that has had bacteria added to it, often sweetened and flavoured with fruit

yoke *n* wooden bar put across the necks of two animals to hold them together; frame fitting over a person's shoulders for carrying buckets; *lit* oppressive force *eg the yoke of the tyrant*; fitted part of a garment to which a fuller part is attached ▷ *v* put a yoke on; unite or link

yokel *n offens* person who lives in the country and is usu simple and old-fashioned

yolk *n* yellow part of an egg that provides food for the developing embryo

Yom Kippur *n* annual Jewish religious holiday

yonder *adj, adv* (situated) over there

yonks *pl n Informal* very long time

yore *n lit* **of yore** a long time ago

Yorkshire pudding *n* baked batter made from flour, milk, and eggs

you *pron* refers to: the person or people addressed; unspecified person or people in general

young *adj* in an early stage of life or growth ▷ *pl n* young people in general; offspring, esp young animals **youngster** *n* young person

your *adj* of, belonging to, or associated with you; of, belonging to, or associated with an unspecified person or people in general **yours** *pron* something belonging to you **yourself** *pron*

youth *n* time of being young; boy or young man; young people as a group **youthful** *adj* **youthfulness** *n* **youth club** club that provides leisure activities for young people **youth hostel** inexpensive lodging place for young people travelling cheaply

yowl *v, n* (produce) a loud mournful cry

yo-yo *n, pl* **-yos** toy consisting of a spool attached to a string, by which it is repeatedly spun out and reeled in

yttrium [**it**-ree-um] *n chem* silvery metallic element used in various alloys

yucca *n* tropical plant with spikes of white leaves

yucky *adj* **yuckier, yuckiest** *slang* disgusting, nasty

Yule *n lit* Christmas (season)

yuppie *n* young highly-paid professional person, esp one who has a materialistic way of life ▷ *adj* typical of or reflecting the values of yuppies

YWCA Young Women's Christian Association

Z

zany [**zane**-ee] *adj* **zanier, zaniest** comical in an endearing way
zap *v* **zapping, zapped** *slang* kill (by shooting); change TV channels rapidly by remote control
zeal *n* great enthusiasm or eagerness **zealot** [**zel**-lot] *n* fanatic or extreme enthusiast **zealous** [**zel**-luss] *adj* extremely eager or enthusiastic **zealously** *adv*
zebra *n* black-and-white striped African animal of the horse family **zebra crossing** pedestrian crossing marked by black and white stripes on the road
zebu [**zee**-boo] *n* Asian ox with a humped back and long horns
Zen *n* Japanese form of Buddhism that concentrates on learning through meditation and intuition
zenith *n* highest point of success or power; point in the sky directly above an observer
zephyr [**zef**-fer] *n* soft gentle breeze
zeppelin *n hist* large cylindrical airship
zero *n, pl* **-ros, -roes** (symbol representing) the number 0; point on a scale of measurement from which the graduations commence; lowest point; nothing, nil ▷ *adj* having no measurable quantity or size **zero in on** *v* aim at; *Informal* concentrate on
zest *n* enjoyment or excitement; interest, flavour, or charm; peel of an orange or lemon
zigzag *n* line or course having sharp turns in alternating directions ▷ *v* **-zagging, -zagged** move in a zigzag ▷ *adj* formed in or proceeding in a zigzag
zinc *n chem* bluish-white metallic element used in alloys and to coat metal
zing *n Informal* quality in something that makes it lively or interesting
Zionism *n* movement to found and support a Jewish homeland in Israel **Zionist** *n, adj*
zip *n* fastener with two rows of teeth that are closed or opened by a small clip pulled between them; *Informal* energy, vigour; short whizzing sound ▷ *v* **zipping, zipped** fasten with a zip; move with a sharp whizzing sound
zircon *n* mineral used as a gemstone and in industry
zirconium *n chem* greyish-white metallic element that is resistant to corrosion
zither *n* musical instrument consisting of strings stretched over a flat box and plucked to produce musical notes

zodiac *n* Imaginary belt in the sky within which the sun, moon, and planets appear to move, divided into twelve equal areas, called signs of the zodiac, each named after a constellation

zombie, zombi *n* person who appears to be lifeless, apathetic, or totally lacking in independent judgment; corpse brought back to life by witchcraft

zone *n* area with particular features or properties; one of the divisions of the earth's surface according to temperature ▷ *v* divide into zones **zonal** *adj*

zoo *n, pl* **zoos** place where live animals are kept for show

zoology *n* study of animals **zoologist** *n* **zoological** *adj* **zoological garden** zoo

zoom *v* move or rise very rapidly; make or move with a buzzing or humming sound **zoom lens** lens that can make the details of a picture larger or smaller while keeping the picture in focus

zucchini [zoo-**keen**-ee] *n, pl* **-ni, -nis** *US & Aust* courgette

Zulu *n* member of a tall Black people of southern Africa; language of this people

zygote *n* fertilized egg cell